D1758588

ADVANCED SOCIAL PSYCHOLOGY

THE STATE OF THE SCIENCE

Edited by

Roy F. Baumeister

Eli J. Finkel

OXFORD
UNIVERSITY PRESS
2010

OXFORD
UNIVERSITY PRESS

Oxford University Press, Inc., publishes works that further
Oxford University's objective of excellence
in research, scholarship, and education.

Oxford New York
Auckland Cape Town Dar es Salaam Hong Kong Karachi
Kuala Lumpur Madrid Melbourne Mexico City Nairobi
New Delhi Shanghai Taipei Toronto

With offices in
Argentina Austria Brazil Chile Czech Republic France Greece
Guatemala Hungary Italy Japan Poland Portugal Singapore
South Korea Switzerland Thailand Turkey Ukraine Vietnam

Published by Oxford University Press, Inc.
198 Madison Avenue, New York, New York 10016

www.oup.com

Library of Congress Cataloging-in-Publication Data
Advanced social psychology : the state of the science / edited by Roy F. Baumeister, Eli J. Finkel.
p. cm.
Includes bibliographical references and index.
ISBN-13: 978-0-19-538120-7
ISBN-10: 0-19-538120-3
1. Social psychology—Textbooks. I. Baumeister, Roy F., 1953– II. Finkel, Eli J.
HM1033.A38 2010
302—dc22 2009050102

9 8 7 6 5 4 3 2

Printed in the United States of America
on acid-free paper

CONTENTS

Part 4 Connections to Related Fields

CONTRIBUTORS

Roy F. Baumeister
Florida State University

Galen V. Bodenhausen
Northwestern University

Marilynn B. Brewer
Ohio State University

Pablo Briñol
Universidad Autónoma de Madrid

Brad J. Bushman
University of Michigan & VU University Amsterdam, the Netherlands

Don Carlston
Purdue University

Charles S. Carver
University of Miami

Robert B. Cialdini
Arizona State University

Leandre R. Fabrigar
Queen's University

Garth J. O. Fletcher
University of Canterbury

Eli J. Finkel
Northwestern University

Vladas Griskevicius
University of Minnesota

Todd F. Heatherton
Dartmouth College

Steven J. Heine
University of British Columbia

Douglas T. Kenrick
Arizona State University

Mary Frances Luce
Duke University

Jon K. Maner
Florida State University

Antony S. R. Manstead
Cardiff University

MICHAEL E. MCCULLOUGH
University of Miami

NICKOLA C. OVERALL
University of Auckland

RICHARD E. PETTY
Ohio State University

HARRY T. REIS
The University of Rochester

JENNIFER A. RICHESON
Northwestern University

BENJAMIN A. TABAK
University of Miami

SHELLEY E. TAYLOR
University of California, Los Angeles

KATHLEEN D. VOHS
University of Minnesota

DUANE T. WEGENER
Purdue University

THALIA WHEATLEY
Dartmouth College

ADVANCED SOCIAL PSYCHOLOGY

Part 1

Background

Chapter 1

Social Psychologists and Thinking about People

Roy F. Baumeister

One of the editors of this textbook belongs to a social program that was created a few years ago. When he asked his new departmental colleagues why they decided to add social psychology to a department that was already large, happy, and successful, they had two answers. First, they did a survey of the top-ranked psychology departments across North America to determine what these departments had that they did not, and social psychology emerged as the top answer. Thus, they considered social psychology an essential ingredient of a high-quality psychology department.

Second, the university administration had also shown considerable interest. Administrators usually seek to break down barriers between fields, so they look for opportunities for scholars with widely different backgrounds to exchange ideas. A social psychologist, they had concluded, was one of those rare specialists who would have something of interest to say to nearly everyone in the university. In other words, almost all fields of inquiry, and certainly all the ones (the majority) that study people, have some interests in common with social psychology.

Social psychology is thus a highly special enterprise. John Cacioppo (2007), as president of the Association for Psychological Science, reported that psychology is a "hub science," in the sense that it has considerable influence on other fields. Social psychology has played an important role in that—and, we think, should be poised to take on an even larger role.

Part of the appeal of social psychology is that it is open to almost anything in the realm of normal human behavior. Many subfields of psychology are defined by a specific focus: on mental illness, on children, or on brain processes. Social psychology has no such specific focus. Anything contributing to an increased understanding of how people in general think, feel, and act is welcome. The opportunities for new ideas, new methods, and new directions seem unlimited. Scholars in many fields keep up with new developments relevant to their own work, but we think social psychologists are especially prone to smile over something they hear or read that may have no bearing on their own work but nonetheless contributes provocative insights to the broad project of understanding people. This focus is also undoubtedly one of the reasons that the deans mentioned above thought that social psychologists were unusually positioned to be able to exchange ideas with professors in almost any other field.

It is therefore with great pleasure that Eli Finkel and I introduce this textbook, *Advanced Social Psychology*. It is intended to provide a basic overview of social psychology for graduate students, upper-level undergraduates, and others. We assume that most readers will have had an undergraduate course in social psychology, if not more, although such a background is not essential. The authors of this book were given the task of providing an introductory overview of their topics—to cover what every graduate student in social psychology ought to know.

As we worked to produce this volume, we were delighted and humbled to read the fine chapters that these experts produced. We will allow them to speak for themselves. In this opening chapter, we will undertake an intellectual exercise, namely to articulate the various images of the human social individual that have informed and guided research in social psychology over the years.

Understanding People

Social psychologists have sometimes seen their task as understanding situations. Yet we think that understates the value of social psychology. You probably were not inspired to become a social psychologist to learn about situations. On the contrary, most people come to social psychology because they are interested in people. Social psychologists study and think endlessly about people. Experiments in social psychology test hypotheses about people. Our field has plenty to say about people.

Most studies in social psychology proceed in very small steps, reporting a few experiments aimed at some narrow aspect of human functioning. Yet underlying those studies are broad assumptions about what types of creatures people really are. By way of introduction to the field, we offer a somewhat haphazard tour through several of these implicit images of humankind as social psychology has imagined them.

In general, psychology involves studies of motivation and cognition, and it is possible to trace the history of psychology as a series of pendulum swings to emphasize one or another. Thus, the Wundtian introspectionist school focused on cognition. The Freudian theory emphasized motivation. The learning in animal learning can be considered to be cognitive, despite the official reluctance to acknowledge that anything inside the mind could be scientifically studied. Drive theory was, however, motivational. And so forth.

Social psychology has likewise varied in terms of espousing "hot" (motivational) and "cold" (cognitive) processes in its history. Hence several of these images of the human person lean heavily toward either cognition or motivation. If we put them all together, we are likely to get a balanced and probably fairly accurate view.

One more point. I have sought to depict these images in a lively manner and to give them somewhat memorable names that might be usable in the occasional seminar discussion. At times, composite images with entertaining names can come to be regarded as caricatures. I hope no theorists will be offended by these depictions and that readers will recognize that they are shorthand summaries that cannot do justice to all the subtleties that individual theorists may appreciate. These are heuristics; please treat them as such.

Ultimately, this chapter is an expression of my own longstanding interest in people, and one that I suspect many social psychologists share. When you read research findings, it is stimulating to step back occasionally and reflect on what they contribute to answering the grand question: "What sort of creatures are human beings?" What follows is a list of some of the answers that social psychologists have pursued.

The Consistency Seeker

We begin with some of the "hot" models that emphasize motivation. Early social psychology emphasized motivation over cognition, although that has been reversed considerably in recent decades.

One of the first big ideas in modern social psychology was that people are motivated to seek consistency. This was a dominant view in the late 1950s and the 1960s and has remained influential ever since. It is a view that emphasizes motivated cognition, or perhaps motivations about cognition. Consistency is, in the final analysis, something cognitive, but the emphasis in early years was in people's motivated strivings to attain and sustain it. Even the theory of cognitive dissonance, which was for a time the most influential theory in social psychology, was really a drive (motivation) theory and not very cognitive by modern standards.

As an image of humankind, the Consistency Seeker goes about his or her business until some sort of inconsistency is encountered, which is disturbing and sets off efforts to restore consistency. Thus, both emotion and motivation are associated with consistency. Inconsistency can arise in many places, such as in conflict between people's actions and their attitudes or in their perceptions of the social world. Having two friends who dislike each other is itself an important source of consistency. ["Balance" was another term for consistency, as in the balance theories by Heider (1958) and others.]

In early and pure forms, the Consistency Seeker idea meant that people are interested in consistency much of the time and are perhaps constantly alert for possible inconsistencies. Later it emerged that people are not all that consistent. People have a great many thoughts, memories, and behaviors, and it would be implausibly laborious to test each new one for possible inconsistencies with all the others. Hence the later versions held that people do not really worry much about inconsistency unless it becomes an issue, for example, when they find themselves doing something that is strikingly inconsistent with what they have said, done, or thought before. In other words, the situation must emphasize the inconsistency to set off the motivation to reduce inconsistency.

The Consistency Seeker today is one of the field's senior citizens. The field respects the idea but has moved on to add other models. That is, consistency seeking is still considered to be an important category of human social behavior, but it is one among many. It is no longer treated as the major or central aspect of human social life.

The Self-Esteem Maximizer

The view that people seek to protect and possibly increase their self-esteem has informed research in social psychology for decades. At first it was related to dissonance theory, several versions of which saw dissonance motivation as centered around maintaining a favorable view of self, because being inconsistent made you look bad. However, concerns about self-esteem soon went far beyond attitude dynamics and dissonance reduction. The motivation to maintain self-esteem was seen as driving task performance and responses to failure, interpersonal strategies, defensive cognitive styles, stress, emotion, risk taking, and much more.

The Self-Esteem Maximizer seeks above all to avoid losing self-esteem. Anything that depicts the self in a bad light and could potentially call for a downward revision in your self-appraisal is seen as threatening. People may avoid certain situations or persons, rationalize events, and even provide themselves with excuses for potential failure, all to prevent the loss of self-esteem. Aggressive responses to criticism are also viewed as driven by concern with self-esteem.

The urge to enhance your favorable view of self is prominent in some versions of the Self-Esteem Maximizer but not in others. It is somewhat more controversial than the urge to avoid losing self-esteem. In part this reflects the influence of the consistency seeker image: To raise your self-esteem is, after all, to change your view of yourself and thus is a form of inconsistency. Self-verification theory, for example, has explicitly rejected the view that people fundamentally want to raise their self-esteem (Swann, 1985), but it strongly avers that people resist losing self-esteem.

The Self-Esteem Maximizer is alive and well in social psychology today. Few social psychological theories dispute that people are sensitive to criticism, enjoy thinking well of themselves, and will adjust their behavior and mental processes to sustain a favorable image of self.

Research on relationships has added another dimension to the Self-Esteem Maximizer: Not only do people want to think that they are great individually, they also want to believe that their close relationships are exceptionally good. People idealize their partners and how well they get along. The self-deceptive aspect of this can explain, among other things, why surveys consistently find that the majority of Americans describe their marriages as quite happy, but half of these marriages end in divorce.

The Terror Manager

A highly distinctive, well-integrated theory of human nature has been advanced under the rubric of Terror Management Theory. This approach was originally inspired by the writings of anthropologist Ernest Becker (1973), who proposed that humans are unique among living things in knowing that they will eventually die. Becker proposed that much human behavior can be understood as a motivated response to the fear of death. Although this was originally presented as a theoretical, even existential argument, it has led to an impressive research program spearheaded by a trio of social psychologists: Tom Pyszczynski, Jeff Greenberg, and Sheldon Solomon. They have refined and updated Becker's notions in light of their experimental findings (see, e.g., Pyszczynski, Greenberg, & Solomon, 1997).

As these theorists argue, the avoidance of death is the "master motive" that underlies most human strivings. To be sure, people are not threatened with death on a regular basis, but in Terror Management Theory the avoidance of reminders of human mortality is the central, overriding fact of human life. The quest for self-esteem, which in the theory of the Self-Esteem Maximizer is the core motive, is considered in this theory to be derived from the fear of death. By building and pursuing self-esteem, people can presumably obliterate thoughts and fears of death. Self-esteem is thus an artificial defense mechanism that helps people forget about death.

Even culture is in this view is considered to be a psychological defense mechanism. That is, people create culture to shield themselves from awareness of death. An important and well-documented response of people who are reminded of death is to increase their loyal support for their cultural worldview.

The notion of death avoidance as the master motive provides a basis for explaining a great many, and potentially all, human actions and strivings. According to Terror Management Theory, sexual activity, achievement motivation, prejudice, emotion, and other phenomena studied by social psychologists are all ways of coping with the threatening idea that we will eventually die, and with the terror that this idea evokes.

The Information Seeker

We turn now from the relatively hot (i.e., motivational) to the colder (i.e., cognitive) images of humankind. These emphasize thinking and processing information as the paramount human activity. Motivation is quietly downplayed in some variations on these approaches, recognized but simply not considered in others, and actively denied (for the most part) in still others.

An early and not very controversial version of the cold, cognitive approach to understanding people depicts them as Information Seekers. The simple assumption behind this theory is that it is important and helpful for people to understand their worlds, and so they constantly go about trying to collect information. The drive to understand the environment is probably present even in simple animals, who benefit from being able to predict events in their physical surroundings. Understanding the social environment is considerably more challenging than understanding the physical environment, and so humans spend much of their time trying to gain information about it. This includes learning and making inferences about other people as well as about social situations and social structures.

The Information Seekers are also interested in gaining information about themselves. To navigate through life effectively, it is most helpful and useful to know as much as possible about both yourself and your world. For example, choosing the right courses of study, the right career, and the right mates depends on finding matches between aspects of the self and aspects of the social world, and so both kinds of knowledge are needed.

The central assumption of the Information Seeker approach was that whenever something happens—you pass a test, get rejected by a romantic partner, meet someone new, have an argument—you respond by trying to determine what it means and what its implications are. Attribution theory, which was one of the dominant theories in social psychology from the late 1960s into the 1980s, took this approach (e.g., Jones, Kanouse, Kelley, Nisbett, Valins, & Weiner, 1972).

Simple curiosity captures the essence of the Information Seeker. Still, in reality, people are more curious about some things than about others. Hence the simplest versions of the Information Seeker, as a person seeking any and all information, are probably not seriously upheld by many social psychologists as the most correct model.

The Motivated Information Seeker is an apt name for the view that combines the basic cognitive, curious, avid learner with the understanding that most individuals have a fairly strong set of preferences for what to learn. Thus, the basic Information Seeker may want to learn the truth about himself or herself, regardless of what it is, but the Motivated Information Seeker (like the Self-Esteem Maximizer) much prefers to hear favorable rather than unfavorable things about the self.

The Information Processor

The simple view of humans as Information Seekers gave way in the 1970s to the realization that information was not simply taken in but rather was subjected to fairly extensive processing. The so-called Cognitive Revolution emerged in social psychology during that decade and became the dominant view during the next one (the 1980s). The image of people as Information Processors was essentially an updated, more sophisticated version of seeing them as Information Seekers.

The image of the Information Seeker depicted humans as scouring their world for information, quickly figuring it out with a couple of attributions, and storing those conclusions for future use. The image of the Information Processor was similar, except that it recognized that considerable inner mental work occurred when the information was first encountered. Instead of an attribution or two, the processing involved selective attention, extensive and fallible interpretation processes, partial encoding into memory and at best modestly reliable retrieval from memory, assimilation of new information to existing knowledge, mental shortcuts, and numerous other processes.

The image of the Information Processor was for a time the coldest of the cold images of the human being that social psychologists had. It borrowed methods and theories from cognitive psychology, a field that has never had much use for motivation, emotion, and other hot processes. Many social psychologists embraced the discipline of thinking in purely cognitive terms and noted that assumptions about motivation were sometimes unnecessary and unsupported. Leading journals for a time insisted that authors could draw a motivational conclusion about their research findings only after they first ruled out all possible cognitive explanations. (The reverse rule, ruling out motivational explanations before positing a purely cognitive one, has never been in force.) For example, why might people take more responsibility for success than failure, in the standard self-serving attributional bias effect (e.g., Jones et al., 1972; Zuckerman, 1979)? The motivational explanation was that people want to believe good things about themselves, so they more readily accept success than failure as a true sign of their worth. But it is also possible to pose a purely cognitive explanation: Perhaps people expect success more than failure (because they succeed more often than they fail), and so failure violates their expectancies in a way that success does not. The violated expectancies cause them to engage in more cognitive processing after failure than success, and the intensified scrutiny will sometimes reveal reasons not to take the failure to heart. In that view, it has nothing to do with wanting to think well of oneself.

Again, the Information Processor has become more of a useful heuristic than something that most social psychologists seriously regard as a thorough, adequate image of the human individual. The facts that some cognitions are motivated, and that motivations can steer and alter the way information is processed, are widely accepted. During a conference debate the influential social psychologist Robert Zajonc once proposed that the image of the human mind as a small computer should be updated to assign more prominence to motivation and emotion, and he suggested the memorable image of a computer covered in barbecue sauce!

Although these new views of the Motivated Information Processor do allow some scope and influence to motivation, they continue to treat it as secondary. Motivation is seen as something that mainly interferes with cognitive processing or, at best, can occasionally focus cognitive processing on things that are important. Still, the Motivated Information Processor is one image of humankind that is still quite popular among researchers today.

The Foolish Mistake Maker

A priority in research and publication in early social psychology, greatly compounded by the Cognitive Revolution, created a variation of the Information Processor, redefining it as someone who processes information *badly*. The priority was that social psychologists searched for counterintuitive findings that went against what most people assumed and expected. Because research on social cognition that showed that people reached the right conclusion was often not very informative about the inner processes involved, a premium was placed on showing instances in which people came to false conclusions or made other errors. Collected together, these created an image of the human being as a Foolish Mistake Maker. (The first draft of this chapter used the label "the Cognitive Dumb-ass," but editorial feedback suggested that this may not be suitable for a professional graduate-level textbook.)

Journalism students learn about "Man Bites Dog" stories. The principle is that a dog biting a man is typical and therefore not newsworthy, but a man biting a dog is unusual and therefore worth reporting. Social psychology, especially in its early years when it struggled to gain respect, had a similar attitude. Showing that people do sensible things for readily understandable reasons was considered not very inspiring and hence not publishable. Showing that people do foolish, self-destructive, or irrational things, possibly for surprising, intuitively disturbing reasons, was a surer path to getting published. Teachers of social psychology have long advised students to seek findings that their grandmothers would not already know to be true.

Hence one important theme throughout the history of social psychology has been to characterize the thoughts and actions of ordinary persons as stupid, biased, and counterproductive. Exposing the dumb things people do has been a reliable path to publication and career advancement for many social psychologists. This approach sometimes produces a mentality comparable to that of so-called "gotcha" journalism, in which researchers design clever experimental procedures that expose their research participants as fools, suckers, and hypocrites. Still, it is important to know the mistakes people make in systematic, predictable ways for this often provides valuable insight, and it would be unfair to stigmatize the entire line of work based on some excesses and unfortunate tendencies.

For example, one well-established principle goes by the name of the Cognitive Miser (Taylor, 1981). The Cognitive Miser is perhaps one aspect of the Foolish Mistake Maker. The essence of being a Cognitive Miser is based on the hypothesis that because people do not like to exert mental effort, they do as little as possible. The lazy, short-cutting style of thought produces some errors. The opposite of the Cognitive Miser is the ruminating person, who thinks too much and too endlessly about something, especially something bad. The Foolish Mistake Maker sometimes thinks too much and sometimes too little, though many mistakes arise not from the amount but from the processes of thinking. Motivation, in particular, has long been regarded by cognitive social psychologists as introducing error into the thought processes, such as in wishful thinking.

The Foolish Mistake Maker remains alive and well as a popular image of humankind in social psychology. There is, we think, a general sense that that is not all that human beings are. There are even reasoned, thoughtful critiques suggesting that much of what is called error and bias should not be thus disparaged, partly because the same inner processes that produce the occasional well-documented errors in studies of social psychology also produce correct answers most of the time (Funder, 1995). But errors are made, and social psychologists thrive on spotting them.

The Nondifferent Individual, or the Situational Responder

During the first half of the twentieth century, as the field of psychology took shape as a standard academic discipline, social psychology was a small, marginally noticed field while personality psychology was a major powerhouse. The personality theorists, such as Freud, Jung, Adler, Erikson, and Maslow, developed grand theories that influenced thinkers from many disciplines. Social psychologists struggled to discover how to do experiments.

For a complicated mixture of reasons, there was a relative shift in power during the 1960s and 1970s, so that social psychology became a large, thriving field, while personality psychology lost much of its clout. The two fields also became closely aligned, as symbolized by the premier journal for both fields, the *Journal of Personality and Social Psychology*, which gradually became the largest journal that the American Psychological Association (APA) publishes. Hence for some time there was a considerable amount of friction and rivalry between personality and social psychologists. We are happy to report that this has diminished considerably, although it can still be glimpsed at times.

Personality came to focus ever more intensely on individual differences, which is to say the study of how people are different. During the periods of most intense friction between the two fields, many social psychologists became fond of downplaying individual differences and pointing to phenomena that suggested that such differences were essentially trivial or irrelevant to behavior. For example, some of the classic articles from this period of social psychology, including the bystander intervention studies and the Stanford prison simulation study, proudly noted that the researchers had tested extensively for individual differences but found none of these to produce any reliable effects.

The view that people are pretty much all the same can be termed the "Nondifferent Individual." The term was chosen to contrast it with the emphasis in personality psychology on individual differences. The underlying theory is that behavior is primarily a response to situations (hence the alternate title of "Situational Responder"). How people think, feel, and act is a direct result of situational pressures and influences. In contrast to the extensive inner depths of the self that some personality theories postulated, this view of humans states that there is not a great deal inside them, other than mechanisms to help them respond to their immediate situation.

Similar to the behaviorist view that refused to talk about mental states, the Nondifferent Individual theory was perhaps an intellectual exercise that made a methodological virtue out of not talking about certain things. Few behaviorists really believed that mental states were not real. In the same way, we suspect, the advocates of the Nondifferent Individual theory probably believed that people do have personality traits that differentiate them. They simply believed that these traits were not terribly important or influential. One of the guiding texts for this movement was Mischel's (1968) *Personality and Assessment*, which famously concluded that personality traits typically predict only about 10% of behavior. Social psychologists helpfully stepped into that apparent gap by suggesting that their research on situational causes could account for the other 90%.

These arguments were overstated, of course. If one trait predicts 10% of the variance, that does not leave 90% for situations. There could be other traits. In addition, there are measurement error and other sources of error variance, which can be considerable. Funder and Ozer (1983) showed that the typical effect size of a situation cause in some classic social psychology experiments was about the same as obtained with a trait measure. Likewise, a giant meta-analysis by Richard, Bond, and Stokes-Zoota (2003) found that the average effect size in experiments in social psychology was even a little smaller, around a fifth of a standard deviation, or 4% of the variance, which again is in the range of what traits predict. Today, most psychologists recognize that both personality traits and situational factors contribute important insights to predicting and understanding human behavior. Still, the Nondifferent Individual remains a popular figure in some styles of thought.

The Impression Manager

Related to the Nondifferent Individual is the idea that people simply try to present themselves to others in ways that make a good impression. As Impression Managers, people again do not have much personal depth (again in contrast to Freudian and many other personality theories) but simply have the inner processes that enable them to adapt to the situation.

The Impression Manager cares greatly about what others think, and so in that sense the theory has a strong motivational component. But other possible motivations were relegated to background status. The Impression Manager can be a chameleon, changing colors to suit the situation. In other versions of the theory, the person has a simple set of basic motivational drives and uses impression management as a means to attain these goals.

The Impression Manager does come equipped with a possibly extensive set of inner mechanisms for discerning what others prefer and for altering his or her own behavior accordingly. Self-presentational strategies and tactics are chosen according to what will work best.

The intellectual lineage of the Impression Manager stems from the writings of Goffman (e.g., 1959), a sociologist who analyzed human interactions as theatrical performances. The view of the self as an actor and role player was apt, because actors in a play say and do things by following a script rather than because they really believe them. An early and influential version in social psychology was put forward as an alternative to cognitive dissonance theory. Tedeschi, Schlenker, and Bonoma (1971) proposed that people do not really change their attitudes to resolve inconsistency—they merely claim to have changed their attitudes so as to appear consistent and thereby make a good impression on the experimenter. The lack of a genuine inner process (other than what was needed for managing the impression made) came to be a controversial but defining feature of the Impression Manager. The contrast with the Consistency Seeker was sharp and made for a lively controversy, because the Consistency Seeker had strong inner commitments to important attitudes, whereas the Impression Manager simply said what was expedient.

Clearly the view of the Impression Manager dovetailed well with that of the Nondifferent Individual, who simply responds to situational forces. In both, the person lacks strong inner values and commitments, other than the value of being accepted. These people simply adapt and respond to the immediate situation.

However, as a general model of human nature, the Impression Manager has largely gone out of fashion. That image too was perhaps more of an intellectual exercise. It is not clear if many social psychologists really believed that people went through life trying to make a good impression, without caring a great deal about the form that the good impression took. To be sure, people were often shown to be surprisingly malleable in response to situations, contrary to the early personality theories that saw each individual as having a powerful, well-defined inner self that strongly resisted change and was the overriding force in dictating behavior. There have even been arguments that people in general have changed across time: The American of the early twentieth century was guided by strong inner convictions, whereas by mid-century he or she was more inclined to go along with the crowd (e.g., Riesman, Glazer, & Denney, 1951).

Even the most ardent advocates of the self-presentation theory soon came to believe that there were powerful inner forces and processes at stake.

Rather than simply presenting yourself in whatever way made a good impression, people carefully selected their public behaviors so as to claim identities for themselves and establish themselves in others' minds the way they themselves wanted to be seen, or at best compromised between presenting themselves according to their own inner values and what the clear preferences of the audience were. Today social psychologists recognize the reality of impression management, but few really think that such processes provide anything close to a thorough account of the human individual and human social behavior. Impression management consists of helpful set of strategies and behaviors that accompany the extensive inner cognitive processes and serve its motivations.

The Naturally Selected Animal

A radically new type of person began to show up in theories of social psychology in the 1980s and has slowly become prominent and influential. The impetus was the influx of biological thinking, with special emphasis on evolutionary theory, as a way to explain social behavior. Prior to this, social psychologists explained that human behavior was the result of immediate situational factors and several types of longer-term influences. Those included socialization, such as media, school, and parental influences; Freudian processes, such as unconscious motivations and the results of childhood experiences; and reinforcement history. They all treated the newborn as largely a blank slate. The idea that people were born with certain innate behavioral tendencies was not widely respected. If anything, the idea of innate tendencies suggested explanations based on instinct, which were seen as old-fashioned and less scientific than explanations based on learning from experience.

The view of humans as Naturally Selected Animals therefore had to fight a long, slow battle to gain respect. However, by the turn of the twenty-first century it had become a, if not *the*, preferred explanation for many behaviors. To be sure, most social psychologists even in the 1950s probably believed in the theory of evolution, but they did not really think evolution had much relevance to social behavior. That is what changed. Many social psychologists today regard human beings as simply another species of animal, and as such they consider human social behavior to be the result of the same evolutionary forces that shaped behavior among all animals.

The Naturally Selected Animal is seen as basically similar to many other animals, although perhaps a bit more complicated in view of its high intelligence, invention of language, and mastery of technology. Still, the same basic principles apply. The Naturally Selected Animal wants to survive and reproduce. Crucially, many behavior patterns have become divorced from their overt connection to survival and reproduction but remain in place because they contributed to survival and reproduction in the past. For example, sexual desire is strong because over the centuries of natural selection, humans with considerable sexual desire were more likely to reproduce than humans who did not desire sex. Today, many people desire sex without reproduction, and in fact quite a few of them take extensive precautions to achieve this, although their patterns of desire are still shaped by what produced the best reproductive results in the past.

Purists among the evolutionary psychology camp insist that reproduction alone is the key to natural selection. Survival is at best a means to make reproduction possible. The emphasis on reproduction has called attention to many differences between men and women, because the contingencies that make for reproductive success are somewhat different for men than for women. Hence the Naturally Selected Animal theory could perhaps be elaborated by suggesting that the Naturally Selected Man and the Naturally Selected Woman are somewhat different versions, with different motivations and different behavioral tendencies.

Still, the Naturally Selected Animal theory offers more than an explanation for sexual behavior. It favors relatives over strangers, forms groups easily, and is interested in dominance (i.e., rising to the top of a group hierarchy). Social psychologists gradually came to realize that evolutionary theory could offer a basis for explaining the majority of human behavior, although proving that those explanations are more correct than other possible explanations is often difficult.

Advocates of the Naturally Selected Animal theory have often found themselves in conflict with social psychologists interested in culture and cultural differences. Although natural and cultural explanations are not necessarily incompatible, in practice thinkers have debated for decades whether particular patterns are innate or learned, and nature–nurture debates have been heated in social psychology too. In particular, the established practice in social psychology was to explain a great many things on the basis of socialization and learning from culture, so there were understandably some conflicts and arguments when a new generation sought to replace or augment those explanations with evolutionary ones.

In many cases, the argument is put in terms of the length of the leash. The assumption is that evolution shaped people to behave in certain ways but left a certain degree of flexibility for adapting to the social environment. Culture can influence behavior up to the length of the leash.

The Cultural Animal

The Cultural Animal view was developed as a synthesis and compromise among many other views, so it is less provocative than most. It was partly an attempt to accept the fundamental fact that the human psyche was shaped by evolution but also to recognize the importance of culture.

The core idea is that the human mind was created by nature, but culture is humankind's biological strategy. That is, nature selected in favor of traits that facilitated survival and reproduction. The human species used culture as its method of solving problems of survival and reproduction. Culture is basically a system that helps groups live together. It is learned behavior that is transmitted through the group (you do not have culture by yourself), and so the prominent features of human psychology are designed to help us participate in these group systems. Thus, crucially, the traits that set humans apart from other animals are based on adaptations to make human social life, including culture, possible.

For example, groups function best if people perform roles in an interlocking system, so humans have selves that can take on and juggle multiple roles. Groups need people to adjust to the rules and standards of the group, so humans are good at self-regulation. Morality is a set of rules created to overcome selfishness and benefit the group. Groups benefit from loyalty and stable relationships, so humans have a need to belong. Cultural groups require shared understandings, so people have empathy and theory of mind (i.e., the mental capacity to appreciate the inner states of others).

Thus, the cultural animal argument rejects the "leash" metaphor that was mentioned with the Naturally Selected Animal theory. The leash argument assumes that nature came first, laying the foundation for human behavior, and culture followed after the evolutionary process was done. Instead, the Cultural Animal argument suggests that *culture influenced evolution*. This does not require that specific cultural practices were produced by evolution, but rather that culture became part of the selection environment, so that traits favorable to culture evolved. For example, following the emergence of human language in the social environment, people who were better able to talk and understand speech became more successful at surviving and reproducing than people who lacked the biological capabilities to use language well.

In short, instead of natural evolution preceding culture, human biology and culture coevolved. This was argued first and persuasively by Boyd and Richerson (1985; Richerson & Boyd, 2005). A very different path led me to arrive at a similar conclusion: I read the social psychology literature and sought to determine which image of the human being best fit the accumulated work of all the people in the field. My conclusion was that the human psyche seemed very well designed, in both cognition and motivation, to participate in complex, information-based social groups, namely culture (Baumeister, 2005).

The other difference between the Cultural Animal view and the Naturally Selected Animal view is one of emphasis. The Naturally Selected Animal explanations focus on how humans are similar to other animals. The Cultural Animal focuses more on how people are different from other animals. Human social life does bear some resemblance to the social lives of other animals, but it also has remarkably unique features, and these can perhaps be understood by considering that evolution favored traits that enabled people to construct this new type of social life.

The importance of culture as a product of human collective efforts is central to both the Cultural Animal and the Terror Manager ideas. The difference is that the Terror Manager is concerned with avoiding the thought of death or mortality, because that idea is what causes the terror that is central to the theory. For the Cultural Animal, a main function of culture is to prevent actual death (not just the idea of it). Culture is the way humans solve the basic natural problems of survival and reproduction.

The Group Member

The study of group processes has a long history in social psychology. Newcomers to the field sometimes think that social psychology is mostly about the study of groups. In reality, however, the long history is one of being respected but politely ignored by much of the field. Social psychologists have preferred to focus on individual persons and even inner processes, thereby sometimes (and in our view unfortunately) overlooking important aspects of human behavior that are found in group processes.

Nevertheless, the study of groups has furnished its own image, or perhaps more precisely an assortment of related images, about the person. Rather than a single version, we will acknowledge several varieties of the image, which is perhaps appropriate for the study of groups. What these versions have in common is that the single person is seen as a member of the group.

The most prevalent theme of the Group Member involves some loss of individuality within the group. Multiple lines of work in social psychology have explored the consequences of immersing oneself in the group to varying degrees. Usually these consequences are seen as bad. The Group Member can become deindividuated, may engage in groupthink, and might even participate in mob violence. These negative effects reveal the group aspect of the Foolish Decision Maker. Or, to put it another way, groups of ordinary people become Foolish Decision Makers. (If they were foolish to start with, they become even more so.) Indeed, the assumption that people degenerate into inferior creatures by virtue of belonging to groups has crept into many other lines of research in social psychology, including social loafing, crowding, social facilitation, and diffusion of responsibility in bystander intervention.

The Group Member need not be a bad person, however. After all, interaction in groups is an almost inevitable part of human social life, especially if we include families as groups (which they most certainly are).

The motivations of the Group Members differ somewhat depending on which of two approaches is taken. One approach considers processes within the group. The Group Member must find ways to be accepted and liked by the other members, which often requires determining how the member is similar to them and can fit in with them (getting along). The Group Member must also seek to rise through the group hierarchy (getting ahead), which may require finding ways to stand out among the group. More recent characterizations of the Group Member involve the cognitive work that is involved in the various steps of entering the group, becoming socialized into full membership, finding a niche or rising through the ranks, exerting leadership, and exiting the group.

The other approach is to look at processes between groups. Intergroup processes have become a dominant focus of social psychology in Europe and Australia and have also been studied elsewhere. The emphasis is on how the individual identifies with the group and relates to members of other groups. The Group Member is thus committed and loyal to his or her group and is competitive with and often prejudiced or even hostile toward other groups.

One further variation on the Group Member might be the ethnically or culturally relative person. In recent years social psychology has paid increasing attention to cultural differences. The implicit view is that people are products of their cultural environment. Thus, this view emphasizes differences between people—not their individual differences, as in personality psychology (individual differences exist but are not seen as highly interesting or important), but their cultural differences.

Most social psychologists are quite convinced that racial, ethnic, and cultural differences have no genetic basis. Hence evidence of such differences poses an implicit challenge to the evolutionary views of people as basically the same. The Naturally Selected Animal and the culturally relative Group Member are not the best of friends in today's social psychology, although they do often manage to compromise.

The Benighted Layperson

One vision of humankind that has a long history in social psychology is that of the everyday person who thinks or does socially undesirable things. We refer to this as the Benighted Layperson. The not-so-hidden implication is that social psychologists need to teach this person how to be a better person, for the good of all.

The Benighted Layperson view has never been the dominant view in the field, partly because it requires consensus that the job of science is to instill social values into the general public, and many social psychologists balk at such an approach. Nonetheless, it is important to recognize that many social psychologists do view their work as a way of contributing to the betterment of society by finding ways to change people whom they regard as needing guidance from wise experts. In fairness, this view is probably more widespread in other social sciences than in psychology. In other fields, strong political views shape the research agenda of many scholars' work. And, also, in fairness, people almost certainly do have numerous faults and other unfortunate tendencies that could benefit from scientific wisdom. The debate is less whether the everyday person is already perfect in every respect than whether social psychologists have the right and/or responsibility to prescribe how people should change.

Which traits of the Benighted Layperson have gotten the most attention from social psychologists? The Benighted Layperson is someone who is prone to holding various prejudices, especially toward women and minorities. The Benighted Layperson is not environmentally friendly, tending instead to waste energy, to fail to recycle properly, to litter, and in other ways to contribute to the degradation of the natural environment. The Benighted Layperson is aggressive, unhelpful, and in other ways does not treat others properly. The Benighted Layperson also does things that are harmful to self, such as smoking and overeating. Some social psychologists view their work as providing insights into ways these people can change these undesirable behaviors.

About These Images

We have discussed some of the primary ways in which social psychologists have thought about the human being. You can spot most of them here and there in the remaining pages of this book. Before closing, we have a few additional remarks.

First, although we have been slightly whimsical about naming and characterizing these different images, we do on the whole respect the need to have some understanding about human nature. Social psychology studies people, and it is inevitable to maintain some assumptions about what those people are like. Social psychology reacted against the elaborated, detailed, systematic theories of the human being, such as those that flourished in personality psychology in the early twentieth century. But it is not really practical for an entire field to do research on people with no assumptions about their fundamental nature.

A second point is that there are some notable omissions from this list. In the 1950s, psychology was dominated by behaviorism and psychodynamic theory, which had quite different views of people; however social psychology never really embraced either of these in anything approximating a pure form. As we said, the elaborate Freudian model, complete with id and superego (not to mention castration anxiety, an Oedipus complex, and penis envy), was never strongly influential in social psychology, although some of Freud's ideas were adopted in the field.

Meanwhile, the behaviorist vision of the human being as an animal whose behavior is the result of conditioning processes—we might refer to this image of humankind as the Behavioristic Super-Rat—was tentatively adopted by some researchers but never really seemed adequate. From its early years in the 1950s, social psychology found it necessary to reject the reigning views, because they were not adequate to explain the phenomena social psychologists were studying. For example, cognitive dissonance and attributional processes did not fit into either the Freudian scheme or the Behavioristic Super-Rat. The behavioristic view of the mind as a "black box" that could not be scientifically studied and was therefore off limits to research simply could not work within a view of social psychology in which attitudes were important concepts. The Cognitive Revolution rendered it fully obsolete.

Last, this list is not exhaustive, and new views may emerge. Today many researchers focus on the brain and there may be a new view of the human being as a set of brain activities and their consequences. Other researchers focus on the active self who makes decisions, self-regulates, and so forth. This will provide an image of the human being as someone who does things. Perhaps in the next edition of this textbook, these will be treated as fully developed images!

References

Baumeister, R. F. (2005). *The cultural animal: Human nature, meaning, and social life.* New York: Oxford University Press.

Becker, E. (1973). *The denial of death.* New York: Academic Press.

Boyd, R., & Richerson, P. J. (1985). *Culture and the evolutionary process.* Chicago, IL: University of Chicago Press.

Cacioppo, J. T. (2007: September). Psychology is a hub science. *APS Observer, 20,* 1–3.

Funder, D. C. (1995). On the accuracy of personality judgment A realistic approach. *Psychological Review, 102,* 652–670.

Funder, D. C., & Ozer, D. J. (1983). Behavior as a function of the situation. *Journal of Personality and Social Psychology, 44,* 107–112.

Heider, F. (1958). *The psychology of interpersonal relations*. New York: Wiley.

Jones, E. E., Kanouse, D. E., Kelley, H. H., Nisbett, R. E., Valins, S., & Weiner, B. (1972). *Attribution: Perceiving the causes of behavior*. Morristown, NJ: General Learning Press.

Mischel, W. (1968). *Personality and assessment*. New York: Wiley.

Pyszczynski, T., Greenberg, J., & Solomon, S. (1997). Why do we need what we need? A terror management perspective on the roots of human social motivation. *Psychological Inquiry, 8*, 1–20.

Richard, F. D., Bond, C. F., & Stokes-Zota, J. J. (2003). One hundred years of social psychology quantitatively described. *Review of General Psychology, 7*, 331–363.

Richerson, P. J., & Boyd, R. (2005). *Not by genes alone: How culture transformed human evolution*. Chicago, IL: University of Chicago Press.

Riesman, D., Glazer, N., & Denney, R. (1951). *The lonely crowd: A study of the changing American character*. New Haven, CT: Yale University Press.

Swann, W. B. (1985). The self as architect of social reality. In B. R. Schlenker (Ed.), *The self and social life* (pp. 100–125). New York: McGraw-Hill.

Taylor, S. E. (1981). The interface of cognitive and social psychology. In J. H. Harvey (Ed.), *Cognition, social behavior, and the environment*. Hillsdale, NJ: Lawrence Erlbaum Associates.

Tedeschi, J. T., Schlenker, B. R., & Bonoma, T. V. (1971). Cognitive dissonance: Private ratiocination or public spectacle? *American Psychologist, 26*, 685–695.

Zuckerman, M. (1979). Attribution of success and failure revisited, or: The motivational bias is alive and well in attribution theory. *Journal of Personality, 47*, 245–287.

Chapter 2

How We Got Here from There: A Brief History of Social Psychology

Harry T. Reis

> She that from whom
> We all were sea-swallow'd, though some cast again
> (And by that destiny) to perform an act
> Whereof what's past is prologue; what to come,
> In yours and my discharge.
>
> —*William Shakespeare, The Tempest*

One of the first lessons I learned teaching introductory Social Psychology was never start with history. History, I quickly realized, is more compelling to those who have lived with its consequences than those who are approaching the field for the first time. In other words, it is easier to appreciate the role of history in shaping a field when we know and appreciate its dominant traditions and themes than when we have no general sense of what the field is about. In writing this chapter for an advanced social psychology textbook I hope that the reader already has some reasonable idea of what social psychology is (perhaps from an introductory course). My further hope is that the reader has some longer-term interest in social psychology. That way, the reader can take advantage of the goals of this chapter: to reveal how our past is prologue to the field's current character and at the same time to help set the stage for where the next generation of young social psychologists will take it.

Social psychologists sometimes find ideas in the field's history (see, for example, Jones, 1985). Contemporary trends, both in science and in the culture at large, are also influential. The social and political zeitgeist has often inspired the field's research and theory, as is evident in the emergence of broad themes in our history: individualism in the early part of the twentieth century; group influence and obedience in the aftermath of World War II; and social inequality, stereotyping, and prejudice in the 1960s and 1970s. Moreover, social psychologists are opportunistic, fast to take advantage of new scientific approaches and tools, as seen, for example, in the rise of cognitive perspectives in the 1970s and biological approaches at the beginning of the twenty-first century. In these and other instances, the field's deep-seated interest in understanding fundamental principles of human social behavior was galvanized by emerging theoretical perspectives, new methodologies, or dramatic events (e.g., the 1964 murder of Kitty Genovese, which spawned research on bystander intervention; Latané & Darley, 1970), and sometimes all three. It is impossible, in other words, to separate historical trends in social psychology from parallel developments in science and culture.

This tendency of social psychological research to be linked to the cultural, political, and scientific zeitgeist has led, in the eyes of some commentators (e.g., Gergen, 1973, 2001), to the claim that social psychology is faddish and noncumulative, in the sense that certain topics or approaches become fashionable and active for a time and then dissipate, not so much because a comprehensive, accurate, and well-documented understanding has been achieved but rather because researchers simply tire of the subject. That interest in one or another research topic waxes and wanes seems indisputable. As Jones (1998) wrote,

> Many social psychologists feel that their field is uniquely or especially vulnerable to faddism. . . . Surely there are bandwagons upon which graduate students and more established scholars climb in all research fields. However, it may be that such labels as "fad" or "fashion" are more easily applied to the social sciences than to the natural sciences because developments in the social sciences tend to be less cumulative and each research concern is therefore more limited by time. In any event, any student of social psychology knows that particular theories or methods or paradigms gain favor, dominate segments of the literature for a period of time, and then recede from view. (p. 9)

Jones went on to describe several factors to which he attributed this waxing and waning. Among the former are the timely interests of innovating researchers, the explanatory power and potential for novel findings provided by new theories or tools, the leadership of prestigious researchers, and (as seems even more true today than in Jones's era) funding priorities. Factors responsible for the waning of research interests include progress in understanding a phenomenon, so that remaining questions provide incrementally smaller yields and are therefore less attractive to young scholars; theoretical or empirical "dead ends" (i.e., once-promising ideas or findings turn out to be mundane, untenable, or artifactual); and what might be called "benign neglect"—diminished interest in the familiar (see Arkin, 2009, for a relevant collection).

If research interests wax and wane, what is the purpose of studying the history of social psychology? Several reasons stand out. First, although trends exist, certain topics do endure. For example, few researchers today study the authoritarian personality, the risky shift, or ingratiation, but bias in perceiving others, persuasion, and social self-regulation have remained persistently popular for more than a half-century. Better appreciation of why research and theory on certain topics continue to evolve while others fade away may provide signposts for researchers considering what to study and how to study it. Also, highlighting broad themes and trends in social-psychological research is a useful way of identifying social psychology's contribution to knowledge relative to other sciences and disciplines (Hinde, 1997).

Second, knowledge in any discipline grows both horizontally and vertically. That is, some advances occur when researchers build on earlier work, whereas other advances arise from entirely new directions (McGuire, 1973). Building, or what Mischel (2006) called becoming a more cumulative science, depends on knowing the history of a phenomenon or theory; new findings deepen, elaborate, or add complexity to what is already known. Discovering new directions also benefits from an awareness of history, because a direction is new only if it can be distinguished from what came before.

Third, in social psychology, unlike many more technical fields, new scholars begin with "entry biases"—preconceived notions, based on "a lifetime of experience in observing and hypothesizing about human behavior" (Cacioppo, 2004, p. 115), grounded in common sense, intuition, and personal theories. Formal theorizing is one method to minimize the harmful effects of these biases, while capitalizing on whatever novel insights they might suggest (Cacioppo, 2004; McGuire, 1997). A good sense of the field's history is also helpful.

For these reasons, this chapter subscribes to a remark widely attributed to Winston Churchill: "(t)he farther backward you look, the farther forward you are likely to see." I propose that future research is likely to be better informed if planned with an awareness of what came before, and is also more likely to fill a useful niche within the broad network of theories that define social psychology. Research conducted without such awareness is more likely to provide isolated results, with ambiguous or even inconsistent links to other principles and theories.

An historical perspective is also conducive to interdisciplinary research, or what Van Lange (2006) described as building bridges between social psychology and other disciplines. Social psychologists have not always capitalized on links to other disciplines, and scholars in other disciplines are sometimes unaware of social-psychological research that bears directly on their interests. If transdisciplinary research is the future of science, as most science administrators believe it is, then the long-term outlook for social psychology depends on our ability to make such bridges explicit and generative. Many such bridges already exist, as Van Lange (2006) illustrates. Awareness of historical trends in theories and research may help illuminate how and why some bridges went nowhere while others opened new territory.

This chapter is organized around six historical periods, catalogued imprecisely according to major research trends that defined the era and distinguished it from preceding periods. These developments reflect far more research and many more contributors than can be mentioned in a brief chapter such as this. For that reason, I emphasize contributions that played pivotal roles in the evolution of social-psychological research and theory. Readers interested in more detailed accounts will find Allport (1954), Goethals (2003), Jahoda (2007), Jones (1985), and Ross, Ward, and Lepper (2010) particularly informative.

Classical Roots

1908 is often listed as the beginning of social psychology because the first two textbooks bearing that name, one by the psychologist William McDougall and the other by the sociologist Edward Alsworth Ross, appeared in that year. This designation is misleading. McDougall and Ross had direct intellectual predecessors in the eighteenth and nineteenth centuries, and their writing featured concepts similar in scope, ideology, and method. Moreover, if social psychology is defined as "an attempt to understand and explain how the thought, feeling, and behavior of individuals are influenced by the actual, imagined, or implied presence of other human beings" (Allport, 1954, p. 5), then it is no overstatement to say that social psychological theorizing dates back to at least the origins of recorded history. This is because members of the species *Homo sapiens* have tried to articulate systematic principles for understanding, predicting, and controlling the ways in which people influence one another at least since cognitive evolution gave us the capacities for self-awareness, symbolic thought, and theory of mind.

For example, one of the oldest known legal codes, the ancient Babylonian Codex Hammurabi (ca. 1760 BCE), contains 282 laws defining properties of interdependence for living in social groups, how responsibilities and rights are linked to social positions, rules for distributive and procedural justice, and attributions for misdeeds. The principle of "an eye for an eye" (known today as the norm of reciprocity) first appears here. The Sanskrit *Bhagavad Gita*, considered the sacred scripture of Hinduism, offers numerous allegorical teachings describing the association between motivation and action, the self, and social and divine influence. In the sixth century, Benedict of Nursia, the founder of western Christian monasticism, compiled 73 "rules" describing how a monastery ought to be run and how a spiritual life ought to be lived. This Rule of Benedict includes many social-psychological ideas, for example, about regulating individual responsibility and interdependence in the monks' activities. Innumerable social psychological principles can be found in the Judeo-Christian Bible, encompassing issues of free will, prosocial and antisocial behavior, self-centered and other-centered motives, the self in relation to others, causal attributions, the nature of human needs and motives (and how to deal with them in social living), forgiveness and guilt, self-regulation, social cognition, and justice motives. Several social-psychological effects are even named after Biblical passages (e.g., the Good Samaritan experiment).

Some have argued that Aristotle was the first social psychologist (e.g., Taylor, 1998). Aristotle maintained that because humans are inherently social, it is necessary to understand how the social environment affects the individual. This general principle led him to numerous specific ideas, such as the role of goals in construing situations, rationality in social judgment and action, and reciprocity of affection as a basis for love and friendship. Nevertheless, Aristotle's predecessors Plato and Socrates also established important wellsprings for the waters of later social-psychological thinking. For example, Plato described the utilitarian functions of groups, introducing constructs later to reemerge as the social contract, the group mind, obedience, conformity, social facilitation, and social loafing. Plato's *Symposium* provides a seminal description of the varieties of love. As for Socrates, the conflict between Socratic rationality and Sophist rhetoric might be considered the first dual process model of persuasion. In short, it seems safe to conclude that there are ample examples of social-psychological theorizing, in character if not in name, throughout antiquity to the present day.

There is little doubt that the social philosophers and early scientists of the Age of Enlightenment played a significant role in setting the stage for modern social psychology (Jahoda, 2007). Many ideas introduced during this period (broadly construed here to start in the latter part of the seventeenth century and end early in the nineteenth century) were instrumental in the later appearance of social-psychological thinking during the latter half of the nineteenth century. Particularly influential examples include the following:

- John Locke's insistence on observation as the basis of both personal and scientific knowledge;
- Rene Descartes' ideas about cognition and the mind/body problem;
- Jeremy Bentham's *hedonic calculus*, which argued that humans act to obtain pleasure and avoid pain;
- Jean Jacques Rousseau's social contract, which explained how people cede certain rights to authorities in order to maintain well-functioning groups;
- Thomas Hobbes's account of power seeking as a basic human motive;
- Georg Hegel's account of the social (group) mind as an entity unto itself, which subsumes individual minds;
- David Hume's attention to reason, as well as his suggestion that sympathy for others provides a foundation for social relations;
- Immanuel Kant's *Critique of Pure Reason*, which suggested that the properties of objects and the way that humans perceive those objects were not one and the same;
- Adam Smith, whose *Wealth of Nations* celebrated self-interest as a moral good, and who proposed a theory of sympathy, in which the act of observing others fosters awareness of one's own behavior and moral motives; and
- Charles Darwin, whose theory of evolution is above all else an account of the role of social relations in reproduction and survival.

None of these scholars used the term social psychology, but their influence on what came later is clear. Insofar as they promulgated principles for a systematic understanding of how individuals function within social groups and society, some even using scientific methods in that quest, they sowed the intellectual seeds that flowered into modern social psychology.

The Emergence of a Field: 1850–1930

As previously explained, assigning a start date to social psychology is an ambiguous enterprise. One reasonable line of demarcation is the first appearance of the term social psychology to identify a field of inquiry. Jahoda (2007) credits an obscure Italian philosopher, Carlo Cattaneo, with coining the term *psicologia sociale* in 1864, to describe the psychology of "associated minds"—how new ideas emerge from the interaction of individual minds. A more influential early user of the term was Gustav Lindner, an Austrian/Czech psychologist whose 1871 textbook discussed at length many matters of "deriving from the mutual effects . . . of individuals in society the phenomena and laws of social life" (Jahoda, 2007, p. 59). Lindner's book included a section entitled "Fundamentals of Social Psychology," and because the book was widely read, it is more likely to be the source of what followed than Cattaneo's article.

Wilhelm Wundt was a substantial intellectual force in the early development of the field. Wundt's 10-volume *Völkerpsychologie* (often loosely translated into English as social psychology, a translation to which Wundt objected because the term "social" at that time connoted culture, whereas Wundt had a more comprehensive intent; Greenwood, 2004), published between 1900 and 1920, was a tour de force of ideas about "those mental products which are created by a community of human life and are, therefore, inexplicable in terms merely of individual consciousness since they presuppose the reciprocal action of many" (Wundt, 1916, p. 2). Wundt is widely considered to be the father of modern experimental psychology, but perhaps curiously, he felt that the experimental approach was not conducive to his *Völkerpsychologie*, which may help explain why Wundtian concepts have not endured in contemporary experimental social psychology. Nevertheless, because Wundt's laboratory in Leipzig was one of the most influential hubs in early psychology, and because Wundt himself was not to be ignored, his writings undoubtedly popularized the study of the individual within group contexts.

Another early landmark was the first social-psychological laboratory experiment, conducted by Norman Triplett at Indiana University in 1897. Stimulated by his observation that bicycle racers rode faster when paced by another rider, Triplett reported results from a study of 40 children asked to wind silk cord onto fishing reels, alternately doing so alone and together (Triplett, 1898). Others picked up on Triplett's use of experimentation to study social-psychological questions, but the experimental method did not become popular until the 1920s, when it was championed by Floyd Allport at Syracuse University. (Indeed, experimentation did not become the predominant method of research in social psychology until the 1950s and 1960s, following Kurt Lewin's influence; McMartin & Winston, 2000.) Allport made two important contributions to the early development of social psychology. The first, already noted, was his conviction that controlled laboratory experimentation would provide the necessary rigor for advancing (social) psychology as a science. The second was his insistence that group phenomena had to be studied in individualist terms:

> There is no psychology of groups which is not essentially and entirely a psychology of individuals. Social psychology . . . *is a part of the psychology*

> *of the individual*, whose behavior it studies in relation to that sector of his environment composed by his fellows. (Allport, 1924, p. 4; italics in the original)

To the extent that social psychology in the 1980s was "largely a North American phenomenon," as E. E. Jones (1985, p. 47) asserted, it was because of Allport's legacy.

Allport's 1924 textbook more nearly resembles contemporary social psychology than its two predecessors, both published in 1908, which are commonly cited as the field's inaugural textbooks. Partly for this reason, Jahoda (2007) considers 1908 to be the end of social psychology's earlier era, rather than the beginning of its new one (notwithstanding the impact of these two textbooks in putting the term *social psychology* on the scholarly map). One of these books, written by the sociologist Edward Alsworth Ross, defined social psychology as concerned with "uniformities due to *social* causes, i.e., to *mental contacts* or *mental interactions* . . . It is *social* only insofar as it arises out of the interplay of minds" (1908, p. 3; italics in the original). What Ross called "uniformities" attributable to the "conditions of life"—features of the environment not subject to mental interplay between persons, such as the physical setting, visual cues, culture, or race—were explicitly excluded. Ross had been notably influenced by earlier sociologists such as Gustave Le Bon and Gabriel Tarde, who popularized concepts such as crowd psychology and the group mind, using suggestion and imitation as mechanisms. Ross sought to explain social influence and control and thus may be considered a bridge between early sociologists and later group-process researchers.

The other inaugural volume, by William McDougall, was somewhat less explicit, charging social psychology with the task of showing "how, given the native propensities and capacities of the individual human mind, all the complex mental life of societies is shaped by them and in turn reacts upon the course of their development and operation in the individual" (1908, p. 18). McDougall emphasized the individual, having been influenced by Darwin. He attributed a prominent role to instincts, which he believed underlie human sociality and more complex forms of social organization. In this emphasis, McDougall faced considerable opposition from the then-emerging followers of behaviorism.

Two additional trends during this period played significant roles in social psychology, although these would not be evident until later. The first, psychoanalytic theory was not particularly influential in early social psychology (with the possible exception of instincts; G. Allport, 1954). Nonetheless, constructs introduced by Sigmund Freud, Carl Jung, Alfred Adler, Karen Horney, and other psychoanalytically oriented psychologists are relevant to modern social psychology, not necessarily in their original forms but rather as contemporaneously reconceptualized. For example, ideas such as motivation outside of awareness, chronic accessibility, subliminal perception, the effects of ego defense on self-regulation, repression, the functional basis of attitudes, the importance of early-life relationships with caregivers, relational conceptions of self, terror management, transference, compensatory behaviors associated with low self-esteem, and the ideal self can all be traced, at least in rudimentary form, to psychoanalytic writings. (See, for example, the December 1994, special issue of the *Journal of Personality* on social cognition and psychoanalysis.) Speculation on the reasons why these concepts took hold in social psychology only after the passage of time go beyond the goals of this chapter. One likely factor is the way in which psychoanalytic observations have been recast into processes and mechanisms that are more amenable to modern psychological theories and methods (e.g., Erdelyi, 1990).

A second development that later bore fruit is the work of William James. James, ever the philosopher-psychologist, had a long and productive career at Harvard University, beginning in 1873 and ending with his death in 1910. James's influence is not particularly visible during this early period of social psychology. Nonetheless, his ideas became important later, when topics such as the self, emotion, and theory of mind became central to the discipline. In particular, James first proposed the "motivated tactician" model of social cognition—that thinking is for doing (Fiske, 1992)—and that the self could vary in response to social context (an idea elaborated by James Mark Baldwin and George Herbert Mead). In some senses, it is striking testimony to James's vision and generativity that although his work was somewhat tangential to social psychology during his time, the field eventually came to him.

To summarize, during the period from 1850 to 1930, social psychology was transformed from a relatively informal conglomeration of ideas about the association of individuals to the groups and societies in which they lived to a viable, self-identified discipline. One sign that the field had come of age was the decision by Morton Prince, then editor of the *Journal of Abnormal Psychology*, to rename that journal as *The Journal of Abnormal Psychology and Social Psychology*, designating Floyd Allport as a co-editor. Their editorial statement nicely summarizes the field's progress:

> At its inception, less than two decades ago, social psychology was variously defined according to different opinions as to its subject matter. The following classes of data were among those stressed in the various definitions: crowd action, the social bases of human nature, the psychological aspects of social formations and movements, and "planes and currents" of thought and action which arise by virtue of the

> association of human beings. Through the enterprise of the pioneers these formulations, supplemented by many incidental contributions from others, have grown into a science having as its field a unique set of natural phenomena, and a wide range of practical application. A distinct method also is emerging, though progress here is necessarily slow owing to the large scale and the intangibility of much of the data. Interest in the subject is rapidly growing, and there are many courses given in it in colleges throughout the country. . . . In view therefore both of the present need of an organ for social psychology and of the mutually helpful contacts between that science and abnormal psychology, The Journal is pleased to announce the extension of its scope to include the former, and cordially invites those who are interested in the advancement of social psychology to join the ranks of its readers and contributors. (Prince & Allport, 1921, pp. 1–5)

Maturation and Migration: 1930–1945

By 1930, social psychology had established itself as an important psychological subdiscipline. As the 1930s began, American social psychology was dominated by the F. Allport-inspired individualist emphasis, whereas European social psychology still reflected earlier notions of a group mind (Franzoi, 2007). All this was to change shortly, for both intellectual and geopolitical reasons.

Notable landmarks in American social psychology in the 1930s included the following: (1) the frustration–aggression hypothesis (Dollard, Doob, Miller, Mowrer, & Sears, 1939), which, derived from stimulus–response concepts, remains social psychology's primary legacy from the behaviorist tradition, along with the later-appearing Social Learning Theory (Bandura & Walters, 1963); (2) interest in the structure and function of attitude, following the growing importance of public opinion research in American society, G. Allport's (1935) seminal chapter in the *Handbook of Social Psychology*, Newcomb's (1943) longitudinal study of attitude change among Bennington College students (conducted between 1935 to 1939), and LaPiere's (1934) classic study demonstrating noncorrespondence between attitudes and action toward outgroup members; (3) Katz and Braley's (1933) study of ethnic stereotypes among Princeton University students, which opened the door to the lasting interest in prejudice and stereotyping in social psychology; and (4) Mead's (1934) theorizing about the role of internalized social experience in the self. It also seems appropriate to cite Henry Murray's (1938) personality theory. Primarily a personality theorist, Murray presaged much of what was to follow by proposing that both situations (press) and dispositions (needs) influenced behavior. By allowing for the existence of numerous needs, in contrast to the more structured conceptions of earlier models, Murray's flexible approach became popular among social psychologists who wanted to study how one or another predisposition (broadly construed to include needs, goals, and motives) affected behavior in social situations.

Significant as these advances were, they pale in comparison to other developments, born in Europe but coming of age in America. Kurt Lewin was a German social psychologist who emigrated to the United States in 1933. Steeped in the Gestalt tradition, Lewin sought to extend its perceptual and cognitive focus to social psychology, particularly to questions about motivation, action, and interaction. Lewin formulated Field Theory (1951)[1] with the intent of describing the social environment in terms of relations between individuals who "'locomoted' through a field of bounded 'regions' impelled by 'forces' or drawn by 'valences' along power 'vectors'" (Jones, 1985, p. 21). These forces were both interpersonal and intrapersonal, leading Lewin to propose that behavior was a function of the person and the environment, represented in his now-famous dictum, $B = f(P, E)$. Even if this dictum is often misconstrued—Lewin did not intend P and E to be separable, additive factors, but rather "*one* constellation of interdependent factors" (1951, p. 240; italics in the original; see Reis, 2008, for further discussion)—it set the stage for examining social behavior in terms of motivational dynamics arising both within and outside the person. In this sense, Lewin's approach may be seen as a hybrid of the American-individualist and European-group mind traditions that were popular at the time. Lewin's goal plainly was to develop a set of quantifiable constructs, using the mathematics of topology, that could be used to formally test propositions about human social relations. Despite the fact that he was not successful in this regard, Lewin's general approach turned out to be extraordinarily influential.

Lewin's lasting influence on social psychology went well beyond his theoretical vision. In 1945, he founded the Research Center for Group Dynamics (RCGD) at the Massachusetts Institute of Technology. Although Lewin died prematurely just 2 years later (in the midst of the RCGD's move to the University of Michigan), the group of social psychologists who worked or trained there under Lewin's far-sighted and inspiring spell were central players in the field's rapid postwar expansion. These included Leon Festinger, Stanley Schachter, Kurt Back, Morton Deutsch, Dorwin Cartwright, Murray Horwitz, Albert Pepitone, John French, Ronald Lippitt, Alvin Zander, John Thibaut, and Harold Kelley. Almost all current social psychologists will find one or more of these figures in their scholarly genogram.

Another enduring impact was Lewin's resolute belief in the value of applied research. In 1943, he asserted that "there is nothing so practical as a good theory"

(Lewin, 1951, p. 169) and he backed this up with the conviction that social psychologists should test their theories in applied settings. Lewin was known for conducting bold "action-oriented" experiments in field settings (for example, his studies during World War II using group pressure to induce American housewives to prepare family meals with more plentiful organ meats, because better quality meat was being used for the troops; Lewin, 1943). Lewin was instrumental in founding the Society for the Psychological Study of Social Issues, in 1936, an organization that continues to be a hub for social psychologists committed to social action.

Lewin's decision to emigrate to the United States, then, turns out to be one of the most important milestones in the history of social psychology. Many other significant European scholars also emigrated to the United States in that era, including Muzafer Sherif (whose pioneering work on social norm development led to Asch's conformity experiments) and Fritz Heider, which led Cartwright (1979) to name Adolph Hitler as the person who most influenced the development of social psychology. World War II had a further influence on the field's progress in that many leading researchers of that or the next generation worked for U.S. government research agencies involved in the war effort, including Lewin himself, Rensis Likert (who advanced survey research methods for the Department of Agriculture), Samuel Stouffer (whose Army experience led directly to the concept of relative deprivation), Murray (who conducted personality assessments for the Office of Special Services), and Carl Hovland (whose evaluations of military training films for the Army led to the Yale tradition of persuasion research). Thus, the impact of the zeitgeist on the development of social psychology is not solely a matter of suggesting research topics; it also involves the movement and activities of the people who do social psychology.

Full Steam Ahead!: 1946–1969

The post-World War II era was a heady time for social psychology. The field was expanding rapidly, fueled by the growth of universities and research. The G.I. Bill, which funded undergraduate and graduate education for soldiers returning from the war effort, created an immediate need for faculty and facilities. Research funding also increased exponentially, particularly in psychology, reflecting greater government investment in science and the mental health needs of returning veterans and others affected by the war. Opportunities were therefore great for the European emigrees and young American social psychologists alike. Social psychology was a relatively new science whose potential resonated with the national mood, and universities were quick to add programs and positions. It was not uncommon in the early postwar era for positions to be offered on the basis of a telephone conversation. Tenure could be achieved in a year or two, and research grants were plentiful.

All these opportunities fed on the ideas and enthusiasms of social psychologists, especially young social psychologists, and it is no overstatement to conclude that their accomplishments largely fulfilled their expectations. The theoretical and empirical achievements of this period were considerable. Researchers expanded on the grand theories of prior periods, adding and fleshing out theoretical models, extending the field's reach to new phenomena, and building an empirical knowledge base to support theory. The laboratory experiment entered its golden age, as researchers found ways to manipulate complex concepts in clever, well-controlled, and highly involving scenarios [e.g., Asch's (1956) conformity experiments or Latané and Darley's (1970) bystander intervention experiments]. It was a good time to be a social psychologist.

Early in this interval, the dominant theme was group dynamics, reflecting the influence of Lewin's students and contemporaries, who fanned out across the country following his death. Much of this research used field-theory concepts and language, although this was usually more an approach than a set of theory-derived propositions. The Lewinian tradition was plainly evident in graduate curricula, embodied in a popular textbook of readings, *Group Dynamics: Theory and Research* (Cartwright & Zander, 1953, 1960, 1968). Among the more influential programs of group-dynamics research among Lewin's disciples were Festinger's (1950) Theory of Informal Social Communication, which identified and described three sources of communication ("pressures toward uniformity") within groups (to establish social reality through consensus, to move toward a goal, and to express emotional states), and Deutsch's (1949) studies of cooperation and competition. Another example (albeit one that did not directly use field-theory terminology and concepts) was Thibaut and Kelley's Interdependence Theory (1959; Kelley & Thibaut, 1978), which provided an elegant theoretical model for explaining how interdependence with respect to outcomes influences individuals' behavior.

By no means was the study of group processes limited to the Lewinians, however. Solomon Asch (1956) was busily conducting experiments on conformity. Asch had been struck by Sherif's (1936) experiments showing the effects of social influence when subjects were confronted with ambiguous stimuli. Asch removed the ambiguity, by asking naive subjects to judge which line among a set of lines was longest. Despite the fact that the correct answer was plainly apparent, confederates would give the wrong response, creating a dilemma for subjects: accept the group consensus or go it alone. Asch's work is often cited for showing "blind conformity," but this is a substantial misconstrual of his approach. Asch believed that disagreement in a group of one's peers, each of whom has as much legitimacy as oneself in making a perceptual judgment, required considering the possibility that one's own judgment might somehow be erroneous: "Not to take it [the group] into account, not to allow one's self to be in any way affected by it, would be willful" (Asch, 1952, p. 484). This important point led to a distinction between private acceptance (informational conformity) and public compliance (normative conformity) as bases for conformity, which was to fuel subsequent research and theory (Deutsch & Gerard, 1955). Research identifying situational and dispositional bases for nonconformity also became important during this period (e.g., Allen, 1975).

Nevertheless, by the mid-1960s, social psychologists were losing interest in group process research (Wittenbaum & Moreland, 2008). In part, this waning may have reflected the emphasis in American social psychology on the individual. European social psychology had been decimated by the war's destruction and the emigration of many important scholars to America. Much of the group research being conducted moved away from studies of within-group processes and instead focused in a much more conceptually limited way on how groups influence the individual, a topic that acquired the label "social influence." For example, research on the "risky shift"—the tendency of individuals to take more risks in group decisions than when deciding alone (Wallach, Kogan & Bem, 1962)—was popular for a time.

Another example was Stanley Milgram's obedience studies (1963, 1965). Arguably, nothing has defined social psychology more sharply in the public mind, for better and for worse, than Milgram's research. Milgram's thinking derived from his penetrating synthesis of the group process and social influence studies that preceded him as well as from his personal observations about the Holocaust (Milgram, 1974). In a series of dramatic experiments that remain controversial to this day (Berger, 2009), Milgram demonstrated how, under certain circumstances, ordinary adults could be induced to deliver lethal electric shocks. Identifying those circumstances, as well as the dispositional factors that interacted with them, became the centerpiece of his research and the research of others. In contrast, public and scholarly attention outside the field largely ignored these moderators, focusing instead on the striking, and to some, morally repugnant, behaviors that Milgram's paradigm had elicited.

Social influence processes were pivotal in other phenomena that became central to the field in the late 1950s and 1960s. For example, at Yale University, Carl Hovland and his colleagues and students began the Yale Communication and Attitude Change Program, which blended Hovland's experience with propaganda during World War II, Hullian learning theory, and group dynamics. The basic premise of the Yale approach to persuasion was to ask, in a somewhat mechanistic way, "Who said what to whom?" This led to numerous studies investigating the factors that predict attitude change, many of which are still cited and applied today. Festinger's interests evolved in a similarly individual-centered direction, as reflected in his Social Comparison Theory (Festinger, 1954). Social Comparison Theory argued that people evaluate their abilities and opinions by considering social reality, which they establish by comparing themselves to similar others. In this theory, we can clearly see the field's move from one concerned with group dynamics to one examining the influence of others on the individual.

Social psychology's bandwidth was also widening during this expansionary era. Social psychological theorizing and methods were being applied to an ever-increasing range of phenomena. Person perception became a major topic, following two important developments: (1) Asch's (1946) work on trait-based impressions, in which he showed that a list of traits such as industrious, skillful, and practical would lead to a very different overall impression if paired with the adjective "warm" than if paired with the adjective "cold;" and (2) the then-innovative "New Look" in perception, which proposed that the act of perception was influenced by motives and expectancies. These models fostered growing interest in understanding the relative contribution of perceivers and percepts in the act of person perception, including enduring questions about bias. Hastorf and Cantril's (1954) classic "They Saw a Game," in which Princeton and Dartmouth students provided strikingly different accounts of rough play in a football game between their two schools, dramatically illustrated principles being studied in several laboratories (Bruner & Tagiuri, 1954). Another, although very different, influence was Cronbach's (1955) seminal critique of simple trait ratings, in which he demonstrated that a single response was actually composed of several distinct components. The complexities that he introduced to the study of accuracy in person perception remain vital (albeit often ignored) today (Funder, 1987; Kenny, 1994).

In 1957, Festinger introduced the Theory of Cognitive Dissonance, which some believe to be the single most influential theory in the history of social psychology (Cooper, 2007). The basic premise of this theory exemplified Festinger's talent for simple yet elegant and generative theorizing: When two cognitions do not fit together, there is pressure to make them fit, which can be resolved through various cognitive or behavioral changes. In its emphasis on cognitive consistency, dissonance theory was not unlike other models popular at the time (e.g., balance theory; see Abelson, Aronson, McGuire, Newcomb, Rosenberg, & Tannenbaum, 1968, for a collection of theories and approaches), but dissonance theory's more dynamic, self-regulatory approach won out. The original theory and experiments led to enthusiastic acceptance on some sides and extensive criticism on other sides, particularly among behaviorists (e.g., Rosenberg, 1965), whose reinforcement principles made very different predictions. It seems safe to say that over time, the cognitive-dissonance position won out, but more important are the changes the theory went through and the various new theories it inspired. Over time, Festinger's propositions were transformed into a theory of behavior justification, postulating that behaviors inadequately explained by external rewards or constraints would engender a need for self-justifying attitude change. Other important work stimulated by the cognitive dissonance tradition includes Bem's model of self-perception (Bem, 1972), reactance theory (Brehm, 1966), self-affirmation theory (Steele, 1988), and research on extrinsic motivation (Deci & Ryan, 1985).

Still other enduring theories and phenomena introduced during this fertile period include Schachter's (1971) two-factor theory of emotion, which popularized emotion as a topic for social-psychological inquiry and introduced ideas about the attribution and misattribution of arousal. Interest in interpersonal attraction and friendship formation grew, spurred by Newcomb's (1961) detailed study of the acquaintance process among new students at the University of Michigan, Byrne's (1971) studies of similarity and attraction, Altman and Taylor's (1973) studies of self-disclosure and social penetration, and, slightly later, Berscheid and Walster's (1974) physical attractiveness research. Stouffer's (1949) seminal book, *The American Soldier*, introduced the concept of relative deprivation, which, integrated with George Homans's (1950) social exchange theory, led J. S. Adams to propose the Equity Theory (1965), all of which fostered lasting interest in social justice research among social psychologists.

Finally, 1968 was the year in which Walter Mischel proposed that the then-dominant stable-trait models of personality, which sought to identify cross-situational consistencies in behavior, be replaced by contextually varying "if–then" models that sought to identify distinctive yet stable patterns of response to particular situations. Mischel's work was an influential reminder of Lewin's famous dictum, and was instrumental to the subsequent popularity of Person × Situation interaction research. Moreover, Mischel's influence reminded the field that personality psychology and social psychology were most effective as a single discipline (a reminder heeded more in principle than in practice).

The zeitgeist continued to play a significant role in the field's evolution, as social psychologists pursued research addressing important events of the day. One of the most compelling examples began in 1964, when Kitty Genovese was brutally stabbed to death outside her Kew Gardens (New York) apartment while 38 witnesses reportedly did nothing to intervene or call the police. Public outrage about urban apathy and callousness was intense. Bibb Latané and John Darley, two young social psychologists residing in the New York City area, proposed and began what became an extensive research program testing a more social-psychological interpretation of factors that determine bystander intervention and nonintervention. Two principles were key: diffusion of responsibility—that bystanders are less likely to feel personally responsible to act if others are present—and situational ambiguity—that bystanders use situational cues, such as the nonresponse of others, to interpret whether the event is truly an emergency. Even though later reports questioned some details about this crime (Rasenberger, 2004), Latané and Darley's research (1970) made bystander intervention an enduring part of the literature. Perhaps more importantly, because their research continues to receive substantial media coverage, it demonstrated to the public the value of social-psychological research.

Another current event, the civil rights movement, also dramatically affected the field's research agenda. Research on the causes and consequences of prejudice and discrimination grew in popularity, serving as a theoretical foundation for later interventions (e.g., the Jigsaw classroom, first used in 1971; Aronson & Patnoe, 1997). *Brown vs. Board of Education of Topeka, Kansas*, the landmark 1954 decision in which the Supreme Court overturned the doctrine of "separate but equal," also energized the field, largely because social science research, as summarized in Kenneth B. Clark's testimony, was cited as particularly influential in the court's decision. Student antiwar protests in the late 1960s also found a resonant chord in social psychology (e.g., Block, Haan, & Smith, 1969), perhaps because social psychologists were at least sympathetic to and often active in the cause.

As the presence of social psychology on university campuses grew, so did the field's infrastructure. Division 8 (Social and Personality Psychology) of the American Psychological Association was formed in 1947, with Gordon Allport as the first Chair. [In 1974, the independent Society for Personality and Social Psychology (SPSP) replaced Division 8 as the field's leading professional organization.] Table 2.1 presents a list of the Presidents of Division 8 and SPSP since then. The Society of Experimental Social Psychology was founded in 1965, because, in the words of its first President, Edwin Hollander, Division 8 had reached "intimidating dimensions" that made "personal contact and communication unwieldy" (1968, p. 280). Hollander envisioned slow growth "to perhaps 100" members[2] (Hollander, 1968, p. 281). European social psychology began to be rebuilt, with significant input from the American-sponsored Committee on Transnational Social Psychology, leading to the formation in 1966 of the European Association of Experimental Social Psychology, with Serge Moscovici as President. Journals also expanded, reflecting the need to disseminate the new research generated by the growing field. The renamed *Journal of Abnormal and Social Psychology* split into two journals in 1965. Daniel Katz, editor of the new *Journal of Personality and Social Psychology* (*JPSP*), remarked:

> It is appropriate with the launching of a new journal to hail the dawn of a new day and to sound a call for revolutionary departures from traditions of the past. . . . Now that the field of social psychology and its sister discipline of personality have a journal all their own, we should take

TABLE 2.1 Past Presidents of Social Psychological Organizations

Division 8, APA (Social and Personality Psychology)		*Society for Personality and Social Psychology*	
1947	Gordon Allport	1974	Urie Bronfenbrenner
1948	Gardner Murphy	1975	Paul Secord
1949	Theodore Newcomb	1976	Marcia Guttentag
1950	Otto Klineberg	1977	Harry Triandis
1951	J. McVicker Hunt	1978	Bibb Latané
1952	Donald MacKinnon	1979	Irwin Altman
1953	O. Hobart Mowrer	1980	Lawrence Wrightsman
1954	Richard Crutchfield	1981	Alice Eagly
1955	Nevitt Sanford	1982	Jerome Singer
1956	Abraham Maslow	1983	Ellen Berscheid
1957	Solomon Asch	1984	Albert Pepitone
1958	Else Frenkel-Brunswik	1985	Walter Mischel
1959	Jerome Bruner	1986	Ladd Wheeler
1960	Ross Stagner	1987	Elliot Aronson
1961	Robert Sears	1988	Edward Jones
1962	Henry Murray	1989	John Darley
1963	Leon Festinger	1990	Marilynn Brewer
1964	Garnder Lindzey	1991	Kay Deaux
1965	Morton Deutsch	1992	Mark Snyder
1966	Roger Brown	1993	Nancy Cantor
1967	Harold Kelley	1994	Susan Fiske
1968	Silvan Tompkins	1995	John Cacioppo
1969	Donald Campbell	1996	Robert Cialdini
1970	Julian Rotter	1997	Mark Zanna
1971	Herbert Kelman	1998	Gifford Weary
1972	Leonard Berkowitz	1999	Shelley Taylor
1973	William McGuire	2000	Abraham Tesser
		2001	Ed Diener
		2002	Claude Steele
		2003	James Blascovich
		2004	Hazel Markus
		2005	Margaret Clark
		2006	Brenda Major
		2007	Harry Reis
		2008	John Dovidio
		2009	Richard Petty
		2010	Jennifer Crocker
		2011	Todd Hetherton

advantage of the fact by . . . dealing more adequately with variables appropriate to our own subject matter. . . . It is our conviction that social psychology is no longer divorced from the other behavioral sciences and

> that in the long run a journal of personality and social psychology can profitably take account of this rapprochement. (1965, pp. 1–2)

Another primary journal formed during this expansionary period was the *Journal of Experimental Social Psychology*, founded in 1965. John Thibaut was the inaugural editor.

As the 1960s came to a close, two trends were apparent. The first concerned personnel. It has sometimes been said that "social psychology is what social psychologists do," and to this point, the social psychologists were, with very few exceptions, white males. Academic institutions were starting to admit more women at all levels, and social psychology was no exception. Looking back on the period 1967–1992, Berscheid speculated that "the proportional increase of women into research positions in social psychology was greater than in any other subarea of psychology" (1992, p. 527). Arguably more important than personnel statistics was the way in which the influx of women intrinsically changed the field, by creating "a single social psychology that has integrated, and has been enriched by, the different experiences and views that female social psychologists have brought to their work" (Berscheid, 1992, p. 527). Progress in integrating the perspectives of nonwhite individuals has been much slower.

The second indisputable trend was that the pace of the field's growth was slowing. Social psychology was young no more. Faculties and enrollments were no longer expanding at a rapid pace, and grant funding would become increasingly competitive. An impressive literature of theory and empirical findings had been established, but future advances would be more challenging.

The Ascent of Social Cognition: 1970–1990

With the benefit of hindsight, it seems only natural that the rapid expansion of social psychology after World War II would inevitably lead to soul-searching about the value of the field's work. In part, this may reflect the prevailing "question authority" attitude of the late 1960s. Perhaps more strikingly, as the growth in resources slowed, and as the field matured from vibrant adolescence into early adulthood, doubts were voiced about its accomplishments and goals, so much so that the early 1970s became known for the "crisis of confidence" that was unmistakably visible in journals and at meetings. Many critiques appeared, ranging from concerns about methodology and the ethics of experimental manipulation (especially involving deception) to more fundamental questions about the value of social-psychological findings and theories.

Two critiques were particularly prominent. In one, Gergen (1973) argued that social psychology should be considered an historical rather than a scientific discipline, because the principles underlying social behavior vary as a function of time and culture. Gergen's position, which dovetailed with growing reservations (noted above) about the dominance of North American white males in social psychology, led many to question the experimental methods and theoretical assumptions that were foundational at the time. The other critique, more evolutionary and ultimately more influential[3] than Gergen's revolutionary charge, was offered by William McGuire. In "The Yin and Yang of Progress in Social Psychology: Seven Koan," McGuire proposed that

> the paradigm that has recently guided experimental social psychology—testing of theory driven hypotheses by means of laboratory manipulated experiments [is dissatisfying] . . . an adequate new paradigm will . . . [involve], on the creative side, deriving hypotheses from a systems theory of social and cognitive structures that takes into account multiple and bidirectional causality among social variables. (1973, p. 446)

Although McGuire's forecast has yet to be realized, it clearly did usher in a new generation of studies focusing on process models and their basic mechanisms, as well as interest in more diverse methods (discussed below). More generally, the crisis of confidence faded away in the late 1970s, as researchers redirected their energy from self-criticism to improving their research.

McGuire's critique was prescient in calling attention to the cognitive structures underlying social behavior. The 1970s heralded the arrival of social cognition as a dominant area of social-psychological research. In large part, this movement reflected the so-called Cognitive Revolution, as psychology distanced itself from the antimentalist behaviorist tradition (which had only an irregular influence within social psychology) and instead whole-heartedly embraced the study of cognitive processes and their impact on behavior. To be sure, there had been earlier examples of social cognition within social psychology (e.g., person perception, attitude structure), but the new-found legitimacy of studying cognitive processes opened the door to a different level of analysis and many new phenomena.

The first of these new social-cognitive phenomena was causal attribution. Seminal groundwork had been laid earlier in three theoretical models. These were Heider's (1958) "common sense psychology," which examined how people make ordinary judgments about causation, in particular describing the constellation of factors that fosters environmental or personal causation; Jones and Davis's (1965) theory of correspondent inferences, which proposed that lay persons ascribe intentionality (and hence dispositional causation) to the extent that actions deviate from what the average person would and could do; and Kelley's (1967) covariation model, which proposed that causal inferences were based on comparative judgments about whether a given action was consistent over time, distinctive among related entities, and unique across persons. Attribution research prospered for a time, and although interest subsequently waned, it set the stage for much of what followed.

In broad perspective, the primary contribution of the new emphasis on social cognition was to situate the major mechanisms for social-psychological explanations of behavior within the mind of the individual. Contemporary social psychology thus moved away from the interpersonal and group-process models favored in earlier approaches, notably those popular in Europe and in sociological social psychology, and toward more individualistic processes as well as the increasingly popular field of cognitive psychology. Social psychological phenomena were seen as being caused proximately by "what the individual makes of the situation" (Kelley, Holmes, Kerr, Reis, Rusbult, & Van Lange, 2003, pp. 5–6) more so than by its distal causes, namely the situation itself. This idea was expressed influentially in Ross and Nisbett's (1991) principle of construal: that causal analysis should focus on the personal and subjective meaning of the situation to the individual actor.

Between 1970 and 1990, social cognition research flourished. Some of the more influential and enduring work of this era includes research on judgment and decision making (which contributed to the development of behavioral economics); studies of social inference processes, such as research on heuristics (Kahneman & Tversky, 1973) and other strategies for organizing and using information; early studies of automaticity (e.g., Winter & Uleman, 1984); formal theories of attitude change, such as the elaboration likelihood model (Petty & Cacioppo, 1986), and of the attitude-behavior association, such as the theory of reasoned action (Fishbein & Ajzen, 1974); various models of social categorization and schema use, including models of person memory (Ostrom, 1989); dual-process models, such as those differentiating deliberative and implemental mind sets (Gollwitzer & Kinney, 1989) or systematic and heuristic processing (e.g., Chaiken, Liberman, & Eagly, 1989); and models differentiating automatic and controlled processes in stereotyping, prejudice, and discrimination (e.g., Devine, 1989). Many other examples might be cited (see Fiske & Taylor, 1991, for a review). The enthusiasm for social cognition was such that Ostrom (1984) could proclaim, not without some credibility, that "social cognition reigns sovereign" (p. 29) over other approaches to understanding social behavior.

This is not to say that other topics were dormant, however. Motivation was becoming more important in social psychology, as exemplified by growing attention to self-regulation. Several major models were formulated during this period, among them Carver and Scheier's control theory (1981), Deci and Ryan's self-determination theory (1985), Higgins's self-discrepancy theory (1987), and terror management theory (Greenberg, Pyszczynski, & Solomon, 1986). More broadly, self-related research expanded from viewing the self as the object of knowledge (i.e., self-esteem, contents of the self-concept) to also considering the self as a causal agent motivated to pursue personal and psychological goals. Numerous "self-"related processes became popular, such as self-evaluation maintenance, self-enhancement, self-verification, and self-assessment (Sedikides & Strube, 1997; Taylor, 1998). Some of this work, under the heading of motivated social cognition, provided a much needed "hot" dynamic contrast to then prevailing "cool" information-processing approaches to social cognition. It was not until the 1990s, however, that these approaches became widely accepted.

Social psychology's net was also widening during this period. Emotion and emotion regulation were becoming increasingly popular topics (Zajonc, 1998), coincident with the founding of the International Society for Research on Emotions in 1984. Research on interpersonal attraction gradually slowed, but was replaced in the 1980s by research on social psychological processes affecting the development, maintenance, and termination of close relationships (Berscheid & Reis, 1998). This vigorous extension was facilitated by a key pair of conferences held in Madison, Wisconsin, in 1982 and 1984, which led to the founding of a new society (now called the International Association for Relationship Research) and two specialty journals. And what about social psychology's original research interest, groups? It became less central than in earlier periods, although groups research was still being conducted, somewhat more in a renaissance of European social psychology than in North America, led by scholars such as Serge Moscovici and Henri Tajfel. Nevertheless, even here the limits of models based in the mind of the individual were plain. As Moreland, Hogg, and Hains (1994) document, research on traditional topics such as group structure, performance, and influence ebbed whereas intergroup relations research (social identity, stereotyping, and prejudice) thrived.

Perhaps more significant than all of these changes in content were changes in the way that research was conducted. Research ethics boards became standard (and, some would say, overzealous), requiring more thorough attention to the protection of research participants' welfare, and raising questions about procedures such as deception and informed consent (McGaha & Korn, 1995). A more substantive change involved the introduction of microprocessors, which made available sophisticated tools for conducting research and analyzing data. For example, computerized technology allowed researchers to measure reaction times within milliseconds or to present stimuli at exposure lengths that could be carefully controlled to be subliminal or supraliminal (Bargh & Chartrand, 2000). These tools afforded unprecedented opportunities to ask questions (e.g., about automaticity or implicit processes) that earlier researchers could barely imagine.

Yet more widespread were changes in data analysis. In 1970, most analyses were conducted using large, cumbersome, malfunction-prone manual calculators. Nearly all published studies presented very simple statistics, largely because analyses involving more than three variables required matrix algebra (which most social psychologists eschewed). By 1990, sophisticated statistical software on mainframe or personal computers was ubiquitous, making complex multivariate procedures routine. Invention thus spawned necessity, in the sense that social psychologists began to rely extensively, and often insist, on research and statistical methods that took advantage of this new found computing power. For example, diary methods such as experience sampling first appeared in the 1970s (see Wheeler & Reis, 1991, for a history), structural equation models became known and useful (Reis, 1982), and Kenny's social relations model transformed studies of person perception (Kenny, 1994). Baron and Kenny's (1986) paper on mediation, the most-cited article in the history of *JPSP*, also changed the way that research is done. Methods for assessing mediation were not just a new tool for social psychologists; they altered the research agenda and broadly helped advance theory by making routine the pursuit of evidence for mediating processes.

Journals were changing, too. In April, 1980, *JPSP* split into its current three independent sections under a single cover. Nominally designed to contend with the distinct expertise that the three areas were presumed to require, as well as the workload created by ever-increasing submissions, the split was a sign of growing specialization and complexity. For similar reasons, several other new journals were founded, including the *European Journal of Social Psychology* and the *Journal of Applied Social Psychology* in 1971, and in 1975, the *Personality and Social Psychology Bulletin*. Reis and Stiller (1982) provided more explicit evidence of the field's increasing complexity. Comparing articles published in *JPSP* in 1968, 1978, and 1988, they found that over time, articles had become longer, had more citations, and reported more studies with more subjects per study, more detailed methods, and more complex statistical analyses.

All these activities suggest that although McGuire seems to have missed the mark in predicting the demise of the laboratory experiment, he was spot-on about much of the rest of it: "deriving hypotheses from a systems theory of social and cognitive structures that takes into account multiple and bidirectional causality among social variables" (1973, p. 446). By 1990, social psychologists were asking multifaceted questions about more intricate concepts, they were using more sophisticated methods to collect and analyze their data, and their publications were growing in length, detail, and complexity. Even if bidirectionality had not yet become endemic—for example, experiments with unidimensional causality continued to dominate over correlational approaches—researchers were thinking in terms of and beginning to test mediational models. All of these signs indicated that social psychology had progressed along the path of becoming an established science (Kuhn, 1962).

Spreading Tentacles, Deeper Roots, and the Move toward Biology: 1990–Today

By 1990, SPSP had about 2800 members. By the end of 2008, membership had doubled, to over 5600. Although some of this increase may be the result of growth in mainstream positions in academic psychology departments, a larger portion likely reflects the spread of social psychology into related disciplines and applied positions. Several such movements are apparent. Social psychological research is increasingly represented in law (e.g., eyewitness testimony, jury decision making), business and economics (e.g., judgment and decision making, motivated social cognition, persuasion), medicine (e.g., motivational processes in health-related behavior, social influences on health and well-being), family studies (e.g., dyadic processes in close relationships), education (e.g., achievement motivation, student–teacher interaction), and politics (e.g., voting behavior). This scholarly diaspora may be seen as a sign of the field's health. The domain of social psychology is the study of how the social context affects behavior, an expertise increasingly sought by basic scientists and applied practitioners in other disciplines. Social psychologists also tend to have excellent skills conceptualizing and conducting research on the effects of social context, which is also valued in various academic and applied settings.

There is no irony in the fact that the influence of social psychology has grown steadily by exporting its theories, methods, and talent to other fields. As Taylor noted, "Whereas social psychology used to be a relatively small field of scholars talking primarily to each other, now we have unprecedented opportunities to collaborate with the other sciences in ways that we would have never imagined even a few years ago" (2004, p. 139). Such outreach is an essential part of scientific relevance in the contemporary world. It has often been argued that the future of science rests in interdisciplinary research programs involving multiple investigators with specialized expertise (sometimes called "big science") to address important problems, and this is no less true in translational and applied settings. The spreading tentacles of social psychology, a trend that, if anything, appears to be accelerating (though it is far from accomplished), thus augurs the field's continued participation in the most important science and applications of the day.

Social psychology's dispersion did not occasion neglect of the field's core. Topics popular or emerging at the beginning of this period, discussed earlier in this chapter, experienced theoretical advances, partly due to the accumulation of research and partly due to the availability of yet more sophisticated methods and tools. For example, programming packages such as E-Prime®, MediaLab®, and DirectRT® enabled any researcher with access to a desktop computer to run complex, precisely timed experiments. Relatively sophisticated social-cognitive protocols, such as lexical decision tasks, subliminal and supraliminal priming, and implicit assessment, became standard, and topics amenable to study by these and similar methods, such as automaticity, dual-process models, the impact of nonconscious goals, motivated social cognition, emotion, and affective influences on judgment and decision making, prospered. To be sure, social psychologists had long been interested in nonconscious processes, but they lacked the tools to study them and the data to theorize about them. The availability of such methods, and the resultant impact on research and (especially) theory, might be considered a hallmark of this period.

Similarly, in the 2000s, the Internet grew in reach and bandwidth, making large, international, and diverse[4] samples accessible for surveys and experiments to all researchers. Newer Internet-based tools, such as social networking sites and immersive virtual worlds, and other microprocessor-based technologies (e.g., ambulatory assessment, virtual reality) are poised to further expand the possibilities (Reis & Gosling, 2009). If the most influential figure in social psychology of the middle twentieth century was Hitler, arguably the most influential figures since 1980 were the inventors of microprocessors.[5]

Indispensable as these new tools may be, Baumeister, Vohs, and Funder (2008) note a downside: Direct observation of behavior has been increasingly supplanted by the study of "self-reports and finger movements"—that is, contemporary social-psychological research is often based on data provided through hand-written self-reports or keystrokes on a computer keyboard. By their tally, only about 15% of the articles published in *JPSP* in 2006 included behavioral measures (compared to about 80% in 1976). Many social psychologists trace their interest in the field to the "golden era" of laboratory experiments, when experimental realism was high and research participants were fully engrossed in experimentally created circumstances. (Think, for example, about Milgram's obedience experiment, Latané and Darley's bystander intervention studies, or Asch's conformity research.) Vivid laboratory experiments of this sort are rare these days, for reasons Baumeister et al. (2008) discuss.

Although many of the substantive advances in social psychology after 1990 represented deepening of what was known about established theories and phenomena, two novel trends were also influential. One of these is greater attention to biology, in particular the biological functions, consequences, and mechanisms of social behavior. For example, because social psychologists were interested in situational causes of behavior, they tended to avoid evolutionary accounts. As evolutionary psychology moved away from accounts featuring inherited, relatively immutable dispositions and toward concepts that asked about flexible behavioral adaptations designed to solve problems of survival and reproduction, social psychologists became more interested. This interest was highlighted in a seminal review by Buss and Kenrick, who noted that

> evolutionary psychology places social interaction and social relationships squarely within the center of the action. In particular, social interactions and relationships surrounding mating, kinship, reciprocal alliances, coalitions, and hierarchies are especially critical, because all appear to have strong consequences for successful survival and reproduction. From an evolutionary perspective, the functions served by social relationships have been central to the design of the human mind. (1998, p. 994)

Since then, evolutionary psychology concepts have appeared regularly in social psychology texts (albeit not without controversy about content; Park, 2007) and are an increasingly valuable source of research hypotheses about, for example, attraction, close relationships, prosocial behavior, aggression, social identity, in-group favoritism, leadership, social cognition, and emotion.

Another example of attention to biology in social psychology is the birth and exceptional growth of social neuroscience, which seeks to identify and understand the neural processes underlying social behavior. To be sure, psychophysiological studies of social behavior, including psychophysiological processes occurring primarily in the brain, are not new (Cacioppo & Petty, 1983). But the rapid advance of cognitive neuroscience in the past two decades has had a profoundly energizing effect. One key in this regard is the development of functional magnetic resonance imaging (fMRI) for noninvasively capturing patterns of brain activation associated with psychological processes. Social neuroscientists use neuroscientific methods to test hypotheses about the neural processes responsible for the phenomena that social psychologists traditionally study at a behavioral level. For example, Beer (2007) examined evidence about activity in the medial prefrontal cortex to determine whether chronic self-evaluation is best represented by accurate self-assessment or self-enhancement; Aron, Fisher, Mashek, Strong, Li, and Brown (2005) used fMRI to support their model of intense romantic love as a motivational state rather than as an emotion; and Decety and Jackson (2006) have used fMRI to better understand the neural and cognitive foundations of empathy. Social neuroscience is misconstrued when it is described as "finding social behavior in the brain." Rather, the goal is to inform social-psychological theory according to what is known about neural function and architecture (i.e., how the brain works and does not work), and simultaneously to better understand how the brain enacts the psychological and social processes that characterize everyday life (Cacioppo, Berntson, Lorig, Norris, Rickett, & Nusbaum, 2003). Though social neuroscience is still very young, there is reason to believe that over time it will do much to better ground social psychological theories of social behavior in a biologically plausible reality.

The second trend that became prominent during the 1990s was culture. Although culture was surely a part of social psychology in the early days (for example, in Wundt's folk psychology), over the years interest in culture waned, probably because of the field's goal of identifying invariant basic processes of social behavior. Nonetheless, as social psychologists reconsidered the impact of culture, partly stimulated by the growth of social psychology outside of North America, research began to accumulate showing that many social psychological processes once thought to be "basic" or "universal" did in fact vary from one culture to another (Fiske, Kitayama, Markus, & Nisbett, 1998). Nowhere was this more evident than in studies of social cognition comparing individualist cultures (North America, Western Europe) with communal cultures (East Asia). In one compelling instance, the so-called "fundamental attribution error" was shown to be characteristic of European-Americans but not of Asians (e.g., Miller, 1984). By now there is sufficient evidence to indicate that cultural influences are relevant to most domains of social psychology.

It is too soon to know which of these trends will continue, which will turn out to be dead ends, and where they will lead social psychology. But if nothing else, they demonstrate that the relentless curiosity of social psychologists has few boundaries.

Conclusions

Past is prologue, Shakespeare wrote, but the future is ours to create. What can this history of social psychology reveal that might usefully guide new investigators preparing to create the field's future? Our progress as a discipline suggests several trends. Social psychologists have always been interested in the same core phenomena—how behavior is affected by the social world in which our lives are embedded—but, as we have seen, the ways in which that interest is explored and expressed have varied markedly. Part of this variability reflects the intellectual, social, and political context of the world in which we live and work. Social psychologists by custom and by inclination tend to rely on the best available conceptual and methodological tools. To be sure, social psychologists are not mere followers of contemporary trends—through research, teaching, and writing, social psychologists contribute to scholarly and popular movements. We might reasonably expect, then, that future social psychologists will continue to explore important questions about timely topics, using state-of-the-art tools.

These trends notwithstanding, the processes and phenomena most central to social psychology have a certain timelessness to them, in the sense that the best principles and theories are general enough to apply to whatever particulars are most prominent at the moment. Whether the principle is Hammurabi's "an eye for an eye," Festinger's theory of cognitive dissonance, or automaticity in social evaluation, the goal is to provide an abstract account of behavior that transcends specific circumstances. For example, good theories of social influence ought to explain social interaction whether it occurs face to face, over the telephone, on Facebook, or by some medium not yet invented. Of course this does not mean that established theories will not be replaced with better ones. A clear sense of history allows new scholars to propose and test better (more accurate, more comprehensive, or more deeply detailed) theories. Isaac Newton famously remarked, "[i]f I have seen a little further it is by standing on the shoulders of giants" (1676). One way in which history informs current progress is by providing a ladder up to the giant's shoulders: identifying what has been determined and providing important clues about what needs to be understood better and what new research directions might be most informative. In this regard, then, I disagree with one distinguished social psychologist's recommendation that new students *not* read the literature, because it would constrain their imagination (see Jost, 2004, for additional information).

An indisputable prediction is that future technological advances in both methods and data analysis will provide innovations that allow social psychologists to ask and answer more probing and, in some instances, entirely new types of questions. As the complexity of these tools grows, so too will specialization, increasing the necessity for collaboration with scholars who possess different expertise. I expect, then, that the trend toward "big science" will continue—multidisciplinary collaborations among researchers with diverse training and expertise. Social psychologists have often been reluctant, perhaps more than scientists in other areas, to initiate such collaborations, but there is little doubt that such participation is needed for the field to thrive (Taylor, 2004). Even more important is the necessity for social psychologists to make visible their expertise so that researchers from other disciplines will invite them to contribute (Reis, 2007). A similar conclusion applies to becoming more involved in the translation and application of basic principles to improve people's lives.

The history of social psychology is the history of people trying to better understand the intrinsically social world in which they live. Studying the field's history represents one step in creating not just the future of the field but all of our futures.

Acknowledgments

For helpful suggestions and comments on an earlier draft of this chapter, I thank David Buss, Bill Graziano, Mike Maniaci, and the editors of this volume.

Footnotes

1. Field theory is actually more a perspective and method than a formal theory, as Lewin himself acknowledged.
2. The current membership in the Society is over 800.
3. Within social psychology, that is. Gergen's writing has had more influence in fields in which textual analysis is more important, such as discourse analysis and communications.
4. Despite the fact that debate continues about the diversity and representativeness of Internet samples (Gosling, Vazire, Srivastava, & John, 2004), there seems little reason to doubt that such samples are more diverse than college freshmen and sophomores.
5. Just who deserves this credit remains a matter of considerable debate, in both historical accounts and the U.S. patent office.

References

Abelson, R. P., Aronson, E., McGuire, W. J., Newcomb, T. M., Rosenberg, M. J., & Tannenbaum, P. H. (Eds.) (1968). *Theories of cognitive consistency: A sourcebook.* Chicago: Rand McNally.

Adams, J. S. (1965). Inequity in social exchange. In L. Berkowitz (Ed.), *Advances in Experimental Social Psychology* (Vol. 2, pp. 267–300). New York: Academic Press.

Ajzen, I., & Fishbein, M. (1974). Factors influencing intentions and the intention-behavior relation. *Human Relations, 27*, 1–15.

Allen, V. L. (1975). Social support for nonconformity. In L. Berkowitz (Ed.), *Advances in Experimental Social Psychology* (Vol. 8, pp. 2–43). New York: Academic Press.

Allport, G. W. (1935). Attitudes. In C. Murchison (Ed.), *A handbook of social psychology*. Worcester, MA: Clark University Press.

Allport, G. W. (1954). The historical background on modern social psychology. In G. Lindzey (Ed.), *Handbook of social psychology* (2nd ed., Vol. 1). Reading, MA: Addison-Wesley.

Altman, I., & Taylor, D. A. (1973). *Social penetration: The development of interpersonal relationships*. New York: Holt, Rinehart & Winston.

Arkin, R. (Ed.). (2009) *Most underappreciated: 50 prominent social psychologists talk about hidden gems*. New York: Oxford University Press.

Aron, A., Fisher, H., Mashek, D., Strong, G., Li, H., & Brown, L. (2005). Reward, motivation and emotion systems associated with early-stage intense romantic love. *Journal of Neurophysiology, 93*, 327–337.

Aronson, E., & Patnoe, S. (1997). *The jigsaw classroom: Building cooperation in the classroom* (2nd ed.). New York: Addison Wesley Longman

Asch, S. E. (1946). Forming impressions of personality. *Journal of Abnormal and Social Psychology, 41*, 258–290.

Asch, S. E. (1952). *Social psychology*. New York: Prentice Hall, Inc.

Asch, S. E. (1956). Studies of independence and conformity: A minority of one against a unanimous majority. *Psychological Monographs, 70*, No. 9 (Whole No. 416).

Bandura, A., & Walters, R. H. (1963). *Social learning and personality development*. New York: Holt, Rinehart, & Winston.

Bargh, J. A., & Chartrand, T. L. (2000). The mind in the middle: A practical guide to priming and automaticity research. In H. T. Reis & C. Judd (Eds.), *Handbook of research methods in social psychology* (pp. 253–285). New York: Cambridge University Press.

Baron, R. M., & Kenny, D. A. (1986). The moderator-mediator variable distinction in social psychological research: Conceptual, strategic, and statistical considerations. *Journal of Personality and Social Psychology, 51*, 1173–1182.

Baumeister, R. F., Vohs, K. D., & Funder, D. C. (2008). Psychology as the science of self-reports and finger movements: Whatever happened to actual behavior? *Perspectives on Psychological Science, 2*, 396–403.

Beer, J. S. (2007). The default self: Feeling good or being right? *Trends in Cognitive Sciences, 11*, 187–189.

Bem, D. (1972). Self-perception theory. In L. Berkowitz (Ed.), *Advances in experimental social psychology* (Vol. 6, pp. 2–62). New York: Academic Press.

Berscheid, E. (1992). A glance back at a quarter century of social psychology. *Journal of Personality and Social Psychology, 63*, 525–533.

Berscheid, E., & Reis, H. T. (1998). Attraction and close relationships. In D. T. Gilbert, S. T. Fiske, & G. Lindzey (Eds.), *The handbook of social psychology* (4th ed., Vol. 2, pp. 193–281). New York: McGraw-Hill.

Berscheid, E., & Walster, E. (1974). Physical attractiveness. *Advances in Experimental Social Psychology, 7*, 157–215.

Block, J. H., Haan, N., & Smith, M. B. (1969). Socialization correlates of student activism. *Journal of Social Issues, 25*, 143–177.

Brehm, J. W. (1966). *A theory of psychological reactance*. New York: Academic Press.

Bruner, J., & Tagiuri, R. (1954). The perception of people. In G. Lindzey (Ed.), *The handbook of social psychology* (Vol. 2, pp. 634–654). Cambridge, MA: Addison-Wesley.

Burger, J. M. (2009). Replicating Milgram: Would people still obey today? *American Psychologist, 64*, 1–11.

Buss, D. M., & Kenrick, D. T. (1998). Evolutionary social psychology. In D. Gilbert & S. Fiske (Eds.), *The handbook of social psychology* (4th ed., Vol. 2, pp. 982–1026). Boston: McGraw-Hill.

Byrne, D. (1971). *The attraction paradigm*. New York: Academic Press.

Cacioppo, J. T. (2004). Common sense, intuition, and theory in personality and social psychology. *Personality and Social Psychology Review, 8*, 114–122.

Cacioppo, J. T., Berntson, G. G., Lorig, T. S., Norris, C. J., Rickett, E., & Nusbaum, H. (2003). Just because you're imaging the brain doesn't mean you can stop using your head: A primer and set of first principles. *Journal of Personality and Social Psychology, 85*, 650–661.

Cacioppo, J. T., & Petty, R. E. (1983). *Social psychophysiology: A sourcebook*. New York: Guilford Press.

Cartwright, D. (1979). Contemporary social psychology in historical perspective. *Social Psychology Quarterly, 42*, 82–93

Cartwright, D., & Zander, A. (1953). *Group dynamics: Theory and research*. New York: Harper & Row.

Cartwright, D., & Zander, A. (1960). *Group dynamics: Theory and research* (2nd ed.). New York: Harper & Row.

Cartwright, D., & Zander, A. (1968). *Group dynamics: Theory and research* (3rd ed.) New York: Harper & Row.

Carver, C. S., & Scheier, M. F. (1981). *Attention and self-regulation: A control-theory approach to human behavior*. New York: Springer.

Chaiken, S., Liberman, A., & Eagly, A. H. (1989). Heuristic and systematic information processing within and beyond the persuasion context. In J. S. Uleman & J. A. Bargh (Eds.), *Unintended thought* (pp. 212–252). New York: Guilford Press.

Cooper, J. M. (2007). Cognitive dissonance: Fifty years of a classic theory. Thousand Oaks, CA: Sage.

Cronbach, L. J. (1955). Processes affecting scores on "understanding of others" and "assumed similarity." *Psychological Bulletin, 52*, 177–193.

Decety, J., & Jackson, P. L. (2006). A social-neuroscience perspective on empathy. *Current Directions in Psychological Science, 15*, 54–58.

Deci, E. L., & Ryan, R. M. (1985). *Intrinsic motivation and self-determination in human behavior*. New York: Plenum Press.

Deutsch, M. (1949). A theory of cooperation and competition. *Human Relations, 2*, 129–152.

Deutsch, M., & Gerard, H. G. (1955). A study of normative and informational social influence upon individual judgment. *Journal of Abnormal and Social Psychology, 51*, 629–636.

Devine, P. G. (1989). Stereotypes and prejudice: Their automatic and controlled components. *Journal of Personality and Social Psychology, 56*, 5–18.

Dollard, J., Doob, L. W., Miller, N. E., Mowrer, O. H., & Sears, R. R. (1939). *Frustration and aggression*. New Haven, CT: Yale University Press.

Erdelyi, M. H. (1990). Repression, reconstruction, and defense: History and integration of the psychoanalytic and experimental frameworks. In J. L. Singer (Ed.), *Repression and dissociation: Implications for personality theory, psychopathology, and health* (pp. 1–31). Chicago: University of Chicago Press.

Festinger, L. (1950). Informal social communication. *Psychological Review, 57*, 271–282.

Festinger, L. (1954). A theory of social comparison processes. *Human Relations, 7*, 117–140.

Festinger, L. (1957). *A theory of cognitive dissonance*. Evanston, IL: Row, Peterson.

Fiske, A. P., Kitayama, S., Markus, H. R., & Nisbett, R. E. (1998). The cultural matrix of social psychology. In D. T. Gilbert, S. T. Fiske, & G. Lindzey (Eds.), *The handbook of social psychology* (4th ed.; Vol. 2, pp. 915–981). New York: McGraw-Hill.

Fiske, S. T. (1992). Thinking is for doing: Portraits of social cognition from daguerreotype to laserphoto. *Journal of Personality and Social Psychology, 63*, 877–889.

Fiske, S. T., & Taylor, S. E. (1991). *Social cognition* (2nd ed.). New York: McGraw-Hill.

Franzoi, S. L. (2007). History of social psychology. In R. F. Baumeister & K. D. Vohs (Eds.), *Encyclopedia of social psychology* (Vol. 1, pp. 431–439). Thousand Oaks, CA: Sage.

Funder, D. C. (1987). Errors and mistakes: Evaluating the accuracy of social judgment. *Psychological Bulletin, 101*, 75–90.

Gergen, K. J. (1973). Social psychology as history. *Journal of Personality and Social Psychology, 26*, 309–320.

Gergen, K. J. (2001). Psychological science in a postmodern context. *American Psychologist, 56*, 803–813.

Goethals, G. R. (2003). A century of social psychology: Individuals, ideas, and investigations. In M. A. Hogg & J. Cooper (Eds.), *The Sage handbook of social psychology* (pp. 3–23). Thousand Oaks, CA: Sage.

Gollwitzer, P. M., & Kinney, R. F. (1989). Effects of deliberative and implemental mindsets on illusion of control. *Journal of Personality and Social Psychology, 56*, 531–542.

Gosling, S. D., Vazire, S., Srivastava, S., & John, O. P. (2004). Should we trust Web-based studies? A comparative analysis of six preconceptions about Internet questionnaires. *American Psychologist, 59*, 93–104.

Greenberg, J., Pyszczynski, T., & Solomon, S. (1986). In R. F. Baumeister (Ed.), *Public self and private self* (pp. 189–212). New York: Springer-Verlag.

Greenwood, J. D. (2004). *The disappearance of the social in American social psychology.* New York: Cambridge University Press.

Hastorf, A., & Cantril, H. (1954). They saw a game: A case study. *Journal of Abnormal and Social Psychology, 49*, 129–134.

Heider, F. (1958). *The psychology of interpersonal relations.* New York: Wiley.

Higgins, E. T. (1987). Self-discrepancy: A theory relating self and affect. *Psychological Review, 94*, 319–340.

Hinde, R. A. (1997). *Relationships: A dialectical perspective.* East Sussex, UK: Psychology Press.

Hollander, E. P. (1968). The society of experimental social psychology: An historical note. *Journal of Personality and Social Psychology, 9*, 280–282.

Homans, G. C. (1950). *The human group.* New York: Harcourt, Brace.

Jahoda, G. (2007). *A history of social psychology: From the eighteenth-century enlightenment to the second world war.* New York: Cambridge University Press.

Jones, E. E. (1985). Major developments in social psychology during the past five decades. In G. Lindzey, & E. Aronson (Eds.), *The handbook of social psychology* (3rd ed., Vol. 1, pp. 47–107). New York: Random House.

Jones, E. E. (1998). Major developments in social psychology during the past five decades. In G. Lindzey & E. Aronson (Eds.), *The handbook of social psychology* (4th ed., Vol. 1, pp. 3–57). New York: Random House.

Jones, E. E., & Davis, K. E. (1965). From acts to dispositions: The attribution process in person perception. In L. Berkowitz (Ed.), *Advances in experimental social psychology* (Vol. 2, pp. 219–266). New York: Academic Press.

Jost, J. T. (2004). A perspectivist looks at the past, present and (perhaps) the future of intergroup relations: A quixotic defense of system justification theory. In J. T. Jost, M. R. Banaji, & D. Prentice (Eds.), *Perspectivism in social psychology: The yin and yang of scientific progress* (pp. 215–230). Washington, DC: APA Press.

Kahneman, D., & Tversky, A. (1973). On the psychology of prediction. *Psychological Review, 80*, 237–251.

Katz, D. (1965). Editorial. *Journal of Personality and Social Psychology*, 1, 1–2.

Katz, D., & Braley, K. W. (1933). Racial stereotypes of 100 college students. *Journal of Abnormal and Social Psychology, 28*, 280–290.

Kelley, H. H. (1967). Attribution theory in social psychology. In D. Levine (Ed.), *Nebraska Symposium on Motivation* (Vol. 15, pp. 192–238). Lincoln, NE: University of Nebraska Press.

Kelley, H. H., Holmes, J. G., Kerr, N. L., Reis, H. T., Rusbult, C. E., & Van Lange, P. A. M. (2003). *An atlas of interpersonal situations*. New York: Cambridge University Press.

Kelley, H. H., & Thibaut, J. W. (1978). *Interpersonal relations: A theory of interdependence*. New York: Wiley.

Kenny, D. A. (1994). *Interpersonal perception: A social relations analysis*. New York: Guilford Press.

Kuhn, T. S. (1962). *The structure of scientific revolutions*. Chicago: University of Chicago Press.

LaPiere, R. T. (1934). Attitudes versus actions. *Social Forces, 13*, 230–237.

Latané, B., & Darley, J. (1970). *The unresponsive bystander: Why doesn't he help?*. New York: Appleton-Century-Crofts.

Lewin, K. (1943). Forces behind food habits and methods of change. Bulletin of The National Research Council and National Academy of Sciences, 108, 35–65.

Lewin, K. (1951). *Field theory in social science*. New York: Harper.

McDougall, W. (1908). *Introduction to social psychology*. Boston: Luce.

McGaha, A., & Korn, J. H. (1995). The emergence of interest in the ethics of psychological research with humans. *Ethics and Behavior, 5*, 147–159

McGuire, W. J. (1973). The yin and yang of progress in social psychology: Seven koan. *Journal of Personality and Social Psychology, 26*, 446–456.

McGuire, W. J. (1997). Creative hypothesis generating in psychology: Some useful heuristics. *Annual Review of Psychology, 48*, 1–30.

McMartin, C., & Winston, A. S. (2000). The rhetoric of experimental social psychology, 1930–1960: From caution to enthusiasm. *Journal of the History of the Behavioral Sciences, 36*, 349–364.

Mead G. H. (1934). *Mind, self, and society*. Chicago: University of Chicago Press.

Milgram, S. (1963). Behavioral study of obedience. *Journal of Abnormal and Social Psychology, 67*, 371–378.

Milgram, S. (1965). Some conditions of obedience and disobedience to authority. *Human Relations, 18*, 57–76.

Milgram, S. (1974). *Obedience to authority*. New York: Harper & Row.

Miller, J. G. (1984). Culture and the development of everyday social explanation. *Journal of Personality and Social Psychology, 46*, 961–978

Mischel, W. (1968). *Personality and assessment*. New York: Wiley.

Mischel, W. (2006). Bridges toward a cumulative psychological science. In P. A. M. Van Lange (Ed.), *Bridging social psychology* (pp. 437–446). Mahwah, NJ: Erlbaum.

Moreland, R. L., Hogg. M. A., & Hains, S. C. (1994). Back to the future: Social psychological research on groups. *Journal of Experimental Social Psychology, 30*, 527–555.

Murray, H. A. (1938). *Explorations in personality*. New York: Oxford University Press.

Newcomb, T. M. (1943). *Personality and social change: Attitude formation in a student community*. New York: Holt, Rinehart & Winston.

Newcomb, T. M. (1961). *The acquaintance process*. New York: Holt, Rinehart & Winston.

Newton, I. (1676). Letter to Robert Hooke. Retrieved from http://en.wikiquote.org/wiki/Isaac_Newton, May 20, 2009.

Ostrom, T. M. (1984). The sovereignty of social cognition. In R. S. Wyer, Jr. & T. K. Srull (Eds.), *Handbook of social cognition* (Vol. 1, pp. 1–38). Hillsdale, NJ: Erlbaum.

Ostrom, T. M. (1989). Three catechisms for social memory. In P. R. Solomon, G. R. Goethals, C. M. Kelley, & B. R. Stephens (Eds.), *Memory: Interdisciplinary approaches* (pp. 201–210). New York: Springer-Verlag.

Park, J. H. (2007). Persistent misunderstandings of inclusive fitness and kin selection: Their ubiquitous appearance in social psychology textbooks. *Evolutionary Psychology, 5*, 860–873.

Petty, R. E., & Cacioppo, J. T. (1986). The elaboration likelihood model of persuasion. In L. Berkowitz (Ed.), *Advances in experimental social psychology* (Vol. 19, pp. 123–205). New York: Academic Press.

Prince, M., & Allport, F. H. (1921). Editorial Announcement. *Journal of Abnormal Psychology and Social Psychology, 16*, 1–5.

Rasenberger, J. (2004). "Kitty, 40 Years Later." *The New York Times* (Final Ed.), Sect. 14, p. 1, col. 2 (Feb. 8, 2004).

Reis, H. T. (1982). An introduction to the use of structural equations: Prospects and problems. In L. Wheeler (Ed.), *Review of personality and social psychology* (Vol. 3, pp. 255–287). Thousand Oaks, CA: Sage.

Reis, H. T. (2008). Reinvigorating the concept of situation in social psychology. *Personality and Social Psychology Review, 12*, 311–329.

Reis, H. T., & Gosling, S. D. (2009). Social psychological methods outside the laboratory. In D. Gilbert, S. Fiske, & G. Lindzey (Eds.), *Handbook of social psychology* (5th ed.). New York: Oxford University Press.

Reis, H. T., & Stiller, J. (1992). Publication trends in JPSP: A three-decade review. *Personality and Social Psychology Bulletin, 18*, 465–472.

Rosenberg, M. J. (1965). When dissonance fails: On eliminating evaluation apprehension from attitude measurement. *Journal of Personality and Social Psychology, 1*, 28–43.

Ross, E. A. (1908). *Social psychology*. New York: McMillan.

Ross, L., & Nisbett, R. E. (1991). *The person and the situation: Perspectives of social psychology*. Philadelphia: Temple University Press.

Ross, L., Ward, A., & Lepper, M. R. (2010). A history of social psychology. In D. Gilbert, S. Fiske, & G. Lindzey (Eds.), *Handbook of social psychology* (5th ed., vol. 1, pp. 3–50). New York: Oxford University Press.

Schachter, S. (1971). *Emotion, obesity, and crime*. New York: Academic Press.

Sedikides, C., & Strube, M. J. (1997). Self-evaluation: To thine own self be good, to thine own self be sure, to thine own self be true, and to thine own self be better.

In M. P. Zanna (Ed.), *Advances in experimental social psychology* (Vol. 29, pp. 209–269). New York: Academic Press.

Sherif, M. (1936). *The psychology of social norms*. New York: Harper Bros.

Steele, C. M. (1988). The psychology of self-affirmation: Sustaining the integrity of the self. In L. Berkowitz (Ed.), *Advances in experimental social psychology, Vol. 21: Social psychological studies of the self: Perspectives and programs* (pp. 261–302). San Diego, CA: Academic Press.

Stouffer, S. A., Suchman, E. A., DeVinney, L. C., Star, S. A., & Williams, R. M., Jr. (1949). *Studies in social psychology in World War II: The American soldier. Vol. 1, Adjustment during army life*. Princeton, NJ: Princeton University Press.

Taylor, S. E. (1998). The social being in social psychology. In D. T. Gilbert, S. T. Fiske, & G. Lindzey (Eds.), *The handbook of social psychology* (4th ed., Vol. 1, pp. 58–95). New York: McGraw-Hill.

Taylor, S. E. (2004). Preparing for social psychology's future. *Journal of Experimental Social Psychology, 40*, 139–141.

Thibaut, J. W., & Kelley, H. H. (1959). *The social psychology of groups*. New York: Wiley.

Triplett, N. (1898). The dynamogenic factors in pacemaking and competition. *American Journal of Psychology, 9*, 507–533.

Van Lange, P. A. M. (Ed.) (2006). *Bridging social psychology*. Mahwah, NJ: Erlbaum.

Wallach, M. A., Kogan, N., & Bem, D. J. (1962). Group influence on individual risk taking. *Journal of Abnormal and Social Psychology, 65*, 75–86.

Wheeler, L., & Reis, H. T. (1991). Self-recording of everyday life events: Origins, types, and uses. *Journal of Personality, 59*, 339–354.

Winter, L., & Uleman, J. S. (1984). When are social judgments made? Evidence for the spontaneousness of trait inferences. *Journal of Personality and Social Psychology, 47*, 237–252.

Wittenbaum, G. M., & Moreland, R. L. (2008). Small-group research in social psychology: Topics and trends over time. *Social and Personality Psychology Compass, 2*, 187–203.

Wundt, W. (1916). *Elements of folk psychology: Outlines of a psychological history of the development of mankind*. London: Allan & Unwin.

Zajonc, R. B. (1998). Emotions. In D. T. Gilbert, S. T. Fiske, & G. Lindzey (Eds.), *The handbook of social psychology* (4th ed., Vol. 2, pp. 591–632). New York: McGraw-Hill.

Part 2

Basic Processes

Chapter 3

Social Cognition

Don Carlston

Social cognition is both a subarea of social psychology and an approach to the discipline as a whole. As a subarea, social cognition encompasses new approaches to classic research on attribution theory (how people explain behavior and events), impression formation (how people form impressions of others), stereotyping (how people think about members of groups), attitudes (how people feel about various things), and the self (how people think about themselves). What binds these areas together is their emphasis on the social implications of peoples' thoughts and subjective perceptions of reality (i.e., their *phenomenology*). Such work fell outside of the mainstream from the 1920s to the 1950s, when behaviorism dominated the field of psychology with an ideology that emphasized objective stimuli and behaviors, while trivializing cognition. But it has been more in vogue since the cognitive revolution of the 1960s, and especially since the social cognitive revolution of the 1980s.

However, the cognitivism of modern social cognition differs from that underlying earlier work in attribution, impression formation, and similar areas. Today's approaches to these issues rely heavily on concepts, theories, and methods borrowed from the field of cognitive psychology, a discipline that has existed only since about 1967, when Neisser published the first cognitive psychology text. In contrast, earlier work necessarily employed concepts, methods, and theories created by social psychologists specifically for the domains of interest. Thus, for example, *balance theory* (Newcomb, 1953) explained some aspects of attitude change and interpersonal attraction by positing that triads of mental concepts are stable when the product of perceived relations among them is positive, and unstable when that product is negative. This balance principle successfully predicted some phenomena, but applied only within a very limited context and relied on a mathematical algorithm that was not generally employed by other psychological theories. Attribution theories, which are discussed later in this chapter, provide additional examples.

The proliferation of such domain-specific "microtheories" was ultimately troubling to some theorists who suggested that because people have only one mind, a single set of concepts and principles ought to explain its role in all psychological domains. In the 1970s, the leading candidate for this "single set of concepts and principles" was the newly emerged field of cognitive psychology, and more particularly, the information-processing model (see below). So it was that by the end of that decade a new subdiscipline had arisen, dedicated to promoting the use of cognitive concepts, theories, and methods in social psychology.

Proponents of social cognition applied their enthusiasm for cognitive psychology to their own research on attribution, impression formation, stereotyping, attitudes, and the self, generating research programs that extended earlier work in those areas in new directions. The first books describing these programs, and the philosophy underlying them, were published around 1980, providing a rough kick-off date for the start of the field (Wyer & Carlston, 1979; Hastie, Ostrom, Ebbesen, Wyer, Hamilton, & Carlston, 1980; Higgins, Herman, & Zanna, 1981). Such volumes characteristically justified the new research programs as an improvement over past approaches that "had run their course" (Hastie et al., 1980, preface), a view that may not have endeared the proponents to those who had been doing the previous course running. But social cognition polarized social psychologists in other ways as well.

Social Cognition as an Approach

The philosophies and practices of the eager new social cognition devotees quickly coalesced into a perspective that some viewed as revolutionary (Ostrom, 1984) and others viewed as misguided and incomplete (Zajonc, 1980a; Forgas, 1983), or sometimes even as arrogant and confrontational (see Ostrom, 1994). The core principles of this approach were that (1) researchers ought to employ general concepts and theories rather than idiosyncratic microtheories; (2) cognitive processes are a major determinant of human judgments and behavior; (3) the information processing model provides a universally useful structure for examining cognition; (4) mediating processes should be measured (generally using methods borrowed from cognitive psychology) rather than just assumed; all of which together imply that (5) there should be one universal set of concepts, principles, and practices underlying most, if not all, psychological theorizing and research.

The construal of social cognition as an approach (see Sherman, Judd, & Park, 1989) explains why it transformed research within those domains that it subsumed (e.g., attribution theory). But it also explains why social cognition enthusiasts saw their principles as applying beyond the borders of their own subdiscipline, arguing that these principles should govern other areas of psychology as well. For example, Ostrom (1984) wrote a controversial chapter in the first *Handbook of Social Cognition* claiming that social cognition deserved sovereignty over other areas of psychology. Although he later suggested that his chapter was meant to be conciliatory (Ostrom, 1994, p. viii), the way that he and others framed their philosophical principles tended to be provocative, whether intentionally or not. Moreover, the argument for a universal set of concepts and principles raised for some the specter of a scientific imperialism, with the social cognition approach threatening to impose its own core principles on the entire field of psychology. This imperialistic attitude did not sit well with everyone. Many senior social psychologists had resisted behaviorist hegemony to construct their own individual cognitive approaches even before there was a formal field of cognitive psychology. Having enjoyed some vindication with the eventual crumbling of the behaviorist empire, they were not inclined to submit to a new, social-cognition-based tyranny.

Conflict between old and new approaches to science is almost inevitable (Kuhn, 1962). In the present case (as, perhaps, with most scientific revolutions), the flames of conflict were fanned by a variety of incidental events and circumstances, including the kinds of incendiary remarks previously noted. The new adherents to social cognition had an evangelical zeal characteristic of those who have recently "found religion." The phrases that Ostrom (1994, p. vii) used to describe the first *Handbook of Social Cognition* applied to the whole subfield: "revolutionary," "confrontational and passionate," and "fists and sinew demanding recognition and acceptance." The zeal of the social cognition devotees produced conferences that some perceived as exclusive, editorships that some perceived as parochial, and demands on resources (e.g., federal grants, journal space, jobs) that some viewed as excessive. In retrospect, it is apparent why non-social-cognitionists sometimes felt threatened, and why coolness, if not actual hostility, sometimes permeated the relationship between social cognition and other subdisciplines. Still, these early reactions dissipated over the years, leaving the younger generation of psychologists wondering what all the fuss was about. New graduate students studied social cognition as a normal part of their curriculum, and often integrated the approach into their own research programs. Over time, many principles of social cognition became so widely accepted that by 1994, Ostrom (p. xii) concluded that social cognition had become "standard science."

As a result, social psychology as a field has changed. Theorists and researchers across the field routinely employ concepts, theories, and methods borrowed from cognitive psychology. Mediating processes are routinely examined using new methods, measures, and statistical techniques. And the subdisciplines of the field are achieving some integration, as domain-specific theories are reinterpreted or replaced by more universal ones. But this hardly means that social cognition now enjoys sovereignty over the entire field—because social cognition did not simply change social psychology, it was also changed by it. To appreciate why this was necessary, we next consider one central aspect of the social cognition approach—the information processing model.

The Information-Processing Model

The information-processing model partitions "cognition" into component processes involving (1) attention and perception, (2) memory, and (3) judgment. Before the model existed, the mind appeared to be an inscrutable "black box," justifying behaviorists' assertions that it was not a proper topic for scientific study and that researchers ought to concentrate instead on more objectively observable data such as behavior. This view dominated American psychology for half of the twentieth century, marginalizing social psychologists who felt that human thought was central to understanding human behavior. However, toward the middle of that century scientists developed the first computer, which provided a useful simplifying metaphor for the inscrutable human mind. If the mind, like the computer, employed input operations (the human equivalent being attention and perception), storage operations (memory), and processing routines (evaluation and judgment), then perhaps these simpler, individual stages would prove more amenable to research than the amalgamated whole. This proved to be, contributing to the demise of behaviorism and the emergence of modern cognitive psychology.

Social cognitionists embraced the information-processing model, not only because it was central to cognitive psychology, but also because it emphasized one problem with the microtheories that had proliferated in social psychology.

These theories focused primarily on the *contents* of the final stage of information processing (evaluation and judgment) with little consideration of the *processes* underlying earlier stages of attention, perception, or memory. Kelley's (1967) influential attribution theory, for example, explained how patterns of actors' behaviors contribute to causal judgments, without taking into account whether all such behaviors are equally attended, how they are interpreted, or whether some are better recalled than others. The social cognition view was that the different subprocesses of cognition needed to be considered in such work. The research areas that arose to do this considering were termed *person perception* and *person memory*, terms sometimes still used to refer to the whole field of social cognition.

It seems evident that attentional, perceptual, and mnemonic processes are important in attribution and other human cognitive processes. But the emphasis in social cognition on the information-processing model nonetheless provoked criticism. For example, Forgas (1983) argued that social cognition ought not to be "merely the information-processing analysis of social domains." As he implied, the major shortcoming of the model was that it was incomplete. Because it was borrowed from cognitive psychology, it reflected the focus of that field, while leaving out a number of concerns central to social psychology. Nowhere in the model are components representing emotion or motivation. Nowhere are processing systems to deal with information that is not attended or remembered, but that nonetheless exerts an influence on human behavior. And nowhere is human behavior itself, the endpoint of interest to most social psychologists.

Such concerns were not fatal to social cognition, but they did force the field to branch out to incorporate components that were missing initially. Emotions and motivations are now represented in many social cognitive theories, although often using processes and principles similar to those designed for "colder" forms of cognitive content. Automatic processes and implicit cognitions are now studied alongside more deliberative and conscious phenomena. And behavior, rather than judgment, is often the ultimate focus of theory and research in the field. As a consequence of such changes, social cognition now looks more like other areas of social psychology, and less like cognitive psychology, than might have been expected in earlier years.

This review focuses first on social cognition as a research area that encompasses earlier core concerns with attribution and impression formation. The social cognition approach will be evident in the ways that research on these topics has evolved and changed. The approach will then be discussed further in relation to core social psychological areas other than social cognition (including several that have their own chapters in this volume).

The Core of Social Cognition

Attribution Theory

Attribution theory, the approach that dominated social psychology in the 1970s, can either be viewed as the last vestige of the old, pre-social-cognition era or as the first harbinger of the new social cognition era. *Attribution theory* is a bit of a misnomer, as the term actually encompasses multiple theories and studies focused on a common issue, namely, how people attribute the causes of events and behaviors. This theory and research derived principally from a single, influential book by Heider (1958) in which he attempted to describe ordinary people's theories about the causes of behavior. His characterization of people as "naive scientists" is a good example of the phenomenological emphasis characteristic of both early social psychology and modern social cognition.

Principal Theories

Two of the most important attribution theories were correspondent inference theory (Jones & Davis, 1965) and covariation theory (Kelley, 1967). Jones and Davis' theory derived principally from Heider's discounting principle, which states that confidence in any cause is diminished to the extent that other causes are plausible. One implication is that people will make fewer trait inferences about someone whose socially appropriate behavior can be explained by their personality *and* by social norms than about someone whose socially *in*appropriate behavior can be explained only by their personality. This prediction was supported by a classic experiment (Jones, Davis, & Gergen, 1961) showing that inferences about a job applicant's traits were stronger when the candidate behaved in a manner contrary to assumed job-seeking norms.

Kelley's covariation theory derived principally from Heider's covariation principle, which states that people explain events in terms of things that are present when the event occurs but absent when it does not. The logic is nicely illustrated by the kind of stimuli that McArthur (1976) used in her test of the theory. Suppose that you learned that Englebert fell asleep in psychology class on Tuesday, but that he also fell asleep in most of his other classes on that day, and that, in fact, he falls asleep in psychology class and most other classes almost every day, though everyone else seems to stay awake. Most likely you would conclude that Englebert is one sleepy guy.

Now suppose that instead, you learned that Englebert was just one of many students who fell asleep in psychology class on Tuesday, although he stayed awake in all other classes, as he usually does. Do you find yourself now blaming Englebert's sleepiness on something about his psychology class—perhaps a boring lecture, a warm room, or a gas leak? In the terms of the theory, the first example suggests that sleeping behavior covaries with the presence of Englebert, whereas the second suggests that such behavior covaries with the presence of the psychology class. Thus the proper cause becomes evident through a mental covariance analysis.

Errors and Biases

Attribution theories were very logical and sensible—and, it turned out, sometimes wrong. In McArthur's (1976) experiment on Kelley's theory, for example, subjects' inferences about a particular actor were predictably affected by the extent to which that person's behavior generalized across different settings (termed *distinctiveness* information) and across different times (*consistency* information), although not by the extent that it generalized across different actors (*consensus* information). In other words, Englebert was viewed as one sleepy guy even if he was just one of many who fell asleep in psychology class. Thus, people sometimes did not appear to be as logical and sensible as the theory said they should be.

Consequently, attribution research began to focus on attributional errors and biases—that is, on subject responses that were less logical than the theories predicted (e.g., Ross, 1977). The implicit message was that the theories provided good baseline descriptions, but that people deviate from these for a variety of reasons. Ultimately, however, some social cognitionists rejected the theories as simply descriptions of what people *should* do rather than what they actually do.

Attribution theories were domain-specific microtheories that typically ignored the information-processing stages of attention, perception, and memory, even though these could alter the information on which people based their attributions. Furthermore, most research in the area, like the two studies described, simply inferred attributional processes and principles from final attribution judgments, rather than from more direct measures of the presumed processes. In other words, attribution theory exhibited many of the deficiencies characteristic of cognitively oriented work in the pre-social-cognition era.

Schema Theory

Although attribution theory was "pre-social-cognition" in some respects, the issues examined and the emphasis on people's phenomenology were quite congenial to the emerging field of social cognition. Moreover, the principles of attribution theory were easily recast in terms more compatible with this emerging field (Hamilton, 1988). Kelley (1987) recognized that his covariance analysis appeared to require more time and work, and even more information, than people ordinarily have when evaluating the causes of events. He therefore suggested a version of attribution theory in which people simply matched an observed event with *causal schemas* they already possessed. Thus, when Englebert falls asleep in psychology class, we might guess from past experience that he has done this before, and that most students typically do not, so that the event fits a "sleepy student" scenario. Application of causal schemas would be expected to require less time, effort, and information than the covariance analysis suggested by the original version of Kelley's theory.

Schema theory was originally described by Bartlett (1932), based on experiments he undertook on people's memory for events. Such cognitively oriented work was out of favor in 1932, and consequently it was largely ignored in the United States until social psychologists discovered Bartlett's legacy years later. His ideas were surprisingly modern in many ways, but his methods and language were not, so we focus here just on his ideas. Bartlett suggested that people have organized conceptions of people, places, events, and other things that they bring to bear in processing new information—conceptions that he called *schemas*. He suggested further that these schemas provide a framework for remembering information, so that things that can be interpreted in terms of the framework are fit to it, and those that cannot are forgotten.

Heider and Simmel (1944) conducted one of the first schema studies in social psychology, showing subjects a short film in which three geometric shapes moved around the screen. Although there was nothing objectively meaningful about the movements of the shapes, subjects generally interpreted the film as a prototypical story about two males fighting over a female. In other words, subjects brought to bear their existing schemas and these affected how the film was remembered. These results are difficult for either correspondent inference theory or Kelley's original covariation theory to explain, although Kelley's later conception of attributional schemas could do so.

Status of Attribution Theory

Attribution work involved more than these two theories. Weiner, Frieze, Kukla, Reed, Rest, and Rosenbaum (1987) proposed a theory of performance attribution that was extensively researched and continues to have an impact in education, sports, and other applied areas. *Attribution* (or *reattribution*) *therapy* has been used in counseling and clinical psychology with some success for years

(Brewin, 1988). And many principles and ideas from attribution theory continue to attract interest and application (Maddux & Yuki, 2006; Sahar, 2008; White, 2005).

Within social cognition, there has always been some ambivalence toward attribution theory. As described earlier, many aspects of the approach are susceptible to the criticisms social cognitionists levied against most earlier forms of cognitive social psychology. In fact, dissatisfaction with attribution theories may have contributed to the rise of social cognition. But whether for positive or negative reasons, attribution theory provided a bridge between the social psychology of the 1960s and the social cognition of the 1980s. It is not surprising, then, that the first social psychology book with *social cognition* in the title had *attribution* in it as well (*Social Cognition, Inference, and Attribution* by Wyer & Carlston, 1979) and that the first text in social cognition (Fiske & Taylor, 1984) devoted a chapter to attribution theory.

Impression Formation

Imagine for a moment that you are interviewing a candidate for a job. Your goal in this situation is logically to form an impression of the candidate, or more specifically, of the candidate's personality, skills, and dedication. This is the prototypical situation with which impression formation research is concerned, although of course the need to form impressions of others applies equally to other situations, ranging from singles bars to dark alleys. Early work on impression formation focused on several issues: the effects of different cues on impressions, the nature and organization of impressions, the processes involved in impression formation, and finally, the accuracy of different people's impressions. The last three issues, which have been most thoroughly reexamined by researchers in social cognition, will serve as the focus of our discussion here. The vast literature on impression cues is touched on elsewhere in this volume (see Finkel & Baumeister, Chapter 12, this volume).

The Organization of Impressions

One of the earliest studies on impression formation was conducted by Asch (1946), who assessed some subjects' traits toward an individual who was "intelligent, skillful, industrious, warm, determined, practical, and cautious" and other subjects' impressions toward an individual who was "intelligent, skillful, industrious, cold, determined, practical, and cautious." Asch noted large differences in these impressions, even though only one trait (warm/cold) differed between the two descriptions. Based on this and similar studies, Asch suggested that "warm/cold" was a central trait, around which other traits tended to be organized. Considerably later, Rosenberg and Sedlak (1972) used newer statistical procedures to systematically plot out a more complete map of the relations that people typically see among traits. Warm and cold traits were closely related to a social/unsocial dimension that aligned with one major axis (with intellective traits representing a second major axis).

Early work on the organization of impressions had two deficiencies in the eyes of social cognition researchers. First, the work assumed, at least implicitly, that impressions consist entirely of trait concepts and their interrelations. And second, the theorized structures were *reflections* of regularities in impression judgments, but not necessarily *representations* of their actual cognitive organization. Later social cognition models of impressions generally involve more diverse kinds of impression-related material, organized in ways thought to reflect the basic nature of underlying memory systems.

Psychologists have long viewed personality principally in terms of traits (e.g., Allport & Odbert, 1936; Thurstone, 1934). At present, for example, the most widely employed theory of personality (the Big Five) classifies people along five trait dimensions: Openness, Extraversion, Conscientiousness, Agreeableness, and Neuroticism (Goldberg, 1993). It was therefore natural for social psychologists to assume that lay people's impressions of others would similarly rely on trait concepts. However, the prominence of attribution theory in the 1970s led researchers to think more about the way that people might represent behaviors they observe, as well as traits that they infer, in memory. As a consequence, several models of impression organization were proposed that involved both traits and behaviors (Carlston, 1980; Hamilton, Katz, & Leirer, 1980; Ostrom, Lingle, Pryor, & Geva, 1980), generally with the former serving to organize the latter.

Impression-Memory Consistency One dilemma raised by these models was the frequently observed lack of relationship between people's impressions of a stimulus person and their memories of that person's behaviors. If you mostly recall a person's positive behaviors, it would seem that you should have a positive impression of that person's traits. And (to turn the example around), if you have a negative impression of someone, it would seem that you should mostly remember their negative behaviors. However, sometimes this expected relationship occurs (Snyder & Uranowitz, 1978) and sometimes it does not (Anderson & Hubert, 1963).

The resolution was suggested by Hastie and Park (1986), who proposed that behavioral memories and trait impressions will be positively related when the impressions are formed *after* relevant behaviors are observed, but that this will not necessarily be so when impressions are formed *as* behaviors are observed. Their logic was that in the former case, impressions are based on those behaviors that can be recalled, but that in the latter case, impressions and memories are formed concurrently, making the relationship between them uncertain. Sometimes the impression and behavioral memories might have completely different implications, as suggested by a classic study by Hastie and Kumar (1979).

The Hastie and Kumar study might be viewed as an investigation into the organization of impressions, pitting schema theory against the information-processing model. These researchers wondered how an existing impression of a target would affect people's memories for new information that was either congruent or incongruent with that impression. Schema theory predicts that material that fits an existing schema (the impression) will be remembered better, because the schema provides a framework for remembering it. But from an information-processing perspective, material that is surprising or unexpected might be better attended and more carefully processed.

In their experiment, Hastie and Kumar told subjects that a target person had some trait (e.g., honesty) and then presented a series of behaviors that were congruent with that trait (e.g., "returned the lost wallet"), incongruent with it (e.g., "stole candy from a baby"), or unrelated to it (e.g., "ate a hamburger at McDonalds"). Results indicated that memory for incongruent behaviors was superior to that for congruent behaviors, and that both were superior to that for unrelated behaviors. Although this confirms the importance of information processing, it does not necessarily challenge schema theory. The superiority of schema-relevant information (both congruent and incongruent) to schema-irrelevant information could be viewed as confirming the importance of an a priori framework for thinking about stimuli.

From an information-processing perspective, the superior recall of incongruent items is consistent with the idea that they received more attention or were processed more thoroughly. However, the prevailing explanation (Hastie & Kumar, 1979; Srull, 1981) is more complicated, suggesting that the result reflects the organization of items in memory. Drawing on associative network models of memory described in both the cognitive literature (Anderson & Bower, 1973; Collins & Loftus, 1975) and the social cognition literature (Wyer & Carlston, 1979), the Hastie–Srull model suggests that incongruent behaviors become associatively linked to more material in memory than congruent behaviors because people perseverate on incongruent information in an attempt to make sense of it. When they later attempt to recall the behaviors, those behaviors with more linkages to more other concepts have a recall advantage. Research has subsequently confirmed many of the implications of this Hastie–Srull model (1981), although some of these results have been controversial (Skowronski & Gannon, 2000).

Associative Network Models Associative network models have also been used in more complex models of impressions. For example, Wyer and Carlston (1979) described an associative network model of impressions in which traits, behaviors, and schemas are connected by associative linkages of varying strengths, reflecting the way that concepts were thought to be represented in memory. Such models have been widely tested (see, for example, Carlston & Skowronski, 1986; Higgins, Bargh, & Lombardi, 1985) and are now among the most common models in social cognition. One of the more complex associative network models of impressions is Carlston's associated systems theory (1994), which proposes that impressions consist of inferred traits, observed behaviors, categorizations, visual images, evaluations, affective and behavioral reactions, and relationships, all organized coherently through their connections with basic brain structures. As discussed below, associative network models also provided useful ways of integrating social cognition with concepts relating to affect, evaluations, and attitudes.

Impression Processes

Theories of human judgment reflect two different viewpoints regarding how people combine the implications of disparate items of information. The *elementist* view is that the separate implications of separate items of information are mentally added or averaged to produce a judgment. The *holistic* view is that different items of available information affect and change each other, so that their combined implications determine judgments, but their separate implications are not very important. You may recognize this latter view as Gestalt theory ("The whole is greater than the sum of the parts"), which was popular in Europe during the era that behaviorism dominated in the United States. The Asch warm/cold study (1946), described above, was an early attempt to pit the elementist and the holistic views against each other. Asch reasoned that if people were just adding or averaging items of information, then changing one of seven descriptive traits (from warm to cold or vice versa) would have little effect on judgments. But if people were considering the seven traits as a whole, then changing one, central trait might have a substantial effect. This is in fact what happened, with subjects given the descriptors *intelligent, skillful, industrious, determined, practical, cautious,* and *warm* viewing the target as successful and hardworking, and those given the same traits and *cold* viewing the target as ambitious and conniving.

The most extensive examination of these issues was provided by Anderson's research on his *information integration model* (1968). Anderson (1974) believed that people simply averaged separate items of information, and he conducted a vast program of research to demonstrate this for a variety of different kinds of information, including that underlying impression judgments. Ultimately he described a complex equation suggesting that people average separate items of information with the implications of their original opinion, weighting each item differently depending on a number of factors.

In 1974, Anderson was co-sponsor of a workshop on mathematical approaches to person perception to which many eventual founders of the social cognition movement were invited (Hastie et al., 1980, preface). During the workshop, these individuals found themselves questioning the adequacy of mathematical models for representing what people really do with impression-related information. As with attribution theory, the information integration approach was a rigorous and logical approach that did not seem to reflect the kinds of mental activities in which people actually engage during impression formation. After the workshop, these dissidents continued to meet regularly to discuss their ideas and research on social cognition. Many of these ideas, involving information processing, schemas, and associative networks, generally reflected the holistic viewpoint more than the elementist one.

Today the holistic view generally dominates, as reflected in recent research on the effects of context on impression judgments. For example, interpretations of facial expressions depended on the context in which they occurred (Aviezer, Hassin, Bentin, & Trope, 2008); reactions to pictures of minority individuals were influenced by brief exposures to pictures suggesting different environments (e.g., a church versus a street corner; Wittenbrink, Judd, & Park, 2001); and subjects' views of a political candidate's personality were affected not only by his behavior, but by his political ideology (Wyer & Watson, 1969). Most theorists today assume that complex, "holistic" interactions may occur among different aspects of a stimulus situation.

The Accuracy of Impressions

Like most people, social psychologists believed that some individuals are more socially perceptive than others. As a consequence, considerable research was conducted to determine what social skills might lead some individuals to form more accurate impressions than others. However, a critique by Cronbach (1955) put a damper on this area for decades by showing that measures of accuracy are affected by a number of artifacts, such as the similarity between the person whose personality is being rated and the person rating that personality. Somewhat later, a review by Cline (1964) confirmed that impression accuracy had less to do with the social sensitivity of the perceiver than with the similarity between rater and ratee. An additional problem with such research was that the criterion for accuracy was often unclear. If you perceive that I am honest, how should we determine if you are right or wrong? Ask me, and I might give an answer less accurate than yours! Ask others and you might get a common stereotype rather than the correct answer. So, research on the accuracy of impression formation largely ground to a halt.

In recent decades, research on impression accuracy has resumed, as a result of several developments. Kenny's Social Relations Model (Kenny & Albright, 1987) provided a method for measuring various factors that contribute to accuracy, including those identified by Cronbach as problematic. And the criterion issue was resolved by comparing subject's personality impressions with the Big Five measure of personality (e.g., Borkenau & Liebler, 1992) or with objective criteria such as sexual orientation (e.g., Rule, Ambady, Adams, & Macrae, 2008). Most research in this area focuses on "first impressions" formed from minimal information about other people. One review of such work (Ambady & Rosenthal, 1992) suggests that observers are as accurate after viewing a very brief "thin slice" of behavior as after 5 minutes of observation, though other research suggests that longer observational periods sometimes produce greater accuracy (Rule et al., 2008). In general, accuracy also depends a great deal on the dimension being judged (e.g., extraversion is more readily perceived than openness) and on the nature of the observational situation (see Gray, 2008, for a review). A very readable review of such work is provided in the book *Blink* by Malcolm Gladwell (2005).

So, to get back to the original question, are some people more socially perceptive than others? It would appear that accuracy in impression formation relates to a number of individual difference variables, including social sensitivity (Carney & Harrigan, 2003) and the need to belong (Pickett, Gardner, & Knowles, 2004). However, different kinds of people appear to be accurate with regard to different attributes under different conditions, so there really is not just one kind of person who is consistently more accurate in forming impressions of others under all circumstances (Hall & Andrzejewski, 2008).

New Issues

In addition to addressing classic issues in impression formation, as described above, social cognition also directed attention to issues that had not previously concerned impression researchers. We will cover two of these, spontaneous trait inference and priming effects, to illustrate some of the new directions suggested by the social cognition approach.

Spontaneous Trait Inference In introducing this section, we cited the job interview as the prototypic impression formation situation. In this context it can be taken as a given that those involved are motivated to form impressions of each other. This may be equally true in singles bars and dark alleys. Thus, the focus of most impression formation research has been on features of the impression formation process, rather than on the question of when impression formation processes will occur. Of course, social psychological laboratories are not interview contexts, singles bars, or dark alleys (though they have been known to house simulations of all three). But because the majority of laboratory experiments on impression formation simply asked subjects to report their impressions, the issue of when they might engage in impression formation, without being asked, was generally avoided.

In 1984, Winter and Uleman published an article that addressed the obvious, but previously unasked, question, "Do people form trait impressions spontaneously?" This is not a question that can be answered by giving subjects trait rating scales, as done in most prior research, because the scales themselves are likely to provoke impression formation. Nor is it a question that can be addressed directly to subjects, since there is ample evidence that people lack the ability to accurately report their own mental processes (Nisbett & Wilson, 1977). So a new research method needed to be devised, and to do so, Winter and Uleman followed the strategy central to social cognition, adapting ideas and methods from cognitive psychology.

Winter and Uleman's research strategy derived from cognitive psychologist Endel Tulving's encoding specificity principle, which states that the best cues for retrieving information from memory are those that relate to the way that information was first processed. Winter and Uleman reasoned that if subjects given behavioral stimuli processed these by thinking about the actor's likely traits, then the traits they thought about would provide the best retrieval cues for the stimulus behaviors. They conducted a study in which subjects were presented with a number of sentences such as "The plumber slips an extra $50 into his wife's purse," and then were asked to recall as many of these as possible, given cues such as "generous" (the trait cue) or "pipes" (an actor cue). The study confirmed that trait cues were more effective in prompting retrieval than either actor cues or no cues, suggesting that people spontaneously thought about implied traits while processing the original sentences.

The Winter and Uleman study elicited considerable attention, much of it critical of their methodological logic (Bassili & Smith, 1986; Wyer & Srull, 1989, p. 146). One pair of critics, Carlston and Skowronski (1994), proposed an alternative method that they believed would disconfirm Winter and Uleman's conclusions. Like Winter and Uleman, Carlston and Skowronski's research was based on an application of cognitive principles, this time Ebbinghaus' (1964) *savings in relearning* principle. Ebbinghaus studied memory long before cognitive psychology existed as a field, and like Bartlett, his work had little impact on social psychology prior to the social cognition era. Among the phenomena that Ebbinghaus observed was the ability of people to relearn previously forgotten material better than they had been able to learn it initially. For example, suppose you were to read a difficult passage from this chapter right now (or even to read it upside down!), and then to try to do this again a few years from now when (unfortunately) you will probably have forgotten ever reading it. According to Ebbinghaus, your initial experience, even though forgotten, will leave memory traces that make it easier for you to repeat the process, or relearn the material, years later.

So Carlston and Skowronski (1994) reasoned that if people spontaneously form trait impressions of actors while reading about those actors' behaviors, they will more easily associate the actors with those traits in the future. In a series of studies, these researchers presented subjects with numerous pairings of actor photos and behavior descriptions with instructions either to form impressions of the actor or to simply familiarize themselves with the materials. Later, subjects tried to memorize an assortment of photo-trait pairs, some of which corresponded with the implications of photo-behavior pairs presented earlier. As expected, subjects instructed to form impressions had an easier time recalling photo-trait pairings that corresponded with information they had been given earlier than they did recalling novel pairings. Contrary to Carlston and Skowronski's expectations, however, an equally strong savings effect was evident among subjects who were *not* told to form impressions. The research thus inadvertently confirmed that people do form trait impressions spontaneously, a conclusion in which we are quite confident because it is now supported by many other studies (e.g., Carlston, Skowronski, & Sparks, 1995; Carlston & Skowronski, 2005) and methods (e.g., Todorov & Uleman, 2002).

Trait Priming Effects Another novel social cognition finding was that peoples' impressions can be altered by priming them with trait concepts. Suppose we told you that "Donald was aware of his ability to do many things well." Would you have a positive or negative impression of Donald? According to research by Higgins, Rholes, and Jones (1977), this probably depends on whether you view Donald as *confident* or *conceited*. Did you think of Donald as confident? If so, could it have anything to do with the fact that you read the word *confident* in the previous paragraph? There is considerable research to suggest such a *priming effect*. In the study by Higgins et al., for example, subjects' views of Donald (who was described partly with the same phrase given above) were manipulated by exposing them to either the word *self-confident* or the word *conceited* in a "unrelated" experiment they completed before reading about Donald.

To fully understand this priming effect, you need to know more about the associative network models described earlier. We noted previously that such models are derived from cognitive models of memory, and that they involve linkages of varying strength among concepts. Specifically, as illustrated in Figure 3.1, concepts in these models are represented by *nodes* and links are construed as *pathways*. Nodes representing concepts that are being thought about become *activated* and then pass *excitation* through connecting pathways to other, associated concept nodes. When enough excitation accumulates at an associated node, that concept is retrieved, and it then spreads excitation to its associates. Stronger pathways conduct more excitation, so more strongly associated concepts are more likely to foster each other's retrieval. (In terms of the figure, for example, thinking of Tiger Woods is likely to activate the professional golfer node, which in turn may activate other golfers such as Phil Mickelson.) And most important in terms of the priming work, once activated, a node loses its excitation only slowly, with any *residual excitation* making it easier for the concept to become reactivated later.

From this perspective, the prior activation of a trait term, even during a separate experiment or task, leaves that term (or, to be more exact, the node representing it) with some residual level of excitation. Later, when an individual

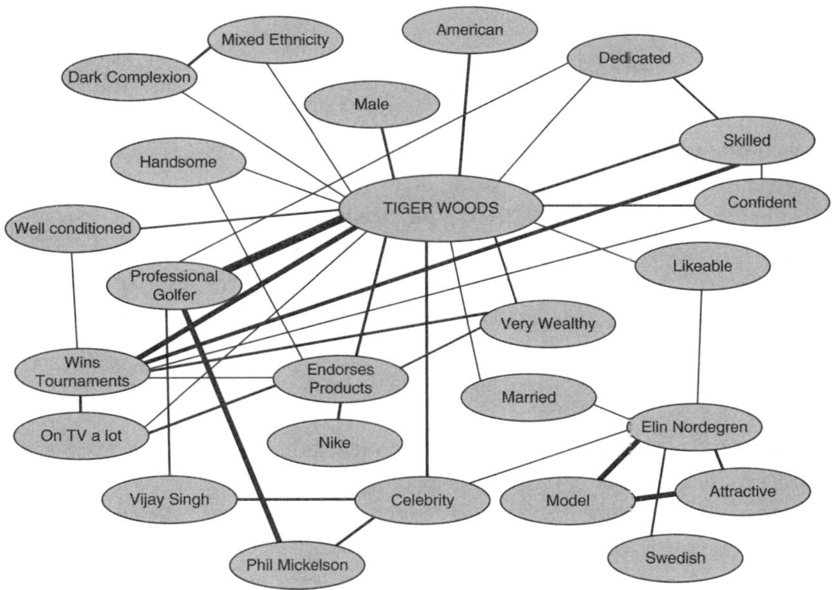

FIGURE 3.1. A portion of an individual's mental representation of golfer Tiger Woods as depicted in an associative network model. Thicker lines represent stronger associations. (Editor's note: This figure was submitted for publication prior to highly publicized events that may alter the associations that some readers have of Tiger woods.)

hears about Donald and begins to search memory for appropriate constructs to use in interpreting Donald's description, the previously activated trait term is likely to come to mind. As a consequence, the individual is more likely to view Donald in a manner consistent with the primed concept.

What if, instead of subtly exposing subjects to the trait word, the researchers had just entered the room with *confident* stamped prominently on their foreheads? Would subjects still have formed impressions consistent with the activated trait term? Probably not. People are generally smart enough to partition out concepts that they know are activated for the wrong reasons (Martin, 1986). In fact, they sometimes bend so far backward to avoid influence that they are actually influenced in the opposite direction (Strack, Schwarz, Bless, Kubler, & Wanke, 1993). In the forehead example, they might be more likely to think of Donald as *conceited* than as *confident,* despite prior exposure to the latter term. What this demonstrates is that memory and judgment are not totally passive activities controlled by the mindless ebb and flow of excitation through an associative network. Nonetheless, the network does underlie human thought and memory, and it does have an impact, perhaps especially when people are not thinking very hard.

Social Cognition and Other Core Topics

As an approach to psychological theorizing and research, social cognition ultimately influenced almost every area of social psychology. (To be fair, almost every area of social psychology also influenced social cognition.) In this section we describe some of those influences, focusing on several central topics in the field. Most of these core topics have their own chapters in this volume, so the current exposition will be kept short, with the intention of illustrating, rather than belaboring, the impact of social cognition.

Nonconscious Processes

An early complaint about the social cognition approach (and also about the attribution approach that preceded it) was that it seemed to (over)emphasize conscious, deliberative cognitive processes, disregarding the kinds of less deliberate, learned responses emphasized by the behaviorists. This was probably a fair criticism, as the victors in the cognitive revolution may have thrown out the baby with the behaviorist bathwater. The information-processing model, which social cognitionists tended to adopt, does seem (at least on the surface) best suited for handling information that is consciously attended and explicitly recalled. So the influence of things not attended or not recalled was initially given short shrift.

But nondeliberative and nonconscious processes were coming to the attention of cognitive psychologists (e.g., Schneider & Shiffrin, 1977) and some models popular among social cognitionists (e.g., schema theory and associative network models) accomplished much of their work outside the range of conscious attention. So the field was somewhat receptive when Bargh (a student of social cognition critic Robert Zajonc) introduced the concept of automaticity to the field in 1982 (see also Bargh, 1984). Following up on earlier work on social "mindlessness" (Langer, Blank, & Chanowitz, 1978) and on cognitive theories of automaticity (e.g., Schneider & Shiffrin, 1977; Posner & Snyder, 1975), Bargh argued that people engage in both controlled and automatic processes, with the latter distinguished from the former by four features. Automatic processes initiate without intention, occur outside of awareness, are difficult to control, and use little of the mind's limited capacity. Bargh (1994) quickly realized that very few processes meet all four criteria, and the theory was revised to suggest that processes are relatively more automatic when they possess more of these features and relatively controlled when they possess fewer.

The critical point is that social cognition expanded to embrace processes that would once have been thought to lie outside its reach. Admittedly, incorporation of Bargh's ideas has not been all hugs and kisses (see, for example, the entire *Advances in Social Cognition*, 1997). But the field now accepts the idea of automaticity, and theories of mental representation now routinely accommodate unconscious ("implicit") representations and processes as well as conscious ("explicit") ones (Carlston, in press). As a result, notions of automaticity and implicitness were less challenges to the validity of social cognition than challenges to expand and refine social cognition theories.

The Self

The Self (see Baumeister, Chapter 5, this volume) is one of the oldest topics in social psychology, having been addressed by William James in 1890. The term has been applied to people's self-concept, as well as to whatever it is that is self-conscious and responsible for control and deliberative processing (see Allport, 1955, for an early treatment). Many psychologists (especially behaviorists) have been uncomfortable with the subjective and seemingly unscientific nature of the self, especially the "whatever it is" part. It is not surprising, then, that self-theorists sought acceptance by periodically recasting the concept in terms of the newly popular psychological constructs of each era (see Linville & Carlston, 1990).

With the emergence of cognitive psychology, this included the "self as schema" (Markus, 1977) and the "self as (associative) cognitive structure" (Bower & Gilligan, 1979.).

Researchers discovered that information is recalled better when initially thought about in relation to the self than when thought about in other ways (Rogers, Kuiper, & Kirker, 1977). This *self-reference effect* (SRE) parallels, but was even stronger than, a *depth of processing* effect that had been documented in cognitive psychology—people who think about the meaning of material remember it better than those who think about it more superficially (Craik & Lockart, 1972). In theory, deeper processing brings material into contact with well-learned knowledge structures (e.g., schemas) that provide a memory framework and potential memory cues. Rogers et al. (1977) therefore posited that the self was a particularly deep and special knowledge structure that bestowed material with particularly good memory cues.

There is now some question as to whether the self-reference effect even exists when the self-reference and comparison tasks are carefully equated (Klein & Kihlstrom, 1986). But during the era when the SRE was most prominent, a number of cognitively oriented researchers attempted to demonstrate the "specialness" of the self-schema. Among these were Higgins, Van Hook, and Dorfman (1988), who tried to show that traits in the self-schema prime other traits that are also part of the schema, and McDaniel, Lapsley, and Milstead (1987), who tried to use a *release from proactive inhibition* task (don't ask) to show that traits in the self-schema are categorized differently from those that are not. These and other similar efforts failed, possibly because the self is really not qualitatively different from other kinds of knowledge (and possibly because trait words, mentioned out of context, are not inherently interpreted as part of the self-concept). Nonetheless, whether "special" or not, it is evident that information about the self is more familiar, better learned, and of more interest to people than are most other kinds of information.

Attitude Structure and Change

In social psychology, the attitudes area (see Fabrigar & Wegener, Chapter 6, this volume; Petty and Briñol, Chapter 7, this volume) is closely related to social cognition, even sharing a section of the leading social psychology journal, the *Journal of Personality and Social Psychology*. Theory and research on attitudes actually predate those on social cognition by decades, and it was generally a cognitive approach in a noncognitive era, although it sometimes made half-hearted efforts to conform with behaviorism (e.g., Staats & Staats, 1958). Some of the early founders of social cognition (e.g., Tom Ostrom and Tony Greenwald) had previously been attitude researchers, as have been some of the winners of the Ostrom Award for Lifetime Contributions to Social Cognition (e.g., Tony Greenwald and Russ Fazio). Thus, even though the social cognition and attitudes areas remain separate subdisciplines, they have had a very symbiotic relationship. As a consequence, there are many areas of overlap, only a few of which will be touched on here.

Early social cognition was criticized for overlooking motivational concerns, which were not inherent in the information processing model. This criticism was probably fair, and explains why social cognition allied itself with the cognitive side of a motivation–cognition debate that played out in the attitude area. This debate pitted dissonance theory (Festinger, 1957), a motivational approach, against self-perception theory (Bem, 1967, 1972), a cognitive approach. Dissonance theory had been one of the most influential theories in social psychology. It suggested that two clashing cognitions (one relating to a belief and another to one's belief-inconsistent behavior) create an uncomfortable state of arousal called *dissonance*. Because dissonance is unpleasant, the theory states, people are motivated to reduce or eliminate it by changing their beliefs. Although simple, the theory has many implications, which busied a generation of attitude researchers (see Cooper & Fazio, 1984; Harmon-Jones & Harmon-Jones, 2008).

Daryl Bem (1967, 1972) suggested that most findings attributed to dissonance could be viewed, instead, as a consequence of a cognitive mechanism, without resorting to motivational constructs. Specifically, he suggested that people often use their own behavior to deduce their beliefs (much as we would use others' behaviors to deduce their beliefs), with the result that after doing so, the two tend to correspond. This *self-perception theory* seemed able to account for most dissonance effects without assuming any motivational processes. Thus began a prolonged battle between dissonance theorists and self-perception theorists over the need for motivational constructs, a battle once thought to be unwinnable (Greenwald, 1975), but ultimately resolved by Fazio, Zanna, and Cooper (1977). In a series of elegant experiments (see also Zanna & Cooper, 1974), these authors showed that dissonance theory applies (and arousal/motivation is important) when a person's beliefs and behavior are quite discrepant, but that self-perception theory applies (and arousal/motivation is not involved) when beliefs and behavior are more consistent. These findings were a bit of a blow to the social cognitionists of that era, suggesting that motivational principles are sometimes important. However, as with the potential threat from automaticity, discussed above, the field of social cognition responded not by admitting defeat, but by expanding to embrace motivational constructs (see below).

The attitude and social cognition areas intersected on other issues as well. Dual processing models, which suggest that people are sometimes thoughtful and sometimes mindless (essentially, on automatic pilot), arose from, and had an impact in, both areas (see Chaiken & Trope, 1999). As with automaticity and dissonance, social cognitive theory expanded to deal with "mindless cognition." As another example, associative network models of memory were applied to the area of attitudes (Fazio, 1986). One interesting implication of this application is that the observation of an attitude object spontaneously activates an attitude or evaluation (Fazio, Sanbonmatsu, Powell, & Kardes, 1986; see also Duckworth, Bargh, Garcia, & Chaiken, 2002). One additional area of overlap, involving "implicit" cognitive representations, is discussed in the next section.

Prejudice and Stereotyping

As with the study of the self and attitudes, the study of prejudice and stereotyping has a venerable tradition in social psychology (see Bodenhausen & Richeson, Chapter 10, this volume). Racial and gender stereotypes were reinterpreted as cognitive schemas during the social cognition era (e.g., Branscombe & Smith, 1990), readily accounting for perceptual and memory biases long known to be associated with stereotyping (Allport, 1954). More recently, prejudice and stereotypes have been viewed as implicit cognitive concepts that sometimes lie outside of awareness and that are activated automatically on exposure to a stereotyped target, potentially leading to prejudiced responses even from egalitarian individuals who normally control their prejudice (Devine, 1989). For example, one study (Bodenhausen, 1990) found that morning people stereotype more in the afternoons and evenings, whereas night people stereotype more in the mornings. In terms of the dual processing theories discussed in the preceding section, people are at their cognitive peak at different times of the day, and when not, they may slip into mindless stereotyping because of beliefs they hold implicitly.

Greenwald, McGhee, and Schwartz (1998) described a cognitively based measure of implicit prejudice that has been widely used and researched (Lane, Banaji, Nosek & Greenwald, 2007), although it remains somewhat controversial (e.g., Blanton & Jaccard, 2006). This measure, the implicit association test (IAT), is based on the premise that it is difficult to simultaneously undertake two cognitive categorization tasks that conflict in terms of feelings about the things being categorized. The task is attractive to social psychologists because it promises to assess how people feel even when their feelings are implicit and outside of awareness. However, the controversy arises because the IAT tends to indicate that almost everyone is prejudiced, leading some to suggest that it may reflect ingrained cultural associations rather than implicit attitudes (Olson & Fazio, 2004).

Of course it is possible that everyone is implicitly prejudiced to some degree, and that the real difference between bigoted and egalitarian individuals is whether they try to control or suppress their prejudice, as Devine (1989) suggested. We have already discussed research showing that prejudice can increase when people's ability to engage in controlled processing is diminished (Bodenhausen, 1990). Other research suggests that the act of exerting control can also backfire, leading prejudice to resurge at a later time (Macrae, Bodenhausen, Milne, & Jetten, 1994). This *rebound effect* is consistent with work by Wegner (1994) that indicates that any attempt to suppress thoughts can backfire by causing the suppressed thoughts to recur stronger than before. To explain such results, Wegner theorized that the act of monitoring our thoughts for a particular concept has the ironic effect of causing that concept to be implicitly rehearsed. In the terms of associative network models described earlier, this rehearsal creates residual activation that makes it easier to remember that concept node in the future.

Judgment and Decision Making

Attempts to document people's errors and biases in the attributional realm were paralleled by attempts to document similar failings in the realm of judgment and decision making (see Vohs & Luce, Chapter 20, this volume). One important program of research was conducted by Kahneman and Tversky (1973; Tversky & Kahneman, 1974). These two theorists identified a variety of simple rules that people use that lead to logical errors, the two most prominent of which were the representativeness heuristic and the availability heuristic.

The idea behind the representativeness heuristic (see Kahneman & Tversky, 1972) is that people make judgments based on whether a stimulus appears to be representative of a particular stimulus or set of circumstances (that is, a schema). As an example, suppose that you were asked whether a well-muscled young man is more likely to be a student or a student and an athlete. Because this stimulus fits your schema of a student-athlete, the representativeness heuristic might lead you to select the second option. However, had you thought about the problem more logically, you might have recognized that the student category includes *all* student-athletes plus many other young men who happen to be well muscled without being athletes. Therefore the probability that this stimulus individual fits the former category has to be higher than the probability that it fits the latter one.

Kahneman and Tversky's (1973) second heuristic, availability, is interesting because it relies on both memory and metamemory (which refers to people's understandings of how their own memory works). This heuristic reflects people's tendency to guess that the ease with which they can recall something reflects the frequency of that thing in the world. Thus, for example, people asked to judge whether more words in the English language begin with "K" or have "K" as the third letter are likely to select the former. It is easier to generate instances based on their first letter ("kite," "kitchen") than on their third ("acknowledge"), so these words are more available in memory, and people assume that they are more frequent. (They are not, as only one-third as many English words actually begin with K.)

The view that people are affected by their own theories about their cognitive processes (known as *metacognition*) has numerous important implications (Flavell, 1976, 1979). One application of metacognition was described earlier in this chapter in relation to the role of awareness in priming. We suggested that people can "partition out concepts that they know are activated for the wrong reasons." Although not labeled as metacognition at the time, such effects hinge on people's beliefs about why particular traits happen to appear in their consciousness.

Emotion

Zajonc' early (1980a) criticism of social cognition stemmed partly from his conviction that affect and emotion are central to human experience. He went so far as to suggest that affect is primary, and that cognition simply follows along, explaining or justifying responses that our affective systems have already determined (Zajonc, 1980b). Thus, it is a mistake for us to imagine that we are sizing someone up, analyzing their behavior, evaluating their personality, and making judgments that will determine our feelings toward them. Rather, according to Zajonc, it is the other way around: We have already determined our feelings, and it is these that will shape our analysis of their behavior and our evaluation of their personality. Zajonc went even further, arguing that affective responses occur even before we recognize what an object is, and that they rely on perceptual features (which he termed "preferenda") different from those that we use to identify or categorize objects (which he termed "discriminenda").

Zajonc supported his argument with research on the implicit effects of repeated exposure (which makes us like things more without knowing why) and on subliminal priming (which can do the same). However, his claims were quite controversial (Lazarus, 1982). Some theorists responded that Zajonc' results were explainable in terms of cognitive mechanisms, without assuming the primacy of affect. One such explanation was that familiarity (even unconscious familiarity) with an object allows it to be processed more easily, creating a *fluency* that is often experienced as pleasant (Reber, Winkielman, & Schwarz, 1998). Such explanations focus on people's subjective interpretations of the cause of their fluency or positive affect, emphasizing again the roles of phenomenology and metacognition.

Although the extreme forms of Zajonc' (1980b) argument met resistance, the importance of human affect and emotional experience is undeniable (see also Forgas, 1983). Consequently, as with automaticity and motivation, social cognitive theory had to adapt. One early effort was Susan Fiske's (1982) schema-based integration of cognition and affect. Another was cognitive psychologist Gordon Bower's (1981) theory that affect can be represented by nodes in an associative network, just as more cognitive constructs can be. From this perspective, experienced affects (moods) can prime memory, resulting in retrieval of memories that are consistent with, and thus linked to, those moods. Fazio's previously described work on the automatic activation of attitudes similarly showed that the subliminal presentation of affectively (or attitudinally) relevant material can facilitate recognition of attitude objects about which we feel similarly. Although such effects were derived from formulations that characterize mood, affect, and evaluation as nodes in an associative network, they are also readily explained by more recent connectionist models that view mood, affect and evaluation as features that combine with other, perceptual features to activate particular constructs (see Carlston, in press). Such models may be increasingly important in the social cognition of the future (Smith, 1996).

Another effort to integrate affect with social cognition was the *affect-as-information* approach (e.g., Clore & Parrott; 1991). This metacognitive approach suggests that people view their own affect as potentially informative about the world, and interpret it in terms of their understanding of the sources and consequences of affective feelings. In a demonstration of this approach, Schwartz and Clore (1983) telephoned people and asked a series of questions about their life satisfaction. The experimenters found an expected relationship between the current local weather and reported satisfaction, with respondents who were experiencing bad weather (and thus presumably were in bad moods) reporting less life satisfaction than those experiencing better weather conditions (and presumably were in better moods). However, before beginning the questioning, some respondents were explicitly asked about the weather they were experiencing. Simply asking this question eliminated the effects of the weather (and thus presumably of mood) on reported life satisfaction. Apparently, knowing that the weather might influence their moods, respondents who had the conditions brought to their attention discounted their moods as a source of information about their life satisfaction, and based their responses on other information.

Notably, both the Bower and the Clore formulations treat affect as they do other, more cognitive constructs, embedding them in an essentially cognitive theory. Forgas (2001) describes a more complex *affect infusion* model, which includes affect-as-information along with several other possible affective and cognitive processing strategies in a more equal partnership. The Forgas approach brings affect into the social cognition fold by employing the information processing model, which he once criticized as incomplete (for its failure to include affect). This nicely illustrates both the influence, and the expansion, of social cognitive theory.

Motivation and Goals

The battle between dissonance and self-perception theory described earlier highlights the historical conflict between motivational and cognitive approaches to human behavior. The reader may recall that the resolution to the dissonance/self-perception battle was essentially to cede each some territory, and to say that both were correct under different circumstances. More recently, however, a different kind of rapprochement has been suggested, which has parallels to the manner in which affect was incorporated into social cognition.

The new approach treats people's motivation and goals as concepts that can interact with other cognitive concepts in associative memory (Bargh, 1990; Kruglanski & Kopetz, 2009). This interaction is nicely illustrated by a study on the effects of subliminal primes on behavior (Strahan, Spencer, & Zanna, 2002). Subjects were induced to feel thirsty (or not), which was presumed to create a goal or motivation to drink. Some subjects were then subliminally primed with thirst-related words, whereas others were not. Finally, as part of a "taste test," subjects were asked to compare two glasses of Kool-Aid, and the experimenters surreptitiously measured how much they drank. The experimenters discovered that if subjects had no motivation to drink (because they were not thirsty), the thirst-related primes had no effect. However, if the subjects had a motivation to drink, they drank more after being primed with thirst-related words than non-thirst-related words. Thus, motivations and cognitions interacted to determine behavior.

Research on the cognitive representation of goals suggests that they are organized hierarchically under superordinate goals and values but above specific means and tasks. Furthermore, they can be primed by, or help to prime, other levels of the goal hierarchy, other noncompeting goals, and other goal-related concepts. Although goals behave much like other kinds of cognitive concepts, they also possess some differences (Bargh & Gollwitzer, 1994; Forster, Liberman, & Friedman, 2007). For example, goals tend to become more activated as their completion nears, but then to switch off suddenly (rather than showing persisting residual excitation) once they are accomplished. It is difficult for traditional associative network models to explain such effects, so the models have had to be stretched to bring motivation and goals under the social cognitive umbrella. This stretching probably makes the social cognitive approach less parsimonious than it once was, but it also has the effect of changing the way that motivationally oriented theorists think about motivation.

Social Cognition Today

The preceding review suggests that the area of social cognition has been expanding to include topics that were previously thought to be noncognitive: automatic processes, implicit representations, affect and emotions, and motivation and goals. This expansion has enriched theory and research in the field, but it has also resulted in a more complex, and a more unwieldy core body of knowledge in social cognition. Some new methods, findings, and principles suggested by this new body of work have yet to be fully assimilated, and it is less clear where the boundaries of the discipline are. Social cognition researchers once focused principally on impression formation (along with attribution and attitudes); however, today they cover everything. Philosophers of science suggest that theories tend to become less parsimonious as they accumulate additional assumptions to accommodate new data that do not fit, and the same may be true of fields as a whole. So social cognition is no longer the coherent set of perspectives and ideals it once was. Still, in time the seams between disparate areas of the field are likely to be smoothed over and new ideas, approaches, methods, and findings are likely to be successfully assimilated.

In the meantime, social cognition is beginning to realize one of its primary objectives: the spread of one universal set of concepts and principles within most, if not all, psychological theorizing and research. Of course, it is possible that social cognitionists may not ultimately determine what that universal set of concepts and principles is. New cognitive approaches such as connectionism do not readily conform to the information processing model. New methods, such as those arising out of social cognitive neuroscience (see Heatherton & Wheatley, Chapter 16, this volume), will undoubtedly result in radical new understandings of human thought processes, posing novel challenges for old social cognition theories. The chances are that social cognition, if it is still called that, will in 10 years look quite different than it does now.

But the core issues that ignited the field will still be important. People's phenomenology will still play a role in how they navigate their social world. Their conscious thoughts and judgments will still matter, although so too will their unconscious thoughts, and other things going on in the brain that we may not even construe as thoughts today. And the science of social psychology will continue to borrow the ideas and tools that it needs from other cutting edge disciplines to construct the most accurate representation possible of the role that people's single, unified mind plays in shaping experiences and behavior. Such developments will be welcome because social cognition never really wanted to rule the world; it only wanted to understand it.

Suggested Further Readings

Carlston, D. E. (In press). Models of implicit and explicit mental representations. In B. Gawronski & B. K. Payne (Eds.), *Handbook of implicit social cognition: Measurement, theory and applications*. New York: Guilford Press.

Gladwell M. (2005). *Blink: The power of thinking without thinking*. Boston, MA: Little, Brown.

Hassin, R., Uleman, J. S., & Bargh, J. A. (Eds.) (2004). *The new unconscious*. New York: Oxford University Press.

References

Allport, G. W. (1954). *The nature of prejudice*. Reading, MA: Addison-Wesley.

Allport, G. W. (1955). *Becoming*. New Haven: Yale University Press.

Allport, G. W., & Odbert, H. S. (1936). Trait names: A psycholexical study. *Psychological Monographs, 47*, 211.

Ambady, N., & Rosenthal, R. (1992). Thin slices of expressive behavior as predictors of interpersonal consequences: A meta-analysis. *Psychological Bulletin, 111*, 256–274.

Anderson, J. R., & Bower, G. H. (1973). *Human associative memory*. Washington, DC: V. H. Winston.

Anderson, N. H. (1968). A simple model for information integration. In R.P. Abelson, E. Aronson, W. J. McGuire, T. M. Newcomb, M. J. Rosenberg, & P. H. Tannenbaum (Eds.), *Theories of cognitive consistency: A sourcebook*. Chicago: Rand McNally.

Anderson, N. H. (1974). Information integration: A brief survey. In D. H. Krantz, R. C. Atkinson, R. D. Luce, & P. Suppes (Eds.), *Contemporary developments in mathematical psychology* (pp. 236–305). San Francisco: Freeman.

Anderson, N. H., & Hubert, S. (1963). Effects of coccomitant verbal recall on order effects in personality impression formation. *Journal of Verbal Learning and Verbal Behavior*, 2, 379–391.

Aviezer, H., Hassin, R. R., Bentin, S., & Trope, Y. (2008). Putting facial expressions back in context. In N. Ambady & J. J. Skowronski (Eds.), *First impressions*. New York: Guilford Press.

Asch, S. E. (1946). Forming impressions of personality. *Journal of Abnormal and Social Psychology, 41*, 1230–1240.

Bargh, J. A. (1982). Attention and automaticity in the processing of self-relevant information. *Journal of Personality and Social Psychology, 43*, 425–436.

Bargh, J. A. (1984). Automatic and conscious processing of social information. In R. S. Wyer, Jr., & T. K. Srull (Eds.), *Handbook of social cognition* (Vol. 3, pp. 1–43). Hillsdale, NJ: Erlbaum.

Bargh, J. A. (1990). Auto-motives: Preconscious determinants of social interaction. In E. T. Higgins & R. M. Sorrentino (Eds.), *Handbook of motivation and cognition: Foundations of social behavior* (Vol. 2: Basic Processes; pp. 93–130). New York: Guilford Press.

Bargh, J. A. (1994). The four horsemen of automaticity: Awareness, intention, efficiency and control in social cognition. In R. S. Wyer, Jr. & T. K. Srull (Eds.), *Handbook of social cognition* (Vol. 1: Basic Processes; pp. 153–208). Hillsdale, NJ: Lawrence Erlbaum Associates.

Bargh, J. A., Chaiken, S., Govender, R., & Pratto, F. (1992). The generality of the automatic attitude activation effect. *Journal of Personality and Social Psychology, 62*(6), 893–912.

Bargh, J. A., & Gollwitzer, P. M. (1994). Environmental control over goal-directed action. *Nebraska Symposium on Motivation, 41*, 71–124.

Bartlett, F. A. (1932). *A study in experimental and social psychology*. New York: Cambridge University Press.

Bassili, J. N., & Smith, M. C. (1986). On the spontaneity of trait attributions: Converging evidence for the role of cognitive strategy. *Journal of Personality and Social Psychology, 50*, 239–246.

Bazil, L. G. D. (1999). The effects of social behavior on fourth- and fifth-grade girls' perceptions of physically attractive and unattractive peers. Unpublished doctoral dissertation.

Beehr, T. A., & Gilmore, D. C. (1982). Applicant attractiveness as a perceived job relevant variable in selection. *Academy of Management Journal, 25*, 607–617.

Bem, D. J. (1967). Self-perception: An alternative interpretation of cognitive dissonance phenomena. *Psychological Review, 74*, 183–200.

Bem, D. J. (1972). Self-perception theory. In L. Berkowitz (Ed.), *Advances in experimental social psychology* (Vol. 6, pp. 1–62). New York: Academic Press.

Berscheid, E., Dion, K. K., Walster, E., & Walster, G. W. (1971). Physical attractiveness and dating choice: A test of the matching hypothesis. *Journal of Experimental Social Psychology, 7*, 173–189.

Blanton, H., & Jaccard, J. (2006). Arbitrary metrics in psychology. *American Psychologist, 61*(1), 27–41.

Bodenhausen, G. V. (1990). Stereotypes as judgmental heuristics: Evidence of circadian variations in discrimination. *Psychological Science, 1*, 319–322.

Borkenau, P., & Liebler, A. (1992). Trait inferences: Sources of validity at zero acquaintance. *Journal of Personality and Social Psychology*, 62, 645–647.

Bower, G. H. (1981). Emotional mood and memory. *American Psychologist, 36*, 129, 148.

Bower, G. H., & Gilligan, S. G. (1979). Remembering information related to one's self. *Journal of Research in Personality, 13*, 420–432.

Branscombe, N. R., & Smith, E. R. (1990). Gender and racial stereotypes in impression formation and social decision-making processes. *Sex Roles*, 22(9–10), 627–647.

Brewin, C. R. (1988). Attribution therapy. In F. N. Watts (Ed.), *New developments in clinical psychology*, Vol. 2 (pp. 20–24) Oxford, England: John Wiley & Sons.

Carlston D. E. (1980). The recall and use of traits and events in social inference processes. *Journal of Experimental Social Psychology, 16*, 303–328.

Carlston, D. E. (1994). Associated systems theory: A systematic approach to the cognitive representation of persons and events. In R. S. Wyer (Ed.), *Advances in social cognition: Vol. 7. Associated systems theory* (pp. 1–78). Hillsdale, NJ: Lawrence Erlbaum Associates.

Carlston, D. E. (2010). Models of implicit and explicit mental representations. In B. Gawronski & B. K. Payne (Eds.), *Handbook of implicit social cognition: Measurement, theory and applications*. New York: Guilford Press. In press.

Carlston, D. E., & Skowronski, J. J. (1986). Trait memory and behavior memory: The effects of alternative pathways on impression judgment response times. *Journal of Personality and Social Psychology*, 50, 1–9.

Carlston, D. E., & Skowronski, J. J. (1994). Savings in the relearning of trait information as evidence for spontaneous inference generation. *Journal of Personality and Social Psychology, 66*, 840–856.

Carlston, D. E., & Skowronski, J. J. (2005). Linking versus thinking: Evidence for the different associative and attributional bases of spontaneous trait transference and spontaneous trait inference. *Journal of Personality and Social psychology, 89*, 884–898.

Carlston, D. E., Skowronski, J. J., & Sparks, C. (1995). Savings in relearning II: On the formation of behavior-based trait associations and inferences. *Journal of Personality and Social Psychology, 69*, 429–436.

Carney, D. R., & Harrigan, J. A. (2003). It takes one to know one: Interpersonal sensitivity is related to accurate assessments of others' interpersonal sensitivity. *Emotion*, 3, 194–200.

Chaiken, S., & Trope, Y. (Eds.) (1999). *Dual-process theories in social psychology*. New York: Guilford Press.

Cline, V. B. (1964). Interpersonal perception. In B. A. Maher (Ed.), *Progress in experimental personality research*. (Vol. 1). New York: Academic Press.

Clore, G. L., & Parrott, W. G. (1991). Moods and their vicissitudes: Thoughts and feelings as information. In J. Forgas (Ed.), *Emotion and social judgment* (pp. 107–123). Oxford: Pergamon.

Collins, A. M., & Loftus, E. F. (1975). A spreading activation model of semantic meaning. *Psychological Review, 82*, 407–428.

Cooper, J., & Fazio, R. H. (1984). A new look at dissonance theory. In L. Berkowitz (Ed.), *Advances in experimental social psychology* (Vol. 17, pp. 229–266). New York: Academic Press.

Craik, F. I. M., & Lockhart, R. S. (1972). Levels of processing: A framework for memory research. *Journal of Verbal Learning and Verbal Behavior, 11*, 671–684.

Cronbach, L. J. (1955). Processes affecting scores on "understanding of others" and "assumed similarity." *Psychological Bulletin, 52*, 177–193.

Cunningham, M. R., Barbee, A. P., & Philhower, C. L. (2002). Dimensions of facial physical attractiveness: The intersection of biology and culture. In G. Rhodes & L. A. Zebrowitz (Eds.), *Facial attractiveness: Evolutionary, cognitive and social perspectives*. Westport, CT: Ablex Publishing.

Darley, J. M., & Gross, P. H. (1983). A hypothesis-confirming bias in labeling effects. *Journal of Personality and Social Psychology, 44*, 20–33.

De Santis, A., and Kayson, W. A. (1999). Defendants' characteristics of attractiveness, race, & sex and sentencing decisions. *Psychological Reports, 81*, 679–683.

Devine, P. G. (1989) Stereotypes and prejudice: Their automatic and controlled components. *Journal of Personality and Social Psychology, 56*, 5–18.

Dion, K. K., Berscheid, E., & Hatfield (Walster), E. (1972). What is beautiful is good. *Journal of Personality and Social Psychology, 24*, 285–290.

Duckworth, K. L., Bargh, J. A., Garcia, M., & Chaiken, S. (2002). The automatic evaluation of novel stimuli. *Psychological Science, 13*, 513–519.

Ebbinghaus, H. (1964). *Memory: A contribution to experimental psychology* (H. A. Ruger & C. E. Bussenius, Trans.). New York: Dover. (Original work published in 1885.)

Fazio, R. H. (1986). How do attitudes guide behavior? In R. M. Sorrentino & E. T. Higgins (Eds.), *Handbook of motivation and cognition: Foundations of social behavior* (pp. 204–243). New York: Guilford Press.

Fazio, R. H., Sanbonmatsu, D. M., Powell, M. C., & Kardes, F. R. (1986). On the automatic activation of attitudes. *Journal of Personality and Social Psychology, 50*, 229–238.

Fazio, R. H., Zanna, M. P., & Cooper, J. (1977). Dissonance and self-perception: An integrative view of each theory's proper domain of application. *Journal of Experimental Social Psychology, 13*, 464–479.

Festinger, L. (1957). *A theory of cognitive dissonance*. Palo Alto, CA: Stanford University Press.

Fiske, S. T. (1982). Schema-triggered affect. In. J. Harvey (Ed.), *Cognition, social behavior, and the environment* (pp. 227–264). Hillsdale, NJ: Erlbaum.

Fiske, S. T., & Taylor, S. E. (1984). *Social cognition*. Reading, MA: Addison-Wesley.

Flavell, J. H. (1976). Metacognitive aspects of problem solving. In L. B. Resnick (Ed.), *The nature of intelligence* (pp. 231–236). Hillsdale, NJ: Erlbaum

Flavell, J. H. (1979). Metacognition and cognitive monitoring: A new area of cognitive-developmental inquiry. *American Psychologist*, *34*(10), 906–911.

Forgas, J. P. (1983). What is social about social cognition? *British Journal of Social Psychology*, *22*(2), 129–144.

Forgas, J. P. (2001). The affect infusion model (AIM): An integrative theory of mood effects on cognition and judgments. In L. L. Martin & G. L Clore (Eds.), *Theories of mood and cognition: A user's guidebook*. (pp. 99–134). Mahwah, NJ: Lawrence Erlbaum.

Forster, J., Liberman, N., & Friedman, R. S. (2007). Seven principles of goal activation: A systematic approach to distinguishing goal priming from priming of non-goal constructs. *Personality and Social Psychology Review*, *11*(3), 211–233.

Gilbert, D. T., & Malone, P. S. (1995). The correspondence bias. *Psychological Bulletin*, *117*, 2138.

Gladwell, M. (2005). *Blink: The power of thinking without thinking*. Boston, MA: Little, Brown.

Goldberg, L. R. (1993). The structure of phenotypic personality traits. *American Psychologist*, *48*, 26–34.

Gray, H. M. (2008). To what extent, and under what conditions, are first impressions valid? In N. Ambady & J. J. Skowronski (Eds.), *First Impressions*. New York: Guilford Press.

Greenwald, A. G. (1975). On the inconclusiveness of "crucial" cognitive tests of dissonance versus self-perception theories. *Journal of Experimental Social Psychology*, *11*, 490–499.

Greenwald, A. G., McGhee, D. E., & Schwartz, J. L. K. (1998). Measuring individual differences in implicit cognition: The implicit association test. *Journal of Personality and Social Psychology*, *74*, 1464–1480.

Hall, J. A., & Andrzewjewski, S. A. (2008). Who draws accurate first impression? Personal correlates of sensitivity to nonverbal cues. In N. Ambady & J. J. Skowronski (Eds.), *First impressions*. New York: Guilford Press.

Hamilton, D. L. (1988). Causal attributions viewed from an information-processing perspective. In D. Bar-Tal & A. W. Kruglanski (Eds.), *The social psychology of knowledge* (pp. 369–385). Cambridge, England: Cambridge University Press.

Hamilton, D. L., Katz, L. B., & Leirer, V. O. (1980). Cognitive representation of personality impressions: Organizational processes in first impression formation. *Journal of Personality and Social Psychology*, *39*, 1050–1063.

Harmon-Jones, E., & Harmon-Jones, C. (2008). Cognitive dissonance theory: An update with a focus on the action-based model. In J. Y. Shaw & W. L. Gardner (Eds.), *Handbook of motivation science* (pp. 71–83). New York: Guilford Press.

Hastie, R., & Kumar, P. A. (1979). Person memory: Personality traits as organizing principles in memory for behaviors. *Journal of Personality and Social Psychology*, *37*(1), 25–38.

Hastie, R., Ostrom, T. M., Ebbesen, E. B., Wyer, R. S., Hamilton, D. L., & Carlston, D. E. (Eds.) (1980). *Person memory: The cognitive basis of social perception* (pp. 1–53). Hillsdale, NJ: Erlbaum.

Hatier, R., & Park, B. (1986). The relationship between memory and judgment depends on whether the judgment task is memory-based or on-line. *Psychological Review, 93*, 258–268.

Heider, F. (1958). *The psychology of interpersonal relations.* New York: Wiley.

Heider, F., & Simmel, M. (1944). An experimental study of apparent behavior. *American Journal of Psychology, 57*, 243–259.

Higgins E. T., Bargh J. A., & Lombardi W. (1985). The nature of priming effects on categorization. *Journal of Experimental Psychology: Learning, Memory and Cognition, 11*, 59–69.

Higgins, E. T., Herman, C. P., & Zanna, M. P. (Eds.) (1981). *Social cognition: The Ontario Symposium* (Vol. 1). Hillsdale, NJ: Lawrence Erlbaum Associates.

Higgins, E. T., Rholes, W. S., & Jones, C. R. (1977). Category accessibility and impression formation. *Journal of Experimental Social Psychology, 13*, 141–154.

Higgins, E. T., Van Hook, E., & Dorfman, D. (1988). Do self attributes form a cognitive structure? *Social Cognition, 6*, 177–207.

Jacobson, M. N. (2004). Effects of victim's and defendant's physical attractiveness on subjects' judgments in a rape case. *Sex Roles, 7*(3), 247–255.

James, W. (1890). *The principles of psychology.* New York: Dover Publications. (Reprinted in 1950.)

Jones, E. E., & Davis, K. E. (1965). From acts to dispositions: The attribution process in person perception. In L. Berkowitz (Ed.), *Advances in experimental social psychology* (Vol. 2, pp. 220–266). New York: Academic Press.

Jones, E. E., Davis, K. E., & Gergen, K. J. (1961). Role playing variations and their informational value for person perception. *Journal of Abnormal and Social Psychology, 63*, 302–310.

Kahneman, D., & Tversky, A. (1972). Subjective probability: A judgment of representativeness. *Cognitive Psychology, 3*, 430–454.

Kahneman, D., & Tversky, A. (1973). On the psychology of prediction. *Psychological Review, 80*, 237–251.

Kelley, H. H. (1967). Attribution theory in social psychology. In D. Levine (Ed.), *Nebraska Symposium on Motivation* (Vol. 15, pp. 192–240). Lincoln: University of Nebraska Press.

Kelley, H. H. (1987). Causal schemata and the attribution process. In E. E. Jones, D. E. Kanouse, H. H. Kelley, R. E. Nisbett, & S. Valins, et al. (Eds.), *Attribution: Perceiving the causes of behavior* (pp. 151–174). Hillsdale, NJ: Lawrence Erlbaum Associates.

Kenny, D. A., & Albright, L. (1987). Accuracy in interpersonal perception: A social relations analysis. *Psychological Bulletin, 102*, 390–402.

Kihlstrom, J. F., & Klein, S. B. (1994). The self as a knowledge structure. In R. S. Wyer, Jr. & T. K. Srull (Eds.), *Handbook of social cognition* (Volume 1: Basic Processes; pp. 153–208). Hillsdale, NJ: Lawrence Erlbaum Associates.

Klein, S. B., & Kihlstrom, J. F. (1986). Elaboration, organization, and the self-reference effect in memory. *Journal of Experimental Psychology: General, 115*, 26–38.

Kruglanski, A. W., & Kopetz, C, (2009). What is so special (and nonspecial) about goals? A view from the cognitive perspective. In G. B. Moskowitz & H. Grant (Eds.), *The psychology of goals*. New York: Guilford Press.

Kuhn, T. S. (1962). *The structure of scientific revolutions*. Chicago: University of Chicago Press.

Lane, K. A., Banaji, M. R., Nosek, B. A., & Greenwald, A. G. (2007). Understanding and using the Implicit Association Test: IV. What we know (so far). In B. Wittenbrink & N. S. Schwarz (Eds.), *Implicit measures of attitudes: Procedures and controversies*. New York: Guilford Press.

Langer, E. J., Blank, A., & Chanowitz, B. (1978). The mindlessness of ostensibly thoughtful action: The role of "placebic" information in interpersonal interaction. *Journal of Personality and Social Psychology*, 36, 635–642.

Langlois, J. H., & Roggman, A. (1990). Attractive faces are only average. *Psychological Science, 1*, 115–121.

Lazarus, R. S. (1982). Thoughts on the relations between emotions and cognition. *American Psychologist, 37*(10), 1019–1024.

Linville, P. W., & Carlston, D.E. (1994). Social cognition of the self. In P. G. Devine, D. L. Hamilton, & T. M. Ostrom (Eds.), *Social cognition: Its impact on social psychology* (pp. 396–403). New York: Academic Press.

Macrae, C. N., Bodenhausen, G. V., Milne, A. B., & Jetten, J. (1994). Out of mind but back in sight: Stereotypes on the rebound. *Journal of Personality and Social Psychology, 67*, 808–817.

Maddux, W. W., & Yuki, M. (2006). The "ripple effect": Cultural differences in perceptions of the consequences of events. *Personality and Social Psychology Bulletin, 32*, 669–684.

Markus, H. (1977). Self-schemata and processing information about the self. *Journal of Personality and Social Psychology, 35*(2), 63–78.

Martin, L. L. (1986). Set/reset: Use and disuse of concepts in impression formation. *Journal of Personality and Social Psychology, 51*, 493–504.

McArthur, L. Z. (1976). The lesser influence of consensus than distinctiveness information on causal attributions: A test of the person-thing hypothesis. *Journal of Personality and Social Psychology, 33*(6), 733–742.

McDaniel, M. A., Lapsley, D. K., & Milstead, M. (1987). Testing the generality and automaticity of self-reference encoding with release from proactive interference. *Journal of Experimental Social psychology, 23*(4), 269–284.

Neisser, U. (1967). *Cognitive psychology*. Englewood Cliffs, NJ: Prentice-Hall.

Newcomb, T. M. (1953). An approach to the study of communicative acts. *Psychological Review, 60*, 393–404.

Nisbett, R. E., & Wilson, T. D. (1977). Telling more than we can know: Verbal reports on mental processes. *Psychological Review, 84*, 231–259.

Olson, M. A., & Fazio, R. H. (2004). Reducing the influence of extrapersonal associations on the implicit association test: Personalizing the IAT. *Journal of Personality and Social Psychology, 86*, 653–667.

Ostrom, T. M. (1984). The sovereignty of social cognition. In R. S Wyer, Jr. & T. K. Srull (Eds.), *Handbook of social cognition* (Vol. 1: Basic Processes; pp. 1–38). Hillsdale, NJ: Lawrence Erlbaum Associates.

Ostrom, T. M., Lingle, J. H., Pryor, J. B., & Geva, N. (1980). Cognitive organization of person impressions. In R. Hastie, T. M. Ostrom, E. B. Ebbesen, R. S. Wyer, D. Hamilton, & D. E. Carlston (Eds.), *Person memory: The cognitive basis of social perception* (pp. 55–88). Hillsdale, NJ: Erlbaum.

Pickett, C. L., Gardner, W. L., & Knowles, M. (2004). Getting a cue: The need to belong enhances sensitivity to social cues. *Personality and Social Psychology Bulletin, 30*, 1095–1107.

Posner, M. I., & Snyder, C. R. R. (1975). Attention and cognitive control. In R. L. Solso (Ed.), *Information processing and cognition: The Loyola symposium* (pp. 55–85). Hillsdale, NJ: Erlbaum.

Reber, R., Winkielman, P., & Schwarz, N. (1998). Effects of perceptual fluency on affective judgments. *Psychological Science, 9*, 45–48.

Rogers, T. B., Kuiper, N. A., & Rogers, P. J. (1979). Symbolic distance and congruity effects for paired-comparison judgment of degree of self-reference. *Journal of Research in Personality, 13*, 433–449.

Rosenberg, S., & Sedlak, A. (1972). Structural representations in implicit personality theory. In L. Berkowitz (Ed.), *Advances in experimental social psychology* (Vol. 10, pp. 235–297).

Ross, L. (1977). The intuitive psychologist and his shortcomings: Distortions in the attribution process. In L. Berkowitz (Ed.), *Advances in experimental social psychology* (Vol. 10, pp. 173–220). New York: Academic Press.

Rule, N. O., Ambady, N., Adams, R. B., Jr., & Macrae, C. N. (2008). Accuracy and awareness in the perception and categorization of male sexual orientation. *Journal of Personality and Social Psychology, 95*(5), 1019–1028.

Sahar, G. (2008). On the importance of attribution theory in political psychology. Paper presented at the annual meetings of the International Society of Political Psychology in Paris France.

Schneider, W., & Shiffrin, R. M. (1977). Controlled and automatic human information processing: 1. Detection, search, and attention. *Psychological Review, 84*, 1–66.

Schwarz, N., & Clore, G. L. (1983). Mood, misattribution, and judgments of well-being: Informative and directive functions of affective states. *Journal of Personality and Social Psychology, 45*, 513–523.

Sherman, S. J., Judd, C. M., and Park, B. (1989). Social cognition. *Annual Review of Psychology*, *40*, 281–326.

Skowronski J. J., & Gannon, K. (2000). Raw conditional probabilities are a flawed index of associative strength: Evidence from a single trait expectancy paradigm. *Basic and Applied Social Psychology*, *22*(1), 9–18.

Smith, E. R. (1996). What do connectionism and social psychology offer each other? *Journal of Personality and Social Psychology*, *70*, 893–912.

Snyder, M., Tanke, E. D., & Berscheid, E. (1977). Social perception and interpersonal behavior: On the self-fulfilling nature of social stereotypes. *Journal of Personality and Social Psychology*, *35*(9), 656–666.

Snyder, M., & Uranowitz, S. W. (1978). Reconstructing the past: Some cognitive consequences of person perception. *Journal of Personality and Social Psychology*, *36*, 941–950.

Srull, T. K. (1981). Person memory: Some tests of associative storage and retrieval models. *Journal of Experimental Psychology: Human Learning and Memory*, *7*, 440–463.

Staats, A. W., & Staats, C. K. (1958). Attitudes established by classical conditioning. *Journal of Abnormal Psychology*, *57*(1), 37–40.

Strack, F., Schwartz, N., Bless, H., Kubler, A., & Wanke, M. (1993). Awareness of the influence as a determinant of assimilation versus contrast. *European Journal of Social Psychology*, *51*, 493–504.

Strahan, E. J., Spence, S. J., & Zanna, M. P. (2002). Subliminal priming and persuasion: Striking while the iron is hot. *Journal of Experimental Social Psychology*, *38*, 556–568.

Thurstone, L. L. (1934). The vectors of the mind. *Psychological Review*, *41*, 1–32.

Todorov, A., & Uleman, J. S. (2002). Spontaneous trait inferences are bound to actors: Evidence from false recognition. *Journal of Personality and Social Psychology*, *83*, 1051–1065.

Tversky, A., & Kahneman, D. (1973). Availability: A heuristic for judging frequency and probability. *Cognitive Psychology*, *5*, 207–232.

Tversky, A., & Kahneman, D. (1974). Judgment under uncertainty: Heuristics and biases. *Science*, *185*, 1124–1131.

Wegner, D. M. (1993). Ironic processes of mental control. *Psychological Review*, *101*, 34–52.

Weiner, B., Frieze, I., Kukla, A., Reed, L., Rest, S., & Rosenbaum, R. M. (1987). In E. E. Jones, D. E. Kanouse, H. H. Kelley, R. E. Nisbett, & S. Valins, et al. (Eds.), *Attribution: Perceiving the causes of behavior*. (pp. 151–174). Hillsdale, NJ: Lawrence Erlbaum Associates.

Winter, L., & Uleman, J. S. (1984). When are social judgments made? Evidence for the spontaneousness of trait inferences. *Journal of Personality and Social Psychology*, *47*, 237–252.

White, N. (2005). Attribution and mitigation of parent and child responsibility: A qualitative analysis. *Psychiatry, Psychology and Law*, *12*, 401411.

Winkielman, P., Halberstadt, J., Fazendeiro, T., & Catty, S. (2006). Prototypes are attractive because they are easy on the mind. *Psychological Science*, *17*, 799–806.

Wittenbrink, B., Judd, C. M., & Park, B. (2001). Evaluative versus conceptual judgments in automatic stereotyping and prejudice. *Journal of Experimental Social Psychology*, *37*(3), 244–252.

Wyer, R. S., Jr. (Ed.), *The automaticity of everyday life: Advances in social cognition* (Vol. 10, pp. 1–61). Hillsdale, NJ: Lawrence Erlbaum Associates.

Wyer, R. S, Jr., & Carlston, D. E. (1979). *Social cognition, inference and attribution*. Hillsdale, NJ: Lawrence Erlbaum Associates.

Wyer, R. S., Jr., & Srull, T. K. (1989). *Memory and cognition in its social context*. Hillsdale, NJ: Lawrence Erlbaum Associates.

Wyer, R. S., Jr., & Watson, S. F. (1969). Context effects in impression formation. *Journal of Personality and Social Psychology*, *12*(1), 22–33.

Zajonc, R. B. (1980a). Cognition and social cognition: A historical perspective. In L. Festinger (Ed.), *Retrospections on social psychology* (pp. 180–204). New York: Oxford University Press.

Zajonc, R. B. (1980b). Feelings and thinking: Preferences need no inferences. *American Psychologist*, 35(2), 151–175.

Zanna, M. P., & Cooper, J. (1974). Disoonance and the pill: An attribution theory approach to studying the arousal properties of dissonance. *Journal of Personality and Social Psychology*, *29*, 703–709.

Zebrowitz, L. A., & Montepare, J. M. (2008). First impression from facial appearance cues. In N. Ambady & J. J. Skowronski (Eds.), *First impressions*. New York: Guilford Press.

Chapter 4

Social Psychology of Emotion

Antony S. R. Manstead

There are grounds for thinking that emotion is deeply social in nature and that social life is imbued with emotion (Parkinson, 1996). First consider the social nature of emotion. It is true that there are emotional responses (such as fear of heights or disgust evoked by bitter tastes) that are evoked by sensory stimuli without any obvious social component, but such emotions are the exception. The majority of the emotions we experience in everyday life have a social origin. The object of emotion is typically social in nature. It may be an individual (someone you love), a social group (a political party you despise), a social event (your favorite sports team winning a competition), or a social or cultural artifact (a piece of music). These social objects are much more likely than nonsocial objects to be the source of our everyday emotions (Scherer, Walbott, & Summerfield, 1986).

Furthermore, many emotions are inherently social, in the sense that they would not be experienced in the absence of others, or appear to have no function other than to bind us to others. Emotions such as compassion, sympathy, maternal love, affection, and admiration depend on other people being physically or psychologically present. Fear of rejection, loneliness, embarrassment, guilt, shame, jealousy, and sexual attraction are emotions that seem to have the primary function of motivating the individual to seek out or cement social relationships.

A final point concerning the link between emotion and social life is that when we experience emotions we have a strong tendency to communicate with others about them. In research on what is called the "social sharing" of emotion, investigators have shown that the majority of emotional experiences are shared with others, and that this is done quite frequently and quite soon after the triggering event (Rimé, Finkenauer, Luminet, Zech, & Philippot, 1998). Moreover, this sharing of emotion with others elicits emotional reactions in listeners, an interesting phenomenon in itself, depending as it does on the listener's tendency to empathize with the sharer (Christophe & Rimé, 1997).

These points make it clear that emotions are typically social in nature: They are about social objects, their function seems to be social, and they have social consequences. A related point is that much of the classic subject matter of social psychology is emotional in nature: Topics such as close relationships, aggression and hostility, altruism and helping behavior, prejudice and stereotyping, and attitudes and persuasion entail concepts and processes that are often explicitly emotional. In short, there is an intimate connection between emotion and social psychology, which helps to account for the prominent role that social psychologists have played in emotion theory and research.

In the rest of this chapter I review the different ways in which social psychologists have advanced our understanding of emotion. I start with appraisal theory, the dominant current theoretical framework in emotion research. I then consider the social functions served by emotion, and how emotions influence social cognition, before turning to fundamentally "social emotions" such as shame and guilt. I go on to address the way in which emotions are expressed in the face. In the following two sections of the chapter I focus on the role of emotion in and between social groups, and on cultural influences on emotion. The chapter closes with a glimpse at some "hot topics" in current research on emotion.

Appraisal and Emotion

The idea that appraisals are fundamental to emotion can be traced to the writings of Magda Arnold (1960; see also Reisenzein, 2006). Arnold argued that whether we find a stimulus emotionally arousing depends on the extent to which the stimulus is personally meaningful. Unless the stimulus matters to us, we will not become emotional. Clearly, what matters to one person may leave another person cold. This emphasis on subjective meaning in appraisal theory led researchers to shift their attention from the objective properties of emotional stimuli to the subjective processes ("appraisal processes") by which perceivers attach significance and meaning to stimuli.

There are several variations on the basic theme of appraisal theory (e.g., Frijda, 1986; Smith & Lazarus, 1993; Roseman, 1984; Scherer, 1984), but they all share the assumption that emotions derive from meaning. Meaning, in turn, derives from appraisals of the significance to an individual of thoughts or events or objects, given a certain set of values and goals. So fundamental is this assumption that it forms the basis of the first in a series of "laws of emotion" formulated by Frijda (1988). The first is the *law of situational meaning*: "Emotions arise in response to the meaning structures of given situations; different emotions arise in response to different meaning structures" (p. 349). In other words, the kind of emotion that someone experiences in a given situation will depend on the meaning they attach to it, such that different people experience different emotions in relation to the same situation.

The second of Frijda's laws of emotion is the *law of concern*: "Emotions arise in response to events that are important to the individual's goals, motives, or concerns" (p. 351). A basic condition for emotion to arise, on this account, is that something happens that is "motivationally relevant" (Smith & Lazarus, 1993). Unless something is at stake, unless an object or an event concerns us, we do not become emotional. We evaluate the personal implications of an object or event in light of our values or goals. It follows that the type of emotion we experience is going to be shaped in important ways by whether the object or event is consistent or inconsistent with these values or goals. This is what Smith and Lazarus (1993) call the assessment of "motivational congruence." Positive emotions are evoked by objects and events that are appraised to be *motivationally congruent*, as well as motivationally relevant; negative emotions are aroused by objects and events that are appraised to be *motivationally incongruent*, as well as motivationally relevant.

What type of positive or negative emotion is experienced depends on further appraisals, one of the most important of which is an attribution-like assessment of who or what is *responsible* for the event in question (Weiner, 1985). An event that is motivationally relevant and incongruent could evoke emotions as disparate as anger (if someone else is seen to be responsible for the event) and guilt (if the self is seen as responsible).

There are several appraisal criteria or dimensions that have been proposed beyond the three discussed (relevance, congruence, and responsibility). The idea is that different emotions are associated with different patterns or profiles of appraisal. The additional appraisal criteria, such as *control* and *power*, help to distinguish between emotional states. Sadness, for example, is theoretically characterized by appraisals of low control and low power, and these appraisals help to distinguish sadness from anger. Scherer (1999) provides a useful overview of the similarities and differences between four influential appraisal theories of emotion, and how these theories conceptualize the relation between specific emotions and appraisal dimensions.

Perhaps the most controversial claim made by appraisal theorists is that appraisals *cause* emotion. Although not all appraisal theorists would go as far as Lazarus (1981) when he wrote "I would argue that there are no exceptions to the principle that emotion is a meaning-centered reaction and hence depends on cognitive mediation" (p. 223), most would agree with the less staunch position adopted by Roseman and Smith (2001). They defend the basic proposition that appraisals cause emotions but accept that appraisals are not necessary for emotions: "For example, it would appear that emotions can be physiologically generated and altered independently of typical appraisal processes, as when endogenous depression is caused by neurotransmitter dysfunction and alleviated by antidepressant drugs. If so, appraisals are not necessary causes of emotion" (p. 16).

Many studies testing predictions derived from appraisal theory involve asking participants to recall emotional events from their own lives and to answer questions designed to elicit their appraisals at the time of the event (e.g., Frijda, Kuipers, & ter Schure, 1989; Smith & Ellsworth, 1985). Although studies of this type have yielded a body of evidence consistent with appraisal theory, they have widely acknowledged limitations. Perhaps the most serious of these is that the studies are correlational in nature, showing that certain kinds of emotional experience are associated with certain kinds of appraisal. Whether these appraisals *preceded*, *accompanied*, or *followed* the emotion is therefore unclear (see Parkinson, 1997; Parkinson & Manstead, 1992, for discussions of these issues).

More compelling evidence of a causal relation between appraisal and emotion comes from experimental studies in which attempts are made to manipulate the nature of the appraisals made by participants to examine the consequences for measures of emotional response. An early example is a study reported by Speisman, Lazarus, Mordkoff, and Davison (1964). Participants were shown an excerpt from a film depicting a rite of passage in the lives of males in aboriginal tribes in Australia, marking the transition from boyhood to manhood. The rite entails operating on the boys' genitals using flintstones. Speisman and colleagues added voiceovers that encouraged viewers to appraise the depicted events in different ways. In the "trauma" condition, the soundtrack emphasized the crude nature of the operation and the pain and suffering experienced by the boys. In the "denial" condition, the soundtrack emphasized the fact that the ceremony was keenly anticipated by the boys and was for them an occasion for joy rather than suffering. In the "intellectualization" condition, the soundtrack encouraged the viewer to adopt the detached perspective of a scientific observer of the ceremony. Figure 4.1 shows the mean skin conductance

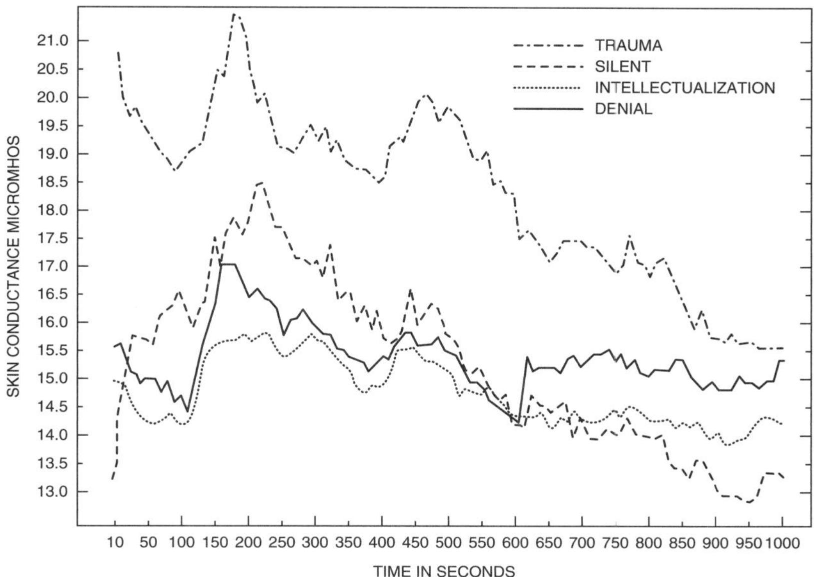

FIGURE 4.1. Mean Skin Conductance Level in Different Soundtrack Conditions of Speisman et al.'s (1964) Experiment. Note: Higher values reflect greater physiological arousal. From Speisman, J. C., Lazarus, R. S., Mordkoff, A., & Davison, L. (1964). Experimental reduction of stress based on ego-defence theory. *Journal of Abnormal and Social Psychology*, *68*, 367–380. Published by the American Psychological Association. Reprinted with permission.

levels (SCL) in the four conditions of the experiment. SCL is one index of autonomic nervous system activity and reflects the type of arousal associated with stress. There are clear between-condition differences showing that the trauma voiceover enhanced SCL whereas the denial and intellectualization conditions attenuated it, relative to the silent control condition.

A limitation of the Speisman et al. (1964) study is that the researchers did not measure appraisal. We therefore have to infer that the different soundtracks did have an impact on appraisals of the events in the film, and that these appraisal changes were responsible for the effects on emotional response. A more recent experimental study addressing some of these issues was reported by Roseman and Evdokas (2004). Participants were told there would be two groups in this study, and that the groups would experience different outcomes. One outcome was always more desirable than the other, because it involved tasting *something pleasant* rather than tasting *nothing* (in the Pleasant condition) or tasting *nothing* rather than tasting *something unpleasant* (in the

Unpleasant condition). Half the participants in the Pleasant condition then learned that they would *definitely* taste something pleasant; the other half learned that they would *probably* taste something pleasant. Likewise, half the participants in the Unpleasant condition learned that they would *definitely* be in the no taste group; the other half learned that they would *probably* be in the no taste group. Participants in the Pleasant condition reported more joy than their counterparts in the Unpleasant condition. More interestingly, those in the Unpleasant condition who were told that they would definitely be in the no taste group reported more relief than those who were told that they would probably be in the no taste group. These results are consistent with appraisal theory; however, some predictions—for example, that those Pleasant condition participants who were told that they would *probably* be in the pleasant taste group would report more hope than their counterparts who believed that they were *definitely* in the pleasant taste group—were not supported. Moreover, even where the predictions were supported, the effect sizes were small, leading the researchers to acknowledge that the emotional states of participants must have been affected by factors other than the manipulations.

Appraisal theory has been hugely influential but has also attracted some criticism. One line of critique has been that appraisal theory is unduly cognitive in its approach (see Izard, 1993). Zajonc (1980) launched a widely cited critique of appraisal theory in which he argued that affective reactions to stimuli could be independent of (and even precede) cognitive responses. Some of the most compelling support for this view derives from research on the "mere exposure effect" (Bornstein, 1989), in which it is shown that the more frequently people have been exposed to a stimulus, the more they like the stimulus, even when the prior exposure was subliminal, thereby ruling out the possibility that the greater liking was "caused" by cognitions such as appraisals of familiarity.

Another line of critique is that in many versions of appraisal theory appraisals and emotions are linearly related, in the sense that appraisals always precede emotions. Frijda (1993) and Lewis (1996) both argue for a reciprocal view of the appraisal–emotion relation in which each factor informs and is informed by the other. Thus Frijda argued that "how events are appraised during emotions appears often to result from cognitive elaboration of the appraisal processes *eliciting* the emotion" (1993, p. 371, emphasis in original). For example, rather than the relation between (own) responsibility and guilt being a straightforward, linear one, the perception that our actions have unintentionally caused harm to others might evoke initial feelings of discomfort that in turn trigger appraisals of (own) responsibility, which in turn might trigger the emotion of guilt (see Berndsen & Manstead, 2007).

A third way in which appraisal theory has been criticized argues that it pays insufficient attention to the inherently social nature of emotion. Although there is nothing in appraisal theory that rules out the influence of social factors, there is little evidence in either theoretical statements or empirical research of a real concern with the social dimension of emotion (Manstead & Fischer, 2001). A well-known theoretical approach to emotion that argues for the role played by social factors is Schachter's (1964) two-factor theory of emotion. Although this is often thought of as a cognitive approach to emotion, the cognitions involved are ones about *other people's emotions*. Thus the nature of the experienced emotion is shaped by the social context. In this account, if you experience physiological arousal without having a clear-cut notion of the source of this arousal, your perceptions of how relevant others are feeling is likely to have an impact on your own emotional experience. The same physiological state could be experienced as different emotions, depending on appraisals of the social context (Schachter & Singer, 1962).

Social Functions of Emotion

The way in which one person's emotions might inform another person is an example of a possible "social function" served by emotion. The notion that emotions are "functional" can be found in many lines of theorizing. The classic perspective on the functionality of emotions is that they increase the probability of the individual's survival and/or reproductive success. The argument is that emotions are functional in the sense that they help the individual to address or overcome problems (Tooby & Cosmides, 2008). Fear is an obvious example. Fear of predators or enemies is adaptive in the sense that individuals who are capable of experiencing fear are more likely to be vigilant and avoidant, and thereby to escape the threat of predation or attack (Öhman, 2008; Tooby & Cosmides, 2008). Although the fear–escape–survival sequence is a clear-cut instance of the way in which emotion directly evokes adaptive behavior, it is worth noting in passing that other examples are not easy to find, a point made by Baumeister, Vohs, DeWall, and Zhang (2007).

Keltner and Haidt (1999) argued that emotions can also be seen as serving *social* functions. Just as individuals who experience fear at the prospect of predation have an adaptive advantage, social systems (dyads, groups, cultures) benefit from the capacity of individuals within these systems to experience and express emotion. An example is the fact that emotional communication enables adult caregivers to inform prelinguistic children about whether it is safe or unsafe to proceed with certain courses of action. Sorce, Emde, Campos, and Klinnert (1985) found that when 12-month-old children were placed on the "shallow" side of a visual cliff, a piece of apparatus with an apparent drop covered by glass, the infants were reluctant to cross to the "deep" side when their mothers wore negative facial expressions, but ready to do so when their mothers wore positive facial expressions. In the developmental psychology literature this phenomenon is known as "social referencing," and is a nice demonstration of how we "coconstruct" appraisals of emotional situations, using others as a resource to help us interpret whether the circumstances are benign or threatening (Walden & Ogan, 1988).

In dyadic relations, then, emotional expressions can serve as incentives (or disincentives) for others' behavior (Keltner & Haidt, 1999; see also van Kleef, De Dreu, & Manstead, 2010). Another adaptive consequence of emotion at this level is that emotions as diverse as empathic distress and romantic love can serve to bind us more closely to others. The economist Robert Frank (1988, 2004) has referred to emotions as "commitment devices," encouraging us to set aside self-interest in favor of the interests of others. In group settings, experiences and expressions of emotion can also lead to individuals working for the interest of the group, rather than their personal interest, thereby enhancing cooperation and coordination, and making it more likely that the group will achieve its goals (see Fessler & Haley, 2003). At the cultural level, media portrayals of how of certain groups or practices evoke widely shared emotional responses serve to create or sustain cultural norms and values (see Doveling, von Scheve, & Konijn, 2010).

Fischer and Manstead (2008) argue that two key social functions are served by emotions. The first is that the experience and expression of many emotions have the effect of establishing or maintaining our relationships with others. The second is that the experience and expression of many emotions have the effect of establishing or maintaining a position relative to others. These functions map broadly onto what Hogan (e.g., Hogan & Kaiser, 2005) and others have called "getting along" versus "getting ahead." That is, some emotions have the effect of promoting interpersonal connectedness and warmth (getting along, or cooperating), whereas others promote interpersonal distance and rivalry (getting ahead, or competing). The second set of emotions, which includes anger, contempt, sociomoral disgust, and pride, may appear to be unlikely candidates for the accolade of being "socially functional." However, it needs to be remembered that unreasonable and reprehensible behavior by others must be confronted and rejected if a society is to function effectively. Also relevant is the point (further developed below) that expressions of anger can serve as warnings of impending aggression, enabling those in dispute to address the source of their conflict without resorting to violence. With regard to pride, it can be argued that for a social group or society to flourish, its members need to be encouraged to achieve to the best of their abilities, and that the social function of pride is precisely to do this (Williams & DeSteno, 2008).

The view that emotions serve social functions runs into many of the same conceptual problems as a general functionalist account (Gross & John, 2002; Oatley & Jenkins, 1992; Parrott, 2001, 2002). Emotions generally have social effects, regardless of whether these effects are intended. However, these social effects are not equivalent to social functions. Fischer and Manstead (2008) argue that the social functions of emotion should be inferred from the social relational goals inherent in the prototypical appraisals and action tendencies of a given emotion (e.g., Roseman, Wiest, & Swartz, 1994). For example, the "getting along" function of emotion is evident in embarrassment (admitting that we have transgressed), love (wanting to be close to the loved one), happiness (sharing positive experiences with others), and sadness (seeking help and support from others), whereas the "getting ahead" function can be seen in anger (seeking to change another person), contempt (seeking to exclude another person), or social fear (seeking distance from another person).

The claim that emotions have social functions does not imply that emotions are always socially functional. Anger, jealousy, and contempt can clearly be socially dysfunctional. Rather than behaviors being changed, the relationship between individuals or between groups may be irreparably damaged, without achieving anything in terms of social control or social standing. The same applies to positive emotions such as pride, happiness, or love: Rather than social bonds being strengthened, others may take exception to what they regard as inappropriate in the circumstances. Social dysfunctionality is especially likely to occur if the social impact of our emotions is not taken into account or if inappropriate appraisals of the social context are made (Parrott, 2001). In general, however, it seems reasonable to hold that emotions typically serve to promote social belongingness and harmony.

Emotion and Social Cognition

Everyone is familiar with the notion that some people have a more "optimistic" way of seeing the world than other people do, and that depression can lead people to see themselves and others in bleaker terms. Emotions affect the way we think, including the way in which we think about social objects such as selves, others, and social entities. Indeed, the evidence that emotions influence cognition is more extensive than the evidence that emotion influences behavior (see Baumeister et al., 2007; Schwarz & Clore, 2007). In what follows I will review research on emotion and social cognition by considering how affect influences both the content of social thinking and the way in which social information is processed.

A key notion in the study of how emotion influences social cognition is that of *congruence*. When we are in a positive or negative mood state, it is argued, we tend to see the world in a way that is congruent with that mood state. Early research tested this prediction by examining whether mood states influence how quickly people name words of the same valence (i.e., positive or negative words, as opposed to neutral ones) as the mood state found inconsistent evidence for this prediction. Research by Niedenthal and her colleagues (e.g., Niedenthal, Halberstadt, & Setterlund, 1997) clarified matters by showing that if we take account of the *specific match* between mood state and emotional words (such that, for example, the influence of *sad mood states* on the naming of *sadness-related* words is studied, as opposed to the influence of sad mood states on words with a negative valence), results are supportive of the prediction. Happy moods facilitate the naming of happiness-related words, but not love-related words; sad moods facilitate the naming of sadness-related words, but not anger-related words. In a parallel line of research, Niedenthal and colleagues have shown similar effects of mood state on the perception of facial expressions of emotion (Niedenthal, Halberstadt, Margolin, & Innes-Ker, 2000).

The congruence notion has also been central to work on mood and memory, where one of the two key phenomena is that people are more likely to retrieve memories that are congruent with their current mood. This is known as *mood-congruent memory*, and refers to the match between *mood state at recall* and *the affective quality of the material being recalled*. The second phenomenon is *mood state-dependent memory*, and refers to people being better able to recall information when they are in the same emotional state as the one in which they were when first exposed to the information. Think of the difference this way: If, when feeling happy, you recall more positive material than negative or neutral material, this would be evidence of mood-congruent memory; but if you were given neutral material to learn when feeling happy, and you were later found to be better able to recall this material when you feel happy than when you feel sad, this would be evidence of mood state-dependent memory. Although both phenomena have attracted considerable research attention, the evidence is quite mixed (see Eich & Macauley, 2000).

In the case of *mood-congruent memory*, where the critical issue is how mood at recall affects what is recalled, it seems that the effect is more robust when there is no other straightforward way to impose a structure on the material that has to be recalled. For example, Fiedler and colleagues (e.g., Fiedler & Stroehm, 1986) have shown that information that can easily be grouped into categories is less susceptible to the influence of mood state at recall than is material that is difficult to classify. The idea is that when material is difficult to classify, the mood you are in at recall provides a way of imposing a structure on it. The fact that you are in a positive mood when asked to recall material means that you remember positive items when they have nothing in common with each other apart from their positivity. However, when the items are easily grouped into categories, you use those groupings to help you recall items, rather than your current mood state.

In the case of *mood state-dependent memory*, where the critical issue is the similarity in mood state at encoding and recall, it seems that the effect is more robust when the material to be learned is generated by the participant rather than provided by the researcher. This is presumably because material generated by the participant is likely to be associated with the participant's own mental state, as opposed to external cues such as the researcher or the physical context in which the material is provided. When the participant is asked to generate material in a happy or sad mood state and is later asked to recall that material when in a happy or sad mood, recall is better when the mood states at encoding and retrieval match than when they do not (Eich & Metcalfe, 1989).

Note that mood-congruent memory is an example of how emotion influences the *content* of social cognition, suggesting that we are more likely to bring to mind thoughts that are congruent with a current emotional state. Mood state-dependent memory, on the other hand, is an example of how emotion influences *the way in which information is processed*; emotion can help us to classify material that is otherwise difficult to structure, and we are better able to recall that material when we are in a similar emotional state because the emotional state serves as a retrieval cue.

The idea that emotion can play more than one role in social cognition, shaping both what we think and how we think, poses a challenge to theorists. Two prominent theoretical models of the relation between emotion and social cognition are the "associative network" model of mood and memory (e.g., Bower, 1981), and the "affect-as-information" model (Clore et al., 2001; Schwarz & Clore, 1983).

In the former, emotion can serve as a "node" in a network of interlinked nodes. When an emotion node is activated by putting someone into an emotional state, this activation spreads to other nodes in the network that are linked to the emotion node. The "affect-as-information" model holds that under certain conditions people make use of their current affective state when making evaluative judgments, such as judgments about life satisfaction or evaluations of consumer products. Both models have a part to play in explaining the relation between emotion and social cognition, but neither model can account for all the known phenomena. A third model, the "affect infusion model" (AIM; Forgas, 1992, 1995), is an attempt to provide a more comprehensive explanation of this relation.

The AIM identifies four strategies for processing social information. These are shown in Figure 4.2. Two of the strategies are "low infusion" strategies,

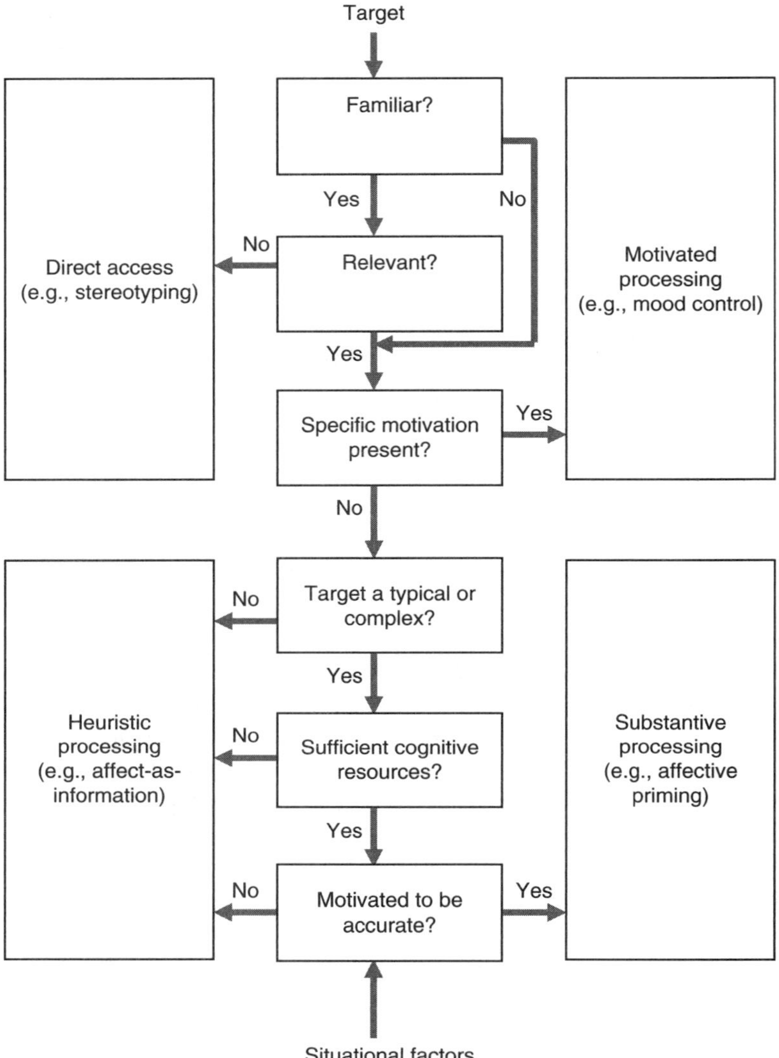

FIGURE 4.2. Schematic representation of the Affect Infusion Model.
Note: Adapted from Forgas, J. P. (1995). Mood and judgment: The affect infusion model (AIM). *Psychological Bulletin*, *117*, 39–66. Published by the American Psychological Association. Adapted with permission.

meaning that affect has little impact on them. These are the "direct access" and "motivated processing" strategies. In the former, the perceiver retrieves a prestored evaluation or judgment about the target. In the latter, the perceiver processes information about the target in a way that serves one or more of the perceiver's goals (for example, to maintain a positive mood state). The remaining two strategies are "high infusion" strategies, meaning that affect has a larger influence. In the "heuristic processing" strategy, simple rules (heuristics) are used to arrive at a judgment. One heuristic may be that if the perceiver feels good, the judgment will be positive (consistent with the affect-as-information model). In the "substantive processing" strategy, the perceiver engages in a more careful analysis of the available information. Here the perceiver's affective state exerts its impact by helping to determine what information is available. This is consistent with the notion that being in a positive mood makes positive material (including positive memories) more salient, consistent with Bower's (1981) theory of how mood affects memory. To make these abstract ideas a little more concrete, imagine that a consumer researcher calls you up to ask questions about your MP3 player. If you have a preformed, unconditionally positive view of your player, you might use that to guide your answers (direct access). If you want to please the researcher, your answers may emphasize the positive qualities of your player (motivated processing). If you do not have especially strong opinions about your player and are not keen to give the matter a lot of thought, the way you answer the questions is likely to be driven in a global way by your current mood, such that if you are in a good mood, you give positive answers (heuristic processing). If you are motivated to think carefully about the player, how you answer each question is likely to depend on your current mood, such that when you are asked questions about the player's reliability, for example, being in a good mood makes instances in which the player jammed or froze come to mind less readily (substantive processing).

As Figure 4.2 shows, which of these strategies is used in a given situation is thought to depend on a variety of factors: the familiarity, relevance, and complexity of the target, along with the perceiver's motivation to be accurate in judging the target, his or her other motivations, and the cognitive resources available for processing the target. There is considerable research evidence that is consistent with the AIM. For example, Petty, Schumann, Richman, and Strathman (1993) found that when people who are low in need for cognition (meaning that they are unwilling to process information carefully) were exposed to persuasive messages about a target, their judgments of the target were influenced directly by their mood state (consistent with heuristic processing); however, when high need for cognition participants were exposed to the same messages, their judgments of the target were determined by the thoughts about the target that came to mind (consistent with substantive processing).

An attractive feature of the AIM is its ability to integrate a variety of processing strategies under one umbrella model, but the ultimate value of the model rests on its ability to make accurate predictions about the conditions under which different processing strategies are engaged.

Social Emotions

As noted earlier, emotions are generally "about" something, in the sense that when we feel emotional it is usually possible to identify what we are feeling emotional about. We are not simply *angry*; we are *angry at someone or about something*. Indeed, other people are often the sources or targets of our emotions. Consistent with Frijda's (1988) law of concern (see above), this reflects the extent to which other people are directly of concern to us, or the extent to which they have the capacity to advance or thwart our concerns. Thus the majority of emotions tend to be social in nature. However, there is one set of emotions that is social in a more fundamental sense. These are emotions that cannot be experienced without the real or imagined presence of others. Anger, fear, sadness, and disgust are often experienced in relation to other people, but they can also be experienced in relation to nonhuman targets. Contrast this with emotions such as shame, guilt, and embarrassment. These cannot be experienced without invoking a social context. It does not make sense to say that we are embarrassed, for example, without invoking the real or imagined presence of others who witness the *faux pas* or blunder that is the source of the embarrassment. Tripping over while walking alone can be a source of irritation or pain, but not of embarrassment (unless we invoke an imaginary audience). Tripping over in the presence of others can be a source of embarrassment. In this sense, emotions such as shame, guilt, embarrassment, envy, and jealousy can justifiably be called "social emotions."

There are several emotions that could reasonably be called "social" in the sense being used here. Sympathy and compassion are emotions that take other human beings as their object, as does *schadenfreude* (pleasure at someone else's setback or suffering). Envy and jealousy also clearly involve others as objects of the emotion, the common theme being social comparison of own outcomes versus the outcomes of one or more others. Here I will consider shame, guilt, and embarrassment as exemplars of social emotions because they can be regarded as a "family" of social emotions relating to the evaluation of the self. Lay people tend to use these emotion terms interchangeably. Indeed, in some languages less distinction is made between shame and embarrassment than is the case in English. In Dutch for example, although there is a word meaning "embarrassment" (*gêne*, borrowed from the French), in everyday discourse speakers use the word *schaamte* (meaning shame) to refer to embarrassment. The fact that embarrassment and shame both invoke negative evaluations of the self in social settings helps to account for this blurring of the distinction in everyday language use, as does the fact that embarrassment and shame (like shame and guilt) can and do cooccur.

The distinction between shame and embarrassment will be clearer if we first consider the relation between shame and guilt. Contemporary emotion theorists tend to unite around the claim (first made by Lewis, 1971) that in shame the entire self is judged to be bad, whereas in guilt a given behavior is judged to be bad. When we feel ashamed, we often talk about feeling "ashamed of myself." When we feel guilty, we typically talk about feeling guilty about having done something that caused hurt or harm. In both cases the trigger for the emotion might be a behavior that is judged to be bad. If this leads to the perception of the self as bad, the resultant emotion should be shame. If instead there is a focus on the negative quality of the behavior, the resultant emotion should be guilt.

Niedenthal, Tangney, and Gavanski (1994) examined this proposal that in shame there is a focus on self whereas in guilt there is a focus on behavior by examining the counterfactual thinking engaged in by participants immediately after incidents that evoked shame or guilt. Counterfactual thinking is the "mental undoing" of something that has happened, and it has been established that when people engage in this mental undoing, they focus on the factors that are seen as causing the outcome. What Niedenthal and colleagues did was to ask participants to write down three counterfactual thoughts that would undo a situation in which guilt or shame was experienced. The researchers found that after recalled or imagined experiences of guilt, participants tended to mentally undo their behaviors. By contrast, after recalled or imagined shame, participants tended to mentally undo themselves. In the first case, the general theme would be "If I hadn't done that . . . ." In the second case, the general theme would be "If I weren't such a (bad/stupid/thoughtless/etc.) person . . . ." Clearly, these findings are consistent with the notion that shame and guilt differ with respect to focus (self versus behavior).

Other researchers have noted differences in the *action tendencies* associated with shame and guilt. In shame people may feel like hiding, running away, or disappearing ("I wanted the ground to swallow me up"). In guilt, by contrast, people may be inclined to apologize and make amends (Frijda et al., 1989). Another approach to the distinction between shame and guilt has entailed a focus on the functions they serve. Tangney and colleagues have developed a measure of shame- and guilt-*proneness*, by which they mean the dispositional tendency to respond to events with shame or with guilt. They then examined correlations between shame- and guilt-proneness, on the one hand, and measures of proneness to respond to setbacks with hostility and aggression, on the other. The researchers noted a consistent tendency for shame-prone individuals to be more likely to react to setbacks with hostile thoughts and behaviors, whereas there was no such relationship between guilt-proneness and hostility. Tangney and colleagues note that the shame–hostility relation has the potential to become self-reinforcing, in the sense that persons who react to shame by becoming angry and hostile to others may later feel ashamed of themselves, leading to more anger and hostility. This led the researchers to conclude that guilt is the more adaptive of the two emotions.

Baumeister, Stillwell, and Heatherton (1994, 1995) also argue that guilt serves social functions. The central point made by these authors is that guilt stems not from judgments of our own behavior made by the self but rather from judgments of our own behavior made by another person in the context of a relationship. In their 1995 paper, these researchers asked participants to write about autobiographical events in which they had angered another person and had then experienced guilt or no guilt. Analyzing the content of the participants' accounts of these events, Baumeister and colleagues noted that the episodes that evoked guilt were ones in which the individual was more likely to have a high regard for the other person, and to see his or her own behavior as selfish. This makes good sense. We feel guilty if we anger someone we care for, and his or her anger leads us to reappraise our own behavior. Moreover, by comparison with the "no guilt" accounts, the "guilt" accounts involved changes in behavior that would benefit the relationship, with the guilty person being more likely to have apologized and to have "learned a lesson." This suggests that guilt serves social (relationship enhancing) functions, as well as being an emotion that has its roots in interpersonal relationships rather than intrapsychic judgments.

Turning to embarrassment, it is now clear why it is more readily confused with shame than with guilt. The behavior that is a source of embarrassment is not one that is likely to upset others; rather, it is one that is incompatible with the identity that we want to project in a given situation. Typically, the source of the embarrassment is a slip or lapse that calls into question our identity as a competent social actor. The presented self is devalued. The source of shame is an action (or inaction) that is seen as undermining the self in a more fundamental way. It is the core self that is devalued. Instead of telling yourself that you *look* stupid to others, you tell yourself that you *are* stupid. There is some dispute in the literature concerning whether this temporary loss of social esteem is a necessary condition for embarrassment to occur (as argued by Manstead & Semin, 1981; Miller, 1996; Miller & Leary, 1992; Schlenker & Leary, 1982), or whether there is a more basic precondition that simply involves actions or events that are incompatible with and disruptive of social roles and scripts, resulting in feeling flustered (Parrott, Sabini, & Silver, 1988; Parrott & Smith,

1991; see Keltner & Busswell, 1997 for an overview). Although there can be little doubt that a temporary loss of social esteem can be a source of embarrassment, the fact that praise can also evoke embarrassment raises doubts about the extent to which loss of social esteem is a necessary condition.

Whether the cause of embarrassment is loss of social esteem or the flustered awkwardness of a disrupted role or script, there is good evidence that displaying embarrassment is a way of coping with embarrassment. Goffman (1967) argued that the embarrassed individual "demonstrates that . . . he is at least disturbed by the fact and may prove worthy at another time" (p. 111). In other words, showing embarrassment implies an acknowledgment of performance failure and a commitment to the norms that have been violated. Consistent with this reasoning, Semin and Manstead (1982) found that someone who accidentally knocked over a supermarket display was rated more positively when he looked embarrassed than when he did not. The display of embarrassment serves the function of communicating that we are not indifferent to social norms. A study by Leary, Landel, and Patton (1996) showed that embarrassment tends to persist until it has served this communicative function. Participants who were discomfited by singing their own version of a well-known schmaltzy song felt more embarrassed if the experimenter failed to interpret their blushing as a sign of embarrassment than if he or she was aware of their embarrassment.

As we have seen, social emotions have humans as their objects or arise because of a real or imagined audience. Although shame, guilt, and embarrassment entail negative evaluations of the self, there are important differences between the three emotions. These differences are found in the antecedents of the emotions, in the phenomenology of the emotions, and in the functions served by the emotions. Shame is driven by appraisals of the self as worthless, is characterized by wanting to disappear from view and thoughts about being a different kind of person, and has a tendency to be socially dysfunctional. Guilt is driven by the appraisal that our behavior has harmed valued others, is characterized by wanting to apologize and thoughts about undoing the harmful behavior, and tends to enhance social relationships. Embarrassment is driven by the appraisal that our behavior has called our identity claim into question, is characterized by wanting to disown the questionable behavior, and tends to evoke positive evaluations from others.

The Expression of Emotion

In any social psychological approach, the ways in which the subjective experience of emotion is expressed in outwardly visible behavioral changes are bound to be a focus of attention. If someone's emotions reflect his or her assessment of whether his or her concerns are being advanced or thwarted, it would be useful for others (whether they have a cooperative or competitive relationship with the individual in question) to know what those emotions are. If emotions are reflected in behavioral changes and a perceiver can interpret these changes reasonably accurately, this should enable the perceiver to adjust his or her own behavior in a way that suits his or her personal goals or furthers the joint goals of perceiver and expresser. In other words, the ability to detect what another person is feeling is likely to have major consequences for social interaction.

Emotions can be expressed in a variety of ways: through language, vocal (but nonverbal) qualities, body posture, hand and arm gestures, and so on. However, one means of expression has captured most of the research attention in this domain, and that is the face. From the earliest hours of life, the face is an important means of mutual engagement and communication between caregiver and infant, and the face continues to play a significant role in social interaction after the child acquires language. Although faces have the capacity to communicate many types of information (see Parkinson, Fischer, & Manstead, 2005, pp. 148–152), there is a widely held assumption that faces are especially useful in communicating emotion.

Scientific interest in the relation between emotion and the face is usually traced to Darwin's (1872/1998) influential book, *The Expression of the Emotions in Man and Animals*. Continuing themes addressed elsewhere in his work, Darwin considered the question of why the facial movements that accompany emotion take the particular form they do. Why do the corners of the mouth turn upward into a smile when we feel happy? Why do the eyes widen when we feel afraid? Darwin's principal explanation for these links between emotion and facial movements was that these movements had, in the course of evolutionary history, served an adaptive function. For example, the wrinkling of the nose when feeling disgust is a component of a retching movement that would expel food or drink that tastes unpleasant. Through repeated association, the movements that originally served the purpose of expelling noxious tastes come to be linked to the underlying emotion that accompanied such tastes, so that elements of these movements occur when someone feels disgust without there being any need to make a "retching" face. Modern research provides support for the idea that the production of facial movements originates in sensory regulation. For example, Susskind, Lee, Cusi, Feiman, Grabski, and Anderson (2008) have shown that the facial movements associated with fear enhance sensory acquisition (larger visual field, faster eye movements, increased nasal volume), whereas those that are associated with disgust have the opposite effect. So there are good reasons for thinking that some facial movements associated with emotion have their origin in changing the way in which we acquire sensory information about the world around us.

Darwin's arguments have two important implications. One is that emotions with facial expressions that have their origin in adaptive movements should be expressed in similar ways across the world, regardless of culture. This is an issue we will return to later, when considering the impact of culture on emotion. The second is that there should be a close and consistent relation between subjective emotion and facial expression. This is the issue that will be considered here.

The most influential modern exponent of the view that at least some emotions are consistently expressed by particular facial movements is Ekman (e.g., 1972, 1973). In his "neurocultural theory," Ekman proposed that the activation of certain emotions triggers a neural program that produces both the subjective experience of the emotion in question and patterned changes in the face and body. The emotions for which this claim is made are happiness, sadness, anger, fear, surprise, and disgust. Contempt was later added to this list (see Ekman & Heider, 1988). However, culture-specific "display rules" can modify the emotion–expression link, such that what appears on the face is an attenuated or exaggerated version of what is actually felt, depending on what is socially appropriate in the circumstances (e.g., maintaining a sad or at least somber expression during a funeral in many Western cultures, regardless of how sad we really feel).

There is a reasonable degree of empirical support for Ekman's neurocultural theory. For example, the studies reported by Ekman, Friesen, and Ancoli (1980) and by Rosenberg and Ekman (1994) show a fair degree of coherence between subjectively reported emotion and objective measures of facial behavior in a film-viewing situation, and an unpublished but often-cited study by Friesen (1972; discussed by Ekman, 1972 & Fridlund, 1994) found evidence consistent with the notion of culture-specific display rules. Japanese and American students viewed unpleasant films (depicting surgical procedures such as limb amputation) alone, and then in the presence of a researcher. Measures of facial behavior show that there was little difference between Japanese and American students in the alone setting, but that the Japanese students showed fewer negative facial expressions in the presence of the researcher. This was interpreted as reflecting the influence of a Japanese display rule proscribing the expression of negative emotions to an authority figure.

However, there are also studies that report weak or inconsistent relations between subjective emotion and facial behavior (e.g., Fernández-Dols & Ruiz-Belda, 1997) or little evidence of the facial movements that would be expected to accompany a specific emotion such as surprise (e.g., Reisenzein, Bördgen, Holtbernd, & Matz, 2006). Moreover, Fridlund (1994) has developed an alternative theoretical position in which he argues that the facial displays that we usually think of as expressing emotion are in fact expressions of social motives. An "angry" face, for example, is in fact a display of the intention to aggress, and will accompany the subjective experience of anger only if the individual has hostile intentions. This relation between social motives or intentions, on the one hand, and facial displays, on the other, has its origins in our evolutionary past, according to Fridlund. Facial displays evolved because they provide conspecifics with information that has adaptive value. If an animal signals its intention to aggress, others who are able to "read" this signal can retreat or protect themselves, or settle up with the potentially aggressive peer and thereby avoid a costly and possibly fatal skirmish. In this way the capacity to display social motives and the capacity to read such displays coevolved. The primary function of facial displays, based on this account, is a communicative one.

Fridlund's (1994) argument implies that facial displays should be more evident when there is an audience to receive them, and there is evidence that facial displays are indeed more frequent in the presence of an audience (Bavelas, Black, Lemery, & Mullett, 1986; Chovil, 1991; Fernández-Dols & Ruiz-Belda, 1995; Fridlund, 1991; Hess, Banse, & Kappas, 1995; Jakobs, Manstead, & Fischer, 1999; Kraut & Johnston, 1979). However, much (but not all) of this evidence relates to smiling, and it may be that smiling is a special case, a facial display that is especially sensitive to the presence or absence of an audience. Furthermore, it is worth noting that some of the studies in which facial displays of smiling were observed to vary as a function of audience presence also found that smiling was correlated with the subjective experience of happiness or amusement (e.g., Hess et al., 1995; Jakobs et al., 1999). This can be regarded as evidence that smiling is related to subjective emotion, as well as social context, although it is hard to rule out completely the possibility that subjective emotion is influenced by social context.

In conclusion, most contemporary emotion researchers would accept that there is a relation between emotion and facial behavior, albeit a somewhat looser relation than that implied by Ekman's neurocultural theory. Most researchers would also reject the notion that facial displays express *either* emotion *or* social motives; there is every likelihood that they do both, and a prime task for future research is to specify the conditions under which facial displays primarily express emotion or primarily communicate social motives.

Emotion in and between Social Groups

A relatively new and distinctively social psychological approach to emotion is one that studies emotions in and between social groups. When commentators speak about a "crowd being angry" or a "nation being in mourning," do they mean that most individuals belonging to these groups experience similar emotions simultaneously, or something more than that?

The possibility that groups "have" emotions may strike you as odd. We tend to assume that emotions are things that happen to individuals. How could there be such a thing as "group emotion?" Here I will use this term to refer to the fact that group membership influences the ways in which people experience and express emotions. This influence manifests itself in the form of similarities in group members' emotional experiences or behaviors, similarities that would not be exhibited if the individuals concerned did not belong to the same group.

It may be helpful to start with a research example of "group emotion." Totterdell (2000) assessed the moods of members of two professional sports teams three times a day for 4 days during a competitive match. Players' moods were more strongly correlated with the current aggregate mood of their own team than with the current aggregate mood of the other team or with the aggregate mood of their own team at other times. These correlations between player mood and team mood were also found to be independent of personal hassles, teammates' hassles, and the match situation between the two teams, effectively ruling out an explanation in terms of shared exposure to common situations.

There are several possible reasons for intragroup similarities of this kind. First, members of a group are likely to be exposed to the same kinds of emotional objects and events—although, as we have just seen, this exposure to common events could not account for Totterdell's findings. Second, in the course of their interactions group members are likely to mutually influence each other's appraisals and emotions. Third, the fact that group members share norms and values is likely to promote similarities in the ways that they appraise events. Fourth, members of a group are likely to define themselves at least partly in terms of this group membership. To the extent that members identify themselves as belonging to a common group, they are likely to have similar interpretations and evaluations of emotional events that have implications for the group as a whole. Finally, a set of people might actually define themselves as a group on the basis that they express or experience a particular emotion, such that if an individual does not feel that emotion, he or she would not join the group or stay in it.

Although there are studies in addition to Totterdell (2000) showing that group members share emotions (e.g., Bartel & Saavedra, 2000; Totterdell, Kellett, Teuchmann, & Briner, 1998), or that groups including a confederate instructed to act happy reported more positive affect than did groups including a confederate instructed to act sad (e.g., Barsade, 2002), there is surprisingly little hard evidence concerning the processes underlying these phenomena.

As noted by Parkinson et al. (2005), explanations can be divided into two groups. "Bottom-up" explanations are ones that entail mutual influence between group members with respect to either emotional expression or the appraisal of events. For example, group members can influence each other's expressions of emotion via a process of "contagion," whereby each member (probably unconsciously) mimics another member's expressions. It is reasonably well established that expressions can have a "feedback" effect on emotion, such that someone who smiles because she or he unconsciously mimics another group member is likely to feel more positive as a result (Neumann & Strack, 2000). This would help to account for similarity of emotion among group members. "Top-down" explanations appeal to the influence of group norms on the ways in which members of a group appraise events and the ways in which they express their emotions. Display rules are in effect group norms about emotional expression, for example, but there are many other ways in which group norms can prescribe or proscribe emotions and emotional expressions (see Parkinson et al., 2005; Thoits, 2004).

Members of social groups are quite likely to share emotions concerning members of other social groups, especially where there is a history of cooperation or competition between the groups involved. To the extent that individuals in their capacity as members of one social group experience and express emotions toward members of another social group, we can speak about "intergroup" or "group-based" emotions (see Iyer & Leach, 2008, for a typology of group-level emotions). Smith (1993) gave a considerable impetus to research on intergroup emotion by providing a theoretical analysis of prejudice as emotion, generally referred to as intergroup emotion theory (IET). In doing so he drew on self-categorization theory (SCT; Turner, Hogg, Oakes, Reicher, & Wetherell, 1987), which argues that when there is competition with an outgroup or when perceivers notice that attributes such as appearance and opinions covary with group membership, there will be a tendency to define the self as a group member rather than as an individual. This is the significance of SCT for intergroup emotion, for self-categorization as a group member should lead to the experience of emotions that are shaped by concerns and appraisals that are group based. In other words, individuals who believe that Group A is being threatened by Group B are likely to react emotionally to this threat to the extent that they define themselves as members of Group A, even if they personally are unaffected by the threat. A real-life example of this is the emotion that most Americans felt in response to the 9/11 attacks on the Twin Towers and the Pentagon, regardless of their proximity to or personal suffering from the attacks. The point is made clearly by research conducted by Dumont, Yzerbyt, Wigboldus, and Gordijn (2003), who examined the emotional reactions of Europeans just 1 week after the 9/11 attacks. They found that responses varied as a function of whether the Belgian participants were led to categorize themselves as *Westerners* rather than *Arabs* (thereby sharing category membership with Americans) or as *Europeans* rather than *Americans* (thereby not sharing category membership with Americans). As predicted, self-reports of fear in response to the attacks were greater in the former (shared category membership) condition.

Another line of research on intergroup emotion has focused on the guilt that members of one group feel in relation to the mistreatment by members of their group of an outgroup. Any country that has been a colonial power provides good conditions for such research, for it is generally not difficult to find aspects of that country's colonial rule that were disadvantageous for the citizens of the colonies in question. Doosje, Branscombe, Spears, and Manstead (1998) examined the group-based guilt felt by Dutch citizens in relation to how their own national group had treated Indonesians during the era when Indonesia was a Dutch colony. Participants read accounts of Dutch treatment of Indonesians that described how the Dutch had done *negative* things, *positive* things, or a *mixture* of negative and positive things. Predictably, group-based guilt was higher when participants read the negative account. More interestingly, reactions to the mixed account depended on the extent to which the participants identified themselves as Dutch. Here strong identifiers reported less guilt than their relatively weak identifying counterparts, suggesting that those who were most highly identified with the national category focused on the positive aspects of Dutch colonial treatment and were therefore less ready to feel guilty about what had happened.

The study by Doosje et al. (1998) and others like it (e.g., Doosje, Branscombe, Spears, & Manstead, 2006; Johns, Schmader, & Lickel, 2005) provide an interesting exception to a more general rule, namely that the more highly you identify with a social group, the stronger should be your emotional responses to issues that are relevant to that identity. This is what would be expected on the basis of Smith's (1993) IET, and is also what has been found in a number of studies researching intergroup emotions other than guilt. For example, anger at the way in which a perpetrator group has treated a victim group is typically greater as a function of how strongly respondents identify with the victim group (Yzerbyt, Dumont, Wigboldus, & Gordijn, 2003). The reason that guilt opposes this general trend is that it is threatening to the identity of a group to acknowledge that it has been responsible for mistreating another group, and this threat is likely to be felt most keenly by those who are highly identified with the perpetrator group. Thus the lesser guilt of high identifiers may simply represent defensive responses to this greater threat (for a careful analysis of the relation between identification and emotion in intergroup relations, see Iyer & Leach, 2008).

To summarize, a relatively new development in emotion research has been a focus on emotions in group and intergroup contexts. A key theoretical construct in these contexts is social identity—the extent to which individuals define themselves in terms of their membership in social groups. When social identity is salient, members of social groups are likely to exhibit emotional similarities and to respond emotionally to events relevant to the wellbeing of the group, even if they personally are unaffected by these events.

Emotion and Culture

There has been a longstanding concern in emotion research with the extent to which emotions are influenced by cultural factors. As we have already seen, Ekman's (1972, 1973) neurocultural theory of facial expression recognized the influence of cultural factors in the form of "display rules," culture-specific norms about when and how to express our feelings. Indeed, the universality or cultural specificity of facial behavior during emotion has been a strong theme in research on cultural influences on emotion. A second major theme in research on cultural variation has been the extent to which there are differences across cultures with respect to norms and values that impact on emotion.

Starting with the question of whether facial behavior during emotion is or is not consistent across cultures, Ekman and Friesen (1971) conducted pioneering research in the highlands of Papua New Guinea, using as participants members of a "preliterate" tribe who had had relatively little exposure to Western culture. These people were shown sets of still photographs of Western facial expressions of emotion and asked to select the one that was appropriate to a short story (such as "His friends have come and he is happy"). The way that most participants made their selections showed that they interpreted the expressions in the same way as Westerners. Research conducted in other cultures has broadly confirmed these findings (see Biehl et al., 1997; Boucher & Carlson, 1980; Ducci, Arcuri, Georgis, & Sineshaw, 1982; Ekman et al., 1987; Haidt & Keltner, 1999; Kirouac & Dore, 1982). In reviewing this research Russell (1994) noted several methodological problems. He concluded that the degree of observed cross-cultural consistency is not sufficient to be able to argue that there is true universality in the way that facial expressions of emotion are interpreted. Instead, he suggested, the evidence is consistent with the concept of "minimal universality," by which he means that there is more consistency across cultures than would be expected if there was *no* shared meanings of facial expressions but less consistency than would be expected if the meanings of facial expressions were the same across all cultures.

Consistent with this notion of "minimal universality" is evidence reviewed by Elfenbein and Ambady (2002), showing that there is what they call an "ingroup advantage" in interpreting facial expressions of emotion. This means that persons of a given culture or ethnicity perform better when interpreting expressions made by members of their own culture or ethnicity than when interpreting expressions made by members of another culture or ethnicity. This observation led Elfenbein and Ambady to propose that people in a given cultural or ethnic group share an "emotion dialect," that is a local variation on a more general, universal theme. Just as there are socioeconomic and regional variations in the way that a national language is spoken, so there are ethnic and cultural variations in the way that faces express emotion. Familiarity with the dialect used by someone who makes facial expressions confers an advantage in recognizing them.

Turning now to the influence of cultural norms and values, one of the most important theoretical notions in this domain is that of *individualism* versus *collectivism* (Hofstede, 1980). Individualistic cultures (broadly speaking, found in Europe, North America, and Australasia) promote personal agency and autonomy; collectivistic cultures (broadly speaking, found in Asia, Africa, and Central and South America) attach importance to group goals and interpersonal relations. It has been argued that these differences in value systems carry implications for notions of self and agency in these different cultures (Markus & Kitayama, 1991), such that members of individualistic cultures tend to have independent self-construals, regarding themselves and others as autonomous beings with a high degree of control over their environment; members of collectivistic cultures, however, tend to have interdependent self-construals, defining themselves and others primarily in terms of roles and relationships and obligations and responsibilities. These differences, in turn, affect the ways in which emotion is experienced and expressed in the two types of culture.

Any characterization of cultural differences in terms of a single dimension runs the risk of oversimplification and overgeneralization, and the individualism–collectivism dimension has been criticized on these grounds (e.g., Schwartz, 1990). The notion that there are differences in emotion between individualistic and collectivistic cultures has nevertheless attracted a reasonable degree of empirical support. For example, Kitayama, Mesquita, and Karasawa (2006) compared the frequency with which emotions are experienced in the United States and Japan. Consistent with the researchers' predictions, in the United States emotions that reflect and reinforce individual autonomy, such as anger and pride, were more prevalent than emotions that emphasize mutual engagement, such as sympathy and respect; the reverse was true in Japan. Thus it would seem that emotions that are compatible with the values that are central in a culture tend to be prevalent, whereas ones that are incompatible with these values tend to be more rare.

Another example of the way in which cultural values impact emotion is shown by research on "honor cultures" (see Cohen & Nisbett, 1994, Cohen, Nisbett, Bowdle, & Schwarz, 1996; Rodriguez Mosquera, Manstead, & Fischer, 2000, 2002). An honor culture is one in which self-esteem is shaped powerfully by the standing of the individual and his or her group (typically the family) in the eyes of others. There is a strong motivation to uphold personal and family honor by conforming to norms of appropriate behavior (which are typically quite different for males and females) and by avoiding humiliation (Miller, 1993).

A series of studies reported by Cohen et al. (1996) compared male American students who had grown up in the American South (theoretically an honor culture) with counterparts who were raised in the American North. All were students at a northern university. The students were invited to come to a research laboratory and to complete a series of questionnaires. At one stage they were asked to move from one room to another and in doing so they had to pass along a corridor in which another person (a research confederate) was standing next to an open file drawer, making it necessary for the confederate to move aside. When the participant returned along the same corridor a few minutes later, again inconveniencing the confederate, the latter bumped into the participant and muttered "asshole." Southerners were more likely than Northerners to react to this insult by acting aggressively, and measures of cortisol (a stress hormone) and testosterone showed that they were more physiologically disturbed and readier to aggress. Thus the value of honor that is central to the culture in which Southerners had been raised had an effect on their behavior in a different cultural context, years later.

In summary, research on cultural variation in emotion has shown that there are interesting and interpretable differences in the emotional lives of people who belong to different cultures. There is a core set of emotions (anger, disgust, sadness, fear, happiness, and surprise) for which there is evidence of at least a certain degree of universality in the way they are facially expressed and the way that their facial expressions are recognized across cultures. Perhaps this reflects the evolutionary significance of facial expressions, either as a way of regulating sensory uptake (Darwin, 1872/1998) or as a way of signaling motives to conspecifics (Fridlund, 1994). However, there is also evidence of cultural variation in facial expression during emotion, suggesting that local norms and practices have an impact on this link (Elfenbein & Ambady, 2002; Russell, 1994). There is also evidence that cultural differences in values related to the individualism–collectivism dimension, such as personal autonomy, interpersonal harmony, and honor, have an impact on the frequency with which people experience emotions that carry social implications (Kitayama et al., 2006), and on the ways in which they react to events that challenge those values (Cohen et al., 1996).

Emotion in Social Psychology Today

Three "hot topics" in current social psychological research on emotion are (1) unconscious emotions, (2) the role of embodiment in emotion perception, and (3) the role of emotions in moral judgments and behaviors. The idea that emotions can be unconscious may seem paradoxical, given that one of the hallmarks of emotion is that we are aware of a subjective feeling state. Yet researchers are starting to show that subliminal exposure to emotional stimuli (such as facial expressions) can influence our behavior. Berridge and Winkielman (2003), for example, found that thirsty participants consumed more of a pleasant tasting drink when they had been primed with happy faces than when they had been primed with sad faces—even though the participants were unaware of the primes and did not differ in self-reported emotion. This shows how subtle the influence of affective states can be, although we might question whether these effects depend on the *valence* of the subliminal stimuli or on their specific emotional content.

Research on the role of embodiment in emotion perception is concerned with the extent to which perceiving an emotional state in another person activates in the perceiver the same sensorimotor states that are entailed in the emotion they are witnessing. In other words, seeing someone else expressing joy or sadness will partly reenact the emotional state in perceivers. Niedenthal, Barsalou, Ric, and Krauth-Gruber (2005) have advanced this argument and Niedenthal (2007) summarizes evidence in favor of this view. One implication is that understanding another person's emotions can be promoted by encouraging the perceiver to mimic the sender's behavior.

Research on the role of emotions in moral judgments and behavior is beginning to combine the efforts of social psychologists, philosophers, economists, and neuroscientists in studying issues such as trust in interpersonal behavior and how emotions affect cooperation and decision making. One example of such an approach is provided by Todorov, Said, Engell, and Oosterhof (2008), who address the question of how we are able to make very fast evaluations of human faces on social dimensions. They show that there is an automatic tendency to evaluate faces on two dimensions: trustworthiness and dominance. The way in which such evaluations are made appears to depend on how structurally similar a neutral face is to a face expressing an emotion that is relevant to one of these dimensions (happiness in the case of trustworthiness, anger in the case of dominance). Based on this account the inferences we make about traits on the basis of faces have their origin in the ways in which faces signal approach intentions and social power. Such inferences then shape social behavior in powerful ways, ranging from social cooperation (Krumhuber et al., 2007) and electoral success (Little et al., 2007) to criminal sentencing decisions (Blair et al., 2004).

Conclusions

Social life is replete with emotion, and emotions are deeply social in nature. Emotions reflect the appraised relationship between an individual and his or her social and physical environment. Thus the same objective set of circumstances may be appraised differently as a function of individual differences and social and cultural affiliations. Emotions can and often do serve social functions, in the sense that they motivate individuals to form and sustain social relationships and to achieve social goals. Emotions also have complex but predictable effects on the ways in which we process social information. Facial and other expressive activity sometimes reflects subjective emotion, but at other times reflects our social motives and intentions. Either way, expressive behavior has the potential to enhance social coordination. Although emotions are experienced and expressed by individuals, the basis for emotions can be the fact that we belong to a social group, just as the object of the emotion can be our own or another social group. Finally, although there is evidence that humans all over the world have much in common with respect to emotion, presumably reflecting the fact that we share a common ancestry and are faced with broadly similar physical and social challenges, there is also evidence that culture has an impact on the experience and expression of emotion.

Acknowledgments

The author thanks Roy Baumeister, Dina Dosmukhambetova, Joe Forgas, and Anja Zimmermann for comments on an earlier draft of this chapter.

References

Arnold, M. B. (1960). *Emotion and personality*. New York: Columbia University Press.

Barsade, S. G. (2002). The ripple effect: Emotional contagion in groups. *Administrative Science Quarterly, 47*, 644–677.

Bartel, C. A., & Saavedra, R. (2000). The collective construction of work group moods. *Administrative Science Quarterly, 45*, 197–231.

Baumeister, R. F., Stillwell, A. M., & Heatherton, T. F. (1994). Guilt: An interpersonal approach. *Psychological Bulletin, 115*, 243–267.

Baumeister, R. F., Stillwell, A. M., & Heatherton, T. F. (1995). Personal narratives about guilt: Role in action control and interpersonal relationships. *Basic and Applied Social Psychology, 17*, 173–198.

Baumeister, R. F., Vohs, K. D., DeWall, C. N., & Zhang, L. (2007). How emotion shapes behavior: Feedback, anticipation, and reflection, rather than direct causation. *Personality and Social Psychology Review, 11*, 167–203.

Bavelas, J. B., Black, A., Lemery, C. R., & Mullett, J. (1986). "I show how you feel:" Motor mimicry as a communicative act. *Journal of Personality and Social Psychology, 50*, 322–329.

Berndsen, M., & Manstead, A. S. R. (2007). On the relationship between responsibility and guilt: Antecedent appraisal or elaborated appraisal? *European Journal of Social Psychology, 37*, 774–792.

Berridge, K. C., & Winkielman, P. (2003). What is an unconscious emotion? The case for unconscious 'liking'. *Cognition and Emotion, 17*, 181–211.

Biehl, M., Matsumoto, D., Ekman, P., Hearn, V., Heider, K., Kudoh, T., & Ton, V. (1997). Matsumoto and Ekman's Japanese and Caucasian Facial Expressions of Emotion (JACFEE): Reliability data and cross-national differences. *Journal of Nonverbal Behavior, 21*, 3–21.

Blair, I. V., Judd, C. M., & Chapleau, K. M. (2004). The influence of Afrocentric facial features in criminal sentencing. *Psychological Science, 15*, 674–679.

Bornstein, R. F. (1989) Exposure and affect: Overview and meta-analysis of research, 1968–1987. *Psychological Bulletin, 106*, 265–289.

Boucher, J. D., & Carlson, G. E. (1980). Recognition of facial expressions in three cultures. *Journal of Cross-Cultural Psychology, 11*, 263–280.

Bower, G. (1981). Mood and memory. *American Psychologist, 36*, 19–148.

Chovil, N. (1991). Social determinants of facial displays. *Journal of Nonverbal Behavior, 15*, 141–154.

Christophe, V., & Rimé, B. (1997). Exposure to social sharing of emotion: Emotional impact, listener responses and secondary social sharing. *European Journal of Social Psychology, 27*, 37–54.

Clore, G. L., Wyer, R. S., Dienes, B., Gasper, K., Gohm, C., & Isbell, L. (2001). Affective feelings as feedback: Some cognitive consequences. In L. L. Martin & G. L. Clore (Eds.), *Theories of mood and cognition: A user's guidebook* (pp. 27–62). Mahwah, NJ: Erlbaum.

Cohen, D., & Nisbett, R. E. (1994). Self-protection and the culture of honor: Explaining southern violence. *Personality and Social Psychology Bulletin, 20*, 551–567.

Cohen, D., Nisbett, R. E., Bowdle, B. F., & Schwarz, N. (1996). Insult, aggression and the southern culture of honor: An "experimental ethnography." *Journal of Personality and Social Psychology, 70*, 945–960.

Darwin, C. (1872/1998). *The expression of the emotions in man and animals.* London: John Murray (3rd 1998 edition edited by P. Ekman and published by Oxford University Press).

Doosje, B., Branscombe, N. R., Spears, R., & Manstead, A. S. R. (1998). Guilty by association: When one's group has a negative history. *Journal of Personality and Social Psychology, 75*, 872–886.

Doosje, B., Branscombe, N. R., Spears, R., & Manstead, A. S. R. (2006). Antecedents and consequences of group-based guilt: The effects of ingroup identification. *Group Processes and Intergroup Relations, 9*, 325–338.

Doveling, K., von Scheve, C., & Konijn, E. A. (Eds.) (2010). *Handbook of emotions and the mass media.* London: Routledge.

Ducci, L., Arcuri, L., Georgis, T., & Sineshaw, T. (1982). Emotion recognition in Ethiopia: The effect of familiarity with Western culture on accuracy of recognition. *Journal of Cross-Cultural Psychology, 13*, 340–351.

Dumont, M., Yzerbyt, V., Wigboldus, D., & Gordijn, E.H. (2003). Social categorization and fear reactions to the September 11th terrorist attacks. *Personality and Social Psychology Bulletin, 29*, 112–123.

Eich, E., & Macaulay, D. (2000). Are real moods required to reveal mood-congruent and mood-dependent memory? *Psychological Science, 11*, 245–248.

Eich, E., & Metcalfe, J. (1989). Mood dependent memory for internal versus external events. *Journal of Experimental Psychology: Learning, Memory, and Cognition, 15*, 443–455.

Elfenbein, H. A., & Ambady, N. (2002). On the universality and cultural specificity of emotion recognition: A meta-analysis. *Psychological Bulletin, 128*, 205–235.

Ekman, P. (1972). Universals and cultural differences in facial expressions of emotion. In J. Cole (Ed.), *Nebraska Symposium on Motivation, 1971* (pp. 207–283). Lincoln, NE: University of Nebraska Press.

Ekman, P. (1973). *Darwin and facial expression.* New York: Academic Press.

Ekman, P., & Friesen, W. V. (1971). Constants across cultures in the face and emotion. *Journal of Personality and Social Psychology, 17*, 124–129.

Ekman, P., Friesen, W. V., & Ancoli, S. (1980). Facial signs of emotional experience. *Journal of Personality and Social Psychology, 39*, 1125–1134.

Ekman, P., Friesen, W. V., O'Sullivan, M., Chan, A., et al. (1987). Universals and cultural differences in the judgments of facial expressions of emotion. *Journal of Personality and Social Psychology, 53*, 712–717.

Ekman, P., & Heider, K. G. (1988). The universality of a contempt expression: A replication. *Motivation and Emotion, 12*, 303–308.

Fernández-Dols, J. M., & Ruiz-Belda, M. A. (1995). Are smiles a sign of happiness? Gold medal winners at the Olympic Games. *Journal of Personality and Social Psychology, 69*, 1113–1119.

Fernández-Dols, J. M., & Ruiz-Belda, M. A. (1997). Spontaneous facial behavior during intense emotional episodes: Artistic truth and optical truth. In J. A. Russell & J. M. Fernández-Dols (Eds.), *The psychology of facial expression* (pp. 255–294). Cambridge, UK: Cambridge University Press.

Fessler, D. M. T., & Haley, K. J. (2003). The strategy of affect: Emotions and human cooperation. In P. Hammerstein (Ed.), *Genetic and cultural evolution of cooperation* (pp. 7–36). Cambridge, MA: MIT Press.

Fiedler, K., & Stroehm, W. (1986). What kind of mood influences what kind of memory: The role of arousal and information structure. *Memory and Cognition, 14*, 181–188.

Fischer, A. H., & Manstead, A. S. R. (2008). Social functions of emotion. In M. Lewis, J. M. Haviland-Jones, & L. Feldman Barrett (Eds.), *Handbook of emotions* (3rd ed., pp. 456–468). New York: Guilford Press.

Forgas J. P. (1992). Affect in social judgment and decisions: A multi-process model. In M. P. Zanna (Ed.), *Advances in experimental social psychology* (Vol. 25, pp. 227–275). San Diego, CA: Academic Press.

Forgas, J. P. (1995). Mood and judgment: The affect infusion model (AIM). *Psychological Bulletin, 117*, 39–66.

Frank, R. H. (1988). *Passions within reason: The strategic role of the emotions.* New York: W. W. Norton.

Frank, R. H. (2004). Introducing moral emotions into models of rational choice. In A. S. R. Manstead, N. H. Frijda, & A. H. Fischer (Eds.), *Feelings and emotions: The Amsterdam Symposium* (pp. 422–440). New York: Cambridge University Press.

Fridlund, A. J. (1991). Sociality of solitary smiling: Potentiation by an implicit audience. *Journal of Personality and Social Psychology, 60*, 229–240.

Fridlund, A. J. (1994). *Human facial expression: An evolutionary view.* San Diego, CA: Academic Press.

Friesen, W. V. (1972). *Cultural differences in facial expressions in a social situation: An experimental test of the concept of display rules.* Unpublished doctoral dissertation, University of California, San Francisco.

Frijda, N. H. (1986). *The emotions.* Cambridge, UK: Cambridge University Press.

Frijda, N. H. (1988). The laws of emotion. *American Psychologist, 43*, 349–358.

Frijda, N. H. (1993). The place of appraisal in emotion. *Cognition and Emotion, 7*, 357–387.

Frijda, N. H., Kuipers, P., & ter Schure, E. (1989). Relations among emotion, appraisal, and emotional action readiness. *Journal of Personality and Social Psychology, 57*, 212–228.

Goffman, E. (1967). *Interaction ritual.* New York: Doubleday Anchor.

Gross, J., & John, O. P. (2002). Wise emotion regulation. In L. Feldman Barrett & P. Salovey (Eds.), *The wisdom of feeling: Psychological processes in emotional intelligence* (pp. 297–319). New York: Guilford Press.

Haidt, J., & Keltner, D. (1999). Culture and emotion: Multiple methods find new faces and a gradient of recognition. *Cognition and Emotion, 13*, 225–266.

Hess, U., Banse, R., & Kappas, A. (1995). The intensity of facial expression is determined by underlying affective state and social situation. *Journal of Personality and Social Psychology, 69*, 280–288.

Hofstede, G. (1980). *Culture's consequences: International differences in work-related values*. Beverly Hills, CA: Sage.

Hogan, R., & Kaiser, R. B. (2005). What we know about leadership. *Review of General Psychology, 9*, 169–180.

Iyer, A., & Leach, C. W. (2008). Emotion in inter-group relations. In W. Stroebe & M. Hewstone (Eds.), *European review of social psychology* (Vol. 19, pp. 86–125). Hove, UK: Psychology Press.

Izard, C. E. (1993). Four systems for emotion activation: Cognitive and noncognitive processes. *Psychological Review, 100*, 68–90.

Jakobs, E., Manstead, A. S. R., & Fischer, A. H. (1999). Social motives and subjective feelings as determinants of facial displays: The case of smiling. *Personality and Social Psychology Bulletin, 25*, 424–435.

Johns, M., Schmader, T., & Lickel, B. (2005). Ashamed to be American? The role of identification in predicting vicarious shame for anti-Arab prejudice after 9/11. *Self and Identity, 4*, 572–587.

Keltner, D., & Buswell, B.N. (1997). Embarrassment: Its distinct form and appeasement functions. *Psychological Bulletin, 122*, 250–270.

Keltner, D., & Haidt, J. (1999). Social functions of emotions at four levels of analysis. *Cognition and Emotion, 13*, 505–521.

Kirouac, G., & Dore, F. Y. (1982). Identification of emotional facial expressions by French speaking subjects in Quebec. *International Journal of Psychology, 17*, 1–7.

Kitayama, S., Mesquita, B., & Karasawa, M. (2006). The emotional basis of independent and interdependent selves: Socially disengaging and engaging emotions in the US and Japan. *Journal of Personality and Social Psychology, 91*, 890–903.

Kraut, R. E., & Johnston, R. E. (1979). Social and emotional messages of smiling: An ethological approach. *Journal of Personality and Social Psychology, 37*, 1539–1553.

Krumhuber, E., Manstead, A. S. R., Cosker, D., Marshall, D., Rosin, P. L., & Kappas, A. (2007). Facial dynamics as indicators of trustworthiness and cooperative behavior. *Emotion, 7*, 730–735.

Lazarus, R. S. (1981). A cognitivist's reply to Zajonc on emotion and cognition. *American Psychologist, 36*, 222–223.

Lazarus, R. S. (1991). *Emotion and adaptation*. New York: Oxford University Press.

Leary, M. R., Landel, J. L., & Patton, K. M. (1996). The motivated expression of embarrassment following a self-presentational predicament. *Journal of Personality, 64*, 619–636.

Lewis, H. B. (1971). *Shame and guilt in neurosis*. New York: International Universities Press.

Lewis, M. D. (1996). Self-organising cognitive appraisals. *Cognition and Emotion, 10*, 1–25.

Little, A. C., Burriss, R. P., Jones, B. C., & Roberts, S. C. (2007). Facial appearance affects voting decisions. *Evolution and Human Behavior, 28*, 18–27.

Manstead, A. S. R., & Fischer, A. H. (2001). Social appraisal: The social world as object of and influence on appraisal processes. In K. R. Scherer, A. Schorr, & T. Johnstone (Eds.), *Appraisal processes in emotion: Theory, methods, research* (pp. 221–232). New York: Oxford University Press.

Manstead, A. S. R., & Semin, G. R. (1981). Social transgressions, social perspectives, and social emotionality. *Motivation and Emotion, 5*, 249–261.

Markus, H. R., & Kitayama, S. (1991). Culture and the self: Implications for cognition, emotion and motivation. *Psychological Review, 98*, 224–253.

Miller, R. S. (1996). *Embarrassment: Poise and peril in everyday life*. New York: Guilford Press.

Miller, R. S., & Leary, M. R. (1992). Social sources and interactive functions of emotions: The case of embarrassment. In M. S. Clark (Ed.), *Emotion and social behavior* (*Review of Personality and Social Psychology*, Vol. 13, pp. 202–221). Newbury Park, CA: Sage.

Miller, W. I. (1993). *Humiliation: And other essays on honor, social discomfort, and violence*. New York: Cornell University Press.

Neumann, R., & Strack, F. (2000). Mood contagion: The automatic transfer of mood between persons. *Journal of Personality and Social Psychology, 79*, 211–223.

Niedenthal, P. M. (2007). Embodying emotion. *Science, 316*, 1002–1005.

Niedenthal, P.M., Barsalou, L.W., Ric, F., & Krauth-Gruber, S. (2005). Embodiment in the acquisition and use of emotion knowledge. In L. Feldman Barrett, P. M. Niedenthal, & P. Winkielman (Eds.), *Emotion and consciousness* (pp. 21–50). New York: Guilford Press.

Niedenthal, P. M., Halberstadt, J. B., Margolin, J., & Innes-Ker, A. H. (2000). Emotional state and the detection of change in facial expression of emotion. *European Journal of Social Psychology 30*, 211–222.

Niedenthal, P.M., Halberstadt, J., & Setterlund, M.B. (1997). Being happy and seeing "happy": Emotional state facilitates visual word recognition. *Cognition and Emotion, 11*, 594–624.

Niedenthal, P.M., Tangney, J., & Gavanski, I. (1994). "If only I weren't" versus "If only I hadn't": Discriminating shame and guilt in counterfactual thinking. *Journal of Personality and Social Psychology, 67*, 585–595.

Oatley, K., & Jenkins, J. M. (1992). Human emotions: Function and dysfunction. *Annual Review of Psychology, 43*, 55–85.

Öhman, A. (2008). Fear and anxiety: Overlaps and dissociations. In M. Lewis, J. M. Haviland-Jones, & L. Feldman Barrett (Eds.), *Handbook of emotions* (3rd ed., pp. 709–729). New York: Guilford Press.

Parkinson, B. (1996). Emotions are social. *British Journal of Psychology, 87*, 663–683.

Parkinson, B. (1997). Untangling the appraisal-emotion connection. *Personality and Social Psychology Review, 1*, 62–79.

Parkinson, B., Fischer, A. H., & Manstead, A. S. R. (2005). *Emotion in social relations: Cultural, group and interpersonal perspectives*. New York: Psychology Press.

Parkinson, B., & Manstead, A. S. R. (1992). Appraisal as a cause of emotion. In M. S. Clark (Ed.), *Emotion and social behavior* (*Review of Personality and Social Psychology*, Vol. 13, pp. 122–149). Newbury Park, CA: Sage.

Parrott, W. G. (2001). Implications of dysfunctional emotions for understanding how emotions function. *Review of General Psychology, 5*, 180–186.

Parrott, W. G. (2002). The functional utility of negative emotions. In L. Feldman Barrett & P. Salovey (Eds.), *The wisdom of feeling: Psychological processes in emotional intelligence* (pp. 341–362). New York: Guilford Press.

Parrott, W. G., Sabini, J., & Silver, M. (1988). The roles of self-esteem and social interaction in embarrassment. *Personality and Social Psychology Bulletin, 14*, 191–202.

Parrott, W. G., & Smith, S. F. (1991). Embarrassment: Actual vs. typical cases, classical vs. prototypical representations. *Cognition and Emotion, 5*, 467–488.

Petty, R. E., Schumann, D. W., Richman, S. A., & Strathman, A. (1993). Positive mood and persuasion: Different roles for affect under high and low elaboration conditions. *Journal of Personality and Social Psychology, 64*, 5–20.

Reisenzein, R. (2006). Arnold's theory of emotion in historical perspective. *Cognition and Emotion, 20*, 920–951.

Reisenzein, R., Bördgen, S., Holtbernd, T., & Matz, D. (2006). Evidence for strong dissociation between emotion and facial displays: The case of surprise. *Journal of Personality and Social Psychology, 91*, 295–315.

Rimé, B., Finkenauer, C., Luminet, O., Zech, E., & Philippot, P. (1998). Social sharing of emotion: New evidence and new questions. In W. Stroebe & M. Hewstone (Eds.), *European review of social psychology* (Vol. 9, pp. 145–189). Chichester, UK: Wiley.

Rodriguez Mosquera, P. M., Manstead, A. S. R., & Fischer, A. H. (2000). The role of honor-related values in the elicitation, experience and communication of pride, shame and anger: Spain and the Netherlands compared. *Personality and Social Psychology Bulletin, 26*, 833–844.

Rodriguez Mosquera, P. M., Manstead, A. S. R., & Fischer, A. H. (2002). The role of honor concerns in emotional reactions to offenses. *Cognition and Emotion, 16*, 143–164.

Roseman, I. J. (1984). Cognitive determinants of emotions: A structural theory. In P. Shaver (Ed.), *Emotions, relationships, and health* (*Review of Personality and Social Psychology*, Vol. 5, pp. 11–36). Beverley Hills, CA: Sage.

Roseman, I. J., & Evdokas, A. (2004). Appraisals cause experienced emotions: Experimental evidence. *Cognition and Emotion, 18*, 1–28.

Roseman, I. J., & Smith, C. A. (2001). Appraisal theory: Overview, assumptions, varieties, controversies. In K. R. Scherer, A. Schorr, & T. Johnstone (Eds.), *Appraisal processes in emotion: Theory, methods, research* (pp. 3–19). New York: Oxford University Press.

Roseman, I. J., Wiest, C., & Swartz, T. S. (1994). Phenomenology, behaviors, and goals differentiate discrete emotions. *Journal of Personality and Social Psychology, 67*, 206–221.

Rosenberg, E. L., & Ekman, P. (1994). Coherence between expressive and experiential systems in emotion. *Cognition and Emotion, 8*, 201–229.

Russell, J. A. (1994). Is there universal recognition of emotion from facial expressions? A review of the cross-cultural studies. *Psychological Bulletin, 115*, 102–141.

Schachter, S. (1964). The interaction of cognitive and physiological determinants of emotional state. In L. Berkowitz (Ed.), *Advances in experimental social psychology* (Vol. 1, pp. 49–80). New York: Academic Press.

Schachter, S., & Singer, J. E. (1962). Cognitive, social, and physiological determinants of emotional state. *Psychological Review, 69*, 379–399.

Scherer, K. R. (1984). Emotion as a multicomponent process: A model and some cross-cultural data. In P. Shaver (Ed.), *Emotions, relationships, and health* (*Review of Personality and Social Psychology*, Vol. 5, pp. 37–63). Beverly Hills, CA: Sage.

Scherer, K. R. (1999). Appraisal theories. In T. Dalgleish & M. Power (Eds.), *Handbook of cognition and emotion* (pp. 637–663). Chichester, UK: Wiley.

Scherer, K. R., Walbott, H. G., & Summerfield, A. B. (1986). *Experiencing emotion: A cross-cultural study*. Cambridge, UK: Cambridge University Press.

Schlenker, B. R., & Leary, M. R. (1982). Social anxiety and self-presentation: A conceptualization and model. *Psychological Bulletin*, 92, 641–669.

Schwartz, S. H. (1990). Individualism-collectivism: Critique and proposed refinements. *Journal of Cross-Cultural Psychology*, 21, 139–157.

Schwarz, N., & Clore, G. L. (1983). Mood, misattribution, and judgments of well-being: Informative and directive functions of affective states. *Journal of Personality and Social Psychology*, 45, 513–523.

Schwarz, N., & Clore, G. L. (2007). Feelings and phenomenal experiences. In E. T. Higgins & A. Kruglanski (Eds.), *Social psychology: A handbook of basic principles* (2nd ed., pp. 385–407). New York: Guilford Press.

Semin, G. R., & Manstead, A. S. R. (1982). The social implications of embarrassment displays and restitution behaviour. *European Journal of Social Psychology, 12*, 367–377.

Smith, C. A., & Ellsworth, P. C. (1985). Patterns of cognitive appraisal in emotion. *Journal of Personality and Social Psychology, 48,* 813–838.

Smith, C. A., & Lazarus, R. S. (1993). Appraisal components, core relational themes, and the emotions. *Cognition and Emotion, 7,* 233–269.

Smith, E. R. (1993). Social identity and social emotions: Toward new conceptualizations of prejudice. In D. M. Mackie, D. Hamilton, & D. Lewis (Eds.), *Affect, cognition, and stereotyping: Interactive processes in group perception* (pp. 297–315). San Diego, CA: Academic Press.

Sorce, J. F., Emde, R. N., Campos, J. J., & Klinnert, M. D. (1985). Maternal emotional signaling: Its effect on the visual cliff behavior of 1-year-olds. *Developmental Psychology, 21,*195–200.

Speisman, J. C., Lazarus, R. S., Mordkoff, A., & Davison, L. (1964). Experimental reduction of stress based on ego-defence theory. *Journal of Abnormal and Social Psychology, 68,* 367–380.

Susskind, J. M., Lee, D. H., Cusi, A., Feiman, R., Grabski, W., and Anderson, A. K. (2008). Expressing fear enhances sensory acquisition. *Nature Neuroscience, 11,* 843–850.

Thoits, P. A. (2004). Emotion norms, emotion work, and social order. In A. S. R. Manstead, N. H. Frijda, & A. H. Fischer (Eds.), *Feelings and emotions: The Amsterdam symposium* (pp. 359–379). New York: Cambridge University Press.

Todorov, A., Said, C. P., Engell, A. D., & Oosterhof, N. N. (2008). Understanding evaluation of faces on social dimensions. *Trends in Cognitive Sciences, 12,* 455–460.

Tooby, J., & Cosmides, L. (2008). The evolutionary psychology of the emotions and their relationship to internal regulatory variables. In M. Lewis, J. M. Haviland-Jones, & L. Feldman Barrett (Eds.), *Handbook of emotions* (3rd ed., pp. 114–137). New York: Guilford Press.

Totterdell, P. (2000). Catching moods and hitting runs: Mood linkage and subjective performance in professional sports teams. *Journal of Applied Psychology, 85,* 848–859.

Totterdell, P., Kellett, S., Teuchmann, K., & Briner, R. B. (1998). Mood linkage in work groups. *Journal of Personality and Social Psychology, 74,* 1504–1515.

Turner, J. C., Hogg, M. A., Oakes, P. J., Reicher, S. D., & Wetherell, M. S. (1987). *Rediscovering the social group: A self-categorization theory.* Oxford, UK: Blackwell.

van Kleef, G. A., De Dreu, C. K. W., & Manstead, A. S. R. (2010). An interpersonal approach to emotion in social decision making: The Emotions as Social Information (EASI) model. In M. P. Zanna (Ed.) *Advances in Experimental Social Psychology* (Vol. 42, pp. 45–96). San Diego, CA: Academic Press.

Walden, T. A., & Ogan, T. A. (1988). The development of social referencing. *Child Development, 59,* 1230–1240.

Weiner, B. (1985). An attributional theory of achievement motivation and emotion. *Psychological Review, 92,* 548–573.

Williams, L., & DeSteno, D. (2008). Pride and perseverance: The motivational role of pride. *Journal of Personality and Social Psychology, 94,* 1007–1017.

Yzerbyt, V., Dumont, M., Wigboldus, D., & Gordijn, E. (2003). I feel for us: The impact of categorization and identification on emotions and action tendencies. *British Journal of Social Psychology, 42,* 533–549.

Zajonc, R. B. (1980). Feeling and thinking: Preferences need no inferences. *American Psychologist, 35,* 151–175.

Chapter 5

The Self

Roy F. Baumeister

If humans evolved from great apes, why are human selves so much more elaborate than those of apes? To answer this question we must first determine what the self essentially is. The self is not a part of the brain, nor is it an illusion, nor is there a "true self" hidden in some magical realm.

Rather, the self is an essential part of the interface between the animal body and the social system. Human social systems—including culture and civilization—are much more complex than the social systems of other great apes. They present more opportunities and more challenges. The human self has to have capabilities and properties that enable it to deal with these.

As a simple example, consider your name. Your name is not a part of your brain, although your brain has to be able to know and use the name. The name is given to you by others. It locates you in the social system: Imagine trying to live in your town without a name! Your name refers to your body but evokes much more, such as group memberships, bank accounts, transcripts, and resumes. It links you to a family, and some people even change their names when they change families (by marrying). Your name tells people how to treat you. (In modern China, which has an acute shortage of names, there are reports of surgery being performed on the wrong person because several hospital patients have identical names. Police work is likewise easily confused by duplicate names.)

Most animals get what they need (food, shelter, and the like) from the physical environment. Humans get it from each other, that is, from their social system. The functions of the self thus include helping the animal self-negotiate the social world to get what it needs. Social needs are also prominent in human behavior, and the self is if anything more important for satisfying them than for satisfying physical needs. The first job of the self is thus to garner social acceptance. Beyond that, the self works to secure and improve its position in the social group. It keeps track of information about itself, works to improve how it is regarded by others, identifies itself with important relationships and roles, and makes choices (most of which are social).

If the self exists at the animal/culture interface, then vastly different cultures would likely produce different versions of selfhood. There is some evidence that this is true. The most studied cultural difference in selfhood describes modern Western selves as emphasizing independence, whereas East Asian selfhood features interdependence (Markus & Kitayama, 1991). That is, Asians base their self-understanding on things that connect them to other people, including family, groups, country, and other relationships. Americans and Western Europeans, in contrast, think of themselves as unique and self-creating. Related to this is a greater emphasis on self-promotion and personal superiority in the West, as compared to more pervasive humility in Asian selves (Heine, Lehmann, Markus, & Kitayama, 1999). For more on this, see Chapter 18 on Cultural Psychology in this volume.

Even within Western culture, there are ample variations. American women are more similar to the Asians than American men, often building interdependent self-concepts (Cross & Madsen, 1997), although it is a mistake to see this as indicating that women are more social than men (Baumeister & Sommer, 1997). The independent thrust of modern Western selfhood probably originated in the political and economic changes that occurred starting in the Renaissance, such as the sharp rise in social mobility (Baumeister, 1987). Medieval Western selfhood, as far as can be reconstructed from the literature and historical evidence, lacked many of the problems and motivations of modern Western selfhood, including concern with self-deception, identity crises, and even the belief in an extensive inner, hidden selfhood. Obviously, the human body did not change greatly from the Middle Ages to modern times, so these extensive historical changes in selfhood almost certainly reflect a response to the changing demands of the social system.

History

Social psychology's interest in self had an odd history with unpromising beginnings. As the history chapter in this volume indicates (Chapter 2), modern social psychology began to take shape in the 1950s. At that time, psychology was dominated by two wildly different paradigms. One was behaviorism, which took a dim view of selfhood. Behavior in that view was a product of reinforcement histories and situational contingencies. There was little room for self-esteem, identity crises, or "black box" invisible entities such as the self.

The other dominant view was Freudian psychoanalysis. It did not quite talk about the self, but did find it useful to talk about the "ego," which was seen in classic Freudian theory as the relatively weak servant of two powerhouse masters, the instinctual drives in the id and the socialized guilt-mongering agent called the superego, which internalized society's rules. The ego, which can be seen as an early theory of self, was a rather pathetic creature trying to carry out the often contradictory demands of these two masters amid the further and often severe constraints of the external world. To be sure, after Freud died there was a movement to revise his theory so as to give more respect and assign more autonomous power to the ego. Across the Atlantic, Gordon Allport (1943) predicted that psychology would devote increasing research attention to the study of ego, and although the term self gradually supplanted the Freudian term ego, he was quite right.

Interest in the self escalated rapidly in the 1960s and 1970s. Quite likely this was fueled by the zeitgeist, which was dominated by youthful rebellion against the establishment and its rules for who to be and how to act, and by the quest to explore and understand inner selves as a crucial pathway to fulfillment and as a vital basis for making life's difficult decisions. By the late 1970s, social psychologists had begun to study many phenomena loosely associated with the self. Incorporating ideas and methods pertinent to the self proved useful in research, and so the evidence accumulated. In the 1980s, before e-mail was available, Anthony Greenwald began distributing an informal newsletter with abstracts of new research findings on the self. His list of addresses on the so-called Self-Interest Group rapidly expanded to include hundreds of researchers who wanted to be kept abreast of the latest work.

Since then, the interest in self has remained a strong theme of social psychology, although the continuity is misleading. The study of self is a large tent containing many other areas of study, and these have waxed and waned over the years. As an incomplete list, consider these terms self-affirmation, self-appraisal, self-awareness, self-concept, self-construal, self-deception, self-defeating behavior, self-enhancement, self-esteem, self-evaluation maintenance, self-interest, self-monitoring, self-perception, self-presentation, self-reference, self-regulation, self-serving bias, and self-verification.

What Is the Self?

In the middle 1990s, faced with the task of producing an integrative overview of research on the self, I searched long and hard for a single core phenomenon or basic root of selfhood, one that could serve as a useful framework for discussing all the work social psychologists had done. I failed. Instead, I reluctantly concluded that at least three important types of phenomena provided three basic roots of selfhood (Baumeister, 1998). This conceptual structure still seems viable and will be the organizational basis for this chapter.

The first basis for selfhood is consciousness turning around toward itself, which is sometimes called "reflexive consciousness." You can be aware of yourself and know things about yourself. For example, you might think about a recent experience of success or failure you have had, including its implications for what possibilities the future may hold for you. You might seek to learn more about yourself by reading your horoscope, by weighing yourself, by timing yourself running a mile, or by taking a magazine quiz. After an accident, you might check your body systematically for injuries. You might read about something that someone did and wonder whether you could do such a thing, whether it be climbing a mountain, learning to paint, shooting someone to death, or winning a Pulitzer prize. All these processes involve how the self is aware of itself and builds a stock of knowledge about itself.

The second basis of selfhood is in interpersonal relations. The self does not emerge from inside the person but rather is formed in interactions and relationships with other people. Moreover, the self functions to create and sustain relationships, to fulfill important roles, and to keep a favored position in the social system. Examples of the interpersonal aspect of self would include getting dressed up for an interview, date, or ceremony, changing your behavior to live up to someone else's expectations, and competing against a rival. You might feel embarrassed on finding that someone has been watching you. You may tell private, personal stories to help a new romantic partner get to know you. You may take on a new identity by joining a group or getting a job. All these involve the self being defined by how it is connected to others and to its efforts to make those relationships strong and satisfying.

The third and final basis of selfhood is making choices and exerting control. You may make yourself keep trying to achieve something despite failure, frustration, and discouragement. You may resist temptation so as to be true to your diet, your wedding vows, or your religious beliefs. You decide what to major in or where to live. You choose your goals and then work toward them even when you might not feel like doing so. You vote, you borrow money and pay it back, you make a promise to a friend and then keep it, and so forth. All these show the self at work, facing and making decisions, following through on previous commitments, and exerting control over itself.

Self-Knowledge

One important part of the self exists mainly inside the individual's own mind. It consists of information. It starts as people pay attention to themselves, and it grows as they develop concepts and ideas about themselves. Self-knowledge has been extensively studied by social psychologists.

Self-Awareness

Self-knowledge would be impossible without self-awareness, which is the basic process by which attention turns around toward its source. An influential early theory by Duval and Wicklund (1972) proposed that awareness could be directed either inward or outward and that inward, self-directed attention would have various motivating effects on behavior. They came up with a startlingly simple way to induce high levels of self-awareness: seating the research participant in front of a mirror. Later refinements included inducing self-awareness with a video camera and with a real or imagined audience (see Carver & Scheier, 1981).

A trait scale that sorted people according to their habitual levels of high or low self-consciousness was also a reliable source of significant differences for many years (Fenigstein, Scheier, & Buss, 1975). Many articles, such as by Carver and Scheier (for reviews, see 1981, 1982), contained one study that used a mirror or camera and a second study that relied on trait differences. The trait scale also promoted a useful conceptual distinction. It measured private self-consciousness, which referred to people's tendency to reflect on their inner selves and be aware of inner states and processes. It also measured public self-consciousness, which meant attunement to how oneself was regarded by others.

Being aware of oneself has many benefits. It improves introspection and awareness of inner states. Attitude self-reports filled out in front of a mirror are more accurate (in the sense that they better predict subsequent behavior) than those filled out with no mirror present, presumably because of the boost in self-awareness (Pryor, Gibbons, Wicklund, Fazio, & Hood, 1976). Self-awareness likewise seems to intensify awareness of our emotional reactions and may intensify the emotions themselves (e.g., Scheier & Carver, 1977). As we shall see later, it improves self-regulation.

Many aspects of the original self-awareness theory gradually faded from use, but one that has gained in importance over the years was comparison to standards (Duval & Wicklund, 1972). Self-awareness is more than just noticing yourself or thinking about yourself: It usually involves an evaluative comparison to a standard. Standards are ideas about how things might or ought to be: ideals, goals, expectations (held by self or others), norms, laws, averages, past or present levels, and more. Even the simplest acts of self-awareness, such as a glance in the mirror, are more than hey, there I am! Instead, they include comparisons to standard: my hair is a mess, that shirt looks better on me than I thought, am I gaining weight?

Comparison to standards motivates people to try to fit the standard (even combing your hair). Hence people often behave better when they are self-aware than when they are not. Increasing self-awareness improves performance and increases socially desirable behavior (Wicklund & Duval, 1971; Diener & Wallbom, 1976; Scheier, Fenigstein, & Buss, 1974).

The other side of the coin is that when behavior or outcomes are bad, people wish to avoid self-awareness. Counterattitudinal behavior, of the sort beloved of dissonance researchers, made participants avoid mirrors, presumably because they did not want to be aware of themselves when acting contrary to their beliefs (Greenberg & Musham, 1981).

Many behavioral patterns are associated with efforts to avoid self-awareness, including although not limited to wishes to stop being aware of the self in connection with unpleasant things such as failures or misdeeds. Hull (1981) proposed that alcohol use reduces self-awareness and that people often drink alcohol precisely for that effect, either to forget their troubles or to reduce inhibitions and celebrate. (Inhibitions often center around self-awareness, because they invoke a particular standard of behavior and censure the self for violating it.) Thus, alcohol does not actually increase desires to misbehave but rather removes the inner restraints against them (Steele & Southwick, 1985; see also Steele & Josephs, 1990).

Binge eating is also associated with loss of self-awareness and may reflect an active attempt to lose awareness of the self by submerging attention in low-level sensory experiences (Heatherton & Baumeister, 1991). Suicidal behavior likewise can be essentially a flight from painful self-awareness (Baumeister, 1991). Escape from self-awareness may also be central to a variety of more unusual behaviors, such as sexual masochism, spiritual meditation, and spurious memories of being abducted by UFOs (Baumeister, 1991; Newman & Baumeister, 1996). The variety of such acts suggests that people have many reasons for wanting to escape the self, possibly because the modern human self is sometimes experienced as burdensome and stressful (Baumeister, 1991; Leary, 2004).

Greenberg and Pyszczynski (1986) proposed that depression is sometimes marked by getting stuck in a state of self-awareness, especially when that state is unpleasant. Even more broadly, Ingram (1990) found that many pathological symptoms are associated with high self-awareness. In general we must assume that the capacity for self-awareness is a positive contribution to many uniquely human psychological achievements and capabilities, but it carries significant costs and drawbacks.

Self-Concepts, Schemas, and Beyond

The traditional term *self-concept* suggests that a person has a single, coherent, integrated idea (concept) that incorporates self-knowledge. Although the term is still sometimes used, the assumption of coherent unity has proven untenable. Instead, people have numerous specific ideas about themselves, and these may be only loosely related and sometimes contradictory. Markus (1977) proposed using the term *self-schema* to refer to each specific idea or piece of information about the self (e.g., "I am shy"). The self-schema term has the added benefit that a person can be aschematic on some dimension, which means not having a specific or clear idea about the self. Thus, someone may have a self-schema as talkative, quiet, in between—or the person may be aschematic, which means not having any opinion as to how talkative or quiet he or she is.

The multiplicity of self-schemas, as well as multiple social identifications, led many researchers for a while to speak of multiple selves, as if each person had many selves. The idea appealed as counterintuitive but presented all sorts of mischief. For example, if you and each of your roommates all have multiple selves, how could you possibly know which shoes to put on in the morning? Mercifully, the talk of multiple selves has largely subsided. Each person may have ideas of different versions of self (e.g., possible future selves; Markus & Nurius, 1986), but these share an important underlying unity.

The diversity of self-knowledge makes people pliable in their self-views. Meehl (1956) coined the term the "Barnum Effect" to refer to people's willingness to accept random feedback from ostensible experts as accurate characterization of their personalities. Laboratory participants can be induced to regard themselves in many different ways with bogus feedback (e.g., Aronson & Mettee, 1968). Most social psychologists believe that horoscopes have no scientific validity, and so something like the Barnum effect is necessary to explain their appeal: If we tell you that you are too wiling to trust strangers, or are sometimes overly critical of partners, you may be willing to think this is correct.

The emerging picture is that a person has a vast store of beliefs about the self, only a few of which are active in focal awareness at any given time.

The term "the phenomenal self" refers to this small portion of self-knowledge that is the current focus of awareness (Jones & Gerard, 1967), although other terms such as working self-concept and spontaneous self-concept have also been used (Markus & Kunda, 1986; McGuire, McGuire, Child, & Fujioka, 1978).

This view provides several useful implications. First, different situations can activate different self-schemas and this produces different versions of self. McGuire et al. (1978; McGuire, McGuire, & Winton, 1979) showed that things such as race and gender stand out in our self-concept precisely when they stand out in the immediate social context by virtue of being unusual. For example, a boy in a roomful of girls is more aware of being a boy than is a boy in a crowd of boys.

Second, people can be manipulated by having them comb through their stock of self-views in a biased manner. Asking people to recall extraverted versus introverted tendencies—because almost everyone has some memories of both kinds—can get them to think of themselves as relatively extraverted or introverted, and their behavior is likely to be altered to be more consistent with those induced views of self (Fazio, Effrein, & Falendar, 1981; Jones, Rhodewalt, Berglas, & Skelton, 1981). These studies provide important basic clues as to how the self-concept can be changed.

Third, they call into question the sometimes popular notions of one "true" self that differs from other ideas of self. For centuries, writers have romanticized the notion that each person has a single true version of self that is buried inside and can be discovered or realized or, alternatively, can be lost and betrayed by insincere or other false behavior. Although people may be wrong about themselves in various particulars, the notion of an inner true self that is discovered by some kind of treasure hunt is probably best regarded as a troublesome myth. Ideas of self come in multiple, sometimes conflicting versions, and the reality of selfhood is likely an emerging project rather than a fixed entity.

Cognitive Roots of Self-Knowledge

Social psychologists have identified several ways that people acquire self-knowledge and self-schemas, although there does not seem to be any grand or integrative theory about this. Students should be aware of these classic contributions, however.

The self-reference effect refers to the tendency for information pertaining to the self to be processed more thoroughly than other information. In the original studies, Rogers, Kuiper, and Kirker (1977) presented participants with various adjectives and asked them a question about each one. Later they were given a surprise recall test. If the question had been "does this word describe you?" the word was remembered better than if a different question had been used (e.g., "Do you know what this word means?" or "Is this a short word?"). Thus, thinking about the word in relation to the self created a stronger memory trace. This was true even if the person's answer had been no. Later work confirmed that the self is a particularly potent hook on which memory can hang information, although it is by no means unique (Greenwald & Banaji, 1989; Higgins & Bargh, 1987).

The self also appears to transfer its generally positive tone to information connected with it. People like things that are associated with the self. For example, people like the letters in their names better than other letters in the alphabet (Nuttin, 1985, 1987). This irrational liking can even subtly sway major life decisions. Pelham, Mirenberg, and Jones (2002) found that people tended to have homes and jobs that contained the letters of their names. People named George were more likely than people named Virginia to move to Georgia. (Guess where people named Virginia were more likely to go!) People named Larry or Laura were more likely to become lawyers than those named Dennis or Denise, who tended instead to become dentists. These effects, to be sure, were quite small, but they were significant, and it is astonishing that they would have any effect at all.

Items seem to gain in value by virtue of being associated with the self. People place a higher cash value on lottery tickets they chose than on ones given to them, even though all tickets have the same objective value (Langer, 1975). People like things more when they own them than when not, even though ownership stemmed from a random gift and they had not used them yet (Beggan, 1992; in this case, the items were insulator sleeves for cold drinks—hardly a major symbol of personal identity!).

Self-perception theory was proposed by Bem (1965, 1972) to explain one process of acquiring self-knowledge. The gist was that people learn about themselves much as they learn about others, namely by observing behaviors and making inferences. The core idea is that people learn about themselves the same way they learn about others: They see what the person (in this case, the self) does and draw conclusions about traits that produce such acts. Such processes may be especially relevant when other sources of self-knowledge, such as direct awareness of your feelings, are not strong or clear.

The most famous application of self-perception theory is the *overjustification effect*. It can be summarized by the expression that "rewards turn play into work." That is, when people perform an activity both because they enjoy doing it (intrinsic motivation) and because they are getting paid or otherwise rewarded (extrinsic motivation), the action is overly justified in the sense that there are multiple reasons for doing it. In such cases, the extrinsic rewards tend to take over and predominate, so that the person gradually comes to feel that he or she is mainly doing it for the sake of the extrinsic rewards. As a result, the person loses the desire or interest in doing it for its own sake.

This effect was first demonstrated by Deci (1971), who showed that students who were paid for doing puzzles subsequently (i.e., after the pay stopped coming) showed less interest in doing them than other students who had done the same tasks without pay. The self-perception aspect became more salient in studies by Lepper, Greene, and Nisbett (1973). In their work, getting rewards reduced children's intrinsic motivation to draw pictures with markers—but only if they knew in advance that they would get a reward. Surprise rewards had no such effect. If you saw someone else painting a picture and getting a surprise reward for it afterward, you would not conclude that the person painted for the sake of the reward, because the person did not know the reward was coming. In contrast, if the person knew about the reward before starting to paint, you might well infer that the person was painting to get the reward. Apparently, people sometimes apply the same logic in learning about themselves.

Motivational Influences on Self-Knowledge

The importance of the self and the diversity of potential information about the self create ample scope for motivations. Self-knowledge does not just happen. Rather, people seek out self-knowledge generally, and they often have highly selective preferences for some kinds of information over others.

Over the years, social psychologists have converged on three main motives that influence self-knowledge, corresponding to three types of preferences. One is a simple desire to learn the truth about the self, whatever it may be. This motive has been called diagnosticity, in that it produces a preference to acquire information that can provide the clearest, most unambiguous information about the self (Trope, 1983, 1986). For example, taking a valid test under optimal conditions has high diagnosticity because it provides good evidence about our knowledge and abilities. Taking an invalid test under adverse conditions, such as in the presence of distracting noise or while intoxicated, has much less diagnosticity.

A second motive is called self-enhancement. It refers to a preference for favorable information about the self (for reviews, see Alicke & Sedikides, 2009; Sedikides & Gregg, 2008). Sometimes the term is used narrowly to refer to acquiring information that will actually entail a favorable upward revision of beliefs about the self. Other usages are broader and include self-protection, that is, preference for avoiding information that would entail a downward revision of beliefs about the self. The idea that people like to hear good things about themselves and prefer to avoid being criticized is consistent with a broad range of findings.

The third motive emphasizes consistency. Consistency motives have a long and influential history in social psychology, such as in research on cognitive dissonance (Festinger, 1957). Applied to the self, the consistency motive has been dubbed self-verification, in the sense that people seek to verify (confirm) whatever they already believe about themselves (see Swann, 1987), even if that information is unflattering. The underlying assumption is that revising your views is effortful and aversive, so people prefer to maintain what they already think.

Much has been written about what happens when the consistency and enhancement motives clash. If a man believes he is incompetent at golf, does he prefer to hear further evidence of that incompetence, or would he like to be told his golf is really pretty good? One resolution has been that emotionally he favors praise but cognitively he may be skeptical of it and hence more apt to believe confirmation (Swann, 1987).

A systematic effort to compare the relative power and appeal of the three motives was undertaken by Sedikides (1993). He concluded that all three motives are genuine and exert influence over self-knowledge. In general, though, he found that the self-enhancement motive was the strongest and the diagnosticity motive the weakest. In other words, people's desire to learn the truth about themselves is genuine, but it is outshone by their appetite for flattery and, to a lesser extent, by their wish to have their preconceptions confirmed.

One area of convergence between the two strongest motives (enhancement and verification) is the resistance to downward change. That is, both motives would make people reluctant to entertain new information that casts the self in a light less favorable than what they already think. Defensive processes should thus be very strong. This brings up self-deception.

Self-Deception

The possibility of self-deception presents a philosophical quandary, insofar as the same person must seemingly be both the deceiver and the deceived. That seemingly implies that the person must both know something and not know it at the same time. Not much research has convincingly demonstrated effects that meet those criteria (Gur & Sackeim, 1979; Sackeim & Gur, 1979).

In contrast, self-deception becomes much more common and recognizable if it is understood more as a kind of wishful thinking, by which a person manages to end up believing what he or she wants to believe without the most rigorous justifications. An often-cited early survey by Svenson (1981) yielded the rather implausible result that 90% of people claimed to be above average drivers. Many subsequent studies have yielded similar (and similarly implausible) statistics (see Gilovich, 1991). Because in principle only about half the population can truly be above average on any normally distributed trait, the surplus of self-rated excellence is generally ascribed to self-deception. In general, self-concepts are more favorable than the objective facts would warrant.

The widespread tendencies for self-deception led Greenwald (1980) to compare the self to a totalitarian regime (the "totalitarian ego") in its willingness to rewrite history and distort the facts so as to portray itself as benevolent and successful. A highly influential review by Taylor and Brown (1988) listed three main positive illusions. First, people overestimate their successes and good traits (and, in a related manner, underestimate and downplay their failures and bad traits). Second, they overestimate how much control they have over their lives and their fate. Third, they are unrealistically optimistic, believing that they are more likely than other people to experience good outcomes and less likely to experience bad ones. Taylor and Brown went on to suggest that these distorted perceptions are part of good mental health and psychological adjustment, and that people who see themselves in a more balanced, realistic manner are vulnerable to unhappiness and mental illness.

How do people manage to deceive themselves? A wide assortment of strategies and tricks has been documented. Here are some. The self-serving bias is a widely replicated pattern by which people assign more responsibility to external causes for failures than for successes (Zuckerman, 1979). People are selectively critical of evidence that depicts them badly while being uncritical of more agreeable feedback (Pyszczynski, Greenberg, & Holt, 1985; Wyer & Frey, 1983). People pay more attention to good than to bad feedback, allowing for better encoding into memory (Baumeister & Cairns, 1992), so they selectively forget failures more than successes (Crary, 1966; Mischel, Ebbesen, & Zeiss, 1976). People compare themselves to targets that make them look good rather than other, more intimidating targets (Crocker & Major, 1989; Wills, 1981). They also persuade themselves that their good traits are unusual whereas their bad traits are widely shared (Campbell, 1986; Marks, 1984; Suls & Wan, 1987).

Another group of strategies involves distorting the meaning of ambiguous traits (Dunning, 2005; Dunning, Meyerowitz, & Holzberg, 1989). Everyone wants to be smart, but there are book smarts, street smarts, emotional intelligence, and other forms, so most people can find some basis for thinking they are smart.

The downside of self-deception would seemingly be an increased risk of failures and other misfortunes stemming from making poor choices. For example, people routinely overestimate how fast they can get things done, with the result that many projects take longer and cost more than originally budgeted

(Buehler, Griffin, & Ross, 1994). Sometimes people procrastinate based on an overconfident expectation about how fast they can get a project done, with the result that last-minute delays or problems force them either to miss the deadline or to turn in subpar work (Ferrari, Johnson, & McCown, 1995; Tice & Baumeister, 1997).

One remarkable way that people seem to reduce the risks and costs of self-deception is to turn positive illusions on and off. Normally they maintain pleasantly inflated views of their capabilities, but when they face a difficult decision involving making a commitment, they seem to suspend these illusions and temporarily become quite realistic about what they can and cannot accomplish. Once the decision is made, they blithely resume their optimistic, self-flattering stance (Gollwitzer & Kinney, 1989; Gollwitzer & Taylor, 1995). The full implications of these findings—that apparently people maintain parallel but different views of self and can switch back and forth among them as is useful for the situation—have yet to be fully explored and integrated into a theory of self.

Self-Esteem and Narcissism

The motivation to protect and enhance self-esteem has figured prominently in social psychology, but self-esteem has also been studied as a trait dimension along which people differ. Over the years, a great many studies have examined how people with high self-esteem differ from those with low self-esteem, typically using the Rosenberg (1965) scale to distinguish the two. It is probably the trait most studied by social psychologists, although at specific times others have been highly popular. Interest has been sustained by belief in practical applications, such as the notion that raising self-esteem among schoolchildren will facilitate learning and good citizenship while reducing drug abuse and problem pregnancies (California Task Force, 1990).

Unfortunately, the fond hopes that boosting self-esteem would make people wiser, kinder, and healthier have largely been disappointed. There are in fact replicable positive correlations between self-esteem and school performance, but high self-esteem appears to be the result rather than the cause of good grades (e.g., Bachman & O'Malley, 1977). If anything, experimental evidence suggests that boosting self-esteem causes students to perform worse subsequently (Forsyth et al., 2007). The long-standing belief that low self-esteem causes violence has likewise been shown to depend mainly on overinterpreted correlations and self-reports. Seriously violent persons, ranging from the Nazi "Master Race" killers and despotic tyrants to wife-beaters, murderers, rapists, and bullies, tend to think very favorably of themselves (Baumeister, Smart, & Boden, 1996).

There does remain some controversy concerning the latter. A New Zealand sample studied by Donnellan et al. (2005) provided comfort to those who believe that low self-esteem contributes to violence, insofar as their survey found that children scoring low in self-esteem were later rated by teachers as more likely to get into fights. However, that sample may be unusual because of its high representation of native Maoris, a downtrodden culture with low self-esteem that romanticizes its violent warrior traditions. Controlled laboratory experiments with ethnically homogeneous, Western samples have consistently failed to find any sign of elevated aggression among people with low self-esteem. On the contrary, high narcissism and high self-esteem contribute most directly to aggression (Bushman et al., 2009; Bushman & Baumeister, 1998; Menon et al., 2007).

One thorough search concluded that two benefits of high self-esteem are well established (Baumeister, Campbell, Krueger, & Vohs, 2003). High self-esteem supports initiative, possibly because it lends confidence to act on our beliefs and assumptions and a willingness to go against the crowd. It also contributes to feeling good and happy. These two benefits take multiple forms, such as promoting persistence in the face of failure and a resilience under stress and adversity.

Many contributions to understanding self-esteem do not depend on searching for benefits of high self-esteem. Campbell (1990) showed that self-esteem levels are associated with differential self-concept clarity. People with high self-esteem have clear and consistent beliefs about themselves, whereas the beliefs of people with low self-esteem are often confused, contradictory, and fluctuating. The lack of a stable image of self may also contribute to the greater emotional lability of people low in self-esteem (Campbell, Chew, & Scratchley, 1991).

Self-esteem can be based on different things. Crocker and Wolfe's (2001) research on contingencies of self-worth has found that identical outcomes may affect people differently depending on whether the underlying dimension is an important basis of each person's self-esteem. For example, academic success will boost self-esteem among some students more than others, insofar as some base their self-esteem on school success and achievement more than others.

Although self-esteem tends to be fairly stable over time, it fluctuates more among some people than others. Kernis and his colleagues have studied this by administering a self-esteem scale repeatedly and determining how much each individual changes. Higher instability of self-esteem (i.e., more change) has been linked to multiple outcomes, including aggression and emotional reactions (Kernis, 1993; Kernis, Cornell, Sun, Berry, & Harlow, 1993; Kernis, Granneman, & Barclay, 1989).

Different levels of self-esteem are associated with different social motivations. People with high self-esteem are attracted to new challenges and opportunities for success. People with low self-esteem favor a cautious, self-protective orientation that seeks to minimize risks, resolve problems, and avoid failures (Baumeister, Tice, & Hutton, 1989; Wood, Heimpel, & Michela, 2003; Wood, Heimbel, Newby-Clark, & Ross, 2005; Wood, Michela, & Giordano, 2000). (The dynamics of self-esteem in close relationships are covered in Chapter 13, this volume, on intimate relationships.)

Given how few direct benefits flow from high self-esteem, why do people care so much about sustaining and even increasing their favorable views of self? The widespread concern is even more surprising given the remarkable range of evidence, reviewed by Crocker and Park (2004), that the pursuit of high self-esteem is often costly and destructive to the individual as well as to other people. The pursuit of high self-esteem can reduce learning, empathy, and prosocial behavior, while increasing aggression and rule-breaking.

One promising answer, proposed by Leary and his colleagues, depicts self-esteem as a sociometer, which is to say an internal measure of how much we are likely to be accepted by others (e.g., Leary, Tambor, Terdal, & Downs, 1995). Self-esteem is typically based on the attributes that make us desirable as a group member or relationship partner: competence, attractiveness, likability, social skills, trustworthiness, reliability, and more. Although having a favorable opinion of yourself may have relatively little benefit, being accepted by others is highly important, and indeed belonging to social groups is central to the biological strategies by which human beings survive and reproduce (Baumeister & Leary, 1995; Baumeister, 2005). Thus, ultimately, concern with self-esteem is nature's way of making people want to be accepted by others. When people cultivate self-esteem by deceiving themselves and overestimating their good traits, rather than by actually trying to be a good person, they are in effect misusing the system for emotional satisfactions and thwarting its purpose.

Viewing self-esteem as a sociometer brings us to the interpersonal aspect of self. Essentially, sociometer theory proposes that self-esteem serves interpersonal functions, and the reasons people care about self-esteem are based on the fundamental importance of being accepted by other people (Leary & Baumeister, 2000). This approach reverses one simple and common approach to understanding psychological phenomena, which is to assume that what happens between people is a result of what is inside them (in this case, that interpersonal behavior is a result of self-esteem). Instead, it contends that the inner processes such as self-esteem emerged or evolved to facilitate social interaction.

In recent years, some interest has shifted from self-esteem to narcissism, which can be understood as a relatively obnoxious form of high self-esteem (although there are a few puzzling individuals who score high in narcissism but low in self-esteem). Narcissism is not just having a favorable view of yourself as superior to others; it also reflects a motivational concern with thinking well of yourself and with getting other people to admire you (Morf & Rhodewalt, 2001).

Interpersonal Self

The interpersonal aspects of self have received only intermittent attention from social psychologists, although by now most would acknowledge their importance. Self-presentation is probably the most interpersonal of the major themes in the study of self. Research on self-presentation spread widely during the 1980s but has tapered off considerably in recent years, partly because many of the basic questions were answered.

Self-Presentation

Self-presentation, also sometimes called impression management, refers to people's efforts to portray themselves in particular ways to others (Schlenker, 1975, 1980). That is, it indicates how people try to make others view them as having certain traits and properties. Most commonly, people seek to make a good impression, but there can be other intended impressions. For example, a violent criminal may seek to convince others that he is dangerous and unpredictable, so that they will do what he says without fighting back or resisting.

Self-presentation first began to influence social psychology when it was put forward as an alternative explanation for research findings that emphasized inner processes. In particular, studies of attitude change and cognitive dissonance had proposed that when people act in ways contrary to their beliefs, they experience an inner state of unpleasant inconsistency, which they resolve by changing their inner attitude to conform to what they have done. Tedeschi, Schlenker, and Bonoma (1971) proposed instead that people merely want to appear consistent, so they might report attitudes consistent with their behavior, even if they did not actually change their attitude. That is, instead of seeking to rationalize their behavior to themselves, they were simply trying to make a good impression on the experimenters. As evidence, self-presentation researchers pointed out that people showed attitude change when their behavior had been viewed by others but not when it was secret or anonymous (Carlsmith, Collins, & Helmreich, 1966; Helmreich & Collins, 1968). The inconsistency and hence the need to rationalize should have been the same regardless of whether others were watching, but the concern with making a good impression would arise only if other people were paying attention.

The controversy over dissonance raged for years. Eventually the conclusion was that people do change attitudes more under public than private conditions, but this involved a genuine inner change rather than just saying something to look good to the experimenter (e.g., Baumeister & Tice, 1984; Cooper & Fazio, 1984; Schlenker, 1980; Tetlock & Manstead, 1985). Dissonance is not our concern here (see Petty & Briñol, Chapter 7, this volume), but that resolution is quite important for the development of self-presentation theory. Self-presentation came to mean more than just saying things that we do not really mean to make a good impression. Rather, inner processes are strongly affected by the interpersonal context. Over the years, researchers continued to show that much inner cognitive and emotional work is done to project the desired image of self (e.g., Vohs, Baumeister, & Ciarocco, 2005; Schlenker & Leary, 1982).

Methodologically, self-presentation research came to rely heavily on comparing behavior in public versus private conditions (Schlenker, 1980). The assumption was that if people behaved differently in public, the difference reflected their concern with how others perceived them and hence showed that they were motivated to send a particular message about themselves. Over the years, a wide variety of phenomena had been shown to change as a function of whether the behavior was public or private, and so the implications were far wider than cognitive dissonance and attitude change. Aggression, helping, reactance, attributions, self-handicapping, prejudice, and many other behaviors showed these differences, indicating that often such behaviors were guided by interpersonal motivations (Baumeister, 1982). Taken together, these shifts pushed social psychology to become more interpersonal, because many of these phenomena had hitherto been discussed and explained in terms of what happens inside the individual mind, but now they had to be acknowledged as influenced by the interpersonal context.

Crucially, though, evidence of self-presentational and interpersonal motives could not be interpreted as denying that genuine inner processes were also at work (such as with cognitive dissonance) (e.g., Tetlock & Manstead, 1985). Instead, it became necessary to understand the inner and the interpersonal as linked. Ultimately, these findings pointed toward the general conclusion that *inner processes serve interpersonal functions*. This is possibly one of the most important general principles in social psychology.

Eventually, self-presentation research became a victim of its own success: Most of the behaviors studied by social psychologists had been shown to differ between public and private situations, and the basic point of the influence of self-presentation had been made over and over. Recent trends toward studying cognitive processes, biological influences on behavior, and prejudice had less relevance to self-presentation. Although the ideas and methods remain viable today, there is little current research going on to extend self-presentation theory.

One of the more creative extensions of self-presentation theory in recent years was a review by Leary, Tchividjian, and Kraxberger (1994) showing that self-presentation can be hazardous to our health. That is, people do things to make a good impression even though they know these things may be harmful. Interest in this work was sparked by Mark Leary's conversation with a friend who continued to sunbathe despite having had skin cancer (which is often caused by high exposure to the sun). Leary discovered that his friend was far from unique, and in fact many people sunbathe even after they have had skin cancer, because they believe that a suntan makes them attractive to others. (A tan itself has a mixed history as a self-presentational tool. In the 1800s, sun-darkened skin was associated with the low or working class, because it meant that the person worked out in the sun. The term "redneck" today still conveys this link between sun exposure and low socioeconomic class. However, in the early 1920s, rich people began to play tennis, thereby getting suntans, and the tanned look became fashionable.)

Moving on beyond sunbathing, Leary et al. (1994) identified a host of things people do that are bad for their health but presumably useful for self-presentation. They ride motorcycles without helmets. They smoke cigarettes. They avoid medical treatments for conditions that are embarrassing or undignified.

The implications of this work are thought provoking. Indeed, one influential theory in social psychology has held that people are mainly motivated by fear of death, and that everything people do is aimed toward the overarching goal of prolonging life and even of avoiding the very thought of death (Pyszczynski, Greenberg, & Solomon, 1997). (In fact, the original statement of this theory was in an edited book about self-presentation; see Greenberg, Pyszczynski, & Solomon, 1986.) Yet the review by Leary et al. (1994) repeatedly showed that many people do things that endanger their lives if those actions help to make a good impression on others. Hence making a good impression can sometimes be a stronger motivation than avoiding death. To be sure, making a good impression is probably an important part of maintaining social acceptance, which itself generally serves the goal of protecting and prolonging life, even if the goals sometimes conflict.

Self-Concept Change and Stability

Can the self-concept change? Of course it can, and does. But demonstrating self-concept change in the laboratory has proven difficult.

Interpersonal context and processes appear to be important in self-concept change. Harter (e.g., 1993) has found that children's self-esteem is most likely to change when the child's social network changes, such as when the child enters a different school or when the family moves. This finding suggests that one source of stability of self-concept is interacting with people who know you and have a stable impression of you.

Laboratory studies have sought to show change in self-concept stemming from interpersonal behavior. When people present themselves in a particular way to strangers, they sometimes internalize how they acted, leading them to view themselves as being the sort of person they presented themselves as being (Jones, Rhodewalt, Berglas, & Skelton, 1991). There are competing views as to how this occurs. One is that to present themselves as ambitious. For example, people must retrieve evidence from memory that would depict themselves as ambitious; then when asked to describe themselves, that information has more weight than it otherwise would.

It seems essential, however, that another person hear and believe the self-presentation. When people present themselves in one way but privately scan their memories for evidence of the opposite trait, the memory scans have little effect on self-concept whereas the self-concept shifts to resemble the version that the other person saw (Schlenker, Dlugolecki, & Doherty, 1994). The decisiveness of the interpersonal context was shown by Tice (1992), who showed that essentially identical behaviors led to self-concept change when witnessed by others but not when they were private or confidential.

Receiving feedback from others may or may not bring about changes in self-concept. People accept favorable feedback more readily than critical feedback (Taylor & Brown, 1988). Apart from favorability, another factor is whether people receive the evaluations passively or can assert themselves interpersonally by disputing the feedback. They are less affected if they can dispute it interpersonally than if they receive it without the opportunity to respond (Swann & Hill, 1982).

One of the most elegant theories linking self-concept stability to interpersonal processes was Tesser's (1988) self-evaluation maintenance (SEM) theory. Two different processes govern how a person's self-esteem is affected by relationship partners. The first is reflection, which means that the partner's achievements and attributes reflect on the self in a consistent manner. That is, your partner's good works reflect well on you and your partner's misdeeds reflect badly on you. The other process is comparison, which reverses the valence: Your partner's successes make you look worse by comparison. Which process predominates depends on several factors. If the partner's attribute is highly relevant to your own career or self-concept, comparison is more important, whereas your partner's successes and failures concerning things irrelevant to your own work foster reflection. The closeness of the relationship intensifies both outcomes. Thus, you are more affected by the successes and failures of your romantic partner than by those of a distant cousin or casual acquaintance.

Executive Function: Self as Agent

The third aspect of self involves what it does, in the sense of how the self acts on the world (and acts on itself). This area of study was slower to develop, as compared with self-knowledge and interpersonal dynamics. Studies on self-regulation, however, has become a major theme of research. It began to increase in the late 1980s and by 2000 had become an ongoing focus of many laboratories. Other aspects of the self as executive function, such as the self as decision maker or as the controller of controlled processes, seem promising areas for further work.

Dual process theories that distinguish between automatic and controlled processes have become widely influential in social psychology. The self is essentially the controller of controlled processes (if not the self, then who else?), and so it plays an important role in such theories. How the self exerts such control is not well understood, and researchers thus far have focused far more effort on the automatic than on the controlled processes, but illuminating the processes of control promises to shed considerable light on this important function of the self. Decision making also involves the self, but that work will be covered in the chapter on decision making (Vohs & Luce, Chapter 20, this volume) rather than here.

Self-Regulation

Self-regulation refers to the self's capacity to alter and change itself and its states, particularly so as to bring them into line with standards such as norms, goals, ideals, or rules. Self-regulation includes diverse areas such as controlling our thoughts and emotions, impulse control and the restraint of problem behavior, and optimizing performance. The everyday term self-control is quite similar to self-regulation and sometimes the terms are used interchangeably, although some researchers make a slight distinction on the basis that self-control refers exclusively to conscious, effortful processes whereas self-regulation also includes nonconscious or automatic regulatory processes, even including the bodily processes that keep the temperature constant and regulate the speed of the heartbeat.

A landmark step in the development of self-regulation theory was Carver and Scheier's (1981, 1982) assertion that self-awareness is essentially for the sake of self-regulation. As you recall, the earlier section on self-awareness pointed out that humans are almost always self-aware in relation to some standard, so that the current state of the self is compared to how it might be. This fact fits well with the idea that self-regulation is the purpose of self-awareness.

Building on that insight, Carver and Scheier (1981, 1982, 1998) imported the concept of the feedback loop from cybernetic theory (e.g., Powers, 1973). The feedback loop is best remembered with its acronym TOTE, which stands for test, operate, test, and exit. Such loops supervise effective self-regulation everywhere. The test involves comparing the current state of the self to the goal or standard. If the test produces an unsatisfactory result, so that the self is not as it should be, then an Operate phase is commenced to correct the problem. From time to time there is another Test phase, to ensure that progress is being made toward the goal. Eventually one of these tests indicates that the self now meets the standard, and the loop is Exited.

The feedback loop incorporates the three essential ingredients of self-regulation. Let us consider each in turn.

Standards The term "regulate" means not just to change but rather to change based on some concept of what ought (or ought not) to be. These concepts are standards. Without standards, self-regulation would have no meaning. Standards can come from external sources such as laws, norms, and expectations, but the self-regulating person internalizes the standard to some degree. The standards are not simply ideas or rules; rather they incorporate the motivational aspect of self-regulation. The amount of effort devoted to self-regulation, and therefore to some degree the success or failure of self-regulation, depends on the extent to which the person embraces the standard and desires to regulate behavior so as to match it.

Standards can be sorted into two main types according to whether the person wants to move toward or away from them (Carver & Scheier, 1998). Positive or ideal standards are ones the person wants to match, and so the purpose of the feedback loop is to reduce the discrepancy between how you are and the standard. For example, a dieter may have a specific target weight (the standard) and strives to lose pounds so as to match that weight. In contrast, negative standards are ones that the person seeks to avoid matching, such as being a liar, a loser, or a drug addict. In these cases, the goal of the feedback loop is to maximize the difference between the actual self and the standard.

An important implication is that the negative standards are more difficult to implement (Carver & Scheier, 1998). It is harder to regulate yourself to not be something than to be something, because there is no obvious direction or goal of change. This can be illustrated by the analogy to a spatial goal. If your goal is to go to Pittsburgh, then you know where you want to be; you can therefore work on changing your location to move closer, and you know when you have successfully arrived there. In contrast, if your goal is to be far away from Pittsburgh, you do not know exactly where to go, and there is no point at which your regulatory task can be pronounced to have reached success. Thus, common self-regulatory tasks such as quitting smoking are by their very nature problematic, because you are never sure you have permanently quit and the steps along the way do not prescribe doing anything specific.

The difference between positive and negative standards has also been the focus of research by E. T. Higgins. In an influential 1987 article, he proposed that standards could be sorted into ideals (how one wanted to be) and oughts (how one is expected to be, which often involves specifics about what not to do and how not to be) and argued, more provocatively, that different emotional reactions were associated with these two types of standards. Specifically, he contended that failure to reach ideals led to low-energy emotions such as sadness and depression, whereas failure to do as one ought to do produced high-energy emotions such as guilt and anxiety (Higgins, 1987). However, the considerable amount of research aimed at pursuing this intriguing theory of emotion produced results that were mixed at best (Tangney, Niedenthal, Covert, & Barlow, 1998).

The impasse prompted Higgins to revise his approach and emphasize a basic distinction between promotion (standards oriented toward gains) and prevention (standards oriented toward nonlosses) (Higgins, 1997). Higgins has also proposed that we can approach or avoid in either a promotion-oriented or prevention-oriented way, which creates a 2 × 2 motivational space. According to his regulatory focus theory, individuals self-regulate differently when they are pursuing promotion-focused versus prevention-focused goals (Higgins, 1997; Higgins & Spiegel, 2004; Molden, Lee, & Higgins, 2008). Promotion-focused goals emphasize advancement, aspiration, and accomplishment, whereas prevention-focused goals emphasize safety, security, and protection. Individuals in a promotion focus experience self-regulatory success as achieving a positive outcome (a gain) and unsuccessful self-regulation as a missed opportunity for a positive outcome (a nongain), whereas individuals in a prevention focus experience self-regulatory success as protecting against a negative outcome (a nonloss) and unsuccessful self-regulation as incurring a negative outcome (a loss). Furthermore, individuals tend to pursue promotion-focused goals with eager self-regulatory strategies and prevention-focused goals with vigilant self-regulatory strategies.

One application of regulatory focus theory to self-regulation research involves the trade-off between speed and accuracy in goal pursuit, with the eagerness of promotion-focused goal pursuit predicting greater speed and diminished accuracy relative to the vigilance of prevention goal pursuit (Förster, Higgins, & Bianco, 2003). In an illustrative study, relative to individuals primed with a prevention focus, those primed with a promotion focus were faster at a proofreading task (indicating eagerness) but less accurate at finding complex grammatical errors (indicating lower vigilance).

Regulatory focus also influences whether individuals tend to view goals as luxuries or necessities. A promotion focus facilitates viewing an adopted goal as one of many opportunities for advancement (i.e., as a luxury), whereas a prevention focus facilitates viewing an adopted goal as the essential means for achieving the goal (i.e., as a necessity). As a result, individuals in a prevention focus tend to initiate goal pursuit faster than do those in a promotion focus (Freitas, Liberman, Salovey, & Higgins, 2002).

In addition to influencing how immediately individuals initiate goal pursuit, regulatory focus also affects how they respond to interruptions of their ongoing goal pursuit. Individuals in a prevention focus show a greater tendency than individuals in a promotion focus to resume an interrupted activity rather than initiate a substitute activity (Liberman, Idson, Camacho, & Higgins, 1999).

Monitoring Monitoring refers to paying attention to and keeping track of the behavior that is to be changed. Just as it is difficult to shoot at a target you cannot see, it is difficult to regulate a behavior that you do not monitor. When people want to improve their self-control, the most effective first steps usually involve improved monitoring: Write down what you spend, weigh yourself daily, count the laps you run, and so forth. Failures of self-control often begin with ceasing to monitor. For example, when dieters go on an eating binge, they lose track of how much they eat much more than other people (Polivy, 1976).

The feedback-loop theory by Carver and Scheier (1981) is essentially a theory of monitoring. As we noted, it made the crucial link between self-awareness and self-regulation. Monitoring thus depends on self-awareness. It is no mere coincidence that loss of self-awareness contributes to poor self-regulation. For example, alcohol reduces self-awareness (Hull, 1981), and alcohol intoxication contributes to almost all known manner of self-control problems. Intoxicated persons spend more money, gamble more, eat more, behave more aggressively, engage in inappropriate sexual activities, and so forth (Baumeister, Heatherton, & Tice, 1994).

Willpower The third ingredient is the capacity to change the self. The folk notion of willpower appears to have some psychological validity, in the sense that the self consists partly of an energy resource that is expended during acts of self-control. Following an initial act of self-control, performance on a second, unrelated self-control task is often impaired, suggesting that some energy was expended during the first task and hence was not available to help with the second task (e.g., Baumeister, Bratslavsky, Muraven, & Tice, 1998). The resultant reduced resources has been dubbed *ego depletion*, because it suggests that some of the self's (ego's) resources have been depleted.

Is the self made partly from energy? For several decades, self theories were mainly cognitive. They focused on self-knowledge and self-awareness and how these influenced information processing. The first ego depletion findings were thus something of an oddity, because the very idea of self as energy was foreign to prevailing views. However, the influx of biological concepts into psychological theory made energy more plausible, insofar as life itself is an energy process and all biological activities depend on energy. Further work with ego depletion has suggested that the self's resources are linked to glucose, which is a chemical in the bloodstream (made from food) that supplies fuel for brain processes. Effective self-control depends on having a sufficient blood glucose level (Gailliot & Baumeister, 2007), and after acts of self-control, blood glucose levels are diminished (Gailliot et al., 2007).

Depleted willpower does not doom the person to poor self-control. People can overcome depletion and perform effectively. Motivational incentives can encourage people to do this (Muraven & Slessareva, 2003), as can positive emotion (Tice, Baumeister, Shmueli, & Muraven, 2007). Thinking at a highly meaningful, abstract level that incorporates long-range perspectives can also improve self-control, even despite depletion (Fujita, Trope, Liberman, & Levin-Sagi, 2006).

Beyond Self-regulation: Executive Function

The idea that the self consists partly of energy, rather than simply concepts, offers a basis for thinking about some of the self's activities beyond self-regulation. The category of executive function (also called agency, as in being an agent) invokes several other things the self does, including making choices, exerting control over the physical and social environment, and taking initiative. In philosophy, questions of agency invoke debates about free will and freedom of action.

There is some evidence that the same energy used for self-control is used for these other activities. After people make choices, their self-control is impaired, which suggests that the same energy is used for both decision making and self-regulation (Vohs et al., 2008). Conversely, after exerting self-control, decision processes are changed and seemingly impaired (Pocheptsova et al., 2009). There is even some evidence that depletion of glucose contributes to irrational decision making (Masicampo & Baumeister, 2008).

The study of executive function is a promising area for advances in the next decade (see Miyake et al., 2000; Suchy, 2009). Planning, decision making, task switching and resumption, goal maintenance and change, information updating and monitoring, and other supervisory processes fall into this category, which is of interest not only to social psychology's self theorists but also to brain researchers, cognitive scientists, and others. A full accounting of how these processes operate and interact will contribute greatly to the understanding of this important aspect of the self.

Self-Determination Theory

Social psychology has a long tradition of studying behavior by assuming that the individual responds to causes that lie outside, in the situation. Rebelling against this view, Deci and Ryan (e.g., 1995) have advocated Self-Determination Theory, which depicts the self as an active agent and which emphasizes causes that lie inside the self. In their view, human behavior produces much more beneficial outcomes when people act from internal causes than when they allow themselves to be pushed by external factors. Of course, the simple dichotomy of internal versus external causes is not rigid, and there are many intermediate causes, such as when people internalize and accept influences from their social worlds, but these are seen as in between. The more internal the cause, the better.

Self-Determination Theory grew out of Deci's (e.g., 1971) research on intrinsic motivation, which was defined as the desire to do something for the sake of enjoyment of the activity itself. It was contrasted with extrinsic motivation, which meant a desire to do something based on the results or outcomes it would bring. This distinction led to the discovery of the overjustification effect (see above).

Self-Determination Theory was developed to respond to the complications surrounding the simple distinction between intrinsic and extrinsic motivation. The core emphasis on the importance of agentic action based on inner values and causes remained central, however. Deci and Ryan (1991, 1995) proposed that people have a fundamental need for autonomy, which can be satisfied only by acting in ways that bring the feeling from which our acts originate within the self, as opposed to being controlled or directed by outside forces. It is not enough to contemplate an external reason to do something and then deliberately decide to go along with it. Instead, it is essential that the very reasons for the action be seen as originating within the self.

Not all researchers accept that autonomy is truly a need, in the sense that people will suffer pathological outcomes if they mainly do what they are told or what the situation requires instead of following their inner promptings. Nonetheless, this controversial position represents an important perspective on human behavior and likely points the way toward the most satisfying and fulfilling ways to live.

Another notable (and less controversial) assertion of Self-Determination Theory is that people have a need for competence. This means learning to control events and to experience yourself as capable and effective. The notion that there is a natural drive to achieve mastery and control is well rooted in psychological theory and implicit in many phenomena, such as findings about learned helplessness (Seligman, 1975) and stress (Brady, 1958). The novel point in Self-Determination Theory is that it is less control than an awareness of the self as capably exerting control that is central to human motivation.

Managing Multiple Goals

Much of self-regulation involves keeping our behavior on track toward goals. Yet people have more than one goal at a time, and so part of managing ourself effectively is juggling the different goals. In recent years, researchers have begun to look at how people manage multiple goals.

Several relevant processes and strategies have been identified. *Goal shielding* refers to the process of protecting our pursuit of one goal from the distracting thoughts and feelings associated with other goals (Shah, Friedman, & Kruglanski, 2002). When people are shielding their pursuit of one goal, they are less prone to think of other goals and less effective at coming up with means of reaching these alternative goals.

Another set of processes involves managing limited amounts of time and effort so as to allocate them where they are most needed. People appraise progress toward various goals. If they think they are ahead of schedule in pursuing one goal, they may decrease their future efforts, a response known as *coasting* (Carver & Scheier, 2009). This allows them to focus their efforts on other goals, for which progress may be more urgent. Notably this is not the same as reducing your efforts when you actually reach or fulfill a goal, because it may happen anywhere along the way, as long as you believe you have made good progress.

Work by Fishbach (e.g., 2009; Fishbach & Dhar, 2005; Fishbach & Zhang, 2009) has focused on the tension between juggling multiple goals (which she calls balancing) and featuring a single primary goal (which she calls highlighting). The greater the commitment to one goal, the more likely it is to be highlighted, which is to say pursued even at the possible cost of neglecting other goals. Meanwhile, when balancing multiple goals, an important factor is how much progress you have made toward each. Focusing on how much is left to do makes you want to zero in on that goal; focusing on how much you have already achieved can make you temporarily satisfied so you can shift efforts elsewhere (as in the concept of coasting).

Conclusions: Looking Ahead

It is safe to say that the self will remain an important focus of theorizing and research in social psychology. Within the broad topic of self, however, the so-called focal areas of study continue to change. Cultural differences in self-construal have continued to provide new research findings. Self-esteem continues to attract interest, most recently in terms of questions about how much it contributes to positive, desirable outcomes and whether it has a downside. Self-regulation remains a thriving focus of research, possibly because it is one of the central activities of the self and therefore is involved at some level in most of the other processes of self. Other aspects of executive function, such as how the self is involved in decision making and initiative, have only begun to be studied, and these seem likely to attract more attention in coming years.

The increased interest in brain processes has not been kind to self research, however. There has not been great success at finding a particular part of the brain that corresponds to self. Quite possibly the brain operates as many distributed, independent processes, whereas the self is a unity constructed for purposes of social action. Reconciling the reality of self in social life with its elusiveness to cognitive neuroscientists will be a fascinating chapter in the history of self theory.

Other puzzles remain. Self-affirmation, which refers to acting or thinking in ways that bolster the self's main values, continues to have an assortment of intriguing effects, but people are not sure just what process produces those effects (e.g., Schmeichel & Vohs, 2009; Steele, 1988). Self-concept change and self change remain important but understudied phenomena. It is clear that self researchers will not run out of questions in the foreseeable future.

References

Alicke, M., & Sedikides, C. (2009). Self-enhancement and self-protection: What they are and what they do. *European Review of Social Psychology, 20*, 1–48.

Allport, G. W. (1943). The ego in contemporary psychology. *Psychological Review, 50*, 451–478.

Aronson, E., & Mettee, D. (1968). Dishonest behavior as a function of differential levels of induced self-esteem. *Journal of Personality and Social Psychology, 9*, 121–127.

Bachman, J. G., & O' Malley, P. M. (1977). Self-esteem in young men: A longitudinal analysis of the impact of educational and occupational attainment. *Journal of Personality and Social Psychology, 35*, 365–380.

Baumeister, R. F. (1982). A self-presentational view of social phenomena. *Psychological Bulletin, 91*, 3–26.

Baumeister, R. F. (1987). How the self became a problem: A psychological review of historical research. *Journal of Personality and Social Psychology, 52*, 163–176.

Baumeister, R. F. (1991). *Escaping the self: Alcoholism, spirituality, masochism, and other flights from the burden of selfhood.* New York: Basic Books.

Baumeister, R. F. (1998). The self. In D. T. Gilbert, S. T. Fiske, & G. Lindzey (Eds.), *Handbook of social psychology* (4th ed., pp. 680–740). New York: McGraw-Hill.

Baumeister, R. F. (2005). *The cultural animal: Human nature, meaning, and social life.* New York: Oxford University Press.

Baumeister, R. F., Bratslavsky, E., Muraven, M., & Tice, D. M. (1998). Ego depletion: Is the active self a limited resource? *Journal of Personality and Social Psychology, 74*, 1252–1265.

Baumeister, R. F., & Cairns, K. J. (1992). Repression and self-presentation: When audiences interfere with self-deceptive strategies. *Journal of Personality and Social Psychology, 62*, 851–862.

Baumeister, R. F., Campbell, J. D., Krueger, J. I., & Vohs, K. D. (2003). Does high self-esteem cause better performance, interpersonal success, happiness, or healthier life-styles? *Psychological Science in the Public Interest, 4*, 1–44.

Baumeister, R. F., Heatherton, T. F., & Tice, D. M. (1994). *Losing control: How and why people fail at self-regulation.* San Diego, CA: Academic Press.

Baumeister, R. F., & Leary, M. R. (1995). The need to belong: Desire for interpersonal attachments as a fundamental human motivation. *Psychological Bulletin, 117*, 497–529.

Baumeister, R. F., Smart, L., & Boden, J. M. (1996). Relation of threatened egotism to violence and aggression: The dark side of high self-esteem. *Psychological Review, 103*, 5–33.

Baumeister, R. F., & Sommer, K. L. (1997). What do men want? Gender differences and two spheres of belongingness: Comment on Cross and Madson (1997). *Psychological Bulletin, 122*, 38–44.

Baumeister, R. F., & Tice, D. M. (1984). Role of self-presentation and choice in cognitive dissonance under forced compliance: Necessary or sufficient causes? *Journal of Personality and Social Psychology, 46*, 5–13.

Baumeister, R. F., Tice, D. M., & Hutton, D. G. (1989). Self-presentational motivations and personality differences in self-esteem. *Journal of Personality, 57*, 547–579.

Beggan, J. K. (1992). On the social nature of nonsocial perception: The mere ownership effect. *Journal of Personality and Social Psychology, 62*, 229–237.

Bem, D. J. (1965). An experimental analysis of self-persuasion. *Journal of Experimental Social Psychology, 1*, 199–218.

Bem, D. J. (1972). Self-perception theory. In L Berkowitz (Ed.), *Advances in experimental social psychology* (Vol. 6, pp. 1–62). New York: Academic Press.

Brady, J. V. (1958). Ulcers in "executive" monkeys. *Scientific American, 199*, 95–100.

Buehler, R., Griffin, D., & Ross, M. (1994). Exploring the "planning fallacy": Why people underestimate their task completion times. *Journal of Personality and Social Psychology, 67*, 366–381.

Bushman, B. J., & Baumeister, R. F. (1998). Threatened egotism, narcissism, self-esteem, and direct and displaced aggression: Does self-love or self-hate lead to violence? *Journal of Personality and Social Psychology, 75*, 219–229.

Bushman, B. J., Baumeister, R. F., Thomaes, S., Ryu, E., Begeer, S., & West, S. G. (2009). Looking again, and harder, for a link between low self-esteem and aggression. *Journal of Personality, 77*, 427–446.

California Task Force to Promote Self-Esteem and Personal and Social Responsibility. (1990). *Toward a state of self-esteem.* Sacramento: California State Department of Education.

Campbell, J. D. (1986). Similarity and uniqueness: The effects of attribute type, relevance, and individual differences in self-esteem and depression. *Journal of Personality and Social Psychology, 50*, 281–294.

Campbell, J. D. (1990). Self-esteem and clarity of the self-concept. *Journal of Personality and Social Psychology, 59*, 538–549.

Campbell, J. D., Chew, B., & Scratchley, L. S. (1991). Cognitive and emotional reactions to daily events: The effects of self-esteem and self-complexity. *Journal of Personality, 59*, 473–505.

Carlsmith, J. M., Collins, B. E., & Helmreich, R. L. (1966). Studies in forced compliance: 1. The effect of pressure for compliance on attitude change produced by face-to-face role playing and anonymous essay writing. *Journal of Personality and Social Psychology, 4*, 1–13.

Carver, C. S., & Scheier, M. F. (1981). Attention and self-regulation: A control theory approach to human behavior. New York: Springer-Verlag.

Carver, C. S., & Scheier, M. F. (1982). Control theory: A useful conceptual framework for personality-social, clinical and health psychology. *Psychological Bulletin, 92*, 111–135.

Carver, C. S., & Scheier, M. F. (1998). *On the self-regulation of behavior.* New York: Cambridge University Press.

Carver, C. S., & Scheier, M. F. (2009). Action, affect, multitasking, and layers of control. In J. Forgas, R. Baumeister, & D. Tice (Eds.), *Psychology of self-regulation* (pp. 109–126). New York: Psychology Press.

Cooper, J., & Fazio, R. H. (1984). A new look at dissonance theory. In L. Berkowitz (Ed.), *Advances in experimental social psychology* (Vol. 17, pp. 229–266). New York: Academic Press.

Crary, W. G. (1966). Reactions to incongruent self-experiences. *Journal of Consulting Psychology, 30*, 246–252.

Crocker, J., & Major, B. (1989). Social stigma and self-esteem: The self-protective properties of stigma. *Psychological Review, 96*, 608–630.

Crocker, J., & Park, L. E. (2004). The costly pursuit of self-esteem. *Psychological Bulletin, 130*, 392–414.

Crocker, J., & Wolfe, C. T. (2001). Contingencies of self-worth. *Psychological Review, 108*, 593–623.

Cross, S. E., & Madson, L. (1997). Models of the self: Self-construals and gender. *Psychological Bulletin, 122*, 5–37.

Deci, E. L. (1971). Effects of externally mediated rewards on intrinsic motivation. *Journal of Personality and Social Psychology, 18*, 105–115.

Deci, E. L., & Ryan, R. M. (1991). A motivational approach to self: Integration in personality. In R. Dienstbier (Ed.), *Nebraska symposium on motivation* (Vol. 38, pp. 237–288). Lincoln: University of Nebraska Press.

Deci, E. L., & Ryan, R. M. (1995). Human autonomy: The basis for true self-esteem. In M. Kernis (Ed.), *Efficacy, agency, and self-esteem* (pp. 31–49). New York: Plenum Press.

Diener, E., & Wallbom, M. (1976). Effects of self-awareness on antinormative behavior. *Journal of Research in Personality, 10*, 107–111.

Donnellan, M. B., Trzesniewski, K. H., Robins, R. W., Moffitt, T. E., & Caspi, A. (2005). Low self-esteem is related to aggression, antisocial behavior, and delinquency. *Psychological Science, 16*, 328–335.

Dunning, D. (2005). *Self-insight: Roadblocks and detours on the path to knowing thyself.* New York: Psychology Press.

Dunning, D., Meyerowitz, J. A., & Holzberg, A. (1989). Ambiguity and self-evaluation: The role of idiosyncratic trait definitions in self-serving assessments of ability. *Journal of Personality and Social Psychology, 57*, 1082–1090.

Duval, S., & Wicklund, R. A. (1972). *A theory of objective self-awareness*. New York: Academic Press.

Fazio, R. H., Effrein, E. A., & Falender, V. J. (1981). Self-perceptions following social interactions. *Journal of Personality and Social Psychology, 41*, 232–242.

Fenigstein, A., Scheier, M. F., & Buss, A. H. (1975). Public and private self-consciousness: Assessment and theory. *Journal of Consulting and Clinical Psychology, 43*, 522–527.

Ferrari, J. R., Johnson, J. L., and McCown, W. G. (1995). *Procrastination and task avoidance: Theory, research, and treatment*. New York: Plenum Press.

Festinger, L. (1957). *A theory of cognitive dissonance*. Stanford, CA: Stanford University Press.

Fishbach, A. (2009). The dynamics of self-regulation. In J. Forgas, R. Baumeister, & D. Tice (Eds.), *Psychology of self-regulation* (pp. 163–181). New York: Psychology Press.

Fishbach, A., & Dhar, R. (2005). Goals as excuses or guides: The liberating effect of perceived goal progress on choice. *Journal of Consumer Research, 32*, 370–377.

Fishbach, A., & Zhang, Y. (2008). Together or apart: When goals and temptations complement versus compete. *Journal of Personality and Social Psychology, 94*, 547–559.

Förster, J., Higgins, E. T., & Bianco, A. T. (2003). Speed/accuracy decisions in task performance: Built-in trade-offs or separate strategic concerns? *Organization Behavior and Human Decision Processes, 90*, 148–164.

Forsyth, D. R., Kerr, N. A., Burnette, J. L., & Baumeister, R. F. (2007). Attempting to improve the academic performance of struggling college students by bolstering their self-esteem: An intervention that backfired. *Journal of Social and Clinical Psychology, 26*, 447–459.

Freitas, A. L., Liberman, N., Salovey, P., & Higgins, E. T. (2002). When to begin? Regulatory focus and initiating goal pursuit. *Personality and Social Psychology Bulletin, 28*, 121–130.

Fujita, K., Trope, Y., Liberman, N., & Levin-Sagi, M. (2006). Construal levels and self-control. *Journal of Personality and Social Psychology, 90*, 351–367.

Gailliot, M. T., & Baumeister, R. F. (2007). The physiology of willpower: Linking blood glucose to self-control. *Personality and Social Psychology Review, 11*, 303–327.

Gailliot, M. T., Baumeister, R. F., DeWall, C. N., Maner, J. K., Plant, E. A., Tice, D. M., Brewer, L. E., & Schmeichel, B. J. (2007). Self-control relies on glucose as a limited energy source: Willpower is more than a metaphor. *Journal of Personality and Social Psychology, 92*, 325–336.

Gilovich, T. (1991). *How we know what isn't so*. New York: Free Press.

Gollwitzer, P. M., & Kinney, R. F. (1989). Effects of deliberative and implemental mind-sets on illusion of control. *Journal of Personality and Social Psychology, 56*, 531–542.

Gollwitzer, P. M., & Taylor, S. E. (1995). Effects of mindset on positive illusions. *Journal of Personality and Social Psychology, 669*, 213–226.

Greenberg, J., & Musham, C. (1981). Avoiding and seeking self-focused attention. *Journal of Research in Personality, 15*, 191–200.

Greenberg, J., & Pyszczynski, J. (1986). Persistent high self-focus after failure and low self-focus after success: The depressive self-focusing style. *Journal of Personality and Social Psychology, 50*, 1039–1044.

Greenberg, J., Pyszczynski, T., & Solomon, S. (1986). The causes and consequences of self-esteem: A terror management theory. In R. Baumeister (Ed.), *Public self and private self* (pp. 189–212). New York: Springer-Verlag.

Greenwald, A. G. (1980). The totalitarian ego: Fabrication and revision of personal history. *American Psychologist, 35*, 603–618.

Greenwald, A. G., & Banaji, M. R. (1989). The self as a memory system: Powerful, but ordinary. *Journal of Personality and Social Psychology, 57*, 41–54.

Gur, R. C., & Sackeim, H. A. (1979). Self-deception: A concept in search of a phenomenon. *Journal of Personality and Social Psychology, 37*, 147–169.

Harter, S. (1993). Causes and consequences of low self-esteem in children and adolescents. In R. Baumeister (Ed.), *Self-esteem: The puzzle of low self-regard* (pp. 87–116). New York: Plenum Press.

Heatherton, T. F., & Baumeister, R. F. (1991). Binge eating as escape from self-awareness. *Psychological Bulletin, 110*, 86–108.

Heine, S. J., Lehman, D. R., Markus, H. R., & Kitayama, S. (1999). Is there a universal need for positive self-regard? *Psychological Review, 106*, 766–794.

Helmreich, R., & Collins, B. E. (1968). Studies in forced compliance: Commitment and magnitude of inducement to comply as determinants of opinion change. *Journal of Personality and Social Psychology, 10*, 75–81.

Higgins, E. T. (1987). Self-discrepancy: A theory relating self and affect. *Psychological Review, 94*, 319–340.

Higgins, E. T. (1997). Beyond pleasure and pain. *American Psychologist, 52*, 1280–1300.

Higgins, E. T., & Bargh, J. A. (1987). Social cognition and social perception. *Annual Review of Psychology, 38*, 369–425.

Higgins, E. T., & Spiegel, S. (2004). Promotion and prevention strategies for self-regulation: A motivated cognition perspective. In R. F. Baumeister & K. D. Vohs (Eds.), *Handbook of self-regulation: Research, theory, and applications* (pp. 171–187). New York: Guilford Press.

Hull, J. G. (1981). A self-awareness model of the causes and effects of alcohol consumption. *Journal of Abnormal Psychology, 90*, 586–600.

Ingram, R. E. (1990). Self-focused attention in clinical disorders: Review and a conceptual model. *Psychological Bulletin, 107*, 156–176.

Jones, E. E., Rhodewalt, F., Berglas, S. C., & Skelton, A. (1981). Effects of strategic self-presentation on subsequent self-esteem. *Journal of Personality and Social Psychology, 41*, 407–421.

Kernis, M. H. (1993). The roles of stability and level of self-esteem in psychological functioning. In R. Baumeister (Ed.), *Self-esteem: The puzzle of low self-regard* (pp. 167–182). New York: Plenum Press.

Kernis, M. H., Cornell, D. P., Sun, C. R., Berry, A., & Harlow, T. (1993). There's more to self-esteem than whether it's high or low: The importance of stability of self-esteem. *Journal of Personality and Social Psychology, 65*, 1190–1204.

Kernis, M. H., Granneman, B. D., & Barclay, L. C. (1989). Stability and level of self-esteem as predictors of anger arousal and hostility. *Journal of Personality and Social Psychology, 56*, 1013–1022.

Langer, E. (1975). The illusion of control. *Journal of Personality and Social Psychology, 32*, 311–328.

Leary, M. R. (2004). *The curse of the self.* New York: Oxford University Press.

Leary, M. R., & Baumeister, R. F. (2000). The nature and function of self-esteem: Sociometer theory. In M. Zanna (Ed.), *Advances in experimental social psychology* (Vol. 32, pp. 1–62). San Diego, CA: Academic Press.

Leary, M. R., Tambor, E. S., Terdal, S. K., & Downs, D. L. (1995). Self-esteem as an interpersonal monitor: The sociometer hypothesis. *Journal of Personality and Social Psychology, 68*, 518–530.

Leary, M. R., Tchividjian, L. R., & Kraxberger, B. E. (1994). Self-presentation can be hazardous to your health: Impression management and health risk. *Health Psychology, 13*, 461–470.

Lepper, M. R., Greene, D., & Nisbett, R. E. (1973). Undermining children's intrinsic interest with extrinsic reward: A test of the "overjustification" hypothesis. *Journal of Personality and Social Psychology, 28*, 129–137.

Liberman, N., Idson, L. C., Camacho, C. J., & Higgins, E. T. (1999). Promotion and prevention choices between stability and change. *Journal of Personality and Social Psychology, 77*(6), 1135–1145.

Marks, G. (1984). Thinking one's abilities are unique and one's opinions are common. *Personality and Social Psychology Bulletin, 10*, 203–208.

Markus, H. R. (1977). Self-schemata and processing information about the self. *Journal of Personality and Social Psychology, 35*, 63–78.

Markus, H. R., & Kitayama, S. (1991). Culture and the self: Implications for cognition, emotion, and motivation. *Psychological Review, 98*, 224–253.

Markus, H. R., & Kunda, Z. (1986). Stability and malleability of the self-concept. *Journal of Personality and Social Psychology, 51*, 858–866.

Markus, H., & Nurius, P. S. (1986). Possible selves. *American Psychologist, 41*, 954–969.

Masicampo, E. J., & Baumeister, R. F. (2008). Toward a physiology of dual-process reasoning and judgment: Lemonade, willpower, and expensive rule-based analysis. *Psychological Science, 19*, 255–260.

McGuire, W. J., McGuire, C. V., Child, P., & Fujioka, T. (1978). Salience of ethnicity in the spontaneous self-concept as a function of one's ethnic distinctiveness in the social environment. *Journal of Personality and Social Psychology, 36*, 511–520.

Meehl, P. E. (1956). Wanted—a good cookbook. *American Psychologist, 11*, 263–272.

Menon, M., Tobin, D. D., Corby, B. C., Menon, M., Hodges, E. V., & Perry, D. G. (2007). The developmental costs of high self-esteem for antisocial children. *Child Development, 78*, 1627–1639.

Mischel, W., Ebbesen, E. B., & Zeiss, A. R. (1976). Determinants of selective memory about the self. *Journal of Consulting and Clinical Psychology, 44*, 92–103.

Miyake, A., Friedman, N. P., Emerson, M. J., Witzki, A. H., Howerter, A., & Wager, T. D. (2000). Contributions to complex "frontal lobe" tasks: A latent variable analysis. *Cognitive Psychology, 41*, 49–100.

Molden, D. C., Lee, A. Y., & Higgins, E. T. (2008). Motivations for promotion and prevention. In J. Shah & W. Gardner (Eds.), *Handbook of motivation science* (pp. 169–187). New York: Guilford Press.

Morf, C. C., & Rhodewalt, F. (2001). Unraveling the paradoxes of narcissism: A dynamic self-regulatory processing model. *Psychological Inquiry, 12*, 177–196.

Muraven, M., & Slessareva, E. (2003). Mechanism of self-control failure: Motivation and limited resources. *Personality and Social Psychology Bulletin, 29*, 894–906.

Newman, L. S., & Baumeister, R. F. (1996). Toward an elaboration of the UFO abduction phenomenon: Hypnotic elaboration, extraterrestrial sadomasochism, and spurious memories. *Psychological Inquiry, 7*, 99–126.

Nuttin, J. M. (1985). Narcissism beyond Gestalt and awareness: The name letter effect. *European Journal of Social Psychology, 15*, 353–361.

Nuttin, J. M. (1987). Affective consequences of mere ownership: The name letter effect in twelve European languages. *European Journal of Social Psychology, 17*, 381–402.

Pelham, B. W., Mirenberg, M. C., & Jones, J. T. (2002). Why Susie sells seashells by the seashore: Implicit egoism and major life decisions. *Journal of Personality and Social Psychology, 82*, 469–487.

Pocheptsova, A., Amir, O., Dhar, R., & Baumeister, R. F. (2009). Deciding without resources: Resource depletion and choice in context. *Journal of Marketing Research, 46*, 344–355.

Polivy, J. (1976). Perception of calories and regulation of intake in restrained and unrestrained subjects. *Addictive Behaviors, 1*, 237–243.

Powers, W. T. (1973). *Behavior: The control of perception*. Chicago, IL: Aldine.

Pryor, J. B., Gibbons, F. X., Wicklund, R. A., Fazio, R. H., & Hood, R. (1977). Self-focused attention and self-report validity. *Journal of Personality, 45*, 514–527.

Pyszczynski, T., Greenberg, J., & Holt, K. (1985). Maintaining consistency between self-serving beliefs and available data: A bias in information processing. *Personality and Social Psychology Bulletin, 11*, 179–190.

Pyszczynski, T., Greenberg, J., & Solomon, S. (1997). Why do we need what we need? A terror management perspective on the roots of human social motivation. *Psychological Inquiry, 8*, 1–20.

Rogers, T. B., Kuiper, N. A., & Kirker, W. S. (1977). Self-reference and the encoding of personal information. *Journal of Personality and Social Psychology, 35*, 677–688.

Rosenberg, M. (1965). *Society and the adolescent self-image*. Princeton, NJ: Princeton University Press.

Sackeim, H. A., & Gur, R. C. (1979). Self-deception, other-deception, and self-reported psychopathology. *Journal of Consulting and Clinical Psychology, 47*, 213–215.

Scheier, M. F., & Carver, C. S. (1977). Self-focused attention and the experience of emotion: Attraction, repulsion, elation, and depression. *Journal of Personality and Social Psychology, 35*, 625–636.

Scheier, M. F., Fenigstein, A., & Buss, A. H. (1974). Self-awareness and physical aggression. *Journal of Experimental Social Psychology, 10*, 264–273.

Schlenker, B. R. (1975). Self-presentation: Managing the impression of consistency when reality interferes with self-enhancement. *Journal of Personality and Social Psychology, 32*, 1030–1037.

Schlenker, B. R. (1980). *Impression management: The self-concept, social identity, and interpersonal relations*. Monterey, CA: Brooks/Cole.

Schlenker, B. R., Dlugolecki, D. W., & Doherty, K. (1994). The impact of self-presentations on self-appraisals and behavior: The roles of commitment and biased scanning. *Personality and Social Psychology Bulletin, 20*, 20–33.

Schlenker, B. R., & Leary, M. R. (1982). Social anxiety and self-presentation: A conceptualization and model. *Psychological Bulletin, 92*, 641–669.

Schmeichel, B. J., & Vohs, K. D. (2009). Self-affirmation and self-control: Affirming core values counteracts ego depletion. *Journal of Personality and Social Psychology, 96*, 770–782.

Sedikides, C. (1993). Assessment, enhancement, and verification determinants of the self-evaluation process. *Journal of Personality and Social Psychology, 65*, 317–338.

Sedikides, C., & Gregg, A. P. (2008). Self-enhancement: Food for thought. *Perspectives on Psychological Science, 3*, 102–116.

Seligman, M. E.P. (1975). *Helplessness: On depression, development, and death*. San Francisco, CA: Freeman.

Shah, J. Y., Friedman, R., & Kruglanski, A. W. (2002). Forgetting all else: On the antecedents and consequences of goal shielding. *Journal of Personality and Social Psychology, 83*, 1261–1280.

Steele, C. M. (1988). The psychology of self-affirmation: Sustaining the integrity of the self. In L. Berkowitz (Ed.), *Advances in experimental social psychology* (Vol. 21, pp. 261–302). New York: Academic Press.

Steele, C. M., & Josephs, R. A. (1990). Alcohol myopia: Its prized and dangerous effects. *American Psychologist, 45*, 921–933.

Steele, C. M., & Southwick, L. (1985). Alcohol and social behavior I: The mediating role of inhibitory conflict. *Journal of Personality and Social Psychology, 48*, 18–34.

Suchy, Y. (2009). Executive functioning: Overview, assessment, and research issues for non-neuropsychologists. *Annals of Behavioral Medicine, 37*, 106–116.

Suls, J., & Wan, C. K. (1987). In search of the false-uniqueness phenomenon: Fear and estimates of social consensus. *Journal of Personality and Social Psychology, 52*, 211–217.

Svenson, O. (1981). Are we all less risky and more skillful than our fellow drivers? *Acta Psychologica, 47*, 143–148.

Swann, W. B. (1987). Identity negotiation: Where two roads meet. *Journal of Personality and Social Psychology, 53*, 1038–1051.

Swann, W. B., & Hill, C. A. (1982). When our identities are mistaken: Reaffirming self-conceptions through social interaction. *Journal of Personality and Social Psychology, 43*, 59–66.

Tangney, J. P., Niedenthal, P. M., Covert, M. V., & Barlow, D. H. (1998). Are shame and guilt related to distinct self-discrepancies? A test of Higgins's (1987) hypothesis. *Journal of Personality and Social Psychology, 75*, 256–268.

Taylor, S. E., & Brown, J. D. (1988). Illusion and well-being: A social psychological perspective on mental health. *Psychological Bulletin, 103*, 193–210.

Tedeschi, J. T., Schlenker, B. R., & Bonoma, T. V. (1971). Cognitive dissonance: Private ratiocination or public spectacle? *American Psychologist, 26*, 685–695.

Tesser, A. (1988). Toward a self-evaluation maintenance model of social behavior. In L. Berkowitz (Ed.), *Advances in experimental social psychology* (Vol. 21, pp. 181–227). San Diego, CA: Academic Press.

Tetlock, P. E., & Manstead, A. S. (1985). Impression management versus intrapsychic explanations in social psychology: A useful dichotomy? *Psychological Review, 92*, 59–77.

Tice, D. M. (1992). Self-presentation and self-concept change: The looking glass self as magnifying glass. *Journal of Personality and Social Psychology, 63*, 435–451.

Tice, D. M., & Baumeister, R. F. (1997). Longitudinal study of procrastination, performance, stress, and health: The costs and benefits of dawdling. *Psychological Science, 8*, 454–458.

Tice, D. M., Baumeister, R. F., Shmueli, D., & Muraven, M. (2007). Restoring the self: Positive affect helps improve self-regulation following ego depletion. *Journal of Experimental Social Psychology, 43*, 379–384.

Trope, Y. (1983). Self-assessment in achievement behavior: In J. Suls & A. Greenwald (Eds.), *Psychological perspectives on the self* (Vol. 2, pp. 93–121). Hillsdale, NJ: Erlbaum.

Trope, Y. (1986). Self-enhancement and self-assessment in achievement behavior. In R. Sorrentino & E. T. Higgins (Eds.), *Handbook of motivation and cognition* (Vol. 2, pp. 350–378). New York: Guilford Press.

Vohs, K. D., Baumeister, R. F., & Ciarocco, N. (2005). Self-regulation and self-presentation: Regulatory resource depletion impairs impression management and effortful self-presentation depletes regulatory resources. *Journal of Personality and Social Psychology, 88*, 632–657.

Vohs, K. D., Baumeister, R. F., Schmeichel, B. J., Twenge, J. M., Nelson, N. M., & Tice, D. M. (2008). Making choices impairs subsequent self-control: A limited resource account of decision making, self-regulation, and active initiative. *Journal of Personality and Social Psychology, 94*, 883–898.

Wicklund, R. A., & Duval, S. (1971). Opinion change and performance facilitation as a result of objective self-awareness. *Journal of Experimental Social Psychology, 7*, 319–342.

Wills, T. A. (1981). Downward comparison principles in social psychology. *Psychological Bulletin, 90*, 245–271.

Wood, J. V., Heimpel, S. A., & Michela, J. L. (2003). Savoring versus dampening: Self-esteem differences in regulating positive affect. *Journal of Personality and Social Psychology, 85*, 566–580.

Wood, J. V., Heimpel, S. A., Newby-Clark, I. R., & Ross, M. (2005). Snatching defeat from the jaws of victory: Self-esteem differences in the experience and anticipation of success. *Journal of Personality and Social Psychology, 89*, 764–780.

Wood, J. V., Michela, J. L., & Giordano, C. (2000). Downward comparison in everyday life: Reconciling self-enhancement models with the mood-cognition priming model. *Journal of Personality and Social Psychology, 79*, 563–579.

Wyer, R. S., & Frey, D. (1983). The effects of feedback about self and others on the recall and judgments of feedback-relevant information. *Journal of Experimental Social Psychology, 19*, 540–559.

Zuckerman, M. (1979). Attribution of success and failure revisited, or: The motivational bias is alive and well in attribution theory. *Journal of Personality, 47*, 245–287.

Chapter 6

Attitude Structure

Leandre R. Fabrigar and Duane T. Wegener

Few concepts have enjoyed as long and influential a role in social psychology and the social sciences more generally as the *attitude* construct (Allport, 1935). Over the years, some social scientists have used the term very broadly to refer to a wide range of subjective judgments, whereas others have used the term more precisely to refer to relatively general evaluative judgments of targets. This long and varied history notwithstanding, in contemporary social psychology, the term attitude is typically used to refer to a relatively general and enduring evaluation of an object or concept on a valence dimension ranging from positive to negative. Thus, attitudes are the good/bad evaluations that we attach to objects in our social world. These evaluations can be attached to almost anything, including people, social groups, physical objects, behaviors, and even abstract concepts.

What Is Attitude Structure?

Because researchers have generally conceptualized attitudes in terms of their valence (positive or negative) and extremity (the magnitude of the deviation of the positive or negative evaluation from neutrality), it is not surprising that traditional attitude measurement techniques have usually represented an attitude as a single numerical value reflecting the position of an attitude object on an evaluative continuum (e.g., see Likert, 1932; Osgood, Suci, & Tannenbaum, 1957; Thurstone, 1928; Thurstone & Chave, 1929). However, even in the early stages of the attitudes literature, theorists recognized that measurement procedures conceptualizing an attitude exclusively in terms of its valence and extremity were inadequate to effectively capture all the relevant properties of an attitude (e.g., see Thurstone, 1928).

Consistent with this reasoning, early attitude theorists proposed a number of properties of attitudes, beyond their valence and extremity, that were important to understanding the impact of attitudes on related thinking and behavior as well as how attitudes could be changed. For instance, early theorists suggested that it was useful to distinguish between different types of evaluative responses comprising attitudes (i.e., affect, cognition, and behavior; e.g., Katz & Stotland,1959; Rosenberg & Hovland, 1960; Smith, 1947), the underlying functions that attitudes might serve (e.g., Katz, 1960; Katz & Stotland, 1959; Smith, Bruner, & White, 1956), the amount of information on which attitudes were based (e.g., Rosenberg & Abelson, 1960), and the extent to which attitudes were linked to other attitudes (e.g., Converse, 1964). In short, attitude theorists have long believed in the importance of understanding the structure of attitudes and related constructs in which attitudes are embedded.

Despite the fact that the term "attitude structure" has been widely used in social psychology, precise definitions of the term have often been lacking. Thus, it is useful to clarify what is typically implied by the term. As noted, attitudes have usually been defined as relatively general and enduring evaluations of objects. Directly following from this definition, some theorists have proposed that an attitude can be conceptualized as a type of knowledge structure stored in memory. More precisely, an attitude can be viewed as a simple two-node semantic network (i.e., an object–evaluation association; Fazio, 1995, 2007), with one node reflecting the representation of the object, the second node the global evaluation of the object, and the link between the two nodes the strength of the association.

Although attitudes can be conceptualized as simple object–evaluation associations, attitude theorists have postulated that people's object–evaluation associations (attitudes) will often be linked in memory to other knowledge structures (see Eagly & Chaiken, 1998; Fabrigar, MacDonald, & Wegener, 2005; Petty & Krosnick, 1995; Pratkanis, Breckler, & Greenwald, 1989). For instance, such linked knowledge structures might include specific attributes or emotional responses linked to the object as well as to the general evaluation of the object (e.g., see Zanna & Rempel, 1988). These knowledge structures might also include functions served by the attitude (e.g., Murray, Haddock, & Zanna, 1996) or metacognitions (i.e., people's beliefs regarding their own thoughts or thought processes) "tagging" the evaluation as relatively valid or invalid (e.g., Petty, 2006). Thus, attitude structure can be described as an object–evaluation association and the knowledge structures linked to it in memory (regardless of whether the associative network metaphor is used to represent the memory structures). The term attitude structure is usually used to refer to various properties reflecting (1) the content of the knowledge structures associated with the attitude, (2) the number of knowledge structures associated with the attitude, (3) the strength of the associative links making up the attitude and its related knowledge structures, and (4) the pattern of associative links among the attitude and its related knowledge structures. Within the context of this general definition, some theorists have further distinguished between two broad categories of attitude structure (Eagly & Chaiken, 1993, 1995, 1998; McGuire, 1989). *Intraattitudinal structure* refers to the structure of a single attitude. *Interattitudinal structure* refers to structures comprising more than one attitude.

An Overview of Structural Properties of Attitudes

There are, of course, many specific structural properties of attitudes that readily fit within the broad definition of attitude structure. One of the great challenges of the 1980s and 1990s in attitude research was to specify which specific features should be important for understanding attitudes and then develop measures and/or manipulations of these properties so their effects could be established. We briefly describe the specific structural properties that have received the most attention and then, in the sections that follow, we turn to research on the effects these properties exert on attitude–behavior consistency and attitude change processes.

Attitude Accessibility

Of the many specific structural properties that have been proposed, probably the most basic is attitude accessibility. Attitude accessibility refers to the strength of the association between the object and the evaluation. When this association is very strong, simply encountering the object is sufficient to automatically activate the evaluation from memory (Fazio, Sanbonmatsu, Powell, & Kardes, 1986). Directly following this logic, attitude accessibility is usually measured by asking people to assess the object using highly evaluative adjectives (e.g., "good" versus "bad") while a computer records the response latencies to these evaluative judgments. Rapid reaction times reflect high accessibility (i.e., a strong object–evaluation association), whereas slow reaction times indicate low accessibility.

Although attitude accessibility has a number of determinants, the most extensively documented is the frequency with which the attitude has been activated (i.e., accessed from long-term memory). Repeated expressions of the attitude strengthen the association between object and evaluation, thus facilitating greater ease of retrieval of the evaluation from memory (Fazio, Chen, McDonel, & Sherman, 1982; Powell & Fazio, 1984). Another factor postulated to influence accessibility is the diagnosticity (i.e., perceived validity) of the information on which the attitude is based. Information from sources seen as highly credible, sensory information about the object, emotional reactions elicited by the object, past behavior toward the object, and direct experience with the object are all classes of information that are likely to be viewed as especially diagnostic (Fazio, 1995).

Content of Attitude-Relevant Information

Another widely explored property of attitude structure is the type of evaluative information with which the attitude is associated. There is of course an almost infinite number of ways that such information might be categorized. However, we will discuss the two systems of categorization that have been especially influential.

Affective/Cognitive/Behavioral Bases Theorists have long speculated that attitudes consist of evaluative responses that are affective, cognitive, or behavioral in nature (e.g., Insko & Schopler, 1967; Katz & Stotland, 1959; Rosenberg & Hovland, 1960; Smith, 1947). Within the context of this *tripartite* perspective, affect refers to the positive and negative feelings associated with the attitude object, cognition reflects the evaluative beliefs about the attitude object, and behavior describes the overt evaluative actions and responses to the attitude object.

In its early form, the tripartite approach implied that people had an attitude only if they had evaluatively consistent affective, cognitive, and behavioral reactions to an attitude object. However, more contemporary versions of the tripartite theory have introduced important revisions (e.g., see Cacioppo, Petty, & Geen, 1989; Petty & Cacioppo, 1986; Zanna & Rempel, 1988). Most notably, cotemporary perspectives postulate that an attitude is not necessarily composed of these three evaluative elements. Rather, the attitude is a separately stored global evaluative summary of one or more of the three types of evaluative information (Cacioppo et al., 1989; Crites, Fabrigar, & Petty, 1994; Zanna & Rempel, 1988). One important implication of both traditional and contemporary versions of the tripartite perspective is that attitudes can vary in the extent to which each base contributes to the attitude (see Breckler & Wiggins, 1989; Crites et al., 1994; Eagly, Mladinic, & Otto, 1994). Such variations could be a result of factors such as personality traits, characteristics of the attitude object, or the modality (e.g., sensory versus written) of information acquisition (e.g., see Fabrigar & Petty, 1999; Haddock, Maio, Arnold, & Huskinson, 2008).

Functional Nature of Attitudes Attitude theorists have long postulated that people hold attitudes because they can serve many useful functions (e.g., Katz, 1960; Katz & Stotland, 1959; Kelman, 1961; Smith et al., 1956). Various theorists proposed somewhat different, but often overlapping functions for attitudes. However, functions that have received the most attention include the knowledge function (i.e., the management and simplification of information processing tasks), utilitarian function (i.e., the achievement of desired goals and avoidance of negative outcomes), ego defensive function (i.e., the maintenance or promotion of self-esteem), the value expressive function (i.e., the expression of values and the self-concept), and the social adjustive function (i.e., the facilitation of identification with similar others and the maintenance of relationships with them).

Although it has not been common to refer to attitude functions as a structural property, they can be viewed as such (see Fabrigar et al., 2005; Fabrigar, Smith, & Brannon, 1999). Specifically, attitudes may serve different functions in part because they are based on or associated with different types of information. For example, an attitude with strong associations in memory to beliefs about important values could result in an attitude that serves a value expressive function. An attitude based on information directly relevant to how important others view the attitude object could serve a social adjustive function. Thus, theories of attitude functions can be viewed as systems for categorizing evaluative information associated with the attitude. Moreover, just as attitude-relevant knowledge can vary in affective, cognitive, or behavioral content, it can also vary in functional content. Such variations may be driven by the nature of the attitude object, personality traits, culture, and social context (e.g., see Shavitt, 1989; Snyder & DeBono, 1989).

Amount and Complexity of Attitude-Relevant Information

A second general way to characterize attitude-relevant information has been in terms of the extensiveness of the evaluative knowledge associated with the attitude. Typically, this has involved either considering the working knowledge associated with the attitude or the dimensional breadth of this information.

Working Knowledge Working knowledge is defined as the number of attitude-relevant beliefs and experiences that are spontaneously activated when encountering an object (Wood, 1982; Wood, Rhodes, & Biek, 1995). Three aspects of this definition merit comment. First, although sometimes viewed as a "cognitive" construct, there is nothing inherent in the definition that restricts it to the cognitive bases of attitudes. Experiences that are activated could have strong affective or behavioral content. Second, this definition does not imply anything about the accuracy of beliefs/experiences (see Biek, 1992, cited in Wood et al., 1995; Scott, 1969). Finally, working knowledge in many cases may be only a subset of the full array of knowledge a person possesses regarding the attitude object (Wood, 1982). Thus, when considered from a structural standpoint, working knowledge is likely to be a function of the number of knowledge structures associated with the attitude and the strength of the associations among the knowledge structures and the attitude. The most common approaches to measuring working knowledge have been to ask people to list their attitude-relevant beliefs and experiences or to subjectively report their level of knowledge.

Researchers have proposed a number of potential determinants of working knowledge (see Wood et al., 1995). For example, because beliefs and experiences must be accessible to be considered part of working knowledge, it logically follows that working knowledge will be partially driven by factors that enhance the accessibility of beliefs or experiences. Frequent exposure to the attitude object (Fazio et al., 1982) and high levels of cognitive elaboration (Petty & Cacioppo, 1986) about the attitude object are both variables that might increase the likelihood that a belief or experience is activated when an attitude object is encountered (see Petty & Briñol, Chapter 7, this volume).

Complexity and Integration Complexity of knowledge refers to the number of distinct dimensions or distinct types of evaluative information associated with the attitude (Scott, 1969; Tetlock, 1989), and integration refers to the extent to which the dimensions are related to one another. Some researchers (e.g., Judd & Lusk, 1984; Scott, 1969; Tesser, Martin, & Mendolia, 1995) have distinguished between relatively complex attitudes based on multiple unrelated dimensions (i.e., attitudes high in differentiation and low in integration) and relatively complex attitudes based on multiple related dimensions (i.e., attitudes are high in differentiation and integration). This later conceptualization is particularly central to the construct of integrative complexity (Tetlock, 1989), which is defined as the number of distinct dimensions underlying an attitude as well as the degree to which these dimensions are linked to one another.

Complexity likely has a number of antecedents. Perhaps most obviously, the greater the amount of information associated with an attitude, the more likely that information will reflect multiple dimensions rather than a single dimension (see Linville, 1982). However, larger amounts of information will not necessarily reflect a larger number of dimensions. A small number of beliefs could reflect multiple dimensions or a large number of beliefs could reflect only a single dimension. Along similar lines, cognitive elaboration is also likely to be related to complexity. Individuals who extensively elaborate about an attitude object are more likely to develop multidimensional evaluative reactions to the object (e.g., see Tetlock, 1983; Tetlock & Kim, 1987). But people could also elaborate information that primarily relates to a single dimension or information that relates to many dimensions.

Ambivalence: Evaluative Inconsistency of Attitude-Relevant Information

Another prominent property of attitude-relevant information is the evaluative consistency of the information. That is, for any given attitude object, that object may be associated with some relatively positive qualities as well as other less positive or even negative qualities. Various types of evaluative inconsistency have been proposed.

Attitudinal Ambivalence Attitudinal ambivalence is present when our evaluative summary of an object includes both positive and negative evaluations (Kaplan, 1972; Scott, 1969; Thompson, Zanna, & Griffin, 1995). Ambivalence can occur when evaluations within a dimension are inconsistent, when one dimension of an attitude object is positive and another dimension is negative, or even when a person's attitude is inconsistent with the attitudes of positively evaluated others (see Fabrigar et al., 2005; Priester & Petty, 2001). *Objective* or *potential* ambivalence is typically assessed by mathematically combining separate reports of the number of positive and negative evaluations associated with an attitude object using one of a several mathematical formulas (e.g., Ambivalence = Conflicting Evaluation × Dominant Evaluation, Ambivalence = Conflicting Evaluation^2/Dominant Evaluation; see Priester & Petty, 1996; Thompson et al., 1995). However, another key property of ambivalent attitudes is that they are experienced as unpleasant, especially when the conflicting reactions are simultaneously accessible and people strongly value cognitive consistency (Newby-Clark, McGregor, & Zanna, 2002) or need to choose a particular attitude-related course of action (van Harreveld, van der Pligt, & de Liver, 2009; cf. Harmon-Jones & Harmon-Jones, 2002). This *subjective* or *felt* ambivalence is typically measured by asking people to report the level of evaluative conflict or discomfort they feel with respect to the object (Priester & Petty, 1996; Tourangeau, Rasinski, Bradburn, & D'Andrade, 1989).

Dimensionality of Ambivalence Attitudinal ambivalence can result from many types of evaluative inconsistency. Within-dimension ambivalence occurs when conflicting evaluative information falls within a single dimension (e.g., when a person has both positive and negative beliefs toward an attitude object or experiences both positive and negative emotions related to an attitude object). Cross-dimension ambivalence refers to evaluative conflicts between two or more distinct dimensions of evaluative information (e.g., when the cognitive dimension is positive and the affective dimension is negative). A variety of subtypes of cross-dimension ambivalence have been proposed (Chaiken, Pomerantz, & Giner-Sorolla, 1995), including affective-cognitive inconsistency (i.e., conflict between affect and cognition), evaluative-affective inconsistency (i.e., conflict between the global attitude and affect), or evaluative-cognitive inconsistency (i.e., conflict between the global attitude and cognition).

Although most studies exploring cross-dimension ambivalence have focused on conflict between affect and cognition, it can occur whenever distinguishable dimensions of attitude-relevant information are inconsistent with one another. For example, attitudes could also be examined in terms of conflicts among attitude functions, conflicts among subdimensions within affect or cognition, or conflicts among subdimensions of a particular attitude function.

Subjective Beliefs about the Attitude as a Structural Property

Attitude structure has often been treated as consisting primarily of direct associations with the attitude object (such as beliefs about the object or past behaviors toward the object). However, people can also hold consequential beliefs about the attitude itself. For example, the attitude could be perceived as serving a particular function (e.g., as expression of a core value or alignment with admired others; Holbrook, Berent, Krosnick, Visser, & Boninger, 2005; Murray et al., 1996). The attitude could also be perceived to be important (Eaton & Visser, 2008), as based on particular types of information (See, Petty & Fabrigar, 2008), or to be held with certainty (Tormala & Rucker, 2007).

In fact, the Meta-Cognitive Model (MCM) of Attitudes directly incorporates perceptions of the attitude's validity into the structure of the attitude (Petty & Briñol, 2006; Petty, Briñol, & DeMarree, 2007). Similar to previous views of the attitude as an association in memory between the attitude object and the evaluation, the MCM portrays attitudes as potentially involving associations between the attitude object and both positive and negative evaluations. In addition, however, the MCM states that validity tags accompany these evaluative associations (i.e., beliefs regarding the accuracy of evaluations) such that the validity tags can influence evaluative responding, especially when those responses are relatively deliberate. Unlike models of attitudes that emphasize on-line assessments of evaluation validity (e.g., Cohen & Reed, 2006; Gawronski & Bodenhausen, 2006), the MCM notes that just as it is adaptive to store evaluations of objects (Fazio, 1995), it should also be adaptive to store assessments of whether the evaluation is "correct" (Festinger, 1954; Petty & Cacioppo, 1986).

When attitude measures or other evaluative responses are relatively automatic (nondeliberative), these responses may be guided by activated evaluative associations. However, when they are more deliberative (i.e., when people think about them more carefully), these responses may be influenced in important ways by the perceptions of validity of the positive versus negative evaluations. This same principle may also apply to the use of perceptions that the attitude is important, that it serves important functions, etc. These "tags" to the evaluation may influence evaluative responding to a greater degree when people respond in more deliberate ways. The concept of relatively deliberative or nondeliberative responding will also be important when we discuss influences of attitude structure on attitude–behavior consistency.

Interattitudinal Structure

All of the previous specific structural properties of attitudes discussed have been intraattitudinal properties. However, it is also possible to conceptualize the structure of attitudes in terms of their associations with attitudes toward different but related attitude objects or in terms of associations among multiple attitudes toward the same object.

Attitude Systems Involving Multiple Objects A number of early cognitive consistency theories postulated that people are motivated to maintain consistency among attitudes toward objects that are related to one another (Abelson & Rosenberg, 1958; Cartwright & Harary, 1956; Festinger, 1957; Heider, 1958). More contemporary research has focused on specific properties of interattitudinal structure such as the degree to which attitudes are linked together in memory and the level of evaluative consistency and strength of those associations (Judd & Downing, 1990; Judd, Drake, Downing, & Krosnick, 1991; Judd & Krosnick, 1989, Lavine, Thomsen, & Gonzales, 1997). In these more contemporary investigations, attitudes have been conceptualized as associative networks, with the nodes characterizing attitude valence (i.e., the evaluation of the object) and the strength of links between objects and evaluations as the strength of the attitude (i.e., the accessibility of the attitude based on frequency of attitude activation). Links among the attitudinal nodes are characterized by implicational relations (consistent or inconsistent) and strength (the probability that the nodes will activate each other). Much of the research on attitude systems has explored the cognitive principles by which people organize related attitudes (e.g., Converse, 1964; Lavine et al., 1997) or variables that moderate interattitudinal linkages such as domain expertise and attitude importance (Judd & Downing, 1990; Judd & Krosnick; 1989).

Attitude Systems Involving Single Objects As discussed previously regarding attitudinal ambivalence, it is possible to hold evaluative associations about a single object that vary in their implications. The Dual Attitude Model (Wilson, Lindsey, & Schooler, 2000) and the Past Attitudes Still There (PAST) Model (Petty, Tormala, Briñol, & Jarvis, 2006; a special case of the MCM model, Petty, 2006; Petty & Briñol, 2006) each extends this possibility to holding two (or more) attitudes toward the same attitude object.

In the Dual Attitude Model, it is assumed that when an attitude changes, the old attitude is not necessarily discarded (cf. Anderson, 1971). It may be retained along with the new attitude. Individuals may simultaneously hold dual attitudes because one is expressed at a conscious level (i.e., the explicit attitude) and the other is expressed at the implicit level (outside awareness, see Greenwald & Banaji, 1995). These attitudes are viewed as stored separately in memory, perhaps in different areas of the brain (e.g., DeCoster, Banner, Smith, & Semin, 2006). In this view, implicit attitudes are the "default" attitudes that are activated automatically, whereas explicit attitudes are expressed only when an individual has sufficient capacity and motivation to override the implicit attitude and retrieve the explicit attitude.

The MCM model also holds that after attitude change, the older attitude will often still exist in memory. However, when an individual changes his or her attitude, that person will "tag" the original attitude as "invalid" (or as held with low confidence). Both the new attitude and the old attitude are still associated with the attitude object in memory, so either (or both) can be activated (depending on principles of activation, such as recency and frequency of activation or relation to memory cues in the environment; Petty et al., 2006).

At first glance, dual (or multiple) attitude structures bear a striking similarity to the intraattitudinal property of ambivalence. Wilson and his colleagues, however, draw a number of distinctions between these two concepts. They note that when ambivalence occurs, tension results as a consequence of two conflicting evaluations that are both in awareness (cf. Newby-Clark et al., 2002). However, in the hypothesized dual attitude structure, social perceivers would not experience unpleasant tension, because the perceiver is aware of only the explicit attitude, not the implicit attitude.

Interestingly, Briñol, Petty, and Wheeler (2003) conducted research showing that increasing discrepancies between traditional self-report measures of self-esteem (Rosenberg, 1965) and automatic [Implicit Association Test (IAT); Greenwald, McGhee, & Schwartz, 1998] measures of self-esteem were associated with stronger associations between self-related words and doubt-related words. However, the same discrepancies were not associated with explicit reports of self-doubt. Also, persuasive messages framed as related to the automatic/deliberative self discrepancies (i.e., a message framed as relevant to self-esteem) were processed to a greater extent as the automatic/deliberative discrepancy increased, but processing of discrepancy-unrelated messages was not influenced by the size of automatic/deliberative discrepancies (Briñol, Petty, & Wheeler, 2006; see also Petty et al., 2006). Even so, the MCM model differs from the dual-attitude approach because, in some circumstances (e.g., when individuals do not access the validity tag), both old and new attitudes can be simultaneously activated and open to awareness. In such instances, individuals can experience "explicit" (subjective) ambivalence.

The Role of Structure in Attitude–Behavior Consistency

Over the years researchers have identified a variety of structural features of attitudes. Why has so much effort been expended in this task? One of the major reasons is that structural properties of attitudes have long been considered as important to understanding when and why attitudes are consequential (i.e., strong; Petty & Krosnick, 1995). Perhaps the aspect of attitude strength most studied is the influence of attitudes on behavior. As we will see, there is now ample evidence to claim that structural properties of attitudes help to determine which attitudes have a marked impact on behavior and which do not.

Structure as a Moderator of Attitude–Behavior Consistency

Accessibility In the context of attitude–behavior consistency, perhaps no attitude property has been examined as extensively as attitude accessibility. Some accessibility studies have explored this structural property by measuring accessibility via response latencies to attitude measures and then testing whether response latencies moderate the ability of attitudinal (valenced) responses to predict behaviors [see Wegener, Downing, Krosnick, & Petty (1995) for descriptions of measures of each of the structural properties discussed in this chapter]. Measured attitude accessibility has moderated attitude–behavior relations in contexts such as voting behavior (Bassili, 1993, 1995; Fazio & Williams, 1986) and consumer product choices (Fazio, Powell, & Williams, 1989; Kokkinaki & Lunt, 1997). Other accessibility studies have manipulated accessibility by varying the frequency of attitude expression or attitude object presentation. Manipulated accessibility has moderated the ability of attitudes to predict behaviors such as decisions to play with puzzles (Fazio et al., 1982) and decisions to donate money to charities (Posavac, Sanbonmatsu, & Fazio, 1997).

Content of Attitude-Relevant Information A smaller body of work has explored the role of content of attitude-relevant information in attitude–behavior consistency. The central premise of this work has been that attitudes will be better predictors of behavior when those attitudes are based on information directly relevant to the goals driving the behavior. For example, Millar and Tesser (1986) found that attitudes based on affect were more predictive of consummatory behaviors (i.e., behaviors performed for their intrinsic reward) rather than instrumental behaviors (i.e., behaviors performed to obtain some goal external to the behavior itself). In contrast, attitudes based on cognition did better at predicting instrumental behaviors than consummatory behaviors (see also Millar & Tesser, 1989). Matching effects between the attitude basis and the behavior have also been demonstrated for distinct dimensions of cognition (Fabrigar, Petty, Smith, & Crites, 2006). For example, consumer choices between competing stores were better predicted by attitudes toward the stores when those attitudes were based on knowledge of products directly relevant to the product being purchased.

Amount of Attitude-Relevant Information Several studies suggest that working knowledge moderates the ability of attitudes to predict behavior. Some studies have tested this hypothesis by asking people to list their knowledge about the attitude object and then examining whether the amount of information listed moderated the ability of attitudes to predict a subsequent behavior. These studies have confirmed that increased knowledge is related to stronger attitude–behavior correlations in the context of environmental attitudes and recycling behavior (Kallgren & Wood, 1986) and voting intentions and subsequent voting behavior (Davidson, Yantis, Norwood, & Montano, 1985). Other studies have used subjective measures of knowledge to demonstrate effects of knowledge on attitude–behavior prediction in voting behavior for community initiatives and in health behaviors (Davidson et al., 1985).

Ambivalence Numerous studies have explored whether ambivalence (of various types) regulates the ability of attitudes to predict behaviors and intentions. For example, in studies that measured overall ambivalence via independent ratings of global positive and negative reactions to the object, increased ambivalence was associated with lower attitude–behavior consistency (Conner, Sparks, Povey, James, Shepherd, & Armitage, 2002; Conner, Povey, Sparks, James, & Shepherd, 2003). Studies specifically measuring ambivalence in evaluative beliefs have produced similar results (Armitage, 2003; Moore, 1973).

Other studies have assessed ambivalence using subjective measures of ambivalence and have also suggested that ambivalence is negatively related to attitude–behavior consistency (Priester, 2002; Sparks, Hedderley, & Shepherd, 1992). Finally, studies measuring cross-dimension ambivalence (more specifically evaluative-cognitive consistency) have produced mixed evidence, with some research indicating that increased ambivalence is associated with decreased attitude–behavior consistency (Norman, 1975) and other studies failing to find an association (Fazio & Zanna, 1978a).

A smaller body of research has tested the role of ambivalence in attitude–behavior consistency by manipulating ambivalence. For example, Armitage (2003) attempted to manipulate ambivalence by assigning participants to a thought condition intended either to make beliefs less ambivalent or to not alter the ambivalence of beliefs. Greater ambivalence among beliefs was associated with lower attitude–behavior consistency. In contrast, Jonas, Diehl, and Bromer (1997) directly manipulated the consistency of beliefs regarding a consumer product and found that increased ambivalence produced higher levels of attitude–behavior consistency. They suggested that attitude–behavior consistency was increased because ambivalence encouraged people to engage in extensive cognitive elaboration of attitude-relevant information so as to resolve the evaluative inconsistencies. In an effort to explain the apparent contradiction between Jonas et al. (1997) and other studies of ambivalence, Sengupta and Johar (2002) proposed that ambivalence should produce higher attitude–behavior consistency when people engage in elaboration of information directed toward forming an integrated attitude. In contrast, they argued that ambivalence should lead to lower attitude–behavior consistency when people are not specifically trying to resolve inconsistencies, either because they are unmotivated or unable to engage in extensive elaboration or because their elaboration is not specifically directed toward integrating evaluative responses.

Subjective Beliefs about the Attitude Numerous studies have measured perceptions of attitude certainty or attitude importance and assessed the extent to which these perceptions moderate the association between attitudes and behavior. For example, increased ratings of importance have been found to be related to stronger attitude–behavior associations in contexts such as class attendance (Rokeach & Kliejunas, 1972), cigarette smoking (Budd, 1986), and voting (Krosnick, 1988a; Schuman & Presser, 1981). Likewise, attitudes held with greater certainty better predict behaviors in domains such as participation in psychological research (Fazio & Zanna, 1978a), choosing to play with puzzles (Fazio & Zanna, 1978b), support for social policies (Franc, 1999), voting in student government elections (Sample & Ward, 1973), and voting in student referendums (Tormala & Petty, 2002).

Processes Underlying Structural Effects on Attitude–Behavior Consistency

Structural properties clearly moderate attitude–behavior associations. However, as pointed out by a number of researchers (e.g., Fazio & Roskos-Ewoldsen, 2005; Fabrigar et al., 2005; Fabrigar, Wegener, & MacDonald, 2010), much less is known about why structural properties influence attitude–behavior relations. In considering this question, it is important to distinguish between prediction and influence. Attitude–behavior consistency is usually defined in terms of prediction (i.e., the strength of association between a measure of attitudes and a subsequent behavior). However, the degree to which an attitude measure predicts a behavior is not synonymous with the degree to which an attitude influences that behavior (Fabrigar et al., 2005, 2010). There are at least two ways in which a measure of attitudes might fail to predict behavior without necessarily implying that the attitude has no influence on the behavior.

First, a measure might simply fail to accurately assess the attitude. For example, in many cases, people might not honestly report attitudes that are seen as undesirable (e.g., racist attitudes). Finding that these reports do not predict behavior in no way implies that people were not relying on their attitudes as guides to behavior. It is entirely possible that attitudes strongly influenced the behaviors and would have been excellent predictors of behavior had people honestly reported the attitudes. Second, even assuming that responses to a measure effectively reflect the attitude at that time, these responses might fail to predict subsequent behavior if the attitude changes during the interval between its initial measurement and the performance of the behavior. For example, we might measure people's attitudes toward a political candidate a week prior to the election. If people's attitudes change before voting, finding that the week-old attitudinal reports are poor predictors of voting would in no way imply that people were voting in ways inconsistent with their attitudes at the time they entered the voting booth. Rather it might indicate that their prior reports were no longer accurate representations of their attitudes. Considering both of these reasons, it follows that two processes by which attitude structure might influence attitude–behavior prediction, independent of any actual effects on the impact of attitudes on behavior, could be by altering the accuracy with which attitudes are measured or the stability of attitudes over time.

Of course, structure may also play a role in regulating the actual influence of attitudes on behavior. In considering why structure might play such a role, it is important to distinguish between behaviors that are deliberative and nondeliberative in nature. As discussed in the Petty and Briñol (Chapter 7, this volume), attitudes can be changed through relatively thoughtful means or relatively nonthoughtful means (e.g., see Chaiken, Liberman, & Eagly, 1989; Chen &

Chaiken, 1999; Petty & Cacioppo, 1986; Petty & Wegener, 1999). So too can behaviors be performed either as a result of very careful deliberation or as a result of very nondeliberative processes (Fazio, 1990; Fazio & Towles-Schwen, 1999). The mechanisms by which structural properties moderate the degree to which attitudes influence behavior may vary depending on the level of deliberation that occurs in the performance of the behavior.

When people are unmotivated or unable to carefully think about their behaviors, attitudes could play a role in influencing behavior in two possible ways (see Fabrigar et al., 2005, 2010). First, the attitude could serve as a direct peripheral cue to infer whether a behavior is appropriate (see Petty & Cacioppo, 1986; Petty & Wegener, 1999). For example, imagine a case in which a person approaches you and invites you to a party, seemingly expecting a response at the time. Thus, you have little opportunity to carefully consider your decision before responding. In such a situation, your attitude toward the person might provide a very quick and easy basis to infer whether you should accept the invitation in the absence of careful consideration of other information about the party (who else will be attending, the nature of the activities at the party, alternative opportunities, etc.). A second process by which attitudes could influence behavior under low deliberation could be by serving as an indirect cue. That is, the attitude could focus attention on attitude-congruent features of the attitude object or behavioral context and these features in turn could serve as simple cues regarding how to behave (Fazio & Dunton, 1997; Fazio, Ledbetter, & Towles-Schwen, 2000; Smith, Fazio, & Cejka, 1996; see also Fazio, 1990; Fazio & Towles-Schwen, 1999). For instance, imagine a situation in which a police officer is called to the scene of a potential crime in which the suspect is a member of a visible minority. A police officer who holds a negative attitude toward the minority group in question might focus on simple visual cues that are negative rather than positive (an aggressive posture rather than a friendly facial expression, the possession of a weapon rather than the nonthreatening manner in which it is being held, etc.); these negative visual cues might cause the officer to make a quick judgment to use deadly force.

Of course, one would expect attitudes to serve as direct or indirect cues to behavior only if they are activated at the time of the behavior (Fazio, 1990; 1995; Fazio & Towles-Schwen, 1999) and there is good reason to expect that a number of structural properties of attitudes might influence the likelihood of attitude activation. Thus, under nondeliberative conditions, structure may moderate the impact of attitudes on behavior via its role in regulating attitude activation.

When people are both able and motivated to deliberate about a behavior, attitudes may influence behavior by serving as an argument or a biasing factor (Petty & Cacioppo, 1986; Petty & Wegener, 1999). If the attitude is judged as an informative guide to the behavior, it might serve as a direct argument regarding a course of action (Fabrigar et al., 2006). For example, the relative evaluation of two different automobiles could be viewed as an argument directly relevant to selecting which vehicle to purchase. However, even if the attitude is not directly relevant to evaluating the merits of a course of action, it could still influence behavior by biasing interpretation of behavior-relevant information (if the behavioral context contains information that is sufficiently ambiguous to permit bias in interpretation; see Chaiken & Maheswaran, 1994). For example, imagine a situation in which a person is choosing between cars from two salespeople. Attitudes toward the salespeople are not directly relevant to evaluating the merits of the cars, but might bias how information about the two vehicles is interpreted.

Of course, just as in low deliberation behaviors, attitudes will not inevitably influence highly deliberative behavior. Attitudes must be activated at the time of the behavior (or of the information processing that leads to behavior) to function as an argument or biasing factor. Thus, structure might moderate the impact of attitudes on behavior by regulating attitude activation. Additionally, structure might also play a role in highly deliberative behaviors for other reasons. For example, we might expect structure to influence the extent to which an attitude is viewed as relevant and as an informative argument to favor or oppose a particular course of action (Fabrigar et al., 2006). Likewise, structure might also affect the extent to which an attitude is seen as a legitimate source of influence on how behavioral information should be interpreted or as an inappropriate source of bias whose influence should be eliminated (cf. Wegener & Petty, 1997).

Importantly, this applicability mechanism will play a role only when behaviors are highly deliberative. Considering the relevance of an attitude to a behavior and disregarding its influence if it is judged uninformative requires substantial cognitive effort. Indeed, research has revealed that people often rely on their attitudes when it is logically inappropriate to do so when they lack the motivation and/or ability to deliberate about their behaviors, but are much less likely to rely on such attitudes when they are able and motivated to carefully consider their actions (Fabrigar et al., 2006; Sanbonmatsu & Fazio, 1990; Schuette & Fazio, 1995).

A final deliberative process through which structure may moderate the influence of attitudes on behavior is by regulating the magnitude of bias that an attitude exerts on the processing of information in a behavioral context. Structure may determine the motivation and ability that a person has to process information relevant to the behavior in a biased manner.

Evidence for Processes Underlying Structural Effects on Attitude–Behavior Consistency

Structure and Behavioral Prediction Processes Although the evidence for a moderating role of structure in attitude–behavior consistency is quite substantial, there is much less evidence for the role of measurement and stability mechanisms in these effects. However, some indirect evidence exists for a few structural properties. For example, with respect to measurement processes and ambivalence, research has suggested that increased ambivalence is related to the greater impact of factors such as priming (MacDonald & Zanna, 1998), mood (Bell & Esses, 1997), and introspection (Erber, Hodges, & Wilson., 1995) on attitudinal judgments. Thus, ambivalence may open people to influences that decrease the extent to which attitude measures are primarily indexing differences in evaluations per se. However, no studies have directly tested whether such potential sources of error in measurement are responsible for the effects of ambivalence on decreased attitude–behavior associations.

Along similar lines, there is also some indirect evidence to support stability processes for a few structural variables. Several studies have documented that greater attitude accessibility (Bargh, Chaiken, Govender, & Pratto, 1992; Grant, Button, & Noseworthy, 1994), decreases in various forms of ambivalence (Chaiken et al., 1995; Erber et al., 1995; Norman, 1975), increased certainty (Bassili, 1996), and higher levels of importance (Krosnick, 1988b) are related to the enhanced stability of attitudes over time. However, these studies did not specifically test if the structure–stability relation was responsible for the effects of these structural properties on attitude–behavior prediction. Likewise, research on working knowledge has indicated that introspecting about attitudes, which is known to both change attitudes and produce weaker attitude–behavior associations, produces decreased attitude–behavior associations for attitudes based on little knowledge, but not for attitudes based on extensive knowledge (Wilson, Kraft, & Dunn, 1989).

Structure and Nondeliberative Attitude–Behavior Consistency To date, there has been little direct evidence for the moderating role of structural properties in regulating the impact of attitudes as direct cues or as indirect cues to nondeliberative behaviors. However, some data suggestive of the possible role of attitude accessibility in moderating attitudes as indirect cues do exist. Studies have shown that activation of attitudes can direct attention to features of an object. For example, Smith et al. (1996) manipulated the accessibility of attitudes toward social categories (e.g., men, women) and demonstrated that increased accessibility enhanced the speed with which people could judge whether a target person was a member of a given category. Fazio et al. (2000) manipulated the accessibility of attitudes toward photos of people using an attitude expression manipulation and then later presented participants with the same photos and photos that had been altered. Increased accessibility produced slower and less accurate judgments of whether photos had been previously viewed. Taken together, these studies demonstrate that making attitudes more accessible (and thus more likely to be activated) does enhance the likelihood that an attitude will direct attention to particular features. However, no studies have then examined whether directive processing of specific features of an object might in turn account for the attitude's impact on subsequent behavior. Additionally, the potential moderating role of other structural features in altering how objects are perceived has not been examined.

Structure and Deliberative Attitude–Behavior Consistency When considering the potential effects of structure for highly deliberative behaviors, accessibility could moderate attitude–behavior consistency is by regulating the likelihood that an attitude is activated and can thus bias elaboration of information relevant to the behavior. Although no studies have directly tested this mechanism, some studies have provided evidence for the first step in this process. In several studies, Fazio and his colleagues manipulated accessibility of attitudes using a repeated attitude expression manipulation and demonstrated that highly accessible attitudes had a greater impact on evaluations of attitude-relevant information than did attitudes low in accessibility (Houston & Fazio, 1989; Schuette & Fazio, 1995). Likewise, Fazio and Williams (1986) measured attitudes toward presidential candidates and the accessibility of these attitudes. They found that high accessibility attitudes were more predictive of evaluations of the candidates' debate performances than were attitudes low in accessibility.

With respect to the potential impact of structure in influencing the extent to which an attitude is judged to be a directly informative guide to the merits of a given behavior, several studies have explored the possible role of content of attitude-relevant information (Fabrigar et al., 2006). In one experiment, these researchers manipulated the cognitive information on which attitudes toward two department stores were based as well as the relevance of purchasing decisions to the information on which the attitudes were based. Attitudes were better predictors of decisions when the information on which the attitudes were based was relevant to the goal of the decision. This result was likely due to influences on perceived attitude applicability. It was unlikely that differences in attitude activation emerged because all attitudes were made highly accessible using a repeated attitude expression procedure. Similarly, no new information was presented with the decision task so as to preclude biased processing of new information relevant to the behavior. Moreover, the matching effect between the attitude basis and the behavior was significantly stronger under highly deliberative conditions than nondeliberative conditions (i.e., when participants were distracted) thereby supporting the deliberative nature of the process.

These same experiments also tested the role of complexity as a determinant of whether attitudes would be judged informative guides to highly deliberative behaviors (Fabrigar et al., 2006). When an attitude is based on a single dimension of knowledge (i.e., the attitude is low in complexity) and that dimension has little direct relevance to the goal of the behavior, the attitude is likely to be judged as an uninformative guide. In contrast, complex attitudes with multiple evaluatively consistent dimensions are viewed as informative guides even when the goal of the behavior has little direct relevance to any of the dimensions of knowledge. This occurs because the object is assumed to be generally good or bad across unknown dimensions. Thus, complex evaluatively consistent attitudes are likely to be judged as useful guides across a wide range of behavioral goals. Consistent these ideas, Fabrigar et al. (2006) found that simple attitudes were excellent predictors of decisions when the knowledge dimension was directly relevant to the decision but were poor predictors when this was not the case. In contrast, evaluatively consistent complex attitudes were found to be relatively good predictors of decisions irrespective of whether the knowledge dimensions were directly relevant to the decision.

Only a few experiments have examined the impact of ambivalence on attitude–behavior consistency under highly deliberative conditions (Fabrigar, Petty, Smith, Wood, & Crites, 2010). Specifically, these experiments tested two possible reasons why cross-dimension ambivalence might result in attitudes being judged as uninformative guides to behavior. First, if a behavior happens to be relevant to a single dimension or a subset of dimensions that are inconsistent with the overall attitude (e.g., the overall evaluation is positive but the relevant dimension is negative), people might judge their global attitudes to be uninformative and thus not rely on them. Second, when inconsistency exists among dimensions, people may be unwilling to extrapolate beyond what they know and thus unwilling to rely on their attitudes when faced with a behavior that is not directly relevant to any dimensions on which their attitudes are based. As expected, Fabrigar et al. (2010) found that complex ambivalent attitudes were poor predictors of decisions relevant to a dimension of knowledge that contradicted the global attitude and poor predictors of decisions that were not relevant to any of the dimensions of knowledge on which the attitude was based. Interestingly, when the decision was relevant to all three dimensions of complex ambivalent attitudes, these attitudes were good predictors. This is because the decision required balancing competing goals and the overall attitude was in fact a summary of these competing dimensions. Thus, it was judged to be an informative guide.

Summary

As these many studies illustrate, there is little doubt that structural properties of attitudes are related to the ability of attitudinal responses to predict behavior. However, very little research has specifically tested the processes we have outlined, and this gap in the literature remains one of the great challenges facing attitude structure researchers. Nonetheless, some evidence does exist for particular processes in the context of some structural properties.

Attitude Structure and Attitude Change Processes

Another reason for interest in attitude structure is its potential role in attitude change. Many attitude researchers have examined the impact of structural properties on attitude change (e.g., see Eagly & Chaiken, 1993, 1998; Petty & Krosnick, 1995; Pratkanis et al., 1989). For example, the literature suggests that attitudes are harder to change when they are more accessible (e.g., Bassili, 1996; Bassili & Fletcher, 1991), associated with high levels of knowledge (e.g., Lewan & Stotland, 1961; Wood, 1982), or associated with low levels of ambivalence (e.g., Armitage & Conner, 2000; Chaiken & Baldwin, 1982). Similarly, attitudes are more resistant to change when associated with high levels of confidence (e.g., Basilli, 1996; Tormala & Petty, 2002) or perceived as personally important (e.g., Fine, 1957). Research on attitude bases has generally supported the idea that affective or cognitive communications (Edwards, 1990; Edwards & von Hippel, 1995; Fabrigar & Petty, 1999) are more persuasive when they match the affective or cognitive basis of the attitude and when they match the perceived basis of the attitude (i.e., the meta-basis; See et al., 2008). Similarly, research on functional matching suggests that messages that address the primary function of the attitude for the person are more likely to result in persuasion (e.g., Shavitt, 1990; Snyder & DeBono, 1985).

However, similar to the research on attitude–behavior consistency, much of this research has not focused on potential mechanisms to account for effects of structural variables. In this section, we briefly outline a conceptual framework for the impact of structure on attitude change that relies heavily on distinctions among low, high, and moderate levels of elaboration in attitude change (see Petty & Briñol, Chapter 7, this volume; Petty & Wegener, 1998a, 1999). The present framework could be applied to any structural variable, but we restrict our discussion to properties for which data currently exist.

A Conceptual Framework for the Role of Structure in Attitude Change

Thoughtfulness and Attitude Change Mechanisms by which structural properties influence persuasion likely vary depending on whether attitude change occurs via relatively thoughtful or nonthoughtful processes [first advanced in the Elaboration Likelihood Model (Petty & Cacioppo, 1981, 1986) and the Heuristic-Systematic Model (Chaiken, 1987; Chaiken et al., 1989)]. These and related models of attitude change generally posit that highly thoughtful processes dominate when individuals are willing and able to carefully consider available information. When motivation and ability are high, attitudes are largely determined by a person's assessments of the "central merits" of the attitude object. Less thoughtful processes dominate when individuals lack the motivation or the capacity to evaluate information carefully. In such cases, people tend to rely on heuristics or other peripheral cues as a simple basis to arrive at an attitude (see Petty & Briñol, Chapter 7, this volume). Thus, as discussed in the following sections, various features of attitude structure might influence the likelihood of the attitude itself serving in a particular role at a given level of elaboration.

Low Elaboration Likelihood When people lack ability or motivation to carefully consider a persuasive appeal, premessage attitudes can serve as peripheral cues to whether the appeal should be accepted (Fabrigar, Petty, Wegener, Priester, & Brooksbank, 2002; described in Wegener, Petty, Smoak, & Fabrigar, 2004). This role of course requires that our premessage attitude is activated at the time of the persuasive message. Various structural properties might influence activation of premessage attitudes and, therefore, the likelihood that they can serve as a cue to accept or reject a message. However, little research on attitude structure has addressed this potential role for premessage attitudes, so the empirical literature primarily examines influences of premessage attitudes in high or moderate elaboration settings.

High Elaboration Likelihood When individuals have the ability and motivation to consider the merits of a persuasive appeal, premessage attitudes can bias evaluation of the message arguments (Fabrigar et al., 2002; described in Wegener et al., 2004). People accept arguments that are compatible with their premessage attitudes, but they reject arguments incompatible with their premessage attitudes (Edwards & Smith, 1996; Lord, Ross, & Lepper, 1979). Attitudes should bias processing only if they are activated, so highly accessible attitudes should be more likely to bias processing (Houston & Fazio, 1989). However, even if attitudes are accessible and activated, people might perceive them as creating inappropriate influences that should be avoided or *corrected* (Wegener & Petty, 1997). Even if the attitude is perceived as applicable and appropriate, attitude-consistent biases will vary depending on our ability to implement the bias (e.g., informational resources) and our motivation to implement it (e.g., consistency pressures). Thus, structural variables can moderate the extent to which premessage attitudes will serve as biasing factors by influencing the likelihood of attitude activation or the likelihood of viewing the attitude as applicable and appropriate for use in processing attitude-relevant information.

Like other persuasion variables, premessage attitudes could also serve to validate our thoughts when elaboration likelihood is high (Briñol & Petty, 2009). For example, just as stereotypes toward a group can validate stereotype-consistent perceptions of a group member (Clark, Wegener, Briñol, & Petty, 2009), an attitude toward the group could validate attitude-consistent thoughts—perhaps especially so when the attitude has one or more structural properties that influence its likelihood of activation or its likelihood of being perceived as a relevant and appropriate guide to thinking or behavior.

Moderate Elaboration Likelihood When elaboration likelihood is not constrained to be particularly high or low, premessage attitudes can influence the extent to which message recipients process the message. Structural properties of attitudes might influence motivation or the ability to process information via their impact on attitude activation, perceived self-relevance of the message, or the person's ability to scrutinize the message. Structural variables could also influence the extent to which certain messages are perceived as threatening to the message recipient or the extent to which the person is motivated to bolster their existing attitudes.

Empirical Research on the Role of Structure in Attitude Change

Accessibility With high levels of elaboration, some research suggests that accessibility can affect the likelihood of premessage attitudes biasing processing. Highly accessible premessage attitudes bias evaluation of presidential debates (Fazio & Williams, 1986) or favorable and unfavorable messages (e.g., about capital punishment; Houston & Fazio, 1989; Schuette & Fazio, 1995) more than inaccessible attitudes.

Under moderate elaboration conditions, attitude accessibility can influence the amount of elaboration given to a persuasive message. Messages have been thought for some time to receive greater processing when they are counterattitudinal rather than proattitudinal (e.g., Cacioppo & Petty, 1979; Edwards & Smith, 1996). However, attitude accessibility moderates this pattern. When a message is counterattitudinal (i.e., opposing the premessage views of message recipients), it receives greater scrutiny when premessage attitudes are accessible rather than inaccessible (Clark, Wegener, & Fabrigar, 2008a; Fabrigar, Priester, Petty, & Wegener, 1998). When the persuasive message is proattitudinal (i.e., consistent with the premessage views of message recipients), however, greater accessibility is associated with less rather than more message scrutiny (Clark et al., 2008a). This research also suggests that high attitude accessibility may be associated with greater perceived threat by counterattitudinal messages, but with greater perceived redundancy of the proattitudinal message with what the person already knows.

Types of Attitude-Relevant Information In high elaboration settings, arguments based on information that matches the affective/cognitive or functional basis of an attitude might be viewed as more compelling than arguments based on mismatching information (assuming that the arguments are relatively strong, or at least ambiguous). In the area of functional matching, Lavine and Snyder (1996, 2000) tested this "biased processing" hypothesis and found that perceptions of message quality mediated the relationship between functional matching status and postmessage attitudes (see also Lavine, Burgess, Snyder, Transue, Sullivan, Haney, & Wagner, 1999).

Although matching effects are most common, sometimes "mismatching arguments" can lead to greater persuasion (e.g., Millar & Millar, 1990; Petty & Wegener, 1998b). Such patterns may point to the importance of factors such as argument strength and the consistency with a person's existing attitude. If elaboration is high, a person may be more able or motivated to counterargue opposing information that matches the basis of the person's current attitude (see Millar & Millar, 1990). Thus, if counterattitudinal arguments are weak, they might actually be less persuasive if they match rather than mismatch the basis of the attitude.

In more moderate elaboration conditions, messages whose content matches the functional or affective/cognitive basis of an attitude may be scrutinized to a greater extent than messages that mismatch the basis of the attitude (Lavine & Snyder, 2000; Petty, Wheeler, & Bizer, 2000; Petty & Wegener, 1998b). In at least some of these settings, matching messages may be perceived as more relevant to the person than mismatching messages (in the functional domain, see DeBono & Packer, 1991). Similar ideas may also help to resolve inconsistencies in the literature on affective/cognitive matching (see Fabrigar & Petty, 1999).

Working Knowledge and Complexity When motivation and ability to think are high (and information is ambiguous enough for biases in processing to occur), effects of knowledge on biased processing may depend on additional variables that motivate people to defend their attitudes. For example, knowledge may provide the ability to process in a biased manner when affect associated with the attitude object provides the motivation to do so (see Biek, Wood, & Chaiken, 1996; Wood et al., 1995). When attitudes are not affect laden, people may be less motivated to preserve their existing attitude and high levels of knowledge may be associated with motivation for accuracy. Similar principles might also apply when knowledge is combined with other strength-related properties (e.g., importance, certainty) that might heighten the motivation to defend our attitude (see also Petty, Tormala, & Rucker, 2003; Wegener et al., 2004). This general approach might also apply to attitudes associated with moral conviction (Skitka, Bauman, & Sargis, 2005; Wright, Cullum, & Schwab, 2008).

When elaboration likelihood is relatively moderate, the amount or complexity of knowledge might influence our motivation or ability to process a persuasive message (and individual differences in amount of knowledge could also be associated with other motivational variables, such as interest, perceived relevance, or perceived importance of the topic). In a variety of studies, high levels of knowledge were associated with greater processing of message content (e.g., Wood & Kallgren, 1988; Wood, Kallgren, & Preisler, 1985). Less knowledgeable people were less likely to critically evaluate new information, relying more on cues such as message length (Wood et. al., 1985) and source characteristics (Wood & Kallgren, 1988).

Ambivalence When elaboration likelihood is high, ambivalence might create countervailing forces regarding the likelihood that an attitude is used in processing. A number of traditional structural reasons suggest that ambivalent attitudes would be less likely to direct information processing. Ambivalent attitudes are less accessible, less extreme, and held with less confidence, which could decrease the likelihood of activation or the perception that the attitude is an appropriate guide for information processing. Even when the attitude is activated and seen as applicable, ambivalence may decrease the ability to effectively counterargue a message (Chaiken & Yates, 1985; Eagly & Chaiken, 1995) because conflicting underlying knowledge might make it difficult to generate strong refutations. Decreased impact of ambivalent attitudes would not always be the outcome, however. If people are motivated to resolve conflict in their attitude-relevant knowledge, then processing can be biased in high elaboration settings to favor the side of the issue that the person already supports (Nordgren, van Harreveld, & van der Pligt, 2006).

Similar motives have long been thought to account for effects of ambivalence on amount of processing (under more moderate levels of elaboration likelihood; Maio, Bell, & Esses, 1996). However, if elaboration is in the service of decreasing ambivalence, then elaboration should be more likely when available information is proattitudinal (and thinking is perceived as likely to resolve the ambivalence) rather than counterattitudinal (when processing is perceived as less likely to resolve the ambivalence; Clark, Wegener, & Fabrigar, 2008b).

Subjective Beliefs about the Attitude Most research on processes underlying effects of subjective beliefs about the attitude has addressed influences on amount of information processing. Some research suggests that perceiving an attitude (Boninger, Krosnick, Berent, & Fabrigar, 1995) or issue (Petty & Cacioppo, 1990) as important increases processing of attitude-relevant information (e.g., Blankenship & Wegener, 2008; Holbrook et al., 2005). The high level of involvement with the attitude object (Petty & Cacioppo, 1990) would increase motivation to process attitude-related information.

Certainty in the attitude can also influence the amount of information processing. As outlined in the Heuristic-Systematic Model (Chaiken et al., 1989), people are thought to use heuristics or to systematically process information with the intent of increasing attitude confidence to meet a desired level of confidence (the sufficiency principle). This idea suggests that people would be likely to increase message processing when their current level of confidence is low. Bohner, Rank, Reinhard, Einwiller, and Erb (1998) showed that people sought additional attitude-relevant information when current confidence was low rather than high, but that this occurred only when people perceived the available information as capable of increasing their attitude confidence.

Other effects of attitude confidence are clearly possible, however. For example, Holland, Verplanken, and van Knippenberg (2003) found that repeated expression of our attitude (a typical manipulation of attitude accessibility) also increases confidence (with accessibility mediating repeated expression effects on reported confidence; see also Petrocelli, Tormala, & Rucker, 2007). Therefore, just as attitude accessibility can have opposing effects on the amount of processing depending on whether the message is proattitudinal or counterattitudinal (Clark et al., 2008a), confidence might also have opposing effects. That is, effects consistent with the sufficiency principle might be more likely with relatively proattitudinal messages (which should be perceived as most capable of increasing confidence). In contrast, higher levels of confidence might motivate greater processing of counterattitudinal messages if the higher level of certainty in the premessage attitude makes the counterattitudinal message more of a threat (cf. Cacioppo & Petty, 1979; Clark et al., 2008a) or if confidence in the attitude also gives us confidence that the attitude can be effectively defended (Albarracín & Mitchell, 2004). Other research showed that high levels of confidence can increase message processing when the message is described as intended to remove doubt and increase confidence (but low levels of confidence result in greater processing when no confidence-related frame was given to the message; Tormala, Rucker, & Seger, 2008; cf. Chaiken et al., 1989).

Summary

Structural aspects of attitudes have important consequences for attitude change. However, much past research has not directly addressed the level of elaboration involved. We organized this literature using the elaboration continuum from the Elaboration Likelihood Model (Petty & Cacioppo, 1986). Much work remains in documenting the specific mechanisms responsible for structural moderation of premessage attitude effects across the elaboration continuum. However, this organization of the literature provides a straightforward way to understand how structural factors might influence the impact of premessage attitudes on attitude change. The approach also generates a number of clear questions to be addressed in future research.

General Discussion: Attitude Structure Research Today and in the Future

Most previous research on attitude structure has focussed on structure as a predictor of attitude strength (especially attitude–behavior consistency). In this sense, attitude structure serves as an important outcome variable in studies of attitude change (Petty & Briñol, Chapter 7, this volume), because interventions are aimed not only at creating attitudes favorable to our preferred view, but also at creating attitudes that will have lasting impact on later thinking and behavior. In accounting for the impact of attitude structure on attitude–behavior consistency, however, much work must be done in documenting how attitude structure influences attitude–behavior consistency. Thus, current research in attitude structure has moved beyond simply establishing that structural properties moderate attitude–behavior consistency (a primary focus of work during the 1970s and 1980s) and has begun to focus increasingly on the psychological processes responsible for these effects. Beyond providing a richer explanatory account of attitude–behavior consistency processes, this increased focus on underlying mechanisms has also produced more sophisticated predictions regarding when structural properties should or should not moderate attitude–behavior consistency (see Fabrigar et al., 2010).

Sometimes, attitude structure may influence the likelihood of attitude measures successfully tapping into the evaluation of interest. This may change the extent to which initial attitude measures predict later behavior even if the later behaviors are still guided by the attitudes that exist at the time. In other situations, structural features may influence how stable the attitude is over time. Thus, attitudes may influence behaviors, but the initial measures of attitudes may not predict later behaviors because the attitude has changed. Attitude structure may also influence the extent to which the attitude guides behaviors. This may depend on the extent to which the behavior itself is relatively deliberative or nondeliberative. When the behavior is nondeliberative, the attitude may serve as a direct or indirect cue to guide behaviors, but this impact will depend, at the very least, on relevant attitudes being activated at the time of the behavior (and perhaps as well on the relative absence of other salient cues). When the behavior is more deliberative, then structural features of the attitudes can also influence the extent to which the attitude serves as an argument to support the behavior or biases processing of behavior-relevant information. For attitudes to serve in these roles, the attitude must be activated at the time of deliberation and behavior, but the attitude must also be viewed as relevant to the behavior and as an appropriate guide for the behavior. Structural properties of the attitudes may influence these perceptions and might also influence motivation and the ability to bolster our attitude through deliberation.

The roles of attitude structure in persuasion parallel the roles of attitude structure in attitude–behavior relations in many ways, because attitude change can be relatively deliberative or nondeliberative, just as behaviors can be. In addition to attitude structure effects on use of our premessage attitude as a cue (under low-elaboration conditions) or on biasing information processing (when elaboration-likelihood is high), attitude structure can also determine how much deliberation is involved in dealing with a persuasive message (when the level of elaboration is not constrained by other factors to be very high or low). One particularly interesting aspect of moderate-elaboration effects of attitude structure is that structurally "weak" attitudes (i.e., inaccessible, low certainty, high ambivalence) can create motives to bolster the attitude that create stronger attitude-consistent influences on processing than when the attitudes are structurally "strong" (i.e., accessible, high confidence, univalent; see also Clark et al., 2008b). Thus, just as in the attitude–behavior consistency literature, current persuasion research in attitude structure is providing increasingly sophisticated insights into the multiplicity of effects that can be produced by a given structural property.

References

Abelson, R. P., & Rosenberg, M. J. (1958). Symbolic psychologic: A model of attitudinal cognition. *Behavioral Science, 3*, 1–13.

Albarracín, D., & Mitchell, A. L. (2004). The role of defensive confidence in preference for proattitudinal information: How believing that one is strong can sometimes be a defensive weakness. *Personality and Social Psychology Bulletin, 30*, 1565–1584.

Allport, G. W. (1935). Attitudes. In C. Murchinson (Ed.), *A handbook of social psychology* (pp. 798–844). Worcester, MA: Clark University Press.

Anderson, N. H. (1971). Integration theory and attitude change. *Psychological Review, 78*, 171–206.

Armitage, C. J. (2003). Beyond attitudinal ambivalence: Effects of belief homogeneity on attitude-intention-behaviour relations. *European Journal of Social Psychology, 33*, 551–563.

Armitage, C. J., & Conner, M. (2000). Attitudinal ambivalence: A test of three key hypotheses. *Personality and Social Psychology Bulletin, 26*, 1421–1432.

Bargh, J. A., Chaiken, S., Govender, R., & Pratto, F. (1992). The generality of the automatic attitude activation effect. *Journal of Personality and Social Psychology, 62*, 893–912.

Bassili, J. N. (1993). Response latency versus certainty as indexes of the strength of voting intentions in a CATI survey. *Public Opinion Quarterly, 57*, 54–61.

Bassili, J. N. (1995). Response latency and the accessibility of voting intentions: What contributes to accessibility and how it affects vote choice. *Personality and Social Psychology Bulletin, 21*, 686–695.

Bassili, J. N. (1996). Meta-judgmental versus operative indexes of psychological attributes: The case of measures of attitude strength. *Journal of Personality and Social Psychology, 71*, 637–653.

Bassili, J. N., & Fletcher, J. F. (1991). Response-time measurement in survey research. *Public Opinion Quarterly, 55*, 331–346.

Bell, D. W., & Esses, V. M. (1997). Ambivalence and response amplification toward native peoples. *Journal of Applied Social Psychology, 27*, 1063–1084.

Biek, M., Wood, W., & Chaiken, S. (1996). Working knowledge, cognitive processing, and attitudes: On the inevitability of bias. *Personality and Social Psychology Bulletin, 22*, 547–556.

Blankenship, K. L., & Wegener, D. T. (2008). Opening the mind to close it: Considering a message in light of important values increases message processing and later resistance to change. *Journal of Personality and Social Psychology, 94*, 196–213.

Bohner, G., Rank, S., Reinhard, M.-A., Einwiller, S., & Erb, H.-P. (1998). Motivational determinants of systematic processing: Expectancy moderates effects of desired confidence on processing effort. *European Journal of Social Psychology, 28*, 185–206.

Boninger, D. S., Krosnick, J. A., Berent, M. K., & Fabrigar, L. R. (1995). The causes and consequences of attitude importance. In R. E. Petty & J. A. Krosnick (Eds.), *Attitude strength: Antecedents and consequences* (pp. 159–189). Mahwah, NJ: Erlbaum.

Breckler, S. J., & Wiggins, E. C. (1989). Affect versus evaluation in the structure of attitudes. *Journal of Experimental Social Psychology, 25*, 253–271.

Briñol, P., & Petty, R. E. (2009). Persuasion: Insights from the self-validation hypothesis. In M.P. Zanna (Ed.), *Advances in experimental social psychology* (Vol. 41, pp. 69–118). San Diego, CA: Academic Press.

Briñol, P., Petty, R. E., & Wheeler, S. C. (2003). Implicit ambivalence: Implications for attitude change. Paper presented at the Attitudinal Incongruence and Information Processing Symposium. Amsterdam, Netherlands.

Briñol, P., Petty, R. E., & Wheeler, S. C. (2006). Discrepancies between explicit and implicit self-concepts: Consequences for information processing. *Journal of Personality and Social Psychology, 91*, 154–170.

Budd, R. J. (1986). Predicting cigarette use: The need to incorporate measures of salience in the theory of reasoned action. *Journal of Applied Social Psychology, 16*, 663–685.

Cacioppo, J. T., & Petty, R. E. (1979). Effects of message repetition and position on cognitive responses, recall, and persuasion. *Journal of Personality and Social Psychology, 37*, 97–109.

Cacioppo, J. T., Petty, R. E., & Geen, T. R. (1989). Attitude structure and function: From the tripartite to the homeostasis model of attitudes. In A. R. Pratkanis, S. J. Breckler, & A. G. Greenwald (Eds.), *Attitude structure and function* (pp. 275–309). Hillsdale, NJ: Erlbaum.

Cartwright, D., & Harary, F. (1956). Structural balance: A generalization of Heider's theory. *Psychological Review, 63*, 277–293.

Chaiken, S. (1987). The heuristic model of persuasion. In M. P. Zanna, J. M. Olson, & C. P. Herman (Eds.), *Social influence: The Ontario symposium* (Vol. 3, pp. 143–177). Hillsdale, NJ: Erlbaum.

Chaiken, S., & Baldwin, M. W. (1981). Affective-cognitive consistency and the effect of salient behavioral information on the self-perception of attitudes. *Journal of Personality and Social Psychology, 41*, 1–12.

Chaiken, S., Liberman, A., & Eagly, A. H. (1989). Heuristic and systematic processing within and beyond the persuasion context. In J. S. Uleman & J. A. Bargh (Eds.), *Unintended thought* (pp. 212–252). New York: Guilford Press.

Chaiken, S., & Maheswaran, D. (1994). Heuristic processing can bias systematic processing: Effects of source credibility, argument ambiguity, and task importance on attitude judgment. *Journal of Personality and Social Psychology, 66*, 460–473.

Chaiken, S., Pomerantz, E. M., & Giner-Sorolla, R. (1995). Structural consistency and attitude strength. In R. E. Petty & J. A. Krosnick (Eds.), *Attitude strength: Antecedents and consequences* (pp. 387–412). Mahwah, NJ: Erlbaum.

Chaiken, S., & Yates, S. M. (1985). Affective-cognitive consistency and thought- induced attitude polarization. *Journal of Personality and Social Psychology, 49*, 1470–1481.

Chen, S., & Chaiken, S. (1999). The Heuristic-Systematic Model in its broader context. In S. Chaiken & Y. Trope (Eds.), *Dual-process theories in social psychology* (pp. 73–96). New York: Guilford Press.

Clark, J. K., Wegener, D. T., Briñol, P., & Petty, R. E. (2009). Discovering that the shoe fits: The self-validating role of stereotypes. *Psychological Science, 20*, 846–852.

Clark, J. K., Wegener, D. T., & Fabrigar, L. R. (2008a). Attitude accessibility and message processing: The moderating role of message position. *Journal of Experimental Social Psychology, 44*, 354–361.

Clark, J. K., Wegener, D. T., & Fabrigar, L. R. (2008b). Attitude ambivalence and message-based persuasion: Motivated processing of proattitudinal information and avoidance of counterattitudinal information. *Personality and Social Psychology Bulletin, 34*, 565–577.

Cohen, J. B., & Reed, A. (2006). A multiple pathway anchoring and adjustment (MPAA) model of attitude generation and recruitment. *Journal of Consumer Research, 33*, 1–15.

Conner, M., Povey, R., Sparks, P., James, R., & Shepherd, R. (2003). Moderating role of attitudinal ambivalence within the theory of planned behaviour. *British Journal of Social Psychology*, *42*, 75–94.

Conner, M., Sparks, P., Povey, R., James, R., Shepherd, R., & Armitage, C. J. (2002). Moderator effects of attitudinal ambivalence on attitude-behavior relationships. *European Journal of Social Psychology*, *32*, 705–718.

Converse, P. E. (1964). The nature of belief systems in the mass public. In D. E. Apter (Ed.), *Ideology and discontent* (pp. 201–261). New York: Free Press.

Crites, S. L., Jr., Fabrigar, L. R., & Petty, R. E. (1994). Measuring the affective and cognitive properties of attitudes: Conceptual and methodological issues. *Personality and Social Psychology Bulletin, 20*, 619–634.

Davidson, A. R., Yantis, S., Norwood, M., & Montano, D. E. (1985). Amount of information about the attitude object and attitude-behavior consistency. *Journal of Personality and Social Psychology*, *49*, 1184–1198.

DeBono, K. G., & Packer, M. (1991). The effects of advertising appeal on perceptions of product quality. *Personality and Social Psychology Bulletin, 17*, 194–200.

DeCoster, J., Banner, M. J., Smith, E. R., & Semin, G. R. (2006). On the inexplicability of the implicit: Differences in information provided by implicit and explicit tests. *Social Cognition, 24*, 5–21.

Eagly, A. H., & Chaiken, S. (1993). *The psychology of attitudes*. Fort Worth, TX: Harcourt, Brace Jovanovich.

Eagly, A. H., & Chaiken, S. (1995). Attitude strength, attitude structure, and resistance to change. In R. E. Petty & J. A. Krosnick (Eds.), *Attitude strength: Antecedents and consequences* (pp. 413–432). Mahwah, NJ: Erlbaum.

Eagly, A. H., & Chaiken, S. (1998). Attitude structure and function. In D. Gilbert, S. Fiske, & G. Lindzey (Eds.), *Handbook of social psychology* (4th ed., pp. 269–322). New York: McGraw-Hill.

Eagly, A. H., Mladinic, A., & Otto, S. (1994). Cognitive and affective bases of attitudes toward social groups and social policies. *Journal of Experimental Social Psychology, 30*, 113–137.

Eaton, A. A., & Visser, P. S. (2008). Attitude importance: Understanding the causes and consequences of passionately held views. *Social and Personality Psychology Compass, 2*, 1719–1736.

Edwards, K. (1990). The interplay of affect and cognition in attitude formation and change. *Journal of Personality and Social Psychology, 59*, 202–216.

Edwards, K., & Smith, E. E. (1996). A disconfirmation bias in the evaluation of arguments. *Journal of Personality and Social Psychology, 71*, 5–24.

Edwards, K., & von Hippel, W. (1995). Hearts and minds: The priority of affective versus cognitive factors in person perception. *Personality and Social Psychology Bulletin, 21*, 996–1011.

Erber, M. W., Hodges, S. D., & Wilson, T. D. (1995). Attitude strength, attitude stability, and the effects of analyzing reasons. In R. E. Petty & J. A. Krosnick (Eds.), *Attitude strength: Antecedents and consequences* (pp. 433–454). Mahwah, NJ: Erlbaum.

Fabrigar, L. R., MacDonald, T. K., & Wegener, D. T. (2005). The structure of attitudes. In D. Albarracín, B. T. Johnson, & M. P. Zanna (Eds.), *Handbook of attitudes and attitude change* (pp. 79–124). Mahwah, NJ: Erlbaum.

Fabrigar, L. R., & Petty, R. E. (1999). The role of the affective and cognitive bases of attitudes in susceptibility to affectively and cognitively based persuasion. *Personality and Social Psychology Bulletin, 25*, 363–381.

Fabrigar, L. R., Petty, R. E., Smith, S. M., & Crites, S. L., Jr. (2006). Understanding knowledge effects on attitude-behavior consistency: The role of relevance, complexity, and amount of knowledge. *Journal of Personality and Social Psychology, 90*, 556–577.

Fabrigar, L. R., Petty, R. E., Smith, S. M., Wood, J. K., & Crites, S. L., Jr. (2010). Exploring the impact of complexity, cross-dimension consistency, and relevance of knowledge on attitude-behavior consistency. Unpublished manuscript, Queen's University, Kingston, Ontario.

Fabrigar, L. R., Petty, R. E., Wegener, D. T., Priester, J., & Brooksbank, L. (2002). *Cue effects and biased processing effects of pre-message attitudes*. Raw data. Queen's University, Kingston, Ontario.

Fabrigar, L. R., Priester, J. R., Petty, R. E., & Wegener, D. T. (1998). The impact of attitude accessibility on elaboration of persuasive messages. *Personality and Social Psychology Bulletin, 24*, 339–352.

Fabrigar, L. R., Smith, S. M., & Brannon, L. A. (1999). Applications of social cognition: Attitudes as cognitive structures. In F. T. Durso, R. S. Nickerson, R. W. Schvaneveldt, S. T. Dumais, D. S. Lindsay, & M. T. H. Chi (Eds.), *Handbook of applied cognition* (pp. 173–206). Chichester, UK: John Wiley & Sons.

Fabrigar, L. R., Wegener, D. T., & MacDonald, T. K. (2010). Distinguishing between prediction and influence: Multiple processes underlying attitude-behavior consistency. In C. R. Agnew, D. E. Carlston, W. G. Graziano, & J. R. Kelly (Eds.), *Then a miracle occurs: Focusing on behavior in social psychological theory and research* (pp. 162–185). New York: Oxford University Press.

Fazio, R. H. (1990). Multiple processes by which attitudes guide behavior: The MODE model as an integrative framework. In L. Berkowitz (Ed.), *Advances in experimental social psychology* (Vol. 23, pp. 75–109). San Diego, CA: Academic Press.

Fazio, R. H. (1995). Attitudes as object-evaluation associations: Determinants, consequences, and correlates of attitude accessibility. In R. E. Petty & J. A. Krosnick (Eds.), *Attitude strength: Antecedents and consequences* (pp. 247–282). Mahwah, NJ: Erlbaum.

Fazio, R. H. (2007). Attitudes as object-evaluation associations of varying strength. *Social Cognition*, *25*, 603–637.

Fazio, R. H., Chen, J., McDonel, E. C., & Sherman, S. J. (1982). Attitude accessibility, attitude-behavior consistency, and the strength of the object-evaluation association. *Journal of Experimental Social Psychology*, *18*, 339–357.

Fazio, R. H., & Dunton, B. C. (1997). Categorization by race: The impact of automatic and controlled components of racial prejudice. *Journal of Experimental Social Psychology*, *33*, 451–470.

Fazio, R. H., Ledbetter, J. E., & Towles-Schwen, T. (2000). On the costs of accessible attitudes: Detecting that the attitude object has changed. *Journal of Personality and Social Psychology*, *78*, 197–210.

Fazio, R. H., Powell, M. C., & Williams, C. J. (1989). The role of attitude accessibility in the attitude-to-behavior process. *Journal of Consumer Research*, *16*, 280–288.

Fazio, R. H., & Roskos-Ewoldsen, D. R. (2005). Acting as we feel: When and how attitudes guide behavior. In T. C. Brock & M. C. Green (Eds.), *Persuasion: Psychological insights and perspectives* (pp. 41–62). Thousand Oaks, CA: Sage Publications.

Fazio, R. H., Sanbonmatsu, D. M., Powell, M. C., & Kardes, F. R. (1986). On the automatic activation of attitudes. *Journal of Personality and Social Psychology*, *50*, 229–238.

Fazio, R. H., & Towles-Schwen, T. (1999). The MODE model of attitude-behavior processes. In S. Chaiken & Y. Trope (Eds.), *Dual-process theories in social psychology* (pp. 97–116). New York: Guilford Press.

Fazio, R. H., & Williams, C. J. (1986). Attitude accessibility as a moderator of the attitude-perception and attitude-behavior relations: An investigation of the 1984 presidential election. *Journal of Personality and Social Psychology*, *51*, 505–514.

Fazio, R. H., & Zanna, M. P. (1978a). Attitudinal qualities relating to the strength of the attitude-behavior relationship. *Journal of Experimental Social Psychology*, *14*, 398–408.

Fazio, R. H., & Zanna, M. P. (1978b). On the predictive validity of attitudes: The roles of direct experience and confidence. *Journal of Personality*, *46*, 228–243.

Festinger, L. (1954). A theory of social comparison processes. *Human Relations*, *7*, 117–140.

Festinger, L. (1957). *A theory of cognitive dissonance*. Stanford, CA: Stanford University Press.

Fine, B. J. (1957). Conclusion-drawing, communicator credibility, and anxiety as factors in opinion change. *Journal of Abnormal and Social Psychology, 54*, 369–374.

Franc, R. (1999). Attitude strength and the attitude-behavior domain: Magnitude and independence of moderating effects of different strength indices. *Journal of Social Behavior and Personality, 13*, 177–195.

Gawronski, B., & Bodenhausen, G. V. (2006). Associative and propositional processes in evaluation: An integrative review of implicit and explicit attitude change. *Psychological Bulletin, 132*, 692–731.

Grant, M. J., Button, C. M., & Noseworthy, J. (1994). Predicting attitude stability. *Canadian Journal of Behavioural Science, 26*, 68–84.

Greenwald, A. G., & Banaji, M. (1995). Implicit social cognition: Attitudes, self-esteem, and stereotypes. *Psychological Review, 102*, 4–27.

Greenwald, A. G., McGhee, D. E., & Schwartz, J. L. K. (1998). Measuring individual differences in implicit cognition: The Implicit Association Test. *Journal of Personality and Social Psychology, 74*, 1464–1480.

Haddock, G., Maio, G. R., Arnold, K., & Huskinson, T. (2008). Should persuasion be affective or cognitive? The moderating effects of need for affect and need for cognition. *Personality and Social Psychology Bulletin, 34*, 769–778.

Harmon-Jones, E., & Harmon-Jones, C. (2002). Testing the action-based model of cognitive dissonance: The effect of action orientation on post-decisional attitudes. *Personality and Social Psychology Bulletin, 28*, 711–723.

Heider, F. (1958). *The psychology of interpersonal relations*. New York: Wiley.

Holbrook, A. L., Berent, M. K., Krosnick, J. A., Visser, P. S., & Boninger, D. K. (2005). Attitude importance and the accumulation of attitude-relevant knowledge in memory. *Journal of Personality and Social Psychology, 88*, 749–769.

Holland, R. W., Verplanken, B., & van Knippenberg, A. (2003). From repetition to conviction: Attitude accessibility as a determinant of attitude certainty. *Journal of Experimental Social Psychology, 39*, 594–601.

Houston, D. A., & Fazio, R. H. (1989). Biased processing as a function of attitude accessibility: Making objective judgments subjectively. *Social Cognition, 7*, 51–66.

Insko, C. A., & Schopler, J. (1967). Triadic consistency: A statement of affective-cognitive-conative consistency. *Psychological Review, 74*, 361–376.

Jonas, K., Diehl, M., & Bromer, P. (1997). Effects of attitudinal ambivalence on information processing and attitude-intention consistency. *Journal of Experimental Social Psychology, 33*, 190–210.

Judd, C. M., & Downing, J. W. (1990). Political expertise and the development of attitude consistency. *Social Cognition, 8*, 104–124.

Judd, C. M., Drake, R. A., Downing, J. W., & Krosnick, J. A. (1991). Some dynamic properties of attitude structures: Context-induced response facilitation and polarization. *Journal of Personality and Social Psychology, 60*, 193–202.

Judd, C. M., & Krosnick, J. A. (1989). The structural bases of consistency among political attitudes: Effects of political expertise and attitude importance. In A. R. Pratkanis, S. J. Breckler, & A. G. Greenwald (Eds.), *Attitude structure and function* (pp. 99–128). Hillsdale, NJ: Erlbaum.

Judd, C. M., & Lusk, C. M. (1984). Knowledge structures and evaluative judgments: Effects of structural variables on judgmental extremity. *Journal of Personality and Social Psychology, 46*, 1193–1207.

Kallgren, C. A., & Wood, W. (1986). Access to attitude-relevant information in memory as a determinant of attitude-behavior consistency. *Journal of Experimental Social Psychology, 22*, 328–338.

Kaplan, K. J. (1972). On the ambivalence-indifference problem in attitude theory and measurement: A suggested modification of the semantic differential technique. *Psychological Bulletin, 77*, 361–372.

Katz, D. (1960). The functional approach to the study of attitudes. *Public Opinion Quarterly, 24*, 163–204.

Katz, D., & Stotland, E. (1959). A preliminary statement to a theory of attitude structure and change. In S. Koch (Ed.), *Psychology: A study of a science: Vol. 3: Formulations of the person and the social context* (pp. 423–475). New York: McGraw-Hill.

Kelman, H. C. (1961). Processes of opinion change. *Public Opinion Quarterly, 25*, 57–78.

Kokkinaki, F., & Lunt, P. (1997). The relationship between involvement, attitude accessibility, and attitude-behaviour consistency. *British Journal of Social Psychology, 36*, 497–509.

Krosnick, J. A. (1988a). The role of attitude importance in social evaluation: A study of policy preferences, presidential candidate evaluations, and voting behavior. *Journal of Personality and Social Psychology, 55*, 196–210.

Krosnick, J. A. (1988b). Attitude importance and attitude change. *Journal of Experimental Social Psychology, 24*, 240–255.

Lavine, H., Burgess, D., Snyder, M., Transue, J., Sullivan, J. L., Haney, B., & Wagner, S. H. (1999). Threat, authoritarianism, and voting: An investigation of personality and persuasion. *Personality and Social Psychology Bulletin, 25*, 337–347.

Lavine, H., & Snyder, M. (1996). Cognitive processing and the functional matching effect in persuasion: The mediating role of subjective perceptions of message quality. *Journal of Experimental Social Psychology, 32*, 580–604.

Lavine, H., & Snyder, M. (2000). Cognitive processes and the functional matching effect in persuasion: Studies of personality and political behavior. In G. R. Maio & J. M. Olson (Eds.), *Why we evaluate: Functions of attitudes* (pp. 97–131). Mahwah, NJ: Erlbaum.

Lavine, H., Thomsen, C. J., & Gonzales, M. H. (1997). The development of inter-attitudinal consistency: The shared-consequences model. *Journal of Personality and Social Psychology, 72*, 735–749.

Lewan, P. C., & Stotland, E. (1961). The effects of prior information on susceptibility to an emotional appeal. *Journal of Abnormal and Social Psychology, 62*, 450–453.

Likert, R. (1932). A technique for the measurement of attitudes. *Archive of Psychology, 140*, 44–53.

Linville, P. W. (1982). The complexity-extremity effect and age-based stereotyping. *Journal of Personality and Social Psychology, 42*, 193–211.

Lord, C. G., Ross, L., & Lepper, M. R. (1979). Biased assimilation and attitude polarization: The effects of prior theories on subsequently considered evidence. *Journal of Personality and Social Psychology, 37*, 2098–2109.

MacDonald, T. K., & Zanna, M. P. (1998). Cross-dimension ambivalence toward social groups: Can ambivalence affect intentions to hire feminists? *Personality and Social Psychology Bulletin, 24*, 427–441.

Maio, G. R., Bell, D. W., & Esses, V. M. (1996). Ambivalence and persuasion: The processing of messages about immigrant groups. *Journal of Experimental Social Psychology, 32*, 513–536.

McGuire, W. J. (1989). The structure of individual attitudes and attitude systems. In A. R. Pratkanis, S. J., Breckler, & A. G. Greenwald (Eds.), *Attitude structure and function* (pp. 37–69). Hillsdale, NJ: Erlbaum.

Millar, M. G., & Millar, K. U. (1990). Attitude change as a function of attitude type and argument type. *Journal of Personality and Social Psychology, 59*, 217–228.

Millar, M., & Tesser, A. (1986). Thought induced attitude change: The effects of schema structure and commitment. *Journal of Personality and Social Psychology, 51*, 259–269.

Millar, M., & Tesser, A. (1989). The effects of affective-cognitive consistency and thought on the attitude-behavior relation. *Journal of Experimental Social Psychology, 25*, 189–202.

Moore, M. (1973). Ambivalence in attitude measurement. *Educational and Psychological Measurement, 33*, 481–483.

Murray, S. L., Haddock, G., & Zanna, M. P. (1996). On creating value-expressive attitudes: An experimental approach. In C. Seligman, J. M. Olson, & M. P. Zanna (Eds.), *The psychology of values* (Ontario Symposium Vol. 8, pp. 107–134). Mahwah, NJ: Erlbaum.

Newby-Clark, I. R., McGregor, I., & Zanna, M. P. (2002). Thinking and caring about cognitive inconsistency: When and for whom does attitudinal ambivalence feel uncomfortable? *Journal of Personality and Social Psychology, 82*, 157–166.

Nordgren, L. F., van Harreveld, F., & van der Plight, J. (2006). Ambivalence, discomfort, and motivated information processing. *Journal of Experimental Social Psychology, 42*, 252–258.

Norman, R. (1975). Affective-cognitive consistency, attitudes, conformity, and behavior. *Journal of Personality and Social Psychology, 32*, 83–91.

Osgood, C. E., Suci, G. J., & Tannenbaum, P. H. (1957). *The measurement of meaning*. Urbana: University of Illinois Press.

Petrocelli, J. V., Tormala, Z. L., & Rucker, D. D. (2007). Unpacking attitude certainty: Attitude clarity and attitude correctness. *Journal of Personality and Social Psychology, 92*, 30–41.

Petty, R. E. (2006). A metacognitive model of attitudes. *Journal of Consumer Research, 33*, 22–24.

Petty, R. E., & Briñol, P. (2006). A meta-cognitive approach to "implicit" and "explicit" evaluations: Comment on Gawronski and Bodenhausen (2006). *Psychological Bulletin, 132*, 740–744.

Petty, R. E., Briñol, P., & DeMarree, K. G. (2007). The meta-cognitive model (MCM) of attitudes: Implications for attitude measurement, change, and strength. *Social Cognition, 25*, 657–686.

Petty, R. E., & Cacioppo, J. T. (1981). *Attitudes and persuasion: Classic and contemporary approaches*. Dubuque, IA: Wm. C. Brown.

Petty, R. E., & Cacioppo, J. T. (1986). *Communication and persuasion: Central and peripheral routes to attitude change*. New York: Springer-Verlag.

Petty, R. E., & Cacioppo, J. T. (1990). Involvement and persuasion: Tradition versus integration. *Psychological Bulletin, 107*, 367–374.

Petty, R. E., & Krosnick, J. A. (Eds.). (1995). *Attitude strength: Antecedents and consequences*. Mahwah, NJ: Erlbaum.

Petty, R. E., Tormala, Z. L., Briñol, P., & Jarvis, W. B. G. (2006). Implicit ambivalence from attitude change: An exploration of the PAST Model. *Journal of Personality and Social Psychology*, 90, 21–41.

Petty, R. E., Tormala, Z. L., & Rucker, D. (2003). An attitude strength perspective on resistance to persuasion. In M. R. Banaji, J. T. Jost, & D. Prentice (Eds.), *The yin and yang of social cognition: Festschrift for William McGuire*. Washington, DC: American Psychological Association.

Petty, R. E., & Wegener, D. T. (1998a). Attitude change: Multiple roles for persuasion variables. In D. Gilbert, S. Fiske, & G. Lindzey (Eds.), *The handbook of social psychology* (4th ed., pp. 323–390). New York: McGraw-Hill.

Petty, R. E., & Wegener, D. T. (1998b). Matching versus mismatching attitude functions: Implications for scrutiny of persuasive messages. *Personality and Social Psychology Bulletin*, 24, 227–240.

Petty, R. E., & Wegener, D. T. (1999). The Elaboration Likelihood Model: Current status and controversies. In S. Chaiken & Y. Trope (Eds.), *Dual-process theories in social psychology* (pp. 41–72). New York: Guilford Press.

Petty, R. E., Wheeler, S. C., & Bizer, G. Y. (2000). Attitude functions and persuasion: An Elaboration Likelihood approach to matched versus mismatched messages. In G. R. Maio & J. M. Olson (Eds.), *Why we evaluate: Functions of attitudes* (pp. 133–162). Mahwah, NJ: Erlbaum.

Posavac, S. S., Sanbonmatsu, D. M., & Fazio, R. H. (1997). Considering the best choice: Effects of the salience and accessibility of alternatives on attitude-decision consistency. *Journal of Personality and Social Psychology*, 72, 253–261.

Powell, M. C., & Fazio, R. H. (1984). Attitude accessibility as a function of repeated attitudinal expression. *Personality and Social Psychology Bulletin, 10*, 139–148.

Pratkanis, A. R., Breckler, S. J., & Greenwald, A. G. (Eds.) (1989). *Attitude structure and function*. Hillsdale, NJ: Erlbaum.

Priester, J. R. (2002). Sex, drugs, and attitudinal ambivalence: How feelings of evaluative tension influence alcohol use and safe sex behaviors. In W. D. Crano & M. Burgoon (Eds.), *Mass media and drug prevention: Classic and contemporary theories and research* (pp. 145–162). Mahwah, NJ: Erlbaum.

Priester, J. R., & Petty, R. E. (1996). The gradual threshold model of ambivalence: Relating the positive and negative bases of attitudes to subjective ambivalence. *Journal of Personality and Social Psychology, 71*, 431–449.

Priester, J. R., & Petty, R. E. (2001). Extending the bases of subjective attitudinal ambivalence: Interpersonal and intrapersonal antecedents of evaluative tension. *Journal of Personality and Social Psychology, 80*, 19–34.

Rokeach, M., & Kliejunas, P. (1972). Behavior as a function of attitude-toward-object and attitude-toward-situation. *Journal of Personality and Social Psychology, 22*, 194–201.

Rosenberg, M. (1965). *Society and the adolescent self-image*. Princeton, NJ: Princeton University Press.

Rosenberg, M. J., & Abelson, R. P. (1960). An analysis of cognitive balancing. In C. I. Hovland & M. J. Rosenberg (Eds.), *Attitude organization and change: An analysis of consistency among components* (pp. 112–163). New Haven, CT: Yale University Press.

Rosenberg, M. J., & Hovland, C. I. (1960). Cognitive, affective, and behavioral components of attitudes. In M. Rosenberg, C. Hovland, W. McGuire, R. Abelson, & J. Brehm (Eds.), *Attitude organization and change* (pp. 1–14). New Haven, CT: Yale University Press.

Sample, J., & Ward, R. (1973). Attitude and prediction of behavior. *Social Forces, 51*, 292–304.

Sanbonmatsu, D. M., & Fazio, R. H. (1990). The role of attitudes in memory-based decision making. *Journal of Personality and Social Psychology, 59*, 614–622.

Schuette, R. A., & Fazio, R. H. (1995). Attitude accessibility and motivation as determinants of biased processing: A test of the MODE model. *Personality and Social Psychology Bulletin, 21*, 704–710.

Schuman, H., & Presser, S. (1981). *Questions and answers: Experiments on question form, wording and context in attitude surveys*. New York: Academic Press.

Scott, W. A. (1969). Structure of natural cognitions. *Journal of Personality and Social Psychology, 12*, 261–278.

See. Y. H. M., Petty, R. E., & Fabrigar, L. R. (2008). Affective and cognitive meta-bases of attitudes: Unique effects on information interest and persuasion. *Journal of Personality and Social Psychology, 94*, 938–955.

Sengupta, J., & Johar, G. V. (2002). Effects of inconsistent attribute information on the predictive value of product attitudes: Toward a resolution of opposing perspectives. *Journal of Consumer Research*, *29*, 39–56.

Shavitt, S. (1989). Operationalizing functional theories of attitude. In A. R. Pratkanis, S. J. Breckler, & A. G. Greenwald (Eds.), *Attitude structure and function* (pp. 311–338). Hillsdale, NJ: Erlbaum.

Shavitt, S. (1990). The role of attitude objects in attitude functions. *Journal of Experimental Social Psychology, 26*, 124–148.

Skitka, L. J., Bauman, C. W., & Sargis, E. G. (2005). Moral conviction: Another contributor to attitude strength or something more? *Journal of Personality and Social Psychology, 88*, 895–917.

Smith, E. R., Fazio, R. H., & Cejka, M. A. (1996). Accessible attitudes influence categorization of multiply categorizable objects. *Journal of Personality and Social Psychology, 71*, 888–898.

Smith, M. B. (1947). The personal setting of public opinions: A study of attitudes toward Russia. *Public Opinion Quarterly, 11*, 507–523.

Smith, M. B., Bruner, J. S., & White, R. W. (1956). *Opinions and personality*. New York: Wiley.

Snyder, M., & DeBono, K. G. (1985). Appeals to images and claims about quality: Understanding the psychology of advertising. *Journal of Personality and Social Psychology, 49*, 586–597.

Snyder, M., & DeBono, K. G. (1989). Understanding the functions of attitudes: Lessons from personality and social behavior. In A. R. Pratkanis, S. J. Breckler, & A. G. Greenwald (Eds.), *Attitude structure and function* (pp. 339–359). Hillsdale, NJ: Erlbaum.

Sparks, P., Hedderley, D., & Shepherd, R. (1992). An investigation into the relationship between perceived control, attitude variability, and the consumption of two common foods. *European Journal of Social Psychology, 22*, 55–71.

Tesser, A., Martin, L., & Mendolia, M. (1995). The impact of thought on attitude extremity and attitude-behavior consistency. In R. E. Petty & J. A. Krosnick (Eds.), *Attitude strength: Antecedents and consequences* (pp. 73–92). Mahwah, NJ: Erlbaum.

Tetlock, P. E. (1983). Accountability and complexity of thought. *Journal of Personality and Social Psychology, 45*, 74–83.

Tetlock, P. E. (1989). Structure and function in political belief systems. In A. R. Pratkanis, S. J. Breckler, & A. G. Greenwald (Eds.), *Attitude structure and function* (pp.129–151). Hillsdale, NJ: Erlbaum.

Tetlock, P. E., & Kim, J. I. (1987). Accountability and judgment processes in a personality prediction task. *Journal of Personality and Social Psychology, 52*, 700–709.

Thompson, M. M., Zanna, M. P., & Griffin, D. W. (1995). Let's not be indifferent about attitudinal ambivalence. In R. E. Petty & J. A. Krosnick (Eds.), *Attitude strength: Antecedents and consequences* (pp. 361–386). Mahwah, NJ: Erlbaum.

Thurstone, L. L. (1928). Attitudes can be measured. *American Journal of Sociology, 33*, 529–554.

Thurstone, L. L., & Chave, E. J. (1929). *The measurement of attitude*. Chicago, IL: The University of Chicago Press.

Tormala, Z. L., & Rucker, D. D. (2007). Attitude certainty: A review of past findings and emerging perspectives. *Social and Personality Psychology Compass, 1*, 469–492.

Tormala, Z. L., & Petty, R. E. (2002). What doesn't kill me makes me stronger: The effects of resisting persuasion on attitude certainty. *Journal of Personality and Social Psychology, 83*, 1298–1313.

Tormala, Z. L., Rucker, D. D., & Seger, C. R. (2008). When increased confidence yields increased thought: A confidence-matching hypothesis. *Journal of Experimental Social Psychology, 44*, 141–147.

Tourangeau, R., Rasinski, K. A., Bradburn, N., & D'Andrade, R. (1989). Belief accessibility and context effects in attitude measurement. *Journal of Experimental Social Psychology, 25*, 401–421.

van Harreveld, F., van der Pligt, J., & de Liver, Y. N. (2009). The agony of ambivalence and the ways to resolve it: Introducing the MAID model. *Personality and Social Psychology Review, 13*, 45–61.

Wegener, D. T., Downing, J., Krosnick, J. A., & Petty, R. E. (1995). Strength-related properties of attitudes: Measures, manipulations, and future directions. In R. E. Petty & J. A. Krosnick (Eds.), *Attitude strength: Antecedents and consequences* (pp. 455–487). Mahwah, NJ: Erlbaum.

Wegener, D. T., & Petty, R. E. (1997). The flexible correction model: The role of naive theories of bias in bias correction. In M. P. Zanna (Ed.), *Advances in experimental social psychology* (Vol. 29, pp. 141–208). San Diego, CA: Academic Press.

Wegener, D. T., Petty, R. E., Smoak, N. D., & Fabrigar, L. R. (2004). Multiple routes to resisting attitude change. In E. S. Knowles & J. A. Linn (Eds.), *Resistance and persuasion* (pp. 13–38). Mahwah, NJ: Erlbaum.

Wilson, T. D., Kraft, D., & Dunn, D. S. (1989). The disruptive effects of explaining attitudes: The moderating effect of knowledge about the attitude object. *Journal of Experimental Social Psychology, 25*, 379–400.

Wilson, T. D., Lindsey, S., & Schooler, T. Y. (2000). A model of dual attitudes. *Psychological Review, 107*, 101–126.

Wood, W. (1982). The retrieval of attitude-relevant information from memory: Effects on susceptibility to persuasion and on intrinsic motivation. *Journal of Personality and Social Psychology, 42*, 798–810.

Wood, W., & Kallgren, C. A. (1988). Communicator attributes and persuasion: Attitude-relevant information in memory. *Personality and Social Psychology Bulletin, 14*, 172–182.

Wood, W., Kallgren, C. A., & Preisler, R. M. (1985). Access to attitude-relevant information in memory as a determinant of persuasion: The role of message attributes. *Journal of Experimental Social Psychology, 21*, 73–85.

Wood, W., Rhodes, N., & Biek, M. (1995). Working knowledge and attitude strength: An information-processing analysis. In R. E. Petty & J. A. Krosnick (Eds.), *Attitude strength: Antecedents and consequences* (pp. 283–313). Mahwah, NJ: Erlbaum.

Wright, J. C., Cullum, J., & Schwab, N. (2008). The cognitive and affective dimensions of moral conviction: Implications for attitudinal and behavioral measures of interpersonal tolerance. *Personality and Social Psychology Bulletin, 34*, 1461–1476.

Zanna, M. P., & Rempel, J. K. (1988). Attitudes: A new look at an old concept. In D. Bar-Tal & A. W. Kruglanski (Eds.), *The social psychology of knowledge* (pp. 315–334). Cambridge, UK: Cambridge University Press.

Chapter 7

Attitude Change

Richard E. Petty and Pablo Briñol

Persuasion plays an essential role in everyday social life. We use the term persuasion to refer to any procedure with the potential to change someone's mind. Although persuasion can be used to change many things such as a person's specific beliefs (e.g., eating vegetables is good for your health), the most common target of persuasion is a person's *attitudes*. Attitudes refer to general evaluations individuals have regarding people (including yourself), places, objects, and issues. Attitudes can be assessed in many ways and are accorded special status because of their presumed influence on people's choices and actions (e.g., attitude change mediates the impact of belief change on behavior change). That is, all else being equal, when making choices people will decide to buy the product they like the most, attend the university they evaluate most favorably, and vote for the candidate they approve of most strongly.

In the typical situation in which persuasion is possible, a person or a group of people (i.e., the recipient) receives a communication (i.e., the message) from another individual or group (i.e., the source) in a particular setting (i.e., the context). The success of a persuasive attempt depends in part on whether the attitudes of the recipients are modified in the desired direction. Designing appropriate strategies for attitude change depends on understanding the basic mechanisms underlying persuasion. Therefore, the primary goal of this chapter is to explain the psychological processes that are responsible for attitude change and provide an overview of the main theories and research findings from social psychology.

Implicit versus Explicit Attitudes

After a long tradition of assessing the impact of persuasion treatments on attitudes using people's responses to self-report measures (e.g., Is fast food good or bad?), more recent work has also assessed attitude change with measures that tap into people's more automatic or gut-level evaluations. Such techniques are often referred to as *implicit measures,* whereas assessments that tap a person's more deliberative and acknowledged evaluations are referred to as *explicit measures*.

Using implicit measures can be important because these measures do not always reveal the same evaluations as explicit self-reports. For example, an explicit measure could reveal that a person claims to dislike cigarettes but an implicit measure might show a more favorable reaction (e.g., stronger associations between cigarettes and positive words than negative words). Implicit measures can be useful because they often bypass social desirability concerns and have been shown to predict spontaneous information processing, judgment, and behavior (see Wittenbrink & Schwarz, 2007; Petty, Fazio, & Briñol, 2009b, for reviews). In contrast, deliberative attitude measures are especially important in predicting behaviors that also are undertaken with some degree of thought (e.g., Dovidio, Kawakami, Johnson, Johnson, & Howard, 1997). Because implicit and explicit measures of attitudes are useful in predicting behavior separately (e.g., Greenwald, Poehlman, Uhlmann, & Banaji, 2009) and in combination (e.g., Briñol, Petty, & Wheeler, 2006), it is useful to understand how each is modified by various persuasion techniques. Before turning to research on attitude change, we will provide a brief discussion of our assumptions regarding attitude structure because it is important for understanding some of the consequences of attitude change that will be described throughout this chapter (see Fabrigar & Wegener, Chapter 6, this volume, for an extended discussion of attitude structure).

Attitude Structure: The Meta-Cognitive Model

In addition to associating attitude objects with general evaluative summaries (e.g., good/bad), people sometimes develop an attitude structure in which attitude objects are separately linked to both positivity and negativity (see also Cacioppo, Gardner, & Berntson, 1997). Furthermore, we assume that people can tag these evaluations as valid or invalid, or held with varying degrees of confidence. Our framework for understanding attitude structure is called the

Meta-Cognitive Model (MCM; Petty & Briñol, 2006a; Petty, Briñol, & DeMarree, 2007). For many attitude objects, one evaluation is dominant and is seen as valid. This evaluation would come to mind on encountering the attitude object, though the speed at which this occurs can vary (e.g., see Bargh, Chaiken, Govender, & Pratto, 1992; Fazio et al., 1986). However, sometimes a person considers both positive and negative evaluations to be valid; this person's attitude is best described as being *explicitly ambivalent* because both positive and negative associations come to mind and are endorsed (e.g., de Liver, van der Plight, & Wigboldus, 2007). At other times, however, people might have two opposite accessible evaluations come to mind, but one is seen as valid and the other is rejected. A denied evaluation can be a past attitude (e.g., I used to like smoking, but now I find it to be disgusting) or an association that was never endorsed but is nonetheless salient due to the person's culture (e.g., from the mass media). One example of the latter is when a person has automatic negative associations to a minority group but recognizes consciously that these associations are inaccurate (e.g., Devine, 1989).

When one evaluation that comes to mind is accepted but the other is rejected, the MCM refers to the attitude structure as one of *implicit ambivalence* (Petty & Briñol, 2009). At the conscious level, people do not report any ambivalence because they accept one evaluation (e.g., cigarettes are bad) but not the other (e.g., cigarettes are good). However, in cases of implicit ambivalence, despite the fact that one evaluation is negated (i.e., the idea that "cigarettes are good" is tagged as "wrong"), both positive and negative evaluations might come to mind spontaneously in the presence of the attitude object. To the extent that the invalidity or "wrong" tag is not retrieved, the person might find him or herself reaching for a cigarette! This conflict at the level of automatic associations can produce some discomfort even though the person does not explicitly endorse opposite evaluations of the same attitude object (Rydell, McConnell, & Mackie, 2008). In one study, for example, when people who had changed their attitudes from negative to positive were given a chance to process information about the attitude object, they engaged in more scrutiny of this information than people who were always positive. That is, even though the individuals who had changed their attitudes clearly rejected their old attitude at the explicit level, they still acted as if they were somewhat ambivalent by engaging in more processing of attitude-relevant information (see Petty, Tormala, Briñol, & Jarvis, 2006).

The MCM holds that automatic evaluative associations only determine explicit self-reports of attitudes to the extent that people endorse these associations. On the other hand, automatic evaluative associations, whether endorsed or not, can affect implicit attitude measures (see also Gawronski & Bodenhausen, 2006). That is, the perceived validity tags tend not to influence implicit measures until these tags become so well learned that that are automatically activated (see Maddux, Barden, Brewer, & Petty, 2005).

Classic Processes of Persuasion

With our definitions of attitudes and persuasion in mind, we can now turn to the classic approaches to understanding attitude change. The earliest studies were guided by relatively simple questions (e.g., is an appeal to the emotions more effective than an appeal to reason?). When the science of persuasion began a century ago, researchers tended to focus on just one outcome for any variable (e.g., positive emotions should always increase persuasion) and only one process by which any variable had its effect (see Petty, 1997). As data accumulated, however, researchers began to recognize that any one variable did not always have the same effect on persuasion (e.g., sometimes positive emotions could decrease persuasion), and each variable could affect attitudes by more than one process. Furthermore, the fact that some attitude changes tended to be relatively durable and impactful (e.g., guiding behavior), but other attitude changes were rather transitory and inconsequential, was puzzling. Contemporary theories of persuasion, such as the Elaboration Likelihood Model (ELM; Petty & Cacioppo, 1986), the Heuristic-Systematic Model (HSM; Chaiken, Liberman, & Eagly, 1989), and the unimodel (Kruglanski & Thompson, 1999) were generated to articulate multiple ways in which variables could affect attitudes in different situations (see Petty & Briñol, 2008, for an historical overview). Before turning to contemporary theories, it is useful to briefly review some of the classic approaches that focused on single processes of persuasion.

Learning and Reception Theories

A prominent early approach to persuasion assumed that the same learning principles that applied to learning how to avoid touching a hot stove were also involved in learning whether to like or dislike something new. Thus, at the simplest level, it was proposed that merely associating some object, person, or issue with something else about which you already felt positively or negatively could make the previously neutral object take on the same evaluation (e.g., Staats & Staats, 1958). We discuss this *classical conditioning* process in more detail later in the chapter.

Perhaps the most influential learning approach stemmed from Carl Hovland's attempt to apply verbal learning principles to persuasion during

World War II (Hovland, Janis, & Kelley, 1953). The core assumption of this approach was that effective influence required a sequence of steps leading to absorption of the content of a message (e.g., exposure, attention, comprehension, learning, retention; see McGuire, 1985). Once the relevant information was learned, people were assumed to yield to it. Thus, the core aspect of persuasion was providing incentives (e.g., an attractive source) to get people to learn the material in a communication so that they would be persuaded by it. In one important variation of this approach proposed by McGuire (1968), the reception phase (e.g., attention, learning) was separated from the yielding phase because several variables could have opposite effects on each step. For example, the intelligence of the message recipient is related positively to learning processes (more intelligence makes it easier to learn), but negatively to yielding (more intelligence makes it less likely to yield to what is learned). The joint action of reception and yielding processes implies that people of moderate intelligence should be easier to persuade than people of low or high intelligence because moderate intelligence maximizes the impact of reception and yielding on persuasion (see Rhodes & Wood, 1992, for a review).

Self-Persuasion Approaches

Despite how sensible the message learning approach seemed, the accumulated evidence showed that message learning could occur in the absence of attitude change and that attitudes could change without learning the specific information in the communication (Petty & Cacioppo, 1981). The *cognitive response approach* (Greenwald, 1968; Petty, Ostrom, & Brock, 1981) was developed to account for this. In contrast to the message learning view, the cognitive response approach proposes that persuasion depends on the thoughts people generate to messages rather than learning the message per se. Thus, appeals that elicit primarily favorable thoughts toward a particular recommendation produce agreement (e.g., "if that new laundry detergent makes my clothes smell fresh, I'll be more popular"), whereas appeals that elicit mostly unfavorable thoughts toward the recommendation are ineffective in achieving attitude change—regardless of the amount of message learning.

A person's thoughts in the absence of any explicit message can also produce attitude change. The persuasive effect of self-generated messages was shown in early research on *role-playing*. For example, in one study, individuals who generated arguments through playing a role (e.g., convincing a friend to quit smoking) were more turned off to cigarettes than those who received the same information passively (Elms, 1966; see also, Janis & King, 1954; Greenwald & Albert, 1968; Huesmann, Eron, Klein, Brice, & Fischer, 1983; Watts, 1967).

In addition to generating messages, other work has shown that people can be persuaded when they try to remember past behaviors, imagine future behaviors, explain some behavior, or merely think about an event. For example, people who are asked to imagine hypothetical events come to believe that these events have a higher likelihood of occurring than before they thought about them (e.g., Anderson, 1983; Anderson, Lepper, & Ross, 1983; Sherman, Cialdini, Schwartzman, & Reynolds, 1985). Similarly, Tesser and his colleagues showed that merely thinking about an attitude object without being told what to think about it can lead to attitude change. In one study, thinking about a person who did something nice led that person to be evaluated more favorably than when distracted from thinking, whereas thinking about a person who was insulting led to more negative evaluations than when distracted (see Tesser, Martin, & Mendolia, 1995). Similar effects have been observed in studies of self-presentation where people generate information about themselves (e.g., Baumeister, 1982; Tice, 1992; Wicklund & Gollwitzer, 1982).

Meta-Cognition

The self-persuasion approaches just mentioned focus on the initial or primary thoughts individuals have about attitude objects. Recent research suggests that people not only have thoughts, but they can have thoughts about their thoughts, or *meta-cognition* (Petty, Briñol, Tormala, & Wegener, 2007). One feature of thoughts that has proven to be useful is the confidence with which people hold their thoughts. That is, two people can have the same favorable thought about the message (e.g., "the proposed tax increase should help our schools"), but one person can have considerably more confidence in the validity of that thought than another person. According to *self-validation theory* (Petty, Briñol, & Tormala, 2002), people should rely on their thoughts more when they have confidence rather than doubt in those thoughts. In support of this idea, Petty et al. (2002) found that when the thoughts in response to a message were primarily favorable, increasing confidence in their validity increased persuasion, but increasing doubt in their validity decreased persuasion. When the thoughts to a message were mostly unfavorable, however, increasing confidence reduced persuasion, but undermining confidence increased persuasion.

An early demonstration of the importance of meta-cognition for persuasion came from research on what is called the *ease of retrieval* effect. In a classic study, Schwarz and colleagues (1991) asked participants to rate their own assertiveness after recalling 6 versus 12 examples of their own assertive behavior. They found that people viewed themselves as more assertive after retrieving just 6 rather than 12 examples. This result was initially surprising because a straightforward application of the self-persuasion approach would have suggested that people generating 12 instances of assertiveness would have judged themselves to be more assertive than those generating 6 instances. So, something other than the mere content of the thoughts generated must have played a role. Schwarz and colleagues reasoned that people also considered the ease with which the thoughts could be retrieved from memory.

Why would ease matter? One possibility suggested by Schwarz and colleagues (1991) is based on the *availability heuristic* (Tversky & Kahneman, 1974). That is, the easier it is to generate information in favor of something (e.g., your own assertiveness), the more supportive information people assume there must be. Although this heuristic explanation makes sense when people have limited ability to think, more recent work has suggested that when people are engaged in thoughtful judgments, ease affects attitudes by affecting thought confidence. Thus, when people have an easy time generating thoughts they are more confident in them and use them more than when they have a difficult time generating them (Tormala, Petty, & Briñol, 2002; Tormala, Falces, Briñol, & Petty, 2007). To date, numerous studies have appeared showing the importance of perceived ease across various issues, and measures, including implicit measures (Gawronski & Bodenhausen, 2005; see Schwarz, 1998, 2004, for reviews).

Motivational Approaches

The approaches just reviewed tend to have in common the idea that attitude change is based on the positive and negative beliefs and emotions that are associated with an attitude object and the perceived validity of these beliefs and emotions. That is, each attitude object is associated with salient information, and people either add up (Fishbein & Ajzen, 1981) or average (Anderson, 1981) this information, either deliberatively or automatically (see Betsch, Plessner, & Schallies, 2004), to arrive at their attitudes. People are sometimes rather impartial in their information-processing activity, carefully assessing whatever is presented for its merits or attempting to generate information on both sides of an issue. At other times, however, people are rather biased in their assessment.

Persuasion theorists have examined a number of motives that lead people away from impartial information processing. Sometimes people want to achieve a particular answer rather objectively weighing all possibilities (Kruglanski & Webster, 1996). As we discuss in more detail later, perhaps the most studied biasing motive is based on the need for cognitive consistency as evident in Festinger's (1957) theory of *cognitive dissonance*. However, other motives can also bias information processing such as a desire to be free and independent or to belong to a group (see Briñol & Petty, 2005, for a discussion). When motives bias thinking, people actively try to generate favorable or unfavorable thoughts. Biased thinking does not require a specific motive, however, as some variables can bias thinking outside of conscious intentions such as when a good mood makes positive thoughts spring to mind (Forgas, 1995; Petty et al., 1993).

Fundamental Processes Underlying Attitude Change

Now that we have described some general orientations to persuasion, we turn to the fundamental processes underlying attitude change. Attitudes are sometimes changed by relatively low thought mechanisms (e.g., conditioning), although at other times they are changed with a great deal of thinking (e.g., role playing). Sometimes the thinking is relatively objective and sometimes it is biased by various motives that are present. Notably, the research on persuasion shows that variables such as using an attractive source or putting people in a good mood sometimes have a positive effect on persuasion and sometimes the effect is negative. To understand these complexities, contemporary multiprocess theories of persuasion were developed. We use one of these theories—the elaboration likelihood model (Petty & Cacioppo, 1986)—to organize the literature.

Elaboration Likelihood Model (ELM) of Persuasion

The ELM (Petty & Cacioppo, 1981, 1986) was developed in an attempt to integrate the literature on persuasion by proposing that there was a limited set of core processes by which variables could affect attitudes, and that these processes required different amounts of thought. Thoughtful persuasion was referred to as following the *central route*, whereas low-thought persuasion was said to follow the *peripheral route*. A common finding in ELM research is that the attitudes of people who are motivated and able to think about a message are influenced by their own thoughts following an assessment of the merits of the appeal, but when they are relatively unmotivated to think, attitudes are influenced by their reaction to simple cues in the persuasion setting (see Petty & Wegener, 1998, for a review).

The ELM is an early example of what became an explosion of dual process (see Chaiken & Trope, 1999) and dual system (see Deutsch & Strack, 2006) theories that distinguished thoughtful (deliberative) from nonthoughtful (gut, experiential, snap) judgments. According to the ELM, the extent of thinking is important not only because it determines the route to persuasion and the process by which a variable affects attitudes, but also because more thoughtful persuasion tends to be more persistent over time, resistant to change, and predictive of behavior than is persuasion produced by low-thought processes (Petty, Haugtvedt, & Smith, 1995). In the remainder of this section we outline the ways in which the ELM specifies that the many source, message, recipient, and context variables can affect the extent of persuasion. We will review each of the five roles that variables can serve in the persuasion process. That is, variables can affect (1) the amount of thinking that takes place, (2) the direction (favorable or unfavorable) of the thinking, (3) structural properties of the thoughts generated, or serve as (4) persuasive arguments for the merits of a proposal, or (5) as simple cues to desirability. We will describe some of the variables that operate in each of these ways.

Amount of Thinking

One of the most fundamental things that a variable can do to influence attitudes is affect the amount of thinking about a communication (Petty, Ostrom, & Brock, 1981). We will review some key variables that affect the extent of thinking.

Motivation to Think Perhaps the most important determinant of a person's motivation to process a message is its perceived personal relevance. Whenever the message can be linked to some aspect of the message recipient's "self," it becomes more personally relevant and more likely to be processed. Linking the message to almost any aspect of the self, such as a person's values, goals, outcomes, and identities, can enhance self-relevance and processing (Blankenship & Wegener, 2008; Fleming & Petty, 2000; Petty & Cacioppo, 1990). In one early demonstration of this, Petty and Cacioppo (1979a) told undergraduates that their university was considering a proposal for comprehensive examinations in their major area as a requirement for graduation. The proposal was said to be under consideration for next year (high relevance) or 10 years in the future (low relevance). The students then received a message on the topic containing either strong (cogent) or weak (specious) arguments. The key result was that enhancing the relevance of the issue led the students to think more about the arguments that were presented. As depicted in Figure 7.1, when the arguments were strong, increasing relevance led to more persuasion as enhanced thinking led people to realize the merits of the arguments. When the arguments were weak, increasing relevance led to reduced persuasion as enhanced thinking led people to see the flaws in the message. In another study showing the power of linking a message to the self, Burnkrant and Unnava (1989) found that simply

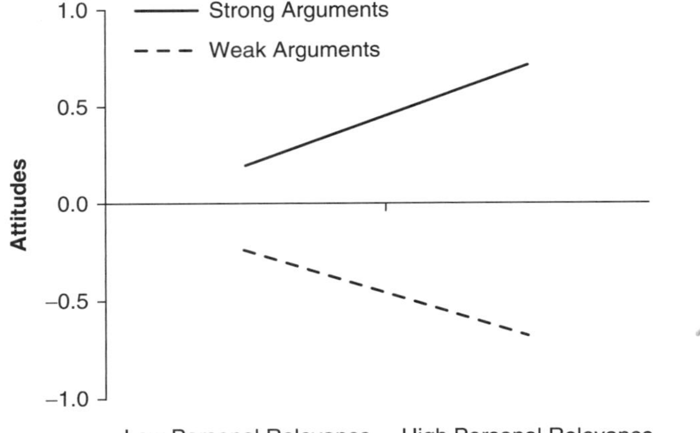

FIGURE 7.1. Personal relevance can increase or decrease persuasion by enhancing message processing. Means represent standardized attitude scores (adapted from Petty & Cacioppo, 1979a).

changing the pronouns in a message from the third person (e.g., "one" or "he and she") to the second person (i.e., "you") was sufficient to increase personal involvement and message processing.

Other ways that have been shown to motivate more thinking when it ordinarily would not have occurred include making people individually accountable for message evaluation (Petty, Harkins, & Williams, 1980), summarizing the key arguments as *questions* rather than as *assertions* (Howard, 1990; Petty, Cacioppo, & Heesacker, 1981; Swasy & Munch 1985), having the message presented by multiple sources rather than just one (Harkins & Petty, 1981), and inducing some sense of doubt or uncertainty regarding the message such as when the proposal is surprising or unexpected (Baker & Petty, 1994; Ziegler, Diehl, & Ruther, 2002). In each case, motivating more thinking led attitudes to be more affected by the quality of the arguments in the message.

Because evaluative conflict is typically experienced as uncomfortable (e.g., Abelson & Ronsenberg, 1958; Higgins, 1987; Newcomb, 1968; Osgood & Tannenbaum, 1955), people attempt to reduce it. Perhaps the most common approach to dealing with feelings of inconsistency is enhanced information processing (e.g., Abelson et al., 1968; Aronson, 1969; Festinger, 1957; Heider, 1958; Hass, Katz, Rizzo, Bailey, & Moore, 1992; Maio, Bell, & Esses, 1996; Nordgren, van Harreveld, & van der Pligt 2006). By considering additional information, individuals presumably hope to gain enough information to resolve or minimize the inconsistency (e.g., Hänze, 2001; Jonas, Diehl, & Bromer, 1997). Or, in a more biased way, they might seek out and think about information that supports their dominant reaction to an issue rather than their subordinate one (Clark, Wegener, & Fabrigar, 2008). As mentioned earlier, the ambivalence that enhances information processing can be explicit or implicit (Briñol et al., 2006; Petty et al., 2006).

Before closing, it is important to note that in addition to the situational factors described, there are also individual differences in people's motivation to think about persuasive communications. Some people like to engage in thoughtful cognitive activities, but others do not. The former are described as being high in *need for cognition* (NC) whereas the latter are low in this trait (Cacioppo & Petty, 1982). Individuals high in NC tend to form attitudes on the basis of an effortful analysis of the quality of the relevant information in the persuasive proposal, whereas people low in NC tend to be more reliant on simple cues (although this pattern can be reversed in some circumstances; See, Petty & Evans, 2009 see Cacioppo, Petty, Feinstein, & Jarvis, 1996; Petty, Briñol, Loersch, & McCaslin, 2009, for reviews).

Ability to Think Having the necessary motivation to process a message is not sufficient for the central route to occur. People must also be able to process it. For example, a complex or long message might require more than one exposure for maximal processing, even if the recipient was highly motivated to think about it (Cacioppo & Petty, 1989; Ratneshwar & Chaiken, 1991). Of course, repetition is just one variable that can exert an impact on a person's ability to think. For example, if a message is accompanied by distraction (Petty, Wells, & Brock, 1976) or if the speaker talks too fast (Briñol & Petty, 2003; Smith & Shaffer, 1995), thinking about the message will be disrupted, leading people to fail to distinguish strong from weak arguments.

Just as there are individual differences in motivation to think about messages, there are also individual differences in ability to think. For example, as general knowledge about a topic increases, people become more able to think about issue-relevant information (Wood, Rhodes, & Biek, 1995), particularly if the knowledge is accessible (e.g., Brucks, Armstrong, & Goldberg, 1988).

Direction or Valence of Thinking

When motivation and ability to think are high, people will engage in careful thought. In such situations, the quality or cogency of the information presented will be an important determinant of whether the thoughts generated are largely favorable or unfavorable. With cogent arguments, thoughts will be predominantly favorable, and with specious arguments, thoughts will be largely unfavorable.[1]

However, as noted earlier, a person's thoughts can also be biased by factors outside of the message itself. Some factors in the persuasion setting, such as being in a positive mood or having the message presented by an expert source, can increase the likelihood that positive thoughts or favorable interpretations of information are generated (e.g., DeSteno, Petty, Wegener, & Rucker, 2000; Petty et al., 1993). Other factors, such as being the target of an explicit persuasion attempt, can increase the likelihood that counterarguing occurs (Petty & Cacioppo, 1979b). This could be why "overheard" communications are often more influential than explicit persuasion attempts (e.g., Walster & Festinger, 1962). In general, biasing influences tend to be more impactful when people are already thinking about the message and the message itself is somewhat ambiguous in its quality (Chaiken & Maheswaran, 1994).

Any time a message takes a position opposed to an existing attitude, people are likely to be biased against it—wanting to reject it. And when a message takes a position in favor of your attitudes, you likely will be biased in favor of it—wanting to accept it. Similarly, if a message is perceived as counter to your outcomes, or values, or identities, you will be biased against it, but if it is perceived to be supportive, you will be biased in favor of it. As noted earlier, when a message is framed as simply relevant to the self (our outcomes, values, or identities), the *amount* of information processing is affected because the message is seen as more personally relevant. But when a message takes a particular position (pro or con) with respect to the self, the *valence* of the processing can be affected (Petty & Cacioppo, 1990).

Motivational Biases As noted earlier, a wide variety of motives have been studied in the persuasion context. For example, consistent with the theory of *psychological reactance* (Brehm, 1966), telling people that they must believe something motivates them to restore freedom by adopting a position counter to that advocated. But telling people that they cannot believe something motivates them to accept what is advocated (see Wicklund, 1974).

As noted earlier, perhaps the most studied motive in the persuasion literature is the need to maintain consistency among attitudes, beliefs, emotions, and behaviors (Festinger, 1957; Heider, 1958; Kiesler, 1971; Rosenberg, 1960), and the most prominent consistency theory is the theory of *cognitive dissonance.* In Festinger's (1954) original formulation of dissonance theory, two elements in a cognitive system (e.g., a belief and an attitude; an attitude and a behavior) were said to be consonant if one followed from the other (e.g., I voted for Candidate X; She has the same positions that I do on the major issues) and dissonant if one belief implied the opposite of the other (e.g., I voted for Candidate X; His political party is opposed to mine). Festinger proposed that the psychological state of dissonance was aversive and that people would be motivated to reduce it.

One of the more interesting dissonance situations occurs when a person's behavior is brought into conflict with his or her attitudes or beliefs. For example, one common way of producing dissonance in the laboratory is by inducing a person to write an essay that is inconsistent with the person's attitude under high choice conditions and with little incentive (e.g., Zanna & Cooper, 1974). Because behavior is usually difficult to undo, dissonance can be reduced by changing beliefs and attitudes to bring them into line with the behavior. Dissonance can result in a reanalysis of the reasons why a person engaged in a certain behavior or made a certain choice, and cause a person to rethink (rationalize) the merits of an attitude object. The end result of this effortful but biased cognitive activity can be a change in attitude toward the object.[2]

In perhaps the most famous dissonance experiment, undergraduates were induced to engage in the quite boring task of turning pegs on a board (Festinger & Carlsmith, 1959). Following this, some of the students were told that the experimenter's assistant was absent today and they were asked to take his place and try to convince a waiting participant that the peg turning task was actually quite interesting and exciting. Some of these students were informed that they would be paid $1 for assuming this role and others were told that the pay was $20 (worth about $8 and $160 in 2010). After agreeing to serve as the accomplice and talking to the waiting student, all participants reported to a psychology department secretary who gave them a presumably standard department survey that asked how interesting they found the experimental task to be. As expected by dissonance theory, the participants who received $1 rated the task as more interesting than those who received $20. This result was expected because the $1 participants had insufficient justification for their behavior, whereas the $20 participants had sufficient justification. Thus, the former participants experienced cognitive dissonance and felt a need to justify their actions (i.e., they convinced themselves that the task really was interesting).

The focus of subsequent research has been on understanding the precise cause of the tension that sometimes accompanies counterattitudinal action. Various theorists have questioned Festinger's view that inconsistency per se produces tension in people or that inconsistency reduction is the motive behind attitude change. Some theorists argue that people must believe that they have freely chosen to bring about some foreseeable negative consequence for themselves or other people (e.g., Cooper & Fazio, 1984; Scher & Cooper, 1989). Other theorists argue that the inconsistency must involve a critical aspect of ourself or a threat to our positive self-concept (e.g., Aronson, 1968; Greenwald & Ronis, 1978; Steele, 1988; Tesser, 1988). Of course, bringing about negative consequences for other people is inconsistent with most people's views of themselves as caring individuals. If people are provided with social support for their actions (Stroebe & Diehl, 1988) or are given an opportunity to restore or bolster their self-esteem in some other manner (Tesser, 2001), dissonance-reducing attitude change is less likely (for a review, see Sherman & Cohen, 2006).[3]

In fact, a strategy of bolstering the esteem of the persuasion target can serve as a general avenue to undermine resistance to persuasion (Knowles & Linn, 2004). That is, one means that has been promulgated to decrease a person's resistance to change is to provide some self-affirmation prior to an attacking message. *Self-affirmation theory* (Steele, 1988) holds that affirming an important aspect of the self prior to receipt of a counterattitudinal message can buffer the self against the threat imposed by the message and thereby increase the likelihood that participants will respond to the message favorably (e.g., Cohen, Aronson, & Steele, 2000).

Ability Biases Although most studies of bias in persuasion contexts fall in the motivational category, ability factors can also produce bias. For example, people who possess accessible attitudes bolstered by considerable attitude-congruent knowledge are better *able* to defend their attitudes than those who have inaccessible attitudes or attitudes with a minimal underlying foundation (Fazio & Williams, 1986; Wood 1982). For some variables, a combination of motivational and ability factors could be at work. For example, being in a positive mood might make it easier for positive thoughts to come to mind (an ability bias; Bower, 1981), but might also motivate people to want to stay in that positive state by generating positive thoughts (e.g., Wegener & Petty, 1994).

Meta-Cognitive Processes

In addition to affecting the amount of thinking and the direction of the thoughts, variables can also have an impact on attitudes by affecting what people think about their thoughts (Petty, Briñol, Tormala, & Wegener, 2007). We describe some of these meta-cognitive factors next.

Expectancy–Value Model Two key aspects of thoughts are the expectancy (i.e., likelihood) and value (i.e., desirability) of consequences considered in a thought. In Fishbein and Ajzen's (1975; 1981) *expectancy–value* formulation, for example, if a person has a thought in response to an advertisement such as "using this new detergent will make my clothes smell fresh," the key aspects of the thought relevant for attitude change are the desirability of smelling fresh and the likelihood that the new detergent will produce this outcome. According to this framework, a persuasive message will be effective to the extent that it produces a change in either the likelihood or the desirability component of a consequence that is linked to the attitude object (e.g., Johnson, Smith-McLallen,

Killeya, & Levin, 2004; see Fabrigar & Wegener, Chapter 6, this volume for further discussion).

Self-Validation Theory Whatever likelihood or desirability is provided for each consequence considered, the thoughts themselves can vary in the confidence with which they are held. For example, if a person thinks that getting his or her clothes clean is highly desirable and the likelihood of this occurring is quite high, but these judgments are not held with much certainty, they will not have as much impact on the person's evaluation of the product as if they were confidently held. In addition to thought certainty being affected by the likelihood and desirability certainties (Petty et al., 2002), as we describe next, it is also affected by numerous other situational and individual factors. Earlier in this chapter we explained how the ease of generation of thoughts could affect their perceived validity (Tormala et al., 2002, 2007), but there are many others.

Other variables that affect perceived validity of thoughts include simple bodily movements. For example, in one study (Briñol & Petty, 2003), undergraduates were asked to move their heads up and down (nodding in a vertical manner) or from side to side (shaking in a horizontal manner) while listening to a message containing strong or weak arguments on the topic of carrying magnetic ID cards around campus. Earlier research had indicated that nodding the head was associated with more favorable attitudes than shaking (Wells & Petty, 1980). One possibility is that nodding imparts a sense of validity to what we are thinking and shaking imparts some doubt. According to this framework, whether nodding is good or bad for persuasion should depend on what people are thinking. Indeed, students who were exposed to a strong message and were generating favorable thoughts showed more persuasion when nodding than shaking. In contrast, students listening to a weak message who were generating mostly negative thoughts showed less persuasion when nodding than shaking. This is because the nodding validated whatever thoughts the students were having, increasing their impact on attitudes.

Many other variables have been shown to affect perceptions of thought validity and thereby attitudes. For example, research has shown that thought confidence is higher when after generating thoughts in response to a persuasive message people learn that the message was generated by an expert versus a nonexpert source. Thought confidence is also increased if people are made to feel happy, powerful, or they are self-affirmed after message processing (see Briñol & Petty, 2009a). In each case, using a confidence manipulation after thought generation caused people to rely more on their thoughts such that when thoughts were primarily positive, increased confidence was associated with more persuasion, but when thoughts were primarily negative, increased confidence was associated with less persuasion.

In the domain of explicit attitudes, confidence in thoughts has been found to be an especially potent determinant of judgment when the amount of thinking at the time of attitude formation or change is relatively high. It is also useful to consider the extent of thinking permitted during response to the attitude measure. In general, if attitudes are not well formed or practiced at the time of attitude measurement, an implicit measure is unlikely to reflect thought confidence effects (Gawronski & Bodenhausen, 2006). However, if the attitude is well formed and practiced at the time of attitude measurement (i.e., people have already considered the confidence in their thoughts in developing their attitudes), the implicit attitude measure is likely to reflect the same factors as the explicit measure (see Briñol, Petty, & McCaslin, 2009).

Flexible Correction Processes Just as enhanced confidence in thoughts leads to greater reliance on them, increased doubt leads people to discard their thoughts. Sometimes, people might be so doubtful of their thoughts that they think the opposite is true. In such cases, doubt can lead to reversed effects with positive thoughts leading to less positive attitudes than negative thoughts. If people have doubt in their thoughts because they fear that their thoughts might have stemmed from some biasing factor in the situation (e.g., an attractive source) or some prejudice they have, they could attempt to explicitly correct for their biased thoughts in accord with the mechanism specified by the *Flexible Correction Model* (FCM; see Wegener & Petty, 1997, for a review). That is, people might estimate the magnitude and direction of the perceived biasing effect on their judgments and attempt to correct for it. To the extent that they correct too much, reverse effects of variables can be obtained (Petty & Wegener, 1993; Wegener & Petty, 1995; Wilson & Brekke, 1994). For example, in one study (Petty, Wegener, & White, 1998), when people became aware that a likable source might be biasing their attitudes, they became more favorable toward the proposal when it was endorsed by a dislikable source. Such explicit corrections typically require relatively high degrees of thinking. However, if certain corrections are practiced repeatedly, they can become less effortful and even automatic (e.g., Glaser & Banaji, 1999; Maddux et al., 2005).

Serving as Arguments

According to the ELM, when the amount of thinking in a persuasion situation is high, people assess the relevance of *all* of the information available. That is, people examine source, message, recipient, and contextual and internally generated information as possible arguments for favoring or disfavoring the attitude object. Interestingly, variables that serve as simple cues when the likelihood of thinking is low can be processed as arguments when thinking is high.

For example, when thinking is low, an attractive source, as a simple cue, would enhance the favorability of attitudes toward almost any advocacy because all that matters when thinking is low is the positive valence of the source. Under high thinking conditions, however, message recipients scrutinize the merits of the information presented so that an attractive source would enhance attitude favorability if it was relevant to the advocacy (e.g., a beauty product), but not when it was irrelevant (e.g., a home loan; see Kruglanski et al., 2005; Miniard, Bhatla, Lord, Dickson, & Unnava, 1991). Of course, what information serves as a cogent argument can vary with individuals and with situations (see Petty & Wegener, 1998).

Serving as Cues

The final role for variables is the most basic—serving as a simple cue. According to the ELM, under low thinking conditions, attitudes are influenced by a variety of low effort processes such as mere association or reliance on simple heuristics and inferences. This is important because it suggests that attitude change does not always require effortful evaluation of the information presented. Next, we briefly describe some of the psychological processes that can produce attitude change with relatively little (if any) effortful thinking.

Attribution Theory In an influential paper introducing *self-perception theory*, Bem (1965) suggested that when people have no special knowledge of their own internal states, they simply infer their attitudes in a manner similar to how they infer the attitudes of others [e.g., "if I (she) walked a mile to Target, I (she) must like that store"]. During much of the 1970s, self-perception theory was thought to provide an alternative account of dissonance effects (Bem, 1972). Subsequent research indicated, however, that both dissonance and self-perception processes can operate, but in different domains. In particular, the underlying "discomfort from inconsistency leading to biased processing" mechanism of dissonance theory operates when a person engages in attitude-discrepant action that is unacceptable to a person whereas self-perception processes are more likely when a person engages in attitude-discrepant but more agreeable behavior (Fazio, Zanna, & Cooper, 1977). Self-perception theory also accounts for some unique attitudinal phenomena. For example, the *overjustification effect* occurs when people come to dislike a previously liked behavior when they are provided with more than sufficient reward for engaging in it (e.g., Lepper, Greene, & Nisbett, 1973; see Deci, 1995).

Use of Persuasion Heuristics The term heuristics refers to simple rules or shortcuts that people can use to simplify decision making (Shah & Oppenheimer, 2008). The *Heuristic/Systematic model* of persuasion (HSM represents an explicit attempt to use heuristics to explain why certain variables such as source expertise or message length have their impact (Chaiken, 1987; Chaiken et al., 1989). That is, the HSM proposes that in contrast to "systematic" (central route) processes, many source, message, and other cues are evaluated by means of simple schemas or cognitive heuristics that people have learned on the basis of past experience and observation.

According to the HSM, the likelihood of careful processing increases whenever confidence in our attitude drops below the desired level (the "sufficiency threshold"). Whenever actual and desired confidence are equal, heuristic processing is more likely. For example, because of prior personal experience, people could base their acceptance of a message on the number of arguments contained in it by invoking the heuristic "the more arguments, the more validity" (a length implies strength heuristic; Petty & Cacioppo, 1984a; Wood, Kallgren, & Preisler, 1985). For the most part, the HSM makes predictions that are similar to the ELM, though the language and specific mechanisms of each theory are a bit different (see Eagly & Chaiken, 1993; Petty & Wegener, 1998, for further discussion).

Conditioning The attribution and heuristic models focus on simple cognitive inferences that can modify attitudes. Other approaches emphasize the role of relatively simple association processes. One of the most direct ways of associating affect with attitude objects is through classical conditioning. In brief, conditioning occurs when an initially neutral stimulus such as an unfamiliar shape (the conditioned stimulus; CS) is associated with another stimulus such as electric shock (the unconditioned stimulus; UCS) that is connected directly or through prior learning to some response such as feeling bad (the unconditioned response; UCR). By pairing the UCS with the CS many times, the CS becomes able to elicit a conditioned response (CR) that is similar to the UCR. Over the past several decades, a wide variety of conditioning stimuli have been used to create positive or negative attitudes including unpleasant odors and temperatures, harsh sounds, pleasant pictures, and elating and depressing films (e.g., Gouaux, 1971; Staats, Staats, & Crawford, 1962; Stuart, Shimp, & Engle, 1987). People have been found to be especially susceptible to conditioning effects when the likelihood of thinking is rather low (Cacioppo, Marshall-Goodell, Tassinary, & Petty, 1992; see also, Shimp, Stuart, & Engle, 1991).

Theorists have suggested that classical conditioning applied to attitudes might actually be a somewhat different phenomenon more appropriately called *evaluative conditioning* (Martin & Levey, 1978). This is because the conditioned attitudes do not follow the same properties as do the behaviors examined in typical classical conditioning paradigms (e.g., the conditioning of a salivary response in dogs). In classical conditioning, the phenomenon works best when there is some awareness of the paring of the CS and UCS so that the UCS comes to signal the appearance of the CS. In evaluative conditioning, this contingency awareness is not necessary. Perhaps because of this, the conditioned response in evaluative conditioning tends not to be extinguished when the UCS is no longer presented, unlike classical conditioning (see De Houwer, Thomas, & Baeyens, 2001, for a review).

If the mechanism of attitude change is not classical conditioning, then what is it? One possibility suggested recently by Jones, Fazio, and Olson (2009) is that evaluative conditioning occurs because of misattribution of the feelings elicited by the UCS to the CS. In a series of studies in which the UCS (pleasant or unpleasant pictures) and CS (Pokémon cartoon characters) were presented simultaneously over many trials, Jones et al. (2009) showed that the easier it was to confuse the source of the affect, the greater the conditioning effect. For example, when the UCS and CS were presented spatially close together, conditioning was greater than when the stimuli were further apart. This research suggests that evaluative conditioning might be reliant on relatively simple misattribution inferences similar to the self-perception and heuristic inferences described earlier.

Mere Exposure The mere exposure effect occurs when attitudes toward stimuli become more favorable as a consequence of their mere repeated presentation without any need to pair the stimuli with other positive stimuli as in evaluative conditioning (Zajonc, 1968). In one representative study, Kunst-Wilson and Zajonc (1980) presented people with a series of polygon images and found that even when these images could not be consciously recognized, the more frequently they were presented, the more they were liked. This effect has been demonstrated with a wide variety of stimuli such as foreign words, photographs, music, ideographs, and nonsense syllables (see Bornstein, 1989, for a review). Moreover, it has been shown that mere exposure can affect mood, and that this mood can spread to other, related stimuli that were not even presented (Monahan, Murphy, & Zajonc, 2000).

Perhaps the most accepted explanation of this effect today relies on the notion of *perceptual fluency*. Much research suggests that previous or repeated exposure to stimuli can make those stimuli easier to process, and that this fluency enhances subsequent liking. Specifically, the feeling of ease of processing is thought to be misattributed to a positive evaluation of the stimulus (Bornstein, 1989; Bornstein & D'Agostino, 1992; Jacoby, Kelley, Brown, & Jasechko, 1989), at least when people perceive fluency as something good (Briñol, Petty, & Tormala, 2006). The fluency process is most likely to occur when the repeated stimuli are not thought about much (e.g., are presented very quickly or are meaningless; see Bornstein, 1989). When the repeated stimuli already have some meaning, or elicit an initial dominant response in one direction or another, repeated exposure can accentuate that dominant response (Brickman, Redfield,

Harrison, & Crandall, 1971). Repeatedly presenting negative information, for instance, can make that information seem more negative (Cacioppo & Petty, 1989; Grush, 1976). One possible reason for these polarization effects is that our positive assessments of positive information might seem more valid or plausible as exposure increases, as do our negative assessments of negative information (Kruglanski, Freund, & Bar-Tal, 1996).

Implicit Change through Automatic Processes Although the research just described on simple mechanisms of attitude change has assessed change using explicit attitude measures, these same mechanisms are capable of affecting implicit measures of attitudes. For example, in one study, Dijksterhuis (2004) found that automatic evaluations of the self were affected by subliminal evaluative conditioning trials in which the word "I" was repeatedly associated with positive or negative trait terms (see also Baccus, Baldwin, & Packer, 2004; Olson & Fazio, 2001; Petty et al., 2006; Walther, 2002).

Perhaps the domain in which researchers have examined implicit changes from seemingly simple processes the most is prejudice (see Bodenhausen & Richeson, Chapter 10, this volume). For example, automatic evaluations of blacks have been shown to be affected by exposure to admired black individuals (e.g., Dasgupta & Greenwald, 2001; Dasgupta & Rivera, 2008). Although some studies likely involve invoking a different attitude object rather than attitude change (e.g., the manipulation makes the subtype of a black professional salient and this subtype is evaluated; see Barden, Maddux, Petty, & Brewer 2004), there are a sufficient number of studies in which it is clear that automatic evaluations of the same attitude object are being modified to conclude that automatic attitudes can be changed by simple associative processes requiring little elaborative thinking (for other illustrations, see Petty & Briñol, in press).

The Influence of Communication Variables on Persuasion

In addition to specifying the general mechanisms of persuasion just reviewed, the ELM postulates that any communication variable (i.e., whether source, message, recipient, or context) influences attitudes by affecting one of these key processes. Because of the very long list of persuasion variables that have been studied and the thousands of published studies, our review of variables is meant to be illustrative of how understanding the basic mechanisms of persuasion is useful in analyzing any possible variable of interest, even if it has never previously been studied.

Source Factors

Consider first the multiple processes by which source factors, such as expertise, attractiveness, race, or gender, can have an impact on persuasion. When the likelihood of thinking was low (e.g., low personal relevance topic), source factors have influenced attitudes by serving as a peripheral cue, affecting implicit (Forehand & Perkins, 2005; McConnell, Rydell, Strain, & Mackie, 2008) as well as explicit attitudes (Petty, Cacioppo, & Goldman, 1981; Chaiken, 1980) in the same direction as their valence.

When the likelihood of thinking is set to be very high (e.g., high personal relevance of the message topic), source factors have taken on other roles. For example, if a source factor is relevant to the merits of a message, it can serve as a persuasive argument. Thus, an attractive endorser can provide persuasive visual evidence for the effectiveness of a beauty product (Petty & Cacioppo, 1984b). Another role that sources can play under high thinking conditions is biasing information processing. For example, Chaiken and Maheswaran (1994) found that when recipients under high thinking conditions received an ambiguous message (i.e., not clearly strong or weak), sources high in expertise led to more favorable thoughts about the message and thus more favorable attitudes than did sources of low expertise. Under high elaboration conditions, source factors have also been shown to influence persuasion by affecting the confidence people have in the validity of their thoughts. As noted earlier, this effect is most likely to occur when the source information follows rather than precedes the persuasive message (Tormala, Briñol, & Petty, 2007).

If the likelihood of thinking is not set to be very high or low by other variables then source factors such as expertise and attractiveness have affected how much thinking people did about the message (e.g., DeBono & Harnish, 1988; Moore, Hausknecht, & Thamodaran, 1986; Puckett, Petty, Cacioppo, & Fisher, 1983). For example, Priester and Petty (1995) demonstrated that if source expertise is high, people process messages more carefully when they come from a source whose trustworthiness is in doubt than from a clearly trustworthy source. If trustworthiness is high, however, then people are more likely to process a message from an expert source than from a source who lacks expertise (Heesacker, Petty, & Cacioppo, 1983; see, Briñol & Petty, 2009b, for an extended review of source factors).

Message Factors

Message variables can also serve in multiple roles. For example, think about the number of arguments that a persuasive message contains. This variable serves as a simple peripheral cue when people are either unmotivated or unable to think about the information (Petty & Cacioppo, 1984a). That is, people can simply count the arguments in a message and agree more with the advocacy as more information is presented, regardless of the cogency of that information. When motivation and ability to think are high, however, the informational items in a message are not simply counted, but instead the information is processed for its quality. Thus, under low thinking conditions when the number of arguments in a message serves as a cue, adding weak reasons in support of a position enhances persuasion, but when the informational items in a message are processed as arguments, adding weak reasons reduces persuasion (Alba & Marmorstein, 1987; Friedrich, Fetherstonhaugh, Casey, & Gallagher, 1996; Petty & Cacioppo, 1984a).

The mere number of arguments is only one of the many message factors that can influence persuasion by serving in different roles in different situations. Other variables include whether the message emphasizes affect or cognition, is complex or not, matches the recipients' characteristics in some way, and argues in favor or against previous views (see Petty & Wegener, 1998). Finally, we note that as was the case with source factors, implicit measures are also affected by message factors (see Petty & Briñol, 2010).

Recipient Factors

There are many recipient variables that are relevant for persuasion, ranging from motives such as the need for cognition (Cacioppo & Petty, 1982), abilities such as intelligence (McGuire, 1968), and individual differences in personality such as self-monitoring (Snyder & DeBono, 1985; see Briñol & Petty, 2005, for a review). Perhaps the recipient factor that has been studied most extensively, however, is a transitory one—the emotions the target of persuasion is experiencing at the time of persuasion. In accord with the ELM, prior research has shown that a person's emotions can serve in all of the roles for variables that we have summarized (see Petty et al., 2003, Briñol, Petty, & Rucker, 2006, for reviews).

Most simply, when thinking is constrained to be low (e.g., distractions present), emotions tend to serve as simple associative cues and produce evaluations consistent with their valence (e.g., Petty et al., 1993). When thinking is high, however, emotions serve in other roles. First, emotions can be evaluated as evidence (e.g., negative emotions such as sadness or fear can lead to positive evaluations of a movie if these are the intended states; e.g., see Martin, 2000). Also, when thinking is high, emotions can bias the ongoing thoughts (e.g., positive consequences seem more likely when people are in a happy than sad state;

e.g., DeSteno et al., 2000). The bias is emotion specific. For example, in one study (DeSteno et al., 2004), participants made to feel sad were more persuaded by a message pointing to sad consequences of a proposal rather than angry ones whereas those participants made to feel angry were more persuaded by a message pointing to angering consequences than sad ones. This is because the consequences seem more likely when the consequence matches rather than mismatches the emotional state.

If an emotion is induced after people have finished thinking about the message, then emotions can affect confidence in our thoughts (Briñol, Petty, & Barden, 2007) because of the certainty appraisals associated with specific emotions. Because emotions such as happiness and anger are associated with certainty, these would validate thoughts, whereas emotions such as sadness would create doubt in thoughts and lead to less use of them (Tiedens & Linton, 2001). Finally, when the likelihood of thinking is not constrained to be high or low, emotions can affect the extent of thinking. Either happiness or sadness could lead to more thinking depending on whether the emotion signals a problem to be solved (Schwarz, Bless, & Bohner, 1991), conveys a sense of uncertainty (Tiedens & Linton, 2001), or invokes a motive to manage one's emotions by thinking (Wegener & Petty, 1994). As was the case with the other variables we have reviewed, recent research has revealed that the emotions experienced by a person can influence implicit measures of attitudes (e.g., Sassenberg & Wieber, 2005).

Consequences of Different Persuasion Processes for Explicit Measures

Now that we have articulated the various mechanisms by which variables can impact persuasion, we turn to the final issue of why we should care about process. Knowing something about the process can indicate whether the attitude change that is produced will be consequential or not. Sometimes a high and a low thought process can result in the same attitude, such as when being in a good mood produces a favorable attitude by serving as a simple associative cue under low thinking but biasing the thoughts generated under high thinking (Petty et al., 1993). According to the ELM, attitudes formed or changed through high thinking processes are more persistent, resistant to change, and predictive of behavior than attitudes changed via low thinking processes. There are both structural and meta-cognitive reasons for this. First, as thinking increases during attitude change, people should acquire more support for their attitudes (knowledge) and their attitudes should become more accessible. Furthermore, people should become more confident in their views. Each of these factors would increase the likelihood that attitudes would be consequential (see Petty et al., 1995, for a review).

Attitude Persistence and Resistance

When attitude changes are based on extensive issue-relevant thinking, they tend to *persist* (endure). For example, research has shown that encouraging self-generation of arguments (e.g., Elms, 1966; Watts, 1967), using interesting or involving communication topics (Ronis et al., 1977), leading recipients to believe that they might have to explain or justify their attitudes to other people (e.g., Boninger et al., 1990; Chaiken, 1980), and having them evaluate a message during its receipt rather than afterward (Mackie, 1987) are all associated with increased persistence of attitude change. Also, people who characteristically enjoy thinking (high need for cognition) show greater persistence of attitude change than people who do not (e.g., Haugtvedt & Petty, 1992; Wegener et al., 2006; see, Petty et al., 2009 for a review).

Resistance refers to the extent to which an attitude change is capable of surviving an attack from contrary information. Although attitude persistence and resistance tend to co-occur, their potential independence is shown in McGuire's (1964) classic work on cultural truisms. Truisms such as "you should brush your teeth after every meal" tend to last forever if not challenged, but are surprisingly susceptible to influence when attacked because people have no practice in defending them. In his work on *inoculation theory*, McGuire (1964) demonstrated that two kinds of bolstering can be effective in facilitating resistance. One relies on providing individuals with a supportive defense of their attitudes (e.g., see Ross, McFarland, Conway, & Zanna, 1983) and a second provides a mild attack and refutation of it (the inoculation). Just as people can be made more resistant to a disease by giving them a mild form of it, people can be made more resistant to discrepant messages by inoculating their initial attitudes (see Petty, Tormala, & Rucker, 2004).

Prediction of Behavior

Once a person's attitude has changed, behavior change requires that the person's new attitudes rather than the old attitudes or previous habits guide action. If a new attitude is based on high thought, it is likely to be highly accessible and come to mind automatically in the presence of the attitude object. Therefore, it will be available to guide behavior even if people do not think much before acting (see Fazio, 1990, 1995). However, even if people do engage in some thought, attitudes based on high thinking are still more likely to guide behavior because these attitudes are held with more certainty and people are more willing to act on attitudes in which they have confidence (e.g., Barden & Petty, 2008; Brown, 1974; Cacioppo, Petty, Kao, & Rodriguez, 1986; Leippe & Elkin, 1987).

Of course, behavior is determined by more than individuals' attitudes even if those attitudes are based on high thought. The *theory of reasoned action* (Fishbein & Ajzen, 1975) highlights social norms (what others think you should do) as an important determinant of behavior, and the *theory of planned behavior* (Ajzen, 1991) points to a person's sense of self-efficacy or competence to perform the behavior (see Ajzen & Fishbein, 2005). These theories make it clear that although attitude change can be an important first step, it might still be insufficient to produce the desired behavioral responses even if appropriate new attitudes were formed by the central route.

Certainty: Strength without More Thinking

We noted earlier that when attitudes change as a result of high thinking processes, they are likely to be held with greater certainty than when they are changed to the same extent by low thinking processes. Certainty generally refers to a sense of validity concerning our attitudes (Gross, Holtz, & Miller, 1995) and is an important construct because it can cause attitude strength. That is, attitudes held with greater certainty are more resistant to change (e.g., Kiesler, 1971), persistent in the absence of a persuasive attack (Bassili, 1996), and more predictive of behavior (Fazio & Zanna, 1978) than attitudes about which there is doubt.

Initial conceptualizations of attitude certainty tended to assume that certainty sprang solely from structural features of attitudes such as having attitudes based on more issue-relevant knowledge, direct experience, or thought (e.g., Fazio & Zanna, 1981). And, indeed, structural factors can play an important role in determining attitude certainty. However, recent research has examined how people sometimes infer greater certainty in the absence of any structural differences. Notably, people can even come to infer greater certainty in their attitudes if they are merely led to believe that they have done much thinking about the attitude object even if they have not (Barden & Petty, 2008). Of greatest importance is that the certainty that comes from simple inferences rather than structural differences can also cause the attitudes to be more consequential (Rucker, Petty, & Briñol, 2008; Tormala & Petty, 2002). Consistent with the meta-cognitive model of attitude structure (Petty et al., 2007), it appears that attaching a sense of validity or certainty to our attitudes by whatever means can have long-term implications.

Attitude Change Today

In this review we have argued that persuasion can be understood by breaking the processes responsible for attitude change into a finite set. These processes relate to some of the classic topics of persuasion (e.g., credibility, emotion), and explain how any one variable can produce opposite outcomes, and how the same outcome can be produced by different processes. We emphasized that understanding the underlying mechanisms of persuasion is important because different processes are associated with different consequences.

Contemporary research has begun to examine the consequences of deliberative and automatic persuasion processes not only for explicit but also for implicit attitude measures. For example, attitude change processes that require thinking deeply about the attitude object are likely to result in attitude representations that are well integrated and connected with other relevant material in memory (see, e.g., McGuire, 1981; Tesser, 1978). High thought attitude change can also spill over and influence related attitudes such as when attempting to change attitudes on abortion leads to changes on the issue of contraception (e.g., Crano & Chen, 1998). Such effects on related attitudes have been especially prevalent in the literature on minority influence whereby the minority does not produce change on the focal issue but does on a related topic (see Moscovici, Mucchi-Faina, & Maass, 1994; Mugny & Perez, 1991). It turns out that implicit measures can also be useful in mapping the interconnections among attitudes. For example, in one study, when a message was aimed at changing attitudes toward the color green, automatic attitudes toward a product associated with this color (*Heineken* beer) were also changed (see Horcajo, Petty, & Briñol, 2009). Research on changing automatic attitudes and understanding their relationship to more deliberative attitudes is likely to increase. One other area that is likely to see an exponential increase in interest concerns how persuasion processes can be mapped with new brain imaging techniques (e.g., see Cunningham, Packer, Kesek, & Van Bavel, 2009). Such measures are likely to add to our knowledge of persuasion just as prior measurement techniques have each led to substantial progress in the field.

Footnotes

1. Although there is relatively little research on what makes an argument cogent or specious, among the factors that contribute are whether the argument presents a consequence that is good or bad for the target and whether this consequence is seen as likely

or unlikely, important or unimportant, unique or already known (see Petty & Wegener, 1993).

2. In contrast to dissonance theory, *balance theory* (Heider, 1958) states that inconsistency pressures sometimes lead to attitude change by a simple inference process rather than because of a reanalysis of the merits of the attitude object. This theory states that balance occurs when people agree with people they like or disagree with people that they dislike and can account for why a person would come to like a candidate more after he or she is endorsed by a favored celebrity (i.e., to restore balance; see Insko 1984, for an extended discussion). A related formulation, congruity theory, states that attitudes toward *both* source and object change to restore "congruity" (Osgood & Tannenbaum, 1955).

3. There are still other approaches to understanding dissonance that might be of interest to readers (e.g., the *self-standards model*: Stone & Cooper, 2001; the *action-based model*: Harmon-Jones & Harmon-Jones, 2008; the *model of ambivalence-induced discomfort*: van Harreveld, van der Pligt, & de Liver, 2009; see Cooper, 2007; Harmon-Jones & Mills, 1999, for reviews).

Suggestions for Further Reading

Briñol, P., & Petty, R. E. (2009). Persuasion: Insights from the self-validation hypothesis. In M. P. Zanna (Ed.), *Advances in experimental social psychology* (Vol. 41, pp. 69–118). New York: Elsevier.

Cooper, J. (2007). Cognitive dissonance: 50 years of a classic theory. London: Sage.

Eagly, A. H., & Chaiken, S. (1993). *The psychology of attitudes*. Fort Worth, TX: Harcourt, Brace, Jovanovich.

Maio, G., & Haddock, G. (2009). *The psychology of attitudes and attitude change*. London: Sage Publications.

Petty, R. E., & Wegener, D. T. (1999). The Elaboration Likelihood Model: Current status and controversies. In S. Chaiken & Y. Trope (Eds.), *Dual process theories in social psychology* (pp. 41–72). New York: Guilford Press.

References

Abelson, R. P., Aronson, E., McGuire, W. J., Newcomb, T. M., Rosenberg, M. J., & Tannenbaum, P. H. (1968). *Theories of cognitive consistency: A sourcebook*. Chicago: Rand McNally.

Abelson, R. P., & Rosenberg, M. J. (1958). Symbolic psycho-logic: A model of attitudinal cognition. *Behavioral Science*, 3, 1–13.

Ajzen, I. (1991). The theory of planned behavior. *Organizational Behavior and Human Decision Processes*, 50, 179–211.

Ajzen, I., & Fishbein, M. (2005). The influence of attitudes on behavior. In D. Albarracín, B. T. Johnson, & M. P. Zanna (Eds.), *The handbook of attitudes* (pp. 173–221). Mahwah, NJ: Erlbaum.

Alba, J. W., & Marmorstein, H. (1987). The effects of frequency knowledge on consumer decision making. *Journal of Consumer Research, 13*, 411–454.

Anderson, C. A. (1983). Imagination and expectation: The effect of imagining behavioral scripts on personal intentions. *Psychological Bulletin*, *93*, 30–56.

Anderson, C. A., Lepper, M. R., & Ross, R. (1983). Perseverance of social theories: The role of explanation in the persistence of discredited information. *Journal of Personality and Social Psychology*, *39*, 1037–1049.

Anderson, N. (1981). Integration theory applied to cognitive responses and attitudes. In R. E. Petty, T. Ostrom, & T. Brock (Eds.), *Cognitive responses in persuasion* (pp. 361–397). Hillsdale, NJ: Erlbaum.

Aronson, E. (1968). Dissonance theory: Progress and problems. In R. P. Abelson, E. Aronson, W. J. McGuire, T. M. Newcomb, M. J. Rosenberg, & P. H. Tannenbaum (Eds.), *Theories of cognitive consistency: A sourcebook* (pp. 5–27). Chicago: Rand McNally.

Aronson, E. (1969). Cognitive dissonance: A current perspective. In L. Berkowitz (Ed.), *Advances in experimental social psychology* (Vol. 4, pp. 1–34). New York: Academic Press.

Baccus, J. R., Baldwin, M. W., & Packer, D. J. (2004). Increasing implicit self-esteem through classical conditioning. *Psychological Science, 15*, 498–502.

Baker, S. M., & Petty, R. E. (1994). Majority and minority influence: Source-position imbalance as a determinant of message scrutiny. *Journal of Personality and Social Psychology*, *67*, 5–19.

Barden, J., Maddux, W. W., Petty, R. E., & Brewer, M. B. (2004). Contextual moderation of racial bias: The impact of social roles on controlled and automatically activated attitudes. *Journal of Personality and Social Psychology, 87*, 5–22.

Barden, J., & Petty, R. E. (2008). The mere perception of elaboration creates attitude certainty: Exploring the thoughtfulness heuristic. *Journal of Personality and Social Psychology, 95*, 489–509.

Bargh, J. A., Chaiken, S., Govender, R., & Pratto, F. (1992). The generality of the automatic attitude activation effect. *Journal of Personality and Social Psychology, 62*, 893–913.

Bassili, J. N. (1996). Meta-judgmental versus operative indices of psychological properties: The case of measures of attitude strength. *Journal of Personality and Social Psychology*, *71*, 637–653.

Baumeister, R. F. (1982). A self-presentational view of social phenomena. *Psychological Bulletin, 91*, 3–26.

Bem, D. J. (1965). An experimental analysis of self-persuasion. *Journal of Experimental Social Psychology*, *1*, 199–218.

Bem, D. J. (1972). Self-perception theory. In L. Berkowitz (Ed.), *Advances in Experimental Social Psychology* (Vol. 6, pp. 1–62). New York: Academic Press.

Betsch, T., Plessner, H., & Schallies, E. (2004). The value-account model of attitude formation. In G. R. Maio & G. Haddock (Eds.), *Contemporary perspectives on the psychology of attitudes* (pp. 252–273). Hove: Psychology Press.

Blankenship, K. L., & Wegener, D. T. (2008). Opening the mind to close it: Considering a message in light of important values increases message processing and later resistance to change. *Journal of Personality and Social Psychology, 94*, 196–213.

Boninger, D. S., Brock, T. C., Cook, T. D., Gruder, C. L., & Romer, D. (1990). Discovery of reliable attitude change persistence resulting from a transmitter turning set. *Psychological Science, 1*, 268–271.

Bornstein, R. F. (1989). Exposure and affect: Overview and meta-analysis of research, 1968–1987. *Psychological Bulletin, 106*, 265–289.

Bornstein, R. F., & D'Agostino, P. R. (1992). Stimulus recognition and the mere exposure effect. *Journal of Personality and Social Psychology, 63*, 545–552.

Bower, G. H. (1981). Mood and memory. *American Psychologist, 36*, 129–148.

Brehm, J. W. (1966). *A theory of psychological reactance*. New York: Academic Press.

Brickman, P., Redfield, J., Harrison, A. A., & Crandall, R. (1972). Drive and pre-disposition as factors in the attitudinal effects of mere exposure. *Journal of Experimental Social Psychology, 8*, 31–44.

Briñol, P., & Petty, R. E (2003). Overt head movements and persuasion: A self-validation analysis. *Journal of Personality and Social Psychology, 84*, 1123–1139.

Briñol, P., & Petty, R. E. (2005). Individual differences in persuasion. In D. Albarracín, B. T. Johnson, & M. P. Zanna (Eds.), *The handbook of attitudes and attitude change* (pp. 575–616). Hillsdale, NJ: Erlbaum.

Briñol, P., & Petty, R. E. (2008). Embodied persuasion: Fundamental processes by which bodily responses can impact attitudes. In G. R. Semin & E. R. Smith (Eds.), *Embodiment grounding: Social, cognitive, affective, and neuroscientific approaches* (pp. 184–207). Cambridge, UK: Cambridge University Press.

Briñol, P., & Petty, R. E. (2009a). Persuasion: Insights from the self-validation hypothesis. In M. P. Zanna (Ed.), *Advances in experimental social psychology* (Vol. 41, pp. 69–118). New York: Elsevier.

Briñol, P., & Petty, R. E. (2009b). Source factors in persuasion: A self-validation approach. *European Review of Social Psychology, 20*, 49–96.

Briñol, P., Petty, R. E., & Barden, J. (2007). Happiness versus sadness as a determinant of thought confidence in persuasion: A self-validation analysis. *Journal of Personality and Social Psychology, 93*, 711–727.

Briñol, P., Petty, R. E., & McCaslin, M. J. (2009). Changing attitudes on implicit versus explicit measures: What is the difference? In R. E. Petty, R. H. Fazio, & P. Briñol (Eds.), *Attitudes: Insights from the new implicit measures* (pp. 285–326). New York: Psychology Press.

Briñol, P., Petty, R. E., & Rucker, D. D. (2006). The role of meta-cognitive processes in emotional intelligence. *Psicothema, 18*, 26–33.

Briñol, P., Petty, R. E., & Tormala, Z. L. (2004). The self-validation of cognitive responses to advertisements. *Journal of Consumer Research, 30*, 559–573.

Briñol, P., Petty, R. E., & Tormala, Z. L. (2006). The malleable meaning of subjective ease. *Psychological Science, 17*, 200–206.

Briñol, P., Petty, R. E., & Wheeler, S. C. (2006). Discrepancies between explicit and implicit self-concepts: Consequences for information processing. *Journal of Personality and Social Psychology, 91*, 154–170.

Brown, D. (1974). Adolescent attitudes and lawful behavior. *Public Opinion Quarterly, 38*, 98–106.

Brucks, M., Armstrong, G. M., & Goldberg, M. E. (1988). Children's use of cognitive defenses against television advertising: A cognitive response approach. *Journal of Consumer Research, 14*, 471–482.

Burnkrant, R. E., & Unnava, R. (1989). Self-referencing: A strategy for increasing processing of message content. *Personality and Social Psychology Bulletin, 15*, 628–638.

Cacioppo, J. T., Gardner, W. L., & Berntson, G. G. (1997). Beyond bipolar conceptualizations and measures: The case of attitudes and evaluative space. *Personality and Social Psychology Review, 1*, 3–25.

Cacioppo, J. T., Marshall-Goodell, B. S., Tassinary, L. G., & Petty, R. E. (1992). Rudimentary determinants of attitudes: Classical conditioning is more effective when prior knowledge about the attitude stimulus is low than high. *Journal of Experimental Social Psychology, 28*, 207–233.

Cacioppo, J. T., & Petty, R. E. (1982). The need for cognition. *Journal of Personality and Social Psychology, 42*, 116–131.

Cacioppo, J. T., & Petty, R. E. (1989). Effects of message repetition on argument processing, recall, and persuasion. *Basic and Applied Social Psychology, 10*, 3–12.

Cacioppo, J. T., Petty, R. E., Feinstein, J., & Jarvis, W. B. G. (1996). Dispositional differences in cognitive motivation: The life and times of individuals varying in need for cognition. *Psychological Bulletin, 119*, 197–253.

Cacioppo, J. T., Petty, R. E., Kao, C., & Rodriguez, R. (1986). Central and peripheral routes to persuasion: An individual difference perspective. *Journal of Personality and Social Psychology, 51*, 1032–1043.

Chaiken, S. (1980). Heuristic versus systematic information processing in the use of source versus message quest in persuasion. *Journal of Personality and Social Psychology, 39*, 752–766.

Chaiken, S. (1987). The heuristic model of persuasion. In M. P. Zanna, J. Olson, & C. P. Herman (Eds.), *Social influence: The Ontario symposium* (Vol. 5, pp. 3–39). Hillsdale, NJ: Erlbaum.

Chaiken, S., Liberman, A., & Eagly, A. H. (1989). Heuristic and systematic processing within and beyond the persuasion context. In J. S. Uleman & J. A. Bargh (Eds.), *Unintended thought* (pp. 212–252). New York: Guilford Press.

Chaiken, S., & Maheswaran, D. (1994). Heuristic processing can bias systematic processing: Effects of source credibility, argument ambiguity, and task importance on attitude judgment. *Journal of Personality and Social Psychology, 66*, 460–473.

Chaiken, S., & Trope, Y. (Eds.) (1999). *Dual process theories in social psychology.* New York: Guilford Press.

Clark, J. K., Wegener, D. T., & Fabrigar, L. R. (2008). Attitudinal ambivalence and message-based persuasion: Motivated processing of proattitudinal information and avoidance of counterattitudinal information. *Personality and Social Psychology Bulletin, 34*, 565–577.

Cohen, G., Aronson, J., & Steele, C. (2000). When beliefs yield to evidence: Reducing biased evaluation by affirming the self. *Personality and Social Psychology Bulletin, 26*, 1151–1164.

Cooper, J. (2007). *Cognitive dissonance: 50 years of a classic theory.* London: Sage.

Cooper, J., & Fazio, R. H. (1984). A new look at dissonance theory. In L. Berkowitz (Ed.), *Advances in Experimental social Psychology* (Vol. 17). New York: Academic Press.

Crano, W. D., & Chen, X. (1998). The leniency contract and persistence of majority and minority influence. *Journal of Personality and Social Psychology, 6*, 1437–1450.

Cunningham, W. A., Packer, D. J., Kesek, A., & Van Bavel, J. J. (2009). Implicit measurement of attitudes: A physiological approach. In R. E. Petty, R. H. Fazio, & P. Briñol (Eds.), *Attitudes: Insights from the new implicit measures* (pp. 485–512). New York: Psychology Press.

Dasgupta, N., & Greenwald, A. G. (2001). On the malleability of automatic attitudes: Combating automatic prejudice with images of admired and disliked individuals. *Journal of Personality and Social Psychology, 81*, 800–814.

Dasgupta, N., & Rivera, L. M. (2008). When social context matters: The influence of long-term contact and short-term exposure to admired outgroup members on implicit attitudes and behavioral intentions. *Social Cognition, 26*, 112–123.

DeBono, K. G., & Harnish, R. J. (1988). Source expertise, source attractiveness, and processing or persuasive information: A functional approach. *Journal of Personality and Social Psychology, 55*, 541–546.

Deci, E. L. (1995). *Why we do what we do.* New York: Putnam.

De Houwer, J. (2009). Comparing measures of attitudes at the functional and procedural level: Analysis and implications. In R. E. Petty, R. H. Fazio, & P. Briñol (Eds.), *Attitudes: Insights from the new implicit measures* (pp. 361–390). New York: Psychology Press.

De Houwer, J., Thomas, S., & Baeyens, F. (2001). Associative learning of likes and dislikes: A review of 25 years of research on human evaluative conditioning. *Psychological Bulletin, 127*, 853–869.

de Liver, Y., van der Pligt, J., & Wigboldus, D. (2007). Positive and negative associations underlying ambivalent attitudes. *Journal of Experimental Social Psychology, 43*, 319–326.

DeSteno, D., Petty, R. E., Rucker, D. D., Wegener, D. T., & Braverman, J. (2004). Discrete emotions and persuasion: The role of emotion-induced expectancies. *Journal of Personality and Social Psychology, 86*, 43–56.

DeSteno, D., Petty, R. E., Wegener, D. T., & Rucker, D. D. (2000). Beyond valence in the perception of likelihood: The role of emotion specificity. *Journal of Personality and Social Psychology, 78*, 397–416.

Deutsch, R., & Strack, F. (2006). Duality models in social psychology: From dual processes to interacting systems. *Psychological Inquiry, 17*, 166–172.

Devine, P. G. (1989). Stereotypes and prejudice: Their automatic and controlled components. *Journal of Personality and Social Psychology, 56*, 5–18.

Dijksterhuis, A. (2004). I like myself but I don't know why: Enhancing implicit self- esteem by subliminal evaluative conditioning. *Journal of Personality and Social Psychology, 86*, 345–355.

Dovidio, J., Kawakami, K., Johnson, C., Johnson, B., & Howard, A. (1997). The nature of prejudice: Automatic and controlled processes. *Journal of Experimental Social Psychology, 33*, 510–540.

Eagly A. H., & Chaiken, S. (1993). *The psychology of attitudes*. Fort Worth, TX: Harcourt, Brace, Jovanovich.

Elms, A. C. (1966). Influence of fantasy ability on attitude change through role playing. *Journal of Personality and Social Psychology, 4*, 36–43.

Fazio, R. H. (1990). Multiple processes by which attitudes guide behavior: The MODE model as an integrative framework. In M. Zanna (Ed.), *Advances in experimental social psychology* (Vol. 23, pp. 75–109). San Diego, CA: Academic Press.

Fazio, R. H. (1995). Attitudes as object-evaluation associations: Determinants, consequences, and correlates of attitude accessibility. In R. E. Petty & J. A. Krosnick (Eds.), *Attitude strength: Antecedents and consequences* (pp. 247–283). Hillsdale, NJ: Erlbaum.

Fazio, R. H., & Olson, M. (2003). Implicit measures in social cognition research: Their meaning and uses. *Annual Review of Psychology, 54*, 297–327.

Fazio, R. H., Sanbonmatsu, D. M., Powell, M. C., & Kardes, F. R. (1986). On the automatic activation of attitudes. *Journal of Personality and Social Psychology, 50*, 229–238.

Fazio, R. H., & Williams, C. J. (1986). Attitude accessibility as a moderator of the attitude-perception and attitude-behavior relations: An investigation of the 1984 presidential election. *Journal of Personality and Social Psychology, 51*, 505–514.

Fazio, R. H., & Zanna, M. P. (1978). Attitudinal qualities relating to the strength of the attitude-behavior relationship. *Journal of Experimental Social Psychology, 14*, 398–408.

Fazio, R. H., & Zanna, M. P. (1981). Direct experience and attitude-behavior consistency. *Advances in Experimental Social Psychology, 14*, 161–202.

Fazio, R. H., Zanna, M. P., & Cooper, J. (1977). Dissonance and self-perception: An integrative view of each theory's proper domain of application. *Journal of Experimental Social Psychology, 13*, 464–479.

Festinger, L. (1954). A theory of social comparison processes. *Human Relations, 7*, 117–140.

Festinger, L. (1957). *A theory of cognitive dissonance*. Stanford, CA: Stanford University Press.

Festinger, L., & Carlsmith, J. M. (1959). Cognitive consequences of forced compliance. *Journal of Abnormal and Social Psychology, 58*, 203–210.

Fishbein, M., & Ajzen, I. (1975). *Belief, attitude, intention, and behavior*. Reading, MA: Addison-Wesley.

Fishbein, M., & Ajzen, I. (1981). Acceptance, yielding and impact: Cognitive processes in persuasion. In R. E. Petty, T. M. Ostrom, and T. C. Brock (Eds.), *Cognitive responses in persuasion* (pp. 339–359). Hillsdale, NJ: Erlbaum.

Fleming, M. A., & Petty, R. E. (2000). Identity and persuasion: An elaboration likelihood approach. In D. J. Terry & M. A. Hogg (Eds.), *Attitudes, behavior, and social context: The role of norms and group membership* (pp. 171–199). Mahwah, NJ: Erlbaum.

Forehand, M. R., & Perkins, A. (2005). Implicit assimilation and explicit contrast: A set/reset model of response to celebrity voiceovers. *Journal of Consumer Research, 32*, 435–441.

Forgas, J. P. (1995). Mood and judgment: The Affect Infusion Model (AIM). *Psychological Bulletin*, 117, 39–66.

Friedrich, J., Fetherstonhaugh, D., Casey, S., & Gallagher, D. (1996). Argument integration and attitude change: Suppression effects in the integration of one-sided arguments that vary in persuasiveness. *Personality and Social Psychology Bulletin, 22*, 179–191.

Gawronski, B., & Bodenhausen, G. V. (2005). Accessibility effects on implicit social cognition: The role of knowledge activation and retrieval experiences. *Journal of Personality and Social Psychology, 89*, 672–685.

Gawronski, B., & Bodenhausen, V. (2006). Associative and propositional processes in evaluation: An integrative review of implicit and explicit attitude change. *Psychological Bulletin, 132*, 692–731.

Glaser, J., & Banaji, M. R. (1999). When fair is foul and foul is fair: Reverse priming in automatic evaluation. *Journal of Personality and Social Psychology, 77*, 669–687.

Gouaux, C. (1971). Induced affective states and interpersonal attraction. *Journal of Personality and Social Psychology, 29*, 37–43.

Greenwald, A. G. (1968). Cognitive learning, cognitive response to persuasion, and attitude change. In A. Greenwald, T. Brock, & T. Ostrom (Eds.), *Psychological foundations of attitudes*. New York: Academic Press.

Greenwald, A. G., & Albert, R. D. (1968). Acceptance and recall of improvised arguments. *Journal of Personality and Social Psychology, 8*, 31–34.

Greenwald, A. G., Poehlman, T. A., Uhlmann, E. L., & Banaji, M. R. (2009). Understanding and using the Implicit Association Test: III. Meta-analysis of predictive validity. *Journal of Personality and Social Psychology, 97*, 17–41.

Greenwald, A. G., & Ronis, D. L. (1978). Twenty years of cognitive dissonance: Case study of the evolution of a theory. *Psychological Review, 85*, 53–57.

Gross, S. R., Holtz, R., & Miller, N. (1995). Attitude certainty. In R. E. Petty & J. A. Krosnick (Eds.), *Attitude strength: Antecedents and consequences* (pp. 215–245). Hillsdale, NJ: Erlbaum.

Grush, J. E. (1976). Attitude formation and mere exposure phenomena: A non-artificial explanation of empirical findings. *Journal of Personality and Social Psychology, 33*, 281–290.

Hänze, M. (2001). Ambivalence, conflict, and decision making: Attitudes and feelings in Germany towards NATO's military intervention in the Kosovo war. *European Journal of Social Psychology, 31*, 693–706.

Harkins, S. G., & Petty, R. E. (1981). The effects of source magnification of cognitive effort on attitudes: An information processing view. *Journal of Personality and Social Psychology, 40*, 401–413.

Harmon-Jones, E., & Harmon-Jones, C. (2008). Action-based model of dissonance: A review of behavioral, anterior cingulate and prefrontal cortical mechanisms. *Social and Personality Psychology Compass, 2/3*, 1518–1538.

Harmon-Jones, E., & Mills, J. S. (Eds.) (1999). *Cognitive dissonance: Progress on a pivotal theory in social psychology*. Washington, DC: American Psychological Association.

Hass, R. G., Katz, I., Rizzo, N., Bailey, J., & Moore, J. (1992). When racial ambivalence evokes negative affect using a disguised measure of feelings. *Personality and Social Psychology Bulletin, 18*, 786–797.

Haugtvedt, C. P., & Petty, R. E. (1992). Personality and persuasion: Need for cognition moderates the persistence and resistance of attitude changes. *Journal of Personality and Social Psychology, 63*, 308–319.

Heesacker, M. H., Petty, R. E., & Cacioppo, J. T. (1983). Field dependence and attitude change: Source credibility can alter persuasion by affecting message-relevant thinking. *Journal of Personality, 51*, 653–666.

Heider, F. (1958). *The psychology of interpersonal relations*. New York: Wiley.

Higgins, E. T. (1987). Self-discrepancy: A theory relating self and affect. *Psychological Review, 94*, 319–340.

Horcajo, J., Petty, R. E., & Briñol, P. (2009). *The effects of minority influence on indirect automatic evaluations*. Unpublished manuscript.

Hovland, C. I., Janis, I. L., & Kelley, H. H. (1953). *Communication and persuasion: Psychological studies of opinion change*. New Haven, CT: Yale University Press.

Howard, D. J. (1990). Rhetorical question effects on message processing and persuasion: The role of information availability and the elicitation of judgment. *Journal of Experimental Social Psychology, 26*, 217–239.

Huesmann, L. R., Eron, L. D., Klein, R., Brice, P., & Fischer, P. (1983). Mitigating the imitation of aggressive behaviors by changing children's attitudes about media violence. *Journal of Personality and Social Psychology, 44*, 899–910.

Jacoby, L. L., Kelley, C. M., Brown, J., & Jasechko, J. (1989). Becoming famous overnight: Limits on the ability to avoid unconscious influences of the past. *Journal of Personality and Social Psychology, 56*, 326–338.

Janis, I. L., & King, B. T. (1954). The influence of role-playing on opinion change. *Journal of Abnormal and Social Psychology, 49*, 211–218.

Johnson, B. T., Smith-McLallen, A., Killeya, L. A., & Levin, K. D. (2004). Truth or consequences: Overcoming resistance to persuasion with positive thinking. In E. S. Knowles & J. A. Linn (Eds.), *Resistance and persuasion*. Mahwah, NJ: Erlbaum.

Jonas, K., Diehl, M., & Bromer, P. (1997). Effects of attitudinal ambivalence on information processing and attitude-intention consistency. *Journal of Experimental Social Psychology, 33*, 190–210.

Jones, C. R., Fazio, R. H., & Olson, M. A. (2009). Implicit misattribution as a mechanism underlying evaluative conditioning. *Journal of Personality and Social Psychology, 96*, 933–948.

Kelman, H. C., & Hovland, C. I. (1953). "Reinstatement" of the communicator in delayed measurement of opinion change. *Journal of Abnormal and Social Psychology, 48*, 327–335.

Kiesler, C.A. (1971). *The psychology of commitment: Experiments linking behavior to beliefs*. New York: Academic Press.

Knowles, E. S., & Linn, J. A. (Eds.) (2004). *Resistance and persuasion*. Mahwah, NJ: Erlbaum.

Kruglanski, A. W., Freund, T., & Bar-Tal, D. (1996). Motivational effects in the mere-exposure paradigm. *European Journal of Social Psychology, 26*, 479–499.

Kruglanski, A. W., Raviv, A., Bar-Tal, D., Raviv, A., Sharvit, K., Ellis, S., Bar, R., Pierro, A., & Mannetti, L. (2005). Says who? Epistemic authority effects in social judgment. In M. P. Zanna (Ed.), *Advances in experimental social psychology* (Vol. 37, pp. 346–392). San Diego, CA: Academic Press.

Kruglanski, A. W., & Thompson, E. P. (1999). Persuasion by a single route: A view from the unimodel. *Psychological Inquiry, 10*, 83–110.

Kruglanski, A.W., & Webster, D.M., (1996). Motivated closing of the mind: Seizing and Freezing. *Psychological Review, 103*, 263–283.

Kunst-Wilson, W. R., & Zajonc, R. B. (1980). Affective discrimination of stimuli that cannot be recognized. *Science, 207*, 557–558.

Leippe, M. R., & Elkin, R. A. (1987). When motives clash: Issue involvement and response involvement as determinants of persuasion. *Journal of Personality and Social Psychology, 52*, 269–278.

Lepper, M. R., Greene, D., & Nisbett, R. E. (1973). Undermining children's intrinsic interest with extrinsic reward: A test of the "over justification" hypothesis. *Journal of Experimental Social Psychology, 28,* 129–137.

Mackie, D. M. (1987). Systematic and nonsystematic processing of majority and minority persuasive communications. *Journal of Personality and Social Psychology, 53,* 41–52.

Maddux, W. W., Barden, J., Brewer, M. B., & Petty, R. E. (2005). Saying no to negativity: The effects of context and motivation to control prejudice on automatic evaluative responses. *Journal of Experimental Social Psychology, 41,* 19–35.

Maio, G. R., Bell, D. E., & Esses, V. M. (1996). Ambivalence and persuasion: The processing of messages about immigrant groups. *Journal of Experimental Social Psychology, 32,* 513–536.

Martin, D. G., & Levey, A. B. (1978). Evaluative conditioning. *Advances in Behavior Research and Therapy, 1,* 57–102.

Martin, L. L. (2000). Moods do not convey information: Moods in context do. In J. P. Forgas (Ed.), *Feeling and thinking: The role of affect in social cognition* (pp. 153–177). Cambridge, UK: Cambridge University Press.

McConnell, A. R., Rydell, R. J., Strain, L. M., & Mackie, D. M. (2008). Forming implicit and explicit attitudes toward individuals: Social group association cues. *Journal of Personality and Social Psychology, 94,* 792–807.

McGuire, W. J. (1964). Inducing resistance to persuasion: Some contemporary approaches. In L. Berkowitz (Ed.), *Advances in experimental social psychology* (Vol. 1, pp. 191–229). New York: Academic Press.

McGuire, W. J. (1968). Personality and attitude change: An information-processing theory. In A. G. Greenwald, T. C. Brock, & T. M. Ostrom (Eds.), *Psychological foundations of attitudes* (pp. 171–196). New York: Academic Press.

McGuire, W. J. (1981). The probabilogical model of cognitive structure and attitude change. In R. E. Petty, T. M. Ostrom, & T. C. Brock (Eds.), *Cognitive responses in persuasion* (pp. 291–307). Hillsdale, NJ: Erlbaum.

McGuire, W. J. (1985). Attitudes and attitude change. In G. Lindzey & E. Aronson (Eds.), *Handbook of social psychology* (3rd ed., Vol. 2, pp. 233–346). New York: Random House.

Miniard, P., Bhatla, S., Lord, K.R., Dickson, P. R., & Unnava. H. R. (1991). Picture-based persuasion processes and the moderating role of involvement. *Journal of Consumer Research, 18,* 92–107.

Monahan, J. L., Murphy, S. T., & Zajonc, R. B. (2000). Subliminal mere exposure: Specific, general, and diffuse effects. *Psychological Science, 11,* 462–466.

Moore, D. L., Hausknecht, D., & Thamodaran, K. (1986). Time pressure, response opportunity, and persuasion. *Journal of Consumer Research, 13,* 85–99.

Moscovici, S., Mucchi-Faina, A., & Maass, A. (1994). *Minority influence.* Chicago, IL: Nelson-Hall Publishers.

Mugny, G., & Perez, J. A. (1991). *The social psychology of minority influence.* Cambridge, UK: Cambridge University Press.

Newcomb, T. M. (1968). Interpersonal balance. In R. Abelson et al. (Eds.), *Theories of cognitive consistency: A sourcebook.* Chicago: Rand McNally.

Nordgren, L. F., van Harreveld, F., & van der Pligt, J. (2006). Ambivalence, discomfort, and motivated information processing. *Journal of Experimental Social Psychology, 42,* 252–258.

Olson, M. A., Fazio, R. H. (2001). Implicit attitude formation through classical conditioning. *Psychological Science, 12,* 413–417.

Osgood, C. E., & Tannenbaum, P. H. (1955). The principle of congruity in the prediction of attitude change. *Psychological Review 62,* 42–55.

Petty, R. E. (1997). The evolution of theory and research in social psychology: From single to multiple effect and process models. In C. McGarty & S. A. Haslam (Eds.), *The message of social psychology: Perspectives on mind in society* (pp. 268–290). Oxford, UK: Blackwell Publishers, Ltd.

Petty, R. E., & Briñol, P. (2006a). Understanding social judgment: Multiple systems and processes. *Psychological Inquiry, 17,* 217–223.

Petty, R. E., & Briñol, P. (2006b). A meta-cognitive approach to "implicit" and "explicit" evaluations: Comment on Gawronski and Bodenhausen (2006). *Psychological Bulletin, 132,* 740–744.

Petty, R. E., & Briñol, P. (2008). Persuasion: From single to multiple to meta-cognitive processes. *Perspectives on Psychological Science, 3,* 137–147.

Petty, R. E., & Briñol, P. (2009). Implicit ambivalence: A meta-cognitive approach. In R. E. Petty, R. H. Fazio, & P. Briñol (Eds.), *Attitudes: Insights from the new implicit measures* (pp. 119–161). New York: Psychology Press.

Petty, R. E., & Briñol, P. (2010). Attitude structure and change: Implications for implicit measures. In B. Gawronski & B. K. Payne (Eds.), *Handbook of implicit social cognition: Measurement, theory, and applications.* New York: Guilford Press.

Petty, R. E., Briñol, P., & DeMarree, K. G. (2007). The meta-cognitive model (MCM) of attitudes: Implications for attitude measurement, change, and strength. *Social Cognition, 25,* 657–686.

Petty, R. E., Briñol, P., Loersch, C., & McCaslin, M. J. (2009). The need for cognition. In M. R. Leary & R. H. Hoyle (Eds.), *Handbook of individual differences in social behavior* (pp. 318–329). New York: Guilford Press.

Petty, R. E., Briñol, P., & Tormala, Z. L. (2002). Thought confidence as a determinant of persuasion: The self-validation hypothesis. *Journal of Personality and Social Psychology, 82,* 722–741.

Petty, R. E., Briñol, P., Tormala, Z. L., & Wegener, D. T. (2007). The role of meta-cognition in social judgment. In E. T. Higgins & A. W. Kruglanski (Eds.), *Social psychology: A handbook of basic principles* (2nd ed., pp. 254–284). New York: Guilford Press.

Petty, R. E., & Cacioppo, J. T. (1979a). Issue-involvement can increase or decrease persuasion by enhancing message-relevant cognitive responses. *Journal of Personality and Social Psychology, 37,* 1915–1926.

Petty, R. E., & Cacioppo, J. T. (1979b). Effects of forewarning of persuasive intent on cognitive responses and persuasion. *Personality and Social Psychology Bulletin, 5*, 173–176.

Petty, R. E., & Cacioppo, J. T. (1981). *Attitudes and persuasion: Classics and contemporary approaches*. Dubuque, IA: Win C. Brown.

Petty, R. E., & Cacioppo, J. T. (1984a). The effects of involvement on responses to argument quantity and quality: Central and peripheral routes to persuasion. *Journal of Personality and Social Psychology, 46*, 69–81.

Petty, R. E., & Cacioppo, J. T. (1984b). Source factors and the elaboration likelihood model of persuasion. *Advances in Consumer Research, 11*, 668–672.

Petty, R. E., & Cacioppo, J. T. (1986). *Communication and persuasion: Central and peripheral routes to attitude change*. New York: Springer-Verlag.

Petty, R. E., & Cacioppo, J. T. (1990). Involvement and persuasion: Tradition versus integration. *Psychological Bulletin, 107*, 367–374.

Petty, R. E., Cacioppo, J. T., & Goldman, R. (1981). Personal involvement as a determinant of argument-based persuasion. *Journal of Personality and Social Psychology, 41*, 847–855.

Petty, R. E., Cacioppo, J. T., & Heesacker, M. (1981). The use of rhetorical questions in persuasion: A cognitive response analysis. *Journal of Personality and Social Psychology, 40*, 432–440.

Petty, R. E., Fazio, R. H., & Briñol, P., (2009a). The new implicit measures: An overview. In R. E. Petty, R. H. Fazio, & P. Briñol (Eds.), *Attitudes: Insights from the new implicit measures* (pp. 3–18). New York: Psychology Press.

Petty, R. E., Fazio, R. H., & Briñol, P. (Eds.) (2009b). *Attitudes: Insights from the new implicit measures*. New York: Psychology Press.

Petty, R. E., Harkins, S. G., & Williams, K. D. (1980). The effects of group diffusion of cognitive effort on attitudes: An information processing view. *Journal of Personality and Social Psychology, 38*, 81–92.

Petty, R. E., Haugtvedt, C., & Smith, S. M. (1995). Elaboration as a determinant of attitude strength: Creating attitudes that are persistent, resistant, and predictive of behavior. In R. E. Petty & J. A. Krosnick (Eds.), *Attitude strength: Antecedents and consequences* (pp. 93–130). Mahwah, NJ: Erlbaum.

Petty, R. E., Ostrom, T. M., & Brock, T. C. (1981). *Cognitive responses in persuasion*. Hillsdale, NJ: Erlbaum.

Petty, R. E., Schumann, D. W., Richman, S. A., & Strathman, A. J. (1993). Positive mood and persuasion: Different roles for affect under high and low elaboration conditions. *Journal of Personality and Social Psychology, 64*, 5–20.

Petty, R. E., Tormala, Z. L., Briñol, P., & Jarvis, W. B. G. (2006). Implicit ambivalence from attitude change: An exploration of the PAST model. *Journal of Personality and Social Psychology, 90*, 21–41.

Petty, R. E., Tormala, Z. L., & Rucker, D. D. (2004). Resisting persuasion by counterarguing: An attitude strength perspective. In J. T. Jost, M. R. Banaji, & D. A. Prentice

(Eds.), *Perspectivism in social psychology: The yin and yang of scientific progress* (pp. 37–51). Washington, DC: American Psychological Association.

Petty, R. E., & Wegener, D. T. (1993). Flexible correction processes in social judgment: Correcting for context-induced contrast. *Journal of Experimental Social Psychology, 29,* 137–165.

Petty, R. E., & Wegener, D. T. (1998). Attitude change: Multiple roles for persuasion variables. In D. Gilbert, S. Fiske, & G. Lindzey (Eds.), *The handbook of social psychology* (4th ed., Vol. 1, pp. 323–390). New York: McGraw-Hill.

Petty, R. E., Wegener, D. T., & White, P. (1998). Flexible correction processes in social judgment: Implications for persuasion. *Social Cognition, 16,* 93–113.

Petty, R. E., Wells, G. L., & Brock, T. C. (1976). Distraction can enhance or reduce yielding to propaganda: Thought disruption versus effort justification. *Journal of Personality and Social Psychology, 34,* 874–884.

Priester, J. M., & Petty, R. E. (1995). Source attributions and persuasion: Perceived honesty as a determinant of message scrutiny. *Personality and Social Psychology Bulletin, 21,* 637–654.

Puckett, J. M., Petty, R. E., Cacioppo, J. T., & Fisher, D. L. (1983). The relative impact of age and attractiveness stereotypes on persuasion. *Journal of Gerontology, 38,* 340–343.

Raden, D. (1989). Are scores on conventional attitude scales confounded with other measures of attitude strength? Findings from the General Social Survey. *Psychological Reports, 64,* 1247–1252.

Ratneshwar, S., & Chaiken, S. (1991). Comprehension's role in persuasion: The case of its moderating effect on the persuasive impact of source cues. *Journal of Consumer Psychology, 18,* 52–62.

Rhodes, N., & Wood, W. (1992). Self-esteem and intelligence affect influenciability: The mediating role of message reception. *Psychological Bulletin, 111,* 156–171.

Ronis, D. L., Baumgardner, M. H., Leippe, M. R., Cacioppo, J. T., & Greenwald, A. G. (1977). In search of reliable persuasion effects: I. A computer-controlled procedure for studding persuasion. *Journal of Personality and Social Psychology, 35,* 548–569.

Rosenberg, M. J. (1960). An analysis of affective-cognitive consistency. In C. I. Hovland, & M. J. Rosenberg (Eds.), *Attitude organization and change: An analysis of consistency among attitude components* (pp. 15–64). New Haven, CT: Yale University Press.

Ross, M., McFarland, C., Conway, M., & Zanna, M. P. (1983). Reciprocal relation between attitudes and behavior recall: Committing people to newly formed attitudes. *Journal of Personality and Social Psychology, 45,* 257–267.

Rucker, D. D., Petty, R. E., & Briñol, P. (2008). What's in a frame anyway? A meta-cognitive analysis of the impact of one versus two sided message framing on attitude certainty. *Journal of Consumer Psychology, 18,* 137–149.

Rydell, R. J., McConnell, A. R., & Mackie, D. M. (2008). Consequences of discrepant explicit and implicit attitudes: Cognitive dissonance and increased information processing. *Journal of Experimental Social Psychology, 44,* 1526–1532.

Sassenberg, K., & Wieber, F. (2005). Don't ignore the other half: The impact of ingroup identification on implicit measures of prejudice. *European Journal of Social Psychology, 35*, 621–632.

Scher, S. J., & Cooper, J. (1989). Motivational basis of dissonance: The singular role of behavioural consequences. *Journal of Personality and Social Psychology, 56*, 899–906.

Schwarz, N. (1998). Accessible content and accessibility experiences: The interplay of declarative and experiential information in judgment. *Personality and Social Psychology Review, 2*, 87–99.

Schwarz, N. (2004). Meta-cognitive experiences in consumer judgment and decision making. *Journal of Consumer Psychology, 14*, 332–348.

Schwarz, N., Bless, H., & Bohner, G. (1991). Mood and persuasion: Affective status influence the processing of persuasive communications. In M. Zanna (Ed.), *Advances in experimental social psychology* (Vol. 24, pp. 161–197). San Diego, CA: Academic Press.

Schwarz, N., Bless, H., Strack, F., Klumpp, G., Rittenauer-Schatka, H., & Simons, A. (1991). Ease of retrieval as information: Another look at the availability heuristic. *Journal of Personality and Social Psychology, 61*, 195–202.

See, Y. H. M., Petty, R. E., & Evans, L. M. (2009). The impact of perceived message complexity and need for cognition on information processing and attitudes. *Journal of Research in Personality, 43*, 880–889..

Shah, A. K., & Oppenheimer, D. M. (2008). Heuristics made easy: An effort reduction framework. *Psychological Bulletin, 134*(2), 207–222.

Sherman, D. K., & Cohen, G. L. (2006). The psychology of self-defense: Self-affirmation theory. In L. M. P. Zanna (Ed.), *Advances in experimental social psychology* (Vol. 38, pp. 183–242). San Diego, CA: Academic Press.

Sherman, S. J., Cialdini, R. B., Schwartzman, D. F., & Reynolds, K. D. (1985). Imagining can heighten or lower the perceived likelihood of contracting a disease: The mediating effect of ease of imagery. *Personality and Social Psychology Bulletin, 16*, 405–418.

Shimp, T. A., Stuart, W. W., & Engle, R. W. (1991). A program of classical conditioning experiments testing variations in the conditioned stimulus and context. *Journal of Consumer Research, 18*, 1–12.

Smith, S. M., & Shaffer, D. R. (1995). Speed of speech and persuasion: Evidence for multiple effects. *Personality and Social Psychology Bulletin, 21*, 1051–1060.

Snyder, M., & DeBono, K. G. (1985). Appeals to image and claims about quality: Understanding the psychology of advertising. *Journal of Personality and Social Psychology, 49*, 586–597.

Staats, A. W., & Staats, C. (1958). Attitudes established by classical conditioning. *Journal of Abnormal and Social Psychology, 67*, 159–167.

Staats, A. W., Staats, A. W., Crawford, H. L. (1962). First-order conditioning. *Journal of Abnormal and Social Psychology, 57*, 37–40.

Steele, C. M. (1988). The psychology of self-affirmation: Sustaining the integrity of the self. In L. Berkowitz (Ed.), *Advances in experimental social psychology* (Vol. 21, pp. 261–302). New York: Academic Press.

Stone, J., & Cooper, J. (2001). A self-standards model of cognitive dissonance. *Journal of Experimental Social Psychology, 37*, 228–243.

Stroebe, W., & Diehl, M. (1988). When social support fails: Supporter characteristics in compliance-induced attitude change. *Personality and Social Psychology Bulletin, 14*, 136–144.

Stuart, E. W., Shimp, T. A., & Engle, R. W. (1987). Classical conditioning of consumer attitudes: Four experiments in an advertising context. *Journal of Consumer Research, 14*, 334–349.

Swasy, J. L., & Munch, J. M. (1985). Examining the target of receiver elaborations: Rhetorical question effects on source processing and persuasion. *Journal of Consumer Research, 11*, 877–886.

Tesser, A. (1978). Self-generated attitude change. In L. Berkowitz (Ed.), *Advances in experimental social psychology* (Vol. 11, pp. 289–338). New York: Academic Press.

Tesser, A. (1988). Toward a self-evaluation maintenance model of social behavior. In L. Berkowitz (Ed.), *Advances in experimental social psychology* (Vol. 21, pp. 181–227). New York: Academic Press.

Tesser, A. (2001). On the plasticity of self-defense. *Current Directions in Psychological Science, 10*, 66–69.

Tesser, A., Martin, L., & Mendolia, M. (1995). The impact of thought on attitude extremity and attitude-behavior consistency. (pp. 73–92). In R. E. Petty & J. A. Krosnick (Eds.), *Attitude strength: Antecedents and consequences*. Mahwah, NJ: Erlbaum Associates.

Tice, D. M. (1992). Self-concept change and self-presentation: The looking glass self is also a magnifying glass. *Journal of Personality and Social Psychology, 63*, 435–451.

Tiedens, L. Z., & Linton, S. (2001). Judgment under emotional certainty and uncertainty: The effects of specific emotions on information processing. *Journal of Personality and Social Psychology, 81*, 973–988.

Tormala, Z. L., Briñol, P., & Petty, R. E. (2007). Multiple roles for source credibility under high elaboration: It's all in the timing. *Social Cognition, 25*, 536–552.

Tormala, Z. L., Falces, C., Briñol, P., & Petty, R. E. (2007). Ease of retrieval effects in social judgment: The role of unrequested cognitions. *Journal of Personality and Social Psychology, 93*, 143–157.

Tormala, Z.L., & Petty, R.E. (2002). What doesn't kill me makes me stronger: The effects of resisting persuasion on attitude certainty. *Journal of Personality and Social Psychology, 83*, 1298–1313.

Tormala, Z. L., Petty, R. E., & Briñol, P. (2002). Ease of retrieval effects in persuasion: A self-validation analysis. *Personality and Social Psychology Bulletin, 28*, 1700–1712.

Tversky, A., & Kahneman, D. (1974). Judgment under uncertainty: Heuristics and biases. *Science, 185*, 1124–1130.

van Harreveld, F., van der Pligt, J., & de Liver, Y. N. (2009). The agony of ambivalence and ways to resolve it: Introducing the MAID model. *Personality and Social Psychology Review, 13*, 45–61.

Walster, E., & Festinger, L. (1962). The effectiveness of "overheard" persuasive communications. *Journal of Personality and Social Psychology, 65*, 395–402.

Walther, E. (2002). Guilty by mere association: Evaluative conditioning and the spreading attitude effect. *Journal of Personality and Social Psychology, 82*, 919–934.

Watts, W. A. (1967). Relative persistence of opinion change induced by active compared to passive participation. *Journal of Personality and Social Psychology, 5*, 4–15.

Wegener, D. T., & Petty, R. E. (1994). Mood management across affective states: The hedonic contingency hypothesis. *Journal of Personality and Social Psychology, 66*, 1034–1048.

Wegener, D. T., & Petty, R. E. (1995). Flexible correction processes in social judgment: The role of naive theories in corrections for perceived bias. *Journal of Personality and Social Psychology, 68*, 36–51.

Wegener, D. T., & Petty, R. E. (1997). The flexible correction model: The role of naive theories of bias in bias correction. In M. P. Zanna (Ed.), *Advances in experimental social psychology* (Vol. 29, pp. 141–208). Mahwah, NJ: Erlbaum.

Wells, G. L., & Petty, R. E. (1980). The effects of overt head movements on persuasion: Compatibility and incompatibility of responses. *Basic and Applied Social Psychology, 1*, 219–230.

Wicklund, R. A. (1974). *Freedom and reactance*. Hillsdale, NJ: Erlbaum.

Wicklund, R. A., & Gollwitzer, P. M. (1982). *Symbolic self-completion*. Hillsdale, NJ: Erlbaum.

Wilson, T. D., & Brekke, N. (1994). Mental contamination and mental correction: Unwanted influences on judgments and evaluations. *Psychological Bulletin, 116*, 117–142.

Wittenbrink, B., & Schwarz, N. (Eds.). (2007). *Implicit measures of attitudes*. New York: Guilford Press.

Wood, W. (1982). Retrieval of attitude relevant information from memory: Effects on susceptibility to persuasion and on intrinsic motivation. *Journal of Personality and Social Psychology, 42*, 798–810.

Wood, W. W., Kallgren, C. A., & Preisler, R. M. (1985). Access to attitude relevant information in memory as a determinant of persuasion: The role of message attributes. *Journal of Personality and Social Psychology, 21*, 73–85

Wood, W., Rhodes, N., & Biek, M. (1995). Working knowledge and attitude strength: An information processing analysis. In R. E. Petty & J. A. Krosnick (Eds.), *Attitude strength: Antecedents and consequences*. Hillsdale, NJ: Erlbaum.

Zajonc, R. B. (1968). Attitudinal effects of mere exposure. *Journal of Personality and Social Psychology, 9*, 1–27.

Zanna, M. P., & Cooper, J. (1974). Dissonance and the pill: An attribution approach to studying the arousal properties of dissonance. *Journal of Personality and Social Psychology, 29*, 703–709.

Ziegler, R., Diehl, M., & Ruther, A. (2002). Multiple source characteristics and persuasion: Source inconsistency as a determinant of message scrutiny. *Personality and Social Psychology Bulletin, 28*, 496–508.

Part 3

Social Relations and Behaviors

Chapter 8

Prosocial Behavior

Michael E. McCullough and Benjamin A. Tabak

Chimpanzees are our closest living relatives, with 96% of our genetic code overlapping theirs (Varki & Nelson, 2007). This deep genetic similarity produces profound physical similarities—and also behavioral ones. These behavioral similarities are nowhere better illustrated than in the realm of prosocial behavior. Chimpanzees, like humans from hunter–gatherer societies, hunt cooperatively. Like humans, they patrol their territories in groups and engage in coordinated group violence against other groups (Wrangham & Peterson, 1996). Within groups, they form coalitions to defeat individuals too powerful for any of the coalition members to defeat on their own (de Waal, 1982), and males join forces to prevent each others' mates from straying (Silk et al., 2005). Individuals also make an effort to reconcile with valuable relationship partners with whom they have recently experienced conflict (Koski, Koops, & Sterck, 2007) and to comfort valuable relationship partners who have recently been the recipients of other individuals' aggressive behavior (Fraser, Stahl, & Aureli, 2008). In addition, chimpanzees recognize when they need a partner to obtain a desirable food item, and they know which potential partners are likely to be most helpful to them (Melis, Hare, & Tomasello, 2006). Evidence also suggests that chimpanzees, like humans, will help others gain access to desired items even when they cannot immediately benefit from a return favor (Warneken, Hare, Melis, Hanus, & Tomasello, 2007; Warneken & Tomasello, 2006).

But we cannot overlook that 4% uniqueness, which indicates that there are approximately 80 million genetic differences between humans and chimpanzees due to base pair differences and nucleotide additions or deletions (Varki & Nelson, 2007). That uniqueness leads to important differences in human and chimpanzee prosocial behavior. For example, chimpanzees show no preference for behaviors that enable others to acquire food when they are attempting to acquire food (Jensen, Hare, Call, & Tomasello, 2006; Silk et al., 2005), but such behavior is common among humans to the point of banality: If I'm going out to get lunch, I just might offer to pick something up for you. Moreover, human infants are better than chimpanzees at inferring humans' needs and then rendering appropriate forms of help (Warneken & Tomasello, 2006). Likewise, even though both humans and chimpanzees help others in some instances, it is humans and not chimpanzees that raise armies for the common defense, seek out training so that they can render more effective emergency aid to others, and endure taxation to provide help for the poor and needy. These important behavioral differences may reflect fundamental qualitative differences in evolved cognitive capacities such as delay of gratification (Stevens, Cushman, & Hauser, 2005), the ability to infer other people's mental states from their behavior and to act empathically on the basis of that knowledge (Liszkowski, Carpenter, & Tomasello, 2008), and the ability to generate and learn from culture (Richerson & Boyd, 2005). In this chapter, we will explore some of the more interesting features of humans' tendencies to engage in helping, sharing, and cooperating—that is, the behaviors collectively known as "prosocial behaviors" (Penner, Dovidio, Piliavin, & Schroeder, 2005). We will describe the classic social–psychological work on this topic, and also some of the more important recent theoretical and empirical advances, beginning with the evolutionary models that are sometimes invoked to explain humans' prosocial tendencies.

Evolutionary Models of Prosocial Behavior

Evolutionary researchers study the body's (brain/mind included) present structures by searching for the functions those structures evolved to serve in the past: Their project is usually (although not always; Andrews, Gangestad, & Matthews, 2002) an adaptationist one (Tooby & Cosmides, 2005; see Maner & Kenrick, Chapter 17, this volume). Adaptationism relies on the fact that individual *organisms* within a population that vary on a trait due to genotypic diversity can incur differing rates of genetic propagation (i.e., *fitness*) if some variants of the *trait* (and, therefore, the genes that contribute to their assembly during development) cause higher rates of reproduction than do others because of their ability to cause organisms to respond to specific adaptive challenges effectively. Because of these phenotype-dependent differences in fitness, small incremental changes in the genes that collectively give rise to the body's mechanisms (e.g., the heart, the fingernails, the brain's reward circuitry) that enhance the fitness of the bearer of those genes can gradually shape the species-typical structure of those mechanisms.

Because of natural selection's relentless favoritism for genes that enhance their bearers' fitness, prosocial behavior has been an evolutionary puzzle since Darwin (1952/1871): Incurring costs (even small costs in the currencies of money, time, or energy should redound to fitness) that benefit *someone else's* fitness (e.g., when someone saves a drowning child or donates blood for a stranger's benefit) at first glance appears to be bad evolutionary bookkeeping. Nevertheless, several evolutionary processes have been identified that can help explain the evolution of mental mechanisms for prosocial behavior in humans (McAndrew, 2002; Nowak, 2006; Wilson & Wilson, 2007). Here, we focus on the models that have (we think) the greatest potential to inform social psychology: kin altruism, direct reciprocity, indirect reciprocity, signaling, and group (or multilevel) selection. What makes these theories useful to social psychology is that they imply that the mind possesses specific functional systems that natural selection designed for their efficacy in producing certain types of prosocial behavior. If we understand the selection pressures we can formulate hypotheses about the operation of the psychological systems that evolved in response to those pressures and the social factors that activate and condition the operation of those systems.

Kin Altruism

Humans regularly endure tremendous energetic costs (e.g., gestation, nursing, feeding, sheltering, clothing, paying for college) to help their offspring and other genetic relatives. The theory of kin altruism explains such behaviors by exploiting the fact that one's fitness is not a function of the number of one's offspring that survive to reproductive maturity, but rather a function of the number of offspring one has *plus* the number of offspring that one's genetic relatives have (Hamilton, 1964). The theory of kin altruism specifies that certain forms of prosocial behavior that are beneficial to the recipient and costly to the helper can evolve when the benefit B to the individual being helped is greater than the cost C to the helper, discounted by a coefficient of relatedness r between the helper and the individual being helped (with $r = 1.0$ being the degree of relatedness between identical twins, $r = 0.5$ between first-degree relatives, $r = 0.25$ between grandparents and their grandchildren, or uncles and aunts and their nieces and nephews, and so on; Hamilton, 1964), which is equivalent to the likelihood that the recipient also possesses the helper's "altruism gene." In other words, specific forms of kin altruism are evolutionarily plausible when $C < rB$.

In support of Hamilton's (1964) model, people report more willingness to provide help (particularly biologically costly help) to closely related genetic relatives than to more distant ones (Bressan, 2009; Burnstein, Crandall, & Kitayama, 1994; Korchmaros & Kenny, 2001; Lieberman, Tooby, & Cosmides, 2007; Stewart-Williams, 2007). Estimates of migrant workers' remittances to their families back at home based on two factors—(1) the fitness costs the worker incurs by sending money back home and (2) the fitness benefits the worker receives via the enhanced fitness of the relatives who benefit from the remittance—account for roughly one-third of the variance in the amounts that those workers actually send home (Bowles & Posel, 2005).

If humans' penchant for prosocial behavior really did evolve in part via kin altruism, then the selection pressure for kin altruism should have left its imprint on the mind's cognitive architecture: If ancestral humans had been unable to reliably identify their genetic relatives, then their prosocial behavior could not have produced beneficial fitness consequences for them via Hamilton's (1964) rule. Lieberman, Tooby, and Cosmides (2007) outlined the workings of a hypothesized "kinship estimator" that computes the degree of relatedness between a potential beneficiary and the benefactor. Among siblings, the kinship estimator appears to use two ancestrally reliable cues: (1) the degree of "maternal perinatal association" (i.e., the amount of time that the individual was in a long-term perinatal relationship with his or her own mother) and (2) the degree of sibling coresidence (i.e., the amount of time that the two individuals lived together during childhood). When these cues imply a high degree of relatedness, the benefactor is more likely to help a person in need (Lieberman et al., 2007). The challenge of identifying one's kin seems trivial here only because we are thinking about humans—a species about which we all feel like experts rather than, say, lemurs (Charpentier, Boulet, & Drea, 2008), a species about which most of us know almost nothing.

The mind should also be sensitive to cues about the remaining reproductive potential of one's kin because it is partly through a relative's future reproductive potential that it is self-serving for people to provide costly help to their kin (Bowles & Posel, 2005). In support of this proposition, Burnstein et al. (1994) found that participants reported more willingness to provide costly help (e.g., saving someone from a fire) to relatives who were healthy (i.e., with greater potential for future reproduction) than to relatives who were not healthy (and whose future reproductive potential was therefore more limited).

Direct Reciprocity

The theory of direct reciprocity posits that mechanisms for prosocial behavior can evolve when the likelihood is greater than zero that the recipient of help will be disposed to help the benefactor in the future if the need arises (Nowak, 2006). Trivers (1971) first coined the term *reciprocal altruism* to describe this form of interaction, and demonstrated mathematically that under some conditions, behavioral systems for reciprocal altruism could evolve in social species.

A widely used paradigm for research on reciprocal altruism is the prisoner's dilemma (Rapoport & Chammah, 1965), in which two participants are presented with a choice either to cooperate with, or to defect against, their partner. If both partners cooperate, they receive a moderate reward (the so-called "reward for mutual cooperation"). If both partners defect, both earn a small payoff called the "punishment for mutual defection." If one individual defects and the other cooperates, the defector receives a large boon called the "temptation to defect" and the cooperator receives the smallest payoff—the "sucker's payoff."

Unconditional defection is the rational course of action in the prisoner's dilemma because it provides the best outcome both when one's partner defects and when one's partner cooperates. However, the prisoner's dilemma becomes more interesting when the two individuals play multiple rounds of the game rather than only one round, allowing them to make choices based on their partners' behavior in previous rounds. In a landmark study in which players from around the world submitted computer programs that would execute strategies for playing this so-called iterated prisoner's dilemma, Axelrod (1980) sought to determine which strategies would score the most points against all of the other strategies that were submitted.

A simple strategy called "tit-for-tat" emerged victorious. Tit-for-tat begins an iterated game with a cooperative move. If the partner also cooperates, then tit-for-tat continues to cooperate. If the partner defects on a given round, however, tit-for-tat will defect on the successive round. If the defecting player ever returns to cooperating, then tit-for-tat will also return to cooperating on the next round. Tit-for-tat has several characteristics that make it effective in iterated games: it is (1) "nice" (i.e., it begins by cooperating), (2) retaliatory (it responds to defection with defection), (3) forgiving (i.e., when a defecting partner returns to cooperation, it returns to cooperation as well, and (4) clear (i.e., its decisions are honest and easy to understand). It does well in iterated games with a wide variety of strategies not by dominating them, but by racking up relatively high tie scores in games with other opponents that are disposed to cooperate and by preventing more selfish strategies from getting the best of itself.

Axelrod and Hamilton (1981) demonstrated that the iterated prisoner's dilemma provides a game-theoretic model for the evolution of Trivers's (1971) reciprocal altruism. Nowak (2006) showed formally that direct reciprocity (as modeled in the prisoner's dilemma) can favor the evolution of cooperation in social species when the probability of a successive round of interaction between two interactants exceeds the ratio of the costs of the altruistic act to the benefactor divided by the value of the benefit to the recipient. The fact that much, if not most, of human social life (especially the social life of small groups of hunter–gatherers and, by extension, our ancestors) involves iterated games rather than single one-shot games may explain why people in (as far as we know) every society studied to date tend to be more generous and prosocial in economic games such as the prisoner's dilemma than standard economic theories for the one-shot prisoner's dilemma predict (Henrich et al., 2005; Hoffman, McCabe, & Smith, 1998; Simpson & Beckes, 2010).

Just as evolutionary psychologists interested in social behavior have deduced that the mind possesses specialized cognitive systems for computing kinship (Lieberman, Tooby, & Cosmides, 2007), they also have deduced that the mind possesses specialized cognitive machinery for detecting individuals who might cheat in the types of social contracts (i.e., "If you'll help me now, I'll help you later") that the prisoner's dilemma attempts to model (Cosmides, 1989; Cosmides & Tooby, 2005). Using a variant of the Wason Selection task (which illustrates that people are not very good at marshaling the right kinds of evidence to test the validity of logical statements of the form if *P*, then *Q*), Cosmides and Tooby (2005) showed that people are more accurate at testing evidence to determine whether particular individuals have cheated on a social contract. People's relatively good skill at detecting cheaters is as true of American undergraduates as it is of people from the Shiwiar, a remote society of hunter/horticulturalists in Amazonian Ecuador (Sugiyama, Tooby, & Cosmides, 2002).

Other researchers have proposed that gratitude might be part of the evolved psychological system that governs reciprocal altruism (McCullough, Kilpatrick, Emmons, & Larson, 2001; McCullough, Kimeldorf, & Cohen, 2008; Trivers, 1971). Gratitude is a reliable emotional response to receiving help from another person that was valuable to the self, costly to the donor, and intentionally rendered (Tesser, Gatewood, & Driver, 1968; Tsang, 2007). The experience of gratitude leads to reciprocation (Bartlett & DeSteno, 2006; Tsang, 2006) and strengthens relationships between benefactors and beneficiaries (Algoe, Haidt, & Gable, 2008).

Forgiveness might also be an important component of the evolved psychological apparatus that facilitates reciprocal altruism, and perhaps also kin altruism as well (McCullough, 2008; McCullough, Kurzban, & Tabak, 2010). In the context of reciprocal altruism in particular, responding to defections by occasionally forgiving them rather than retaliating can help to preserve cooperation when there is a possibility that individuals might make mistakes in implementing their prosocial intentions, or might mistake their partners' prosocial intentions for selfish ones (Van Lange, Ouwerkerk, & Tazelaar, 2002). People who forgive their relationship partners for interpersonal transgressions experience greater restorations of positive relations (Karremans & Van Lange, 2004; Tsang, McCullough, &

Fincham, 2006) and elicit prosocial behavior from partners who have transgressed (Kelln & Ellard, 1999; Wallace, Exline, & Baumeister, 2008). In support of the contention that the capacity to forgive was naturally selected on the basis of selection pressure for the maintenance of valuable relationships, people are more forgiving of relationships in which the transgressor and victim are close and committed (Finkel, Rusbult, Kumashiro, & Hannon, 2002; McCullough et al., 1998) and in which transgressors have communicated (e.g., through apologies or other expressions of remorse) their inability or unwillingness to harm the victim in the future (McCullough, Worthington, & Rachal, 1997), though these effects are more difficult to demonstrate experimentally between strangers in laboratory settings (Lount, Zhong, & Murnighan, 2008; Risen & Gilovich, 2007).

At the neural level, mutual cooperation during prisoner's dilemmas is supported by brain regions involved in motivating the pursuit of reward (e.g., nucleus accumbens, caudate nucleus, ventromedial frontal/orbitofrontal cortex, and rostral anterior cingulate cortex; Rilling et al., 2002; Rilling, Sanfey, Aronson, Nystrom, & Cohen, 2004), and is partially dependent on serotonin (Wood, Rilling, Sanfey, Bhagwagar, & Rogers, 2006).

Social psychologists have identified several other factors that influence cooperation in prisoner's dilemma-type situations. For example, the ability to communicate (and, therefore, coordinate) with an interaction partner fosters cooperation in prisoner's dilemma-like contexts (Kiesler, Sproull, & Waters, 1996; Steinfatt, 1973), especially when people can make mistakes in implementing their prosocial intentions (Tazelaar, Van Lange, & Ouwerkerk, 2004). In addition, people cooperate more with ingroup members than with outgroup members when sharing limited resources (Van Vugt, Snyder, Tyler, & Biel, 2000), perhaps because ingroup members are seen as more trusting than outgroup members (Turner, Oakes, Reicher, & Wetherell, 1987).

Indirect Reciprocity

The evolution of direct reciprocity requires a relatively high probability of future interactions among individuals who are taking turns helping each other, but there is a kind of prosocial behavior that can evolve even when the benefactor and beneficiary have zero likelihood of meeting again. *Indirect reciprocity* occurs when a benefactor acquires a good reputation for providing help to people in need; this encourages other individuals to help the benefactor in the future (Nowak, 2006). Experimental evidence shows that people tend to help, donate, or cooperate more frequently with individuals who have reputations for having been helpful or cooperative with others in the past (Seinen & Schram, 2006; Wedekind & Milinski, 2000).

According to Nowak (2006), when the probability q of knowing a benefactor's history of helpfulness toward others exceeds the ratio of the costliness of the benefactor's act of helping relative to its benefit to the recipient (c/b), natural selection favors the evolution of mechanisms that promote indirect reciprocity. Indirect reciprocity seems like an important candidate for explaining prosocial behavior in humans because our languages are replete with personality descriptors for conveying information about other people's generosity (e.g., soft-hearted) and stinginess (e.g., tight-fisted). Moreover, people are indeed more prosocial when their partners have the ability to spread information to others about their generosity and selfishness (Piazza & Bering, 2008; Sommerfeld, Krambeck, Semmann, & Milinski, 2007).

Signaling Theory

Signaling theory seeks to explain the evolution of prosocial behavior by virtue of its ability to convey information to others about a benefactor's hidden (i.e., genotypic) qualities (McAndrew, 2002), such as his or her intelligence, physical strength, resourcefulness, or value as a mate or coalition member (Gintis, Smith, & Bowles, 2001; Smith & Bleige Bird, 2001). A differential preference for associating with individuals who have signaled such hidden traits might provide benefits to benefactors that offset the costs of the generous behavior itself. In a signaling account of prosocial behavior, signalers receive fitness benefits from sending information, receivers benefit from decoding it and using it, and both signalers and receivers have evolved psychological systems that are dedicated to these purposes (Maynard Smith & Harper, 2003).

In support of signaling models for prosocial behavior, Iredale, Van Vugt, and Dunbar (2008) found that men were more generous in donating their earnings from a laboratory task to charity when a female observer was present than when a male observer or no observer was present, which led the researchers to propose that generosity in such contexts might result from a system design to advertise an otherwise hidden psychological quality (e.g., empathy or the ability to share) that was relevant to their mate value. Likewise, people are more cooperative with attractive than unattractive members of the opposite sex, and such cooperative behaviors makes cooperators seem particularly attractive (Farrelly, Lazarus, & Roberts, 2007).

Group (or Multilevel) Selection Theory

Another evolutionary model that has influenced recent research on prosocial behavior is the theory of group selection, increasingly known as "multilevel selection theory." For the first 60 years of the twentieth century, many biologists assumed that natural selection took place at the level of both individuals and groups, but with the publication of Williams's (1966) *Adaptation and Natural Selection*, the concept of group selection became anathema to evolutionary biologists on the grounds that, even if theoretically plausible, the assumptions governing its tenability were so restrictive as to make it ignorable in practice.

The assumptions of group selection have been revisited in recent years (Wilson & Wilson, 2007), and Williams himself (1992) went on to soften his position on the ignorability of group selection as an evolutionary force. Wilson and Wilson (2007) summarized the foundational claim of multilevel selection in this way: "Selfishness beats altruism within groups. Altruistic groups beat selfish groups" (p. 345). In the same way that individual-selection models of altruism posit that fitness benefits redound to individuals with prosocial phenotypes as a result of their prosocial behavior, group-selection or multilevel selection models posit that some fitness benefit redounds to *groups* with high levels of prosocial behavior relative to other groups. As a result, groups with higher levels of prosocial behavior will become more common whereas groups with lower levels of prosocial behavior will become less common.

Nowak (2006) explained that the mathematical feasibility of group-selection models of prosocial behavior requires more restrictive assumptions than other models do (for example, one must assume that as soon as a group reaches a certain size, it splits in two and one of the two resultant groups replaces another group within a population, with the consequence that the number of groups within a population remains constant). Although critical tests of the utility of multilevel (or group selection) theory for explaining the evolution of prosocial behavior in humans are difficult to specify, group-selection accounts of altruism require that altruists (1) can identify each other, (2) tend to preferentially associate with each other, and (3) outcompete groups of nonaltruists. These requirements appear to be fulfilled in social relations among children and adults (Gürerk, Irlenbusch, & Rockenbach, 2006; Pradel, Euler, & Fetchenhauer, 2009; Sheldon, Sheldon, & Osbaldiston, 2000).

Intermezzo on the Current Difficulty of Reconciling Functionalist and Nonfunctionalist Accounts of Prosocial Behavior

Social-psychological research on prosocial behavior predates psychologists' more recent interest in applying evolutionary concepts to prosocial behavior.

It can be jarring to move from the tight selectionist and functionalist logic of evolutionarily informed research on prosocial behavior to the constructs and theoretical apparatus that have historically driven social–psychological research on prosocial behavior, so readers should prepare for an abrupt transition to a rather different approach to the social psychology of prosocial behavior. Terminology is also used quite differently. For example, what biologists mean by *altruism* is very different from how that term is used in the mainstream social psychology literature.

It would be good to see some reconciliation between these two approaches to studying prosocial behavior, but the difficulty of doing so is compounded by the fact that the research fields with an interest in the evolution of prosocial behavior (e.g., economics, anthropology, ecology, and evolutionary biology) have themselves not reached consensus on many basic issues. For example, there is no consensus on how specific forms of prosocial behavior should be named and defined, how carefully the costs and benefits to interactants should be specified, the extent to which short-term benefits can be taken as proxies for lifetime reproductive fitness, and even whether a behavior should be described as "prosocial" if it did not evolve in response to selection pressures for prosocial behavior (West, Griffin, & Gardner, 2006). To wit, consider the elephant's production of dung (which dung beetles can then use to their benefit). Is the elephant behaving prosocially toward the dung beetle by producing dung? One should answer affirmatively unless one has defined prosocial behavior at the outset as "the output of a behavioral system that *evolved* to deliver benefits to others" (West, Griffin, & Gardner, 2006). One can hardly criticize social psychologists for failing to make more incisive contributions to the interdisciplinary science of prosocial behavior when those more evolutionarily minded disciplines' own conceptual house is in such disarray. We will not solve these problems here, but we will point out some places in which more conceptual clarity might help social psychology increase its impact on the interdisciplinary science of prosocial behavior.

Reciprocity and Fairness: Two Norms for Prosocial Behavior

One cannot go far in the history of research on the social psychology of prosocial behavior without encountering the concept of norms. Norms are written or unwritten rules for appropriate behavior that people internalize through direct punishment, direct reinforcement, or social learning (Batson, 1998; Gürerk, Irlenbusch, & Rockenbach, 2006; Weber & Murnighan, 2008), and they are regularly enforced in hunter–gatherer groups whose lives closely resemble those of ancestral humans (Boehm, 2008). Social psychologists have concentrated on two norms that help to explain many of the prosocial behaviors that are favored and for which violations are regularly punished cross-culturally: the norm of reciprocity and the norm of fairness.

The Norm of Reciprocity

The norm of reciprocity is the obligation to benefit (and refrain from harming) people from whom one has received benefits in the past (Gouldner, 1960). There is also a norm of negative reciprocity, thought to be equally universal and influential, that compels people to return harm for harm (Eisenberger, Lynch, Aselage, & Rohdieck, 2004). Reciprocity norms are believed to be cross-culturally universal features of humans' moral sensibilities (Brown, 1991; Triandis, 1978), and may reflect how the evolved psychological processes that govern effective reciprocal altruism (Axelrod, 1984) give rise to culture.

In an early study of the reciprocity norm, Pruitt (1968) showed that the amount of helping that people reciprocate in laboratory situations is (1) a direct function of the amount they had previously been given, (2) an inverse function of the total amount of resources the benefactor had to give, and (3) a direct function of the amount of resources the benefactor would have to give in the future. These findings suggest that people are motivated to provide benefits in order to repay debts—especially generous ones—and also to maintain their standing as good candidates for future exchange.

The Norm of Fairness

The norm of fairness reflects a deep aversion to unequal treatment. Brosnan and de Waal (2003) trained capuchin monkeys to exchange tokens for food, and they showed that after monkeys who had been trained to exchange tokens for pieces of cucumber witnessed other monkeys who were able to trade tokens for grapes (a more highly valued food item) the monkeys either (1) refused to continue trading tokens or (2) rejected the cucumber pieces completely. Likewise, people are much less cooperative in iterated prisoner's dilemmas when their partners systematically receive better payoffs than they do (Sheposh & Gallo, 1973). Anger and resentment are associated with feeling underbenefited (Hassebrauck, 1986), as is increased disapproval of the overbenefited partner (Sheposh & Gallo, 1973). Conversely, enhancing people's confidence that a public good will be distributed fairly among contributors increases contributions (Eek & Anders, 2003).

According to equity theory (Walster, Berscheid, & Walster, 1973; Walster, Walster, & Berscheid, 1978), people are motivated to preserve equity, which these theorists define as a state in which the ratio of outcomes to inputs is equal for all of the individuals involved in a relationship. A prediction from equity theory about Brosnan and de Waal's (2003) capuchin monkeys trading tokens for money is that the monkey receiving cucumber (the worse outcome) instead of grapes (the better outcome) could potentially be satisfied with that arrangement if the experimenters reduced the number of tokens needed to trade per unit of cucumber so that the two monkeys' ratios of outcomes (value received) to inputs (number of tokens traded) were equal. Things can be equitable even if they are not identical.

When people's cost/benefit ratios become markedly lower than those of their partners (i.e., when they are overbenefited), they often feel guilty (Austin, McGinn, & Susmilch, 1980) and become motivated to reduce the inequity. One prosocial thing partners who are feeling overbenefited might do to reduce the inequity is to try to help their partners increase their benefits or reduce their inputs. They might also engage in indirect prosocial behavior. Wayment (2004), for example, found that people who reported higher levels of survivor guilt and grief following the September 11 terrorist attacks engaged in collective helping more so than people who reported less survivor guilt and grief. Relatedly, Berscheid and Walster (1967) showed that people are motivated to provide benefits to people they have inadvertently harmed in proportion to the amount of harm done. Conversely, people who feel underbenefited relative to their inputs may respond to the perceived inequity in many ways, including reducing their effort, trying to renegotiate a better deal, or exiting the relationship and trying to find a new one.

Equity theory has been modified substantially since its initial formulation and has well-known limitations. For example, equity concerns are less salient in relationships with high degrees of interpersonal commitment and self-other overlap and in relationships for which partners have poor alternatives (Buunk & Bakker, 1997; Medvene, Teal, & Slavich, 2000; Rusbult, 1980, 1983). Nevertheless, equity retains *some* degree of importance even in highly committed relationships (Sprecher, 2001), especially when partners have an exchange orientation to the relationship or to relationships in general (Buunk & Van Yperen, 1991). It is also clear that people differ in the extent to which they are oriented toward a communal view of relationships (Clark, Ouellette, Powell, & Milberg, 1987), and these individual differences should be considered as important moderators of people's responses to inequity. Recently, Tabibnia, Satpute, and Lieberman (2008) made some progress in identifying brain regions that support calculations of fairness and unfairness in social exchange (viz., areas involved in reward computation and emotion regulation).

Motives for Prosocial Behavior

Social psychologists often study prosocial behavior by examining the motives that stimulate it. One of the greatest distinctions is between prosocial behavior that is motivated by so-called egoistic concerns and behavior that is motivated by so-called altruistic concerns (and it is here we see the term "altruism" used very differently from its usage in biology). Batson, Ahmad, Powell, and Stocks (2008) described three types of egoistic motivations for prosocial behavior: (1) the motivation to receive material, social, and self-administered rewards (such as payment, gifts, credit for future help from reciprocal altruism partners, enhanced self-esteem, or imagined religious rewards); (2) the motivation to avoid material, social, and self-administered punishments (e.g., fines/imprisonment, attacks, social sanctions for violating norms, or shame); and (3) the motivation to reduce aversive arousal (including distress associated with witnessing other people's pain and suffering).

Rather than assuming that every instance of helping has an egoistic motivation at its root, theorists from the altruistic tradition in social psychology hypothesize instead that "at least some of us, to some degree, under some circumstances, help with an ultimate goal of benefiting the person in need" (Batson, Ahmad, & Lishner, 2009, p. 417). (Evolutionarily minded readers will notice, too, the very different way in which the concept of "ultimate" is used in this quotation. Evolutionary thinkers would typically look for the ultimate causes of prosocial behavior in the selectionist models we enumerated earlier—all of which, ultimately, turn on the fact that mechanisms designed for prosocial behavior could have evolved only because their ultimate cause was that they increased the fitness of their bearer, on average, during evolution.) The number of egoistic models for prosocial motivation that have been advanced over the years is overwhelming, so here we limit ourselves to describing two of the more influential ones, plus an altruistic alternative and some of the critiques that have been leveled against it.

The Negative State Relief Model

Cialdini, Darby, and Vincent (1973) proposed a "negative state relief" model that specifies that people help others to reduce their own distress by experiencing the countervailing positive emotions that come from helping someone in need. These researchers found that people who had either (1) harmed someone or (2) witnessed someone experiencing harm (both of which presumably led to negative moods, although for different reasons) subsequently engaged in more prosocial behavior than did people in a control group who had not perpetrated or witnessed any transgressions against others—but only if they had not experienced an intervening situation that improved their moods (i.e., the receipt of money or social approval). Furthermore, there is evidence that under certain conditions, helping can elevate one's mood (Gebauer, Riketta, Broemer, & Maio, 2008; Midlarsky, 1991; Williamson & Clark, 1989). Conversely, several studies have also shown that inducing positive affect increases helping behaviors (Carlson, Charlin, & Miller, 1988), perhaps because people want to ensure that their good moods will not be spoiled by someone else's suffering (Batson, Ahmad, Powell, & Stocks, 2008).

The Arousal: Cost-Reward Model

Piliavin and colleagues (Dovidio, Piliavin, Gaertner, Schroeder, & Clark, 1991; Piliavin, Dovidio, Gaertner, & Clark, 1981) developed the "arousal: cost-reward theory" to explain when people are likely to help in emergency situations. The negative state relief model, however, involves helping to enhance one's mood—regardless of the reason for the bad mood; based on the arousal: cost-reward theory, emergency helping is the result of a motivation to eliminate the negative affect specifically due to witnessing the physical or emotional distress of the person in need.

The arousal: cost-reward theory specifies three conditions under which emergency assistance should be most likely. First, the more aversive arousal people feel in an emergency situation, the more likely they will be to provide help (Dovidio, 1984; Gaertner & Dovidio, 1977). Second, people will be more likely to help when the victim and the helper share similarities, common group identities, or feelings of relatedness or closeness. Third, the model specifies that emergency helping will be more likely when the costs of doing so are low relative to the hedonic rewards that will come from helping. When the costs of helping become too high—for example, if the person in need is bleeding and the helper may have to come in contact with blood (Piliavin & Piliavin, 1972), or when their levels of arousal are heightened by the fact that the person in need is of a different race than they are (Kunstman & Plant, 2008), people may choose other methods for reducing their negative arousal (e.g., trying to ignore the person's plight or leaving the scene) (Dovidio, Piliavin, Gaertner, Schroeder, & Clark, 1991).

The Empathy-Altruism Hypothesis

Batson and colleagues have repeatedly tested the hypothesis that humans have an "altruistic motivation" for helping that is reliably elicited by empathy for the person in need. Batson et al. (2009) define empathy as "an other-oriented emotional response elicited by and congruent with the perceived welfare of someone else" (p. 418). Empathy for another person can be enhanced by observing or imagining the person's affective state (de Vignemont & Singer, 2006), by sharing emotions, feelings or sensations (Preston & de Waal, 2002), by valuing another person's welfare (Batson, Eklund, Chermok, Hoyt, & Ortiz, 2007; Batson, Turk, Shaw, & Klein, 1995), and by recognition of kinship, similarity, or closeness (Cialdini, Brown, Lewis, Luce, & Neuberg, 1997). In the laboratory, empathy for complete strangers is elicited most commonly (and with the least apparent risk of confounding with other processes) through a two-step process: first, exposing a participant to someone else's need; and second, instructing the participant to imagine how the person in need is feeling (Batson, 1991; Batson, Turk, Shaw, & Klein, 1995). At the neural level the experience of empathy for someone in distress is supported by some of the same brain regions that are involved in the distress that people feel when experiencing pain or discomfort (e.g., bilateral anterior insula and rostral anterior cingulate cortex; Singer et al., 2004).

Empathy reliably elicits helping (Coke, Batson, & McDavis, 1978), but this fact does not imply that the motivation underlying empathy-induced helping is to improve the welfare of the person in need: The underlying goal could be, for example, reducing one's own empathic arousal, or avoiding social or self-imposed punishments associated with failing to help, or gaining social or self-approval. Batson and colleagues (and their detractors) have conducted more than 30 experiments to evaluate these motivations over the past several decades. In one of the earliest studies (Batson, Duncan, Ackerman, Buckley, & Birch, 1981), they induced empathy in participants by telling half of the sample that they had values and interests similar to a confederate named Elaine, who would be receiving random electric shocks as part of the experimental procedure. Before the study began, Elaine and the experimenter had a conversation (that they intended the participant to overhear) in which Elaine described her apprehension about receiving the shocks due to a traumatic event that she had experienced in the past. After two trials participants were then asked if they would be willing to trade places with Elaine to help her avoid more suffering.

To test an egoistic explanation derived from negative state relief theory, the researchers manipulated how difficult it was for the participants to escape the situation (in the easy escape condition, participants could finish the study after the first two trials; in the difficult escape condition, participants could not leave until all 10 trials were completed). Participants in the low-empathy group were more likely to opt out when doing so was easy; however, when it was difficult, half of them agreed to trade places with Elaine. In support of the empathy-altruism hypothesis, the majority of those in the high-empathy group agreed to trade places with Elaine irrespective of whether it was easy for them to escape.

Other experiments using perspective-taking manipulations of empathy (for review see Batson, 1991) have likewise demonstrated that inducing empathy causes people to help even when escape is easy, which suggests that participants are able to accomplish their empathically induced goal only by helping the participant (rather than by escaping the situation). These results cast doubt on the tenability of the hypothesis that the motivation underlying empathically induced helping is the escape of aversive arousal (Batson, Ahmad, Powell, & Stocks, 2008). Batson et al. (2009) likewise concluded that experiments testing the possibility that empathy-induced helping was motivated by the goal of avoiding social or self-administered punishments for failing to help have consistently supported the empathy-altruism hypothesis.

Research on the possibility that empathically induced helping has as its goal the rewards (either self-administered or from other people) associated with helping someone else has been a bit more controversial, with some researchers claiming confirmation (Cialdini et al., 1987; Schaller & Cialdini, 1988; Smith, Keating, & Stotland, 1989) and others claiming refutation based on methodological limitations in the studies that supposedly supported the egoistic alternative, along with experimental data that surmount those methodological limitations (Batson et al., 1988, 1991; Dovidio, Allen, & Schroeder, 1990; Schroeder, Dovidio, Sibicky, Matthews, & Allen, 1988). Nevertheless, even Cialdini and colleagues (1997) have acknowledged that the argument for the existence of an altruistic motivation in human nature "does appear to have won the war in important respects" (p. 482).

Who Provides Help?

Some people are more prosocial than others. Some stop at the scene of accidents to render first aid, or donate to charities, or volunteer in their communities. Others do not. Researchers have tried to explain these individual differences in terms of (1) prosocial personality traits; (2) sex differences; and (3) genetic and neuroendocrine factors.

Prosocial Personality Traits

Individual differences in trait empathy are associated with individual differences in prosocial behavior (Davis et al., 1999) and empathy and other prosocial traits are stable over time (Eisenberg et al., 2002). Based on findings such as these, Penner, Fritzsche, Craiger, and Freifeld (1995) proposed that the prosocial personality consists primarily of a suite of personality traits including (1) a sense of responsibility, (2) empathy, and (3) the self-perception that one is capable of being helpful across diverse situations. In addition, believing in a "just world" (Furnham, 2003)—the idea that people ultimately get what they deserve—may influence prosociality. People who believe in a just world may help others when they believe that others deserve their help (Zuckerman, 1975)—though they may be less likely to help people whose plights they perceive to be largely self-created (Lerner, 1970, 1980).

Bierhoff, Klein, and Kramp's (1991) study illustrates some of these points. They studied the personality differences between a group of 34 people who had stopped to render aid at traffic accidents and a group of 36 other people (matched on age, sex, and socioeconomic status) who had witnessed similar accidents but had not stopped to help. Helpers described themselves as having more internal loci of control, stronger beliefs in a just world, and higher empathy. Similarly, Oliner and Oliner (1988) and Fagin-Jones and Midlarsky (2007) found that non-Jews who had aided or rescued Jews during the Holocaust reported more empathy and feelings of social responsibility (and were more likely to see all people as equal) than did a group of age- and sex-matched non-Jews who did not.

The prosocial traits proposed by Penner et al. (1995) overlap to some extent with the "Big Five" (John, 1990) or "Five-Factor" (McCrae & Costa, 1987) personality dimension known as Agreeableness (Penner et al., 1995), which itself is a reliable predictor of prosocial behavior (e.g., Graziano, Habashi, Sheese, & Tobin, 2007). Highly agreeable people tend to be more aware of the mental states of others, which may be one of the mechanisms responsible for their prosociality (Nettle & Liddle, 2008). Graziano and colleagues (2007) also found that people high in Agreeableness tended to offer more help across a wider range of situations. Agreeable people also engage in more active implicit emotion regulation when confronted with aggressive or antisocial stimuli, which helps them to respond more prosocially to such stimuli (Meier, Robinson, & Wilkowski, 2006).

Sex Differences

Men render more aid in social psychology experiments (when helping is measured in terms of behaviors such as giving money to a stranger, stopping a man from stealing someone's calculator, or helping someone who has dropped some envelopes) than women. In a meta-analysis of the extant studies, which evaluated 12 different predictors of between-study variation in effect size, Eagly and Crowley (1986) found that a medium-sized gender difference favoring men

($d = 0.52$) could be expected in a study with typical values on all 12 moderators. They also found that this effect would be expected to be even larger in experiments conducted outside university campuses.

But the fact that men tend to provide more help in social–psychological experiments should not be taken as evidence that men are more prosocial across the board than women. Women have more empathy for others than men (Eisenberg & Lennon, 1983), and longitudinal studies also indicate that girls demonstrate higher levels of prosocial behavior than boys (Gregory, Light-Hauserman, Rijsdijk, & Eley, 2009; Zahn-Waxler, Schiro, Robinson, Emde, & Schmitz, 2001). Women also provide more emotional and instrumental social support to people in their social networks (including family and friends) than do men—particularly under times of stress (Taylor et al., 2000). Additionally, they perform more caregiving (particularly in terms of personal care and household tasks) for older adults than do men (Miller & Cafasso, 1992). On the basis of gender differences such as these, Taylor and colleagues (Taylor, 2002; Taylor, Dickerson, & Klein, 2002; Taylor et al., 2000) have hypothesized evolved sex differences in biological systems designed to mobilize nurturance and social support, which arose due to selection pressure for women to provide care for their offspring during stress (see Taylor, Chapter 19, this volume).

Women are also more likely to provide heroic, life-threatening forms of care to strangers than the laboratory experiments indicate. Although men are overwhelmingly more likely to engage in life-threatening acts of heroism of the sort that might win them a nomination for a Carnegie Hero Fund Award (these awards are given to civilian adults who voluntarily, and outside of job responsibilities, knowingly risk their lives to rescue unrelated individuals form life-threatening situations such as fires, drownings, and attacks by animals or criminals) relative to any conceivable base rate for their presence in the settings that give rise to such emergencies, Becker and Eagly (2004) demonstrated that there are several forms of risky helping behaviors for which women are over-represented. For example, among unmarried people in Poland, the Netherlands, and France during World War II (i.e., when married couples are excluded from the calculations), unmarried non-Jewish women were approximately 10% more likely than unmarried non-Jewish men to risk their life, freedom, or safety to rescue Jews from the Holocaust (these and all comparable statistics below are adjusted for men's and women's representation in the general population). Becker and Eagly also documented that women are approximately 13% more likely than men to donate kidneys, approximately 16% more likely than men to serve in the Peace Corps, and about twice as likely to serve as physicians with *Doctors of the World* relative to their representation among all physicians in the United States.

From these data, Becker and Eagly made the point that although men's physical strength, capacity for fast action, (possibly) better training for informal lifesaving (e.g., through the Boy Scouts or military training), and differential responsiveness to the reputational incentives associated with being publicly acknowledged as heroes might lead them to engage in more emergency helping in many public settings, women's tendency to help more than men in the other risky situations that Becker and Eagly documented might reflect women's higher levels of empathy or (we take them to mean, as a by-product of) a female-specific adaptation for providing nurturance to offspring during times of stress (see also Taylor et al., 2000).

Genetic and Neuroendocrine Factors

Behavioral-genetic studies indicate that prosocial behavior (at least as measured by self-reports and informant reports of traits such as trust, empathy, cooperation, and altruism) has a substantial genetic component (Gillespie, Cloninger, Heath, & Martin, 2003; Gregory, Light-Hauserman, Rijsdijk, & Eley, 2009; Matthews, Batson, Horn, & Rosenman, 1981; Rushton, Fulker, Neale, Nias, & Eysenck, 1986). Additive genetic factors appear to account for roughly 40% to 70% of the variation in adults' prosocial behavior, with the remainder largely attributable to nonshared environmental factors (Gregory, Light-Hauserman, Rijsdijk, & Eley, 2009).

With the widened availability of genomic methods to behavioral scientists, researchers have begun to identify several genes that are associated with prosocial behavior. In a sample of 354 multisibling families, Bachner-Melman and colleagues (2005) found associations between selflessness (e.g., less concern for one's own needs, greater attendance to the needs of others) and the dopamine D4 and dopamine D5 receptor polymorphisms. Other researchers have found evidence that individual differences in the receptor genes for vasopressin and oxytocin are associated with individual differences in prosocial behavior (Israel et al., 2009; Knafo et al., 2008).

Who Receives Help?

In social psychology experiments, women in need receive more help than men in need. Based on a meta-analysis of data from 36 experiments, Eagly and Crowley (1986) estimated that women receive 0.46 standard deviations more help than men in similar need situations, but after controlling for 11 potential moderators of between-study variability in their meta-analytic results, Eagly and Crowley found that women could be expected to receive a whopping 1.69 standard deviations more help than men generally receive.

People also tend to help people with whom they are similar (Park & Schaller, 2005). In addition, people are more likely to give help to members of groups to which they belong. For example, white people wait longer to provide emergency help (i.e., they provide help less immediately) to a black person than they do to a white person—particularly in high-emergency situations (Kunstman & Plant, 2008).

Finally, both men and women provide more help to attractive people than to unattractive people (Benson, Karabenick, & Lerner, 1976; Dovidio & Gaertner, 1983; Farrelly, Lazarus, & Roberts, 2007; West & Brown, 1975). Stürmer, Snyder, and Omoto (2005) found that the attractiveness of the target to be helped was a particularly important mediator of helping when that person (who was of the same gender as the participant) was a member of a group to which the participant did not belong (e.g., when the potential helper was heterosexual and the potential target of helping was same-gender homosexual, and vice versa). When the helper and target of helping were from the same social group (i.e., when both were either heterosexual or homosexual) empathy predicted helping better than did attractiveness.

Environmental and Situational Factors

There are many environmental and situational factors that influence prosocial behavior. For example, all over the world, people in cities are significantly less helpful than people in rural areas (Steblay, 1987). Levine, Martinez, Brase, and Sorenson (1994) conducted a study of helping behaviors in 36 U.S. cities and found that population density was a more important predictor than overall population size. A common explanation for this finding is that with increased population density, people become fatigued by unwanted distractions and interruptions and therefore begin to psychologically close themselves off to interactions with strangers, which causes them to become less responsive to people who might be in need of help (Milgram, 1970).

In a cross-cultural study of helping in 23 large world cities (e.g., Budapest, Rio de Janeiro, Tel Aviv, New York), Levine, Norenzayan, and Philbrick (2001) found substantial cross-cultural differences in the extent to which people would (1) stop to pick up a pen that a confederate had dropped, (2) help or offer to help a confederate wearing a leg brace to pick up a pile of magazines he had dropped, and (3) help a seemingly blind confederate cross the street. The best predictor of cross-cultural differences in helping was purchasing power parity (PPP), which measures economic development. Cities in nations with the highest PPP had the lowest rates of helping ($r = -0.43$ with the mean of all three measures of helping). Rates of helping were not significantly correlated with the cities' population sizes, pedestrians' mean walking speed (used as a proxy for pace of life), or culture-level measures of individualism and collectivism. Levine et al. (2001) suggested that with economic development comes the replacement of traditional value systems that emphasized the importance of helping strangers.

Time Pressure

Time pressure also influences emergency helping. In an influential early study on this topic, Darley and Batson (1973) assigned seminary students to low, moderate, and high "hurry" conditions. The students, who were on their way to give a talk about the Good Samaritan parable (a story in the Christian Bible about a man who stopped to help someone from a different ethnic group who was very ill) or about a control topic, passed a confederate who looked unwell. Darley and Batson found that 80% of seminarians who were not rushed stopped to help, whereas only 10% of those who were running late stopped to help. The topic of the seminarians' upcoming talks did not significantly influence what they did (but see Greenwald, 1975, who argued that there was in fact an important effect for the topic of the talk that was masked by low statistical power. We wonder why no one ever noted Greenwald's suggestion and explored the issue further.).

Ambiguity of Need

Shotland and Straw (1976) conducted an experiment in which they staged an altercation between a man and a woman. If the woman shouted "get away from me; I don't know you," bystanders helped 65% of the time. In contrast, if the women shouted "Get away from me; I don't know why I ever married you," bystanders helped 19% of the time.

The Bystander Effect

This takes us to the *bystander effect*—the tendency for people to render less assistance in an emergency as the number of other bystanders increases.

Latané and Darley's (1968, 1970) initial work in this area was stimulated by a *New York Times* account of the murder of a young woman in Queens, New York, named Kitty Genovese. According to the original report, Genovese was fatally assaulted outside of her apartment, and 38 of her neighbors heard the 30-minute-long altercation without a single one lifting a hand to intervene. As the standard telling of the story goes, the assailant left the scene and came back on two different occasions shortly afterward to continue the attack. However, recent research based on legal documents and testimony from the attacker's murder trial calls into question many details of the canonical Kitty Genovese story. For example, there were two attacks rather than three; the number of eyewitnesses was fewer than 38; several witnesses did call the police after the first attack; none of the witnesses would have had the field of view to see the complete 30-minute episode; the second and fatal attack took place indoors where only a few witnesses would have been able to hear or see any part of it; and the first attack was, in fact, ended by bystander intervention—someone shouted out of a window so that the perpetrator ran off, presumably ending the altercation from many bystanders' points of view (Manning, Levine, & Collins, 2007). Nevertheless, the story is still a powerful one that inspired scores of studies on the bystander effect and its boundary conditions.

Latané and Darley (1970) proposed that people must successfully negotiate a series of decisions—often under conditions of considerable chaos and emotional arousal—before rendering aid in a group setting (Batson, 1998; Latané & Nida, 1981). They hypothesized that the presence of other people biases each of these decisions toward the choice that would reduce the likelihood of prosocial behavior. First, people must notice that something is happening that requires intervention. If bystanders are uncertain about whether to help, they tend to look to others for guidance. Unfortunately, because no one wants to be embarrassed by overreacting to a situation that is in actuality not an emergency, it is thought that most people inhibit their expressions of emotion in such situations. As a result, looking to others for cues that an emergency is indeed happening inhibits bystander intervention. This is a phenomenon that Latané and Darley (1970) called *pluralistic ignorance*. Another important social process in these situations is *social influence*, in which other people's inaction causes people to conclude that a situation does not, in fact, require intervention. In an experiment involving a confederate whom participants believed was blind, Ross and Braband (1973) found that bystanders continued to react to odorless smoke even if the presumably blind confederate did not. However, bystanders reacted less often when the presumably blind confederate did not react to a woman's scream (i.e., which did not require eyesight).

Having recognized a need, bystanders must then decide they have a personal responsibility to take action. Darley and Latané (1968) conducted an experiment in which participants engaged in a discussion, when a confederate began to feign a seizure and called for help. Nearly every participant who believed that no one else could hear what was happening tried to help the confederate, whereas participants in larger groups (six persons) tended not to help. Conversely, participants are more likely to help—even when in the presence of others—if they perceive that the other bystanders are unable to help (Bickman, 1971). When people know that they are the only ones who are in a position to help, the personal costs of nonintervention become higher, as they know that they will be to blame if the person's need remains unrelieved.

Finally, even if people decide that they should take action, they may believe that they are incompetent to do so. In the presence of groups, lack of perceived competence can deter offers of help. Cramer et al. (1988) conducted a study in which half of the participants were registered nurses and the others were general education students. With the use of confederate bystanders who were instructed not to react, participants passed a worker on a ladder and then heard a noise as if the worker had fallen. The nurses helped when in the presence of others or when alone, whereas the general education students were more likely to help if they were alone.

Other variables can also reduce the bystander effect. When groups are cohesive, rather than simply an aggregation of strangers, larger groups can actually increase helping behavior relative to smaller groups (Rutkowski, Gruder, & Romer, 1983). When people are seated face to face, and can easily observe each others' facial and nonverbal reactions to a potential emergency situation (and so that others can see theirs), helping is higher in the presence of others than when people are seated back to back and thus cannot see each other's nonverbal expressions of concern (Darley, Teger, & Lewis, 1973). Finally, people help more in the presence of friends than in the presence of strangers (Latané & Rodin, 1969) and may even help more when the group shares a common identity with the person in need of help: Men and women both are more likely to help a woman in distress if they have been seated among a group of strangers who were all women (Levine & Crowther, 2008).

Despite these boundary conditions, the bystander effect is robust. Across nearly 50 laboratory experiments, approximately 75% of people tried to render aid to someone in need when alone, whereas only 53% of people did so in the presence of others (Latané & Nida, 1981). But the person in need has a different question: "Will I receive help?" According to Latané and Nida's (1981) meta-analysis, in situations in which bystanders are able to see, and be seen by, other potential helpers, only 70% of people in need receive help. In contrast, people in need receive help 82% of the time when there is a single bystander.

Volunteering

Volunteering is one of the most widely practiced prosocial behaviors. In the United States, approximately 26% of the population (i.e., 62 million people) volunteered at least once between September 2007 and September 2008 (U.S. Department of Labor, 2009). Volunteering is evidently beneficial for psychological well-being and physical health (Brown, Nesse, Vinokur, & Smith, 2003; Musick, Herzog, & House, 1999; Oman, Thoresen, & McMahon, 1999; Thoits, 2001). Hansen, Larson, and Dworkin (2003) also found that participation in volunteer activities was associated with personal development (e.g., identity) as well as interpersonal development (e.g., prosocial norms and ties to the community) among an ethnically diverse sample of youth. Among the different types of organizations in which people volunteer, more time is devoted to volunteering for religious organizations (35.1% of all volunteers; U.S. Department of Labor, 2009).

Some of the best predictors of volunteer activity are the extent to which one feels that volunteering has become an important part of one's identity and the extent to which one feels that other people are aware of one's volunteer activities and expect one to continue working as a volunteer (Finkelstein, Penner, & Brannick, 2005). Volunteering is also associated with higher levels of self-reported empathy, a generally positive orientation toward helping, and religiosity (Penner, 2002; Penner & Finkelstein, 1998). Clary and Snyder (1999) furthermore suggested that people can have any of six motivations for volunteering (i.e., expressing one's values, gaining knowledge or understanding, growing or developing psychologically, gaining career-relevant experience, strengthening one's social relationships, or reducing one's own negative feelings or addressing one's own personal problems). Matching people with volunteer opportunities that allow them to fulfill their motivations produces greater satisfaction with the experience and increases their intention to volunteer in the future (Clary & Snyder, 1999; Clary et al., 1998; Clary, Snyder, Ridge, Miene, & Haugen, 1994). Also, it is important to note that requiring people to volunteer (e.g., through service learning requirements in high schools) who are not initially motivated to do so reduces their intention to volunteer in the future (Clary et al., 1998).

Fostering Prosocial Behavior

A considerable amount of research has addressed the factors that foster prosocial behavior in children and adults. Parental modeling of prosocial behavior is an important element of prosocial development (Rushton, 1975). Another aspect of parenting that may foster prosocial behavior is providing reasoned explanations when asking children to change their behavior (Hoffman, 1970; Krevans & Gibbs, 1996). Similarly, parental authoritativeness, positivity (indexed by emotionally positive, noncoercive methods of discipline), and emotional availability also appear to play a role in prosocial development (Hastings, Zahn-Waxler, Robinson, Usher, & Bridges, 2000; Knafo et al., 2008; Moreno, Klute, & Robinson, 2008).

Rosenhan and White (1967) conducted a study of fourth and fifth graders in which the children played a game once in the presence of an adult model and once without this model. Every time the model won, the model donated half of the earnings to charity. Children who had witnessed the model's behavior, and particularly those who had also given to charity while in the model's presence, tended to donate to charity when playing alone. Similarly, Rushton (1975) studied 7- to 11-year-old children who had witnessed an adult model play a game and donate a portion of his or her earnings (i.e., tokens) to charity. Two months later the children played one of three games that varied in similarity to the original game. The children who viewed the modeling behavior 8 weeks earlier behaved more prosocially (i.e., donated more to charity) across all three game conditions. In addition, children who had been "preached" to during the task about the importance of giving money to the charity donated more money 8 weeks later (even though preaching did not influence donations immediately following the game 8 weeks earlier).

In addition, Bryan and Test (1967) found that after drivers saw someone stop by the side of the road to help a woman change a flat tire, they were more likely to stop and help a woman in a similar situation. Likewise, exposure to prosocially oriented television programs (Hearold, 1986) and video games (Gentile et al., 2009) can increase prosocial behavior in children and adolescents, perhaps through social learning or direct reinforcement: Video games are fun, so playing a video game in which characters have prosocial goals can make helping fun.

Explicit attempts to educate people about prosocial behavior can also make a difference. For example, educating others about the bystander effect has been shown to increase helping behavior in students (67% versus 27% who did not hear the lecture; Beaman, Barnes, & Klentz, 1978). Finally, research suggests that subtly priming people with social stimuli such as geometric configurations that resemble eyes or faces (Bateson, Nettle, & Roberts, 2006; Haley & Fessler, 2005; Rigdon, Ishii, Watabe, & Kitayama, 2010), reminders of God or religion (Pichon, Boccato, & Saroglou, 2007; Shariff & Norenzayan, 2007), and even secular institutions such as contracts and police that regulate prosocial behavior (Shariff & Norenzayan, 2007) increase generosity, cooperation, and charitable giving. These effects are obtained in both laboratory and field experiments, suggesting that some of the lowest-hanging fruit in social psychologists' efforts to increase prosocial behavior in the real world might be best be obtained through subtle, nonpreachy stimuli that activate prosocial cognition and behavior without conscious awareness.

Prosocial Behavior Today

Nearly 50 years of research on the social psychology of prosocial behavior has produced a broad and fascinating set of facts and theories about the factors that promote and inhibit prosocial behavior, as well as interventions that might be applied in the real world to increase prosocial behavior. These concepts continue to attract the attention of social psychologists, and they should. We are confident that high-quality social–psychological work on prosocial behavior will continue much in the same fashion it has for the past five decades.

Which is not to say that there is no room for new conceptual directions, because there is. Humans' penchant for prosocial behavior is one of the great puzzles of evolutionary theorizing, and there is considerable room for further social–psychological research devoted to uncovering the mind's functional circuitry for producing prosocial behavior. By thinking explicitly about the selection pressures that might have given rise to prosocial behavior and the types of psychological machinery that would be required to produce prosocial solutions in response to those selection pressures, social psychologists may be able to make important new strides in understanding how humans manage to be so prosocial, how those tendencies are thwarted, and the cognitive tools that the mind might possess for producing such remarkable behavior.

Moreover, many important issues in the mainstream social–psychological literature are ripe for evolutionary recasting. From what selection pressures did Batsonian altruistic motivation arise? Does the role of blood in discouraging emergency helping reflect a conflict between evolved mechanisms for disgust and evolved mechanisms for reciprocal altruism? Are men so much more likely to render emergency aid in highly public settings because of a desire to signal their value as protectors and providers to a choosy pool of prospective mates? Can the bystander effect be better conceptualized as a public goods problem (i.e., it benefits me if we have a system in which people can get help, but not if I'm the one who has to do the helping)—which would render it highly amenable to evolutionary analysis? The field is filled with opportunities such as these. Careful reliance on well-established evidentiary criteria for testing adaptationist hypotheses (Andrews, Gangestad, & Matthews, 2002; Williams, 1966; see

Maner & Kenrick, Chapter 17, this volume) is essential for doing this job well, and would help put the social psychology of prosocial behavior on a broader theoretical footing that will improve its relevance to both social psychology and the interdisciplinary science of prosocial behavior.

Acknowledgments

Preparation of this chapter was supported by the Center for the Study of Law and Religion at Emory University. The authors gratefully acknowledge Rob Kurzban, who provided helpful feedback on a previous version of this chapter.

References

Algoe, S. B., Haidt, J., & Gable, S. L. (2008). Beyond reciprocity: Gratitude and relationships in everyday life. *Emotion, 8*, 425–429.

Andrews, P. W., Gangestad, S. W., & Matthews, D. (2002). Adaptationism—How to carry out an exaptationist program. *Behavioral and Brain Sciences, 25*, 489–504.

Austin, W., McGinn, N. C., & Susmilch, C. (1980). Internal standards revisited: Effects of social comparisons and expectancies on judgments of fairness and satisfaction. *Journal of Experimental Social Psychology, 16*, 426–441.

Axelrod, R. (1980). More effective choice in the Prisoner's Dilemma. *Journal of Conflict Resolution, 24*, 379–403.

Axelrod, R. (1984). *The evolution of cooperation*. New York: Basic Books.

Axelrod, R., & Hamilton, W. D. (1981). The evolution of cooperation. *Science, 211*, 1390–1396.

Bachner-Melman, R., Gritsenko, I., Nemanov, L., Zohar, A. H., Dina, C., & Ebstein, R. P. (2005). Dopaminergic polymorphisms associated with self-report measures of human altruism: A fresh phenotype for the dopamine D4 receptor. *Molecular Psychiatry, 10*, 333–335.

Bartlett, M. Y., & DeSteno, D. (2006). Gratitude and prosocial behavior: Helping when it costs you. *Psychological Science, 17*, 319–325.

Bateson, M., Nettle, D., & Roberts, G. (2006). Cues of being watched enhance cooperation in a real-world setting. *Biology Letters, 2*, 412–414.

Batson, C. D. (1991). *The altruism question: Toward a social-psychological answer*. Hillsdale, NJ: Erlbaum.

Batson, C. D. (1998). Altruism and prosocial behavior. In D. Gilbert, S. Fiske, & G. Lindzey (Eds.), *Handbook of social psychology* (Vol. 2, pp. 282–316). New York: McGraw-Hill.

Batson, C. D., Ahmad, N., & Lishner, D. A. (2009). Empathy and altruism. In C. R. Snyder & S. J. Lopez (Eds.), *Oxford handbook of positive psychology* (2nd ed., pp. 417–426). New York: Oxford University Press.

Batson, C. D., Ahmad, N., Powell, A. A., & Stocks, E. L. (2008). Prosocial motivation. In J. Shah & W. Gardner (Eds.), *Handbook of motivation science* (pp. 135–149). New York: Guilford Press.

Batson, C. D., Batson, J. G., Slingsby, J. K., Harrell, K. L., Peekna, H. M., & Todd, R. M. (1991). Empathic joy and the empathy-altruism hypothesis. *Journal of Personality and Social Psychology, 61*, 413–426.

Batson, C. D., Duncan, B. D., Ackerman, P., Buckley, T., & Birch, K. (1981). Is empathic emotion a source of altruistic motivation? *Journal of Personality and Social Psychology, 40*, 290–302.

Batson, C. D., Dyck, J. L., Brandt, J. R., Batson, J. G., Powell, A. L., McMaster, M. R., et al. (1988). Five studies testing two new egoistic alternatives to the empathy-altruism hypothesis. *Journal of Personality and Social Psychology, 55*, 52–77.

Batson, C. D., Eklund, J. H., Chermok, V. L., Hoyt, J. L., & Ortiz, B. G. (2007). An additional antecedent of empathic concern: Valuing the welfare of the person in need. *Journal of Personality and Social Psychology, 93*, 65–74.

Batson, C. D., Turk, C. L., Shaw, L. L., & Klein, T. R. (1995). Information function of empathic emotion: Learning that we value the other's welfare. *Journal of Personality and Social Psychology, 68*, 300–313.

Beaman, A. L., Barnes, P. J., & Klentz, B. (1978). Increasing helping rates through information dissemination: Teaching pays. *Personality and Social Psychology Bulletin, 4*, 406–411.

Becker, S. W., & Eagly, A. H. (2004). The heroism of women and men. *American Psychologist, 59*, 163–178.

Benson, P. L., Karabenick, S. A., & Lerner, R. M. (1976). Pretty pleases: The effects of physical attractiveness, race, and sex on receiving help. *Journal of Experimental Social Psychology, 12*, 409–415.

Berscheid, E., & Walster, E. (1967). When does a harmdoer compensate a victim? *Journal of Personality and Social Psychology, 6*, 435–441.

Bickman, L. (1971). The effect of another bystander's ability to help on bystander intervention in an emergency. *Journal of Experimental Social Psychology, 7*, 367–379.

Bierhoff, H. W., Klein, R., & Kramp, P. (1991). Evidence for the altruistic personality from data on accident research. *Journal of Personality, 59*, 263–280.

Boehm, C. (2008). Purposive social selection and the evolution of human altruism. *Cross-Cultural Research, 42*, 319–352.

Bowles, S., & Posel, D. (2005). Genetic relatedness predicts South African migrant workers' remittances to their families. *Nature, 434*, 380–383.

Bressan, P. (2009). Biologically costly altruism depends on emotional closeness among step but not half or full sibling. *Evolutionary Psychology, 7*, 118–132.

Brosnan, S. F., & de Waal, F. B. M. (2003). Monkeys reject unequal pay. *Nature, 425*, 297–299.

Brown, D. E. (1991). *Human universals.* Boston, MA: McGraw-Hill.

Brown, S. L., Nesse, R. M., Vinokur, A. D., & Smith, D. M. (2003). Providing social support may be more beneficial than receiving it: Results from a prospective study of mortality. *Psychological Science, 14*, 320–327.

Bryan, J. H., & Test, M. A. (1967). Models and helping: Naturalistic studies in aiding behavior. *Journal of Personality and Social Psychology, 6*, 400–407.

Burnstein, E., Crandall, C., & Kitayama, S. (1994). Some neo-Darwinian decision rules for altruism: Weighing cues for inclusive fitness as a function of the biological importance of the decision. *Journal of Personality and Social Psychology, 67*, 773–789.

Buunk, B. P., & Bakker, A. B. (1997). Responses to unprotected extradyadic sex by one's partner: Testing predictions from interdependence and equity theory. *Journal of Sex Research, 34*, 387–397.

Buunk, B. P., & Van Yperen, N. W. (1991). Referential comparisons, relational comparisons, and exchange orientation: Their relation to marital satisfaction. *Personality and Social Psychology Bulletin, 17*, 709–717.

Carlson, M., Charlin, V., & Miller, N. (1988). Positive mood and helping behavior: A test of six hypotheses. *Journal of Personality and Social Psychology, 55*, 211–229.

Charpentier, M. J., Boulet, M., & Drea, C. M. (2008). Smelling right: The scent of male lemurs advertises genetic quality and relatedness. *Molecular Ecology, 17*, 3225–3233.

Cialdini, R. B., Brown, S. L., Lewis, B. P., Luce, C., & Neuberg, S. L. (1997). Reinterpreting the empathy-altruism relationship: When one into one equals oneness. *Journal of Personality and Social Psychology, 73*, 481–494.

Cialdini, R. B., Darby, B. L., & Vincent, J. E. (1973). Transgression and altruism: A case for hedonism. *Journal of Experimental Social Psychology, 9*, 502–516.

Cialdini, R. B., Schaller, M., Houlihan, D., Arps, K., Fultz, J., & Beaman, A. L. (1987). Empathy-based helping: Is it selflessly or selfishly motivated? *Journal of Personality and Social Psychology, 52*, 749–758.

Clark, M. S., Ouellette, R., Powell, M. C., & Milberg, S. (1987). Recipient's mood, relationship type, and helping. *Journal of Personality and Social Psychology, 53*, 94–103.

Clary, E. G., & Snyder, M. (1999). The motivations to volunteer: Theoretical and practical considerations. *Current Directions in Psychological Science, 8*, 156–159.

Clary, E. G., Snyder, M., Ridge, R. D., Copeland, J., Stukas, A. A., Haugen, J., et al. (1998). Understanding and assessing the motivations of volunteers: A functional approach. *Journal of Personality and Social Psychology, 74*, 1516–1530.

Clary, E. G., Snyder, M., Ridge, R. D., Miene, P., & Haugen, J. (1994). Matching messages to motives in persuasion: A functional approach to promoting volunteerism. *Basic and Applied Social Psychology, 24*, 1129–1146.

Coke, J. S., Batson, C. D., & McDavis, K. (1978). Empathic mediation of helping: A two-stage model. *Journal of Personality and Social Psychology, 36*, 752–766.

Cosmides, L. (1989). The logic of social exchange: Has natural selection shaped how humans reason? Studies with the Wason selection task. *Cognition, 31*, 187–276.

Cosmides, L., & Tooby, J. (2005). Neurocognitive adaptations designed for social exchange. In D. M. Buss (Ed.), *Handbook of evolutionary psychology* (pp. 584–627). Hoboken, NJ: Wiley.

Cramer, R. E., McMaster, M. R., Bartell, P. A., & Dragna, M. (1988). Subject competence and the minimization of the bystander effect. *Journal of Applied Social Psychology, 18*, 1133–1148.

Darley, J. M., & Batson, C. D. (1973). "From Jerusalem to Jericho": A study of situational and dispositional variables in helping behavior. *Journal of Personality and Social Psychology, 27*, 100–108.

Darley, J. M., & Latané, B. (1968). Bystander intervention in emergencies: Diffusion of responsibility. *Journal of Personality and Social Psychology, 8*, 377–383.

Darley, J. M., Teger, A. I., & Lewis, L. D. (1973). Do groups always inhibit individuals' responses to potential emergencies? *Journal of Personality and Social Psychology, 26*, 395–399.

Darwin, C. (1952). *The descent of man, and selection in relation to sex*. Chicago, IL: University of Chicago Press. Original published in 1871.

Davis, M. H., Mitchell, K. V., Hall, J. A., Lothert, J., Snapp, T., & Meyer, M. (1999). Empathy, expectations, and situational preferences: Personality influences on the decision to volunteer helping behaviors. *Journal of Personality, 67*, 469–503.

de Vignemont, F., & Singer, T. (2006). The empathetic brain: How, when, and why? *Trends in Cognitive Sciences, 10*, 435–441.

de Waal, F. B. M. (Ed.). (1982). *Chimpanzee politics: Power and sex among the apes*. New York: Harper & Row.

Dovidio, J. F. (1984). Helping behavior and altruism: An empirical and conceptual overview. In L. Berkowitz (Ed.), *Advances in experimental social psychology* (pp. 361–427). New York: Academic Press.

Dovidio, J. F., Allen, J. L., & Schroeder, D. A. (1990). The specificity of empathy-induced helping: Evidence for altruistic motivation. *Journal of Personality and Social Psychology, 59*, 249–260.

Dovidio, J. F., & Gaertner, S. L. (1983). The effects of race, status, and ability on helping behavior. *Journal of Applied Social Psychology, 13*, 191–205.

Dovidio, J. F., Piliavin, J. A., Gaertner, S. L., Schroeder, D. A., & Clark, R. D. (1991). The arousal: Cost-reward model and the process of intervention: A review of the evidence. In M. S. Clark (Ed.), *Prosocial behavior* (pp. 86–118). Newbury Park, CA: Sage.

Eagly, A. H., & Crowley, M. (1986). Gender and helping behavior: A meta-analytic review of the social psychological literature. *Psychological Bulletin, 100*, 283–308.

Eek, D., & Anders, B. (2003). The interplay between greed, efficiency, and fairness in public-goods dilemmas. *Social Justice Research, 16*, 195–215.

Eisenberg, N., & Lennon, R. (1983). Sex differences in empathy and related capacities. *Psychological Bulletin, 94*, 100–131.

Eisenberg, N., Guthrie, I. K., Cumberland, A., Murphy, B. C., Shepard, S. A., Zhou, Q., et al. (2002). Prosocial development in early adulthood: A longitudinal study. *Journal of Personality and Social Psychology, 82*, 993–1006.

Eisenberger, R., Lynch, P., Aselage, J., & Rohdieck, S. (2004). Who takes the most revenge? Individual differences in negative reciprocity norm endorsement. *Personality and Social Psychology Bulletin, 30*, 787–799.

Fagin-Jones, S., & Midlarsky, E. (2007). Courageous altruism: Personal and situational correlates of rescue during the Holocaust. *Journal of Positive Psychology, 2*, 136–147.

Farrelly, D., Lazarus, J., & Roberts, G. (2007). Altruists attract. *Evolutionary Psychology, 5*, 313–329.

Finkel, E. J., Rusbult, C. E., Kumashiro, M., & Hannon, P. A. (2002). Dealing with a betrayal in close relationships: Does commitment promote forgiveness? *Journal of Personality and Social Psychology, 82*, 956–974.

Finkelstein, M. A., Penner, L. A., & Brannick, M. T. (2005). Motive, role identity, and prosocial personality as predictors of volunteer activity. *Social Behavior and Personality, 33*, 403–418.

Fraser, O. N., Stahl, D., & Aureli, F. (2008). Stress reduction through consolation in chimpanzees. *Proceedings of the National Academy of Sciences, 105*, 8557–8562.

Furnham, A. (2003). Belief in a just world: Research progress over the past decade. *Personality and Individual Differences, 34*, 795–817.

Gaertner, S. L., & Dovidio, J. F. (1977). The subtlety of white racism, arousal, and helping behavior. *Journal of Personality and Social Psychology, 35*, 691–707.

Gebauer, J. E., Riketta, M., Broemer, P., & Maio, G. R. (2008). Pleasure and pressure based prosocial motivation: Divergent relations to subjective well-being. *Journal of Research in Personality, 42*, 399–420.

Gentile, D. A., Anderson, C. A., Yukawa, S., Ihori, N., Saleem, M., Ming, L. K., et al. (2009). The effects of prosocial video games on prosocial behavior: International evidence from correlational, longitudinal, and experimental studies. *Personality and Social Psychology Bulletin, 35*, 752–763.

Gillespie, N. A., Cloninger, C. R., Heath, A. C., & Martin, N. G. (2003). The genetic and environmental relationship between Cloninger's dimensions of temperament and character. *Personality and Individual Differences, 35*, 1931–1946.

Gintis, H., Smith, E. A., & Bowles, S. (2001). Costly signaling and cooperation. *Journal of Theoretical Biology, 213*, 103–119.

Gouldner, A. W. (1960). The norm of reciprocity: A preliminary statement. *American Sociological Review, 25*, 161–178.

Graziano, W. G., Habashi, M. M., Sheese, B. E., & Tobin, R. M. (2007). Agreeableness, empathy, and helping: A person x situation perspective. *Journal of Personality and Social Psychology, 93*, 583–599.

Greenwald, A. G. (1975). Does the Good Samaritan parable increase helping? A comment on Darley and Batson's no-effect conclusion. *Journal of Personality and Social Psychology, 32*, 578–583.

Gregory, A., Light-Hauserman, J., Rijsdijk, F., & Eley, T. (2009). Behavioral genetic analyses of prosocial behavior in adolescents. *Developmental Science, 12*, 165–174.

Gürerk, O., Irlenbusch, B., & Rockenbach, B. (2006). The competitive advantage of sanctioning institutions. *Science, 312*, 108–111.

Haley, K. J., & Fessler, D. M. T. (2005). Nobody's watching? Subtle cues affect generosity in an anonymous economic game. *Evolution and Human Behavior, 26*, 245–256.

Hamilton, W. D. (1964). The genetical evolution of social behaviour. I, II. *Journal of Theoretical Biology, 7*, 1–52.

Hansen, D. M., Larson, R. W., & Dworkin, J. B. (2003). What adolescents learn in organized youth activities: A survey of self-reported developmental experiences. *Journal of Research on Adolescence, 13*, 25–55.

Hassebrauck, M. (1986). Ratings of distress as a function of degree and kind of inequity. *Journal of Social Psychology, 126*, 269–270.

Hastings, P. D., Zahn-Waxler, C., Robinson, J., Usher, B., & Bridges, D. (2000). The development of concern for others in children with behavior problems. *Developmental Psychology, 36*, 531–546.

Hearold, S. (1986). A synthesis of 1043 effects of television on social behavior. In G. Comstock (Ed.), *Public communication and behavior* (Vol. 1, pp. 65–133). Orlando, FL: Academic Press.

Henrich, J., Boyd, R., Bowles, S., Camerer, C., Fehr, E., Gintis, H., et al. (2005). "Economic man" in cross-cultural perspective: Behavioral experiments in 15 small-scale societies. *Behavioral and Brain Sciences, 28*, 795–855.

Hoffman, E., McCabe, K. A., & Smith, V. L. (1998). Behavioral foundations of reciprocity: Experimental economics and evolutionary psychology. *Economic Inquiry, 36*, 335–352.

Hoffman, M. L. (1970). Conscience, personality, and socialization techniques. *Human Development, 13*, 90–126.

Iredale, W., Van Vugt, M., & Dunbar, R. I. M. (2008). Showing off in humans: Male generosity as a mating signal. *Evolutionary Psychology 6*, 386–392.

Israel, S., Lerer, E., Shalev, I., Uzefovsky, F., Riebold, M., Liaba, E., et al. (2009). The oxytocin receptor (OXTR) contributes to prosocial fund allocations in the dictator game and the social value orientations task. *PLoS One Biology, 4*, e5535.

Jensen, K., Hare, B., Call, J., & Tomasello, M. (2006). What's in it for me? Self-regard precludes altruism and spite in chimpanzees. *Proceedings of the Royal Society of London, Series* B–Biological Sciences, 273, 1013–1021.

John, O. P. (1990). The "Big Five" factor taxonomy: Dimensions of personality in the natural language and in questionnaires. In L. A. Pervin (Ed.), *Handbook of personality: Theory and research* (pp. 66–100). New York: Guilford Press.

Karremans, J. C., & Van Lange, P. A. M. (2004). Back to caring after being hurt: The role of forgiveness. *European Journal of Social Psychology, 34*, 207–227.

Kelln, B. R. C., & Ellard, J. H. (1999). An equity theory analysis of the impact of forgiveness and retribution on transgressor compliance. *Personality and Social Psychology Bulletin, 25*, 864–872.

Kiesler, S., Sproull, L., & Waters, K. (1996). A prisoner's dilemma experiment on cooperation with people and human-like computers. *Journal of Personality and Social Psychology, 70*, 47–65.

Knafo, A., Israel, S., Darvasi, A., Bachner-Melman, R., Uzefovsky, F., Cohen, L. H., et al. (2008). Individual differences in allocation of funds in the dictator game associated with length of the arginine varopressin 1a receptor RS3 promoter region and correlation between RS3 length and hippocampal mRNA. *Genes, Brain and Behavior, 7*, 266–275.

Korchmaros, J. D., & Kenny, D. A. (2001). Emotional closeness as a mediator of the effect of genetic relatedness on altruism. *Psychological Science, 12*, 262–265.

Koski, S. E., Koops, K., & Sterck, E. H. M. (2007). Reconciliation, relationship quality, and postconflict anxiety: Testing the integrated hypothesis in captive chimpanzees. *American Journal of Primatology, 69*, 158–172.

Krevans, J., & Gibbs, J. C. (1996). Parents' use of inductive discipline: Relations to children's empathy and prosocial behavior. *Child Development, 67*, 3263–3277.

Kunstman, J. W., & Plant, E. A. (2008). Racing to help: Racial bias in high emergency helping situations. *Journal of Personality and Social Psychology, 95*, 1499–1510.

Latané, B., & Darley, J. M. (1968). Group inhibition of bystander intervention in emergencies. *Journal of Personality and Social Psychology, 10*, 215–221.

Latané, B., & Darley, J. M. (1970). *The unresponsive bystander: Why doesn't he help?* New York: Appleton-Century-Crofts.

Latané, B., & Nida, S. (1981). Ten years of research on group size and helping. *Psychological Bulletin, 89*, 308–324.

Latané, B., & Rodin, J. (1969). A lady in distress: Inhibiting effects of friends and strangers on bystander intervention. *Journal of Experimental Social Psychology, 5*, 189–202.

Lerner, M. J. (1970). The desire for justice and reactions to victims. In J. Macaulay & L. Berkowitz (Eds.), *Altruism and helping behavior* (pp. 205–229). New York: Academic Press.

Lerner, M. J. (1980). *The belief in a just world: A fundamental delusion.* New York: Plenum.

Levine, M., & Crowther, S. (2008). The responsive bystander: How social group membership and group size can encourage as well as inhibit bystander intervention. *Journal of Personality and Social Psychology, 95*, 1429–1439.

Levine, R. V., Martinez, T. S., Brase, G., & Sorenson, K. (1994). Helping in 36 U. S. cities. *Journal of Personality and Social Psychology, 67*, 69–82.

Levine, R. V., Norenzayan, A., & Philbrick, K. (2001). Cross-cultural differences in helping strangers. *Journal of Cross-Cultural Psychology, 32*, 543–560.

Lieberman, D., Tooby, J., & Cosmides, L. (2007). The architecture of human kin detection. *Nature, 445*, 727–731.

Liszkowski, U., Carpenter, M., & Tomasello, M. (2008). Twelve-month-olds communicate helpfully and appropriately for knowledgeable and ignorant partners. *Cognition, 108*, 732–739.

Lount, R. B., Zhong, C.-B. S. N., & Murnighan, J. K. (2008). Getting off on the wrong foot: The timing of a breach and restoration of trust. *Personality and Social Psychology Bulletin, 34*, 1601–1612.

Manning, R., Levine, M., & Collins, A. (2007). The Kitty Genovese murder and the social psychology of helping. *American Psychologist, 62*, 555–562.

Matthews, K. A., Batson, C. D., Horn, J., & Rosenman, R. H. (1981). Principles in his nature which interest him in the fortune of others...": The heritability of empathic concern for others. *Journal of Personality, 49*, 237–247.

Maynard Smith, J., & Harper, D. (2003). *Animal signals*. Oxford: Oxford University Press.

McAndrew, F. T. (2002). New evolutionary perspectives on altruism: Multilevel-selection and costly-signaling theories. *Current Directions in Psychological Science, 11*, 79–82.

McCrae, R. R., & Costa, P. T. (1987). Validation of the five-factor model of personality across instruments and observers. *Journal of Personality and Social Psychology, 52*, 81–90.

McCullough, M. E. (2008). *Beyond revenge: The evolution of the forgiveness instinct*. San Francisco: Jossey-Bass.

McCullough, M. E., Kilpatrick, S. D., Emmons, R. A., & Larson, D. B. (2001). Is gratitude a moral affect? *Psychological Bulletin, 127*, 249–266.

McCullough, M. E., Kimeldorf, M. B., & Cohen, A. D. (2008). An adaptation for altruism? The social causes, social effects, and social evolution of gratitude. *Current Directions in Psychological Science, 17*, 281–285.

McCullough, M. E., Kurzban, R., & Tabak, B. A. (2010). Evolved mechanisms for revenge and forgiveness. In M. Mikulincer & P. R. Shaver (Eds.), *Understanding and reducing aggression, violence, and their consequences*. Washington, DC: American Psychological Association.

McCullough, M. E., Rachal, K. C., Sandage, S. J., Worthington, E. L., Brown, S. W., & Hight, T. L. (1998). Interpersonal forgiving in close relationships. II: Theoretical elaboration and measurement. *Journal of Personality and Social Psychology, 75*, 1586–1603.

McCullough, M. E., Worthington, E. L., & Rachal, K. C. (1997). Interpersonal forgiving in close relationships. *Journal of Personality and Social Psychology, 73*, 321–336.

Medvene, L. J., Teal, C. R., & Slavich, S. (2000). Including the other in self: Implications for judgments of equity and satisfaction in close relationships. *Journal of Social and Clinical Psychology, 19*, 396–419.

Meier, B. P., Robinson, M. D., & Wilkowski, B. M. (2006). Turning the other cheek: Agreeableness and the regulation of aggression-related primes. *Psychological Science, 17*, 136–142.

Melis, A. P., Hare, B., & Tomasello, M. (2006). Chimpanzees recruit the best collaborators. *Science, 311*, 1297–1300.

Midlarsky, E. (1991). Helping as coping. In M. S. Clark (Ed.), *Prosocial behavior* (pp. 238–264). Thousand Oaks, CA: Sage.

Milgram, S. (1970). The experience of living in cities. *Science, 167*, 1461–1468.

Miller, B., & Cafasso, L. (1992). Gender differences in caregiving: Fact or artifact? *The Gerontologist, 32*, 498–507.

Moreno, A., Klute, M., & Robinson, J. (2008). Relational and individual resources as predictors of empathy in early childhood. *Social Development, 17*, 613–637.

Musick, M. A., Herzog, A. R., & House, J. S. (1999). Volunteering and mortality among older adults: Findings from a national sample. *Journals of Gerontology Series B: Psychological Sciences and Social Sciences, 54*, S173–S180.

Nettle, D., & Liddle, B. (2008). Agreeableness is related to social-cognitive, but not social-perceptual, theory of mind. *European Journal of Personality, 22*, 323–335.

Nowak, M. (2006). Five rules for the evolution of cooperation. *Science, 314*, 1560–1563.

Oliner, S. P., & Oliner, P. M. (1988). *The altruistic personality: Rescuers of Jews in Nazi Europe*. New York: Free Press.

Oman, D., Thoresen, C. E., & McMahon, K. (1999). Volunteerism and mortality among the community-dwelling elderly. *Journal of Health Psychology, 4*, 301–316.

Park, J. H., & Schaller, M. (2005). Does attitude similarity serve as a heuristic cue for kinship? Evidence of an implicit cognitive association. *Evolution and Human Behavior, 26*, 158–170.

Penner, L. A. (2002). Dispositional and organizational influences on sustained volunteerism: An interactionist perspective. *Journal of Social Issues, 58*, 447–467.

Penner, L. A., & Finkelstein, M. A. (1998). Dispositional and structural determinants of volunteerism. *Journal of Personality and Social Psychology, 74*, 525–537.

Penner, L. A., Dovidio, J. F., Piliavin, J. A., & Schroeder, D. A. (2005). Prosocial behavior: Multilevel perspectives. *Annual Review of Psychology, 56*, 365–392.

Penner, L. A., Fritzsche, B. A., Craiger, J. P., & Freifeld, T. R. (1995). Measuring the prosocial personality. In J. Butcher & C. D. Spielberger (Eds.), *Advances in personality assessment* (pp. 147–163). Hillsdale, NJ: Erlbaum.

Piazza, J., & Bering, J. M. (2008). Concerns about reputation via gossip promote generous allocations in an economic game. *Evolution and Human Behavior, 29*, 172–178.

Pichon, I., Boccato, G., & Saroglou, V. (2007). Nonconscious influences of religion on prosociality: A priming study. *European Journal of Social Psychology, 37*, 1032–1045.

Piliavin, J. A., & Piliavin, I. M. (1972). Effect of blood on reactions to a victim. *Journal of Personality and Social Psychology, 23*, 353–361.

Piliavin, J. A., Dovidio, J. F., Gaertner, S. L., & Clark, R. D. (1981). *Emergency Intervention*. New York: Academic Press.

Pradel, J., Euler, H. A., & Fetchenhauer, D. (2009). Spotting altruistic dictator game players and mingling with them: The elective assortation of classmates. *Evolution and Human Behavior, 30*, 103–113.

Preston, S. D., & de Waal, F. B. M. (2002). Empathy: Its ultimate and proximate bases. *Behavioral and Brain Sciences, 25*, 1–20.

Pruitt, D. G. (1968). Reciprocity and credit building in a laboratory dyad. *Journal of Personality and Social Psychology, 8*, 143–147.

Rapoport, A., & Chammah, A. M. (1965). *The prisoner's dilemma*. Ann Arbor: University of Michigan Press.

Richerson, P. J., & Boyd, R. (2005). *Not by genes alone: How culture transformed human evolution*. Chicago: University of Chicago Press.

Rigdon, M., Ishii, K., Watabe, M., & Kitayama, S. (2009). Minimal social cues in the dictator game. *Journal of Economic Psychology, 30*, 358–367.

Rilling, J. K., Gutman, D. A., Zeh, T. R., Pagnoni, G., Berns, G. S., & Kilts, C. D. (2002). A neural basis for social cooperation. *Neuron, 35*, 395–405.

Rilling, J. K., Sanfey, A. G., Aronson, J. A., Nystrom, L. E., & Cohen, J. D. (2004). Opposing BOLD responses to reciprocated and unreciprocated altruism in putative reward pathways. *Neuroreport, 15*, 2539–2543.

Risen, J. L., & Gilovich, T. (2007). Target and observer differences in the acceptance of questionable apologies. *Journal of Personality and Social Psychology, 92*, 418–433.

Rosenhan, D., & White, G. M. (1967). Observation and rehearsal as determinants of prosocial behavior. *Journal of Personality and Social Psychology, 5*, 424–431.

Ross, A. S., & Braband, J. (1973). Effect of increased responsibility on bystander intervention: II. The cue value of a blind person. *Journal of Personality and Social Psychology, 25*, 254–258.

Rusbult, C. E. (1980). Commitment and satisfaction in romantic associations: A test of the investment model. *Journal of Experimental Social Psychology, 16*, 172–186.

Rusbult, C. E. (1983). A longitudinal test of the investment model: The development (and deterioration) of satisfaction and commitment in heterosexual involvements. *Journal of Personality and Social Psychology, 45*, 101–117.

Rushton, J. P. (1975). Generosity in children: Immediate and long-term effects of modeling, preaching, and moral judgment. *Journal of Personality and Social Psychology, 31*, 459–466.

Rushton, J. P., Fulker, D. W., Neale, M. C., Nias, D. K. B., & Eysenck, H. J. (1986). Altruism and aggression: The heritability of individual differences. *Journal of Personality and Social Psychology, 50*, 1192–1198.

Rutkowski, G. K., Gruder, C. L., & Romer, D. (1983). Group cohesiveness, social norms, and bystander intervention. *Journal of Personality and Social Psychology, 44*, 545–552.

Schaller, M., & Cialdini, R. B. (1988). The economics of empathic helping: Support for a mood-management motive. *Journal of Experimental Social Psychology, 24*, 163–181.

Schroeder, D. A., Dovidio, J. F., Sibicky, M. E., Matthews, L. L., & Allen, J. L. (1988). Empathy and helping behavior: Egoism or altruism? *Journal of Experimental Social Psychology, 24*, 333–353.

Seinen, I., & Schram, A. (2006). Social status and group norms: Indirect reciprocity in a repeated helping experiment. *European Economic Review, 50*, 581–602.

Shariff, A. F., & Norenzayan, A. (2007). God is watching you: Supernatural agent concepts increase prosocial behavior in an anonymous economic game. *Psychological Science, 18*, 803–809.

Sheldon, K. M., Sheldon, M. S., & Osbaldiston, R. (2000). Prosocial values and group orientation within an N-person prisoner's dilemma game. *Human Nature, 11*, 387–404.

Sheposh, J. P., & Gallo, P. S. (1973). Asymmetry of payoff structure and cooperation in the prisoner's dilemma game. *Journal of Conflict Resolution, 17*, 371–373.

Shotland, R. L., & Straw, M. K. (1976). Bystander response to an assault: When a man attacks a woman. *Journal of Personality and Social Psychology, 34*, 990–999.

Silk, J. B., Brosnan, S. F., Vonk, J., Henrich, J., Povinelli, D. J., Richardson, A. S., et al. (2005). Chimpanzees are indifferent to the welfare of unrelated group members. *Nature, 437*, 1357–1359.

Simpson, J. A., & Beckes, L. (2009). Evolutionary perspectives on prosocial behavior. In M. Mikulincer & P. R. Shaver (Eds.), *Prosocial motives, emotions, and behavior: The better angels of our nature*. Washington, DC: American Psychological Association.

Singer, T., Seymour, B., O'Doherty, J., Kaube, H., Dolan, R. J., & Frith, C. D. (2004). Empathy for pain involves the affective but not sensory components of pain. *Science, 303*, 1157–1162.

Smith, E. A., & Bleige Bird, R. (2001). Turtle hunting and tombstone opening: Public generosity as costly signaling. *Evolution and Human Behavior, 21*, 245–261.

Smith, K. D., Keating, J. P., & Stotland, E. (1989). Altruism reconsidered: The effect of denying feedback on a victim's status to empathic witnesses. *Journal of Personality and Social Psychology, 57*, 641–650.

Sommerfeld, R. D., Krambeck, H., Semmann, D., & Milinski, M. (2007). Gossip as an alternative for direct observation in games of indirect reciprocity. *Proceedings of the National Academy of Sciences, 104*, 17435–17440.

Sprecher, S. (2001). A comparison of emotional consequences of and change in equity over time using global and domain-specific measures of equity. *Journal of Social and Personal Relationships, 18*, 477–501.

Steblay, N. M. (1987). Helping behavior in rural and urban environments: A meta-analysis. *Psychological Bulletin, 102*, 346–356.

Steinfatt, T. M. (1973). The prisoner's dilemma and a creative alternative game: The effects of communications under conditions of real reward. *Simulation and Games, 4*, 389–409.

Stevens, J. R., Cushman, F. A., & Hauser, M. D. (2005). Evolving the psychological mechanisms for cooperation. *Annual Review of Ecology, Evolution, and Systematics, 36*, 499–518.

Stewart-Williams, S. (2007). Altruism among kin vs. nonkin: Effects of cost of help and reciprocal exchange. *Evolution and Human Behavior, 28*, 193–198.

Stürmer, S., Snyder, M., & Omoto, A. M. (2005). Prosocial emotions and helping: The moderating role of group membership. *Journal of Personality and Social Psychology, 88*, 532–546.

Sugiyama, L., Tooby, J., & Cosmides, L. (2002). Cross-cultural evidence of cognitive adaptations for social exchange among the Shiwiar of Ecuadorian Amazonia. *Proceedings of the National Academy of Sciences, 99*, 11537–11542.

Tabibnia, G., Satpute, A. B., & Lieberman, M. D. (2008). The sunny side of fairness: Preference for fairness activates reward circuitry (and disregarding unfairness activates self-control circuitry). *Psychological Science, 19*, 339–347.

Taylor, S. E. (2002). *The tending instinct: Women, men, and the biology of our relationships*. New York: Times Books.

Taylor, S. E., Dickerson, S. S., & Klein, L. C. (2002). Toward a biology of social support. In C. R. Snyder & S. J. Lopez (Eds.), *Handbook of positive psychology* (pp. 556–569). New York: Oxford University Press.

Taylor, S. E., Klein, L. C., Lewis, B. P., Gruenewald, T. L., Gurung, R. A. R., & Updegraff, J. A. (2000). Biobehavioral responses to stress in females: Tend-and-befriend, not fight-or-flight. *Psychological Review, 107*, 411–429.

Tazelaar, M. J. A., Van Lange, P. A. M., & Ouwerkerk, J. W. (2004). How to cope with "noise" in social dilemmas: The benefits of communication. *Journal of Personality and Social Psychology, 87*, 845–859.

Tesser, A., Gatewood, R., & Driver, M. (1968). Some determinants of gratitude. *Journal of Personality and Social Psychology, 9*, 233–236.

Thoits, P. H., L. (2001). Volunteer work and well-being. *Journal of Health and Social Behavior, 42*, 115–131.

Tooby, J., & Cosmides, L. (2005). Conceptual foundations of evolutionary psychology. In D. M. Buss (Ed.), *Handbook of evolutionary psychology* (pp. 5–67). Hoboken, NJ: Wiley.

Triandis, H. C. (1978). Some universals of social behavior. *Personality and Social Psychology Bulletin, 4*, 1–6.

Trivers, R. L. (1971). The evolution of reciprocal altruism. *Quarterly Review of Biology, 46*, 35–57.

Tsang, J. (2006). Gratitude and prosocial behaviour: An experimental test of gratitude. *Cognition and Emotion, 20*, 138–148.

Tsang, J. (2007). Gratitude for small and large favors: A behavioral test. *Journal of Positive Psychology, 2*, 157–167.

Tsang, J., McCullough, M. E., & Fincham, F. (2006). The longitudinal association between forgiveness and relationship closeness and commitment. *Journal of Social and Clinical Psychology, 25*, 448–472.

Turner, J. C. H., Oakes, P. J., Reicher, S. D., & Wetherell, M. S. (1987). *Rediscovering the social group: A self-categorization theory*. Oxford, UK: Basil Blackwell.

U.S. Department of Labor. (2009). Volunteering in the United States, 2008. Retrieved 30 May, 2009, from http://www.bls.gov/news.release/volun.nro.htm.

Van Lange, P. A. M., Ouwerkerk, J., & Tazelaar, M. (2002). How to overcome the detrimental effects of noise in social interaction: The benefits of generosity. *Journal of Personality and Social Psychology, 82*, 768–780.

Van Vugt, M., Snyder, M., Tyler, T., & Biel, A. (2000). *Cooperation in modern society: Promoting the welfare of communities, states, and organisations*. London: Routledge.

Varki, A., & Nelson, D. L. (2007). Genomic comparisons of humans and chimpanzees. *Annual Review of Anthropology, 36*, 191–209.

Wallace, H. M., Exline, J. J., & Baumeister, R. F. (2008). Interpersonal consequences of forgiveness: Does forgiveness deter or encourage repeat offenses? *Journal of Experimental Social Psychology, 44*, 453–360.

Walster, E., Berscheid, E., & Walster, G. W. (1973). New directions in equity research. *Journal of Personality and Social Psychology, 25*, 151–176.

Walster, E., Walster, G. W., & Berscheid, E. (1978). *Equity: Theory and research*. Boston: Allyn & Bacon.

Warneken, F., Hare, B., Melis, A. P., Hanus, D., & Tomasello, M. (2007). Spontaneous altruism by chimpanzees and young children. *PLoS Biology, 5*, 1414–1420.

Warneken, F., & Tomasello, M. (2006). Altruistic helping in human infants and young chimpanzees. *Science, 311*, 1301–1303.

Wayment, H. A. (2004). It could have been me: Vicarious victims and disaster-focused distress. *Personality and Social Psychology Bulletin, 30*, 515–528.

Weber, J. M., & Murnighan, J. K. (2008). Suckers or saviors? Consistent contributors in social dilemmas. *Journal of Personality and Social Psychology, 95*, 1340–1353.

Wedekind, C., & Milinski, M. (2000). Cooperation through image scoring in humans. *Science, 288*, 850–852.

West, S. A., Griffin, A. S., & Gardner, A. (2006). Social semantics: Altruism, cooperation, mutualism, strong reciprocity, and group selection. *Journal of Evolutionary Biology, 20*, 415–432.

West, S. G., & Brown, T. J. (1975). Physical attractiveness, the severity of the emergency and helping: A field experiment and interpersonal simulation. *Journal of Experimental Social Psychology, 11*, 531–538.

Williams, G. C. (1966). Adaptation and natural selection. A critique of some current evolutionary thought. Princeton, NJ: Princeton University Press.

Williams, G. C. (1992). *Natural selection: Domains, levels, and challenges.* New York: Oxford University Press.

Williamson, G. M., & Clark, M. S. (1989). Providing help and desired relationship type as determinants of changes in moods and self evaluations. *Journal of Personality and Social Psychology, 56*, 722–734.

Wilson, D. S., & Wilson, E. O. (2007). Rethinking the theoretical foundation of sociobiology. *Quarterly Review of Biology, 82*, 327–348.

Wood, R. M., Rilling, J. K., Sanfey, A. G., Bhagwagar, Z., & Rogers, R. D. (2006). Effects of tryptophan depletion on the performance of an iterated prisoner's dilemma game in healthy adults. *Neuropsychopharmacology, 31* 1075–1084.

Wrangham, R. W., & Peterson, D. (1996). *Demonic males: Apes and the origins of human violence.* New York: Houghton Mifflin.

Zahn-Waxler, C., Schiro, K., Robinson, J. L., Emde, R. N., & Schmitz, S. (2001). Empathy and prosocial patterns in young MZ and DZ twins: Development and genetic and environmental influences. In R. Emole (Ed.), *Infancy to early childhood: Genetic and environmental influences on developmental change* (pp. 141–162). Oxford, UK: Oxford University Press.

Zuckerman, M. (1975). Belief in a just world and altruistic behavior. *Journal of Personality and Social Psychology, 31*, 972–976.

Chapter 9

Aggression

Brad J. Bushman and Bruce D. Bartholow

> War may sometimes be a necessary evil. But no matter how necessary, it is always an evil, never a good. We will not learn how to live together in peace by killing each other's children.
>
> — *Jimmy Carter, former U.S. President*

If you look at the news, it may seem as if the world is a more violent place now than ever before. But in the media, "if it bleeds it leads." The media provide a violent, distorted reflection of reality. Television characters are 1000 times more likely to be murdered than real people (Robson, 1992). Quantitative studies of body counts, such as the proportion of prehistoric skeletons with axe and arrowhead wounds, suggest that prehistoric societies were far more violent than our own. Even though many more people can be killed with a bomb than with an axe, the death rates per battle were about 20 times higher in ancient tribal wars than in twentieth-century wars (Pinker, 2007). Even if we compare twentieth-century wars with more recent wars, such as those fought during the Middle Ages, the death counts were much higher then than now (e.g., Eisner, 2001; Gurr, 1981). For example, the estimated numbers of murders in England dropped from 24 per 100,000 in the fourteenth century to 0.6 per 100,000 by the early 1960s. The major decline in violence seems to have occurred in the seventeenth century during the "Age of Reason," beginning in the Netherlands and England and then spreading to other European countries (Pinker, 2007). In fact, global violence has been steadily falling since the middle of the twentieth century (Human Security Brief, 2007). The number of battle deaths in interstate wars has declined from more than 65,000 per year in the 1950s to less than 2000 per year in the 2000s. There are also global declines in the number of armed conflicts and combat deaths, the number of military coups, and the number of deadly violence campaigns waged against civilians.

A number of other observations are consistent with the view that human violence is decreasing. Pinker (2007) notes: "Cruelty as entertainment, human sacrifice to indulge superstition, slavery as a labor-saving device, conquest as the mission statement of government, genocide as a means of acquiring real estate, torture and mutilation as routine punishment, . . . —all were unexceptionable features of life for most of human history. But, today, they are rare to nonexistent in the West, far less common elsewhere than they used to be, concealed when they do occur, and widely condemned when they are brought to light."

Although we would like to, social psychologists cannot take credit for the significant reduction in violence that has occurred over time. Social psychologists have, however, conducted numerous studies that shed light on specific factors that increase and decrease aggression among humans today. We discuss the findings from these studies in this chapter. We begin by defining the terms *aggression* and *violence*. Next, we describe different theoretical explanations for aggression. We describe environmental, pharmacological, physiological, and neuropsychological factors that influence aggression. Next, we discuss different approaches for reducing aggression. Finally, we describe what topics are hot in the area of aggression today and what topics might be hot in the future.

Social Psychological Definitions of Aggression and Violence

In sports and in business, the term "aggressive" is frequently used when the terms "assertive," "enthusiastic," or "confident" would be more accurate. For example, an aggressive salesperson tries really hard to sell you something. The salesperson is not trying to harm you. In social psychology, the term *aggression* is generally defined as any behavior that is intended to harm another person who does not want to be harmed (e.g., Baron & Richardson, 1994). This definition contains several important features. Aggression is an external behavior that you can see. For example, you can see a person hit someone, curse someone, try to destroy someone's reputation by spreading gossip, or leave a really small tip for a waiter. (These behaviors represent different forms of aggression, which we address in detail in the next section.) Aggression is not an emotion that occurs inside a person, such as an angry feeling. Aggression is not a thought that occurs inside someone's brain, such as mentally rehearsing a murder you would like to commit. Aggression is a social behavior because it involves at least two people. Also, aggression is intentional, although not all intentional behaviors that hurt others are aggressive behaviors. For example, a dentist might intentionally give a patient a shot of Novocain (and the shot hurts!), but the goal is to help rather than hurt the patient.

Social psychologists and laypeople also differ in their use of the term *violence*. A meteorologist might call a storm "violent" if it has intense winds, rain, thunder, and lightning. In social psychology, *violence* is aggression that has extreme physical harm, such as injury or death, as its goal. One child intentionally pushing another child down is an act of aggression but is not an act of violence. One person intentionally hitting, kicking, shooting, or stabbing another person is an act of violence. Violence is a subset of aggression. All violent acts are aggressive, but not all aggressive acts are violent. The U.S. Federal Bureau of Investigation (FBI) classifies four crimes as violent: murder, assault, rape, and robbery. Social psychologists would also classify other physically aggressive acts as violent even if they do not meet the FBI definition of a violent crime, such as slapping someone really hard across the face. But a husband who swears at his wife would not be committing an act of violence by this definition.

Forms and Functions of Aggression

Different Forms of Aggression: Physical, Verbal, Relational, Direct, Indirect, Displaced, Passive, and Active Aggression

We believe it is useful to distinguish between forms and functions of aggression. By *forms* we mean how the aggressive behavior is expressed, such as physical verses verbal, direct versus indirect, and active versus passive (Buss, 1961). *Physical aggression* involves harming others with body parts or weapons (e.g., hitting, kicking, stabbing, or shooting them). *Verbal aggression* involves harming others with words (e.g., yelling, screaming, swearing, name calling). *Relational aggression* (also called *social aggression*) is defined as intentionally harming another person's social relationships, feelings of acceptance by others, or inclusion within a group (e.g., Crick & Grotpeter, 1995). Some examples of relational aggression include saying bad things about people behind their backs, withdrawing affection to get what you want, excluding others from your circle of friends, and giving someone the "silent treatment." Relational aggression is similar to the concept of ostracism. *Ostracism* refers to being excluded, rejected, and ignored by others (Williams, 2001).

The different forms of aggression can be expressed directly or indirectly (Lagerspetz, Bjorkqvist, & Peltonen, 1988). With *direct aggression*, the victim is physically present. With *indirect aggression*, the victim is physically absent. For example, physical aggression can be direct (e.g., choking a person) or indirect (e.g., puncturing the tires of a person's car when they aren't looking). Likewise, verbal aggression can be direct (e.g., cursing a person face-to-face) or indirect (e.g., spreading rumors about a person who is not present).

In *displaced aggression*, a substitute aggression target is used (e.g., Marcus-Newhall, Pedersen, Carlson, & Miller, 2000). The substitute target has not done anything to provoke an aggressive response, but just happens to be in the wrong place at the wrong time. For example, a man is berated by his boss at work and "suffers in silence" rather than retaliating. When he gets home, he yells at his children instead. Sometimes the substitute target is not entirely innocent, but has committed a minor or trivial offense. In this case, the aggression is called *triggered displaced aggression* (Pedersen, Gonzales, & Miller, 2000). For example, perhaps the man's children left toys in the family room rather than putting them away. Triggered displaced aggression is especially likely to occur when the aggressor ruminates about the initial offense (Bushman, Bonacci, Pedersen, Vasquez, & Miller, 2005) and when the aggressor does not like the substitute target (e.g., Pederson, Bushman, Vasquez, & Miller, 2008). People displace aggression for two main reasons. First, directly aggressing against the initial provoker may not be possible because the source is unavailable (e.g., the provoker has left the area) or because the source is an intangible entity (e.g., hot temperature). Second, fear of retaliation or punishment from the provoker may inhibit direct aggression. For example, the employee who was reprimanded by his boss may be reluctant to retaliate because he does not want to lose his job.

The form of aggression may be active or passive. With *active aggression*, the aggressor responds in a harmful manner (e.g., hitting, cursing). With *passive aggression*, the aggressor fails to respond in a helpful manner. For example, the aggressor might "forget" to deliver an important message to the person. It is often difficult to establish blame with passive acts of aggression, which frequently is a desirable feature from the aggressor's perspective.

Direct and active forms of aggression can be quite risky, leading to injury or even death. Thus, most people would rather use indirect and passive forms of aggression.

Different Functions of Aggression: Reactive and Proactive Aggression

Aggressive acts may also differ in their function. Consider two examples. In the first example, a husband finds his wife and her secret lover together in bed. He takes his rifle from the closet and shoots and kills them both. In the second example, a "hitman" uses a rifle to kill another person for money. The form of aggression is the same in both examples (i.e., physical aggression caused by shooting and killing victims with a rifle). However, the motives appear quite different. In the first example, the husband appears to be motivated by anger. He is enraged when he finds his wife making love to another man, so he shoots them both. In the second example, the "hitman" appears to be motivated by money. The "hitman" probably does not hate his victim and probably is not angry with the person. He might not even know his victim, but he kills the man anyway because he wants the money. To capture different functions or motives for aggression, researchers have made a distinction between reactive aggression (also called hostile, affective, angry, impulsive, or retaliatory aggression) and proactive aggression (also called instrumental aggression; e.g., Buss, 1961; Dodge & Coie, 1987; Feshbach, 1964). *Reactive aggression* is "hot," impulsive, angry behavior that is motivated by a desire to harm someone. Harming the person is the end goal. *Proactive aggression* is "cold," premeditated, calculated behavior that is motivated by some other goal (obtaining money, restoring your image, restoring justice). Harming the other person is a means to some other end goal. Some social psychologists have argued that it is difficult (if not impossible) to distinguish between reactive and proactive aggression because they are highly correlated and because motives are often mixed (Bushman & Anderson, 2001a). For example, what if the husband who finds his wife making love to another man hires a hitman to kill them both? Would this be reactive or proactive aggression?

Theoretical Approaches to the Study of Aggression

Although aggression was probably adaptive for our ancient ancestors, it seems maladaptive today. Aggression breeds more aggression, thereby creating a "downward spiral" of aggression (Slater, Henry, Swaim, & Anderson, 2003). Even though aggressive people often get what they want in the short run, there are many unintended consequences associated with aggression in the long run (e.g., relationships can be damaged; retaliation can occur). We might therefore ask: Why do humans behave aggressively? Is it because our brains are old and the aggressive tendencies that were so useful for our ancient ancestors are difficult to override now? Is it because of biological abnormalities or poor upbringing? Is it because of frustration or some other factor? In this section we review the major psychological theories of aggression.

Instinctive/Psychoanalytic Theories

First given scientific prominence by Darwin (1871), instinct theory viewed aggressive behavior as motivated by neither the seeking of pleasure nor the avoidance of pain, but rather as an evolutionary adaptation that had enabled our ancient ancestors to survive better. According to this view, aggression is instinctive in humans just as it is in many other animals. Aggression has several adaptive functions, from an evolutionary perspective. Aggression helps to disperse populations over a wide area, thereby ensuring maximum use of available natural resources. Aggression helps animals to successfully compete for limited resources in their environment and, consequently, is beneficial to their individual survival and to their ability to reproduce. Because it is closely related to mating, aggression also helps ensure that only the strongest individuals will pass their genes on to the next generation. The existence of innate, relatively automatic, aggressive responses has been demonstrated for many species (e.g., Lorenz, 1966). For example, for the male Stickleback fish, a red object triggers attack 100% of the time (Timbergen, 1952). However, no parallel innate aggressive response has been demonstrated for humans (Hinde, 1970).

In his early writings, Sigmund Freud proposed that all human behavior stems from a life or self-preservation instinct, which he called *eros*. Freud did not acknowledge the presence of an independent instinct to explain the darker side of human nature. He wrote: "I cannot bring myself to assume the existence of a special aggressive instinct alongside the familiar instincts of self-preservation and of sex, on an equal footing with them" (Freud, 1909/1961, p. 140). The atrocities of World War I changed his mind. By 1920, Freud had proposed the existence of an independent death or self-destruction instinct, which he called *thanatos*. The life instinct supposedly counteracts the death instinct and preserves life by diverting destructive urges outward toward others in the form of aggressive acts (Freud, 1933/1950).

Frustration–Aggression Theory

In 1939, psychologists from Yale University published an important book titled *Frustration and Aggression* (Dollard, Doob, Miller, Mowrer, & Sears, 1939). In this book, the authors proposed that aggression was due to frustration rather than to an aggressive instinct, as Freud had proposed. Frustration is an unpleasant emotion that arises when a person is being blocked from achieving a goal. Their theory was summarized in two bold statements: (1) "the occurrence of aggressive behavior always presupposes the existence of frustration" and (2) "the existence of frustration always leads to some form of aggression." In their view, frustration depended on an "expected" or "hoped for" goal being denied, and was not simply the absence of achieving a goal.

This theory seemed to explain a large amount of everyday occurrences of aggression, but it soon became apparent to the authors that not every frustration led to observable aggression. Miller (1941), one of the original authors, was the first to revise frustration–aggression theory. He explained that frustrations actually stimulate a number of different inclinations other than an inclination to aggress, such as an inclination to escape or to find a way around the obstacle to the goal. The inclination that eventually dominates, he proposed, is the one that is most successful in reducing frustration. In other words, people learn through experience to respond to frustrations in a number of different ways. If aggression has been an effective response in the past, then people will tend to use it whenever they become frustrated. This idea opened the door for learning theory explanations of aggression (see the next section).

In 1989, Leonard Berkowitz revised frustration–aggression theory by proposing that all unpleasant events—instead of only frustration—deserve to be recognized as important causes of aggression. The idea is that unpleasant events (including frustrations) automatically produce primitive fight-or-flight reactions. This fight-or-flight response is an adaptive stress-reducing response that occurs in humans and other animals (Cannon, 1915). When we experience an unpleasant event, we want to stop it or leave. Thus, anything that makes us feel bad automatically produces aggressive tendencies. Whether aggression occurs depends on how the unpleasant event is interpreted and on the presence of aggressive cues. For example, if a person has just seen a violent movie and is pushed from behind while exiting the theater, he or she may very well act in an aggressive manner.

Learning Theory Models

The earliest learning theory explanations for individual differences in aggressiveness focused on operant and classical conditioning processes. *Operant conditioning theory*, developed by behaviorists such as Edward Thorndike (1901) and B. F. Skinner (e.g., Ferster & Skinner, 1957), proposed that people are more likely to repeat behaviors that have been rewarded and are less likely to repeat behaviors that have been punished. Classical conditioning theory, developed by Ivan Pavlov (1927), proposes that through repeated pairing of an unconditioned stimulus with a conditioned stimulus, the unconditioned stimulus eventually elicits a response similar to the one elicited by the conditioned stimulus? Dogs that heard a bell (conditioned stimulus) every time they received food (unconditioned stimulus) eventually salivated when they heard the bell alone (conditioned response). Research showed that children who are reinforced for behaving aggressively learn to behave aggressively. Children also learn to discriminate between situations in which aggression pays and situations in which it does not. Through stimulus generalization they apply what they have learned to new situations (Sears, Whiting, Nowlis, & Sears, 1953). These processes explained how aggressive behavior could be learned (e.g., Eron, Walder, & Lefkowitz, 1971).

By the early 1960s, however, it became clear that operant and classical conditioning processes could not fully explain individual differences in aggression. Bandura theorized that people learn to behave aggressively by observing and imitating others (e.g., Bandura, Ross, & Ross 1961, 1963; Bandura, 1977). In several classic experiments, he tested his *observational learning theory* (also called *social learning theory*) by showing that young children imitated specific aggressive acts they observed in aggressive models. Bandura also developed the concept of *vicarious learning* of aggression by showing that children were especially likely to imitate models that had been rewarded for behaving aggressively (Bandura, 1965; Bandura et al., 1963). He argued that the imitation was the key to social learning. The child does not just imitate whatever behaviors he or she observes. What is important is how the child interprets the observed behavior, and how competent the child feels in carrying out the behavior (Bandura, 1986). These cognitions provide a basis for stability of behavior tendencies across a variety of situations. Watching one parent hit the other parent may not only increase a child's likelihood of hitting, but may also increase the child's belief that hitting is an acceptable response when someone makes you angry.

More recent research helps us better understand observational learning processes. Human and primate young have an innate tendency to imitate what they observe (Meltzoff, 2005; Meltzoff & Moore, 1977). They imitate expressions in early infancy and they imitate behaviors by the time they can walk. Thus, the hitting, grabbing, pushing behaviors that young children see around them or in the mass media are generally immediately mimicked unless the child has been taught not to (Bandura, 1977; Bandura, Ross, & Ross, 1961, 1963). Furthermore, automatic imitation of expressions on others' faces can lead to the automatic activation of the emotion that the other was experiencing. For example, observing angry expressions can stimulate angry emotions in viewers (Prinz, 2005; Zajonc, Murphy, & Inglehart, 1989).

The demonstration in the mid-1990s of the existence of "mirror neurons" that fire either when an action is observed or when it is executed provided a strong basis for understanding why children imitate others (Gallese, Fadiga, Fogassi, & Rizzolatti, 1996; Iacoboni, Woods, Brass, Bekkering, Mazziotta, & Rizzolatti, 1999; Rizzolatti, 2005). The immediate "mimicry" of aggressive behaviors does not require a complex cognitive representation of the observed act, but only a simple "mirror" representation of it.

Theories Based on Physiological Arousal

Many stimuli that increase aggression (e.g., provocation, heat, media violence) also increase arousal levels, suggesting that arousal may have a role in stimulating aggression. But why would arousal increase aggression? There are at least four possible reasons. First, high levels of arousal may be experienced as aversive (e.g., Mendelson, Thurston, & Kubzansky, 2008), and may therefore stimulate aggression in the same way as other aversive stimuli (Berkowitz, 1989). Second, arousal narrows our span of attention (Easterbrook, 1959). If aggressive cues are salient in the situation, then people will focus most of their attention on the aggressive cues, which will facilitate aggression. Third, arousal increases the dominant response, which is defined as the most common response in that situation (Zajonc, 1965). Thus, people who are characteristically aggressive will be even more inclined to behave aggressively when they are aroused than when they are not aroused. Fourth, arousal may be mislabeled as anger in situations involving provocation, thus producing anger-motivated aggressive behavior. This mislabeling of arousal has been demonstrated in several studies by Dolf Zillmann, who has named it *excitation transfer* (Zillmann, 1979, 1988). Excitation-transfer theory assumes that physiological arousal, however it is produced, dissipates slowly. If two arousing events are separated by a short amount of time, some of the arousal caused by the first event may transfer to the second event. In other words, arousal from the first event may be misattributed to the second event. If the second event increases anger, then the additional arousal should make the person even angrier. Excitation-transfer theory also suggests that anger may be extended over long periods of time, if the person has attributed his or her heightened arousal to anger and ruminates about it. Thus, even after the arousal has dissipated the person may remain ready to aggress for as long as the self-generated label of "anger" persists.

Social-Cognitive, Information-Processing Models of Aggression

Two important cognitive information-processing models were proposed in the 1980s. One model, developed by Rowell Huesmann and his colleagues (Huesmann, 1982, 1988, 1998; Huesmann & Eron, 1984), focuses primarily on scripts. In a play or movie, a script tells the actor what to say and do. In memory, a *script* defines situations and guides behavior: The person first selects a script to represent the situation and then assumes a role in the script. One example is a restaurant script (i.e., enter restaurant, go to table, look at menu, order food, eat food, pay for food, leave tip, exit restaurant; see Abelson, 1981). Scripts can be learned by direct experience or by observing others (e.g., parents, siblings, peers, mass media characters). Huesmann proposed that when children observe violence in the mass media, they learn scripts for aggressive behavior.

What determines which of the many scripts in a person's memory will be retrieved on a given occasion? One factor involves the principle of encoding specificity. According to this principle, the recall of information depends in large part on the similarity of the recall situation to the situation in which encoding occurred (Tulving & Thomson, 1973). As a child develops, he or she may observe cases in which violence is used to solve interpersonal conflicts. The observed information is then stored in memory, possibly to be retrieved later when the child is involved in a conflict situation. Whether the script is retrieved will depend partly on the similarity between cues present at the time of encoding and those present at the time of retrieval. If the cues are similar, the child may retrieve the script and use it as a guide for behavior.

The second model, developed by Dodge and his colleagues (Dodge, 1980; 1986, 1993; Dodge & Frame, 1982; Fite, Goodnight, Bates, Dodge, & Pettit, 2008), focuses primarily on attributions. *Attributions* are the explanations people give about why others behave the way they do. Dodge and his colleagues have found that aggressive people have a *hostile attribution bias*—they tend to perceive ambiguous actions by others as hostile, which can lead them to respond in hostile ways themselves. For example, if a person bumps into them, they might infer that the person did it intentionally to hurt or challenge them. A meta-analytic review showed a strong relationship between hostile attribution of intent and aggressive behavior (Orobrio de Castro, Veerman, Koops, Bosch, & Monshouwer, 2002).

Although the two models differ in their details, both view aggression as the outcome of a social problem-solving process in which situational factors are evaluated, social scripts are retrieved or attributions are made, and these scripts or attributions are evaluated (often nonconsciously) until one is selected to guide a response.

General Aggression Model

In an attempt to build a broad model of aggression that encompasses other aggression theories, Craig Anderson and his colleagues developed the General

Aggression Model (e.g., Anderson & Bushman, 2002). In the model, certain person and situation *inputs* are risk factors for aggression. Person inputs include anything the person brings to the situation, such as biological sex, genetic predispositions, personality traits, attitudes, beliefs, and values. Situation inputs include all external factors that can influence aggression, such as aggressive cues, unpleasant situations, and external motives for aggression (e.g., money, recognition from others). These personal and situational factors influence the person's internal state, such as aggressive thoughts, angry feelings, physiological arousal levels, and brain activity. These internal states are all interconnected. The internal states influence the decisions the person makes. These decisions influence whether the person will behave aggressively.

Environmental/Situational Triggers of Aggression

Often aggression can be triggered by factors external to the person, such as events that occur in the environment. In the next two sections, we review some of the most common external triggers, and the internal states they often produce, that can prompt aggressive responding. Although we have chosen to separate environmental triggers (this section) from internal triggers (the next section) given the theoretical distinction between them, it is often difficult to unambiguously assign particular stimuli to only one of these two categories. In addition, although there are numerous external events that can trigger aggression, we have classified them into three categories: (1) *provocations*, (2) *aggression-related cues*, and (3) *intangible entities*.

Most people understand what provocation is, but it is useful to provide a definition. A provocation is any action taken by one person that makes another person angry. Provocations need not be intentional. For example, someone could inadvertently mention a sensitive topic during a conversation without realizing that the remarks might make their partner angry. Whether intentional or not, provocations are perhaps the most reliable predictor of aggression. A considerable amount of research has investigated the influence of provocation on aggression (e.g., Giancola et al., 2002a, 2002b; Bettencourt, Talley, Benjamin, & Valentine, 2006). In laboratory studies, provocation has been operationalized in a number of ways, including personal insults (e.g., Berkowitz, 1960; Caprara, Passerini, Pastorelli, Renzi, & Zelli, 1986; Caprara & Renzi, 1981), intensity of electric shock or noxious noise administered to a participant (e.g., Bushman, 1995; Giancola & Zeichner, 1995b; Taylor, 1967), magnitude of penalties assessed during a competitive task (e.g., Bjork, Dougherty, & Moeller, 1997; Bjork et al., 2000), and exclusion from some activity (e.g., Geen, 1968;

Rule & Percival, 1971). The basic (and unsurprising) conclusion from this work is that people are much more likely to be aggressive if they have been provoked than if they have not.

The second broad category of external triggers includes cues that have been associated with aggression (e.g., weapons, violent media). In an early experiment (Berkowitz & LePage, 1967), participants who had been insulted by a confederate were seated at a table that had a shotgun and a revolver on it, or, in the control condition, badminton racquets and shuttlecocks. The items on the table were described as part of another experiment that the other researcher had supposedly forgotten to put away. The participant was supposed to decide what level of electric shock to deliver to a confederate (aggression measure). The experimenter told participants to ignore the items, but apparently they could not. Participants who saw the guns were more aggressive than were participants who saw the sports items. This so-called "weapons effect" has been replicated numerous times (see Carlson et al., 1990; Turner, Simons, Berkowitz, & Frodi, 1977). The weapons effect appears to be due to increased accessibility of aggressive thoughts (Anderson, Benjamin, & Bartholow, 1998; Bartholow, Anderson, Carnagey, & Benjamin, 2005). Due to their common cooccurrence, strong associations between guns and violence form in long-term memory. Perceiving a gun can activate these associations, temporarily making aggression-related thoughts highly accessible. Participants in one study responded more quickly to aggressive words after seeing photos of guns than after seeing photos of plants (Anderson et al., 1998). Subsequent work showed that the weapons effect differs for people who have experience with guns (e.g., hunters, target shooters) compared to people who have no experience with guns (Bartholow et al., 2005). Specifically, sport-shooters showed the typical weapon-priming and behavioral weapons effects in the presence of assault guns but not in the presence of hunting guns. In contrast, participants without prior sport-shooting experience did not show this differentiation.

Of course, weapons are just one example of cues that can become associated with aggression in long-term memory. Another example is alcohol-related cues, such as photos of alcohol bottles or words such as "vodka" and "beer." Research has consistently shown that people—drinkers and nondrinkers alike—associate alcohol consumption with a number of psychological, emotional, and behavioral effects, including increased aggression (e.g., Goldman, 1999; Stacy, Widaman, & Marlatt, 1990). These "alcohol outcome expectancies" are conceptualized as constructs in long-term memory that develop through both direct drinking experience and through indirect experiences (e.g., observing others drinking, the media). Using a variety of cue exposure methods and aggression-related outcome measures, Research has shown that exposure to alcohol-related cues—even words presented too briefly to be recognized — can elicit increased aggression, particularly among individuals whose alcohol outcome expectancies include the idea that drinking alcohol makes people aggressive (e.g., Bartholow & Heinz, 2006; Friedman, McCarthy, Bartholow, & Hicks, 2007; Subra, Muller, Bègue, Bushman, Delmas, in press). Importantly, these effects occur even though participants do not drink a single drop of alcohol or even a placebo beverage (i.e., one that they believe contains alcohol).

Similarly, hot temperatures are often linked to aggression and violence in memory. This belief has even crept into the English language, as indicated by common phrases such as "hot temper, "hot headed," "hot under the collar," and "my blood is boiling." Recent research has shown that words associated with hot temperatures (e.g., boiling, roasted) increase aggressive thoughts and hostile perceptions (DeWall & Bushman, 2009).

Another important source of external triggers for aggression is mass media. Content analyses have shown that television programs, movies, video games, and other popular forms of entertainment media contain considerable amounts of violence (Gentile & Walsh, 2002; National Television Violence Study, 1998). In 1972, the Surgeon General issued a warning on violent TV programs stating: "It is clear to me that the *causal relationship* between televised violence and antisocial behavior is sufficient to warrant appropriate and *immediate* remedial action" (Steinfeld, 1972). In the years since this warning was issued, hundreds of studies have shown a link between violent media exposure and aggression (see Anderson et al., 2010; Anderson et al., 2003; Bushman & Huesmann, 2006).

Recently, researchers have begun to investigate the boundary conditions for media violence effects, particularly those associated with violent video games. For example, one study showed that violent video games increase aggressive thoughts, feelings, and behavior immediately after game play, but that the effects do not last longer than 15 minutes (Sestir & Bartholow, 2010). However, if players ruminate about the violence in the game, the effects can last at least 24 hours (Bushman & Gibson, 2010). In addition, the cumulative effects of exposure to media violence can last for many years (e.g., Huesmann, Moise, Podolski, & Eron, 2003).

Intangible entities are triggers that make people feel bad but cannot be attributed to a particular person or obvious cue. One example is hot temperature. In the mid-1700s, Montesquieu wrote of an apparent link between climate differences and crime, noting, "in the northern climates you will find people with few vices . . . as you move toward the countries of the south, you will believe you have moved away from morality itself: the liveliest passions will increase crime" (1748/1989, p. 234). Montesquieu's observations were correct: Hot temperatures are linked to violent and aggressive behavior (see Anderson, 1989; Anderson & Anderson, 1996; Anderson, Bushman, & Groom, 1997). Other intangible entities are loud noises, including traffic noise (Gaur, 1988). Noise is especially likely to increase aggression when it is uncontrollable (Geen, 1978; Geen & McCown, 1984) and when it is paired with other factors that increase aggression, such as provocation (Donnerstein & Wilson, 1976) or violent media (Geen & O'Neal, 1969). Irritants in the air that we breathe can make us more aggressive, such as foul odors (Rotton, Frey, Barry, Milligan, & Fitzpatrick, 1979), secondhand smoke (Jones & Bogat, 1978), and air pollution (Rotton & Frey, 1985).

Internal Triggers

One reason external factors increase aggression is that they increase aggressive thoughts and angry feelings. For example, research suggests that provocation from an external source leads to increased aggression primarily by increasing anger. Why is anger likely to increase aggression? One possible reason is that angry people aggress in the hope that doing so will help them feel better. Research has consistently shown that people who feel bad often try to remedy or repair their moods (Morris & Reilly, 1987). Because many people believe that venting is a healthy way to reduce anger and aggression they might vent by lashing out at others to improve their mood. One series of studies replicated the standard finding that anger increases aggression, but also found an interesting (and revealing) exception: When participants believed that their angry mood would not change for the next hour no matter what they did (ostensibly because of side effects of a pill they had taken), anger did not lead to aggression (Bushman et al., 2001). The implication of this finding is that anger does not *directly* or *inevitably* cause aggression. Rather, angry people attack others because they believe that lashing out will help them get rid of their anger and enable them to feel better.

Pain is another internal state that has been linked to the propensity to aggress. Numerous studies conducted on animals (e.g., Azrin, Hutchinson, & McLaughlin, 1965; Hutchinson, 1983; Ulrich, 1966) have shown that experiencing physical pain elicits aggressive responses. Similar findings have been reported with humans (e.g., Anderson, Anderson, Dill, & Deuser, 1998; Berkowitz, Cochran, & Embree, 1981). A number of hypotheses have been offered to explain why pain increases aggression. Perhaps the most interesting are the contrasting views that pain-induced aggression is (1) merely defensive versus (2) motivated by retribution. Studies using both animal (e.g., Azrin et al., 1965) and human (e.g., Berkowitz et al., 1981) participants support the latter view, showing that, for example, an animal will expend effort (e.g., by pulling a chain) to gain access to the target of their aggression.

Not only does physical pain increase aggression, but psychological or emotional pain, such as interpersonal rejection (i.e., feeling as though your relationship to another person is not valued by or is not important to that other person) or social exclusion, has similar effects (Buckley, Winkel, & Leary, 2004). The underlying neurocognitive mechanisms of social pain are similar to those for physical pain (see Eisenberger, Lieberman, & Williams, 2003; MacDonald & Leary, 2005). Rejected people aggress for a host of reasons: to improve their mood, to establish (or reestablish) efficacy, control, or social influence, and to seek revenge (Leary et al., 2006). Recent research shows that Tylenol reduces emotional pain was well as physical pain (DeWall et al., in press).

Like unpleasant feelings (e.g., anger, frustration), aggressive cognitions hold a prominent place in many theories of aggression (e.g., Dodge, 1986; Huesmann, 1998; Lindsay & Anderson, 2000). As reviewed in the previous section, a number of external triggers (e.g., guns, alcohol, temperature, media violence) increase the accessibility of aggressive thoughts. Aggressive thoughts, in turn, increase the likelihood of aggressive behaviors, either through simple priming (see Bartholow et al., 2005) or via their place in aggressive behavioral scripts (e.g., Huesmann, 1998) or by biasing their interpretation of others' behaviors (e.g., Dodge, 1986).

Chemical/Pharmacological Influences on Aggression

Hormones and Neurotransmitters

Like most behaviors, aggression is mediated by changes in chemical reactions and interactions within the brain. Two naturally occurring chemicals in the brain, testosterone and serotonin, have been closely linked with aggression. Testosterone, a male sex hormone, is a simple chemical arrangement of carbon rings, a derivative of the molecule cholesterol. Although both males and females have testosterone, males have much more of it. Testosterone levels are at their lifetime peak during puberty, and they begin to decline around the age of 23. Testosterone has repeatedly been linked to aggression in both sexes. In a review of this work, Sapolsky (1998) provided a concise description of the seemingly direct association between testosterone and aggression: "Remove the source of testosterone in species after species and levels of aggression typically plummet. Reinstate normal testosterone levels afterward with injections of synthetic testosterone, and aggression returns" (p. 150).

Research indicates both long-term and short-term effects of testosterone on aggression (Archer, 1991). In the long run, testosterone seems to affect the development and organization of various collections of cells in the brain that are associated with sex-typed behaviors (ranging from sex to hunting—see Cosmides & Tooby, 2006) as well as affecting bodily structures (e.g., muscles, height) that influence the likelihood and success of aggressive behaviors. In the short run, testosterone may increase aggression by increasing feelings of dominance. Although both effects are well established in animals, only the long-term effects are well established in humans (Brain & Susman, 1997; Reinisch, 1981).

Serotonin is another naturally occurring chemical in the brain that is known to influence aggression, particularly impulsive aggression. Serotonin (also known by its chemical name 5-hydroxytryptamine, or 5-HT) is called the "feel good" neurotransmitter. People who do not have enough serotonin may feel bad and may therefore behave more aggressively. Although serotonin can act in other parts of the body (e.g., the digestive system), in the brain it is important in modulating a number of emotional and behavioral responses, including anger, mood, and aggression. In correlational studies, levels of serotonin in the brain have been negatively related to violence in both epidemiological (Moffitt et al., 1998) and clinical samples (Goveas et al., 2004). Similar results have been reported with nonhuman primates (see Higley et al., 1992; Westergaard et al., 1999).

Perhaps the best evidence of the influence of serotonin on aggression comes from experimental laboratory studies showing that short-term reduction in serotonin levels, achieved by decreasing dietary tryptophan, increases aggressive responding, whereas increasing serotonin levels via dietary supplements of tryptophan decreases aggressive responding (e.g., Cleare & Bond, 1995; Marsh et al., 2002; Pihl et al., 1995). Similar results have been obtained by increasing serotonin levels using drugs such as D-fenfluramine (see Cherek & Lane, 2001) and paroxetine (Berman, McCloskey, Fanning, Schumacher, & Coccaro, 2009). Other studies have shown that long-term use of medications that increase levels of serotonin reduces impulsive aggression in patients with personality disorders (e.g., Coccaro & Kavoussi, 1997; Salzman et al., 1995).

The question of just *how* serotonin influences aggression has been the subject of considerable debate and theorizing. Most theories agree that serotonin does not decrease aggression directly, but does so indirectly by its effects on other processes such as irritability, impulsivity, and information processing (e.g., Berman et al., 1997). This idea is supported by research showing that serotonin influences impulsive (but not planned) aggression (see Berman et al., 1997), and the recent idea that factors such as alcohol increase aggression by reducing inhibitory control through decreases in the levels of serotonin (see McCloskey, Berman, Echevarria, & Coccaro, 2009).

Alcohol and Other Drugs of Abuse

In addition to considering how naturally occurring chemicals in the brain influence aggression, it is also important to consider how chemicals that people ingest influence aggression. By far the chemical that has received the most attention is alcohol. Considerable evidence indicates that consumption of alcohol increases aggression (for reviews see Bushman & Cooper, 1990; Giancola, 2000; Ito et al., 1998). A number of theories have been proposed to explain alcohol's aggression-enhancing effects, most of which emphasize the effects of the drug on disrupting cognitive processing (see Giancola, 2000; Steele & Josephs, 1990). Perhaps the most influential of these theories has been the "alcohol myopia" theory (Steele & Josephs, 1990), which posits that alcohol narrows the range of cues to which people pay attention so that they focus mainly on the most noticeable ones. For example, after a few drinks, a bar patron might be especially likely to focus attention on a highly salient, apparent provocation (e.g., being pushed in the back) and to ignore or poorly process other, more peripheral cues that might inhibit an aggressive response (e.g., that the "push" was accidental, or that the provocateur is much larger and stronger). Evidence from some recent experiments supports the myopia theory (e.g., Denson, Aviles, Pollock, Earleywine, Vasquez, & Miller, 2008; Giancola & Corman, 2007).

Another similar theory posits that alcohol disrupts executive functions (Giancola, 2000). Although exactly which processes are considered executive functions is a matter of continuing debate (see Miyake et al., 2000), all models generally agree that the ability to inhibit behavior is central to executive functioning. According to the executive impairment model of alcohol-related aggression, alcohol increases aggression by reducing inhibitory control. In other words, alcohol increases aggression not by "stepping on the gas" but by paralyzing the brakes. Numerous studies have shown that alcohol impairs inhibition (see Bartholow, Dickter, & Sestir, 2006; Fillmore & Vogel-Sprott, 1999, 2000; Giancola, 2000, 2004) and that inhibition is critical for withholding aggression (see Berkowitz, 1993).

It is important to note that alcohol consumption is not uniformly associated with increased aggression. A number of factors moderate the effects of alcohol on aggression. For example, alcohol is more likely to increase aggression in men than in women (see Giancola, 2002a; Gussler-Burkhardt & Giancola, 2005; Hoaken & Pihl, 2000), and alcohol is especially likely to increase aggression in men who are predisposed to behave aggressively (Giancola, 2002b,c; Giancola, Saucier, & Gussler-Burkhardt, 2003) and in individuals who expect alcohol to increase aggression (see Giancola 2006).

Considerably less research has been conducted on the aggression-related effects of other drugs of abuse, particularly in humans. However, human studies that do exist provide evidence that cocaine exposure, for instance, is associated with increased aggression. For example, preadolescence boys (although not girls) prenatally exposed to cocaine were more aggressive than nonexposed boys and girls (Bennett, Bendersky, & Lewis, 2007). Other work with cocaine-dependent patients found similar results (see Denison, Paredes, & Booth, 1997), although causal relations are not entirely clear in such correlational studies. For obvious ethical and legal reasons it is very difficult for researchers to conduct controlled, randomized laboratory experiments on the effects of cocaine in humans. Still, the available experimental evidence indicates that acute cocaine administration leads to increased aggression in laboratory tasks (e.g., Licata, Taylor, Berman, & Cranston, 1993).

Despite the relative dearth of experimental studies with humans, effects of both acute and chronic cocaine exposure on aggression have been studied extensively with animals. Considerable research has shown that rats, hamsters, and other rodents chronically exposed to cocaine, particularly during adolescence, are more aggressive than nonexposed animals (e.g., DeLeon, Grimes, Connor, & Melloni, 2002; Harrison, Connor, Nowak, & Melloni, 2000; Knyshevski, Ricci, McCann, & Melloni, 2005). A number of studies have linked these effects to systems involving serotonin (e.g., Knyshevski et al., 2005; Ricci, Knyshevski, & Melloni, 2005). This research is consistent with other findings showing that reduced levels of serotonin in humans are associated with increased aggression (e.g., Cleare & Bond, 1995; Marsh et al., 2002; Pihl et al., 1995).

Neuropsychological and Physiological Correlates of Aggression and Violence

In previous sections we have discussed how research in neuroscience investigating the effects of brain chemicals (e.g., serotonin, testosterone) and ingested substances (e.g., alcohol) has increased our understanding of aggression. In this section we extend this review by linking this work with research evidence on the relationships between brain processes, including both brain structure and function, and aggression (for a general overview of the link between brain processes and social processes, see Heatherton and Wheatley, Chapter 16, this volume).

Frontal Lobe Function and Aggression

We noted previously that alcohol consumption might increase aggression by impairing executive functioning (Giancola, 2000). This hypothesis stems from the more general idea that impaired executive functioning is linked to aggression (Giancola, 1995; Giancola, Mezzich, & Tarter, 1998; Seguin & Zelazo, 2005). Neuropsychological and functional brain imaging research has identified the frontal lobes, and, in particular, the prefrontal cortex (i.e., the part of the brain located just behind the forehead), as the source of executive functioning (see Roberts, Robbins, & Weiskrantz, 1998). Generally speaking, frontal lobe function is negatively related to aggression and violence in both normal (e.g., Giancola, 1995; Giancola & Zeichner, 1994) and clinical populations (e.g., Giancola, Mezzich, & Tarter, 1998a,b). Additionally, damage to the prefrontal cortex has been linked to increased aggression and antisocial behavior (e.g., Grafman et al., 1996). The "frontal lobes" are not, however, a unitary structure. Ongoing research is beginning to specify which structure(s) within the frontal lobes are implicated in aggression, and why.

Aggression is characteristic of some psychiatric disorders, especially disorders involving poor impulse control (Seo, Patrick, & Kennealy, 2008). The link is particularly strong for disorders involving low levels of serotonin. Dysfunctional interactions between serotonin and dopamine systems in the prefrontal cortex appear especially important in understanding links between impulsive aggression and other psychiatric conditions. Abnormally low serotonin function could represent a biochemical trait that predisposes affected individuals to impulsive aggression. The importance of this and related work is in the potential to identify so-called "endophenotypes" for aggression and violence. An endophenotype is essentially an intermediate phenotype, occurring between the ultimate causes (e.g., genetic variation) and ultimate outcomes (e.g., psychiatric diagnosis) of a condition of interest. Endophenotypes are thought to be state independent, meaning they are manifest in affected individuals regardless of whether the relevant syndrome or condition (e.g., antisocial personality disorder) has emerged. Thus, identifying endophenotypes for aggression and violence could be very important in the search for ways to identify people who are at risk for extreme aggression (e.g., school shooters) before they have had a chance to wreak too much havoc, providing opportunities for intervention and treatment.

Contributions of Electrophysiological, Functional Brain Imaging and Genetic Research

Recently, some researchers have begun to investigate brain responses elicited by external and internal cues to aggression. Work of this type is important to establish links between aggression-related triggers and the neural processes that give rise to overt behavioral expression of aggression. One study examined the desensitization effects of violent video games on the brains of young men who played either many violent games or many nonviolent games (Bartholow, Bushman, & Sestir, 2006). Chronic exposure to violent games was expected to be associated with muted brain responses to images depicting violence in the real world, and this brain response was expected to be related to increased aggressive behavior. Participants completed survey measures of violent media exposure, trait hostility, and irritability, and then viewed a series of violent, negative but nonviolent, and neutral pictures while event-related brain potentials (ERPs) were recorded. Briefly, ERPs represent electrical responses generated by the brain (primarily the cortex) during information processing. A particular component (i.e., voltage deflection) of the ERP, the P300 (which occurs approximately 300 milliseconds, or three-tenths of a second, following the onset of a stimulus), has been associated in previous research with the activation of approach and avoidance motivational systems in response to positive and negative images (e.g., Ito, Larsen, Smith, & Cacioppo, 1998; Schupp et al., 2000). Chronic violent video game exposure was expected to be associated with desensitization to violence, as reflected by smaller P300 responses to violent images. As expected, there was a negative association between violent game exposure and the size of the P300 elicited by violent pictures. This relationship remained even after individual differences in trait hostility and irritability were statistically controlled. Moreover, the P300 response elicited by violent pictures predicted aggressive behavioral responses in a subsequent laboratory task, suggesting that desensitization at the neural level is associated with increased aggressive responding (see also Funk et al., 2004).

Functional magnetic resonance imaging (fMRI) has been used to study the specific neural structures involved in processing violence and in regulating aggressive responding. fMRI involves the measurement of blood flow to specific brain structures in response to specific stimuli or events, which can be used as an index of how much activity in those structures is elicited by those stimuli. Recent evidence suggests that exposure to violent media may be linked to decreases in the activity of brain structures needed for the regulation of aggressive behavior. For example, the anterior cingulate cortex (ACC), located in the medial frontal lobe, is vital for self-regulation, as it appears to serve as one seat of the interface between affect and cognition during the monitoring of ongoing action (see Bush, Luu, & Posner, 2000). More specifically, the ACC appears to serve an action-monitoring function (see Botvinick et al., 2001), alerting other areas of the prefrontal cortex when increased control is needed to regulate behavior. Recent work used fMRI to test potential links between exposure to violent games, ACC activity, and aggression (Weber, Ritterfeld, & Mathiak, 2006). It was found that engaging in virtual violence during game play was associated with decreased activation of the ACC and, in particular, the rostral (anterior) part of the ACC, which has been linked to integration of emotional information (see Bush et al., 2000). These data are consistent with ERP findings (Bartholow et al., 2006) in suggesting that exposure to violence leads to suppression of affective information processing, which could interfere with the regulation of aggressive responding (see also Sterzer, Stadler, Krebs, Kleinschmidt, & Poustka, 2003).

Other brain imaging studies also point to areas in the prefrontal cortex as important for regulating anger and aggression. These data are consistent with the neuropsychological data reviewed previously. For example, participants in one study were insulted and induced to ruminate while fMRI was used to measure the flow of blood to different parts of their brains (Denson, Pedersen, Ronquillo, & Nandy, 2009). The results showed that activity in areas of the prefrontal cortex was positively related to self-reported feelings of anger and to individual differences in self-reported aggression. In another study, women received injections of testosterone while viewing slides depicting angry and happy faces (Hermans, Ramsey, & Van Honk, 2008). The results showed consistent activation to angry versus happy faces in brain areas known to be involved in reactive aggression, such as the amygdala and hypothalamus. Heightened activation was also found in the orbitofrontal cortex, a region of the brain linked to impulse control. Testosterone appears to enhance responsiveness in neural circuits believed to be involved in interpersonal aggression, providing some of the first direct evidence in humans for the seat of testosterone's effects in the brain.

Recently, Raine (2008) reviewed the genetic and brain imaging literatures related to violent and antisocial behavior and proposed a model whereby specific genes result in structural and functional brain alterations that, in turn, predispose individuals to behave in an aggressive manner. In the model, the prefrontal cortex (as well as limbic structures, such as the amygdala) is especially important for understanding aggression and violence. The model, however, goes beyond previous work by focusing on how environmental influences may alter gene expression in these areas "to trigger the cascade of events that translate genes into antisocial behavior" (2008, p. 323). For example, a common polymorphism (i.e., an individual difference in the form or expression of a biological process) in the monoamine oxidase A (MAOA) gene, which produces an enzyme important for breaking down neurotransmitters such as serotonin and dopamine, has been associated with both antisocial behavior (Moffitt et al., 2002) and reduced volume of brain structures, such as the amygdala and orbitofrontal cortex, important for emotion and self-regulation. These structures are known to be compromised in antisocial people. Future treatments for violent, antisocial behavior could therefore include drug therapy to regulate levels of MAOA activity.

In summary, the available biochemical, neuropsychological, and brain imaging data all indicate areas of the prefrontal cortex and limbic structures known to be important for self-regulation, impulse control, and processing of emotional information are also important for regulating aggressive behavior. Moreover, considerable research in both humans and animals points to serotonin as a key neurotransmitter for this regulatory process, with low levels of serotonin reliably producing high levels of aggression.

What If Anything Can be Done to Reduce Aggression?

People do not have to learn how to behave aggressively—it comes quite naturally. What people have to learn is how to control aggressive tendencies. Because aggression directly interferes with our basic needs of safety and security, it is important to find interventions that reduce it. The fact that there is no single cause for aggression makes it difficult to design effective interventions. A treatment that works for one person may not work for another. Indeed, some people (e.g., psychopaths) may not respond to any intervention. We do not want to sound pessimistic, but many people have started to accept the fact that aggression and violence may be an inevitable part of our society.

This being said, there certainly are interventions that can reduce aggression and violence. There are two important general points we would like to emphasize. First, successful interventions target as many causes of aggression as possible, and attempt to tackle them collectively. Interventions that are narrowly focused at removing a single cause of aggression, however well conducted, are likely to fail. Second, aggressive behavior problems are best treated in childhood, when they are still malleable. It is much more difficult to alter aggressive behaviors when they are part of an adult personality than when they are still in development. Thus, interventions should target aggressive children before they grow up to become aggressive adolescents and adults. In this section we discuss some interventions that have been used to reduce aggression. Before we discuss the effective interventions, we first debunk two ineffective ones: catharsis and punishment.

Catharsis

The term catharsis dates back to Aristotle, who taught in *Poetics* that viewing tragic plays gave people emotional release from negative emotions such as pity and fear. In Greek drama, the heroes did not just grow old and die of natural causes—they were often murdered. In modern times, Sigmund Freud revived the ancient concept of catharsis. Freud believed that if people repressed their negative emotions, they could develop psychological systems such as hysteria and neuroses (e.g., Breuer & Freud, 1893–1895). Freud's ideas are the foundation of the hydraulic model of anger, which suggests that frustrations lead to anger. Anger, in turn, builds up inside an individual like hydraulic pressure inside a closed circuit until it is vented. If the anger is not vented, the build-up of anger will presumably cause the individual to explode in an aggressive rage. People can presumably vent their anger by engaging in aggressive activities such as yelling, screaming, swearing, punching a pillow, throwing objects, tearing phone books, kicking trash cans, and slamming doors.

Almost as soon as researchers started testing the catharsis theory, it ran into trouble. In one early experiment (Hornberger, 1959), participants who had been insulted by a confederate either pounded nails with a hammer for 10 minutes or did nothing. Next, all participants had a chance to criticize the confederate who had insulted them. According to catharsis theory, the act of pounding nails should reduce anger and subsequent aggression. However, the opposite was true: Participants who pounded nails were *more* hostile toward the confederate afterward than were the participants who did nothing. Subsequent research has found similar results (e.g., Geen & Quanty, 1977). Other research has shown that venting does not reduce aggression even among people who believe in the value of venting, and even among people who report feeling better after venting (Bushman, Baumeister, & Stack, 1999). Indeed, venting increases aggression, even against innocent bystanders (Bushman et al., 1999).

One variation of venting is physical exercise. Although physical exercise is good for your heart, it is not good for reducing anger (Bushman, 2002). Angry people are physiologically aroused, and physical exercise just keeps the arousal level high. To reduce anger, people should try to reduce their level of arousal.

Punishment

Most cultures assume that punishment is an effective way to reduce aggression. *Punishment* is defined as inflicting pain (*positive punishment*) or removing pleasure (*negative punishment*) for a misdeed to reduce the likelihood that the punished individual would repeat the misdeed (or related misdeeds) in the future. Parents use it, organizations use it, and governments use it. But does it work? Today, aggression researchers think punishment does more harm than good. This is because punishment only temporarily suppresses aggression, and it has several undesirable side effects (Baron & Richardson, 1994; Berkowitz, 1993; Eron et al., 1971). Punishment models the behavior it seeks to prevent. For example, suppose a father sees an older brother beating up his younger brother. The father starts spanking the older boy while proclaiming, "I'll teach you not to hit your little brother!" Yes, the father is indeed teaching the older boy something; he is teaching him that it is okay to behave aggressively as long as you are an authority figure. In addition, because punishment is aversive, it can classically condition children to avoid their parents, and in the short run can instigate retaliatory aggression. Longitudinal studies have shown that children who are physically punished by their parents at home are more aggressive outside the home, such as in school (e.g., Lefkowitz. Huesmann, & Eron, 1978).

Developing Nonaggressive Ways of Behaving

Most aggression treatment programs can be divided into one of two broad categories, depending on whether aggression is viewed as proactive or reactive (Berkowitz, 1993, pp. 358–370). Recall that proactive aggression is cold blooded and is a means to some other end, whereas reactive aggression is hot blooded and is an end in itself.

Approaches to Reducing Proactive Aggression

People often resort to aggression because they think it is the easiest and fastest way to achieve their goals. Psychologists who view aggression as proactive behavior use *behavior modification* learning principles to teach aggressive people to use nonaggressive behaviors to achieve their goals, and it works (e.g., Patterson, Reid, Jones, & Conger, 1975). In behavior modification it is useful to replace an undesirable behavior with a desirable one. A major problem with punishment is that it does not teach the aggressor new, nonaggressive forms of behavior. One way to eliminate an undesirable behavior is to replace it with a desirable behavior (called *differential reinforcement of alternative behavior*). The idea is that by reinforcing nonaggressive behavior, aggressive behavior should decrease. Other effective programs include social skills training, in which people are taught how to better read verbal and nonverbal behaviors in social interactions (e.g., Pepler, King, Craig, Byrd, & Bream, 1995). Exposure to prosocial role models also reduces aggression and increases helping (e.g., Spivey & Prentice-Dunn, 1990), even if the models are film or TV characters (for a meta-analytic review see Mares & Woodward, 2005).

Approaches to Reducing Reactive Aggression

Other approaches to reducing aggression focus on decreasing emotional reactivity using relaxation and cognitive-behavioral techniques (for a meta-analytic review see DiGuiseppe & Tafrate, 2003). Most relaxation-based techniques involve deep breathing, visualizing peaceful images, or tightening and loosening muscle groups in succession. People practice relaxing after imaging or experiencing a provocative event. In this way, they learn to calm down after they have been provoked. Cognitive-based techniques focus on how a potentially provocative event is interpreted and how to respond to such events. For example, people rehearse statements in their mind such as "Stay calm. Just continue to relax" and "You don't need to prove yourself." It is especially effective to combine relaxation and cognitive techniques (e.g., Novaco, 1975).

Aggression Research Today and in the Future

We do not have a crystal ball, and predictions of the future can be hazardous. Indeed, in Dante's Inferno, futurists and fortune-tellers are consigned to the eighth circle of hell. Despite Dante's warning, we will make a few speculations. Social neuroscience is a hot topic today (see Heatherton and Wheatley, Chapter 16, this volume), and will probably become even hotter in the future. The link between brain activity and human aggression is a promising area of current and future research, both in terms of understanding the brain structures that are implicated in aggressive responding (e.g., Weber et al., 2006) and in terms of the effects of internal and external triggers on neural responses and how these relate to aggression (e.g., Bartholow et al., 2006). A related area of work that holds considerable promise for greatly improving our ability to predict who will be violent under what circumstances is behavioral genetics. As briefly reviewed in a previous section, researchers are beginning to discover variations in the regulation of neurochemicals linked to aggression and violence that ultimately have genetic causes and that can be targeted for pharmacological and behavioral interventions to reduce their influence on the expression of aggressive behavior (e.g., Seo et al., 2008). Another promising research direction is self-control. Aggression often starts when self-control stops (e.g., DeWall, Baumeister, Stillman, & Gailliot, 2007; Finkel, DeWall, Slotter, Oaten, & Foshee, 2009). A third promising research direction is apology and forgiveness (e.g., McCullough, 2008). Hopefully social psychologists will be at the forefront, conducting research on these and other important topics that ultimately have the potential to make the world a less violent, more peaceful place.

References

Abelson, R. P. (1981). Psychological status of the script concept. *American Psychologist, 36*, 715–729.

Anderson, C. A. (1989). Temperature and aggression: Ubiquitous effects of heat on the occurrence of human violence. *Psychological Bulletin, 106*, 74–96.

Anderson, C. A., & Anderson, K. B. (1996). Violent crime rate studies in philosophical context: A destructive testing approach to heat and southern culture of violence effects. *Journal of Personality and Social Psychology, 70*, 740–756.

Anderson, K.B., Anderson, C.A., Dill, K.E., & Deuser, W.E. (1998). The interactive relations between trait hostility, pain, and aggressive thoughts. *Aggressive Behavior, 24*, 161–171.

Anderson, C. A., Benjamin, A. J. Jr., & Bartholow, B. D. (1998). Does the gun pull the trigger? Automatic priming effects of weapon pictures and weapon names. *Psychological Science, 9*, 308–314.

Anderson, C. A., Berkowitz, L., Donnerstein, E., Huesmann, R. L., Johnson, J., Linz, D., Malamuth, N., & Wartella, E. (2003). The influence of media violence on youth. *Psychological Science in the Public Interest, 4*, 81–110.

Anderson. C. A., & Bushman, B. J. (1997). External validity of "trivial" experiments: The case of laboratory aggression. *Review of General Psychology, 1*, 19–41.

Anderson, C. A., & Bushman, B. J. (2002). Human aggression. *Annual Review of Psychology, 53*, 27–51.

Anderson, C. A., Bushman, B. J., & Groom, R. W. (1997). Hot years and serious and deadly assault: Empirical tests of the heat hypothesis. *Journal of Personality and Social Psychology, 73*, 1213–1223.

Anderson, C. A, Deuser, W. E., & DeNeve, K. (1995). Hot temperatures, hostile affect, hostile cognition, and arousal: Tests of a general model of affective aggression. *Personality and Social Psychology Bulletin, 21*, 434–448.

Anderson, C. A., Shibuya, A., Ihori, N., Swing, E. L., Bushman, B. J., Sakamoto, A., Rothstein, H. R., Saleem, M., & Barlett, C. P. (2010). Violent video game effects on aggression, empathy, and prosocial behavior in Eastern and Western countries: A meta-analytic review. Psychological Bulletin, *136(2)*, 151–173.

Archer, J. (1991). The influence of testosterone on human aggression. *British Journal of Psychology, 82*, 1–28.

Archer, J., & Benson, D. (2008). Physical aggression as a function of perceived fighting ability and provocation: An experimental investigation. *Aggressive Behavior, 34*, 9–24.

Azrin, N. H., Hutchinson, R. R., & McLaughlin, R. (1965). The opportunity for aggression as an operant reinforcer during aversive stimulation. *Journal of the Experimental Analysis of Behavior, 8*, 171–180.

Bandura, A. (1965). Influence of models' reinforcement contingencies on the acquisition of imitative responses. *Journal of Abnormal and Social Psychology, 66*, 575–582.

Bandura, A. (1973). *Aggression: A social learning theory analysis.* Englewood Cliffs, NJ: Prentice-Hall.

Bandura, A. (1977). *Social learning theory.* Englewood Cliffs, NJ: Prentice-Hall.

Bandura, A. (1986). *Social foundations of thought and action: A social-cognitive theory.* Englewood Cliffs, NJ: Prentice-Hall.

Bandura, A., Ross, D., & Ross, S. A. (1961). Transmission of aggression through imitation of aggressive models. *Journal of Abnormal and Social Psychology, 63*, 575–582.

Bandura, A., Ross, D., & Ross, S. A. (1963). Vicarious reinforcement and imitative learning. *Journal of Abnormal and Social Psychology, 67*, 601–607.

Baron, R. A., & Richardson, D. R. (1994). *Human aggression* (2nd ed.). New York: Plenum.

Bartholow, B. D., Anderson, C. A., Carnagey, N. L., & Benjamin, A. J. Jr. (2005). Interactive effects of life experience and situational cues on aggression: The weapons priming effect in hunters and nonhunters. *Journal of Experimental Social Psychology, 41*, 48–60.

Bartholow, B. D., Bushman, B. J., & Sestir, M. A. (2006). Chronic violent video game exposure and desensitization: Behavioral and event-related brain potential data. *Journal of Experimental Social Psychology, 42*, 532–539.

Bartholow, B.D., Dickter, C.L., & Sestir, M.A. (2006). Stereotype activation and control of race bias: Cognitive control of inhibition and its impairment by alcohol. *Journal of Personality and Social Psychology, 90*, 272–287.

Bartholow, B. D., & Heinz, A. (2006). Alcohol and aggression without consumption: Alcohol cues, aggressive thoughts, and hostile perception bias. *Psychological Science, 17*, 30–37.

Bennett, D., Bendersky, M., & Lewis, M. (2007). Preadolescent health risk behavior as a function of prenatal cocaine exposure and gender. *Journal of Development and Behavioral Pediatrics, 28*, 467–472.

Berkowitz, L. (1960). Some factors affecting the reduction of overt hostility. *The Journal of Abnormal and Social Psychology, 60*, 14–21.

Berkowitz, L. (1989). Frustration-aggression hypothesis: Examination and reformulation. *Psychological Bulletin, 106*, 59–73.

Berkowitz, L. (1993). *Aggression: Its causes, consequences, and control.* New York: McGraw- Hill.

Berkowitz L., Cochran, S. T., & Embree, M. C. (1981). Physical pain and the goal of aversively stimulated aggression. *Journal of Personality and Social Psychology, 40*, 687–700.

Berkowitz, L., & LePage, A. (1967). Weapons as aggression-eliciting stimuli. *Journal of Personality and Social Psychology, 7*, 202–207.

Berman, M. E., McCloskey, M. S., Fanning, J. R., Schumacher, J. A., & Coccaro, E. F. (2009). Serotonin augmentation reduces response to attack in aggressive individuals. *Psychological Science, 20*(6), 714–720.

Berman, M. E., Tracy, J. I., & Coccaro, E. F. (1997). The serotonin hypothesis of aggression revisited. *Clinical Psychology Review, 17*, 651–665.

Bettencourt, B. A., & Miller, N. (1996). Gender differences in aggression as a function of provocation: A meta-analysis. *Psychological Bulletin, 119*, 422–447.

Bettencourt, B. A., Talley, A., Benjamin, A. J., & Valentine, J. (2006). Personality and aggressive behavior under provoking and neutral conditions: A meta-analytic review. *Psychological Bulletin, 132*, 751–777.

Bjork, J. M., Dougherty, D. M., & Moeller, F. G. (1997). A positive correlation between self-ratings of depression and laboratory-measured aggression. *Psychiatry Research, 69*, 33–38.

Bjork, J. M., Dougherty, D. M., Moeller, G., & Swann, A. C. (2000). Differential behavioral effects of plasma trytophan depletion and loading in aggressive and nonagressive men. *Neuropsychopharmacology, 22*, 357–369.

Botvinick, M. M., Braver, T. S., Barch, D. M., Carter, C. S., & Cohen, J. D. (2001). Conflict monitoring and cognitive control. *Psychological Review, 108*, 624–652.

Brain, P.F., & Susman, E. J. (1997). Hormonal aspects of aggression and violence. In D. M. Stoff, J. E. Breiling, & J. D. Maser (Eds.), *Handbook of antisocial behavior* (pp. 314–323). Hoboken, NJ: Wiley & Sons.

Breuer, J., & Freud, S. (1893–1895/1955). *Studies on hysteria.* Standard edition, Vol. II. London: Hogarth.

Buckley, K. E., Winkel, R. E., & Leary, M. R. (2004). Emotional and behavioral responses to interpersonal rejection: Anger, sadness, hurt, and aggression. *Journal of Experimental Social Psychology, 40*, 14–28.

Bush, G., Luu, P., & Posnter, M. I. (2000). Cognitive and emotional influences in anterior cingulate cortex. *Trends in Cognitive Sciences, 4*, 215–222.

Bushman, B. J. (1995). Moderating role of trait aggressiveness in the effects of violent media on aggression. *Journal of Personality and Social Psychology, 69*, 950–960.

Bushman, B. J. (2002). Does venting anger feed or extinguish the flame? Catharsis, rumination, distraction, anger, and aggressive responding. *Personality and Social Psychology Bulletin, 28*, 724–731.

Bushman, B. J., & Anderson, C. A. (2001a). Is it time to pull the plug on the hostile versus instrumental aggression dichotomy? *Psychological Review, 108*, 273–279.

Bushman, B. J., & Anderson, C. A. (2001b). Media violence and the American public: Scientific facts versus media misinformation. *American Psychologist, 56*, 477–489.

Bushman, B. J., Baumeister, R. F., & Phillips, C. M. (2001). Do people aggress to improve their mood? Catharsis beliefs, affect regulation opportunity, and aggressive responding. *Journal of Personality and Social Psychology, 81*, 17–32.

Bushman, B. J., Baumeister, R. F., & Stack, A. D. (1999). Catharsis, aggression, and persuasive influence: Self-fulfilling or self-defeating prophecies? *Journal of Personality and Social Psychology, 76*, 367–376.

Bushman, B. J., Bonacci, A. M., Pedersen, W. C., Vasquez, E. A., & Miller, N. (2005). Chewing on it can chew you up: Effects of rumination on triggered displaced aggression. *Journal of Personality and Social Psychology, 88,* 969–983.

Bushman, B. J., & Cooper, H. M. (1990). Alcohol and human aggression: An integrative research review. *Psychological Bulletin, 107,* 341–354.

Bushman, B., J., & Gibson, B. (2010). Violent video games cause an increase in aggression long after the game has been turned off. Manuscript under review.

Bushman, B. J., & Huesmann, L. R. (2006). Short-term and long-term effects of violent media on aggression in children and adults. *Archives of Pediatrics & Adolescent Medicine, 160,* 348–352

Bushman, B. J., Wang, M. C., & Anderson, C. A. (2005). Is the curve relating temperature to aggression linear or curvilinear? Assaults and temperature in Minneapolis reexamined. *Journal of Personality and Social Psychology, 89,* 62–66.

Buss, A. H. (1961). *The psychology of aggression.* New York: Wiley.

Cannon, W. B. (1915). *Bodily changes in pain, hunger, fear and rage: An account of recent researches into the function of emotional excitement.* New York Appleton.

Caprara, G. V., Passerini, S., Pastorelli, C., Renzi, P., & Zelli, A. (1986). Instigating and measuring interpersonal aggression and hostility: A methodological contribution. *Aggressive Behavior, 12,* 237–247.

Caprara, G. V., & Renzi, P. (1981). The frustration-aggression hypothesis vs. irritability. *Recherches de Psychologie Sociale, 3,* 75–80.

Carlson, M., Marcus-Newhall, A., & Miller, N. (1990). Effects of situational aggressive cues: A quantitative review. *Journal of Personality and Social Psychology, 58,* 622–633.

Carnagey, N. L., & Anderson, C. A. (2003). Theory in the study of media violence: The General Aggression Model. In D. Gentile (Ed.), *Media violence and children* (pp. 87–106), Westport, CT: Praeger.

Cherek, D.R., & Lane, S.D. (2001). Acute effects of D-fenfluramine on simultaneous measures of aggressive escape and impulsive responses of adult males with and without a history of conduct disorder. *Psychopharmacology (Berl), 157,* 221–227.

Cleare, A. J., & Bond, A. J. (1995). The effect of tryptophan depletion and enhancement on subjective and behavioural aggression in normal male subjects. *Psychopharmacology, 118,* 72–81.

Coccaro, E. F., & Kavoussi, R. J. (1997). Fluoxetine and impulsive aggressive behavior in personality-disordered subjects. *Archives of General Psychiatry 54,* 1081–1088.

Cosmides, L., & Tooby, J. (2006). Origins of domain specificity: The evolution of functional organization. In J. L Bermudez (Ed.), *Philosophy of psychology: Contemporary readings* (pp. 539–555), New York: Routledge.

Crick, N. R., & Grotpeter, J. K. (1995). Relational aggression, gender, and social-psychological adjustment. *Child Development, 66,* 710–722.

Darwin, C. (1871/1948). *Origin of species.* New York: Modern Library.

DeLeon, K. R., Grimes, J. M., Connor, D. F., & Melloni, R. H. (2002). Adolescent cocaine exposure and offensive aggression: Involvement of serotonin neural signaling and innervation in male Syrian hamsters. *Behavioural Brain Research, 133*, 211–220.

Denison, M. E., Paredes, A., & Booth, J. B. (1997). Alcohol and cocaine interactions and aggressive behaviors. *Recent Developments in Alcoholism, 13*, 283–303.

Denson, T. F., Pedersen, W. C., Ronquillo, J., & Nandy, A. S. (2009). The angry brain: Neural correlates of anger, angry rumination, and aggressive personality. *Journal of Cognitive Neuroscience, 21*, 734–444.

DeWall, C. N., Baumeister, R. F., Stillman, T. F., & Gailliot, M. T. (2007). Violence restrained: Effects of self-regulation and its depletion on aggression. *Journal of Experimental Social Psychology, 43*, 62–76.

DeWall, C, N., & Bushman, B. J. (2009). Hot under the collar in a lukewarm environment: Hot temperature primes increase aggressive thoughts and hostile perceptions. *Journal of Experimental Social Psychology, 45*(4), 1045–1047.

DeWall C. N., MacDonald, G., Webster, G. D., Masten, C., Baumeister, R. F., Powell, C., Combs, D., Schurtz, D. R., Stillman, T. F., Tice, D. M., & Eisenberger, N. I. (in press). Tylenol reduces social pain: Behavioral and neural evidence. Psychological Science.

DiGuiseppe, R., & Tafrate, R. C. (2003). Anger treatment for adults: A meta-analytic review. *Clinical Psychology: Science and Practice, 10*, 70–84.

Dodge, K. A. (1980). Social cognition and children's aggressive behavior. *Child Development, 51*, 620–635.

Dodge, K. A. (1986). A social information processing model of social competence in children. In M. Perlmutter (Ed.), *The Minnesota Symposium on Child Psychology, Vol. 18* (pp. 77–125). Hillsdale, NJ: Erlbaum.

Dodge, K. A. (1993). Social-cognitive mechanisms in the development of conduct disorder and depression. *Annual Review of Psychology, 44*, 559–584.

Dodge, K. A., & Coie, J. D. (1987). Social-information-processing factors in reactive and proactive aggression in children's peer groups. *Journal of Personality and Social Psychology, 53*, 1146–1158.

Dodge, K. A., & Frame, C. L. (1982). Social cognitive biases and deficits in aggressive boys. *Child Development, 53*, 620–635.

Dollard, J., Doob, L. W., Miller, N. E., Mower, O. H., & Sears, R. R. (1939). *Frustration and aggression*. New Haven, CT: Yale University Press.

Donnerstein, E., & Wilson, D. W. (1976). Effects of noise and perceived control on ongoing and subsequent aggressive behavior. *Journal of Personality and Social Psychology, 34*, 774–781.

Easterbrook, J. A. (1959). The effect of emotion on the utilization and the organization of behavior. *Psychological Review, 66*, 183–201.

Eisenberger, N. I., Lieberman, M. D., & Williams, K. D. (2003). Does Rejection Hurt? An fMRI Study of Social Exclusion. *Science, 302*, 290–292.

Eron, L. D., Walder, L. O., & Lefkowitz, M. M. (1971). *The learning of aggression in children*. Boston: Little Brown.

Ferster, C. B., & Skinner, B. F. (1957). *Schedules of reinforcement*. New York: Appleton-Century-Crofts.

Feshbach, S. (1964). The function of aggression and the regulation of aggressive drive. *Psychological Review, 71*, 257–272.

Fillmore, M. T., & Vogel-Sprott, M. (1999). An alcohol model of impaired inhibitory control and its treatment in humans. *Experimental and Clinical Psychopharmacology, 7*, 49–55.

Fillmore, M. T., & Vogel-Sprott, M. (2000). Response inhibition under alcohol: Effects of cognitive and motivational control. *Journal of Studies on Alcohol, 61*, 239–246.

Finkel, E. J., DeWall, C. N., Slotter, E. B., Oaten, M., & Foshee, V. A. (2009). Self-regulatory failure and intimate partner violence perpetration. *Journal of Personality and Social Psychology, 97*, 483–489.

Fite, J. E., Goodnight, J. A., Bates, J. E., Dodge, K. A., & Pettit, G. S. (2008). Adolescent aggression and social cognition in the context of personality: Impulsivity as a moderator of predictions from social information processing. *Aggressive Behavior, 34*(5), 511–520. Freud, S. (1909/1961). *Analysis of a phobia in a five-year-old boy* (standard ed.). London: Norton.

Freud, S. (1933/1950). Why war? In *Collected Works of Sigmund Freud*, Vol. 16. London: Imagio.

Friedman, R. S., McCarthy, D. M., Bartholow, B. D., & Hicks, J. (2007). Interactive effects of alcohol outcome expectancies and alcohol cues on non-consumptive behavior. *Experimental and Clinical Psychopharmacology, 15*, 102–114.

Funk, J. B., Bechtoldt-Baldacci, H., Pasold, T., & Baumgartner, J. (2004). Violence exposure in real-life, video games, television, movies, and the internet: Is there desensitization? *Journal of Adolescence, 27*, 23–39.

Gallese, V., Fadiga, L., Fogassi, L., & Rizzolatti, G. (1996). Action recognition in the premotor cortex. *Brain, 119*, 593–609.

Gaur, S. D. (1988). Noise: Does it make you angry? *Indian Psychologist, 5*, 51–56.

Geen, R. G. (1968). Effects of frustration, attack, and prior training in aggressiveness upon aggressive behavior. *Journal of Personality and Social Psychology, 9*, 316–321.

Geen, R. G. (1978). Effects of attack and uncontrollable noise on aggression. *Journal of Research in Personality, 12*, 15–29.

Geen, R. G., & McCown, E. J. (1984). Effects of noise and attack on aggression and physiological arousal. *Motivation and Emotion, 8*, 231–241.

Geen, R. G., & O'Neal, E. C. (1969). Activation of cue-elicited aggression by general arousal. *Journal of Personality and Social Psychology, 11*, 289–292.

Geen, R. G., & Quanty M. B. (1977). The catharsis of aggression: An evaluation of a hypothesis. In L. Berkowitz (Ed.), *Advances in experimental social psychology* (Vol. 10, pp. 1–37). New York: Academic Press.

Gentile, D. A. & Walsh, D. A. (2002). A normative study of family media habits. *Journal of Applied Developmental Psychology, 23*, 157–178.

Giancola, P. R. (1995). Evidence for dorsolateral and orbital prefrontal cortical involvement in the expression of aggressive behavior. *Aggressive Behavior, 21*, 431–450.

Giancola, P. R. (2000). Executive functioning: A conceptual framework for alcohol-related aggression. *Experimental and Clinical Psychopharmacology, 8*, 576–597.

Giancola, P. R. (2002a). Alcohol-related aggression in men and women: The influence of dispositional aggressivity. *Journal of Studies on Alcohol, 63*, 696–708.

Giancola, P. R. (2002b). The influence of trait anger on the alcohol-aggression relation in men and women. *Alcoholism: Clinical and Experimental Research, 26*, 1350–1358.

Giancola, P. R. (2002c). Irritability, acute alcohol consumption, and aggressive behavior in men and women. *Drug and Alcohol Dependence, 68*, 263–274.

Giancola, P. R. (2004). Executive functioning and alcohol-related aggression. *Journal of Abnormal Psychology, 113*, 541–555.

Giancola, P. R. (2006). The influence of subjective intoxication, breath alcohol concentration, and expectancies on the alcohol-aggression relation. *Alcoholism: Clinical and Experimental Research, 30*, 844–850.

Giancola, P. R., & Corman, M. D. (2007). Alcohol and aggression: A test of the attention-allocation model. *Psychological Science, 18*, 649–655.

Giancola, P. R., Helton, E. L., Osborne, A. B., Terry, M. K., Fuss, A. M., & Westerfield, J. A. (2002). The effects of alcohol and provocation on aggressive behavior in men and women. *Journal of Studies on Alcohol, 63*, 64–73.

Giancola, P. R., Mezzich, A. C., & Tarter, R. E. (1998a). Executive cognitive functioning, temperament, and antisocial behavior in conduct-disordered adolescent females. *Journal of Abnormal Psychology, 107*, 629–641.

Giancola, P. R., Mezzich, A. C., & Tarter, R. E. (1998b). Disruptive, delinquent, and aggressive behavior in adolescent females with a psychoactive substance use disorder: Relation to executive cognitive functioning. *Journal of Studies on Alcohol, 59*, 560–567.

Giancola, P.R., Saucier, D.A., & Gussler-Burkhardt, N.L. (2003). The effects of affective, behavioral, and cognitive components of trait anger on the alcohol-aggression relation. *Alcoholism: Clinical and Experimental Research, 27*, 1944–1954.

Giancola, P. R., & Zeichner, A. (1995). Construct validity of a competitive reaction-time aggression paradigm. *Aggressive Behavior, 21*, 199–204.

Giancola, P. R., & Zeichner, A. (1994). Neuropsychological performance on tests of frontal-lobe functioning and aggressive behavior in men. *Journal of Abnormal Psychology, 103*, 832–835.

Goldman, M. S. (1999). Risk for substance abuse: Memory as a common etiological pathway. *Psychological Science, 10*, 196–198.

Goveas, J.S., Csernansky, J.G., & Coccaro, E. F. (2004). Platelet serotonin content correlates inversely with life history of aggression in personality-disordered subjects. *Psychiatry Research, 126*, 23–32.

Grafman, J., Schwab, K., Warden, D., Pridgen, A., Brown, H.R., & Salazar, A.M. (1996). Frontal lobe injuries, violence, and aggression: a report of the Vietnam Head Injury Study. *Neurology, 46*, 1231–1238.

Gurr, T. R. (1981). Historical trends in violent crime: A critical review of the evidence. *Crime and Justice, 3*, 295.

Gussler-Burkhardt, N. L., & Giancola, P. R. (2005). A further investigation of gender differences in alcohol-related aggression. *Journal of Studies on Alcohol, 66*, 413–422.

Harrison, R. J., Connor, D. F., Nowak, C., & Melloni, R. H. (2000). Chronic low-dose cocaine treatment during adolescence facilitates aggression in hamsters. *Physiology & Behavior, 69*, 555–562.

Hermans, E., Ramsey, N., & van Honk, J. (2008). Exogenous Testosterone Enhances Responsiveness to Social Threat in the Neural Circuitry of Social Aggression in Humans. *Biological Psychiatry, 63*, 263–270.

Higley, J. D., et al. (1992). Cerebrospinal Fluid Monoamine and Adrenal Correlates of Aggression in Free-Ranging Rhesus Monkeys. *Archives of General Psychiatry, 49*, 436–441.

Hinde, R. A. (1970). *Animal behavior.* New York: McGraw-Hill.

Hoaken, P. N. S., & Pihl, R. O. (2000). The effects of alcohol intoxication on aggressive responses in men and women. *Alcohol and Alcoholism, 35*, 471–477.

Hornberger, R. H. (1959). The differential reduction of aggressive responses as a function of interpolated activities. *American Psychologist, 14*, 354.

Huesmann, L. R. (1982). Information processing models of behavior. In N. Hirschberg & L. Humphreys (Eds.), *Multivariate applications in the social sciences* (pp. 261–288). Hillsdale, NJ: Erlbaum.

Huesmann, L. R. (1988). An information processing model for the development of aggression. *Aggressive Behavior, 14*, 13–24.

Huesmann, L. R. (1998). The role of social information processing and cognitive schemas in the acquisition and maintenance of habitual aggressive behavior. In R. G. Geen & E. Donnerstein (Eds.), *Human aggression: Theories, research, and implications for policy* (pp. 73–109). New York: Academic Press.

Huesmann, L. R., Moise, J., Podolski, C. P. & Eron, L. D. (2003). Longitudinal relations between childhood exposure to media violence and adult aggression and violence: 1977–1992. *Developmental Psychology, 39*, 201–221.

Huesmann, L. R., & Eron, L. D. (1984). Cognitive processes and the persistence of aggressive behavior. *Aggressive Behavior, 10*, 243–251.

Human Security Brief (2007). Retrieved July 29, 2009 from http://www .humansecuritybrief.info/.Hutchinson, R. R. (1983). The pain-aggression relationship and its expression in naturalistic settings. *Aggressive Behavior, 9*, 229–242.

Iacoboni, M., Woods, R., Brass, M., Bekkering, H., Mazziotta, J., & Rizzolatti, G. (1999). Cortical mechanisms of human imitation. *Science, 286*, 2526–2528.

Ito, T. A., Larsen, J. T., Smith, K., & Cacioppo, J. T. (1998). Negative information weighs more heavily on the brain: The negativity bias in evaluative categorization. *Journal of Personality and Social Psychology, 75*, 887–900.

Jones, J. W., & Bogat, G. A. (1978). Air pollution and human aggression. *Psychological Reports, 43*, 721–722.

Knyshevski, I., Ricci, L. A., McCann, T. E., & Melloni, R. H. (2005). Serotonin type-1A receptors modulate adolescent, cocaine-induced offensive aggression in hamsters. *Physiology & Behavior, 85*, 167–176.

Lagerspetz, K. M., Bjorkqvist, K., & Peltonen, T. (1988). Is indirect aggression typical of females? Gender differences in aggressiveness in 11- to 12-year-old children. *Aggressive Behavior, 14*, 403–414.

Leary, M. R., Tewnge, J. M., & Quinlivan, E. (2006). Interpersonal rejection as a determinant of anger and aggression. *Personality and Social Psychology Review, 10*, 111–132.

Lefkowitz, M. M., Huesmann, L. R., & Eron, L. D. (1978). Parental punishment: A longitudinal analysis of effects. *Archives of General Psychiatry, 35*, 186–191.

Licata, A., Taylor, S., Berman, M., & Cranston, J. (1993). Effects of cocaine on aggression in humans. *Pharmacology, Biochemistry, & Behavior, 45*, 549–552.

Lindsay, J. L., & Anderson, C. A. (2000). From antecedent conditions to violent actions: A general affective aggression model. *Personality and Social Psychology Bulletin, 26*, 533–547.

Lorenz, K. (1966). *On aggression* (M. K. Wilson, trans.). New York: Harcourt, Brace.

Macdonald G., & Leary, M. R. (2005). Why does social exclusion hurt? The relationship between social and physical pain. *Psychological Bulletin, 131*, 202–223. Marcus-Newhall, A., Pedersen, W. C., Carlson, M., & Miller, N. (2000). Displaced aggression is alive and well: A meta-analytic review. *Journal of Personality and Social Psychology, 78*, 670–689.

Mares, M. L., & Woodard, E. (2005). Positive effects of television on children's social. interactions: A meta-analysis. *Media Psychology, 7*, 301–322.

Marsh, D.M., Dougherty, D.M., Moeller, F.G., Swann, A.C., & Spiga, R. (2002). Laboratory-measured aggressive behavior of women: acute tryptophan depletion and augmentation. *Neuropsychopharmacology, 26*, 660–671.

McCloskey, M. S., Berman, M. E., Echevarria, D. J., & Coccaro, E. F. (2009). Effects of Acute Alcohol Intoxication and Paroxetine on Aggression in Men. *Alcoholism: Clinical and Experimental Research, 33*, 581–90.

McCullough, M. (2008). *Beyond revenge: The evolution of the forgiveness instinct.* New York: John Wiley & Sons.

Meltzoff, A. N. (2005). Imitation and other minds: The "Like Me" hypothesis. In S. Hurley & N. Chater (Eds.), *Perspectives on imitation: From mirror neurons to memes* (Vol. 2, pp. 55–78). Cambridge, MA: MIT Press.

Meltzoff, A. N., & Moore, K. M. (1977). Imitation of facial and manual gestures by human neonates. *Science, 109*, 77–78.

Mendelson, T., Thurston, R. C., & Kubzansky, L. D. (2008). Arousal and stress: Affective and cardiovascular effects of experimentally-induced social status. *Health Psychology, 27*(4), 482–489.

Miller, N. E. (1941). The frustration-aggression hypothesis. *Psychological Review, 48*, 337–342.

Miyake, A., Friedman, N.P., Emerson, M.J., Witzki, A.H., Howerter, A., & Wager, T. (2000). The unity and diversity of executive functions and their contributions to complex "frontal lobe" tasks: A latent variable analysis. *Cognitive Psychology, 41*, 49–100.

Moffitt, T., Brammer, G., Caspi, A., Fawcett, J., Raleigh, M., Yuwiler, A., & Silva, P. (1998). Whole Blood Serotonin Relates to Violence in an Epidemiological Study. *Biological Psychiatry, 43*, 446–457.

Moffitt, T. E., Caspi, A., Harrington, H., & Milne, B. J. (2002). Males on the life-course-persistent and adolescence-limited antisocial pathways: Follow-up at age 26 years. *Development and Psychopathology, 14*, 179–207.

Montesquieu, C. (1989). *The spirit of the laws* (A. Cohler, B Miller, & H. Stone, Trans.). New York: Cambridge University Press (Original work published in 1748).

Morris, W. N., & Reilly, N. P. (1987). Toward the self-regulation of mood: Theory and research. *Motivation and Emotion, 11*, 215–249.

National Television Violence Study, (1998). *National Television Violence Study (Vol. 3)*. Santa Barbara: University of California, Santa Barbara, Center for Communication and Social Policy.

Novaco, R. W. (1975). *Anger control: The development and evaluation of an experimental treatment*. Lexington, MA: Lexington Books.

Olweus, D. (1979). The stability of aggressive reaction patterns in males: A review. *Psychological Bulletin, 86*, 852–875.

Orobio de Castro, B., Veerman, J. W., Koops, W., Bosch, J. D., & Monshouwer, H. J. (2002). Hostile attribution of intent and aggressive behavior: A meta-analysis. *Child Development, 73*, 916–934.

Patterson, G. R., Reid, J. B., Jones, R. R., & Conger, R. E. (1975). *A social learning approach to family intervention. Vol. 1: Families with aggressive children*. Eugene, OR: Castalia.

Pavlov, I. P. (1927). *Conditioned reflexes: An investigation of the physiological activity of the cerebral cortex*. Translated and Edited by G. V. Anrep. London: Oxford University Press.

Pedersen, W. C., Bushman, B. J., Vasquez, E. A., & Miller, N. (2008). Kicking the (barking) dog effect: The moderating role of target attributes on triggered displaced aggression. *Personality and Social Psychology Bulletin, 34*(10), 1382–1395.

Pedersen, W. C., Gonzales, C., & Miller, N. (2000). The moderating effect of trivial triggering provocation on displaced aggression. *Journal of Personality and Social Psychology, 78*, 913–927.

Pepler, D., King, G., Craig, W., Byrd, B., & Bream, L. (1995). The development and evaluation of a multisystem social skills group training program for aggressive children. *Child & Youth Care Forum, 24*(5), 297–313.

Pihl, R. O., Young, S. N., Harden, P., Plotnick, S., Chamberlain, B., & Ervin, F. R. (1995). Acute effect of altered tryptophan levels and alcohol on aggression in normal human males. *Psychopharmacology, 119*, 353–360.

Pinker, S. (2007). A history of violence. *The New Republic, 236*(12), 18.

Prinz, J. J. (2005). Imitation and moral development. In S. Hurley & N. Chater (Eds.), *Perspectives on imitation: From mirror neurons to memes* (Vol. 2, pp. 267–282). Cambridge, MA: MIT Press.

Raine, A. (2008). From genes to brain to antisocial behavior. *Current Directions in Psychological Science, 17*, 323–328.

Reinisch, J. M. (1981). Prenatal exposure to synthetic progestins increases potential for aggression in humans. *Science, 211*, 1171–1173.

Ricci, L. A., Knyshevski, I., & Melloni, R. H. (2005). Serotonin type 3 receptors stimulate offensive aggression in Syrian hamsters. *Behavioural Brain Research, 156*, 19–29.

Rizzolatti, G. (2005). The mirror neuron system and imitation. In S. Hurley & N. Chatter (Eds.), *Perspectives on imitation: From mirror neurons to memes* (Vol. 1, pp. 55–76). Cambridge, MA: MIT Press.

Roberts, A. C., Robbins, T. W., & Weiskrantz, L. (Eds.) (1998). *The prefrontal cortex: Executive and cognitive functions*. New York: Oxford University Press.

Robson, B. (1992). Attacking violence. Minneapolis/St. Paul Magazine. Downloaded 12 April 2009 from http://74.125.95.132/search?q=cache:iAc6MicVx8UJ:www.nmctlp.org/nmfccla/files/stopviolence/Turn%2520off%2520the%2520violence%25201.ppt+%22Attacking+Violence%22+Britt+Robson&cd=1&hl=en&ct=clnk&gl=us&client=firefox-a.

Rotton, J., Frey, J., Barry, T., Milligan, M., & Fitzpatrick, M. (1979). The air pollution experience and physical aggression. *Journal of Applied Social Psychology, 9*, 397–412.

Rotton, J., & Frey, J. (1985). Air pollution, weather, and violent crimes: Concomitant time-series analysis of archival data. *Journal of Personality and Social Psychology, 49*, 1207–1220.

Rule, B. G., & Percival, E. (1971). The effects of frustration and attack on physical aggression. *Journal of Experimental Research in Personality, 5*, 111–118.

Salzman, C., et al. (1995). Effect of Fluoxetine on Anger in Symptomatic Volunteers with Borderline Personality Disorder. *Journal of Clinical Psychopharmacology, 15*, 23–29.

Sapolsky, R. M. (1998). Why zebras don't get ulcers: An updated guide to stress, stress-related diseases, and coping. New York: W.H. Freeman.

Schupp, H. T., Cuthbert, B. N., Bradley, M. M., Cacioppo, J. T., Ito, T. A., & Lang, P. J. (2000). Affective picture processing: The late positive potential is modulated by motivational relevance. *Psychophysiology, 37*, 257–261.

Sears, R. R., Whiting, J. W., Nowlis, V., & Sears, P. S. (1953). Some child-rearing antecedents of aggression and dependency in young children. *Genetic Psychology Monographs, 47*, 135–236.

Séguin, J. R. & Zelazo, P. D. (2005). Executive function in early physical aggression. In R. E. Tremblay, W. W. Hartup, & J. Archer (Eds.), *Developmental origins of aggression* (pp. 307–329). New York: Guilford.

Seo, D., Patrick, C. J., Kennealy, P. J. (2008). Role of serotonin and dopamine system interactions in the neurobiology of impulsive aggression and its comorbidity with other clinical disorders. *Aggression and Violent Behavior, 13*, 383–395.

Sestir, M. A., & Bartholow, B. D. (2010). Violent and nonviolent video games produce opposing effects on aggressive and prosocial outcomes. Manuscript under review.

Slater, M. D., Henry, K. L., Swaim, R. C., & Anderson, L. L. (2003). Violent media content and aggressiveness in adolescents: A downward spiral model. *Communication Research, 30*, 713–736.

Stacy, A. W., Widaman, K. F., & Marlatt, G. A. (1990). Expectancy models of alcohol use. *Journal of Personality and Social Psychology, 58*, 918–928.

Steele, C. M., & Josephs, R. A. (1990). Alcohol myopia: Its prized and dangerous effects. *American Psychologist, 45*, 921–933.

Steinfeld, J. (1972). *Statement in hearings before Subcommittee on Communications of Committee on Commerce* (United States Senate, Serial #92–52, pp. 25–27). Washington, DC: U.S. Government Printing Office.

Sterzer, P., Stadler, C., Krebs, A., Kleinschmidt, A., & Poustka, F. (2003). Reduced anterior cingulated activity in adolescents with antisocial conduct disorder confronted with affective pictures. *NeuroImage, 19*(Suppl. 1), 123.

Subra, B., Muller, D., Bègue, L., Bushman, B. J., & Delmas, F. (in press). Effects of alcohol and weapon cues on aggressive thoughts and behaviors. *Personality and Social Psychology Bulletin*.

Taylor, S. P. (1967). Aggressive behavior and physiological arousal as a function of provocation and the tendency to inhibit aggression. *Journal of Personality, 35*, 297–310.

Thorndike, E. L. (1901). Animal intelligence: An experimental study of the associative processes in animals. *Psychological Review Monograph Supplement, 2*, 1–109.

Timbergen, N. (1952). The curious behavior of the Stickleback. *Scientific American, 187*, 22–26.

Tulving, E., & Thomson, D. M. (1973). Encoding specificity and retrieval processes in episodic memory. *Psychological Review, 80*, 352–373.

Turner, C. W., Simons, L. S., Berkowitz, L., & Frodi, A. (1977). The stimulating and inhibiting effects of weapons on aggressive behavior. *Aggressive Behavior, 3*, 355–378.

Ulrich, R. (1966). Pain as a cause of aggression. *American Zoologist, 6*, 643–662.

Weber, R., Ritterfield, U., & Mathiak, K. (2006). Does Playing Violent Video Games Induce Aggression? Empirical Evidence of a Functional Magnetic Resonance Imaging Study. *Media Psychology, 8*, 39–60.

Westergaard, G. C., Mehlman, P. T., Suomi, S. J., & Higley, J. D. (1999). CSF 5-HIAA and aggression in female macaque monkeys: species and interindividual differences. *Psychopharmacology, 146*, 440–446.

Williams, K. D. (2001). *Ostracism: The power of silence*. New York: Guilford.

Zajonc, R. B. (1965). Social facilitation *Science, 149*, 269–274.

Zajonc, R. B., Murphy, S. T., & Inglehart, M. (1989). Feeling and facial efference: Implications of vascular theory of emotions. *Psychological Review, 96*, 395–416.

Zillmann, D. (1979). *Hostility and aggression*. Hillsdale, NJ: Erlbaum.

Zillmann, D. (1988). Cognitive-excitation interdependencies in aggressive behavior. *Aggressive Behavior 14*, 51–64.

Chapter 10

Prejudice, Stereotyping, and Discrimination

Galen V. Bodenhausen and Jennifer A. Richeson

The Problem

Stereotyping, prejudice, and discrimination are phenomena that inspire heated debate among the general public as well as among scholars. Which acts should be considered discriminatory? When can we conclude that a particular decision or a social policy preference is based on prejudice? What role does prejudice play in producing racial and gender disparities? When is it rational or justifiable to base decisions, at least in part, on the sex or the race of a person being evaluated? Also of great interest are questions concerning how society should respond to these problems and whether we have already addressed them in a satisfactory manner. Social psychologists dive into this fray armed with the scientific method, hoping to collect evidence that can shed light on these enduring concerns. In particular, we seek to understand why stereotypes and prejudice arise in the minds of perceivers, as well as how and under what conditions they are likely to influence perceivers' overt behavior. As well, we examine the effects these phenomena exert on the lives of their targets, seeking to identify the vulnerabilities and resiliencies that mediate the consequences that emerge. Perhaps most ambitiously, we attempt to document how prejudice and stereotypes can influence the course of social interactions that cross group boundaries, as well as how their negative effects can be effectively countered. Much has been learned in the course of these investigations, and we aim to provide a compelling sampler of this scholarship in this chapter. The sheer volume of research in this domain, however, means that our sample must necessarily be selective and incomplete.

Conceptual Definitions

Supreme Court Justice Potter Stewart is remembered for his claim that although he could not readily define pornography, he knew it when he saw it. The same may hold for prejudice, but even when the evidence seems clear-cut, claims of prejudice are often hotly contested. Consider a pair of salient examples that cover the gamut from words to deeds: A well known comedian responds angrily to a black heckler, invoking lynching and the "n-word" repeatedly. The tirade is captured on video and goes viral on YouTube; nevertheless, the comedian adamantly insists that he is not a racist. Or consider the case of two men who meet a young gay man in a bar and subsequently offer him a ride home. Instead of taking him home, they rob and torture him and leave him tied to a fence, eventually to die after suffering for more than 18 hours. To many, this incident constitutes a prototypic hate crime, yet the defendants denied that their actions were motivated by prejudice; rather, they claimed that they were merely reacting to unwanted sexual advances, their judgment clouded by the influence of illicit drugs. It is not surprising that people accused of prejudice and stereotyping would seek to deflect such unflattering (and, in some cases, criminal) characterizations. But how can we know what is and what is not prejudice?

A classic definition was provided by Allport (1954, p. 9), who wrote that "prejudice is an antipathy based on a faulty and inflexible generalization. It may be felt or expressed. It may be directed toward a group as a whole or toward an individual because he is a group member." Many contemporary psychologists would endorse the general features of this definition, which invokes the process of categorization (generalization) and subsequent indiscriminate dislike or animosity toward the relevant category and its members. An important part of the attribution of prejudice lies in correctly identifying the relevant category toward which antipathy is targeted. For example, people may not be prejudiced against women in general, but they may be quite prejudiced against women who occupy social roles traditionally prescribed for men (Eagly & Diekman, 2005). Some prejudice takes the form of patronizing or condescending reactions, when groups are assumed to be incompetent or dependent (Glick et al., 2000). Expanding on Allport's definition, we might expect that antipathy will characterize the prejudice that is directed at groups that are viewed as lacking on moral dimensions, whereas disdain will be directed at groups that are viewed as lacking on competence dimensions. Another complicating factor concerns the phenomenon of ethnocentrism, or ingroup favoritism more generally. As Brewer (1999) has argued, people often show favoritism toward members of their own group without necessarily feeling animus toward other groups, yet a positive bias toward your own group at the expense of others feels like a form of prejudice too. Definitional clarity may emerge if we regard such situations as embodying discrimination rather than prejudice. Discrimination can be defined as the differential treatment of individuals, based on their membership in a particular group. Such treatment can often be motivated by prejudice, but it may also result from ethnocentric feelings that are devoid of animus.

Although this definition of discrimination seems straightforward, whether a person has been treated in a particular way *because of his or her group membership* is often ambiguous. Consider the evidence summarized by Benokraitis (1997) indicating that although about one-third of the population of the United States consists of white men, this group accounts for 85% of tenured professors, 85% of partners at law firms, 90% of the U.S. Senate, and 95% of the CEOs of Fortune 500 companies. This evidence certainly seems to point toward systematic discrimination against women and nonwhite people, but how can we be sure? In the absence of laws and explicit policies that either ban or limit the number of women and nonwhite individuals in these domains, forces other than and/or in addition to discrimination may be at work. One possibility, for example, is that women and nonwhite people are simply significantly less interested in these types of careers. To establish that discrimination is involved, in other words, we need to go further than merely documenting group differences and disparities, which could arise for a variety of reasons. Some scholars attempt to use statistical evidence to determine whether groups are treated differently (e.g., Persico, 2009). Suppose that we want to know whether police are engaging in unfair racial or gender profiling. We could collect evidence regarding the rates at which motor vehicles are stopped and searched as a function of the driver's racial group or sex. We might, for example, discover that the police are more likely to search cars with drivers from a particular ethnic group, but it would remain possible that some other factor(s) might happen to be correlated with race (e.g., type of vehicle, registration status), and these correlated factors determined police decisions. Or perhaps there are real group differences in the likelihood of perpetrating a given type of offense. Statistical models can be developed that attempt to control for such considerations. Persico and Todd (2008) developed and tested such a model using police vehicle searches in Maryland. They examined the overall hit rate of correctly identifying cars carrying contraband as a function of the driver's ethnic identity. The hit rate for black motorists who were searched was 0.34, indicating that the majority of black drivers who were stopped had no illegal items in their cars. However, the hit rate for white motorists was quite comparable (0.32), suggesting in this case that the police were similarly accurate in identifying offenders of both racial groups. The hit rate for Hispanic motorists, however, was just 0.11, suggesting that this group may in fact be unfairly profiled by police, resulting in their being stopped without justification to a greater extent than the other groups. As Persico (2009) notes, discrimination is most evident when members of different groups who are otherwise "similarly situated" are treated differently. The degree to which two individuals are similarly situated in the real world can be difficult to determine, so social psychologists often turn to carefully controlled laboratory experiments to examine the role of group membership when all else is in fact equal.

Legal definitions of discrimination place particular importance on the notion of intentionality (Nelson, Berrey, & Nielsen, 2008). That is, a legal entity must intend to engage in disparate treatment for an allegation of discrimination to be supported. Quite apart from the difficulty of establishing what someone's past intentions were, this stance overlooks the fact that many kinds of decisions, including legal ones, can be made in a manner that reflects mindless routines (e.g., Hanay López, 2000) that can reproduce discriminatory outcomes without any conscious intention on the part of the decision maker. For example, a personnel manager may rely on the "old boys' network" to identify qualified candidates simply because that is what has always been done in the past, without considering that this approach disadvantages groups that are not already well connected within that network. Or decision makers may be influenced in ways they do not consciously appreciate by automatic mental associations that color their impressions of others (Krieger, 1995). Although lacking in intent, are these any less consequential forms of discrimination? One of the major themes of contemporary research on discrimination concerns the possible role of automatic mental processes in its genesis.

Discrimination can also take subtle forms and need not consist of blatant exclusion. Carbado, Fisk, and Gulati (2008) argued for the existence of "discrimination by inclusion," in which people from diverse social groups are included (e.g., in an organization) but nevertheless subjected to disparate treatment. Sometimes the basis for initial inclusion can be problematic (e.g., hiring recent Latino/a immigrants because they are expected to be more compliant and less likely to complain or agitate for better conditions than majority group members). Moreover, even when they have been included in an organization, members of targeted groups can still receive differential treatment often consisting of "cool neglect" (Fiske, 2002) rather than overt hostility. Cortina (2008) proposed that contemporary discrimination in the workplace often takes the form of selective incivility, which includes acts that are disrespectful but ambiguous in their underlying intent (e.g., ignoring, interrupting, or failing to include members of the targeted group).

Stereotypes represent the third component of our analysis. A stereotype can be defined as a generalized belief about the characteristics of a group, and stereotyping represents the process of attributing these characteristics to particular individuals only because of their membership in the group. Whereas prejudice involves a global evaluative response to a group and its members, stereotyping consists of a much more specific, descriptive analysis. Stereotypes need not be overtly negative, and indeed, many common stereotypes have ostensibly positive connotations (e.g., the notion that African Americans are naturally athletic or that Asians are mathematically gifted). However, the stereotypes we hold of other groups are rarely uniformly positive, and any positive traits we may associate with a particular group are likely to be accompanied by more ominous associations (Fiske, Cuddy, Glick, & Xu, 2002). Fiske et al. found that when groups are stereotyped as competent, they tend to also be viewed as cold; on the other hand, when groups are stereotyped as warm and likable, they are often also viewed as being incompetent.

In the most minimal sense, stereotypes represent the features ascribed to social groups. However, stereotypes tend to be embedded in causal theories. As a result, stereotypes involve not just beliefs about what a group is like, but also causal chains that relate group characteristics to one another (Wittenbrink, Gist, & Hilton, 1997; Murphy & Medin, 1985). For example, members of a group might be stereotyped as poor because they are unskilled, unskilled because they failed in their educational pursuits, and educational failures because they are lazy and do not apply themselves. The stereotypic characteristics of the group are not simply a list of unrelated features, but rather they constitute a coherent account for why the group is the way it is perceived to be. Such causal chains commonly start from the implicit assumption of an ultimate cause, which is the group's inherent "essence" (Rothbart & Taylor, 1992). Psychological essentialism (Medin & Ortony, 1989) is the assumption that categories are imbued with a defining essence that is responsible for producing the observed characteristics of category members. In the case of many important kinds of social groups, such as gender and ethnic groups, psychological essentialism is linked to genetic determinism (Keller, 2005). Thus, stereotypes are often embedded in naive ontologies that imply that group characteristics are innate and immutable (Haslam, Rothschild, & Ernst, 2000).

Operational Definitions

The measurement of prejudice and stereotyping has a long and interesting history. Self-report measures of these phenomena have been employed by psychologists since the early part of the twentieth century, allowing an interesting window on how they have changed over time (e.g., Madon et al., 2001). However, because bigotry is widely viewed as repugnant, researchers have long recognized the possibility that self-reported intergroup attitudes and stereotypes might reflect "faking" rather than candid, honest responses (Sigall & Page, 1971). As a consequence, scholars sought less reactive measures of these phenomena (Crosby, Bromley, & Saxe, 1980). These measures have flourished in recent decades. They include relatively more subtle and indirect kinds of self-report questionnaires, physiological measures such as facial electromyogram (EMG) and amygdala activation, a growing variety of reaction time measures, and direct behavioral observation, such as interpersonal distancing and nonverbal rapport (for a comprehensive review, see Olson, 2009).

In recent times, the rationale for employing indirect measures of prejudice and stereotyping has expanded beyond concerns about social desirability biases. In particular, researchers have argued that self-report measures and many kinds of indirect measures may be tapping different facets of the underlying phenomena. Whereas self-report measures capture how individuals thoughtfully deliberate about their intergroup impressions, indirect measures may capture more spontaneous and automatic responses to other social groups. From this perspective, the convergences and divergences between indirect and self-reported measures constitute a topic of considerable interest in its own right (Dovidio, Kawakami, Smoak, & Gaertner, 2009). Controversies are raging regarding the validity of direct and indirect measures of prejudice, but as we shall see, the idea that there is an important distinction between deliberate and automatic forms of prejudice and stereotyping now seems to be quite widely accepted.

Stereotyping, prejudice, and discrimination are interlocking phenomena, and scholars have been interested in sketching a general model of how they relate to one another. One view holds that stereotypes give rise to prejudice (i.e., people develop antipathy toward a group based on the characteristics the group is assumed to possess), and in turn, prejudice gives rise to discrimination (i.e., people treat group members disadvantageously because of the antipathy or disdain they feel toward the group). In other words, cognitive appraisals give rise to affective reactions, which then shape intentions and behavior. Such an approach follows the assumptions of the theory of reasoned action (Fishbein & Ajzen, 1975) and related approaches linking beliefs, attitudes, and behavior. Although much research is consistent with this view, a great deal of recent research has shown that other patterns are also possible. For example, as previously mentioned, discrimination can be based on ingroup favoritism rather than prejudice toward the outgroup (Brewer, 1999), and it can occur by relatively mindless routes (Bertrand, Chugh, & Mullainathan, 2005; Hanay López,

2008; Langer, Bashner, & Chanowitz, 1985). Indeed, an explosion of research has recently explored the possibility that these phenomena can sometimes be manifested in a manner that is quite distinct from reasoning processes. It is to this issue that we now turn our attention.

Deliberate versus Automatic Prejudice, Stereotyping, and Discrimination

Over the past century, there has been a sharp shift in public opinion regarding issues surrounding prejudice and stereotyping, prompting many scholars to propose models that can capture the psychological differences that characterize modern or contemporary forms of these phenomena, in contrast to their old-fashioned forms (Dovidio & Gaertner, 1986). In bygone eras, most bigots explicitly endorsed policies that maintain racial and sex discrimination, reasoning from an ideology of racial or gender superiority to justify these policy preferences. A number of compelling historical forces, such as the civil rights movement and the public exposure of the genocidal atrocities of the Nazis, produced a dramatic shift in the palatability of these racial and gender ideologies (Schuman, Steeh, Bobo, & Krysan, 1997). To be sure, old-fashioned racism and sexism have not been extinguished. For example, a sizable minority of white Americans still believe that racial disparities in education and income can be explained, at least in part, by genetic differences (more than 40% in one national survey; Huddy & Feldman, 2009), yet the consensus among biologists is that race is not a biologically valid construct because human genetic variation is "continuous, complexly structured, constantly changing, and predominantly within 'races'" (Goodman, 2000, p. 1699). Race is thus a social rather than a biological reality, and racial disparities cannot be plausibly dismissed as genetically determined or innate. The role of race in the 2008 Presidential election in the United States was much discussed and debated (Peery & Bodenhausen, 2009), but one direct indicator of the continuing existence of blatant racism is the fact that within the Democratic primary (in which both candidates had generally similar policy orientations), exit polls conducted in 31 states showed that 14% of white voters explicitly indicated that race was a factor in their vote—and these individuals overwhelming voted for Clinton; in states such as Mississippi and West Virginia, as many as one in five primary voters voted against Obama for explicitly racial reasons (Huddy & Feldman, 2009). It is clearly premature to be unconcerned about old-fashioned forms of prejudice, or to view them as characterizing only a very small fringe fraction of the populace.

Much of the focus of recent social psychological research has been on the possibility that there are more subtle forms of prejudice and stereotyping that characterize many, if not most, members of contemporary society. Gaertner and Dovidio (1986), in their theory of aversive racism, proposed that most members of contemporary society endorse egalitarianism and are loath to be considered, or to consider themselves, to be prejudiced. However, their egalitarian aspirations are hampered by the fact that they often tend to possess lingering prejudiced feelings. In the contest between negative affect and egalitarianism, egalitarianism tends to win out whenever the role of race is obvious and clear-cut. Under such circumstances, the aversive racist will take pains to avoid behaving in an ostensibly biased manner. However, negative, prejudicial affect can still "leak out" and produce discriminatory behavior, particularly when the affect is misattributed to some nonracial factor. An impressive array of research has supported the basic tenets of aversive racism theory (Dovidio & Gaertner, 2004).

In an extraordinarily influential paper, Devine (1989) argued that prejudiced feelings and egalitarian beliefs coexist in the minds of most if not all members of contemporary society. The difference between them is that the egalitarian beliefs are assumed to operate in a controlled manner, meaning that their activation and use are subject to the intentions and efforts of the individual. In contrast, prejudiced feelings are assumed to operate in an automatic manner, meaning that they become activated spontaneously, without intention or effort. Devine provocatively proposed that even when people explicitly disavow prejudice and stereotypes, they may nevertheless fall prey to their automatic activation, which occurs much like an autonomous mental reflex. From this perspective, automatic prejudiced reactions are likely to prevail unless controlled processes are subsequently brought to bear in reining them in.

Origins of Intergroup Biases

If people truly aspire to egalitarianism, why do they still possess prejudiced feelings? This question raises important issues regarding the origins of prejudice and stereotyping. Evidently, an important part of the story lies outside the realm of our reasoned ideologies. A common assumption is that the sociocultural environment conditions individuals who live within it to develop stereotypic and prejudicial associations regarding a variety of social groups. According to this view, racist sentiments are still present in many individuals in contemporary society because these sentiments have been repeatedly (even if unwittingly) reinforced over the course of development by agents of socialization such as our parents (Rohan & Zanna, 1996), other adults (Castelli, De Dea, & Nesdale, 2008), or the mass media (Harris, 2004). This approach suggests that intergroup biases will emerge incrementally over the course of ontogeny, as a child gains greater exposure to socializing forces and comes to internalize the view of other groups that is pervasive in the social environment. In contrast to this view, recent research suggests that automatic biases emerge very rapidly and indeed are present at high levels in very early childhood (Dunham, Baron, & Banaji, 2008). This latter evidence suggests that rapid affective conditioning processes lie at the heart of the development of automatic biases toward other groups. Only those individuals who are less susceptible to affective conditioning may escape from the formation of automatic prejudice (Livingston & Drwecki, 2007).

Intergroup Dynamics

But why are the affective experiences that individuals associate with other groups so often negative? The world would surely be a much more enjoyable place if different groups coexisted in harmony and mutual respect. So why is prejudice so commonplace? As Rodney King memorably asked, can't we all just get along? Research has implicated a multitude of relevant factors. Evolutionary analyses have emphasized the role of adaptive xenophobia and intergroup conflict in producing a readiness to view outgroups negatively (Schaller & Neuberg, 2008). Whether or not we adopt an evolutionary perspective, intergroup dynamics certainly can set the stage for prejudice and stereotyping (see Brewer, Chapter 15, this volume). Cuddy, Fiske, and Glick (2008) have argued that the core of stereotypical content can be explained by two key dimensions of intergroup relations—relative status and competition. Groups that have lower status will tend to be stereotyped as incompetent (unintelligent, lazy, etc.), whereas those with higher status will be stereotyped in opposite terms. Groups that are perceived as competing with our own group will be perceived as unlikable (cold, dishonest, etc.), whereas groups that are perceived as cooperative and unthreatening will tend to be stereotyped as warm, likable, etc. Clearly, the ways that social groups are historically situated vis-à-vis one another will have a major impact on the types of stereotypes and affective reactions they tend to elicit.

Motivational Forces

Beyond the intergroup level, motivational forces within the individual can also contribute to the tendency to form negative stereotypes and prejudices.

Several of the classic Freudian defense mechanisms have been proposed to contribute to negative intergroup biases. Displacement refers to the tendency to redirect unacceptable impulses or to vent our frustrations on a target other than the original source of the frustration (e.g., when acting against the real source would be taboo or dangerous). Displacement is closely related to the tendency to engage in scapegoating, or the process of blaming another group for your misfortunes. In his seminal analysis of prejudice, Allport (1954) considered scapegoating to be a key psychological process in the production of particularly toxic intergroup animosities. Projection is another defense mechanism that is often linked to stereotyping. It involves seeing our undesirable qualities in others. People are threatened by the idea of possessing negative characteristics, so they actively suppress thoughts about these undesirable qualities. As an ironic consequence of this suppression, the inhibited concepts tend to be quite cognitively accessible (Newman, Duff, & Baumeister, 1997) and the behavior of outgroup members, to the extent it is sufficiently ambiguous, will tend to be perceived as embodying these accessible concepts (see Govorun, Fuegen, & Payne, 2006). Beyond the psychodynamic realm, ordinary self-enhancement motives have also been implicated in the generation of intergroup bias. In particular, perceiving outgroups in ways that establish the relative superiority of the ingroup should gratify self-enhancement motives via downward social comparison (e.g., Tajfel, 1974). One of Tajfel's key insights was that even in the absence of competition or conflict between groups, the basic desire for a comparatively positive social identity in itself could be sufficient to produce intergroup bias.

Ordinary Cognitive Processes

Yet another general perspective on the origins of prejudice and stereotyping emphasizes the role of ordinary cognitive processes. The cognitive analysis starts from the assumption that representations of social groups arise from basic processes of categorization (Hamilton, 1981; Turner, Hogg, Oakes, Reicher, & Wetherell, 1987). In the process of forming such representations, certain cognitive biases are evident. One is the tendency to accentuate between-category differences, while minimizing within-category variability (Krueger & Rothbart, 1990). By itself, this kind of bias would not explain why outgroups tend to become associated with negative stereotypes, but Hamilton and Gifford (1976) proposed a basic cognitive mechanism that could explain the negative bias in stereotype formation in the case of minority groups—distinctiveness-based illusory correlation. The basic notion is that distinctive stimuli tend to receive enhanced processing and thus are more memorable and exert a disproportionate influence on judgments. Minority groups are more distinctive than majority groups (in strictly numerical terms), and negative behavior is more distinctive than positive behavior. When members of a minority group perform a negative behavior, it would be doubly distinctive and thus highly likely to be noticed and remembered. Although Hamilton and Gifford's account has been the subject of controversy, the various alternative accounts that have been generated comport with the more general theme that ordinary cognitive processes can give rise to the tendency to form negative stereotypes about minority groups.

Effects of Prejudice and Stereotypes on Judgment and Behavior

Stereotyping and prejudice generate such deep interest not because of an abiding concern about the private thoughts and feelings people may have, but because of the assumption that these private reactions can influence overt decisions and actions in ways that have important consequences for their targets. In this section we review some of the extensive evidence documenting these effects and delineating the psychological processes through which they unfold.

Effects on Judgments and Decisions

Explicit judgments and decisions are subject to deliberation and control, so individuals who aspire to be unprejudiced should theoretically have the option to disregard prejudices and stereotypes in reaching conclusions about others. Unfortunately, however, people are often completely unaware of a range of factors that can influence their judgments in noteworthy ways (Nisbett & Wilson, 1977), and intergroup biases appear to constitute an important category of this kind of subtle influence. Based on the previously noted evidence that stereotypes and prejudice can be activated automatically, it would not be surprising to discover that they influence the judgments even of ostensibly egalitarian decision makers. Because of the rapidity and spontaneity with which they can be activated, stereotypes and prejudice can color initial reactions and potentially bias the processing of subsequently encountered evidence. Bodenhausen (1988) presented evidence in the context of legal judgments that stereotypes form the basis for an initial judgment and that relevant case evidence was subsequently assimilated toward the implications of this stereotypic prejudgment, thereby biasing the decision that was ultimately reached; in contrast, when stereotypes were activated after the relevant case evidence had been processed, no stereotypic biases where evident in the decisions that were rendered. Along similar lines, Gawronski, Geschke, and Banse (2003) showed that even when given the same behavioral information about targets, people judged them more negatively when they were known to be a member of an ethnic outgroup (versus ingroup member), to the extent that they held independently assessed automatic prejudice toward the ethnic group. Presumably their automatically activated prejudice resulted in the assimilation of the presented behavioral information toward this biased image of the outgroup.

The extent to which biased deliberation of this sort will be evident is known to be moderated by several factors. For example, when people are under time pressure or are otherwise lacking in the cognitive resources needed to systematically evaluate individuating information or to control their prejudiced reactions, judgmental biases are more likely to be evident. A number of specific variables have been shown to bear on the motivation and/or the ability to go beyond our initial prejudicial impulses in making judgments, including individual differences in the motivation to control prejudice (Plant & Devine, 1998), the need for cognition (Florack, Scarabis, & Bless, 2001), concurrent emotional states (Bodenhausen, Mussweiler, Gabriel, and Moreno, 2001), ego depletion (Govorun & Payne, 2006), and circadian arousal levels (Bodenhausen, 1990). Collectively, the research shows that people who are susceptible to biased reactions are nevertheless able to control their automatic intergroup biases, provided that they have both the momentary motivation and cognitive capacity to engage in relevant controlled processes.

Effects on Interpersonal Behavior

In the realm of intergroup relations, interpersonal interactions are where the rubber hits the road. When members of different social groups interact with each other, how will their prejudices and stereotypes influence their behavior? We will explore the dynamics of intergroup interactions in some detail, but first we highlight some of the more insidious forms that behavioral influences can take. One quite interesting and initially surprising behavioral effect of stereotypes lies in the phenomenon of "automatic behavior" (Dijksterhuis & Bargh, 2001). When stereotypes of a particular group become activated, they tend to elicit a corresponding behavioral response. For example, thinking about the elderly tends to elicit slower walking speeds and greater forgetfulness. The mechanisms producing such effects, and their functional basis, have been much discussed and debated. Some theorists, such as Dijksterhuis and Bargh, have suggested that the activation of relevant concepts directly triggers corresponding responses, because the representations involved in perceiving and understanding a behaviorally relevant concept (such as slowness or forgetfulness) are also involved in executing related behavior. Others have argued that automatic behavior reflects the application of accessible concepts to the momentarily active representation of the self (Wheeler, DeMarree, & Petty, 2007). Still others have proposed that automatic behavior of this sort reflects a motivated preparation to interact with members of the stereotyped group (Cesario, Plaks, & Higgins, 2006).

Another noteworthy behavioral manifestation of stereotypes and prejudice is the self-fulfilling prophecy (Darley & Fazio, 1980). In interracial interaction, for example, the biased expectations individuals have regarding the other person may lead them to behave in a manner that will elicit the expected kind of behavior. For instance, if we expect an interaction partner to be unpleasant, we may start the interaction by behaving in an aloof or cold manner, which in turn may elicit an unpleasant response (which might never have occurred but for our initial coldness). This process can unfold quite automatically, in that stereotypic expectations can be activated unintentionally, and moreover, as just noted, they can also trigger corresponding "automatic behavior" on the part of the person holding the expectancy (Chen & Bargh, 1997).

Just as with judgments, behaviors need not inevitably reflect the biasing influence of automatic stereotypes and prejudices. Research has identified boundary conditions that generally accord with the moderating processes that are known to govern the expression of bias in judgment. For example, Dasgupta and Rivera (2006) found that heterosexual people who possessed automatic antigay prejudice were likely to produce unfriendly nonverbal behavior in an interaction with a gay confederate, but this effect was eliminated when individuals had "behavioral control" over their nonverbal responses (i.e., when they had a sense of awareness and a feeling of control over these displays). Taken as a whole, the research confirms that stereotypes and prejudice *can* lead to discriminatory judgments and behavior, as many scholars have theorized, but this kind of outcome is far from inevitable in the contemporary context of individuals who strive to be egalitarian.

Countering the Influence: Self-Regulation of Bias

Although stereotyping and prejudice are ubiquitous, both social norms and internal standards to be nonprejudiced (Dunton & Fazio, 1997; Plant & Devine, 1998) lead individuals to attempt to control their expression. Indeed, despite initial theories suggesting that biased responding may be inevitable on encountering a stigmatized group member (Allport, 1954; Bargh, 1999; Devine, 1989), considerable research suggests that it is possible for social perceivers to control the initial activation of prejudiced associations as well as to curb the influence of prejudicial associations, once activated, on judgments and behavior.

Whether intergroup biases will be expressed depends on the interaction of automatically-activated mental associations and executive control (Devine, 1989; Fazio, 1990; Payne, 2001, 2005; see also Conrey, Sherman, Gawronski, Hugenberg, & Groom, 2005). Thus, there are two routes through which we can attempt to reduce the expression of prejudice. The first is to reduce the extent to which individuals automatically (and perhaps unconsciously) evaluate members of low-status (i.e., stigmatized) social groups negatively and/or stereotypically. Certainly, without automatically activated biases, individuals will be less likely to behave in prejudiced ways. The second route involves increasing individuals' motivation, ability, and/or opportunity to control the expression of biased mental associations that have been activated. In the sections that follow, we review research pertaining to each of these two routes.

Controlling the Initial Activation of Biased Associations

Although it was previously thought that the automatic activation of stereotypical mental associations on encountering a relevant group member was both widespread and inevitable (Bargh, 1999; Devine, 1989), recent research suggests otherwise. The extent to which biased mental associations become activated for perceivers depends on a number of factors, including chronic individual differences such as the perceivers' explicit attitudes and motivation to respond in nonbiased ways (e.g., Devine, Plant, Amodio, & Harmon-Jones, 2002; Lepore & Brown, 1997; Wittenbrink, Judd, & Park, 1997), features of the social context (e.g., Barden et al., 2004; Wittenbrink et al., 2001), and individuals' situational goals and information-processing capacity (e.g., Gilbert & Hixon, 1991; Macrae, Bodenhausen, Milne, Thorne, & Castelli, 1997; Wheeler & Fiske, 2005). Given that individuals cannot readily change their chronic attitudes and motivations, shift their goals and motivational states, increase their processing capacity, and control the contexts in which they encounter members of stigmatized groups, scholars have looked to more acute strategies to regulate the expression of bias.

One of the best-studied bias regulation procedures is stereotype suppression—the deliberate attempt by individuals to prevent prejudicial thoughts from entering their consciousness (Macrae, Bodenhausen, Milne, & Jetten, 1994; Monteith, Sherman, & Devine, 1998). Although suppression is an intuitively appealing strategy that is relatively easy to implement, considerable research has documented its unintended consequences (see Monteith et al., 1998). Specifically, shortly after suppression, the suppressed idea can become hyperaccessible due to the mind's efforts to monitor for the "restricted" content (Wegner, 1994). In one of the first demonstrations of stereotype hyperaccessibility following suppression, Macrae et al. (1994) had participants compose an essay about a "day-in-the-life" of a skinhead. Half of the participants were instructed to avoid the influence of stereotypes when writing their essay and the other half was given no specific instruction. In a subsequent reaction-time task, participants who had suppressed stereotypes while writing the essay exhibited significantly greater activation of skinhead stereotypes compared to participants in the no-instruction condition. In other words, suppressing skinhead stereotypes caused them to become even more accessible than they would have been if participants had never attempted to suppress them.

Although this stereotype rebound effect is troubling, other work suggests that under the right conditions, at least some individuals are able to employ a suppression strategy successfully (Gollwitzer, Fujita, & Oettingen, 2004; Monteith, Spicer, & Tooman, 1998). For instance, individuals with more practice and/or internal motivation to control the expression of prejudice are better able to suppress stereotypes without falling prey to stereotype rebound (Gordijn, Hindriks, Koomen, Dijksterhuis, & van Knippenberg, 2004). Furthermore, even high-prejudice individuals can avoid postsuppression rebound if the norms of the environment are sufficiently strong to require continued suppression and the prejudiced individuals have ample cognitive resources (Monteith et al., 2008).

A bias control strategy having seemingly more general efficacy is perspective taking—the active attempt to imagine the thoughts, feelings, and experiences of another individual. In one demonstration, nonblack individuals who took the perspective of a member of a socially devalued group while writing a "day-in-the-life" essay about a black male target individual subsequently expressed less automatic prowhite (antiblack) evaluative bias on a response-latency measure (A. R. Todd, 2009). Furthermore, because perspective taking does not entail the active suppression of unwanted associations, it is not vulnerable to rebound effects. Indeed, comparing the effects of stereotype suppression and perspective taking, Galinsky and Moskowitz (2000) discovered that whereas stereotype suppressers exhibited heightened stereotype accessibility, participants instructed to adopt the perspective of an outgroup member did not. Thus, perspective taking may be a more successful strategy for undermining the activation of biased mental associations compared with suppression, although its implementation during intergroup interactions may be less straightforward than suppression (A. R. Todd, 2009; Vorauer, Martens, & Sasaki, 2009).

Controlling the Application of Biased Associations

Although the automatic activation of biased associations on encountering a relevant group member is not inevitable, for many it is quite a regular occurrence. What, then, can individuals do to avoid having their decisions and behaviors tainted by these prejudiced associations? The dominant assumption is that individuals must engage in self-control to stop prejudice from affecting their subsequent responses regarding stigmatized group members. The term executive function refers to the constellation of higher-order cognitive processes involved in the planning, execution, and regulation (i.e., control) of behavior (Baddeley, 1986; Norman & Shallice, 1986). Similar to its role in regulating other types of behavior, executive function has been shown to play a fundamental role in controlling the expression of prejudice (e.g., Conrey et al., 2005; Cunningham et al., 2004; Macrae, Bodenhausen, Schloersheidt, & Milne, 1999; Payne, 2005; Richeson et al., 2003; Richeson & Trawalter, 2005; von Hippel & Gonsalkorale, 2005).

Indeed, the most comprehensive model of prejudice regulation, advanced by Monteith and colleagues (Monteith, 1993; Monteith & Mark, 2005, 2009), heavily implicates executive control. Specifically, Monteith's Self-Regulation of Prejudice (SRP) model proposes an iterative process through which individuals first learn to control the expression of biased mental associations and, over time, become less biased. The SRP model assumes that for most individuals, encounters with members of low-status sociocultural groups result in the automatic (and, perhaps unconscious) activation of biased thoughts and feelings that, in turn, typically results in discriminatory behaviors. For people who endorse egalitarian values, however, discrepancies between these values and biased behavior lead to five consequences that serve to "put the breaks" on prejudice: (1) behavioral inhibition, (2) negative self-directed affect, (3) retrospective reflection, (4) the development of cues for control, and (5) prospective reflection.

Imagine, for instance, a white woman who is low in explicit racial prejudice, but nevertheless mistakes an African American woman for a store employee while she is out shopping one afternoon. The white woman is likely to stop what she was doing (i.e., inhibit all behavior) and feel embarrassed and guilty (i.e., negative self-directed affect) initially, then attempt to figure out where she erred (i.e., engage in retrospective reflection) to avoid similarly prejudiced responses and the resultant negative self-directed affect in the future. Such retrospective reflection, Monteith and colleagues argue, will lead the woman to focus on features of the situation that are correlated with the prejudiced response (e.g., needing assistance from a store clerk, the African American shopper's race) that will ultimately become cues for control. The relevant features of the situation, that is, will eventually become cues that biased responding is likely and, thus, act as a signal to the woman that she should exercise control to ensure that she does not actually engage in discriminatory behavior. After these cues for control are developed, the woman will be able to engage in prospective reflection when she finds herself in situations in which those cues are present. In other words, she will become more aware of the potential for bias and, thus, be better able to generate nonbiased responses.

Although control of prejudice is quite promising in that it does not require individuals to undo strongly held (perhaps unconscious) associations, it is not without its pitfalls. First, on detecting the potential for unwanted bias, people may not be able to negate its influence (e.g., Wegener & Petty, 1997; Wilson & Brekke, 1994). People may either overcorrect for their perceived bias, perhaps behaving in patronizing ways with members of stigmatized groups, or their efforts at correction may be insufficient or incomplete, behaving in ways that subtly reveal their bias (Dovidio, Kawakami, & Gaertner, 2002). Thus, unless individuals are skillful enough to (1) identify precisely the magnitude of their bias and (2) correct for it effectively, becoming more aware of the potential for biased responding may not successfully eliminate it.

Also of great consequence is the fact that resources for executive control are limited. Specifically, research suggests that executive functioning draws on a limited resource (Engle, Conway, Tuholski, & Shisler, 1995; Norman & Shallice, 1986) and, thus, individuals can focus only on a limited number of tasks at one time. Furthermore, Baumeister and colleagues' self-control strength model (e.g., Baumeister, Vohs, & Tice, 2007; Muraven & Baumeister, 2000) suggests that tasks that require executive control temporarily deplete a common central executive resource, leaving individuals less able to perform optimally on subsequent executive control tasks. Taken together, this work suggests that the efficacy of efforts to control the expression of biased mental associations is bounded by the inherent limits of this cognitive resource.

In sum, the presence of members of culturally devalued groups often triggers the activation of stereotypical thoughts and biased evaluations. Although stereotype suppression can be effective in reducing stereotype activation, at least for some individuals, recent research suggests that perspective taking may be a more reliable route to undermine the activation of biased mental associations. After such associations are activated, however, research reveals the important role of self-regulatory processes (i.e., executive control) in undermining their ability to taint individuals' judgments and behavior.

The Target's Perspective: The Experience of Stigma

Our review thus far has largely focused on the processes that give rise to, and support the control of, stereotyping and prejudice—topics that take the perspective of nonstigmatized social perceivers evaluating members of stigmatized social groups. This section considers the social psychological processes associated with being a target of stereotyping and prejudice.

Being the target of negative stereotypes, prejudice, and discrimination is one of the primary mechanisms of stigmatization (Crocker, Major, & Steele, 1998; Goffman, 1963). Discrimination affects the socioeconomic status, physical health, and psychological well-being of members of stigmatized groups through any number of sociological and psychological processes. Nevertheless, social-psychological research points to identity threat—concerns about group devaluation—as a primary factor shaping the cognition, affect, and behavior of members of stigmatized groups (Branscombe, Schmitt, & Harvey, 1999; Major & O'Brien, 2005; Shelton, Richeson, & Vorauer, 2006).

Research has found, for instance, that stigmatized individuals often stereotypically believe that nonstigmatized individuals are prejudiced against their group (Monteith & Spicer, 2000). It is this stereotype, ironically, that fuels stigmatized group members' prejudice against the nonstigmatized outgroup (Livingston, 2002). In addition to shaping stigmatized group members' intergroup attitudes, concerns about being the target of prejudice can lead some members of stigmatized groups to become vigilant for signs of prejudice (Inzlicht, Kaiser, & Major, 2008; Kaiser, Vick, & Major, 2006; Mendoza-Denton, Downey, Purdie, Davis, & Pietrzak, 2002; Pinel, 1999). Although such heightened awareness can lead members of stigmatized groups to perceive negative treatment where there is none (Kleck & Strenta, 1980), it can also result in greater efficiency and accuracy at detecting prejudice cues when they do appear (Richeson & Shelton, 2005). Taken together, this work reveals the power of stigma to shape cognition and perception (see also Feldman Barrett & Swim, 1998).

In addition, the threat of group devaluation can lead stigmatized group members to question their legitimacy and belonging in an environment (Walton & Cohen, 2007) and undermine the ability of individuals to perform to the best of their ability (Inzlicht & Ben Zeev, 2000; Steele, Spencer, & Aronson, 2002). For instance, African Americans perform worse on academic tests that are described as diagnostic of intelligence—activating the stereotype that African Americans are academically inferior to whites—compared with tests described as nondiagnostic (Steele & Aronson, 1995). Similarly, women perform worse on math tests after reading about genetic (i.e., internal and stable), compared with experiential (i.e., external and unstable), gender differences in math ability (Dar-Nimrod & Heine, 2006).

A number of mechanisms have been offered to explain why identity threat undermines performance (Schmader, Johns, & Forbes, 2008). For instance, research suggests that individuals appraise situations in which group stereotypes are salient as "threatening" rather than "challenging" (Blascovich, Spencer, Quinn, & Steele, 2001), which induces anxiety (Ben-Zeev, Fein, & Inzlicht, 2005) and triggers a maladaptive pattern of physiological arousal (Vick, Seery, Blascovich, & Weisbuch, 2008), all of which can undermine task performance. Furthermore, contending with identity threat has been shown to undermine performance because it usurps cognitive resources that would otherwise be devoted to completing the task (Beilock, Rydell, & McConnell, 2007; Inzlicht, McKay, & Aronson, 2006; Krendl, Richeson, Kelley, & Heatherton, 2008; Schmader & Johns, 2003).

Not surprisingly, stigmatized individuals who are highly identified with their group (Schmader, 2002) and with the performance domain (Aronson et al., 1999) and who are extremely sensitive to group stigmatization (Brown & Pinel, 2002) are particularly likely to fall prey to social identity threat. Moreover, the accumulation of such threatening experiences has been theorized to lead individuals to psychologically disengage from important domains in which their groups are stereotyped to perform poorly (e.g., academics for blacks; Steele, 1997). Needless to say, psychological disengagement is likely to have widespread negative consequences, such as contributing to the well-known academic achievement gaps between members of stigmatized and nonstigmatized groups.

Stigma can also have deleterious consequences for mental and physical health. Extant research has found that members of stigmatized groups who perceive that they have been discriminated against have poorer mental and physical health (Sellers & Shelton, 2003; Williams, Neighbors, & Jackson, 2003). For instance, Cole and colleagues (Cole, Kemeny, & Taylor, 1997) found that the HIV virus advanced more rapidly during a 9-year period in HIV+ gay men who were higher in sensitivity to antigay prejudice (i.e., high in stigma sensitivity) than in their less stigma-sensitive counterparts. Although the pathways through which stigma may affect health are largely unknown (but see Clark, Anderson, Clark, & Williams, 1999; Dickerson & Kemeny, 2004), research suggests that as with other stressors, stigmatization triggers physiological reactions that with repeated activation contribute to ill health (McEwen, 2000).

One of the most controversial issues in the stigma literature is the extent to which members of stigmatized groups endorse and/or internalize the negative stereotypes regarding their groups. Although conventional wisdom suggests that members of such groups must have lower self-esteem compared with their nonstigmatized counterparts, the research on this question has proved to be mixed. Early research did suggest that African American children may have lower self-esteem than white children (Clark & Clark, 1947). As the research accumulated, however, the evidence, primarily from self-report measures, did not support the claim that blacks had lower self-esteem than whites (Grey-Little

& Hafdahl, 2000). Recent research employing more unobtrusive, indirect measures, however, has begun to challenge the idea that members of stigmatized groups do not internalize their stigma. Jost and colleagues argue that members of stigmatized groups, much like nonstigmatized group members, are motivated to justify the status quo of group hierarchy (Jost, Banaji, & Nosek, 2004; Jost, Pelham, & Carvallo, 2002). Consistent with this claim, research on automatic racial bias has found that unlike whites and other members of nonstigmatized groups, blacks and members of stigmatized groups often fail to demonstrate automatic ingroup favoritism and sometimes even demonstrate outgroup favoritism (see also Dasgupta, 2004 for a review). Although the extent to which outgroup favoritism is observed in stigmatized groups continues to be debated, what is clear is that the internalization of negative group stereotypes is harmful to the health and well-being of stigmatized group members (Allport, 1954). In a number of elegant studies, for instance, Levy and colleagues have shown that older adults who endorse negative aging stereotypes die sooner than older adults with more positive views of aging (Levy, Slade, Kunkel, & Kasl, 2002).

At this point, the growing literature on the experience of stigma supports several broad conclusions. Members of stigmatized groups are aware of the negative societal stereotypes regarding their groups, and even if they do not endorse those stereotypes, they must contend with the possibility that they will taint their interactions with nonstigmatized group members. The threat of (and actual) group devaluation, furthermore, often shapes stigmatized group members' cognitions about, attitudes toward, and behaviors with members of nonstigmatized groups. It also has important implications for stigmatized individuals' health and well-being.

The Experience of Contact

Much of the social psychological research on prejudice, stereotyping, and the experience of social stigma has employed research paradigms in which people read or think about members of other groups. Recent work, however, is beginning to consider how the processes of mind that give rise to stereotyping and prejudice and/or reactions to stigma unfold within actual intergroup encounters. Emerging models of the interaction dynamics between members of nonstigmatized and members of stigmatized groups posit that individuals' experiences are largely shaped by their attitudes and stereotypical beliefs (both deliberate and automatic) and their concerns about the potential influence of prejudice (Hebl & Dovidio, 2005; Shelton & Richeson, 2006a). In other words, prejudice and concerns about prejudice shape cognitive, affective, and behavioral dynamics of intergroup interactions.

Stereotypes and Attitudes

It should come as no surprise that individuals' attitudes and stereotypical beliefs affect the way intergroup interactions unfold. Indeed, individuals who harbor negative stereotypes about the group membership of their interaction partners often display behavior that conforms to their stereotypical beliefs. For instance, young adults tend to believe that older adults are mentally slow and incompetent (Hummert, Garstka, Shaner, & Strahm, 1994) and, during interactions with older adults, they often use diminutive language and speak in an altered tone of speech similar to that used with children and pets (Ryan, Bourhis, & Knops, 1991). As previously noted, stereotyped targets often behave in stereotype-consistent ways in response to the treatment they receive during intergroup interactions (Snyder, Tanke, & Berscheid, 1977; Word, Zanna, & Cooper, 1974).

Although stereotypes often have predictable effects on behavior during intergroup interactions, the effects of individuals' attitudes are more complex. Recent work suggests that individuals' unconscious attitudes and beliefs shape their behavior in ways that are dissociable from the attitudes they explicitly hold (Dovidio et al., 2002; Fazio, Jackson, Dutton, & Williams, 1995). Specifically, deliberated attitudes shape behaviors that are relatively controllable, such as how favorably a person in a wheelchair is evaluated by nonstigmatized interaction partners (Dovidio, Kawakami, Johnson, Johnson, & Howard, 1997). Automatic attitudes, by contrast, influence behavior that is relatively difficult to monitor and control, for instance the nonverbal manner with which an individual interacts with a physically disabled job candidate (e.g., smiling less or displaying less eye contact—a behavioral signal of interest; see Fazio et al., 1995; McConnell & Liebold, 2001).

Because most individuals harbor positive explicit attitudes, but relatively negative automatic evaluative reactions, toward many stigmatized groups, verbal aspects of their communications with stigmatized group members are positive, whereas nonverbal aspects are often relatively negative (e.g., Dovidio et al., 2002; Fazio et al., 1995; McConnell & Leibold, 2001). In other words, individuals' nonverbal behaviors often reveal automatically activated biased mental associations that are more negative than their explicitly held egalitarian values. Because members of stigmatized groups tend to focus on their interaction partners' nonverbal rather than verbal behavior, however, their interaction experiences are typically more negative than their interaction partners either intend or even realize (Dovidio et al., 2002). For instance, contending with verbal–nonverbal mixed messages during intergroup interactions has recently been shown to be cognitively depleting (Murphy, Richeson, Shelton, Rheinschmidt, & Berkseiger, 2010).

Unlike the complex and complicated effects of intergroup attitudes, negative attitudes (both automatic and deliberated) have fairly straightforward effects on individuals' affective outcomes. It is therefore not surprising that the more negative an individual's attitudes about a particular social group, the less positive his or her interaction experiences with a member of that group (see e.g., Richeson, Trawalter, & Shelton, 2005; Shelton & Richeson, 2006b). Indeed, negative attitudes and beliefs regarding outgroups often lead individuals to experience feelings of threat and anxiety during intergroup interactions (Mackie, Devos, & Smith, 2000; Stephan & Stephan, 1985). It is also the case that our interaction partner's attitudes can influence an individual's affective experiences during the interaction. For example, Vorauer and Kumhyr (2001) found that First Nations participants (i.e., members of the Aboriginal Canadian tribes) experienced more discomfort after interacting with high-prejudiced compared to low-prejudiced white partners. Similarly, Murphy et al. (2010) found that blacks reported more depressive affect after interacting with a racially biased white partner than with a nonprejudiced white partner. Taken together, this work reveals the multiple dynamics of intergroup interactions that are shaped, in part, by individuals' stereotypes and attitudes.

Motivations and Goals

Although stereotypes and attitudes certainly have profound effects on interaction dynamics, research suggests that motivations can both attenuate as well as completely alter their influence. Both chronic egalitarian values and pressure from the social context to behave in nonprejudiced ways (Plant & Devine, 1998) affect the expression of bias by members of nonstigmatized groups during intergroup interactions (Vorauer & Turpie, 2004). For instance, Shelton (2003) found that although whites who were instructed to avoid prejudice reported that they felt more anxious during the interaction than whites who were not given this instruction, analyses of their nonverbal behavior revealed that they behaved less anxiously (they fidgeted less) than whites who were not so instructed. Motivation to behave in nonprejudiced ways can also moderate the influence of automatic associations on behavior during intergroup interactions (Dasgupta & Rivera, 2006). The desire of individuals to behave in egalitarian ways thus can override the typical consequences of automatic mental associations.

The motivation of nonstigmatized group members to respond without prejudice, however, can also result in paradoxical behavioral outcomes. The effort required to control the expression of bias during intergroup interactions is cognitively demanding (Richeson et al., 2003; Richeson & Trawalter, 2005), and, as a consequence, can lead individuals to behave in ways that differ from their intentions (Apfelbaum, Sommers, & Norton, 2008). First, the arousal associated with the potential to reveal bias during intergroup interactions can lead even those with egalitarian values to avoid such interactions when possible (Plant & Devine, 2003; Snyder, Kleck, Strenta, & Mentzer, 1979). Second, when nonstigmatized individuals with low levels of explicit bias cannot avoid intergroup interactions, preoccupation with avoiding prejudiced behavior can undermine efforts to communicate their largely positive, egalitarian beliefs (Shelton, Richeson, & Salvatore, 2005; Vorauer & Turpie, 2004). For instance, when whites are concerned about acting in prejudiced ways, they may focus their attention on managing their verbal behaviors (i.e., what they say), which are easier to monitor and control than many nonverbal aspects of behavior (e.g., blinking); however, as mentioned previously, members of stigmatized groups typically focus on nonverbal behavior when assessing the beliefs and intentions of nonstigmatized interaction partners (Dovidio et al., 2002). Consequently, concerns about appearing prejudiced may make members of nonstigmatized groups appear more biased than they actually are (Shelton et al., 2005; Vorauer & Turpie, 2004).

In addition, concerns about behaving inappropriately can lead individuals to feel anxious during intergroup interactions (Devine & Vasquez, 1998) and to construe intergroup interactions as psychologically threatening, triggering maladaptive physiological reactivity (Blascovich, Mendes, Hunter, Lickel, & Kowai-Bell, 2001). Indeed, considerable research has found that nonstigmatized individuals often display nonverbal signs of anxiety and discomfort (e.g., excessive blinking) more during intergroup, compared with intragroup, interactions (Dovidio et al., 1997; Fazio et al., 1995; Kleck, 1968; Richeson & Shelton, 2005; Trawalter & Richeson, 2008; Trawalter, Richeson, & Shelton, 2009; West, Shelton, & Trail, 2009). Similarly, recent evidence suggests that physiological threat reactivity disallows the types of fluid behaviors that promote positive interpersonal interactions (Mendes, Blascovich, Hunter, Lickel, & Jost, 2007). The experience of anxiety during intergroup interactions, furthermore, often undermines the benefit of contact for improving intergroup attitudes (Pettigrew & Tropp, 2008), and the effort required to regulate the expression of anxiety during intergroup interactions taxes individuals' cognitive resources (Richeson & Trawalter, 2005).

The social context can also provide an incentive for individuals to attempt to control the expression of prejudiced behavior. Indeed, when discrimination is discouraged by social norms and/or prohibited by the law, individuals are unlikely to respond in an overtly prejudicial fashion (but see also Pager, 2003). For instance, Hebl, Foster, Mannix, and Dovidio (2002) found no evidence of discrimination in formal actions made by potential employers toward gay men and lesbians (e.g., permission to complete a job application, job callbacks); however, these employers' less controllable, informal behaviors (e.g., amount of time spent with gay versus straight applicants) revealed considerable discrimination. Contextual pressure to behave in nonprejudiced ways can also backfire. Individuals who are motivated to behave in nonprejudiced ways because of external pressures (such as the fear of social disapproval) are especially likely to behave anxiously during interracial interactions (Trawalter, Adam, Chase-Lansdale, & Richeson, 2009). These individuals have also been found to display race-based patterns of selective attention to photographs of blacks that are thought to reflect anxious reactions to black individuals (Richeson & Trawalter, 2008); they are also most susceptible to reacting with increased negativity toward stigmatized groups (Plant & Devine, 2001). Although rooted in anxiety, such reactions can lead these individuals to behave more positively with other white individuals than with racial minorities. In sum, this research suggests that the restriction of overt bias may actually serve to increase the likelihood that individuals will respond differently, albeit subtly, to members of stigmatized groups than they do to members of nonstigmatized groups.

To avoid being the target of prejudice, stigmatized group members exhibit similar behavior during intergroup interactions. When members of stigmatized groups expect to be the target of prejudice, they become vigilant for signs of prejudice (Inzlicht et al., 2008; Kaiser et al., 2006; Kleck & Strenta, 1980), which is likely to result in (1) increased detection of interaction partners' actual biased behaviors (Dovidio et al., 2002; Richeson & Shelton, 2005), (2) increased attribution of interaction partners' ambiguous behaviors to prejudice (e.g., Inzlicht et al., 2008), and (3) reduced expression of positive, affiliative behavior (Frable, Blackstone, & Scherbaum, 1990; see also Ickes, 1984)—a recipe for a negative interaction.

Nevertheless, there is also research suggesting that under some conditions, concern about being the target of prejudice can facilitate smooth intergroup interactions. Specifically, this work finds that concerns about being the target of prejudice lead stigmatized individuals to employ compensatory strategies, such as smiling more and being more engaged in the interaction, to cope with or even ward off actual or anticipated discrimination during the interaction (Miller & Myers, 1998). Shelton, Richeson, and Salvatore (2005) found, for instance, that ethnic minorities who were concerned about the potential bias of a white interaction partner were more involved during the interactions compared with ethnic minorities who were less concerned, and, as a result, were better liked by their white interaction partners (see also Miller & Malloy, 2003). In other words, concern about being the target of prejudice can result in either positive or negative behavior during intergroup interactions. Irrespective of the effects on behavior, however, the evidence seems to be unequivocal that the more stigmatized individuals are concerned about being the target of prejudice during intergroup interactions, the more negative their emotional reactions (e.g., Hyers & Swim, 1998; Page-Gould, Mendoza-Denton, & Tropp, 2008; Shelton, 2003; Shelton et al., 2005; Tropp, 2003).

In sum, research on the effects of concerns about either appearing prejudiced or being the target of prejudice suggests that such concerns can result both in behavior that facilitates and in behavior that disrupts positive intergroup interactions. The effects of attitudes and motivations on interaction dynamics, furthermore, can be quite complex, often resulting in divergent experiences for participants and their partners (Shelton & Richeson, 2006a). That is, one participant may have a positive interaction experience while the other has a quite negative experience.

Prejudice, Stereotyping, and Discrimination Today

Although scholars have been assiduously researching the psychology of prejudice for many decades, much remains to be explored and discovered, and many controversies remain unresolved. We conclude by highlighting a few of the most novel and contentious issues.

Unconscious Prejudice and Stereotyping?

As described, much recent scholarly attention has been devoted to the relatively automatic forms that stereotyping and prejudice can take. Automaticity is a multifaceted phenomenon that includes a number of defining features. In general, automatic mental processes are ones that occur spontaneously, rapidly, efficiently, and inevitably when triggering cues are encountered (Bargh, 1994; Moors & De Houwer, 2006). Automaticity is a matter of degree, and automatic processes may contain various mixtures of these qualities. An additional quality of automaticity that has been the focus of much discussion and debate is implicitness or unconsciousness. Some scholars have provocatively asserted that prejudice and stereotyping commonly occur unconsciously (e.g., Banaji, Lemm, & Carpenter, 2001). Certainly, cognitive psychologists have established beyond any doubt that unconscious mental processes can influence task performance and other kinds of behavior (e.g., Underwood, 1996). Nevertheless, the postulation of unconscious prejudice has been met with strong resistance from some scholars (e.g., Blanton & Jaccard, 2008). It is crucial to appreciate that there are several distinct claims regarding the role of conscious awareness in stereotyping and prejudice, and each one needs to be evaluated on its own terms. Specifically, people may potentially lack awareness of (1) the reasons for their automatic reactions to other groups, (2) the stimuli that trigger automatic reactions in a given situation, (3) the consequences of their automatic reactions, and (4) the very existence of their automatic reactions (see Gawronski, Hofmann, & Wilber, 2006). Research using subliminal stimuli makes a strong case that automatic reactions can be triggered in the absence of awareness of the triggering stimulus. It is also not particularly controversial to claim that people may lack full insight into the causes and the consequences of their attitudes and beliefs. Indeed, people may often be influenced by stereotypes yet feel that their judgments have not been tainted by such associations (see Bodenhausen & Todd, 2010). What is most thorny, and most difficult to establish definitively, is the notion that people are routinely unaware of the existence of stereotypic or prejudicial associations, whether they are personally endorsed or not (see Han, Olson, & Fazio, 2006; Nosek & Hansen, 2008). It is a most intriguing possibility that calls out for more investigation.

The Neurobiology of Bias

Another emerging trend in current research involves employing neuroimaging techniques, particularly electroencephalography (EEG) and functional magnetic resonance imaging (fMRI), to investigate the neural basis of intergroup bias (e.g., Amodio, 2008; Amodio & Lieberman, 2009). This work has largely found that people exhibit different patterns of neural activity in response to ingroup compared with outgroup individuals (Golby, Gabrieli, Chiao, & Eberhardt, 2001; Harris & Fiske, 2006; Hart et al., 2000; Krendl, Macrae, Kelley, Fugelsang, & Heatherton, 2006; Phelps et al., 2000; Richeson et al., 2003; Van Bavel, Packer, & Cunningham, 2008; see also Eberhardt, 2005; Ito & Bartholow, 2009 for reviews). The work examining neural correlates of bias thus far has largely contributed to our understanding of the automatic activation (Cunningham et al., 2004; Hart et al., 2000; Wheeler & Fiske, 2005) and subsequent attempts to control (Amodio, Devine, & Harmon-Jones, 2008; Amodio et al., 2004; Beer et al., 2008; Cunningham et al., 2004; Richeson et al., 2003) the expression of anti-black racial bias. Indeed, research suggests that the amygdala—a brain region known to be responsive to potentially threatening and important socioemotional stimuli—is involved in the automatic evaluation of black individuals

(Cunningham et al., 2004; Lieberman, Hariri, Jarcho, Eisenberger, & Bookheimer, 2005; Phelps et al., 2000), whereas the anterior cingulate cortex (ACC) and prefrontal cortex (PFC)—brain regions known to be involved in conflict monitoring and cognitive control—support the regulation of biased attitudes and beliefs (Amodio et al., 2004; Cunningham et al., 2004; Lieberman et al., 2007; Richeson et al., 2003). Taken together, in other words, the research has thus far served to support prevailing social psychological models of prejudice, specifying the neural correlates that underlie the cognitive component processes implicated by them. That said, the social neuroscience approach to the study of prejudice will prove useful only if (1) it is able to generate new predictions and (2) patterns of neural activity are shown to predict behavior outside of the MRI scanner, for instance, during actual intergroup interactions (Dovidio, Pearson, & Orr, 2008).

Although this focus on the activation and control of bias has proved insightful, research should not be limited to this pursuit. Some of the most compelling results are likely to come from studies that examine the role of group membership in modulating patterns of neural activity that are associated with basic social information processing, such as face processing (see, e.g., Chiao et al., 2008; Golby et al., 2001), theory of mind, and the experience of empathy. Future investigations of this type may prove particularly fruitful and useful to both social psychology and cognitive neuroscience. Finally, similar to the disproportionate focus on nonstigmatized social perceivers of stigmatized targets, future work needs to consider the neural correlates of being the target of prejudice and discrimination (e.g., Derks, Inzlicht, & Kang, 2008; Krendl et al., 2008).

The Accuracy and Rationality of Stereotyping

Because of its association with discrimination and injustice, stereotyping is often viewed as a defective form of thinking. However, a rational, Bayesian approach to judgment requires decision makers to make use of base rate information. To the extent that stereotypes capture actual group differences (i.e., base rates), it would indeed be irrational for people *not* to rely on them in forming judgments. Clearly, the normative rationality of using stereotypes hinges entirely on their accuracy. If devoid of accuracy, their use will likely have only a corrupting influence on judgment and choice. Scholars have diverged markedly in their expectations about the accuracy of stereotypes. Some argue that it is vital for survival to form generally accurate impressions of the social environment; from this perspective, stereotypes represent our way of representing the general differences that actually exist between groups (see Lee, Jussim, & McCauley, 1995). Without disputing the general adaptiveness of human cognition, other scholars—dating back to Allport's (1954) seminal work—have argued that noteworthy cognitive and motivational processes can and do introduce systematic bias into the representation of group differences, some of which we have previously reviewed.

Evidence that stereotypes can sometimes be accurate is primarily found in research on sex differences, which has shown that lay perceptions of the differences between men and women often align with meta-analytically estimated "real" sex differences (e.g., Swim, 1994). Of course, people in our culture typically have extensive contact with both sexes throughout their lives, so it is perhaps not surprising that they can develop relatively well-calibrated group impressions under these conditions. Nevertheless, it is also clear that the general accuracy of sex stereotypes seen at an aggregated level belies an underlying heterogeneity of accuracy among individuals; Hall and Carter (1999) found pronounced individual differences in the accuracy of sex stereotypes, with greater accuracy being found among respondents who had less rigid cognitive styles and greater interpersonal sensitivity. To the extent that stereotypes are indeed accurate, it remains unclear whether this accuracy arises because the mind has merely "captured" existing differences, or rather has played an active role in creating expected differences, via the aforementioned self-fulfilling prophecy cycle (Darley & Fazio, 1980). Measuring the accuracy of stereotypes is a fairly tricky matter in any case (see Judd & Park, 1993), but the issue of stereotype accuracy will likely remain controversial.

The Generality versus Specificity of Prejudice

Finally, an important direction for future research concerns differentiating the shared psychological components of different forms of prejudice and stereotyping (e.g., ageism, racism, sexism, heterosexism, antisemitism) from the elements that may be specific and unique to particular varieties of intergroup bias. Much research has proceeded in a relatively ghettoized manner, with sexism researchers (e.g., Swim & Hyers, 2009), racism researchers (e.g., Zárate, 2009), and ageism researchers (e.g., Nelson, 2009) developing their own distinct models of the form of prejudice of greatest focal interest to them. Much has been learned from this approach, and it is inevitable that different psychological issues will emerge in different domains, making it necessary to consider each case separately. Nevertheless, a systematic consideration of what is constant and what is variable across different types of prejudice is a matter that deserves more attention. The "BIAS map" introduced by Cuddy, Fiske, and Glick (2008) represents one attempt to place prejudice toward different groups within a common conceptual framework, explaining the particular features of each type of prejudice as a function of how a given group is viewed on the dimensions of warmth–coldness and competence. Research involving this kind of ambitious, integrative scope represents an important direction for future scholarship.

We can look back over the abundant research on prejudice and stereotyping and discern many important advances, and we hope we have done justice to these scholarly accomplishments in our necessarily brief survey. Much has been learned, but the pressing problems of intergroup conflict and social disparities have certainly not been resolved, and the ongoing threats they pose to social cohesion provide no room for complacency. We fully anticipate that social psychologists will continue to make important contributions to the understanding and amelioration of these significant social problems.

References

Allport, G. (1954). *The nature of prejudice*. New York: Doubleday Anchor Books.

Amodio, D. M. (2008). The social neuroscience of intergroup relations. *European Review of Social Psychology, 19*, 1–54.

Amodio, D. M., Devine, P. G., & Harmon-Jones, E. (2008). Individual differences in the regulation of intergroup bias: The role of conflict monitoring and neural signals for control. *Journal of Personality and Social Psychology, 94*, 60–74.

Amodio, D. M., Harmon-Jones, E., Devine, P. G., Curtin, J. J., Hartley, S. L., & Covert, A. E. (2004). Neural signals for the detection of unintentional race bias. *Psychological Science, 15*, 88–93.

Amodio, D. M., & Lieberman, M. D. (2009). Pictures in our heads: Contributions of fMRI to the study of prejudice and stereotyping. In T. D. Nelson (Ed.), *Handbook of prejudice, stereotyping, and discrimination* (pp. 347–366). New York: Psychology Press.

Apfelbaum, E. P., Sommers, S. R., & Norton, M. I. (2008). Seeing race and seeming racist? Evaluating strategic colorblindness in social interaction. *Journal of Personality and Social Psychology, 95*, 918–932.

Aronson, J., Lustina, M. J., Good, C., Keough, K., Steele, C. M., & Brown, J. (1999). When white men can't do math: Necessary and sufficient factors in stereotype threat. *Journal of Experimental Social Psychology, 35*, 29–46.

Baddeley, A. D. (1986). *Working memory*. London: Oxford University Press.

Banaji, M. R., Lemm, K. M., & Carpenter, S. J. (2001). The social unconscious. In A. Tesser & N. Schwarz (Eds.), *Blackwell handbook of social psychology: Intraindividual processes* (pp. 134–158). Malden, MA: Blackwell Publishers.

Barden, J., Maddux, W., Petty, R. E., & Brewer, M. B. (2004). Contextual moderation of racial bias: The impact of social roles on controlled and automatically activated attitudes. *Journal of Personality and Social Psychology, 87*, 5–22.

Bargh, J. A. (1994). The four horsemen of automaticity: Awareness, intention, efficiency, and control in social cognition. In R. S. Wyer, Jr., & T. K. Srull (Eds.), *Handbook of social cognition* (2nd ed., Vol. 1, pp. 1–40). Hillsdale, NJ: Erlbaum.

Bargh, J. A. (1999). The cognitive monster: The case against the controllability of automatic stereotype effects. In S. Chaiken & Y. Trope (Eds.), *Dual process theories in social psychology* (pp. 361–382). New York: Guilford Press.

Baumeister, R. F., Vohs, K. D., & Tice, D. M. (2007). The strength model of self-control. *Current Directions in Psychological Science, 16,* 351–355.

Beer, J. S., Stallen, M., Lombardo, M. V., Gonsalkorale, K., Cunningham, W. A., & Sherman, J. W. (2008). The Quadruple Process model approach to examining the neural underpinnings of prejudice. *NeuroImage, 43,* 775–783.

Beilock, S. L., Rydell, R. J., & McConnell, A. R. (2007). Stereotype threat and working memory: Mechanisms, alleviation, and spill over. *Journal of Experimental Psychology: General, 136,* 256–276.

Benokraitis, N. V. (1997). Sex discrimination in the 21st century. In N. V. Benokraitis (Ed.), *Subtle sexism: Current practice and prospects for change* (pp. 5–33). Thousand Oaks, CA: Sage.

Ben-Zeev, T., Fein, S., & Inzlicht, M. (2005). Stereotype threat and arousal. *Journal of Experimental Social Psychology, 41,* 174–181.

Bertrand, M., Chugh, D., & Mullainathan, S. (2005). Implicit discrimination. *The American Economic Review, 95,* 94–98.

Blanton, H., & Jaccard, J. (2008). Unconscious racism: A concept in pursuit of a measure. *Annual Review of Sociology, 34,* 277–297.

Blascovich, J., Mendes, W. B., Hunter, S. B., Lickel, B., & Kowai-Bell, N. (2001). Perceiver threat in social interactions with stigmatized individuals. *Journal of Personality and Social Psychology, 80,* 253–267.

Blascovich, J., Spencer, S. J., Quinn, D., & Steele, C. M. (2001). African Americans and high blood pressure: The role of stereotype threat. *Psychological Science, 12,* 225–229.

Bodenhausen, G. V. (1988). Stereotypic biases in social decision making and memory: Testing process models of stereotype use. *Journal of Personality and Social Psychology, 55,* 726–737.

Bodenhausen, G. V. (1990). Stereotypes as judgmental heuristics: Evidence of circadian variations in discrimination. *Psychological Science, 1,* 319–322.

Bodenhausen, G. V., Mussweiler, T., Gabriel, S., & Moreno, K. N. (2001). Affective influences on stereotyping and intergroup relations. In J. P. Forgas (Ed.), *Handbook of affect and social cognition* (pp. 319–343). Mahwah, NJ: Erlbaum.

Bodenhausen, G. V., & Todd, A. R. (2010). Automatic aspects of judgment and decision making. In B. Gawronski & B. K. Payne (Eds.), *Handbook of implicit social cognition.* New York: Guilford Press.

Bodenhausen, G. V., Todd, A. R., & Richeson, J. A. (2009). Controlling prejudice and stereotyping: Antecedents, mechanisms, and contexts. In T. D. Nelson (Ed.),

Handbook of prejudice, stereotyping, and discrimination (pp. 111–135). New York: Psychology Press.

Branscombe, N. R., Schmitt, M. T., & Harvey, R. D. (1999). Perceiving pervasive discrimination among African Americans: Implications for group identification and well-being. *Journal of Personality and Social Psychology, 77*, 135–149.

Brewer, M. B. (1999). The psychology of prejudice: Ingroup love or outgroup hate? *Journal of Social Issues, 55*, 429–444.

Brown, R. P., & Pinel, E. C. (2002). Stigma on my mind: Individual differences in the experience of stereotype threat. *Journal of Experimental Social Psychology, 39*, 626–633.

Carbado, D., Fisk, C., & Gulati, M. (2008). After inclusion. *Annual Review of Law and Social Science, 4*, 83–102.

Castelli, L., De Dea, C., & Nesdale, D. (2008). Learning social attitudes: Children's sensitivity to the nonverbal behaviors of adult models during interracial interactions. *Personality and Social Psychology Bulletin, 34*, 1504–1513.

Cesario, J., Plaks, J. E., & Higgins, E. T. (2006). Automatic social behavior as motivated preparation to interact. *Journal of Personality and Social Psychology, 90*, 893–910.

Chen, M., & Bargh, J. A. (1997). Nonconscious behavioral confirmation processes: The self-fulfilling consequences of automatic stereotype activation. *Journal of Experimental Social Psychology, 33*, 541–560.

Chiao, J. Y., Iidaka, T., Gordon, H. L., Nogawa, J., Bar, M., Aminoff, E., Sadato, N., & Ambady, N. (2008). Cultural specificity in amygdala response to fear faces. *Journal of Cognitive Neuroscience, 20*, 2167–2174

Clark, C., Anderson, N. B., Clark, V. R., & Williams, D. R. (1999). Racism as a stressor for African Americans. A biopsychosocial model. *American Psychologist, 54*, 805–816.

Clark, K., & Clark, M. (1947). Racial identification and preference in Negro children. In T. M. Newcomb & E. L. Hartley (Eds.), *Readings in social psychology* (pp. 169–178). New York: Holt.

Cole, S. W., Kemeny, M. E., & Taylor, S. E. (1997). Social identity and physical health: Accelerated HIV progression in rejection-sensitive gay men. *Journal of Personality and Social Psychology, 72*, 320–335.

Conrey, F. R., Sherman, J. W., Gawronski, B., Hugenberg, K., & Groom, C. (2005). Separating multiple processes in implicit social cognition: The Quad-Model of implicit task performance. *Journal of Personality and Social Psychology, 89*, 469–487.

Cortina, L. M. (2008). Unseen injustice: Incivility as modern discrimination in organizations. *Academy of Management Review, 33*, 55–75.

Crocker, J., Major, B., & Steele, C. M. (1998). Social stigma. In S. Fiske, D. Gilbert, & G. Lindzey (Eds.), *Handbook of social psychology* (4th ed., Vol. 2, pp. 504–553). Boston, MA: McGraw-Hill.

Crosby, F., Bromley, S., & Saxe, L. (1980). Recent unobtrusive studies of black and white discrimination and prejudice: A literature review. *Psychological Bulletin, 87*, 546–563.

Cuddy, A. J. C., Fiske, S. T., & Glick, P. (2008). Warmth and competence as universal dimensions of social perception: The stereotype content model and the BIAS map. *Advances in Experimental Social Psychology, 40*, 61–149.

Cunningham, W. A., Johnson, M. K., Raye, C. L., Gatenby, J. C., Gore, J. C., & Banaji, M. R. (2004). Separable neural components in the processing of black and white faces. *Psychological Science, 15*, 806–813.

Darley, J., & Fazio, R. (1980). Expectancy confirmation processes arising in the social interaction sequence. *American Psychologist, 35*, 867–881.

Dar-Nimrod, I., & Heine, S. J. (2006). Exposure to scientific theories affects women's math performance. *Science, 314*, 435.

Dasgupta, N. (2004). Implicit ingroup favoritism, outgroup favoritism, and their behavioral manifestations. *Social Justice Research, 17*, 143–169.

Dasgupta, N., & Rivera, L. M. (2006). From automatic antigay prejudice to behavior: The moderating role of conscious beliefs about gender and behavioral control. *Journal of Personality and Social Psychology, 91*, 268–280.

Derks, B., Inzlicht, M., & Kang, S. (2008). The neuroscience of stigma and stereotype threat. *Group processes and Intergroup Relations, 11*, 163–181.

Devine, P. G. (1989). Stereotypes and prejudice: Their automatic and controlled components. *Journal of Personality and Social Psychology, 56*, 5–18.

Devine, P. G., Plant, A. E., & Amodio, D. M., & Harmon-Jones, E., & Vance, S. L. (2002). The regulation of implicit race bias: The role of motivations to respond without prejudice. *Journal of Personality and Social Psychology, 82*, 835–848.

Devine, P. G., & Vasquez, K. A. (1998). The rocky road to positive intergroup relations. In J. L. Eberhardt & S. T. Fiske (Eds.), *Confronting racism: The problem and the response* (pp. 234–262). Thousand Oakes, CA: Sage.

Dickerson, S., & Kemeny, M. E. (2004). Acute stressors and cortisol responses: A theoretical integration and synthesis of laboratory research. *Psychological Bulletin, 130*, 355–391.

Dijksterhuis, A., & Bargh, J. A. (2001). The perception-behavior expressway: Automatic effects of social perception on social behavior. *Advances in Experimental Social Psychology, 33*, 1–40.

Dovidio, J. F., & Gaertner, S. L. (Eds.) (1986). *Prejudice, discrimination, and racism.* Orlando, FL: Academic Press.

Dovidio, J. F., & Gaertner, S. L. (2004). Aversive racism. In M. P. Zanna (Ed.), *Advances in experimental social psychology* (Vol. 36, pp. 1–52). San Diego, CA: Elsevier Academic Press.

Dovidio, J. F., Kawakami, K., & Gaertner, S. L. (2002). Implicit and explicit prejudice and interracial interaction. *Journal of Personality and Social Psychology, 82*, 62–68.

Dovidio, J. F., Kawakami, K., Johnson, C., Johnson, B., & Howard, A. (1997). On the nature of prejudice: Automatic and controlled processes. *Journal of Experimental Social Psychology, 33*, 510–540.

Dovidio, J. F., Kawakami, K., Smoak, N., & Gaertner, S. L. (2009). The nature of contemporary racial prejudice: Insights from implicit and explicit measures of attitudes. In R. E. Petty, R. H. Fazio, & B. Briñol (Eds.), *Attitudes: Insights from the new implicit measures* (pp. 165–192). New York: Psychology Press.

Dovidio, J. F., Pearson, A. R., & Orr, P. (2008). Social psychology and neuroscience: Strange bedfellows or a healthy marriage? *Group Processes & Intergroup Relations, 11*, 247–263.

Dunham, Y., Baron, A. S., & Banaji, M. R. (2008). The development of implicit intergroup cognition. *Trends in Cognitive Sciences, 12*, 248–253.

Dunton, B. C., & Fazio, R. H. (1997). An individual difference measure of motivation to control prejudiced reactions. *Personality and Social Psychology Bulletin, 23*, 316–326.

Eagly, A. H., & Diekman, A. B. (2005). What is the problem? Prejudice as an attitude-in-context. In J. F. Dovidio, P. Glick, & L. Rudman (Eds.), *On the nature of prejudice: Fifty years after Allport* (pp. 19–35). Malden, MA: Blackwell.

Eberhardt, J. L. (2005). Imaging race. *American Psychologist, 60*, 181–190.

Engle, R. W., Conway, A. R. A., Tuholski, S. W., & Shisler, R. J. (1995). A resource account of inhibition. *Psychological Science, 6*, 122–125.

Fazio, R. H. (1990). Multiple processes by which attitudes guide behavior: The MODE model as an integrative framework. In M. P. Zanna (Ed.), *Advances in experimental social psychology* (Vol. 23, pp. 75–109). New York: Academic Press.

Fazio, R. H., Jackson, J. R., Dunton, B. C., & Williams, C. J. (1995). Variability in automatic activation as an unobtrusive measure of racial attitudes: A bona fide pipeline? *Journal of Personality and Social Psychology, 69*, 1013–1027.

Feldman Barrett, L., & Swim, J. K. (1998). Appraisals of prejudice and discrimination. In J. K. Swim & C. Stangor (Eds.), *Prejudice: The target's perspective* (pp. 11–36). San Diego: Academic Press.

Fishbein, M., & Ajzen, I. (1975). *Belief, attitude, intention, and behavior: An introduction to theory and research.* Reading, MA: Addison-Wesley.

Fiske, S. T. (2002). What we know now about bias and intergroup conflict, the problem of the century. *Current Directions in Psychological Science, 11*, 123–128.

Fiske, S. T., Cuddy, A. J. C., Glick, P., & Xu, J. (2002). A model of (often mixed) stereotype content: Competence and warmth follow respectively from perceived status and competition. *Journal of Personality and Social Psychology, 82*, 878–902.

Florack, A., Scarabis, M., & Bless, H. (2001). When do associations matter? The use of automatic associations toward ethnic groups in person judgments. *Journal of Experimental Social Psychology, 37*, 518–524.

Frable, D. E., Blackstone, T., & Scherbaum, C. (1990). Marginal and mindful: Deviants in social interactions. *Journal of Personality and Social Psychology, 59*, 140–149.

Gaertner, S. L., & Dovidio, J. F. (1986). The aversive form of racism. In J. F. Dovidio & S. L. Gaertner (Eds.), *Prejudice, discrimination, and racism* (pp. 61–89). Orlando, FL: Academic Press.

Galinsky, A. D., & Moskowitz, G. B. (2000). Perspective-taking: Decreasing stereotype expression, stereotype accessibility, and in-group favoritism. *Journal of Personality and Social Psychology, 78*, 708–724.

Gawronski, B., Geschke, D., & Banse, R. (2003). Implicit bias in impression formation: Associations influence the construal of individuating information. *European Journal of Social Psychology, 33*, 573–589.

Gawronski, B., Hofmann, W., & Wilbur, C. J. (2006). Are "implicit" attitudes unconscious? *Consciousness and Cognition, 15*, 485–499.

Gilbert, D. T., & Hixon, J. G. (1991). The trouble of thinking: Activation and application of stereotypic beliefs. *Journal of Personality and Social Psychology, 60*, 509–517.

Glick, P., Fiske, S. T., Mladinic, A., Saiz, J., Abrams, D., Masser, B., et al. (2000). Beyond prejudice as simple antipathy: Hostile and benevolent sexism across cultures. *Journal of Personality and Social Psychology, 79*, 763–775.

Goffman, E. (1963). *Stigma: Notes on the management of spoiled identity*. New York: Prentice Hall.

Golby, A. J., Gabrieli, J. D. E., Chiao, J. Y., & Eberhardt, J. L. (2001). Differential fusiform responses to same- and other-race faces. *Nature Neuroscience, 4*, 845–850.

Gollwitzer, P. M., Fujita, K., & Oettingen, G. (2004). Planning and the implementation of goals. In R. F. Baumeister & K. D. Vohs (Eds.), *Handbook of self-regulation: Research, theory and applications* (pp. 211–228). New York: Guilford Press.

Goodman, A. H. (2000). Why genes don't count (for racial differences in health). *American Journal of Public Health, 90*, 1699–1702.

Gordijn, E. H., Hindriks, I., Koomen, W., Dijksterhuis, A., & Knippenberg, A. V. (2004). Consequences of stereotype suppression and internal suppression motivation: A self-regulation approach. *Personality and Social Psychology Bulletin, 30*, 212–224.

Govorun, O., Fuegen, K., & Payne, B. K. (2006). Stereotypes focus defensive projection. *Personality and Social Psychology Bulletin, 32*, 781–793.

Govorun, O., & Payne, B. K. (2006). Ego-depletion and prejudice: Separating automatic and controlled components. *Social Cognition, 24*, 111–136.

Grey-Little, B., & Hafdahl, A. R. (2000). Factors influencing racial comparisons of self-esteem: A quantitative review. *Psychological Bulletin, 126*, 26–54.

Hall, J. A., & Carter, J. D. (1999). Gender-stereotype accuracy as an individual difference. *Journal of Personality and Social Psychology, 77*, 350–359.

Hamilton, D. L. (Ed.) (1981). *Cognitive processes in stereotyping and intergroup behavior*. Hillsdale, NJ: Erlbaum.

Hamilton, D. L., & Gifford, R. K. (1976). Illusory correlation in interpersonal perception: A cognitive basis of stereotypic judgments. *Journal of Experimental Social Psychology, 12*, 392–407.

Han, H. A., Olson, M. A., & Fazio, R. H. (2006). The influence of experimentally created associations on the Implicit Association Test. *Journal of Experimental Social Psychology, 42*, 259–272.

Hanay López, I. (2000). Institutional racism: Judicial conduct and a new theory of racial discrimination. *Yale Law Journal, 109*, 1717–1884.

Harris, R. J. (2004). *A cognitive psychology of mass communication* (4th ed.). Mahwah, NJ: Erlbaum.

Harris, L. T., & Fiske, S. T. (2006). Dehumanizing the lowest of the low: Neuro-imaging responses to extreme outgroups. *Psychological Science, 17*, 847–853.

Hart, A. J., Whalen, P. J., Shin, L. M., McInerney, S. C., Fischer, H., & Rauch, S. L. (2000). Differential response in the human amygdala to racial outgroup vs. ingroup face stimuli. *Neuroreport, 11*, 2351–2355.

Haslam, N., Rothschild, L., & Ernst, D. (2000). Essentialist beliefs about social categories. *British Journal of Social Psychology, 39*, 113–127.

Hebl, M. R., & Dovidio, J. F. (2005). Promoting the "social" in the examination of social stigmas. *Personality and Social Psychology Review, 9*, 156–182.

Hebl, M. R., Foster, J., Mannix, L. M., & Dovidio, J. F. (2002). Formal and interpersonal discrimination: A field study understanding of applicant bias. *Personality and Social Psychological Bulletin, 28,* 815–825.

Huddy, L., & Feldman, S. (2009). On assessing the political effects of racial prejudice. *Annual Review of Political Science, 12*, 423–447.

Hummert, M. L., Garstka, T. A., Shaner, J. L., & Strahm, S. (1994). Stereotypes of the elderly held by young, middle-aged, and elderly adults. *Journal of Gerontology: Psychological Sciences, 49,* 240–249.

Hyers, L., & Swim, J. (1998). A comparison of the experiences of dominant and minority group members during an intergroup encounter. *Group Processes and Intergroup Relations, 1*, 143–163.

Ickes, W. (1984). Compositions in black and white: Determinants of interaction in interracial dyads. *Journal of Personality and Social Psychology, 47*, 330–341.

Inzlicht, M., & Ben-Zeev, T. (2003). Do high-achieving female students underperform in private? The implications of threatening environments on intellectual processing. *Journal of Educational Psychology, 95*, 796–805.

Inzlicht, M., Kaiser, C. R., & Major, B. (2008). The face of chauvinism: How prejudice expectations shape perceptions of facial affect. *Journal of Experimental Social Psychology, 44*, 758–766.

Inzlicht, M., McKay, L., & Aronson, J. (2006). Stigma as ego depletion: How being the target of prejudice affects self-control. *Psychological Science, 17*, 262–269.

Ito, T. A., & Bartholow, B. D. (2009). The neural correlates of race. Trends *in Cognitive Sciences, 19*, 524–531.

Jost, J. T., Banaji, M. R., & Nosek, B. A. (2004). A decade of system justification theory: Accumulated evidence of conscious and unconscious bolstering of the status quo. *Political Psychology, 25*, 881–919.

Jost, J. T., Pelham, B. W., & Carvallo, M. R. (2002). Nonconscious forms of system justification: Implicit and behavioral preferences for higher status groups. *Journal of Experimental Social Psychology, 38,* 586–602.

Judd, C. M., & Park, B. (1993). Definition and assessment of accuracy in social stereotypes. *Psychological Review, 100,* 109–128.

Kaiser, C. R., Vick, S. B., & Major, B. (2006). Prejudice expectations moderate preconscious attention to cues that are threatening to social identity. *Psychological Science, 17,* 332–338.

Keller, J. (2005). In genes we trust: The biological component of psychological essentialism and its relationship to mechanisms of motivated cognition. *Journal of Personality and Social Psychology, 88,* 686–702.

Kleck, R. E. (1968). Physical stigma and nonverbal cues emitted in face-to-face interaction. *Human Relations, 21,* 19–28.

Kleck, R. E., & Strenta, A. (1980). Perceptions of the impact of negatively valued physical characteristics on social interaction. *Journal of Personality and Social Psychology, 39,* 861–873.

Krendl, A. C., Macrae, C. N., Kelley, W. M., Fugelsang, J. F., & Heatherton, T. F. (2006). The good, the bad, and the ugly: An fMRI investigation of the functional anatomic correlates of stigma. *Social Neuroscience, 1,* 5–15.

Krendl, A. C., & Richeson, J. A., Kelley, W. M., & Heatherton, T. F. (2008). The negative consequences of threat: An fMRI investigation of the neural mechanisms underlying women's underperformance in math. *Psychological Science, 19,* 168–175.

Krieger, L. H. (1995). The content of our categories: A cognitive bias approach to discrimination and equal employment opportunity. *Stanford Law Review, 47,* 1161–1248.

Krueger, J., & Rothbart, M. (1990). Contrast and accentuation effects in category learning. *Journal of Personality and Social Psychology, 59,* 651–663.

Langer, E. J., Bashner, R. S., & Chanowitz, B. (1985). Decreasing prejudice by increasing discrimination. *Journal of Personality and Social Psychology, 49,* 113–120.

Lee, Y.-T., Jussim, L. J., & McCauley, C. R. (Eds.) (1995). *Stereotype accuracy: Toward appreciating group differences.* Washington, DC: American Psychological Association.

Lepore, L., & Brown, R. (1997). Category and stereotype activation: Is prejudice inevitable? *Journal of Personality and Social Psychology, 72,* 275–287.

Levy, B. R., Slade, M. D., Kunkel, S. R., & Kasl, S. V. (2002). Longevity increased by positive self-perceptions of aging. *Journal of Personality and Social Psychology 83,* 261–270.

Lieberman, M. D., Eisenberger, N. I., Crockett, M. J., Tom, S. M., Pfeifer, J. H., & Way, B. M. (2007). Putting feelings into words: Affect labeling disrupts amygdala activity to affective stimuli. *Psychological Science, 18,* 421–428.

Lieberman, M. D., Hariri, A., Jarcho, J. M., Eisenberger, N. I ., & Bookheimer, S. Y. (2005). An fMRI investigation of race-related amygdala activity in African-American and Caucasian-American individuals. *Nature Neuroscience, 8*, 720–722.

Livingston, R. W. (2002). The role of perceived negativity in the moderation of African Americans' implicit and explicit racial attitudes. *Journal of Experimental Social Psychology, 38*, 405–413.

Livingston, R. W., & Drwecki, B. B. (2007). Why are some individuals not racially prejudiced? Susceptibility to affective conditioning predicts nonprejudice toward blacks. *Psychological Science, 18*, 816–823.

Mackie, D. M., Devos, T., & Smith, E. R. (2000). Intergroup emotions: Explaining offensive action tendencies in an intergroup context. *Journal of Personality and Social Psychology, 79*, 602–616.

Macrae, C. N., Bodenhausen, G. V., Milne, A. B., & Jetten, J. (1994). Out of mind but back in sight: Stereotypes on the rebound. *Journal of Personality and Social Psychology, 67*, 808–817.

Macrae, C. N., Bodenhausen, G. V., Milne, A. B., Thorne, T. M. J., & Castelli, L. (1997). On the activation of social stereotypes: The moderating role of processing objectives. *Journal of Experimental Social Psychology, 33*, 471–489.

Macrae, C. N., Bodenhausen, G. V., Schloerscheidt, A. M., & Milne, A. B. (1999). Tales of the unexpected: Executive function and person perception. *Journal of Personality and Social Psychology, 76*, 200–213.

Madon, S., Guyll, M., Aboufadel, K., Montiel, E., Smith, A., Palumbo, P., & Jussim, L. (2001). Ethnic and national stereotypes: The Princeton trilogy revisited and revised. *Personality and Social Psychology Bulletin, 27*, 996–1010.

Major, B., & O'Brien, L. T. (2005). The social psychology of stigma. *Annual Review of Psychology, 56*, 393–421.

McConnell, A. R., & Leibold, J. M. (2001). Relations between the Implicit Association Test, explicit racial attitudes, and discriminatory behavior. *Journal of Experimental Social Psychology, 37*, 435–442.

McEwen, B. S. (2000). The neurobiology of stress: From serendipity to clinical relevance. *Brain Research, 886*, 172–189.

Medin, D. L., & Ortony, A. (1989). Psychological essentialism. In S. Vosniadou & A. Ortony (Eds.), *Similarity and analogical reasoning* (pp. 179–195). New York: Cambridge University Press.

Mendes, W. B., Blascovich, J., Hunter, S., Lickel, B., & Jost, J. T. (2007). Threatened by the unexpected: Challenge and threat during inter-ethnic interactions. *Journal of Personality and Social Psychology, 92*, 698–716.

Mendoza-Denton, R., Downey, G., Purdie, V., Davis, A., & Pietrzak, J. (2002). Sensitivity to status-based rejection: Implications for African-American students' college experience. *Journal of Personality and Social Psychology, 83*, 896–918.

Miller, C. T. & Myers, A. (1998). Compensating for prejudice: How heavyweight people (and others) control outcomes despite prejudice. In J. K. Swim & C. Stangor (Eds.), *Prejudice: The target's perspective* (pp. 191–218). San Diego, CA: Academic Press.

Miller, S., & Malloy, T. E. (2003). Interpersonal behavior, perception, and affect in status-discrepant dyads: Social interaction of gay and heterosexual men. *Psychology of Men and Masculinity, 4*, 121–135.

Monteith, M. J. (1993). Self-regulation of prejudiced responses: Implications for progress in prejudice reduction efforts. *Journal of Personality and Social Psychology, 65*, 469–485

Monteith, M. J., & Mark, A. (2005). Changing one's prejudice ways: Awareness, affect, and self-regulation. *European Review of Social Psychology, 16*, 113–154.

Monteith, M. J., & Mark, A. (2009). The self-regulation of prejudice. In T. Nelson (Ed.), *Handbook of prejudice, stereotyping, and discrimination* (pp. 507–524). New York: Psychology Press.

Monteith, M. J., Sherman, J., & Devine, P. G. (1998). Suppression as a stereotype control strategy. *Personality and Social Psychology Review, 2*, 63–82.

Monteith, M. J., & Spicer, C. V. (2000). Contents and correlates of whites' and blacks' racial attitudes. *Journal of Experimental Social Psychology, 36*, 125–154.

Monteith, M. J., & Spicer, C. V., & Tooman, G. (1998). Consequences of stereotype suppression: Stereotypes on AND not on the rebound. *Journal of Experimental Social Psychology, 34*, 355–377.

Moors, A., & De Houwer, J. (2006). Automaticity: A theoretical and conceptual analysis. *Psychological Bulletin, 132*, 297–326.

Muraven, M., & Baumeister, R. F. (2000). Self-regulation and depletion of limited resource: Does self-control resemble a muscle? *Psychological Bulletin, 126*, 247–259.

Murphy, G. L., & Medin, D. L. (1985). The role of theories in conceptual coherence. *Psychological Review, 92*, 289–316.

Murphy, M. C., Richeson, J. A., Shelton, J. A., Rheinschmidt, M., & Bergsieker, H. (2010). *Cognitive costs of subtle v. blatant prejudice during interracial interaction*. Submitted for publication.

Nelson, R. L., Berrey, E. C., & Nielsen, L. B. (2008). Divergent paths: Conflicting conceptions of employment discrimination in law and the social sciences. *Annual Review of Law and Social Science, 4*, 103–122.

Nelson, T. D. (2009). Ageism. In T. D. Nelson (Ed.), *Handbook of prejudice, stereotyping, and discrimination* (pp. 431–440). New York: Psychology Press.

Newman, L. S., Duff, K., & Baumeister, R. F. (1997). A new look at defensive projection: Suppression, accessibility, and biased person perception. *Journal of Personality and Social Psychology, 72*, 980–1001.

Nisbett, R. E., & Wilson, T. D. (1977). Telling more than we can know: Verbal reports on mental processes. *Psychological Review, 84*, 231–259.

Norman, D. A., & Shallice, T. (1986). Attention to action: Willed and automatic control of behavior. In R. J. Davidson, G. E. Schwartz, & D. Shapiro (Eds.), *Consciousness and self-regulation: Advances in research and theory* (Vol. 4, pp. 1–18). New York: Plenum Press.

Nosek, B. A., & Hansen, J. J. (2008). The associations in our heads belong to us: Searching for attitudes and knowledge in implicit evaluation. *Cognition and Emotion, 22*, 553–594.

Olson, M. A. (2009). Measures of prejudice. In T. D. Nelson (Ed.), *Handbook of prejudice, stereotyping, and discrimination* (pp. 367–386). New York: Psychology Press.

Page-Gould, E., Mendoza-Denton, R., & Tropp, L. R. (2008). With a little help from my cross-group friend: Reducing anxiety in intergroup contexts through cross-group friendship. *Journal of Personality and Social Psychology, 95*, 1080–1094.

Pager, D. (2003). The mark of a criminal record. *American Journal of Sociology, 108*, 937–975.

Payne, B. K. (2001). Prejudice and perception: The role of automatic and controlled processes in misperceiving a weapon. *Journal of Personality and Social Psychology, 81*, 181–192.

Payne, B. K. (2005). Conceptualizing control in social cognition: How executive control modulates the expression of automatic stereotyping. *Journal of Personality and Social Psychology, 89*, 488–503.

Peery, D., & Bodenhausen, G. V. (2009). Ambiguity and ambivalence in the voting booth and beyond: A social-psychological perspective on racial attitudes and behavior in the Obama era. *Du Bois Review, 6*, 71–82.

Persico, N. (2009). Racial profiling? Detecting bias using statistical evidence. *Annual Review of Economics, 1*. 1–16.

Persico, N., & Todd, P. E. (2008). The hit rates test for racial bias in motor vehicle searches. *Justice Quarterly, 25*, 37–53.

Pettigrew, T. F., & Tropp, L. R. (2008). How does intergroup contact reduce prejudice? Meta-analytic tests of three mediators. *European Journal of Social Psychology, 38*, 922–934.

Phelps, E. A., O'Connor, K. J., Cunningham, W. A., Funayama, E. S., Gatenby, J. C., Gore, J. C., & Banaji, M. R. (2000). Performance on indirect measures of race evaluation predicts amygdala activation. *Journal of Cognitive Neuroscience, 12*, 729–738.

Pinel, E. C. (1999). Stigma consciousness: The Psychological legacy of social stereotypes. *Journal of Personality and Social Psychology, 76*, 114–128.

Plant, E. A., & Devine, P. G. (1998). Internal and external motivation to respond without prejudice. *Journal of Personality and Social Psychology, 75*, 811–832.

Plant, E. A., & Devine, P. G. (2001). Responses to other-imposed pro-black pressure: Acceptance or backlash? *Journal of Experimental Social Psychology, 37*, 486–501.

Plant, E. A., & Devine, P. G. (2003). The antecedents and implications of interracial anxiety. *Personality and Social Psychology Bulletin, 29*, 790–801.

Richeson, J. A., Baird, A. A., Gordon, H. L., Heatherton, T. F., Wyland, C. L., Trawalter, S., & Shelton, J. N. (2003). An fMRI examination of the impact of interracial contact on executive function. *Nature Neuroscience, 6*, 1323–1328.

Richeson, J. A., & Shelton, J. N. (2003). When prejudice does not pay: Effects of interracial contact on executive function. *Psychological Science, 14*, 287–290.

Richeson, J. A., & Shelton, J. N. (2005). Thin slices of racial bias. *Journal of Nonverbal Behavior, 29*, 75–86.

Richeson, J. A., & Trawalter, S. (2005). Why do interracial interactions impair executive function? A resource depletion account. *Journal of Personality and Social Psychology, 88*, 934–947.

Richeson, J. A., & Trawalter, S. (2008). The threat of appearing prejudiced and race-based attentional biases. *Psychological Science, 19*, 98–102.

Richeson, J. A., Trawalter, S., & Shelton, J. N. (2005). African American's implicit racial attitudes and the depletion of executive function after interracial interactions. *Social Cognition, 23*, 336–352.

Rohan, M. J., & Zanna, M. P. (1996). Value transmission in families. In C. Seligman, J. M. Olson, & M. P. Zanna (Eds.), *The psychology of values: The Ontario symposium* (Vol. 8, pp. 253–276). Mahwah, NJ: Erlbaum.

Rothbart, M., & Taylor, M. (1992). Category labels and social reality: Do we view social categories as natural kinds? In G. R. Semin & K. Fiedler (Eds.), *Language, interaction, and social cognition* (pp. 11–36). London: Sage.

Ryan, E. B., Bourhis, R. Y., & Knops, U. (1991). Evaluative perceptions of patronizing speech addressed to elders. *Psychology and Aging, 6*, 442–450.

Schaller, M., & Neuberg, S. L. (2008). Intergroup prejudices and intergroup conflicts. In C. Crawford & D. Krebs (Eds.), *Foundations of evolutionary psychology* (pp. 401–414). New York: Erlbaum.

Schmader, T. (2002). Gender identification moderates stereotype threat effects on women's math performance. *Journal of Experimental Social Psychology, 38*, 194–201.

Schmader, T., & Johns, M. (2003). Converging evidence that stereotype threat reduces working memory capacity. *Journal of Personality and Social Psychology, 84*, 440–452.

Schmader, T., Johns, M., & Forbes, C. (2008). An integrated process model of stereotype threat effects on performance. *Psychological Review, 115*, 336–356.

Schuman, H., Steeh, C., Bobo, L., & Krysan, M. (1997). *Racial attitudes in America* (2nd ed.). Cambridge, MA: Harvard University Press.

Sellers, R. M., & Shelton, J. N. (2003). The role of racial identity in perceived racial discrimination. *Journal of Personality and Social Psychology, 84*, 1079–1092.

Shelton, J. N. (2003). Interpersonal concerns in social encounters between majority and minority group members. *Group Processes and Intergroup Relations, 6*, 171–185.

Shelton, J. N., & Richeson, J. A. (2006a). Interracial interactions: A relational approach. *Advances in Experimental Social Psychology, 38*, 121–181.

Shelton, J. N., & Richeson, J. A. (2006b). Ethnic minorities' racial attitudes and contact experiences with white people. *Cultural Diversity and Ethnic Minority Psychology, 12*, 149–164.

Shelton, J. N., Richeson, J. A., & Salvatore, J. (2005). Expecting to be the target of prejudice. Implications for interethnic interactions. *Personality and Social Psychology Bulletin, 31*, 1189–1202.

Shelton, J. N., Richeson, J. A., & Vorauer, J. D. (2006). Threatened identities and interethnic interactions. *European Review of Social Psychology, 17*, 321–358.

Sigall, H., & Page, R. (1971). Current stereotypes: A little fading, a little faking. *Journal of Personality and Social Psychology, 18*, 247–255.

Snyder, M. L., Kleck, R. E., Strenta, A., & Mentzer, S. J. (1979). Avoidance of the handicapped: An attributional ambiguity analysis. *Journal of Personality and Social Psychology, 37*, 2297–2306.

Snyder, M. L., Tanke, E. D., & Berscheid, E. (1977). Social perception and interpersonal behaviour: On the self-fulfilling nature of social stereotypes. *Journal of Personality and Social Psychology, 35*, 656–666.

Steele, C. M. (1997). A threat in the air: How stereotypes shape intellectual identity and performance. *American Psychologist, 52*, 613–629.

Steele, C. M., & Aronson, J. (1995). Stereotype threat and the intellectual test performance of African Americans. *Journal of Personality and Social Psychology, 69*, 797–811.

Steele, C. M., Spencer, S. J., & Aronson, J. (2002). Contending with bias: The psychology of stereotype and social identity threat. In M. P. Zanna (Ed.), *Advances in experimental social psychology* (Vol. 34, pp. 277–341). San Diego, CA: Academic Press.

Stephan, W. G., & Stephan, C. W. (1985). Intergroup anxiety. *Journal of Social Issues, 41*, 157–175.

Swim, J. K. (1994). Perceived versus meta-analytic effect sizes: An assessment of the accuracy of gender stereotypes. *Journal of Personality and Social Psychology, 70*, 1126–1141.

Swim, J. K., & Hyers, L. L. (2009). Sexism. In T. D. Nelson (Ed.), *Handbook of prejudice, stereotyping, and discrimination* (pp. 407–430). New York: Psychology Press.

Tajfel, H. (1974). Social identity and intergroup behavior. *Social Science Information, 13*, 65–93.

Todd, A. R. (2009). *Combating contemporary racial biases: On the virtues of perspective taking*. Unpublished doctoral dissertation, Northwestern University.

Todd, T. D. (2009). Ageism. In T. D. Nelson (Ed.), *Handbook of prejudice, stereotyping, and discrimination* (pp. 431–440). New York: Psychology Press.

Trawalter, S., Adam, E. K., Chase-Lansdale, P. L., & Richeson, J. A. (2009). *Prejudice concerns get under the skin: External motivation to respond without prejudice shapes behavioral and physiological responses to interracial contact.* Unpublished manuscript. Northwestern University.

Trawalter, S., & Richeson, J. A. (2008). Let's talk about race, baby! When whites' and blacks' interracial contact experiences diverge. *Journal of Experimental Social Psychology, 44*, 1214–1217.

Trawalter, S., Richeson, J. A., & Shelton, J. N. (2009). Predicting behavior during interracial interactions: A stress and coping approach.*Review of Personality and Social Psychology, 13*, 243–268.

Tropp, L. R. (2003). The psychological impact of prejudice: Implications for intergroup contact. *Group Processes and Intergroup Relations, 6*, 131–149.

Turner, J. C., Hogg, M. A., Oakes, P. J., Reicher, S. D., & Wetherell, M. (1987). *Rediscovering the social group: A self-categorization theory*. Oxford, England: Basil Blackwell.

Underwood, G. (Ed.) (1996). *Implicit cognition*. New York: Oxford University Press.

Van Bavel, J. J., Packer, D. J, & Cunningham, W. A. (2008). The neural substrates of in-group bias: A functional magnetic resonance imaging investigation. *Psychological Science, 11*, 1131–1139.

Vick, S. B., Seery, M. D., Blascovich, J., & Weisbuch, M. (2008). The effect of gender stereotype activation on challenge and threat motivational states. *Journal of Experimental Social Psychology, 44*, 624–630.

von Hippel, W., & Gonsalkorale, K. (2005). "That is bloody revolting!" Inhibitory control of thoughts better left unsaid. *Psychological Science, 16*, 497–500.

Vorauer, J. D., & Kumhyr, S. M. (2001). Is this about you or me? Self- versus other-directed judgments and feelings in response to intergroup interaction. *Personality and Social Psychology Bulletin, 27*, 706–719.

Vorauer, J. D., Martens, V., & Sasaki, S. J. (2009). When trying to understand detracts from trying to behave: Effects of perspective taking in intergroup interaction. *Journal of personality and social psychology, 96*, 811–827.

Vorauer, J. D., & Turpie, C. (2004). Disruptive effects of vigilance on dominant group members' treatment of outgroup members: Choking versus shining under pressure. *Journal of Personality and Social Psychology, 27*, 706–709.

Walton, G. M., & Cohen, G. L. (2007). A question of belonging: Race, social fit, and achievement. *Journal of Personality and Social Psychology, 92*, 82–96.

Wegener, D. T., & Petty, R. E. (1997). The flexible correction model: The role of naive theories of bias in bias correction. In M. P. Zanna (Ed.), *Advances in experimental social psychology* (Vol. 29, pp. 141–208). Mahwah, NJ: Erlbaum.

Wegner, D. M. (1994). Ironic processes of mental control. *Psychological Review, 101*, 34–52.

West, T., Shelton, J. N., & Trail, T. (2009). Relational anxiety and interracial interactions. *Psychological Science, 20*, 298–292.

Wheeler, M. E., & Fiske, S. T. (2005). Controlling racial prejudice and stereotyping: Social cognitive goals affect amygdala and stereotype activation. *Psychological Science, 16*, 56–63.

Wheeler, S. C., DeMarree, K. G., & Petty, R. E. (2007). Understanding the role of the self in prime-to-behavior efforts: The active self account. *Personality and Social Psychology Review, 11*, 234–261.

Williams, D. R., Neighbors, H. W., & Jackson, J. S. (2003). Racial/ethnic discrimination and health: Findings from community studies. *American Journal of Public Health, 93*, 200–208.

Wilson, T. D., & Brekke, N. (1994). Mental contamination and mental correction: Unwanted influences on judgments and evaluations. *Psychological Bulletin, 116*, 117–142.

Wittenbrink, B., Gist, P. L., & Hilton, J. L. (1997). Structural properties of stereotypic knowledge and their influences on the construal of social situations. *Journal of Personality and Social Psychology, 72*, 526–543.

Wittenbrink, B., Judd, C. M., & Park, B. (2001). Spontaneous prejudice in context: Variability in automatically activated attitudes. *Journal of Personality and Social Psychology, 81*, 815–827.

Wittenbrink, B., Judd, C. M., & Park, B. (1997). Evidence for racial prejudice at the implicit level and its relationship with questionnaire measures. *Journal of Personality and Social Psychology, 72*, 262–274.

Word, C. O., Zanna, M. P., & Cooper, J. (1974). The nonverbal mediation of self-fulfilling prophecies in interracial interaction. *Journal of Experimental Social Psychology, 10*, 109–120.

Zárate, M. A. (2009). Racism in the 21st century. In T. D. Nelson (Ed.), *Handbook of prejudice, stereotyping, and discrimination* (pp. 387–406). New York: Psychology Press.

Chapter 11

Social Influence

Robert B. Cialdini and Vladas Griskevicius

> Blandishing persuasion steals the mind even of the wise.
>
> —*Homer*

For nearly a century, social psychologists have been investigating the process of social influence, wherein one person's attitudes, cognitions, or behaviors are changed through the doings of another. Because other authors within this volume have addressed social influences on attitudes and cognitions (Fabrigar & Wegener, Chapter 6, this volume; Petty & Briñol, Chapter 7, this volume), our focus will be on the realm of behavior change and on the factors that cause one individual to comply with another's request for action of some sort. In the process, we will consider a set of six psychological principles that appear to influence behavioral compliance decisions most powerfully. Briefly, these principles involve pressures to comply because of tendencies to (1) return a gift, favor, or service, (2) be consistent with prior commitments, (3) follow the lead of similar others, (4) accommodate the requests of those we know and like, (5) conform to the directives of legitimate authority, and (6) seize opportunities that are scarce or dwindling in availability.

Social Influence on Compliance

Focusing on Powerful Effects

Within academic social psychology, research into the behavioral compliance process has emphasized two questions: "Which principles and techniques reliably affect compliance?" and "How do these principles and techniques work to affect compliance as they do?" The first of these questions is concerned with the identification of real effects, whereas the second is concerned with their theoretical/conceptual bases. Almost without exception, the vehicle that has been used to answer these two questions has been the controlled experiment. And this is understandable, as controlled experimentation provides an excellent context for addressing issues such as whether an effect is real (i.e., reliable) and which theoretical account best explains its occurrence.

However, a somewhat different approach is called for when our concern with the compliance process is more than purely academic, as is the case for most of us who find ourselves either interested investigators or interested observers of the interpersonal influence interactions of daily life. We want to know more than whether a particular influence exists and what causes it. We want to know, as well, how powerful it is in the course of naturally occurring behavior, so that we can better decide whether the effect is especially worthy of our attention and study. That is, we want to know whether a particular technique has the ability to change compliance decisions meaningfully over a wide range of everyday situations and circumstances.

Regrettably, when the question of primary interest includes a determination of the power of possible influences on natural compliance behavior, the controlled experiment becomes less suited to the job. The high levels of experimental rigor and precision that allow us to determine that an effect is genuine and theoretically interpretable simultaneously decrease our ability to assess the potency of that effect. That is, because the best-designed experiments (1) eliminate or control all sources of influence except the one under study and (2) possess highly sensitive measurements techniques that may register whisper-like effects so small as to never make a difference when other (extraneous) factors are allowed to vary naturally, as they typically do in the social environment. What's more, such ecologically trivial effects can be replicated repeatedly in the antiseptic environment of the controlled experiment, giving the mistaken impression of power, when, in reality, all that has been demonstrated is the reliability of the effects.

Thus, rigorous experimentation should not be used as the primary device for deciding which compliance-related influences are powerful enough to be submitted to rigorous experimentation for further study. Some other starting point should be found to identify the most potent influences on the compliance process. Otherwise, valuable time could well be spent seeking to investigate and to apply effects that are only epiphenomena of the controlled experimental setting.

The Development of Powerful Compliance Inducers

A crucial question thus becomes, "How are the most powerful compliance principles and tactics determined?" One answer involves the systematic observation of the behaviors of commercial compliance professionals.

Who are the commercial compliance professionals, and why should their actions be especially informative as to the identification of powerful influences on everyday compliance decisions? They can be defined as those individuals whose business or financial well-being is dependent on their ability to induce compliance (e.g., salespeople, fund-raisers, advertisers, political lobbyists, cult recruiters, negotiators, con artists). With this definition in place, we can begin to recognize why the regular and widespread practices of these professionals would be noteworthy indicators of the powerful influences on the compliance process: Because the livelihoods of commercial compliance professionals depend on the effectiveness of their procedures, those professionals who use procedures that work well to elicit compliance responses will survive and flourish. Furthermore, they will pass these successful procedures on to the succeeding generations (trainees). However, those practitioners who use unsuccessful compliance procedures will either drop them or quickly go out of business; in either case, the procedures themselves will not be passed on to newer generations.

The result is that over time and over the range of naturally occurring compliance contexts, the strongest and most adaptable procedures for generating compliance will rise, persist, and accumulate. Furthermore, these procedures will point a careful observer toward the major principles that people use to decide when to comply. Several years ago, one of the authors of this chapter resolved to become such an observer. What emerged from this period of systematic observation was a list of six principles on which compliance professionals appeared to base most of their psychological attempts: (1) reciprocity, (2) consistency, (3) social validation, (4) liking, (5) authority, and (6) scarcity. A full account of the origins, workings, and prevalence of these six principles is available elsewhere (Cialdini, 2009; see also Goldstein, Martin, & Cialdini, 2008). The remainder of this chapter offers a summary description of these principles and of the social scientific theory and evidence regarding how and why each principle functions to motivate compliance.

The Principles of Influence

Goal-Directed Nature of Behavior

Before discussing each principle in detail, it is useful to consider why these principles are so powerful at influencing human behavior. An important thread that links all of the principles is related to the fact that human behavior is goal directed. Our actions are aimed at achieving goals on several levels (Kenrick, Griskevicius, Neuberg, & Schaller, 2010; also see Maner & Kenrick in the current volume). At a surface level, for instance, people behave so as to attain a variety of moment-to-moment or day-to-day goals: A person might want to make a good impression on a teacher or save enough money to buy a car. At a deeper level, behavior promotes ultimate or evolutionary motives, including survival and reproduction. Indeed, part of the reason why the principles discussed in this chapter are effective at influencing behavior is because they promote adaptive behavior. That is, the sense of obligation to reciprocate a gift, the tendency to value scarce items, the inclination to turn to similar others or to experts in times of uncertainty, and the desire to say "yes" to people we like all have likely evolutionary bases (Sundie, Cialdini, Griskevicius, & Kenrick, 2006).

Here we consider how the six principles of influence help achieve at least three human goals: affiliation, accuracy, and consistency (Cialdini & Trost, 1998; Cialdini & Goldstein, 2004). Humans are fundamentally motivated to affiliate, creating and maintaining meaningful social relationships with others (Baumeister & Leary, 1995). Reciprocating favors and saying yes to those we like is an adaptive strategy for affiliation. Humans are similarly motivated to make accurate decisions that will help further their other goals in the most effective manner. When the best course of action is unclear, it is adaptive to follow the advice of authority or the behavior of similar others. People also have a strong need to behave in a manner that is consistent with their actions, statements, commitments, and beliefs.

Reciprocity

> Pay every debt as if God wrote the bill.
>
> —*Ralph Waldo Emerson*

One of the most powerful norms in all human cultures is that for reciprocity (Cialdini, 2009; Gouldner, 1960), which obligates individuals to return the form of behavior that they have received from another. Not only does the norm apply to all cultures, but it applies broadly to various behaviors within those cultures. For instance, we report liking those who report liking us (Condon & Crano, 1988); we cooperate with cooperators and compete against competitors (Rosenbaum, 1980); we self-disclose to those who have self-disclosed to us (Cunningham, Strassberg, & Haan, 1986); we yield to the persuasive appeals of those who have previously yielded to one of our persuasive appeals (Cialdini, Green, & Rusch, 1992); we try to harm those who have tried to harm us (Dengerink, Schnedler, & Covey, 1978); and in negotiations, we make concessions to those who have offered concessions to us (Thompson, 2009). The rule of reciprocity helps us build trust with others and pushes us toward equity in our relationships (Kelln & Ellard, 1999; Pilluta, Malhotra, & Murnighan, 2003). Although the rule tends to operate most reliably in public domains, it is so deeply ingrained in most individuals that it powerfully directs behavior in private settings (Burger, Sanchez, Imberi, & Grande, 2009; Whatley et al., 1999) and virtual environments (Eastwick & Gardner, 2009).

A widely shared feeling of future obligation made an enormous difference in human social evolution. For the first time in evolutionary history, one individual could give any of a variety of resources—help, gifts, tools, goods—without actually giving them away. Sophisticated and coordinated systems of gift giving, defense, and trade became possible, bringing immense benefit to the societies that possessed them (Leakey & Lewin, 1978; Ridley, 1997). With such clearly adaptive consequences for all cultures, it is not surprising that reciprocity is not only a human universal (Brown, 1991; Gintis et al., 2003), but it is prevalent in many other social species (see Sundie et al., 2006).

A *reciprocation rule* for compliance can be worded as follows: *One should be more willing to comply with a request from someone who has previously provided a favor or concession.* Under this general rule, people will feel obligated to provide gifts, favors, services, and aid to those who have given them such things first (Goldstein, Griskevicius, & Cialdini, 2010; Singer, Van Holwyk, & Maher, 2000), sometimes even returning larger favors than those they have received (Regan, 1971). For example, restaurant servers who give two candies to guests along with the check increase their tips by 14.1% (Strohmetz et al., 2002). A number of sales and fund-raising tactics also use this factor to advantage: The compliance professional initially gives something to the target person, thereby causing the target person to be more likely to give something in return. Often, this "something in return" is the target person's compliance with a substantial request.

The unsolicited gift, accompanied by a request for a donation, is a commonly used technique that employs the norm for reciprocity. One example is organizations sending free gifts through the mail. Such groups count on the fact that most people will not go to the trouble of returning the gift and will feel uncomfortable about keeping it without reciprocating in some way. For instance, the Disabled American Veterans organization reports that its simple mail appeal for donations produces a response rate of about 18%. But when the mailings also includes an unsolicited gift (gummed, individualized address labels), the success rate nearly doubles to 35% (Smolowe, 1990). People often feel obligated to reciprocate even the smallest of gifts. For example, one study showed that people were more than twice as likely to fill out a lengthy survey when the request asking to complete the survey was accompanied by a handwritten Post-It Note (Garner, 2005). Although such a note does not constitute a sizable gift, people recognize the extra effort and personal touch that this gesture requires, and they feel obligated to reciprocate by agreeing to the request. Indeed, those who filled out the survey when it came with a handwritten sticky note returned it more promptly and provided more detailed answers (Garner, 2005).

The sense of discomfort that attends an unpaid debt not only explains why people will often agree to perform a return favor that is larger than the one they received. It also explains why people frequently refrain from asking for a needed favor if they will not be in a position to repay it (DePaulo, Nadler, & Fisher, 1983; Riley & Eckenrode, 1986): The saddle of unmet social debt weighs heavily, and we will go to considerable lengths to remove or avoid it to protect ourselves from the social disapproval associated with taking without giving in return (Wedekind & Milinski, 2000).

The features of the rule for reciprocation account nicely for the twin outcomes of a study by Rand Corporation researchers Berry and Kanouse (1987). They found that by paying physicians first, it was possible to increase the likelihood that the doctors would complete and return a long questionnaire they received in the mail. If a check for $20 accompanied the questionnaire, 78% of the physicians filled out the survey and sent it back as requested. But if they learned that the $20 check was to be sent to them after they complied, only 66% did so. By giving the check the character of a noncontingent gift rather than a reward for compliance, the researchers enhanced their success substantially.

The second reciprocation-related finding concerned only the physicians who received the check up front. As indicated, most complied with the questionnaire request, but some did not. Although most (95%) of the doctors who had complied cashed their checks, only 26% of those who did not comply did so. If they were not in a position to reciprocate the $20 gift, they were not of a mind to accept it, making the "accompanying gift" technique a highly cost-effective one for the researchers.

A crucial aspect of successful reciprocity-based influence techniques involves activating the sense of obligation. The creation of obligation necessitates that the individual who desires to influence another needs to be the first to provide a gift. It is noteworthy that this important aspect of reciprocity-based influence techniques is often misemployed. For example, numerous commercial organizations offer donations to charity in return for the purchase of products or services—a general strategy falling under the rubric of "cause-related marketing." Yet such tit-for-tat appeals often fail to engage reciprocity properly because influence agents do not provide benefits first and then allow recipients to return the favor. The suboptimal nature of such messages can be clearly seen in a field experiment in hotels, in which we varied messages that urged guests to reuse their towels. Messages that promised a donation to an environmental cause if guests first reused their towels were no more effective than standard proenvironmental messages (Goldstein, Griskevicius, & Cialdini, 2010). Consistent with the obligating force of reciprocity, however, a message informing guests that the hotel had already made a donation increased towel reuse by 26%.

Reciprocal Concessions A variation of the norm for reciprocation of favors is that for reciprocation of concessions. A reciprocal concessions procedure (or *door-in-the-face technique*) for inducing compliance has been documented repeatedly (e.g., Cialdini, Vincent, Lewis, Catalan, Wheeler, & Darby, 1975; Eastwick & Gardner, 2009; for meta-analyses, see O'Keefe & Hale, 1998, 2001). A requester uses this procedure by beginning with an extreme request that is usually rejected and then retreating to a more moderate favor—the one the requester had in mind from the outset. In doing so, the requester hopes that the retreat from an extreme to a moderate request will spur the target person to make a reciprocal concession by moving from initial rejection of the larger favor to acceptance of the smaller one. This reciprocal concessions strategy has been successfully used in fund-raising contexts where, after refusing a larger request for donations, people become substantially more likely than before to give the average contribution (e.g., Reingen, 1978). Cialdini and Ascani (1976) also used this technique in soliciting blood donors. They first requested a person's involvement in a long-term donor program. When that request was refused, the solicitor made a smaller request for a one-time donation. This pattern of a large request (that is refused) followed by a smaller request significantly increased compliance with the smaller request, as compared to a control condition of people who were asked only to perform the smaller one-time favor (a 50% versus a 32% compliance rate).

Of special interest to university students is evidence that the door-in-the-face technique can greatly increase a professor's willingness to spend time helping a student (Harari, Mohr, & Hosey, 1980). In that study, only 59% of faculty members were willing to spend "15 to 20 minutes" to meet with a student on an issue of interest to the student—when that was the only request the student made. However, significantly more faculty members (78%) were willing to agree to that same request if they had first refused the student's request to spend "2 hours a week for the rest of the semester" meeting with the student.

Related to the door-in-the-face technique is the *that's-not-all technique* investigated by Burger (1986), which is frequently used by sales operators. An important procedural difference between the two techniques is that in the that's-not-all tactic, the target person does not turn down the first offer before a better second offer is provided. After making the first offer but before the target can respond, the requester betters the deal with an additional item or a price reduction. Burger (1986) found this approach to be useful in selling more goods during a campus bake sale. One reason that this technique works appears to be the target person's desire to reciprocate for the better deal.

Social Validation

> If you can keep your head when people all around you are losing theirs, you probably haven't grasped the situation.
>
> —*Jean Kerr*

People frequently use the beliefs, attitudes, and actions of others, particularly similar others, as a standard of comparison against which to evaluate the correctness of their own beliefs, attitudes, and actions. Thus, it is common for individuals to decide on appropriate behaviors for themselves in a given situation by searching for information as to how similar others have behaved or are behaving in that situation (e.g., Asch, 1956; Goldstein, Cialdini, & Griskevicius, 2008; Darley & Latane, 1970). This simple principle of behavior accounts for an amazingly varied army of human responses. For instance, research has shown that New Yorkers use it in deciding whether to return a lost wallet (Hornstein, Fisch, & Holmes, 1968), that hotel guests use it when deciding whether to reuse their towels (Goldstein, Cialdini, & Griskevicius, 2008), that children with a fear of dogs use it in deciding whether to risk approaching a dog (Bandura & Menlove, 1968), that amusement park visitors use it to decide whether to litter in a public place (Cialdini, Reno, & Kallgren, 1990), that audience members use it in deciding whether a joke is funny (Provine, 2000), that National Park visitors use it when deciding whether to commit theft (Cialdini, 2003), that pedestrians use it in deciding whether to stop and stare at an empty spot in the sky (Milgram, Bickman, & Berkowitz, 1969), and, on the alarming side, that troubled individuals use it in deciding whether to commit suicide (Phillips & Carstensen, 1988).

Much of this evidence can be understood in terms of Festinger's (1954) *social comparison theory*, which states that (1) people have a constant drive to evaluate themselves (i.e., the appropriateness of their abilities, beliefs, feelings, and behaviors); (2) if available, people will prefer to use objective cues to make these evaluations; (3) if objective evidence is not available, people will rely on social comparison evidence instead; and (4) when seeking social comparison evidence for self-evaluations, people will look to similar others as the preferred basis for comparison. So, if, while sitting in a seminar, you find yourself feeling the room getting uncomfortably warm, social comparison theory would make some predictions about how you would likely behave. First, you ought to feel a need to assess the appropriateness of your feeling, which should manifest itself as a search for validating information. If, by chance, there is a thermometer on the wall immediately behind your chair, your first inclination would be to glance at it to obtain objective verification of your perception. But should no thermometer be present, you would have to resort to social information; so, you might nudge a classmate (a similar other) and whisper something to the effect of "Does it feel warm in here to you?" Only then, and only if the evidence confirmed your perception, would you likely feel justified in taking congruous action (e.g., asking that the thermostat be adjusted or a window be opened).

When the goal is to evaluate the correctness of an opinion or action, research has generally supported Festinger's theory. Social comparison is most likely to occur in situations that are objectively unclear (Sechrist & Stangor, 2007; Zitek & Hebl, 2007) and is most likely to be directed at similar others (Goldstein, Cialdini, & Griskevicius, 2008; Miller, 1984; Platow et al., 2005). For example, people are strongly influenced by the behavior of others when deciding whether to conserve energy in their homes (Schultz, Nolan, Cialdini, Goldstein, & Griskevicius, 2007). However, the influence of others' conservation behaviors increased as those others became more similar to the actual home resident: Whereas other citizens of the state had an effect on conservation, behavior was more strongly influenced by the residents of the same city, and even more strongly influenced by the residents of their own neighborhood (Nolan, Schultz, Cialdini, Goldstein, & Griskevicius, 2008). Thus, when people are unsure, they are most likely to look to and accept the beliefs and behaviors of similar others as valid indicators of what they should believe and do themselves.

The *social validation rule* for compliance can be stated as follows: *We should be more willing to comply with a request for behavior if it is consistent with what similar others are thinking or doing.* Our tendency to assume that an action is more correct if others are doing it is exploited in a variety of settings. Bartenders often "salt" their tip jars with a few dollar bills at the beginning of the evening to simulate tips left by prior customers and, thereby, to give the impression that tipping with folded money is proper barroom behavior (Griskevicius, Cialdini, & Goldstein, 2008). Church ushers sometimes prime collection baskets for the same reason and with the same positive effect on proceeds. Evangelic preachers are known to seed their audiences with "ringers," who are rehearsed to come forward at a specified time to give witness and donations. For example, an Arizona State University research team that infiltrated the Billy Graham organization reported on such advance preparations prior to one of his Crusade visits. "By the time Graham arrives in town and makes his altar call, an army of 6,000 await with instructions on when to come forth at varying intervals to create the impression of spontaneous mass outpouring" (Altheide & Johnson, 1977). Advertisers love to inform us when a product is the "fastest growing" or "largest selling" because they do not have to convince us directly that the product is good; they need only say that many others think so, which seems proof enough (Griskevicius, Goldstein, Mortensen, Sundie, Cialdini, & Kenrick, 2009). The producers of charity telethons devote inordinate amounts of time to the incessant listing of viewers who have already pledged contributions. The message being communicated to the holdouts is clear: "Look at all the people who have decided to give; it *must* be the correct thing to do" (see Surowiecki, 2005).

One tactic that compliance professionals use to engage the principle of social validation has been put to a scientific test. Called the *list technique,* it involves asking for a request only after the target person has been shown a list of similar others who have already complied. Reingen (1982) conducted several experiments in which college students or home owners were asked to donate money or blood to charitable cause. Those individuals who were initially shown a list of similar others who had already complied were significantly more likely to comply themselves. What's more, the longer the list, the greater was the effect.

Consistency

> It is easier to resist at the beginning than at the end.
>
> —*Leonardo da Vinci*

Social psychologists have long understood the strength of the consistency principle to direct human action. Prominent early theorists such as Leon Festinger (1957), Fritz Heider (1958), and Theodore Newcomb (1953) have viewed the desire for consistency as a prime motivator of our behavior. Other theorists (e.g., Baumeister, 1982) have recognized that the desire to *appear* consistent exerts considerable influence over our behavior as well. If we grant that the power of consistency is formidable in directing human action, an important practical question immediately arises: How is that force engaged? Social psychologists think they know the answer—commitment. If a person can get you to make a commitment (that is, to take a stand, to go on record), that person will have set the stage for your consistency with that earlier commitment. Once a stand is taken, there is a natural tendency to behave in ways that are stubbornly consistent with the stand (Burger & Caldwell, 2003; Greenwald, Carnot, Beach, & Young, 1987; Howard, 1990).

A *consistency rule* for compliance can be worded as follows: *After committing yourself to a position, you should be more willing to comply with requests for behaviors that are consistent with that position.* Any of a variety of strategies may be used to generate the crucial instigating commitment. One such strategy is the *foot-in-the-door technique* (Freedman & Fraser, 1966; Schwartzwald, Bizman, & Raz, 1983; see Burger, 1999). A solicitor using this procedure will first ask for a small favor that is almost certain to be granted. The initial compliance is then followed by a request for a larger, *related* favor. It has been repeatedly found that people who have agreed to the initial small favor are more willing to do the larger one (see Beaman et al., 1983, for a review), seemingly to be consistent with the implication of the initial action. For instance, home owners who had agreed to accept and wear a small lapel pin promoting a local charity were, as a consequence, more likely to contribute money to that charity when canvassed during a subsequent donation drive (Pliner, Hart, Kohl, & Saari,1974).

Freedman and Fraser (1966) have argued that the foot-in-the-door technique is successful because performance of the initially requested action causes individuals to see themselves as possessing certain traits. This explanation has received much support (e.g., Burger & Guadagno, 2003; Burger & Caldwell, 2003; Dolinski, 2000). For example, in the study by Piner and colleagues (1974), after taking and wearing the charity pin, subjects would be expected to see themselves as favorable toward charitable causes. Later, when asked to perform the larger, related favor of contributing to that charity, subjects would be more willing to do so to be consistent with the "charitable" trait they had assigned to themselves. Support for this interpretation comes from a study showing that children are not influenced by the foot-in-the-door technique until they are old enough to understand the idea of a stable personality trait (around 6 to 7 years). Once children are old enough to understand the meaning of a stable trait, the foot-in-the-door tactic becomes effective, especially among those children who prefer consistency in behavior (Eisenberg, Cialdini, McCreath, & Shell, 1987).

Other, more unsavory techniques induce a commitment to an item and then remove the inducements that generated the commitment. Remarkably, the commitment frequently remains. For example, the *bait-and-switch procedure* is used by some retailers who may advertise certain merchandise (e.g., a room of furniture) at a special low price. When the customer arrives to take advantage of the special, he or she finds the merchandise is low quality or sold out.

However, because customers have by now made an active commitment to getting new furniture at that particular store, they are more willing to agree to examine and, consequently, to buy alternative merchandise there (Joule, Gouilloux, & Weber, 1989).

A similar strategy is often employed by car dealers in the *low-ball technique*, which proceeds by obtaining a commitment to an action and *then* increasing the costs of performing the action (Cialdini, Cacioppo, Bassett, & Miller, 1978). The automobile salesperson who "throws the low ball" induces the customer to decide to buy a particular model car by offering a low price on the car or an inflated one on the customer's trade-in. After the decision has been made (and, at times, after the commitment is enhanced by allowing the customer to arrange financing, take the car home overnight, etc.), something happens to remove the reason the customer decided to buy. Perhaps a price calculation error is found, or the used car assessor disallows the inflated trade-in figure. By this time, though, many customers have experienced an internal commitment to that specific automobile and proceed with the purchase. Experimental research has documented the effectiveness of this tactic in settings beyond automobile sales (e.g., Brownstein & Katzev, 1985; Guegen et al., 2002; Joule, 1987). Additional research indicates that the tactic is effective primarily when used by a single requester (Burger & Petty, 1981), when the commitment is public (Burger & Cornelius, 2003), and when the initial commitment is freely made (Aronson & Mills, 1959; Cialdini, Cacioppo, Bassett,& Miller, 1978).

One thing that these procedures (and others like them) have in common is the establishment of an earlier commitment that is consistent with a later action desired by the compliance professional. The need for consistency then takes over to compel performance of the desired behavior. Even preliminary leanings that occur before a final decision has to be made can bias us toward consistent subsequent choices (Brownstein, Read, & Simon, 2004; Russo, Carlson, & Meloy, 2006).

Another approach to employing the commitment/consistency principle also has gained popularity among commercial compliance professionals. Rather than inducing a new commitment to their product or service, many practitioners point out existing commitments within potential customers that are consistent with the product or service being offered—a tactic called the *labeling technique* (see Tybout & Yalch, 1980; Cialdini et al., 1998). In this way, desirable existing commitments are made more visible to the customer, and the strain for consistency is allowed to direct behavior accordingly. For example, insurance agents are frequently taught to stress to new home owners that the purchase of an expensive house reflects an enormous personal commitment to their home and the wellbeing of their family. Consequently, they argue it would be consistent with such a commitment to home and family to purchase home and life insurance in amounts that befit the size of this commitment. Research of various kinds indicates that this sort of sensitization to commitments and to consequent inconsistencies can be effective in producing belief, attitude, and behavior change. Ball-Rokeach, Rokeach, and Grube (1984) demonstrated long-term behavioral effects from a television program that focused viewers on their personal commitments to certain deep-seated values (e.g., freedom, equality), on the one hand, and their current beliefs and behaviors, on the other. Not only did uninterrupted viewers of this single program evidence enhanced commitment to these values, but they were significantly more likely to donate money to support causes consistent with the values 2 to 3 months after the program had aired.

A more manipulative tactic than merely focusing people on their existing values is to put them in a situation in which to refuse a specific request would be inconsistent with a value that people wish to be known as possessing (Greenwald, Camot, Beach, & Young, 1987; Sherman, 1980). One such tactic is the *legitimization-of-paltry favors* (or even-a-penny-would-help) *technique* (Cialdini & Schroeder, 1976). Most people prefer to behave in ways that are consistent with a view of themselves as helpful, charitable individuals. Consequently, a fundraiser who makes a request that legitimizes a paltry amount of aid ("Could you give a contribution, even a penny would help") makes it difficult for a target to refuse to give at all; to do so risks appearing to be a very unhelpful person. Notice that this procedure does not specifically request a trivial sum; that would probably lead to a profusion of pennies and a small total take. Instead, the request simply makes a minuscule form of aid acceptable, thereby reducing the target's ability to give nothing and still remain consistent with the desirable image of a helpful individual. After all, how could a person remain committed to a helpful image after refusing to contribute when "even a penny would help"?

Experimental research done to validate the effectiveness of the technique has shown it to be successful in increasing the percentage of charity contributors (Cialdini & Schroeder, 1976; Reeves, Macolini, & Martin, 1987). What's more, in each of these studies the even-a-penny procedure proved profitable because subjects did not actually give a penny but provided the donation amount typically given to charities. Thus, the legitimization-of-paltry-favors approach appears to work by getting more people to agree to give (so as to be consistent with a helpful image); but the decision of how much to give is left unaffected by the mention of a paltry amount. The consequence is increased proceeds.

A last commitment-based tactic deserves mention—one that we might call the "How are you feeling?" technique. Have you noticed that callers asking you to contribute to some cause or another these days seem to begin things by inquiring as to your current health and well-being? "Hello, Mr./Ms. Target person?" they say. "How are you feeling this evening?" Or, "How are you doing today?" The caller's intent with this sort of introduction is not only to seem friendly and caring. It is to get you to respond—as you normally do to such polite, superficial inquiries—with a polite, superficial comment of your own: "Just fine" or "Real good" or "I'm doing great, thanks." Once you have publicly stated that all is well, it becomes much easier for the solicitor to corner you into aiding those for whom all is not well: "I'm glad to hear that, because I'm calling to ask if you'd be willing to make a donation to help out the unfortunate victims of. . . ."

The theory behind this tactic is that people who have just asserted that they are doing/ feeling fine—even as a routine part of a sociable exchange—will consequently find it awkward to appear stingy in the context of their own admittedly favored circumstances. If all this sounds a bit far-fetched, consider the findings of consumer researcher Daniel Howard (1990), who put the theory to the test. Dallas, Texas, residents were called on the phone and asked if they would agree to allow a representative of the Hunger Relief Committee to come to their homes to sell them cookies, the proceeds from which would be used to supply meals for the needy. When tried alone, that request (labeled the standard solicitation approach) produced only 18% agreement. However, if the caller initially asked "How are you feeling this evening?" and waited for a reply before proceeding with the standard approach, several noteworthy things happened. First, of the 120 individuals called, most (108) gave the customary a favorable replay ("Good," "Fine," "Real well," etc.). Second, 32% of the people who got the how-are-you-feeling-tonight question agreed to receive the cookie seller at their homes, nearly twice the success rate of the standard solicitation approach. Third, true to the consistency principle, almost everyone who agreed to such a visit did in fact make a cookie purchase when contacted at home (89%).

Liking

> The main work of a trial attorney is to make the jury like his client.
>
> —*Clarence Darrow*

A fact of social interaction to which each of us can attest is that people are more favorably inclined toward the needs of those they know and like. Consequently, a *friendship/liking rule for compliance can be worded as follows: We should be more willing to comply with the requests of friends or other liked individuals.* Could there be any doubt that this is the case after examining the remarkable success of the Tupperware Corporation and their "home party" demonstration concept (Frenzen & Davis, 1990)? The demonstration party for Tupperware products is hosted by an individual, usually a woman, who invites to her home an array of friends, neighbors, and relatives, all of whom know that their hostess receives a percentage of the profits from every piece sold by the Tupperware representative, who is also there. In this way, the Tupperware Corporation arranges for its customers to buy from and *for* a friend rather than from an unknown salesperson. So favorable has been the effect on proceeds ($3 million in sales per day!) that the Tupperware Corporation has wholly abandoned its early retail outlets, and a Tupperware party begins somewhere every 2.7 seconds (Cialdini, 2009). Indeed, the success of this strategy has inspired many companies to use parties to sell their products, including cosmetics, arts and crafts, and even video games. Most influence agents, however, attempt to engage the friendship/liking principle in a different way: Before making a request, they get their targets to like *them*. But how do they do it? It turns out that the tactics that practitioners use to generate liking cluster around certain factors that have been shown by controlled research to increase liking (for an additional discussion of the predictors of liking and interpersonal attraction, see Finkel & Baumeister, Chapter 12, this volume).

Physical Attractiveness Although it is generally acknowledged that good-looking people have an advantage in social interaction, research findings indicate that we may have greatly underestimated the size and reach of that advantage (e.g., Lynn & Simons, 2000; McCall, 1997). There appears to be a positive reaction to good physical appearance that generalizes to favorable trait perceptions such as a talent, kindness, honesty, and intelligence (see Langolis et al., 2000, for a review). As a consequence, attractive individuals are more persuasive in terms of both changing attitudes (Chaiken, 1979) and getting what they request (Benson, Karabenic, & Lerner, 1976). For instance, a study of Canadian Federal elections found that attractive candidates received more than two and a half times the votes of unattractive ones (Efran & Patterson, 1976). Equally impressive results seem to pertain to the judicial system (see reviews by Castellow, Wuensch, & Moore, 1990; Downs & Lyons, 1991). In a Pennsylvania study, researchers rated the physical attractiveness of 74 separate male defendants at the start of their criminal trials. When, much later, the researchers checked the results of these cases via court records, they found that the better-looking men received significantly lighter sentences. In fact, the attractive defendants were twice as likely to avoid incarceration as the unattractive defendants (Stewart, 1980). When viewed in light of such powerful effects, it is not surprising that extremely attractive models are employed to promote products and services, that sales trainers frequently include appearance and grooming tips in their presentations, or that, commonly, con men are handsome and con women are pretty.

Similarity We like people who are similar to us (Burger et al., 2004; Carli, Ganley, & Pierce-Otay, 1991). This fact seems to hold true whether the similarity occurs in the area of opinions, personality traits, background, or lifestyle. Not only has research demonstrated that even trivial similarities can increase liking and have profound effects on important decisions such as careers and marriage partners (e.g., Garner, 2005; Pelham, Mirenberg, & Jones, 2002; Jones, Pelham, Carvallo, & Mirenberg, 2004), but perceived attitude similarity between yourself and a stranger can automatically activate kinship cognitions, inducing a person to behave prosocially toward that similar other (Park & Schaller, 2005). Consequently, those who wish to be liked to increase our compliance can accomplish that purpose by appearing similar to us in any of a wide variety of ways. For that reason, it would be wise to be careful around salespeople who *seem* to be just like us. Many sales training programs urge trainees to "mirror and match" the customer's body posture, mood, and verbal style, as similarities along each of these dimensions have been shown to lead to positive results (Maddux, Mullen, & Galinski, 2008; van Baaren, Holland, Steenaert, & van Knippenberg, 2003). Similarity in dress provides still another example. Several studies have demonstrated that we are more likely to help those who dress like us. In one study, done in the early 1970s when young people tended to dress either in "hippie" or "straight" fashion, experimenters donned hippie or straight attire and asked college students on campus for a dime to make a phone call. When the experimenter was dressed in the same way as the student, the request was granted in over two-thirds of the instances; but when the student and requester were dissimilarly dressed, a dime was provided less than half of the time (Emswiller, Deaux, & Willits, 1971). Another experiment shows how automatic our positive response to similar others can be. Marchers in a political demonstration were found not only to be more likely to sign the petition of a similarly dressed requester but to do so without bothering to read it first (Suedfeld, Bochner, & Matas, 1971).

Compliments Praise and other forms of positive estimation also stimulate liking (e.g., Howard et al., 1995, 1997; Gordon, 1996; Vonk, 2002). The actor Maclain Stevenson once described how his wife tricked him into marriage: "She said she liked me." Although designed for a laugh, the remark is as much instructive as humorous. The simple information that someone fancies us can be a bewitchingly effective device for producing return liking and willing compliance. Although there are limits to our gullibility—especially when we can be sure that the flatterer's intent is manipulative (Jones & Wortman, 1973)—we tend as a rule to believe praise and to like those who provide it. Evidence for the power of praise on liking comes from a study (Drachman, deCarufel, & Insko, 1978) in which men received personal comments from someone who needed a favor from them. Some of the men got only positive comments, some only negative comments, and some got a mixture of good and bad. There were three interesting findings. First, the evaluator who offered only praise was liked best. Second, this was so even though the men fully realized that the flatterer stood to gain from their liking of him. Finally, unlike the other types of comments, pure praise did not have to be accurate to work. Compliments produced just as much liking for the flatterer when they were untrue as when they were true. Because of this, salespeople are educated in the art of praise. A potential customer's home, clothes, car, taste, etc., are all frequent targets for compliments.

Cooperation Cooperation is another factor that has been shown to enhance positive feelings and behavior (e.g., Bettencourt, Brewer, Croak, & Miller, 1992; Paolini, Hewstone, & Cairns, 2004). Those who cooperate in achieving a common goal are more favorable and helpful to each other as a consequence. That is why compliance professionals often strive to be perceived as cooperating partners with a target person (Rafaeli & Sutton, 1991). Automobile sales managers frequently set themselves as "villains" so that the salesperson can "do battle" on the customer's behalf. The cooperative, pulling together kind of relationship that is consequently produced between the salesperson and customer naturally leads to a desirable form of liking that promotes sales.

Scarcity

> The way to love anything is to realize that it might be lost.
> —*Gilbert Keith Chesterton*

Opportunities seem more valuable to us when they are less available (Lynn, 1991; McKensie & Chase, 2010). Interestingly, this is often true even when the opportunity holds little attraction for us on its own merits. Take, as evidence, the experience of Florida State University students who, like most undergraduates, rated themselves as dissatisfied with the quality of their cafeteria's food. Nine days later, they had changed their minds, rating that food significantly better than they had before. It is instructive that no actual improvement in food service had occurred between the two ratings. Instead, earlier in the day of the second rating students had learned that because of a fire, they could not eat at the cafeteria for 2 weeks (West, 1975).

There appear to be two major sources of the power of scarcity. First, because we know that the things that are difficult to possess are typically better than those that are easy to possess, we can often use an item's availability to help us quickly and correctly decide on its quality (Lynn, 1992). Thus, one reason for the potency of scarcity is that, by assessing it, we can obtain a quick indication of an item's value.

In addition, there is a unique, secondary source of power within scarcity: As the things we can have become less available, we lose freedoms; and we *hate* to lose the freedoms we already have. This desire to preserve our established prerogatives is the centerpiece of *psychological reactance theory* (Brehm, 1981; Burgoon, Alvaro, Grandpre, & Voulodakis, 2002) developed to explain the human response to diminishing personal control. According to the theory, whenever our freedoms are limited or threatened, the need to retain those freedoms makes us want them (as well as the goods and services associated with them) significantly more than we previously did. So, when increasing scarcity—or anything else—interferes with our prior access to some item, we will *react against* the interference by wanting and trying to possess the item more than before.

One naturally occurring example of the consequences of increased scarcity can be seen in the outcome of a decision by county officials in Miami to ban the use and possession of phosphate detergents. Spurred by the tendency to want what they could no longer have, the majority of Miami consumers came to see phosphate cleaners as better products than before. Compared to Tampa residents, who were not affected by the Miami ordinance, the citizens of Miami rated phosphate detergents as gentler, more effective in cold water, better whiteners and fresheners, and more powerful on stains. After passage of the law, they had even come to believe that phosphate detergents poured more easily than the detergents used by Tampa consumers (Mazis, 1975).

This sort of response is typical of individuals who have lost an established freedom and is crucial to an understanding of how psychological reactance and scarcity work on us. When our freedom to have something is limited, the item becomes less available, and we experience an increased desire for it. However, we rarely recognize that psychological reactance has caused us to want the item more; all we know is that we *want* it. Still, we need to make sense of our desire for the item, so we begin to assign it positive qualities to justify the desire. After all, it is natural to suppose that if we feel drawn to something, it is because of the merit of the thing. In the case of the Miami antiphosphate law—and in other instances of newly restricted availability—that is a faulty supposition. Phosphate detergents clean, whiten, and pour no better after they are banned than before. We just assume they do because we desire them more.

Other research has suggested that in addition to commodities, limited access to information makes the information more desirable and more influential (Brock, 1968; Brock & Bannon, 1992). One test of Brock's thinking found good support in a business setting. Wholesale beef buyers who were told of an impending imported beef shortage purchased significantly more beef when they were informed that the shortage information came from certain "exclusive" contacts that the importer had (Knishinsky, 1982). Apparently, the fact that the scarcity news was itself scarce made it more valued and persuasive.

Additional evidence—from the literature on censorship—suggests that restricting information can empower that information in unintended ways. Individuals typically respond to censorship by wanting to receive the banned information to a greater extent and by becoming more favorable to it than before the ban (e.g., Brown, 2008; Worchel, 1992). Especially interesting is the finding that people will come to believe in banned information more even though they have not received it (Worchel, Arnold, & Baker, 1975).

A *scarcity rule* for compliance can be worded as follows: *We should try to secure those opportunities that are scarce or dwindling.* With scarcity operating powerfully on the worth assigned to things, it is not surprising that compliance professionals have a variety of techniques designed to convert this power to compliance. Probably the most frequently used technique is the "limited number" tactic in which the customer is informed that membership opportunities, products, or services exist in a limited supply that cannot be guaranteed to last for long.

Related to the limited number tactic is the "deadline" technique in which an official time limit is placed on the customer's opportunity to get what is being offered. Newspaper ads abound with admonitions to the customer regarding the folly of delay: "Last three days." "Limited time offer." "One week only sale." The purest form of a decision deadline—right now—occurs in a variant of the deadline technique in which customers are told that unless they make an immediate purchase decision, they will have to buy the item at a higher price, or they will not be able to purchase it at all. We found this tactic used in numerous compliance settings. For example, a large child photography company urges parents to buy as many poses and copies as they can afford because "stocking limitations force us to burn the unsold pictures of your children within 24 hours." A prospective health club member or automobile buyer might learn that the deal offered by the salesperson is good for that one time; should the customer leave the premises, the deal is off. One home vacuum cleaner sales company instructs its trainees to tell prospects that "I have so many other people to see that I have the time to visit a family only once. It's company policy that even if you decide later that you want this machine, I can't come back and sell it to you." For anyone who thought about it carefully, this was nonsense: The company and its representatives are in the business of making sales, and any customer who called for another visit would be accommodated gladly. The real purpose of the can't-come-back-again claim was to evoke the possibility of loss that is inherent in the scarcity rule for compliance.

The idea of potential loss plays a large role in human decision making (see Vohs & Luce, Chapter 20, this volume). In fact, people seem to be more motivated by the thought of losing something than by the thought of gaining something of equal value (Hobofoll, 2001; Tversky & Kahneman, 1981). For instance, home owners told about how much money they could lose from inadequate insulation are more likely to insulate their homes than those told about how much money they could save (Gonzales, Aronson, & Costanzo, 1988). Similar results have been obtained on college campuses where students experienced much stronger emotions when asked to imagine losses rather than gains in their romantic relationships or grade point averages (Ketelaar, 1995).

Authority

> Follow an expert.
>
> —*Virgil*

Legitimately constituted authorities are extremely influential persons (e.g., Aronson, Turner, & Carlsmith, 1963; Blass, 2004; Burger, 2009; Milgram, 1974). Whether they have acquired their positions through knowledge, talent, or fortune, their positions bespeak of superior information and power. For each of us this has always been the case. Early on, these people (e.g., parents, teachers) knew more than us, and we found that taking their advice proved beneficial—partly because of their greater wisdom and partly because they controlled our rewards and punishments. As adults, the authority figures have changed to employers, judges, police officers, and the like, but the benefits associated with doing as they say have not. For most people, then, conforming to the dictates of authority figures produces genuine practical advantages. Consequently, it makes great sense to comply with the wishes of properly constituted authorities. It makes so much sense, in fact, that people often do so when it makes no sense at all.

Take, for example, the strange case of the "rectal earache" reported by two professors of pharmacy, Michael Cohen and Neil Davis (1981). A physician ordered eardrops to be administered to the right ear of a patient suffering pain and infection there. But instead of completely writing out the location "right ear" on the prescription, the doctor abbreviated it so that the instructions read "place in R ear." On receiving the prescription, the duty nurse promptly put the required number of eardrops into the patient's anus. Obviously, rectal treatment of an earache made no sense. Yet neither the patient nor the nurse questioned it.

Of course, the most dramatic research evidence for the power of legitimate authority comes from the famous Milgram experiment in which 65% of the subjects were willing to deliver continued, intense, and dangerous levels of electric shock to a kicking, screeching, pleading other subject simply because an authority figure—in this case a scientist—directed them to do so. Although almost everyone who has ever taken a psychology course has learned about this experiment, Milgram (1974) conducted a series of variations on his basic procedure that are less well known but equally compelling in making the point about the powerful role that authority played in causing subjects to behave so cruelly. For instance, in one variation, Milgram had the scientist and the victim switch scripts so that the scientist told the subject to stop delivering shock to the victim, while the victim insisted bravely that the subject continue for the good of the experiment. The results couldn't have been clearer: Not a single subject gave even one additional shock when it was a nonauthority who demanded it. Even more than 30 years later, replications of Milgram's classic studies continue to demonstrate the power of authority (Burger, 2009).

An *authority rule* for compliance can be worded as follows: *We should be more willing to follow the suggestions of someone who is a legitimate authority.* Authorities may be seen as falling into two categories: authorities with regard to the specific situation and more general authorities. Compliance practitioners employ techniques that seek to benefit from the power invested in authority figures of both types. In the case of authority relevant to a specific situation, we can note how often advertisers inform their audiences of the level of expertise of product manufacturers (e.g., "Fashionable men's clothiers since 1841"; "Babies are our business, our only business"). At times, the expertise associated with a product has been more symbolic than substantive, for instance, when actors in television commercials wear physicians' white coats to recommend a product. In one famous coffee commercial, the actor involved, Robert Young, did not need a white coat, as his prior identity as TV doctor Marcus Welby, M.D., provided the medical connection. It is instructive that the mere symbols of a physician's expertise and authority are enough to trip the mechanism that governs authority influence. One of the most prominent of these symbols, the bare title "Dr.," has been shown to be devastatingly effective as a compliance device among trained hospital personnel. In what may be the most frightening study we know, a group of physicians and nurses conducted an experiment that documented the dangerous degree of blind obedience that hospital nurses accorded to an individual whom they had never met, but who claimed in a phone call to be a doctor (Hofling, Brotzman, Dalrymple, Graves, & Pierce, 1966). Ninety-five percent of those nurses were willing to administer an unsafe level of a drug merely because a caller they thought was a doctor requested it.

In the case of influence that generalizes outside of relevant expertise, the impact of authority (real and symbolic) appears equally impressive. For instance, researchers have found that when wearing a security guard's uniform, a requester could produce more compliance with requests (e.g., to pick up a paper bag in the street, to stand on the other side of a Bus Stop sign) that were irrelevant to a security guard's domain of authority (Bickman, 1974; Bushman, 1988). Less blatant in its connotation than a uniform, but nonetheless effective, is another kind of attire that has traditionally bespoken of authority status in our culture—the well-tailored business suit. Take as evidence the results of a study by Lefkowitz, Blake, and Mouton (1955), who found that three and a half times as many people were willing to follow a jaywalker into traffic when he wore a suit and tie versus a work shirt and trousers.

Con artists frequently make use of the influence inherent in authority attire. For example, a gambit called the bank examiner scheme depends heavily on the automatic deference most people assign to authority figures, or those merely dressed as such. Using the two uniforms of authority we have already mentioned, a business suit and guard's outfit, the con begins when a man dressed in a conservative three-piece suit appears at the home of a likely victim and identifies himself as an official of the victim's bank. The victim is told of suspected irregularities in the transactions handled by one particular teller and is asked to help trap the teller by drawing out all of his or her savings at the teller's window. In this way, the examiner can "catch the teller red-handed" in any wrongdoing. After cooperating, the victim is to give the money to a uniformed bank guard waiting outside, who will then return it to the proper account. Often, the appearance of the "bank examiner" and uniformed "guard" are so impressive that the victim never thinks to check on their authenticity and proceeds with the requested action, never to see the money or those two individuals again. Authority cues are similarly used in many types of email or other online scams, in which a seemingly trustworthy source asks for the victim's private information.

Social Influence Today

Throughout this chapter we have noted that part of the reason why the principles of influence discussed here are so powerful is because they all promote adaptive behavior in the evolutionary sense. That is, the sense of obligation to reciprocate a gift, the tendency to value scarce items, the inclination to turn to similar others or to experts in times of uncertainty, and the desire to say "yes" to people we like all have likely evolutionary sources. However, only recently have researchers begun to examine the nature of social influence by explicitly drawing on an evolutionary perspective (e.g., Sundie et al., 2006; see Maner & Kenrick, Chapter 17, this volume). An evolutionary approach offers powerful theories to generate unique hypotheses about social influence. For example, by considering the kinds of recurring social problems that humans have evolved to solve (protecting ourselves from danger, attracting mates, etc.; see Kenrick et al., 2010), this perspective points to conditions under which specific influence principles should be more effective and to conditions under which specific principles might be ineffective. For example, activating motives of self-protection causes the principle of social validation to be more powerful, whereby a person is especially influenced by what many others are doing when that person is in a state of fear (e.g., Griskevicius et al., 2006, 2009). Social validation information appears to be much less influential, however, when a person is concerned about attracting a mate, leading people to sometimes do the exact opposite of what many others are doing.

An evolutionary perspective is also useful in helping address another important gap in the social influence literature. Specifically, the overwhelming majority of social influence research informs us primarily about the strategies that are effective in influencing relative strangers, such as when a salesperson attempts to influence a customer whom he has never met. From an evolutionary perspective, however, interactions with unfamiliar individuals were a rare occurrence throughout human evolution. Instead, our ancestors needed to influence people with whom they were familiar, such as siblings, parents, friends, leaders, mates, and offspring. Even today, many of our efforts at influence concern trying to persuade people who we know quite well, yet little is known about the nature of the influence process between individuals highly familiar with each other. An evolutionary perspective suggests that the influence process may differ depending on the specific relationship between the influence agent and target (e.g., a parent trying to influence his or her child; an employee trying to influence his or her boss; a person of one sex trying to influence a person of the opposite sex). From an evolutionary perspective, different types of relationships are associated with specific types of opportunities and specific types of threats (Schaller, Park, & Kenrick, 2007). And because these opportunities and costs within each type of relationship have remained similar throughout evolutionary history, people are likely to use different psychologies when interacting with strangers than when interacting with siblings, parents, leaders, mates, or offspring. By understanding the nature and function of such relationships, we can gain insight into the types of influence strategies that are likely to be successful within a specific relationship versus the types of strategies that are likely to lead to resistance and resentment (e.g., see Oriña, Wood, & Simpson, 2002).

Summary

At the outset of this chapter it was suggested that an important question for anyone interested in understanding resisting or harnessing the process of interpersonal influence is, "Which are the most powerful principles that motivate us to comply with another's request?" It was also suggested that one way to assess such power would be to examine the practices of commercial compliance professionals for their pervasiveness. That is, if compliance practitioners made widespread use of certain principles, this would be evidence for the natural power of these principles to affect everyday compliance. Six psychological principles emerged as the most popular in the repertoires of the compliance pros: reciprocity, social validation, consistency, liking, scarcity, and authority. Close examination of the principles revealed broad professional usage that could be validated and explained by controlled experimental research. As with most research perspectives, additional work needs to be done before we can have high levels of confidence in the conclusions. However, there is considerable evidence at this juncture to indicate that these six principles engage central features on the human condition in the process of motivating compliance.

Suggestions for Further Reading

Burger, J. M. (2009). Replicating Milgram: Would people still obey today? *American Psychologist, 64,* 1–11.

Cialdini, R. B. (2009). *Influence: Science and practice* (5th ed.). Boston, MA: Allyn & Bacon.

Cialdini, R. B., & Goldstein, N. J. (2004). Social influence: Compliance and conformity. *Annual Review of Psychology, 55,* 591–621.

Garner, R. (2005). Post-It Note persuasion: A sticky influence. *Journal of Consumer Psychology, 15,* 230–237.

Goldstein, N. J., Cialdini, R. B., & Griskevicius, V. (2008). A room with a viewpoint: Using social norms to motivate environmental conservation in hotels. *Journal of Consumer Research, 35,* 472–482.

Goldstein, N. J., Martin, S., & Cialdini, R. B. (2008). *Yes! 50 scientifically proven ways to be persuasive.* New York: Free Press.

Griskevicius, V., Cialdini, R. B., & Goldstein, N. J. (2008). Applying (and resisting) peer influence. *MIT/Sloan Management Review, 49,* 84–88.

Oriña, M. M., Wood, W., & Simpson, J. A. (2002). Strategies of influence in close relationships. *Journal of Experimental Social Psychology, 38,* 459–472.

References

Altheide, D. L., & Johnson, J. M. (1977). Counting souls: A study of counseling at evangelical crusades. *Pacific Sociological Review, 20,* 323–348.

Aronson, E., & Mills, J. (1959). The effect of severity of initiation on liking for a group. *Journal of Abnormal and Social Psychology, 59*, 177–181.

Aronson, E., Turner, J. A., & Carlsmith, J. M. (1963). Communicator credibility and communication discrepancy as a determinant of opinion change. *Journal of Abnormal and Social Psychology, 67*, 31–36.

Asch, S. E. (1956). Studies of independence and conformity: I. A minority of one against a unanimous majority. *Psychological Monographs, 70(9)*.

Ball-Rokeach, S., Rokeach, M., & Grube, J. W. (1984). *The great American values test.* New York: Free Press.

Bandura, A., & Menlove, F. L. (1968). Factors determining vicarious extinction of avoidance behavior through symbolic modeling. *Journal of Personality and Social Psychology, 8*, 99–108.

Baumeister, R. F. (1982). A self-presentational view of social phenomena. *Psychological Bulletin, 91*, 3–26.

Baumeister, R. F., & Leary, M. R. (1995). The need to belong: Desire for interpersonal attachments as a fundamental human motivation. *Psychological Bulletin, 177*, 497–529.

Beaman, A. L., Cole C. M., Preston, M., Klentz, B., & Steblay, N. M. (1983). Fifteen years of food-in-the-door research: A meta-analysis. *Personality and Social Psychology Bulletin, 9*, 181–196.

Benson, P. L., Karabenic, S. A., & Lerner, R. M. (1976). Pretty pleases: The effects of physical attractiveness on race, sex, and receiving help. *Journal of Experimental Social Psychology, 12*, 409–415.

Berry, S. H., & Kanouse, D. E. (1987). Physician response to a mailed survey: An experiment in timing of payment. *Public Opinion Quarterly, 51*, 102–114.

Bettencourt, B. A., Brewer, M. B., Croak, M. R., & Miller, N. (1992). Cooperation and the reduction of intergroup bias. *Journal of Experimental Social Psychology, 28*, 301–319.

Bickman, L. (1974). The social power of a uniform. *Journal of Applied Social Psychology, 4*, 47–61.

Blass, T. (2004). The man who shocked the world: The life and legacy of Stanley Milgram. New York: Basic Books.

Brehm, S. S. (1981). Psychological reactance and the attractiveness of unattainable objects: Sex differences in children's responses to an elimination of freedom. *Sex Roles, 7*, 937–949.

Brock, T. C. (1968). Implications of commodity theory for value change. In A. G. Greenwald, T. C. Brock, & T. M. Ostrom (Eds.), *Psychological foundations of attitudes.* New York: Academic Press.

Brock, T. C., & Bannon, L. A. (1992). Liberalization of commodity theory. *Basic and Applied Social Psychology, 13*, 135–143.

Brown, D. E. (1991). *Human universals.* New York: McGraw-Hill.

Brown, M. (2008). Montana high school cancels climate speech (January 17, 2008). *MiamiHerald.com.* Retrieved from http://www.miamiherald.com/news/nation/AP/story/383710.

Brownstein, R., & Katzev, R. (1985). The relative effectiveness of three compliance techniques in eliciting donations to a cultural organization. *Journal of Applied Social Psychology, 15*, 564–574.

Brownstein, A., Read, S. J., & Simon, D. (2004). Bias at the racetrack: Effects of individual and task importance on predecision reevaluation of alternatives. *Personality and Social Psychology Bulletin, 30,* 891–904.

Burger, J. M. (1986). Increasing compliance by improving the deal: The that's-not-all technique. *Journal of Personality and Social Psychology, 51*, 277–283.

Burger, J. M. (1999). The foot-in-the-door compliance procedure: A multiple-process analysis and review. *Personality and Social Psychology Review, 3,* 303–325.

Burger, J. M. (2009). Replicating Milgram: Would people still obey today? *American Psychologist, 64,* 1–11.

Burger, J. M., & Caldwell, D. C. (2003). The effects of monetary incentives and labeling on the foot-in-the-door effect: Evidence for a self-perception process. *Basic and Applied Social Psychology, 25,* 235–241.

Burger, J. M., & Cornelius, T. (2003). Raising the price of agreement: Public commitment and the low-ball compliance procedure. *Journal of Applied Social Psychology, 33,* 923–934.

Burger, J. M., & Guadagno, R. E. (2003). Self-concept clarity and the foot-in-the-door procedure. *Basic and Applied Social Psychology, 25,* 79–86.

Burger, J. M., Messian, N., Patel, S., del Prado, A., & Anderson, C. (2004). What a coincidence! The effects of incidental similarity on compliance. *Personality and Social Psychology Bulletin, 30,* 35–43.

Burger, J. M., & Petty, R. E. (1981). The low-ball compliance technique: Task or person commitment? *Journal of Personality and Social Psychology, 40,* 492–500.

Burger, J.,M., Sanchez, J., Imberi, J. E., & Grande, L. R. (2009). The norm of reciprocity as an internalized social norm: Returning favors even when no one finds out. *Social Influence, 4,* 11–17.

Burgoon, M., Alvaro, E., Grandpre, J., & Voulodakis, M. (2002). Revisiting the theory of psychological reactance. In J. P. Dillard and M. Pfau (Eds.), *The persuasion handbook: Theory and practice* (pp. 213–232). Thousand Oaks, CA: Sage.

Bushman, B. A. (1988). The effects of apparel on compliance. *Personality and Social Psychology Bulletin, 14*, 459–467.

Carli, L. L., Ganley, R., & Pierce-Otay, A. (1991). Similarity and satisfaction in roommate relationships. *Personality and Social Psychology Bulletin, 17,* 419–426.

Castellow, W. A., Wuensch, K. L., & Moore, C. H. (1990). Effects of physical attractiveness of the plaintiff and defendant in sexual harassment judgments. *Journal of Social Behavior and Personality,* 5, 547–562.

Chaiken, S. (1979). Communicator physical attractiveness and persuasion. *Journal of Personality and Social Psychology, 37*, 1387–1397.

Cialdini, R. B. (2003). Crafting normative messages to protect the environment. *Current Directions in Psychological Science, 12*, 105–109.

Cialdini, R. B. (2008). *Influence: Science and practice* (5th ed.). Boston, MA: Allyn & Bacon.

Cialdini, R. B., & Ascani, K. (1976). Test of a concession procedure for inducing verbal, behavioral, and further compliance with a request to give blood. *Journal of Applied Psychology, 61*, 295–300.

Cialdini, R. B., Cacioppo, J. T., Bassett, R., & Miller, J. A. (1978). Low-ball procedure for producing compliance: Commitment then cost. *Journal of Personality and Social Psychology, 36*, 463–476.

Cialdini, R. B., Eisenberg, N., Green, B. L., Rhoads, K. v. L., & Bator, R. (1998). Undermining the undermining effect of reward on sustained interest. *Journal of Applied Social Psychology, 28*, 249–263.

Cialdini, R. B., Eisenberg, N., Shell, R., & McCreath, H. (1987). Commitments to help by children: Effects on subsequent prosocial attributions. *British Journal of Social Psychology, 26*, 237–245.

Cialdini, R. B., & Goldstein, N. J. (2004). Social influence: Compliance and conformity. *Annual Review of Psychology, 55*, 591–621.

Cialdini, R. B., Green, B. L., & Rusch, A. J. (1992). When tactical pronouncements of change become real change: The case of reciprocal persuasion. *Journal of Personality and Social Psychology, 63*, 30–40.

Cialdini, R. B., Reno, R. R., & Kallgren, C. A. (1990). A focus theory of normative conduct: Recycling the concept of norms to reduce littering in public places. *Journal of Personality and Social Psychology, 58*, 1015–1026.

Cialdini, R. B., & Schroeder, D. A. (1976). Increasing compliance by legitimizing paltry contributions: When even a penny helps. *Journal of Personality and Social Psychology, 34*, 599–604.

Cialdini, R. B., & Trost, M. R., (1998) Social influence: Social norms, conformity, and compliance. In D. T. Gilbert & S. T. Fiske (Eds.), *The handbook of social psychology: Vol. 2* (4th ed., pp. 151–192). Boston: McGraw-Hill.

Cialdini, R. B., Vincent, J. E., Lewis, S. K., Catalan, J., Wheeler, D., & Darby, B. L. (1975). Reciprocal concessions procedure for inducing compliance: The door-in-the-face technique. *Journal of Personality and Social Psychology, 31*, 206–215

Cohen, M., & Davis, N. (1981). *Medication errors: Causes and prevention.* Philadelphia: G. F. Stickley Co.

Condon, J. W., & Crano, W. D. (1988). Inferred evaluation and the relation between attitude similarity and interpersonal attraction. *Journal of Personality and Social Psychology, 54*, 789–797.

Cunningham, J. A., Strassberg, D. S., & Haan, B. (1986). Effects of intimacy and sex-role congruency of self-disclosure. *Journal of Social and Clinical Psychology, 4*, 393–401.

Darley, J. M., & Latane, B. (1970). Norms and normative behavior: Field studies of social interdependence. In J. Macaulay & L. Berkowitz (Eds.), *Altruism and helping behavior*. New York: Academic Press.

Dengerink, H. A., Schnedler, R. W., & Covey, M. K. (1978). Role of avoidance in aggressive responses to attack and no attack. *Journal of Personality and Social Psychology, 36*, 1044–1053.

DePaulo, B. M., Nadler, A., & Fisher, J. D. (Eds.). (1983). *New directions in helping: Vol. 2. Help seeking*. New York: Academic Press.

Dolinski, D. (2000). On inferring one's beliefs from one's attempt and consequences for subsequent compliance. *Journal of Personality and Social Psychology, 78*, 260–272.

Downs, A. C., & Lyons, P. M. (1991). Natural observations of the links between attractiveness and initial legal judgements. *Personality and Social Psychology Bulletin, 17*, 541–547.

Drachman, D., DeCarufel, A., & Insko, C. (1978). The extra credit effect in interpersonal attraction. *Journal of Experimental Social Psychology 14*, 458–469.

Eastwick, P. W., & Gardner, W. I. (2009). Is it just a game? Evidence for social influence in the virtual world. *Social Influence, 4*, 18–32.

Efran, M. G., & Patterson, E. W. J. (1976). *The politics of appearance*. Unpublished manuscript, University of Toronto.

Eisenberg, N. E., Cialdini, R. B., McCreath, H., & Shell, R. (1987). Consistency-based compliance: When and why do children become vulnerable? *Journal of Personality and Social Psychology, 52*, 1174–1181.

Emswiller, T., Deaux, K., & Willits, J. E. (1971). Similarity, sex, and requests for small favors. *Journal of Applied Social Psychology, 1*, 284–291.

Festinger, L. (1954). A theory of social comparison processes. *Human Relations, 7*, 117–140.

Festinger, L. (1957). *A theory of cognitive dissonance*. Stanford: Stanford University Press.

Freedman, J. L., & Fraser, S. C. (1966). Compliance without pressure: The foot-in-the-door technique. *Journal of Personality and Social Psychology, 4*, 195–203.

Frenzen, J. R., & Davis, H. L. (1990). Purchasing behavior in embedded markets. *Journal of Consumer Research, 17*, 1–12.

Garner, R. (2005). Post-It Note persuasion: A sticky influence. *Journal of Consumer Psychology, 15*, 230–237.

Gintis, H., Bowles, S., Boyd, R., & Fehr, E. (2003). Explaining altruistic behavior in humans. *Evolution and Human Behavior, 24*, 153–172.

Goldstein, N. J., Cialdini, R. B., & Griskevicius, V. (2008). A room with a viewpoint: Using social norms to motivate environmental conservation in hotels. *Journal of Consumer Research, 35*, 472–482.

Goldstein, N. J., Griskevicius, V., & Cialdini, R. B. (2010). Reciprocity by Proxy: Harnessing the Power of Obligation to Foster Cooperation Submitted for publication.

Goldstein, N. J., Martin, S., & Cialdini, R. B. (2008). *Yes! 50 scientifically proven ways to be persuasive.* New York: Free Press.

Gonzales, M. H., Aronson, E., & Costanzo, M. (1988). Increasing the effectiveness of energy auditors: A field experiment. *Journal of Applied Social Psychology, 18,* 1046–1066.

Gordon, R. A. (1996). Impact of ingratiation on judgments and evaluations: a meta-analytic investigation. *Journal of Personality and Social Psychology, 71,* 54–70.

Gouldner, A. W. (1960). The norm of reciprocity: A preliminary statement. *American Sociological Review, 25,* 161–178.

Greenwald, A. F., Carnot, C. G., Beach, R., & Young, B. (1987). Increasing voting behavior by asking people if they expect to vote. *Journal of Applied Psychology, 72,* 315–318.

Griskevicius, V., Cialdini, R. B., & Goldstein, N. J. (2008). Applying (and resisting) peer influence. *MIT/Sloan Management Review, 49,* 84–88.

Griskevicius, V., Goldstein, N. J., Mortensen, C. R., Cialdini, R. B., & Kenrick, D. T. (2006). Going along versus going alone: When fundamental motives facilitate strategic (non)conformity. *Journal of Personality and Social Psychology, 91*(2), 281–294.

Griskevicius, V., Goldstein, N. J., Mortensen, C. R., Sundie, J. M., Cialdini, R. B., & Kenrick, D. T. (2009). Fear and loving in Las Vegas: Evolution, emotion, and persuasion. *Journal of Marketing Research, 46,* 384–395.

Gueguen, N., Pascual, A., & Dagot, L. (2002). Lowball and compliance to a request: An application in a field setting. *Psychological Reports, 91,* 81–84.

Harari, H., Mohdr, D., & Hosey, K. (1980). Faculty helpfulness to students: A comparison of compliance techniques. *Personality and Social Psychology Bulletin, 6,* 373–377.

Heider, F. (1958). *The psychology of interpersonal relations.* New York: Wiley.

Hobofoll, S. E. (2001). The influence of culture, community, and the nested-self in the stress process. *Applied Psychology: An International Review, 50,* 337–421.

Hofling, C. K., Brotzman, E., Dalrymple, S., Graves, N., & Pierce, C. M. (1966). An experimental study of nurse-physician relationships. *Journal of Nervous and Mental Disease, 143,* 171–180.

Hornstein, H. A., Fisch, E., & Holmes, M. (1968). Influence of a model's feeling about his behavior and his relevance as a comparison other on observers' helping behavior. *Journal of Personality and Social Psychology, 10,* 222–226.

Howard, D. J. (1990). The influence of verbal responses to common greetings on compliance behavior: The foot-in-the-mouth effect. *Journal of Applied Social Psychology, 20,* 1185–1196.

Howard, D. J., Gengler, C. E., & Jain, A. (1995). What's in a name? A complimentary means of persuasion. *Journal of Consumer Research, 22,* 200–211.

Howard, D. J., Gengler, C. E., & Jain, A. (1997). The name remembrance effect: A test of alternative explanations. *Journal of Social Behavior and Personality,12,* 801–810.

Jones, E. E., & Wortman, C. (1973). *Ingratiation: An attributional approach.* Morristown, NJ: General Learning Corp.

Jones, J. T., Pelham, B. W., Carvallo, M., & Mirenberg, M. C. (2004). How do I love three? Let me count the Js: Implicit egoism and interpersonal attraction. *Journal of Personality and Social Psychology, 87*, 665–683.

Joule, R. V. (1987). Tobacco deprivation: The foot-in-the-door technique versus the low-ball technique. *European Journal of Social Psychology, 17*, 361–365.

Joule, R. V., Gouilloux, F., & Weber, F. (1989). The lure: A new compliance procedure. *Journal of Social Psychology, 129*, 741–749.

Kelln, B. R. C., & Ellard, J. H. (1999). An equity theory analysis of the impact of forgiveness and retribution on transgressor compliance. *Personality and Social Psychology Bulletin, 25*, 864–872.

Kenrick, D. T., Griskevicius, V., Neuberg, S. L., & Schaller, M. (2010). Renovating the pyramid of needs: Contemporary extensions built upon ancient foundations. *Perspectives on Psychological Science.* In press.

Ketelaar, T. (1995). *Emotions as mental representations of gains and losses: Translating prospect theory into positive and negative affect.* Paper presented at the meeting of the American Psychological Society, New York.

Knishinsky, A. (1982). *The effects of scarcity of material and exclusivity of information on industrial buyer perceived risk in provoking a purchase decision.* Doctoral dissertation, Arizona State University, Tempe.

Langlois, J. H., Kalakanis, A., Rubenstein, A. J., Larson, A., Hallam, M., & Smoot, M. (2000). Maxims or myths of beauty: A meta-analytic and theoretical review. *Psychological Bulletin, 126*, 390–423.

Leakey, R., & Lewin, R. (1978). *People of the lake.* New York: Anchor Press.

Lefkowitz, M., Blake, R. R., & Mouton, J. S. (1955). Status factors in pedestrian violation of traffic signals. *Journal of Abnormal and Social Psychology, 51*, 704–706.

Lynn, M. (1991). Scarcity effects on value. *Psychology and Marketing, 8*, 43–57.

Lynn, M. (1992). Scarcity's enhancement of desirability. *Basic and Applied Social Psychology, 13*, 67–78.

Lynn, M., & Simons, T. (2000). Predictors of male and female servers' average tip earnings. *Journal of Applied Social Psychology, 30*, 241–252

Maddux, W. W., Mullen, E., & Galinsky, A. D. (2008). Chameleons bake bigger pies and take bigger pieces: Strategic behavioral mimicry facilitates negotiation outcomes. *Journal of Experimental Social Psychology, 44*(2), 461–468.

Mazis, M. B. (1975). Antipollution measures and psychological reactance theory: A field experiment. *Journal of Personality and Social Psychology, 31*, 654–666.

McCall, M. (1997). Physical attractiveness and access to alcohol: What is beautiful does not get carded. *Journal of Applied Social Psychology, 27*, 453–462.

McKensie, C. R. M., & Chase, V. M. (2010). Why rare things are precious: The importance of rarity in lay inference. In P. M. Todd, G. Gigerenzer, & The ABC Research

Group (Eds.), *Ecological rationality: Intelligence in the world.* Oxford, UK: Oxford University Press.

Milgram, S. (1974). *Obedience to authority.* New York: Harper & Row.

Milgram, S., Bickman, L., & Berkowitz, L. (1969). Note on the drawing power of crowds of different size. *Journal of Personality and Social Psychology, 13,* 79–82.

Miller, C. T. (1984). Self-schemas, gender, and social comparison: A clarification of the related attributes hypothesis. *Journal of Personality and Social Psychology, 46,* 1222–1229.

Newcomb, T. (1953). An approach to the study of communicative acts. *Psychological Review, 60,* 393–404.

Nolan, J. P., Schultz, P. W., Cialdini, R. B., Goldstein, N. J., & Griskevicius, V. (2008). Normative social influence is underdetected. *Personality and Social Psychology Bulletin, 34,* 913–923.

O'Keefe, D. J., & Hale, S. L. (1998). The door-in-the-face influence strategy: A random-effects meta-analytic review. In M. E. Roloff (Ed.), *Communication yearbook* (pp. 1–33). Thousand Oaks, CA: Sage.

O'Keefe D. J., & Hale S. L. (2001). An odds-ratio-based meta-analysis of research on the door-in-the-face influence strategy. *Communication Reports,14,* 31–38.

Oriña, M. M., Wood, W., & Simpson, J. A. (2002). Strategies of influence in close relationships.

Paolini, S., Hewstone, M., & Cairns, E., (2004). Effects of direct and indirect cross-group friendships on judgments of Catholics and Protestants in Northern Ireland: The mediating role of an anxiety-reduction mechanism. *Personality and Social Psychology Bulletin, 30,* 770-786.

Park, J. H., & Schaller, M. (2005). Does attitude similarity serve as a heuristic cue for kinship? Evidence of an implicit cognitive association. *Evolution and Human Behavior, 26,* 158–170.

Pelham, B. W., Mirenberg, M. C., & Jones, J. T. (2002). Why Susie sells seashells by the seashore: Implicit egoism and major life decisions. *Journal of Personality and Social Psychology, 82,* 469–487.

Phillips, D. P., & Carstensen, L. L. (1988). The effect of suicide stories on various demographic groups, 1968–1985. *Suicide and Life-Threatening Behavior, 18,* 100–114.

Pilluta, M. M., Malhotra, D., & Murnighan, K. (2003). Attributions of trust and the calculus of reciprocity. *Journal of Experimental Social Psychology, 39,* 448–455.

Platow, M. J., Haslam, S. A., Both, B., Chew, I., Cuddon, M., Goharpey, N., Maurer, J., Rosini, S., Tsekouras, A., & Grace, D. M. (2005). "It's not funny if *they're* laughing": Self-categorization, social influence, and responses to canned laughter. *Journal of Experimental Social Psychology, 41,* 542–550.

Pliner, P. H., Hart, H., Kohl, J., & Saari, D. (1974). Compliance without pressure: Some further data on the foot-in-the-door technique. *Journal of Experimental Social Psychology, 10,* 17–22.

Provine, R. (2000). *Laughter: A scientific investigation.* New York: Viking.

Rafaeli, A., & Sutton, R. I. (1991). Emotional contrast strategies as means of social influence. *Academy of Management Journal, 34*, 749–775.

Reeves, R. A., Macolini, R. M., & Martin, R. C. (1987). Legitimizing paltry contributions: On-the-spot vs. mail-in requests. *Journal of Applied Social Psychology, 17*, 731–738.

Regan, D. T. (1971). Effects of a favor and liking on compliance. *Journal of Experimental Social Psychology, 7*, 627–639.

Reingen, P. H. (1978). On inducing compliance with requests. *Journal of Consumer Research, 5*, 96–102.

Reingen, P. H. (1982). Test of a list procedure for inducing compliance with a request to donate money. *Journal of Applied Psychology, 67*, 110–118.

Ridley, M. (1997). *The origin of virtue.* London: Penguin Books.

Riley, D., & Eckenrode, J. (1986). Social ties: Subgroup differences in costs and benefits. *Journal of Personality and Social Psychology, 51*, 770–778.

Rosenbaum, M. E. (1980). Cooperation and competition. In P. B. Paulus (Ed.), *The psychology of group influence* (pp. 23–41). Hillsdale, NJ: Erlbaum.

Russo, J. E., Carlson, K. A., & Meloy, M. G. (2006). Choosing an inferior alternative. *Psychological Science, 17*, 899–904.

Schaller, M., Park, J. H., & Kenrick, D. T. (2007). Human evolution and social cognition. In R. I. M. Dunbar & L. Barrett (Eds.), *The Oxford handbook of evolutionary psychology*. Oxford, UK: Oxford University Press.

Schultz, P. W., Nolan, J. P., Cialdini, R. B., Goldstein, N. J., & Griskevicius, V. (2007). The constructive, destructive, and reconstructive power of social norms. *Psychological Science, 18*(5), 429–434.

Schwartzwald, J., Bizman, A., & Ray, M. (1983). The foot-in-the-door paradigm: Effects of request size on donation probability and donation generosity. *Personality and Social Psychology Bulletin, 9*, 443–450.

Sechrist, G. B., & Stangor, C. (2007). When are intergroup attitudes based on perceived consensus information? The role of group familiarity. *Social Influence, 2*, 211–235.

Sherman, S. J. (1980). On the self-erasing nature of errors of prediction. *Journal of Personality and Social Psychology, 39*, 211–221.

Singer, E., Van Hoewyk, J., & Maher, M. P. (2000). Experiments with incentives in telephone surveys. *Public Opinion Quarterly, 64*, 171–188.

Smolowe, J. (1990). Contents require immediate attention. *Time*, November 26, p. 64.

Stewart, J. E., II. (1980). Defendant's attractiveness as a factor in the outcome of trials. *Journal of Applied Social Psychology, 10*, 348–361.

Strohmetz, D. B., Rind, B., Fisher, R., & Lynn, M. (2002). Sweetening the till: The use of candy to increase restaurant tipping. *Journal of Applied Social Psychology, 32*, 300–309.

Suedfeld, P., Bochner, S., & Matas, C. (1971). Petitioner's attire and petition signing by peace demonstrators: A field experiment. *Journal of Applied Social Psychology, 1*, 278–283.

Sundie, J. M., Cialdini, R. B., Griskevicius, V., & Kenrick, D. T. (2006). In M. Schaller, J. A. Simpson, & D. T. Kenrick (Eds.), *Evolutionary social influence* (pp. 287–316). New York: Psychology Press.

Surowiecki, J. (2005). *The wisdom of crowds.* New York: Doubleday Press.

Thompson, L. L. (2009). *The heart and soul of the negotiator.* Upper Saddle River, NJ: Prentice Hall.

Tversky, A., & Kahneman, D. (1974). Judgment under uncertainty: Heuristics and biases. *Science, 185*, 1123–1131.

Tversky, A. & Kahneman, D. (1981). The framing of decisions and psychology of choice. *Science, 211*, 453-458.

Tybout, A. M., & Yalch, R. F. (1980). The effect of experience: A matter of salience? *Journal of Consumer Research, 6*, 406–413.

van Baaren, R. B., Holland, R. W., Steenaert, B., & van Knippenberg, A. (2003). Mimicry for money: Behavioral consequences of imitation. *Journal of Experimental Social Psychology, 39*, 393–398.

Vonk, R. (2002). Self-serving interpretations of flattery: why ingratiation works. *Journal of Personality and Social Psychology, 82*, 515–526.

Wedekind, C., & Milinski, M. (2000). Cooperation through image scoring in humans. *Science, 288*, 850–852.

West, S. G., (1975). Increasing the attractiveness of college cafeteria food. *Journal of Applied Psychology, 10*, 656–658.

Whatley, M.A., Webster, M.J., Smith, R.H., & Rhodes, A. (1999). The effect of a favor on public and private compliance: How internalized is the norm of reciprocity? *Basic and Applied Social Psychology, 21*, 251–259.

Worchel, S. (1992). Beyond a commodity theory analysis of censorship: When abundance and personalism enhance scarcity effects. *Basic and Applied Social Psychology, 13*, 79–93.

Worchel, S., Arnold, S. E., & Baker, M. (1975). The effect of censorship on attitude change: The influence of censor and communicator characteristics. *Journal of Applied Social Psychology, 5*, 222–239.

Zitek, E. M., & Hebl, M. R. (2007). The role of social norm clarity in the influenced expression of prejudice over time. *Journal of Experimental Social Psychology, 43*, 867–876.

Chapter 12

Attraction and Rejection

Eli J. Finkel and Roy F. Baumeister

Few experiences are more all-consuming than intense interpersonal attraction or intense interpersonal rejection. Most of us can readily remember attraction and rejection experiences that dominated our life for a while. Regarding attraction, perhaps we recall the mental preoccupation with our first love or the strong desire to form a friendship with a fellow collegiate dorm resident. Regarding rejection, perhaps we recall the time when we were ostracized by everybody at a party or the time when the love of our life left us for another partner. As these examples illustrate, attraction involves an individual's positive evaluation of others and the desire to approach them, whereas rejection involves others' negative evaluation of an individual and the tendency to exclude him or her. The present chapter reviews the scientific work on attraction and rejection, beginning with attraction.

Attraction

What Is Attraction?

Scholars have not arrived at a consensual definition of attraction. Perhaps the most influential definition over the past several decades is that interpersonal attraction is "an individual's tendency or predisposition to evaluate another person . . . in a positive (or negative) way" (Berscheid & Walster, 1978, p. 20). Scholars adopting this definition primarily conceptualize attraction as an attitude, with affective, behavioral, and cognitive components. Over time, scholars have increasingly complemented this attitudinal conceptualization by emphasizing the motivational aspects of attraction, observing that attraction characterizes not only perceivers' evaluations of targets, but also their desire to initiate contact or to establish intimacy with them (e.g., Simpson & Harris, 1994; see Graziano & Bruce, 2008).

Attraction scholars focus on relationships that are not (yet) close, although they also examine attraction-relevant processes conducted in close relationship contexts (e.g., research distinguishing strangers who become close friends from strangers who do not). We refer to the person who inspires attraction in somebody else as the "target" and the person who experiences attraction as the "perceiver." In reality, of course, both interactants are frequently in both of these roles simultaneously; we adopt this terminology for clarity of exposition. We discuss the history of research on interpersonal attraction and theoretical perspectives driving this research before reviewing the predictors of attraction.

Historical Perspective

We can roughly divide empirical research on attraction into four historical epochs: (1) pre-1960, (2) 1960s–1970s, (3) 1980–2005, and (4) 2005–present. Although social theory of human relations—including classic work on friendship (Aristotle, 330 BC/1991) and love (Capellanus, 1184/1960)—is millennia old, the pre-1960s epoch included only a few empirical studies of attraction. Notable among these were studies on assortive mating (Harris, 1912), social popularity (Moreno, 1934), relationship power (Waller, 1938), mate preferences (Hill, 1945), human sexuality (Kinsey, Pomeroy, & Martin, 1948; Kinsey, Pomeroy, Martin, & Gebhard, 1953), and the effects of physical proximity on attraction (Festinger, Schachter, & Back, 1950). These studies did not cohere into an organized field of inquiry, but they set the stage for social psychologists to pursue an intensive research emphasis on interpersonal attraction.

In the second epoch, approximately the 1960s and 1970s, research on attraction blossomed from a smattering of disparate findings to a major research area within social psychology. Newcomb (1961) and Byrne (1961) launched this epoch with landmark publications establishing the theoretical and methodological foundations for research linking similarity to attraction. Shortly thereafter, scholars investigated a broad range of attraction topics, including the effects of the target's physical attractiveness (Walster, Aronson, Abrahams, & Rottman, 1966; Huston, 1973), the effects of the perceiver's physiological arousal (Berscheid & Walster, 1974; Dutton & Aron, 1974), whether targets tend to reciprocate perceivers' attraction (Walster, Walster, Piliavin, & Schmidt, 1973), whether individuals who are "too perfect" are less likable than individuals who have benign imperfections (Aronson, Willerman, & Floyd, 1966), and whether perceivers are more attracted to targets who grow to like them over time than to targets who have liked them from the beginning (Aronson & Linder, 1965). Indeed, the empirical yield of attraction research was substantial enough to warrant a book entitled *Interpersonal Attraction*, which Berscheid and Walster first published in 1969 and revised in 1978.

In the third epoch, from approximately 1980 to 2005, "The field of interpersonal attraction, as an organized literature, largely faded into the background, supplanted but not replaced by a field called 'close relationships'" (Graziano & Bruce, 2008, p. 272; see Berscheid, 1985; Reis, 2007). For diverse reasons, including the skyrocketing divorce rates of the era, scholars became increasingly interested in understanding what makes established relationships, such as marriages and dating relationships, satisfying versus dissatisfying and stable versus unstable (see Fletcher & Overall, Chapter 13, this volume). Meanwhile, evolutionary psychology emerged as a new approach to studying interpersonal attraction and became influential in the absence of a coherent scholarly field of attraction (Buss, 1989; Buss & Schmitt, 1993; Gangestad & Simpson, 2000; see Maner & Kenrick, Chapter 17, this volume). Evolutionarily oriented psychologists have launched many new directions in attraction research, particularly regarding sex differences.

The fourth epoch, from approximately 2005 to the present, has witnessed a resurgence of interest in attraction research, as scholars have capitalized on technological and methodological advances in dating practices and social networking in the real world. For example, scholars have studied attraction through online dating (Fiore, Taylor, Mendelsohn, & Hearst, 2008; Hitsch, Hortaçsu, & Ariely, in press; Sprecher, Schwartz, Harvey, & Hatfield, 2008), speed-dating (Finkel, Eastwick, & Matthews, 2007; Fisman, Iyengar, Kamenica, & Simonson, 2006; Kurzban & Weeden, 2005), and social networking Web sites (McKenna, 2008; Tong, Van Der Heide, Langwell, & Walther, 2008; Walther, Van Der Heide, Kim, Westerman, & Tong, 2008). Interest in these technological and methodological advances has helped fuel a broader renaissance of research on attraction, with many current approaches addressed in the recent *Handbook of Relationship Initiation* (Sprecher, Wenzel, & Harvey, 2008).

Theoretical Perspectives

Despite the recent renaissance of attraction scholarship, the field remains a theoretical morass. Dozens of theories have guided research, and scholars have devoted little effort toward linking these far-flung theories into an integrated framework.

This theoretical disorganization notwithstanding, we can extract a few organizing themes (see Graziano & Bruce, 2008). In the 1960s and 1970s, a large proportion of attraction research fell into one (or both) of two broad theoretical traditions. The first encompassed *reinforcement theories*, which were guided by the idea that perceivers are attracted to targets who are rewarding to them. Attraction scholars working in this tradition borrowed ideas from general theories—such as social exchange theory (Blau, 1964; Homans, 1974), equity theory (Adams, 1965; Walster, Walster, & Berscheid, 1978), and interdependence theory (Kelley & Thibaut, 1978; Thibaut & Kelley, 1959)—and also developed more specific variants targeted toward attraction. According to one such theory, "liking for a person will result under those conditions in which an individual experiences *reward in the presence of that person*, regardless of the relationship between the other person and the rewarding event or state of affairs" (Lott & Lott, 1974, p. 172; emphasis in original; see also Byrne & Clore, 1970). Illustrative of research in this tradition is work demonstrating that perceivers in physically uncomfortable environments (e.g., hot or crowded rooms) are less attracted to strangers than are perceivers in more comfortable environments (Griffitt, 1970; Griffitt & Veitch, 1971).

The second broad theoretical tradition encompassed *cognitive consistency theories*, which were guided by the idea that perceivers are motivated to seek congruence among their thoughts, feelings, and interpersonal relationships. As with the reinforcement approach, scholars working in this tradition borrowed ideas from general theories—particularly cognitive dissonance theory (Festinger, 1957) and balance theory (Heider, 1958)—and also developed more specific variants targeted toward attraction. For example, not only do perceivers tend to like targets who like them, they also tend to like targets who share their own sentiments toward third parties (e.g., they like targets who dislike somebody they also dislike) (Aronson & Cope, 1968).

Although reinforcement and cognitive consistency theories have continued to influence attraction research, a number of additional theoretical perspectives have become influential in recent decades. Of these, the most influential has been *evolutionary psychology*, which David Buss and his collaborators introduced to study attraction dynamics in the mid-to-late 1980s (Buss, 1989; Buss & Barnes, 1986). Evolutionary psychology is guided by the idea that people's thoughts, feelings, and behaviors are influenced by evolved biological mechanisms (see Chapter 17, this volume). Scholars have derived a panoply of new attraction hypotheses from this evolutionary approach (e.g., Buss & Schmitt, 1993; Eastwick, 2009; Gangestad & Simpson, 2000), and many of these hypotheses have been empirically supported.

Additional theories that have influenced the study of attraction include attachment theory (Eastwick & Finkel, 2008b), reactance theory (Pennebaker et al., 1979), and communal-exchange theory (Clark & Mills, 1979). In addition, in the concluding chapter of the *Handbook of Relationship Initiation*, Perlman (2008) discusses a long list of perspectives addressed by authors in that volume, including theories of uncertainty reduction, information management, self-expansion, relationship goal pursuits, social penetration, dialectic processes, scripts, and gender.

Predictors of Attraction

We now explore the predictors of attraction: What makes a perceiver become attracted to a target? We divide this exploration into sections on (1) target factors, (2) perceiver factors, (3) relationship factors, and (4) environmental factors.

Target Factors: Who Is Attractive? Scholars have identified a broad range of factors that make some targets more attractive than others. Some of these target effects are stable individual differences, whereas others are situationally induced or time varying. In terms of stable individual differences, one of the most important and well-studied target factors is *physical attractiveness*. In one early demonstration of the power of physical attractiveness, college students attended an evening-long dance party with a randomly assigned partner they had not previously met (Walster et al., 1966). The *only* variable that predicted attraction was the target's physical attractiveness. Although scholars have now identified other target factors that promote attraction (see below), this early study established the target's physical attractiveness as a major predictor of perceivers' attraction, and decades of subsequent research have done little to soften this conclusion (Eastwick & Finkel, 2008a; Feingold, 1990; Langlois et al., 2000; Reis, Nezlek, & Wheeler, 1980).

At first glance, these results appear to contradict the robust finding that perceivers tend to become romantically involved with targets who are approximately equal to them in attractiveness (Berscheid, Dion, Walster, & Walster, 1971; White, 1980; see Feingold, 1988). However, this matching effect appears to be driven by perceivers desiring to date extremely attractive targets but settling for targets of comparable attractiveness to themselves because they typically cannot attract the most gorgeous targets (Burley, 1983; Huston, 1973; Kalick & Hamilton, 1986). This settling logic becomes especially plausible when we consider that there is widespread agreement about which targets are attractive. This agreement emerges not only across cultures (Cunningham, Roberts, Barbee, Druen, & Wu, 1995; Jones & Hill, 1993), but also when the perceivers are very young children (e.g., 3-month-old infants) whose attraction was assessed by recording how long they looked at attractive and unattractive faces (Langlois et al., 1987; also see Slater et al., 1998).

What characteristics make a target physically attractive? In terms of faces, targets are perceived as warm and friendly when they exhibit a large smile, dilated pupils, highly set eyebrows, full lips, and a confident posture (see Cunningham & Barbee, 2008). In addition, men tend to be attracted to women with sexually mature features such as prominent cheekbones, whereas women tend to be attracted to men with sexually mature features such as a broad jaw (Cunningham, Barbee, & Philhower, 2002; Rhodes, 2006). One clever line of research using computer morphing procedures to produce composite versions of human faces (see Fig. 12.1) demonstrated that such faces become more attractive when they consist of a larger number of human faces. One explanation for this effect is that such composites seem most familiar to the perceivers because they approximate an average of the targets perceivers have encountered in their everyday lives, which make the composites easy to process (Langlois, Roggman, & Musselman, 1994; Langlois, Roggman, & Rieser-Danner, 1990; Rhodes, Harwood, Yoshikawa, Nishitani, & MacLean, 2002; Rubenstein, Langlois, & Roggman, 2002). A second explanation is that such composites are symmetrical, a feature that perceivers find attractive in its own right (Fink, Neave, Manning, & Grammer, 2006; Mealey, Bridgstock, & Townsend, 1999; Rhodes, Sumich, & Byatt, 1999).

Moving from faces to bodies, men tend to be most attracted to women with waist-to-hip ratios of approximately 0.7, whereas women tend to be most attracted to men with waist-to-hip ratios of approximately 0.9 (Furnham, Petrides, & Constantinides, 2005; Singh, 1993, 1995, 2004). Men's waist-to-hip ratio preferences tend to be stronger than women's, although the degree to which men's preferences are cross-culturally universal has been challenged by recent evidence that men in less sexually egalitarian cultures such as Greece and Japan place more importance on women's waist-to-hip ratio than do men in more egalitarian cultures such as Great Britain and Denmark (Cashdan, 2008). Shocking recent evidence demonstrates that men also tend to prefer women with relatively large breasts, especially when they are accompanied by a relatively trim waist (Furnham, Swami, & Shah, 2006; Voracek & Fisher, 2006), and women seem to prefer men with broad shoulders, especially when they are accompanied by a relatively trim waist (Hughes & Gallup, 2003). Women also tend to prefer tall men over short men (Hitsch et al., in press; Salska et al., 2008).

In addition to their physical attractiveness, targets are more attractive to the extent that they possess certain *psychological dispositions*. Scholars have identified a broad range of target characteristics that are appealing to perceivers; three of the most important are warmth/trustworthiness, attractiveness/vitality, and

FIGURE 12.1. Composite male and female faces (on left of figure), along with photographs of the 16 individual faces incorporated into each composite. We thank faceresearch.org for supplying the composites and the photographs.

status/resources (Fletcher, Simpson, Thomas, & Giles, 1999; Simpson, Fletcher, & Campbell, 2001).

A third stable factor influencing how attractive targets are is the degree to which they anticipate that perceivers will like them or reject them (Curtis & Miller, 1986). Targets who anticipate that perceivers will like them behave more warmly during their interactions, which in turn predicts perceivers' liking for them (Stinson, Cameron, Wood, Gaucher, & Holmes, 2009).

Shifting from dispositional to situational factors, targets who are *familiar* are more attractive than targets who are not (but see Norton, Frost, & Ariely, 2007). In an early study (Hartley, 1946), research participants provided their impressions of various national groups, some of which were fictitious (e.g., Danerians). Participants generally disliked the unfamiliar groups, assuming they possessed unappealing characteristics. Similarly, research on the "mere exposure effect" (Zajonc, 1968, 2001) suggests that individuals tend to experience greater attraction toward familiar stimuli (including familiar people) than toward unfamiliar stimuli. This effect emerges in the absence of any other features frequently confounded with familiarity (e.g., quantity or quality of social contact) and without perceivers even being aware they have gained familiarity. In one study, female research assistants posed as students in a lecture course, attending 0, 5, 10, or 15 of the 40 lectures; these research assistants did not speak to the other students when attending the course (Moreland & Beach, 1992). The more classes the women attended, the more attractive students rated them to be.

Perceivers also tend to be more attracted to targets who *ingratiate* than to targets who do not, particularly when the ingratiation attempt is directed toward the perceiver rather than toward a third party observer (Gordon, 1996). This perceiver–observer discrepancy appears to result from perceivers' self-enhancement motives and is not moderated by perceivers' self-esteem (Vonk, 2002). In addition, perceivers tend to be more attracted (1) to targets who *self-disclose* to them than to targets who do not (Collins & Miller, 1994) and (2) to appealing (but not unappealing) targets who exhibit benign *pratfalls*, such as spilling coffee on themselves, than to appealing targets who do not (Aronson et al., 1966; see Deaux, 1972).

Finally, male perceivers tend to find female targets more attractive—in terms of both physical appearance (Roberts et al., 2004) and scent (Havlíček, Dvořáková, Bartoš, & Flegr, 2006; Singh & Bronstad, 2001)—when these targets are *ovulating* than when they are not. This effect could emerge in part because women dress better when they are ovulating than when they are not (Haselton & Gangestad, 2006; Haselton, Mortezaie, Pillsworth, Bleske-Rechek, & Frederick, 2007; Schwarz & Hassebrauck, 2008). However, the effect remains robust when clothing is held constant. A recent study of lap dancers working at "gentlemen's clubs" demonstrated that the dancers earned approximately $335 (U.S. currency) in tips throughout the evening from male customers when they were in the fertile phase of the menstrual cycle (when they were ovulating), $260 in the luteal phase (when they were neither ovulating nor menstruating), and $185 in the menstrual phase (Miller, Tybur, & Jordan, 2007). These effects were limited to women who were naturally cycling, which suggests that they were caused by hormonal shifts across the menstrual cycle. Women who were taking oral contraceptives earned less money than naturally cycling women who were ovulating did.

Perceiver Factors: Who Becomes Attracted? In addition to targets differing in how attractive they are, perceivers differ in their tendency to become attracted to targets. As with target effects, some of these perceiver effects are stable individual differences, whereas others are situationally induced or time varying. In terms of stable individual differences, *physically unattractive perceivers* tend to view targets as more attractive (Montoya, 2008) and tend to have lower standards for a potential partner (Buss & Shackelford, 2008) than physically attractive perceivers do, although some research suggests that physically unattractive perceivers merely lower their standards for whom they would date while still accurately assessing targets' attractiveness (Lee, Loewenstein, Ariely, Hong, & Young, 2008).

Similarly, perceivers with low *comparison standards* (low expectations regarding what they deserve or can get from a relationship) tend to view targets as more attractive than do perceivers with high comparison standards. Although individuals vary in the degree to which their comparison standards are stably high or low, a given individual's comparison standards can also fluctuate over time. In one study, for example, male participants rated a photographed female as less attractive after watching a television show depicting gorgeous women (*Charlie's Angels*) than after watching a television show that did not (Kenrick & Gutierres, 1980). A striking follow-up study showed that men who had just viewed *Playboy* centerfolds rated their wife as less attractive and even rated themselves as less in love with her than did men looking at magazines that did not depict beautiful women; these effects did not emerge for women's evaluations of their husband just after they had viewed *Playgirl* (Kenrick, Gutierres, & Goldberg, 1989).

Another individual difference variable influencing perceivers' tendencies to become attracted to targets is *perceiver sex*. At least in the romantic domain, men tend to experience greater attraction than women, especially when considering short-term involvements. For example, men were somewhat more likely than women (58% versus 48%) to accept a date from an opposite-sex research confederate who approached them on campus, and they were *much* more likely to accept an offer to go home with (63% versus 7%) or to "go to bed with" (71% versus 0%) the confederate (Clark, 1990; Clark & Hatfield, 1989). Several speed-dating studies have yielded compatible results, with men "yessing" a larger proportion of their partners than women (Fisman et al., 2006; Kurzban & Weeden, 2005; Todd, Penke, Fasolo, & Lenton, 2007; but see Finkel & Eastwick, 2009).

Shifting from dispositional to situational factors, perceivers can misattribute their *physiological arousal* from a nonromantic source to a romantic one (Berscheid & Walster, 1974; see Schachter & Singer, 1962). In a classic field study, an attractive female experimenter approached men immediately after they had walked across either a low, stable bridge or a high, swaying one (Dutton & Aron, 1974). The high bridge presumably inspired greater fear in most people than the low one did, and, consistent with the misattribution idea, the men who had walked across the high bridge exhibited greater romantic attraction to the experimenter than did the men who had walked across the latter one (also see Meston & Frohlich, 2003). Scholars have employed a range of arousal manipulations (e.g., fear, aerobic exercise, sexual arousal) to replicate this effect for physically attractive targets (see Foster, Witcher, Campbell, & Green, 1998). However, the effect reverses for unattractive targets, with physiologically aroused perceivers rating such targets as less attractive than physiologically unaroused perceivers do (Foster et al., 1998).

Additional situational variables that increase perceivers' attraction to targets include (1) perceivers being in a happy mood rather than a sad mood (Gouaux, 1971; Veitch & Griffitt, 1976); (2) perceivers experiencing fear caused by a noninterpersonal stimulus and believing that affiliating can reduce the impact of the stressor (Schachter, 1959; see Rofé, 1984); (3) perceivers' level of self-disclosure, with greater self-disclosure causing greater attraction to the target of the self-disclosure (Collins & Miller, 1994); (4) perceivers' level of alcohol consumption, with greater consumption predicting greater attraction (Jones, Jones, Thomas, & Piper, 2003; Parker, Penton-Voak, Attwood, & Munafò, 2008); (5) perceivers keeping the relationship secret (Wegner, Lane, & Dimitri, 1994); and (6) perceivers physically approaching targets rather than being physically approached by them (Finkel & Eastwick, 2009).

Relationship Factors: What Dyadic Characteristics Promote Attraction? Attraction is determined by more than just the characteristics of the target, on the one hand, and the characteristics of the perceiver, on the other. Many important predictors of attraction are dyadic, or relational, involving the interplay between the target's and the perceiver's characteristics. In this section, we review relational predictors relevant to the *attributes* of the target and the perceiver and the *interpersonal dynamics* emerging between them.

PERCEIVER × TARGET ATTRIBUTES In reviewing research on the link between the target's and the perceiver's attributes and attraction, we focus on the expansive literature investigating the link between similarity and attraction. As discussed, Newcomb and Byrne both published landmark studies on similarity and attraction in 1961. Newcomb (1961) randomly assigned University of Michigan transfer students to be roommates and discovered that the more similar the students were before moving in together, the more they liked each other by the end of the academic year. Byrne (1961) innovated a novel laboratory paradigm (his "bogus stranger" paradigm) to glean experimental evidence that perceivers are attracted to targets who are similar to them. A decade later, Byrne (1971) reviewed the extant literature, concluding that attraction is a linear function of attitudinal similarity: As the proportion of similar to dissimilar attitudes increases, so too does attraction to the target.

The similarity–attraction effect exists not only for attitudinal similarity (see also Griffitt & Veitch, 1974), but also for demographic similarity (Hitsch et al., in press; McPherson, Smith-Loving, & Cook, 2001; Watson et al., 2004), personality similarity (Gonzaga, Campos, & Bradbury, 2007), and, remarkably, even similarity in the letters in the perceiver and the target's names (Jones, Pelham, Carvallo, & Mirenberg, 2004). Furthermore, similarity effects are not limited to positive characteristics; antisocial individuals tend to be attracted to other antisocial individuals (Krueger, Moffitt, Caspi, Bleske, & Silva, 1998), and depressive individuals tend to be attracted to other depressive individuals (Locke & Horowitz, 1990).

Some scholars have argued that perceivers experience the strongest attraction to targets who are similar to the perceivers' "ideal self" (the person they aspire to become) rather than to the perceivers' actual self (LaPrelle, Hoyle, Insko, & Bernthal, 1990). Some evidence, however, suggests a boundary condition on perceivers' attraction to a target who is similar to their ideal self: Cognitive attraction increases as the target approaches and even exceeds the perceiver's ideal self, but affective attraction declines as the target exceeds perceiver's ideal self, most likely because such a target is threatening to perceivers (Herbst, Gaertner, & Insko, 2003).

Although the link between similarity and attraction is robust (for a meta-analytic review, see Montoya, Horton, & Kirchner, 2006), it is not universal. For example, abundant evidence suggests that complementarity on the dominance–submissiveness dimension predicts greater attraction than similarity on that dimension (Dryer & Horowitz, 1997; Markey & Markey, 2007; Tiedens & Fragale, 2003; see Winch, 1958).

PERCEIVER × TARGET INTERACTION DYNAMICS In addition to this research exploring the interplay between the perceiver's and the target's attributes, much research has also explored the interplay between the perceiver and the target's interaction dynamics. Perhaps the most extensively researched topic in this domain is *reciprocity of attraction*. Scholars have long demonstrated that perceivers tend to like targets who like them more than targets who do not (Backman & Secord, 1959; Curtis & Miller, 1986). Kenny and his colleagues have distinguished between two distinct forms of reciprocity: generalized and dyadic (Kenny, 1994; Kenny & Nasby, 1980; Kenny & La Voie, 1984). Whereas the *generalized reciprocity* correlation indexes the degree to which likers tend to be liked (i.e., whether perceivers who tend to like targets on average tend to be liked by those targets on average), the *dyadic reciprocity* correlation indexes the degree to which uniquely liking a given target more than other targets predicts being uniquely liked by that target in return (i.e., whether perceivers who selectively like certain targets more than others tend to be liked by those certain targets more than those targets like other people). One interesting feature of this work is that dyadic reciprocity effects tend to be positive in both platonic and romantic contexts (with perceivers who uniquely like or desire a target also being uniquely liked or desired by that target), whereas generalized reciprocity effects are positive in platonic contexts (with perceivers who generally like targets being liked by those targets) but negative in romantic contexts (with perceivers who generally desire targets not being desired by those targets) (Kenny, 1994; Eastwick, Finkel, Mochon, & Ariely, 2007; see Finkel & Eastwick, 2008).

A second line of research on the attraction-relevant effects of perceiver × target interaction dynamics involves *nonconscious mimicry*, which refers to unintentional behavioral synchrony between a perceiver and a target. Perceivers like targets who mimic them more than targets who do not (Chartrand & Bargh, 1999). People seem to have an unconscious intuition of this effect, as they tend to mimic others when they want to be liked (Cheng & Chartrand, 2003; Lakin & Chartrand, 2003; Lakin, Jefferis, Cheng, & Chartrand, 2003).

A third line of research involves *transference*, which refers to a cognitive process through which aspects of a perceiver's relationship with one target are automatically applied to the perceiver's relationship with another (Andersen, Reznik, & Manzella, 1996; see Freud, 1912/1958). In one study, perceivers became more attracted to targets who resembled positive than negative significant others in their life, an effect that was not due to the simple positivity or negativity of the targets' characteristics (Andersen et al., 1996).

A fourth line of research involves *instrumentality*, which refers to the degree to which perceivers find a given target useful in helping them progress in their current goal pursuits. Perceivers are more attracted to a target who is instrumental for a specific goal (but not to a target who is not) when that goal is currently active than when it is not (Fitzsimons & Shah, 2008). This preference for instrumental targets when a particular goal is relevant appears to be especially strong for perceivers with high power (Bargh, Raymond, Pryor, & Strack, 1995; Gruenfeld, Inesi, Magee, & Galinsky, 2008).

A fifth line of research involves *exchange and communal norms*, which refer to expectations that dyadic partners should give benefits contingently or noncontingently, respectively (see Clark, Lemay, Graham, Pataki, & Finkel, 2010). Perceivers are more attracted to a target who behaves in a manner consistent with the norm they prefer for that relationship. In a landmark experiment, male perceivers eager to follow an exchange norm with a female target were more attracted to her when she reciprocated a benefit they had provided than when she did not, whereas male perceivers eager to follow a communal norm were more attracted to her when she did not reciprocate their benefit than when she did (Clark & Mills, 1979).

Environmental Factors: What Situational Circumstances Promote Attraction? In addition to effects of the target, the perceiver, and their interaction, perceivers' attraction to targets is also influenced by environmental factors. In this section, we review attraction predictors emerging from the social *environment* and the *physical environment.*

THE SOCIAL ENVIRONMENT One aspect of the social environment that influences the degree to which perceivers are attracted to a given target is the degree to which the members of the perceivers' *social network* like or dislike that target. Early research on a phenomenon entitled "the Romeo and Juliet effect" built on the theory of psychological reactance (Brehm, 1966) to suggest that perceivers (e.g., teenagers) become increasingly attracted to a given target when members of their social network (e.g., parents) disapprove of the relationship (Driscoll, Davis, & Lipetz, 1972). Subsequent research, however, has failed to support this intriguing idea. Indeed, just the opposite is frequently the case: Perceivers experience greater attraction to a given target when members of their social network approve of the relationship (e.g., Sprecher & Felmlee, 1992), although some evidence suggests that the effect of perceivers' social networks on their relationship with a given target is stronger for female than for male perceivers (Leslie, Huston, & Johnson, 1986; Sprecher & Felmlee, 1992). Indeed, female perceivers appear to be more influenced than male perceivers by the opinions of others, even when these others are strangers (Graziano, Jensen-Campbell, Schebilske, & Lundgren, 1993).

A second aspect of the social environment that influences attraction pertains to *cultural norms*, which refer to widespread beliefs within certain cultural or historical contexts about who is attractive. For example, although women are more attracted than men to potential romantic partners who have good earning prospects and are older than themselves, and men are more attracted than women to potential romantic partners who are physically attractive and are younger than themselves (Buss, 1989), these sex differences are substantially weaker to the extent that the power imbalance between men and women within the culture is smaller (Eagly & Wood, 1999).

Another line of research also examines cross-cultural differences, although it does not examine cultural norms, per se. It links the amount of food that exists in a certain culture to men's preferences for women's body shapes. Males prefer heavier women to lighter women when food is in short supply, and they prefer lighter women to heavier women during times of plenty (Tovée, Swami, Furnham, & Mangalparsad, 2006). Evidence that such effects are due to hunger, rather than to some other factor confounded with food supplies, comes from recent studies demonstrating that men rated heavier women as more attractive when the men were entering the campus dining hall for dinner (when they were hungry) than when they were leaving after eating dinner (when they were satiated) (Nelson & Morrison, 2005; Swami & Tovée, 2006).

A third aspect of the social environment that influences attraction is *perceived scarcity*, which refers to perceivers' subjective experience that access to potential targets is dwindling. In a first demonstration of this effect, bar patrons reported on the physical attractiveness of opposite-sex patrons at 9:00 pm, 10:30 pm, and 12:00 am, with this last assessment shortly before the 12:30 am closing time (Pennebaker et al., 1979). Perceivers viewed the targets in the bar as increasingly attractive as closing time approached. Although one study failed to replicate this effect (Sprecher et al., 1984), several other studies have replicated it (e.g., Gladue & Delaney, 1990), especially for perceivers who were not currently in a relationship (Madey et al., 1996).

THE PHYSICAL ENVIRONMENT One of the most extensively researched aspects of the physical environment that predicts attraction is *proximity*, which refers to the degree to which the perceiver and target are close to rather than far from each other in physical space. A famous early demonstration of the power of proximity comes from a study of a campus housing complex at the Massachusetts Institute of Technology (Festinger et al., 1950). This study not only demonstrated that people are more likely to befriend others who live near them than those who do not, it also spoke to the large magnitude of the effect. For example, people were about twice as likely to become close friends with somebody who lived next door to them (approximately 20 feet away) than to somebody who lived two doors down (approximately 40 feet away). Although the proximity effect has been replicated many times (e.g., Ebbeson, Kjos, & Konečni, 1976; Latané, Liu, Nowak, Bonevento, & Zheng, 1995; Nahemow & Lawton, 1975; Segal, 1974), even in initial encounters (Back, Schmulke, & Egloff, 2008), proximity does not always lead to liking; indeed, people are also much more likely to be enemies with somebody who lives near them than with somebody who lives farther away (Ebbeson et al., 1976).

In addition to these robust effects of physical proximity, a broad range of environmental variables influences attraction by making the context of the social interaction pleasant as opposed to unpleasant. As mentioned previously, perceivers experience greater attraction to targets when interacting with them in a comfortable room than in a hot or crowded room (Griffitt, 1970; Griffitt & Veitch, 1971). The same goes for a number of additional environmental factors, including listening to pleasant or unpleasant music (May & Hamilton, 1980).

Rejection

We now turn from attraction to rejection. This shift in content is accompanied by a shift in the design variable. Attraction is typically studied as a dependent variable, whereas rejection is most commonly studied as an independent variable—that is, researchers mostly explore the *causes* of attraction but the *consequences* of rejection. We discuss rejection research methods and theoretical perspectives on rejection before reviewing the consequences of being rejected; we then discuss loneliness and explore why people are rejected.

Methods of Rejection Research

Rejection research emerged in a rather brief time, as several different strands converged to stimulate research. Baumeister and Leary's (1995) review article on the need to belong led them to begin to explore the consequences of having that need thwarted (which is what rejection does). Around the same time, Williams had begun to reflect on ostracism and to conduct some initial studies, later summarized in his 2002 book. Loneliness research had been going on for some time, but it also received a new boost around this time, especially in connection with work by Cacioppo and colleagues, later summarized in his 2008 book with Patrick.

As with almost any research topic, progress depends on having good methods. Multiple procedures have assisted researchers in exploring the effects of rejection, although most of them use stranger interactions and rejections (so we should be cautious in generalizing to cases of rejection by important, long-term relationship partners). In one method (e.g., Leary, Tambor, Terdal, & Downs, 1995; Nezlek, Kowalski, Leary, Blevins, & Holgate, 1997; Twenge, Baumeister, Tice, & Stucke, 2001), a group of strangers engages in a get-acquainted conversation and then is told that they will pair off for the next part. Each is asked to list two desired partners, and then everyone goes to a separate room. The experimenter visits each room and gives bogus feedback that everyone, or no one, has selected you as a desirable partner. Thus, rejection means being chosen by no one as a desirable partner.

In another procedure, people take a personality test by questionnaire and are given feedback that includes the ostensible prediction that you will end up alone in life (e.g., Twenge et al., 2001). In a third procedure, two participants exchange get-acquainted videos, and then the experimenter tells the participant that after seeing your video, the other person does not want to meet you (as opposed to saying the other person had to leave because of a dentist appointment) (e.g., DeWall, Baumeister, & Vohs, 2008). A fourth procedure asks people to recall or imagine experiences of rejection (e.g., DeWall & Baumeister, 2006).

The first study on ostracism sent the participant into a room with two confederates posing as participants (Williams & Sommer, 1997). All were instructed to remain silent. One confederate pretended to discover a ball and started tossing it to the others. In the control condition, all three threw the ball back and forth for several minutes. In the ostracism condition, the confederates briefly included the participant in the game and then gradually stopped throwing the ball to him or her. Later, a computerized version of this game called "Cyberball" was developed, and it has proven very popular as a convenient and inexpensive substitute for using live confederates (e.g., Eisenberger, Lieberman, & Williams, 2003; see also Van Beest & Williams, 2006).

Ostracism procedures may manipulate more than rejection. Williams (2001) has argued all along that ostracism thwarts not just the need to belong but also other needs, including desires for control and understanding (meaning). If so, ostracism procedures cannot be considered pure manipulations of social rejection, and their effects may or may not stem from the interpersonal rejection aspect. However, a recent meta-analysis found that at least some effects of ostracism were indistinguishable from those of other rejection manipulations (Blackhart, Knowles, Nelson, & Baumeister, 2009).

Loneliness is mostly studied as an individual difference measure, assessed by questionnaire. Several scales are available for measuring loneliness per se, including the UCLA Loneliness Scale (Russell et al., 1980). There are also scales to measure the degree of perceived social support.

General Theory

Approaches to rejection have generally been based on the assumption that people have a strong, basic drive to form and maintain social bonds. Most theories of personality and human nature have recognized this to some degree (e.g., Freud, 1930; Maslow, 1968). Recent assertions of the need to belong, such as that of Baumeister and Leary (1995), have not really discovered or posited a new motivation but rather have given it more prominence and primacy among motivations. Regardless, given that rejection thwarts this pervasive and powerful drive, it should be upsetting and disturbing to people, and it should set in motion other behaviors aimed at forming other bonds or strengthening the remaining ones.

A link to self-esteem has been proposed by Leary and colleagues (e.g., Leary, Tambor, Terdal, & Downs, 1995; also Leary & Baumeister, 2000).

Self-esteem is puzzling because people seem highly motivated to maintain and enhance self-esteem, yet high self-esteem has relatively few palpable advantages. Why do people care so much about something that has so little apparent benefit? Leary's answer is that self-esteem, albeit perhaps not important in and of itself, is closely tied to something that is important, namely belongingness. According to him, self-esteem functions as a sociometer—an inner gauge of our likelihood of having sufficient social ties. High self-esteem is generally associated with believing that you have traits that bring social acceptance, including likability, competence, attractiveness, and moral goodness. Hence rejection tends to reduce self-esteem, whereas acceptance increases it.

Thus, people seem designed by nature to want to connect with others. Some people may seem to like to be alone, but usually still desire to have a few friends and close relationships. (Even religious hermits typically maintain a close bond with at least one person who visits regularly and provides some companionship.) In prison, solitary confinement may seem a more attractive alternative than being with other prisoners and suffering the associated risks of assault and rape, but in fact solitary confinement is highly stressful and damaging (Rebman, 1999), and most prisoners seek to avoid it if they can.

People who are rejected or otherwise alone suffer more mental and physical health problems than other people (Baumeister & Leary, 1995). In some cases, it could be argued that the problems led to the rejection, but other cases make that seem implausible. Being alone is bad for the person. Indeed, mortality from all causes of death is significantly higher among people who are relatively alone in the world than among people with strong social ties (House, Landis, & Umberson, 1988). Lonely people take longer than others to recover from stress, illness, and injuries (Cacioppo & Hawkley, 2005). Even a cut on the finger, administered in a carefully controlled manner in a laboratory study, heals more slowly than normal in a lonely person.

Consequences of Rejection

We now explore the consequences of attraction: What happens to people who are rejected? We divide this exploration into sections on (1) behavioral consequences; (2) cognitive, motivational, and self-regulatory consequences; and (3) emotional consequences.

Behavioral Consequences Rejection produces strong effects on behavior. Many published studies report effects larger than a standard deviation, which is quite unusual for laboratory experiments in social psychology. Rejection studies produce large, significant effects. Most likely, the strong effects reflect the high motivational importance of belongingness.

The potential link between feeling rejected and turning violent gained national prominence from widely publicized episodes in which high school students brought guns to school and fired on classmates and teachers. A compilation and analysis of these cases indicated that most of the school shooters had felt rejected by their peers, and the feelings of rejection had fueled their violent tendencies (Leary, Kowalski, Smith, & Phillips, 2003). Laboratory experiments confirmed that participants who were randomly assigned to experience rejection by other participants became highly aggressive toward other participants, even toward innocent third parties who had not provoked them in any other way (Twenge, Baumeister, Tice, & Stucke, 2001). Only new persons who praised the rejected person were exempted from the aggressive treatment.

Parallel to the increase in aggression, rejected people show a broad decrease in prosocial behavior. In multiple studies, rejected people were less generous in donating money to worthy causes, less willing to do a favor that was asked of them, less likely to bend over and pick up spilled pencils, and less likely to cooperate with others on a laboratory game (the Prisoner's Dilemma) (Twenge, Baumeister, DeWall, Ciarocco, & Bartels, 2007).

Cognitive, Motivational, and Self-Regulatory Consequences The behavioral effects of rejection were puzzling in some ways. The underlying theory, after all, was that people are driven by a need to belong, and rejection thwarts that need, so rejected people should be trying even more to find new ways of connecting with others. Instead, they seemed to become unfriendly, aggressive, and uncooperative. Why?

Alongside the antisocial behaviors noted in the preceding section, some researchers have found signs that rejected people may become interested in forming new social bonds. They show heightened interest in other people's interpersonal activities. For example, Gardner, Pickett, and Brewer (2000) administered a laboratory rejection experience and then let participants read other people's diaries. The rejected persons showed relatively greater interest in the diary writers' social lives, such as going on a date or playing tennis with someone. Another investigation found that rejected persons were especially likely to seek and notice smiling faces (DeWall, Maner, & Rouby, 2009). For example, they were quicker than others to spot a smiling face in a crowd of faces, and they tended to look longer at smiling faces than neutral faces, relative to other participants.

Some actual signs of trying to form a new social connection were found by Maner, DeWall, Baumeister, and Schaller (2007). In these studies, rejected persons were more interested than others in joining a campus service to facilitate meeting people. They also bestowed more rewards on future interaction partners than other people did, possibly to get the person in a good mood.

None of these findings indicates that rejected persons rush off to make new friends. Rather, the findings suggest that they are cautiously interested in finding people who seem likely to accept them. Perhaps the best integration is to suggest that rejected people want to be accepted but also want to avoid being rejected again. They may want the other person to make the first move, and then they may respond positively. If others do not seem promising, the rejected people may be especially antisocial.

Ostracized people, too, seem quite positively responsive to friendly gestures and overtures by others (e.g., Williams & Zadro, 2005). For example, on an Asch conformity task, ostracized people conformed more (i.e., were more likely to give the wrong answer endorsed by other group members) than other participants (Williams, Cheung, & Choi, 2000). This could indicate that they hope to win friends by going along with the group.

Rejection appears to affect cognitive processes other than attention to friendliness. It seems to have a strong, though presumably temporary, effect on our intelligence. One series of studies found substantial drops in IQ scores among rejected persons (Baumeister, Twenge, & Nuss, 2002). Perhaps surprisingly, rejected people did quite well with simple intellectual tasks, being able to concentrate well enough to read a passage and answer questions about it correctly. But performance on more complicated mental tasks such as logical reasoning and extrapolation was seriously impaired. The implication is that rejection impairs controlled but not automatic processes.

However, an alternative explanation for a number of these findings is that rejected and ostracized people simply do not want to exert themselves. They may become passive and not bother putting forth the effort needed to think for themselves.

Self-regulation also appears to be impaired among rejected persons, and these findings reinforce the theory that rejected people do not want to bother. This line of work was stimulated in part by Cacioppo's observation that lonely people often have poor attention control (see Cacioppo & Patrick, 2008), as indicated by poor performance on dichotic listening. In a dichotic listening task the participant puts on headphones, and different voices are heard in different ears, so that the person must screen out one voice and focus on what the other one is saying. Rejected persons show similar deficits, and they also self-regulate poorly on other tests of self-control (Baumeister, DeWall, Ciarocco, & Twenge, 2005). However, they remain capable of performing perfectly well, for example, when a cash incentive is available for good performance.

These studies suggest that humans want to be accepted but recognize that they have to pay a price for belongingness, such as exerting themselves to self-regulate and behave properly. If they believe they are being rejected, they lose their willingness to pay that price and make those efforts. Hence they become passive, lazy, and uncooperative. But if they see an opportunity to be accepted again, they are quite capable of pulling themselves together and making the right efforts.

Emotional Consequences Rejection makes people feel bad. A literature review on anxiety concluded that the most common and widespread cause is being rejected or otherwise excluded from groups or relationships (Baumeister & Tice, 1990). Baumeister and Leary (1995) went so far as to suggest that a basic function of emotions is to promote interpersonal connection, insofar as most negative emotions have some link to threat or damage to relationships (think of grief, jealousy, anger, sadness, and anxiety), whereas any event that conveys social acceptance, such as forming or solidifying social bonds, typically results in positive emotion.

The link between rejection and emotion seemed obvious. As sometimes happens, however, the data did not cooperate. Some early studies of interpersonal rejection found no sign of changes in mood or emotion (e.g., Twenge et al., 2001). Even when emotional differences were found, they often failed to mediate the (often large) behavioral effects (e.g., Buckley, Winkel, & Leary, 2004; Williams et al., 2000). At first it was assumed that researchers had used the wrong scale or that participants simply refused to acknowledge their distress, but evidence with multiple measures continued to produce the same pattern.

At the same time, links to physical pain were emerging. A study of what people mean when they say their "feelings are hurt" found that hurt feelings essentially signify being rejected or excluded, or at least a step in that direction (Leary, Springer, Negel, Ansell, & Evans, 1998). In this case, whether the person intended to hurt you may be irrelevant. Rather, your hurt feelings depend on how much you value the relationship and how strongly you got the impression that the other person did not value it as much as you do (Leary, 2005). (Your feelings may be hurt when someone's actions imply not she does not value her relationship with you.) Brain scans indicated that similar brain sites were activated when people were rejected during the Cyberball game as were activated when people suffered physical pain (Eisenberger, Lieberman, & Williams, 2003).

Perhaps most remarkably, a review by MacDonald and Leary (2005) showed that being rejected often causes a feeling of numbness. The review mainly emphasized research with animals. For example, when rat pups are excluded from the litter, they develop some loss of sensitivity to physical pain (Kehoe & Blass, 1986; Naranjo & Fuentes, 1985; Spear, Enters, Aswad, & Louzan, 1985). This research pointed to something Panksepp had theorized decades earlier (Herman & Panksepp, 1978; Panksepp, Herman, Conner, Bishop, & Scott, 1978; Panksepp, Vilberg, Bean, Coy, & Kastin, 1978). When animals evolved to become social, they needed biological systems to respond to social events, and rather than developing entirely new systems in the body to deal with the social world, evolution piggybacked the social responses onto the already existing systems. Hence social rejection activated some of the same physiological responses as physical injury, just as Eisenberger et al. (2003) later showed.

Physical injury does not always cause maximum pain right away. A shock reaction often numbs the pain for a brief period. Possibly this developed so that an injured animal could make its way to safety without being distracted by intense pain. Regardless, the shock or numbness reaction offered a possible explanation for the lack of immediate emotion reported by many studies of rejection.

The links between rejection, emotion, and physical pain were explored most directly in a series of experiments by DeWall and Baumeister (2006). Consistent with the ideas of MacDonald and Leary (2005) and Panksepp (1998), rejected participants in those studies showed low sensitivity to pain: Rejected participants were slower than others to report that something hurt and slower to complain that it became intolerable. Moreover, the lack of sensitivity to pain correlated closely with a lack of self-reported emotional reaction to pain. This generalized to other emotional phenomena, such as feeling sympathy for someone experiencing misfortune.

A comprehensive review of the effects of rejection was provided in a meta-analysis by Blackhart et al. (2009). Their results showed conclusively that rejection does produce significant changes in emotion. The reason many researchers had failed to report significant results was that the effect was rather weak, and so the small to medium samples used in most studies lacked the statistical power to detect these. But when results from many studies were combined, it was clear that rejected people did feel worse than accepted ones—and even, though just barely, worse than neutral controls. Accepted people felt better than controls, though this effect, too, was weak.

Yet feeling worse does not necessarily mean feeling bad. When Blackhart et al. (2009) compiled data on just how bad people felt, it emerged that rejected people typically reported emotional states that were near the neutral point on the scale and, if anything, slightly on the positive side.

Does that mean rejection is not upsetting? Hardly. The laboratory studies examined one-time, immediate reactions to rejection experiences that mainly involve strangers. Being rejected repeatedly and by people you love may be more immediately upsetting. Even the neutral reactions in the laboratory studies are likely just temporary states, akin to how the body goes into shock right after an injury but feels considerable pain later on.

All of this has made for an intriguing mixture. In the next decade there will almost certainly be further advances in exploring the inner effects of rejection.

It appears that being rejected produces an immediate reaction that is not quite what anyone expected. There is a shift away from a positive mood and happy emotions toward a neutral state, but it is not entirely the same as the numbness of shock, either. Impaired emotional responsiveness appears to be one way of characterizing it. Most researchers assume that genuine distress does emerge at some point, but it has been surprisingly hard to get rejected people to say that they feel really bad right now. Meanwhile, the impairment of emotional responsiveness may prove a useful tool for researchers who wish to study the effects of emotion on other factors, such as judgment and cognition.

Loneliness

The laboratory studies of immediate reactions to carefully controlled rejection experiences can be augmented by studying people who feel rejected and socially excluded over a long period of time. The largest body of work on such effects concerns loneliness. Being left out of social relationships makes people lonely.

Recent work has begun to discredit the stereotype of lonely persons as social misfits or unattractive, socially inept losers. Lonely and nonlonely people are quite similar in most respects, including attractiveness, intelligence, and social skills. In fact, lonely people spend about the same amount of time as other people in social interaction (Cacioppo & Patrick, 2008). In general, then, loneliness is not a lack of contact with other people (Wheeler, Reis, & Nezlek, 1983). Rather, it seems to reflect a dissatisfaction with the quality of the interaction. Lonely people do spend time with others but they typically are not satisfied with those interactions, and they come away feeling that something important was lacking (Cacioppo & Hawkley, 2005). If rejection causes loneliness, then, it is not so much an explicit refusal to have anything to do with the person, but rather a more subtle refusal to provide the kind of close relationship and meaningful interactions that the person wants.

If there is one core characteristic that seems to produce loneliness, it is that lonely people are less emotionally empathic than other people (Pickett & Gardner, 2005). That is, they seem relatively deficient in their ability to understand other people's emotional states. Even with this finding, however, it is not yet fully clear what is cause and what is effect. Conceivably the difficulty in establishing an empathic connection with another person's emotions could be the result of loneliness rather than its cause.

Once we define loneliness as a lack of certain kinds of satisfying relationships, we can begin to ask what those relationships are. Marriage and family are obviously important bonds to many people, and married people are somewhat less likely than single people to be lonely (Peplau & Perlman, 1982; Russell,

Peplau, & Cutrona, 1980). The new mobility of modern life also takes its toll in terms of loneliness; people who move far from home for college or work are more likely to be lonely (Cacioppo et al., 2000).

For people with no close ties to romantic partners or best friends, what other sorts of bonds can reduce loneliness? For men but not women, feeling connected to a large organization reduces loneliness (Gardner et al., 2005). For example, men can feel a bond to their university, their employer, or even a sports team, and this helps prevent loneliness, but this does not work for women. The reason, very likely, is that the social inclinations of women tend to focus very heavily on close, intimate social connections. Men like those intimate relationships, but they are also oriented toward large groups and organizations (Baumeister & Sommer, 1997).

Some people even form pseudorelationships with celebrities or fictional characters such as people on television shows. Women who watch many situation comedies feel less lonely than other women, even when both have the same quantity of real friends and lovers (Kanazawa, 2002). Other people are able to reduce loneliness by feeling connected to nonhuman living things, such as a dog or even a plant.

If the causes of loneliness are only slowly becoming clear, its consequences seem better known, and they are not good (see Cacioppo & Patrick, 2008). By middle age, lonely people drink more alcohol than other people, exercise less, and eat less healthy food. They sleep as much as others but not as well. Their lives are no more stressful than other people's lives in any objective sense, but subjectively they feel more stress. They enjoy the good things in life less than other people, and they suffer more from the bad things.

Why Rejection Occurs

Why do people reject each other? There are many answers. Studies of rejection among children focus on three main things (e.g., Juvonen & Gross, 2005). The first is being aggressive. Children who do not want to risk being hurt avoid other children who are aggressive. This seems ironic in the context of what we noted above, namely that being rejected causes people to become more aggressive. Aggression is seen as incompatible with human social life, and so aggressive people are rejected, just as rejection fosters aggression.

A second reason is that isolation seems to breed more isolation. Some children tend to withdraw from others and keep to themselves, and other children respond to this by avoiding them all the more. This can create an unfortunate spiral leading to loneliness and many of the problems that go with it. Children may believe that the loner is rejecting them, and so they respond by rejecting the loner in return.

The third reason is deviance. The early part of this chapter showed that similarity leads to attraction. Dissimilarity leads to rejection. Children who are different are prone to be rejected by others. Regardless of whether they look different, talk differently, have an unusual family, or act in unusual ways, differentness invites rejection. Children at both extremes of intellectual ability are rejected, which again suggests that being different from the average or typical is enough to cause rejection.

Marrying one person may necessitate rejecting others. But which ones? A seemingly simple answer is that people reject others who do not measure up to their standards and expectations. As previously confirmed, although most people are attracted to desirable partners, they pair off with partners whose attributes, including intelligence and looks, are similar to theirs. In short, you may fall in love with a fabulous, gorgeous, wealthy person, but unless you are equally fabulous (and gorgeous and wealthy), that person will reject you, leaving you disappointed. The process may be repeated until you find someone who is about your equal. Baumeister and Wotman (1992) labeled the process "falling upward": you fall for people better than you, which leads to romantic disappointment.

A disturbing implication of falling upward is that the people who reject you must somehow be better than you. This is only partly accurate. To be sure, the more desirable partner in most mismatches rejects the less desirable one. Moreover, the first reaction to being rejected is often to view it as a negative assessment of your romantic appeal: "What's wrong with me?" But there are many sources of slippage. For one thing, most people overvalue how attractive they are, so the person who rejects you may not be objectively better—he or she merely regards himself or herself as better. For another, local variations in sex ratio change people's relative attractiveness (Guttentag & Secord, 1983). During or after a major war, for example, there is often a shortage of men at home, and the women must settle for partners far less desirable than they would otherwise expect. Furthermore, many capricious factors can influence attraction (Lykken & Tellegen, 1993). The fact that you smell a bit like someone's mother or talk like someone's ex-partner could be enough to make that person reject you, even if you are fabulous in other respects (Andersen et al., 1996).

An early study on romantic rejection by Folkes (1982) explored women's reasons for refusing a date with a man. The reasons the women told the researchers were not, however, the reasons they reported telling the men. They differed along all three of the major dimensions of attribution theory (Kelley, 1967; see Carlston, Chapter 3, this volume). The reasons they gave to the man who asked them out tended to be unstable, external (to the man), and specific, whereas their actual reasons tended to be stable, internal, and global. For example, she might say she was busy that particular night. Such an excuse is unstable (it applies to only that night; tomorrow might be different), external (it has nothing to do with him), and specific (it is one narrow issue). In reality, she might decline the invitation because she finds him unattractive (which is a permanent, general aspect of him).

Romantic rejection sometimes involves more than declining a date. One person may have developed strong romantic feelings toward the other, who does not feel the same way. This is called *unrequited love*. Studies indicate that the two roles have very different experiences (e.g., Baumeister, Wotman, & Stillwell, 1993; Hill, Blakemore, & Drumm, 1997). Rejecters often have a difficult time refusing love that they really do not want. They feel guilty, so they make excuses or avoid the other person rather than clearly stating the reasons for refusing the other's advances. They do not want to hurt the other person's feelings—and as we saw earlier, hurt feelings are a response to discovering that the other person does not desire or value a connection with you to the extent that you want. Sure enough, unrequited love often precipitates feelings of low self-esteem and self-doubt among the rejected persons.

In general, rejection may not be inevitable, but it can still serve important social goals. The fact that people reject those who are different suggests a basic drive to keep the social group full of people who are alike. Like children, adults reject people who are different from them (Wright et al., 1986). They have a more negative reaction to deviance among members of their group than among outsiders (Hogg, 2005). Indeed, given exactly the same amount of deviance, groups reject insiders more than outsiders (Marques & Yzerbyt, 1988). Even just performing badly at a task is more troubling, and hence more likely to cause rejection, when it is by a member of the group than by someone outside the group (Marques & Paez, 1994; Marques, Abrams, & Serôdio, 2001). To be sure, it works both ways: Good performance by ingroup members is appreciated and rewarded more than equally good performance by someone outside the group.

Thus, it seems that people want their groups to be homogeneous, and they reject members of the group who seem different or who act differently. Although diversity has many benefits, people still seem to feel and act as if it is best to have a group of people who are fundamentally similar. Rejection can thus be a way of strengthening the group by eliminating people who seem not to fit. People understand this and therefore may try harder to conform to the group to avoid being rejected. Even the threat of being rejected is often enough to make people behave in ways that benefit the group (Kerr et al., 2009).

Thus, rejection can serve a valuable function in solidifying the group in two ways. It gets rid of people who do not fit in or who otherwise detract from the group. And it motivates the people in the group to behave properly, cooperate with others, and contribute to the group, so that they will not be rejected.

Attraction and Rejection Today

Attraction research has ebbed and flowed over the past 50 years, whereas rejection research, which rose to prominence over the past 15 years, has received a steady stream of attention. Despite these different historical trajectories, both areas of research are currently flourishing. Attraction research has become increasingly influential and interdisciplinary in recent years as its interface with technology and with big business has grown. For example, economists have recently employed speed-dating (Fisman et al., 2006) and online dating (Hitsch et al., in press) procedures to understand mate selection processes, and communications researchers have examined behavior on social networking Web sites (e.g., Facebook) to examine diverse aspects of interpersonal attraction (Tong et al., 2008; Walther et al., 2008). Rejection research has benefited from a broad array of methodological innovations and a recent foray into applying emerging theory to real-world cases of rejection, including the application to school shootings (Leary et al., 2003).

As we look to the next decade, attraction research would benefit from greater theoretical integration, and rejection research would benefit from a greater emphasis on rejection in close, long-term relationships (and perhaps from integration with relationships research on topics such as betrayal and breakup). Given the flurry of attention being paid to both topics, we anticipate that scholars will make major strides toward addressing these limitations—and toward extending these research topics in exciting new directions.

Acknowledgments

The authors thank Paul Eastwick, Gráinne Fitzsimons, and Sue Sprecher for their insightful comments on a draft of this chapter.

References

Adams, J. S. (1965). Inequity in social exchange. In L. Berkowitz (Ed.), *Advances in experimental social psychology* (Vol. 2, pp. 266–300). New York: Academic Press.

Andersen, S. M., Reznik, I., & Manzella, L. M. (1996). Eliciting facial affect, motivation, and expectancies in transference: Significant-other representations in social relations. *Journal of Personality and Social Psychology*, *71*, 1108–1129.

Aristotle (330 BC/1991). Rhetoric (II.4). In M. Pakaluk (Ed.), *Other selves: Philosophers on friendship* (pp. 72–76). Indianapolis, IN: Hackett.

Aronson, E., & Cope, V. (1968). My enemy's enemy is my friend. *Journal of Personality & Social Psychology, 8*, 8–12.

Aronson, E., & Linder, D. (1965). Gain and loss of esteem as determinants of interpersonal attractiveness. *Journal of Experimental Social Psychology, 1*, 156–172.

Aronson, E., Willerman, B., & Floyd, J. (1966). The effect of a pratfall on increasing interpersonal attractiveness. *Psychonomic Science, 4*, 227–228.

Back, M. D., Schmulke, S. C., & Egloff, B. (2008). Becoming friends by chance. *Psychological Science, 19*, 439–440.

Backman, C. W., & Secord, P. F. (1959). The effect of perceived liking on interpersonal attraction. *Human Relations, 12*, 379–384.

Bargh, J. A., Raymond, P., Pryor, J. B., & Strack, F. (1995). Attractiveness of the underling: An automatic power–sex association and its consequences for sexual harassment and aggression. *Journal of Personality and Social Psychology, 68*, 768–781.

Baumeister, R. F., DeWall, C. N., Ciarocco, N. J., & Twenge, J. M. (2005). Social exclusion impairs self-regulation. *Journal of Personality and Social Psychology, 88*, 589–604.

Baumeister, R. F., & Leary, M. R. (1995). The need to belong: Desire for interpersonal attachments as a fundamental human motivation. *Psychological Bulletin, 117*, 497–529.

Baumeister, R. F., & Sommer, K. L. (1997). What do men want? Gender differences and two spheres of belongingness: Comment on Cross and Madson (1997). *Psychological Bulletin, 122*, 38–44.

Baumeister, R. F., & Tice, D. M. (1990). Anxiety and social exclusion. *Journal of Social and Clinical Psychology, 9*, 165–195.

Baumeister, R. F., Twenge, J. M., & Nuss, C. (2002). Effects of social exclusion on cognitive processes: Anticipated aloneness reduces intelligent thought. *Journal of Personality and Social Psychology, 83*, 817–827.

Baumeister, R. F., & Wotman, S. R. (1992). *Breaking hearts: The two sides of unrequited love*. New York: Guilford Press.

Baumeister, R. F., Wotman, S. R., & Stillwell, A. M. (1993). Unrequited love: On heartbreak, anger, guilt, scriptlessness, and humiliation. *Journal of Personality and Social Psychology, 64*, 377–394.

Berscheid, E. (1985). Interpersonal attraction. In G. Lindzey & E. Aronson (Eds.), *The handbook of social psychology* (3rd ed., Vol. 2, pp. 413–484). New York: Random House.

Berscheid, E., Dion, K. K., Walster, E., & Walster, G. W. (1971). Physical attractiveness and dating choice: A test of the matching hypothesis. *Journal of Experimental Social Psychology, 7*, 173–189.

Berscheid, E., & Walster, E. (1969/1978). *Interpersonal attraction*. Reading, MA: Addison-Wesley.

Berscheid, E., & Walster, E. (1974). A little bit about love. In T. Huston (Ed.), *Foundations of interpersonal attraction* (pp. 355–381). New York: Academic Press.

Blackhart, G. C., Knowles, M. L., Nelson, B. C., & Baumeister, R. F. (2009). Rejection elicits emotional reactions but neither causes immediate distress nor lowers self-esteem: A meta-analytic review of 192 studies on social exclusion. *Personality and Social Psychology Review, 13,* 269–309.

Blau, P. M. (1964). *Exchange and power in social life.* New York: Wiley.

Brehm, J. W. (1966). *A theory of psychological reactance.* New York: Academic Press.

Buckley, K. E., Winkel, R. E., & Leary, M. R. (2004). Emotional and behavioral responses to interpersonal rejection: Anger, sadness, hurt, and aggression. *Journal of Experimental Social Psychology, 40,* 14–28.

Burley, N. (1983). The meaning of assortative mating. *Ethology and Sociobiology, 4,* 191–203.

Buss, D. M. (1989). Sex differences in human mate preferences: Evolutionary hypotheses tested in 37 cultures. *Behavioral and Brain Sciences, 12,* 1–49.

Buss, D. M., & Barnes, M. L. (1986). Preferences in human mate selection. *Journal of Personality and Social Psychology, 50,* 559–570.

Buss, D. M., & Schmitt, D. P. (1993). Sexual strategies theory: An evolutionary perspective on human mating. *Psychological Review, 100,* 204–232.

Buss, D. M., & Shackelford, T. K. (2008). Attractive women want it all: Good genes, economic investment, parenting proclivities, and emotional commitment. *Evolutionary Psychology, 6,* 134–146.

Byrne, D. (1961). Interpersonal attraction and attitude similarity. *Journal of Abnormal and Social Psychology, 62,* 713–715.

Byrne, D. (1971). *The attraction paradigm.* New York: Academic Press.

Byrne, D., & Clore, G. L. (1970). A reinforcement-affect model of evaluative responses. *Personality: An International Journal, 1,* 103–128.

Cacioppo, J. T., Ernst, J. M., Burleson, M. H., McClintock, M. K., Malarkey, W. B., Hawkley, L. C., Kowalewski, R. B., Paulsen, A., Hobson, J. A., Hugdahl, K., Spiegel, D., Berntson, G. G. (2000). Lonely traits and concomitant physiological processes: The MacArthur Social Neuroscience Studies. *International Journal of Psychophysiology, 35,* 143–154.

Cacioppo, J. T., & Hawkley, L. C. (2005). People thinking about people: The vicious cycle of being a social outcast in one's own mind. In K. D. Williams, J. P. Forgas, & W. von Hippel (Eds.), *The social outcast: Ostracism, social exclusion, rejection, and bullying.* New York: Psychology Press.

Cacioppo, J. T., & Patrick, W. (2008). *Loneliness: Human nature and the need for social connection.* New York: Norton.

Capellanus, A. (1184/1960). *The art of courtly love.* (J. J. Parry, Trans.). New York: Columbia University Press.

Cashdan, E. (2008). Waist-to-hip ratio across cultures: Trade-offs between androgen- and estrogen-dependent traits. *Current Anthropology, 49*, 1099–1107.

Chartrand, T. L., & Bargh, J. A. (1999). The chameleon effect: The perception-behavior link and social interaction. *Journal of Personality and Social Psychology, 76*, 893–910.

Cheng, C. M., & Chartrand, T. L. (2003). Self-monitoring without awareness: Using mimicry as a nonconscious affiliation strategy. *Journal of Personality and Social Psychology, 85*, 1170–1179.

Clark, M. S., Lemay, E. P., Graham, S. M., Pataki, S. P., & Finkel, E. J. (2010). Ways of giving and receiving benefits in marriage: Norm use and attachment related variability. *Psychological Science*. In press.

Clark, M. S., & Mills, J. (1979). Interpersonal attraction in exchange and communal relationships. *Journal of Personality and Social Psychology, 37*, 12–24.

Clark, R. D. III. (1990). The impact of AIDS on gender differences in the willingness to engage in casual sex. *Journal of Applied Social Psychology, 20*, 771–782.

Clark, R. D. III, & Hatfield, E. (1989). Gender differences in receptivity to sexual offers. *Journal of Psychology and Human Sexuality, 2*, 39–55.

Collins, N. L., & Miller, L. C. (1994). Self-disclosure and liking: A meta-analytic review. *Psychological Bulletin, 116*, 457–475.

Cunningham, M. R., & Barbee, A. P. (2008). Prelude to a kiss: Nonverbal flirting, opening gambits, and other communication dynamics in the initiation of romantic relationships. In S. Sprecher, A. Wenzel, & J. Harvey (Eds.), *Handbook of relationship initiation* (pp. 97–120). New York: Psychology Press.

Cunningham, M. R., Barbee, A. P., & Philhower, C. L. (2002). Dimensions of facial physical attractiveness: The intersection of biology and culture. In G. Rhodes & L. A. Zebrowitz (Eds.), *Facial attractiveness: Evolutionary, cognitive, and social perspectives* (pp. 193–238). Westport, CT: Ablex.

Cunningham, M. R., Roberts, A. R., Barbee, A. P., Druen, P. B., & Wu, C. (1995). "Their ideas of beauty are, on the whole, the same as ours": Consistency and variability in the cross-cultural perception of female physical attractiveness. *Journal of Personality and Social Psychology, 68*, 261–279.

Curtis, R. C., & Miller, K. (1986). Believing another likes or dislikes you: Behaviors making the beliefs come true. *Journal of Personality and Social Psychology, 51*, 284–290.

Deaux, K. (1972). To err is humanizing: But sex makes a difference. *Representative Research in Social Psychology, 3*, 20–28.

DeWall, C. N., & Baumeister, R. F. (2006). Alone but feeling no pain: Effects of social exclusion on physical pain tolerance and pain threshold, affective forecasting, and interpersonal empathy. *Journal of Personality and Social Psychology, 91*, 1–15.

DeWall, C. N., Baumeister, R. F., & Vohs, K. D. (2008). Satiated with belongingness? Effects of acceptance, rejection, and task framing on self-regulatory performance. *Journal of Personality and Social Psychology, 95*, 1367–1382.

DeWall, C. N., Maner, J. K., & Rouby, D. A. (2009). Social exclusion and early-stage interpersonal perception: Selective attention to signs of acceptance. *Journal of Personality and Social Psychology, 96*, 729–741.

Driscoll, R., Davis, K. E., & Lipetz, M. E. (1972). Parental interference and romantic love: The Romeo and Juliet effect. *Journal of Personality and Social Psychology, 24*, 1–10.

Dryer, D.C., & Horowitz, L. M. (1997). When do opposites attract? Interpersonal complementarity versus similarity. *Journal of Personality and Social Psychology, 72*, 592–603.

Dutton, D. G., & Aron, A. P. (1974). Some evidence for heightened sexual attraction under conditions of high anxiety. *Journal of Personality and Social Psychology, 30*, 510–517.

Eagly, A. H., & Wood, W. (1999). The origins of sex differences in human behavior. *American Psychologist, 54*, 408–423.

Eastwick, P. W. (2009). Beyond the Pleistocene: Using phylogeny and constraint to inform the evolutionary psychology of human mating. *Psychological Bulletin, 135*, 794–821.

Eastwick, P. W., & Finkel, E. J. (2008a). Sex differences in mate preferences revisited: Do people know what they initially desire in a romantic partner? *Journal of Personality and Social Psychology, 94*, 245–264.

Eastwick, P. W., & Finkel, E. J. (2008b). The attachment system in fledgling relationships: An activating role for attachment anxiety. *Journal of Personality and Social Psychology, 95*, 628–647.

Eastwick, P. W., Finkel, E. J., Mochon, D., & Ariely, D. (2007). Selective versus unselective romantic desire: Not all reciprocity is created equal. *Psychological Science, 18*, 317–319.

Ebbeson, E. B., Kjos, G. L., & Konečni, V. J. (1976). Spatial ecology: Its effects on the choice of friends and enemies. *Journal of Experimental Social Psychology, 12*, 505–518.

Eisenberger, N. I., Lieberman, M. D., & Williams, K. D. (2003). Does rejection hurt? An fMRI study of social exclusion. *Science, 302*, 290–292.

Feingold, A. (1988). Matching for attractiveness in romantic partners and same-sex friends: A meta-analysis and theoretical critique. *Psychological Bulletin, 104*, 226–235.

Feingold, A. (1990). Gender differences in effects of physical attractiveness on romantic attraction: A comparison across five research paradigms. *Journal of Personality and Social Psychology, 59*, 981–993.

Festinger, L. (1957). *A theory of cognitive dissonance*. Evanston, IL: Row, Peterson.

Festinger, L., Schachter, S., & Back, K. (1950). *Social pressures in informal groups: A study of human factors in housing*. Stanford, CA: Stanford University Press.

Fink, B., Neave, N., Manning, J. T., & Grammer, K. (2006). Facial symmetry and judgements of attractiveness, health and personality. *Personality and Individual Differences, 41*, 491–499.

Finkel, E. J., & Eastwick, P. W. (2008). Speed-dating. *Current Directions in Psychological Science, 17*, 193–197.

Finkel, E. J., & Eastwick, P. W. (2009). Arbitrary social norms and sex differences in romantic selectivity. *Psychological Science, 20*, 1290–1295.

Finkel, E. J., Eastwick, P. W., & Matthews, J. (2007). Speed-dating as an invaluable tool for studying romantic attraction: A methodological primer. *Personal Relationships, 14*, 149–166.

Fiore, A. T., Taylor, L. S., Mendelsohn, G. A., & Hearst M. (2008). Assessing attractiveness in online dating profiles. In *Proceedings of Computer-Human Interaction 2008* (pp. 797–806). New York: ACM Press.

Fisman, R., Iyengar, S. S., Kamenica, E., & Simonson, I. (2006). Gender differences in mate selection: Evidence from a speed dating experiment. *Quarterly Journal of Economics, 121*, 673–697.

Fitzsimons, G. M., & Shah, J. Y. (2008). How instrumentality shapes relationship evaluations. *Journal of Personality and Social Psychology, 95*, 319–337.

Fletcher, G. J. O., Simpson, J. A., Thomas, G., & Giles, L. (1999). Ideal in intimate relationships. *Journal of Personality and Social Psychology, 76*, 72–89.

Folkes, V. S. (1982). Communicating the reasons for social rejection. *Journal of Experimental Social Psychology, 18*, 235–252.

Foster, C. A., Witcher, B. S., Campbell, W. K., & Green, J. D. (1998). Arousal and attraction: Evidence for automatic and controlled processes. *Journal of Personality and Social Psychology, 74*, 86–101.

Freud, S. (1912/1958). The dynamics of transference. In J. Strachey (Ed., and trans.), *The standard edition of the complete psychological works of Sigmund Freud* (Vol. 12, pp. 97–108). London: Hogarth Press.

Freud, S. (1930) *Civilization and its discontents.* (J. Riviere, trans.). London: Hogarth Press.

Furnham, A., Petrides, K. V., & Constantinides, A. (2005). The effects of body mass index and waist-to-hip ratio on ratings of female attractiveness, fecundity, and health. *Personality and Individual Differences, 38*, 1823–1834.

Furnham, A., Swami, V., & Shah, K. (2006). Body weight, waist-to-hip ratio and breast size correlates of ratings of attractiveness and health. *Personality and Individual Differences, 41*, 443–454.

Gangestad, S. W., & Simpson, J. A. (2000). The evolution of human mating: Trade-offs and strategic pluralism. *Behavioral and Brain Sciences, 23*, 573–644.

Gardner, W. L., Pickett, C. L., & Brewer, M. B. (2000). Social exclusion and selective memory: How the need to belong influences memory for social events. *Personality and Social Psychology Bulletin, 26*, 486–496.

Gardner, W. L., Pickett, C. L., & Knowles, M. (2005). Social snacking and shielding Using social symbols, selves, and surrogates in the service of belonging needs. In K. D. Williams, J. P. Forgas, & W. von Hippel (Eds.), *The social outcast: Ostracism, social exclusion, rejection, and bullying*. New York: Psychology Press.

Gladue, B. A., & Delaney, H. (1990). Gender differences in perception of attractiveness of men and women in bars. *Personality and Social Psychology Bulletin, 16*, 378–391.

Gonzaga, G. C., Campos, B., & Bradbury, T. (2007). Similarity, convergence, and relationship satisfaction in dating and married couples. *Journal of Personality and Social Psychology, 93*, 34–48.

Gordon, R. A. (1996). Impact of ingratiation on judgments and evaluations: A meta-analytic investigation. *Journal of Personality and Social Psychology, 71*, 54–70.

Gouaux, C. (1971). Induced affective states and interpersonal attraction. *Journal of Personality and Social Psychology, 20*, 37–43.

Graziano, W. G., & Bruce, J. W. (2008). Attraction and the initiation of relationships: A review of the empirical literature. In S. Sprecher, A. Wenzel, & J. Harvey (Eds.), *Handbook of relationship initiation* (pp. 269–295). New York: Guilford Press.

Graziano, W. G., Jensen-Campbell, L. A., Shebilske, L. J., Lundgren, S. R. (1993). Social influence, sex differences, and judgments of beauty: Putting the *interpersonal* back in interpersonal attraction. *Journal of Personality and Social Psychology, 63*, 522–531.

Griffitt, W. (1970). Environmental effects on interpersonal affective behavior: Ambient effective temperature and attraction. *Journal of Personality and Social Psychology, 15*, 240–244.

Griffitt, W., & Veitch, R. (1971). Hot and crowded: Influences of population density and temperature on interpersonal affective behavior. *Journal of Personality and Social Psychology, 17*, 92–98.

Griffitt, W., & Veitch, R. (1974). Preacquaintance attitude similarity and attraction revisited: Ten days in a fall-out shelter. *Sociometry, 37*, 163–173.

Gruenfeld, D. H., Inesi, M. E., Magee, J. C., & Galinsky, A. D. (2008). Power and the objectification of social targets. *Journal of Personality and Social Psychology, 95*, 111–127.

Guttentag, M., & Secord, P. F. (1983). *Too many women? The sex ratio question*. Beverly Hills, CA: Sage.

Harris, J. A. (1912). Assortive mating in man. *Popular Science Monthly, 80*, 476–492.

Hartley, E. L. (1946). *Problems in prejudice*. New York: King's Crown Press.

Haselton, M. G., & Gangestad, S. W. (2006). Conditional expression of women's desires and men's mate guarding across the ovulatory cycle. *Hormones and Behavior, 49*, 509–518.

Haselton, M. G., Mortezaie, M., Pillsworth, E. G., Bleske-Rechek, A., & Frederick, D. A. (2007). Ovulatory shifts in female ornamentation: Near ovulation, women dress to impress. *Hormones and Behavior, 51*, 40–45.

Havlíček, J., Dvořáková, R., Bartoš, L., & Flegr, J. (2006). Non-advertized does not mean concealed: Body odour changes across the human menstrual cycle. *Ethology, 112*, 81–90.

Heider, F. (1958). *The psychology of interpersonal relations*. New York: Wiley.

Herbst, K. C., Gaertner, L., & Insko, C. A. (2003). My head says yes but my heart says no: Cognitive and affective attraction as a function of similarity to the ideal self. *Journal of Personality and Social Psychology, 84*, 1206–1219.

Herman, B. H., & Panksepp, J. (1978). Effects of morphine and naloxone on separation distress and approach attachment: Evidence for opiate mediation of social affect. *Pharmacology, Biochemistry & Behavior, 9*, 213–220.

Hill, C. A., Blakemore, J., & Drumm, P. (1997). Mutual and unrequited love in adolescence and adulthood. *Personal Relationships, 4*, 15–23.

Hill, R. (1945). Campus values in mate-selection. *Journal of Home Economics, 37*, 554–558.

Hitsch, G. J., Hortaçsu, A., & Ariely, D. (In press). What makes you click?—Mate preferences in online dating. *Quantitative Marketing and Economics.*

Hogg, M. A. (2005). All animals are equal but some animals are more equal than others: Social identity and marginal membership. In K. D. Williams, J. P. Forgas, & W. von Hippel (Eds.), *The social outcast: Ostracism, social exclusion, rejection, and bullying*. New York: Psychology Press.

Homans, G. C. (1974). *Social behavior: Its elementary forms*. New York: Harcourt Brace Jovanovich.

House, J. S., Landis, K. R., & Umberson, D. (1988). Social relationships and health. *Science, 241*, 540–545.

Hughes, S. M., & Gallup, G. G., Jr. (2003). Sex differences in morphological predictors of sexual behavior: Should to hip and waist to hip ratios. *Evolution and Human Behavior, 24*, 173–178.

Huston, T. L. (1973). Ambiguity of acceptance, social desirability, and dating choice. *Journal of Experimental Social Psychology, 9*, 32–42.

Jones, B. T., Jones, B. C., Thomas, A. P., & Piper, J. (2003). Alcohol consumption increases attractiveness ratings of opposite-sex faces: A third route to risky sex. *Addiction, 98*, 1069–1075.

Jones, D., & Hill, K. (1993). Criteria of facial attractiveness in five populations. *Human Nature, 4*, 271–296.

Jones, J. T., Pelham, B. W., Carvallo, M., & Mirenberg, M. C. (2004). How do I love thee? Let me count the Js: Implicit egotism and interpersonal attraction. *Journal of Personality and Social Psychology, 87*, 665–683.

Juvonen, J., & Gross, E. F. (2005). The rejected and the bullied: Lessons about social misfits from developmental psychology. In K. D. Williams, J. P. Forgas, & W. von Hippel (Eds.), *The social outcast: Ostracism, social exclusion, rejection, and bullying*. New York: Psychology Press.

Kalick, S. M., & Hamilton, T. E. (1986). The matching hypothesis reexamined. *Journal of Personality and Social Psychology, 51*, 673–682.

Kanazawa, S. (2002). Bowling with our imaginary friends. *Evolution and Human Behavior, 23*, 167–171.

Kehoe, P., & Blass, E. M. (1986). Opioid-mediation of separation distress in 10-day-old rats: Reversal of stress with maternal stimuli. *Developmental Psychobiology, 19*, 385–398.

Kelley, H. H. (1967). Attribution theory in social psychology. In D. Levine (Ed.), *Nebraska symposium on motivation* (Vol. 15, pp. 192–238). Lincoln: University of Nebraska Press.

Kelley, H. H., & Thibaut, J. W. (1978). *Interpersonal relations: A theory of interdependence*. New York: Wiley.

Kenny, D. A. (1994). *Interpersonal perception: A social relations analysis*. New York: Guilford Press.

Kenny, D. A., & La Voie, L. (1984). The social relations model. In L. Berkowitz (Ed.), *Advances in experimental social psychology* (Vol. 18, pp. 141–182). New York: Academic Press.

Kenny, D. A., & Nasby, W. (1980). Splitting the reciprocity correlation. *Journal of Personality and Social Psychology, 38*, 249–256.

Kenrick, D. T., & Gutierres, S. E. (1980). Contrast effects and judgments of physical attractiveness: When beauty becomes a social problem. *Journal of Personality and Social Psychology, 38*, 131–140.

Kenrick, D. T., Gutierres, S. E., & Goldberg, L. L. (1989). Influence of popular erotica on judgments of strangers and mates. *Journal of Experimental Social Psychology, 25*, 159–167.

Kerr, N. L., Rumble, A. C., Park, E. S., Ouwerkerk, J. W., Parks, C. D., Gallucci, M., & Van Lange, P. A. M. (2009). "How many bad apples does it take to spoil the whole barrel?" Social exclusion and toleration for bad apples. *Journal of Experimental Social Psychology, 45*, 603–613.

Kinsey, A. C., Pomeroy, W. B., & Martin, C. E. (1948). *Sexual behavior in the human male*. Philadelphia: Saunders.

Kinsey, A. C., Pomeroy, W. B., Martin, C. E., & Gebhard, P. H. (1953). *Sexual behavior in the human female*. Philadelphia: Saunders.

Krueger, R. F., Moffitt, T. E., Caspi, A., Bleske, A., & Silva, P. A. (1998). Assortative mating for antisocial behavior: Developmental and methodological implications. *Behavior Genetics, 28*, 173–186.

Kurzban, R., & Weeden, J. (2005). Hurrydate: Mate preferences in action. *Evolution and Human Behavior, 26*, 227–244.

Lakin, J., & Chartrand, T. L. (2003). Using nonconscious behavioral mimicry to create affiliation and rapport. *Psychological Science, 14*, 334–339.

Lakin, J. L., Jefferis, V. E., Cheng, C. M., & Chartrand, T. L. (2003). The Chameleon Effect as social glue: Evidence for the evolutionary significance of nonconscious mimicry. *Journal of Nonverbal Behavior, 27*, 145–162.

Langlois, J. H., Kalakanis, L., Rubenstein, A. J., Larson A., Hallam, M., & Smoot, M. (2000). Maxims or myths of beauty? A meta-analytic and theoretical review. *Psychological Bulletin, 126*, 390–423.

Langlois, J. H., Roggman, L. A., Casey, R. J., Ritter, J. M., Rieser-Danner, L. A., & Jenkins. V. Y. (1987). Infant preferences for attractive faces: Rudiments of a stereotype? *Developmental Psychology, 23*, 363–369.

Langlois, J. H., Roggman, L. A., & Musselman, L. (1994). What is average and what is not average about attractive faces. *Psychological Science, 5*, 214–220.

Langlois, J. H., Roggman, L. A., & Rieser-Danner, L. A. (1990). Infants' differential social responses to attractive and unattractive faces. *Developmental Psychology, 26*, 153–159.

LaPrelle, J., Hoyle, R. H., Insko, C. A., & Bernthal, P. (1990). Interpersonal attraction and descriptions of the traits of others: Ideal similarity, self similarity, and liking. *Journal of Research in Personality, 24*, 216–240.

Latané, B., Liu, J. H., Nowak, A., Bonevento, M., & Zheng, L. (1995). Distance matters: Physical space and social impact. *Personality and Social Psychology Bulletin, 21*, 795–805.

Leary, M. R. (2005). Varieties of interpersonal rejection. In K. D. Williams, J. P. Forgas, & W. von Hippel (Eds.), *The social outcast: Ostracism, social exclusion, rejection, and bullying* (pp. 35–52). New York: Psychology Press.

Leary, M. R., & Baumeister, R. F. (2000). The nature and function of self-esteem: Sociometer theory. In M. Zanna (Ed.), *Advances in experimental social psychology* (Vol. 32, pp. 1–62). San Diego, CA: Academic Press.

Leary, M. R., Kowalski, R. M., Smith, L., & Phillips, S. (2003). Teasing, rejection, and violence: Case studies of the school shootings. *Aggressive Behavior, 29*, 202–214.

Leary, M. R., Springer, C., Negel, L., Ansell, E., & Evans, K. (1998). The causes, phenomenology, and consequences of hurt feelings. *Journal of Personality and Social Psychology, 74*, 1225–1237.

Leary, M. R., Tambor, E. S., Terdal, S. K., & Downs, D. L. (1995). Self-esteem as an interpersonal monitor: The sociometer hypothesis. *Journal of Personality and Social Psychology, 68*, 518–530.

Lee, L., Loewenstein, G., Ariely, D., Hong, J., & Young, J. (2008). If I'm not hot, are you hot or not: Physical attractiveness evaluation and dating preferences as a function of one's own attractiveness. *Psychological Science, 19*, 669–677.

Leslie, L., Huston, T. L., & Johnson, M. P. (1986). Parental reactions to dating relationships: Do they make a difference? *Journal of Marriage and the Family, 48*, 57–66.

Locke, K. D., & Horowitz, L. M. (1990). Satisfaction in interpersonal interactions as a function of similarity in level of dysphoria. *Journal of Personality and Social Psychology, 58*, 823–831.

Lott, B. E., & Lott, A. J. (1974). The role of reward in the formulation of positive interpersonal attitudes. In T. L. Huston (Ed.), *Foundations of interpersonal attraction* (pp. 171–192). New York: Academic Press.

Lykken, D. T., & Tellegen, A. (1993). Is human mating adventitious or the result of lawful choice? A twin study of mate selection. *Journal of Personality and Social Psychology, 65*, 56–68.

MacDonald, G., & Leary, M. R. (2005). Why does social exclusion hurt? The relationship between social and physical pain. *Psychological Bulletin, 131*, 202–223.

Madey, S. F., Simo, M., Dillworth, D., & Kemper, D. (1996). They do get more attractive at closing time, but only when you are not in a relationship. *Basic and Applied Social Psychology, 18*, 387–393.

Maner, J. K., DeWall, C. N., Baumeister, R. F., & Schaller, M. (2007). Does social exclusion motivate interpersonal reconnection? Resolving the "porcupine problem." *Journal of Personality and Social Psychology, 92*, 42–55.

Markey, P. M., & Markey, C. N. (2007). Romantic ideals, romantic obtainment, and relationships experiences: The complementarity of interpersonal traits among romantic partners. *Journal of Social and Personal Relationships, 24*, 517–533.

Marques, J. M., Abrams, D., & Serôdio, R. G. (2001). Being better by being right: Subjective group dynamics and derogation of in-group deviants when generic norms are undermined. *Journal of Personality and Social Psychology, 81*, 436-447.

Marques, J. M., & Paez, D. (1994). The 'black sheep effect': Social categorization, rejection of ingroup deviates and perception of group variability. *European Review of Social Psychology, 5*, 37–68.

Marques, J. M., & Yzerbyt, V. Y. (1988). The black sheep effect: Judgmental extremity in inter- and intra-group situations. *European Journal of Social Psychology, 18*, 287–292.

Maslow, A. H. (1968). *Toward a psychology of being*. New York: Wiley.

May, J. L., & Hamilton, P. A. (1980). Effects of musically evoked affect on women's interpersonal attraction toward and perceptual judgments of physical attractiveness of men. *Motivation and Emotion, 4*, 217–228.

McKenna, K. Y. A. (2008). MySpace or your place: Relationship initiation and development in the wired and wireless world. In S. Sprecher, A. Wenzel, & J. Harvey (Eds.), *Handbook of relationship initiation* (pp. 235–247). New York: Guilford Press.

McPherson, M., Smith-Loving, L., & Cook, J. M. (2001). Birds of a feather: Homophily in social networks. *Annual Review of Sociology, 27*, 415–444.

Mealey L., Bridgstock, R., & Townsend, G. C. (1999). Symmetry and perceived facial attractiveness: A monozygotic co-twin comparison. *Journal of Personality and Social Psychology, 76*, 151–158.

Meston, C. M., & Frohlich, P. F. (2003). Love at first fright: Partner salience moderates roller-coaster-induced excitation transfer. *Archives of Sexual Behavior, 32*, 537–544.

Miller, G., Tybur, J. M., & Jordan, B. D. (2007). Ovulatory cycle effects on tip earnings by lap dancers: Economic evidence for human estrus? *Evolution and Human Behavior, 28*, 375–381.

Montoya, R. M. (2008). I'm hot, so I say you're not: The influence of objective physical attractiveness on mate selection. *Personality and Social Psychology Bulletin, 34*, 1315–1331.

Montoya, R. M., Horton, R. S., & Kirchner, J. (2006). Is actual similarity necessary for attraction? A meta-analysis of actual and perceived similarity. *Journal of Social and Personal Relationships*, 25, 889–922.

Moreland, R. L., & Beach. S. R. (1992). Exposure effects in the classroom: The development of affinity among students. *Journal of Experimental Social Psychology, 28*, 255–276.

Moreno, J. L. (1934). *Who shall survive? A new approach to the problem of human interrelationships*. Washington, DC: Nervous and Mental Disease Publishing.

Nahemow, L., & Lawton, M.P. (1975). Similarity and propinquity in friendship formation. *Journal of Personality and Social Psychology*, 32, 205–213.

Naranjo, J. R., & Fuentes, J. A. (1985). Association between hypoalgesia and hypertension in rats after short-term isolation. *Neuropharmacology, 24*, 167–171.

Nelson, L. D., & Morrison, E. L. (2005). The symptoms of resource scarcity: Judgments of food and finances influence preferences for potential partners. *Psychological Science, 16*, 167–173.

Newcomb, T. M. (1961). *The acquaintance process*. New York: Holt, Rinehart, & Winston.

Nezlek, J. B., Kowalski, R. M., Leary, M. R., Blevins, T., & Holgate, S. (1997). Personality moderators of reactions to interpersonal rejection: Depression and trait self-esteem. Personality and Social Psychology Bulletin, 23, 1235–1244.

Norton, M. I., Frost, J. H., & Ariely, D. (2007). Less is more: The lure of ambiguity, or why familiarity breeds contempt. *Journal of Personality and Social Psychology*, 92, 97–105.

Panksepp, J. (1998). *Affective neuroscience: The foundations of human and animal emotions*. London: Oxford University Press.

Panksepp, J., Herman, B., Conner, R., Bishop, P., & Scott, J. P. (1978). The biology of social attachments: Opiates alleviate separation distress. *Biological Psychiatry, 9*, 213–220.

Panksepp, J., Vilberg, T., Bean, N. J., Coy, D. H., & Kastin, A. J. (1978). Reduction of distress vocalization in chicks by opiate-like peptides. *Brain Research Bulletin, 3*, 663–667.

Parker, L. L. C., Penton-Voak, I. S., Attwood, A. S., & Munafò, M. R. (2008). Effects of acute alcohol consumption on ratings of attractiveness of facial stimuli: Evidence of long-term encoding. *Alcohol & Alcoholism, 43*, 636–640.

Pennebaker, J. W., Dyer, M. A., Caulkins, R. S., Litowitz, D. L., Ackreman, P. L., Anderson, D. B., & McGraw, K. M. (1979). Don't the girls get prettier at closing time: A country and western application to psychology. *Personality and Social Psychology Bulletin*, *5*, 122–125.

Peplau, L. A., & Perlman, D. (Eds.). (1982). *Loneliness: A sourcebook of current theory, research, and therapy*. New York: Wiley.

Perlman, D. (2008). Ending the beginning of relationships. In S. Sprecher, A. Wenzel, & J. Harvey (Eds.), *Handbook of relationship initiation* (pp. 217–234). New York: Guilford Press.

Pickett, C. L., & Gardner, W. L. (2005). The social monitoring system: Enhanced sensitivity to social cues and information as an adaptive response to social exclusion and belonging need. In K. D. Williams, J. P. Forgas, & W. von Hippel (Eds.), *The social outcast: Ostracism, social exclusion, rejection, and bullying*. New York: Psychology Press.

Rebman, C. (1999). Eighth amendment and solitary confinement: The gap in protection from psychological consequences. *DePaul Law Review*, *49*, 567–620.

Reis, H. T. (2007). Steps toward the ripening of relationship science. *Personal Relationships*, *14*, 1–23.

Reis, H. T., Nezlek, J., & Wheeler, L. (1980). Physical attractiveness in social interaction. *Journal of Personality and Social Psychology*, *38*, 604–617.

Rhodes, G. (2006). The evolutionary psychology of facial beauty. *Annual Review of Psychology*, *57*, 199–226.

Rhodes, G., Harwood, K., Yoshikawa, S., Nishitani, M., & MacLean, I. (2002). The attractiveness of average faces: Cross-cultural evidence and possible biological basis. In G. Rhodes & L. A. Zebrowitz (Eds.), *Facial attractiveness: Evolutionary, cognitive and social perspectives* (pp. 35–58). Westport, CT: Ablex.

Rhodes, G., Sumich, A., & Byatt, G. (1999). Are average facial configurations attractive only because of their symmetry? *Psychological Science*, *10*, 52–58.

Roberts, S. C., Havlicek, J., Flegr, J., Hruskova, M., Little, A. C., Jones, B. C., Perrett, D. I., & Petrie, M. (2004). Female facial attractiveness increases during the fertile phase of the menstrual cycle. *Proceedings of the Royal Society of London Series B*, *271*(S5), S270–S272.

Rofé, Y. (1984). Stress and affiliation: A utility theory. *Psychological Review*, *91*, 235–250.

Rubenstein, A. J., Langlois, J. H., & Roggman, L. A. (2002). What makes a face attractive and why: The role of averageness in defining facial beauty. In G. Rhodes & L. A. Zebrowitz (Eds.), *Facial attractiveness: Evolutionary, cognitive and social perspectives* (pp. 1–33). Westport, CT: Ablex.

Russell, D., Peplau, L. A., & Cutrona, C. E. (1980). The revised UCLA Loneliness Scale: Concurrent and discriminant validity evidence. *Journal of Personality and Social Psychology*, *39*, 472–480.

Salska, I., Frederick, D. A., Pawlowski, B., Reilly, A. H., Laird, K. T., & Rudd, N. A. (2008). Conditional mate preferences: Factors influencing preferences for height. *Personality and Individual Differences*, *44*, 203–215.

Schachter, S. (1959). *The psychology of affiliation: Experimental studies of the sources of gregariousness*. Stanford, CA: Stanford University Press.

Schachter, S., & Singer, J. E. (1962). Cognitive, social, and physiological determinants of emotional state. *Psychological Review, 69*, 379–399.

Schwarz, S., & Hassebrauck, M. (2008). Self-perceived and observed variations in women's attractiveness throughout the menstrual cycles—a diary study. *Evolution and Human Behavior, 29*, 282–288.

Segal, M. W. (1974). Alphabet and attraction: An unobtrusive measure of the effect of propinquity in a field setting. *Journal of Personality and Social Psychology, 30*, 654–657.

Simpson, J. A., Fletcher, G. J. O., & Campbell, L. (2001). The structure and ideal functions of ideal standards in close relationships. In G. J. O. Fletcher & M. S. Clark (Eds.), *Blackwell handbook of social psychology: Interpersonal processes* (pp. 86–106). Malden, MA: Blackwell.

Simpson, J. A., & Harris, B. A. (1994). Interpersonal attraction. In A. L. Weber & J. H. Harvey (Eds.), *Perspectives on close relationships* (pp. 45–66). Boston: Allyn & Bacon.

Singh, D. (1995). Female judgment of male attractiveness and desirability for relationships: Role of waist-to-hip ratio and financial status. *Journal of Personality and Social Psychology, 69*, 1089–1101.

Singh, D. (2004). Mating strategies of young women: Role of physical attractiveness. *Journal of Sex Research, 41*, 43–54.

Singh, D., & Bronstad, P. M. (2001). Female body odour is a potential cue to ovulation. *Proceedings of the Royal Society of London Series B, 268*, 797–801.

Slater, A., Von der Schulenburg, C., Brown, E., Badenoch, M., Butterworth, G., Parsons, S., & Samuels, C. (1998). Newborn infants prefer attractive faces. *Infant Behavior and Development, 21*, 345–354.

Spear, L. P., Enters, E. K., Aswad, M. A., & Louzan, M. (1985). Drug and environmentally induced manipulations of the opiate and serotonergic systems alter nociception in neonatal rat pups. *Behavioral and Neural Biology, 44*, 1–22.

Sprecher, S., DeLamater, J., Neuman, N., Neuman, M., Kahn, P., Orbuch, D., & McKinney, K. (1984). Asking questions in bars: The girls (and boys) may not get prettier at closing time and other interesting results. *Personality and Social Psychology Bulletin, 10*, 482–488.

Sprecher, S., & Felmlee, D. (1992). The influence of parents and friends on the quality and stability of romantic relationships: A three-wave longitudinal investigation. *Journal of Marriage and Family, 54*, 888–900.

Sprecher, S., Schwartz, P., Harvey, J., & Hatfield, E. (2008). TheBusinessofLove.com: Relationship initiation at Internet matchmaking services (pp. 249–265). In S. Sprecher, A. Wenzel, & J. Harvey (Eds.), *Handbook of relationship initiation* (pp. 269–295). New York: Guilford Press.

Sprecher, S., Wenzel, A., & Harvey, J. (2008). *Handbook of relationship initiation.* New York: Guilford Press.

Stinson, D. A., Cameron, J. J., Wood, J. V., Gaucher, D., & Holmes, J. G. (2009). Deconstructing the "reign of error": Interpersonal warmth explains the self-fulfilling prophecy of anticipated acceptance. *Personality and Social Psychology Bulletin, 35*, 1165–1178.

Swami, V., & Tovée, M. J. (2006). Does hunger influence judgments of female physical attractiveness? *British Journal of Psychology, 97*, 353–363.

Thibaut, J. W. ,& Kelley, H. H. (1959). *The social psychology of groups.* New York: Wiley.

Tiedens, L., & Fragale, A. (2003). Power moves: Complementarity in dominant and submissive nonverbal behavior. *Journal of Personality and Social Psychology,* 84, 558–568.

Todd, P. M., Penke, L., Fasolo, B., & Lenton, A. P. (2007). Different cognitive processes underlie human mate choices and mate preferences. *Proceedings of the National Academy of Sciences, 104*, 15011–15016.

Tong, S. T., Van Der Heide, B., Langwell, L., & Walther, J. B. (2008). Too much of a good thing? The relationship between number of friends and interpersonal impressions on Facebook. *Journal of Computer-Mediated Communication, 13*, 531–549.

Tovée, M. J., Swami, V., Furnham, A., & Mangalparsad, R. (2006). Changing perceptions of attractiveness as observers are exposed to a different culture. *Evolution and Human Behavior, 27*, 443–456.

Twenge, J. M., Baumeister, R. F., DeWall, C. N., Ciarocco, N. J., & Bartels, J. M. (2007). Social exclusion decreases prosocial behavior. *Journal of Personality and Social Psychology, 92*, 56–66.

Twenge, J. M., Baumeister, R. F., Tice, D. M., & Stucke, T.S. (2001). If you can't join them, beat them: Effects of social exclusion on aggressive behavior. *Journal of Personality and Social Psychology, 81*, 1058–1069.

Van Beest, I., & Williams, K. (2006). When inclusion costs and ostracism pays, ostracism still hurts. *Journal of Personality and Social Psychology, 91*, 918–928.

Veitch, R., & Griffitt, W. (1976). Good news-bad news: Affective and interpersonal effects. *Journal of Applied Social Psychology, 6*, 69–75.

Vonk, R. (2002). Self-serving interpretations of flattery: Why ingratiation works. *Journal of Personality and Social Psychology, 82*, 515–526.

Voracek, M., & Fisher, M. L. (2006). Success is all in the measures: Androgenousness, curvaciousness, and starring frequencies in adult media actresses. *Archives of Sexual Behavior, 35*, 297–304.

Waller, W. (1938). *The family: A dynamic interpretation.* New York: Gordon.

Walster, E., Aronson, V., Abrahams, D., & Rottman, L. (1966). Importance of physical attractiveness in dating behavior. *Journal of Personality and Social Psychology, 4*, 508–516.

Walster, E., Walster, G. W., & Berscheid, E. (1978). *Equity: Theory and research.* Boston: Allyn & Bacon.

Walster, E., Walster, G. W., Piliavin, J., & Schmidt, L. (1973). "Playing hard to get": Understanding an elusive phenomenon. *Journal of Personality and Social Psychology, 26*, 113–121.

Walther, J. B., Van Der Heide, B., Kim, S., Westerman, D., & Tong, S. T. (2008). The role of friends' appearance and behavior on evaluations of individuals on Facebook: Are we known by the company we keep? *Human Communication Research, 34*, 28–49.

Watson, D., Klohnen, E. C., Casillas, A. Simms, E. N., Haig, J., & Berry, D. S. (2004). Match makers and deal breakers: Analyses of assortative mating in newlywed couples. *Journal of Personality, 72*, 1029–1068.

Wegner, D. M., Lane, J. D., & Dimitri, S. (1994). The allure of secret relationships. *Journal of Personality and Social Psychology, 66*, 287–300.

Wheeler, L., Reis, H. T., & Nezlek, J. (1983). Loneliness, social interaction, and sex roles. *Journal of Personality and Social Psychology, 45*, 943–953.

White, G. L. (1980). Physical attractiveness and courship progress. *Journal of Personality and Social Psychology, 39*, 660–668.

Williams, K. D. (2001). *Ostracism: The power of silence.* New York: Guilford Press.

Williams, K. D., Cheung, C. K. T., & Choi, W. (2000). CyberOstracism: Effects of being ignored over the Internet. *Journal of Personality and Social Psychology, 79*, 748–762.

Williams, K. D., & Sommer, K. L. (1997). Social ostracism by coworkers: Does rejection lead to loafing or compensation? *Personality and Social Psychology Bulletin, 23*, 693–706.

Williams, K. D., & Zadro, L. (2005). Ostracism: The indiscriminate early detection system. In K. D. Williams, J. P. Forgas, & W. von Hippel (Eds.), *The social outcast: Ostracism, social exclusion, rejection, and bullying.* New York: Psychology Press.

Winch, R. F. (1958). *Mate selection: A study of complementary needs.* New York: Harper.

Wright, J. C., Giammarino, M., & Parad, H. W. (1986). Social status in small groups: Individual-group similarity and the social "misfit." *Journal of Personality and Social Psychology, 50*, 523–536.

Zajonc, R. B. (1968). Attitudinal effects of mere exposures. *Journal of Personality and Social Psychology, 9*, 1–27.

Zajonc, R. B. (2001). Mere exposure: A gateway to the subliminal. *Current Directions in Psychological Science, 10*, 224–228.

Chapter 13

Intimate Relationships

Garth J. O. Fletcher and Nickola C. Overall

How do people know they are in good relationships? Why do some people have problems with intimacy? What is the nature and origin of love? Does good communication really produce successful relationships? These are just some of the intriguing questions that social psychologists attempt to answer. Indeed, the study of intimate relationships has become one of the most important domains in social psychology over the past three decades or so.

But what are intimate relationships? Answering this question is not as easy as it seems. One key concept developed by Kelley and colleagues (Kelley & Thibaut, 1978; Kelley et al., 1983) describes relationships in terms of interdependence. In close, intimate relationships the well-being and psychological processes of one individual are intertwined with the same processes in another person. Not surprisingly, therefore, successful intimate relationships are characterized by relatively high levels of trust, knowledge, commitment, and intimacy.

However, intimate relationships themselves can be divided into two categories: platonic friendships and romantic relationships (this chapter focuses on nonfamilial intimate relationship). Romantic relationships differ from intimate platonic friendships in two major ways. First, romantic relationships contain elements of sexual attraction and passion, and second, individuals are typically involved in just one romantic attachment at a time. Friendships can be intense and are of great psychological importance in people's lives, but most research in social psychology has been devoted to understanding romantic relationships. Accordingly, we will focus on this domain in this chapter.

First, we present a brief historical synopsis to help understand the scientific work in relationships in the proper context. Then we cover five key areas that have dominated social psychological research in intimate relationships for the past 20 years: interdependence theory, social cognition, love, attachment, and communication.

A Brief History

A social psychological approach to intimate relationships focuses on the interaction between two individuals, paying close attention to both behavior and what goes on in people's minds (emotions and cognitions). Up to the late 1970s, social psychological research into relationships concentrated on interpersonal attraction, namely, the factors that lead people to be attracted to one another at the initial stages of relationship development. This research was largely atheoretical and the results read like a laundry list of variables that influence attraction including similarity, proximity, and physical attractiveness (for an overview of research on initial attraction see Finkel & Baumeister, Chapter 12, this volume).

In the 1980s the psychological zeitgeist shifted toward the greater complexity inherent in the development, maintenance, and dissolution phases of dyadic romantic relationships. This shift was prompted by several key developments in the 1970s. First, Gottman and other clinical psychologists began research that, for the first time, observed and carefully measured the dyadic interchanges of married couples in an attempt to predict divorce (Gottman, 1979). Second, Rubin (1973) and others became interested in love, and devised reliable scales that could measure the concept. Third, Kelley et al. (1983) led a team of social psychologists in producing a seminal book published in 1983 titled *Close Relationships*, which presented the first full-blooded treatment of intimate relationships from an interactional, social psychological perspective.

The explosion of social psychological research in intimate relationships over the past two decades has been marked by five major developments. First, there has been a continuing stream of research inspired by the early work by Kelley and others on the nature and process of interdependence in romantic relationships. Second, considerable attention has been given to understanding the inner workings of the intimate relationship mind via the role that social cognition (beliefs, cognitive processes, etc.) and emotions play in intimate relationships. Third, the topic of love has attracted considerable attention. Fourth, there has been a burgeoning interest in how attachment and bonding processes contribute to adult romantic relationships. Finally, prompted in part by the development of new statistical and methodological tools, the study of communication has provided an increasingly illuminating analysis of interaction in intimate relationships. We discuss each area in turn before discussing new developments. Finally we pull the threads together to provide a brief synthesis of this work.

Interdependence Theory

The genesis of interdependence theory can be traced to the books produced by Kelley and Thibaut, published from 1959 to 1979 (Kelley, 1979; Kelley & Thibaut, 1978; Thibaut & Kelley, 1959). This approach has various interlocking components. Overall, the theory is framed in terms of costs versus rewards. However, the subsequent relationship evaluations and decisions (e.g., "should I go or should I stay") are not based on the objective nature of such benefits, but rather on the perceived consistency between perceptions of the benefits and two different kinds of standards—expectations about what benefits are deserved (comparison level or CL) and the available alternatives (comparison level alternatives or CLalt). If the perceived benefits are higher than CL and CLalt, then this should produce higher levels of relationship satisfaction and commitment, respectively. Keeping the benefits constant, however, but moving CL or CLalt higher than the perceived benefits should reduce relationship satisfaction or relationship commitment.

A second key feature of this theory concerns the way in which two partners coordinate their interaction to sustain cooperation and concern for the other, rather than selfishly pursuing benefits for the self. Using concepts drawn from game theory, this aspect of the theory deals with the type of power and influence individuals have over each other and how couples respond to each other when their interests conflict or overlap. The two most basic mutual forms of control are termed fate control and behavior control. Fate control is a function of what each partner decides to do for the other (regardless of what the recipient says or does). An example of this category is arranging a surprise party for our partner—the partner does not exert any control over this event. Relationships in which such forms of control are pervasive are problematic because the recipient will be deprived of control and is likely to feel dissatisfied. An example of mutual behavior control might be negotiating who will do what in organizing a joint party in a situation in which the individuals have equal power and the outcome (organizing a successful party) is equally desirable for both parties. Of course, situations in real life are often blends of the two processes (Kelley, 1979), but this approach posits that there is a set number of prototypical situations in social life that encourages competition or cooperation and that poses different problems and opportunities (see Kelley, et al. 2003).

The third feature of the theory concerns the central role played by interpersonal attributions, such as trust, commitment, and attitudes to the other. These facilitate and render automatic the shift from a selfish frame of mind (termed the given matrix in the theory) to a relationship or partner-serving orientation (termed the effective matrix) and are thought to be important in maintaining successful relationships (see Rusbult &Van Lange, 2003).

It is hard to exaggerate the importance that this general theory has had in the study of intimate relationships in social psychology. This is not because the specific details of the theory have all been accepted as they were originally formulated, but rather because the three main planks of the approach—interdependence, mutual responsiveness, and interpersonal attributions—have continued to guide the questions, theories, and research generated to study intimate relationships. We document this claim in the remainder of this chapter.

The Intimate Relationship Mind

Figure 13.1 shows a general model that more or less encompasses the existing work in the area. As can be seen, the causal processes can go in both directions. Moreover, although the model is drawn with the causal processes proceeding in a linear fashion, in reality they may often occur simultaneously. We will start with the goals (shown on the left side of Fig. 13.1) and proceed to each component in turn.

Relationship Goals

If an alien anthropologist appeared on earth, listened to pop music for a day or two, and browsed through a random assortment of self-help books, movies, and novels, it would quickly conclude that humans are obsessed with love, sex, and intimate relationships. Indeed, research has confirmed that finding a mate and forming a warm, intimate relationship (to love and be loved) are recognized by most people as key goals in their lives (see Reis & Downey, 1999). Other kinds of life goals, that at first glance seem not to be about intimate relationships, are also linked to this search for a satisfying sexual relationship including the drive for status, attractiveness, fitness, and good health. The reason is that these qualities are highly valued in mates in sexual relationships (Fletcher, Simpson, Thomas, & Giles, 1999). And, of course, raising children

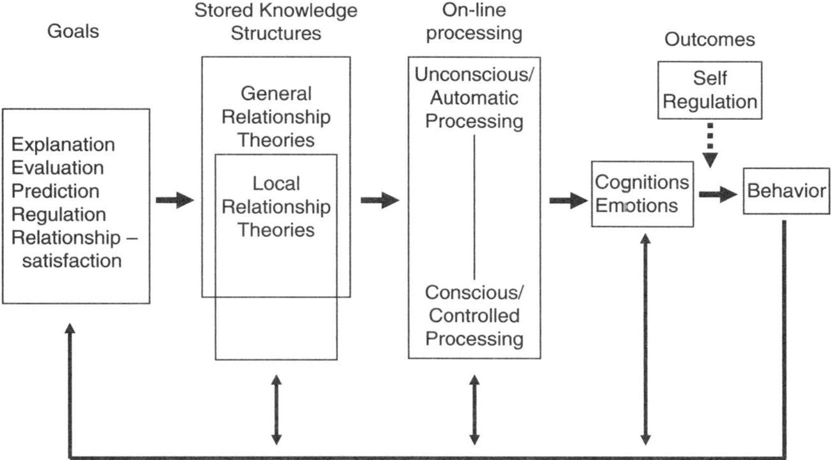

FIGURE 13.1. The Intimate Relationship Mind

and enjoying family life are also often (but not always) linked to the goal of finding and retaining a mate.

The five general goals listed in Figure 13.1 (explanation, evaluation, prediction, regulation, and achieving relationship satisfaction) are activated the moment a potential partner is met, and they remain potent throughout the course of the relationship. As already noted, one of the main goals in life is to have a satisfying sexual relationship. However, even a cursory analysis of this goal reveals its complexity. First, such goals vary from a one-night stand to a life-long commitment. Second, as relationships change over time so does the nature of the goals (Stephen might simply be after a good time initially, but this goal will change after his love and commitment for Mary deepens over time). Third, the way in which people achieve satisfying intimate relationships varies as a function of how they cope with a conundrum posed by developing a close sexual relationship, namely, the potential of relationships to provide succor and support versus pain and rejection. To put it another way, intimate relationships pose an approach–avoidance problem.

This conundrum, inherent in intimate relationships, has been recognized repeatedly in social psychology. It can be found, for example, as a central component in three theories we discuss later in the chapter: attachment theory, regulatory focus theory, and risk regulation theory. We simply note here that these three theories share a common proposition that individuals vary in the way they set their relationship goals along a dimension that ranges from the confident desire to promote closeness and commitment to the defensive need to protect the self from potential rejection and thus to restrict intimacy and dependence to manageable levels.

The five goals listed will often interact with one another instead of acting independently. For example, Gable and Poore (2008) had people in long-term dating relationships beeped randomly for 10 days to report their positive and negative thoughts about the relationship; participants also reported how satisfied they were with the relationship at the end of each day. Their results suggested that people tend to evaluate their relationship satisfaction in different ways depending on whether they are dominated by goals that involve approaching positive outcomes in intimate relationships or avoiding negative outcomes. For those adopting an approach orientation, daily judgments of relationship satisfaction were a function of the frequency of positive thoughts. In contrast, relationship satisfaction for those participants dominated by the need to avoid unpleasant outcomes was a function of the incidence of negative thoughts.

Lay Relationship Theories

We move next to the stored knowledge structures (see Fig. 13.1) that exist in the service of the goals. Regardless of the way in which such knowledge structures are conceptualized, scientists agree that people do not store and retrieve exact replicas of every interpersonal experience. Instead, experiences are organized into generalized representations that summarize regularities encountered over time, including beliefs, expectations, interpersonal goals, and behavioral strategies. Whenever a relationship-relevant event occurs (from simply thinking of a close other to receiving a compliment from your partner), such lay theories are activated automatically, guiding how the event is mentally processed and influencing both accompanying emotions and resultant behavior.

We distinguish between two levels of lay intimate theories: *general relationship theories* that summarize knowledge specifically relevant to close relationships and *local theories* that represent models of specific intimate relationships such as our husband or ex-girlfriend. We briefly describe each in turn, and analyze how they help drive the ABCs (Affect, Behavior, and Cognition) of psychological phenomena in intimate relationships.

General relationship theories contain beliefs, expectations, and concepts that are concerned with intimate, sexual relationships. These theories can be idiosyncratic, to some extent, depending on individual experiences. Nevertheless, relationship theories are derived from both culturally shared sources of information (e.g., media) and from hard-wired evolutionary adaptations (see Maner & Kenrick, Chapter 17, this volume). Thus, many core features of general relationship theories are similar across individuals. For example, people hold similar theories regarding the nature and roles of emotions in relationships, such as love, anger, and jealousy (Fitness, 1996), and have similar conceptualizations of concepts such as commitment (Fehr, 1999) and mate selection criteria (Fletcher et al., 1999). A key point here is that people bring these expectations and beliefs with them from the beginning of specific relationships.

Other types of general lay relationship theories have the same structure across individuals, although the actual content may differ. We have already noted that there are stable individual differences in relationship goals. In addition, there is good evidence that the same is true for attachment models, ideal standards, and what Knee, Patrick, and Lonsbary (2003) terms "growth and destiny beliefs." That is, individuals differ in the extent to which they believe and trust others will be available and responsive in times of need (Mikulincer & Shaver, 2007), the importance they place on such standards as physical attractiveness in evaluating a potential or existent mate (Fletcher et al., 1999), and the extent to which they believe relationship success is determined by destiny or through overcoming challenges (Knee et al., 2003). Individual differences in the content of these lay theories (partly) determine how the same relationship events are perceived and responded to. For example, individuals who ascribe to destiny beliefs are less satisfied with their relationships in the face of negative partner behavior or relationship experiences. In contrast, individuals who view relationship problems as challenges to be overcome remain relatively satisfied and committed when their partners do not live up to their ideals or when they experience conflict within their relationships (Knee et al., 2003).

Regardless of their particular content, lay relationship theories pervasively influence affect, behavior, and cognition within relationships. Consider the following short account of Mary and Stephen, in the course of their first date.

> Mary notices that Stephen dresses well and has a good job. This fits nicely with Susan's theory about the ideal man. However, caring and sensitivity are also critical for Mary; she seeks a long-term relationship, and her last boyfriend was so concerned about his career she felt he didn't have enough time for her. Similar feelings have plagued Mary's previous relationships, and deep down she fears that no one will ever really love her. As the discussion turns to their interests, Mary finds they have a lot of in common—"that's good," she thinks, "similarity is important in relationships." Maybe there is hope after all.

As this tale suggests, people enter social situations with preexistent mental dispositions (theories about relationships) that help to produce interpretations and explanations of behavior, evaluations of the partner and the relationship, and finally decisions about the course of the relationship. If Mary and Stephen's relationship continues they will both develop elaborate local relationship theories including accounts of the other's personality, attributes, and attitudes, and mental models of their relationship, including the how and the why of their levels of closeness, their communication, and developing problems.

Another type of general theory that predates, but influences, local relationship theories concerns the self. Indeed, as local relationship theories develop over time they steadily become entwined with representations and evaluations of the self (Aron, Aron, & Norman, 2001). That is, people start thinking in terms of "we" rather than "I" and "you." Another way in which the self is linked to relationship outcomes is via self-esteem. Self-esteem can be thought of as an attitude toward the self (a local theory of the self) and is sensitive to how other people view and react to the self. In an influential theory, Leary and colleagues (Leary, Tambor, Terdal, & Downs, 1995; Leary, 2001) posited that self-esteem is essentially like a gauge (or sociometer) that monitors the extent to which the individual is well regarded by others. Evidence has steadily accumulated supporting this theory in intimate relationship contexts. For example, self-esteem is positively correlated with self-perceived mate value, such as attractiveness (Anthony, Holmes, & Wood, 2007), and with secure attachment representations (Bylsma, Cozzarelli, & Sumer, 1997).

Murray and her colleagues have shown that lower self-esteem is associated with underplaying the amounts of love and satisfaction actually reported by the partner (Murray, Holmes, & Griffin, 2000). Recent diary studies by Murray and others also document the subtle and dynamic nature of associated processes over short periods of time (typically 3 weeks) in romantic relationships (Murray, Holmes, Bellavia, Griffin, & Dolderman, 2002; Murray, Bellavia, Rose, & Griffin, 2003; 2006; Murray, Griffin, Rose, & Bellavia, 2003). These studies suggest that when the partner is perceived to be insensitive or transgressing in some way, low self-esteem motivates withdrawal from the relationship, the production of uncharitable attributions, and a decline in relationship satisfaction.

The take-home message is that local relationship theories are generated according to the way in which they overlap with preexistent general relationship theories. Thus, relationship evaluations are produced (in part) as a function of the extent to which perceptions and experiences match prior expectations and beliefs. This insight is taken directly from interdependence theory. However, recent research and theorizing has extended this idea and showed that greater discrepancies between ideal standards and perceptions of the partner in existing relationships on specific dimensions (such as warmth, attractiveness, and status) are linked with lower relationship satisfaction (Fletcher et al., 1999), higher rates of relationship dissolution (Fletcher, Simpson, & Thomas, 2000), and more strenuous attempts to change the partner (Overall, Fletcher, & Simpson, 2006).

At the center of lay local relationship theories is a set of relationship evaluative judgments that are continuously updated on the basis of relevant information. The most studied evaluative categories include overall satisfaction, passion, commitment, trust, closeness or intimacy, and love. Social psychologists and others have carried out huge amounts of research on such constructs, and there are many self-report scales designed to measure relationship quality judgments. Just one of the most popular scales developed in 1976 by Spanier (the Dyadic Adjustment Scale) had been cited 2529 times in research articles (at present). These kinds of judgments play a critical role in generating relationship behavior, cognition, and emotion.

As romantic relationships develop, intimacy and closeness change. Reis and colleagues (Reis & Shaver, 1988; Reis & Patrick, 1996), taking a leaf out of interdependence theory, argue that a key element in developing intimacy is the way in which the partner responds; specifically, to what extent does the partner communicate that he or she understands, validates, and cares for the other? The associated types of attributions (what you think your partner thinks and feels about you), sometimes termed "reflected appraisals," are important in intimate relationships, consistent with Reis' ideas (Reis, Clark, & Holmes, 2004).

On-Line Processing

The relationship mind not only stores knowledge and theories but also thinks, daydreams, perceives, and feels in episodic bursts. We have labeled this component "on-line processing" in Figure 13.1. Although the examples used may leave the impression that people always consciously draw on their theories, relationship theories are also routinely accessed unconsciously (Fletcher, Rosanowski, & Fitness, 1994). In addition, the on-line cognitive processing itself may be unconscious and automatic. This level of efficiency is necessary. A single interpersonal interaction requires many streams of cognitive processing to occur simultaneously. Partners must encode the verbal and nonverbal behavior (including facial expressions, eye contact, and gestures), while controlling their own behavior, making rapid judgments, and blending their thoughts, emotions, and behavior into a smoothly coordinated interaction. This is achievable only if considerable processing is conducted automatically and unconsciously.

There is considerable direct evidence for this thesis based on studies that use techniques that require individuals to carry out two tasks at the same time, thus loading their cognitive resources (e.g., Fletcher et al., 1994), or studies that assess the power of subliminal perception (Mikulincer, Gillath, & Shaver, 2002). Murray and Holmes (2009) review research showing that people automatically respond to the goal of enhancing intimacy. For example, subliminal priming of the name of an accepting other increases the willingness to disclose (Gillath et al., 2006) and forgive transgressions (Karremans & Aarts, 2007). Exposing people to stress also seems to automatically trigger the goal of seeking support from a current romantic partner (Mikulincer, Gillath & Shaver, 2002).

The extent to which relationship events are subject to in-depth conscious analysis will vary considerably depending on the stage of the relationship, individual differences, and the situational context. In long-term, stable relationships a great deal of communication becomes routine, resulting in over learned and stereotypical sequences of behavior. Two types of events have been shown to cause people to return to conscious, controlled cognition (often accompanied by emotion)—negative events and unexpected events (Berscheid, 1983; Fletcher & Thomas, 1996).

Emotions

The study of social cognition in intimate relationships can ill afford to ignore the role of emotions, given that relationship cognition is often "hot cognition," shot through with affect and evaluations (see Fig. 13.1). The functions of emotions in relationships are no different from their role generally (Fitness, Fletcher, & Overall, 2003). First, emotions (such as fear, anger, or love) both attract attention and provide the motivation to attain a goal. Second, they provide information that helps people decide how to attain goals. Thus, in relationship settings feelings of love are associated with the desire to be physically close to the partner and to express such urges, and feelings of anger are associated with the desire to confront the partner and seek redress (Fitness & Fletcher, 1993).

However, negative emotions provide a problem in relationships, given that their expression is likely to accelerate the demise of relationships. Thus, individuals actively control and manage the expression of emotions such as jealousy or anger (Fletcher, Thomas, & Durrant, 1999). Indeed, the expression of emotions serves a range of communication goals that are important in intimate relationships. Drawing on Darwin's (1872) pioneering account, Clark and her colleagues have argued, for example, that the expression of emotions such as anxiety and sadness signals the need for comfort and support from the partner, whereas the expression of anger sets the scene for the partner to seek forgiveness (Clark, Fitness, & Brissette, 2001). Emotions are, thus, tied to both social cognition and the way that couples interact and negotiate issues within their relationships.

At the general level individuals hold theories about the nature of emotions as they play out in intimate relationships, such as anger and love. These are often referred to as scripts, because they involve interactional sequences that unfold predictably over time (Fitness, 1996). For example, the prototypical script for anger (as revealed in participants' reports of anger episodes in their relationships) involves the partner triggering the emotion by treating the target unfairly, the target feeling muscle tension and a strong urge to express the emotion, the partner responding in kind (angrily), the target feeling tense or depressed afterward, the target perceiving reasonable control over the self, and the target believing it was mainly the partner's fault. Finally, the partner should eventually respond by asking for forgiveness (Fitness & Fletcher, 1993). Use of these scripts allows individuals to read and interpret the emotions not only of their partners but also of themselves.

We draw two main conclusions. First, emotions and cognitions are thoroughly intertwined, and work together in normal social cognition. Thus, if Stephen buys Mary a rose, she is likely to feel love or gratitude, but if Mary realizes that Stephen knows she is allergic to roses, than she may feel contempt or anger. Second, studies of rare forms of brain damage that incapacitate emotions, but leave other abilities and functions intact, have shown that people develop crippling deficits in social intelligence and managing interpersonal relationships (Damasio, 1994). Damasio's explanation is that without emotions individuals are deprived of critical information. Thus, emotions are indispensable rather than inimical to rationality and good decision-making.

Damasio's explanation has the ring of truth when applied to intimate relationships. Imagine, for example, making decisions and judgments in relationship contexts while experiencing no emotions or feelings. If you go on a date with someone, how do you decide whether to go out on another date? How do you respond when your partner tells you he or she loves you? If you do decide that your partner can be trusted or not trusted, is warm or cold, is patient or bad tempered, how do you act on those judgments? Without emotions or affective tone, individuals would become rudderless ships, similar to the patients described by Damasio who suffered from specific damage to regions of the brain centrally involved in emotions and affect.

Self-Regulation

And so we come to the final step in the model—behavior and the self-regulation of behavior (see Fig. 13.1). If everyone openly expressed every passing cognition and emotion honestly, many relationships would implode. Consider revelations such as "I wish your penis was bigger," "I always liked your sister more than you," "I stole some money from you years ago," or even "Actually, you do look fat in those trousers". Fortunately, as shown in our model (Fig. 13.1), the expression of thoughts and feelings are routinely controlled and censored in relationships.

This censoring process is revealed in many ways. For example, studies investigating the private thoughts and feelings that partners report while having discussions about relationship problems reveal that the behavior exhibited during these problem-solving discussions is relatively positive compared to the underlying set of reported cognitions and emotions, which presents a bleaker picture (Fletcher & Fitness, 1990; Fletcher & Thomas, 2000). The same research shows that the two spheres (thoughts/emotions and behavior) are correlated, but that the negativity of the thoughts and feelings are typically softened and packaged for public consumption, although it may translate in subtle ways into nonverbal behavior (see, for example, Fletcher & Fitness, 1990).

Moreover, people often lie in relationships. DePaula and Kashy (1998) asked people to keep a diary of the lies they told to others over 1 week. In that period those in nonmarital romantic relationships told on average close to one lie in every three interactions, whereas for married individuals this rate dropped to just under one lie for every 10 interactions. Many of these lies were white lies designed to protect the feelings of the other person (e.g., "you look great in those trousers"), but many were also classified as protecting the self in some way (e.g., "I said I did not know why the computer crashed because I didn't want to admit I caused the problem").

We noted previously that intimate relationships pose an approach–avoidance problem. There is increasing evidence that the way in which people regulate the self emphasizes goals of approaching positive outcomes and of avoiding negative outcomes in relationship contexts (see Finkel, Molden, Johnson, & Eastwick, 2009, for a review). These authors review research suggesting, for example, that promotion-focused individuals (who are oriented toward approaching gains and avoiding nongains) are more likely than prevention-focused individuals (who are oriented toward approaching nonlosses and avoiding losses) to perceive more romantic alternatives and to pursue them more vigorously.

We have more to say about self-regulation in intimate relationships in the later section dealing with communication. However, with this brief sketch of the intimate relationship mind as background, we move to discussing the work on attachment, love, and communication.

Attachment

Human infants and their caretakers are born to bond. The first psychologist to grasp and exploit this point—John Bowlby—produced a detailed version of what has come to be known as "attachment theory," which he detailed in three volumes from 1969 to 1980 (Bowlby, 1969, 1973, 1980). Based on observations of both human infants and other mammalian species, Bowlby discovered a standard sequence of responses produced by infants when separated from their caregiver—protest, despair, and detachment.

The most important elaboration of attachment theory, especially for later work dealing with adult intimate relationships, was provided by Ainsworth who developed the "strange situation" laboratory procedure in the 1960s and 1970s (Ainsworth, Blehar, Waters, & Wall, 1978). This procedure stressed infants by separating them from their mother, leaving them in the presence of a stranger. Ainsworth found a pattern that has since been generally replicated many times; the most common response of the infants tested (categorized as *secure*) was to cry when the mother left, seek comfort when she returned, and then settle down and continue playing with the toys. However, approximately 20% of the infants tested (who were categorized as *avoidant*) did not pay much attention to their mothers, were not particularly distressed when the mother left, and more or less ignored the mother on return. The remaining 10% to 15% of the infants tested (who were categorized as *anxious* or *ambivalent*) tended to behave in a contradictory fashion when the mother returned, whining, crying, and seeking physical contact, yet resisting and hanging back at the same time.

Bowlby's theory did not just deal with infant–adult attachment, but is also a theory of personality development over the life span. Bowlby (1973) was convinced that based on early pivotal experiences with mothers or caretakers, infants develop working cognitive models of attachment (expectations, attitudes, emotional reactions, and so forth) that are carried into adulthood. These working models, he postulated, should exert profound psychological influences throughout adult life on the nature of intimate relationships forged with both adults and children.

However, it was not until 1987 that Hazan and Shaver published the first systematic research applying attachment theory to adult intimate relationships. This article proved to be the big bang of adult attachment research, initiating a massive surge of theorizing and research focused on attachment in adult romantic relationships (for a recent review, see Mikulincer & Shaver, 2007). Hazan and Shaver argued that romantic love represents a reprise of the intense intimacy bonds generated in infant–caregiver attachments, and thus should resemble the patterns found in the developmental research.

Hazan and Shaver (1987) initially developed self-report measures of the three attachment working models, which they derived from the work of Bowlby and Ainsworth. From the following paragraphs participants were instructed to choose the one that best described themselves in terms of the feelings they typically experienced in romantic adult relationships:

> **Secure**: I find it relatively easy to get close to others and I am comfortable depending on them and having them depend on me.

I don't often worry about being abandoned or about someone getting too close to me.

Avoidant: I am somewhat uncomfortable being close to others. I find it difficult to trust them completely, difficult to allow myself to depend on them. I am nervous when anyone gets too close, and love partners often want me to be more intimate than I feel comfortable being.

Anxious: I find that others are reluctant to get as close to me as I would like. I often worry that my partner doesn't really love me or won't want to stay with me. I want to merge completely with another person, and this desire sometimes scares people away.

They found that the proportions of participants who endorsed each working model were similar to the figures obtained with infants from the Ainsworth strange situation, and that secure people reported more positive relationships with their parents than did avoidant or anxious participants (Hazan & Shaver, 1987). The barrage of research that followed this article has replicated these findings, but has, inevitably, complicated the attachment picture.

The Hazan and Shaver (1987) measurement method assumed that people fit into either one attachment working model or the other. This may seem like a reasonable assumption, but it has turned out to be wrong. Other researchers have developed multi-item scales that do not assume the categories are mutually exclusive. Factor analyses of these scales have consistently revealed the existence of two relatively independent attachment dimensions: secure versus avoidant on one dimension and the degree of attachment anxiety (high versus low) on the other dimension (Mikulincer & Shaver, 2007).

One important question studied has been the extent to which attachment working models are stable over time. Most studies examining stability of attachment from infancy (using the Ainsworth strange situation) to adulthood have reported correlations of 0.22 to 0.27 (Simpson, Winterfield, Rholes, & Orina, 2007; Fraley & Brumbaugh, 2004). This might not seem high, but given the power of the intervening experiences and events that might influence attachment, correlations of this size are impressive. Moreover, changes over long developmental periods do not seem to be a product of random noise; for example, some studies have found that suffering long illnesses or having parents who subsequently divorce was associated with a shift to more insecure working models, whereas individuals whose parents stayed together were more likely to shift to a secure working model (Lewis, Feiring, & Rosenthal, 2000).

Other studies that have investigated the stability of adult attachment working models in intimate sexual relationships reveal reasonable levels of consistency across periods of 6 months or a year, with about 30% of participants changing their dominant working model over time (see Baldwin & Fehr, 1995). Again, these shifts are not just a function of measurement noise. For example, Kirkpatrick and Hazan (1994) tracked 177 adults over a 4-year period, and reported that 50% of those individuals who reported they were originally secure (using the original categorical measure) and who experienced a relationship breakup switched to an avoidant working model. To summarize, the evidence indicates that across the life span attachment working models are relatively stable, but are also exquisitely attuned to external influences, especially intimate relationship experiences.

For Bowlby (1973), working models were internal cognitive representations that summarized the child's previous attachment experiences, both emotional and behavioral. Working models comprise beliefs about others and the self, and produce expectations and attitudes that can be used to predict consequences for future relationships. Working models, thus, provide the mechanism and the link between childhood and adult relationships. Specifically, consistent with Bowlby's prediction, when individuals or relationships are put under stress, higher levels of avoidance in working models increase the fear of rejection, which leads to withdrawal and a reluctance to seek or offer support (Collins & Feeney, 2004; Simpson, Rholes, & Nelligan; 1992). However, there is also evidence that working models differentiate among different categories of relationship partners in adulthood. For example, there is good evidence that different working models can apply to family, friends, and romantic relationships, although it is also true that attachment working models are positively correlated across these groups (Baldwin, Keelan, Fehr, Enns, & Koh-Rangarajoo, 1996; Overall, Fletcher, & Friesen, 2003).

Attachment working models are related to the goals already described (see Fig. 13.1). For example, research has shown that when more secure individuals explain negative behaviors from their partners (e.g., failing to comfort them when they were depressed), they are more inclined to produce charitable attributions apparently designed to maintain their belief in the essential warmth and trustworthiness of their partner (e.g., the partner had a bad cold). In contrast, more anxious individuals adopt a more negative pattern and emphasize their partner's indifference to their needs and lack of commitment (Collins, Ford, Guichard, & Allard, 2006). These findings by Collins et al. were not produced by differences in relationship satisfaction between secure and anxious individuals, because they found that these effects remained strong after statistically controlling for the impact of relationship satisfaction.

Finally, there is evidence that attachment working models are used to regulate behavior. In a pioneering piece of research, Simpson, Rholes, and Nelligan (1992) revisited Bowlby's hypothesis that the attachment systems should be initiated when individuals are placed under stress (indeed, this is the basis for the strange situation procedure developed by Ainsworth). Thus, Simpson and colleagues surreptitiously observed the behavior of couples sitting in a waiting room, after the woman in each couple had been stressed by information about an upcoming experiment, which never actually took place, but which supposedly involved painful experiences. The more stressed the women became, the more their attachment working models (assessed prior to the experiment) seemed to influence their behavior; for example, more secure women sought more support whereas more avoidant women avoided seeking support from their partner, to the extent of expressing irritation if their partners asked what was wrong or proffered support.

To summarize, attachment working models operate like highly accessible general or local relationship lay theories. When triggered, they automatically influence relationship judgments or decisions. More specifically, the activation of a relationship threat automatically calls up attachment working models. The nature of those attachment working models (which may be specific to particular targets) will then partly determine the subsequent emotions, cognitions, and behavioral responses.

Love

The nature of romantic love and its origins are all too often proclaimed as a mystery or as beyond the reach of science. In fact, scientific investigation into the phenomenon of love is rapidly demonstrating that the opposite is true, with (social) psychology in the vanguard of contemporary research (Reis & Aron, 2008).

Romantic love is not simply an invention of Western cultures. Jankowiak and Fischer (1992) found good evidence (based on folk tales, ethnographies, evidence of elopement, and so forth) that romantic love exists in 147 of 166 cultures studied. This is a conservative figure, given that in 18 of the 19 love-absent cultures the ethnographic accounts were uninformative rather than definitive, and in only one culture did an ethnographer claim that romantic love did not actually exist. Moreover, romantic love is not simply a product of modern cultures—the power and addictive nature of love have been noted in poetry and literature going back 3000 years (Fowler, 1994).

Romantic love has other features that mark it out as basic and universal. It has a specific neuropsychological signature, including the release of hormones such as oxytocin and dopamine (Fisher, 2004). Like all hormones these substances have multiple functions in the brain and in the body; when they are released in the brain, they operate as neurotransmitters with oxytocin being associated with bonding and affiliation behavior and dopamine associated with rewards and pleasure. Moreover, both these neurotransmitters tend to be focused on the same part of the brain (the nucleus accumbens), and thus are implicated in the development of mate attraction and bonding (Insel, 2000; Aragona et al., 2006).

Monogamy is rare among mammalian species, with only 3% to 5% forming long-term pair bonds. In species that do so, such as humans, there is evidence that both males and females have extensive receptors for oxytocin (or a closely related neuropeptide called vasopressin). In contrast, in species in which the males are promiscuous, only the females possess such extensive receptors in the brain for this neuropeptide (which is thought to be associated with the need for females to bond with immature, defenseless offspring) (Insel, 2000).

Romantic love also has characteristic behavioral displays and interactions that have their precursors in adult–infant interactions. Interactions between infants and doting parents reveal that parents seem fascinated with the infant's appearance, maintain much eye contact, express considerable affection, indulge in horse-play, and are exquisitely attuned to the needs of the infant. The same behavioral interactions are equally descriptive of couples head over heels in love (Shaver, Morgan, & Wu, 1996). In a series of studies Gonzaga and colleagues have shown that couples display distinctive affiliation behaviors toward each other when, for example, discussing their first date—head nods, smiles, positive hand movements, and leaning toward the partner (see Gonzaga & Haselton, 2008, for a review). Moreover, this pattern of behaviors is distinct from the way in which other closely related emotions, such as happiness, desire, or arousal, are expressed.

There also exists a plausible evolutionary account that specifies the functions that love has evolved to meet (Gonzaga & Haselton, 2008). Compared to other primates, humans have exceptionally large brains and thus heads; to achieve egress though the birth canal they must be born at an unusually undeveloped stage (for a mammal). As a result, humans are dependent on their parents and other relatives for exceptionally long periods of time before attaining adulthood (compared to other animals including primates) and also require a tremendous amount of informal and formal education from their parents to acquire the social, cultural, and practical knowledge necessary for survival and reproductive success. Accordingly, as brain size and childhood length steadily increased over the last million or so years of *Homo* evolution, there were probably strong selection pressures toward the development of (relatively) monogamous pair bonding (Fisher, 2004; also see Maner & Kenrick, Chapter 17, this volume).

Thus, love is an evolutionary device designed to encourage couples to stay together long enough to enable their children to reach adulthood. Reproductive success counts only if the progeny make it to adulthood and pass their parents' genes (in turn) to their offspring. The existence of a stable monogamous couple in a hunter–gatherer lifestyle also allows for a potentially valuable division of labor, with the man being the dominant provider and the woman being the dominant caregiver (although in hunter–gatherer cultures both genders typically perform both functions). In brief, in the human ancestral environment, two parents were better than one (Gonzaga & Haselton, 2008).

This sort of evolutionary account is consistent with evidence that the most important standards across cultures (for both men and women) for mates in long-term relationships consistently concern a partner's warmth and trustworthiness (Buss, 1989). However, recent research suggests that romantic love is not one thing, but is based around two or three distinct psychological (and biological) components. Shaver, Hazan, and Bradshaw (1988) conceptualized adult romantic love in terms of Bowlby's (evolutionary) treatment of attachment systems in humans. Bowlby argued for the existence of three basic behavioral systems that bond dyads together: attachment, caregiving, and sex. Thus, Shaver et al. (p. 93) wrote that saying "I love you" can mean any or all of the following (note the role of emotions in the descriptions).

- ***Love as attachment***: "I am emotionally dependent on you for happiness, safety, and security; I feel anxious and lonely when you're gone, relieved and stronger when you're near. I want to be comforted, supported emotionally, and taken care of by you. Part of my identity is based on my attachment to you."
- ***Love as caregiving***: "I get great pleasure from supporting, caring for, and taking care of you; from facilitating your progress, health, growth, and happiness. Part of my identity is based on caring for you, and if you were to disappear I would feel sad, empty, less worthwhile, and perhaps guilty."
- ***Love as sexual attraction***: "I am sexually attracted to you and can't get you out of my mind. You excite me, 'turn me on,' make me feel alive, complete my sense of wholeness. I want to see you, devour you, touch you, merge with you, lose myself in you, 'get off on you.'"

Berscheid and Walster (1978) provided an influential attempt to conceptualize (sexual) love in terms of two basic factors: companionate love and passionate love. Companionate love captures the former two categories (attachment and caregiving), whereas passionate love is akin to sexual attraction. Research using a prototype approach (Fehr, 1994), or the use of factor analysis to identify latent factors (Aron & Westbay, 1996), suggests that laypeople think about love based on the same kinds of distinctions, namely, in terms of intimacy (or attachment), commitment (or caregiving), and passion (or sexual attraction) (also see Sternberg, 1986).

If love is a commitment device, as an evolutionary approach suggests, then it should function to end the search for alternative mates. Indeed, there is good evidence this is just what happens. For example, Johnson and Rusbult (1989) showed that higher levels of commitment in romantic relationships are associated with the tendency to derogate attractive alternatives. Moreover, these processes appear to operate in an unconscious, automatic fashion. In one study (Maner, Gailliot, & Miller, 2009), participants were primed with mate selection goals. For those who were single this increased their attention to attractive pictures of the opposite sex, whereas for those in existing romantic relationships the opposite was the case.

There is also considerable evidence that when people are in love, they idealize their partners and put a rose-colored spin on judgments of them and their relationships. For example, people routinely rate the chances that their own marriages will fail as considerably lower than their perceptions of the population base rates (Fowers, Lyons, Montel, & Shaked, 2001), and keep doubts about their relationship at bay by restructuring judgments or rewriting their relationship stories (see Murray, 2001). And as love prospers and grows more intense, individuals increasingly exaggerate their similarity with their partners (Murray et al., 2002), the extent to which their relationships have improved over time (Karney & Frye, 2002), and the extent to which their real-life partners resemble archetypal ideals (Murray, Holmes, & Griffin, 1996).

However, there are also strong arguments and evidence suggesting that love may not be so blind. The fact that many long-term romantic relationships dissolve suggests that the motivating power of love to promote positive bias has its limitations. Moreover, a broad array of empirical evidence suggests that lay judgments of partners and relationships are firmly tied to reality. For example, relationship evaluations strongly predict both interactive behavior (e.g., Fletcher & Thomas, 2000) and relationship dissolution (see Karney & Bradbury, 1995), and are shared across partners (e.g., Campbell, Simpson, Kashy, & Fletcher, 2001). And studies using a range of external criteria or benchmarks (including self-reports of the partner, observer ratings of interactive behavior, and the predicted future or recalled past states of the relationship) reveal quite good levels of accuracy in relationship and partner judgments (for a recent review see Fletcher & Boyes, 2008).

One way of resolving this apparent contradiction is that there may be two independent ways of measuring the accuracy of judgments in intimate relationships: *mean-level bias* and *tracking accuracy.* Consider the following example (adapted from Fletcher, 2002). Mary rates her partner Stephen (using 1–7 Likert scales) as being extremely sensitive (7), very warm (6), very sexy (6), and moderately ambitious (5). Now imagine that we have gold standard criteria that show, in reality, that Stephen is two units less positive than Mary's ratings (5, 4, 4, and 3, respectively). This pattern shows that Mary is positively biased (she is on average two units more positive than Stephen is on each trait). However, it is also apparent that Mary is accurately tracking Stephen's traits for this example; as Mary's traits become more or less positive so do Stephen's judgments (if you put this simple data set into a statistics program you will see that the correlation between the two sets of scores is a perfect 1.0). It is also possible for Mary to be biased and tracking inaccurately, or, be unbiased and tracking accurately, or, finally, to be unbiased and tracking inaccurately (you could try manipulating the scores in a data file to achieve each of these results).

Thus, it is possible for people to have the best of both worlds in romantic relationships and to be both positively biased and accurate at the same time. To illustrate, consider some recent research on the so-called "affective forecasting error" in relationship contexts (Eastwick, Finkel, Krishnamurti, & Loewenstein, 2008). Prior evidence has indicated a robust tendency in nonrelationship contexts for people to predict greater levels of negative or positive affect, following negative or positive events, than actually happen (an example of mean-level bias). The research by Eastwick et al. found the same effect when individuals first predicted and then experienced the affective outcomes associated with a dating relationship break up; people experienced significantly less distress than they predicted (effect size $r = 0.66$). However, they also evinced significant tracking accuracy of their emotional reactions ($r = 0.44$). And the forecasting (mean-level) error disappeared for those who were not in love with their partners when making the forecasts, or indicated a week prior to the break up that it was likely they would start a new romantic relationship, or who initiated the break up. In short, only those who were significantly invested in the relationship predicted more distress than they experienced when the relationship actually dissolved. It is hard to resist the conclusion that this bias has a functional basis, given that it should motivate individuals who have much at stake to maintain and improve their romantic relationship, and perhaps retain their mates.

There is also evidence that bias in people's judgments will depend on their goals. A study by Rusbult, Van Lange, Wildschut, Yevetich, and Verette (2000) showed that people who were instructed to be as accurate as possible had less positive bias when describing their relationships. Moreover, the correlations between relationship commitment and positive bias were strongest in a relationship threat condition (0.61), moderate in the control condition (0.37), and weakest when an accuracy goal was primed (0.17).

Communication

As noted previously, the defining feature of intimate relationships is interdependence; one partner's desires, goals, and happiness depend on the desires, goals and behavior of the other partner (Kelley & Thibaut, 1978). Inevitably, however, situations will arise in which partners' goals clash (e.g., negotiating household chores or amount of time spent together) and one partner behaves negatively (e.g., is critical or withdraws from affection) or disregards the others' needs (e.g., fails to provide necessary support or refuses to accept an apology). Thus, one key question is how couples maintain satisfying relationships in the face of conflict. Motivated by the assumption that marital distress is caused by destructive reactions to conflict, researchers in the 1970s studied the communication behaviors partners exchange when discussing relationship problems. This approach has yielded hundreds of studies that employ arguably the most time-consuming and sophisticated methodological and analytic techniques within the field.

The standard paradigm involves recording couples discussing an unresolved relationship issue and then measuring communication behavior using extensive coding systems (see Heyman, 2001). For example, the Marital Interaction Coding System (MICS; Weiss & Summers, 1983) involves assigning each person's comments and behavior each time they speak or within every 10-second block to one of 28 categories, such as whether the individual criticizes, puts down, or interrupts his or her partner, proposes solutions and compromises, or displays humor and physical affection. Single codes are then counted across the interaction and combined to measure broad dimensions of behavior, such as overall levels of hostility. Comparisons between distressed and nondistressed couples have revealed that couples who are less satisfied tend to be more likely to criticize, express more hostility, interrupt, defensively withdraw, propose fewer positive solutions, and express less positive affect such as humor, smiling, and affection (for reviews of this vast literature see Gottman, 1998; Gottman & Notarius, 2000; Weiss & Heyman, 1997).

This initial work was expanded by employing longitudinal designs to test whether destructive communication predicted important relationship outcomes, such as declines in relationship satisfaction or divorce. In 1995, Karney and Bradbury conducted a meta-analytic review of these studies and found that the presence of negative interaction behavior was linked to a greater probability of divorce and reduced satisfaction of both partners over time. In contrast, positive interaction behavior was associated with more happiness and a lower likelihood of divorce. The message from this massive literature supports the intuitions of the pioneers—engaging in hostile, critical, or demanding communication behavior produces relationship dysfunction, whereas expressing positive affect to soften conflict interactions promotes relationship quality.

But why is negative communication so toxic for intimate relationships? Two interaction patterns seem to play a central role in this process. First, Gottman (1994, 1998) reported that a particularly unhealthy dyadic exchange is negative reciprocity—when negative behavior by one partner is met with intensified negative behavior by the other (Gottman, 1998). Second, Christensen and his colleagues found that critical, blaming, and demanding communication from the person who wants change (more often the woman) often elicits defensive withdrawal from the targeted partner (more often the man) and this demand-withdraw pattern predicts poorer problem resolution and reduced relationship satisfaction (Christensen & Heavey, 1990; Heavey, Layne, & Christensen, 1993; Klinetob & Smith, 1996). In short, hostile and blaming communications, as a response to conflict or relationship problems, tend to drive negative interactions that can all too readily spiral downward over time.

This pattern highlights a key point: The consequences for the relationship of a given communication attempt will be partly determined by how the other partner responds (a point we return to later). In the 1990s there were two shifts from the (clinical) focus on overt behaviors. First, as previously noted, there was increasing emphasis on the role that beliefs and perceptions play in understanding communication and relationship maintenance (Fletcher & Fincham, 1991). For example, reflecting a theme from interdependence theory, the explanations that individuals generate for relationship events are linked to relationship satisfaction. The standard finding, across many studies, shows that unhappy intimates attribute negative partner behavior to undesirable personality traits and intentions (e.g., "he is uncaring and selfish"), but attribute positive partner behavior to external factors, such as a having a rare good day (e.g., Bradbury & Fincham, 1992). Happy partners, in contrast, attribute negative behaviors to external attributions (having a hard day at work) but attribute positive behaviors to stable, internal traits (caring and unselfish). Moreover, the former, uncharitable attributional pattern is associated with destructive communication during problem-solving discussions, such as less support and agreement and more criticism, withdrawal, and negative reciprocity (Bradbury & Fincham, 1992; Bradbury, Beach, Fincham, & Nelson, 1996; Miller & Bradbury, 1995).

Exploring the links between cognition and behavior also provides a window into how personal traits influence communication within intimate relationships. For example, as previously noted, chronic expectations of rejection associated with attachment anxiety lead to perceptions that the partner's actions, such as the failure to reciprocate a cuddle, are designed to reject and hurt the partner (Collins, et al., 2006). Furthermore, this attribution bias leads anxious individuals to react with greater hostility and anger during problem-solving discussions (Simpson, Rholes, & Phillips, 1996) and these destructive reactions tend to escalate conflict during daily life (Campbell, Simpson, Boldry, & Kashy, 2005). Finally, consistent with the above communication patterns, hostile and defensive behavior arising from expectations of rejection evoke anger and dissatisfaction in the partner (Downey, Frietas, Michaelis, & Khouri, 1998). As can be seen, this work has effectively tracked down some of the key mechanisms that explain why insecure attachment undermines relationship satisfaction and stability.

The second shift, referred to previously, involved recognizing that communication is important in maintaining relationships when faced with any kind of relationship threat, not just in situations of overt conflict. For example, Caryl Rusbult and colleagues (Rusbult, Zembrodt, & Gunn, 1982) detailed four typical responses (EVLN) people described when feeling dissatisfied in their relationship.

Exit: Active behaviors that are destructive for the relationship, such as ending or threatening to terminate the relationship, and abusing, criticizing, or derogating the partner.

Voice: Constructive active behaviors such as attempting to improve conditions by discussing problems, suggesting solutions, and altering problematic behavior.

Loyalty: Passively waiting and hoping for improvement, forgiving and forgetting partner offences, and maintaining faith in the partner even when faced with hurtful actions.

Neglect: Passive destructive responses such as allowing the relationship to deteriorate by ignoring or spending less time with the partner and avoiding discussions of problems.

This typology captures many of the overt communication behaviors examined in dyadic conflict discussions previously described. For example, exit incorporates behaviors such as hostility, anger, and criticism, and neglect encapsulates withdrawal. In addition, research using this typology to examine peoples' responses to negative partner behavior reveals that communication within everyday interactions (not just laboratory-based ones) produces similar effects. Couples who tend to engage in exit and neglect report lower problem resolution and reduced satisfaction and commitment (Drigotas, Whitney, & Rusbult, 1995; Rusbult, Johnson, & Morrow, 1986a, b; Rusbult, Verette, Whitney, Slovik, & Lipkus, 1991).

Furthermore, a pattern of responding that represents the opposite of the negative reciprocity and demand-withdraw patterns identified in the laboratory plays an important role in the maintenance of relationship well-being. Accommodation—the tendency to inhibit destructive exit and neglect responses when faced with negative partner behavior and instead react constructively with voice and loyalty—is associated with increases in relationship satisfaction (Rusbult, Bissonnette, Arriaga, & Cox, 1998). This is because accommodation builds trust and commitment (Weiselquist, Rusbult, Foster, & Agnew, 1999) and eases problematic interactions by maintaining feelings of acceptance and intimacy (Overall & Sibley, 2008).

Thus far, it is beginning to look as if sweetness and accommodation are the recipes for relationship success. However, more recent work has suggested that things are not this simple. Some studies have reported that negative communication predicts relative *increases* in relationship satisfaction across time (e.g., Cohan & Bradbury, 1997; Heavey et al., 1993, 1995; Karney & Bradbury, 1997), which suggests the exact opposite of the standard finding. Such findings (often called reversal effects), at face value, seem odd if not bizarre.

However, it turns out that the distinction between active and passive communication embodied in the EVLN typology may provide the solution to this puzzle. Recall that voice and exit involve individuals actively addressing and attempting to solve the problem (voice) or directly expressing their anger and discontent (exit). In contrast, loyalty and neglect are passive responses because individuals avoid the problem by withdrawing from the relationship (neglect) or passively waiting for the problem to solve itself (loyalty).

First, these reversal effects are restricted to negative behaviors that are active and direct, such as criticism and blame. Similarly, some research has shown that constructive but passive behavior, such as using humor to minimize conflict or being loyal and waiting for things to improve, is associated with lower relationship satisfaction (Cohan & Bradbury, 1997) and has a weaker effect on solving the problem compared to active voice-type responses (Drigotas et al., 1995; Overall, Sibley & Travaglia, 2010; Rusbult et al., 1986a, b). Second, expressing anger and hostility clearly communicates the nature and severity of the problem, thus perhaps motivating partners to bring about change and therefore leading to successful problem resolution. Positive loyal responses, in contrast, may reduce conflict in the short term, but leave the problem unaddressed (Holmes & Murray, 1996).

In support of this explanation, recent research has found that using active exit-type communication behavior, such as being demanding and derogating the partner, generates significant partner change over time (Overall, Fletcher, Simpson, & Sibley, 2009). This research also found that active constructive behavior, such as directly discussing causes and solutions, is associated with a greater change in targeted problems over time, whereas loyalty-type responses, such as using positive affect to soften conflict, fail to produce the desired change.

However, this does not mean that being obnoxious is good for relationships. Although a critical, blaming approach might prompt greater change in the partner, the well-established patterns of negative reciprocity and demand-withdraw suggest that this approach will nevertheless elicit hostility and defensive reactions in the partner. These destructive effects are unlikely to be fleeting, and the positive changes that are produced by active communication may counterbalance—but *not* reverse—the negative impact of these behaviors. Thus, improving problem resolution might best be accomplished by using active strategies that also communicate care and regard, such as directly discussing problems and suggesting solutions, as long as the message is not gift-wrapped to the point that it appears as if the communicator does not really care whether the situation changes or not (see Overall et al., 2009).

In summary, the examination of how couples communicate when managing dissatisfaction and conflict in their relationships has revealed a sizable list of behaviors that are likely to be damaging to the relationship. These fall within the general categories of critical hostility, reciprocating negativity, and defensive withdrawal. However, the research also suggests that the link between negative communication and poor relationship outcomes is not straightforward. Instead, highlighting the truly dyadic nature of behavior in intimate relationships, the impact of specific communications depends on how the partner responds, including whether the partner attacks, retreats, or accommodates and/or makes desired changes. Moreover, the same communication behavior might have different, and sometimes opposing, consequences. For example, hostile and demanding communication may be more likely to prompt change but at the cost of generating feelings of negativity (even hatred) in the partner.

Relationships Today: Caveats and Conclusions

One question often asked of social psychologists working in this area concerns the future of contemporary intimate relationships, given the way in which individuals are bombarded with information about relationships, along with images of beautiful people and their beautiful partners. The availability of personal computers and the Internet has also rendered this information a mouse-click away for most people, and introduced on-line Internet dating, which has rapidly become a popular way to meet potential partners (see Finkel & Baumeister, Chapter 12, this volume).

Our answer is two-fold. First, humans are cultural animals, born to live and learn within cultures (Baumeister, 2005). Thus, the kind of cultural shifts we have (and are) witnessing since the last ice age—from about 11,000 years ago when *Homo sapiens* started the long march from an ancient hunter–gatherer life style to the contemporary information age—is bound to exert massive influences on personal intimate relationships. However, human nature is not just a cultural product but is forged in the evolutionary past, which is why the topics dealt with in this chapter have a universal, timeless quality about them. Evolutionary processes have left biological and psychological footprints all over the intimate relationship mind.

Intimate relationships are complex and multifaceted, as we have seen. It would be wrong to assume that social psychology can provide all the tools and means to understand how and why they work; for that we need an interdisciplinary approach that combines biology, zoology, evolutionary psychology, cross-cultural psychology, the study of culture, developmental psychology, and neuropsychology. And although social psychologists inevitably study specific topics in depth, including love or communication, such intimate relationship domains are thoroughly intertwined as this chapter makes clear.

Nevertheless, we believe that social psychology will continue to provide the cornerstone of future interdisciplinary endeavors because it combines the major elements of the proximal psychological system that powerfully predicts and explains personal experience in intimate relationships. Social psychologists build process models that combine individual differences in what people bring with them into local intimate relationships (traits, attitudes, beliefs, and resources) with subsequent cognitive and affective processes and behavioral interactions. Moreover, such models detail how these psychological systems change and function over time.

Social psychologists build theories and test hypotheses, but so do laypeople, especially about phenomena that have special significance in their lives. And intimate relationships have primary significance or centrality in people's everyday lives. Thus, the scientist must take lay theories and beliefs about intimate relationships seriously. Even if they are wrong or muddled (as they sometimes are) they still exert powerful causal influences on everyday relationship behavior.

At the beginning of this chapter we enumerated a series of questions of the sort asked by social psychologists in the study of intimate relationships: How do people know they are in good relationships? Why do some people have problems with intimacy? What is the nature and origin of love? Does good communication really produce successful relationships? Because (social) psychology is a science, answering such fascinating questions is a work in progress. Nevertheless, we trust we have provided some idea of both the state of the play and where the science, fueled by human curiosity, is leading us.

References

Ainsworth, M. D. S., Blehar, M. C., Waters, E., & Wall, S. (1978). *Patterns of attachment: A psychological study of the strange situation*. Hillsdale, NJ: Erlbaum.

Anthony, D. B., Holmes, J. G., & Wood, J. V. (2007). Social acceptance and self-esteem: Tuning the sociometer to interpersonal value. *Journal of Personality and Social Psychology, 92*, 1024–1039.

Aragona, B. J., Liu, Y., Yu, Y. J., Curtis, J. T., Detwiler, J. M., Insel, T. R., & Wang, Z. X. (2006). Nucleus accumbens dopamine differentially mediates the formation and maintenance of monogamous pair bonds. *Nature Neuroscience, 9*, 133–139.

Aron, A., Aron, E. N., & Norman, C. (2001). Self-expansion model of motivation and cognition in close relationships and beyond. In G. J. O. Fletcher & M. S. Clark (Eds.), *Blackwell handbook of social psychology: Interpersonal processes* (pp. 478–501). Oxford, UK: Blackwell.

Aron, A., & Westbay, L. (1996). Dimensions of the prototype of love. *Journal of Personality and Social Psychology, 70*, 535–551.

Baldwin, M. W., & Fehr, B. (1995). On the instability of attachment style ratings. *Personal Relationships, 2*, 247–261.

Baldwin, M. W., Keelan, J. P. R., Fehr, B., Enns, V., & Koh-Rangarajoo, E. (1996). Social-cognitive conceptualization of attachment working models: Availability and accessibility effects. *Journal of Personality & Social Psychology, 71*, 94–109.

Baumeister, R. F. (2005). *The cultural animal: Human nature, meaning, and social life*. New York: Oxford University Press.

Berscheid, E. (1983). Emotion. In H. H. Kelley, E. Berscheid, A. Christensen, J. Harvey, T. Huston, G. Levinger, D. McClintock, L. Peplau, & D. Peterson (Eds.), *Close relationships* (pp. 110–168). San Francisco, CA: Freeman.

Berscheid, E., & Walster, E. H. (1978). *Interpersonal attraction* (2nd ed.). Reading, MA: Addison-Wesley.

Bowlby, J. (1969). *Attachment and loss*: Vol. 1. *Attachment*. New York: Basic Books.

Bowlby, J. (1973). *Attachment and loss*: Vol. 2. *Separation: Anger and anxiety*. New York: Basic.

Bowlby, J. (1980). *Attachment and loss*: Vol. 3. *Loss*. New York: Basic Books.

Bradbury, T. N., Beach, S. R. H., Fincham, F. D., & Nelson, G. M. (1996). Attributions and behavior in functional and dysfunctional marriages. *Journal of Consulting and Clinical Psychology, 64*, 569–576.

Bradbury, T. N., & Fincham, F. D. (1992). Attributions and behavior in marital interaction. *Journal of Personality and Social Psychology*, 63, 613–628.

Bradbury, T. N., & Karney, B.R. (1993). Longitudinal study of marital interaction and dysfunction: Review and analysis. *Clinical Psychology Review, 13*, 15–27.

Buss, D. M. (1989). Sex differences in human mate preferences: Evolutionary hypotheses testing in 37 cultures. *Behavioral and Brain Sciences*, 12, 1–49

Bylsma, W. H., Cozzarelli, C., & Sumer, N. (1997). Relation between adult attachment styles and global self-esteem. *Basic and Applied Social Psychology, 19*, 1–16.

Campbell, L., Simpson, J.A., Boldry, J., & Kashy, D.A. (2005). Perceptions of conflict and support in romantic relationships: The role of attachment anxiety. *Journal of Personality and Social Psychology, 88*, 510–531.

Campbell, L., Simpson, J. A., Kashy, D. A., & Fletcher, G. J. O. (2001). Ideal standards, the self, and flexibility of ideals in close relationships. *Personality and Social Psychology Bulletin, 27*, 447–462

Christensen, A., & Heavey, C.L. (1990). Gender and social structure in the demand/ withdraw pattern of marital conflict. *Journal of Personality and Social Psychology*, 59, 73–81.

Clark, M. S., Fitness, J., & Brisette, I. (2001). Understanding people's perceptions of relationships is crucial to understanding their emotional lives. In G. J. O. Fletcher & M. Clark (Eds.), *Blackwell handbook of social psychology: Interpersonal processes* (pp. 252–278). Malden, MA: Blackwell.

Cohan, C. L., & Bradbury, T. N. (1997). Negative life events, marital interaction, and the longitudinal course of newlywed marriage. *Journal of Personality and Social Psychology, 73*, 114–128.

Collins, N. L., & Feeney, B. C. (2004). Working models of attachment shape perceptions of social support: Evidence from experimental and observational studies. *Journal of Personality and Social Psychology, 87*, 363–383.

Collins, N. L., Ford, M. B., Guichard, A. C., & Allard, L. M. (2006). Working models of attachment and attribution processes in intimate relationships. *Personality and Psychological Bulletin, 32*, 210–219.

Damasio, A. R. (1994). *Descartes' error: Emotion, reason and the human brain*. New York: G. P. Putnam.

Darwin, C. (1872). *The expression of the emotions in man and animals*. London: Murray.

DePaulo, B. M. & Kashy, D. A. (1998). Everyday lies in close and casual relationships. *Journal of Personality and Social Psychology, 74, 63-79*.

Downey, G., Frietas, A.L., Michaelis, B., & Khouri, H. (1998). The self-fulfilling prophecy in close relationships: Rejection sensitivity and rejection by romantic partners. *Journal of Personality and Social Psychology*, 75, 545–560.

Drigotas, S. M., Whitney, G. A., & Rusbult, C. E. (1995). On the peculiarities of loyalty: A diary study of responses to dissatisfaction in everyday life. *Personality and Social Psychology Bulletin*, 21, 596–609.

Eastwick, P. W., Finkel, E. J., Krishnamurti, T., & Loewenstein, G. (2008). Mispredicting distress following romantic breakup: Revealing the time course of the affective forecasting error. *Journal of Experimental Social Psychology, 44*, 800–807.

Fehr, B. (1994). Prototype-based assessment of laypeople's views of love. *Personal Relationships, 1*, 309–331.

Fehr, B. (1999). Layperson's perception of commitment. *Journal of Personality and Social Psychology, 76*, 90–103.

Finkel, E. J., Molden, D. C., Johnson, S. E., & Eastwick, P. W. (2009). Regulatory focus and romantic alternatives. In J. Forgas, R. F. Baumeister, & D. M. Tice (Eds.), *Psychology of self-regulation: Cognitive, affective, and motivational processes* (319-355). London: Psychology Press.

Fisher, H. (2004). *Why we love: The nature and chemistry of romantic love*. New York: Holt.

Fitness, J. (1996). Emotion knowledge structures in close relationships. In G. J. O. Fletcher & J. Fitness (Eds.), *Knowledge structures in close relationships: A social psychological approach* (pp. 195–218). Mahwah, NJ: Erlbaum.

Fitness, J., & Fletcher, G. J. O. (1993). Love, hate, anger and jealousy in close relationships: A cognitive appraisal and prototype analysis. *Journal of Personality and Social Psychology, 65*, 942–958.

Fitness, J., Fletcher, G. J. O., & Overall, N. (2003). Interpersonal Attraction and Intimate Relationships. In M. Hogg & J. Cooper (Eds.). *Sage handbook of social psychology* (pp. 258-276). London: Sage.

Fletcher, G. J. O. (2002). *The new science of intimate relationships*. Cambridge, UK: Blackwell.

Fletcher, G. J. O., & Boyes, A. D. (2008). Is love blind? Reality and illusion in intimate relationships. In J. Forgas & J. Fitness (Eds.), *Social relationships: Cognitive, affective and motivational processes* (pp. 101–114). Cambridge, UK: Cambridge University Press.

Fletcher, G. J. O., & Fincham, F. D. (Eds.) (1991). *Cognition in close relationships*. Hillsdale, NJ: Erlbaum.

Fletcher, G. J. O., & Fitness, J. (1990). Occurrent social cognition in close relationships: The role of proximal and distal variables. *Journal of Personality and Social Psychology, 59*, 464–474.

Fletcher, G. J. O., Rosanowski, J., & Fitness, J. (1994). Automatic processing in intimate contexts: The role of close-relationship beliefs. *Journal of Personality and Social Psychology, 67*, 888–97.

Fletcher, G. J. O., Simpson, J., & Thomas, G. (2000). Ideals, perceptions and evaluations in early relationship development. *Journal of Personality and Social Psychology, 79*, 933–940.

Fletcher, G. J. O., Simpson, J. A., Thomas, G., & Giles, L. (1999). Ideals in intimate relationships. *Journal of Personality and Social Psychology, 76*, 72–89.

Fletcher, G. J. O., & Thomas, G. (1996). Close relationship lay theories: Their structure and function. In G. J. O. Fletcher & J. Fitness (Eds.), *Knowledge structures in close relationships* (pp. 3–24). Mahwah, NJ: Erlbaum.

Fletcher, G. J. O., & Thomas, G. (2000). Behavior and on-line cognition in marital interaction: A longitudinal study. *Personal Relationships, 7,* 111–130.

Fletcher, G. J. O., Thomas, G., & Durrant, R. (1999). Cognitive and behavioral accommodation in relationship interaction. *Journal of Social and Personal Relationships, 16,* 705–730.

Fowers, B. J., Lyons, E., Montel, K. H., & Shaked, N. (2001). Positive illusions about marriage among married and single individuals. *Journal of Family Psychology, 15,* 95–109.

Fowler, B. H. (1994). *Love lyrics of ancient Egypt.* Chapel Hill: University of North Carolina Press.

Fraley, C. F., & Brumbaugh, C. C. (2004). A dynamical systems approach to conceptualizing and studying stability and change in attachment security. In W. S. Rholes & J. A. Simpson (Eds.), *Adult attachment: Theory, research, and clinical implications* (pp. 86–132). New York: Guilford Press.

Gable, S. L., & Poore, J. (2008). Which thoughts count? Algorithms for evaluating satisfaction in relationships. *Psychological Science, 19,* 1030–1036.

Gillath, O., Mikulincer, M., Fitzsimons, G. M., Shaver, P. R., Schachner, D. A., & Bargh, J. A. (2006). Automatic activation of attachment-related goals. *Personality and Social Psychology Bulletin, 32,* 1375–1388.

Gonzaga, G. C., & Haselton, M. G. (2008). The evolution of love and long-term bonds. In J. P. Forgas & J. Fitness (Eds.), *Social relationships: Cognitive, affective and motivational Processes* (pp. 39–54). Cambridge, UK: Cambridge University Press

Gottman, J. M. (1979). *Marital interaction: Experimental investigations.* New York: Academic Press.

Gottman, J.M. (1994). *What predicts divorce?* Hillsdale, NJ: Erlbaum.

Gottman, J. M. (1990). How marriages change. In G. R. Patterson (Ed.), *Depression and aggression in family interaction* (pp. 75–101). Hillsdale, NJ: Erlbaum.

Gottman, J. M. (1998). Psychology and the study of marital processes. *Annual Review of Psychology, 49,* 169–197.

Gottman, J. M., & Notarius, C. I. (2000). Decade review: Observing marital interaction. *Journal of Marriage and the Family, 62,* 927–947.

Hazan, C., & Shaver, P. (1987). Romantic love conceptualized as an attachment process. *Journal of Personality and Social Psychology, 52,* 511–24.

Heavey, C. L., Christensen, A., & Malamuth, N.M. (1995). The longitudinal impact of demand and withdrawal during marital conflict. *Journal of Consulting and Clinical Psychology, 63,* 797–801.

Heavey, C. L., Layne, C., & Christensen, A. (1993). Gender and conflict structure in marital interaction: A replication and extension. *Journal of Consulting and Clinical Psychology, 61,* 16–27.

Heyman, R. E. (2001). Observation of couple conflicts: Clinical assessment applications, stubborn truths, and shaky foundations. *Psychological Assessment, 13,* 5–35.

Holmes, J. G., & Murray, S. L. (1996). Conflict in close relationships. In E. T. Higgins & A. Kruglanski (Eds.), *Social psychology: Handbook of basic principles* (pp. 622–654). New York: Guilford Press.

Insel, T. R. (2000). Toward a neurobiology of attachment. *Review of General Psychology, 4*, 176–185.

Jankowiak, W. R., & Fischer, E. F. (1992). A cross-cultural perspective on romantic love. *Ethnology, 31*, 149–155.

Johnson, D. J., & Rusbult, C. E. (1989). Resisting temptation: Devaluation of alternative partners as a means of maintaining commitment in close relationships. *Journal of Personality and Social Psychology, 72*, 1075–1092.

Karney, B. R., & Bradbury, T. N. (1995). The longitudinal course of marital quality and stability: A review of theory, method and research. *Psychological Bulletin, 118*, 3–34.

Karney, B. R., & Bradbury, T. N. (1997). Neuroticism, marital interaction, and the trajectory of marital satisfaction. *Journal of Personality and Social Psychology, 72*, 1075–1092.

Karney, B. R., & Frye, N. E. (2002). "But we've been getting better lately": Comparing prospective and retrospective views of relationship development. *Journal of Personality and Social Psychology, 82*, 222–238.

Karremans, J. C., & Aarts, H. (2007). The role of automaticity in determining the inclination to forgive close others. *Journal of Experimental Social Psychology, 43*, 902–917.

Kelley, H. H. (1979). *Personal relationships: Their structures and processes*. New York: Wiley.

Kelley, H. H., Berscheid, E., Christensen, A., Harvey, J. H., Huston, T. L., Levinger, G., McClintock, E., Peplau, L. A., & Peterson, D. R. (1983). *Close relationships*. San Francisco, CA: Freeman.

Kelley, H. H., & Thibaut, J. W. (1978). *Interpersonal relations*. New York: Wiley.

Kirkpatrick, L. A., & Hazan, C. (1994). Attachment styles and close relationships: A four-year prospective study. *Personal Relationships, 1*, 123–142.

Klinetob, N. A., & Smith, D. A. (1996). Demand-withdraw communication in marital interaction: Tests of interpersonal contingency and gender role hypotheses. *Journal of Marriage and the Family, 58*, 945–957.

Knee, C. R., Patrick, H., & Lonsbary, C. (2003). Implicit theories of relationships: Orientation toward evaluation and cultivation. *Personality and Social Psychology Review, 7*, 41–55.

Leary, M. R. (2001). The self we know, the self we show, self-esteem, self-presentation, and the maintenance of interpersonal relationships. In G. J. O. Fletcher & M. S. Clark (Eds.), *Blackwell handbook of social psychology: Interpersonal processes* (pp. 457–477). Oxford, UK: Blackwell.

Leary, M. R., Tambor, E. S., Terdal, S. K., & Downs, D. L. (1995). Self-esteem as an interpersonal monitor: The sociometer hypothesis. *Journal of Personality and Social Psychology, 68*, 518–530.

Lewis, M., Feiring, C., & Rosenthal, S. (2000). Attachment over time. *Child Development, 71*, 707–720.

Maner, J. K., Gailliot, & Miller, S. L. (2009). The implicit cognition of relationship maintenance: Inattention to attractive alternatives. *Journal of Experimental Social Psychology, 45*, 174–179.

Mikulincer, M., Gillath, O., & Shaver, P. R. (2002). Activation of the attachment system in adulthood: Threat-related primes increase the accessibility of mental representations of attachment figures. *Journal of Personality and Social Psychology, 83*, 881–895.

Mikulincer, M., & Shaver, P. R. (2007). *Attachment in adulthood: Structure, dynamics, and change*. New York: Guilford Press.

Miller, G.E., & Bradbury, T.N. (1995). Refining the association between attributions and behavior in marital interaction. *Journal of Family Psychology, 9*, 196-208.

Murray, S. L. (2001). Seeking a sense of conviction: Motivated cognition in close relationships. In G. J. O. Fletcher & M. S. Clark (Eds.), *Blackwell handbook of social psychology: Interpersonal processes* (pp. 107–126). Malden, MA: Blackwell.

Murray, S. L., Bellavia, G. M., Rose, P., & Griffin, D. W. (2003). Once hurt, twice hurtful: How perceived regard regulates daily marital interactions. *Journal of Personality and Social Psychology, 84*, 126–147.

Murray, S. L., Griffin, D. W., Rose, P., & Bellavia, G. M. (2003). Calibrating the sociometer: The relational contingencies of self-esteem. *Journal of Personality and Social Psychology, 85*, 63–84.

Murray, S. L., Griffin, D. W., Rose, P., & Bellavia, G. M. (2006). For better or worse? Self-esteem and the contingencies of acceptance in marriage. *Personality and Social Psychology Bulletin, 32*, 866–880.

Murray, S. L., & Holmes, J. G. (2009). The architecture of interdependent mind: A motivation-management theory of mutual responsiveness. *Psychological Review, 116*, 908-928.

Murray, S. L., Holmes, J. G., Bellavia, G., Griffin, D. W., & Dolderman, D. (2002). Kindred spirits? The benefits of egocentrism in close relationships. *Journal of Personality and Social Psychology, 82*, 563–581.

Murray, S. L., Holmes, J. G., & Griffin, D. W. (1996). The self-fulfilling nature of positive illusions in romantic relationships: Love is not blind, but prescient. *Journal of Personality and Social Psychology, 71*, 1155–1180.

Murray, S. L., Holmes, J. G., & Griffin, D. W. (2000). Self-esteem and the quest for felt security: How perceived regard regulates attachment processes. *Journal of Personality and Social Psychology, 78*, 478–498.

Overall, N. C., Fletcher G. J. O., & Friesen, M. (2003). Mapping the intimate relationship mind: Comparisons between three models of attachment representations. *Personality and Social Psychology Bulletin, 29*, 1479–1493.

Overall, N. C., Fletcher, G. J. O., & Simpson, J. A. (2006). Regulation processes in intimate relationships: The role of ideal standards. *Journal of Personality and Social Psychology, 91*(4), 662–685.

Overall, N. C., Fletcher, G. J. O., Simpson, J. A., & Sibley, C. G. (2009). Regulating partners in intimate relationships: The costs and benefits of different communication strategies. *Journal of Personality and Social Psychology, 96,* 620–639.

Overall, N. C., & Sibley, C. G. (2008). When accommodation matters: Situational dependency within daily interactions with romantic partners. *Journal of Experimental Social Psychology, 44,* 238–249.

Overall, N. C., Sibley, C. G. & Travaglia, K. (2010). Loyal but ignored: The benefits and costs of constructive communication behavior. *Personal Relationships, 17, 127-148.*

Reis, H. T., & Aron, A. (2008). Love: What it is, why does it matter, and how does it operate? *Perspectives on Psychological Science, 3,* 80–86.

Reis, H. T., Clark, M. S., & Holmes, J. G. (2004). Perceived partner responsiveness as an organizing construct in the study of intimacy and closeness. In D. J. Mashek & A. P. Aron (Eds.), *Handbook of closeness and intimacy* (pp. 201–225). Mahwah, NJ: Erlbaum.

Reis, H. T., & Downey, G. (1999). Social cognition in relationships: Building essential bridges between two literatures. *Social Cognition, 17,* 97–117.

Reis, H. T., & Patrick, B. C. (1996). Attachment and intimacy: Component processes. In E. T. Higgens & A. Kruglanski (Eds.). *Social psychology: Handbook of basic principles* (pp. 367–389). New York: Guilford Press.

Reis, H. T., & Shaver, P. R. (1988). Intimacy as an interpersonal process. In S. Duck (Ed.), *Handbook of personal relationships: Theory, research, and interventions* (pp. 367–389). Chichester, UK: Wiley.

Rubin, Z. (1973). *Liking and loving: An invitation to social psychology.* New York: Holt, Rinehart & Winston.

Rusbult, C. E., Bissonnette, V. L., Arriaga, X. B., & Cox, C. L. (1998). Accommodation processes during the early years of marriage. In T. N. Bradbury (Ed.), *The developmental course of marital dysfunction* (pp. 74–113). New York: Cambridge University Press.

Rusbult, C. E., Johnson, D. J., & Morrow, G. D. (1986a). Impact of couple patterns of problem solving on distress and nondistress in dating relationships. *Journal of Personality and Social Psychology, 50,* 744–753.

Rusbult, C. E., Johnson, D. J., & Morrow, G. D. (1986b). Determinants and consequences of exit, voice, loyalty, and neglect: Responses to dissatisfaction in adult romantic involvements. *Human Relations, 39,* 45–63.

Rusbult, C. E., & Van Lange, P. A. M. (2003). Interdependence, interaction, and relationships. *Annual Review of Psychology, 54,* 351–375.

Rusbult, C. E., Van Lange, P. A. M., Wildschut, T., Yovetich, N. A., & Verette, J. (2000). Perceived superiority in close relationships: Why it exists and persists. *Journal of Personality and Social Psychology, 79,* 521–545.

Rusbult, C. E., Verette, J., Whitney, G. A., Slovik, L. F., & Lipkus, I. (1991). Accommodation processes in close relationships: Theory and preliminary empirical evidence. *Journal of Personality and Social Psychology, 60,* 53–78.

Rusbult, C. E., Zembrodt, I. M., & Gunn, L. K. (1982). Exit, voice, loyalty, and neglect: Responses to dissatisfaction in romantic involvements. *Journal of Personality and Social Psychology, 43,* 1230–1242.

Shaver, P. R., Hazan, C., & Bradshaw, D. (1988). Love as attachment: The integration of three behavioral systems. In R. J. Sternberg & M. L. Barnes (Eds.), *The psychology of love* (pp. 68–99). New Haven, CT: Yale University Press.

Shaver, P. R., Morgan, H. J., & Wu, S. (1996). Is love a "basic" emotion? *Personal Relationships, 3,* 81–96.

Simpson, J. A., Rholes, W. S., & Nelligan, J. S. (1992). Support seeking and support giving within couples in an anxiety-provoking situation: The role of attachment styles. *Journal of Personality and Social Psychology, 62,* 434–446.

Simpson, J. A., Rholes, W. S., & Phillips, D. (1996). Conflict in close relationships: An attachment perspective. *Journal of Personality and Social Psychology, 71,* 899–914.

Simpson, J. A., Winterfield, H. A., Rholes, W. S., & Orina, A. M. (2007). Working models of attachment and reactions to different forms of caregiving from romantic partners. *Journal of Personality and Social Psychology, 93,* 466–477.

Spanier, G. B. (1976). Measuring dyadic adjustment: New scales for assessing the quality of marriage and similar dyads. *Journal of Marriage and the Family, 38,* 15–28.

Sternberg, R. J. (1986). A triangular theory of love. *Psychological Review, 93,* 119–135.

Thibaut, J. W., & Kelley, H. H. (1959). *The social psychology of groups.* New York: Wiley.

Weiss, R. L., & Heyman, R. E. (1997). A clinical-research overview of couple's interactions. In W. K. Halford & H. J. Markman (Eds.), *Clinical handbook of marriage and couples interventions* (pp. 13–41). Chichester, UK: Wiley.

Weiss, R. L., & Summers, K. J. (1983). Marital Interaction Coding System-III. In E. Filsinger (Ed.), *Marriage and family assessment* (pp. 35–115). Beverly Hills, CA: Sage.

Wieselquist, J., Rusbult, C. E., Foster, C. A., & Agnew, C. R. (1999). Commitment, pro-relationship behavior, and trust in close relationships. *Journal of Personality and Social Psychology, 77,* 942–966.

Chapter 14

Group Processes

Donelson R. Forsyth and Jeni Burnette

Social behavior is often group behavior. People are in many respects individuals seeking their personal, private objectives, yet they are also members of social collectives that bind members to one another. The tendency to join with others is perhaps the most important single characteristic of humans. The processes that take place within these groups influence, in fundamental ways, their members and society-at-large. Just as the dynamic processes that occur in groups—such as the exchange of information among members, leading and following, pressures put on members to adhere to the group's standards, shifts in friendship alliances, and conflict and collaboration—change the group, so do they also change the group's members. In consequence, a complete analysis of individuals and their social relations requires a thorough understanding of groups and their dynamics.

Studying Groups

Audiences, bands, cliques, clubs, committees, crews, crowds, congregations, dance troupes, families, fraternities, gangs, juries, military squads, mobs, orchestras, professional associations, queues, support groups, and teams are just a few of the groups that enfold and surround us. But do all of these collections of people qualify as groups in the social psychological sense of the word?

Groups differ from one another in many ways. Some, such as the crew of an airliner or students in a graduate seminar, are small, but others are so large they include thousands of members. Some groups form spontaneously and exist only briefly, whereas others are deliberately created, elaborately structured, and enduring (Arrow, McGrath, & Berdahl, 2000). Some, such as teams, are devoted to accomplishing tasks, whereas others seem to have no clear purpose. Despite these wide variations, groups sustain and are sustained by relationships among their members. A family is a group because the members are connected, not just genetically, but by social and emotional bonds. People who work together are linked not only by the tasks that they must complete collectively, but also by friendships, alliances, and shared antagonisms. Thus, a group is two or more individuals who are connected by and within social relationships (Forsyth, 2010).

Perceiving Groups

Not all collections of individuals are groups. People waiting on a subway platform may, for example, just be a set of individuals gathered together by chance as they wait for a train. But they may be a group, particularly if the same individuals tend to gather at the same platform at the same time each workday to catch the same train (Milgram, 1992). Groups, then, are as much subjective, social reality as they are objective, physical reality. As the concept of *entitativity* suggests, perceptual factors such as similarity, proximity, and common fate influence both members' and nonmembers' perceptions of a group's unity (Campbell, 1958). When members are similar to one another, frequently together rather than apart, and experience shared outcomes then most would conclude the aggregation is an entity—a group.

People's intuitive distinctions among various kinds of groups hinge, to an extent, on variations in entitativity. People are more likely to consider aggregations marked by strong bonds between members, frequent interactions among members, and clear boundaries to be groups, but they are less certain that aggregations such as crowds, waiting lines, or categories qualify as groups (Lickel, Hamilton, Wieczorkowska, Lewis, Sherman, & Uhles, 2000, Study 3). The four basic categories of groups in Table 14.1—small intimate groups, more socially oriented groups, collectives, and categories—capture most people's thinking with regard to groups and associations, but the line between group and nongroup is often a fuzzy one.

These intuitive construals, even though subjective, influence how people respond to social collectives. A collection of individuals literally becomes a

TABLE 14.1 **Four Types of Groups**

Type of Group	*Characteristics*	*Examples*
Primary groups	Small in size, moderate in duration and permeability, but characterized by substantial levels of interaction among the members, who considered them to be very important to them personally	Families, romantic couples, and close friends, street gangs
Social groups	Groups in public settings, such as employment settings and goal-focused groups in a variety of nonemployment situations	Employees at a restaurant, people who work in a factory, committees, support groups, juries, study groups
Associations	Aggregations of individuals that formed spontaneously; some last only a brief period of time and have permeable boundaries, whereas others are marked by very weak relationships among members or very limited interaction among them	People gathered at a bus stop waiting for the next bus; an audience in a movie theater, residents in a large neighborhood, students in a large college class
Categories	Aggregates of individuals who were similar to one another in terms of gender, ethnicity, religion, and nationality	"Women," "Catholics," "lawyers," "Canadians," "feminists"

Source: Forsyth (2010).

group when the members, or others outside the group, label the collective a group. Group members are much more likely to identify with such groups (Castano, Yzerbyt, & Bourguignon, 2003), and this tendency is particularly strong when people feel uncertain about themselves and the correctness of their beliefs (Hogg, Sherman, Dierselhuis, Maitner, & Moffitt, 2007). When, for example, researchers regularly reminded individuals working in isolation that they were members of a group they eventually accepted the label of group and felt badly when told their group had performed poorly (Zander, Stotland, & Wolfe, 1960). Groups that are high in entitativity tend to be more cohesive groups (Zyphur & Islam, 2006) and their members report enhanced feelings of social well-being (Sani, Bowe, & Herrera, 2008). Entitativity is also related to both stereotyping and prejudice, since it influences perceivers' perceptions of people who are members of groups and categories (Rydell, Hugenberg, Ray, & Mackie, 2007). When perceivers think an aggregate of individuals is a group they are more likely to treat it like a group, and this treatment increases the group's actual unity (Alter & Darley, 2009).

The Reality of Groups

Scholars have debated the connection between the individual and the group for centuries. When the social sciences such as psychology and sociology emerged as their own unique disciplines in the late 1800s, each one recognized the importance of understanding group processes, but with that shared focus on groups came differences in *level of analysis*. Some researchers adopted an *individual-level perspective*, for they considered people to be autonomous, self-reliant creatures who struggle against the group's influence. Others favored a *group-level perspective* that assumed each person is a constituent in an encompassing group, organization, or society, and that each person's reactions shape and are shaped by the group and its processes (Steiner, 1974). Reconciling these two potentially compatible views is, in many respects, social psychology's "master problem" (Allport, 1962).

The group-level explanation of people's thoughts, emotions, and actions is not as intuitively appealing as an individual-level analysis to those who are acculturated to a Western world view. Even though people speak of concepts such as teamwork, synergy, leadership, and cliques in their discussions of contemporary issues, they tend to translate these group-level processes into individualistic ones. Displaying a kind of group-level *fundamental attribution error* (FAE)—the tendency to assume other people's actions are caused by their personal, individual qualities rather than external, situational forces (Ross, 1977)—perceivers are slow to admit that an explanation that stresses group-level causes is as accurate as one that stresses individualistic causes. In consequence, they are often surprised when the same individual acts differently when he or she changes groups; after all, if personal, individualistic qualities are the primary causes of behavior then group-level process should play only a minor role in determining outcomes (Darley, 1992).

A multilevel perspective amends these tendencies by recognizing the profound impact of groups on members' thoughts, feelings, and actions (Forsyth & Burnette, 2005). Repeatedly researchers have discovered that cognitive processes are not private and personal but shared and interpersonal. People base their estimates and opinions on the statements made by other group members rather than on evidence of their own senses (Asch, 1957; Sherif, 1936). Groups prompt their members to endorse certain ideas and attitudes, and even nonconformists tend to eventually take on the standards of the groups to which they belong (Newcomb, 1943). Disagreeing with other members can trigger cognitive dissonance, and as a result people's thoughts change to reduce this unpleasant mental state (Matz & Wood, 2005). People also process information collectively, through discussion and other group communication processes, and so basic cognitive processes such as planning, evaluating, judging, decision making, and problem solving are undertaken, not by individuals, but by groups (Hinsz, Tindale, & Vollrath, 1997).

Turning to emotions, groups directly and indirectly influence members' affect and emotional adjustment. Members' feelings about themselves and their identities depend on inclusion in social groups that sustain their sense of satisfaction and well-being. Groups create affectively rich relationships between people and they are often the source of the motivational drive needed to accomplish difficult, taxing goals. Emotions are also sometimes contagious in groups, with the feelings of one individual passing rapidly from one member of the group to the next. These group-level emotions become more intense when individuals identify with their group, and can be shared among members who did not even experience the emotion-provoking event (Smith, Seger, & Mackie, 2007; Vider, 2004). Even members of more task-focused groups, such as teams and task forces, become increasingly similar in their overall mood the longer they remain together (Kelly, 2001).

Group influence is perhaps most conspicuous at the behavioral level. People, both knowingly and unwittingly, will amend their actions and preferences to match the actions of others (Semin, 2007). Groups can literally transform their members, to the point that the behavior of a person in a group may have no connection to that person's behavior when alone. Milgram's work (1963), for example, can be considered a study of group influence, for once the participants took their place in a hierarchical group structure, they obediently followed the orders of the group's leader. Similarly, individuals who join religious or political groups that stress secrecy, obedience to leaders, and dogmatic acceptance of unusual or atypical beliefs (cults) often display fundamental and unusual changes in behavior (Kelman, 2006).

A Multilevel Perspective on Groups

Rather than favor either an individual-level perspective or a group-level perspective, a multilevel approach assumes group dynamics are shaped by processes that range along the micro-meso-macro continuum. *Microlevel* factors include the qualities, characteristics, and actions of the individual members. *Mesolevel* factors are group-level qualities of the groups themselves, such as their cohesiveness, their size, their composition, and their structure. *Macrolevel* factors are the qualities and processes of the larger collectives that enfold the groups, such as communities, organizations, or societies. Groups, then, are nested at the mesolevel where the bottom-up microlevel variables meet the top-down macrolevel variables (Hackman, 2003).

A multilevel approach requires that social psychologists share the study of groups with researchers in a variety of scientific disciplines and professions.

Groups were originally studied primarily by social psychologists within psychology and sociology, but in time investigators in other fields—communication studies, organizational behavior, political science, economics, and anthropology—began to explore issues related to group formation, processes, and performance. For example, those who study organizations discovered that these larger social entities actually depend on the dynamics of small subgroups within the organization. Social scientists examining global issues such as the development and maintenance of culture found themselves turning their attention toward small groups as the unit of cultural transmission. Researchers in business and industry interested in workgroups and teams drew heavily on studies of groups performing tasks in the laboratory. Social psychology can claim the group as one of its key subjects of study, but it must share groups with all the other social sciences, including sociology, anthropology, economics, and business.

The multilevel approach also requires that researchers implement specialized methodological and statistical procedures in their work. Because the individuals they study are nested in groups that are also nested in organizations, researchers must be careful not to attribute effects caused by group-level processes to individual-level processes and vice versa. If data are collected from individual group members, researchers must check for group-level interdependencies by computing intraclass correlations (ICC), average deviation scores (e.g., rWG scores), or within-and-between analysis (WABA) statistics. These analyses will indicate if the individual can serve as the unit of analysis or if interdependency among the members' data make aggregated group-level analyses more appropriate. Advanced statistical procedures, such as hierarchical linear modeling (HLM), are capable of disentangling cause–effect relationships and processes that operate simultaneously at two or more levels (Zyphur, Kaplan, & Christian, 2008). These advances, taken together, highlight the growing methodological sophistication of group researchers as they identify ways to deal with the challenge of studying individuals nested in groups (Sadler & Judd, 2001).

Group Formation

Groups form through a combination of personal, situational, and interpersonal processes. Some people are more likely than others to seek the company of others, and when they do a group is born. Groups also come into existence through deliberate planning or when the press of environmental circumstances brings people together, repeatedly, and these associations kindle attractions (Correll & Park, 2005).

Attachment to Groups

Baumeister and Leary (1995) suggest human's tendency to seek social connections and avoid isolation is generated by a basic *need to belong* to social groups: All "human beings have a pervasive drive to form and maintain at least a minimum quantity of lasting, positive, and impactful interpersonal relationships" (p. 497). People's need to belong is thoroughly satisfied by a group that actively seeks them out, but any group that accepts the person is preferred to one that refuses to permit entry (Leary, 2007). Individuals who are made to feel as though they will be excluded from groups display a number of dysfunctional side-effects, including increased aggression, risk-taking, procrastination, and tentativeness when interacting with others (Blackhart, Nelson, Knowles, & Baumeister, 2009; Burnette & Forsyth, 2008; Twenge, Baumeister, DeWall, Ciarocco, & Bartels, 2007).

Although few individuals live out their lives isolated from others, people differ in their proclivity to seek out and maintain group memberships. This difference is due, in part, to past experiences, for those who report prior positive outcomes are more likely to seek out membership in the future (Brinthaupt, Moreland, & Levine, 1991; Pavelshak, Moreland, & Levine, 1986). Personality differences also influence the willingness to join groups. Extraversion, a key aspect identified in most theories of personality, is a particularly influential determinant of group behavior (Asendorpf & Wilpers, 1998). Extraverts may seek out groups because such interactions are stimulating and they appreciate stimulating experiences more than introverts (Eysenck, 1990). Groups may also seek out extraverts rather than introverts. Some qualities, such as intelligence, morality, and friendliness, are difficult to judge during initial encounters, but observers are particularly good at detecting extraversion in others (Albright, Kenny, & Malloy, 1988).

Attachment orientation is another important predictor of who joins groups (Smith, Murphy, & Coats, 1999). For example, individuals who are anxious about their group experiences—particularly those who feel they are unworthy of membership—will eschew group membership. People with anxious group attachment styles also spend less time in their groups, engage in fewer collective activities, and are less satisfied with the level of support they receive from the group. Those with avoidant group attachment styles report feeling that the group is less important to them and spend more of their time alone rather than with others (Brown, Silvia, Myin-Germeys, & Kwapil, 2007).

Affiliation in Groups

Festinger (1950, 1954), in his theory of social comparison, suggested that people affiliate with others because other people are excellent sources of information about social reality. When people find themselves in ambiguous situations, conventional sources of information do not provide enough information to erase their doubts and apprehensions. In such cases, they join with other people to compare their personal viewpoint to those expressed by others, and so determine if they are "correct," "valid," or "proper" (Forsyth, 2000).

Schachter (1959) confirmed the informational value of groups for members in a series of studies of women's reactions when they were led to believe they would be given electric shocks. In one study the women in the low-anxiety condition were told the shocks would be so mild that they would "resemble more a tickle or a tingle than anything unpleasant" (p. 14). However, those in the high-anxiety condition were told that the shocks would be painful. When given the choice to wait alone or with others, 63% of the women in the high-anxiety condition chose to wait with others, compared to only 33% of the women in the low-anxiety condition. Schachter (1959) concluded: "Misery loves company". In a second study some women who expected to receive painful electric shock were given the opportunity to wait with other women who were about to receive shocks. Those in the control condition were told they could wait with women queuing to meet an advisor. Schachter felt that if the women believed that the others could not provide them with social-comparison information, there would be no reason to join them. The findings confirmed his analysis, leading him to conclude, "Misery doesn't love just any kind of company, it loves only miserable company" (p. 24).

Social Identity and Groups

Other group members are not only fonts of information during times of uncertainty but sources of identity and self-definition. Groups are often very willing to provide members with descriptive feedback about their personal qualities and capabilities, and so can correct misperceptions and enhance self-authenticity. Additionally, a substantial portion of the sense of self entails group-level qualities and characteristics. This collective self or social identity includes all those qualities that spring from one's membership in social groups: families, cliques, neighborhoods, tribes, cities, countries, regions. Even demographic qualities, such as sex or age, can influence the collective self provided group members categorize themselves on the basis of these qualities. Social identity theory assumes that people ascribe the characteristics of the typical group member to themselves when the group becomes central to their identity (Hogg, 2001).

Groups also provide a variety of means for maintaining and enhancing a sense of self-worth. Because the self-concept is defined, at least partially, by the groups to which people belong, joining prestigious or successful groups can boost self-esteem (Branscombe, 1998). Adolescents, for example, often seek out membership in high-status cliques, and those who manage to gain acceptance report feeling very satisfied with themselves and their group (Brown & Lohr, 1987). Individuals are more interested in joining and maintaining membership in groups that succeed at the tasks they attempt rather than fail (Leary & Forsyth, 1986). In consequence, personal self-esteem is linked to *collective self-esteem*: a person's assessment of the quality of the groups to which he or she belongs (Crocker & Luhtanen, 1990).

Groups and Survival

By joining with others in groups, members satisfy not only their need for self-worth but also their need for belonging, information, control, and identity. Moreland (1987), in his theory of social integration, concluded that groups tend to form whenever "people become dependent on one another for the satisfaction of their needs" (p. 104). The advantages of group life may be so great that humans may be genetically ready to prefer membership in a group to isolation. From an evolutionary psychology perspective, because groups increased humans' overall fitness for countless generations, individuals who carried genes that promoted solitude seeking were weeded out, whereas those with genes that prompted them to join groups survived. This process of natural selection culminated in the creation of a modern human who seeks out membership in groups instinctively (Buss, 1996; Simpson & LaPaglia, 2010; Van Vugt & Schaller, 2008).

Networks of Association

Group behavior is usually orderly and predictable rather than disorganized and capricious. In any group some people make the assignments and others carry them out. Some members are liked by nearly everyone but others are barely tolerated. Some people talk to many others in the group but others hardly speak. These regularities reflect the group's *structure*: the underlying pattern of relationships among members (Cartwright & Zander, 1968; Troyer & Younts, 2010).

Status Networks

Few groups treat all members equally. Just as some group members are permitted to lead and others must follow, so some group members are afforded more authority than the rank-and-file. These stable status networks—these pecking orders—are often hierarchical and centralized (Tiedens, Unzueta, & Young, 2007).

Expectation-states theory provides an explanation for the gradual emergence of status networks even in groups with no formally appointed leaders (e.g., Berger & Zelditch, 1998). The theory assumes group members intuitively take note of one another's personal qualities that they assume are indicative of ability, skill, or prestige. Specific-status characteristics are qualities that group members think signal each individual's level of ability at the task to be performed in the given situation. On a mountain climbing expedition, for example, athletic ability may be a specific-status characteristic, whereas a degree from Harvard Business School may be an indicator of skill among the members of a bank's board of directors. Diffuse-status characteristics are more general qualities often related to social category membership that the members think are relevant to ability and evaluation. The members' beliefs about the link between these qualities and skill may be completely inaccurate, but group members may nonetheless assume that these characteristics are good indicators of leadership potential. Those who possess specific and diffuse status rise upward in the group's status hierarchy (Driskell & Mullen, 1990; Ridgeway, 2006).

Sociometric Relations

Members of groups are linked to one another not only in status hierarchies, but also in networks of likes, dislikes, affection, and even hatred (Maassen, Akkermans, & van der Linden, 1996). This network of likes and dislikes among the members is often called the group's sociometric structure. This term derives from *sociometry*, which is a method for measuring social relationships in groups developed by researcher and theorist Jacob Moreno (1953). Researchers who use this method typically ask group members to identify which members of the group they like or dislike most. Their choices are then summarized statistically or in a graph such as the one shown in Figure 14.1. Popular individuals are singled out by most of the others to be the target of much affection, isolates are neglected by most of the group, outcasts are rejected by the majority of the group, whereas the average members are liked by several others in the group (Coie, Dodge, & Coppotelli, 1982; Newcomb, Bukowski, & Pattee, 1993).

Sociometric relations tend to be organized rather than random configurations of liking and disliking. Most attraction relations are reciprocal; if person A likes B then B likes A. As Heider's (1958) balance theory suggests, the relations in groups usually fit together to form a coherent, unified whole. A dyad, for example, is balanced only if liking (or disliking) is mutual. Similarly, triads

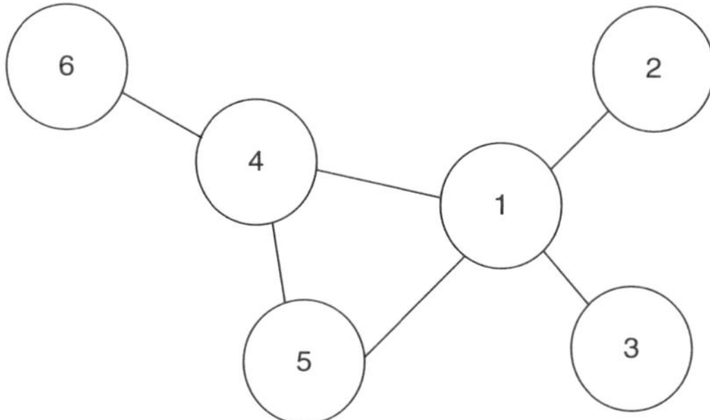

FIGURE 14.1. Sociometric structure of a group.

and larger groups are balanced only if (1) all the relationships are positive or (2) an even number of negative relationships occurs in the group. Conversely, groups are unbalanced if they contain an odd number of negative relations (Gawronski, Walther, & Blank, 2005).

Communication Flow in Groups

The flow of information from one person to another in groups is often structured by the group's communication network. Patterns of communication among group members, similar to other structural features of groups, are sometimes deliberately set in place when the group is organized. Many companies, for example, adopt a centralized, hierarchical communication network that prescribes how information is passed up to superiors, down to subordinates, and horizontally to equals. Even if no formal attempt is made to organize communication, an informal communication network will usually take shape over time.

Communication networks often parallel status and attraction patterns (Shelly, Troyer, Munroe, & Burger, 1999), although they tend to become more centralized as groups increase in size. With centralized networks, one of the positions in the group has a very high degree of centrality—it is located at the crossroads (the *hub*) of communications—relative to the other positions in the group. Groups with this type of structure tend to use the hub position as the data-processing center, and its occupant typically collects information, synthesizes it, and then sends it back to others. In decentralized structures the number of channels at each position is roughly equal, so no one position is more "central" than another (Shaw, 1964).

Early studies of communication networks suggested that groups with centralized networks outperformed groups with decentralized networks (Bavelas, 1950; Leavitt, 1951). However as Shaw (1964) noted, the benefit of centralization depends on network saturation. When a group is working on a problem, exchanging information, and making a decision, the central position in the network can best manage the inputs and interactions of the group. As work progresses and the number of communications being routed through the central member increases, however, a saturation point can be reached, at which point the individual can no longer efficiently monitor, collate, or route incoming and outgoing messages. Because the "greater the saturation the less efficient the group's performance" (Shaw, 1964, p. 126), when the task is simple, centralized networks are more efficient than decentralized networks; when the task is complex, decentralized networks are superior. As a consequence, groups tend to gravitate naturally to more decentralized network structures when the tasks they must accomplish become more complex and multifaceted (Brown & Miller, 2000).

Social Network Analysis

The study of relations among individuals in groups, organizations, and even larger collectives is termed *social network analysis* (SNA). Figure 14.1 illustrates an application of SNA to groups. Each network member, or node, is represented as a point or circle, and the lines connecting nodes indicate who is linked to whom—by a line of communication or by friendship. Directed relations, such as liking, are capped with arrows to indicate the direction of nonsymmetrical relationships, whereas nondirected relations such as those in Figure 14.1 have no directional indicators (Freeman, 2004).

SNA yields information about group structure as well as each individual's location in the structure. Group-level, or sociocentric, views capture characteristics of the entire network whereas member-level, egocentric studies look at the individuals within the network (Knoke & Yang, 2008). The *density* of a group, for example, is determined by how many people are linked to one another out of the total possible number of links. The group in Figure 14.1, for example, includes six members, and so a total of 15 relationships would be required to link every member to every other member. (The formula, $n(n - 1)/2$, where n is the number of members, defines the number of relationships needed to create a completely interlinked group.) Because this group contains only six relationships, its density is 6/15, or 0.40. *Centrality*, in contrast, is an individual-level, or egocentric index, and is defined by how many connections a person has relative to others. Person 1 in Figure 14.1, for example, has the highest *degree centrality*, for Person 1 is connected to four other members, whereas Person 6 has the lowest. SNA provides researchers with the means to quantify the extent to which members are embedded in their group as well as a tool for studying the impact of structural variations on various interpersonal outcomes (e.g., Paxton & Moody, 2003).

Group Cohesion

In physics, the strength of the molecular attraction that holds particles of matter together is known as cohesiveness. In psychology, a group's cohesiveness is the strength of the relationships linking the members to one another and to the group itself (Dion, 2000). Even though theorists and researchers continue to debate the nature of this construct, most agree that what unifies the members of one group may be different from the factors that cause another group to form a cohesive unit. Social cohesion, for example, traces a group's cohesion back to attraction—both between specific group members and to the group itself (Festinger, Schachter, & Back, 1950; Hogg, 1992). Other cohesive groups, in contrast, may promote a strong sense of group loyalty and unity (e.g., Henry, Arrow, & Carini, 1999), and still others may be marked by heightened emotionality and *esprit de corps* (Smith et al., 2007). Regardless of the source of cohesion, researchers note that the strength of relationships is the overarching component of a group's cohesion (Dion, 2000)

In most instances, cohesion is associated with increases in member satisfaction and decreases in turnover and stress. For example, the staff of an office will likely enjoy their work more if their group is a cohesive one, and they may even outperform an equally talented, but less cohesive, group. This cohesion–performance relationship, however, is a complex one. Meta-analytic studies suggest that cohesion improves teamwork among members, but that performance quality influences cohesion more than cohesion influences performance (Mullen & Copper, 1994). The work group may not be successful because it is cohesive, but instead it may be cohesive because it has succeeded in the past. Also, cohesiveness that is based on attraction to specific members of the group has less of an effect on performance than does shared commitment to the group's task, so team building will not be effective unless it includes suggestions on improving workgroup efficiency. Cohesive groups can also be dramatically unproductive if the group's norms stress low productivity rather than high productivity (Seashore, 1954).

Leadership and Power

The leader is the individual in the group who guides others in their pursuits, often by organizing, directing, coordinating, supporting, and motivating their efforts. In some cases the group's leader is formally recognized, However, in many groups the leader gains authority implicitly, as other group members come to rely on him or her to guide the group.

Studies of leaders in all kinds of group situations—flight crews, politics, schools, military units, and religious groups—suggest that groups prosper when guided by good leaders (Hogan & Kaiser, 2005). The ingredients for "effective leadership," however, are often debated, for leadership involves finding the right balance between (1) keeping the members working at their tasks and improving relationships and (2) providing guidance without robbing members of their autonomy.

Leadership Styles

The leadership role usually includes two interrelated components: task orientation and relationship orientation. The task-oriented leader focuses on the problem at hand by defining problems for the group, establishing communication networks, providing feedback as needed, planning, motivating action, coordinating members' actions, and so on. Relationship leaders focus on the quality of the relationships among the members of the group by boosting morale, increasing cohesion, managing conflict, showing concern and consideration for group members, and additional factors (Yukl, 2010).

Which leader will be more effective: the one who can get the job done or the one with relationship skills? Researchers and theorists agree on one conclusion: It depends on the nature of the group situation. Fiedler's (1978, 1981) *contingency theory* of leadership, for example, assumes that most people are, by nature, either task-oriented leaders or relationship-oriented leaders; few can shift from one style of leadership to the other. Importantly, however, different styles work better in different situations. If the group situation is very favorable for the leader or very unfavorable for the leader (say, because the group members do not get along with the leader and the leader has little power), the task-oriented leader will perform most effectively. In contrast, the relationship leader should be more effective in moderately favorable or moderately unfavorable situations.

Other theories, in contrast, assume that effective leaders should exhibit varying amounts of task-oriented and relationship-oriented leadership depending on the situation they face. Situational leadership theory, for example, assumes that groups require more or less task and relational guidance depending on their degree of development (Hersey & Blanchard, 1982). Newly formed groups, groups beginning a new project, and groups with many new members are immature, and they require a high task/low relationship leader. As the group matures and begins working adequately on the task, the leader can increase the relationship behavior and adopt a high/high style. Still later in the group's development, the leader can decrease on both types of leadership, starting first with task emphasis. Unlike Fiedler's contingency theory model, the situational model recommends that leaders adjust their style until it fits the circumstances (Hersey & Blanchard, 1982). Situational leadership theory's emphasis on adaptability as a cardinal trait in a leader is consistent with studies that have identified people who seem to rise to positions of leadership in all settings. These individuals are often intelligent, energetic, and socially skilled, but above all they are flexible: They can read the demands of the situation and adjust their actions so that they meet those demands (Kirkpatrick & Locke, 1991; Zaccaro, Foti, & Kenny, 1991).

Participatory Leadership

Leaders differ in how much control they exert over the group (Hollander & Offermann, 1990; Sankowsky, 1995).Which leader is most effective: the one who takes charge and directs the group with a strong hand or the one who consults with group members and lets them share the reins of leadership? Lewin, Lippitt, and White (1939) examined this question in one of the first studies to create groups in a laboratory setting for experimental purposes. They examined the reactions of small groups of boys working on craft projects after school to one of three types of adult leaders. In some groups, the leader made all the decisions for the group without consulting the boys. This directive, *autocratic leader* told the boys what to do, he often criticized them, and he remained aloof from the group. Other groups were guided by a participatory, *democratic leader* who let them make decisions as he provided guiding advice. He explained long-term goals and steps to be taken to reach the goals, but he rarely criticized the boys or gave orders. Other groups were given a *laissez-faire leader* who allowed the boys to work in whatever way they wished. He provided information on demand, but he did not offer information, criticism, or guidance spontaneously.

The boys responded very differently to these three types of leaders. Groups with autocratic leaders spent more time working than groups with democratic leaders, which in turn spent more time working than groups with the laissez-faire leaders—provided the leader remained in the room. Groups with a democratic leader kept working when their leader left but the boys working under the direction of an autocratic leader did not. Laissez faire and democratic groups were also less aggressive than autocratic groups. In autocratic groups, observers noted high rates of hostility among members, more demands for attention, more destructiveness, and a greater tendency to single out one group member to serve as the target of verbal abuse.

Lewin, Lippitt, and White's (1939) findings suggest that autocratic (directive) and democratic (participatory) leaders have both strengths and weaknesses. The strongly directive leader often succeeds in pushing the group to high levels of productivity, although at an interpersonal cost as conflict increases. The groups with a participatory leader were not as productive or efficient in their work, but members were more satisfied with their group and more involved (Stogdill, 1974). Laissez-faire leaders increased members' sense of autonomy, but their productivity was especially low. In conclusion, each type of leadership method may be appropriate in certain situations. If the group members are unmotivated and working on well-defined tasks, then a strong, directive style may work best. A directive approach is also warranted when the issues to be settled are minor ones, the group's acceptance will not impact them in any way, and the group members are, themselves, autocratic. In general, however, group members will be much happier if they are involved in group decisions. The decisions, too, will probably be better if the leader is puzzled by the issues and group members have information that might be relevant (Pearce & Conger, 2003; Vroom, 2003).

Women and Leadership

Leaders differ physically and psychologically from their subordinates. Leaders tend to be older, taller, and heavier than the average group member. They are generally more accomplished at the tasks facing the group and they tend to talk more than the average member. Leaders are outgoing rather than shy and dominant rather than submissive. Leaders, too, are more often men than women (Eagly & Carli, 2007; Hoyt & Chemers, 2008).

Even though the gender gap in leadership has narrowed in recent years, it has not closed. More men than women work outside the home, and their over-representation in organizations and business settings provides them with far more leadership opportunities than are available to women. The number of women working in managerial roles has risen steadily over the years, but women make up only about 5% of management and only 1% of upper management. The reasons women are not equally represented in the highest ranks of leadership in corporations are many. For example, some researchers argue that there is a leadership labyrinth of obstacles for women to overcome (Eagly & Carli, 2007).

Additional factors may include the fact that women are aware of existing stereotypes that suggest they lack leadership aptitude (Crocker, Major, & Steele, 1998), which makes them vulnerable to *stereotype threat*. Stereotypes can undermine performance when a person is in a situation that could confirm an attitude that disparages the abilities of his or her own social group. This stereotype threat contributes to the underperformance of individuals belonging to a range of negatively stereotyped groups (e.g., Davies, Spencer, & Steele, 2005). Different work experiences and family roles also shape women and men's perspective on leadership and often influence leadership approaches and emergence. For example, gender differences influence men and women's actions in small group settings, with men five times more likely to enact leadership behaviors than women in small, mixed sex leaderless groups (Walker, Ilardi, McMahon, & Fennell, 1996) and to emerge as leaders (Bartol & Martin, 1986).

As in many social psychological processes, individual perceptions—even though mistaken—generate a series of reactions that fundamentally shape social outcomes. As *social role theory* explains, people in most cultures, when asked to describe women, speak of their expressive qualities, including nurturance, emotionality, and warmth. They expect a "she" to be sentimental, affectionate, sympathetic, soft-hearted, talkative, gentle, and feminine. When describing men, they stress their instrumental qualities, including productivity, energy, and strength (Eagly & Karau, 2002). But when group members are asked to describe the qualities needed in a leader, their implicit leadership theories prompt them to emphasize the instrumental side of leadership rather the more relational side (Forsyth & Nye, 2008).

The Effects of Power

Power and leadership typically go together. Leaders, no matter how they gain their position and maintain it, use forms of influence that range from persuasion to coercion to guide others in their pursuits. French and Raven (1959), when describing the typical sources of a leader's influence, identified five key foundations: the leader's capacity to reward others (reward power) and punish others (coercive power), the authority vested in their position (legitimate power), their followers' feelings of respect and admiration (referent power), and their superior experience and skill (expert power).

Power is, fundamentally, a group-level process, for it involves some members of a group conforming to the requirements of others in situations that vary from the cooperative and collaborative to those rife with conflict, tension, and animosity. As an evolutionary account of human gregariousness would suggest, group members accept influence from others because such behavioral responses are adaptive. As long as the group's leaders are perceived to be motivated by group-level goals, then those lower in the status hierarchy tend to do as they are told by those with higher status (Tiedens et al., 2007). Power in social species, then, is a dynamic, negotiated process rather than a top-down chain of influence (Keltner, Van Kleef, Chen, & Kraus, 2008). As Milgram (1974, p. 124) explained, "Each member's acknowledgement of his place in the hierarchy stabilizes the pack."

Probably for as long as humans have aggregated in groups, they have puzzled over the nature of power and its influence on those who have it, those who lack it, and those who seek it. Keltner and his colleagues (2003, 2008), synthesizing previous analyses, theorize that power—having power, using power, even thinking about power—transforms individuals' psychological states (Keltner, Gruenfeld, & Anderson, 2003; Keltner et al., 2008). Their approach/inhibition model assumes that power activates: it triggers increases in action, self-promotion, energy, and environmental scanning. The lack of power, in contrast, triggers inhibition and is associated with reaction, self-protection, vigilance, loss of motivation, and an overall reduction in activity. In consequence, powerful people tend to be active group members whose increased drive, energy, motivation, and emotion help the group overcome difficulties and reach its goals. Powerful group members are more proactive than those with little power, and they tend to pursue goals appropriate to the given situation (Guinote, 2008). Researchers have demonstrated the proactive tendencies of the powerful by first priming a sense of power or powerlessness. Some participants were asked to think back to a time when they had power over other individuals, whereas others thought of a time when they had little power. The participants were then seated at a table positioned too close to an annoying fan blowing directly on them. A majority of the participants primed with power took steps to solve the problem: they moved the fan or turned it off. Most of the participants primed with powerlessness, in contrast, just put up with this irritation (Galinsky, Gruenfeld, & Magee, 2003).

Power also leads to enhanced executive functioning. For example, those primed with power plan, make decisions, set goals, and monitor information flow more rapidly and effectively (Smith, Jostmann, Galinsky, & van Dijk, 2008). Even when distracted by irrelevant information, powerful individuals make better decisions than less powerful group members, apparently because they can think in more abstract terms (Smith, Dijksterhuis, & Wigboldus, 2008). Powerful people also tend to be happier group members. Their moods are elevated, they report higher levels of positive emotions such as happiness and satisfaction, and they are more optimistic and enthusiastic (Berdahl & Martorana, 2006).

But these positive consequences of power are counterbalanced by the liabilities of power. Powerful people are proactive, but in some cases their actions are risky, inappropriate, or unethical. Simply being identified as the leader of a group prompts individuals to claim more than the average share of the resources, as members believe the leadership role entitles them to take more than others (De Cremer & Van Dijk, 2005). When individuals gain power, their self-evaluations grow more favorable, whereas their evaluations of others grow more negative. If they believe that they have a mandate from their group or organization, they may do things they are not empowered to do. When individuals feel powerful, they sometimes treat others unfairly, particularly if they are more self-centered than focused on the overall good of the group. Some individuals associate power with sexuality, and so when they are empowered, they engage in inappropriate sexual behaviors, including sexual harassment (Galinsky, Jordan, & Sivanathan, 2008; Keltner et al., 2008). Power's darker side lends credence to Lord Acton's famous warning: "Power tends to corrupt, and absolute power corrupts absolutely."

Performing: Working in Groups

Researchers have studied a variety of aspects of groups, but McGrath's (1997) historical analysis of the field identifies three basic "schools of thought" that organize researchers' efforts and interests. The *systems perspective* considers groups to be complex sets of interdependent components that influence members' thoughts, feelings, and actions. The *structural perspective* examines the way that groups create enduring patterns and consistencies in social settings, including norms, roles, and regularized patterning in communication and influence. The third school of thought, the *functional perspective*, considers groups to be tools, for people use groups to achieve goals that require collaboration among many. Groups assemble to lift, build, or move things that individuals cannot. When critical decisions and selections must be made—judgments of criminal guilt or innocence, choices between diverse alternatives, or identification of previous errors—people turn to groups rather than make such determinations individually. Yet, at the same time people ridicule the benefits of work groups and teams with sarcasms such as, "an elephant is a mouse designed by a committee," "a committee is a group that keeps minutes and wastes hours," and "too many cooks spoil the broth." Groups can push members to reach the peak of their capabilities but they can also promote mediocrity as well (Larson, 2010; Nijstad, 2009).

Social Facilitation

Do people perform more effectively when alone or when part of a group? Social psychologists have been studying this question for over a century, beginning with Norman Triplett (1898). He noted that bicyclists in races were fastest when they competed against other racers rather than when they raced alone against the clock, and hypothesized that the presence of others leads to psychological stimulation that enhances performance. To test this idea he conducted the first laboratory study in the field of social psychology. He arranged for 40 children to play a game that involved turning a small reel as quickly as possible. He carefully measured how quickly they turned the reel, and confirmed that children performed best when they played the game in pairs compared to when they played alone (see Strube, 2005, for a reanalysis of Triplett's data).

Triplett (1898) succeeded in sparking interest in a phenomenon known now as *social facilitation*: the enhancement of an individual's performance when that person works in the presence of other people. It remained for Zajonc (1965), however, to specify when social facilitation does and does not occur. Zajonc (1965), after reviewing prior research, noted that the facilitating effects of an audience usually occur only when the task requires the person to perform dominant responses, ones that are well-learned or based on instinctive behaviors. If the task requires nondominant responses—novel, complicated, or untried behaviors that the organism has never performed before or has performed only infrequently—then the presence of others inhibits performance (see Figure 14.2). Hence, students write poorer quality essays on complex philosophical questions when they labor in a group rather than alone (Allport, 1924), but they make fewer mistakes in solving simple, low-level multiplication problems with an audience or a coactor than when they work in isolation (Dashiell, 1930).

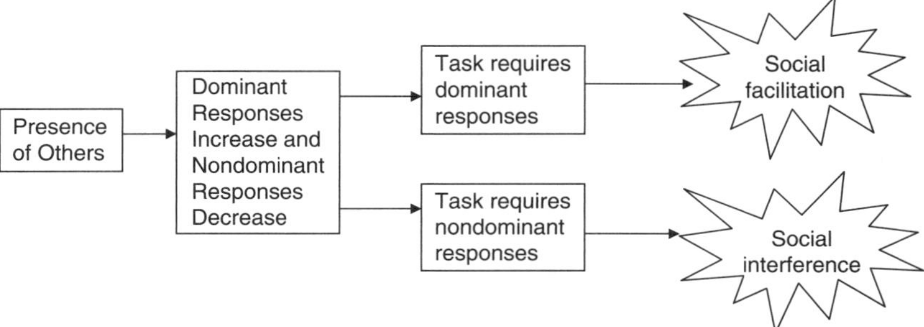

FIGURE 14.2. Zajonc's (1965) model of social facilitation. If the dominant response is appropriate in the situation, the presence of others is facilitating. If, however, the situation calls for a nondominant response, the presence of others will interfere with performance.

Bond and Titus (1983), in their review of 241 studies of social facilitation, confirmed Zajonc's (1965) insight by finding that facilitation occurs primarily when people perform simple tasks that require dominant responses. And Zajonc and his colleagues themselves confirmed this clarification in a study of some unusual subjects: cockroaches (Zajonc, Heingartner, & Herman, 1969). Zajonc, noting that roaches, by instinct, run from bright lights, designed two mazes with a start box near a light and a goal box hidden from the light. The simple maze was just a straight runway from the start to the goal. In the more complex maze, the roaches had to turn to the right to reach their goal. Zajonc reasoned that when other roaches are present the roaches should perform more efficiently in the simple maze than in the complex one. As predicted, cockroaches escaped the light more quickly in pairs than when alone provided the maze was simple. If the maze was complex, they escaped more quickly when alone than when with another cockroach. Zajonc and his colleagues also found that having an observer roach that watched from a small plastic cubicle located by the maze facilitated performance of the simple task but interfered with performance of the complex task.

Three processes—arousal, evaluation apprehension, and distraction-conflict—combine to create social facilitation effects (Aiello & Douthitt, 2001). First, as Zajonc (1965, 1980) noted, the mere presence of others introduces an element of uncertainty into any situation, and so elevates arousal. Once aroused, individuals tend to perform more dominant responses and fewer nondominant responses. The nature of this arousal is also different, depending on the nature of the task (Blascovich, Mendes, Hunter, & Salomon, 1999). When the task is easy, people display a *challenge response.* At the physiological level, they appear to be ready to respond to the challenge that they face (elevated heart rate and activation of the sympathetic nervous system). But when the task is difficult, people display a *threat response;* they appear to be stressed rather than ready for effective action.

Second, arousal is particularly likely when people are concerned about being evaluated by others (Cottrell, 1972). People know, from experience, that most observers are judging the quality of their work, and so the presence of an audience increases feelings of evaluation apprehension. As a consequence, individuals who display a negative orientation toward social situations tend to show a decline in performance in social settings, whereas those with a more positive orientation show a gain in performance (Uziel, 2007).

Third, a number of researchers suggest that cognitive processes account for social facilitation effects. These distraction-conflict theories note that others can be distracting, as attention is divided between the task and others' reactions. This distraction taxes the performer's cognitive resources and prevents him or her from processing task-related information thoroughly. If the task is a simple one, this distraction is overcome by working harder, and performance improves. But if the task is so complex that the increase in motivation is unable to offset the negative consequences of attentional conflict, then the presence of others will lead to decrements in performance (Baron, 1986; Guerin, 1983).

Social Loafing

Groups usually outperform individuals. One person playing soccer against a team of 11 will lose. Groups estimating the temperature of a room will be more accurate than an individual making the same estimate (Surowiecki, 2004). Students taking a multiple choice test as a team will get a higher score than a single individual taking the same test (Littlepage, 1991; Steiner, 1972).

Groups, though, display a curious tendency toward underachievement. The soccer team with superb athletes sometimes seems to play without any energy or excitement. Each student in a learning team may not do all that he or she can to help the group reach its goals. This inefficiency was documented by French agricultural engineer Max Ringelmann nearly a century ago. Say, hypothetically, an average individual working alone was able to lift 100 pounds. Therefore, two people working together should be able to lift nearly 200 pounds, three 300 pounds, and so on. But Ringelmann found that dyads managed to pull only about 1.9 times as much as one person, triads only 2.5 times as much, and eight-person groups a woeful 3.9 times the individual level. This tendency for groups to become less productive as their size increases is known as the *Ringelmann effect* (Kravitz & Martin, 1986).

Ringelmann traced this loss of productivity to two causes—one interpersonal and one motivational. First, when people work together they sometimes have trouble coordinating their individual activities and contributions, so they never reach the maximum level of efficiency (Diehl & Stroebe, 1987). Three people, lifting a heavy weight, for example, invariably pull and pause at slightly different times, so their efforts are uncoordinated. In consequence, they are stronger than a single person, but not three times as strong. Second, people just do not expend as much physical effort when working on a collective endeavor, nor do they expend as much cognitive effort trying to solve problems. They display *social loafing* (Latané, Williams, & Harkins, 1979; Petty, Harkins, & Williams, 1980).

Latané and colleagues (1979) examined both coordination losses and social loafing by arranging for students to cheer or clap alone or in groups of varying sizes. The students cheered alone or in two- or six-person groups, or they were led to believe they were in two- or six-person groups (those in the "pseudo-groups" wore blindfolds and headsets that played masking sound). As Figure 14.3 indicates, groups generated more noise than solitary participants, but the

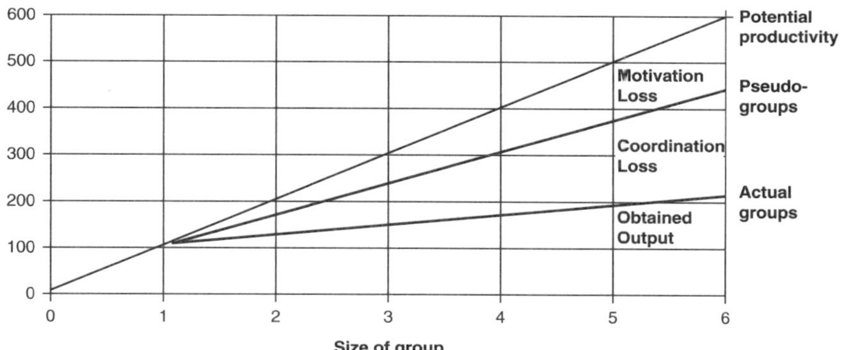

FIGURE 14.3. Social loafing in groups. Latané and his colleagues examined the two major causes of the Ringelmann effect by leading people to think they were working in groups when they actually were not. The people in these pseudogroups suffered from motivation loss, but not from coordination loss since they were actually working alone.

productivity dropped as the groups became larger in size. In dyads, each participant worked at only 66% of capacity, and in six-person groups at 36%. Productivity also dropped when participants believed they were in groups. If participants thought that one other person was shouting with them, they shouted only 82% as intensely, and if they thought five other people were shouting, they reached only 74% of their capacity. These losses in productivity were not due to problems with coordination but to a reduction in effort—to social loafing (Latané et al., 1979; Experiment 2).

Social loafing is not a rare phenomenon. People working on all types of physical and mental tasks—including brainstorming, evaluating employees, monitoring equipment, interpreting instructions, and formulating causal judgments—are less productive when working in a group situation than when working alone. Group members, however, rarely notice their loss of productivity. When people in groups are asked whether they are working as hard as they can, they generally claim that they are doing their best even when they are loafing. Either people are not aware or are simply unwilling to admit that they are loafing (Karau & Williams, 1993).

Reducing Social Loafing

Studies of social loafing suggest ways to increase the productivity of individuals working on collective tasks. Williams, Harkins, and Latané (1981) succeeded in eliminating social loafing in their noise-making paradigm by making each person's contribution seem identifiable. Just as the belief that you are being evaluated can facilitate performance on simple tasks, the belief that your contribution can be identified and evaluated will likely make you work much harder (Harkins & Jackson, 1985; Jackson & Latané, 1981). Social loafing is also minimized when subjects think that objective standards exist that can be used to evaluate their personal performance (Harkins & Szymanski, 1989; Szymanski & Harkins, 1987).

Social loafing can also be reduced if group members believe that their contribution to the project is important and if they personally value the group's goals. People should be made to believe that their contributions are unique and essential for the group's success. By breaking down large groups into smaller ones, for example, leaders can reduce feelings of anonymity and increase involvement (Kameda, Stasson, Davis, Parks, & Zimmerman, 1992). Loafing also becomes less likely when group members expend more effort to avoid the stigma associated with being the group's weakest performer. This tendency is known as the Köhler effect, after the investigator who noticed the performance gains of weaker individuals striving to keep up with the accomplishments of others in the group (Kerr, Messé, Seok, Sambolec, Lount, & Park, 2007; Weber & Hertel, 2007).

Group Decision Making

People often turn to groups when they must make key decisions, for groups can draw on more resources than one individual. Groups can generate more ideas and possible solutions by discussing the problem. Groups, too, can evaluate the options that they generate during discussion more objectively. Before accepting a solution, a group may stipulate that a certain number of people must favor it, or that it meets some other standard of acceptability. People generally believe that a group's decision will be superior to an individual's decision.

Groups, however, do not always make good decisions. Juries sometimes render verdicts that run counter to the evidence presented. Community groups take radical stances on issues before thinking through all the ramifications. Military strategists concoct plans that seem, in retrospect, ill-conceived and short-sighted. Three processes that can warp a group's decisions—group polarization, the shared information bias, and groupthink—are considered next.

Polarization in Groups

Common sense notions suggest that groups exert a moderating, subduing effect on their members. However, in the early 1960s social psychologists began to question this assumption. By asking individuals to make judgments alone and then in groups, they found a surprising shift in the direction of greater risk after group interaction (Stoner, 1961; Wallach, Kogan, & Bem, 1962). Moreover, this group shift carried over when members gave their private choices following the group discussion. This change was dubbed the *risky shift*.

Subsequent study indicated that risky shifts after group discussion are part of a larger, more general process. When people discuss issues in groups, they tend to decide on a more extreme course of action than would be suggested by the average of their individual judgments. Group discussion leads to *group polarization*: judgments are more extreme in the same direction as the average of individual judgments made prior to the discussion (Myers, 1982). For example, in France, where people generally like their government but dislike Americans, group discussion improved their attitude toward their government but exacerbated their negative opinions of Americans (Moscovici & Zavalloni, 1969). Similarly, prejudiced people who discussed racial issues with other prejudiced individuals became even more negative. Conversely, when mildly prejudiced persons discussed racial issues with other mildly prejudiced individuals, they became less prejudiced (Myers & Bishop, 1970).

As with social facilitation, several cognitive and interpersonal processes probably combine to generate group polarization (Isenberg, 1986; Kaplan & Miller, 1983). As group members discuss possible choices, the one favored by the majority of members will likely be supported with more and better arguments. Members who were initially ambivalent will be persuaded by the arguments, and as a result the entire group will become polarized (persuasive-argument theory; Burnstein & Vinokur, 1973, 1977). As group members compare their judgments to those of others, they shift their position when they realize that the attitudes of others are stronger (or more extreme) than their attitudes (social comparison theory; Blascovich, Ginsburg, & Howe, 1975, 1976). Groups may also become polarized when they implicitly adopt a majority-rules scheme and adopt the solution when more than 50% of the group expresses approval of that solution. If a majority, no matter how slim, favors a more extreme choice, then the group will polarize (social decision scheme theory; Davis, Kameda, & Stasson, 1992).

Shared Information Bias

When group members share their knowledge with each other in extensive discussions, these conversations often focus on information that the majority of the members already have. Instead of revealing unique pieces of information gleaned from personal experience or unique expertise, the group members discuss ideas that they share in common (Stasser, 1992; Stasser, Talor, & Hanna, 1989).

This *shared information bias* is inconsequential if the group is discussing a problem that is well known to all group members or that has an obvious solution. If, however, the group must access the unshared information to make a good decision, then the bias can lead the group astray. If a group is working on a problem and the shared information suggests that Alternative A is correct, but the unshared information favors Alternative B, then the group will discover this so-called hidden profile only if it discusses the unshared information (Larson, 2010; Wittenbaum, 2010).

Groupthink

Groups sometimes make spectacularly bad decisions. In 1961 a special advisory committee to President John F. Kennedy planned and implemented a covert invasion of Cuba at the Bay of Pigs that ended in total disaster. In 1986 NASA carefully, and incorrectly, decided to launch the Challenger space shuttle in temperatures that were too cold, and it crashed. Experts in the Bush administration weighed the risks of a war in Iraq carefully, and then proceeded with it only to find that the human and financial costs far exceeded their expectations.

Intrigued by these types of blunders, Janis (1982) carried out a number of case studies of such groups: the military experts that planned the defense of Pearl Harbor, Kennedy's Bay-of-Pigs planning group, and the presidential team that escalated the war in Vietnam. Each group, he concluded, fell prey to a distorted style of thinking that rendered its members incapable of making a rational decision. Janis labeled this syndrome *groupthink*: "a mode of thinking that people engage in when they are deeply involved in a cohesive in-group, when the members' strivings for unanimity override their motivation to realistically appraise alternative courses of action" (1982, p. 9).

Symptoms of Groupthink To Janis, groupthink is a disease that infects healthy groups, rendering them inefficient and unproductive. And like the physician who searches for symptoms that distinguish one disease from another, Janis has identified a number of symptoms that occur in groupthink situations. These danger signals, which should serve to warn members that they may be falling prey to groupthink, include overestimating the group's capabilities, biased perceptions, pressures to conform, and defective decision strategies. Groups that have fallen into the trap of groupthink are stumbling, yet the members usually assume that everything is working well. They think that nothing can stop them from reaching their goals (illusions of invulnerability) and they are morally vindicated to take action (illusions of morality).

During groupthink, members misperceive the motivations and intentions of other people, often assuming people who oppose their plan are untrustworthy or manipulative. Groupthink groups also display a high level of conformity. Even members who begin to question the group's decision privately engage in self-censorship; they hide their misgivings when they discuss the issue openly. As a result, many members may privately disagree with what is occurring in the group, yet publicly everyone expresses total agreement with the group's policies.

Causes of Groupthink In addition to identifying the warning signs of groupthink, Janis (1982) pointed out aspects of the situation and the group that serve as antecedents to this negative decisional syndrome. One cause, cohesion, serves as a necessary condition for groupthink, for only highly unified groups will display the pressures to conform that promote groupthink. Cohesive groups have many advantages over groups that lack unity, but when cohesiveness intensifies, members become more likely to accept the goals, decisions, and norms of the group without reservation. Pressures to conform also increase as members become reluctant to say or do anything that goes against the grain of the group, and the number of internal disagreements—necessary for good decision making—decreases. Noncohesive groups can also make terrible decisions, "especially if the members are engaging in internal warfare" (Janis, 1982, p. 176), but they do not fall prey to groupthink.

Other causal conditions include the degree of isolation, leadership methods, and the degree of stress. Kruglanski's group-centrism theory, for example, suggests that groups are more likely to make decisional mistakes when they encounter situations that interfere with their capacity to process information—time pressures, severe ambiguity, noise, or fatigue (Kruglanski, Pierro, Mannetti, & De Grada, 2006). In such situations, a group strives for cognitive closure, and its members are willing to accept the authority of strong, focused leaders. Baron's (2005) ubiquity model of group decision making shares a number of points of agreement with Janis's (1982) approach, but Baron suggests it is not group cohesion that increases groupthink symptoms but rather a threat to a shared social identity that may result should the group fail (Haslam, Ryan, Postmes, Spears, Jetten, & Webley, 2006).

Groups need not sacrifice cohesiveness to avoid the pitfall of groupthink. Rather, limiting premature seeking of concurrence, correcting misperceptions and errors, and improving the group's decisional methods can collectively help reduce poor decisions (Janis, 1982).

Groups over Time

Groups, like all living things, change over time. A group may begin as unrelated individuals, but in time roles develop and friendships form. New members join the group and old members leave. The group may become more cohesive or begin to loose its unity (see Table 14.2 for a summary).

These changes, however, follow a predictable pattern (Wheelan, 2005). In most groups the same types of issues arise over time, and once resolved the group can continue to develop. Tuckman (1965, Tuckman & Jenson, 1977) maintained that this group development often involves five stages. In the *forming phase* the group members become oriented toward one another. In the *storming phase* the group members find themselves in conflict, and some solution is sought to improve the group environment. In the *norming phase* standards for behavior and roles develop that regulate behavior. In the *performing phase* the group has reached a point at which it can work as a unit to achieve desired goals. The *adjourning phase* ends the sequence of development; the group disbands. Throughout these stages groups tend to oscillate back and forth between the task-oriented issues and the relationship issues, with members sometimes working hard but at other times strengthening their interpersonal bonds (Bales, 1965).

Individuals also experience change as they pass through the group: They are gradually assimilated into a group, remain in a group for a time, and then separate from the group. Moreland and Levine's (1982) model of group socialization, shown in Figure 14.4, describes this process. During the investigation

TABLE 14.2 **Stages of Group Development**

Stage	*Major Processes*	*Characteristics*
Orientation: *Forming*	Members become familiar with each other and the group; dependency and inclusion issues; acceptance of leader and group consensus	Communications are tentative, polite; concern for ambiguity, group's goals; leader is active; members are compliant
Conflict: *Storming*	Disagreement over procedures; expressions of dissatisfaction; tension among members; antagonism toward the leader	Criticism of ideas; poor attendance; hostility; polarization and coalition formation
Structure: *Norming*	Growth of cohesiveness and unity; establishment of roles, standards, and relationships; increased trust, communication	Agreement on procedures; reduction in role ambiguity; increased "we-feeling"
Work: *Performing*	Goal achievement; high task orientation; emphasis on performance and production	Decision making; problem solving; mutual cooperation
Dissolution: *Adjourning*	Termination of roles; completion of tasks; reduction of dependency	Disintegration and withdrawal; increased independence and emotionality; regret

Sources: Tuckman (1965) and Forsyth (2010).

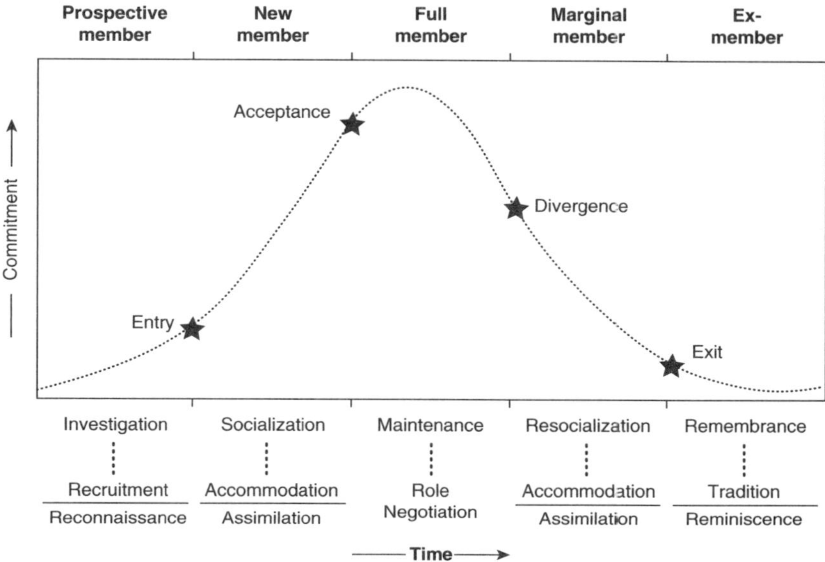

FIGURE 14.4. Moreland and Levine's (1982) theory of group socialization.

stage prospective members are still outsiders: They are interested in joining the group, but are not yet committed to it. Once the group accepts them as members, socialization begins as they take on different responsibilities depending on their role within the group. Even though they are full-fledged members at this point, changes continue as their roles and responsibilities change. During this maintenance phase, members may have to learn new ways of doing things or accept responsibilities that they would rather avoid. If this maintenance is successful they remain in this stage until the group or their membership ends as scheduled. If, however, they fail to adapt to changes appropriately, then group members may attempt resocialization, in which group members are reminded that they must abide by the group's norms. If they fail, they will probably leave the group. In any case, once membership in the group is concluded the former members pass through yet another stage, remembrance. They are no longer members, but still remember, sometimes with fondness and sometimes with regret, the time when they belonged to the group.

Future of Group Research

Social psychologists are intrigued by a variety of topics and phenomena, including attitudes and prejudices, liking and loving, altruism and aggression, and the way perceivers process information about their social worlds, but the study of groups and their processes remains the cornerstone of a social psychological approach to understanding human interaction. Although researchers have explored many intriguing aspects of groups, this chapter has explored only a small fraction of the insights yielded by those investigations: the compelling need of individuals to be part of a group, and the far-reaching effects that result when that need is denied; a group's astonishing capacity to transform its members, prompting them to act in ways that they never would were they acting as individuals; the tendency for groups to create consistencies among the relationships of members, with the result that communication, influence, and even attraction become patterned and predictable; the group's willingness to allow some members to assume responsibility for, and control over, the group's activities; a group's capacity to bring individuals together in the pursuit of shared goals, with results that are sometimes admirable but also, in some cases, appalling; and the way groups, like all living organisms, change and develop as they form, mature, and dissolve.

Despite researchers' success in studying groups, much more work needs to be done in exploring the nature and functioning of groups. It is ironic that although scientists have studied aspects of the physical world for centuries, only in the past 100 years have they turned their attention to human experiences, and human groups in particular. Yet theories and studies of groups repeatedly confirm the important role they play in all aspects of social life. Groups are the key to understanding people—why they think, feel, and act the way they do. On a practical level, much of the world's work is done by groups, so by understanding groups we move toward making them more efficient. If we want to improve productivity in a factory, problem solving in a boardroom, or learning in the classroom, we must understand groups. An understanding of groups is also essential if we are to solve societal problems such as racism, sexism, and international conflict. Any attempt to change society will succeed only if the groups within that society change. As society adjusts to a more technological and globally united world, and as economic success is increasingly determined by group decisions and work team efforts, a clear understanding of group processes will become increasingly relevant, practical, and essential (Forsyth & Burnette, 2005).

References

Aiello, J. R., & Douthitt, E. A. (2001). Social facilitation: From Triplett to electronic performance monitoring. *Group Dynamics: Theory, Research, and Practice, 5*, 163–180.

Albright, L., Kenny, D. A., & Malloy, T. E. (1988). Consensus in personality judgments at zero acquaintance. *Journal of Personality and Social Psychology, 55*, 387–395.

Allport, F. H. (1924). *Social psychology*. Boston: Houghton Mifflin.

Allport, F. H. (1962). A structuronomic conception of behavior: Individual and collective. I. Structural theory and the master problem of social psychology. *Journal of Abnormal and Social Psychology, 64*, 3–30.

Alter, A. L., & Darley, J. M. (2009). When the association between appearance and outcome contaminates social judgment: A bidirectional model linking group homogeneity and collective treatment. *Journal of Personality and Social Psychology, 97*, 776–795.

Arrow, H., McGrath, J. E., & Berdahl, J. L. (2000). Small groups as complex systems: Formation, coordination, development, and adaptation. Thousand Oaks, CA: Sage.

Asch, S. E. (1957). An experimental investigation of group influence. In *Symposium on preventive and social psychiatry*. Washington, DC: U.S. Government Printing Office.

Asendorpf, J. B., & Wilpers, S. (1998). Personality effects on social relationships. *Journal of Personality and Social Psychology, 74*, 1531–1544.

Bales, R. F. (1965). The equilibrium problem in small groups. In A. P. Hare, E. F. Borgatta, & R. F. Bales (Eds.), *Small groups: Studies in social interaction*. New York: Knopf.

Baron, R. S. (1986). Distraction-conflict theory: Progress and problems. *Advances in Experimental Social Psychology, 19*, 1–40.

Baron, R. S. (2005). So right it's wrong: Groupthink and the ubiquitous nature of polarized group decision making. *Advances in Experimental Social Psychology, 37*, 219–253.

Bartol, K. M., & Martin, D. C. (1986). Women and men in task groups. In R. D. Ashmore & F. K. DelBoca (Eds.), *The social psychology of female-male relations* (pp. 259–310). New York: Academic Press.

Baumeister, R. F., & Leary, M. R. (1995). The need to belong: Desire for interpersonal attachments as a fundamental human motivation. *Psychological Bulletin, 117*, 497–529.

Bavelas, A. (1950). Communication patterns in task-oriented groups. *Journal of the Acoustical Society of America, 22*, 725–730.

Berdahl, J. L., & Martorana, P. (2006). Effects of power on emotion and expression during a controversial group discussion. *European Journal of Social Psychology, 36*, 497–509.

Berger, J., & Zelditch, M., Jr. (1998). *Status, power, and legitimacy: Strategies and theories*. New Brunswick, NJ: Transaction.

Blackhart, G. C., Nelson, B. C., Knowles, M. L., & Baumeister, R. F. (2009). Rejection elicits emotional reactions but neither causes immediate distress nor lowers self-esteem: A meta-analytic review of 192 studies on social exclusion. *Personality and Social Psychology Review, 13*, 269–309.

Blascovich, J., Ginsburg, G. P., & Howe, R. C. (1975). Blackjack and the risky shift, II: Monetary stakes. *Journal of Experimental Social Psychology, 11*, 224–232.

Blascovich, J., Ginsburg, G. P., & Howe, R. C. (1976). Blackjack, choice shifts in the field. *Sociometry, 39*, 274–276.

Blascovich, J., Mendes, W. B., Hunter, S. B., & Salomon, K. (1999). Social "facilitation" as challenge and threat. *Journal of Personality and Social Psychology, 77*, 68–77.

Bond, C. F., & Titus, L. J. (1983). Social facilitation: A meta-analysis of 241 studies. *Psychological Bulletin, 94*, 265–292.

Branscombe, N. R. (1998). Thinking about one's gender group's privileges or disadvantages: Consequences for well-being in women and men. *British Journal of Social Psychology, 37*, 167–184.

Brinthaupt, T. M., Moreland, R. L., & Levine, J. M. (1991). Sources of optimism among prospective group members. *Personality and Social Psychology Bulletin, 17*, 36–43.

Brown, B. B., & Lohr, N. (1987). Peer group affiliation and adolescent self-esteem: An integration of ego-identity and symbolic-interaction theories. *Journal of Personality and Social Psychology, 52*, 47–55.

Brown, L. H., Silvia, P. J., Myin-Germeys, I., & Kwapil, T. R. (2007). When the need to belong goes wrong: The expression of social anhedonia and social anxiety in daily life. *Psychological Science, 18*, 778–782.

Brown, T. M., & Miller, C. E. (2000). Communication networks in task-performing groups: Effects of task complexity, time pressure, and interpersonal dominance. *Small Group Research, 31*, 131–157.

Burnette, J. L., & Forsyth, D. R. (2008). "I didn't do it:" Responsibility biases in open and closed groups. *Group Dynamics: Theory, Research, and Practice, 12*, 210–222.

Burnstein, E., & Vinokur, A. (1973). Testing two classes of theories about group-induced shifts in individual choice. *Journal of Experimental Social Psychology, 9*, 123–137.

Burnstein, E., & Vinokur, A. (1977). Persuasive arguments and social comparison as determinants of attitude polarization. *Journal of Experimental Social Psychology, 13*, 315–332.

Buss, D. M. (1996). The evolutionary psychology of human social strategies. In E. T. Higgins & A. W. Kruglanski (Eds.), *Social psychology: Handbook of basic principles* (pp. 3–38). New York: Guilford Press.

Campbell, D. T. (1958). Common fate, similarity, and other indices of the status of aggregates of persons as social entities. *Behavioral Science, 3*, 14–25.

Cartwright, D., & Zander, A. (Eds.). (1968). *Group dynamics: Research and theory* (3rd ed.). New York: Harper & Row.

Castano, E., Yzerbyt, V., & Bourguignon, D. (2003). We are one and I like it: The impact of ingroup entitativity on ingroup identification. *European Journal of Social Psychology, 33*, 735–754.

Coie, J. D., Dodge, K. A., & Coppotelli, H. (1982). Dimensions and types of social status: A cross-age perspective. *Developmental Psychology, 18*, 557–570.

Correll, J., & Park, B. (2005). A model of the ingroup as a social resource. *Personality and Social Psychology Review, 9*, 341–359.

Cottrell, N. B. (1972). Social facilitation. In C. G. McClintock (Ed.), *Experimental social psychology* (pp. 185–236). New York: Holt, Rinehart & Winston.

Crocker, J., & Luhtanen, R. (1990). Collective self-esteem and ingroup bias. *Journal of Personality and Social Psychology, 58*, 60–67.

Crocker, J., Major, B., & Steele, C. (1998). Social stigma. in D. T. Gilbert & S. T. Fiske (Eds.), *The handbook of social psychology* (Vol. 2, 4th ed., pp. 504–553). New York: McGraw-Hill.

Darley, J. (1992). Social organization for the production of evil. *Psychological Inquires, 3*, 199–218.

Dashiell, J. F. (1930). An experimental analysis of some group effects. *Journal of Abnormal and Social Psychology, 25*, 190–199.

Davies, P., Spencer, P. J., & Steele, C. M. (2005). Clearing the air: Identity safety moderates the effects of stereotype threat on women's leadership aspirations. *Journal of Personality and Social Psychology, 88*, 276–287.

Davis, J. H., Kameda, T., & Stasson, M. (1992). Group risk taking: Selected topics. In J. F. Yates (Ed.), *Risk-taking behavior* (pp. 163–199). Chichester, UK: Wiley.

De Cremer, D., & Van Dijk, E. (2005). When and why leaders put themselves first: Leader behavior in resource allocations as a function of feeling entitled. *European Journal of Social Psychology, 35*, 553–563.

Diehl, M., & Stroebe, W. (1987). Productivity loss in brainstorming groups: Toward the solution of a riddle. *Journal of Personality and Social Psychology, 53*, 497–509.

Dion, K. L. (2000). Group cohesion: From "field of forces" to multidimensional construct. *Group Dynamics: Theory, Research, and Practice, 4*, 7–26.

Driskell, J. E., & Mullen, B. (1990). Status, expectations, and behavior: A meta-analytic review and test of theory. *Personality and Social Psychology Bulletin, 16*, 541–553.

Eagly, A. H., & Carli, L. L. (2007). *Through the labyrinth: The truth about how women become leaders*. Boston: Harvard Business School Press.

Eagly, A. H., & Karau, S. J. (2002). Role congruity theory of prejudice toward female leaders. *Psychological Review, 109*, 573–598.

Eysenck, H. (1990). Biological dimensions of personality. In L. A. Pervin (Ed.), *Handbook of personality: Theory and research* (pp. 244–276). New York: Guilford Press.

Festinger, L. (1950). Informal social communication. *Psychological Review, 57*, 271–282.

Festinger, L. (1954). A theory of social comparison processes. *Human Relations, 7*, 117–140.

Festinger, L., Schachter, S., & Back, K. (1950). *Social pressures in informal groups*. New York: Harper.

Fiedler, F. E. (1978). The contingency model and the dynamics of the leadership process. *Advances in Experimental Social Psychology, 12*, 59–112.

Fiedler, F. E. (1981). Leadership effectiveness. *American Behavioral Scientist, 24*, 619–632.

Forsyth, D. R. (2000). Social comparison and influence in groups. In J. Suls & L. Wheeler (Eds.), *Handbook of social comparison: Theory and research* (pp. 81–103). Dordrecht, Netherlands: Kluwer Academic Publishers.

Forsyth, D. R. (2010). *Group dynamics* (5th ed.). Belmont, CA: Wadsworth/Thompson.

Forsyth, D. R., & Burnette, J. L. (2005). The history of group research. In S. Wheelan (Ed.), *The handbook of group research and practice* (pp. 3–18). Thousand Oaks, CA: Sage.

Forsyth, D. R., & Nye, J. L. (2008). Seeing and being a leader: The perceptual, cognitive, and interpersonal roots of conferred influence. In C. L. Hoyt, G. R. Goethals, & D. R. Forsyth (Eds.), *Leadership at the crossroads: Leadership and psychology* (Vol. 1, pp. 116–131). Westport, CT: Praeger.

Freeman, L. C. (2004). The development of social network analysis: A study in the sociology of science. Vancouver, British Columbia: Empirical Press.

French, J. R. P., Jr., & Raven, B. (1959). The bases of social power. In D. Cartwright (Ed.), *Studies in social power*. Ann Arbor, MI: Institute for Social Research.

Galinsky, A. D., Gruenfeld, D. H., & Magee, J. C. (2003). From power to action. *Journal of Personality and Social Psychology, 85*, 453–466.

Galinsky, A. D., Jordan, J., & Sivanathan, N. (2008). Harnessing power to capture leadership. In C. L. Hoyt, G. R. Goethals, & D. R. Forsyth (Eds.), Leadership at the crossroads: Leadership and psychology (Vol. 1, pp. 283–299). Westport, CT: Praeger.

Gawronski, B., Walther, E., & Blank, H. (2005). Cognitive consistency and the formation of interpersonal attitudes: Cognitive balance affects the encoding of social information. *Journal of Experimental Social Psychology, 41*, 618–626.

Guerin, B. (1983). Social facilitation and social monitoring: A test of three models. *British Journal of Social Psychology, 22*, 203–214.

Guinote, A. (2008). Power and affordances: When the situation has more power over powerful than powerless individuals. *Journal of Personality and Social Psychology, 95*, 237–252.

Hackman, J. R. (2003). Learning more by crossing levels: Evidence from airplanes, hospitals, and orchestras. *Journal of Organizational Behavior, 24*, 905–922.

Harkins, S. G., & Jackson, J. M. (1985). The role of evaluation in eliminating social loafing. *Personality and Social Psychology Bulletin, 11*, 457–465.

Harkins, S. G., & Szymanski, K. (1989). Social loafing and group evaluation. *Journal of Personality and Social Psychology, 56*, 934–941.

Haslam, S. A., Ryan, M. K., Postmes, T., Spears, R., Jetten, J., & Webley, P. (2006). Sticking to our guns: Social identity as a basis for the maintenance of commitment to faltering organizational projects. *Journal of Organizational Behavior, 27*, 607–628.

Heider, F. (1958). The psychology of interpersonal relations. New York: Wiley.

Henry, K. B., Arrow, H., & Carini, B. (1999). A tripartite model of group identification: Theory and measurement. *Small Group Research, 30*, 558–581.

Hersey, P., & Blanchard, K. H. (1982). *Management of organizational behavior* (4th ed.). Upper Saddle River, NJ: Prentice Hall.

Hinsz, V. B., Tindale, R. S., & Vollrath, D. A. (1997). The emerging conceptualization of groups as information processors. *Psychological Bulletin, 121*, 43–64.

Hogan, R., & Kaiser, R. B. (2005). What we know about leadership . *Review of General Psychology, 9*, 169–180.
Hogg, M. A. (1992). *The social psychology of group cohesiveness: From attraction to social identity*. New York: New York University Press.
Hogg, M. A. (2001). Social categorization, depersonalization, and group behavior. In M. A. Hogg & R. S. Tindale (Eds.), *Blackwell handbook of social psychology: Group processes* (pp. 56–85). Malden, MA: Blackwell.
Hogg, M. A., Sherman, D. K., Dierselhuis, J., Maitner, A. T., & Moffitt, G. (2007). Uncertainty, entitativity, and group identification. *Journal of Experimental Social Psychology, 43*, 135–142.
Hollander, E. P., & Offermann, L. R. (1990). Power and leadership in organizations: Relationships in transition. *American Psychologist, 45*, 179–189.
Hoyt, C. L., & Chemers, M. M. (2008). Social stigma and leadership: A long climb up a slippery ladder. In C. L. Hoyt, G. R. Goethals, & D. R. Forsyth (Eds.), *Leadership at the crossroads: Leadership and psychology* (Vol. 1, pp. 165–180). Westport, CT: Praeger.
Isenberg, D. J. (1986). Group polarization: A critical review and meta-analysis. *Journal of Personality and Social Psychology, 50*, 1141–1151.
Jackson, J. M., & Latané, B. (1981). All alone in front of all those people: Stage fright as a function of number and type of co-performances and audience. *Journal of Personality and Social Psychology, 40*, 73–85.
Janis, I. L. (1982). *Groupthink: Psychological studies of policy decisions and fiascos* (2nd ed.). Boston: Houghton Mifflin.
Kameda, T., Stasson, M. F., Davis, J. H., Parks, C. D., & Zimmerman, S. K. (1992). Social dilemmas, subgroups, and motivation loss in task-oriented groups: In search of an "optimal" team size in division of work. *Social Psychology Quarterly, 55*, 47–56.
Kaplan, M. F., & Miller, C. E. (1983). Group discussion and judgment. In P. B. Paulus (Ed.), *Basic group processes* (pp. 65–94). New York: Springer-Verlag.
Karau, S. J., & Williams, K. D. (1993). Social loafing: A meta-analytic review and theoretical integration. *Journal of Personality and Social Psychology, 65*, 681–706.
Kelly, J. R. (2001). Mood and emotion in groups. In M. A. Hogg & R. S. Tindale (Eds.), *Blackwell handbook of social psychology: Group processes* (pp. 164–181). Malden, MA: Blackwell.
Kelman, H. C. (2006). Interests, relationships, identities: Three central issues for individuals and groups in negotiating their social environment. *Annual Review of Psychology, 57*, 1–26.
Keltner, D., Gruenfeld, D. H., & Anderson, C. (2003). Power, approach, and inhibition. *Psychological Review, 110*, 265–284.
Keltner, D., Van Kleef, G. A., Chen, S., & Kraus, M. W. (2008). A reciprocal influence model of social power: Emerging principles and lines of inquiry. *Advances in Experimental Social Psychology, 40*, 151–192.

Kerr, N. L., Messé, L. A., Seok, D., Sambolec, E. J., Lount, R. B. Jr., & Park, E. S. (2007). Psychological mechanisms underlying the Köhler motivation gain. *Personality and Social Psychology Bulletin, 33*, 828–841.

Kirkpatrick, S. A., & Locke, E. A. (1991). Leadership: Do traits matter? *Academy of Management Executive, 5*, 48–60.

Knoke, D., & Yang, S. (2008). *Social network analysis* (2nd ed.). Los Angeles: Sage.

Kravitz, D. A., & Martin, B. (1986). Ringelmann rediscovered: The original article. *Journal of Personality and Social Psychology, 50*, 936–941.

Kruglanski, A. W., Pierro, A., Mannetti, L., & De Grada, E. (2006). Groups as epistemic providers: Need for closure and the unfolding of group-centrism. *Psychological Review, 113*, 84–100.

Larson, J. R., Jr. (2010). *In search of synergy in small group performance*. New York: Psychology Press.

Latané, B., Williams, K., & Harkins, S. (1979). Many hands make light the work: The causes and consequences of social loafing. *Journal of Personality and Social Psychology, 37*, 822–832.

Leary, M. R. (2007). Motivational and emotional aspects of the self. *Annual Review of Psychology, 58*, 317–344.

Leary, M. R., & Forsyth, D. R. (1986). Attributions of responsibility for collective endeavors. *Review of Personality and Social Psychology, 8*, 167–188.

Leavitt, H. J. (1951). Some effects of certain communication patterns on group performance. *Journal of Abnormal and Social Psychology, 46*, 38–50.

Lewin, K., Lippitt, R., & White, R. (1939). Patterns of aggressive behavior in experimentally created "social climates." *Journal of Social Psychology, 10*, 271–299.

Lickel, B., Hamilton, D. L., Wieczorkowska, G., Lewis, A., Sherman, S. J., & Uhles, A. N. (2000). Varieties of groups and the perception of group entitativity. *Journal of Personality and Social Psychology, 78, 223–246.*

Littlepage, G. E. (1991). Effects of group size and task characteristics on group performance: A test of Steiner's model. *Personality and Social Psychology Bulletin, 17*, 449–456.

Maassen, G. H., Akkermans, W., & van der Linden, J. L. (1996). Two-dimensional sociometric status determination with rating scales. *Small Group Research, 27*, 56–78.

Matz, D. C., & Wood, W. (2005). Cognitive dissonance in groups: The consequences of disagreement. *Journal of Personality and Social Psychology, 88*, 22–37.

McGrath, J. E. (1997). Small group research: That once and future field. *Group Dynamics: Theory, Research & Practice, 1*, 7–27.

Milgram, S. (1963). Behavioral study of obedience. *Journal of Abnormal and Social Psychology, 67*, 371–378.

Milgram, S. (1974). *Obedience to authority*. New York: Harper & Row.

Milgram, S. (1992). *The individual in a social world: Essays and experiments* (2nd ed.). New York: McGraw-Hill.

Moreland, R. L. (1987). The formation of small groups. *Review of Personality and Social Psychology, 8*, 80–110.
Moreland, R. L., & Levine, J. M. (1982). Socialization in small groups: Temporal changes in individual-group relations. *Advances in Experimental Social Psychology, 15*, 137–192.
Moreno, J. L. (1953). *Who shall survive? A new approach to the problem of human interrelations* (revised ed.). Washington, DC: Nervous and Mental Disease Publishing Co.
Moscovici, S., & Zavalloni, M. (1969). The group as a polarizer of attitudes. *Journal of Personality and Social Psychology, 12*, 125–135.
Mullen, B., & Copper, C. (1994). The relation between group cohesiveness and performance: An integration. *Psychological Bulletin, 115*, 210–227.
Myers, D. G. (1982). Polarizing effects of social interaction. In H. Brandstätter, J. H. Davis, & G. Stocker-Kreichgauer (Eds.), *Group decision making*. New York: Academic Press.
Myers, D. G., & Bishop, G. D. (1970). Discussion effects on racial attitudes. *Science, 169*, 778–789.
Newcomb, A. F., Bukowski, W. M., & Pattee, L. (1993). Children's peer relations: A meta-analytic review of popular, rejected, neglected, controversial, and average sociometric status. Psy*chological Bulletin, 113*, 99–128.
Newcomb, T. M. (1943). *Personality and social change*. New York: Dryden.
Nijstad, B. A. (2009). *Group performance*. New York: Psychology Press.
Pavelshak, M. A., Moreland, R. L., & Levine, J. M. (1986). Effects of prior group memberships on subsequent reconnaissance activities. *Journal of Personality and Social Psychology, 50*, 56–66.
Paxton, P., & Moody, J. (2003). Structure and sentiment: Explaining emotional attachment to group. *Social Psychology Quarterly, 66*, 34–47.
Pearce, C. L., & Conger, J. A. (Eds.). (2003). *Shared leadership: Reframing the hows and whys of leadership*. Thousand Oaks, CA: Sage.
Petty, R. E., Harkins, S. G., & Williams, K. D. (1980). The effects of group diffusion of cognitive effort on attitudes: An information-processing view. *Journal of Personality and Social Psychology, 38*, 81–92.
Ridgeway, C. L. (2006). Status construction theory. In P. J. Burke (Ed.), Contemporary social psychological theories (pp. 301–323). Stanford, CA: Stanford University Press.
Ross, L. (1977). The intuitive psychologist and his shortcomings: Distortions in the attribution process. *Advances in Experimental Social Psychology, 10*, 173–220.
Rydell, R. J., Hugenberg, K., Ray, D., & Mackie, D. M. (2007). Implicit theories about groups and stereotyping: The role of group entitativity. *Personality and Social Psychology Bulletin, 33*, 549–558.
Sadler, M. S., & Judd, C. M. (2001). Overcoming dependent data: A guide to the analysis of group data. In M. A. Hogg & R. S. Tindale (Eds.), *Blackwell handbook of social psychology: Group processes* (pp. 497–524). Malden, MA: Blackwell.

Sani, F., Bowe, M., & Herrera, M. (2008). Perceived collective continuity and social well-being: Exploring the connections. *European Journal of Social Psychology, 38*, 365–374.

Sankowsky, D. (1995). Charismatic leader as narcissist: Understanding the abuse of power. *Organizational Dynamics, 23*, 57–71.

Schachter, S. (1959). *The psychology of affiliation.* Stanford, CA: Stanford University Press.

Seashore, S. E. (1954). *Group cohesiveness in the industrial work group.* Ann Arbor, MI: Institute for Social Research.

Semin, G. R. (2007). Grounding communication: Synchrony. In A. W. Kruglanski & E. T. Higgins (Eds.), *Social psychology: Handbook of basic principles* (2nd ed., pp. 630–649). New York: Guilford Press.

Shaw, M. E. (1964). Communication networks. *Advances in Experimental Social Psychology, 1*, 111–147.

Shelly, R. K., Troyer, L., Munroe, P. T., & Burger, T. (1999). Social structure and the duration of social acts. *Social Psychology Quarterly, 62*, 83–95.

Sherif, M. (1936). *The psychology of social norms.* New York: Harper & Row.

Simpson, J. A., & LaPaglia, J. (2010). Evolutionary psychology. In J. M. Levine & M. A. Hogg (Eds.), Encyclopedia of group processes & intergroup relations (Vol. 1, pp. 258–262). Los Angeles: Sage.

Smith, E. R., Murphy, J., & Coats, S. (1999). Attachment to groups: Theory and management. *Journal of Personality and Social Psychology, 77*, 94–110.

Smith, E. R., Seger, C. R., & Mackie, D. M. (2007). Can emotions be truly group level? Evidence regarding four conceptual criteria. *Journal of Personality and Social Psychology, 93*, 431–446.

Smith, P. K., Dijksterhuis, A., & Wigboldus, D. H. J. (2008). Powerful people make good decisions even when they consciously think. *Psychological Science, 19*, 1258–1259.

Smith, P. K., Jostmann, N. B., Galinsky, A. D., & van Dijk, W. W. (2008). Lacking power impairs executive functions. *Psychological Science, 19*, 441–447.

Stasser, G. (1992). Pooling of unshared information during group discussions. In S. Worchel, W. Wood, & J. A. Simpson (Eds.), *Group process and productivity* (pp. 48–67). Thousand Oaks, CA: Sage.

Stasser, G., Taylor, L. A., & Hanna, C. (1989). Information sampling in structured and unstructured discussions of three- and six-person groups. *Journal of Personality and Social Psychology, 57*, 67–78.

Steiner, I. D. (1972). *Group process and productivity.* New York: Academic Press.

Steiner, I. D. (1974). Whatever happened to the group in social psychology? *Journal of Experimental Social Psychology, 10*, 94–108.

Stogdill, R. M. (1974). *Handbook of leadership.* New York: Free Press.

Stoner, J. A. F. (1961). *A comparison of individual and group decisions involving risk.* Unpublished master's thesis. Cambridge, MA: Massachusetts Institute of Technology.

Strube, M. J. (2005). What did Triplett really find? A contemporary analysis of the first experiment in social psychology. *American Journal of Psychology, 118,* 271–286.

Surowiecki, J. (2004). *The wisdom of crowds.* New York: Anchor.

Szymanski, K., & Harkins, S. G. (1987). Social loafing and self-evaluation with a social standard. *Journal of Personality and Social Psychology, 53,* 891–897.

Tiedens, L. Z., Unzueta, M. M., & Young, M. J. (2007). An unconscious desire for hierarchy? The motivated perception of dominance complementarity in task partners. *Journal of Personality and Social Psychology, 93,* 402–414.

Triplett, N. (1898). The dynamogenic factors in pacemaking and competition. *American Journal of Psychology, 9,* 507–533.

Troyer, L., & Younts, C. W. (2010). Group structure. In J. M. Levine & M. A. Hogg (Eds.), *Encyclopedia of group processes & intergroup relations* (Vol. 1, pp. 381–385). Los Angeles: Sage.

Tuckman, B. W. (1965). Developmental sequences in small groups. *Psychological Bulletin, 63,* 384–399.

Tuckman, B. W., & Jensen, M. A. C. (1977). Stages of small group development revisited. *Group and Organizational Studies, 2,* 419–427.

Twenge, J. M., Baumeister, R. F., DeWall, C. N., Ciarocco, N. J., & Bartels, J. M. (2007). Social exclusion decreases prosocial behavior. *Journal of Personality and Social Psychology, 92,* 56–66.

Uziel, L. (2007). Individual differences in the social facilitation effect: A review and meta-analysis. *Journal of Research in Personality, 41,* 579–601.

Van Vugt, M., & Schaller, M. (2008). Evolutionary approaches to group dynamics: An introduction. *Group Dynamics: Theory, Research, and Practice, 12,* 1–6.

Vider, S. (2004). Rethinking crowd violence: Self-categorization theory and the Woodstock 1999 riot. *Journal for the Theory of Social Behavior, 34,* 141–166.

Vroom, V. H. (2003). Educating managers in decision making and leadership. *Management Decision, 10,* 968–978.

Walker, H. A., Ilardi, B. C., McMahon, A. M., & Fennell, M. L. (1996). Gender, interaction, and leadership. *Social Psychology Quarterly, 59,* 255–272.

Wallach, M. A., Kogan, N., & Bem, D. J. (1962). Group influence on individual risk taking. *Journal of Abnormal and Social Psychology, 65,* 75–86.

Weber, B., & Hertel, G. (2007). Motivation gains of inferior group members: A meta-analytical review. *Journal of Personality and Social Psychology, 93,* 973–993.

Wheelan, S. (2005). The developmental perspective. In S. Wheelan (Ed.), *The handbook of group research and practice* (pp. 119–132). Thousand Oaks, CA: Sage.

Williams, K. D., Harkins, S., & Latané, B. (1981). Identifiability as a deterrent to social loafing: Two cheering experiments. *Journal of Personality and Social Psychology, 40*, 303–311.

Wittenbaum, G. M. Hidden profile task. In J. M. Levine & M. A. Hogg (Eds.), *Encyclopedia of group processes & intergroup relations* (Vol. 1, pp. 398–400). Los Angeles: Sage.

Yukl, G. (2010). *Leadership in organizations* (7th ed.). Upper Saddle River, NJ: Prentice Hall.

Zaccaro, S. J., Foti, R. J., & Kenny, D. A. (1991). Self-monitoring and trait-based variance in leadership: An investigation of leader flexibility across multiple group situations. *Journal of Applied Psychology, 76*, 308–315.

Zajonc, R. B. (1965). Social facilitation. *Science, 149*, 269–274.

Zajonc, R. B. (1980). Compresence. In P. B. Paulus (Ed.), *Psychology of group influence* (pp. 35–60). Mahwah, NJ: Erlbaum.

Zajonc, R. B., Heingartner, A., & Herman, E. M. (1969). Social enhancement and impairment of performance in the cockroach. *Journal of Personality and Social Psychology, 13*, 83–92.

Zander, A., Stotland, E., & Wolfe, D. (1960). Unity of group, identification with group, and self-esteem of members. *Journal of Personality, 28*, 463–478.

Zyphur, M. J., & Islam, G. (2006). *Toward understanding the existence of groups: The relationship between climate strength and entitativity.* IBMEC Working Paper (WPE–12–2006). Retrieved from http://www.ibmecsp.edu.br/ December 15, 2008.

Zyphur, M. J., Kaplan, S. A., & Christian, M. S. (2008). Assumptions of cross-level measurement and structural invariance in the analysis of multilevel data: Problems and solutions. *Group Dynamics: Theory, Research, and Practice, 12*, 127–140.

Chapter 15

Intergroup Relations

Marilynn B. Brewer

In the 1990s, the demise of the Soviet Union brought an end to the "Cold War" era with its focus on relations between two political superpowers. In its aftermath, an apparent resurgence of ethnic conflict throughout the world gave rise to the idea that local group loyalties and intergroup hostilities were never far below the surface. The media began talking about the "new tribalism" that seemed to be emerging everywhere. As public interest in these issues grew, so did the resurgence of interest in theory and research on intergroup relations within social psychology in Europe and in the United States. By the turn of the millennium, concern about issues of intergroup relations has become even more intense for social scientists and laypersons alike. In addition to organized conflict carried on by nations against nations, states against subgroups within their own populations, and ethnic and religious conflicts within nations, acts of international terrorism by small groups of extremists have riveted attention and concern across the globe. It is more clear than ever that group identities play a major role in human behavior—impelling heroic action on behalf of *ingroups*, as well as horrific atrocities against designated *outgroups*. Social–psychological understanding of these processes has also grown as the study of intergroup relations took center stage within the discipline.

The salience and extremity of intergroup hostility and violence lead to the impression that the study of intergroup relations is equivalent to the study of intergroup conflict. However, although escalation of conflict and hostility between groups is the form of intergroup relationships of most concern in the real world, social-psychological research on intergroup behavior starts with other, more subtle, forms of responding that reflect differences in disposition toward others as a function of their group membership. Understanding intergroup relations invokes most areas of social-psychological inquiry—from the study of person perception, social attitudes, aggression, self-esteem, social comparison, equity, cooperation, and competition to conformity and compliance. From research in all of these areas we have a wealth of information about the cognitive and motivational foundations of intergroup behavior.

Defining Intergroup Relations

It is a basic fact of human existence that people are organized into social groups. We are all members of many different types of groups, ranging from small, face-to-face groupings of family and friends, to large social categories such as gender, religion, and nationality. As a consequence, much of our interaction with others takes place in a group setting, where we are not only individual persons but representatives of our respective social groups. For social psychologists, the classic definition of intergroup situations is that provided by Sherif (1966): "Whenever individuals belonging to one group interact, collectively or individually, with another group or its members in terms of their group identification, we have an instance of intergroup behavior" (p. 12). What this definition implies is that intergroup relations can occur at the level of two persons interacting (the dyadic level) as well as the level of exchanges between groups as a whole (the intergroup level).

The essence of the social-psychological approach to the study of intergroup relations is to understand the causes and consequences of the distinction between ingroups (those groups to which an individual belongs) and outgroups (social groups that do not include the individual as a member)—the apparently universal propensity to differentiate the social world into "us" and "them." In general, feelings, beliefs, and interpersonal behaviors tend to be more positive when they involve members of the same group (ingroup behavior) than when they occur between groups. An intergroup orientation arises when ingroup–outgroup differentiation is engaged in connection with particular social categorizations. Attitudes and behavior toward members of the ingroup and outgroup then follow from the level of the individual's attachment to the ingroup and his or her assessment of the nature of the outgroup *in relation to* the ingroup.

It is this relational aspect of intergroup behavior that distinguishes the study of intergroup relations from the study of prejudice as an individual attitude toward specific groups or social categories (cf. Bodenhausen and Richeson, Chapter 10, this volume). Ingroup–outgroup differentiation involves thinking of social groups or categories in us–them terms. Category membership alone is not sufficient to engage this intergroup orientation. Ingroup activation involves an additional process of *self*-categorization (Turner et al., 1987) or social identification whereby the sense of self is extended to the group as a whole. Similarly, a social category becomes an outgroup only when the self is actively disassociated from the group, in a "not-me" sense. Thus, to understand intergroup relations, we first need to understand the processes and motivations underlying an individual's attachment to his or her social groups and the conditions under which ingroup–outgroup differentiation becomes engaged.

Social Identity and Ingroup Bias

Social identity is defined as "that part of an individual's self-concept which derives from his knowledge of his membership of a social group . . . together with the value and emotional significance attached to that membership" (Tajfel, 1981, p. 255). Social identity theory, as articulated by Tajfel (1978) and Turner (1975), represents the convergence of two traditions in the study of intergroup attitudes and behavior—social categorization [as represented in the work by Doise (1978), Tajfel (1969), and Wilder (1986)] and social comparison [as exemplified by Lemaine (1974) and Vanneman & Pettigrew (1972)]. The theoretical perspective rests on two basic premises:

1. Individuals organize their understanding of the social world on the basis of categorical distinctions that transform continuous variables into discrete classes; categorization has the effect of minimizing perceived differences *within* categories and accentuating intercategory differences.
2. Because individuals are members of some social categories and not others, social categorization carries with it implicit *ingroup–outgroup* (we–they) distinctions; because of the self-relevance of social categories, the ingroup–outgroup classification is a superimposed category distinction with affective and emotional significance.

These two premises provide a framework for conceptualizing any social situation in which a particular ingroup–outgroup categorization is made salient. In effect, the theory posits a basic *intergroup schema* with the following characteristic features:

1. Assimilation within category boundaries and contrast between categories such that all members of the ingroup are perceived to be more

similar to the self than members of the outgroup (the *intergroup accentuation* principle).
2. Positive affect (trust, liking) selectively generalized to fellow ingroup members but not outgroup members (the *ingroup favoritism* principle).
3. Intergroup social comparison and perceived competition between ingroup and outgroup for positive value (the *social competition* principle) (Turner, 1975).

Social identity theory in conjunction with self-categorization theory (Turner et al., 1987) provides a comprehensive view of group behavior and the cognitive processes that underlie a range of intergroup and group phenomena. The basic tenet of these theories is that group behaviors derive from cognitive representations of the self in terms of a shared social category membership, in which there is effectively no psychological separation between the self and the group as a whole. This phenomenon is referred to as *depersonalization of self-representation*, whereby the cognitive representation of the self shifts from *personal self* to *collective self* (Hogg & Abrams, 1988; Hogg & Turner, 1987). In self-categorization terms, social identity entails "a shift towards the perception of self as an interchangeable exemplar of some social category and away from the perception of self as a unique person" (Turner, Hogg, Oakes, Reicher, & Wetherell, 1987, p. 50). As a consequence of this shift in level of self-categorization, self-interest becomes equated with ingroup interests, and the welfare and status of the ingroup become primary motivations.

Mere Categorization and Intergroup Behavior

In a laboratory setting in Bristol, England, Henri Tajfel and his colleagues undertook initial experiments with the so-called "minimal intergroup situation" (Tajfel, 1970: Tajfel, Billig, Bundy, & Flament, 1971) in which individuals are assigned to arbitrary social categories. In these experiments, participants chose to allocate higher rewards to members of their own category relative to members of the outgroup category, even in the absence of any personal identification of group members, any past history, or any direct benefit to the self. The results provided a powerful demonstration that merely classifying individuals into arbitrary distinct social categories was sufficient to produce ingroup–outgroup discrimination and bias, even in the absence of any interactions with fellow group members or any history of competition or conflict between the groups.

Since the initial minimal group experiments, hundreds of studies in the laboratory and the field have documented ingroup favoritism in myriad forms

(Brewer, 1979; Brewer & Campbell, 1976; Diehl, 1990; Mullen, Brown, & Smith, 1992). In addition to the allocation bias demonstrated by Tajfel, preferential treatment and evaluation of ingroups relative to outgroups appear in evaluations of group products (e.g., Gerard & Hoyt, 1974), application of rules of fairness (Ancok & Chertkoff, 1983; Ng, 1984; Platow, McClintock, & Liebrand, 1990), attributions for positive and negative behavior (Hewstone, 1990; Weber, 1994), and willingness to trust and cooperate (Brewer & Kramer, 1986; Miller, Downs, & Prentice, 1998; Wit & Kerr, 2002; Yuki, Maddux, Brewer, & Takemura, 2005). There is considerable evidence that such ingroup favoritism is considered normative in its own right (Blanz, Mummendey, & Otten, 1997; Platow, O'Connell, Shave, & Hanning, 1995) and that it is activated automatically when a group identity is salient (Otten & Moskowitz, 2000; Otten & Wentura, 1999).

These studies succeeded in confirming the power of we–they distinctions to produce differential evaluation, liking, and treatment of other persons depending on whether they are identified as members of the ingroup category or not. The laboratory experiments with the minimal intergroup situation demonstrated that ethnocentric loyalty and bias clearly do not depend on kinship or an extensive history of interpersonal relationships among group members, but can apparently be engaged readily by symbolic manipulations that imply shared attributes or a common fate. What appears to be critical for ingroup attachment is a distinctive identification of who is "us" and who is "them"—a rule of exclusion as well as inclusion.

Ethnocentrism and Ingroup Positivity

The hallmark of ingroup identification is ingroup positivity, positive feelings about the ingroup and fellow ingroup members. There is even ample evidence that positive affect and positive evaluation are activated automatically by an ingroup label or whenever a group (even a minimal group) is associated with the self (Perdue, Dovidio, Gurtman, & Tyler,1990; Otten, 2002; Farnham, Greenwald, & Banaji, 1999; Rudman, Greenwald, & McGhee, 2001).

This idea that ingroups are inevitably positively regarded accords with the concept of "ethnocentrism" as introduced by Sumner (1906) several decades earlier. Ethnocentrism was described by Sumner as a universal characteristic of human social groups whereby

> a differentiation arises between ourselves, the we-group, or ingroup, and everybody else, or the others-group, outgroups. The insiders in a we-group are in a relation of peace, order, law, government, and industry, to each other . . . Ethnocentrism is the technical name for this view of things in

> which one's own group is the center of everything, and all others are scaled and rated with reference to it . . . Each group nourishes its own pride and vanity, boasts itself superior, exalts its own divinities, and looks with contempt on outsiders. . . . (Sumner, 1906, pp. 12–13)

This does not mean, however, that ingroup evaluations are indiscriminantly positive on all dimensions of assessment. When there is objective evidence of outgroup achievement or a consensual status hierarchy in which the outgroup is recognized to be of higher status than the ingroup, then some degree of outgroup positivity (relative to the ingroup) is frequently obtained (Jost, 2001). However, ingroup positivity is consistently found on traits or attributes that are self-defining or self-relevant (Otten, 2002), and on traits reflecting basic moral values (e.g., warmth, trustworthiness, cooperativeness) (Leach, Ellemers, & Barreto, 2007). On these basic value dimensions, ingroup positivity appears to be essentially universal (Brewer, 2001; LeVine & Campbell, 1972).

Motives Underlying Ingroup Attachment and Positivity

Self-esteem The motivational concept most associated with social identity theory is that of self-esteem enhancement. To the extent that individuals identify with a social group, they derive benefit from their group's successes and achievements, even when the individual has not contributed directly to the group's accomplishment. Thus, ingroup status and achievements become a source of self-esteem that goes beyond what can be achieved by the individual alone. This is the basis for the social identity theory idea that group members are motivated to seek *positive distinctiveness* in comparing their ingroups to outgroups (Turner, 1975). However, it is not clear from the social identity literature whether positive self-esteem was being invoked as a motive for social identity itself or as a motive for ingroup favoritism *given that* social identity had been engaged. Whatever the original intent, subsequent research on the role of self-esteem in ingroup bias has generally supported the idea that enhanced self-esteem may be a *consequence* of achieving a positively distinct social identity, but there is little evidence that the need to increase self-esteem motivates social identification in the first place (Rubin & Hewstone, 1998). To the contrary, there is considerable evidence that individuals often identify strongly with groups that are disadvantaged, stigmatized, or otherwise suffer from negative intergroup comparison (e.g., Branscombe, Ellemers, Spears, & Doosje, 1999; Crocker, Luhtanen, Blaine, & Broadnax, 1994; Jetten, Branscombe, Schmitt, & Spears, 2001; Turner, Hogg, Turner, & Smith, 1984). Some experimental research indicates that social identification with a group may actually be increased when the group is threatened or stigmatized (Jetten, Branscombe, Schmitt, & Spears, 2001; Turner et al., 1984).

Cognitive Motives: Uncertainty Reduction Given the inadequacy of self-esteem as an explanation for why social identity is engaged, other motives have been proposed that do not require positive ingroup status as a basis for attachment to groups and self-definition as a group member. One proposal is that group identity meets fundamental needs for reducing uncertainty and achieving meaning and clarity in social contexts (Hogg & Abrams, 1993; Hogg & Mullin, 1999). In support of this hypothesis, Hogg and his colleagues (Grieve & Hogg, 1999; Mullin & Hogg, 1998) have generated compelling evidence that identification and ingroup bias are increased under conditions of high cognitive uncertainty and reduced or eliminated when uncertainty is low. And it is undoubtedly true that one function that group memberships and identities serve for individuals is that of providing self-definition and guidance for behavior in otherwise ambiguous social situations (Deaux , Reid, Mizrahi, & Cotting, 1999; Vignoles, Chryssochoou, & Breakwell, 2000). However, group identity is only one of many possible modes of reducing social uncertainty. Roles, values, laws, etc. serve a similar function without necessitating social identification processes. Thus, uncertainty reduction alone cannot account for the pervasiveness of group identification as a fundamental aspect of human life.

Security and Belonging Uncertainty reduction as a theory of social identity places the explanation for group identification in a system of cognitive motives that includes needs for meaning, certainty, and structure. An alternative perspective is that the motivation for social identification arises from even more fundamental needs for security and safety. Consistent with this idea, Baumeister and Leary (1995) postulate a universal need for *belonging* as an aspect of human nature derived from our vulnerability as lone individuals who require connection with others to survive. But belonging alone cannot account for the selectivity of social identification, as any and all group memberships should satisfy the belonging motive. The theory of "optimal distinctiveness" (Brewer, 1991) thus postulates that the need for belonging and inclusion is paired with an opposing motive—the need for differentiation—that together regulate the individual's social identity and attachment to social groups.

The basic premise of the optimal distinctiveness model is that the two identity needs (inclusion/assimilation and differentiation/distinctiveness) are independent and work in opposition to motivate group identification. Optimal identities are those that satisfy the need for inclusion *within* the ingroup and simultaneously serve the need for differentiation through distinctions *between* the ingroup and outgroups. In effect, optimal social identities involve *shared distinctiveness* (Stapel & Marx, 2007). Individuals will resist being identified with social categorizations that are either too inclusive or too differentiating but will define themselves in terms of social identities that are optimally distinctive. Equilibrium is maintained by correcting for deviations from optimality. A situation in which a person is overly individuated will excite the need for assimilation, motivating the person to adopt a more inclusive social identity. Conversely, situations that arouse feelings of overinclusion will activate the need for differentiation, resulting in a search for more exclusive or distinct identities.

Evidence for competing social motives comes from empirical demonstrations of efforts to achieve or restore group identification when these needs are not met. Results of experimental studies have shown that activation of the need for assimilation or the need for differentiation increases the importance of distinctive group memberships (Pickett, Silver, & Brewer, 2002), and any threat to inclusion enhances self-stereotyping on group-characteristic traits (Brewer & Pickett, 1999; Pickett, Bonner, & Coleman, 2002; Spears, Doosje, & Ellemers, 1997). Furthermore, assignment to distinctive minority group categories engages greater group identification and self-stereotyping than does membership in large, inclusive majority groups (Brewer & Weber, 1994; Leonardelli & Brewer, 2001; Simon & Hamilton, 1994). Thus, there is converging evidence that group attachment is regulated by motives for both inclusion and distinctiveness.

Also consistent with optimal distinctiveness theory, threats to group distinctiveness (e.g., too much similarity to outgroups or ambiguity of group boundaries) arouse concern about restoring ingroup boundaries and intergroup differentiation (Hornsey & Hogg, 1999; Jetten, Spears, & Manstead, 1998; Jetten, Spears, & Postmes, 2004; Roccas & Schwartz, 1993). Research on the "ingroup overexclusion effect" (Castano, Yzerbyt, Bourguignon, & Seron, 2002; Leyens & Yzerbyt, 1992; Yzerbyt, Leyens, & Bellour, 1995) demonstrates that group members tend to take more time and employ more stringent criteria when deciding if someone is a potential ingroup member than when deciding if the person is a potential outgroup member. This overexclusion effect is enhanced when distinctiveness motives have been aroused (Brewer & Pickett, 2002).

Ingroup Positivity and Outgroup Derogation

There is a widespread assumption in the social–psychological literature that high levels of social identification and ingroup positivity are associated with derogation and hostility toward outgroups. However, despite a common belief that ingroup positivity and outgroup derogation are reciprocally related, empirical research demonstrates little consistent relation between the two. Indeed, results from both laboratory experiments and field studies indicate that variations in ingroup positivity and social identification do not systematically correlate with degree of bias or negativity toward outgroups (Brewer, 1979; Hinkle & Brown, 1990; Kosterman & Feshbach, 1989; Struch & Schwartz, 1989).

Experiments with the minimal intergroup situation also provided additional evidence that ingroup favoritism is prior to, and not necessarily associated with, outgroup negativity or hostility. Brewer (1979) reported that most minimal group studies that assessed ratings of the ingroup and outgroup separately found that categorization into groups leads to enhanced ingroup ratings in the absence of decreased outgroup ratings. Furthermore, the ingroup favoritism that is exhibited in the allocation of positive resources in the minimal intergroup situation (Tajfel et al., 1971) is essentially eliminated when allocation decisions involve the distribution of negative outcomes or costs (e.g., Mummendey et al., 1992), suggesting that individuals are willing to differentially benefit the ingroup compared to outgroups but are reluctant to harm outgroups more directly.

Subsequent research in both laboratory and field settings has come to acknowledge the important distinction between ingroup bias that reflects beneficence and positive sentiments toward the ingroup that are withheld from outgroups ("subtle" prejudice) and discrimination that reflects hostility, derogation, and intent to harm the outgroup ("blatant" prejudice) (Pettigrew & Meertens, 1995). This is not to say that ingroup-based discrimination is benign or inconsequential. Indeed, many forms of institutional racism and sexism are probably attributable to discrimination based on ingroup preference rather than prejudice against outgroups (Brewer, 1996). Nonetheless, the absence of positive regard and the lack of trust for outgroups that are characteristic of most ingroup–outgroup differentiation can be conceptually and empirically distinguished from the presence of active hostility, distrust, and hate for outgroups that characterize virulent prejudice. Thus, ingroup identity alone is not sufficient to predict attitudes and behavior toward outgroups and we must look beyond social identity theory to account for intergroup hostility and conflict.

Theories of Intergroup Conflict

Traditional Theories: Realistic Group Conflict and Relative Deprivation

Traditional theories of intergroup relations trace hostility and conflict with outgroups to the nature of the structural relations between group interests. Realistic group conflict theory (LeVine & Campbell, 1972, Chapter 3) posits that conflict derives from competition between groups for material resources and power. Within social psychology one of the most influential proponents of Realistic Group Conflict Theory was Sherif (e.g., Sherif, 1966). In a famous series of field experiments conducted in the context of a boys' summer camp (known as the "Robber's Cave" experiments), he and his colleagues showed how the behavior of a group of strangers could be predictably transformed by first dividing them into groups and then arranging for those groups to compete with one another for valued resources (Sherif, Harvey, White, Hood, & Sherif, 1961). During and after competition the boys exhibited hostile intergroup behavior and showed marked ingroup favoritism in friendship choices and judgments. Consistent with the conflict of interests approach, when the researchers changed the structural arrangements so that the groups were placed in a series of cooperative encounters (in which group interests were compatible and interdependent), the intergroup behavior became more amicable and the favoritism declined.

Subsequent research largely confirmed these basic findings. In laboratory studies when the interdependence between groups is experimentally controlled to be either negative, neutral, or positive the results are quite consistent: There is usually more ingroup bias, less intergroup liking, and greater intergroup discrimination when groups are objectively in competition than when they are independent or must cooperate over some common goal (e.g. Kahn & Ryen, 1972; Rabbie & Wilkins, 1971; Rabbie, Benoist, Oosterbaan, & Visser, 1974; Worchel, Andreoli, & Folger, 1977). In field settings a similar correspondence between objective or perceived goal relationships linking groups and intergroup attitudes has been observed. Evaluative or affective judgments of outgroups are generally correlated with perceptions of groups being positively or negatively interdependent (Brown & Abrams, 1986; Esses, Jackson, & Armstrong, 1998; Struch & Schwartz, 1989).

Realistic Group Conflict Theory provides a powerful explanation for many instances of intergroup discrimination and conflict. Moreover it has the advantage of being able to account for changes in levels of prejudice over time or across different social contexts reflecting changing economic and political relations between the groups concerned. Nevertheless, there are, as Turner (1981) has noted, a number of empirical and theoretical difficulties with the perspective. First, functional interdependence per se may not be sufficient to determine intergroup behavior unless some degree of ingroup identification is also present. Consistent with this conclusion, Struch and Schwartz (1989) found that the correlation between perceived conflicts of interests among religious groups in Israel and levels of intergroup hostility were higher for those respondents who identified strongly with their religious ingroup than it was for those who identified less strongly.

A more serious issue in Realistic Group Conflict Theory concerns whether the negative interdependence that it assumes to underlie hostilities need always be based on real conflicts over concrete things such as land, money, or political power. It could derive from perceived conflicts or competition over some rather less tangible assets such as prestige or "to be the winner." Sherif was deliberately vague on this point, defining group interests as "a real or imagined threat to the safety of the group, an economic interest, a political advantage, a military consideration, prestige, or a number of others" (Sherif, 1966, p. 15). Allowing perceived conflicts to have causal status similar to actual conflicts poses a theoretical problem. If perceptions of competing goals can underlie intergroup hostility, and if such perceptions are not always correlated with the groups' actual material interests, where do they come from? Apart from actual structural relations between groups, there may be additional social–psychological origins for subjective competitive orientations and perceived threats from outgroups.

Realistic Conflict Updated: Integrated Threat Theory

A more recent approach to conceptualizing how perceptions of ingroup–outgroup relations may lead to outgroup negativity is integrated threat theory (Stephan & Stephan, 2000). This model distinguishes four different sources of experienced threat from a specific outgroup: *realistic threats* (threats to the existence, power, or material well-being of the ingroup or ingroup members), *symbolic threats* (threats to the ingroup worldview arising from perceived group differences in morals, values, and standards), *intergroup anxiety* (personal fear or discomfort experienced in connection with actual or anticipated interactions with members of the outgroup), and *negative stereotypes* (beliefs about outgroup characteristics that imply unpleasant or conflictual interactions and negative consequences for the self or the ingroup). Field tests of this model have found that ratings of realistic threat, symbolic threat, and intergroup anxiety are significant predictors of negative interracial attitudes and that these threat perceptions mediate the effects of other predictor variables such as ingroup identification, intergroup contact, and status differences (Riek, Mania, & Gaertner, 2006; Stephan et al., 2002).

The nature of symbolic threat is of particular interest because of the role that symbolic threats to group identity apparently play in many intractable intergroup conflicts (Bar-Tal, 2007; Rouhana & Bar-Tal, 1998). Concerns for symbolic threats to group values and icons or lack of respect and recognition are often conceptualized as the subjective "irrational" bases of intergroup hostility and fear, posed in opposition to concerns for objective or "realistic" threats to material welfare and group existence. But objective assessments of conflict of interest and subjective perceptions of identity threat are inextricably intertwined. Especially in the modern world, competition over resources (e.g., land, power) has as much to do with the identity meaning of those resources as it does actual group survival (e.g., Ledgerwood, Liviatan, & Carnevale, 2007). Many intractable conflicts are characterized by conceptualizations of group identity in which the identities of the groups involved become oppositional, such that a key component of each group's identity is based on negation of the other (Kelman, 1999). The role of such symbolic identity concerns in sustaining intractable conflicts is of particular importance because the costs of extensive and protracted conflict in terms of material resources and human lives defy rational choice theories of group behavior. Members of both groups generally recognize that they would be collectively better off if the conflicts were resolved. Yet deeply held identity concerns stand as a barrier to negotiated resolution (Kelman, 1999, 2001).

Intergroup Comparison, Relative Deprivation, and Social Change

The social identity theory approach to understanding intergroup relations places particular attention on comparisons between the status and outcomes of the ingroup and those of relevant outgroups. Considerable research on social justice supports the idea that individuals' feelings of being deprived or disadvantaged are based on the comparisons they make rather than the absolute value of their own condition. Feelings of resentment and the sense of injustice that arises from perceiving that you have less than what you deserve compared to others are called *relative deprivation.*

The concept of relative deprivation was developed by social scientists during World War II to explain some paradoxic findings that emerged in the study of morale among American soldiers (Stouffer, Suchman, DeVinney, Stat, & Williams, 1949). Researchers found, for instance, that soldiers in air force units, in which rates of promotion were quite high, had more complaints about the promotion system than did soldiers in the military police, where promotions were few and far between. Equally surprising, they found that black soldiers who were stationed in southern states in the United States (where overt discrimination based on race was very visible) had higher morale than black soldiers stationed in the less racist northern states. Stouffer and his colleagues explained these anomalous results in terms of different standards of comparison being used by soldiers in different units. Compared to peers who were advancing at a rapid rate, air force soldiers who had not yet been promoted felt deprived, even though their objective chances of promotion were higher than those of soldiers in other units. Similarly, the high morale of black soldiers stationed in the South may have derived from comparisons with black civilians who fared very poorly; black soldiers in the North, on the other hand, may have felt deprived relative to civilian blacks in that region who were earning higher wages in war-related factory jobs.

Parallel to relative deprivation at the personal level is what Runciman (1966) called *fraternal deprivation*. Fraternal deprivation arises from comparisons between the outcomes of your ingroup as a whole and those of more advantaged groups. Whereas personal deprivation depends on interpersonal comparisons with similar others, fraternal deprivation involves intergroup comparisons between dissimilar groups and becomes a source of resentment and potential conflict with groups perceived as being unjustly more advantaged than the ingroup.

Relative deprivation may be experienced even by those who are objectively advantaged but feel they are losing by comparison to previous expectations. This principle was dramatically illustrated by behavior of young members of the upper castes of India in a series of incidents in 1990. During one period that year, scores of middle-class youths (members of the Brahmin, Kshatriya, and Vaishya castes) committed suicide in protest against government policies that open more jobs to the poor. By any objective standards, the upper castes were doing quite well, even in the presence of government economic reforms designed to benefit the disadvantaged castes. Yet the perception that their own caste was losing position relative to the lower castes created a sense of comparative disadvantage that was sufficient to motivate dramatic protest against the reforms.

Perceptions of unjust ingroup deprivation can spur collective action on the part of disadvantaged group members to improve the status and outcomes of the ingroup. Theories of social identity, social comparison, and relative deprivation all suggest that members of lower-status groups will be discontented with the resources and valuation attached to their collective identity and will be motivated toward social change. Yet it seems to take a great deal more than perceived discrepancies and status differentials to mobilize collective action.

In reviewing the options available to members of low-status social categories to achieve positive distinctiveness, Tajfel and Turner (1986) distinguished three different avenues of responding to negative social identity, each with different implications for collective movements:

1. *Individual mobility*. With this option, individuals dissociate themselves from the lower-status ingroup and seek identification with the higher-status outgroup. This route to achieving positive social identity is most likely in social systems characterized by permeability of group boundaries and high opportunity for upward social mobility.

2. *Social creativity.* Group members may achieve positive distinctiveness by redefining the bases of intergroup comparison, choosing new dimensions on which the ingroup can be assigned higher values than relevant outgroups, or changing the valuation attached to existing comparisons. The "black is beautiful" movement in the United States is an example of this latter strategy. This option essentially leaves the social relationships between groups unchanged, but alters the implications for group self-esteem.
3. *Social competition.* Finally, low-status group members may seek to change the structure of intergroup dominance and status differentials by engaging in direct competition with higher-status outgroups. It is only under this condition that perceptions of relative deprivation will lead to intergroup conflict.

Tajfel and Turner (1986) distinguish three different aspects of the status relationships among groups that determine what mode of adaptation disadvantaged group members are likely to pursue. These are the perceived *permeability* of group boundaries and the perceived stability and *legitimacy* of the status differences between groups. Permeability refers to the extent to which group members can expect to be able to move from one group to another, or shift their social identity, on an individual basis. According to social identity theory, under conditions of high permeability members of lower status groups will tend to prefer membership in the higher status outgroup and seek social mobility as a strategy for improving positive social identity (van Knippenberg & Ellemers, 1990). Experimental studies have confirmed that manipulations of perceived permeability interact with group status to affect ingroup identification. Members of low-status groups express more dissatisfaction with their group membership and less ingroup preference when group boundaries are permeable rather than impermeable (Ellemers et al., 1988). However, when individuals could potentially change their group affiliation (high permeability), members of high-status groups increase their commitment to their current group membership. Under the risk of losing their attractive group membership, members of permeable high-status groups express significantly stronger ingroup identification than when group membership is fixed (Ellemers, Doosje, van Knippenberg, & Wilke, 1992).

Permeability creates instability of group membership but does not necessarily alter the status relationships between the groups as a whole. More important for social identity is the perceived stability or security of the status or dominance hierarchy itself (Sidanius, 1993; Sidanius & Pratto, 1999; Tajfel & Turner, 1986; van Knippenberg & Ellemers, 1993). When status differentials are perceived to be unstable or illegitimate, members of lower status groups exhibit significantly stronger ingroup identification than when status relationships are stable (Caddick, 1982; Ellemers, van Knippenberg, & Wilke, 1990). Although perceived injustice at the personal level often motivates individuals to dissociate from low-status ingroups, perceived collective injustice enhances group identification and efforts to improve the status position of the group as a whole (Ellemers, Wilke, & van Knippenberg, 1993; Taylor, Moghaddam, Gamble, & Zellerer, 1987; Wright, Taylor, & Moghaddam, 1990).

At the same time, perceived instability of the status hierarchy threatens the positive distinctiveness of high-status groups. In experiments manipulating both group size and group status, discrimination in intergroup allocations is particularly high for minority high-status groups (Mullen, Brown, & Smith, 1992). Sachdev and Bourhis (1991) argue that this is because when the dominant group is in the minority, the status structure is inherently more unstable than when the majority is dominant. Secure status differentials may reduce the salience of intergroup comparisons and discrimination, but insecurity heightens the motivation to maintain status distinctions on the part of high-status group members. Thus, conditions of social change increase the motivation for intergroup conflict, distrust, and heightened discrimination for groups in all positions of the status hierarchy.

Intergroup Emotions Theory

The general idea that intergroup attitudes are shaped by the perceived relationship between the ingroup and outgroup (in particular, whether the existence of the outgroup poses a threat to the ingroup) is consistent with recent theories of prejudice as intergroup emotion (Smith, 1993). Emotional reactions to a particular outgroup can include positive emotions (e.g., admiration, respect) as well as a range of negative emotions (e.g., fear, disgust, anxiety, and hate). In Dijker's (1987) examination of the relation between emotions and attitudes toward two minority groups in the Netherlands, although both types of emotion predicted evaluation of the outgroups, positive emotions were more predictive of attitudes toward one group and negative emotions were more predictive of attitudes toward the other. Similarly, in an investigation of the relationship between positive and negative emotional responses toward seven minority groups in the United States, both types of emotion predicted prejudice toward these groups (Stangor, Sullivan, & Ford, 1991, Study 1).

In addition to distinguishing between positive and negative emotions as components of intergroup attitudes, researchers have begun to recognize the importance of distinguishing among different types of negative emotions in intergroup contexts. Distinct emotions reflect different underlying causes and lead to different types of behavior. Smith (1993) has suggested that five specific emotions are most likely to be aroused in intergroup situations: fear, disgust, contempt, anger, and jealousy. Of these, fear and disgust can be distinguished as emotions that imply avoidance or movement away from the outgroup, whereas contempt and anger imply movement against the outgroup (although fear can also elicit the attack response if the perceiver feels trapped or cornered and unable to effectively flee the source of fear). Attitudes that are driven by the former emotional states are likely to have different cognitive contents and behavioral implications than attitudes that are associated with the latter forms of emotion.

Mackie, Devos, and Smith (2000) demonstrated, across three empirical studies, that (1) for groups that are defined by a basic value conflict, anger and fear can be differentiated as distinct negative emotional responses to the outgroup, (2) appraisals of relative ingroup strength determine the degree of reported anger toward the outgroup, and (3) the level of felt anger mediates the relationship between strength appraisals and participants' desire to confront, oppose, or attack members of the outgroup. Based on these findings, Mackie et al. concluded that intergroup attitudes and behavior are channeled by the specific emotions that are elicited in response to appraisals of a particular outgroup in relation to the ingroup.

According to appraisal theories of emotion, the type of emotion directed toward outgroups may be a function of the degree of conflict of interest that is perceived to exist between the outgroup and the ingroup. When the perceived conflict or threat is relatively low, negative emotions toward outgroups are likely to be associated with appraisals of status and legitimacy. The perception that the outgroup is different from the ingroup in ways that are devalued or illegitimate gives rise to feelings of moral superiority, intolerance, and concomitant emotions of contempt and disgust toward relevant outgroups. The emotions associated with moral superiority may justify some negative discrimination against outgroups, but do not necessarily lead directly to hostility or conflict. The emotions of contempt and disgust are associated with avoidance rather than attack, so intergroup peace may be maintained through segregation and mutual avoidance. As perceived conflict increases, avoidant emotions such as anxiety and disgust may be replaced by emotions such as anger, which instigate active hostility and aggression. Thus, the nature of the appraisal of the intergroup situation and the specific emotion that is engaged determine whether outgroup negativity gives rise to intergroup conflict.

Changing Intergroup Relations: Cooperative Contact

Whether realistic or perceived, the idea that an outgroup constitutes a threat to the welfare, values, or position of the ingroup is the primary basis of intergroup negativity and hostility. From that perspective, the route to improved intergroup relations lies in changing the perception of the outgroup vis-à-vis the ingroup. Ever since Sherif's classic Robber's Cave experiments, social psychologists have advocated cooperative intergroup contact as an effective strategy for improving intergroup relations. The key idea behind the "contact hypothesis" (Allport, 1954) is that isolation and segregation perpetuate intergroup hostility and negative attitudes. Interpersonal contact with members of the outgroup provides an opportunity for disconfirming negative expectations and building positive relations that can influence attitudes toward the outgroup as a whole.

Of course, mere contact between members of hostile groups does not always have such benign or positive outcomes. For contact to be an effective means of improving intergroup relations, at least two requirements have to be met. First, the contact must occur under conditions that reduce intergroup anxiety and promote positive interpersonal experiences (Voci & Hewstone, 2003). Second, group membership must be sufficiently salient in the contact situation so that the positive experience generalizes to the group as a whole (Brown, Vivian, & Hewstone, 1999; Hewstone & Brown, 1986; Ensari & Miller, 2002).

To meet the first requirement, the original contact hypothesis was qualified to include a number of preconditions for positive contact. According to Allport (1954), the four most important of these qualifying conditions were (1) integration has the support of authority, fostering *social norms* that favor intergroup acceptance, (2) the situation has high "acquaintance potential," promoting *intimate contact* among members of both groups, (3) the contact situation promotes *equal status* interactions among members of the social groups, and (4) the situation creates conditions of *cooperative interdependence* among members of both groups. Of these qualifiers, personalized contact and cooperation have received the most attention in both field and laboratory research (Pettigrew, 1998).

From Robbers Cave onward, many field studies of intergroup contact have confirmed that intergroup cooperation leads to more friendliness and less ingroup bias than situations that do not promote or require cooperative interaction. Probably the most extensive application of the contact hypothesis has been the implementation of cooperative learning programs in desegregated school classrooms. There is a sizable body of evidence that demonstrates the effectiveness of cooperative learning groups for increasing attraction and interaction between members of different social categories (Aronson et al., 1978; Johnson & Johnson, 1981; Slavin, 1985). Meta-analyses of studies in ethnically mixed classrooms confirm the superiority of cooperative learning methods over individualistic or competitive learning in promoting cross-ethnic friendships and reduced prejudice (Johnson, Johnson, & Maruyama, 1984).

Issues of Generalization

One concern about the validity of the contact hypothesis is whether findings obtained under relatively benign conditions can be generalized to real-world social groups with a history of conflict and hostility, inequalities of status and power, and political struggle. With established groups, resistance to contact and cooperative interdependence may be strong enough to make questions of the conditions of contact moot, and the history of outcomes of forced desegregation and contact is mixed at best (e.g., Cook, 1985; Gerard, 1983; Gerard & Miller, 1975; Stephan, 1986).

Another issue is whether any positive effects of contact, when they do occur, are generalized from the immediate contact experience to attitudes toward the outgroup as a whole. Many laboratory experiments on contact effects are limited in that they assess only attitudes toward ingroup and outgroup participants within the contact setting. Presumably, however, the ultimate goal of contact interventions is reduction of prejudice toward whole social groups, not simply creation of positive attitudes toward specific group members, so promoting generalization may be as important as conditions of the contact itself.

In what is probably the most comprehensive laboratory test of interracial contact effects, Cook (1971, 1984) conducted a series of experiments in which highly prejudiced white subjects worked with a black confederate in an ideal contact situation (equal status, cooperative interdependence, with high acquaintance potential and equalitarian social norms) over an extended period of time. Perceptions of the black co-worker were measured at the completion of the contact experience, and general racial attitudes were assessed before, immediately after, and up to 3 years following the experimental sessions. Across all variations of this experiment, white participants displayed predominantly positive behaviors toward their black co-worker and expressed highly favorable evaluations in the postexperimental questionnaires. Whether liking for this individual member of the outgroup resulted in changed attitudes toward blacks and race-related issues, however, varied across the experiments and for different attitude measures.

One major reason why generalization fails is that the newly positively valued outgroup member is regarded as an exception and not as typical or representative of the outgroup in general (Allport, 1954; Rothbart & John, 1985; Wilder, 1984). In Cook's studies, significant differences in postcontact attitude change among those who participated in the contact experience compared to control subjects were obtained only in an initial experiment in which what Cook (1984) referred to as a "cognitive booster" was introduced during the course of the experiment. This added element was a guided conversation (led by a research confederate) in which the negative effects of discriminatory policies and practices were directly connected to the now-liked black co-worker. This booster served to make salient the co-worker's category membership and to establish a link between feelings toward this individual and members of the group as a whole. In a later, conceptually related experiment, van Oudenhoven, Groenewoud, and Hewstone (1996) found that Dutch students' evaluations of Turkish people in general were more positive after an episode of cooperative interaction with an individual Turkish person when his ethnicity was explicitly mentioned during the cooperative session than when ethnicity remained implicit only. Again, the explicit linkage appears to be a necessary mechanism for generalized contact effects.

Results from a recent meta-analysis of data from years of contact research suggests that, overall, positive contact experiences do generalize to intergroup attitudes (Pettigrew & Tropp, 2006). Collapsing findings across a wide range of field and laboratory studies with different types of groups, the average effect of contact on measures of prejudice toward the outgroup proved to be significant—more contact was associated with less prejudice. Furthermore, consistent with the tenets of the qualified contact hypothesis, contact in the form of interpersonal friendships proved to have a greater effect on average than contact in less personalized contexts (Pettigrew & Tropp, 2006). Thus, contact does seem to have a robust prejudice-reducing effect overall, despite considerable variation in its effects under specific circumstances.

Theoretical Underpinnings of Contact Effects

Although it is encouraging to learn that the effects of contact on intergroup attitudes are more likely to be positive than negative, this result does not indicate how to manage contact situations to ensure such beneficial outcomes. In his review of the current status of contact research, Pettigrew (1998) suggested that the challenge is to distinguish between factors that are *essential* to the processes underlying positive contact experiences and their generalization, and those that merely *facilitate* (or inhibit) the operation of these processes. To make this distinction, contact researchers needed a more elaborate theory of what the underlying processes are and how they mediate the effects of intergroup contact under different conditions. One advance toward a more integrative theory of intergroup relations was achieved when contact research was combined with concepts of social categorization and social identity theory to provide a theoretical framework for understanding the cognitive mechanisms by which cooperative contact is presumed to work (see Brewer & Miller, 1984; Brown & Hewstone, 2005; Gaertner, Mann, Murrell, & Dovidio, 1989; Hewstone & Brown, 1986; Hewstone, 1996; Wilder, 1986).

Based on the premises of social identity theory, three alternative models for contact effects have been developed and tested in experimental and field settings, namely Decategorization, Recategorization, and Mutual Differentiation. The first two models seek to change attitudes and perceptions by altering the salience of ingroup–outgroup social categorization in the contact situation. The third model addresses how intergroup attitudes can be changed while ingroup–outgroup differentiation remains salient.

Decategorization: The Personalization Model The first model is essentially a formalization and elaboration of the assumptions implicit in the contact hypothesis itself (Brewer & Miller, 1984; Miller 2002). A primary consequence of salient ingroup–outgroup categorization is the deindividuation of members of the outgroup. The personalization perspective on the contact situation implies that intergroup interactions should be structured so as to reduce the salience of category distinctions and promote opportunities to get to know outgroup members as individual persons. Attending to personal characteristics of group members not only provides the opportunity to disconfirm category stereotypes, it also breaks down the monolithic perception of the outgroup as a homogeneous unit (Wilder, 1978). In this scheme, the contact situation encourages attention to information at the individual level that replaces category identity as the most useful basis for classifying participants.

Repeated personalized contacts with a variety of outgroup members should, over time, undermine the value and meaningfulness of the social category stereotype as a source of information about members of that group. This is the process by which contact experiences are expected to generalize—via reducing the salience and meaning of social categorization in the long run (Brewer & Miller, 1988).

A number of experimental studies provide evidence supporting this perspective on contact effects (Bettencourt, Brewer, Croak, & Miller, 1992; Marcus-Newhall, Miller, Holtz, & Brewer, 1993). Miller, Brewer, and Edwards (1985), for instance, demonstrated that a cooperative task that required personalized interaction with members of the outgroup resulted not only in more positive attitudes toward outgroup members in the cooperative setting but also toward other outgroup members shown on a videotape, compared to task-focused rather than person-focused cooperative contact.

The personalization model is also supported by early empirical evidence for the effects of extended, intimate contact on racial attitudes. More recently, extensive data on effects of intergroup friendships have been derived from surveys in Western Europe regarding attitudes toward minority immigrant groups (Hamberger & Hewstone, 1997; Pettigrew, 1997; Pettigrew & Meertens, 1995). Across samples in France, Great Britain, the Netherlands, and Germany, Europeans with outgroup friends scored significantly lower on measures of prejudice, particularly affective prejudice (Pettigrew, 1998). This positive relationship did not hold for other types of contact (work or residential) that did not involve formation of close personal relationships with members of the outgroup. Although there is clearly a bidirectional relationship between positive attitudes and extent of personal contact, path analyses indicate that the path from friendship to reduction in prejudice is stronger than the other way around (Pettigrew, 1998).

Recategorization: The Common Ingroup Identity Model The second social categorization model of intergroup contact and prejudice reduction is also based on the premise that reducing the salience of ingroup–outgroup category distinctions is the key to positive effects. In contrast to the decategorization approaches previously described, recategorization is not designed to reduce or eliminate categorization but rather to create group categorization at a higher level of category inclusiveness. Specifically, the "common ingroup identity model" (Gaertner, Dovidio, Anastasio, Bachman, & Rust, 1993; Gaertner & Dovidio, 2000) proposes that intergroup bias and conflict can be reduced by factors that transform participants' representations of memberships from two groups to one more inclusive group. With common ingroup identity, the cognitive and motivational processes that initially produced ingroup favoritism are redirected to benefit the former outgroup members.

Among the antecedent factors proposed by the common ingroup identity model are the features of contact situations (Allport, 1954) that are necessary for intergroup contact to be successful (e.g., interdependence between groups, equal status, equalitarian norms). From this perspective, cooperative interaction, for example, enhances positive evaluations of outgroup members, at least in part, because cooperation transforms members' representations of the memberships from "us" and "them" to a more inclusive "we." To test this hypothesis directly, Gaertner, Mann, Dovidio, Murrell, and Pomare (1990) conducted a laboratory experiment that brought two three-person laboratory groups together under conditions designed to vary independently the members' representations of the aggregate as one group or two groups (by varying factors such as seating arrangement) and the presence or absence of intergroup cooperative interaction. Supportive of the hypothesis, the introduction of cooperative interaction increased participants' perceptions of one group and also reduced their bias in evaluative ratings relative to those who did not cooperate during the contact period. In further support for the common ingroup identity model, this effect of cooperation was mediated by the extent to which members of both groups perceived themselves as one group.

Outside of the laboratory, survey studies conducted in natural settings across very different intergroup contexts offered converging support for the proposal that the features specified by the contact hypothesis can increase intergroup harmony in part by transforming members' representations of the memberships from separate groups to one more inclusive group (Gaertner, Dovidio, & Bachman, 1996; Gaertner, Rust, Dovidio, Bachman, & Anastasio, 1994; Gaertner et al., 2000).

Challenges to the Decategorization/Recategorization Models Although the structural representations of the contact situation advocated by the decategorization (personalization) and recategorization (common ingroup identity) models are different, the two approaches share common assumptions about the need to reduce category differentiation and associated processes. Because both models rely on reducing or eliminating the salience of intergroup differentiation, they involve structuring contact in a way that will challenge or threaten existing social identities. Both cognitive and motivational factors conspire to create resistance to the dissolution of category boundaries or to reestablish category distinctions across time. Although the salience of a common superordinate identity or personalized representations may be enhanced in the short run, these may be difficult to maintain across time and social situations.

Preexisting social-structural relationships between groups may also create strong forces of resistance to changes in category boundaries. Cognitive restructuring may be close to impossible (at least as a first step) for groups already engaged in deadly hostilities. Even in the absence of overt conflict, asymmetries between social groups in size, power, or status create additional sources of resistance. When one group is substantially numerically smaller than the other in the contact situation, the minority category is especially salient and minority group members may be particularly reluctant to accept a superordinate category identity that is dominated by the other group. Another major challenge is created by preexisting status differences between groups, in which members of both high- and low-status groups may be threatened by contact and assimilation (Hornsey & Hogg, 2000a; Riek, Mania, & Gaertner, 2006).

The Mutual Differentiation Model These challenges to processes of decategorization and recategorization led Hewstone and Brown (1986; Brown & Hewstone, 2005) to recommend an alternative approach to intergroup contact wherein cooperative interactions between groups are introduced without degrading the original ingroup–outgroup categorization. To promote positive intergroup experience, Hewstone and Brown recommended that the contact situation be structured so that members of the respective groups have distinct but complementary roles to contribute toward common goals. In this way, both groups can maintain positive distinctiveness within a cooperative framework. This strategy allows group members to maintain their social identities and positive distinctiveness while avoiding insidious intergroup comparisons. Thus, the intergroup contact model does not seek to change the basic category structure of the intergroup contact situation, but to change the intergroup affect from negative to positive interdependence and evaluation.

Evidence in support of this approach comes from the results of an experiment by Brown and Wade (1987) in which work teams composed of students from two different faculties engaged in a cooperative effort to produce a two-page magazine article. When the representatives of the two groups were assigned separate roles in the team task (one group working on figures and layout and the other group working on text), the contact experience had a more positive effect on intergroup attitudes than when the two groups were not provided with distinctive roles (see also Deschamps & Brown, 1983; Dovidio, Gaertner, & Validzic, 1998).

Hewstone and Brown (1986) argued that generalization of positive contact experiences is more likely when the contact situation is defined as an *intergroup* situation rather than an interpersonal interaction. Generalization in this case is direct rather than requiring additional cognitive links between positive affect toward individuals and representations of the group as a whole. This position is supported by evidence that cooperative contact with a member of an outgroup leads to more favorable generalized attitudes toward the group as a whole when category membership is made salient during contact (e.g., Brown, Vivian, & Hewstone, 1999; Hewstone et al., 2005; van Oudenhoven, Groenewoud, & Hewstone, 1996).

Although ingroup–outgroup category salience is usually associated with ingroup bias and the negative side of intergroup attitudes, cooperative interdependence is assumed to override the negative intergroup schema, particularly if the two groups have differentiated, complementary roles to play. The affective component of the model, however, is potentially unstable. Salient intergroup boundaries are associated with mutual distrust (Insko & Schopler, 1987) and intergroup anxiety (Greenland & Brown, 1999; Islam & Hewstone, 1993), which undermine the potential for cooperative interdependence and mutual liking over any length of time. By reinforcing perceptions of group differences, the differentiation model risks reinforcing negative beliefs about the outgroup, and the potential for fission and conflict along group lines remains high.

Hybrid Models: An Integration of Approaches

As reviewed, each of the cognitive–structural models of intergroup contact and prejudice reduction has its weaknesses and limitations, particularly when we seek to generalize beyond small group interactions in laboratory settings. These criticisms have led a number of writers to suggest that some combination of all three models may be necessary to create conditions for long-term attitude change (e.g., Brewer & Gaertner, 2001; Brown & Hewstone, 2005; Gaertner et al., 2000; Hewstone, 1996; Pettigrew, 1998). More integrative models of intergroup contact take advantage of the fact that individuals are members of multiple social groups, which implies different social identities and ingroup loyalties.

Nested Dual Identities In recent work regarding the development of a common ingroup identity, it has been proposed that embracing a more inclusive superordinate identity does not necessarily require each group to forsake its original group identity completely (Gaertner, Rust, Dovidio, Bachman, & Anastasio, 1994). Instead, group members may simultaneously perceive themselves as members of different groups but also as part of the same team or superordinate entity. For example, in a multiethnic high school, minority students who identified themselves in terms of both their ethnic group and their American identity (e.g., Korean-American) had lower intergroup affective bias than minority students who identified themselves only in terms of their ethnicity. Dual identified students were also more likely to endorse the statement "Although there are different groups at school, it feels like we are playing on the same team" (Gaertner et al., 1994).

Other studies indicate that the intergroup benefits of a strong superordinate identity remain relatively stable even when the strength of the subordinate identity is equivalently high (Huo, Smith, Tyler, & Lind, 1996; Smith & Tyler, 1996). This suggests that identification with a more inclusive social group does not require individuals to deny their ethnic identity. In addition, a dual identity can also lead to even more positive outgroup attitudes than those associated with a superordinate identity alone (Hornsey & Hogg, 2000b). In terms of promoting more harmonious intergroup interactions, a dual identity capitalizes on the benefits of common ingroup membership as well those accrued from mutual differentiation between the groups.

On the other hand, dual identities are not always associated with positive relations between subgroups within the superordinate category. Mummendey and Wenzel (1999) make a convincing case that under some circumstances, making a shared superordinate category salient can lead to enhanced derogation of other subgroups when both subgroup and superordinate group identities are strong. This can happen if the values and attributes of the ingroup are projected onto the superordinate group, in which case subgroups that differ from these attributes come to be seen as *deviant* (rather than just "different") and a potential source of symbolic threat to the ingroup and the superordinate group. In studies of national groups in the European Union, Mummendey and Waldzus (2004) demonstrated that individuals who profess dual identification (strong national identity and European identity) also exhibit higher ingroup projection, which in turn is associated with negative attitudes toward other subgroup nations. Thus, ironically, nested dual identities may enhance rather than reduce ingroup bias and discrimination against other subgroups.

Cross-Cutting Identities Nested categories at different levels of inclusiveness represent only one form of multiple ingroup identities. Individuals may also be members of social categories that overlap only partially, if at all. Many bases of social category differentiation—gender, age, religion, ethnicity, occupation—represent cross-cutting cleavages. From the standpoint of a particular person, other individuals may be fellow ingroup members on one dimension of category differentiation but outgroup members on another. (For instance, for a woman business executive, a male colleague is an ingroup member with respect to occupation but an outgrouper with respect to her gender identification.) It is possible that such orthogonal social identities are kept isolated from each other so that only one ingroup–outgroup distinction is activated in a particular social context. But there are reasons to expect that simultaneous activation of multiple ingroup identities is possible and has the potential to reduce prejudice and discrimination based on any one category distinction.

Evidence from both anthropology (e.g., Gluckman, 1955) and political sociology (e.g., Coser, 1956) has long suggested that societies characterized by cross-cutting loyalty structures are less prone to schism and internal intergroup conflict than societies characterized by a single hierarchical loyalty structure. More recently, social psychologists have also begun to consider the implications of such multiple cross-cutting social identities for reduction of ingroup bias at the individual level (Deschamps & Doise, 1978; Brown & Turner, 1979; Marcus-Newhall et al., 1993; Roccas & Brewer, 2002; Vanbeselaere, 1991).

Experimental studies with both natural and artificial categories have demonstrated that adding a cross-cutting category distinction reduces ingroup bias and increases positive attitudes toward crossed category members compared to simple ingroup–outgroup differentiation (Vanbeselaere, 1991) or compared to situations in which category distinctions are convergent or superimposed (Bettencourt & Dorr, 1998; Marcus-Newhall et al., 1993; Rust, 1996). In these studies, cooperative interaction in the context of cross-cutting social identities and roles increases intracategory differentiation and reduces perceived intercategory differences, resulting in less category-based evaluations of individual group members. Furthermore, the benefits of cross-categorization may be enhanced when both category distinctions are embedded in a common superordinate group identity (Rust, 1996; Gaertner et al., 1999). Thus, crossed categorization and recategorization may work together to produce enhanced inclusiveness and reduced intergroup discrimination.

Intergroup Relations Today: Implications for Pluralistic Societies

The principles of social categorization, ingroup favoritism, and outgroup prejudice discussed in this chapter have important implications for promoting positive intergroup relations within a context in which groups must live together interdependently. The same basic principles apply whether we are considering departments or companies combined within an organization, diverse ethnic or religious groups within a nation, or nation-states within an international community. In any of these contexts, the goals of contact and cooperation compete with natural tendencies toward ingroup–outgroup differentiation, separation, and exclusion. Processes that reduce the social meaning of category boundaries and associated us–them distinctions are in tension with pluralistic values that seek to maintain cultural variation and distinct social identities. The tension between differentiation and integration must be recognized and acknowledged in any complex social system. Exclusive focus on either assimilation or separation as the solution to intergroup discrimination and conflict is neither desirable nor realistic (Verkuyten, 2006). New directions in the social psychology of intergroup relations involve putting the study of intergroup processes back into the context of the social and political systems within which they are embedded and the multiple social identities that characterize our complex social world.

References

Allport, G. (1954). *The nature of prejudice*. Cambridge, MA: Addison-Wesley.

Ancok, D., & Chertkoff, J. M. (1983). Effects of group membership, relative performance, and self-interest on the division of outcomes. *Journal of Personality and Social Psychology, 45*, 1256–1262.

Aronson, E., Blaney, N., Stephan, C., Sikes,J., & Snapp, M. (1978). *The jigsaw classroom*. Beverly Hills, CA: Sage.

Bar-Tal, D. (2007). Sociopsychological foundations of intractable conflicts. *American Behavioral Scientist, 50*, 1430–1453.

Baumeister, R. F., & Leary, M. R. (1995). The need to belong: Desire for interpersonal attachments as a fundamental human motivation. *Psychological Bulletin, 117*, 497–529.

Bettencourt, B. A., & Dorr, N. (1998). Cooperative interaction and intergroup bias: Effects of numerical representation and cross-cut role assignment. *Personality and Social Psychology, 24*, 1276–1293

Bettencourt, B. A ., Brewer, M. B., Croak, M. R., & Miller, N. (1992). Cooperation and the reduction of intergroup bias: The role of reward structure and social orientation. *Journal of Experimental Social Psychology, 28*, 301–319.

Blanz, M., Mummendey, A., & Otten, S. (1997). Normative evaluations and frequency expectations regarding positive and negative outcome allocations between groups. *European Journal of Social Psychology, 27*, 165–176.

Branscombe, N. R., Ellemers, N., Spears, R., & Doosje, B. (1999). The context and content of social identity threat. In N. Ellemers, R. Spears, & B. Doosje (Eds.), *Social identity: Context, commitment, content* (pp. 35–58). Oxford, UK: Blackwell

Brewer, M. B. (1979). Ingroup bias in the minimal intergroup situation: A cognitive-motivational analysis. *Psychological Bulletin, 86*, 307–324.

Brewer, M. B. (1991). The social self: On being the same and different at the same time. *Personality and Social Psychology Bulletin, 17*, 475–482.

Brewer, M. B. (1996). In-group favoritism: The subtle side of intergroup discrimination. In D. Messick & A. Tenbrunsel (Eds.), *Codes of conduct: Behavioral research into business ethics* (pp. 160–170). New York: Russell Sage Foundation.

Brewer, M. B. (2001). Ingroup identification and intergroup conflict: When does ingroup love become outgroup hate? In R. Ashmore, L. Jussim, & D. Wilder (Eds.), *Social identity, intergroup conflict, and conflict reduction* (pp. 17–41). New York: Oxford University Press.

Brewer, M. B., & Campbell, D. T. (1976). *Ethnocentrism and intergroup attitudes: East African evidence.* New York: Halsted-Press (Sage).

Brewer, M. B., & Gaertner, S. L. (2001). Toward reduction of prejudice: Intergroup contact and social categorization. In R. Brown & S. Gaertner (Eds.), *Blackwell handbook of social psychology: Intergroup processes* (pp. 451–472). Oxford, UK: Blackwell.

Brewer, M. B., & Kramer, R. M. (1986). Choice behavior in social dilemmas: Effects of social identity, group size, and decision framing. *Journal of Personality and Social Psychology, 50*, 543–549.

Brewer, M., & Miller, N. (1984). Beyond the contact hypothesis: Theoretical perspectives on desegregation. In N. Miller & M. Brewer (Eds.), *Groups in contact: The psychology of desegregation* (pp. 281–302). New York: Academic Press.

Brewer, M. B., & Miller, N. (1988). Contact and cooperation: When do they work? In P. Katz and D. Taylor (Eds.), *Eliminating racism: Means and controversies* (pp. 315–326). New York: Plenum Press.

Brewer, M. B., & Pickett, C. A. (1999). Distinctiveness motives as a source of the social self. In T. Tyler, R. Kramer, & O. John (Eds.), *The psychology of the social self* (pp. 71–87). Mahwah, NJ: Erlbaum.

Brewer, M. B., & Pickett, C. L. (2002). The social self and group identification: Inclusion and distinctiveness motives in interpersonal and collective identities. In J. Forgas & K. Williams (Eds.), *The social self: Cognitive, interpersonal, and intergroup perspectives* (pp. 255–271). Philadelphia: Psychology Press.

Brewer, M. B., & Weber, J. G. (1994). Self-evaluation effects of interpersonal versus intergroup social comparison. *Journal of Personality and Social Psychology, 66*, 268–275.

Brown, R. J., & Abrams, D. (1986). The effects of intergroup similarity and goal interdependence on intergroup attitudes and task performance. *Journal of Experimental Social Psychology, 22*, 78–92.

Brown, R. J., & Hewstone, M. (2005). An integrative theory of intergroup contact. In M. Zanna (Ed.), *Advances in experimental social psychology* (Vol. 37, pp. 256–343). New York: Elsevier.

Brown, R. J., & Turner, J. C. (1979). The criss-cross categorization effect in intergroup discrimination. *British Journal of Social and Clinical Psychology, 18*, 371–383.

Brown, R. J., Vivian, J., & Hewstone, M. (1999). Changing attitudes through intergroup contact: The effects of group membership salience. *European Journal of Social Psychology, 29*, 741–764.

Brown, R. J., & Wade, G. (1987). Superordinate goals and intergroup behaviour: The effect of role ambiguity and status on intergroup attitudes and task performance. *European Journal of Social Psychology, 17*, 131–142.

Caddick, B. (1982). Perceived illegitimacy and intergroup relations. In H. Tajfel (Ed.), *Social identity and intergroup relations* (pp. 137–154). Cambridge, UK: Cambridge University Press.

Castano, E., Yzerbyt, V. Y., Bourguignon, D., & Seron, E. (2002). Who may come in? The impact of ingroup identification on ingroup-outgroup categorization. *Journal of Experimental Social Psychology, 38*, 315–322.

Cook, S. W. (1971). *The effect of unintended interracial contact upon racial interaction and attitude change.* (Final Report, Project No. 5–1320.) Washington, DC: U.S. Department of Health, Education, and Welfare.

Cook, S. W. (1984). Cooperative interaction in multiethnic contexts. In N. Miller & M. Brewer (Eds.), *Groups in contact: The psychology of desegregation* (pp. 155–185). New York: Academic Press.

Cook, S. W. (1985). Experimenting on social issues: The case of school desegregation. *American Psychologist, 40*, 452–460.

Coser, L. A. (1956). *The functions of social conflict*. New York: Free Press.

Crocker, J., Luhtanen, R., Blaine, B., & Broadnax, S. (1994). Collective self-esteem and psychological well-being among white, black, and Asian college students. *Personality and Social Psychology Bulletin, 20*, 503–513.

Deaux, K., Reid, A., Mizrahi, K., & Cotting, D. (1999). Connecting the person to the social: The functions of social identification. In T. Tyler, R. Kramer, & O. John (Eds.), *The psychology of the social self* (pp. 91–113). Mahwah, NJ: Erlbaum.

Deschamps, J.-C., & Brown, R. J. (1983). Superordinate goals and intergoup conflict. *British Journal of Social Psychology, 22*, 189–195.

Deschamps, J-C., & Doise, W. (1978). Crossed category memberships in intergroup relations. In H. Tajfel (Ed.), *Differentiation between social groups* (pp. 141–158). Cambridge, UK: Cambridge University Press.

Diehl, M. (1990). The minimal group paradigm: Theoretical explanations and empirical findings. *European Review of Social Psychology,1*, 263–292.

Dijker, A. J. M. (1987). Emotional reaction to ethnic minorities. *European Journal of Social Psychology, 17*, 305–325.

Doise, W. (1978). *Groups and individuals: Explanations in social psychology*. Cambridge, UK: Cambridge University Press.

Dovidio, J. F., Gaertner, S. L., & Validzic, A. (1998). Intergroup bias: Status differentiation and a common ingroup identity. *Journal of Personality and Social Psychology, 75*, 109–120.

Ellemers, N., Doosje, B., van Knippenberg, A., & Wilke, H. (1992). Status protection in high status minority groups. *European Journal of Social Psychology, 22*, 123–140.

Ellemers, N., van Knippenberg, A., de Vries, N., & Wilke, H. (1988). Social identification and permeability of group boundaries. *European Journal of Social Psychology, 18*, 497–513.

Ellemers, N., van Knippenberg, A., & Wilke, H. (1990). The influence of permeability of group boundaries and stability of group status on strategies of individual mobility and social change. *British Journal of Social Psychology, 29*, 233–246.

Ellemers, N., Wilke, H., & van Knippenberg, A. (1993). Effects of the legitimacy of low group or individual status on individual and collective identity enhancement strategies. *Journal of Personality and Social Psychology, 64*, 766–778.

Ensari, N., & Miller, N. (2002). The out-group must not be so bad after all: The effects of disclosure, typicality, and salience on intergroup bias. *Journal of Personality and Social Psychology, 83*, 313–329.

Esses, V. M., Jackson, L. M., & Armstrong, T. L. (1998). Intergroup competition and attitudes toward immigrants and immigration: An instrumental model of group conflict. *Journal of Social Issues, 54*, 699–724.

Farnham, S. D., Greenwald, A. G., & Banaji, M. R. (1999). Implicit self-esteem. In D. Abrams & M. Hogg (Eds.), *Social identity and social cognition* (pp. 230–248). Oxford, UK: Blackwell.

Gaertner, S. L., & Dovidio, J. F. (2000). *Reducing intergroup bias: The common ingroup identity model*. Philadelphia: Psychology Press.

Gaertner, S. L., Dovidio, J. F., Anastasio, P. A., Bachman, B. A., & Rust, M. C. (1993). The Common Ingroup Identity Model: Recategorization and the reduction of intergroup bias. *European Review of Social Psychology, 4*, 1–26.

Gaertner, S. L., Dovidio, J. F., & Bachman, B. A. (1996). Revisiting the contact hypothesis: The induction of a common ingroup identity. *International Journal of Intercultural Relations, 20*, 271–290.

Gaertner, S. L., Dovidio, J. F., Banker, B., Houlette, M., Johnson, K., & McGlynn, E. (2000). Reducing intergroup conflict: From superordinate goals to decategorization, recategorization, and mutual differentiation. *Group Dynamics, 4*, 98–114.

Gaertner, S. L., Dovidio, J. F., Nier, J. A., Ward, C. M., & Banker, B. S. (1999). Across cultural divides: The value of a superordinate identity. In D. Prentice & D. Miller (Eds.), *Cultural divides: Understanding and overcoming group conflict*. New York: Sage.

Gaertner, S. L., Mann, J. A., Dovidio, J. F., Murrell, A. J., & Pomare, M. (1990). How does cooperation reduce intergroup bias? *Journal of Personality and Social Psychology, 59*, 692–704.

Gaertner, S. L., Mann, J. A., Murrell, A. J., & Dovidio, J. F. (1989). Reduction of intergroup bias: The benefits of recategorization. *Journal of Personality and Social Psychology, 57*, 239–249.

Gaertner, S. L., Rust, M. C., Dovidio, J. F., Bachman, B. A., & Anastasio, A. (1994). The contact hypothesis: The role of a common ingroup identity on reducing intergroup bias. *Small Groups Research, 25*, 224–290.

Gerard, H. B. (1983). School desegregation: The social science role. *American Psychologist, 38*, 869–887.

Gerard, H. B., & Hoyt, M. (1974). Distinctiveness of social categorization and attitude toward in-group members. *Journal of Personality and Social Psychology, 29*, 836–842.

Gerard, H. B., & Miller, N. (1975). *School desegregation: A long-term study*. New York: Plenum Press.

Gluckman, M. (1955). *Customs and conflict in Africa*. London: Blackwell

Greenland, K., & Brown, R. J. (1999). Categorization and intergroup anxiety in contact between British and Japanese nationals. *European Journal of Social Psychology, 29*, 503–521.

Grieve, P. G., & Hogg, M. A. (1999). Subjective uncertainty and intergroup discrimination in the minimal group situation. *Personality and Social Psychology Bulletin, 25*, 926–940.

Hamberger, J., & Hewstone, M. (1997). Inter-ethnic contact as a predictor of prejudice: Tests of a model in four West European nations. *British Journal of Social Psychology, 36*, 173–190.

Hewstone, M. (1990). The `ultimate attribution error'? A review of the literature on intergroup causal attribution. *European Journal of Social Psychology, 20*, 311–335.

Hewstone, M. (1996). Contact and categorization: Social psychology interventions to change intergroup relations. In C. N. Macrae, C. Stangor, & M. Hewstone (Eds.), *Stereotypes and stereotyping* (pp. 323–368). New York: Guilford Press.

Hewstone, M., & Brown, R. J. (1986). Contact is not enough: An intergroup perspective on the "contact hypothesis." In M. Hewstone & R. Brown (Eds.), *Contact and conflict in intergroup encounters* (pp. 1–44). Oxford, UK: Basil Blackwell.

Hewstone, M., Cairns, Voci, A., Paolini, S., McLernon, F., Crisp, R., et al. (2005). Intergroup contact in a divided society: Challenging segregation in Northern Ireland. In D. Abrams, J. M. Marques, & M. A . Hogg (Eds.), *The social psychology of inclusion and exclusion* (pp. 265–292). Philadelphia: Psychology Press.

Hinkle, S., & Brown, R. (1990). Intergroup comparisons and social identity: Some links and lacunae. In D. Abrams & M. Hogg (Eds.), *Social identity theory: Construction and critical advances* (pp. 48–70). London: Harvester Wheatsheaf.

Hogg, M. A., & Abrams, D. (1988). *Social identifications.* London: Routledge.

Hogg, M. A., & Abrams, D. (1993). Towards a single-process uncertainty-reduction model of social motivation in groups. In M. Hogg & D. Abrams (Eds.), *Group motivation: Social psychological perspectives* (pp. 173–190). Hemel Hempstead, UK: Harvester Wheatsheaf.

Hogg, M. A., & Mullin, B-A. (1999). Joining groups to reduce uncertainty: Subjective uncertainty reduction and group identification. In D. Abrams & M. A . Hogg (Eds.), *Social identity and social cognition* (pp. 249–279). Oxford, UK: Blackwell.

Hogg, M. A., & Turner, J. C. (1987). Intergroup behaviour, self-stereotyping, and the salience of social categories. *British Journal of Social Psychology, 26*, 325–340.

Hornsey, M. J., & Hogg, M. A. (1999). Subgroup differentiation as a response to an overly-inclusive group: A test of optimal distinctiveness theory. *European Journal of Social Psychology, 29*, 543–550.

Hornsey, M. J., & Hogg, M. A. (2000a) Assimilation and diversity: An integrative model of subgroup relations. *Personality and Social Psychology Review, 4*, 143–156.

Hornsey, M. J., & Hogg, M. A. (2000b). Subgroup relations: A comparison of mutual intergroup differentiation and common ingroup identity models of prejudice reduction. *Personality and Social Psychology Bulletin, 26*, 242–256.

Huo, Y., Smith, H., Tyler, T. R., & Lind, E. A. (1996). Superordinate identification, subgroup identification, and justice concerns: Is separatism the problem; is assimilation the answer? *Psychological Science, 7*, 40–45.

Insko, C. A., & Schopler, J. (1987). Categorization, competition, and collectivity. In C. Hendrick (Ed.), *Group processes. Review of personality and social psychology* (Vol. 8, pp. 213–251). Beverly Hills, CA: Sage.

Islam, M. R., & Hewstone, M. (1993). Dimensions of contact as predictors of intergroup anxiety, perceived outgroup variability and outgroup attitude: An integrative account. *Personality and Social Psychology Bulletin, 19*, 700–710.

Jetten, J., Branscombe, N. R., Schmitt, M. T., & Spears, R. (2001). Rebels with a cause: Group identification as a response to perceived discrimination from the mainstream. *Personality and Social Psychology Bulletin, 27*, 1204–1213.

Jetten, J., Spears, R., & Manstead, A. S. R. (1998). Intergroup similarity and group variability: The effects of group distinctiveness on the expression of in-group bias. *Journal of Personality and Social Psychology, 74*, 1481–1492.

Jetten, J., Spears, R., & Postmes, T. (2004). Intergroup distinctiveness and differentiation: A meta-analytic integration. *Journal of Personality and Social Psychology, 86*, 862–879.

Johnson, D. W., & Johnson, R. T. (1981). Effects of cooperative and individualistic learning experiences on interethnic interaction. *Journal of Educational Psychology, 73*, 444–449.

Johnson, D. W., Johnson, R., & Maruyama, G. (1984). Goal interdependence and interpersonal attraction in heterogeneous classrooms: A metaanalysis. In N. Miller & M. Brewer (Eds.), *Groups in contact: The psychology of desegregation* (pp. 187–212). New York: Academic Press.

Jost, J. T. (2001). Outgroup favoritism and the theory of system justification: An experimental paradigm for investigating the effects of socio-economic success on stereotype content. In G. Moskowitz (Ed.), *Cognitive social psychology: The Princeton symposium on the legacy and future of social cognition* (pp. 89–102). Hillsdale, NJ: Erlbaum.

Kahn, A., & Ryen, A. (1972). Factors influencing the bias towards one's own group. *International Journal of Group Tensions, 2*, 33–50.

Kelman, H. C. (1999). The interdependence of Israeli and Palestinian national identities: The role of the other in existential conflicts. *Journal of Social Issues, 55*, 581–600.

Kelman, H. C. (2001). The role of national identity in conflict resolution. In R. D. Ashmore, L. Jussim, & D. Wilder (Eds.), *Social identity, intergroup conflict, and conflict reduction* (pp. 187–212). New York: Oxford University Press.

Kosterman, R., & Feshbach, S. (1989). Toward a measure of patriotic and nationalistic attitudes. *Political Psychology, 10*, 257–274.

Leach, C. W., Ellemers, N., & Barreto, M. (2007). Group virtue: The importance of morality (vs. competence and sociability) in the positive evaluation of in-groups. *Journal of Personality and Social Psychology, 93*, 234–249.

Ledgerwood, A., Liviatan, I., & Carnevale, P. (2007). Group-identity completion and the symbolic value of property. *Psychological Science, 18*, 873–878.

Lemaine, G. (1974). Social differentiation and social originality. *European Journal of Social Psychology, 4*, 17–52.

Leonardelli, G., & Brewer, M. B. (2001). Minority and majority discrimination: When and why. *Journal of Experimental Social Psychology, 37*, 468–485.

LeVine, R. A., & Campbell, D. T. (1972). Ethnocentrism: Theories of conflict, ethnic attitudes and group behavior. New York: Wiley.

Leyens, J-P., & Yzerbyt, V. (1992). The ingroup overexclusion effect: Impact of valence and confirmation on stereotypical information search. *European Journal of Social Psychology, 22*, 549–569.

Mackie, D. M., Devos, T., & Smith, E. R. (2000). Intergroup emotions: Explaining offensive action tendencies in an intergroup context. *Journal of Personality and Social Psychology, 79*, 602–616.

Marcus-Newhall, A., Miller, N., Holtz, R., & Brewer, M. B. (1993). Crosscutting category membership with role assignment: A means of reducing intergroup bias. *British Journal of Social Psychology, 32*, 125–146.

Miller, D. T., Downs, J. S., & Prentice, D. A. (1998). Minimal conditions for the creation of a unit relationship: The social bond between birthday mates. *European Journal of Social Psychology, 28*, 475–481.

Miller, N. (2002). Personalization and the promise of contact theory. *Journal of Social Issues, 58*, 387–410.

Miller, N., Brewer, M. B., & Edwards, K. (1985). Cooperative interaction in desegregated settings: A laboratory analogue. *Journal of Social Issues, 41*(3), 63–79.

Mullen, B., Brown, R., & Smith, C. (1992). In-group bias as a function of salience, relevance, and status: An integration. *European Journal of Social Psychology, 22*, 103–122.

Mullin, B-A., & Hogg, M. A. (1998). Dimensions of subjective uncertainty in social identification and minimal intergroup discrimination. *British Journal of Social Psychology, 37*, 345–365.

Mummendey, A., Simon, B., Dietze, C., Grunert., M., Haeger, G., Kessler, S., et al. (1992). Categorization is not enough: Intergroup discrimination in negative outcome allocations. *Journal of Experimental Social Psychology, 28*, 125–144.

Mummendey, A., & Waldzus, S. (2004). National differences and European plurality: Discrimination or tolerance between European countries. In R. Herrmann, T. Risse, & M. Brewer (Eds.), *Transnational identities: Becoming European in the EU* (pp. 59–72). Lanham, MD: Rowman & Littlefield.

Mummendey, A., & Wenzel, M. (1999). Social discrimination and tolerance in intergroup relations. *Personality and Social Psychology Review, 3*, 158–174.

Ng, S. H. (1984). Equity and social categorization effects on intergroup allocation of rewards. *British Journal of Social Psychology, 23*, 165–172.

Otten, S. (2002). I am positive and so are we: The self as determinant of favoritism toward novel ingroups. In J. Forgas & K. Williams (Eds.), *The social self: Cognitive, interpersonal, and intergroup processes* (pp. 273–291). New York: Psychology Press.

Otten, S., & Moskowitz, G. B. (2000). Evidence for implicit evaluative in-group bias: Affect-biased spontaneous trait inference in a minimal group paradigm. *Journal of Experimental Social Psychology, 36*, 77–89.

Otten, S., & Wentura, D. (1999). About the impact of automaticity in the minimal group paradigm: Evidence from affective priming tasks. *European Journal of Social Psychology, 29*, 1049–1071.

Perdue, C., Dovidio, J., Gurtman, M., & Tyler, R. (1990). Us and them: Social categorization and the process of ingroup bias. *Journal of Personality and Social Psychology, 59*, 475–486.

Pettigrew, T. F. (1997). Generalized intergroup contact effects on prejudice. *Personality and Social Psychology Bulletin, 23*, 173–185.

Pettigrew, T. F. (1998). Intergroup contact theory. *Annual Review of Psychology, 49*, 65–85.

Pettigrew, T. F., & Meertens, R. W. (1995). Subtle and blatant prejudice in Western Europe. *European Journal of Social Psychology, 25*, 57–75.

Pettigrew, T. F., & Tropp, L. R. (2006). A meta-analytic test of intergroup contact theory. *Journal of Personality and Social Psychology, 90*, 751–783.

Pickett, C. L., Bonner, B. L., & Coleman, J. M. (2002). Motivated self-stereotyping: Heightened assimilation and differentiation needs result in increased levels of positive and negative self-stereotyping. *Journal of Personality and Social Psychology, 82*, 543–562.

Pickett, C. L., Silver, M. D., & Brewer, M. B. (2002). The impact of assimilation and differentiation needs on perceived group importance and judgments of group size. *Personality and Social Psychology Bulletin, 28*, 546–558.

Platow, M. J., McClintock, C. G., & Liebrand, W. G. (1990). Predicting intergroup fairness and in-group bias in the minimal group paradigm. *European Journal of Social Psychology, 20*, 221–239.

Platow, M. J., O'Connell, A., Shave, R., & Hanning, P. (1995). Social evaluations of fair and unfair allocations in interpersonal and intergroup situations. *British Journal of Social Psychology, 34*, 363–381.

Rabbie, J. M., Benoist, F., Oosterbaan, H., & Visser, L. (1974). Differential power and effects of expected competitive and cooperative intergroup interaction on intragroup and outgroup attitudes. *Journal of Personality and Social Psychology, 30*, 46–56.

Rabbie, J. M., & Wilkins, G. (1971). Intergroup competition and its effect on intragroup and intergroup relations. *European Journal of Social Psychology*, 1, 215–234.

Riek, B. M., Mania, E. W., & Gaertner, S. L. (2006). Intergroup threat and outgroup attitudes: A meta-analytic review. *Personality and Social Psychology Review, 10*, 336–353.

Roccas, S., & Brewer, M. B. (2002). Social identity complexity. *Personality and Social Psychology Review, 6*, 88–106.

Roccas, S., & Schwartz, S. (1993). Effects of intergroup similarity on intergroup relations. *European Journal of Social Psychology, 23*, 581–595.

Rothbart, M., & John, O. P. (1985). Social categorization and behavioral episodes: A cognitive analysis of the effects of intergroup contact. *Journal of Social Issues, 41*(3), 81–104.

Rouhana, N. N., & Bar-Tal, D. (1998). Psychological dynamics of intractable ethnonational conflicts: The Israeli-Palestinian case. *American Psychologist, 53*, 761–770.

Rubin, M., & Hewstone, M. (1998). Social identity theory's self-esteem hypothesis: A review and some suggestions for clarification. *Personality and Social Psychology Review, 2*, 40–62.

Rudman, L. A., Greenwald, A. G., & McGhee, D. E. (2001). Implicit self-concept and evaluative implicit gender stereotypes: Self and ingroup share desirable traits. *Personality and Social Psychology Bulletin, 27*, 1164–1178.

Runciman, W. C. (1966). *Relative deprivation and social justice: A study of attitudes to social inequality in twentieth century England.* Berkeley, CA: University of California Press.

Rust, M. C. (1996). *Social identity and social categorization.* Unpublished doctoral dissertation. University of Delaware, Newark, DE.

Sachdev, I., & Bourhis, R. (1991). Power and status differentials in minority and majority group relations. *European Journal of Social Psychology, 21,* 1–24.

Sherif, M. (1966). *In common predicament: Social psychology of intergroup conflict and cooperation.* New York: Houghton Mifflin.

Sherif, M., Harvey, O. J., White, B. J., Hood, W. R., & Sherif, C. W. (1961). *Intergroup conflict and cooperation: The Robbers Cave experiment.* Norman, OK: University of Oklahoma Book Exchange.

Sidanius, J. (1993). The psychology of group conflict and the dynamics of oppression: A social dominance perspective. In S. Iyengar & W. McGuire (Eds.), *Explorations in political psychology* (pp. 183–219). Durham, NC: Duke University Press.

Sidanius, J., & Pratto, F. (1999). *Social dominance: An intergroup theory of social hierarchy and oppression.* New York: Cambridge University Press.

Simon, B., & Hamilton, D. H. (1994). Social identity and self-stereotyping: The effects of relative group size and group status. *Journal of Personality and Social Psychology, 66,* 699–711.

Slavin, R. E. (1985). Cooperative learning: Applying contact theory in desegregated schools. *Journal of Social Issues, 41*(3), 45–62.

Smith, E. R. (1993). Social identity and social emotions: Toward new conceptualizations of prejudice. In D. Mackie & D. Hamilton (Eds.), *Affect, cognition, and stereotyping* (pp. 297–315). San Diego, CA: Academic Press.

Smith, H. J., & Tyler, T. R. (1996). Justice and power: When will justice concerns encourage the advantaged to support policies which redistribute economic resources and the disadvantaged to willingly obey the law? *European Journal of Social Psychology, 26,* 171–200.

Spears, R., Doosje, B., & Ellemers, N. (1997). Self-stereotyping in the face of threats to group status and distinctiveness: The role of group identification. *Personality and Social Psychology Bulletin, 23,* 538–553.

Stangor, C., Sullivan, M. W., & Ford (1991). Affective and cognitive determinants of prejudice. *Social Cognition, 9,* 359–380.

Stapel, D. A., & Marx, D. M. (2007). Distinctiveness is key: How different types of self-other similarity moderate social comparison effects. *Personality and Social Psychology Bulletin, 33,* 439–448.

Stephan, W. G. (1986). The effects of school desegregation: An evaluation 30 years after *Brown.* In M. Saks & L. Saxe (Eds.), *Advances in applied social psychology* (Vol. 3, pp. 181–206). Hillsdale, NJ: Erlbaum.

Stephan, W. G., Boniecki, K. A., Ybarra, O., Bettencourt, A., Ervin, K. S., Jackson, L. A., et al. (2002). The role of threats in the racial attitudes of blacks and whites. *Personality and Social Psychology Bulletin, 28*, 1242–1254.

Stephan, W. G., & Stephan, C. W. (2000). An integrated threat theory of prejudice. In S. Oskamp (Ed.), *Reducing prejudice and discrimination* (pp. 23–45). Mahwah, NJ: Erlbaum.

Stouffer, S., Suchman, E., DeVinney, L., Stat, S., & Williams, R. (1949). *The American soldier: Adjustments during Army life* (Vol. 1). Princeton, NJ: Princeton University Press.

Struch, N., & Schwartz, S. H. (1989). Intergroup aggression: Its predictors and distinctness from in-group bias. *Journal of Personality and Social Psychology, 56*, 364–373.

Sumner, W. G. (1906). *Folkways.* New York: Ginn.

Tajfel, H. (1969). Cognitive aspects of prejudice. *Journal of Social Issues, 25*, 79–97.

Tajfel, H. (1970). Experiments in intergroup discrimination. *Scientific American, 223*(2), 96–102.

Tajfel, H. (1978). *Differentiation between social groups: Studies in the social psychology of intergroup relations.* London: Academic Press.

Tajfel, H. (1981). *Human groups and social categories.* Cambridge, UK: Cambridge University Press.

Tajfel, H., Billig, M., Bundy, R., & Flament, C. (1971). Social categorization and intergroup behaviour. *European Journal of Social Psychology, 1*, 149–178.

Tajfel, H., & Turner, J. C. (1986). The social identity theory of intergroup behavior. In S. Worchel & W. Austin (Eds.), *Psychology of intergroup relations* (pp. 7–24). Chicago: Nelson-Hall.

Taylor, D. M., Moghaddam, F. M., Gamble, I., & Zellerer, E. (1987). Disadvantaged group responses to perceived inequality: From passive acceptance to collective action. *Journal of Social Psychology, 127*, 259–272.

Turner, J. C. (1975). Social comparison and social identity: Some prospects for intergroup behaviour. *European Journal of Social Psychology, 5*, 5–34.

Turner, J. C . (1981). The experimental social psychology of intergroup behaviour. In J. Turner & H. Giles (Eds.), *Intergroup behaviour* (pp. 66–101). Oxford, UK: Blackwell.

Turner, J. C., Hogg, M., Oakes, P., Reicher, S., & Wetherell, M. (1987). *Rediscovering the social group: A self-categorization theory.* Oxford, UK: Basil Blackwell.

Turner, J. C., Hogg, M., Turner, P., & Smith, P. (1984). Failure and defeat as determinants of group cohesiveness. *British Journal of Social Psychology, 23*, 97–111.

Vanbeselaere, N. (1991). The different effects of simple and crossed categorizations: A result of the category differentiation process or of differential category salience? *European Review of Social Psychology*, 2, 247–278.

van Knippenberg, A., & Ellemers, N. (1990). Social identity and intergroup differentiation processes. *European Review of Social Psychology, 1*, 137–169.

van Oudenhoven, J. P., Groenewoud, J. T., & Hewstone, M. (1996). Cooperation, ethnic salience and generalisation of interethnic attitudes. *European Journal of Social Psychology, 26,* 649–661.

Vanneman, R. D., & Pettigrew, T. F. (1972). Race and relative deprivation in the urban United States. *Race, 13,* 461–486.

Verkuyten, M. (2006). Multicultural recognition and ethnic minority rights: A social identity perspective. *European Review of Social Psychology, 17,* 148–184.

Vignoles, V. L., Chryssochoou, Z., & Breakwell, G. M. (2000). The distinctiveness principle: Identity, meaning, and the bounds of cultural relativity. *Personality and Social Psychology Review, 4,* 337–354.

Voci, A., & Hewstone, M. (2003). Intergroup contact and prejudice toward immigrants in Italy: The mediational role of anxiety and the moderation role of group salience. *Group Processes and Intergroup Relations, 6,* 37–54.

Weber, J. G. (1994). The nature of ethnocentric attribution bias: In-group protection or enhancement? *Journal of Experimental Social Psychology, 30,* 482–504.

Wilder, D. A. (1978). Reduction of intergroup discrimination through individuation of the outgroup. *Journal of Personality and Social Psychology, 36,* 1361–1374.

Wilder, D. A. (1984). Intergroup contact: The typical member and the exception to the rule. *Journal of Experimental Social Psychology, 20,* 177–194.

Wilder, D. A. (1986). Social categorization: Implications for creation and reduction of intergroup bias. In L. Berkowitz (Ed.), *Advances in experimental social psychology* (Vol. 19, pp. 291–355). New York: Academic Press.

Wit, A. P., & Kerr, N. L. (2002). "Me versus just us versus us all": Categorization and cooperation in nested social dilemmas. *Journal of Personality and Social Psychology, 83,* 616–637.

Worchel, S., Andreoli, V., & Folger, R. (1977). Intergroup cooperation and intergroup attraction: The effect of previous interaction and outcome of combined effort. *Journal of Experimental Social Psychology, 13,* 131–140.

Wright, S. C., Taylor, D. M., & Moghaddam, F. M. (1990). Responding to membership in a disadvantaged group: From acceptance to collective protest. *Journal of Personality and Social Psychology, 58,* 994–1003.

Yuki, M., Maddux, W. W., Brewer, M. B., & Takemura, K. (2005). Cross-cultural differences in relationship- and group-based trust. *Personality and Social Psychology Bulletin, 31,* 48–62.

Yzerbyt, V. Y., Leyens, J-P., & Bellour, F. (1995). The ingroup overexclusion effect: Identity concerns in decisions about group membership. *European Journal of Social Psychology*, 25, 1–16.

Part 4

Connections to Related Fields

Chapter 16

Social Neuroscience

Todd F. Heatherton and Thalia Wheatley

> [People have] through the adaptive capacities of the cortex, attained the levels of intelligence and the power of inhibition and control which are prerequisite for civilized society. The chief contributions of the cortex to social behavior may be summarized as follows: (1) It underlies all solutions of human problems, which are also social problems, and makes possible their preservation in language, customs, institutions, and inventions. (2) It enables each new generation to profit by the experience of others in learning this transmitted lore of civilization. (3) It establishes habits of response in the individual for social as well as for individual ends, inhibiting and modifying primitive self-seeking reflexes into activities which adjust the individual to the social as well as to the non-social environment. Socialized behavior is thus the supreme achievement of the cortex.
>
> —*(Allport, 1924, p. 31)*

In arguably the first major textbook on social psychology, Floyd Allport (1924) chose to begin with an examination of the physiological basis of human behavior. It is not surprising, therefore, that the topic of social neuroscience should stand with other research areas in any comprehensive coverage of social psychology. Yet, for most of the past century, relatively few social psychologists have emphasized its biological nature (with notable exceptions to be discussed shortly). Within the past decade or so, however, a biological revolution has taken place within many areas of psychological science, including social psychology, with an increasing emphasis on the use of neuroscience methods to understand human behavior. The field of neuroscience reflects the interdisciplinary effort to understand the structure, function, physiology, biology, biochemistry, and pathology of the nervous system. From a psychological perspective, however, the term neuroscience typically is used to refer primarily to the study of the brain. Of interest is how the brain gives rise to affect, cognition, and behavior.

Social neuroscience, a term first used by John Cacioppo and colleagues (e.g., Cacioppo & Berntson, 1992), is an emerging field that uses the methods of neuroscience to understand how the brain processes social information. It involves scholars from widely diverse areas (e.g., social and personality psychology, neuroscience, psychiatry, philosophy, anthropology, economics, and sociology) working together and across levels of analysis to understand fundamental questions about human social nature. The core challenge of social neuroscience is to elucidate the neural mechanisms that support social thought and behavior. From this perspective, just as there are dedicated brain mechanisms for breathing, seeing, and hearing, the brain has evolved specialized mechanisms for processing information about the social world, including the ability to know ourselves, to know how others respond to us, and to regulate our actions in order to coexist with other members of society. The problems that are studied by social neuroscience have been of central interest to social psychologists for decades, but the methods and theories that are used reflect recent discoveries in neuroscience. Although in its infancy, there has been rapid progress in identifying the neural basis of many social behaviors, such as attitudes (Cunningham & Zelazo, 2007), stereotyping (Eberhardt, 2005; Quadflieg et al., 2009), conformity (Berns et al., 2005), and cross-cultural factors (Adams et al., 2010; Chiao et al., 2010; for reviews see Adolphs, 2009; Amodio & Frith, 2006; Cacioppo et al., 2007; Heatherton, Macrae, & Kelley, 2004; Mitchell & Heatherton, 2009; Lieberman, 2009; Ochsner, 2007; Todorov, Harris, & Fiske, 2006).

Our goal in this chapter is to sketch a brief history of the field of social neuroscience, describe the major techniques—including their strengths and limitations—used to study the social brain, briefly discuss some of the brain regions and structures that are likely to be of greatest interests to social psychologists, describe the neural basis of select components that make up the social brain, and explain why understanding the brain may be useful for understanding social minds and behaviors.

History of Social Neuroscience

Although a rise in the use of neuroscience methods has accelerated over the past decade or so, it is important to understand how it has permeated psychological thinking as we look at how those methods can be useful for studying social cognition and behavior.

The Intellectual Backdrop

By the beginning of the twentieth century, anatomists had a reasonably good understanding of the basic structures of the brain. What was less clear, however, is how these structures worked to produce thought and behavior—much less how the brain created complex mental activities such as those associated with attitudes, prejudice, or love. A key question was whether different parts of the brain did different things or whether the entire brain acted in unison to perform its vital functions. This issue remains at the heart of social neuroscience, in that ascribing particular functions to specific brain regions might make intuitive sense, but it also might be quite misleading if activity in that brain area reflects general mechanisms that might be true for many different functions (Cacioppo, Berntson, & Nusbaum, 2008; Ochsner, 2007). The major question that remains is how specific brain regions contribute to social cognition (see Mitchell, 2009) as well as how activity across distributed brain areas produces social thoughts and actions.

Some of the earliest proponents of functional localization were the phrenologists, such as Franz Gall and Johann Spurzheim, who identified social constructs such as self-esteem as being reflected by enlargements on the skull (the area to feel for bumps in the skull indicating high self-esteem is just at the crown at the back of your head). Although the theory that brain functions are associated with specific patterns of bumps on the skull is now discredited, the idea that discrete regions of the brain are specialized for different tasks was quite insightful. Early case histories of individuals with brain damage also provided considerable evidence for localized functions. For social and personality psychologists, the most important early case was that of Phineas Gage, a 25-year-old railroad foreman from New Hampshire who suffered extensive damage to his frontal lobes when a blast charge he was preparing accidentally ignited and propelled his tamping iron—an iron bar roughly 1 yard long and 3.2 inches in diameter that was used to prepare explosive charges—through his left cheekbone, into his brain, and out the top of his head. Physicians of the period were initially incredulous at the possibility that anyone could sustain such a massive trauma to the brain and survive, but Gage seemed otherwise unaffected by the blast, conversing casually with both his workers and his physician John Harlow (Macmillan, 2000). Following this extraordinary accident, remarkable changes in Gage's personality and social behavior were noted. Formerly thought of as honest, reliable, and deliberate (Harlow, 1868), Gage was afterward described as "gross, profane, coarse, and vulgar, to such a degree that his society was intolerable to decent people" (Anonymous, 1851; attributed to Harlow, see Macmillan, 2000, p. 348). Importantly, then, Gage's injuries produced specific social deficits without impairing other capacities, such as language or intelligence. The evidence from these early reports seemed clear: localized brain damage causes specific impairments.

Yet psychologists such as Karl Lashley in the early twentieth century continued to argue that all parts of the cortex contributed equally to mental abilities through mass action, an idea known as equipotentiality. In a series of learning studies, Lashley removed cortical tissue from rats to see if he could disrupt their ability to remember how to navigate through mazes. He found that it was the amount of tissue removed rather than where it was located that impaired learning. However, had Lashley removed subcortical tissue he would have come to a much different conclusion. It is now well established that subcortical structures such as the hippocampus and the amygdala are critical to learning and memory.

One reason the debate about whether psychological processes are located in specific parts of the brain or distributed throughout the brain continued so long was because researchers did not have methods for studying ongoing mental activity in the working brain. The invention of brain-imaging methods in the 1970s and 1980s changed that swiftly and decidedly. Functional brain imaging, the use of imaging techniques to observe ongoing mental activity, was pioneered by Marcus Raichle and his colleagues (i.e., Peter Fox, Michael Posner, and Steven Petersen) in the mid-1980s. Although early imaging work used positron emission tomography (PET), functional magnetic resonance imaging (fMRI) was developed in the early 1990s and now serves as the dominant brain imaging method. In the past decade there has been an explosion of research linking specific brain areas with particular behaviors and mental processes (for reviews see the various chapters in Gazzaniga, 2009). We now know that there is some localization of function, but that many different brain regions participate to produce behavior and mental activity (Adolphs, 2009; Lieberman, 2009). That is, although there is considerable support for the general idea of specialization, almost every behavior involves the joint activity of many brain regions. As we discuss later, identifying specific functions for discrete brain structures remains an ongoing challenge for functional neuroimaging approaches to studying social behavior.

The Rise of Social Neuroscience

Within social psychology, efforts to understand bodily involvement in social phenomena also has a long history, such as the use of skin conductance measures to indicate whether experimental conditions produced arousal (e.g., Lanzetta & Kleck, 1970), the assessment of changes in various facial muscles for understanding emotionality (e.g., Cacioppo & Petty, 1981), and the measurement of heart rate and other cardiac activity to understand specific psychological states (e.g., Berntson, Cacioppo, & Quigley, 1991), such as whether people feel threatened or challenged by environmental events (Tomaka, Blascovich, Kelsey, & Leitten, 1993; Mendes, Blascovich, Hunter, Lickel, & Jost, 2007). Indeed, early descriptions of social neuroscience emphasized psychophysiological arousal and response (Cacioppo, Berntson, & Crites, 1999).

In the mid-1990s Stan Klein and John Kihlstrom (1998) argued that the study of various neurological conditions could provide novel assessments of social functions by examining what happens to relevant social behaviors when particular systems are impaired. For example, Klein (2004) has tested numerous amnesic patients who cannot provide episodic memories but whose self-descriptions match those who know them well. That is, a young woman might not remember a single episode when she was outgoing, but she is able to provide a reasonably accurate assessment of whether she is an extravert. Even with exciting possibilities, relatively few social psychologists have developed research programs studying neurological patients. One notable exception is Jennifer Beer's work on patients who sustained damage to their orbitofrontal cortex, the brain region that lies just above the eye orbits and directly behind the forehead. This research made it clear that this region is vital for social emotions such as embarrassment (Beer et al., 2003).

What has dramatically increased interest in social neuroscience is the new generation of brain imaging techniques that allows researchers to watch the working mind in action (Heatherton et al., 2004; Lieberman, 2009; Macrae, Heatherton, & Kelley, 2004; Ochsner, 2007; Ochsner & Lieberman, 2001), which has led some to prefer the term social cognitive neuroscience to social neuroscience (see Lieberman, 2009; Ochsner 2007); however, most researchers use the terms interchangeably. The advent of imaging led to an explosion of research on social cognition, with a resulting boom in special issues of various journals devoted to the topic, specialized conferences both large and small, grant initiatives from several institutes of the National Institutes of Health and from the National Science Foundation, and the launching of two new journals in 2006 focusing on social neuroscience (*Social Cognitive and Affective Neuroscience* and *Social Neuroscience*). Several recent literature reviews have appeared (Amodio & Frith, 2006; Cacioppo et al., 2007; Lieberman, 2009;

Mitchell & Heatherton, 2009; Ochsner, 2007) as well as methodological critiques raising concerns about the value of imaging for elucidating psychological processes (Aue, Lavelle, & Cacioppo, 2009; Cacioppo et al., 2003; Vul et al., 2009). The goal of the next section is to consider the extent to which neuroscience methods are useful for social psychologists to test their theories and study the social brain in action.

Methods of Social Neuroscience

Researchers have only recently been able to study the working brain as it performs its vital mental functions, including social cognition. Although a multitude of different methods have been developed, they tend to group into two categories. The first group relies on measuring the electrical activity (and its associated magnetic consequences) in the brain. These methods are optimized for assessing the timing of brain activity (i.e., they are high in temporal resolution) but are limited in their ability to localize the origins of the brain activity (i.e., they are low in spatial resolution). The second category is based on tracking the blood flow (and its correlates) that accompanies neuronal activity. Methods in this group, such as PET and fMRI, are relatively high in spatial resolution, but because of the rather sluggish nature of blood flow, they are low in temporal resolution. Here we describe some of the major techniques that are used in social neuroscience.

Electroencephalography (EEG) and Event-Related Potential (ERP)

EEG was the first noninvasive method of brain mapping developed for humans. It is based on the principle that neural activity produces electrical potentials that can be measured and that the sum of these potentials indicates the relative activity of the brain. EEG records these electrical signals in real time through electrodes that are strategically placed on the scalp. Because EEGs register all brain activity the signal is noisy and it cannot provide information about specific changes in brain activity in response to a stimulus or cognitive task. This problem is remedied by using event-related potentials (ERP), an offshoot of EEG. During ERP experiments, the trials are repeated numerous times and the EEG signals following those trials are averaged together to create an average waveform of the brain's response to the experimental event. Perhaps the most important feature of ERP is that it provides a relatively precise record of brain activity. The use of ERP methods has provided psychologists with insights into a number of important social behaviors, including identifying unique patterns that are associated with perceiving members of an outgroup, at least for those who score high on measures of racial prejudice (Ito, Thompson, & Cacioppo, 2004). An excellent review of findings in social neuroscience using ERP describes the method as being useful for understanding person perception, stereotyping, attitudes and evaluative processes, and self-regulation (Bartholow & Amodio, 2009).

A technique related to ERP that also provides better spatial resolution is magnetoencephalography (MEG), which measures magnetic fields that are produced by the electrical activity of the brain. Unlike EEG, MEG does not require electrodes but rather uses special sensors that detect magnetic fields. MEG has the same temporal resolution as ERP, but because magnetic signals are not distorted by the skull, as are EEG signals, its signal localization is considerably better. In a study of the effects of social exclusion on self-control failure using MEG, Campbell and colleagues (2006) found that social exclusion affected frontal lobe regions typically involved in executive control of attention. Unfortunately, MEG is not widely available and is considerably more expensive than EEG.

Functional Neuroimaging

The brain imaging methods that have produced the greatest scientific enthusiasm in recent times measure metabolic processes rather than electrical activity. Brain activity is associated with changes in the flow of blood as it carries oxygen and nutrients to activated brain regions. Brain imaging methods track this flow of blood to understand which areas of the brain are most active for a given task. PET, the first imaging method developed, involves tracking the brain's metabolic activity by using a relatively harmless radioactive substance that is injected into the bloodstream. A PET scanner detects this radiation as blood travels through the brain and therefore can be used to map out brain activity in real time in three-dimensional space. The resulting image identifies the neural structures engaged in specific cognitive tasks. PET has at least one major disadvantage. The use of radioactive substances places an inherent limitation on the number of trials that can be used, and accordingly tends to have low power. Moreover, it can take a long time to image the entire brain and so trials themselves need to last for an extended period. For reasons of safety as well as the ability to use many more trials, most current brain imaging is conducted using fMRI, to which we now turn.

Similar to PET, fMRI measures brain activity by tracking metabolism associated with blood flow, but it does so noninvasively (that is, nothing is injected into the bloodstream). Thus, a single fMRI study can contain hundreds of trials, thereby greatly enhancing the power of the study. fMRI does not measure blood flow directly. Rather, it employs a strong magnetic field to assess changes in the blood–oxygen level-dependent (BOLD) response at particular cortical sites after they have become active, which is an indirect measure of blood flow. Specifically, the BOLD signal is derived from the ratio of oxygenated to deoxygenated blood at cortical locations throughout the brain.

Transcranial Magnetic Stimulation (TMS)

It is commonly known that functional neuroimaging data only "suggest" brain regions that may be engaged during a given behavior; correlations between behavior and localized brain activity cannot establish a causal brain–behavior linkage. One way to address such a hypothesis would be to conduct a lesion study in which specific brain regions were damaged while leaving other areas relatively intact. Ethics committees, however, tend not to encourage lesioning our undergraduate research participants. Fortunately, TMS allows reversible experimental disruption of neural activity in relatively circumscribed cortical regions while individuals engage in a cognitive task (Jahanshahi & Rothwell, 2000; Walsh & Cowey, 2000; Wig, Grafton, Demos, & Kelley, 2005). During TMS, a powerful electrical current flows through a wire coil that is placed on the scalp over the area to be stimulated. As electrical current flows through the coil, a powerful magnetic field is produced that interferes with neural functions in specific regions of the brain. If multiple pulses of TMS are given over an extended time (known as repeated TMS), the disruption can carry over beyond the period of direct stimulation. Recent studies using TMS to create a virtual lesion in the superior temporal sulcus (STS) have demonstrated interference in the perception of eye gaze direction (Pourtois et al., 2004), reduced accuracy in detecting biological motion from point light displays (Grossman, Battelli, & Pascual-Leone, 2005), and interference with processing facial expressions indicating anger (Harmer, Thilo, Rothwell, & Goodwin, 2001).

Conceptual Concerns for Using Imaging Methods

In spite of the enthusiastic adoption of the methods of neuroscience to study social psychological constructs, there remain important conceptual issues regarding this approach (see Vul et al., 2009). Space limits preclude a full discussion of such concerns, but we provide a few examples. Perhaps the most central issue is that scientists do not yet fully understand the specific neural basis of brain imaging signals. Although several explanations have been proposed for the BOLD response, the precise mechanism remains unspecified at the neuronal level. Another problem we discussed earlier is that most imaging methods are necessarily correlational and therefore prone to all the inherent limitations of correlational methods. The advent of tools such as TMS may make it possible to examine causality, but TMS is limited to cortical areas near the skull and therefore will not be useful for many mental processes that involve deeper structures. Assessing patients who have brain injury can provide complementary evidence for the causal involvement of a brain region for a given psychological function.

The final conceptual issue we note is the difficulty in localizing specific psychological functions to discrete brain regions. There have now been several thousand imaging studies of a variety of psychological functions. What is clear is that there is no one-to-one mapping between brain region and psychological function. Indeed, some brain regions are activated across numerous cognitive and social tasks (see Mitchell, 2009; Ochsner, 2007). Thus, when a researcher finds a particular activation in an imaging study it is not always obvious what that activation indicates. Although the literature contains sufficient evidence that there is specialization of brain function, it can be challenging to determine the specific function associated with a particular activation (Lieberman, 2009). An area may be activated across a broad array of disparate cognitive tasks because those different tasks share some common psychological process (i.e., semantic processing, memory, selecting among competing stimuli). In these cases, the activation may have little to do with the research question of greatest interest to the investigator. As in all areas of science, the value of any imaging study depends on the care with which the experimental tasks are designed. In the ideal world appropriate comparisons conditions are used that differ from the experimental conditions in as few dimensions as possible. Moreover, researchers have to be vigilant to the possibility that their manipulations may be confounded with other psychological processes.

Building a Social Brain

How do you build a social brain? Or what does the brain need to do to allow it to be social? In this section we describe a conceptual framework for understanding the social brain (Krendl & Heatherton, 2009; Mitchell & Heatherton, 2009). The overarching assumption is that the brain evolved over millions of years as an organ that solves adaptive problems, which for humans are frequently social in nature. Early human ancestors needed to recognize faces of friends and foe, identify potential mates and evaluate them in terms of desirability, understand the nature of group relations, and so on. Importantly, humans have evolved a fundamental need to belong which encourages behavior that helps people be good group members (Bowlby, 1969; Baumeister & Leary, 1995). Effective groups shared food, provided mates, and helped care for offspring. As such, human survival has long depended on living within groups; banishment from the group was effectively a death sentence. Baumeister and Leary (1995) argued that the need to belong is a basic motive that activates behavior and influences cognition and emotion, and that it leads to ill effects when not satisfied. Indeed, even today not belonging to a group increases a person's risk for a number of adverse consequences, such as illnesses and premature death (see Cacioppo et al., 2006).

Initial findings using neuroimaging have shown that unique neural regions are associated with processing social information as compared to general semantic knowledge. For instance, Mitchell, Heatherton, and Macrae (2002) showed that when participants make semantic judgments about words that could either describe a person (e.g., assertive, fickle) or an object such as fruit (e.g., sundried, seedless), various brain regions, particularly the medial prefrontal cortex, were uniquely associated with person judgments. Similarly, Mason, Banfield, and Macrae (2004) found that when participants made judgments about whether an action (e.g., running, sitting, or biting) could be performed by a person or a dog, the medial prefrontal cortex was once again associated with judgments only about people. Thus, the brain seems to treat other humans as a special class of stimuli (Norris et al., 2004). Here we examine the implications of that notion.

The Building Blocks of the Social Brain

Converging evidence suggests that the human brain comes hard-wired to find other humans interesting. Within 48 hours of life, newborns attend more to faces than any other objects, listen longer to human voices than other sounds, and gaze longer at upright versus upsidedown displays of biological motion (Goren, Sarty, & Wu, 1975; Johnson, Dziurawiec, Ellis, & Morton, 1991; Simion, Regolin, & Bulf, 2008; Vouloumanos & Werker, 2007). Because babies lack knowledge about the world, this initial interest in other beings is likely driven by simple, perceptual cues. Indeed, two dots and a line are enough to grab an infant's attention, but only if those shapes are presented in the configuration of a face: two dots for eyes and a line for the nose (Goren, Sarty, & Wu, 1975). However primitive, having an innate set of "life detectors" affords two important benefits. First, it increases the chance of survival by ensuring that infants detect those who are likely to feed, protect, or eat them. The second, perhaps less obvious, benefit is that cleaving the world into animate and inanimate halves establishes the foundation on which social thought is built (Wheatley, Milleville, & Martin, 2007).

The layering of social understanding on a framework of animacy is demonstrated across child development. By 5 months of age, infants infer goal-directedness in a moving human hand but not a moving rod (Woodward, 1998) and by 18 months they attribute intentions to human actors but not machines (Meltzoff, 1995). Thus, early on, thoughts, feelings, and actions are imputed only to the subset of the world that can think, feel, and act in return. In this way, the initial step of detecting life conserves precious cognitive energy—a finite resource that people are loath to expend (Fiske & Taylor, 1991). Detecting animacy avoids such effort-wasting missteps as greeting doors or wondering why the lamp is such a poor conversationalist. Evidence from neuroscience suggests that these "life detectors" are housed in two regions of the temporal lobe: the ventral temporal cortex for the detection of human form (faces, bodies) and the lateral temporal cortex for the detection of human dynamics (sound, motion).

Detecting Faces Faces pack a wealth of information into a relatively small space: they identify people and can be evaluated along many dimensions including attractiveness, maturity, and trustworthiness. Consistent with its usefulness, expertise in facial recognition develops early and appears to hold a privileged status in the human brain. Indeed, one of the most robust findings in social neuroscience is that viewing faces activates a particular section of cortex more than any other kind of stimuli including nonface objects, scrambled faces, and inverted faces (Ishai, Ungerleider, Martin, Maisog, & Haxby, 1997; Kanwisher, McDermott, & Chun, 1997; McCarthy, Puce, Gore, & Allison, 1997). This region is located bilaterally (one per hemisphere) on the underside of the human brain and is dubbed the fusiform face area (FFA) given its heightened response to faces.

Lesions to the FFA can create prosopagnosia: the selective inability to recognize the identity of faces (Duchaine & Nakayama, 2005; Tranel, Damasio, & Damasio, 1998). However, despite difficulties in recognizing even highly familiar faces consciously, prosopagnosic patients can identify people by voice and show a heightened emotional response (skin conductance) to familiar others indicating an unconscious level of recognition (von Kriegstein, Kleinschmidt, & Giraud, 2006). Thus, even when conscious facial recognition fails, other brain regions aid the all-important task of identifying people in the environment.

The structural properties of a face provide not only the identity of a person but also the raw material for attraction. Regardless of whether a book should be judged by its cover, research suggests that people cannot help but do just that. In one study, subjects were asked to report the identity of various faces while lying in an fMRI scanner. Although subjects were not judging attractiveness at the time, hemodynamic activity in the orbitofrontal cortex (OFC) correlated with subjects' later ratings of the attractiveness of those faces. OFC, a region associated with the evaluation of reward, was activated more by faces later deemed attractive relative to faces deemed unattractive (O'Doherty et al., 2003). As might be predicted, sexual preference modulates this activity: male faces evoked a greater response in this region for homosexual men and heterosexual women while female faces evoked a greater response for heterosexual men and homosexual women (Kranz & Ishai, 2006). However, the magnitude of OFC activity to attractive faces may not be equivalent across genders. In a recent study, the OFC of male viewers was activated more by attractive females than vice versa, supporting the hypothesis that heterosexual males find attractive, opposite-sex faces more rewarding than do their female counterparts. However, other reward regions such as the nucleus accumbens were activated in response to attractive faces similarly across genders (Cloutier et al., 2008).

Recently, other face-sensitive regions of the cortex have been identified that may work in tandem with the FFA to support other percepts and inferences based on the invariant features of a face (e.g., gender—Kriegeskorte, Formisano, Sorger & Goebel, 2007; trustworthiness—Oosterhof & Todorov, 2008). However, the face is more than a collection of features; it also provides a canvas for facial expressions that convey transitory emotional and mental states.

Decoding Expressions: Faces A person's facial expressions telegraph intentions and emotions. These expressions can last several seconds (imagine winning the lottery or finding out that your new roommate keeps ferrets), but the majority are subtle and fleeting. Indeed, the most telling expressions are often very brief: a sneer, a glimmer of recognition, or a flicker of raised eyebrows can announce our true feelings in an instant (Ekman, 1992). Social intelligence requires a sensitive and rapid system to decode these social cues. Neuroimaging studies using high temporal resolution ERP has found that some neural responses to emotional facial expressions are so rapid (<100 ms) that they may be processed even before achieving conscious awareness. Consistent with evolutionary pressures, this rapid system appears to be especially geared to detect expressions of threat (e.g., the large eye-whites of fearful faces—Whalen et al., 2004).

At a slower timescale, decoding expressions may also rely on the ability to simulate another's emotional state (Damasio, 1994). Somatosensory cortices associated with having cutaneous, kinesthetic, and visceral sensations appear to be active during emotion recognition. Damage to this region has been associated with impaired touch sensation and impaired recognition for multiple emotions (Adolphs et al., 2000). Furthermore, the insular cortex associated with the perception of taste is recruited during the recognition of facial expressions of disgust (Phillips et al., 1997). Patients with reduced activity in somatosensory regions have difficulty accessing their own bodily state and exhibit flat affect. This overlap is consistent with the idea that emotion recognition may depend in part on activating circuits involved in learning our own emotional states.

Decoding Expressions: Bodies and Voices Faces are not the only way to determine what someone is thinking or feeling. Body language and tone of voice are also important social cues. In the past decade, many studies have converged on one region in the brain as the hub for understanding human movement: the STS (Allison et al., 2000, Beauchamp et al., 2002; Grossman et al., 2005; Haxby, Hoffman, & Gobbini, 2000). Consistent with a layering of social understanding on the detection of biological properties, the STS in adult subjects seems to be particularly tuned to human movement that expresses social meaning (Castelli, Happé, & Frith, 2002; Haxby et al., 2000; Martin & Weisberg, 2003). Those with compromised functioning in this region (e.g., autism) are less accurate at decoding emotional compared to neutral movements (Dakin & Frith, 2005).

The same region implicated in detecting human movement is adjacent to the region supporting the detection of human voice. Several studies have shown that a region near the STS is activated by the sound of other human beings relative to similarly complex nonspeech sounds and supports the ability to understand emotional intonation (Beaucousin et al., 2007; von Kriegstein & Giraud, 2004). In normal daily life, the ability to hear emotion in a person's voice is taken for granted, but losing that ability (aprosodia) can have devastating social consequences. A recent meta-analysis found that schizophrenia patients were more than one standard deviation below the mean of healthy controls in recognizing tone of voice cues to emotion. The impairment was so large that the authors concluded it to be "one of the most pervasive disturbances in schizophrenia that may contribute to social isolation" (Hoekert et al., 2007, p. 135). In sum, the superior temporal cortex appears to be particularly attuned to the detection of human voice and movement and instrumental in decoding these stimuli for social meaning.

The human brain appears to have specialized regions of cortex for the detection and understanding of human faces, movement, and voice. These regions are highly interconnected not only with each other, but as nodes within larger, interacting circuits that support the full breadth of social understanding including self-identity, ability to empathize, and regulation of our behavior in accordance with social norms. We now discuss a conceptual model of the neural basis of such components.

Components of the Social Brain

Given the fundamental need to belong, there needs to be a social brain system that monitors for signs of social inclusion/exclusion and alters behavior to forestall rejection or resolve other social problems (see Krendl & Heatherton, 2009). Such a system requires four components, each of which is likely to have a discrete neural signature. First, people need self-awareness—to be aware of their behavior so as to gauge it against societal or group norms. Second, people need to understand how others are reacting to their behavior so as to predict how others will respond to them. In other words they need "theory of mind" or the capacity to attribute mental states to others. This implies the need for a third mechanism, which detects threat, especially in complex situations. Finally, there needs to be a self-regulatory mechanism for resolving discrepancies between what we know about that self and what is expected of ourself, which motivates behavior to resolve any conflict that exists.

This does not mean that other psychological processes are unimportant for social functioning. Indeed, capacities such as language, memory, and vision, along with motivational and basic emotional states, are generally important for functioning within the social group. However, they are not necessary for a person to be a good group member; the blind and deaf can contribute substantially to their groups. By contrast, people with disturbances in the primary components of self, theory of mind, threat detection, or self-regulation have fundamental and often specific impairments in social function. Recall the case of Phineas Gage who had severe social impairments while having most of his mental faculties intact.

Unlike many other aspects of cognition, almost everything we know about the social brain has been uncovered in the past decade and a half. Fortunately, the emergence of social neuroscience has been both rapid and far reaching, and thus, despite its infancy, this approach has netted a substantial number of reliable and surprising empirical findings about how the brain gives rise to human sociality.

Awareness and Knowledge about the Self

The concept of self forms the foundation for the social brain. Survival in human social groups requires people to monitor their behavior and thoughts to assess whether those thoughts and behaviors are in keeping with prevailing group (social) norms. According to Baumeister (1998), "the capacity of the human organism to be conscious of itself is a distinguishing feature and is vital to selfhood" (p. 683). The topic of self may be among the most near and dear to social and personality psychologists. In social neuroscience, the study of self-reflection has provided one of the best examples of how neuroimaging might be especially useful as a tool to resolve theoretical debates when traditional behavioral methods are unable to do so. Because this is an important demonstration of the value of imaging, we present this material in considerable detail before summarizing what social neuroscience has learned about the brain mechanisms that support self-reflection.

In the 1980s, a major debate in social psychology was whether information processed about the self is treated in the same manner as any other type of information (Bower & Gilligan, 1979; Klein & Kihlstrom, 1986; Klein & Loftus, 1988; Maki & McCaul, 1985; Markus, 1977; Rogers, Kuiper, & Kirker, 1977). The first line of evidence in favor of the view that self is special emerged from the pioneering work of Tim Rogers and his colleagues (1977), who showed that when trait adjectives (e.g., happy) were processed with reference to the self (e.g., "does happy describe you?"), subsequent memory performance was better than when the items were processed only for their general meaning (e.g., "does happy mean the same as optimistic?"). This self-referential effect in memory has been demonstrated many times (Symons & Johnson, 1997) and shows that information processed about the self is special. Indeed, even people who can remember very little can often remember information that is self-relevant. Recall that people with severe amnesia retain the ability to accurately describe whether specific traits are true of the self (Klein, 2004). Patient K.R., for instance, suffered from profound Alzheimer's disease, yet she was still able to identify self-relevant personality traits accurately (Klein, Cosmides, & Costabile, 2003). So why is information about the self particularly memorable?

During the 1980s, social and cognitive psychologists debated two theories for the self-reference superiority effect in memory. Rogers (1977) proposed that the self is a unique cognitive structure that possesses special mnemonic abilities, leading to the enhanced memorability of material processed in relation to self. Other researchers argued that self plays no special or unique role in cognition, but that the memory enhancement that accompanies self-referential processing can be interpreted as a standard depth-of-processing effect (Greenwald & Banaji, 1989; Klein & Kihlstrom, 1986). The wealth of personal information that resides in memory encourages the elaborative encoding of material that is processed in relation to self. In turn, this elaborative encoding enhances the memorability of self-relevant information. From this perspective, the self is quite ordinary; it just elicits greater elaboration during encoding.

Research on this question eventually withered, in part because the opposing theories made identical behavioral predictions, namely, better memory for items that were processed in a self-referential manner. Herein lies the tremendous advantage of using brain imaging. Neuroimaging techniques are ideally suited for resolving debates for which competing theories make identical behavior predictions. An initial attempt to examine the neural substrates of the self-reference effect used PET. Unfortunately, as discussed, there is a limit to the number of trials that can be presented using PET, and the researchers did not obtain a statistically significant self-reference effect (Craik et al., 1999). Nonetheless, their results were intriguing in that during self-reference processing trials, they did find distinct activations in frontal regions, notably the medial prefrontal cortex (MPFC) and areas of the right prefrontal cortex. Observing the power limitation of PET, Kelley and colleagues used event-related fMRI in an attempt to identify the neural signature of self-referential mental activity (Kelley et al., 2002). In a standard self-reference paradigm, participants judged trait adjectives in one of three ways: self ("does the trait describe you?), other ("does the trait describe George Bush?"), and case ("is the trait presented in uppercase letters"?). These judgments produced the expected significant differences in subsequent memory performance (i.e., self > other > case).

More importantly, however, they enabled the researchers to test the competing explanations that have been offered for the self-reference effect in memory. Previous functional imaging studies have identified multiple regions within the left frontal cortex that are responsive to elaborate semantic encoding (Buckner, Kelley, & Petersen, 1999; Demb et al., 1995; Gabrieli et al., 1996; Kapur et al., 1996; Kelley et al., 1998; Wagner et al., 1998). Thus, if the self-reference effect simply reflects the operation of such a process, one would expect to observe elevated levels of activation in these left frontal areas when traits are judged in relation to self. If, however, the effect results from the properties of a unique cognitive self, we might expect self-referential mental activity to engage brain regions that are distinct from those involved in general semantic processing. The left inferior frontal region, notable for its involvement in semantic processing tasks, did not discriminate between self and other trials. Instead, Kelley et al. (2002) observed selective activity in areas of prefrontal cortex, notably the MPFC, suggesting that this region might be involved in the self-referential memory effect. In a later study, Macrae and colleagues (2004) demonstrated that activity in MPFC could predict whether a person would subsequently remember terms encoded with reference to self, providing more compelling evidence of a link between the activity in MPFC and self-memory processes.

Since these early studies, social neuroscience has made excellent strides in identifying brain regions that are involved in processing information about the self (Krendl & Heatherton, 2009; Lieberman, 2009). Both neuroimaging and neurological patients have implicated ventral regions of the MPFC as contributing importantly to conceptual aspects of selfhood (along with a consistent collection of other brain structures along the cortical midline; see Northoff et al., 2006). For example, a considerable number of neuroimaging studies have replicated the involvement of this MPFC region in tasks that require participants to judge their own personality traits (Fossati et al., 2003, 2004; Heatherton et al., 2006; Johnson et al., 2002; Macrae, Moran, Heatherton, Banfield, & Kelley,

2004; Moran, Macrae, Heatherton, Wyland, & Kelley, 2006; Ochsner et al., 2004; Pfeifer, Lieberman, & Dapretto, 2007; Schmitz, Kawahara-Baccus, & Johnson, 2004; Zysset, Huber, Ferstl, & von Cramon, 2002) or report on their preferences and opinions (Ames, Jenkins, Banaji, & Mitchell, 2008; Jenkins, Macrae, & Mitchell, 2008; Mitchell, Macrae, & Banaji, 2006), compared to judging these characteristics in others. Although the cognitive aspects of self-reflection involve MPFC, the emotional consequences of those responses (i.e., whether the response indicates positive or negative things about the rater) appear to be coded in the ventral anterior cingulate cortex, which is just adjacent to MPFC (Moran et al., 2006). This area is important for interpersonal relations, which we discuss later in this chapter. The issue of whether the self is somehow "special" remains somewhat contentious (see Gillihan & Farah, 2005), but the imaging literature is quite clear regarding tasks that involve self-awareness: they activate MPFC in imaging studies (Gusnard, 2005).

The extent to which we include others in our self-concept has been a topic of particular interest for social psychologists. Theories of intimacy and personal relationships might suggest that the self-reference effect is affected by the closeness of a relationship with the other used as a target. Indeed, Aron and colleagues define closeness as the extension of self into other and suggest that our cognitive processes about a close other develop to include that person as part of the self (Aron & Aron, 1996; Aron, Aron, Tudor, & Nelson, 1991; Aron & Fraley, 1999). Neuroimaging provides an interesting context for examining this question. The available studies provide mixed evidence regarding overlap in making trait judgments for self and others, with some studies finding overlapping patterns of activation in MPFC (Ochsner et al., 2005; Schmitz, Kawahara-Baccus, & Johnson, 2004; Seger, Stone, & Keenan, 2004) and others finding MPFC activity only for self and not for a highly familiar other (Heatherton et al., 2006). It is possible that methodological issues may account for this discrepancy, as the studies used different targets and different types of imaging designs. One intriguing finding is that Chinese participants tend to activate MPFC when answering questions about themselves or their mothers, whereas Western participants activated MPFC more for self than for their mothers (Zhu et al., 2007), supporting the idea that collectivist cultures involve cognitive interdependencies (Markus & Kitayama, 1991). However, since the MPFC is a rather large area, and different parts may be sensitive to different task parameters or MPFC may be performing common functions across different types of tasks (see Mitchell, 2009; Ochsner, 2007), additional research is necessary to understand more fully how self-representation overlaps with representation of others.

It is interesting to note that converging evidence from patient research indicates that frontal lobe lesions, particularly to the MPFC and adjacent structures, have detrimental consequences for personality, mood, motivation, and self-awareness. Patients with frontal lobe lesions show dramatic deficits in recognizing their own limbs, engaging in self-reflection and introspection, and even reflecting on personal knowledge. Indeed, frontal lobe patients are particularly impaired in social emotions (Beer et al., 2003). Likewise, damage to this region can lead to deficits in the organization of knowledge about our preferences. Fellows and Farah (2007) reported that when asked to indicate their attitudes toward various stimuli, patients with MPFC lesions show unusually large discrepancies between testing sessions, suggesting that damage to this region leads either to failures to retrieve knowledge of our attitudes or instability in otherwise stable aspects of selfhood.

It is important to be clear that that there is no specific "self" spot of the brain, no single brain region that is responsible for all psychological processes related to self. Rather, psychological processes are distributed throughout the brain, with contributions from multiple subcomponents determining discrete mental activities that come together to give rise to the human sense of self (Turk, Heatherton, Macrae, Kelley, & Gazzaniga, 2003). Various cognitive, sensory, motor, somatosensory, and affective processes are essential to self, and these processes likely reflect the contribution of several cortical and subcortical regions. Indeed, some have argued that the most important psychological processes that produce activation of MPFC involve inferential processing, whether about the self or anything else (Legrand & Ruby, 2009). More recently, Jason Mitchell (2009) proposed that any type of social cognition that involves internally generated "fuzzy" representations that are inexact and subject to revision, such as judging attitudes about self or others, or even objects in general, activates MPFC.

Mentalizing and Theory of the Mind

One of the most important attributes of the social brain is the ability to infer the mental states of others to predict their actions (Amodio & Frith, 2006; Gallagher & Frith, 2003; Mitchell, 2006). The underlying assumption—that behavior is caused by mental states—has been called taking an "intentional stance," "theory of mind," and "mind perception" (Epley & Waytz, 2009) and is an important developmental milestone. Testing whether young children possess theory of mind usually involves telling them stories in which false beliefs must be inferred. In one well-known example, a child is shown two dolls: Sally and Ann. Sally has a basket and Ann has a box. The child watches as Sally puts a marble in the basket and leaves. While Sally is gone, "naughty" Ann takes the marble out of the basket and puts it in the box. Then Sally returns. The child is asked: "Where will Sally look for the marble?" The correct response requires understanding that Ann moved the marble *unbeknownst to* Sally and that Sally thus holds a false belief that the marble is still in the basket. Healthy and IQ-matched Downs syndrome children succeed at this task around the age of 4 years (Baron-Cohen, Leslie, & Frith, 1985). Before that time, children have difficulty grasping the idea that a person can believe something decoupled from reality.

It is perhaps not surprising that patients with impoverished social relationships do poorly on theory of mind tasks. Four-year-old autistic children have a failure rate of 80% on the Sally-Ann task (Baron-Cohen, Leslie, & Frith, 1985). If the task involves the added difficulty of understanding what a person thinks about *another* person's beliefs or thoughts (i.e., second-order mental state attribution), the failure rate in autistic individuals is very high (Baron-Cohen, 1989). Although autistic individuals may develop strategies using nonmentalistic representations to pass some of these tests, difficulty inferring another's thoughts is an enduring and debilitating indicator of autism. Research with patients and healthy adults has converged on three brain areas that are consistently modulated by tasks requiring the inference of mental states: the temporal poles, the temporal parietal junction (TPJ), and the MPFC. Healthy adult volunteers recruit these areas when inferring mental states from facial expressions in photographs, attributing mental states to animations of geometric shapes, and imputing mental states to characters in stories (Frith & Frith, 1999).

Temporal Poles The temporal poles are the farthest forward ends of the temporal lobes. Lesions of this region in monkeys yield grossly abnormal social behavior and result in the loss of normal emotional attachments to the monkeys' infants and peers. Damage to this region in humans also leads to severe socioemotional deficits including depression, socially inappropriate behavior, and a lack of empathy (Olson, Plotzker, & Ezzyat, 2007).

In the intact adult brain, the temporal poles are especially active when people imagine or read about social situations. Given the connections of this area to the medial temporal lobe memory system, it has been suggested that this region evaluates incoming social information based on our past experience. In this way, the temporal poles allow people to construct and evaluate social norms. Consistent with this view, patients with TP lesions have particular difficulty predicting how people will behave in social and emotional circumstances even if they know them quite well (Frith, 2008; Olson, Plotzker, & Ezzyat, 2007).

STS/TPJ As discussed previously, numerous studies have linked the superior temporal sulcus with the perception of human movement, particularly socially meaningful human movement. The tendency to impute social meaning to motion cues was demonstrated in an early social psychological study by Fritz Heider and Mary-Ann Simmel (1944). In this seminal study, subjects spontaneously inferred intent, emotion, gender, and even personality in simple animations of interacting geometric shapes. Some researchers have speculated that there are adjacent but distinct areas within this region of cortex that support three related but dissociable functions: recognition of human movement, recognition of mental states from motion cues, and the ability to understand another's mind regardless of whether motion cues are present. The latter ability appears to be associated primarily with the most posterior region of the superior temporal sulcus, also known as the temporal parietal junction, or TPJ. This region has been implicated in mental perspective taking (Saxe & Powell, 2006) as well as physical perspective taking. Disruption to this region produces impairments in the ability to imagine how one's body looks from another's perspective (Blanke et al., 2005). Thus, this region supports the ability to contemplate spatial and mental perspectives different from our own (Saxe & Kanwisher, 2003; Mitchell, 2008).

Medial Prefrontal Cortex The area consistently activated by mentalizing is the MPFC, although typically an area slightly higher than observed for self-referential processing. In separate studies, activity in this region has been associated with the perception of pain and anxiety, as well as autobiographical memory and esthetic judgment (Jacobsen, Schubotz, Höfel, & von Cramon, 2006; Janata, 2009; Macrae, Moran, Heatherton, Banfield, & Kelley, 2004; Peyron, Laurent, & Garcia-Larrea, 2000; Simpson, Drevets, Snyder, Gusnard, & Raichle, 2001). Across these seemingly disparate studies, however, a common denominator has emerged: MPFC appears to support the ability to *attend to* the mental states that give rise to experience, that is, to create an explicit representation of what we think or feel *about* X. Recent research suggests that this area is also important for taking the perspective of another person (i.e., "how would you feel if you were person X"). This suggests that being able to represent our own subjective experience plays a central role in the ability to understand the subjective experience of others (Jenkins, Macrae, & Mitchell, 2008; Mitchell, Banaji, & Macrae, 2005; Mitchell, Heatherton, & Macrae, 2002).

Detection of Threat

One value of having theory of mind is that it supports a third mechanism, which is threat detection, a process particularly useful in complex situations such as may be encountered in dealing with ingroup or outgroup members.

Ingroup Threats If humans have a fundamental need to belong, then there ought to be mechanisms for detecting inclusionary status (Leary, Tambor, Terdal, & Downs, 1995; Macdonald & Leary, 2005). Put another way, given the importance of group inclusion, humans need to be sensitive to signs that the group might exclude them. Indeed, there is evidence that people feel anxious when they face exclusion from their social groups (Baumeister & Tice, 1988). Thus, feeling socially anxious or worrying about potential rejection should lead to heightened social sensitivity. Indeed, research has demonstrated that people who worry most about social evaluation (i.e., the shy and lonely) show enhanced memory for social information, are more empathetically accurate, and show heightened abilities to decode social information (Gardner, Pickett, & Brewer, 2000; Gardner, Pickett, Jefferis, & Knowles, 2005; Pickett, Gardner, & Knowles, 2004). Lonely people show a pattern of activation in theory of mind regions that indicates they spontaneously reflect more when viewing distressed than happy people (Cacioppo et al., 2008).

Social psychologists have documented the pernicious effects of interpersonal rejection threat on mood, behavior, and cognition (Smart & Leary, 2009). There have recently been a series of neuroimaging studies that have examined social rejection. Most prominent is the study by Naomi Eisenberger and her colleagues (2003) who found that the dorsal anterior cingulate cortex (dACC) was responsive during a video game designed to elicit feelings of social rejection when virtual interaction partners suddenly and surprisingly stopped cooperating with the research participant. Since this initial study, other studies have also implicated the anterior cingulate cortex, although some of them find a more ventral (lower) rather than dorsal (higher) region. For instance, one study found that social feedback about acceptance or rejection was associated with differential activity in the ventral anterior cingulate cortex (vACC; Somerville, Heatherton, & Kelley, 2006) and another found vACC activity for rejected adolescents (Masten et al., 2009). One interesting study using paintings portraying rejection imagery observed a pattern somewhat different than found in either of the previous studies (Kross, Egner, Ochsner, Hirsch, & Downey, 2007). Although these authors also found dACC to be responsive to rejection imagery, the response was in a different area of dACC from that found by Eisenberger et al. and the relation between feelings of rejection and activity in this area was opposite that reported by Eisenberger et al. Another recent study (Burklund, Eisenberger, & Lieberman, 2007) found a relationship between both dACC and vACC activity and rejection sensitivity during emotional processing, albeit the vACC activity was in a region different from that reported by Somerville et al. (2006). The somewhat disparate findings of these studies indicate the need for further research to more clearly identify the neural correlates of states of social distress, especially in terms of the functional roles of dACC and vACC in processing and responding to threat cues.

Similarly, Krendl, Richeson, Kelley, and Heatherton (2008) found vACC activation during a stereotype threat task. They conducted an fMRI study in which women were reminded of gender stereotypes about math ability while they were completing difficult math problems. Women showed an increase in vACC activity while performing difficult math problems after a social threat was induced (reminding them of gender stereotypes), whereas in the absence of a social threat, women instead showed heightened activation over time in regions associated with math learning, and no change in vACC activation. Not surprisingly, women who were threatened exhibited a decrease in math performance over time whereas women who were not threatened improved in performance over time. Given the above findings, it is reasonable to conclude that the vACC is engaged in social and emotional processing.

Outgroup Threats Not all threats, however, are related to social exclusion. Just as people naturally fear dangerous animals (i.e., poisonous snakes and spiders, tigers and wolves), they also face harm from other humans. Indeed, other group members can transmit disease, act carelessly and place bystanders at risk, waste or steal vital group resources, or poach one's mate. Similarly, people from other groups can also be dangerous when competition for scarce resources leads to intergroup violence. Hence, there is also a need for mechanisms that detect threats from people from outgroups.

The most common area identified as relevant to threat from outgroup members is the amygdala (for a review, see Eberhardt, 2005). In perhaps the first social neuroscience study that used functional neuroimaging, cognitive neuroscientist Elizabeth Phelps, social psychologist Mahzarin Banaji, and their colleagues used fMRI to study racial attitudes. They showed white college students pictures of unfamiliar black and white faces while they scanned brain activity (Phelps et al., 2000). For those subjects who score high on an implicit measure of racial bias, the unfamiliar black faces activated the amygdala, a brain structure that is involved in fear responses. Many other studies have associated amygdala activity with negative response to African-Americans (Cunningham et al., 2004; Phelps et al., 2000; Richeson et al., 2003). Wheeler and Fiske (2005) found that the types of judgments that participants make about faces affect amygdala activity. For instance, when white participants were asked to evaluate black faces, amygdala activity was observed only when the target was socially categorized (e.g., "Is this individual over 21 years old?"), and not when participants were asked to individuate the target ("Would this individual like this vegetable?").

It is important to the note that the amygdala is only one of several neural areas engaged during the evaluation of an outgroup member. Emerging research from neuroimaging has revealed that areas of the prefrontal cortex involved in cognitive control are also engaged in these tasks. For instance, Cunningham and colleagues (2004) showed that the amygdala responded to pictures of black faces when presented very quickly (30 ms). However, when the faces were presented for a longer period of time (525 ms), the amygdala response was dampened, and instead increased activation was observed in the prefrontal cortex. The authors argued that the heightened activation in the prefrontal cortex may have been inhibiting the automatic response elicited by the amygdala.

Richeson and colleagues (2003) also found that white participants engage prefrontal control mechanisms (i.e., the dorsolateral prefrontal cortex and anterior cingulate cortex) in response to viewing black faces. However, they found that the activation of these areas was positively correlated with antiblack bias. In other words, they found that white individuals with greater antiblack bias recruit some of these cognitive control areas to a greater extent than white individuals with less antiblack bias. They argue that this heightened activation results from the attempts of the more biased whites to mask their prejudice (see also Richeson & Shelton, 2003).

People who possess stigmatizing conditions that make them seem less than human, such as the homeless, also activate regions of the amygdala (Harris & Fiske, 2006), as do the physically unattractive and people with multiple facial piercings (Krendl et al., 2006). Considered together, it is clear that evaluating outgroup members involves activity of the amygdala. So, what does the amygdala do in the social context? It has long been thought to play a special role in responding to stimuli that elicit fear (Blanchard & Blanchard, 1972; Feldman Barrett & Wager, 2006; LeDoux, 1996). From this perspective, affective processing in the amygdala is a hard-wired circuit that has developed over the course of evolution to protect animals from danger. For example, much data support the notion that the amygdala is robustly activated in response to primary biologically relevant stimuli (e.g., faces, odors, and tastes), even when these stimuli remain below the subjects' reported level of awareness (e.g., Morris et al., 1998; Whalen et al., 1998).

However, many recent imaging studies have observed amygdala activity to stimuli of both negative and positive valence, indicating that the amygdala is not solely concerned with fear. Indeed, some have argued that the amygdala is important for drawing attention to novel stimuli that have biological relevance. For instance, Stephan Hamann and colleagues (2004) found that activity within the amygdala increased when both men and women viewed sexually arousing stimuli, such as short film clips of sexual activity or pictures of opposite-sex nudes. Under this argument, it is plausible that the amygdala plays a role in processing social emotions because they have direct relevance in maintaining long-term social relations, which has been argued to reflect a fundamental need that is biologically relevant. Whalen (1998, 2007) has argued that the amygdala is especially concerned with ambiguous stimuli that provide insufficient information to discern the nature of the threat. This may be why faces expressing fear activate the amygdala to a greater extent than do angry faces (Whalen et al., 2001).

Self-Regulation

A unique aspect of human behavior is the ability to regulate and control thoughts and actions, an ability commonly referred to as self-regulation. Self-regulation allows people to make plans, choose from alternatives, focus attention on the pursuit of goals, inhibit competing thoughts, and regulate social behavior (Baumeister, Heatherton, & Tice, 1994; Baumeister & Vohs, 2004; Metcalfe & Mischel, 1999; Wegner, 1994). Extensive evidence from neuroimaging and patient research demonstrates that the prefrontal cortex is imperative in successfully engaging self-regulatory processes, as befitting its label as "chief executive" of the brain (Goldberg, 2001). Abundant patient and neuroimaging research has identified discrete brain regions within the prefrontal cortex that are critical for self-regulation (for review, see Banfield, Wyland, Macrae, Münte, & Heatherton, 2004), primarily the dorsolateral prefrontal cortex (DLPFC; involved in modulating cognitive control), the orbitofrontal cortex (OFC; involved in integrating cognitive and affective information), and the anterior cingulate cortex (ACC; involved in conflict resolution).

The DLPFC has been associated with planning, novelty processing, choice, the control of memory and working memory, and language function (see D'Esposito et al., 1995; Dronkers, Redfern, & Knight, 2000; Fuster, Brodner, & Kroger, 2000; Goldman-Rakic, 1987). Damage to this area often results in patients' inability to inhibit certain behaviors (Pandya & Barnes, 1987). Damage to the OFC, which controls our behavioral and emotional output and how we interact with others (Dolan, 1999), often results in striking, and sometimes aggressive, behavioral changes (e.g., Rolls, Hornak, Wade, & McGrath, 1994). Damage to the OFC usually results in personality changes such as indifference, impaired social judgment and responsiveness, poor self-regulation, lack of impulse control, and poor judgment and insight (Damasio, 1994; Stone, Baron-Cohen, & Knight, 1998; Stuss & Alexander, 2000). Patients with OFC damage often cannot inhibit desires for instant gratification and thus may commit thefts or exhibit sexually aggressive behavior (Blumer & Benson, 1975; Grafman et al., 1996).

The ACC is essential for initiating actions, evaluating conflicts, and inhibiting prepotent responses, processes heavily involved in self-regulation (Kerns et al., 2004). The ACC is functionally dissociated into the dorsal (higher) ACC that evaluates cognitive conflict and the ventral (lower) ACC that evaluates emotional conflict (Bush, Luu, & Posner, 2000). Recall that the ventral ACC is active during social evaluation and rejection. The ACC is often engaged whenever any kind of "supervisory input" is required (Badgaiyan & Posner, 1998). In fact, it is widely accepted that the ACC is somehow involved in evaluating the degree and nature of conflict, whereas other parts of the brain (particularly the

PFC) may be involved in resolving the conflict itself (Botvinick, Cohen, & Carter, 2004; Cohen, Botvinick, & Carter, 2000; Kerns et al., 2004).

Emerging neuroimaging research has sought to identify more clearly the neural structures in self-regulation by examining the structures engaged in emotion and cognitive regulation. Ochsner, Bunge, Gross, and Gabrieli (2002) showed participants highly negative pictures and instructed them to either "attend" (study the picture and be aware of, but not try to alter, their feelings toward it) or "reappraise" (reinterpret the picture in such a way that it would no longer elicit a negative response) the photograph. The authors found that reappraising the photographs led to a decreased subjective negative affect, and this was reflected in a reduction of activity in the amygdala and OFC, and increased activation in the lateral and medial prefrontal cortex, as well as in the anterior cingulate cortex. Importantly, Ochsner et al. (2004) later observed that activity in the amygdala decreased when participants actively decreased their negative affect to the picture, and increased when they increased their negative affect.

Another important form of self-regulation that is critical for daily living is mental control (Wegner, 1989). Successfully controlling the contents of consciousness is a difficult task—worries intrude when people least desire them and it is not uncommon for the mind to wander when people should be focused on a particular task or objective. Functional neuroimaging studies have implicated the ACC in efforts to control personal thoughts (Wyland, Kelley, Macrae, Gordon, & Heatherton, 2003). More specifically, the ACC plays an important role in suppressing unwanted thoughts (Mitchell et al., 2007), such that it is transiently engaged following the occurrence of unwanted thoughts, whereas the dorsolateral PFC is most active during efforts to suppress those thoughts. This finding is in keeping with the important role of prefrontal regions in executive functions more generally, all of which are necessary for successful self-regulation (Miller & Cohen, 2001), and it also supports Wegner's (1994) model of ironic mental control. Since the case of Phineas Gage, we have known that damage to certain prefrontal regions is associated with a lack of impulse control and self-regulatory difficulties more generally. The role of lateral PFC regions in regulating social emotions appears to be among the most robust findings in social neuroscience.

Summary

Over the past two decades, the integration of cognitive neuroscience and social psychology has led to new insights into the neural basis of human social cognition. In beginning to examine the neural support of social behavior, researchers have sought to identify the neural bases of cognitive processes that allow humans to tap into the minds of others. It seems likely that the methods of cognitive neuroscience will contribute to our understanding of the social brain.

Acknowledgments

The work described in this chapter was supported by Grants NIMH 59282 and NIDA 022582. The authors would like to thank Jane V. Tucker for assistance with this chapter as well as Anne Krendl, Dylan Wagner, and Jason Mitchell for helpful discussions.

References

Adams, R. B., Rule, N. O., Franklin, R. G., Wang, E. J., Stevenson, M. R., Yoshikawa, S., Nomura, M., Sato, W., Kveraga, K., & Ambady, N. (2010). Cross-cultural reading the mind in the eyes: An fMRI investigation. *Journal of Cognitive Neuroscience, 22*, 97–108.

Adolphs, R. (2009). The social brain: Neural basis of social knowledge. *Annual Review of Psychology, 60*, 693–716.

Adolphs, R., Damasio, H., Tranel, D., Cooper, G., & Damasio, A. R. (2000). A role for somatosensory cortices in the visual recognition of emotion as revealed by three-dimensional lesion mapping. *Journal of Neuroscience, 20* (7), 2683–2690.

Allison, T., Puce, A., & McCarthy, G. (2000). Social perception from visual cues: Role of the STS region. *Trends in Cognitive Sciences, 4* (7), 267–278.

Allport, F. H. (1924). *Social psychology.* Cambridge, MA: Riverside Press.

Ames, D. L., Jenkins, A. C., Banaji, M. R., & Mitchell, J. P. (2008). Taking another's perspective increases self-referential neural processing. *Psychological Science, 19*, 642–644.

Amodio, D. M., & Frith, C. D. (2006). Meeting of the minds: The medial frontal cortex and social cognition. *Nature, 7*, 268–277.

Anonymous. (1851). Remarkable case of injury. *American Phrenological Journal, 13*, 89.

Aron, A., & Aron, E. N. (1996). *Self and self-expansion in relationships.* Hillsdale, NJ: Lawrence Erlbaum Associates, Inc.

Aron, A., Aron, E. N., Tudor, M., & Nelson, G. J. (1991). Close relationships as including other in the self. *Journal of Personality and Social Psychology, 60* (2), 241–253.

Aron, A., & Fraley, B. (1999). Relationship closeness as including other in the self: Cognitive underpinnings and measures. *Social Cognition. Special Issue: Social cognition and relationships, 17* (2), 140–160.

Atkinson, A. P., Dittrich, W. H., Gemmell, A. J., & Young, A. W. (2004). Emotion perception from dynamic and static body expressions in point-light and full-light displays. *Perception, 33* (6), 717–746.

Aue, T., Lavelle, L. A., & Cacioppo, J. T. (2009). Great expectations: What can fMRI research tell us about psychological phenomena? *International Journal of Psychophysiology, 73* (1), 10–16.

Badgaiyan, R., & Posner, M. (1998). Mapping the cingulate cortex in response selection and monitoring. *NeuroImage, 7*, 255–260.

Banfield, J. F., Wyland, C. L., Macrae, C. N., Münte, T. F., & Heatherton, T. F. (2004). *The cognitive neuroscience of self-regulation*. New York: Guilford Press.

Baron-Cohen, S. (1989). The autistic child's theory of mind: A case of specific developmental delay. *Journal of Child Psychology and Psychiatry, 30*, 285–297.

Baron-Cohen, S., Leslie, A. M., & Frith, U. (1985). Does the autistic child have a 'theory of mind'? *Cognition, 21*, 37–46.

Bartholow, B. D., & Amodio, D. M. (2009). Using event-related brain potentials in social psychological research: A brief review and tutorial. In E. Harmon-Jones & S. Beer (Eds.), *Methods in social neuroscience*. New York: Guilford Press.

Baumeister, R. F. (1998). *The self* (4th ed., Vol. 2). New York: McGraw-Hill.

Baumeister, R. F., Heatherton, T. F., & Tice, D. M. (1994). *Losing control: How and why people fail at self-regulation*. San Diego, CA: Academic Press.

Baumeister, R. F., & Leary, M. R. (1995). The need to belong: Desire for interpersonal attachments as a fundamental human motivation. *Psychological Bulletin, 117* (3), 497–529.

Baumeister, R. F., & Tice, D. M. (1988). Metatraits. *Journal of Personality, 56* (3), 571–598.

Baumeister, R. F., & Vohs, K. D. (2004). *Handbook of self-regulation: Research, theory, and applications*. New York: Guilford Press.

Beauchamp, M. S., Lee, K. E., Haxby, J. V., & Martin, A. (2002). Parallel visual motion processing streams for manipulable objects and human movements. *Neuron, 34* (1), 149–159.

Beaucousin, V., Lacheret, A., Turbelin, M., Morel, M., Mazoyer, B., & Tzourio-Mazoyer, N. (2007). FMRI study of emotional speech comprehension. *Cerebral Cortex, 17* (2), 339–352.

Beer, J. S., Heerey, E. A., Keltner, D., Scabini, D., & Knight, R. T. (2003). The regulatory function of self-conscious emotion: Insights from patients with orbitofrontal damage. *Journal of Personality and Social Psychology, 85*, 594–604.

Berns, G. S., Chappelow, J., Zink, C. F., Pagnoni, G., Martin-Skurski, M. E., & Richards, J. (2005). Neurobiological correlates of social conformity and independence during mental rotation. *Biological Psychiatry, 58* (3), 245–253.

Berntson, G. G., Cacioppo, J. T., & Quigley, K. S. (1991). Autonomic determinism: The modes of autonomic control, the doctrine of autonomic space, and the laws of autonomic constraint. *Psychological Review, 98* (4), 459–487.

Blanchard, D. C., & Blanchard, R. J. (1972). Innate and conditioned reactions to threat in rats with amygdaloid lesions. *Journal Comparative and Physiological Psychology, 81* (2), 281–290.

Blanke, O., Mohr, C., Michel C. M., Pascual-Leone, A., Brugger, P., Seeck, M., et al. (2005). Linking out-of-body experience and self processing to mental own-body imagery at the temporoparietal junction. *Journal of Neuroscience, 25*, 550–557.

Blumer, D., & Benson, D. (1975). *Personality changes with frontal and temporal lesions.* New York: Grune & Stratton.

Botvinick, M. M., Cohen, J. D., & Carter, C. S. (2004). Conflict monitoring and anterior cingulate cortex: An update. *Trends in Cognitive Sciences, 8* (12), 539–546.

Bower, G. H., & Gilligan, S. G. (1979). Remembering information related to one's self. *Journal of Research in Personality, 13*, 420–432.

Bowlby, J. (1969). *Attachment and loss* (Vol. 1). New York: Basic Books.

Buckner, R. L., Kelley, W. M., & Petersen, S. E. (1999). Frontal cortex contributes to human memory formation. *Nature Neuroscience, 2*, 311–314.

Burklund, L. J., Eisenberger, N. I., & Lieberman, M. D. (2007). The face of rejection: Rejection sensitivity moderates dorsal anterior cingulated activity to disapproving facial expressions. *Social Neuroscience, 2*, 238–253.

Bush, G., Luu, P., & Posner, M. I. (2000). Cognitive and emotional influences in anterior cingulate cortex. *Trends in Cognitive Sciences, 4* (6), 215–222.

Cacioppo, J. T., Amaral, D. G., Blanchard, J. J., Cameron, J. L., Carter, C. S., Crews, D., Fiske, S., Heatherton, T., Johnson, M. K., Kozak, M. J., Levenson, R. W., Lord, C., Miller, E. K., Ochsner, K., Raichle, M. E., Shea, M. T., Taylor, S. E., Young, L. J., & Quinn, K. J. (2007). Social neuroscience: Progress and implications for mental health. *Perspectives on Psychological Science, 2* (2), 99–123.

Cacioppo, J. T., & Berntson, G. G. (1992). Social psychological contributions to the decade of the brain: Doctrine of multilevel analysis. *American Psychologist, 47* (8), 1019–1028.

Cacioppo, J. T., Berntson, G. G., & Crites, S. L., Jr. (1996). In E. T. Higgins & A. Kruglanski (Eds.), *Social psychology: Handbook of basic principles* (pp. 72–101). New York: Guilford Press.

Cacioppo, J. T., Berntson, G. G., Lorig, T. S., Norris, C. J., Rickett, E., & Nusbaum, H. (2003). Just because you're imaging the brain doesn't mean you can stop using your head: A primer and set of first principles. *Journal of Personality and Social Psychology, 85*, 650–661.

Cacioppo, J. T., Berntson, G. G., & Nusbaum, H. C. (2008). Neuroimaging as a new tool in the toolbox of psychological science. *Current Directions in Psychological Science, 17* (2), 62–67.

Cacioppo, J. T., Hughes, M. E., Waite, L. J., Hawkley, L. C., & Thisted, R. A. (2006). Loneliness as a specific risk factor for depressive symptoms: Cross-sectional and longitudinal analyses. *Psychology and Aging, 21,* 140–151.

Cacioppo, J. T., & Petty, R. E. (1981). Electromyograms as measures of extent and affectivity of information processing. *American Psychologist, 36* (5), 441–456.

Campbell, W. K., Krusmark, E. A., Dyckman, K. A., Brunell, A. B., McDowell, J. E., Twenge, J. M., & Clementz, B. A. (2006). A magnetoencephalography investigation of neural correlates for social exclusion and self-control. *Social Neuroscience, 1* (2), 124–134.

Castelli, F., Happé, F., & Frith, U. (2002). Movement and mind: A functional imaging study of perception and interpretation of complex intentional movement patterns. *NeuroImage, 12,* 314–325.

Chiao, J. Y., Harada, T., Komeda, H., Li, Z., Mano, Y., Saito, D., Parrish, T. B., Sadato, N., & Iidaka, T. (2010). Dynamic cultural influences on neural representations of the self. *Journal of Cognitive Neuroscience, 22* (1), 1–11.

Clarke, T. J., Bradshaw, M. F., Field, D. T., Hampson, S. E., & Rose, D. (2005). The perception of emotion from body movement in point-light displays of interpersonal dialogue. *Perception, 34* (10), 1171–1180.

Cloutier, J., Heatherton, T. F., Whalen, P. J., & Kelley, W. M. (2008). Are attractive people rewarding? Sex differences in the neural substrates of facial attractiveness. *Journal of Cognitive Neuroscience, 20* (6), 941–951.

Cohen, J. D., Botvinick, M., & Carter, C. S. (2000). Anterior cingulate and prefrontal cortex: Who's in control? *Nature Neuroscience, 3,* 421–423.

Craik, F. I. M., Moroz, T. M., Moscovitch, M., Stuss, D. T., Winocur, G., Tulving, E., & Kapur, S. (1999). In search of the self: A positron emission tomography study. *Psychological Science, 10* (1), 26–34.

Cunningham, W. A., Johnson, M. K., Raye, C. L., Gatenby, C. J., Gore, J. C., & Banaji, M. R. (2004). Separable neural components in the processing of black and white faces. *Psychological Science, 15,* 806–813.

Cunningham, W. A., & Zelazo, P. D. (2007). Attitudes and evaluations: A social cognitive neuroscience perspective. *Trends in Cognitive Sciences, 11* (3), 97–104.

Dakin, S., & Frith, U. (2005). Vagaries of visual perception in autism. *Neuron, 48,* 497–507.

Damasio, A. R. (1994). Descartes' error and the future of human life. *Scientific American, 271,* 144.

Demb, J. B., Desmond, J. E., Wagner, A. D., Vaidya, C. J., Glover, G. H., & Gabrieli, J. D. E. (1995). Semantic encoding and retrieval in the left inferior prefrontal cortex: A functional MRI study of task difficulty and process specificity. *Journal of Neuroscience, 15,* 5870–5878.

D'Esposito, M., Detre, J. A., Alsop, D. C., Shin, R. K., Atlas, S., & Grossman, M. (1995). The neural basis of the central executive system of working memory. *Nature, 378,* 279–281.

Dolan, R. J. (1999). On the neurology of morals. *Nature Neuroscience, 2,* 927–929.

Dronkers, N. F., Redfern, B. B., & Knight, R. T. (2000). *The neural architecture of language disorders.* Cambridge, MA: MIT Press.

Duchaine, B., & Nakayama, K. (2005). Dissociations of face and object recognition in developmental prosopagnosia. *Journal of Cognitive Neuroscience, 17,* 249–261.

Duchaine, B., Parker, H., & Nakayama, K. (2003). Normal emotion recognition in a prosopagnosic. *Perception, 32,* 827–838.

Eberhardt, J. L. (2005). Imaging race. *American Psychologist, 60,* 181–190.

Eisenberger, N. I., Lieberman, M. D., & Williams, K. D. (2003). Does rejection hurt? An fMRI study of social exclusion. *Science, 302* (5643), 290–292.

Ekman, P. (1992). Facial expressions of emotion: An old controversy and new findings. *Philosophical Transactions of the Royal Society, London, B335,* 63–69.

Epley, N., & Waytz, A. (2009). Mind perception. In S. T. Fiske, D. T. Gilbert, & G. Lindzey (Eds.), *The handbook of social psychology* (5th ed.). New York: Wiley.

Feldman Barrett, L., & Wager, T. D. (2006). The structure of emotion: Evidence from neuroimaging studies. *Current Directions in Psychological Science, 15,* 79–83.

Fellows, L. K., & Farah, M. J. (2007). The role of ventromedial prefrontal cortex in decision making: Judgment under uncertainty or judgment per se? *Cerebral Cortex, 17* (11), 2669–2674.

Fiske, S. T., & Taylor, S. E. (1991). *Social cognition* (2nd ed.). New York: McGraw-Hill.

Fossati, P., Hevenor, S. J., Graham, S. J., Grady, C., Keightley, M. L., Craik, F., et al. (2003). In search of the emotional self: An fMRI study using positive and negative emotional words. *American Journal of Psychiatry, 160* (11), 1938–1945.

Fossati, P., Hevenor, S. J., Lepage, M., Graham, S. J., Grady, C., Keightley, M. L., et al. (2004). Distributed self in episodic memory: Neural correlates of successful retrieval of self-encoded positive and negative personality traits. *NeuroImage, 22* (4), 1596–1604.

Frith, C. (2008). The social brain. In N. Emery, N. Clayton, and C. Frith (Eds.), *Social intelligence: From brain to culture.* Oxford: Oxford University Press.

Frith, C. D., & Frith, U. (1999). Interacting minds—a biological basis. *Science, 286,* 1692–1695.

Fuster, J. M., Brodner, M., & Kroger, J. K. (2000). Cross-modal and cross-temporal associations in neurons of frontal cortex. *Nature, 405,* 347–351.

Gabrieli, J. D. E., Desmond, J. E., Demb, J. B., Wagner, A. D., Stone, M. V., Vaidya, C. J., et al. (1996). Functional magnetic resonance imaging of semantic memory processes in the frontal lobes. *Psychological Science, 7,* 278–283.

Gallagher, H. L., & Frith, C. D. (2003). Functional imaging of 'theory of mind.' *Trends in Cognitive Sciences, 7* (5), 77–83.

Gardner, W. L., Pickett, C. L., & Brewer, M. B. (2000). Social exclusion and selective memory: How the need to belong influences memory for social events. *Personality and Social Psychology Bulletin, 26,* 486–496.

Gardner, W. L., Pickett, C. L., Jefferis, V., & Knowles, M. (2005). On the outside looking in: Loneliness and social monitoring. *Personality and Social Psychology Bulletin, 31,* 1549–1560.

Gazzaniga, M. S. (Ed.) (2009). *The cognitive neurosciences* (4th ed.). Cambridge, MA: MIT Press.

Gillihan, S. J., & Farah, M. J. (2005). Is self special? A critical review of evidence from experimental psychology and cognitive neuroscience. *Psychological Bulletin, 13* (1), 76–97.

Goldberg, E. (2001). *The executive brain: The frontal lobes and the civilized mind.* New York: Oxford University Press.

Goldman-Rakic, P. S. (1987). Development of cortical circuitry and cognitive function. *Child Development, 58,* 601–622.

Goren, C., Sarty, M., & Wu, P. (1975). Visual following and pattern discrimination of face-like stimuli by newborn infants. *Pediatrics, 56,* 544–549.

Grafman, J., Schwab, K., Warden, D., Pridgen, A., Brown, H. R., & Salazar, A. M. (1996). Frontal lobe injuries, violence, and aggression: A report of the Vietnam Head Injury Study. *Neurology, 46,* 1231–1238.

Greenwald, A. G., & Banaji, M. R. (1989). The self as a memory system: Powerful, but ordinary. *Journal of Personality and Social Psychology, 57* (1), 41–54.

Grossman, E. D., Battelli, L., & Pascual-Leone, A. (2005). Repetitive TMS over posterior STS disrupts perception of biological motion. *Vision Research, 45* (22), 2847–2853.

Gusnard, D. A. (2005). Being a self: Considerations from functional imaging. *Consciousness and Cognition, 14,* 679–697.

Hamann, S., Herman, R. A., Nolan, C. L., & Wallen, K. (2004). Men and women differ in amygdala response to visual sexual stimuli. *Nature Neuroscience, 7* (4), 411–416.

Harlow, J. M. (1868). Recovery from the passage of an iron bar through the head. *Publications of the Massachusetts Medical Society, 2,* 327–347.

Harmer, C. J., Thilo, K. V., Rothwell, J. C., & Goodwin, G. M. (2001). Transcranial magnetic stimulation of medial-frontal cortex impairs the processing of angry facial expressions. *Nature Neuroscience, 4* (1), 17–18.

Harris, L. T., & Fiske, S. T. (2006). Dehumanizing the lowest of the low: Neuroimaging responses to extreme out-groups. *Psychological Science, 17,* 847–853.

Haxby, J. V., Hoffman, E. A., & Gobbini, M. I. (2000). The distributed human neural system for face perception. *Trends in Cognitive Sciences, 4,* 223–233.

Heatherton, T. F., Macrae, C. N., & Kelley, W. M. (2004). What the social brain sciences can tell us about the self. *Current Directions in Psychological Science, 13* (5), 190–193.

Heatherton, T. F., Wyland, C., Macrae, C. N., Denny, B. T., Demos, K. D., & Kelley, W. M. (2006). Friends among us? Medial prefrontal activity is specific for self-referential processing. Unpublished manuscript.

Heberlein, A. S., & Adolphs, R., Tranel, D., & Damasio, H. (2004). Cortical regions for judgments of emotions and personality traits from point-light walkers. *Journal of Cognitive Neuroscience, 16,* 1143–1158.

Heider, F., & Simmel, M. (1944). An experimental study of apparent behavior. *American Journal of Psychology, 57,* 243–259.

Hoekert, M., Kahn, R. S., Pijnenborg, M., & Aleman, A. (2007). Impaired recognition and expression of emotional prosody in schizophrenia: Review and meta-analysis. *Schizophrenia Research, 96,* 135–145.

Ishai, A., Ungerleider, L., Martin, A., Maisog, J. M. & Haxby, J. V. (1997). fMRI reveals differential activation in the ventral object vision pathway during the perception of faces, houses, and chairs. *NeuroImage, 5,* S149.

Ito, T. A., Thompson, E., & Cacioppo, J. T. (2004). Tracking the timecourse of social perception: The effects of racial cues on event-related brain potentials. *Personality and Social Psychology Bulletin, 30* (10), 1267–1280.

Jacobsen, T., Schubotz, R. I., Höfel, L., & von Cramon, D. Y. (2006). Brain correlates of aesthetic judgment of beauty. *NeuroImage, 29,* 276–285.

Jahanshahi, M., & Rothwell, J. (2000). Transcranial magnetic stimulation studies of cognition: An emerging field. *Experimental Brain Research, 131* (1), 1–9.

Janata, P. (2009). The neural architecture of music-evoked autobiographical memories. *Cerebral Cortex, 19*(11), 2579–2594.

Jenkins, A. C., Macrae, C. N., & Mitchell, J. P. (2008). Repetition suppression of ventromedial prefrontal activity during judgments of self and others. *Proceedings of the National Academy of Sciences, 105,* 4507–4512.

Johansson, G. (1973). Visual perception of biological motion and a model for its analysis. *Perception and Psychophysics, 14,* 201–211.

Johnson, M. H., Dziurawiec, S., Ellis, H. & Morton, J. (1991). Newborns' preferential tracking of face-like stimuli and its subsequent decline. *Cognition, 40,* 1–19.

Johnson, S. C., Baxter, L. C., Wilder, L. S., Pipe, J. G., Heiserman, J. E., & Prigatano, G. P. (2002). Neural correlates of self-reflection. *Brain, 125* (Pt. 8), 1808–1814.

Kanwisher, N., McDermott, J., & Chun, M. M. (1997). The fusiform face area: A module in human extrastriate cortex specialized for face perception. *Journal of Neuroscience, 17,* 4302– 4311.

Kapur, S., Tulving, E., Cabeza, R., McIntosh, A. R., Sylvain, H. A., Fergus, I. M., et al. (1996). The neural correlates of intentional learning of verbal materials: A PET study in humans. *Cognitive Brain Research, 4*(4), 243–249.

Kelley, W. M., Macrae, C. N., Wyland, C. L., Caglar, S., Inati, S., & Heatherton, T. F. (2002). Finding the self?: An event-related fMRI study. *Journal of Cognitive Neuroscience, 14* (5), 785–794.

Kelley, W. M., Miezin, F. M., McDermott, K. B., Buckner, R. L., Raichle, M. E., Cohen, N. J., et al. (1998). Hemispheric specialization in human dorsal frontal cortex and medial temporal lobe for verbal and nonverbal memory encoding. *Neuron, 20* (5), 927–936.

Kerns, J. G., Cohen, J. D., MacDonald, A. W., Cho, R. Y., Stenger, V. A., & Carter, C. S. (2004). Anterior cingulate conflict monitoring and adjustments in control. *Science, 303* (5660), 1023–1026.

Klein, S. B. (2004). *The cognitive neuroscience of knowing one's self* (Vol. 3). Cambridge: Massachusetts Institute of Technology.

Klein, S. B., Cosmides, L., & Costabile, K. A. (2003). Preserved knowledge of self in a case of Alzheimer's dementia. *Social Cognition, 21*, 157–165.

Klein, S. B., & Kihlstrom, J. F. (1986). Elaboration, organization, and the self-reference effect in memory. *Journal of Experimental Psychology: General, 115*, 26–38.

Klein, S. B., & Kihlstrom, J. F. (1998). On bridging the gap between social-personality psychology and neuropsychology. *Personality & Social Psychology Review, 2*, 228–242.

Klein, S. B., & Loftus, J. (1988). The nature of self-referent encoding: The contributions of elaborative and organizational processes. *Journal of Personality and Social Psychology, 55*, 5–11.

Kranz, F., & Ishai, A. (2006). Face perception is modulated by sexual preference. *Current Biology, 16*, 63–68.

Krendl, A. K., & Heatherton, T. F. (2009). Self versus others/self-regulation. In G. G. Berntson & J. T. Cacioppo (Eds.), *Handbook of neuroscience for the behavioral sciences*. Hoboken, NJ: John Wiley & Sons.

Krendl, A. C., Macrae, C. N., Kelley, W. M., Fugelsang, J. F., & Heatherton, T. F. (2006). The good, the bad, and the ugly: An fMRI investigation of the functional anatomic correlates of stigma. *Social Neuroscience, 1*, 5–15.

Krendl, A. C., Richeson, J. A., Kelley, W. M., & Heatherton, T. F. (2008). The negative consequences of threat: An fMRI investigation of the neural mechanisms underlying women's underperformance in math. *Psychological Science, 19* (2), 168–175.

Kriegeskorte, N., Formisano, E., Sorger, B., & Goebel, R. (2007). Individual faces elicit distinct response patterns in human anterior temporal cortex. *Proceedings of the National Academy of Sciences, 104*, 20600–20605.

Kross, E., Egner, T., Ochsner, K., Hirsch, J., & Downey, G. (2007). Neural dynamics of rejection sensitivity. *Journal of Cognitive Neuroscience, 19*, 945–956

Lanzetta, J. T., & Kleck, R. E. (1970). Encoding and decoding of nonverbal affect in humans. *Journal of Personality and Social Psychology, 16* (1), 12–19.

Leary, M. R., Tambor, E. S., Terdal, S. K., & Downs, D. L. (1995). Self-esteem as an interpersonal monitor: The sociometer hypothesis. *Journal of Personality and Social Psychology, 68* (3), 518–530.

LeDoux, J. E. (1996). *The emotional brain*. New York: Simon & Schuster.

Legrand, D., & Ruby, P. (2009). What is self-specific? Theoretical investigation and critical review of neuroimaging results. *Psychological Review, 116* (1), 252–282.

Lieberman, M. D. (2009). Social cognitive neuroscience. In S. T. Fiske, D. T. Gilbert, & G. Lindzey (Eds.), *The handbook of social psychology* (5th ed.). New York: Wiley.

Macdonald, G., & Leary, M. R. (2005). Why does social exclusion hurt? The relationship between social and physical pain. *Psychological Bulletin, 131*, 202–223.

Macmillan, M. (2000). *An odd kind of fame: Stories of Phineas Gage*. Cambridge, MA: MIT Press.

Macrae, C. N., Heatherton, T. F., & Kelley, W. M. (2004). *A self less ordinary: The medial prefrontal cortex and you* (3rd ed.). Cambridge, MA: MIT Press.

Macrae, C. N., Moran, J. M., Heatherton, T. F., Banfield, J. F., & Kelley, W. M. (2004). Medial prefrontal activity predicts memory for self. *Cerebral Cortex, 14* (6), 647–654.

Maki, R. H., & McCaul, K. D. (1985). The effects of self-reference versus other reference on the recall of traits and nouns. *Bulletin of the Psychonomic Society, 23*, 169–172.

Markus, H. (1977). Self-schemata and processing information about the self. *Journal of Personality and Social Psychology, 35*, 63–78.

Markus, H. R., & Kitayama, S. (1991). Culture of the self: Implications for cognition, emotion, and motivation. *Psychological Review, 98* (2), 224–253.

Martin, A., & Weisberg, J. (2003). Neural foundations for understanding social and mechanical concepts. *Cognitive Neuropsychology, 20* (3–6), 575–587.

Mason, M. F., Banfield, J. F., & Macrae, C. N. (2004). Thinking about actions: The neural substrates of person knowledge. *Cerebral Cortex, 14*, 209–214.

Masten, C. L., Eisenberger, N. I., Borofsky, L.A., Pfeifer, J.H., McNealy, K., Mazziotta, J.C., et al. (2009). Neural correlates of social exclusion during adolescence: Understanding the distress of peer rejection. *Social Cognitive Affective Neuroscience, 4*, 143–157.

McCarthy, G., Puce, A., Gore, J. C., & Allison, T. (1997). Face-specific processing in the human fusiform gyrus. *Journal of Cognitive Neuroscience, 9*, 604–609.

Meltzoff, A. N. (1995). Understanding the intention of others: Re-enactment of intended acts by 18-month-old children. *Developmental Psychology, 31*, 838–850.

Mendes, W. B., Blascovich, J., Hunter, S., Lickel, B., & Jost, J. (2007). Threatened by the unexpected: Challenge and threat during inter-ethnic interactions. *Journal of Personality and Social Psychology, 92*, 698–716.

Metcalfe, J., & Mischel, W. (1999). A hot/cool-system analysis of delay of gratification: Dynamics of willpower. *Psychological Review, 106* (1), 3–19.

Miller, E. K., & Cohen, J. D. (2001). An integrative theory of prefrontal cortex function. *Annual Review of Neuroscience, 24*, 167–202.

Mitchell, J. P. (2006). Mentalizing and Marr: An information processing approach to the study of social cognition. *Brain Research, 1079* (1), 66–75.

Mitchell, J. P. (2008). Activity in right temporo-parietal junction is not selective for theory-of-mind. *Cerebral Cortex, 18*, 262–271.

Mitchell, J. P. (2009). Social psychology as a natural kind. *Trends in Cognitive Sciences, 13* (6), 246–251.

Mitchell, J. P., Banaji, M. R., & Macrae, C. N. (2005). General and specific contributions of the medial prefrontal cortex to knowledge about mental states. *NeuroImage, 28* (4), 757–762.

Mitchell, J. P., & Heatherton, T. F. (2009). Components of a social brain. In M.S. Gazzaniga (Ed.), *The cognitive neurosciences* (4th ed., pp. 951–958). Cambridge, MA: MIT Press.

Mitchell, J. P., Heatherton, T. F., Kelley, W. M., Wyland, C. L., Wegner, D. M., & Neil Macrae, C. (2007). Separating sustained from transient aspects of cognitive control during thought suppression. *Psychological Science, 18* (4), 292–297.

Mitchell, J. P., Heatherton, T. F., & Macrae, C. N. (2002). Distinct neural systems subserve person and object knowledge. *Proceedings of the National Academy of Sciences, 99*, 15238–15243.

Mitchell, J. P., Macrae, C. N., & Banaji, M. R. (2006). Dissociable medial prefrontal contributions to judgments of similar and dissimilar others. *Neuron, 50*, 655–663.

Moran, J. M., Macrae, S. N., Heatherton, T. F., Wyland, C. L., & Kelley, W. M. (2006). Neuroanatomical evidence for distinct cognitive and affective components of self. *Journal of Cognitive Neuroscience, 18*, 1586–1594.

Morris, J. S., Öhman, A., & Dolan, R. J. (1998). Conscious and unconscious emotional learning in the human amygdala. *Nature, 393*, 467–470.

Norris, C. J., Chen, E. E., Zhu, D. C., Small, S. L., & Cacioppo, J. T. (2004). The interaction of social and emotional processes in the brain. *Journal of Cognitive Neuroscience, 16*, 1818–1829.

Northoff, G., Heinzel, A., de Greck, M., Bermpohl, F., Dobrowolny, H., & Panskepp, J. (2006). Self-referential processing in our brain. *NeuroImage, 31* (1), 440–457.

Ochsner, K. N. (2007). Social cognitive neuroscience: Historical development, core principles, and future promise. In A. Kruglanski & E. T. Higgins (Eds.), *Social psychology: A handbook of basic principles* (2nd ed., pp. 39–66). New York: Guilford Press.

Ochsner, K. N., Beer, J. S., Robertson, E. R., Cooper, J. C., Gabrieli, J. D., Kihsltrom, J. F., et al. (2005). The neural correlates of direct and reflected self-knowledge. *NeuroImage, 28* (4), 797–814.

Ochsner, K. N., Bunge, S. A., Gross, J. J., & Gabrieli, J. D. (2002). Rethinking feelings: An FMRI study of the cognitive regulation of emotion. *Journal of Cognitive Neuroscience, 14*, 1215–1229.

Ochsner, K. N., & Lieberman, M. D. (2001). The emergence of social cognitive neuroscience. *American Psychologist, 56*, 717–734.

Ochsner, K. N., Ray, R. D., Cooper, J. C., Robertson, E. R., Chopra, S., Gabrieli, J. D. E., et al. (2004). For better or for worse: Neural systems supporting the cognitive down- and up-regulation of negative emotion. *NeuroImage, 2*, 483–499.

O'Doherty, J., Winston, J., Critchley, H., Perret, D., Burt, D., & Dolan, R. (2003). Beauty in a smile: The role of orbitofrontal cortex in facial attractiveness. *Neuropsychologia, 41*, 147–155.

Olson, I. R., Plotzker, A., & Ezzyat, Y. (2007). The enigmatic temporal pole: A review of findings on social and emotional processing. *Brain, 130*, 1718–1731.

Oosterhof, N. N., & Todorov, A. (2008). The functional basis of face evaluation. *Proceedings of the National Academy of Sciences of the USA, 105*, 11087–11092.

Pandya, D. N., & Barnes, C. L. (1987). *Architecture and connections of the frontal lobe.* New York: IRBN Press.

Peyron, R., Laurent, B., & Garcia-Larrea, L. (2000). Functional imaging of brain responses to pain. A review and meta-analysis. *Clinical Neurophysiology, 30,* 263–288.

Pfeifer, J. H., Lieberman, M. D., & Dapretto, M. (2007). "I know you are but what am ?!": Neural bases of self- and social knowledge in children and adults. *Journal of Cognitive Neuroscience, 19,* 1323–1337.

Phelps, E. A., O'Connor, K. J., Cunningham, W. A., Funayama, E. S., Gatenby, J. C., Gore, J. C., et al. (2000). Performance on indirect measures of race evaluation predicts amygdala activation. *Journal of Cognitive Neuroscience, 12,* 729–738.

Phillips, M. L., Young, A. W., Senior, C., Brammer, M., Andrew, C., Calder, A. J., et al. (1997). A specific neural substrate for perceiving facial expressions of disgust. *Nature, 389,* 495–498.

Pickett, C. L., Gardner, W. L., & Knowles, M. (2004). Getting a cue: The need to belong and enhanced sensitivity to social cues. *Personality and Social Psychology Bulletin, 30,* 1095–1107.

Pollick, F. E., Lestou, V., Ryu, J., & Cho, S. B. (2002). Estimating the efficiency of recognizing gender and affect from biological motion. *Vision Research, 42* (20), 2345–2355.

Pourtois, G., Sander, D., Andres, M., Grandjean, D., Reveret, L., Olivier, E., et al. (2004). Dissociable roles of the human somatosensory and superior temporal cortices for processing social face signals. *European Journal of Neuroscience, 20* (12), 3507–3515.

Quadflieg, S., Turk, D. J., Waiter, G. D., Mitchell, J. P., Jenkins, A. C., & Macrae, C. N. (2009). Exploring the neural correlates of social stereotyping. *Journal of Cognitive Neuroscience, 21* (8), 1560–1570.

Richeson, J. A., Baird, A. A., Gordon, H. L., Heatherton, T. F., Wyland, C. L., Trawalter, S., et al. (2003). An fMRI investigation of the impact of interracial contact on executive function. *Nature Neuroscience, 6,* 1323–1328.

Richeson, J. A., & Shelton, J. N. (2003). When prejudice does not pay: Effects of interracial contact on executive function. *Psychological Science, 14,* 287–290.

Rogers, T. B., Kuiper, N. A., & Kirker, W. S. (1977). Self-reference and the encoding of personal information. *Journal of Personality and Social Psychology, 35,* 677–688.

Rolls, E. T., Hornak, J., Wade, D., & McGrath, J. (1994). Emotion-related learning in patients with social and emotional changes associated with frontal lobe damage. *Journal of Neurology, Neurosurgery & Psychiatry, 57* (2), 1518–1524.

Saxe, R., & Kanwisher, N. (2003). People thinking about thinking people: The role of the temporo-parietal junction in theory of mind. *NeuroImage, 19,* 1835–1842.

Saxe, R., & Powell, L. J. (2006). It's the thought that counts: Specific brain regions for one component of theory of mind. *Psychological Science, 17,* 692–699.

Schmitz, T. W., Kawahara-Baccus, T. N., & Johnson, S. C. (2004). Metacognitive evaluation, self-relevance, and the right prefrontal cortex. *NeuroImage, 22* (2), 941–947.

Seger, C. A., Stone, M., & Keenan, J. P. (2004). Cortical activations during judgments about the self and an other person. *Neuropsychologia, 42* (9), 1168–1177.

Simion, F., Regolin, L., & Bulf, H. (2008). A predisposition for biological motion in the newborn baby. *Proceedings of the National Academy of Sciences, 105*, 809–813.

Simpson, J. R. Jr., Drevets, W. C., Snyder, A. Z., Gusnard, D. A., & Raichle, M. E. (2001). Emotion-induced changes in human medial prefrontal cortex: II. During anticipatory anxiety. *Proceedings of the National Academy of Sciences, 98*, 688–693.

Smart Richman, L., & Leary, M. R. (2009). Reactions to discrimination, stigmatization, ostracism, and other forms of interpersonal rejection: A multimotive model. *Psychological Review, 116* (2), 365–383.

Somerville, L. H., Heatherton, T. F., & Kelley, W. M. (2006). Disambiguating anterior cingulate cortex function: Differential response to experiences of expectancy violation and social rejection. *Nature Neuroscience, 9*, 1007–1008.

Stone, V. E., Baron-Cohen, S., & Knight, R. T. (1998). Frontal lobe contributions to theory of mind. *Journal of Cognitive Neuroscience, 10* (5), 640–656.

Stuss, D. T., & Alexander, M. P. (2000). Executive functions and the frontal lobes: A conceptual view. *Psychology Research, 63* (3–4), 289–298.

Symons, C. S., & Johnson, B. T. (1997). The self-reference effect in memory: A meta-analysis. *Psychological Bulletin, 121*, 371–394.

Todorov, A., Harris, L. T., & Fiske, S. T. (2006). Toward socially inspired social neuroscience. *Brain Research, 1079* (1), 76–85.

Tomaka, J., Blascovich, J., Kelsey, R. M., & Leitten, C. L. (1993). Subjective, physiological, and behavioral effects of threat and challenge appraisal. *Journal of Personality and Social Psychology, 65* (2), 248–260.

Tranel, D., Damasio, A. R., & Damasio, H. (1998). Intact recognition of facial expression, gender and age in patients with impaired recognition of face identity. *Neurology, 38*, 690–696.

Turk, D. J., Heatherton, T. F., Macrae, C. N., Kelley, W. M., & Gazzaniga, M. S. (2003). Out of contact, out of mind: The distributed nature of the self. *Annals of the New York Academy of Sciences, 1001*, 65–78.

von Kriegstein, K., & Giraud, A. L. (2004). Distinct functional substrates along the right superior temporal sulcus for the processing of voices. *NeuroImage, 22*, 948–955.

von Kriegstein, K., Kleinschmidt, A., & Giraud, A. L. (2006). Voice recognition and cross-modal responses to familiar speakers' voices in prosopagnosia. *Cerebral Cortex, 16*, 1314–1322.

Vouloumanos, A., & Werker, J. F. (2007). Listening to language at birth: Evidence for a bias for speech in neonates. *Developmental Science, 10*, 159–164.

Vul, E., Harris, C., Winkielman, P., & Pashler, H. (2009). Puzzlingly high correlations in fMRI studies of emotion, personality, and social cognition. *Perspectives on Psychological Science, 4* (3), 274–290.

Wagner, A. D., Schacter, D. L., Rotte, M., Koutstaal, W., Maril, A., Dale, A. M., et al. (1998). Building memories: Remembering and forgetting of verbal experiences as predicted by brain activity. *Science, 281*, 1188–1191.

Walsh, V., & Cowey, A. (2000). Transcranial magnetic stimulation and cognitive neuroscience. *Nature Reviews Neuroscience, 1* (1), 73–79.

Wegner, D. M. (1989). *White bears and other unwanted thoughts: Suppression, obsession, and the psychology of mind control.* New York: Guilford Press.

Wegner, D. M. (1994). Ironic processes of mental control. *Psychological Review, 10* (1), 34–52.

Whalen, P. J. (1998). Fear, vigilance, and ambiguity: Initial neuroimaging studies of the human amygdala. *Current Directions in Psychological Science, 7,* 177–188.

Whalen, P. J. (2007). The uncertainty of it all. *Trends in Cognitive Sciences, 11,* 499–500.

Whalen, P. J., Kagan, J., Cook, R. G., Davis, F. C., Kim, H., Polis, S., et al. (2004). Human amygdala responsivity to masked fearful eye whites. *Science, 306* (5704), 2061.

Whalen, P. J., Rauch, S. L., Etcoff, N. L., McInerney, S. C., Lee, M. B., & Jenike, M. A. (1998). Masked presentations of emotional facial expressions modulate amygdala activity without explicit knowledge. *Journal of Neuroscience, 18* (1), 411–418.

Whalen, P. J., Shin, L. M., McInerney, S. C., Fischer, H., Wright, C. I., & Rauch, S. L. (2001). A functional MRI study of human amygdala responses to facial expressions of fear versus anger. *Emotion, 1* (1), 70–83.

Wheatley, T., Milleville, S. C., & Martin, A. (2007). Understanding animate agents: Distinct roles for the social network and mirror system. *Psychological Science, 18,* 469–474.

Wheeler, M. E., & Fiske, S. T. (2005). Controlling racial prejudice: Social-cognitive goals affect amygdala and stereotype activation. *Psychological Science, 16,* 56–63.

Wig, G. S., Grafton, S. T., Demos, K. E., & Kelley, W. M. (2005). Reductions in neural activity underlie behavioral components of repetition priming. *Nature Neuroscience, 8* (9), 1228–1233.

Woodward, A. L. (1998). Infants selectively encode the goal object of an actor's reach. *Cognition, 69,* 1–34.

Wyland, C. L., Kelley, W. M., Macrae, C. N., Gordon, H. L., & Heatherton, T. F. (2003). Neural correlates of thought suppression. *Neuropsychologia, 41* (14), 1863–1867.

Zhu, Y., Zhang, L., Fan, L., & Han, S. (2007). Neural basis of cultural influence on self-representation. *NeuroImage, 34,* 1310–1316.

Zysset, S., Huber, O., Ferstl, E., & von Cramon, D. Y. (2002). The anterior frontomedian cortex and evaluative judgment: An fMRI study. *NeuroImage, 15,* 983–991.

Chapter 17

Evolutionary Social Psychology

Jon K. Maner and Douglas T. Kenrick

Women in long-term romantic relationships are sometimes inclined to cheat on their partner with another man, particularly when the woman is ovulating and when the other man displays signs of high genetic quality. On the other side of this equation, when women are ovulating, their male partners tend to guard those women from other men inclined to compete for the women's affections. People learn to fear snakes and spiders more quickly than they do guns and knives, even though the latter pose much greater threats to physical safety. When a woman encounters a strange man who physically resembles her, she is likely to judge that man as a desirable friend but not as a desirable sexual partner—as trustworthy but not lustworthy.

These research findings, and many others like them, are difficult to explain—even in hindsight—with most conventional social psychological theories. Yet each was predicted from the framework of evolutionary social psychology (DeBruine, 2005; Haselton & Gangestad, 2006; Öhman & Mineka, 2001). An evolutionary perspective implies that many thoughts, feelings, and behaviors of people are caused, in part, by biological mechanisms that have been shaped by thousands of generations of evolution. From romantic relationships, friendship, and prosocial behavior to fear, aggression, and intergroup prejudice, the principles of evolutionary psychology can provide a deeper understanding of most important topics in social psychology (see Buss, 2005; Cosmides, Tooby, & Barkow, 1992; Crawford & Krebs, 2008; Gangestad & Simpson, 2007; Kenrick, Maner, & Li, 2005).

A Bit of History

Since the time of Charles Darwin, scientists have recognized that the human body is a product of biological evolution, but not until the 1970s did scientists begin to seriously explore the possibility that biological evolution also influences human psychology and behavior. E. O. Wilson's book *Sociobiology* (1975) ushered in the perspective of evolutionary psychology—an approach in which psychologists use what they know about human biological evolution to inform their understanding of the contemporary human mind. A relative newcomer on the social psychology scene, evolutionary psychology has become a major explanatory force that unites into one conceptual framework many diverse findings within the field.

The initial advent of evolutionary psychology was colored by controversy. Many thought that although evolution might underlie human physical characteristics (such as opposable thumbs and upright posture), it was less obvious how evolution might provide a foundation for cognition and behavior. At the time, most traditional approaches to psychological science relied heavily on explanations involving unconstrained learning—a process that could be directly observed and manipulated. The notion that who we are is constrained by relatively innate biological processes did not complement the zeitgeist view of the mind as a blank slate, and many doubted that the more ultimate perspective of evolutionary psychology could produce testable hypotheses about human behavior. If we cannot observe human evolution directly, how could we ever know whether a pattern of cognition and behavior was produced by evolution (see Conway & Schaller, 2002)?

Fortunately, controversy often contributes to scientific progress, as a theory's proponents search for new findings to address critics' skepticism. The evolutionary approach has generated many new findings and ideas, and the field's top journals have since published hundreds of social psychological studies testing evolutionarily informed hypotheses about the whole range of social psychological phenomena, from altruism to xenophobia (e.g., Griskevicius et al., 2007; Navarette et al., 2009; Schaller & Murray, 2008). In the following sections, we outline some of the basic assumptions and conceptual tools of an evolutionary approach, and detail a subset of important evolutionarily relevant empirical findings.

What Is Evolutionary Social Psychology?

Evolutionary psychology is not limited to any particular domain of scientific inquiry. It is not a single theory or hypothesis. Rather, evolutionary psychology is an overarching meta-theoretical perspective. It comprises a set of assumptions that governs how scientists approach questions about psychological phenomena (Buss, 1995; Ketelaar & Ellis, 2000). These assumptions (e.g., that cognition is produced in part by underlying biological processes and that human biology has been shaped by a long history of evolutionary forces) are scientifically noncontroversial, and are based on a vast storehouse of knowledge within the biological sciences. When applied to the conceptual landscape of social psychology, these assumptions focus scientific inquiry on specific kinds of research questions and generate specific kinds of answers to those questions.

The broad perspective of evolutionary psychology provides a set of conceptual tools that can be used to deduce specific mid-level theories, models, and hypotheses about social psychological phenomena. It is these theories, models, and hypotheses (not the overarching perspective of evolution) that offer specific predictions pertaining to social psychological phenomena. Rarely do evolutionary psychologists frame their specific research questions in terms of very broad considerations such as survival and reproduction. Rather, research questions tend to be framed so that they test mid-level theories that provide a more specific portrait of the influences of evolution on psychology and behavior. Tinbergen (1963) made an important distinction between historical evolutionary hypotheses (concerned with questions such as when mammalian females shifted from laying eggs to bearing live young) and functional evolutionary hypotheses (concerned with questions such as the functional implications of how males versus females invest in their offspring). Evolutionary psychology is generally concerned with the latter level of analysis (Kenrick, Griskevicius, Neuberg, & Schaller, 2010, in press).

Partly because its assumptions are rooted in the biological sciences (rather than the traditional social sciences), evolutionary social psychology has sometimes been incorrectly viewed as an *alternative* to the basic assumptions of social psychology. An evolutionary approach, however, is very much consistent with the defining themes of social psychology (Neuberg, Kenrick, & Schaller, 2009). Evolutionary social psychology, for example, incorporates the power of the situation, assuming that proximate triggers for action typically lie in the immediate social context. Evolutionary social psychology is also an interactionist perspective, in recognizing that thoughts, feelings, and behavior emerge as an interactive function of variables inside the person (e.g., individual differences, specific motives) and the situation (e.g., salient contextual variables). Thus, an evolutionary perspective is not meant to replace traditional social psychological perspectives. Far from it. The perspective of evolutionary psychology supplements traditional approaches by providing a deeper explanatory framework that helps explain psychological phenomena in terms of their root causes.

For critics of an evolutionary approach, the notion that biology constrains thought and behavior often conjures images of genetic determinism—a picture in which psychology is determined at birth by a genetic blueprint. Quite the contrary. As evolutionary psychologists are quick to point out, an evolutionary perspective rejects any simplistic "nature versus nurture" approach to the causes of social behavior. Rather, it acknowledges, and seeks to unpack, the fascinating and dynamic interactions among evolved psychological mechanisms, developmental processes, learning, and culture. When asked the question: "Where does evolution have its effects?" an evolutionary psychologist would be remiss in not mentioning genes, but clearly the answer is far more complex. Our evolutionary heritage unfolds as we learn and grow, interact with our culture, and develop knowledge structures based on our experiences. Thus, an evolutionary approach replaces both a blank slate view and a genetic determinist view with a view of the mind as a coloring book: some of the basic foundations of the human mind are predetermined, just as the lines in a coloring book are already written in. But the richness of human experience, learning, and culture is needed to color in those lines to make an actual human being (Kenrick, Nieuweboer, & Buunk, 2010).

Thus, an evolutionary approach does not imply that human behaviors are robotically determined by instinctive mechanisms over which people have no conscious control or that are impervious to environmental inputs (e.g., Barrett, Frederick, Haselton, & Kurzban, 2006). People can and often do exercise control over powerful and fundamental emotional and motivational inclinations, including anger, fear, and sexual arousal. Furthermore, most psychological mechanisms reflect the operation of flexible trade-offs, determined in interaction with current environmental conditions and past learning experiences (Gangestad & Simpson, 2000; Kenrick, Li, & Butner, 2003). Contrary to an all-too-common misconception, an evolutionary perspective does not discount the role of social learning. Indeed, the capacity for learning is itself based on a set of evolutionary adaptations (Moore, 2004), and many specific psychological processes that are rooted in evolved mechanisms are still responsive to cultural context and social learning histories (Kurzban, Cosmides, & Tooby, 2001; Maner et al., 2005). Rather than being "hardwired" to respond to social situations in certain ways, the human mind evolved to be especially adept at learning those elements of the social environment that are relevant to solving evolutionarily fundamental challenges, and to respond flexibly when those elements come into play.

Important Assumptions and Conceptual Tools

Some individual organisms have characteristics that enable them, compared to other members of their species, to more successfully exploit the prospects and avoid the perils presented by their environment. As a consequence, these organisms tend to be more successful at reproducing and thus transmitting their genes to future generations. Over many generations of differential reproductive success, this process—*natural selection*—produces organisms possessing those characteristics that previously conferred relatively high reproductive fitness.

The mind has also been shaped by the process of *sexual selection*, which refers to the idea that some individuals are better able to compete with members of their own sex over access to potential mating partners. In some cases, traits that are selected for because they enhance reproductive success may be neutral with respect to survival or they may even hinder survival. A classic example is the peacock's tail: A peacock's tail draws attention and is physically unwieldy, thus making the bird more vulnerable to predation. However, an ornate tail enhances the peacock's attractiveness to potential mating partners. This example highlights the critical importance of *trade-offs* in evolutionary processes. A trait that improves reproductive fitness in one way can work against reproductive fitness in another. The existence of such conflicting design criteria helps set the stage for an immensely complex set of psychological characteristics.

Reproductive Fitness Is the Engine That Drives Evolution

Evolutionary approaches begin with the assumption that many social psychological processes have been shaped by evolution to serve some function. The *ultimate* function of evolved psychological processes is to promote reproduction—the perpetuation of genes into subsequent generations. Although reproduction is the ultimate function of evolved psychological and behavioral processes, this does not mean that each episode of thought or behavior directly promotes reproductive success. First, not all psychological and behavioral processes reflect evolved mechanisms. Many processes, for example, can reflect by products of evolved mechanisms. What television shows people choose to watch, the languages they speak, and whether they prefer chocolate or vanilla ice cream have not been specifically designed by evolution, although they may reflect byproducts of underlying evolved mechanisms.

Second, even processes that have been designed through evolution to serve some adaptive function do not necessarily enhance reproduction in an immediate sense. To assert that psychological mechanisms were designed by evolution to promote reproductive fitness is sometimes misunderstood to imply that all behavior is ultimately about sex. Although successful reproduction requires mating, successful reproduction involves a diverse array of other challenges including protecting yourself from predators and other forms of physical harm, avoiding contagious diseases, avoiding rejection and social exclusion, navigating status hierarchies, caring for offspring, and so on (Bugental, 2000; Tooby & Cosmides, 1990; Kenrick, Li, & Butner, 2003; Kenrick, Maner, Butner, Li, Becker, & Schaller, 2002).

Indeed, even individuals who never reproduce directly may still increase their reproductive fitness through a variety of indirect means. Reproductive fitness is not defined by the production of offspring but by the successful reproduction of genes. Actions that have implications for the survival and reproduction of close genetic relatives, therefore, have indirect implications for our own reproductive fitness (this illustrates the concept of *inclusive fitness*; Hamilton, 1964). Under some conditions, for instance, some birds actually fare better by helping their siblings raise offspring than by mating on their own (Trivers, 1985). People and other animals may also enhance their own reproductive fitness by performing behaviors that promote the survival and reproduction of close kin (Burnstein, Crandall, & Kitayama, 1994; Faulkner & Schaller, 2007; Hrdy, 1999), even if it means putting their own survival at risk (Sherman, 1977). Consequently, evolutionary analyses apply not only to the small set of behaviors bearing directly on sex and mating, but to a much greater proportion of human social cognition and behavior.

Adaptations Are Designed to Solve Recurrent Social Problems

The physical and psychological characteristics produced through natural and sexual selection are known as *adaptations*. Adaptations, which are features of an organism that were selected because they enhanced the reproductive fitness of the organism's ancestors, are designed to solve specific adaptive challenges that arose consistently in ancestral environments. In this chapter, we focus on (1) adaptive problems defined by the recurring threats and opportunities presented by human social ecologies; and (2) the cognitive, emotional, and behavioral mechanisms that evolved to help ancestral humans solve those challenges.

What kinds of recurring social problems did early humans face? There is some convergence in the various answers that have been offered to this question (e.g., Bugental, 2000; Kenrick, Li, & Butner, 2003). Like many other social species, humans must often avoid sources of harm, including harm from predators, intrasexual rivals, and members of hostile outgroups. Humans must also avoid contact with sources of disease including pathogens potentially carried by other people. To reproduce, humans must solve challenges pertaining to the formation of new romantic and sexual relationships. Like the (relatively few) mammals that include long-term pair-bonding as a predominant mating strategy, humans must solve challenges associated with maintaining and protecting long-term romantic relationships. Like other animals that invest heavily in offspring, humans must also solve problems related to child rearing. Like other highly social species, humans must solve problems associated with forming and maintaining lasting coalitions of allies. Because many human social structures are organized hierarchically, humans must also solve problems associated with the attainment of social status and dominance.

Each of these broad classes of problems can be divided into hierarchically linked subproblems. For instance, maintaining coalitions of allies requires people to solve the problem of successful social exchange. As such, individuals must be able to identify individuals with traits that facilitate or hinder successful exchange, detect people who might be cheaters or nonreciprocators, discourage cheating and free-riding, and so on (e.g., Cosmides & Tooby, 2005; Cottrell, Neuberg, & Li, 2007; Fehr, Fischbacher, & Gachter, 2002). To solve challenges associated with forming new romantic partnerships, individuals must also solve myriad subproblems including the ability to discriminate between individuals according to their fertility, parental potential, genetic quality, and degree of kinship (e.g., Gangestad & Simpson, 2000; Kenrick & Keefe, 1992; Lieberman, Tooby, & Cosmides, 2007). Most adaptations are designed to solve these types of specific subproblems.

Adaptations Are Functionally Specialized and Domain Specific

Traditional psychological theories presume that the mind reflects an information processor designed to encode and integrate many different forms of information according to the same basic rules, similar to a computer with a single operating system. In contrast, most evolutionary approaches presume that natural selection produces numerous relatively specialized, domain-specific psychological mechanisms, similar to the range of different software applications that can be run on a computer (Cosmides & Tooby, 2005; Kenrick, Sadalla, & Keefe, 1998). In fact, both viewpoints may be right. Some mental processes appear to be domain general, in the sense that they work the same way across many different domains. The ability to exert self-control over your own behavior, for example, appears to work the same way whether you are dieting, presenting yourself in a particular way to others, or studying (Muraven & Baumeister, 2000). Above and beyond such general processes, however, many mental phenomena operate in ways that are functionally specific (Klein et al., 2002). Just as computer software comes in many different packages, some designed to process text, others designed to organize information into a spreadsheet, and still others designed to interface with the web, many mental processes are designed to serve highly specific functions (Barrett & Kurzban, 2006; Fodor, 1983; Kurzban & Aktipis, 2007; Pinker, 1997; Sherry & Schacter, 1987).

To give an example of domain specificity from a noncognitive system, humans do not have a single all-purpose "survival system" that addresses the problems of extracting nutrients from food and moving those nutrients throughout the body. Instead, humans possess functionally distinct (albeit linked) digestive, circulatory, and respiratory systems. These domain-specific systems are themselves comprised of functionally distinct sub-systems designed to perform specific tasks (e.g., the digestive system's salivary glands, stomach, and intestines). Similarly, rather than having a single "social survival system" that addresses all fitness-relevant problems presented by social ecologies (problems of status attainment, coalition formation, child-rearing, and the like), an evolutionary perspective presumes that the human psyche is made up of functionally distinct (albeit linked) cognitive, emotional, and behavioral mechanisms—each designed to serve a specific set of fitness-relevant functions.

Functionally specific psychological mechanisms may perform more effectively than a single all-purpose information-processing system (Cosmides & Tooby, 2005). Mechanisms that serve specific functions would be better equipped to deal with the huge influx of information from the environment, because they would be designed to process only a very narrow and specific portion of that information. Human threat-avoidance mechanisms, for example, are built to associate fear with natural sources of threat such as snakes, spiders, and angry faces. Because snakes, spiders, and angry people have posed threats throughout evolutionary history, some of their meaning comes already built into the cognitive system (Kaschak & Maner, 2009). As a result, people are especially efficient at learning to fear those things (Öhman & Mineka, 2001).

Thus, a view of the mind as domain specific implies that psychological mechanisms that govern cognition and behavior in one social domain may be very different from those that govern cognition and behavior in other social domains (e.g., Ackerman & Kenrick, 2008; Kenrick, Sundie, & Kurzban, 2008; Neuberg & Cottrell, 2006). The focus on recurrent fitness-relevant problems encourages attention not only to specific underlying processes, but to the specific *content* of those processes (e.g., whether a social exchange process involves sharing information among friends, trading food between members of different groups, or helping a family member in a fistfight). The result is a set of hypotheses that is often more highly specific and nuanced than sets deduced from other perspectives in psychology.

Evolutionary Social Psychology by Domains

The bottom line of evolution by natural selection is differential reproductive success. Successful reproduction involves a diverse array of tasks—making friends, negotiating status hierarchies, forming and maintaining long-term relationships, and taking care of your children (Kenrick, Griskevicius, Neuberg, & Schaller, In press). Adaptationist reasoning—bolstered by cognitive, behavioral, and neurophysiological evidence (Panksepp, 1982; Plutchik, 1980)—suggests that much of human behavior may be organized around a fairly limited set of fundamental motives, each linked to a particular adaptive challenge posed by ancestral environments. Based on several recent reviews (Bugental, 2000; Buss, 1999; Fiske, 1992; Kenrick et al., 2002, 2003; Kenrick, Neuberg, & Cialdini, 1999), we will organize the remainder of our discussion around five key domains of social life—coalition formation, status, self-protection, mating, and parental care. We consider evidence for some of the cognitive and behavioral mechanisms that may have evolved to help people succeed in each of these domains.

Coalition Formation

Humans have a fundamental need for social belonging that is rooted deeply within human evolutionary history (Baumeister & Leary, 1995). For most of human history, our ancestors lived in small highly interdependent groups (Caporeal, 1997; Dunbar, 1993; Sedikides & Skowronski, 1997). Successful cooperation among group members greatly increased each person's probability of surviving, prospering, and eventually reproducing. This was particularly true during times of need (e.g., food shortages) (Hill & Hurtado, 1996). The evolutionary literature on social affiliation has important implications for understanding cooperation, prosocial behavior, exchange, reciprocity, and the psychology of kinship.

Alliances with Kin Social psychologists tend not to focus much on differences between interactions among kin versus nonkin (Daly, Salmon, & Wilson, 1997). However, there are important differences between these kinds of relationships. Research with humans and other species, for example, suggests substantially lower thresholds for engaging in various types of cooperative behavior among individuals who are genetically related (e.g., Ackerman, Kenrick, & Schaller, 2008; Burnstein et al., 1994; Essock-Vitale & McGuire, 1985; Neyer & Lang, 2003). From the perspective of inclusive fitness theory (Hamilton, 1964), it is easy to see why people tend to align themselves with their kin—a benefit shared with a kin member implies indirect genetic benefits to oneself, and costs exacted on the self by kin are also indirect costs to the kin member.

Kinship provides one foundation for understanding the evolution of prosocial behavior as well as variability in prosocial behavior across different circumstances. The logic of inclusive fitness provides an explanation for one form of altruism—nepotism. Evidence of nepotistic altruism is found widely across the animal kingdom (Greenberg, 1979; Holmes & Sherman, 1983; Suomi, 1982). Compared to dizygotic twins, monozygotic (identical) twins are more cooperative in economic decision-making games (Segal & Hershberger, 1999). In other contexts, too, people are more inclined to help genetically related kin, and this tendency is bolstered under conditions that have direct implications for the kin member's survival and reproductive fitness (Burnstein et al., 1994; Neyer & Lang, 2003; Stewart-Williams, 2008).

The evolved psychology of kinship even has important implications for prosocial behavior among total strangers. As with many other animals, ancestral humans were often unable to directly identify kin—people cannot "see" genes—but instead inferred kinship implicitly on the basis of superficial cues such as familiarity and similarity (Lieberman et al., 2007; Park et al., 2008). Consequently, people may respond prosocially to individuals who appear either familiar or highly similar in some way—even when they know, rationally, that the individuals are total strangers. For instance, just as facial similarity promotes trust (DeBruine, 2002), it also promotes cooperative behavior in a public goods game (Krupp, DeBruine, & Barclay, 2008). Emotions may also serve as heuristic cues to kinship. Empathy likely evolved as part of a system for aiding kin in distress (Preston & de Waal, 2002; Maner & Gailliot, 2007), and thus kinship may be implicitly connoted by the emotional experience of empathy—even when the empathy is elicited by nonkin (Hoffman, 1981; Krebs, 1987; Park et al., 2008). This suggests that the often-observed relation between empathy and helping behavior among strangers (see Batson, 1991) may be rooted, in part, in the evolved psychology of kinship.

Alliances with Nonkin Why would people form coalitions with nonkin? Theories of reciprocal altruism provide one answer (Axelrod & Hamilton, 1981; Trivers, 1971). According to these theories, our ancestors would have benefited from cooperating with others to the extent that those people were likely to reciprocate. In this way, each member of reciprocal exchange relationship reaps benefits in the long term. Indeed, whereas close kin cooperate with relatively less regard for past reciprocation, sharing between progressively less related individuals becomes more linked to a history of reciprocal sharing (e.g., Fiske, 1992; Trivers, 1971). Across societies, the norm of reciprocal exchange is universal (Brown, 1991; Fiske, 1992).

Because people cannot see the future, they cooperate with group members based on the *probability* that those group members will later reciprocate. Hence, it behooves people to attend carefully to signs that a member of their group is not a good candidate for future reciprocation or that this member is likely to draw more resources from the group than he or she is willing to give back. Indeed, evidence suggests that people are quite vigilant to potential deceit and evidence of social cheating (Cosmides & Tooby, 1992; Mealey, Daood, & Krage, 1996). Conversely, recent evolutionary analyses of what attributes people value most in group members highlight the universal value placed on trustworthiness (Cottrell, Neuberg, & Li, 2007).

Social Exclusion and Social Anxiety What happens when the powerful need for social belonging is thwarted? Being excluded by other people can be very distressing and anxiety provoking and can precipitate neurophysiological responses resembling physical pain (Eisenberger, Liberman, & Williams, 2003; MacDonald & Leary, 2005). This makes sense from the standpoint that throughout much of evolutionary history, being excluded from your group led to disastrous consequences, even death. The threat of social exclusion can promote a variety of psychological changes aimed at restoring a person's level of social belonging (Maner, DeWall, Baumeister, & Schaller, 2007; Maner, Miller, Schmidt, & Eckel, in press). When threatened with the possibility of social exclusion, people become highly attuned to other people in ways that might help facilitate social connectons (DeWall, Maner, & Rouby, 2009; Gardner et al., 2000; Williams et al., 2000), although negative and antisocial responses to exclusion have also been observed (e.g., Baumeister et al., 2005; DeWall, Twenge, Gitter, & Baumeister, 2009; Leary et al., 2006).

Evolutionary considerations suggest that social anxiety—the tendency to anticipate and to fear negative social evaluation—may have evolved as a mechanism designed to help people avoid social exclusion (Buss, 1990; Maner, 2009). Anxiety leads people to avoid doing potentially embarrassing things and taking social risks, and thus helps people avoid negative social attention and potential rejection or ostracism (see also Allen & Badcock, 2003).

Status

Like the social structures of other species, the social structures of many human societies are organized hierarchically, with some individuals enjoying higher status than others (Barkow, 1989; Eibl-Eibesfeldt, 1989). Social status, a basic aspect of most social groups, refers to a person's position in a social hierarchy, such that people high in status have greater influence over others and greater access to group resources. Even in face-to-face interactions between complete strangers, relative status differences emerge quickly and spontaneously, often on the basis of very limited social information (Fisek & Ofshe, 1970).

Links among Status, Dominance, and Prestige Having high social status is associated with an array of adaptive rewards such as access to group assets, friends, mates, respect, praise, admiration, happiness, and health (Archer, 1988; Eibl-Eibesfeldt, 1989; Keltner et al., 2003). Evolutionary theories suggest that status brings reproductive success across many species: high-status individuals are better able to obtain mating partners and to provide care to offspring than low-status individuals (e.g., Ellis, 1995; Sadalla, Kenrick, & Vershure, 1987). Having status may also increase the likelihood that your mate will be willing and able to devote time and energy to caring for your offspring (Eibl-Eibesfeldt, 1989).

Henrich and Gil-White (2001) suggested that dominance and prestige provide two different routes to attaining status. Dominance involves influencing and controlling other people via force. In many nonhuman primates this involves physical force and so depends largely on physical size and fighting ability. In humans, dominance depends less on physical force and more on enlisting allies and manipulating rewards and punishments to influence other people. Prestige, on the other hand, typically comes from having expertise, knowledge, or wisdom, usually in a domain that is useful to the group. Unlike people with dominance, people with prestige have influence because they are listened to and respected, not because they force others to do what they want. Deference to prestigious people is freely conferred. Notably, it is possible to have prestige without dominance (e.g., a well-respected emeritus faculty member), just as it is possible to have dominance without prestige (e.g., a nefarious and disliked dictator). Both dominance and prestige serve as routes through which people can climb to the top of a social hierarchy. The difference lies in whether status is attained through force (dominance) or through knowledge and expertise (prestige).

Because there are many benefits to having high status, some have argued that striving for status is a fundamental human motive (Bugental, 2000; McClelland, 1975), and many behaviors are designed to help an individual gain status. For example, people will sometimes behave prosocially as a means of achieving high social status (Griskevicius et al., 2007, 2010; Reykowski, 1980). Males, in particular, sometimes use violence as a means of increasing their status (Archer, 1994; Griskevicius et al., 2007). Many social psychological studies have noted that people present themselves to others in ways designed to increase their own status (Allen et al., 1979; Bushman, 1993); however, an evolutionary analysis provides a deeper explanation as to why people are so motivated to achieve status. For both sexes, the advantages of gaining and maintaining status included access to material resources and extended social alliances. These advantages, in turn, translated into increased reproductive success: resources could be invested in offspring and allies assisted in caring for and protecting them.

The evolutionary literature on status has also been applied to the study of leadership (Boehm, 1999; van Vugt, 2006). It sometimes can be difficult to get group members to work together. Group leaders, by virtue of their leadership position, possess status and influence, can help solve this social coordination problem, and enable groups to manage fundamental challenges such as protecting themselves from rival outgroups, acquiring resources, and defusing conflicts within the group. The prevalence of leadership throughout history and across species suggests that leadership and followership can provide stable strategies for an effective group. However, recent evolutionarily inspired work has noted that there may also be a fundamental motivational conflict between leaders and their followers (Maner & Mead, in press; van Vugt, Hogan, & Kaiser, 2008). Leaders typically are given power, defined in terms of their ability to control group resources and influence people (see Keltner, Gruenfeld, & Anderson, 2003), whereas followers lack power. van Vugt and colleagues (2008) proposed that this power asymmetry results in a basic ambivalence in the relationship between leaders and followers. Followers need leaders to achieve their goals, but giving up some of their power makes them vulnerable to exploitation. Consequently, followers may be motivated to decrease the power gap between themselves and leaders. Having power provides many benefits, so leaders, on the other hand, may be motivated to increase the power gap between themselves and followers, and to use their power for personal gain. This motivational conflict may have negative consequences for group functioning, as leaders sometimes use their power in corrupt and selfish ways (e.g., Kipnis, 1972).

Gender Differences in Fitness Payoffs for Status Striving From an evolutionary perspective, males gain an additional set of benefits from striving for status. Due to their high level of parental investment, women tend to be highly selective in choosing their long-term mates, and tend to place a premium on the social status of potential long-term romantic partners (Li, Bailey, Kenrick, & Linsenmeier, 2002; Sadalla et al., 1987). High status men are able to offer their mates relatively greater protection and access to resources, both of which were useful in caring for offspring. Consequently, compared to females, males are more motivated to seek high levels of social dominance (Hill & Hurtado, 1996) and are more likely to worry about possible loss of status relative to other group members (Daly & Wilson, 1988; Gutierres, Kenrick, & Partch, 1999; Maner, Miller, Schmidt, & Eckel, 2008).

Eagly and Wood (1999) argued that differences in status striving may stem from the male gender role's emphasis on power and status versus the female gender role's emphasis on nurturance. They suggest that men's and women's gender roles differ across societies because of two fundamental evolved differences: men are physically larger and women carry and nurse offspring (Wood & Eagly, 2007). Thus, they posit an interaction between an evolved mechanism and the development of cultural norms, which is in some ways consistent with evolutionary models of gender role norms (Kenrick, 1987; Kenrick, Trost, & Sundie, 2004). In positing a causal link between social roles and various gender differences in social behavior, Eagly and Wood's biosocial model provides a proximate account of gender differences (Kenrick & Li, 2000). The biosocial model even links social roles to underlying biological processes, for example, arguing that hormones such as testosterone help prepare men and women for the social roles they fill in their society. An evolutionary perspective, however, provides a deeper level of explanation that specifies the root causes of underlying biological processes that can account for gender differences, for example, by linking men's higher levels of testosterone to their greater focus on dominance and intrasexual competition, characteristics found in males across many species (Mazur & Booth, 1998). Nevertheless, the work by Eagly and Wood and others indicates an increasing tendency for social psychologists to develop theories that consider the links between evolution and the development of culture (see also Schaller et al., 2010).

Self-Protection

The need to protect yourself from harm is perhaps the most fundamental of human motivations. Ancestral humans frequently encountered threats from members of hostile outgroups (Baer & McEachron, 1982) and intragroup competition over status and material resources led to recurrent threats from ingroup members (Daly & Wilson, 1988). Moreover, some threats take the form of contagious disease, and are transmitted via interpersonal contact (Kurzban & Leary, 2001; Park, Schaller, & Crandall, 2007). Thus, threats can come from many places and, consequently, psychological mechanisms are designed specifically to help people detect and avoid those threats (see Öhman & Mineka, 2001, for a review).

The Evolved Fear Module Psychological processes are very sensitively tuned to evolutionarily relevant cues in the environment that can signal the presence of possible threats (Haselton & Nettle, 2006). An angry facial expression, for example, often signals that a person is inclined toward aggressive behavior and may take violent physical action (Parkinson, 2005). Indeed, expressions of anger are cross-culturally universal—they are recognized the world over as a sign of impending threat (Ekman & Friesen, 1976; Ekman, 1982). Consequently, people selectively attend to angry faces and quickly and accurately detect angry-looking faces among distracter faces in a variety of visual search tasks (e.g., Becker, Kenrick, Neuberg, Blackwell, & Smith, 2007; Fox, Russo, Bowles, & Dutton, 2001; Hansen & Hansen, 1988).

The effects of natural selection can be seen in the process by which people learn to associate perceptions of threat with particular types of stimuli. To the extent that particular threats have posed recurrent dangers to humans throughout evolutionary history, people may be particularly adept at learning to fear those threats. In a series of classical conditioning experiments, people were submitted to electric shocks while they viewed images of threatening stimuli—ancestrally dangerous stimuli such as snakes and spiders, as well as more contemporary threat stimuli such as guns and knives (see Öhman & Mineka, 2001). The researchers measured how quickly people came to associate the shocks with the images with which they were paired (as indicated, for example, by physical startle responses). People demonstrated more efficient conditioned fear responses to stimuli such as snakes and spiders—stimuli that have posed physical threats to humans throughout history—than they did to guns and knives, even though the latter arguably present more immediate and common dangers to people in modern society.

These findings provide a good illustration of the interaction between evolution and learning. They fit with Seligman's (1971) preparedness theory, which suggests that people come biologically prepared to learn particular associations—those bearing especially on survival—with a very high degree of efficiency. Indeed, people do not come into the world preprogrammed with a store of ready-to-use knowledge at their disposal. Rather, people are born into the world biologically prepared to learn certain things more easily and efficiently than others. They are especially adept at learning things that can help them seize important adaptive opportunities and avoid forms of threat.

Intergroup Processes Throughout evolutionary history, people were threatened by members of potentially hostile outgroups (Baer & McEachron, 1982; Daly & Wilson, 1988). Consequently, a variety of self-protective processes are directed selectively at avoiding outgroup members. For example, self-protective goals can lead people to see anger in the faces of outgroup members, even when those faces are perceived as neutral in other contexts (Maner et al., 2005). Although people tend to remember the faces of outgroup members less well than the faces of ingroup members, that pattern is reversed when the outgroup members display an angry facial expression—angry outgroup faces are remembered particularly well, presumably because they are perceived as posing a particularly dire threat (Ackerman et al., 2006). Moreover, the presentation of one angry-looking outgroup member leads people to see subsequent outgroup members as more threatening; the same does not hold true for perceptions of ingroup members (Shapiro et al., 2009). Thus, people display forms of vigilance to members of coalitional outgroups as sources of physical danger.

Cottrell and Neuberg (2005) proposed an evolutionarily inspired "sociofunctional" theory of intergroup prejudice. Their approach emphasized the domain specificity of intergroup processes, hypothesizing that prejudice reflects not a general propensity to negatively evaluate outgroups, but rather a set of domain-specific evaluations that reflect the existence of different forms of outgroup threat. That is, different outgroups pose different kinds of threat, which in turn evoke highly specific adaptive emotional and behavioral responses. Some groups are perceived as posing threats to physical safety; other groups are thought to pose threats to the security of our economic resources; still other groups are presumed to threaten a group's ability to socialize its young. In each case, the specific type of perceived threat evokes a highly specific pattern of emotion (fear, anger, disgust, pity) and behavior (avoidance, ostracism, aggression). And in each case, the pattern of psychological responses maps onto forms of recurrent intergroup threats faced by humans throughout history.

Vigilance toward sources of outgroup threat is exacerbated by contextual cues that, throughout history, have signaled increased vulnerability to forms of harm. In a number of studies, for example, Schaller and his colleagues examined the implications of ambient darkness on outgroup prejudice. Darkness affords greater susceptibility to harm, and tends to evoke fear and anxiety. As a result, being in the dark can increase vigilance toward members of outgroups that are heuristically associated with physical threat. Compared to control participants, for example, participants seated in a dark laboratory room displayed greater danger-related stereotypes about African Americans, a group that is stereotypically viewed as threatening by many white North Americans (Schaller, Park, & Mueller, 2003).

Research on racial prejudice provides another excellent illustration that evolution works via the constraints it places on learning (i.e., "nature via nurture"; Ridley, 2003). Humans, like other primates, tend to be xenophobic (Holloway, 1974). Toward that end, people possess basic mechanisms for parsing people into coalitional categories of "us" and "them," and for rapidly learning whatever cues reliably make that distinction. The specific cues used for this purpose, however, are highly variable, implying that coalitional distinctions depend importantly on local learning environments (Kurzban et al., 2001). Although much of the recent research on prejudice in America focuses on prejudice toward particular racial groups, an evolutionary perspective provides a wider lens with which to conceptualize intergroup processes. From an evolutionary perspective, ethnic and racial distinctions provide only one of many possible characteristics that people may use to define the boundaries between ingroup and outgroup.

Disease Avoidance Although modern medical advances have dramatically reduced the likelihood that infection with pathogens will lead to death, throughout most of evolutionary history infection spelled disaster for the infected individual. As a result, humans possess a number of emotional and cognitive mechanisms designed to help avoid contact with potential sources of contagion.

The emotion of disgust plays a key role in promoting adaptive avoidance of potential contagion (e.g., Rozin & Fallon, 1987). Disgust serves as a rich source of information (cf. Schwarz & Clore, 1983), signaling that a substance, food, or person is potentially hazardous. Disgust responses are deeply rooted in human biology and in the capacity for learning. Many cases of single trial conditioned taste aversion, for example, have been documented wherein taste aversion is conditioned to novel tastes; this is highly functional because it helps isolate the food most likely to have caused the illness (e.g., Garcia & Koelling, 1966).

Researchers have shown that concerns about disease lead people to display vigilance to other people who display cues that are heuristically associated with disease, even though those cues may not be truly indicative of disease (e.g., Kurzban & Leary, 2001; Zebrowitz & Collins, 1997). Physical abnormalities or disabilities, for example, promote avoidance of people as if they were a source of contagious infection (Park, Faulkner, & Schaller, 2003).

An intriguing set of evolutionary hypotheses pertains to disease avoidance mechanisms that emerge at particular points in a woman's menstrual cycle. Fessler and colleagues have argued that although avoidance of contagion is important for both men and women, infection presents a particularly pernicious problem for women (e.g., Fessler, 2001, 2002; also Fessler & Navarrete, 2003). So that their body does not reject an unborn offspring, women's immune systems are suppressed when likelihood of pregnancy is high. Fessler tested this hypothesis by examining disgust and avoidance of potential sources of pathogens in women across their menstrual cycle. They observed an increase in sensitivity to disgusting stimuli in the luteal phase of the menstrual cycle—the period immediately following possible fertilization in which the immune system is suppressed (Fessler, 2001).

Mating

Because reproductive success is the engine that drives evolutionary processes, and because success in mating is essential for reproductive success, the vestiges of human evolution are highly apparent in the way people approach challenges involved in mating (e.g., Buss, 1989b; Miller, 2000). Evolutionary research on mating can be organized into two primary domains: relationship selection and relationship maintenance. Relationship selection refers to a person's choice of potential partners and the priority they place on long-term, committed relationships and short-term, casual sexual relationships. Relationship maintenance refers to processes involved in helping people protect their long-term relationships; this includes avoiding the temptation of attractive relationship alternatives and warding off intrasexual competitors.

Relationship Selection Almost all human societies have some form of institutionalized long-term bonding such as marriage (Daly & Wilson, 1983). At the same time, people often engage in short-term casual sexual relationships, with little or no intention of staying together for the long term (e.g., Marshall & Suggs, 1971). Decisions about whether to pursue a long-term or short-term relationship depend in part on an individual's sociosexual orientation (Gangestad & Simpson, 2000; Simpson & Gangestad, 1991; Jackson & Kirkpatrick, 2007), which refers to a person's general inclination to pursue committed long-term relationships and/or short-term sexual relationships. An orientation toward short-term mating is referred to as being sociosexually unrestricted, whereas an orientation toward long-term mating is referred to as being sociosexually restricted.

There is variability in sociosexuality both among individuals (with some people being more unrestricted than others) and between the sexes. On average, men tend to be somewhat more unrestricted than women; they are relatively more inclined to pursue short-term sexual relationships and to desire sex without commitment. Women, in contrast, are relatively more inclined to seek long-term commitment (Clark & Hatfield, 1989; Simpson & Gangestad, 1991). Evolutionary theorists have attributed this to sex differences in minimum obligatory parental investment (Trivers, 1972). Because human females, like other mammalian females, incubate their young, they are required to make a more substantial investment of time and resources than males. Thus, throughout evolutionary history, the benefit-to-cost ratio of casual sex has been lower for women than for men (although new forms of birth control have changed some of the costs of casual sex). As such, women tend to be relatively more cautious and choosy in selecting their romantic partners (e.g., Buss & Schmitt, 1993).

A complete account of sex differences in sociosexuality takes into consideration not only how the sexes differ on average, but also how individuals interact with each other and actually decide on which type of relationship to pursue (Gangestad & Simpson, 2000). Indeed, there is substantial variability within each sex with regard to people's romantic strategies. Kenrick, Li, and Butner (2003) suggested that each sex bases its decisions of which strategy (short-term versus long-term strategy) to pursue on an implicit comparison of sex ratios in the local environment. Sex ratios can be thought of as a comparison of opposite sex people (i.e., available mates) to same sex people (i.e., intrasexual competitors). In any local environment, a strategy becomes more desirable to the extent that there are more available mates responding to that strategy and fewer same-sex competitors using that strategy (see also Guttentag & Secord, 1983).

Evolutionary analyses also provide a basis for predicting sex differences in the types of characteristics valued in short-term and long-term partners

(Li & Kenrick, 2006; Li, Bailey, Kenrick, & Linsenmeier, 2002). With regard to short-term relationships, both men and women are highly attentive to the physical attractiveness of a potential partner (e.g., Maner et al., 2003; Maner, Gailliot, Rouby, & Miller, 2007). Physical attractiveness can signal a number of characteristics relevant to reproductive fitness. Highly symmetrical people, for example, typically are judged to be attractive, and symmetry can signal the presence of a strong immune system and a person's overall level of genetic fitness (Gangestad & Simpson, 2000). Mating with an attractive man should increase the likelihood that a woman will have more genetically fit offspring (Fisher, 1958; Scheib et al., 1999). Moreover, a man's physical attractiveness often signals his level of social dominance (e.g., via markers of testosterone; Cunningham, Barbee, & Pike, 1990), and women tend to prioritize dominance in their male partners (Buss, 1989a). Characteristics such as health and youth, which are related to perceptions of female attractiveness, may signal a woman's level of fertility (Buss & Schmitt, 1993; Kenrick et al., 1990; Li et al., 2002). From an evolutionary perspective, men have an evolved preference for healthy, young mates because such a preference would have increased the likelihood that a male ancestor would have fathered healthy offspring and, in turn, successfully passed his genes on to subsequent generations (Kenrick & Keefe, 1992; Singh, 1993).

The characteristics people value in long-term mates are somewhat different than what they seek in short-term mates. When considering marriage partners, for example, there is some evidence that women tend to prefer status and access to resources somewhat more than men and men tend to prefer physical attractiveness somewhat more than women (e.g., Buss, 1989b; Buss & Barnes, 1986; McGinnis, 1958; Sprecher, Sullivan, & Hatfield, 1994). Evolutionary theorists have suggested that these sex differences reflect the fact that men and women have faced somewhat different adaptive problems (Buss, 1989b; Symons, 1979). Because fertility tends to peak in a woman's early to mid-20s, and drop off rapidly after 35, men may be especially drawn to women displaying physical markers of sexual maturity and youth (Singh, 1993; Symons, 1979). Male reproductive potential, on the other hand, is not as constrained by fertility as it is by the ability to provide resources. Thus, women may be especially attentive to cues signaling a man's status in the social hierarchy and his ability to provide resources for her and her offspring (Buss, 1989a; Maner, DeWall, & Gailliot, 2008; Sadalla et al., 1987).

The evolutionary literature on sex differences in mating preferences has been challenged on the grounds that (1) it has relied too much on self-report measures and responses to hypothetical scenarios and (2) self-reported mating preferences may not correspond well with preferences demonstrated in a face-to-face mating context. Eastwick and Finkel (2008) used a speed dating paradigm to show that men and women's actual preferences did not conform to their self-reported preferences and, in their study, little evidence for sex differences in actual choices were found (see also Finkel & Eastwick, 2009). On the other hand, Todd and his colleagues (2007) also used a speed dating paradigm to show that although men's and women's preferences did not conform to evolutionary predictions, their actual mate choices did, with men being less choosy than women and valuing physical attractiveness more than women. In addition, other studies have used non-self-report measures to ascertain people's attraction to particular kinds of mates and have found, for example, that men are more inclined than women to visually attend to attractive members of the opposite sex (Maner et al., 2003), whereas women are more inclined than men to visually attend to high status members of the opposite sex (Maner, DeWall, & Gailliot, 2008). One thing is clear: the debate over the existence and origin of sex differences in mating is ongoing, as researchers continue to use a variety of methods to investigate mating preferences and choices.

Relationship Maintenance Because human infants are helpless and slow to develop, sustained input from both parents helps ensure the offspring's survival (Geary, 1998; Hrdy, 1999). Although human mating arrangements vary from culture to culture, all include long-term relationships in which both the male and female contribute to the offspring's welfare (Daly & Wilson, 1983). From an evolutionary perspective, the maintenance of long-term relationships serves key social affiliation and child-rearing functions that enhance reproductive success (Buss, 1999; Hazan & Diamond, 2000).

Humans, like many other sexually reproducing species, sometimes display a tendency toward polygamy and may be disinclined to maintain romantic relationships that are completely monogamous (Baresh & Lipton, 2007; Betzig, 1985). One challenge, therefore, involves the temptation of desirable relationship alternatives. For people who are already in a romantic relationship, attention to other desirable people can threaten their satisfaction with and commitment to their existing romantic partnership (Kenrick, Neuberg, Zierk, & Krones, 1994; Miller, 1997; Johnson & Rusbult, 1989). Evolutionary theories help generate predictions about which particular members of the opposite sex might threaten a person's commitment to a current relationship partner. Theories of short-term mating suggest that both men and women place a premium on the physical attractiveness of extra-pair relationship partners (Gangestad & Thornhill, 1997; Greiling & Buss, 2000; Haselton & Gangestad, 2006; Li & Kenrick, 2006; Scheib, 2001). Consequently, highly attractive members of the opposite sex can threaten commitment to a current partner, and psychological mechanisms designed to reduce threats posed by relationship alternatives tend to focus selectively on the attractiveness of alternative partners. For example, people in committed romantic relationships sometimes "devalue" alternative partners by judging them to be less physically attractive than single people do (e.g., Lydon, Fitzsimons, & Naidoo, 2003; Lydon, Meana, Sepinwall, Richards, & Mayman, 1999; Simpson, Gangestad, & Lerma, 1990). Negative evaluations of alternative partners can help reduce perceived relationship threats and aid in maintaining commitment to a current partner. In addition, because relationship alternatives threaten individuals' commitment, people sometimes display attentional biases such that as soon as physically attractive alternatives are perceived, attention is repelled and people look away (Maner, Gailliot, & Miller, 2009).

The emotion of romantic love has been conceptualized as an adaptation designed to help people maintain commitment to a long-term relationship (Frank, 1988, 2001). Feelings of romantic love reduce people's interest in alternative partners and help ensure their satisfaction and commitment to a current partner (Gonzaga et al., 2001). Consistent with this literature, priming people with thoughts and feelings of love for their partner helps them suppress thoughts about (Gonzaga et al., 2008) and stay inattentive to (Maner, Rouby, & Gonzaga, 2008) attractive relationship alternatives.

Although psychological mechanisms generally operate to help people protect their long-term relationships, those mechanisms are sensitive to the costs and benefits of staying in a relationship. For example, if a couple has offspring, it raises the threshold for decisions to leave a relationship for an alternative mate (Essock-Vitale & McGuire, 1989; Rasmussen, 1981). On the other hand, the availability of desirable alternatives tends to lower the decision threshold to leave a relationship (Guttentag & Secord, 1983; Kenrick et al., 1994).

Another challenge people face in maintaining a long-term relationship involves preventing their partner from being unfaithful. From an evolutionary perspective, warding off romantic rivals and preventing a partner from engaging in extra-pair relationships is a key part of ensuring your own reproductive success (e.g., Buss & Shackelford, 1997; Haselton & Gangestad, 2006). Just as psychological processes help maintain commitment to a relationship, they also help prevent partner infidelity (Amato & Booth, 2001; Finkel, 2007; Shackelford et al., 2005; Sheets, Fredendall, & Claypool, 1997; Wilson & Daly, 1996).

The threat of infidelity may promote adaptive cognitive processes designed to ward off potential intrasexual rivals. Moreover, an evolutionary perspective is useful for identifying the specific types of relationship rivals that might be most appealing to your mate. As mentioned previously, people tend to seek out extra-pair mates who are physically attractive. Consequently, when primed with the threat of infidelity, members of both sexes attend vigilantly to same-sex interlopers who are physically attractive (Maner, Miller, Rouby, & Gailliot, 2009).

Despite this similarity between men and women, there is also evidence for sex differences in jealousy. Buss, Larsen, Westen, and Semelroth (1992) proposed that although both sources of infidelity evoke jealousy in both sexes, men respond more strongly when their partner appears to be sexually attracted to others, whereas women are relatively more sensitive to emotional infidelity (see also Becker, Sagarin, Guadagno, Millevoi, & Nicastle, 2004; Easton, Schipper, & Shackelford, 2007; Sagarin, 2005; Schützwohl, 2008). From an evolutionary perspective, this sex difference reflects innate jealousy modules designed to deal with sex-specific challenges related to paternal uncertainty (for men) and paternal investment (for women) (Buss, 2002). Because fertilization occurs within a woman's body, men can never be certain that they are the father of their mate's offspring. As a result, the prospect of a woman's sexual infidelity may be particularly distressing for a man because it could lead him to invest time and resources in raising another man's offspring. In contrast to men, women can be certain of their maternity; thus, sexual infidelity should be somewhat less disconcerting for women than for men. Women, however, have faced a different threat—having their long-term mate direct resources toward other women. As a consequence, a man's emotional infidelity may be particularly distressing because it can signal a high likelihood of diverting resources to other women and their offspring.

The evolutionary approach to sex differences in jealousy has been controversial and has been criticized on both methodological and theoretical grounds. First, some have argued that methods designed to assess sex differences in jealousy (e.g., forcing people to choose which type of infidelity is more distressing) overestimate the size of the sex difference because, in fact, both types of infidelity tend to be highly distressing to both sexes (e.g., Harris, 2003, 2005). In addition, researchers have questioned whether the sex difference reflects different evolved mechanisms in men and women, or simply differences in the inferences men and women make based on the kind of infidelity. DeSteno and Salovey (1996), for example, suggested the "double-shot" hypothesis: a woman might think that if her husband is emotionally attached to another woman, he is probably having sex with her, and thus this double shot of infidelity is particularly distressing. Thus, even when acknowledging the existence of sex differences in jealousy, there is still debate as to their underlying cause.

Parental Care

Parental care is critical to the survival of human offspring (Geary, 2000; Hrdy, 1999). The desire to nurture offspring, however, is not constant across all parents. Decisions about caring for any particular offspring are contingent on a variety of factors that affect the costs and benefits of parental investment (Alexander, 1979; Daly & Wilson, 1980). An evolutionary logic suggests that decisions pertaining to child nurturance depend on various factors including the perceived genetic relatedness to the parent, the ability of parental investment to be converted to reproductive success, and the opportunity costs of investing.

Because a given offspring shares 50% of each parent's genes, and because offspring have the opportunity to someday reproduce, it makes sense that evolutionary processes have selected for behaviors that promote the survival and, ultimately, the reproductive success of offspring. However, there are more subtle distinctions that factor into the decision to invest. Consider the following: Mothers tend to invest more in their offspring than fathers. Maternal grandparents tend to invest more than paternal grandparents. Biological parents invest more in their children than stepparents, and are 40 times less likely to abuse them (Daly & Wilson, 1985) and up to several hundred times less likely to kill them than stepparents (Daly & Wilson, 1988).

These differences in investment are consistent with theories that emphasize the role of genetic relatedness. Only women can be completely sure which offspring are theirs; men can never be 100% sure. Thus, it makes sense that mothers invest more than fathers, and that relatives on the maternal side invest more than relatives on the paternal side. In addition, because investing in other men's offspring is unwise from a reproductive standpoint, it makes sense from an evolutionary perspective that the behavior of stepparents toward stepchildren is not equal to that of biological parents toward their own children.

Parental investment in male offspring may have a higher rate of both return and risk than investment in female offspring (Daly & Wilson, 1988; Trivers & Willard, 1973). Although there is rarely a shortage of males willing to mate with a female, a male typically needs to compete against other males to gain access to mates. In addition, whereas females are physically limited to having children at a relatively slow rate across a shorter reproductive lifespan, males are not constrained by internal gestation and menopause. Rather, male reproductive success varies greatly across men, ranging from those at the bottom of a status hierarchy who have no mates to those at the top, who have been known to sire up to several hundred children (e.g., Betzig, 1992; Daly & Wilson, 1988). Because of this differential in risk and return, it may be advantageous for a family with abundant resources to invest in sons, but for resource-poor families to allocate what they have to their daughters (Trivers & Willard, 1973). In support of this reasoning, a study of families in North America found differences in investment patterns between low- and high-income families (Gaulin & Robbins, 1991). Among the findings, low-income mothers were more likely to breast feed their daughters than their sons, whereas the opposite pattern was true for mothers in affluent families. Low-income mothers also had another child sooner if the first was a son, whereas high-income mothers had another child sooner if the first was a daughter.

Finally, parental investment is reproductively advantageous to the extent that alternative uses of such time and resources are not more lucrative. Because men are not constrained by childbearing and nursing, the pursuit of other mating relationships is a more viable option to them than it is for women. Indeed, tribal evidence from Africa shows that among the Aka pygmies, men of high status have more wives and spend less time on parenting than men of low status (Hewlett, 1991). People may also be more willing to abandon a given investment when the time horizon for making other investments is relatively long. Evidence from records of infanticide show that women are more likely to kill their infants when those women are younger and unwed with no men acknowledging fatherhood (Daly & Wilson, 1988).

Evolutionary Social Psychology Today

Relative to many other approaches in psychology, evolutionary approaches are the new kid on the block. Each year, the field of evolutionary social psychology sees significant new advances in theory and method. Here we mention only two.

One of the current emphases involves the integration of evolution, learning, and culture (e.g., Kenrick, Nieuweboer, & Buunk, 2010). Evolutionary psychologists are quick to point out that evolved psychological mechanisms work in conjunction with learning, and that learning occurs within a rich context of cultural information. Researchers have begun to deliver on the promise of an integrative evolutionary psychology by directly examining the interaction of evolution and culture (Tooby & Cosmides, 1992). For example, several lines of research suggest that people's mating strategies are adaptively tuned to the prevalence of disease-causing pathogens in the environment (e.g., Gangestad, Haselton, & Buss, 2006). In more pathogen-rich environments (e.g., hot and humid areas near the equator), people place greater value on the physical attractiveness of potential romantic partners, as attractiveness can signal the strength of a person's immune system (Gangestad & Buss, 1993). In addition, higher levels of polygyny are found in pathogen-rich environments because it may be more reproductively advantageous for a woman to become the second wife of an attractive man with a strong immune system than to become the first wife of a less fit man (Low, 1990). Such findings suggest that aspects of the physical environment interact with evolved biological mechanisms to produce different normative mating patterns, which can emerge in the form of large-scale differences among cultures. Similarly, using an evolutionary analysis, Schaller and Murray (2008) showed that basic units of personality such as sociosexual orientation, extraversion, and openness to experience vary predictably with the prevalence of pathogens in local cultural environments. New cross-cultural research is providing unique opportunities to examine the environmental and cultural contingencies that influence the here-and-now manifestation of evolved mental processes (Henrich et al., 2006; Marlowe et al., 2008).

One source of debate in this area involves the distinction between "evoked" culture and "transmitted" culture. Evoked culture refers to the process through which ecological variables directly activate genetic mechanisms, as in the previous mating-related examples. Transmitted culture instead refers to the process through which cultural norms travel from individual to individual via learning processes (e.g., imitation, mimicry, and story-telling; e.g., Tomasello, Kruger, & Ratner, 1993). Although there is little doubt that both systems interact to produce culture (Norenzayan, 2006; see also Henrich & Gil-White, 2001; Richerson & Boyd, 2005), it is less clear exactly how this interaction occurs, and what aspects of cultural variation are evoked versus transmitted. Research today is attempting to address these issues.

A second (and related) set of new developments pertains to the conceptual integration of situational and evolutionary causes (Kenrick, Griskevicius, Neuberg, & Schaller, 2010). Whereas traditional psychological theories tend to focus on proximate factors within the person or immediate situation, evolutionary theories tend to focus on background factors that help explain the underlying functions of particular psychological mechanisms. New evolutionarily inspired research bridges these two approaches by considering not only how particular cognitive mechanisms are linked to the recurrent adaptive challenges encountered by humans living in social groups, but also how immediate psychological factors (e.g., temporarily activated motives, individual differences, acute biological processes) shape adaptive social cognition.

For example, researchers have begun to document a number of interesting changes that occur across women's menstrual cycles. During ovulation (their peak period of fertility) women dress more attractively, act in flirtatious ways, and seek out men displaying cues to high genetic fitness (Haselton & Gangestad, 2006; Penton-Voak et al., 1999). Women at the peak of their reproductive fertility are even more likely to cheat on their current partner, as long as the man they are cheating with is more sexually attractive than their current partner (Pillsworth & Haselton, 2006). Conversely, men prefer the scent of women who are ovulating, and men who smell the scent of an ovulating women display high levels of testosterone, a hormone that promotes sexual courtship (Miller & Maner, 2010). Other recent research is integrating social psychological theories of priming with evolutionary theories of adaptive psychological processes. Findings from these priming studies suggest that the temporary activation of important goal states promotes the engagement of adaptive psychological processes ultimately designed to enhance reproductive success (Ackerman et al., 2009; Griskevicius et al., 2006a,b; Maner et al., 2005, 2007).

Closing Remarks

Darwin's theory of evolution by natural selection is likely the grandest of unifying theories in the life sciences. And it has great integrative potential for social psychology. Embracing an evolutionary perspective, however, does not challenge the findings of traditional social psychology; nor does it mean that social psychologists should send their laboratory participants home, march off to a remote part of the globe to live with a tribe of hunter-gatherers, dig up australopithecine bones, or commune with chimpanzees. Embracing an evolutionary explanation does not mean giving up research on ongoing phenomenology or learning processes or culture. In fact, because we carry the vestiges of ancestral adaptations, one of the best ways to gather evidence regarding the adaptive significance of human behavior is to study contemporary humans in modern environments (Buss & Kenrick, 1998).

How "ultimate" do our explanations for behavior need to be? When searching for causes, we can in theory go as far back as the beginning of life or the Big Bang. However, such an explanation would hardly be useful. A more satisfactory stop point is one that connects current behaviors to their adaptive function—the particular way in which behaviors served ancestral survival and reproduction. A causal explanation that simply points to "differential reproduction" would, by this reasoning, be going a step too far up the causal ladder. It would fail to distinguish the explanation for a bird's hollow skeletal structure from a shark's ability to sense prey by generating electromagnetic fields. We want to understand the particulars—how is it that these very different adaptations solved specific challenges posed by the organism's ecology. A more useful level of explanation would, for example, connect the bird's lightweight bones to intrinsic flight constraints set by an animal's strength-to-weight ratio, and a hammerhead's uniquely shaped head to its need to sweep the ocean floor in search of prey hiding under the sand. Being able to lift one's body into the air and finding hidden prey were different needs that birds' and sharks' physical design features were differentially adapted to solve. Thus, an adaptationist account seeks to explain how an animal's cognitive and behavioral mechanisms are connected to the specific demands and opportunities its ancestors regularly confronted.

The debate is no longer about nature *or* nurture. Both genes and learning play a strong role in shaping people's behavior. Only by spanning the continuum from proximate to ultimate levels of explanation will psychologists be able to paint a full picture of a psychological phenomenon. Considering multiple levels of causation leads to a depth of understanding not possible by considering only one level of analysis at a time. For example, experimental social psychological studies suggest that nonverbal indicators of social dominance increase the sexual attractiveness of males, but not females (e.g., Sadalla et al., 1987). Comparative studies conducted with other species indicate a link between an animal's testosterone level and his or her social rank (e.g., Rose, Bernstein, & Holaday, 1971). Physiological studies indicate that males typically produce more testosterone than females (Mazur & Booth, 1998). Correlational studies indicate that individuals with high testosterone also exhibit more anti-socially competitive behavior, particularly when other paths to social success are blocked (Dabbs & Morris, 1990). Together, these and other sources of evidence provide a whole network of findings that fit together to tell a compelling story about sexual selection and gender differences (Geary, 1998). No one source of data is superior to others, and none is superfluous—each is necessary to understand a complicated but ultimately sensible natural process. Although data from psychological studies are not by themselves sufficient, they are, in alliance with data from other disciplines and methods, necessary for complete explanations of behavior.

References

Ackerman, J. M., Becker, D. V., Mortensen, C. R., Sasaki, T., Neuberg, S. L., & Kenrick, D. T. (2009). A pox on the mind: Disjunction of attention and memory in the processing of physical disfigurement. *Journal of Experimental Social Psychology, 45*, 478–485.

Ackerman, J. M., & Kenrick, D. T. (2008). The costs of benefits: Help-refusals highlight key trade-offs of social life. *Personality & Social Psychology Review, 12*, 118–140.

Ackerman, J. M., Kenrick, D. T., & Schaller, M. (2007). Is friendship akin to kinship? *Evolution & Human Behavior, 28*, 365–374.

Ackerman, J. M., Shapiro, J. R., Neuberg, S. L., Kenrick, D. T., Becker, D. V., Griskevicius, V., Maner, J. K., & Schaller, M. (2006). They all look the same to me (unless they're angry): From outgroup homogeneity to outgroup heterogeneity. *Psychological Science, 17*, 836–840.

Alcock, J. (2001). *The triumph of sociobiology*. New York: Oxford University Press.

Alexander, R. D. (1979). *Darwinism and human affairs*. Seattle: University of Washington Press.

Allen, K. M., Madison, D. L., Porter, L. W., Renwick, P. A., & Mayes, B. T. (1979). Organizational politics: Tactics and characteristics of its actors. *California Management Review, 22*, 77–83.

Allen, N. B., & Badcock, P. B. T. (2003). The social risk hypothesis of depressed mood. *Psychological Bulletin, 129*, 887–913.

Amato, P. R., & Booth, A. (2001). The legacy of parents' marital discord: Consequences for children's marital quality. *Journal of Personality and Social Psychology, 81*, 627–638.

Archer, J. (1988). The sociobiology of bereavement: A reply to Littlefield and Rushton. *Journal of Personality and Social Psychology, 55*, 272–278.

Archer, J. (1994). Introduction: Male violence in perspective. In J. Archer (Ed.), *Male violence* (pp. 1–22). New York: Routledge.

Axelrod, R., & Hamilton, W. D. (1981). The evolution of cooperation. *Science, 211*, 1390–1396.

Baer, D., & McEachron, D. L. (1982). A review of selected sociobiological principles: Application to hominid evolution I: The development of group structure. *Journal of Social & Biological Structures, 5*, 69–90.

Baresh, D. P., & Lipton, J. E. (2001). *The myth of monogamy: Fidelity and infidelity in animals and people*. New York: W. H. Freeman.

Barkow, J. (1989). *Darwin, sex, and status: Biological approaches to mind and culture*. Toronto: University of Toronto Press.

Barrett, H. C., Frederick, D. A., Haselton, M. G., & Kurzban, R. (2006). Can manipulations of cognitive load be used to test evolutionary hypotheses? *Journal of Personality and Social Psychology, 91*, 513–518.

Barrett, H. C., & Kurzban, R. (2006). Modularity in cognition: Framing the debate. *Psychological Review, 113*, 628–647.

Batson, C. D. (1991). *The altruism question: Towards a social social-psychological answer*. Hillsdale, NJ: Erlbaum.

Baumeister, R. F., & Leary, M. R. (1995). The need to belong: Desire for interpersonal attachments as a fundamental human motivation. *Psychological Bulletin, 117*, 497–529.

Baumeister, R. F., Dewall, C. N., Ciarocco, N. J., & Twenge, J. M. (2005). Social exclusion impairs self-regulation. *Journal of Personality and Social Psychology, 88*, 589–604.

Becker, D. V., Kenrick, D. T., Neuberg, S. L., Blackwell, K. C., & Smith, D. M. (2007). The confounded nature of angry men and happy women. *Journal of Personality and Social Psychology, 92*, 179–190.

Becker, V. D., Sagarin, B. J., Guadagno, R. E., Millevoi, A., & Nicastle, L. D. (2004). When the sexes need not differ: Emotional responses to the sexual and emotional aspects of infidelity. *Personal Relationships, 11*, 529–538.

Betzig, L. (1985). Despotism and differential reproduction: A Darwinian view of history. New York: Aldine de Gruyter.

Betzig, L. (1992). Roman polygyny. *Ethology and Sociobiology, 13*, 309–349.

Boehm, C. (1999). *Hierarchy in the forest*. London: Harvard University Press.

Brown, D. E. (1991). *Human universals*. New York: McGraw-Hill.

Bugental, D. B. (2000). Acquisition of the algorithms of social life: A domain-based approach. *Psychological Bulletin, 126*, 187–219.

Burnstein, E., Crandall, C., & Kitayama, S. (1994). Some neo-Darwinian decision rules for altruism: Weighing cues for inclusive fitness as a function of the biological importance of the decision. *Journal of Personality and Social Psychology, 67*, 773–389.

Bushman, B. J. (1993). Human aggression while under the influence of alcohol and other drugs: An integrative research review. *Current Directions in Psychological Science, 2*, 148–152.

Buss, D. M. (1989a). Conflict between the sexes: Strategic interference and the evocation of anger and upset. *Journal of Personality & Social Psychology, 56*, 735–747.

Buss, D. M. (1989b). Sex differences in human mate preferences: Evolutionary hypotheses tests in 37 cultures. *Behavioral and Brain Sciences, 12*, 1–49.

Buss, D. M. (1990). The evolution of anxiety and social exclusion. *Journal of Social and Clinical Psychology, 9*, 196–210.

Buss, D. M. (1995). Psychological sex differences: Origins through sexual selection. *American Psychologist, 50*, 164–168.

Buss, D. M. (1999). Evolutionary psychology: A new paradigm for psychological science. In D. H. Rosen & M. C. Luebbert (Eds.), *Evolution of the psyche. Human evolution, behavior and intelligence* (pp. 1–33). Westport, CT: Praeger Publisher/Greenwood Publishing.

Buss, D. M. (2000). *Jealousy: The dangerous passion*. New York: Free Press.

Buss, D. M. (2002). Human mate guarding. *Neuroendocrinology Letter Special Issue, 23*, 23–29.

Buss, D. M. (2005). *The handbook of evolutionary psychology*. Hoboken, NJ: Wiley.

Buss, D. M., & Barnes, M. (1986). Preferences in human mate selection. *Journal of Personality and Social Psychology, 50*, 559–570.

Buss, D. M., & Kenrick, D. T. (1998). Evolutionary social psychology. In D. T. Gilbert, S. T. Fiske, & G. Lindzey (Eds.), *Handbook of social psychology* (Vol. 2, 4th ed., pp. 982–1026). New York: McGraw-Hill.

Buss, D. M., Larsen, R. J., Westen, D., &; Semmelroth, J. (1992). Sex differences in jealousy: Evolution, physiology, and psychology. *Psychological Science, 3*, 251–255.

Buss, D. M., & Schmitt, D. P. (1993). Sexual strategies theory: A contextual evolutionary analysis of human mating. *Psychological Review, 100*, 204–232.

Buss, D. M., & Shackelford, T. K. (1997). From vigilance to violence: Mate retention tactics in married couples. *Journal of Personality and Social Psychology, 72*, 346–361.

Caporeal, L. R. (1997). The evolution of truly social cognition: The core configurations model. *Personality and Social Psychology Review, 1*, 276–298.

Clark, R. D., & Hatfield, E. (1989). Gender differences in receptivity to sexual offers. *Journal of Psychology and Human Sexuality, 2*, 39–55.

Conway, L. G., & Schaller, M. (2002). On the verifiability of evolutionary psychological theories: An analysis of the psychology of scientific persuasion. *Personality and Social Psychology Review, 6*, 152–166.

Cosmides, L., & Tooby, J. (1992). Cognitive adaptations for social exchange. In J. Barkow, L. Cosmides, & J. Tooby (Eds.), *The adapted mind* (pp. 163–228). New York: Oxford University Press.

Cosmides, L., & Tooby, J. (2005). Neurocognitive adaptations designed for social exchange. In D. M. Buss (Ed.), *The handbook of evolutionary psychology.* New York: Wiley.

Cosmides, L., Tooby, J., & Barkow, J. (1992). Evolutionary psychology and conceptual integration. In J. Barkow, L. Cosmides, & J. Tooby (Eds.), *The adapted mind: Evolutionary psychology and the generation of culture.* New York: Oxford University Press.

Cottrell, C. A., & Neuberg, S. L. (2005). Different emotional reactions to different groups: A sociofunctional threat-based approach to 'prejudice.' *Journal of Personality and Social Psychology, 88*, 770–789.

Cottrell, C. A., Neuberg, S. L., & Li, N. P. (2007). What do people desire in others? A sociofunctional perspective on the importance of different valued characteristics. *Journal of Personality and Social Psychology, 92*, 208–231.

Crawford, C., & Krebs, D. (2008). *Foundations of evolutionary psychology.* New York: Erlbaum.

Cunningham, M. R., Barbee, A. P., & Pike, C. L. (1990). What do women want? Facialmetric assessment of multiple motives in the perception of male facial physical attractiveness. *Journal of Personality and Social Psychology, 59*, 61–72.

Dabbs, J., Jr., & Morris, R. (1990). Testosterone, social class, and antisocial behavior in a sample of 4,462 men. *Psychological Science, 1*, 209–211.

Daly, M., Salmon, C., & Wilson, M. (1997). Kinship: The conceptual hole in psychological studies of social cognition and close relationships. In J. A. Simpson & D. T. Kenrick (Eds.), *Evolutionary social psychology* (pp. 265–296). Mahwah, NJ: Erlbaum.

Daly, M., & Wilson, M. (1980). Discriminative parental solicitude: A biological perspective. *Journal of Marriage & Family, 42*, 277–288.

Daly, M., & Wilson, M. I. (1983). *Sex, evolution and behavior: Adaptations for reproduction* (2nd ed.). Boston, MA: Willard Grant Press.

Daly, M., & Wilson, M. I. (1985). Child abuse and other risks of not living with both parents. *Ethology & Sociobiology*, 6, 197–210.

Daly, M., & Wilson, M. (1988). *Homicide.* Hawthorne, NY: Aldine de Gruyter.

DeBruine, L. M. (2002). Facial resemblance enhances trust. *Proceedings of the Royal Society of London B, 269*, 1307–1312.

DeBruine L. M. (2005). Trustworthy but not lust-worthy: Context-specific effects of facial resemblance. *Proceedings of the Royal Society of London, B, 272*, 919–922.

DeSteno, D. A., & Salovey, P. (1996). Evolutionary origins of sex differences in jealousy? Questioning the 'fitness' of the model. *Psychological Science, 7*, 367–372.
DeWall, C. N., Maner, J. K., & Rouby, D. A. (2009). Social exclusion and early-stage interpersonal perception: Selective attention to signs of acceptance. *Journal of Personality and Social Psychology, 96*, 729–741.
DeWall, C. N., Twenge, J. M., Gitter, S. A., & Baumeister, R. F. (2009). It's the thought that counts: The role of hostile cognition in shaping aggressive responses to social exclusion. *Journal of Personality and Social Psychology, 96*, 45–59.
Dunbar, R.I.M. (1993). Coevolution of neocortex size, group size and language in humans. *Behavioral Brain Sciences*, 16, 681-735.
Eagly, A. H., & Wood, W. (1999). The origins of sex differences in human behavior: Evolved dispositions versus social roles. *American Psychologist, 54*, 408–423.
Easton, J. A., Schipper, L. D., & Shackelford, T. K. (2007). Morbid jealousy from an evolutionary psychological perspective. *Evolution and Human Behavior, 28*, 399–402.
Eastwick, P. W., & Finkel, E. J. (2008). Sex differences in mate preferences revisited: Do people know what they initially desire in a romantic partner? *Journal of Personality and Social Psychology, 94*, 245–264.
Eibl-Eibesfeldt, I. (1989). *Human ethology*. New York: Aldine de Gruyter.
Eisenberger, N. I., Lieberman, M. D., & Williams, K. D. (2003). Does rejection hurt? An fMRI study of social exclusion. *Science, 302*, 290–292.
Ekman, P. (1982). *Emotion in the human face* (2nd ed.) Cambridge: Cambridge University Press.
Ekman, P., & Friesen, W. (1976). *Pictures of facial affect*. Palo Alto, CA: Consulting Psychologists Press.
Ellis, L. (1995). Dominance and reproductive success among nonhuman animals. *Ethology and Sociobiology, 16*, 257–333.
Essock-Vitale, S., & McGuire, M. (1985). Women's lives viewed from an evolutionary perspective. II. Patterns of helping. *Ethology and Sociobiology, 6*, 155–173.
Faulkner, J., & Schaller, M. (2007). Nepotistic nosiness: Inclusive fitness and vigilance of kin members' romantic relationships. *Evolution and Human Behavior, 28*, 430–438.
Fehr, E., Fischbacher, U., & Gachter, S. (2002). Strong reciprocity, human cooperation and the enforcement of social norms. *Human Nature, 13*, 1–25.
Fessler, D. M.T. (2001). Luteal phase immunosuppression and meat eating. *Rivista di Biologia/Biology Forum* 94(3), 403–426.
Fessler, D. M.T. (2002). Reproductive immunosuppression and diet: An evolutionary perspective on pregnancy sickness and meat consumption. *Current Anthropology* 43(1), 19–39, 48–61.
Fessler, D. M.T., & Navarrete, C. D. (2003). Meat is good to taboo: Dietary proscriptions as a product of the interaction of psychological mechanisms and social processes. *Journal of Cognition and Culture* 3(1), 1–40.

Finkel, E. J. (2007). Impelling and inhibiting forces in the perpetration of intimate partner violence. *Review of General Psychology, 11*, 193–207.

Finkel, E. J., & Eastwick, P. W. (2009). Arbitrary social norms influence sex differences in romantic selectivity. *Psychological Science, 20*, 1290–1295.

Fisek, M. H., & Ofshe, R. (1970). The process of status evolution. *Sociometry, 33*, 327–346.

Fisher, R. A. (1958). *The genetical theory of natural selection* (2nd ed.). New York: Dover.

Fiske, A. P. (1992). The four elementary forms of sociality: Framework for a unified theory of social relations. *Psychological Review, 99*, 689–723.

Fodor, J. A. (1983). *The modularity of mind: An essay on faculty psychology*. Cambridge, MA: MIT Press.

Fox, E., Russo, R., Bowles, R., & Dutton, K. (2001). Do threatening stimuli draw or hold visual attention in subclinical anxiety? *Journal of Experimental Psychology: General, 130*, 681–700.

Frank, R. H. (1988). *Passions within reason: The strategic role of the emotions.* New York: Norton.

Frank, R. H. (2001). Cooperation through emotional commitment. In R. M. Nesse (Ed.), *Evolution and the capacity for commitment* (pp. 57–76). New York: Russell Sage.

Gangestad, S. W., & Buss, D. M. (1993). Pathogen prevalence and human mate preferences. *Ethology and Sociobiology, 14*, 89–96.

Gangestad, S. G., Haselton, M. G., & Buss, D. M. (2006a). Evolutionary foundations of cultural variation: Evoked culture and mate preferences. Target article. *Psychological Inquiry, 17*, 75–95.

Gangestad, S. G., Haselton, M. G., & Buss, D. M. (2006b). Toward an integrative understanding of evoked and transmitted culture: The importance of specialized psychological design. *Psychological Inquiry, 17*, 138–151.

Gangestad, S. W., & Simpson, J. A. (2000). The evolution of human mating: Trade-offs and strategic pluralism. *Behavioral and Brain Sciences, 23*, 573–644.

Gangestad, S. W., & Simpson, J. A. (2007). *The evolution of mind: Fundamental questions and controversies*. New York: Guilford Press.

Gangestad, S. W., & Thornhill, R. (1997). The evolutionary psychology of extra-pair sex: The role of fluctuating asymmetry. *Evolution and Human Behavior, 18*, 69–88.

Garcia, J., & Koelling, R. A. (1966). Relation of cue to consequence in avoidance learning. *Psychonomic Science, 4*, 123–124.

Gardner, W. L., Pickett, C. L., & Brewer, M. B. (2000). Social exclusion and selective memory. How the need to belong influences memory for social events. *Personality and social Psychology Bulletin, 26*, 486–496.

Gaulin, S., & Robbins, C. (1991). Trivers-Willard effect in contemporary North American society. *American Journal of Physical Anthropology, 85*, 61–69.

Geary, D. C. (1998). *Male, female: The evolution of human sex differences*. New York: American Psychological Association.

Geary, D. C. (2000). Evolution and proximate expression of human paternal investment. *Psychological Bulletin, 126*, 55–77.

Gonzaga, G. C., Haselton, M. G., Smurda, J., Davies, M., & Poore, J. C. (2008). Love, desire, and the suppression of thoughts of romantic alternatives. *Evolution and Human Behavior, 29*, 119–126.

Gonzaga, G. C., Keltner, D., Londahl, E. A., & Smith, M. D. (2001). Love and the commitment problem in romantic relations and friendship. *Journal of Personality and Social Psychology, 81*, 247–262.

Greenberg, L. (1979). Genetic component of bee odor in kin recognition. *Science, 206*, 1095–1097.

Greiling, H., & Buss, D. M. (2000). Women's sexual strategies: The hidden dimension of extra-pair mating. *Personality and Individual Differences, 28*, 929–963.

Griskevicius, V., Cialdini, R. B., & Kenrick, D. T. (2006a). Peacocks, Picasso, and parental investment: The effects of romantic motives on creativity. *Journal of Personality and Social Psychology, 91*, 63–76.

Griskevicius, V., Goldstein, N. J., Mortensen, C. R., Cialdini, R. B., & Kenrick, D. T. (2006b). Going along versus going alone: When fundamental motives facilitate strategic (non)conformity. *Journal of Personality and Social Psychology, 91*, 281–294.

Griskevicius, V., Tybur, J. M., Sundie, J. M., Cialdini, R. B., Miller, G. F., & Kenrick, D. T. (2007). Blatant benevolence and conspicuous consumption: When romantic motives elicit strategic costly signals. *Journal of Personality and Social Psychology, 93*, 85–102.

Griskevicius, V., Tybur, J. M., & Van den Bergh, B. (2010). Going green to be seen: Status, reputation, and conspicuous conservation. *Journal of Personality and Social Psychology. 98, 392–404.*

Gutierres, S. E., Kenrick, D. T., & Partch, J. J. (1999). Beauty, dominance, and the mating game: Contrast effects in self-assessment reflect gender differences in mate selection. *Personality and Social Psychology Bulletin, 25*, 1126–1134.

Guttentag, M., & Secord, P. F. (1983). *Too many women? The sex ratio question*. Beverly Hills, CA: Sage Publications.

Hamilton, W. D. (1964). The genetical evolution of social behavior: I & II. *Journal of Theoretical Biology, 7*, 1–32.

Hansen, C. H., & Hansen, R. D. (1988). Finding the face in the crowd: An anger superiority effect. *Journal of Personality and Social Psychology, 54*, 917–924.

Harris, C. R. (2003). A review of sex differences in sexual jealousy, including self-report data, psychophysiological responses, interpersonal violence, and morbid jealousy. *Personality and Social Psychology Review, 7*, 102–128.

Harris, C. R. (2005). Male and female jealousy, still more similar than different: Reply to Sagarin (2005). *Personality and Social Psychology Review, 9*, 76–86.

Haselton, M. G., & Gangestad, S. W. (2006). Conditional expression of women's desires and men's mate guarding across the ovulatory cycle. *Hormones and Behavior, 49*, 509–518.

Haselton, M. G., & Nettle, D. (2006). The paranoid optimist: An integrative evolutionary model of cognitive biases. *Personality and Social Psychology Review, 10*, 47–66.

Hazan, C., & Diamond, L. M. (2000). The place of attachment in human mating. *Review of General Psychology, 4*, 186–204.

Henrich, J., & Gil-White, F. J. (2001). The evolution of prestige: Freely conferred deference as a mechanism for enhancing the benefits of cultural transmission. *Evolution and Human Behavior, 22*, 165–196.

Henrich J., McElreath, R., Barr, A., Ensminger, J., Barret, C., Bolyanatz, A., Camilo Cardenas, J., Gurven, M., Gwako, E., Henrich, N., Lesorogol, C., Marlowe, F., Tracer, D., and Ziker, J. (2006). Costly punishment across human societies. *Science*, 312, 1767–1770.

Hewlett, B. S. (1991). *Intimate fathers: The nature and context of Aka pygmy paternal infant care*. Ann Arbor: University of Michigan Press.

Hill, K., & Hurtado, A. M. (1996). *Ache life history*. Hawthorne, NY: Aldine de Gruyter.

Hoffman, M. (1981). Is altruism part of human nature? *Journal of Personality and Social Psychology, 40*, 121–137.

Holloway, R. L. (1974). On the meaning of brain size. A review of H. J. Jerison's 1973 *Evolution of the Brain and Intelligence. Science, 184*, 677–679.

Holmes, W. G., & Sherman , P. W. (1983). Kin recognition in animals. *American Scientist, 71*, 46–55.

Hrdy, S. H. (1999). *Mother Nature: A history of mothers, infants, and natural selection*. New York: Pantheon.

Jackson, J. J., & Kirkpatrick, L. A. (2007). The structure and measurement of human mating strategies: Toward a multidimensional model of sociosexuality. *Evolution and Human Behavior, 28*, 382–391.

Johnson, D. J., & Rusbult, C. E. (1989). Resisting temptation: Devaluation of alternative partners as a means of maintaining commitment in close relationships. *Journal of Personality and Social Psychology, 57*, 967–980.

Kaschak, M. P., & Maner, J. K. (2009). Embodiment, evolution, and social cognition: An integrative framework. *European Journal of Social Psychology, 39*, 1236–1244.

Keltner, D., Gruenfeld, D. H., & Anderson, C. (2003). Power, approach, and inhibition. *Psychological Review, 110*, 265–284.

Kenrick, D. T. (1987). Gender, genes, and the social environment: A biosocial interactionist perspective. In P. Shaver & C. Hendrick (Eds.), *Review of personality and social psychology* (Vol. 7). Newbury Park, CA: Sage.

Kenrick, D. T., Becker, D. V., Butner, J., Li, N. P., &. Maner, J. K. (2003). Evolutionary cognitive science: Adding what and why to how the mind works. In J. Fitness &

K. Sterelny (Eds.), *From mating to mentality: Evaluating evolutionary psychology* (pp. 13–38). New York: Psychology Press.

Kenrick, D. T., Griskevicius, V., Neuberg, S. L., & Schaller, M. (2010). Renovating the pyramid of needs: Contemporary extensions built upon ancient foundations. *Perspectives on Psychological Science*, 5(in press).

Kenrick, D. T., & Keefe, R. C. (1992). Age preferences in mates reflect sex differences in mating strategies. *Behavioral & Brain Sciences, 15*, 75– 91.

Kenrick, D. T., & Li. N. (2000). The Darwin is in the details. *American Psychologist, 55*, 1060–1061.

Kenrick, D. T., Li, N. P., & Butner, J. (2003). Dynamical evolutionary psychology: Individual decision-rules and emergent social norms. *Psychological Review, 110*, 3–28.

Kenrick, D. T., Maner, J. K., Butner, J., Li, N. P., Becker, D. V., & Schaller, M. (2002). Dynamical evolutionary psychology: Mapping the domains of the new interactionist paradigm. *Personality and Social Psychology Review, 6*, 347–356.

Kenrick, D. T., Maner, J. K., & Li, N. P. (2005). Evolutionary social psychology. In D. Buss (Ed.), *The handbook of evolutionary psychology.* Hoboken, N.J: John Wiley & Sons.

Kenrick, D. T., Neuberg, S. L., & Cialdini, R. B. (1999). *Social psychology: Unraveling the mystery*. Boston: Allyn & Bacon.

Kenrick, D. T., Neuberg, S. L., Zierk, K., & Krones, J. (1994). Evolution and social cognition: Contrast effects as a function of sex, dominance, and physical attractiveness. *Personality & Social Psychology Bulletin, 20*, 210–217.

Kenrick, D. T., Nieuweboer, S., & Buunk, A. P. (2010). Universal mechanisms and cultural diversity: Replacing the blank slate with a coloring book. In M. Schaller, S. Heine, A. Norenzayan, T. Yamagishi, & T. Kameda (Eds.), *Evolution, culture, and the human mind* (pp. 257–272). Mahwah, NJ: Lawrence Erlbaum Associates.

Kenrick, D. T., Sadalla, E. K., Groth, G., & Trost, M. R. (1990). Evolution, traits, and the stages of human courtship: Qualifying the parental investment model. *Journal of Personality, 58*, 97–116.

Kenrick, D. T., Sadalla, E. K., & Keefe, R. C. (1998). Evolutionary cognitive psychology: The missing heart of modern cognitive science. In C. Crawford & D. L. Krebs (Eds.), *Handbook of Evolutionary Psychology* (pp. 485–514). Hillsdale, NJ: Erlbaum.

Kenrick, D. T., Sundie, J. M. & Kurzban, R. (2008). Cooperation and conflict between kith, kin, and strangers: Game theory by domains. In C. Crawford & D. Krebs (Eds.), *Foundations of evolutionary psychology* (pp. 353–370). New York: Lawrence Erlbaum Associates.

Kenrick, D. T., Trost, M. R., & Sundie, J. M. (2004). Sex-roles as adaptations: An evolutionary perspective on gender differences and similarities. In A. H. Eagly, A. Beall, & R. Sternberg (Eds.), *Psychology of Gender* (pp. 65–91). New York: Guilford Press.

Ketelaar, T., & Ellis, B. J. (2000). Are evolutionary explanations unfalsifiable? Evolutionary psychology and the Lakatosian philosophy of science. *Psychological Inquiry, 11*, 1–21.

Kipnis, D. (1972). Does power corrupt? *Journal of Personality & Social Psychology, 24,* 33–41.

Klein, S. B., Cosmides, L., Tooby, J., & Chance, S. (2002). Decisions and the evolution of memory: Multiple systems, multiple functions. *Psychological Review, 109,* 306–329.

Krebs, D. (1987). The challenge of altruism in biology and psychology. In C. Crawford, M. Smith, & D. Krebs (Eds.), *Sociobiology and psychology: Ideas, issues, and applications* (pp. 81–118). Hillsdale, NJ: Erlbaum.

Krupp, D. B., DeBruine, L. M., & Barclay, P. (2008). A cue of kinship promotes cooperation for the public good. *Evolution and Human Behavior, 29,* 49–55.

Kurzban, R., & Aktipis, C. A. (2007). Modularity and the social mind: Are psychologists too self-ish? *Personality and Social Psychology Review, 11,* 131–149.

Kurzban, R., & Leary, M. R. (2001). Evolutionary origins of stigmatization: The functions of social exclusion. *Psychological Bulletin, 127,* 187–208.

Kurzban, R., Tooby, J., & Cosmides, J. (2001). Can race be erased? Coalitional computation and social categorization. *Proceedings of the National Academy of Sciences, 98,* 15387– 15392.

Leary, M. R., Twenge, J. M., & Quinlivan, E. (2006). interpersonal rejection as a determinant of anger and aggression. *Personality and Social Psychology Review, 10,* 111–132.

Li, N. P., Bailey, J. M., Kenrick, D. T., & Linsenmeier, J. A. (2002). The necessities and luxuries of mate preferences: Testing the trade-offs. *Journal of Personality and Social Psychology, 82,* 947–955.

Li, N. P., & Kenrick, D. T. (2006). Sex similarities and differences in preferences for short-term mates: What, whether, and why. *Journal of Personality and Social Psychology, 90,* 468–489.

Lieberman, D., Tooby, J., & Cosmides, L. (2007). The architecture of human kin detection. *Nature, 445,* 727–731.

Low, B. S. (1990). Marriage systems and pathogen stress in human societies. *American Zoologist, 30,* 325–340.

Lydon, J. E., Fitzsimons, G. M., & Naidoo, L. (2003). Devaluation versus enhancement of attractive alternatives: A critical test using the calibration paradigm. *Personality and Social Psychology Bulletin, 29,* 349–359.

Lydon, J. E., Meana, M., Sepinwall, D., Richards, N., & Mayman, A. (1999). The commitment calibration hypothesis: When do people devalue attractive alternatives? *Personality and Social Psychology Bulletin, 25,* 152–161.

MacDonald, G., & Leary, M. R. (2005). Why does social exclusion hurt? The relationship between social and physical pain. *Psychological Bulletin, 131,* 202–223.

Maner, J. K. (2009). Anxiety: Proximate processes and ultimate functions. *Social and Personality Psychology Compass, 3,* 798–811.

Maner, J. K., DeWall, C. N., Baumeister, R. F., & Schaller, M. (2007). Does social exclusion motivate interpersonal reconnection? Resolving the "porcupine problem." *Journal of Personality and Social Psychology, 92,* 42–55.

Maner, J. K., DeWall, C. N., & Gailliot, M. T. (2008). Selective attention to signs of success: Social dominance and early stage interpersonal perception. *Personality and Social Psychology Bulletin, 34*, 488–501.

Maner, J. K., & Gailliot, M. T. (2007). Altruism and egoism: Prosocial motivations for helping depend on relationship context. *European Journal of Social Psychology, 37*, 347–358.

Maner, J. K., Gailliot, M. T., & Miller, S. L. (2009). The implicit cognition of relationship maintenance: Inattention to attractive alternatives. *Journal of Experimental Social Psychology, 45*, 174–179.

Maner, J. K., Gailliot, M. T., Rouby, D. A., & Miller, S. L. (2007). Can't take my eyes off you: Attentional adhesion to mates and rivals. *Journal of Personality and Social Psychology, 93*, 389–401.

Maner, J. K., Kenrick, D. T., Becker, D. V., Delton, A. W., Hofer, B., Wilbur, C., & Neuberg, S. (2003). Sexually selective cognition: Beauty captures the mind of the beholder. *Journal of Personality and Social Psychology, 85*, 1107–1120.

Maner, J. K., Kenrick, D. T., Neuberg, S. L., Becker, D. V., Robertson, T., Hofer, B., Delton, A., Butner, J., & Schaller, M. (2005). Functional projection: How fundamental social motives can bias interpersonal perception. *Journal of Personality and Social Psychology, 88*, 63–78.

Maner, J. K., & Mead, N. (in press). The essential tension between leadership and power: When leaders sacrifice group goals for the sake of self-interest. *Journal of Personality and Social Psychology*

Maner, J. K., Miller, S. L., Rouby, D. A., & Gailliot, M. T. (2009). Intrasexual vigilance: The implicit cognition of romantic rivalry. *Journal of Personality and Social Psychology, 97*, 74–87.

Maner, J. K., Miller, S. L., Schmidt, N. B., & Eckel, L. A. (2008). Submitting to defeat: Social anxiety, dominance threat, and decrements in testosterone. *Psychological Science, 19*, 264–268.

Maner, J. K., Miller, S. L., Schmidt, N. B., & Eckel, L. A. (2010). The endocrinology of exclusion: Rejection elicits motivationally tuned changes in progesterone. *Psychological Science* 21, 581–588.

Maner, J. K., Rouby, D. A., & Gonzaga, G. (2008). Automatic inattention to attractive alternatives: The evolved psychology of relationship maintenance. *Evolution & Human Behavior, 29*, 343–349.

Marlowe, F. W., Berbesque, J. C., Barr, A., Barrett, C., Bolyanatz, A., Cardenas, J. C., Ensminger, J., Gurven, M., Gwako, E., Henrich, J., Henrich, N., Lesorogol, C., McElreath, R., & Tracer, D. (2008). More 'altruistic' punishment in larger societies. *Proceedings of the Royal Society Biology, 275*, 587–590.

Marshall, D. S., & Suggs, R. G. (1971). *Human sexual behavior: Variations in the ethnographic spectrum*. New York: Basic Books.

Mazur, A., & Booth, A. (1998). Testosterone and dominance in men. *Behavioral and Brain Sciences, 21*, 353–397.

McClelland, D. C. (1975). *Power: The inner experience*. Oxford, England: Irvington.

McGinnis, R. (1958). Campus values in mate selection: A repeat study. *Social Forces, 36*, 368–373.

Mealey, L., Daood, C., & Krage, M. (1996). Enhanced memory for faces of cheaters. *Ethology and Sociobiology, 17*, 119–128.

Miller, G. F. (2000). *The mating mind: How sexual choice shaped the evolution of human nature*. New York: Doubleday.

Miller, R. S. (1997). Inattentive and contented: Relationship commitment and attention to alternatives. *Journal of Personality and Social Psychology, 73*, 758–766.

Miller, S. L., & Maner, J. K. (2010). Scent of a woman: Male testosterone responses to female olfactory ovulation cues. *Psychological Science* 21, 276–283.

Moore, B. R. (2004). The evolution of learning. *Biological Review, 79*, 301–335.

Muraven, M. R., & Baumeister, R. F. (2000). Self-regulation and depletion of limited resources: Does self-control resemble a muscle? *Psychological Bulletin, 126*, 247–259.

Navarrete, C. D., Olsson, A., Ho, A., Mendes, W., Thomsen, L., & Sidanius, J. (2009). Fear extinction to an outgroup face: The role of target gender. *Psychological Science, 20*, 155–158.

Neuberg, S. L. (2003). Sexually selective cognition: Beauty captures the mind of the beholder. *Journal of Personality and Social Psychology, 85*, 1107–1120.

Neuberg, S. L., & Cottrell, C. A. (2006). Evolutionary bases of prejudices. In M. Schaller, J. A. Simpson, & D. T. Kenrick (Eds.), *Evolution and social psychology* (pp. 163–187). Psychology Press: New York.

Neuberg, S. L, Kenrick, D. T., & Schaller, M. (2009). Evolutionary social psychology. In S. T. Fiske, D. T. Gilbert, & G. Lindzey (Eds.), *Handbook of social psychology* (5th ed.). New York: John Wiley & Sons.

Neyer, F. J., & Lang, F. R. (2003). Blood is thicker than water: Kinship orientation across adulthood. *Journal of Personality and Social Psychology, 84*, 310–321.

Norenzayan, A. (2006). Evolution and transmitted culture. *Psychological Inquiry, 17*, 123–128.

Öhman, A, & Mineka, S. (2001). Fears, phobias, and preparedness: Toward an evolved module of fear and fear learning. *Psychological Review, 108*, 483–522.

Panksepp, J. (1982). Toward a general psychobiological theory of emotions. *Behavioral & Brain Sciences, 5*, 407–467.

Park, J. H., Faulkner, J., & Schaller, M. (2003). Evolved disease-avoidance processes and contemporary anti-social behavior: Prejudicial attitudes and avoidance of people with physical disabilities. *Journal of Nonverbal Behavior, 27*, 65–87.

Park, J. H., Schaller, M., & Crandall, C. S. (2007). Pathogen-avoidance mechanisms and the stigmatization of obese people. *Evolution and Human Behavior, 28*, 410–414.

Park, J., Schaller, M., & Van Vugt, M. (2008). The psychology of human kin recognition: Heuristic cues, erroneous inferences, and their implications. *Review of General Psychology, 12*, 215–235.

Parkinson, B. (2005). Do facial movements express emotions or communicate motives? *Personality and Social Psychology Review, 9*, 278–311.

Penton-Voak, I. S., Perrett, D. I., Casteles, D. L., Kobayashi, T., Burt, D. M., Murray, L. K., & Minamisawa, R. (1999). Female preference for male faces changes cyclically. *Nature, 399*, 741–742.

Pillsworth, E. G., & Haselton, M. G. (2006). Male sexual attractiveness predicts differential ovulatory shifts in female extra-pair attraction and male mate retention. *Evolution and Human Behavior, 27*, 247–258.

Pinker, S. (1997). *How the mind works*. New York: W. W. Norton.

Plutchik, R. (1980). A general psychoevolutionary theory of emotion. In R. Plutchik & H. Kellerman (Eds.), *Emotions: Theory, research, and experience* (Vol. 1). New York: Academic Press.

Preston, S. D., and de Waal, F. B. M. (2002). Empathy: Its ultimate and proximate bases. *Behavioral and Brain Sciences, 25*, 1–71.

Rasmussen, D. R. (1981). Pair bond strength and stability and reproductive success. *Psychological Review, 88*, 274–290.

Reykowski, J. (1980). Origin of prosocial motivation: Heterogeneity of personality development. *Studia Psychologia, 22*, 91–106.

Richerson, P. J., & Boyd, R. (2005). *Not by genes alone: How culture transformed human evolution*. Chicago: University of Chicago Press.

Ridley, M. (2003). Nature via nurture: Genes, experience, and what makes us human. New York: HarperCollins.

Rose, R. M., Bernstein, I. S., & Holaday, J. W. (1971). Plasma testosterone, dominance rank, and aggressive behavior in a group of male rhesus monkeys. *Nature, 231*, 366.

Rozin, P., & Fallon, A. (1987). A perspective on disgust. *Psychological Review, 94*, 23–41.

Sadalla, E. K., Kenrick, D. T., & Venshure, B. (1987). Dominance and heterosexual attraction. *Journal of Personality and Social Psychology, 52*, 730–738.

Sagarin, B. J. (2005). Reconsidering evolved sex differences in jealousy: Comment on Harris (2003). *Personality & Social Psychology Review, 9*, 62–75.

Schaller, M., & Murray, D. R. (2008). Pathogens, personality and culture: Disease prevalence predicts worldwide variability in sociosexuality, extraversion, and openness to experience. *Journal of Personality and Social Psychology, 95*, 212–221.

Schaller, M., Norenzayan, A., Heine, S. J., Yamagishi, T., & Kameda, T. (2010). *Evolution, culture, and the human mind*. New York: Psychology Press.

Schaller, M., Park, J. H., & Mueller, A. (2003). Fear of the dark: Interactive effects of beliefs about danger and ambient darkness on ethnic stereotypes. *Personality and Social Psychology Bulletin, 29*, 637–649.

Scheib, J. E. (2001). Context-specific mate choice criteria: Women's trade-offs in the contexts of long-term and extra-pair mateships. *Personal Relationships, 8*, 371–389.

Scheib, J. E., Gangestad, S. W., & Thornhill, R. (1999). Facial attractiveness, symmetry, and cues of good genes. *Proceedings of the Royal Society of London, B, 266*, 1913–1917.

Schützwohl, A. (2008). The crux of cognitive load: Constraining deliberate and effortful decision processes in romantic jealousy. *Evolution and Human Behavior, 29*, 127–132.

Schwarz, N., & Clore, G. L. (1983). Mood, misattribution, and judgments of well-being: Informative and directive functions of affective states. *Journal of Personality and Social Psychology, 45*, 513–523.

Sedikides, C., & Skowronski, J. J. (1997). The symbolic self in evolutionary context. *Personality and Social Psychology Review, 1*, 80–102.

Segal, N. L., & Hershberger, S. L. (1999). Cooperation and competition in adolescent twins: Findings from a prisoner's dilemma game. *Evolution and Human Behavior, 20*, 29–51.

Seligman, M. E. P. (1971). Phobias and preparedness. *Behavior Therapy, 2*, 307–320.

Shackelford, T. K., Goetz, A. T., Buss, D. M., Euler, H. A., & Hoier, S. (2005). When we hurt the ones we love: Predicting violence against women from men's mate retention. *Personal Relationships, 12*, 447–463.

Shapiro, J., Ackerman, J., Neuberg, S. L., Maner, J. K., Becker, D. V., & Kenrick, D. T. (2009). Following in the wake of anger: When not discriminating is discriminating. *Personality & Social Psychology Bulletin, 35*, 1356–1367.

Sheets, V. L., Fredendall, L. L., & Claypool, H. M. (1997). Jealousy evocation, partner reassurance and relationship stability: An exploration of the potential benefits of jealousy. *Evolution and Human Behavior, 18*, 387–402.

Sherman, P. W. (1977). Nepotism and the evolution of alarm calls. *Science, 197*, 1246–1253.

Sherry, D. F., & Schacter, D. L. (1987). The evolution of multiple memory systems. *Psychological Review, 94*, 439–454.

Simpson, J. A., & Gangestad, S. W. (1991). Individual differences in sociosexuality: Evidence for convergent and discriminant validity. *Journal of Personality and Social Psychology, 67*, 870–883.

Simpson, J. A., Gangestad, S. W., & Lerma, M. (1990). Perception of physical attractiveness: Mechanisms involved in the maintenance of romantic relationships. *Journal of Personality and Social Psychology, 59*, 1192–1201.

Singh, D. (1993). Adaptive significance of waist-to-hip ratio and female attractiveness. *Journal of Personality and Social Psychology, 65*, 293–307.

Spencer, J. P., Blumberg, M. S., McMurray, B., Robinson, S. R., Samuelson, L. K., & Tomblin, J. B. (2009). Short arms and talking eggs: Why we should no longer abide the nativist-empiricist debate. *Child Development Perspectives, 3*, 79–87.

Sprecher, S., Sullivan, Q., & Hatfield, E. (1994). Mate selection preferences: Gender differences examined in a national sample. *Journal of Personality and Social Psychology, 66*, 1074–1080.

Stewart-Williams, S. (2008). Human beings as evolved nepotists: Exceptions to the rue and effects of cost of help. *Human Nature, 19*, 414–425.

Suomi, S. J. (1982). Sibling relationships in nonhuman primates. In M. E. Lamb & B. Sutton-Smith (Eds.), *Sibling relationships.* Mahwah NJ: Erlbaum.

Symons, D. (1979). *The evolution of human sexuality.* New York: Oxford University Press.

Tinbergen, N. (1963). On the aims and methods of ethology. *Zeitschrift für Tierpsychologie, 20,* 410–433.

Todd, P. M., Penke, L., Fasolo, B., & Lenton, A. P. (2007). Different cognitive processes underlie human mate choices and mate preferences. *Proceedings of the National Academy of Sciences USA, 104,* 15011–15016.

Tooby, J., & Cosmides, L. (1990). On the universality of human nature and the uniqueness of the individual: The role of genetics and adaptation. *Journal of Personality, 58,* 17–67.

Tooby, J., & Cosmides, L. (1992). The psychological foundations of culture. In J. Barkow, L. Cosmides, & J. Tooby (Eds.), *The adapted mind: Evolutionary psychology and the generation of culture.* New York: Oxford University Press.

Tomasello, M., Kruger, A. C., & Ratner, H. H. (1993). Cultural learning. *Behavioral and Brain Sciences, 16,* 495–552.

Trivers, R. L. (1971). The evolution of reciprocal altruism. *Quarterly Review of Biology, 46,* 35–37.

Trivers, R. L. (1972). Parental investment and sexual selection. In B. Campbell (Ed.), *Sexual selection and the descent of man* (pp. 136–179). Chicago: Aldine-Atherton.

Trivers, R. L. (1985). *Social evolution.* Menlo Park: Benjamin/Cummings.

Trivers, R. L., & Willard, D. E. (1973). Natural selection of parental ability to vary the sex ratio of offspring. *Science, 197,* 90–92.

van Vugt, M. (2006). Evolutionary origins of leadership and followership. *Personality and Social Psychology Review, 10,* 354–371.

van Vugt, M., Hogan, R., & Kaiser, R. (2008). Leadership, followership, and evolution: Some lessons from the past. *American Psychologist, 63,* 182–196.

Williams, K. D., Cheung, C. K.T., & Choi, W. (2000). Cyberostracism: Effects of being ignored over the internet. *Journal of Personality and Social Psychology, 79,* 748–762.

Wilson, E. O. (1975). *Sociobiology: The new synthesis.* Cambridge, MA: Harvard University Press.

Wilson, M., and Daly, M. (1996). Male sexual proprietariness and violence against wives. *Current Directions in Psychological Science, 5,* 2–7.

Wood, W., & Eagly, A. H. (2007). Social structural origins of sex differences in human mating. In S. W. Gangestad & J. A. Simpson (Eds.), *Evolution of the mind: Fundamental questions and controversies* (pp. 383–390). New York: Guilford Press.

Zebrowitz, L. A., & Collins, M. A. (1997). Accurate social perception at zero acquaintance: The affordances of a Gibsonian approach. *Personality and Social Psychology Review, 1,* 203–222.

Chapter 18

Cultural Psychology

Steven J. Heine

Introduction

Imagine what it must have been like. About 8 million years ago, rustling about the savannas of East Africa, there lived a family of apes. They had their ape-like concerns, struggling to get enough food, avoid the lions, negotiate the power hierarchy in their troupe, groom themselves, and take care of their offspring. Their lives would have looked awfully ordinary if we could see them now, and it is doubtful that there would have been any signs of the things that would happen to their descendants. Some of the descendants of those apes would evolve into what we recognize today as the species of chimpanzees and bonobos—clever apes living in small pockets of the jungles of central Africa. Some of the other descendants of these apes would evolve into a species whose members have gone on to populate the furthest reaches of the planet, split the atom, paint the Sistine Chapel, and invent the iPhone. What factors have determined the different trajectories of these biologically similar species? Many of the answers to this question have to do with culture.

Humans are a cultural species. That is, we depend critically on cultural learning in virtually all aspects of our lives. Whether we are trying to manage our resources, woo a mate, protect our family, enhance our status, or form a political alliance—goals that are pursued by people in all cultures—we do so in culturally particular ways (Richerson & Boyd, 2005). Of course, there are many psychological phenomena that appear similarly across cultures; there are also many that reveal pronounced differences (for a review see Norenzayan & Heine, 2005). The point is that all psychological phenomena, whether largely similar or different across cultures, remain entangled in cultural meanings. The challenge for understanding the mind of a cultural species is that it requires a rich knowledge of how the mind is shaped by cultural learning. The field of cultural psychology has emerged in response to this challenge.

Cultural psychologists share the key assumption that not all psychological processes are so inflexibly hardwired into the brain that they appear in identical ways across cultural contexts. Rather, psychological processes are seen to arise from evolutionarily shaped biological potentials becoming attuned to the particular cultural meaning system within which the individual develops. At the same time, cultures can be understood to emerge through the processes by which humans interact with and seize meanings and resources from them. In this way, culture and the mind can be said to be mutually constituted (Shweder, 1990). An effort to understand either one without considering the other is bound to be incomplete.

Why Is Studying Culture Important for Social Psychology?

One important set of questions that social psychologists address concerns how people make sense of their social worlds. However, when we use the term "people" we immediately have the challenge of determining "which people?" Social psychology surely would be a far more straightforward enterprise if the phenomena that we studied all emerged in identical ways across all cultural contexts. However, it is perhaps not surprising to social psychologists that many ways of thinking do importantly vary across cultural contexts, as this chapter will reveal, as in many ways culture can be seen as the social situation writ large. On the one hand, pronounced cultural variance has been identified in fundamental psychological phenomena such as perceptions of fairness (e.g., Henrich et al., 2005), approach-avoidance motivations (e.g., Lee, Aaker, & Gardner, 2000), attention (Chua, Boland, & Nisbett, 2005), preferences for formal reasoning (e.g., Norenzayan, Smith, Kim, & Nisbett, 2002b), the need for high self-esteem (e.g., Heine, Lehman, Markus, & Kitayama, 1999), and moral reasoning (e.g., Miller & Bersoff, 1992). At the same time, there are many key psychological phenomena for which varying degrees of universality have been compellingly established, such as facial expressions of emotions (Ekman, Sorenson, & Friesen, 1969), various mating preferences (Buss, 1989), sex differences in violence (Daly & Wilson, 1988), and the structure of personality (McCrae et al., 2005). Some psychological phenomena are manifest in more culturally variable ways than others, and it is typically not clear a priori which phenomena should be the most similar across cultures. Hence, if we are interested in assessing the universality of a particular phenomenon it is necessary to examine data from a wide array of samples.

Social psychologists do not always hypothesize about or assess the degree of universality in psychological processes, but when they do a major obstacle is the limited nature of the database. For example, a recent review of all papers published in the *Journal of Personality and Social Psychology* from 2003 to 2007 (Arnett, 2008) found that 94% of the samples were from Western countries, with 62% coming from the United States. Moreover, 67% of the American samples (and 80% of the non-American samples) were done by undergraduates in psychology courses at research universities. Similar geographic proportions were found for other fields in psychology. Curiously, this American dominance of psychology is unparalleled by other disciplines—a larger proportion of citations come from American researchers in psychology than they do for any of the other 19 sciences that were compared in one extensive international survey (May, 1997). Although it remains an interesting question to consider why psychology is more American than other sciences, the biased nature of the database means that often we simply do not know whether a given psychological phenomenon is universal because it likely has not been investigated in a sufficient range of cultural contexts (although there are a number of important cross-cultural research programs that are exceptions).

However, what is even more problematic for identifying the universality of psychological processes is that the psychological database does not just represent a narrow sample of the world's population, it often represents an *unusual* sample. The results of studies conducted on American undergraduates are frequently outliers within the context of an international database for many of the key domains in the behavioral sciences (Henrich, Heine, & Norenzayan, 2010). The available cross-cultural data find that for a number of fundamental psychological phenomena (such as some visual illusions, decisions in behavioral economic games, moral reasoning, self-concept, worldview defense, social motivations, analytic reasoning, spatial perception) (1) people from industrialized societies respond differently than those from small-scale societies, (2) people from Western industrialized societies demonstrate more pronounced responses than those from non-Western societies, (3) Americans show yet more extreme responses than other Westerners, and (4) the responses of contemporary American college students are even more different than those of non-college-educated American adults (Henrich et al., 2010). We have termed samples of American college students "WEIRD samples" (i.e., they are samples of Western, Educated, Industrialized, Rich, and Democratic societies), as the results from these samples are frequently (but not always) statistical outliers for many of the phenomena that psychologists study.

What do the unusual responses of such WEIRD samples mean for social psychologists? Do they mean that we need to avoid studying American undergraduates? Definitely not! There have always been and continue to be many good reasons for American researchers to study the most convenient samples for them as this allows researchers to test hypotheses about the nature of psychological phenomena, understand how these phenomena relate to each other, identify underlying mechanisms, and reveal the situations in which these phenomena occur—that is, studying WEIRD samples is not a problem for most of what social psychologists have always been interested in doing (for more discussion of this point see Mook, 1983). However, psychologists are often interested in generalizing far beyond their samples and in constructing universal theories. This goal is hindered when researchers rely solely on a database that is limited to a narrow and somewhat unrepresentative slice of human diversity (see Norenzayan & Heine, 2005, for methodological strategies for inferring universality from data from a limited number of cultures). Hence, to develop a universal theory of human nature it is of critical importance that samples other than exclusively WEIRD ones are included.

Another reason that the study of culture is important for psychology is that it increases our understanding of the nature of the psychological processes themselves. For example, take the case of the Mueller-Lyer illusion in Figure 18.1. Most likely the line on the left looks longer than the line on the right. However, people who were raised in subsistence environments do not see a difference in the length of these lines (Segall, Campbell, & Herskiovits, 1963). This instance of cultural variation provided a means to understanding why people even see this as an illusion. Apparently, being exposed to carpentered corners in the early years of life organizes the visual system such that we come to rely on the angles of corners to infer relative distance. In the absence of cultural variation for this illusion it is quite likely that researchers would not have learned that this illusion develops as a function of the environmental input of a carpentered world. Similar to how neuroscientists often study the cognitive deficits that people with brain injuries have as a tool for discovering what parts of the brain are associated with what types of cognitive abilities, cultural psychologists can also learn more about particular psychological phenomena by identifying cultures that engage in these phenomena relatively more or less than those in another culture. Learning about the minds of people from other cultures better helps us understand our own minds.

FIGURE 18.1. The Mueller-Lyer Illusion. People who were exposed to carpentered corners in their childhood tend to see the left line as looking longer than the right line, which is the nature of the illusion. In contrast, those who were not exposed to carpentered corners during their childhood do not see these two lines as an illusion: the lines appear the same length to them.

It is for these reasons that cultural psychology has been interested in exploring differences in various psychological processes between cultures (see Baumeister, 2005, for a discussion of how culture in psychology can also be fruitfully studied by considering similarities across cultures). In the following sections, I review the evidence for cultural variability in a number of key research programs in social psychology.

The Self-Concept

Much cultural psychological research extends from research on the self-concept. This research has largely focused on distinctions between independent and interdependent self-concepts and how these different self-views manifest with respect to self-consistency and flexibility, insider and outsider phenomenological experiences, and incremental and entity theories of self. Further, this section discusses the psychological experiences of those with multicultural selves.

Independent versus Interdependent Self-Concepts

People are not born with a particular self-concept; rather, the process of becoming a self is contingent on people interacting with and seizing meanings from their cultural environments. Because people are exposed to very different cultural experiences around the world, it follows that they will come to develop different kinds of self-concepts. As Clifford Geertz (1973) famously asserted, "we all begin with the natural equipment to live a thousand kinds of life but end in the end having lived only one" (p. 45).

Evidence for the cultural foundation of the self-concept comes from a number of sources. For example, many studies have assessed the structure of people's self-concepts by having people freely describe aspects of themselves using the Twenty Statements Test (Kuhn & McPartland, 1954). Such studies reveal that people from various Western cultural contexts, such as Australia, Britain, Canada, and Sweden, tend to describe themselves most commonly with statements that reflect their inner psychological characteristics, such as their attitudes, personality traits, and abilities. In contrast, people from various non-Western cultural contexts, such as Cook Islanders, Native Americans, Malaysians, Kenyans, Puerto Ricans, Indians, and various East Asian populations, show a greater tendency, relative to Westerners, to describe themselves by indicating relational roles and memberships that they possess (see Heine, 2008, for a review). Such cultural differences are already evident among kindergarten-aged children (Wang, 2004), revealing how early cultural experiences come to shape the self-concept.

These different patterns of responses in self-descriptions suggest that there are at least two different ways in which people might conceive themselves. One way, as evident in the most common responses of Westerners, is that the self can largely derive its identity from its inner attributes– a self-contained model of self that Markus and Kitayama (1991) labeled an independent self-concept. These attributes are assumed to reflect the essence of an individual in that they are viewed as stable across situations and across the lifespan, they are perceived to be unique (in that no on else is expected to have the same configuration of attributes), they are viewed as significant for regulating behavior, and individuals feel obligated to publicly advertise themselves in ways consistent with these attributes. A second way that people can conceptualize themselves, as was more common among the responses of those from non-Western cultures, is to view the self as largely deriving its identity from its relations with significant others; this model is termed an interdependent self-concept (Markus & Kitayama, 1991). With this view of self, people recognize that their behavior is contingent on their perceptions of other's thoughts, feelings, and actions, they attend to how their behaviors affect others, and they consider their relevant roles within each social context. The interdependent self is not a separate and distinct entity, but is embedded in a larger social group.

Because the self-concept is central to the ways that people process and interpret much information (Markus, 1977), it is perhaps not surprising that this distinction in self-concepts (which relates to individualism–collectivism; Triandis, 1989) has been related to a wide variety of different psychological processes. For example, cultural variation in independence and interdependence has been linked to cultural differences in motivations for uniqueness (e.g., Kim & Markus, 1999), self-enhancement (e.g., Heine et al., 1999), feelings of agency (e.g., Morling, Kitayama, & Miyamoto, 2002), kinds of emotional experiences (e.g., Mesquita, 2001), perspectives on relationships (e.g., Adams, 2005), and analytic versus holistic reasoning styles (e.g., Nisbett, Peng, Choi, & Norenzayan, 2001). At present, the distinction between independent and interdependent selves stands as the most fruitful way of making sense of many cultural differences in psychological processes (Oyserman, Coon, & Kemmelmeier, 2002). It is possible that other cultural dimensions will be found that have comparable degrees of explanatory power for making sense of cultural differences in various ways of thinking, but thus far independence and interdependence have attracted the most research interest.

Self-Consistency versus Flexibility

The idea that people strive to maintain a consistent self-concept has been central to many seminal theories regarding the self (e.g., Festinger, 1957; Heider, 1958; Swann, Wenzlaff, Krull, & Pelham, 1992); however, much of this research has targeted cultural samples in which independent self-concepts predominate. This fact matters because the independent self is viewed as a relatively bounded and autonomous entity, complete in and of itself, that is perceived to exist separately from others and the surrounding social context (Markus & Kitayama, 1991). Because independent selves are viewed as similar to objects in that they are viewed as whole, unified, integrated, stable, and inviolate entities (Shweder et al., 1998), core representations of the self tend to remain largely uninfluenced by the presence of others (although situations may activate different aspects of the working self-concept; Markus & Kunda, 1986). The independent self is experienced as relatively unchanging and constant across situations, and people are often willing to make rather costly sacrifices to preserve a semblance of self-consistency (for example, see Freedman & Fraser, 1966).

In contrast, for people with interdependent views of self, an individual's relationships and roles take precedence over abstracted and internalized attributes, such as attitudes, traits, and abilities. Hence, a person with an interdependent self who changes situations finds himself or herself in new roles bearing different obligations, and these should lead to different experiences of the self. Indeed, much research with participants from cultures in which interdependent selves are common reveals less evidence for a self-concept that is consistent across contexts compared with cultures in which independent selves predominate. For example, Kanagawa, Cross, and Markus (2001) found that Japanese (but not American) self-descriptions varied significantly depending on who was in the room when participants completed their questionnaires (that the interdependent self is grounded in its immediate context presents a real challenge to studying it—in what contexts lies the real interdependent self?). These cultural differences in consistency have also been observed in people's affective experiences: European-Americans show less variability in their emotions across situations than do Japanese, Hispanic Americans, and Indians (Oishi, Diener, Scollon, & Biswas-Diener, 2004). It is important to note, however, that whereas the self-concepts among non-Westerners appear more variable across contexts than those of Westerners, it is not the case that non-Westerners have unstable self-concepts. Rather, non-Westerners appear to develop a number of stable but context-specific self-views that depend on the relationships and roles that are activated in a given context, that are as stable across time as the self-concepts of Westerners (English & Chen, 2007).

Cultural differences in self-consistency are also apparent in that East Asians endorse more contradictory self-views than Westerners. For example, Chinese self-evaluations are more ambivalent (they contain both positive and negative statements) than those of Americans (Spencer-Rodgers, Peng, Wang, & Hou, 2004). Similarly, East Asians tend to endorse contradictory items about their personalities; for example, Koreans are more likely than Americans to state that they are both introverted and extraverted (Choi & Choi, 2002), and Japanese were more likely than Canadians to endorse both positively worded and reverse-scored items regarding the Big Five personality traits (Hamamura, Heine, &

Paulhus, 2008). Such contradictory self-knowledge is more readily available, and is simultaneously accessible, among East Asian participants than among Americans (Spencer-Rodgers, Boucher, Mori, Wang, & Peng, 2009).

Whereas psychological consistency has been linked with well-being among Westerners, the benefits of being consistent across situations are less apparent for East Asians. Suh (2002) found that whereas consistency across situations was associated with greater degrees of well-being, social skills, and being liked by others for Americans, these relations were far weaker for Koreans. Well-being and positive feelings about the self do not seem to be as tethered to a consistent identity for East Asians as they do for North Americans.

The above studies converge in demonstrating that people from cultures characterized by interdependent views of self have weaker tendencies for self-consistency than do those from cultures characterized by independent views of self. However, one alternative perspective is that people with interdependent selves have different kinds of consistency needs. For example, although there is little evidence that East Asians strive to keep their attitudes and behaviors consistent (Kashima, Siegal, Tanaka, & Kashima, 1992) or to reduce dissonance to the extent Westerners do (Heine & Lehman, 1997; Hiniker, 1969), East Asians do show some consistency motivations when others are involved. For example, Asian-Canadians will rationalize decisions that they make for others even though they do not rationalize the decisions that they make for themselves (Hoshino-Browne et al., 2005; also see Kitayama, Snibbe, Markus, & Suzuki, 2004). Likewise, Cialdini, Wosinska, and Barrett (1999) found that although the intentions of American participants were more consistent with their own past behaviors, Polish participants were more likely to be consistent with the behavior of others. In sum, people from more interdependent cultures aspire for consistency when they consider themselves in relation to others.

Insider versus Outsider Phenomenological Experiences

Self-concepts also vary in terms of the perspective that people habitually adopt. On the one hand, people may prioritize their own perspective, thereby making sense of the world in terms of how it unfolds for them. Alternatively, people may prioritize the perspective of an audience, and attend to the world and themselves in terms of how they imagine it appears to others. Cohen, Hoshino-Browne, and Leung (2007) refer to these two perspectives as insider and outsider phenomenological experiences. In interdependent cultural contexts, in which individuals need to adjust themselves to better fit in with the ingroup, it becomes crucial to know how they are being evaluated by others. In independent cultural contexts, in contrast, in which people's identity rests largely on the inner attributes that they possess, there is a cultural imperative to "know oneself" and to elaborate on their unique perspective.

There is much recent evidence for this cultural difference in phenomenological experiences. For example, Cohen and Gunz (2002) demonstrated that East Asians are more likely to recall memories of themselves when they were at the center of attention from a third-person perspective than are Westerners. Apparently, East Asians' attention to an audience leaks into and distorts their memories of themselves. Similarly, East Asians outperformed Westerners on a visual task in which they needed to take the perspective of their partner, making fewer visual fixations on objects that were not visible to their partner (Wu & Keysar, 2007). The perspective of an audience is also made more salient when people see themselves in a mirror (Duval & Wicklund, 1972), and research finds that the self-evaluations and behaviors of East Asians are less impacted by the presence of a mirror (suggesting that they habitually considered themselves from the perspective of an audience) than was the case for North Americans (Heine, Takemoto, Moskalenko, Lasaleta, & Henrich, 2008).

Multicultural Selves

Much cross-cultural research has also explored the self-concepts of those with multiple cultural experiences. If culture shapes the self, how do people from multiple cultural backgrounds represent the self? There are two complementary perspectives on this. One is that multicultural people have multiple self-concepts that are simultaneously accessible, and their typical thoughts and responses reflect a blending of these. Evidence for this can be seen in that Asian-Americans, for example, tend to perform intermediately on many psychological tasks compared with European-Americans and Asians in Asia (e.g., Heine & Hamamura, 2007; Norenzayan, Smith, Kim, & Nisbett, 2002b).

A second perspective is that multicultural people sequentially activate their different self-concepts, depending on situation or primes; this perspective is known as frame-switching (Hong, Morris, Chiu, & Benet-Martinez, 2000). For example, in one study Hong Kong Chinese were primed with either Chinese, American, or neutral thoughts by showing them cultural icons (or neutral images), and were subsequently asked to make attributions for the behaviors of computerized images of fish (Hong et al., 2000). Those who were primed with American icons made fewer external attributions for the fish's behavior than those who were primed with Chinese icons, with the attributions of those in the neutral prime condition falling in between. That is, Hong Kong Chinese sometimes access Western ways of thinking and sometimes they access Chinese ways of thinking. This kind of frame-switching is not equally likely for all biculturals; people are more likely to frame-switch if they see their dual cultural identities as integrated than if they see them in opposition (Benet-Martinez, Leu, Lee, & Morris, 2002), and if they were second-generation as opposed to first-generation immigrants (Tsai, Ying, & Lee, 2000).

The existence of frame-switching suggests that people can have multiple knowledge structures—that is networks of associated ideas. Activation of one part of the network (such as seeing an American icon) facilitates the activation of another part of that same network [such as preferring to explain people's (or fish's) behavior in terms of internal dispositions]. Although there is much evidence now that multiculturals often frame-switch, an obvious question to consider is whether such frame-switching effects are limited to those with multicultural experiences? The kinds of ideas that have been primed in frame-switching studies (such as thoughts regarding interdependence, external attributions, cooperation with ingroup members) would seem to be thoughts that are accessible to people everywhere, given that humans are such a highly social species. If people do have different networks of ideas associated with concepts such as interdependence than they do with concepts such as independence, then monocultural people should also frame-switch when different knowledge networks are activated. Indeed, many studies find that people with largely monocultural experiences also frame-switch (e.g., Kuhnen, Hannover, & Schubert, 2001; Trafimow, Triandis, & Goto, 1991; for a meta-analysis see Oyserman & Lee, 2008). For example, whereas much research finds that East Asians display more pronounced prevention motivations than Westerners (e.g., Elliot, Chirkov, Kim, & Sheldon, 2001), priming European-Americans with interdependent thoughts leads them to become more prevention oriented as well (Lee et al., 2000). That is, interdependent-primed European-Americans showed prevention motivations that were closer to those of nonprimed East Asians than were European-Americans who were not primed with interdependence. This indicates that the relations between interdependence and prevention motivations exist across cultural groups, so that anyone, multicultural or not, who thinks interdependent thoughts should also become more prevention oriented. Frame-switching thus is not limited to multiculturals. Nonetheless, multiculturals do show more extreme degrees of frame-switching than do monoculturals (Gardner, Gabriel & Dean, 2004), suggesting that the knowledge networks of multiculturals regarding ideas such as independence and interdependence are more clearly demarcated than they are for monoculturals.

Multicultural people appear to differ from monocultural people in another way—they tend to be more creative. When people adapt to different cultural environments they need to adopt a flexible style in how they approach problems, and this has been shown to be associated with enhanced creativity on a number of different creative tasks (Leung, Maddux, Galinsky, & Chiu, 2008; Maddux & Galinsky, 2009). This is particularly true among those with higher levels of identity integration (i.e., those who perceive compatibility between their two cultural identities; Cheng, Sanchez-Burks, & Lee, 2008).

Motivation

People's motivations are influenced by their cultural experiences. A number of key motivations have been found to appear differently across cultures, including motivations for self-enhancement, approach-avoidance motivations, agency and control, motivations to fit in or to stick out, achievement motivations, and motivations for honor.

Motivations for Self-Enhancement and Self-Esteem

Much research has focused on people's motivation for self-enhancement, that is, a desire to view yourself positively. This research reveals that most Westerners desire to view themselves in positive terms. For example, the majority of North Americans have high self-esteem (Baumeister, Tice, & Hutton, 1989), show much evidence for unrealistically positive views of themselves (e.g., Greenwald, 1980; Taylor & Brown, 1988), and engage in various compensatory self-protective responses when they encounter threats to their self-esteem (e.g., Steele, 1988, Tesser, 2000).

In contrast, however, evidence for self-enhancement motivations is less pronounced in many interdependent cultural contexts. For example, Mexicans (Tropp & Wright, 2003), Native Americans (Fryberg & Markus, 2003), Chileans (Heine & Raineri, 2009), and Fijians (Rennie & Dunne, 1994) show less evidence for self-enhancement than do Westerners. Evidence for self-serving biases is particularly weak in East Asian cultures (e.g., Mezulis, Abramson, Hyde, & Hankin, 2004). A meta-analysis on self-enhancing motivations among Westerners and East Asians found significant cultural differences in every study for 30 of the 31 methods that were used [the one exception is comparisons of self-esteem using the Implicit Associations Test (IAT); Greenwald & Farnham, 2000; see Falk, Heine, Yuki, & Takemura, 2009]. Whereas the average effect size for self-enhancing motivations was large ($d = 0.86$) within the Western samples, these motivations were largely absent among the East Asian samples ($d = -0.02$) with Asian-Americans falling in between ($d = 0.33$). Apparently, East Asians possess little motivation to self-enhance, and in many situations they instead appear especially attentive to negative information about themselves that allows for self-improvement (Heine et al., 1999).

There are a number of alternative explanations that have been offered to account for this cultural difference. One possibility is that East Asians are more motivated to enhance their group selves rather than their individual selves, and comparisons of people's individual self-enhancing tendencies thus obscure their group self-enhancing motivations. However, as of yet, there are no published studies indicating that East Asians enhance their group selves more than Westerners, whereas several studies find that Westerners show more group enhancement than East Asians (see Heine, 2003, for a review).

A second possibility is that East Asians will self-enhance in domains that are especially important to them. Some evidence in support of this alternative account has been found using the "Better-than-Average Effect" paradigm (e.g., Sedikides, Gaertner, & Vevea, 2005, 2007); however, studies using other methods reveal that East Asians are more self-critical for important traits than they are for less important ones (e.g., Heine & Renshaw, 2002; Kitayama, Markus, Matsumoto, & Norasakkunkit, 1997). The most extensive meta-analysis on this topic finds no correlation between self-enhancement and importance for East Asians, $r = -0.01$, in contrast to a positive correlation for Westerners, $r = 0.18$ (Heine, Kitayama, & Hamamura, 2007). The "Better-than-Average Effect" yields different results from other self-enhancement methodologies apparently because of the difficulties that people have in considering distributed targets (such as the average person) in contrast to specific targets (such as the self or your best friend; Hamamura, Heine, & Takemoto, 2007; Klar & Giladi, 1997; Krizan & Suls, 2008).

A third alternative account is that East Asians are presenting themselves self-critically, but are privately evaluating themselves in a self-enhancing manner (e.g., Kurman, 2003). Evidence with the IAT measure of self-esteem is largely consistent with this account (see Falk et al., 2009, for a review), although studies that employ hidden behavioral measures in anonymous situations reveal cultural differences similar to those that employ questionnaires (e.g., Heine et al., 2001; Heine, Takata, & Lehman, 2000). That the IAT measure of self-esteem has thus far failed to show reliable correlations with other implicit or explicit measures of self-esteem or external criteria (see Bosson, Swann, & Pennebaker, 2000; Hofmann, Gawronski, Gschwendner, Le, & Schmitt, 2005) makes it difficult to evaluate the conflicting results from these studies.

Variation in self-esteem has also been identified across historical periods. A meta-analysis from 1965 to 1995 of studies using the Rosenberg (1965) self-esteem scale with American college students found that self-esteem scores had increased substantially over that time ($d = 0.6$; Twenge & Campbell, 2001). These increases in self-esteem parallel increases in independence over the same time-period (as measured in terms of people's changing habits of interacting with others and belonging to groups; Putnam, 2000). Given that independence correlates with self-esteem within cultures (e.g., Heine et al., 1999), it is possible that self-esteem has been in increasing in the United States because people are living more independent lifestyles.

Approach and Avoidance Motivations

There are also cultural differences in approach and avoidance motivations between East Asians and Westerners. Given that both self-enhancement and approach motivations reflect concerns about obtaining positive benefits for the self, and that both self-improvement and avoidance motivations entail attending to potential costs to the self, it is possible that these motivations might share a common basis (Heine, 2005; Higgins, 2008). Much research finds that, in general, East Asians show relatively more evidence for avoidance motivation, and relatively less evidence for approach motivation, compared to Westerners. For example, compared with North Americans, East Asians embrace more personal avoidance goals (Elliot et al., 2001), rate opportunities to lose as more important than opportunities to win (Lee et al., 2000), persist on a task more after failure and less after success (Heine et al., 2001; Oishi & Diener, 2003), perform better while attending to weaknesses or losses (Peters & Williams, 2006), are motivated more by negative role models (Lockwood, Marshall, & Sadler, 2005), recall events better if they contain avoidance information, and consider book reviews more helpful if those reviews contain avoidance information (Hamamura, Meijer, Heine, Kamaya, & Hori, 2009). One account for these cultural differences is that "face" is a critical resource in East Asian cultural contexts, and because face is more easily lost than it is gained, people come to habitually attend to avoidance information (Heine, 2005).

Agency and Control

The ways that people attend to their needs and desires are shaped by the theories that they embrace regarding where they can exert control. As previously discussed, Dweck and colleagues (e.g., Dweck & Leggett, 1988) discuss implicit theories that people have regarding the malleability of their selves: namely, incremental and entity theories of self. In addition, people also have implicit theories about the malleability of the world. For example, we can see the world as something that is fixed and that is beyond our ability to change (an entity theory of the world) or we can think of the world as flexible and responsive to our efforts to change (an incremental theory of the world; Chiu, Dweck, Tong, &

Fu, 1997). To the extent that people have implicit theories that the world is malleable but that selves are stable, they should have experiences of control different from people who view their selves as malleable but the world as largely impervious to change (Su et al., 1999). Those who tend to see the world as malleable and their selves as stable will be more likely to maintain a sense of primary control, in which they strive to shape existing realities to fit their perceptions, goals, or wishes. In contrast, those who are more likely to see the world as stable and their selves as malleable will be more likely to engage in secondary control strategies. People strive to achieve secondary control by aligning themselves with existing realities, leaving the realities unchanged, but exerting control over their psychological impact (see Rothbaum, Weisz, & Snyder, 1982).

In hierarchical collectivistic cultures, the lone individual is somewhat powerless to exert change on the social world (e.g., Chiu et al., 1997). Power and agency tend to be concentrated in groups (e.g., Menon, Morris, Chiu, & Hong, 1999), and thus there are many domains in which people are unable to exert much direct influence. Likewise, East Asians are more likely to have a flexible and incremental view of themselves (Heine et al., 2001). When the self is perceived to be more mutable than the social world, it follows that people would be quite willing to adjust themselves to better fit in with the demands of their social worlds.

In contrast, people from Western cultures tend to stress the malleability of the world relative to the self (Su et al., 1999). When individuals are viewed as the center of experience and action, they accordingly should feel a stronger sense of primary control. This view that the self is an immutable entity, working within the context of a mutable world, sustains a perception of primary control. Indeed, much research finds that people from Western cultures are more likely to use primary control strategies and are less likely to use secondary control strategies than people from East Asian cultures (e.g., Morling. Kitayama, & Miyamoto, 2002; Weisz, Rothbaum, & Blackburn, 1984).

In collectivist contexts power rests more with groups than it does with individuals. Accordingly, East Asians tend to view groups as more agentic than Westerners. For example, in their reporting of rogue traders in various stock scandals, Japanese newspapers are more likely than American newspapers to describe the scandal in terms of the organizations that were involved as opposed to the individual traders (Menon et al., 1999). People look to explain events in the world in which they perceive the most agency to lie, and in collectivist societies this tends to be in groups.

Cultural differences in agency are also evident in the ways that people make choices. People in interdependent contexts should be more concerned with the goals of their groups, and thus be more willing to adjust their behaviors (and reduce their choices) to coordinate the actions of the group toward those goals.

One stark example of this cultural difference is that in many interdependent cultures today (and perhaps in a majority of cultures several centuries ago), critical life decisions, such as who to marry or what job to pursue, have been made by families rather than by the individuals themselves (e.g., Lee & Stone, 1980).

Examples of how perceptions of choice differ across cultures have been demonstrated in a number of studies. For example, Indians have been found to differ in their choice-making from Americans, in that the Indians are slower to make choices, are less likely to choose according to their preferences, and are less motivated to express their preferences in their choices (Savani, Markus, & Conner, 2008). Cultural variation in choice-making does not differ only between those from Eastern and Western cultural contexts—middle-class Americans, specifically, seem quite unusual in their high desire for choice (Schwartz, 2004). For example, in a survey of people from six Western countries, only Americans preferred making a choice from 50 ice cream flavors compared with 10 flavors (Rozin, Fischler, Shields, & Masson, 2006). Furthermore, people from American working class cultures are less protective of their choices (i.e., they do not seem as bothered when an experimenter denies them their original choice) compared with middle class Americans (Snibbe & Markus, 2005). In sum, the ways that people make choices, and express agency more generally, differ in a number of important ways across cultures.

Motivations to Fit in or to Stick Out

People have competing motivations to fit in with others or to stick out from a crowd. Asch (1956) famously documented a motivation to conform with a unanimous majority in his line-comparison studies. This conformity paradigm has been replicated well over 100 times in 17 different countries. A meta-analysis of these studies revealed one clear trend: although Americans show much conformity, people from collectivistic cultures conform even more (Bond & Smith, 1996). Motivations to fit in appear to be stronger in cultural contexts that encourage people to maintain strong relationships with others.

In contrast to a motivation to conform, we can also consider people's motivations to stick out and to be unique. In general, it appears that people from independent cultural contexts have a stronger motivation for uniqueness; a desire to be viewed as distinct from others should be facilitated by evidence that you are unique. For example, Kim and Markus (1999) found that when given a choice of pens, European-Americans were more likely to choose a minority-colored pen whereas East Asians were more likely to choose a majority-colored pen. Parallel differences in pen preferences have also been observed in contrasts of middle-class and working-class Americans (Stephens, Markus, & Townsend, 2007). Likewise, advertisements targeting East Asians and working-class Americans are more likely to emphasize themes of connection with others than are advertisements that target middle-class Americans, which are more likely to emphasize uniqueness (Kim & Markus, 1999; Stephens et al., 2007).

Motivations for Honor

Much cross-cultural research has investigated motivations for honor, particularly between the southern and northern United States (Cohen, Nisbett, Bowdle, & Schwarz, 1996; Nisbett, 1993; Nisbett & Cohen, 1996; some research has also explored the stronger honor motivations among Turks; Cross, 2009). Nisbett and Cohen (1996) proposed that the southern United States has a culture of honor, that is, a culture in which people (especially men) strive to protect their reputation through aggression. They argue that cultures of honor are common in contexts in which people's wealth is vulnerable and there is little institutionalized protection (such as in inner cities, various Middle Eastern herding cultures, and some small-scale African societies; e.g., Anderson, 1999; Galaty & Bonte, 1991). In the case of the southern United States, a culture of honor emerged because herding was a key component of the South's early economy, and herders have vulnerable wealth (livestock can easily be stolen, and the sparse population of herding lands made it difficult to police). The establishment of a personal reputation for aggressive revenge for insults therefore emerged to prevent herd-rustling. Although herding is no longer the primary economic activity of most Southerners, Nisbett and Cohen argue that these cultural norms have persisted as a culture of honor represents a stable equilibrium point (see Cohen, 2001).

There are a variety of different kinds of data that converge in support of this thesis. For example, archival data reflect that the relatively greater amount of violence in the South is largely limited to argument-related violence (in which the defense of your honor is often implicated), and this is especially common in the rural herding regions of the South (Nisbett & Cohen, 1996). Similarly, survey data reveal that Southerners are more likely than Northerners to offer violent solutions to problems, but only if those involve a threat to an individual's or family's honor (Cohen & Nisbett, 1994). Experimental evidence further reveals that when Southerners are insulted they are more likely than Northerners to be angry, show heightened cortisol and testosterone responses (these hormone levels tend to increase with aggression), and act more physically aggressive (Cohen et al., 1996). Likewise, field studies reveal that Southerners, compared with Northerners, are warmer toward someone who committed violence in defense of their honor (but not for other kinds of violent acts; Cohen & Nisbett, 1997). Much evidence thus converges on the notion that the southern United States maintains more of a culture of honor than the northern United States (also see Vandello & Cohen, 2003, for further explorations of behavioral correlates of a culture of honor).

Relationships

Central to the distinction between independent and interdependent self-concepts is the notion that culture shapes the ways that people relate to others. This section reviews how the self-concept is related to the way that people distinguish between ingroups and outgroups, how people with more independent self-concepts tend to have more opportunities for forming new relationships and dissolving older relationships than do those with more interdependent self-concepts, and how this difference in relational mobility is associated with various aspects of people's relationships.

The interdependent self, as discussed, is importantly sustained and defined by its significant relationships within the ingroup (Markus & Kitayama, 1991). This suggests that an interdependent individual's ingroup relationships represent a unique class within the universe of potential relationships that the individual might have. An interdependent self cannot be interdependent with everyone, and the self-defining nature of ingroup relationships suggests that these relationships should hold a particularly privileged position. In contrast, the independent self is a self-contained entity that remains quite similar regardless of its interaction partners, and there are fewer consequences associated with distinguishing between ingroup and outgroup members in many situations. As such, the demarcation of ingroups from outgroups should be more salient and stable in interdependent cultural contexts.

Much evidence supports this reasoning. For example, Iyengar and Lepper (1999) found that whereas European-Americans reacted negatively when choices were made for them by someone else, regardless of whether the choicemaker was their mother or a stranger, Asian-American children reacted negatively only when the choicemaker was a stranger. When their mother had made the choice for them they were just as willing to work on the task as when they had chosen it for themselves. As another example, whereas Americans showed evidence for social loafing regardless of whether they were working with ingroup or outgroup members, both Israeli and Chinese loafed only with outgroup members. In contrast, they showed evidence for social striving (i.e., working harder than they did as individuals) when working with ingroup members (Earley, 1993). The distinction between ingroup and outgroup members varies in salience across cultures, and this raises the possibility that minimal group designs might be less effective at eliciting a sense of shared belongingness among people with interdependent self-concepts.

Relationships also vary across cultures in terms of the ease with which people can form them. Relationships among those in independent cultures are entered into, and are maintained, on a somewhat mutually voluntary basis. In such contexts, people have relatively high relational mobility (Falk et al., 2009; Yuki et al., 2008; also see Oishi, Lun, & Sherman, 2007) and individuals can seek new relationships or dissolve unsatisfying older relationships. Importantly, a relationship must in some way benefit the independent individual or they would not devote the efforts necessary to cultivating it. Hence, people in independent contexts actively seek positive and rewarding relationships and will often not devote much effort or resources to any relationship that does not appear to be beneficial, or may allow those relationships to wither (Adams, 2005; Anderson, Adams, & Plaut, 2008; Baumeister, 2005; Heine, Foster, & Spina, 2009; Schug, Yuki, Horikawa, & Takemura, 2009). The Western social psychological literature on relationships tends to be focused largely on the formation and dissolution of relationships, suggesting that conditional relationships have thus far been the primary focus of inquiry—indeed, there are relatively few references to less contingent relationships, such as those with kin (cf. Lieberman, Tooby, & Cosmides, 2007).

In contrast, relationships among those from interdependent cultures are often viewed in less conditional terms. We are born into a relatively fixed interpersonal network and over the course of a lifetime an individual subsequently joins a select few interpersonal networks that remain somewhat stable over the years. There are relatively few opportunities to form new relationships or to dissolve existing ones at any given point in time, and this holds true regardless of whether the relationships are rewarding. As a consequence, people with more interdependent selves (particularly in West African contexts) tend to have more ambivalent feelings toward friendship (Adams & Plaut, 2003), are more likely to say that they have enemies (often from within their own ingroups) than those with more independent selves (Adams, 2005), and have a weaker relationship between physical attractiveness and positive life outcomes (Anderson et al., 2008). The lower relational mobility of people from interdependent cultures is also associated with people showing a weaker similarity-attraction effect (Schug et al., 2009) and weaker self-enhancing motivations (Falk et al., 2009; Yuki et al., 2008).

Cognition and Perception

Many psychologists assume that research from the area of cognition and perception targets the most basic and fundamental psychological processes. Given this perspective, it is interesting that cross-cultural research on cognition and perception reveals some of the clearest evidence for cultural variation. Research contrasting analytic and holistic ways of thinking reveals much cultural variation in how people attend to objects and fields, how they reason, and how they explain the behavior of others.

Analytic versus Holistic Thinking

Nisbett and colleagues (Nisbett, 2003; Nisbett, Peng, Choi, & Norenzayan, 2001) explored whether a variety of cognitive and perceptual tasks glossed under the labels of analytic and holistic thinking varied across cultural contexts, particularly between North American and East Asian cultures. By analytic thinking they mean a focus on objects, which are perceived as existing independently from their contexts, and are understood in terms of their underlying attributes. These attributes are further used as a basis to categorize objects, and a set of fixed abstract rules are used for predicting and explaining their movements and actions. In contrast, by holistic thinking Nisbett and colleagues are referring to an orientation to the context. This is an associative way of thinking in which people attend to the relations among objects and among the objects and the surrounding context. These relations are used to explain and predict the behavior of objects. Furthermore, in holistic thinking there is an emphasis on knowledge that is gained through experience rather than through the application of fixed abstract rules. Numerous studies have now been conducted that demonstrate how cultures vary in these two ways of thinking (for reviews see Henrich et al., 2010; Nisbett et al., 2001; Norenzayan, Choi, & Peng, 2007). In general, analytic thinking is especially common in Western cultures whereas holistic thinking is more normative in the rest of the world, particularly in East Asia where most of the cross-cultural research has been conducted. This distinction between analytic and holistic thinking has been studied in a number of different ways.

Attention to Objects and Fields

A variety of different experimental paradigms have revealed that Americans and other Westerners attend less to the background than people from other non-Western societies, with the likely exception of migratory foragers. For example, Witkin and Berry (1975) summarized a wide range of evidence from work with migratory and sedentary foraging populations (Arctic, Australia, and Africa), sedentary agriculturalists, and industrialized westerners, and found that only the West and migratory foragers appeared at the field independent end of the spectrum. Field independence is the tendency to separate objects from their background fields. Recent work using a variety of measures of field independence show that Westerners are more field independent than people from a variety of other non-Western cultures (Ji, Peng, & Nisbett, 2000; Kitayama, Duffy, Kawamura, & Larsen, 2003; Kühnen, Hannover, & Schubert, 200; Norenzayan, 2008).

Further evidence for a greater attention to objects can be seen in studies in which people are asked whether they have seen a focal object before in scenes in which the background has been switched. For example, in one study Japanese and Americans were shown pictures of animals in natural contexts (e.g., a wolf in a forest) and were later shown pictures of the same animals, sometimes with the original background and sometimes with a different background (e.g., a wolf in a desert). The researchers found that the Japanese participants' recall for the animals was worse than it was for Americans if the background has been replaced with a new one (Masuda & Nisbett, 2001), indicating that they were attending to the field. This difference in attention toward the field has also been found in the eye movements of people as measured with eye-trackers in both social and nonsocial scenes (Chua, Boland, & Nisbett, 2005; Masuda, Ellsworth, Mesquita, Leu, Tanida, & Van de Veerdonk, 2008). In these studies, the attention of Americans rarely leaves the focal object, whereas, after an initial 1000 milliseconds or so of attending to the focal object, East Asians are more likely to shift their gaze to the background.

This cultural difference in attention to the field is further evident in different artistic traditions between the West and East Asia; East Asian paintings tend to have a horizon that is approximately 15% higher than it is in Western paintings (the higher horizon calls attention to the depth of the setting and allows for the different objects and places in a scene to be seen in relation to each other) and Western portraits include focal figures that are approximately three times as large as those in East Asian portraits. Furthermore, when American college students draw a scene, or take a photograph of someone, they are more likely to draw a lower horizon, include fewer objects in their drawings, and zoom in to photograph a larger focal figure than do Japanese students (Masuda, Gonzales, Kwan, & Nisbett, 2008). In sum, these findings converge to show that Westerners perceive the world in some importantly different ways than people from other cultural contexts.

Reasoning Styles

Westerners are more likely to group objects on the basis of categories and rules, whereas people from many other cultural groups are more likely to group objects based on similarity or functional relationships (e.g., Ji, Zhang, & Nisbett, 2004; Knight & Nisbett, 2007). In a similar vein, Norenzayan and colleagues found that the Chinese were more likely to group objects if they shared a strong family resemblance, whereas Americans were more likely to group the same objects if they could be assigned to that group on the basis of a deterministic rule (Norenzayan et al., 2002b). These cultural differences in reasoning appear to be a product of social interdependence; even within the same linguistic and geographic regions of Turkey, farmers and fishermen, who have more socially connected lifestyles, showed more evidence for holistic reasoning on this same task (and on other related tasks) than did herders, who are more isolated (Uskul, Kitayama, & Nisbett, 2008).

Furthermore, as previously discussed, cultures differ with respect to how people reason about contradiction. A holistic orientation suggests that everything appears fundamentally connected and in flux, which suggests that real contradiction might not be possible. The Aristotelian law of contradiction, in which "A" cannot equal "not A" is not as compelling if "A" is connected with "not A" and if "A" and "not A" are always changing. This "naive dialecticism," which is more common among East Asians, is associated with a greater tolerance for contradiction compared with Westerners across a variety of tasks (see Peng & Nisbett, 1999). The fluid and contradictory nature of East Asian beliefs is also reflected in their predictions of future changes. Whereas Westerners tend to make rather linear future predictions for change (e.g., if the stock market has been dropping over the past year it will probably continue to drop next year), East Asian future predictions are considerably more nonlinear (Ji, Nisbett, & Su, 2001). This less linear view of the future may be because East Asians perceive events as having a broader net of consequences compared with Westerners (Maddux & Yuki, 2006).

Explaining the Behavior of Others

Given these cultural differences in attention and reasoning, we might expect that Westerners would be inclined to explain events by reference to properties of the person, whereas non-Westerners would be inclined to explain the same events with reference to interactions between the person and the field. A number of classic studies, which were initially conducted exclusively with Western participants, found that when asked to explain the behavior of others, people largely attend to the person's disposition to explain the behavior, even when there are compelling situational constraints available (e.g., Jones & Harris, 1967). However, research in non-Western cultures often reveals a somewhat different pattern. Geertz (1975) described how Balinese do not tend to conceive of people's behaviors in terms of underlying dispositions, but instead see it as emerging out of the roles that they have. Miller (1984) found that Indian adults tended to favor situational information over dispositional accounts. Several studies conducted with East Asians and Americans revealed that whereas Americans attend to dispositions first, regardless of how compelling the situational information may be (Gilbert & Malone, 1995), East Asians are more likely than Americans to infer that behaviors are controlled by the situation (Norenzayan et al., 2002a) and to attend to situational information (Morris & Peng, 1994; Miyamoto & Kitayama, 2002), particularly when that information is salient (Choi & Nisbett, 1998). Similarly, East Asians are less likely than Americans to use trait adjectives when describing someone's behaviors (Maass, Karasawa, Politi, & Suga, 2006). In sum, whereas considering dispositional information over situational information tends to be found cross-culturally, this correspondence bias is attenuated in non-Western cultures (Choi, Nisbett, & Norenzayan, 1999).

Emotion

The relation between culture and emotional experience has attracted much research interest. Two aspects of emotions have received the most amount of study across cultures: facial expressions of emotion and people's subjective reports of their emotions, including people's reports of the intensity of their emotional experiences, emotion terms, and kinds of emotional experiences. Furthermore, the nature of positive emotional experiences, such as subjective well-being and happiness, has been extensively studied across cultures.

Emotions and Facial Expressions

Darwin was one of the first scientists to consider whether emotional facial expressions were universal features of the human species or were the products of cultural learning (Darwin, 1872/1965). He noted a number of similarities in the facial expressions of various primates and humans and proposed that these expressions should be shared by all humans. Ekman and colleagues, who extensively followed up on Darwin's hypothesis, conducted several studies to investigate whether emotional expressions are universally shared. For example, Ekman and Friesen (1971) showed a series of photos corresponding to what they referred to as a set of "basic emotions" (viz., anger, disgust, fear, happiness, sadness, and surprise) to participants from Argentina, Brazil, Chile, Japan, and the United States and asked them to match the expressions to emotion terms. Whereas chance performance would have been 16.7% correct, participants tended to get between 80% and 90% of the questions correct, regardless of cultural background, indicating much universality in recognition of the expressions. Cross-cultural similarities in emotion recognition are also found in cultural groups that have had little contact with each other, such as between Westerners and the Fore of New Guinea (Ekman, Sorenson, & Freisen, 1969). This evidence, combined with findings that the same facial expressions that adults make are made by very young infants (Izard, 1994), including those who are congenitally blind (reviewed in Ekman, 1973), demonstrates that facial expressions for the basic emotions are innate. Some other emotions, in particular, contempt, shame, embarrassment, pride, and interest, have also believed to be universally recognized (e.g., Keltner, 1995). For example, a bodily posture associated with feelings of pride appears to be universally recognized and is spontaneously produced across cultures (Tracy & Robins, 2008), including those who are congenitally blind (Tracy & Matsumoto, 2008).

Although this research reveals that people are able to recognize the facial expressions of many emotions across cultures, people are more accurate in recognizing emotional expressions made by people from their own cultural background. A meta-analysis of all the past research on cross-cultural recognition of facial expressions found that, on average, people are about 9% more accurate in judging the facial expressions of people from their own culture than those of another culture (with, on average, people showing about 58% accuracy overall; Elfenbein & Ambady, 2002). Furthermore, people are able to reliably distinguish between the nationality of targets when they are making emotional but not when they are making neutral expressions. For example, American participants could reliably distinguish between Australian and American faces, but only when they were expressing emotions (Marsh, Elfenbein, & Ambady, 2007).

Moreover, across cultures people appear to attend to different parts of the face when deciphering facial expressions. Yuki, Maddux, and Masuda (2007) proposed that in cultures in which there were stronger cultural norms to regulate emotional expressions, such as in Japan, people would be more likely to attend to those aspects of the face that were more difficult to regulate (i.e., the eyes). In contrast, in cultures in which there are weaker norms for emotional regulation, such as in the United States, people would attend to the largest visual cues (i.e., the mouth). Indeed, studies found that independent manipulations of the mouth and eyes in facial expressions affected Japanese and Americans differently—Japanese attended more to the eyes than Americans whereas Americans attended more to the mouth than Japanese (Yuki et al., 2007).

Whereas Ekman and colleagues argued that the capacity to produce and recognize particular facial expressions is identical across cultures, cultural variation is anticipated in the form of "display rules" (Ekman & Friesen, 1969). Display rules are the culturally specific rules that govern what facial expressions are appropriate in a given situation and how intensely they should be displayed. There is much evidence that cultures differ in the degree to which emotions are expressed. For example, in response to recalled situations in which participants report feeling the same amount of happiness, Hmong Americans are less likely to smile than are European-Americans (Tsai, Chentsova-Dutton, Freire-Bebeau, & Przymus, 2002). The ways in which emotions are expressed thus vary across cultures. This notion of display rules assumes that even though people in different cultures vary considerably in how strongly they express certain emotions, they may be experiencing the same underlying feelings.

In addition to governing the intensity with which emotions are expressed, display rules are also seen to shape the *kinds* of facial expressions that people might display. For example, Indians often express their embarrassment by biting their tongues, which is distinct from a prototypical expression of embarrassment (Keltner, 1995), and the tongue bite is not reliably produced or recognized in many other cultures. This suggests that the tongue bite represents an expression that is voluntarily produced rather than reflexively generated (Haidt & Keltner, 1999); this is termed an example of a ritualized display. The notion of display rules adds considerable complexity to the task of interpreting emotional expressions across cultures. It is not always obvious whether we are presenting a universal facial expression or enacting a cultural display rule. Furthermore, as people's facial expressions can affect their emotional experience (e.g., Strack, Martin, & Stepper, 1988), it is possible that cultures differ not only in their display rules, but also in their emotional experiences.

Intensity of Emotional Experience

Much cross-cultural research in emotions has targeted similarities and differences in the facial expressions of people. What does evidence regarding people's emotional experiences indicate about cultural similarities and differences? One study found that consistent with the evidence that display rules for intensity are relatively more dampened in Japan than in the United States, Americans reported feeling their emotions longer and more intensely than Japanese (Matsumoto, Kudoh, Scherer, & Wallbott, 1988). Similarly, in a diary study

Japanese participants were about three times as likely as Americans to report that they had not been feeling any emotions when prompted (Mesquita & Karasawa, 2002; also see Kitayama, Markus, & Kurokawa, 2000). These studies suggest that the cultural display rules governing the relative deamplifying and masking of emotions in Japan might be leading them to experience fewer and less intense emotions compared to Americans.

Suppressing some emotions (particularly anger) has been found to lead to less cardiac regulation of heart rate, and thus a slower recovery of the heart rate following an initial angering event (e.g., Brosschot & Thayer, 1998). However, in East Asian cultural contexts, in which inhibition of emotional expressions is more common, people's heart rate recovers more quickly following an angering event. This appears to be due to the fact that East Asian participants are more likely to reappraise events in a less anger-provoking way (Anderson & Linden, 2006; also see Butler, Lee, & Gross, 2007).

Kinds of Emotional Experiences

Independent and interdependent self-concepts provide a useful framework to make sense of cultural variation in emotional experiences. The self-concept should shape how an emotionally relevant situation is appraised. Those with interdependent selves are more concerned with maintaining a sense of interpersonal harmony, and thus should consider how events in the world impact close others as well as themselves. Those with independent selves, in contrast, should focus more intently on how events impact them, or how events might serve to distinguish them from others. Mesquita (2001) contrasted people from a more interdependent culture (Surinamese and Turkish immigrants to Holland) with those from a more independent culture (mainstream Dutch citizens of Holland), and found that the Surinamese and Turks expressed more relational concerns and were more concerned with how situations affected others compared with the Dutch. Moreover, the Surinamese and Turks were more likely than the Dutch to ensure that others attended to the same events, thereby sharing the experience with the participants.

Along a similar line, Kitayama et al. (2000) compared descriptions of daily emotional experiences among Japanese and Americans. People reported how frequently they experienced various emotions that varied both in terms of their valence and in terms of the extent to which they were interpersonally engaged. The findings revealed that general positive feelings were especially correlated with the frequency with which the person felt positive interpersonally engaged emotions (e.g., respect, friendly feelings) among Japanese, whereas general positive feelings for Americans were especially correlated with the frequency with which the person felt positive interpersonally disengaged emotions (e.g., pride, feeling on top of the world). In sum, what makes people feel good varies across cultures (also see Kitayama, Mesquita, & Karasawa, 2006, for similar findings).

Emotion and Language

Although there is a set of basic emotions that is recognized comparably around the world, there is much cultural variability in the terms that people use to describe their emotions (see Russell, 1991, for a review). Across cultures people categorize their emotions in very different ways. For example, the Buganda of Uganda do not make a distinction between sorrow and anger. The Gidjingali aborigines of Australia use one word, *gurakadj*, to express both shame and fear. Samoans use one word, *alofa*, to express both love and pity. The Utku Eskimos do not distinguish between feelings of kindness and gratitude. The Ifaluk in Micronesia do not even have a specific word for "emotion," but instead lump all internal states together (Lutz, 1988). It largely remains an open question as to whether these cultural differences in emotion terms are mirrored by cultural differences in emotional experiences (for conflicting views on this point see Pinker, 1994; Russell, 1991).

Cultural Variation in Subjective Well-Being and Happiness

Is there variability in people's happiness and subjective well-being across cultures? Indeed, pronounced cultural differences consistently emerge in multinational surveys, with the most common pattern being that the nations that cluster toward the "happy" pole are Scandinavian and Nordic countries, much of Latin America, various English-speaking countries, and Western Europe. On the low end are the former Soviet republics and some impoverished countries in Africa and South Asia (Diener & Diener, 1995; Diener, Diener, & Diener, 1995; Inglehart & Klingemann, 2000).

Many factors influence the overall satisfaction that people have with their lives. Wealth as assessed by GDP positively correlates with the overall well-being of a country. However, this relation is not linear; money and happiness are most closely connected at very low levels of wealth, where a little extra money can make the difference between surviving or not. For example, income and life satisfaction are correlated at 0.45 among respondents in the slums of Calcutta (Biswas-Diener & Diener, 2002). In contrast, above an average GDP of 40% of that of the United States, there is no longer any clear relation between money and subjective well-being (Diener et al., 1995). In addition, human rights and overall equality of a country are associated with greater subjective well-being (Diener et al., 1995).

There are also some factors that predict life satisfaction differently across cultures. Suh, Diener, Oishi, and Triandis (1998) found that life satisfaction is more highly correlated with overall positive affect in individualistic cultures than in collectivist ones. On the other hand, people in collectivist cultures showed a higher correlation between their life satisfaction scores and being respected by others for living up to cultural norms, compared with people from individualistic cultures.

Furthermore, the kinds of positive emotions that people desire also varies across cultures. Some work by Tsai and colleagues (e.g., Tsai, Knutson, & Fung, 2006) reveals that Americans seek out positive emotions that are high in arousal more than East Asians, whereas East Asians prefer low arousal positive emotions more than Americans. Evidence for this cultural difference comes from a variety of sources. For example, a comparison of facial expressions that were shown in characters in American and Taiwanese children's storybooks revealed that the American faces more often showed feelings of excitement and had significantly larger smiles than the Taiwanese faces. Moreover, European-American preschool children preferred the pictures of excited faces more than the Taiwanese preschoolers did; they also felt more similar to the characters who were engaged in high arousal activities than did Taiwanese children (Tsai, Louie, Chen, & Uchida, 2006). In sum, cultures vary in their happiness, in part, because they appear to have quite different ideas about what happiness is and from what it is derived (also see Falk, Dunn, & Norenzayan, 2010).

To summarize the cross-cultural research on emotions, there is much similarity across cultures with respect to facial expressions of emotions (although there is some important variability here too). In the domain of emotional experience, in contrast, the evidence for cultural variation is more pronounced.

Conclusions

Humans are a cultural species and a rich understanding of how human minds operate would be facilitated by a psychological science that is attentive to people's cultural experiences. Research in cultural psychology has grown substantially, particularly in the past two decades. This growing database has revealed that many key psychological processes, some of which were hitherto viewed as psychological universals, manifest in distinct ways across cultures. Furthermore, although some psychological phenomena appear in more invariant forms across cultures than others, it is often not clear which phenomena should be expected to vary the most. Pronounced cultural variation has been identified in many fundamental psychological phenomena, and thus it is crucial to seek cross-cultural data before confidently making inferences about the cultural generalizability of a phenomenon (Henrich et al., 2010).

Such evidence for cultural variability in basic processes emphasizes how many psychological phenomena do not unfold reflexively, regardless of context, but are importantly shaped by engagement in the particular scripts, practices, and situations that each culture provides. In this way, psychological processes can be seen as entangled with "meaning"—and because particular meanings can vary substantially across cultural contexts, so must the psychological process (Bruner, 1990; Heine, Proulx, & Vohs, 2006).

A serious shortcoming of the cultural psychological database thus far is that a large portion of it is constituted by comparisons of North American and East Asian college students. Although there have been good theoretical and methodological reasons to build on the differences that have been identified between these groups, much of the world remains largely unexplored territory. In particular, the role of culture in psychological functioning should become especially evident when small-scale societies are studied, which differ from the industrialized West in many profound ways. Much excellent and influential work has already been conducted with such groups (e.g., Atran, Medin, & Ross, 2005; Cole, Gay, & Glick, 1968; Gordon, 2004; Henrich et al., 2005; Segall et al., 1963), much of it done to make arguments for psychological universals (e.g., Barrett & Behne, 2005; Ekman et al., 1969; Levenson, Ekman, Heider, & Friesen, 1992).

Attention to other cultural samples will likely uncover some psychological phenomena that are less familiar to Western psychologists. For example, the notion of "face" is far more elaborated and takes on different meanings within East Asia than in the West, and this leads to specific psychological predictions that can be tested (e.g., Chang & Holt, 1994; Heine, 2005; Ting-Toomey, 1994). Likewise, a type of dialectical thinking that emphasizes constant change and is tolerant of apparent contradiction (distinct from the Hegelian dialectic) likely would not have been investigated among Westerners if it had not first been identified among Chinese (e.g., Peng & Nisbett, 1999). It is very likely that there are numerous other examples in other cultural contexts (e.g., *simpatia* in Hispanic contexts; Sanchez-Burks, Nisbett, & Ybarra, 2000; Triandis, Marin, Lisansky, & Betancourt, 1984), and these phenomena would stand to greatly advance our understanding of cultural variation and the universality of psychological processes.

There will likely continue to be much interest in using cultural variation in psychological processes as a means to identify the underlying mechanisms.

Such research has already increased our understanding of mechanisms in ways would not have been possible had the research been restricted to monocultural samples. This search for mechanisms has adopted a variety of methods, such as employing trait measures to mediate the cultural differences (e.g., Diener & Diener, 1995; Singelis, Bond, Lai, & Sharkey, 1999; but see Heine & Norenzayan, 2006, for discussion regarding limitations in this), priming cultural constructs (e.g., Adams, 2005; Spencer-Rodgers et al., 2004), varying degrees of exposure to certain cultural experiences (e.g., Koo & Choi, 2005), situation sampling (e.g., Kitayama et al., 1997; Morling et al., 2002), experimental methods that assess people's default thoughts across cultures (e.g., Heine et al., 2001), and triangulation strategies that contrast multiple groups that vary in different sets of cultural variables (e.g., Medin & Atran, 2004). These and other methods will surely continue to be used to identify the mechanisms underlying cultural differences.

In sum, studying the psychology of people from different cultures does not provide only information relevant to those other cultures. Such research also serves to identify psychological phenomena that researchers might miss if they limited their research to Western samples, and it serves as an important tool to identify mechanisms that underlie psychological processes.

References

Adams, G. (2005). The cultural grounding of personal relationship: Enemyship in West African worlds. *Journal of Personality and Social Psychology, 88,* 948–968.

Adams, G., & Plaut, V. C. (2003). The cultural grounding of personal relationship: Friendship in North American and West African worlds. *Personal Relationships, 10,* 333–348.

Anderson, E. (1999). *Code of the street: Decency, violence, and the moral life of the inner city.* New York: Norton.

Anderson, J. C., & Linden, W. (2006). *The influence of culture on cardiovascular response to anger.* Citation poster session presented at the annual meeting of the American Psychosomatic Society, Denver, CO.

Anderson, S. L., Adams, G., & Plaut, V. C. (2008). The cultural grounding of personal relationship: The importance of attractiveness in everyday life. *Journal of Personality and Social Psychology, 95,* 352–368.

Arnett, J. (2008). The neglected 95%: Why American psychology needs to become less American. *American Psychologist, 63,* 602–614.

Asch, S. (1956). Studies of independence and conformity. A minority of one against a unanimous majority. *Psychological Monographs, 70* (9, Whole No. 416).

Atran, S., Medin, D. L., & Ross, N. O. (2005). The cultural mind: Environmental decision making and cultural modeling within and across populations. *Psychological Review, 112*, 744–776.

Barrett, H. C., & Behne, T. (2005). Children's understanding of death as the cessation of agency: A test using sleep versus death. *Cognition, 96*, 93–108.

Baumeister, R. F. (2005). *The cultural animal.* Oxford: Oxford University Press.

Baumeister, R. F., Tice, D. M., & Hutton, D. G. (1989). Self-presentational motivations and personality differences in self-esteem. *Journal of Personality, 57*, 547–579.

Benet-Martinez, V., Leu, J., Lee, F., & Morris, M. W. (2002). Negotiating biculturalism: Cultural frame switching in biculturals with oppositional versus compatible cultural identities. *Journal of Cross-Cultural Psychology, 33*, 492–516.

Bond, R., & Smith, P. B. (1996). Culture and conformity: A meta-analysis of studies using Asch's (1952b, 1956) line judgment task. *Psychological Bulletin, 119*, 111–137.

Bosson, J. K., Swann, W. B., & Pennebaker, J. W. (2000). Stalking the perfect measure of implicit self-esteem: The blind men and the elephant revisited? *Journal of Personality and Social Psychology, 79*, 631–643.

Brosschot, J. F., & Thayer, J. F. (1998). Anger inhibition, cardiovascular recovery, and vagal function: A model of the link between hostility and cardiovascular disease. *Annals of Behavior Medicine, 20*, 326–332.

Bruner, J. (1990). *Acts of meaning.* Cambridge, MA: Harvard University Press.

Buss, D. M. (1989). Sex differences in human mate preferences: Evolutionary hypotheses tested in 37 cultures. *Behavioral and Brain Sciences, 12*, 1–49.

Butler, E. A., Lee, T. L., & Gross, J. J. (2007). Emotion regulation and culture: Are the social consequences of emotion suppression culture-specific? *Emotion, 7*, 30–48.

Chang, H.-C., & Holt, G. R. (1994). A Chinese perspective on face as inter-relational concern. In S. Ting-Toomey (Ed.), *The challenge of facework: Cross-cultural and interpersonal issues* (pp. 95–132). Albany, NY: SUNY Press.

Cheng, C., Sanchez-Burks J., & Lee, F. (2008). Connecting the dots within: Creative performance and identity integration. *Psychological Science, 19*, 1178–1184.

Chiu, C., Dweck, C. S., Tong, J. U., & Fu, J. H. (1997). Implicit theories and conceptions of morality. *Journal of Personality and Social Psychology, 73*, 923–940.

Choi, I., & Choi, Y. (2002). Culture and self-concept flexibility. *Personality and Social Psychology Bulletin, 28*, 1508–1517.

Choi, I., & Nisbett, R. E. (1998). Situational salience and cultural differences in the correspondence bias and in the actor-observer bias. *Personality and Social Psychology Bulletin, 24*, 949–960.

Choi, I., Nisbett, R. E., & Norenzayan, A. (1999). Causal attribution across cultures: Variation and universality. *Psychological Bulletin, 125*, 47–63.

Chua, H. F., Boland, J. E., & Nisbett, R. E. (2005). Cultural variation in eye movements during scene perception. *Proceedings of the National Academy of Sciences, 102*, 12629–12633.

Cialdini, R. B., Wosinska, W., & Barrett, D. W. (1999). Compliance with a request in two cultures: The differential influence of social proof and commitment/consistency on collectivists and individualists. *Personality and Social Psychology Bulletin, 25*, 1242–1253.

Cohen, D. (2001). Cultural variation: Considerations and implications. *Psychological Bulletin, 127*, 451–471.

Cohen, D., & Gunz, A. (2002). As seen by the other . . . : Perspectives on the self in the memories and emotional perceptions of Easterners and Westerners. *Psychological Science, 13*, 55–59.

Cohen, D., Hoshino-Browne, E., & Leung, A. (2007). Culture and the structure of personal experience: Insider and outsider phenomenologies of the self and social world. In M. P. Zanna (Ed.), *Advances in experimental social psychology* (Vol. 39). San Diego: Academic Press.

Cohen, D., & Nisbett, R. E. (1994). Self-protection and the culture of honor: Explaining southern homicide. *Personality and Social Psychology Bulletin, 20*, 551–567.

Cohen, D., & Nisbett, R. E. (1997). Field experiments examining the culture of honor: The role of institutions in perpetuating norms about violence. *Personality and Social Psychology Bulletin, 23*, 1188–1199.

Cohen, D., Nisbett, R. E., Bowdle, B. F., & Schwarz, N. (1996). Insult, aggression, and the Southern culture of honor: An "experimental ethnography." *Journal of Personality and Social Psychology, 70*, 945–960.

Cole, M., Gay, J., & Glick, J. (1968). Some experimental studies of Kpelle quantitative behavior. *Psychonomic Monograph Supplements, 2*, 173–190.

Daly, M., & Wilson, M. (1988). *Homicide*. New York: Aldine de Gruyter.

Darwin, C. (1872/1965). *The expression of emotions in man and animals*. Chicago: University of Chicago Press.

Diener, E., & Diener, M. (1995). Cross-cultural correlates of life satisfaction and self-esteem. *Journal of Personality and Social Psychology, 68*, 653–663.

Diener, E., Diener, M., & Diener, C. (1995). Factors predicting the subjective well-being of nations. *Journal of Personality and Social Psychology, 69*, 851–864.

Duval, S., & Wicklund, R. (1972). *A theory of objective self-awareness*. New York: Academic Press.

Dweck, C. S., & Leggett, E. L. (1988). A social-cognitive approach to motivation and personality. *Psychological Review, 95*, 256–273.

Earley, P. C. (1993). East meets West meets Mideast: Further explorations of collectivistic and individualistic work groups. *Academy of Management Journal, 36*, 319–348.

Ekman, P. (1973). Universal facial expressions in emotion. *Studia Psychologica, 15*, 140–147.

Ekman, P., & Friesen, W. V. (1969). The repertoire of nonverbal behavior: Categories, origins, usage, and coding. *Semiotica, 1*, 49–98.

Ekman, P., & Friesen, W. V. (1971). Constants across cultures in the face and emotion. *Journal of Personality and Social Psychology, 17*, 124–129.

Ekman, P., Sorenson, E. R., & Friesen, W. (1969). Pancultural elements in facial displays of emotion. *Science, 164*, 86–88.

Elfenbein, H. A., & Ambady, N. (2002). On the universality and cultural specificity of emotion recognition: A meta-analysis. *Psychological Bulletin, 128*, 203–235.

Elliot, A. J., Chirkov, V. I., Kim, Y., & Sheldon, K. M. (2001). A cross-cultural analysis of avoidance (relative to approach) personal goals. *Psychological Science, 12*, 505–510.

English, T., & Chen, S. (2007). Culture and self-concept stability: Consistency across and within contexts among Asian-American and European-Americans. *Journal of Personality and Social Psychology, 93*, 478–490.

Falk, C. F., Dunn, E. W., & Norenzayan, A. (2010). *Cultural variation in the importance of expected emotions for decision-making.* Unpublished manuscript, University of British Columbia.

Falk, C. F., Heine, S. J., Yuki, M., & Takemura, K. (2009). Why do Westerners self-enhance more than East Asians? *European Journal of Personality, 23*, 183–209.

Festinger, L. (1957). *A theory of cognitive dissonance.* Stanford, CA: Stanford University Press.

Frager, R. (1970). Conformity and anti-conformity in Japan. *Journal of Personality and Social Psychology, 15*, 203–210.

Freedman, J. L., & Fraser, S. C. (1966). Compliance without pressure: The foot-in-the-door technique. *Journal of Personality and Social Psychology, 4*, 195–202.

Fryberg, S. A., & Markus, H. R. (2003). On being American Indian: Current and possible selves. *Self and Identity, 2*, 325–344.

Galaty, J. G., & Bonte, P. (Eds.). (1991). *Herders, warriors, and traders: Pastoralism in Africa.* Boulder, CO: Westview Press.

Gardner, W. L., Gabriel, S., & Dean, K. K. (2004). The individual as „melting pot": The flexibility of bicultural self-construals. *Cahiers de Psychologie Cognitive/Current Psychology of Cognition, 22*, 181–201.

Geertz, C. (1973). *The Interpretation of cultures.* New York: Basic Books.

Geertz, C. (1975). On the nature of anthropological understanding. *American Scientist, 63*, 4–53.

Gilbert, D. T., & Malone, P. S. (1995). The correspondence bias. *Psychological Bulletin, 117*, 21–38.

Gordon, P. (2004). Numerical cognition without words: Evidence from Amazonia. *Science, 306*, 496–499.

Greenwald, A. G. (1980). The totalitarian ego: Fabrication and revision of personal history. *American Psychologist, 35*, 603–618.

Greenwald, A. G., & Farnham, S. D. (2000). Using the implicit association test to measure self-esteem and self-concept, *Journal of Personality and Social Psychology, 79*, 1022–1038.

Haidt, J., & Keltner, D. (1999). Culture and facial expression: Open-ended methods find more expressions and a gradient of recognition. *Cognition and Emotion, 13*, 225–266.

Hamamura, T., Heine, S. J., & Paulhus, D. L. (2008). Cultural differences in response styles: The role of dialectical thinking. *Personality and Individual Differences, 44*, 932–942.

Hamamura, T., Heine, S. J., & Takemoto, T. (2007). Why the better-than-average effect is a worse-than-average measure of self-enhancement. An investigation of conflicting findings from studies of East Asian self-evaluations. *Motivation and Emotion, 31*, 247–259.

Hamamura, T., Meijer, Z., Heine, S. J., Kamaya, K., & Hori, I. (2009). Approach-avoidance motivations and information processing: A cross-cultural analysis. *Personality and Social Psychology Bulletin, 35*, 454–462.

Heider, F. (1958). *The psychology of interpersonal relations*. New York: John Wiley.

Heine, S. J. (2003). Self-enhancement in Japan? A reply to Brown and Kobayashi. *Asian Journal of Social Psychology, 6*, 75–84.

Heine, S. J. (2005). Constructing good selves in Japan and North America. In R. M. Sorrentino, D. Cohen, J. M. Olson, & M. P. Zanna (Eds.), *Culture and social behavior: The Tenth Ontario Symposium*. (pp. 95–116). Hillsdale, NJ: Lawrence Erlbaum.

Heine, S. J. (2008). *Cultural psychology*. New York: W. W. Norton.

Heine, S. J., Foster, J. A., & Spina, R. (2009). Do birds of a feather universally flock together? Cultural variation in the similarity-attraction effect. *Asian Journal of Social Psychology, 12*, 247–258.

Heine, S. J., & Hamamura, T. (2007). In search of East Asian self-enhancement. *Personality and Social Psychology Review, 11*, 4–27.

Heine, S. J., Kitayama, S., & Hamamura, T. (2007). The inclusion of additional studies yields different conclusions: A reply to Sedikides, Gaertner, & Vevea (2005), JPSP. *Asian Journal of Social Psychology, 10*, 49–58.

Heine, S. J., Kitayama, S., Lehman, D. R., Takata, T., Ide, E., Leung, C., & Matsumoto, H. (2001). Divergent consequences of success and failure in Japan and North America: An investigation of self-improving motivations and malleable selves. *Journal of Personality and Social Psychology, 81*, 599–615.

Heine, S. J., & Lehman, D. R. (1997). Culture, dissonance, and self-affirmation. *Personality and Social Psychology Bulletin, 23*, 389–400.

Heine, S. J., Lehman, D. R., Markus, H. R., & Kitayama, S. (1999). Is there a universal need for positive self-regard? *Psychological Review, 106*, 766–794.

Heine, S. J., & Norenzayan, A. (2006). Towards a psychological science for a cultural species. *Perspectives on Psychological Science, 1*, 251–269.

Heine, S. J., Proulx, T., & Vohs, K. D. (2006). Meaning maintenance model: On the coherence of social motivations. *Personality and Social Psychology Review, 10*, 88–110.

Heine, S. J., & Raineri, A. (2009). Self-improving motivations and culture: The case of Chileans. *Journal of Cross-Cultural Psychology, 40*, 158–163.

Heine, S. J., & Renshaw, K. (2002). Interjudge agreement, self-enhancement, and liking: Cross-cultural divergences. *Personality and Social Psychology Bulletin, 28*, 578–587.

Heine, S. J., Takata, T., & Lehman, D. R. (2000). Beyond self-presentation: Evidence for self-criticism among Japanese. *Personality and Social Psychology Bulletin, 26*, 71–78.

Heine, S. J., Takemoto, T., Moskalenko, S., Lasaleta, J., & Henrich, J. (2008). Mirrors in the head: Cultural variation in objective self-awareness. *Personality and Social Psychology Bulletin, 34*, 879–887.

Henrich, J., Boyd, R., Bowles, S., Camerer, C., Fehr, E., Gintis, H., McElreath, R., Alvard, M., Barr, A., Ensminger, J., Henrich, N., Hill, K., Gil-White, F., Gurven, M., Marlowe, F. W., Patton, J. Q., & Tracer, D. (2005). 'Economic Man' in cross-cultural perspective: Behavioral experiments in 15 small-scale societies. *Behavioral & Brain Sciences, 28*, 795–855.

Henrich, J., Heine, S. J., & Norenzayan, A. (2010). The weirdest people in the world. *Behavioral and Brain Sciences.*

Hiniker, P. J. (1969). Chinese reactions to forced compliance: Dissonance reduction or national character. *Journal of Social Psychology, 77*, 157–176.

Hofmann, W., Gawronski, B., Gschwendner, T., Le, H., & Schmitt, M. (2005). A meta-analysis on the correlation between the impolict association test and explicit self-report measures. *Personality and Social Psychology Bulletin, 31*, 1369–1385.

Hong, Y., Morris, M. W., Chiu, C., & Benet-Martinez, V. (2000). Multicultural minds: A dynamic constructivist approach to culture and cognition. *American Psychologist, 55*, 705–720.

Hoshino-Browne, E., Zanna, A. S., Spencer, S. J., Zanna, M. P., Kitayama, S., & Lackenbauer, S. (2005). On the cultural guises of cognitive dissonance: The case of Easterners and Westerners. *Journal of Personality and Social Psychology, 89*, 294–310.

Inglehart, R., & Klingemann, H. (2000). Genes, culture, democracy, and happiness. In E. Diener & E. Suh (Eds.), *Culture and subjective well-being* (pp. 165–184). Cambridge, MA: MIT Press.

Iyengar, S. S., & Lepper, M. R. (1999). Rethinking the value of choice: A cultural perspective on intrinsic motivation. *Journal of Personality and Social Psychology, 76*, 349–366.

Izard, C. E. (1994). Innate and universal facial expressions: Evidence from developmental and cross-cultural research. *Psychological Bulletin, 115*, 288–299.

Ji, L. J., Nisbett, R. E., & Su, Y. (2001). Culture, change, and prediction. *Psychological Science, 12*, 450–456.

Ji, L. J., Peng, K., & Nisbett, R. E. (2000). Culture, control, and perception of relationships in the environment. *Journal of Personality and Social Psychology, 78*, 943–955.

Ji, L. J., Zhang, Z., & Nisbett, R. E. (2004). Is it culture or is it language? Examination of language effects in cross-cultural research on categorization. *Journal of Personality and Social Psychology, 87*, 57–65.

Jones, E. E., & Harris, V. A. (1967). The attribution of attitudes. *Journal of Experimental Social Psychology, 3*, 1–24.

Kanagawa, C., Cross, S. E., & Markus, H. R. (2001). "Who am I?": The cultural psychology of the conceptual self. *Personality and Social Psychology Bulletin, 27*, 90–103.

Kashima, Y., Siegal, M., Tanaka, K., & Kashima, E. S. (1992). Do people believe behaviors are consistent with attitudes? Towards a cultural psychology of attribution processes. *British Journal of Social Psychology, 31*, 111–124.

Kim, H. S., & Markus, H. R. (1999). Deviance or uniqueness, harmony or conformity? A cultural analysis. *Journal of Personality and Social Psychology, 77*, 785–800.

Kitayama, S., Duffy, S., Kawamura, T., & Larsen, J. T. (2003). Perceiving an object and its context in different cultures: A cultural look at New Look. *Psychological Science, 14*, 201–206.

Kitayama, S., Markus, H. R., & Kurokawa, M. (2000). Culture, emotion, and well-being: Good feelings in Japan and the United States. *Cognition and Emotion, 14*, 93–124.

Kitayama, S., Markus, H. R., Matsumoto, H., & Norasakkunkit, V. (1997). Individual and collective processes in the construction of the self: Self-enhancement in the United States and self-criticism in Japan. *Journal of Personality and Social Psychology, 72*, 1245–1267.

Kitayama, S., Mesquita, B., & Karasawa, M. (2006). Cultural affordances and emotional experience: Socially engaging and disengaging emotions in Japan and the United States. *Journal of Personality and Social Psychology, 91*, 890–903.

Kitayama, S., Snibbe, A.C., Markus, H.R., & Suzuki, T. (2004). Is there any "free" choice? Self and dissonance in two cultures. *Psychological Science, 15*, 527–533.

Klar, Y., & Giladi, E. E. (1997). No one in my group can be below the group's average" A robust positivity bias in favor of anonymous peers. *Journal of Personality and Social Psychology, 73*, 885–901.

Knight, N., & Nisbett, R. E. (2007). Culture, class and cognition: Evidence from Italy. *Journal of Cognition and Culture, 7*, 283–291.

Koo, M., & Choi, I. (2005). Becoming a holistic thinker: Training effect of oriental medicine on reasoning. *Personality and Social Psychology Bulletin, 31*, 1264–1272.

Krizan, X., & Suls, J. (2008). Losing sight of oneself in the above-average effect: When egocentrism, focalism, and group diffuseness collide. *Journal of Experimental Social Psychology, 44*, 929–942.

Kuhn, M. H., & McPartland, T. (1954). An empirical investigation of self-attitudes. *American Sociological Review, 19*, 68–76.

Kühnen, U., Hannover, B., & Schubert, B. (2001). The semantic-procedural interface model of the self: The role of self-knowledge for context-dependent versus context-independent modes of thinking. *Journal of Personality and Social Psychology, 80*, 397–409.

Kurman, J. (2003). Why is self-enhancement low in certain collectivist cultures? An investigation of two competing explanations. *Journal of Cross-Cultural Psychology, 34*, 496–510.

Lee, A. Y., Aaker, J. L., & Gardner, W. L. (2000). The pleasures and pains of distinct self-construals: The role of interdependence in regulatory focus. *Journal of Personality and Social Psychology, 78*, 1122–1134.

Lee, G. R., & Stone, L. H. (1980). Mate-selection systems and criteria: Variation according to family structure. *Journal of Marriage and the Family, 42*, 319–326.

Leung, A. K., & Cohen, D. (2007). The soft embodiment of culture: Camera angles and motion through time and space. *Psychological Science, 18*, 824–830.

Leung, A. K., Maddux, W. W., Galinsky, A. D., & Chiu, C. (2008). Multicultural experience enhances creativity: The when and how. *American Psychologist, 63*, 169–181.

Levenson, R. W., Ekman, P., Heider, K., & Friesen, W. V. (1992). Emotion and autonomic nervous system activity in the Minangkabau of West Sumatra. *Journal of Personality and Social Psychology, 62*, 972–988.

Lieberman, D., Tooby, J., & Cosmides, L. (2007). The architecture of human kin detection. *Nature, 445*, 727–731.

Lockwood, P., Marshall, T. C., & Sadler, P. (2005). Promoting success or preventing failure: Cultural differences in motivation by positive and negative role models. *Personality and Social Psychology Bulletin, 31*, 379–392.

Lutz, C. (1988). *Unnatural emotions*. Chicago: University of Chicago Press.

Maass, A., Karasawa, M., Politi, F., & Suga, S. (2005). Do verbs and adjectives play different roles in different cultures? A cross-linguistic analysis of person representation. *Journal of Personality and Social Psychology, 90*, 734–750.

Maddux, W. W., & Galinsky, A. D. (2009). Cultural barriers and mental borders: Living in and adapting to foreign cultures facilitates creativity. *Journal of Personality and Social Psychology, 96*, 1047–1061.

Maddux, W. W., & Yuki, M. (2006). The "ripple effect": Cultural differences in perceptions of the consequences of events. *Personality and Social Psychology Bulletin, 32*, 669–683.

Mandel, N. (2003). Shifting selves and decision making: The effects of self construal priming on consumer risk taking. *Journal of Consumer Research, 30*, 30–40.

Markus, H. (1977). Self-schemata and processing information about the self. *Journal of Personality and Social Psychology, 35*, 63–78.

Markus, H. R., & Kitayama, S. (1991). Culture and the self: Implications for cognition, emotion, and motivation. *Psychological Review, 98*, 224–253.

Markus, H. R., & Kunda, Z. (1986). Stability and malleability of the self-concept. *Journal of Personality and Social Psychology, 51*, 858–866.

Marsh, A. A., Elfenbein, H. A., & Ambady, N. (2007). Separated by a common language: Nonverbal accents and cultural stereotypes about Americans and Australians. *Journal of Cross-Cultural Psychology, 38*, 284–301.

Masuda, T., Ellsworth, P. C., Mesquita, B., Leu, J., Tanida, S., & van de Veerdonk, E. (2008). Placing the face in context: Cultural differences in the perception of facial emotion. *Journal of Personality and Social Psychology, 94*, 365–381.

Masuda, T., Gonzalez, R., Kwan, L., & Nisbett, R. E. (2008). Culture and aesthetic preference: Comparing the attention to context of East Asians and European Americans. *Personality and Social Psychology Bulletin, 34*, 1260–1275.

Masuda, T., & Nisbett, R. E. (2001). Attending holistically vs. analytically: Comparing the context sensitivity of Japanese and Americans. *Journal of Personality and Social Psychology, 81*, 922–934.

Matsumoto, D., Kudoh, T., Scherer, K., & Wallbott, H. (1988). Antecedents of and reactions to emotions in the United States and Japan. *Journal of Cross-Cultural Psychology, 19*, 267–286.

May, R. M. (1997). The scientific wealth of nations. *Science, 275*, 793–796.

McCrae, R. R., Terraciano, A., and 78 members of the Personality Profiles of Cultures Project. (2005). Universal features of personality traits from the observer's perspective: Data from 50 cultures. *Journal of Personality and Social Psychology, 88*, 547–561.

Medin, D. L., & Atran. S. (2004). The native mind: Biological categorization, reasoning and decision making in development and across cultures. *Psychological Review, 111*, 960–983.

Menon, T., Morris, M. W., Chiu, C., & Hong, Y. (1999). Culture and the construal of agency: Attribution to individual versus group dispositions. *Journal of Personality and Social Psychology, 76*, 701–717.

Mesquita, B. (2001). Emotions in collectivist and individualist contexts. *Journal of Personality and Social Psychology, 80*, 68–74.

Mesquita, B., & Karasawa, M. (2002). Different emotional lives. *Cognition and Emotion, 17*, 127–141.

Mezulis, A. H., Abramson, L. Y., Hyde, J. S., & Hankin, B. L. (2004). Is there a universal positive bias in attributions?: A meta-analytic review of individual, developmental, and cultural differences in the self-serving attributional bias. *Psychological Bulletin, 130*, 711–747.

Miller, J. G. (1984). Culture and the development of everyday social explanation. *Journal of Personality and Social Psychology, 46*, 961–978.

Miller, J. G., & Bersoff, D. M. (1992). Culture and moral judgment: How are conflicts between justice and interpersonal responsibilities resolved? *Journal of Personality and Social Psychology, 62*, 541–554.

Miyamoto, Y., & Kitayama, S. (2002). Cultural variation in correspondence bias: The critical role of attitude diagnosticity of socially constrained behavior. *Journal of Personality and Social Psychology, 83*, 1239–1248.

Mook, D. G. (1983) In defense of external invalidity. *American Psychologist, 38*, 379–387.

Morling, B., Kitayama, S., & Miyamoto, Y. (2002). Cultural practices emphasize influence in the United States and adjustment in Japan. *Personality and Social Psychology Bulletin, 28*, 311–323.

Morris, M., & Peng, K. (1994). Culture and cause: American and Chinese attributions for social and physical events. *Journal of Personality and Social Psychology, 67*, 949–971.

Nisbett, R. E. (2003). *The geography of thought*. New York: Free Press.

Nisbett, R. E., & Cohen, D. (1996). *Culture of honor: The psychology of violence in the south*. Boulder, CO: Westview Press.

Nisbett, R. E., Peng, K., Choi, I., & Norenzayan, A. (2001). Culture and systems of thought: Holistic vs. analytic cognition. *Psychological Review, 108*, 291–310.

Norenzayan, A. (2008). *Middle Eastern cognition in cross-cultural context.* Unpublished manuscript, University of British Columbia.

Norenzayan, A., Choi, I., & Nisbett, R. E. (2002a). Cultural similarities and differences in social inference: Evidence from behavioral predictions and lay theories of behavior. *Personality and Social Psychology Bulletin, 28,* 109–120.

Norenzayan, A., Choi, I., & Peng, K. (2007). Perception and cognition. In S. Kitayama & D. Cohen (Eds.), *Handbook of cultural psychology* (pp. 569–594). New York: Guilford Press.

Norenzayan, A., & Heine, S. J. (2005). Psychological universals: What are they and how can we know? *Psychological Bulletin, 131,* 763–784.

Norenzayan, A., Smith, E. E., Kim, B., & Nisbett, R. E. (2002b). Cultural preferences for formal versus intuitive reasoning. *Cognitive Science, 26,* 653–684.

Oishi, S., & Diener, E. (2003). Culture and well-being: The cycle of action, evaluation, and decision. *Personality and Social Psychology Bulletin, 29,* 939–949.

Oishi, S., Diener, E., Scollon, C. N., & Biswas-Diener, R. (2004). Cross-situational consistency of affective experiences across cultures. *Journal of Personality and Social Psychology, 86,* 460–472.

Oishi, S., Lun, J., & Sherman, G. D. (2007). Residential mobility, self-concept, and positive affect in social interactions. *Journal of Personality and Social Psychology, 93,* 131–141.

Oyserman, D., Coon, H. M., & Kemmelmeier, M. (2002). Rethinking individualism and collectivism: Evaluation of theoretical assumptions and meta-analyses. *Psychological Bulletin, 128,* 3–72.

Oyserman, D., & Lee, S. W. S. (2008). Does culture influence what and how we think: Effects of priming individualism and collectivism. *Psychological Bulletin, 134,* 311–342.

Peng, K., & Nisbett, R. E. (1999). Culture, dialectics, and reasoning about contradiction. *American Psychologist, 54,* 741–754.

Peters, H. J., & Williams, J. M. (2006). Moving cultural background to the foreground: An investigation of self-talk, performance, and persistence following feedback. *Journal of Applied Sport Psychology, 18,* 240–253.

Pinker, S. (1994). *The language instinct.* New York: Harper-Collins.

Putnam, R. D. (2000). *Bowling alone: The collapse and revival of American community.* New York: Simon & Schuster.

Richerson, P. J., & Boyd, R. (2005). *Not by genes alone.* Chicago: University of Chicago Press.

Rosenberg, M. (1965). *Society and the adolescent self-image.* Princeton, NJ: Princeton University Press.

Rothbaum, F., Weisz, J. R., & Snyder, S. S. (1982). Changing the world and changing the self: A two-process model of perceived control. *Journal of Personality and Social Psychology, 42,* 5–37.

Rozin, P., Fischler, C., Shields, C., & Masson, E. (2006). Attitudes towards large numbers of choices in the food domain: A cross-cultural study of five countries in Europe and the USA. *Appetite, 46*, 304–308..

Russell, J. A. (1991). Culture and the categorization of emotions. *Psychological Bulletin, 110*, 426–450.

Sanchez-Burks, J., Nisbett, R. E., & Ybarra, O. (2000). Cultural styles, relational schemas and prejudice against outgroups. *Journal of Personality and Social Psychology, 79*, 174–189.

Savani, K., Markus, H. R., & Conner, A. L. (2008). Let your preference be your guide? Preferences and choices are more tightly linked for North Americans than for Indians. *Journal of Personality and Social Psychology, 95*, 861–876.

Schug, J., Yuki, M., Horikawa, H., & Takemura, K. (2009). Similarity attraction and actually selecting similar others: How cross-societal differences in relational mobility affect interpersonal similarity in Japan and the United States. *Asian Journal of Social Psychology, 12*, 95–103.

Schwartz, B. (2004). *The paradox of choice: Why more is less*. New York: Harper-Collins.

Sedikides, C., Gaertner, L., & Vevea, J. (2005). Pancultural self-enhancement reloaded: A meta-analytic reply to Heine (2005). *Journal of Personality and Social Psychology, 89*, 539–551.

Segall, M. H., Campbell, D. T., & Herskiovits, M. J. (1963). Cultural differences in the perception of geometric illusions. *Science, 193*, 769–771.

Shweder, R. A. (1990). Cultural psychology: What is it? In J. W. Stigler, R. A. Shweder, & G. Herdt (Eds.), *Cultural psychology: Essays on comparative human development* (pp. 1–43). Cambridge: Cambridge University Press.

Shweder, R. A., Goodnow, J., Hatano, G., LeVine, R. A., Markus, H., & Miller, P. (1998). The cultural psychology of development: One mind, many mentalities. In W. Damon & R. M. Lerner (Eds.), *Handbook of child psychology* (Vol. 1, pp. 865–937). New York: John Wiley.

Singelis, T. M., Bond, M. H., Lai, S. Y., & Sharkey, W. F. (1999). Unpackaging culture's influence on self-esteem and embarrassability: The role of self-construals. *Journal of Cross-Cultural Psychology, 30*, 315–331.

Snibbe, A. C., & Markus, H. R. (2005). You can't always get what you want: Social class, agency, and choice. *Journal of Personality and Social Psychology, 88*, 703–720.

Spencer-Rodgers, J., Boucher, H. C., Mori, S. C., Wang, L., & Peng, K. (2009). The dialectical self-concept: Contradiction, change, and holism in East Asian cultures. *Personality and Social Psychology Bulletin, 35*, 29–44.

Spencer-Rodgers, J., Peng, K., Wang, L., & Hou, Y. (2004). Dialectical self-esteem and East-West differences in psychological well-being. *Personality and Social Psychology Bulletin, 30*, 1416–1432.

Steele, C. M. (1988). The psychology of self-affirmation: Sustaining the integrity of the self. In L. Berkowitz (Ed.), *Advances in experimental social psychology* (Vol. 21, pp. 261–302). San Diego, CA: Academic Press.

Stephens, N. M., Markus, H. R., & Townsend, S. S. M. (2007). Choice as an act of meaning: The case of social class. *Journal of Personality and Social Psychology, 93*, 814–830.

Strack, F., Martin, L. L., & Stepper, S. (1988). Inhibiting and facilitating conditions of the human smile: A nonobtrusive test of the facial feedback hypothesis. *Journal of Personality and Social Psychology, 54*, 768–777.

Su, S. K., Chiu, C.-Y., Hong, Y.-Y., Leung, K., Peng, K., & Morris, M. W. (1999). Self organization and social organization: American and Chinese constructions. In T. R. Tyler, R. Kramer, & O. John (Eds.), *The psychology of the social self* (pp. 193–222). Mahwah, NJ: Lawrence Erlbaum.

Suh, E. M. (2002). Culture, identity consistency, and subjective well-being. *Journal of Personality and Social Psychology, 83*, 1378–1391.

Suh, E., Diener, E., Oishi, S., & Triandis, H. C. (1998). The shifting basis of life satisfaction judgments across cultures: Emotions versus norms. *Journal of Personality and Social Psychology, 74*, 482–493.

Swann, W. B., Wenzlaff, R. M., Krull, D. S., & Pelham, B. W. (1992). Allure of negative feedback: Self-verification strivings among depressed persons. *Journal of Abnormal Psychology, 101*, 293–306.

Taylor, S. E., & Brown, J. D. (1988). Illusion and well-being: A social psychological perspective on mental health. *Psychological Bulletin, 103*, 193–210.

Tesser, A. (2000). On the confluence of self-esteem maintenance mechanisms. *Personality and Social Psychology Review, 4*, 290–299.

Ting-Toomey, S. (Ed.) (1994). *The challenge of facework: Cross-cultural and interpersonal issues*. Albany: State University of New York Press.

Tracy, J. L., & Matsumoto, D. (2008). The spontaneous display of pride and shame: Evidence for biologically innate nonverbal displays. *Proceedings of the National Academy of Science, 105*, 11655–11660.

Tracy, J. L., & Robins, R. W. (2008). The nonverbal expression of pride: Evidence for cross-cultural recognition. *Journal of Personality and Social Psychology, 94*, 516–530.

Trafimow, D., Triandis, H. C., & Goto, S. G. (1991). Some tests of the distinction between the private self and the collective self. *Journal of Personality and Social Psychology, 60*, 649–655.

Triandis, H. C. (1989). The self and social behavior in differing cultural contexts. *Psychological Review, 96*, 506–520.

Triandis, H. C., Marin, G., Lisansky, J., & Betancourt, H. (1984). Simpatia as a cultural script of Hispanics. *Journal of Personality and Social Psychology, 47*, 1363–1375.

Tropp, L. R., & Wright, S. C. (2003). Evaluations and perceptions of self, ingroup, and outgroup: Comparisons between Mexican-American and European-American children. *Self and Identity, 2*, 203–221.

Tsai, J. L., Chentsova-Dutton, Y., Freire-Bebeau, L., & Przymus, D. E. (2002). Emotional expression and physiology in European-Americans and Hmong Americans. *Emotion, 2*, 380–397.

Tsai, J. L., Knutson, B. K., & Fung, H. H. (2006). Cultural variation in affect valuation. *Journal of Personality and Social Psychology, 90*, 288–307.

Tsai, J. L., Louie, J. Y., Chen, E. E., & Uchida, Y. (2006). Learning what feelings to desire: Socialization of ideal affect through children's storybooks. *Personality and Social Psychology Bulletin, 32*, 1–14.

Tsai, J. L., Ying, Y., & Lee, P. A. (2000). The meaning of "being Chinese" and "being American: Variation among Chinese American young adults." *Journal of Cross-Cultural Psychology, 31*, 302–332.

Twenge, J. M., & Campbell, W. K. (2001). Age and birth cohort differences in self-esteem: A cross-temporal meta-analysis. *Personality and Social Psychology Review, 5*, 321–344.

Uskul, A. K., Kitayama, S., & Nisbett, R. E. (2008). Ecocultural basis of cognition: Farmers and fishermen are more holistic than herders. *Proceedings of the National Academy of Sciences, 105*, 8552–8556.

Vandello, J. A., & Cohen, D. (2003). Male honor and female fidelity: Implicit cultural scripts that perpetuate domestic violence. *Journal of Personality and Social Psychology, 84*, 997–1010.

Wang, Q. (2004). The emergence of cultural self-constructs: Autobiographical memory and self-description in European American and Chinese children. *Developmental Psychology, 40*, 3–15.

Weisz, J. R., Rothbaum, F. M., & Blackburn, T. C. (1984). Standing out and standing in: The psychology of control in America and Japan. *American Psychologist, 39*, 955–969.

Witkin, H. A., & Berry, J. W. (1975). Psychological differentiation in cross-cultural perspective. *Journal of Cross-Cultural Psychology, 6*, 4–87.

Wu, S., & Keysar, B. (2007). Cultural effects on perspective taking. *Psychological Science, 18*, 600–606.

Wundt, W. (1921). *Elements of folk psychology*. London: Allen & Unwin.

Yuki, M., Maddux, W. W., & Masuda, T. (2007). Are the windows to the soul the same in the East and West? Cultural differences in using the eyes and mouth as cues to recognize emotions in Japan and the United States. *Journal of Experimental Social Psychology, 43*, 303–311.

Yuki, M., Schug, J. R., Horikawa, H., Takemura, K., Sato, K., Yokota, K., & Kamaya, K. (2008). *Development of a scale to measure perceptions of relational mobility in society*. Unpublished manuscript, Hokkaido University.

Chapter 19

Health Psychology

Shelley E. Taylor

Health psychology is a relatively recent branch of psychology, formalized in the late 1970s. It adopts a definition of health as "a complete state of physical, mental, and social wellbeing, and not merely the absence of disease or infirmity" (World Health Organization, 1948). As such, the field is guided by a biopsychosocial model that addresses health promotion and maintenance, including the development and practice of health habits; the prevention and treatment of illness; the etiology and correlates of health, illness, and dysfunction; and psychological perspectives on the healthcare system and the formulation of health policy. Thus, the field covers the psychological, social, and biological factors that lead to the enhancement of health, the prevention and treatment of illness, and the evaluation and modification of health policies in directions consistent with these underlying values (Taylor, 2009a).

Why did the field of health psychology develop? A primary factor was the change in illness patterns that occurred in the United States and other developed countries over the past century. There has been a shift in the major causes of morbidity and mortality, from acute disorders, such as tuberculosis, pneumonia, and infectious diseases, to chronic illnesses, especially heart disease, cancer, and diabetes.[1] These are diseases in which psychological and social factors are clearly implicated as causes. Diet, smoking, and lack of exercise contribute to the development of heart disease, diabetes, and some cancers, for example. Accordingly, these are also diseases in which psychological and social processes are heavily implicated in prevention, such as the need to modify health habits, communication patterns with healthcare providers, and adherence to treatment recommendations, among other issues. Chronic diseases are slow-developing disorders with which people live for a long time and that often cannot be cured but rather managed by patient and healthcare providers collaborating together. How to make that collaboration successful is also a task of social psychologists interested in health psychology.

Social psychologists were some of the founding figures in health psychology and have made substantial contributions to areas such as the practice of health behaviors, stress and coping, adherence to treatment regimens, discoveries of the underlying causes of complex disorders, and the management of chronic diseases. This chapter addresses all of these topics, but begins with a framework for understanding stress, because stress and reactions to it are heavily implicated in the diseases of modernity that affect our population, and increasingly, other countries around the world as well.

Stress

Everyone has an intuitive appreciation of stress. It is being late for an important appointment, realizing you ran a stoplight and a hidden camera just took a picture of your license plate, or finding out that your parents need your help at home during examination time. Stress is formally defined as a negative emotional experience accompanied by predictable biochemical, physiological, cognitive, and behavioral changes directed either toward altering the stressful event or accommodating to its effects (Baum, 1990).

Although researchers initially focused on stressful events themselves, called stressors, increasingly researchers have recognized that stress is the consequence of a person's appraisal processes. Primary appraisal determines the meaning of the event (Lazarus & Folkman, 1984). Events may be perceived as positive, neutral, or negative in their consequences and are further appraised for their possible harm, threat, or challenge. Secondary appraisal involves the assessment of our coping abilities and resources, namely whether they will be sufficient to meet the harm, threat or challenge of the event. Ultimately, the subjective experience of stress is a balance between primary and secondary appraisal. When people feel able to deal with difficult situations, they experience a sense of challenge, but when resources are perceived to be insufficient to address the event, they experience threat (cf. Tomaka, Blascovich, Kelsey, & Leitten, 1993). Stress, then, results from the process of appraising events as harmful, threatening, or challenging, of assessing potential responses, and of responding to those events.

Models of Stress

Several important theoretical models have guided the study of stress. The first was Walter Cannon's (1932) description of the *fight-or-flight response*. Cannon proposed that when an organism perceives a threat, the body is rapidly aroused and motivated via the sympathetic nervous system and the endocrine system to attack the threat or to flee from it. In current times, fight refers to aggressive or assertive responses to stress, whereas flight may be manifested in social withdrawal or withdrawal through substance use, such as alcohol or drugs. On the one hand, the fight-or-flight response is adaptive because it mobilizes the organism for a quick response, but on the other hand, it may be harmful because long-term stress disrupts emotional and physiological functioning and, as will shortly be noted, lays the groundwork for health problems.

Another seminal contribution to research on stress was Hans Selye's (1956) work on the *general adaptation syndrome*. Selye exposed rats to a variety of stressors and observed their physiological responses. To his surprise, all stressors, regardless of type, produced essentially the same pattern of physiological changes, which led to an enlarged adrenal cortex, shrinking of the thymus and lymph glands, and ulceration of the stomach and duodenum. From these observations, he argued that when an organism confronts a stressor, it mobilizes itself for action. Selye termed this pattern of responses the general adaptation syndrome and maintained that it is nonspecific with respect to the stressor. The general adaptation syndrome consists of three phases. In the first phase, alarm, the organism is mobilized to meet the threat. In the second phase, resistance, the organism makes an effort to cope with the threat, as through confrontation. The third phase, exhaustion, occurs if the organism fails to overcome the threat and depletes its physiological resources in the process of trying. Over time, with repeated or prolonged exposure to stress, wear-and-tear on biological systems lays the groundwork for disease.

A third guiding model in the field of stress builds on the observation that animals, whether human or nonhuman, do not only fight, flee, or grow exhausted in response to stress; they also affiliate with each other and protect their offspring in times of stress. Taylor and colleagues (Taylor et al., 2000) termed this pattern *tend and befriend*. The theory maintains that in addition to fight-or-flight, humans respond to stress with social affiliation and protective behavior toward offspring. These responses appear to particularly characterize women's responses to stress, although men also affiliate in response to stress.

Tend and befriend has its origins in evolutionary theory and maintains that during the time that human responses to stress evolved, men and women faced somewhat different adaptive challenges, which led to different responses to threat. Whereas men were responsible for hunting and protection, women were responsible for foraging and childcare. Because these activities were largely sex segregated, women's responses to stress would have evolved to protect not only the self but offspring as well. Whereas fight-or-flight is a mechanism that addresses individual self-protection, tend and befriend is a response to stress that benefits both the self and offspring. That is, the chances that both self and offspring will survive a threat unscathed are greatly enhanced if we are affiliated with a social group for joint protection and comfort. Like the fight-or-flight mechanism, tend and befriend may depend on underlying biological mechanisms, in particular the hormone oxytocin and endogenous opioid peptides. Oxytocin acts as an impetus for affiliation (Taylor et al., 2006) and induces levels of calm and relaxation (e.g., Light, Grewen, & Amico, 2005), responses that may depend on downstream opioid peptides.

Biological Bases of Stress Responses

The underlying physiology of the stress response depends heavily on two interrelated stress systems, namely the sympathetic adrenomedullary (SAM) system and the hypothalamic pituitary adrenal (HPA) axis. Stress engages sympathetic arousal, which leads to the secretion of epinephrine and norepinephrine. These catecholamines, in turn, lead to increased blood pressure, heart rate, sweating, and constriction of blood vessels, among other changes. The HPA axis releases corticotropin releasing factor (CRF), which stimulates the pituitary to secrete adrenocorticotropin hormone (ACTH), which in turn, stimulates the adrenal cortex to release glucocorticoids, including cortisol. Cortisol acts to conserve stores of carbohydrates and helps control inflammation in the case of injury. It also helps restore the body to a steady state following stress.

Although these systems are protective on the short term, over the long term, repeated or chronic activation of these systems can compromise their functioning. A concept that addresses this damage is *allostatic load* (McEwen & Stellar, 1993). Allostatic load refers to the fact that physiological systems fluctuate to meet demands from stress, a state called allostasis, but over time, the physiological costs of chronic exposure to fluctuating or heightened neural or neuroendocrine responses increase, and allostatic load builds up. Signs of allostatic load, that is the long-term costs of chronic or repeated stress, include decreases in cell-mediated immunity, the inability to shut off cortisol in response to stress, lowered heart rate variability, elevated epinephrine level, a high waist-to-hip ratio reflecting abdominal fat, low hippocampal volume (which is believed to result from repeated stimulation of the HPA axis), problems with memory (an indirect measure of hippocampal functioning), high plasma fibrinogen, and elevated blood pressure (Seeman, McEwen, Rowe, & Singer, 2001). Most of these changes occur over the lifespan naturally, and so allostatic load may be thought of as accelerated aging of the organism in response to stress. Over time, this wear and tear leads to susceptibility to chronic illnesses and an increased risk of death (Karlamangla, Singer, & Seeman, 2006). This buildup interacts both with genetically based risk factors and with lifestyle factors, and so if people cope with stress via a high fat diet, less frequent exercise, or smoking, for example, the buildup of allostatic load may be hastened.

Although the proceeding discussion may be an unexpected coverage of more biology than the average social psychologist wants, it is increasingly difficult to do good health psychology research without some awareness of these systems and the biological models that guide them—hence, this background.

What Makes Events Stressful

Although events are not inherently stressful, some events are more likely to be appraised as such than others. *Negative events* produce more stress than positive events. Although both have the potential to cause stress (e.g., think of the stress involved in planning a wedding or having a baby), negative events bear a stronger relationship to both psychological distress and adverse physical symptoms than do positive ones.

Uncontrollable or unpredictable events are perceived to be more stressful than controllable, predictable ones. When people feel that they can predict, modify, or terminate an aversive event, or that they have access to someone who can, the event is experienced as less stressful.

Ambiguous events are often perceived as more stressful than clear cut events. When a potential stressor cannot be well defined (e.g., ambiguous feedback from a boss), a person has difficulty taking action. He or she must instead devote energy to understanding the stressor. The ability to take confrontative action is usually associated with less stress and better coping.

Overloaded people are more stressed than people with fewer tasks to perform (e.g., Cohen & Williamson, 1988). People also appear to be more vulnerable to stress when stressful events occur in central life domains (Swindle & Moos, 1992).

The question arises as to whether people can adapt to stress. We all know people who seem to lead chronically stressful lives and yet, to all appearances, are none the worse for it. There is some evidence that people can habituate to stress, especially relatively low-level stressors. Arguably, New York City is a stressful place to live just by the nature of the traffic, noise, crowding, and other characteristics of the physical environment. Nonetheless, many people thrive and appear to habituate easily to this background stress. More serious ongoing stressors, however, such as a deteriorating marriage or a high-stress job, are more difficult to adapt to and impair cardiovascular, neuroendocrine, and immune system functioning, and thus lead to an increased risk for disease (Matthews, Gump, & Owens, 2001).

People are also perfectly capable of creating their own stress. Anticipating a stressful event, whether it occurs or not, can be as stressful as actually experiencing it. For example, studies of students anticipating examinations find that on days when students are worrying about the examination, their psychological and biological stress levels are as high as those seen during the examination itself (e.g., Sausen, Lovallo, Pincomb, & Wilson, 1992). There are reliable aftereffects of stress as well, such that performance and attention span are limited following a stressful event (e.g., Glass & Singer, 1972). Thus, the experience of stress is heavily psychological and can occur over a long time frame involving both the anticipation of stress as well as its aftermath.

On an extreme level, people who have been exposed to very serious stressors, such as childhood sexual abuse, rape, or wartime combat may experience posttraumatic stress disorder (PTSD), which may permanently alter stress regulatory systems and psychological functioning in response to normal events. PTSD usually requires clinical intervention (e.g., Nemeroff et al., 2006).

Increasing evidence suggests that stress experienced early in life, especially from low childhood socioeconomic status or a harsh early family environment marked by conflict or cold, nonnurturant behavior, can produce alterations in biological stress responses (Repetti, Taylor, & Saxbe, 2007). Early stress also disrupts the development of emotion regulation skills and social competence skills in ways that have lifelong effects on the risk for mental and physical health disorders. By contrast, offspring that grow up in highly nurturant families typically develop good emotion regulation and social competence skills that help them cope with stress (e.g., Taylor, Lerner, Sherman, Sage, & McDowell, 2003a,b).

How Is Stress Studied

Health psychologists have developed many ways to measure stress and to assess its effects on psychological and physical functioning. One common method is to bring people into the laboratory, expose them to short-term stressful events (such as counting backward quickly by sevens or delivering an impromptu speech to an unresponsive audience), and observe the impact of that stress on their physiological, neuroendocrine, and psychological responses. This *acute stress paradigm* consistently reveals that people assigned to perform these stressful tasks experience both psychological distress and strong indications of sympathetic activity and elevated cortisol (e.g., Kirschbaum, Klauer, Filipp, & Hellhammer, 1995). This stress paradigm has proved useful in identifying factors that moderate the stress response. For example, people react more strongly to these laboratory stressors if they also have chronic stress going on in their lives at well (Pike et al., 1997). By contrast, people who experience social support regularly on a daily basis react less strongly to these laboratory circumstances (e.g., Eisenberger, Taylor, Gable, Hilmert, & Lieberman, 2007).

Another useful paradigm intentionally exposes people to viruses, and then assesses whether they become ill and how ill they become as a function of how much stress they are experiencing and what coping abilities they have. Cohen and colleagues (1999), for example, measured levels of psychological stress in a group of adults, infected them with an influenza virus by swabbing their nose with cotton soaked in a viral culture, and measured their symptoms and the proinflammatory cytokine [interleukin-6 (IL-6)] that may link stress through the immune system to illness. They found that people experiencing more stress had greater symptoms of illness and increased production of IL-6. However, people who were exposed to the virus but who reported having a supportive social environment were less likely to get ill, had less severe viral infections if they did, and recovered more quickly (Cohen, Doyle, Skoner, Rabin, & Gwaltney, 1997).

Sometimes researchers want a general indication of background stress. Assessment of *stressful life events* can be a helpful method for this kind of research. Stressful life events range from cataclysmic ones, such as the death of a parent, to more mundane but problematic events, such as moving to a new home. In some research that uses this method, participants respond to standardized lists of stressful life events that have already been evaluated in terms of how much stress or change they typically cause and indicate how many they have experienced over a fixed period of time, such as in the preceding 6 months (e.g., Holmes & Rahe, 1967). In other cases, people are asked to indicate how much stress they have been through recently and list and rate the specific events. In both cases, research demonstrates a modest relationship between stress experienced and the likelihood of adverse health outcomes (e.g., Turner & Avison, 1992; Schroeder & Costa, 1984). However, as noted earlier, some people will appraise a particular event, such as being fired from work, as a catastrophe, whereas others may see it as an unexpected opportunity. Because people vary so much in what they consider to be stressful, many researchers believe that perceived stress is a better indicator of experienced stress than instruments that assess particular events (Cohen, Kamarck, & Mermelstein, 1983).

Stress has also increasingly been studied in the environments in which people normally live. For example, most adults work, and work can be both a common source of stress in everyday life as well as a potentially preventable source of stress. Work-related factors that increase the experience of stress include work overload, namely feeling that you are required to work too long and too hard at too many tasks; role conflict, which occurs when a person receives conflicting information about work tasks or standards from different people; the inability to develop satisfying social relationships at work (Buunk, Doosje, Jans, & Hopstaken, 1993); a lack of perceived control over work-related tasks (e.g., Kivimäki et al., 2006); and difficulty finding or holding a job.

A particularly influential model of job stress draws on basic social psychological principles of demands and control. First developed by Karasek and colleagues (1981), the model details conditions that lead to job stress. Specifically, high psychological demands on the job coupled with little decision latitude (such as low job control) cause job strain, which in turn has been related to the development of coronary artery disease. When high demands and low control are combined with little social support at work, the risk for coronary artery disease is even greater (Muhonen & Torkelson, 2003). High-demand/high-control jobs also entail a certain degree of stress but are often perceived to be challenging and exciting rather than stressful. Low-demand/low-control jobs tend to breed disaffection in the workplace because these jobs are typically boring. Low-demand/high-control jobs can be satisfying, but in a low key way.

Considerable research has also been devoted to stress that involves juggling multiple roles. These issues are particularly acute for women, as the number of mothers of young children in the workforce is estimated to be more than 50% (Department for Professional Employees, April 2006). Because concessions to working parents are rarely made at work, at least in the United States, and because mothers continually bear a disproportionate share of household and childcare tasks (Emmons, Biernat, Teidje, Lang, & Wortman, 1990), home and work responsibilities have the potential to conflict with each other.

Despite the potential for women to suffer role conflict and role overload by combining these roles, there appear to be protective effects of combining work and home responsibilities (Waldron, Weiss, & Hughes, 1998). Early work by Linville (1985) found that having multiple activities that contribute to personal identity and self-esteem means that a setback in one domain can be buffered by feelings of competence or satisfaction in another. Although it is clear that juggling heavy responsibilities at work and home reduces the enjoyment of both sets of tasks and may contribute to depression, combining motherhood and employment can lead to women's improved wellbeing, improved self-esteem, feelings of self-efficacy, life satisfaction, and better health (Verbrugge, 1983; Weidner, Boughal, Connor, Pieper, & Mendell, 1997). Whether the effects of multiple roles are positive or negative depends heavily on the personal and social resources that are available. We next turn to coping resources and processes that may ameliorate the experience of stress.

Coping with Stress

How do people manage the stressful events that threaten to engulf them? In this section, we discuss individual differences that contribute to coping processes, general propensities to cope via approach or avoidance, and one of the most important resources that people possess, namely social support.

Coping is defined as the thoughts and behaviors that people use to manage the internal and external demands of situations that have been appraised as stressful (Folkman & Moskowitz, 2004; Taylor & Stanton, 2007). The relationship between coping and stress is a dynamic one, occurring through a series of transactions between a person who has a set of resources, values, and commitments, and a particular environment with its own resources, demands, and constraints (Folkman & Moskowitz, 2004). As such, coping is not a one-time action that people undertake to deal with a specific stressor, typically, but is rather an evolving process.

Negativity, Stress, and Coping

Some people are predisposed to experience events as stressful. Negative affectivity is a dispositional, pervasive negative mood marked by anxiety, depression, and hostility (Watson & Clark, 1984). People who are high in negative affectivity (or neuroticism) are more likely to express distress and unhappiness across a wide range of situations (Gunthert, Cohen, & Armeli, 1999). Negative affectivity is related both to poor health and to the belief that you have poor health. For example, negative emotions influence the course of asthma, arthritis, ulcers, headaches, and coronary artery disease, among other disorders, and thus, negative affectivity has been considered the cornerstone of a "disease-prone personality" (e.g., Friedman & Booth-Kewley, 1987). Negative affectivity is associated with elevated cortisol, and high levels of adrenocortical activity may provide a pathway linking negative affectivity to adverse health outcomes (Polk, Cohen, Doyle, Skoner, & Kirschbaum, 2005).

But negative affectivity may also make it difficult to assess illness, because people who are high in negative affectivity report more distressing physical symptoms, such as headaches, stomachaches, and various pains, especially when under stress, even if there is no evidence of an underlying physiological disorder (e.g., Cohen, Doyle, Turner, Alper, & Skoner, 2003). People high in negative affectivity may also use health services more, even when they do not need them, thereby contributing to the appearance, if not the reality, of illness (Cohen & Williamson, 1991).

Coping Resources

Positive emotional functioning has been associated with better mental and physical health (e.g., Cohen & Pressman, 2006; Pressman & Cohen, 2005). For example, a positive emotional style has been tied to lower cortisol levels (Polk et al., 2005), better responses to vaccinations (Marsland, Cohen, Rabin, & Manuck, 2006), and resistance to illness following exposure to a flu virus (Cohen, Alper, Doyle, Treanor, & Turner, 2006), among other healthful outcomes.

Related to a positive emotional style are several specific coping resources, including optimism, a sense of mastery or control, self-esteem, and related resources. Dispositional optimism, typically assessed by the Life Orientation Test (LOT)-R (Scheier, Carver, & Bridges, 1994), has been consistently tied to mental and physical health benefits (Segerstrom, 2007). Those who score high on this scale answer positively to items such as "Overall, I expect more good things to happen to me than bad." Optimists have a more positive mood, which may be physiologically protective. Optimism promotes more active and persistent coping efforts, which may improve long-term prospects for psychological adjustment and health (Segerstrom, Castañeda, & Spencer, 2003), and can speed recovery from illness and treatment (e.g., Scheier et al., 1989).

Psychological control or mastery involves the belief that we can determine our own behavior, influence the environment, and bring about desired outcomes (Thompson, 1981). It is related to self-efficacy, which is the more narrow perception that we have the ability to take a specific action to obtain a specific outcome in a specific situation (Bandura, 1991). Control or mastery has been linked to a lower risk for mortality (e.g., Surtees, Wainwright, Luben, Khaw, & Day, 2006) and better asthma control (Chen, Fisher, Bacharier, & Strunk, 2003), among other beneficial health outcomes. So powerful are its effects that psychological control has been used extensively in interventions to promote good health habits and to help people cope with stressful events, such as surgery and other noxious medical procedures. For example, by creating control-based interventions that provide information, relaxation, and cognitive behavioral skills, such as learning to think differently about the unpleasant sensations of a noxious medical procedure, patients are able to cope more successfully with medical tests and surgeries (Ludwick-Rosenthal & Neufeld, 1988).

Self-esteem and self-affirmation also aid effective coping, particularly at low levels of stress (Whisman & Kwon, 1993). In an experimental study, Creswell and colleagues (2005) had some people focus on and write about their important values and other people focus on less important values (a self-affirmation manipulation) (Steele, 1988). All participants then went through laboratory stressors, including mental arithmetic and delivering a speech to an unresponsive audience.

Those who had affirmed their important personal values had lower biological responses to stress, and among those with high dispositional self-esteem, experienced less psychological stress as well. Related resources include dependability, trust, lack of impulsivity, self-confidence, a sense of coherence about life, and conscientiousness, all of which have also been found to buffer people against stress (see Taylor, 2009a, for a review).

The beneficial effects of individual differences in these and related psychosocial resources on health appear to be mediated via the decreased neuroendocrine and physiological reactivity that people experience in response to stress when they believe they have the resources to manage it (e.g., Taylor, Lerner, Sherman, Sage, & McDowell, 2003a). Coping resources can lead to lower levels of activation of brain regions implicated in stress responses, including the amygdala and the dorsal anterior cingulate cortex (Eisenberger et al., 2007), patterns of activity that affect physiological and neuroendocrine responding. Coping resources have also been tied to greater activity in cortical regions, including the ventrolateral prefrontal cortex and the medial prefrontal cortex, which have been implicated in the regulation of threat responses (Taylor et al., 2008).

Social Support

Social support is perhaps the most significant coping resource that people possess. It is the perception or experience that you are loved and cared for by others, esteemed and valued, and part of a social network of mutual assistance and obligations (Wills, 1991). Social support may assume any of several forms. Tangible assistance involves the provision of material support, such as services, financial assistance, or goods. Informational support from others helps people to understand a stressful event better and determine what resources and coping strategies must be mustered to deal with it. Emotional support is provided when a person is reassured by close others that he or she is a valuable individual who is cared for by others (Wills, 1991).

Although the types of support just described involve the actual provision of help or solace by one person to another, in fact, many of the benefits of social support come from the perception that social support is available; that is, people carry their support networks around in their heads. Indeed, when we receive help from another and are aware of it, self-esteem may be threatened because the act of social support suggests a dependence on others or potentially a need to reciprocate (Bolger, Zuckerman, & Kessler, 2000). When we receive help from another but are unaware of it, that help is most likely to benefit the recipient, a type of support called invisible support (Bolger & Amarel, 2007).

Without question, social support is the most health-promoting resource uncovered by health psychologists. It has health-protective effects on par with or exceeding such well-established predictors of health as cholesterol and smoking. And, correspondingly, people who are socially isolated (Hawkley, Burleson, Berntson, & Cacioppo, 2003), who are chronically shy (Naliboff et al., 2004), or who anticipate rejection by others (Cole, Kemeny, Fahey, Zack, & Naliboff, 2003) experience elevated mental and physical health risks. Social isolation is also a risk factor for early death for both humans and animals (House, Landis, & Umberson,1988).

Social support probably exerts its health-protective effects by some of the same routes as other psychosocial resources, that is, by reducing physiological and neuroendocrine responses to stress. For example, biological responses to laboratory stressors are typically more subdued when a supportive companion is present than when no companion is present (Christenfeld, 1997). One possible reason is that warm social contact can release oxytocin, which has been tied to lower stress responses (Grewen, Girdler, Amico, & Light, 2005). Even undergoing stressful events in the presence of a pet can keep our heart rate and blood pressure lower and lead to faster physiological recovery following stress. Dogs appear to be more adept at providing social support than other pets (Allen, Blascovich, & Mendes, 2002).

Social support can lower the likelihood of illness, speed recovery from illness or treatment when it occurs, and reduce the risk of prolonged illness or risk of mortality due to serious disease (House, Landis, & Umberson, 1988; Rutledge, Matthews, Lui, Stone, & Cauley, 2003). A substantial literature attests to the mental and physical health benefits of perceived and actual social support (see Taylor, 2009b for a review).

Social support appears to have genetic bases in either the ability to construe social support as available or to establish supportive social networks (Kessler, Kendler, Heath, Neale, & Eaves, 1992). During stressful times these genetic predispositions may be activated, leading people to experience social support as available to them.

On the whole, the evidence for the beneficial effects of social support is overwhelming. It is beneficial during nonstressful as well as stressful times (direct effects hypothesis), but may be especially beneficial during periods of high stress (the buffering hypothesis). It is more effective when it matches the needs that a person has (the matching hypothesis; Cohen & McKay, 1984) than if the wrong person provides the wrong kind of social support (Dakof & Taylor, 1990). When would-be support providers fail to provide the kind of support that is needed or react in an unsupportive manner, they actually aggravate the negative event. Negative interactions can have a more adverse effect on well-being than positive interactions can have on improving it (Rook, 1984).

There are significant gender and cultural variations in how social support is experienced or used. Women are somewhat more likely to draw on their social networks for coping with stress than are men (Taylor, 2002, for a review). East Asians and Asian-Americans appear to profit more from social support that is implicit, that is, achieved through the awareness of knowing that one is part of a network consisting of mutual obligations; European Americans, by contrast, appear to benefit from explicit social support, that is, actually making use of their network to ask for help or comfort (Taylor, Welch, Kim, & Sherman, 2007). These qualifications notwithstanding, social support is a profoundly important resource that merits research attention and cultivation.

Coping Style

In addition to individual differences in resources, people have general ways of responding across situations that reflect coping styles, that is, general propensities to deal with stressful events in a particular way. Many frameworks for characterizing coping processes have been advanced (Skinner, Edge, Altman, & Sherwood, 2003). For example, coping strategies are often organized according to their intended function, such as resolving the stress (i.e., problem-focused coping) or palliating event-related distress (i.e., emotion-focused coping).

An important framework is approach-avoidance. Reflecting a core motivational construct in psychology (e.g., Davidson, Jackson, & Kalin, 2000), the approach-avoidance continuum characterizes coping efforts and maps easily onto broader theories of biobehavioral functioning. Examples of approach-oriented coping are problem solving, seeking social support, and creating outlets for emotional expression. Coping through avoidance includes both cognitive and behavioral strategies, such as the use of alcohol, drugs, or television to withdraw from stress.

Consistently, researchers find that the use of avoidance-oriented coping typically predicts elevated distress and less effective coping. Avoidance-oriented coping may preempt more effective active coping efforts, involve damaging behaviors, such as substance use, or induce intrusion of stress-related thoughts and emotions. Approach-based coping, however, is typically associated with more beneficial health and mental health outcomes, and has been advanced as an explanation for the generally beneficial effects of psychosocial resources on health and mental health (Taylor & Stanton, 2007).

In addition to addressing coping resources and broad coping styles, health psychologists have measured specific coping strategies that people use when they are managing the stressful events of daily life. One widely used measure developed by Carver and colleagues (Carver, Scheier, & Weintraub, 1989) is the COPE. It assesses the specific coping strategies of active coping, planning, positive reframing, acceptance, humor, religion, using emotional support from others, using instrumental support from others, self-distraction, denial, venting, substance use, behavioral disengagement, and self-blame. For example, a person might name a specific stressor and answer questions such as "I've been taking action to try to make the situation better," an item that assesses active coping. Perusal of these scales reveals that they map well onto the approach-avoidance continuum just described and also distinguish between social coping strategies and individual ones.

Many people are unable to develop effective coping strategies on their own, and so a variety of interventions have been developed to enable them to do so, including mindfulness training (e.g., Brown & Ryan, 2003), cognitive-behavioral stress management interventions (e.g., Antoni et al., 2001), and writing interventions that encourage emotional expression (e.g., Pennebaker, 1997; Lepore & Smyth, 2002). For example, Burton and King (2008) asked undergraduates to write either about a personal trauma, a positive life experience, or a control topic for 2 minutes each day for 2 days. Both the trauma group and the positive experience group reported fewer health complaints during follow-up than the control condition. This intervention is especially notable not only for being theoretically based, but for showing how a very brief intervention may provide benefits.

Modifying Health Risks

People are better able to deal with risks to their health and better able to avoid illness if they practice good health behaviors and adhere to their physicians' recommendations. These are areas to which social psychological theory and research have also made substantial contributions.

Health behaviors are behaviors undertaken by people to enhance or maintain their health. A health habit is a health behavior that is firmly established, often performed automatically without awareness, and often instilled during childhood. Health behaviors may include wearing a seatbelt, brushing your teeth, or consuming a healthy diet. The importance of health habits for good health cannot be overestimated. Sleeping 7 to 8 hours a night, not smoking, having no more than one or two alcoholic drinks each day, getting regular exercise, being no more than 10% overweight, and maintaining a good diet that is modest in meat consumption and high in vegetables, fruits, and whole grains delay the onset of chronic diseases and mortality. Instilling good health habits such as these is the task of primary prevention.

Social Influence and Health Behaviors

Social influence processes are important for instilling and modifying health behaviors. Families, friends, and workplace companions may motivate either good or poor health behaviors depending on social opinion. For example, peer pressure often leads to smoking in adolescence, but may influence people to stop smoking in adulthood. Social networks are critical to habits such as smoking and obesity (Cristakis & Fowler, 2007, 2008). In addition, health habits are strongly affected by early socialization, especially the influence of parents as role models and those who control children's environments.

A number of teachable moments may be identified during which health behavior interventions are particularly likely to succeed. For example, many teachable moments arise in early childhood when children are covered by insurance companies for well baby care, and pediatricians can use these moments to teach new parents how to instill basic health habits. Early dental visits may be used to teach both parents and children the importance of correct brushing. First pregnancy is a teachable moment for modifying health habits such as diet and smoking, because many women are motivated to preserve the health of their unborn child. As such, they may be especially motivated to curb bad health habits at this time.

There are also predictable windows of vulnerability for health habits, many of which occur in junior high school, when students are first exposed to smoking, drugs, alcohol, and dietary choices outside of the control of their parents. Social psychologists have devised interventions implemented through the schools that can help students avoid the temptations that lead to these health-compromising behaviors (Evans, Powers, Hersey, & Renaud, 2006). For example, several such interventions make use of peer role models who influence the behavior of younger students by teaching them how to resist the influence of cigarette manufacturers or negative peer group role models.

Attitude Change and Health Behaviors

Applications to health have been undertaken since the beginning of social psychological research on attitude formation and attitude change (for general overviews of attitudes research, see Fabrigar & Wegener, Chapter 6, this volume, and Petty & Briñol, Chapter 7, this volume). From these many studies, a number of generalizations can be drawn:

1. Communications should be colorful and vivid rather than steeped in statistics and jargon. If possible, they should also use case histories

(Taylor & Thompson, 1982). For example, a vivid account of the health benefits of regular exercise, coupled with a case history of someone who took up bicycling after a heart attack, may be persuasive to someone at risk for heart disease.

2. The communicator should be expert, prestigious, trustworthy, likable, and similar to the audience (McGuire, 1964). For example, a health message will be more persuasive if it comes from a respected, credible physician rather than from the proponent of the latest health fad.
3. Strong arguments should be presented at the beginning and end of a message, not buried in the middle (Zimbardo & Ebbesen, 1969).
4. Messages should be short, clear, and direct (Zimbardo & Ebbesen, 1969).
5. Messages should state conclusions explicitly (Zimbardo & Ebbesen, 1969). For example, a communication extolling the virtues of a low-cholesterol diet should explicitly advise the reader to alter his or her diet to lower cholesterol.
6. Extreme messages produce more attitude change, but only up to a point. Very extreme messages are discounted (Zimbardo & Ebbesen, 1969). For example, a message that urges people to exercise for at least half an hour 3 days a week will be more effective than one that recommends several hours of exercise a day.
7. For illness detection behaviors (such as HIV testing or obtaining a mammogram), emphasizing the problems that may occur if the behavior is not undertaken will be most effective (for example, Banks et al., 1995; Kalichman & Coley, 1996). For health promotion behaviors (such as sunscreen use), emphasizing the benefits to be gained may be more effective (Rothman & Salovey, 1997).
8. If the recipient of the message has an approach orientation, then messages phrased in terms of benefits are more successful (e.g., calcium will keep your bones healthy). People who have an avoidance orientation will be more influenced by messages that stress the risks of not performing a health behavior (e.g., a low calcium intake will increase bone loss) (Mann, Sherman, & Updegraff, 2004).
9. If the audience is receptive to changing a health habit, then the communication should include only favorable points, but if the audience is not inclined to accept the message, the communication should discuss both sides of the issue (Zimbardo & Ebbesen, 1969). For example, messages to smokers ready to stop should emphasize the health risks of smoking. Smokers who have not yet decided to stop may be more persuaded by a communication that points out its risk while acknowledging and rebutting its pleasurable effects.

Attitudinal approaches to changing health habits often make use of *fear appeals.* This approach assumes that if people are fearful that a particular habit is hurting their health, they will change their behavior to reduce their fear. Common sense suggests that the relationship between fear and behavior change should be direct: The more fearful an individual is, the more likely he or she should be to change the relevant behavior. However, research has found that this relationship does not always hold (Leventhal, 1970). Persuasive messages that elicit too much fear may actually undermine health behavior change (Becker & Janz, 1987). Moreover, research suggests that fear alone may not be sufficient to change behavior. Sometimes fear can affect intentions to change health habits (for example, Sutton & Eiser, 1984), but it may not produce long-lasting changes in health habits unless it is coupled with recommendations for action or information about the efficacy of the health behavior (Self & Rogers, 1990).

Providing information does not ensure that people will perceive that information accurately, however. When people receive negative information about risks to their health, they may process that information defensively (Millar & Millar, 1996). Instead of making appropriate health behavior changes, the person may reinterpret the problem as less serious or more common than he or she had previously believed (for example, Croyle, Sun, & Louie, 1993), particularly if the person intends to continue the behavior (Gerrard, Gibbons, Benthin, & Hessling, 1996). Smokers, for example, know that they are at a greater risk for lung cancer than nonsmokers, but they see lung cancer as less likely or problematic and smoking as more common than do nonsmokers.

The Health Belief Model

The most influential attitude theory of why people practice health behaviors is the *health belief model* (Rosenstock, 1966). This model states that whether a person practices a particular health behavior can be understood by knowing two factors: whether the person perceives a personal health threat and whether the person believes that a particular health practice will be effective in reducing that threat.

The perception of a personal health threat is influenced by at least three factors: general health values, which include interest and concern about health; specific beliefs about personal vulnerability to a particular disorder; and beliefs about the consequences of the disorder, such as whether or not they are serious. Thus, for example, people may change their diet to include low-cholesterol foods if they value health, feel threatened by the possibility of heart disease, and perceive that the threat of heart disease is severe (Brewer et al., 2007).

Whether a person believes a health measure will reduce the threat has two subcomponents: whether the individual thinks a health practice will be effective and whether the cost of undertaking that measure exceeds the benefits of the measure (Rosenstock, 1974). For example, the man who feels vulnerable to a heart attack and is considering changing his diet may believe that dietary change alone would not reduce the risk of a heart attack and that changing his diet would interfere with his enjoyment of life too much to justify taking the action. Thus, although his belief in his personal vulnerability to heart disease may be great, if he lacks the belief that a change of diet would reduce his risk, he would probably not make any changes.

The health belief model explains people's practice of health habits quite well. It predicts preventive dental care (Ronis, 1992), breast self-examination (Champion, 1990), dieting for obesity (Uzark, Becker, Dielman, & Rocchini, 1987), and AIDS risk-related behaviors (Aspinwall, Kemeny, Taylor, Schneider, & Dudley, 1991), among many other behaviors. Typically, health beliefs are a modest determinant of intentions to adopt these health measures.

The health belief model also predicts some of the circumstances under which people's health behaviors will change. Interventions that draw on the health belief model have generally supported its predictions. Emphasizing perceived vulnerability and simultaneously increasing the perception that a particular health behavior will reduce the threat are somewhat successful in changing smoking behavior (Eiser, van der Plight, Raw, & Sutton, 1985), encouraging preventive dental behavior (Ronis, 1992), and adopting measures to prevent osteoporosis (Klohn & Rogers, 1991). However, the health belief model focuses heavily on beliefs about risk, rather than emotional responses to perceived risk, which may better predict behavior (e.g., Lawton, Conner, & Parker, 2007; Peters, Slovic, Hibbard, & Tusler, 2006; Weinstein et al., 2007). In addition, the health belief model leaves out an important component of health behavior change: the perception that we will be able to engage in the health behavior.

Self-Efficacy

An important determinant of the practice of health behaviors is a sense of *self-efficacy:* the belief that we are able to control particular behaviors (Bandura, 1991; Murphy, Stein, Schlenger, Maibach, & NIMH Multisite HIV Prevention Trial Group, 2001). For example, smokers who believe they will not be able to break their habit probably will not try to quit, however much they think that smoking is risky and that stopping smoking is desirable. Self-efficacy affects health behaviors as varied as abstinence from smoking (Prochaska & DiClemente, 1984), weight control (Strecher, DeVellis, Becker, & Rosenstock, 1986), condom use

(Wulfert & Wan, 1993), and dietary change (Schwarzer & Renner, 2000). Typically, research finds a strong relationship between perceptions of self-efficacy and both initial health behavior change and long-term maintenance of change.

The Theory of Planned Behavior

Although health beliefs help clarify when people will change their health habits, increasingly health psychologists are turning their attention to the analysis of action. A theory that links health attitudes directly to behavior is Ajzen's *theory of planned behavior* (Ajzen & Madden, 1986; Fishbein & Ajzen, 1975).

According to this theory, a health behavior is the direct result of a behavioral intention. Behavioral intentions are themselves made up of three components: attitudes toward the specific action, subjective norms regarding the action, and perceived behavioral control. Attitudes toward the action are based on beliefs about the likely outcomes of the action and evaluations of those outcomes. Subjective norms are what a person believes *others* think that person should do (normative beliefs) and the motivation to comply with those normative references. Perceived behavioral control occurs when a person is able to perform the contemplated action and believes that the action undertaken will have the intended effect; this component of the model is very similar to self-efficacy. These factors combine to produce a behavioral intention and, ultimately, behavior change. To take a simple example, smokers who believe that smoking causes serious health outcomes, who believe that other people think they should stop smoking, who are motivated to comply with those normative beliefs, and who believe that they are capable of stopping smoking will be more likely to try to stop smoking than individuals who do not hold these beliefs.

The theory of planned behavior is a useful addition to understanding health behavior change processes for two reasons. First, it provides a model that links beliefs directly to behavior. Second, it provides a fine-grained picture of people's intentions with respect to a particular health habit. It predicts a broad array of health behaviors, such as condom use among students (Sutton, McVey, & Glanz, 1999), sunbathing and sunscreen use (Hillhouse, Stair, & Adler, 1996), use of oral contraceptives (Doll & Orth, 1993), and consumption of soft drinks among adolescents (Kassem & Lee, 2004).

Limitations of Attitude Change Approaches

Despite the success of theories that link beliefs to the modification of health habits, attitudinal approaches are not very successful in explaining spontaneous behavior change, nor do they predict long-term behavior change very well. An additional complication is that communications designed to change people's attitudes about their health behaviors sometimes evoke defensive or irrational processes: People may perceive a health threat to be less relevant than it really is (Liberman & Chaiken, 1992), they may falsely see themselves as less vulnerable than others (Clarke, Lovegrove, Williams, & Macpherson, 2000), and they may see themselves as dissimilar to those who have succumbed to a particular health risk (Thornton, Gibbons, & Gerrard, 2002). Continued practice of a risky behavior may itself lead to changes in perception of a person's degree of risk, inducing a false sense of complacency (Halpern-Felsher et al., 2001).

Moreover, thinking about disease can produce a negative mood (Millar & Millar, 1995), which may, in turn, lead people to ignore or defensively interpret their risk. Although some research has found that inaccurate risk perception can be modified by information and educational interventions (Kreuter & Strecher, 1995), other reports suggest that unrealistic optimism is peculiarly invulnerable to feedback (Weinstein & Klein, 1995).

Because health habits are often deeply ingrained and difficult to modify, attitude-change procedures may not go far enough in simply providing the informational base for altering health habits (Ogden, 2003). Attitude-change procedures may instill the motivation to change a health habit but not provide the preliminary steps or skills necessary to actually alter behavior and maintain behavior change (Bryan, Fisher, & Fisher, 2002). Consequently, health psychologists have also turned to therapeutic techniques that typically draw on the principles of cognitive behavioral therapy (Antoni et al., 2001).

Finally, it is important to bear in mind that each health habit has a specific social, psychological, and cultural context that often needs to be addressed when an intervention is implemented. For example, interventions that draw on individualistic values and needs may be most successful for modifying the health behaviors of European-Americans, whereas interventions that draw on social values may be more successful among Latinos (Fitzgibbon, Stolley, Avellone, Sugerman, & Chavez, 1996). Accordingly, successful interventions need to identify what these dimensions are and address those components of the health behavior as well as the aspects of the intervention directly addressed by the theoretical model.

As an example, consider the modification of behaviors related to HIV infection. Most interventions begin by educating a target population about risky activity, providing information about AIDS and modes of transmission, and drawing on one or more of the theories just described for designing persuasive communications. There may, however, be particular teachable moments when AIDS education is particularly valuable. For example, gay men who have lost a partner are more likely to engage in unprotected anal intercourse in the following months, and at the beginning of a new relationship, people are especially likely to practice risky behaviors. Consequently, interventions may be especially successful at these times. Cultural sensitivity is essential to modifying risky sexual behavior. For example, an intervention by Jemmott, Jemmott, and Fong (1992) was designed to appeal especially to inner-city African American adolescents, using materials specifically developed to be interesting to them; the intervention was implemented by young African Americans. Another issue that arises when using social psychological theories to design interventions is whether there are cofactors or environmental factors that influence the behavior that need to be simultaneously addressed. An example is alcohol consumption during risky sexual activity. Alcohol is known to disinhibit sexual behavior, and so, effective interventions may need to simultaneously address the alcohol component as well (Morgenstern et al., 2007).

The overall message is that, whereas attitude-change studies conducted in the laboratory often create pure conditions to test specific hypotheses derived from the theories, interventions conducted in the real world are often aimed at the multitude of factors that influence the health habit so that the intervention will actually work.

Adherence to Treatment

Adherence to complex treatment regimens is often required for the modification of health behaviors and the management of chronic conditions, and the likelihood of adherence depends critically on patient–practitioner communication. Changes in the structure of the healthcare delivery system have brought this issue increasingly to the fore, as patients express dissatisfaction with their often-fragmented managed care. Because patients typically do not have the medical expertise to judge whether their care is technically competent, they often judge the quality of their care based on how much they like the practitioner, including how friendly, apparently caring, and polite he or she was (Bogart, 2001).

Accordingly, social psychologists have been heavily involved in interventions to attempt to eliminate the common complaints that patients report. These include inattentiveness, use of jargon, baby talk, depersonalization, and brusque, rushed visits. In addition, communication patterns appear to be especially eroded when physicians encounter patients whom they would prefer not to treat. These may include the elderly and members of minority groups. Studies show that physicians give less information, are less supportive, and demonstrate less proficient clinical care with African American and Latino patients and patients of lower socioeconomic status than is true for more advantaged and white patients (van Ryn & Fu, 2003). Satisfaction tends to be higher when patients are seen by practitioners of the same race or ethnicity (Laveist & Nuru-Jeter, 2002). Sexism, likewise, is a problem, in that medical intervention is sometimes regarded as less important for female than male patients (Martin & Lemos, 2002). Women may be stereotyped as seeking treatment for psychological distress, such as depression or anxiety. Communication interventions may help to reduce problems such as these.

Communication interventions are most successful if the recommendations can be learned easily, incorporated into medical routines easily, and implemented almost automatically. For example, greeting patients, addressing them by name, telling them where they can hang up their clothes if an examination is warranted, explaining the purpose of a procedure before and while it is going on, saying goodbye, and using the patient's name are simple behaviors that may add mere seconds to a visit. The author's own physician also made short notes in his charts about things to talk about during visits and inquired faithfully about the author's dog long after the dog had died. Nonetheless, actions such as these are seen as signs of warmth and supportiveness by patients (DiMatteo, 2004).

Simple communication interventions can also improve adherence to treatment. Asking the patient to repeat what needs to be done, keeping recommendations as simple as possible, writing them down as well as communicating them orally, emphasizing the importance of adherence, acknowledging the patient's efforts to adhere, involving family members when possible, using short words and short sentences that include concrete, specific language, and finding out what the patient's worries are or what potential barriers to treatment might be also help to improve nonadherence (Taylor, 2009a).

Alerting practitioners to how effective they can be as agents of behavior change is important. Practitioners are highly credible sources for patients with knowledge of medical issues, and they are typically well respected by patients. The practitioner is in a better position to effect behavior change and encourage adherence than many other people in the patient's life. By making messages simple and tailoring them to personal needs, the practitioner can help the patient decide to adhere and figure out how to implement recommendations in his or her life. The private face-to-face nature of the interaction between the healthcare practitioner and the patient provides an effective setting for holding attention, repeating and clarifying instructions, extracting commitments for adherence from the patient, and assessing potential sources of resistance.

Drawing on the six bases of power originally articulated by French and Raven (1959) yields the insight that health practitioners, especially physicians, can use these sources of power in their communications with patients (Raven, 1992). Physicians have legitimate power, namely the right to request that patients undertake particular actions. They have information power, in that physicians can control the persuasive power of a message. They have expertise, by virtue of special knowledge. For most patients, physicians also hold reward power, in that approval from your physician for achieving positive outcomes is likely to be rewarding. Physicians have the potential for coercive power by indicating that unpleasant tests or hospitalization may be necessary if the patient fails to follow the physician's recommendations. Finally, physicians have referent power because patients may want to foster a positive relationship with the physician and thus voluntarily adhere to the behaviors that are recommended (Raven, 1992). The practitioner can also keep the patient under at least partial surveillance and monitor progress at subsequent visits.

The importance of communication during medical visits has not been fully recognized. But with research, much of which was conducted by social psychologists, training institutions have become more receptive to the importance of training programs such as these. The payoffs for the often minimal amount of time invested in communication training can be very high. Good communication has been tied directly to patient satisfaction with care, a disinclination to sue in discretionary medical malpractice cases, and adherence to treatment. Social psychologists have been involved in many of the interventions that are now widely adopted in medical school curricula for training physicians in these simple, basic steps.

Health Psychology Today

At present, health psychology is moving in multiple directions, as both basic research and applications of the principles described here represent vibrant areas of research. One of the challenges facing health psychology is to identify the pathways whereby social psychological variables have robust effects on health and illness. For example, social support is, arguably, the most potent social psychological variable affecting health that has been identified to date, and yet we still know relatively little about what aspects of social support exert these effects and the pathways by which they do so. Similarly, variables such as optimism and neuroticism have been clearly linked to health outcomes, and yet the mechanisms by which these relations exist remain sketchy. This is a challenge for future work.

Related to this issue is how health psychologists integrate multiple levels of analysis to reach an understanding of these pathways. Increasingly, research is bringing together perspectives from genetics, neuroendocrine functioning, immune functioning, and biomedical markers of disease to elucidate these underlying mechanisms. Among other issues, this integrative approach requires that social psychologists entering the field ask themselves hard questions: How much must we know about the functioning of biological systems, such as the expression of genes, the functioning of neuroendocrine systems, and the immune system, to make meaningful contributions to this multidisciplinary field?

Another significant issue in the field concerns the mechanics by which health psychologists can most efficiently change the health behaviors of as many people as possible in a cost-effective manner. How can we determine what is effective in changing behavior and how can we apply this to a short-term, inexpensive, easily-implemented intervention with enduring effects? Sometimes the challenges facing the investigator attempting to change behavior requires abandoning a pure theoretical orientation in favor of what works. This can go against the basic research training and emphasis on theory that mark good social psychological training. It may also mean that is it not always possible to identify which aspects of an intervention produce the desired effects. Research that moves back and forth between the laboratory and the field, however, has the potential to test basic theory in the laboratory and then package its products with other effective intervention techniques for implementation in the field.

The field of health psychology is a broad and diverse one and includes inputs from all branches of psychology. This chapter has emphasized the contributions of social psychology. These include the dynamics of stress and the development of effective coping resources and ways of coping, the modification of health risks through interventions that draw on principles of social influence and attitude change, the understanding of the social and cultural environments within which health behaviors are enacted, and the development of interventions to improve communication between patients and practitioners, which has payoffs for satisfaction with care and adherence to complex treatment regimens.

Yet the role for social psychologists in health psychology is not inherently limited to these applications. Social psychologists have increasingly been involved in the teams that develop interventions and evaluate them, because they have expertise concerning the dynamics of social interactions that underlie most interventions. Consequently, the role of social psychologists in health psychology is an ever expanding one that will bring important changes and insights in future decades, as we learn more about the determinants of good and poor health.

Acknowledgments

Preparation of this manuscript was supported by grants from NIA (AG-030309) and NSF (SES-0525713 and BCS-0729532).

Footnotes

1. Morbidity refers to the number of cases of a disease that exist at a given point in time. Mortality refers to the number of deaths due to particular causes.

Suggestions for Further Reading

Cohen, S., Alper, C. M., Doyle, W. J., Treanor, J. J., & Turner, R. B. (2006). Positive emotional style predicts resistance to illness after experimental exposure to rhinovirus or influenza A virus. *Psychosomatic Medicine, 68,* 809–815.

Creswell, J. D., Welch, W. T., Taylor, S. E., Sherman, D. K., Gruenewald, T., & Mann, T. (2005). Affirmation of personal values buffers neuroendocrine and psychological stress responses. *Psychological Science, 16,* 846–851.

Cristakis, N. A., & Fowler, J. H. (2008). The collective dynamics of smoking in a large social network. *New England Journal of Medicine, 358,* 2249–2258.

DiMatteo, M. R. (2004). Social support and patient adherence to medical treatment: A meta-analysis. *Health Psychology, 23,* 207–218.

Folkman, S., & Moskowitz, J. T. (2004). Coping: Pitfalls and promise. *Annual Review of Psychology, 55,* 745–774.

Low, C. A., Stanton, A. L., & Danoff-Burg, S. (2006). Expressive disclosure and benefit-finding among breast cancer patients: Mechanisms for positive health effects. *Health Psychology, 25,* 181–189.

McEwen, B. S., & Lasley, E. N. (2004). *The end of stress as we know it.* Washington, DC: Joseph Henry Press.

Taylor, S. E. (2009). Social support: A review. In H. S. Friedman (Ed.), *Oxford handbook of health psychology*. New York: Oxford University Press.

References

Ajzen, I., & Madden, T. J. (1986). Prediction of goal-directed behavior: Attitudes, intentions, and perceived behavioral control. *Journal of Experimental Social Psychology, 22,* 453–474.

Allen, K., Blascovich, J., & Mendes, W. B. (2002). Cardiovascular reactivity and the presence of pets, friends, and spouses: The truth about cats and dogs. *Psychosomatic Medicine, 64,* 727–739.

Antoni, M. H., Lehman, J. M., Kilbourne, K. M., Boyers, A. E., Culver, J. L., Alferi, S. M., et al. (2001). Cognitive-behavioral stress management intervention decreases the prevalence of depression and enhances benefit finding among women under treatment of early-stage breast cancer. *Health Psychology, 20,* 20–32.

Aspinwall, L. G., Kemeny, M. E., Taylor, S. E., Schneider, S. G., & Dudley, J. P. (1991). Psychosocial predictors of gay men's AIDS risk-reduction behavior. *Health Psychology, 10,* 432–444.

Bandura, A. (1991). Self-efficacy mechanism in physiological activation and health-promotion behavior. In J. Madden IV (Ed.), *Neurobiology of learning, emotion, and affect* (pp. 229–269). New York: Raven Press.

Banks, S. M., Salovey, P., Greener, S., Rothman, A. J., Moyer, A., Beauvais, J., & Spel, E. (1995). The effects of message framing on mammography utilization. *Health Psychology, 14,* 178–184.

Baum, A. (1990). Stress, intrusive imagery, and chronic distress. *Health Psychology, 9,* 653–675.

Becker, M. H., & Janz, N. K. (1987). On the effectiveness and utility of health hazard/health risk appraisal in clinical and nonclinical settings. *Health Services Research, 22,* 537–551.

Bogart, L. M. (2001). Relationship of stereotypic beliefs about physicians to health-care relevant behaviors and cognitions among African American women. *Journal of Behavioral Medicine, 245,* 573–586.

Bolger, N., & Amarel, D. (2007). Effects of social support visibility on adjustment to stress: Experimental evidence. *Journal of Personality and Social Psychology, 92,* 458–475.

Bolger, N., Zuckerman, A., & Kessler, R. C. (2000). Invisible support and adjustment to stress. *Journal of Personality and Social Psychology, 79,* 953–961.

Brewer, N. T., Chapman, G. B., Gibbons, F. X., Gerrard, M., McCaul, K. D., & Weinstein, N. D. (2007). Meta-analysis of the relationship between risk perception and health behavior: The example of vaccination. *Health Psychology, 26,* 136–145.

Brown, K. W., & Ryan, R. M. (2003). The benefits of being present: Mindfulness and its role in psychological well-being. *Journal of Personality and Social Psychology, 84,* 822–848.

Bryan, A., Fisher, J. D., & Fisher, W. A. (2002). Tests of the mediational role of preparatory safer sexual behavior in the context of the theory or planned behavior. *Health Psychology, 21,* 71–80.

Burton, C. M., & King, L. A. (2008). Effects of (very) brief writing on health: The two-minute miracle. *British Journal of Health Psychology, 13,* 9–14.

Buunk, B. P., Doosje, B. J., Jans, L. G. J. M., & Hopstaken, L. E. M. (1993). Perceived reciprocity, social support, and stress at work: The role of exchange and communal orientation. *Journal of Personality and Social Psychology, 65,* 801–811.

Cannon, W. B. (1932). *The wisdom of the body.* New York: Norton.

Carver, C. S., Scheier, M. F., & Weintraub, J. K. (1989). Assessing coping strategies: A theoretically based approach. *Journal of Personality and Social Psychology, 56,* 267–283.

Champion, V. L. (1990). Breast self-examination in women 35 and older: A prospective study. *Journal of Behavioral Medicine, 13*, 523–538.

Chen, E., Fisher, E. B., Bacharier, L. B., & Strunk, R. C. (2003). Socioeconomic status, stress, and immune markers in adolescents with asthma. *Psychosomatic Medicine, 65*, 984–992.

Christenfeld, N. (1997). Memory for pain and the delayed effects of distraction. *Health Psychology, 16*, 327–330.

Clarke, V. A., Lovegrove, H., Williams, A., & Macpherson, M. (2000). Unrealistic optimism and the health belief model. *Journal of Behavioral Medicine, 23*, 367–376.

Cohen, S., Alper, C. M., Doyle, W. J., Treanor, J. J., & Turner, R. B. (2006). Positive emotional style predicts resistance to illness after experimental exposure to rhinovirus or influenza A virus. *Psychosomatic Medicine, 68*, 809–815.

Cohen, S., Doyle, W., & Skoner, D. (1999). Psychological stress, cytokine production, and severity of upper respiratory illness. *Psychosomatic Medicine, 61*, 175–180.

Cohen, S., Doyle, W. J., Skoner, D. P., Rabin, B. S., & Gwaltney, J. M., Jr. (1997). Social ties and susceptibility to the common cold. *Journal of the American Medical Association, 277*, 1940–1944.

Cohen, S., Doyle, W. J., Turner, R. B., Alper, C. M., & Skoner, D. P. (2003). Emotional style and susceptibility to the common cold. *Psychosomatic Medicine, 65*, 652–657.

Cohen, S., Kamarck, T., & Mermelstein, R. (1983). A global measure of perceived stress. *Journal of Health and Social Behavior, 24*, 385–396.

Cohen, S., & McKay, G. (1984). Social support, stress, and the buffering hypothesis: A theoretical analysis. In A. Baum, S. E. Taylor, & J. Singer (Eds.), *Handbook of psychology and health* (Vol. 4, pp. 253–268). Hillsdale, NJ: Erlbaum.

Cohen, S., & Pressman, S. D. (2006). Positive affect and health. *Current Directions in Psychological Science, 15*, 122–125.

Cohen, S., & Williamson, G. M. (1988). Perceived stress in a probability sample of the United States. In S. Spacapan & S. Oskamp (Eds.), *The social psychology of health* (pp. 31–67). Newbury Park, CA: Sage.

Cohen, S., & Williamson, G. M. (1991). Stress and infectious disease in humans. *Psychological Bulletin, 109*, 5–24.

Cole, S. W., Kemeny, M. E., Fahey, J. L., Zack, J. A., & Naliboff, B. D. (2003). Psychological risk factors for HIV pathogenesis: Mediation by the autonomic nervous system. *Biological Psychiatry, 54*, 1444–1456.

Creswell, J. D., Welch, W. T., Taylor, S. E., Sherman, D. K., Gruenewald, T., & Mann, T. (2005). Affirmation of personal values buffers neuroendocrine and psychological stress responses. *Psychological Science, 16*, 846–851.

Cristakis, N. A., & Fowler, J. H. (2007). The spread of obesity in a large social network over 32 years. *New England Journal of Medicine, 357*, 370–379.

Cristakis, N. A., & Fowler, J. H. (2008). The collective dynamics of smoking in a large social network. *New England Journal of Medicine, 358*, 2249–2258.

Croyle, R. T., Sun, Y. C., & Louie, D. H. (1993). Psychological minimization of cholesterol test results: Moderators of appraisal in college students and community residents. *Health Psychology, 12,* 503–507.

Dakof, G. A., & Taylor, S. E. (1990). Victims' perceptions of social support: What is helpful from whom? *Journal of Personality and Social Psychology, 58,* 80–89.

Davidson, R. J., Jackson, D. C., & Kalin, N. H. (2000). Emotion, plasticity, context, and regulation: Perspectives from affective neuroscience. *Psychological Bulletin, 126,* 890–909.

Department for Professional Employees. (2006). *Fact Sheet 2006, Professional Women: Vital Statistics.* Retrieved on April 13, 2007 from http://www.dpeaflcio.org/programs/factsheets/fs_2006_Professional_Women.htm#_edn14.

DiMatteo, M. R. (2004). Social support and patient adherence to medical treatment: A meta-analysis. *Health Psychology, 23,* 207–218.

Doll, J., & Orth, B. (1993). The Fishbein and Ajzen theory of reasoned action applied to contraceptive behavior: Model variants and meaningfulness. *Journal of Applied Social Psychology, 23,* 395–341.

Eisenberger, N. I., Taylor, S. E., Gable, S. L., Hilmert, C. J., & Lieberman, M. D. (2007). Neural pathways link social support to attenuated neuroendocrine stress responses. *NeuroImage, 35,* 1601–1612.

Eiser, J. R., van der Plight, J., Raw, M., & Sutton, S. R. (1985). Trying to stop smoking: Effects of perceived addiction, attributions for failure, and expectancy of success. *Journal of Behavioral Medicine, 8,* 321–342.

Emmons, C., Biernat, M., Teidje, L. B., Lang, E. L., & Wortman, C. B. (1990). Stress, support, and coping among women professionals with preschool children. In J. Eckenrode & S. Gore (Eds.), *Stress between work and family* (pp. 61–93). New York: Plenum Press.

Evans, W. D., Powers, A., Hersey, J., & Renaud, J. (2006). The influence of social environment and social image on adolescent smoking. *Health Psychology, 25,* 26–33.

Fishbein, M., & Ajzen, I. (1975). *Belief, attitude, intention, and behavior: An introduction to theory and research.* Reading, MA: Addison-Wesley.

Fitzgibbon, M. L., Stolley, M. R., Avellone, M. E., Sugerman, S., & Chavez, N. (1996). Involving parents in cancer risk reduction: A program for Hispanic American families. *Health Psychology, 15,* 413–422.

Folkman, S., & Moskowitz, J. T. (2004). Coping: Pitfalls and promise. *Annual Review of Psychology, 55,* 745–774.

French, J. R. P., & Raven, B. (1959). The bases of social power. In D. Cartwright & A. Zander (Eds.), *Group dynamics* (pp. 150–167). New York: Harper & Row.

Friedman, H. S., & Booth-Kewley, S. (1987). The "disease-prone" personality: A meta-analytic view of the construct. *American Psychologist, 42,* 539–555.

Gerrard, M., Gibbons, F. X., Benthin, A. C., & Hessling, R. M. (1996). A longitudinal study of the reciprocal nature of risk behaviors and cognitions in adolescents: What you do shapes what you think, and vice versa. *Health Psychology, 15,* 344–354.

Glass, D. C., & Singer, J. E. (1972). *Urban stress.* New York: Academic Press.

Grewen, K. M., Girdler, S. S., Amico, J., & Light, K. C. (2005). Effects of partner support on resting oxytocin, cortisol, norepinephrine, and blood pressure before and after warm partner contact. *Psychosomatic Medicine, 67,* 531–538.

Gunthert, K. C., Cohen, L. H., & Armeli, S. (1999). The role of neuroticism in daily stress and coping. *Journal of Personality and Social Psychology, 77,* 1087–1100.

Halpern-Felsher, B. L., Millstein, S. G., Ellen, J. M., Adler, N. E., Tschann, J. M., & Biehl, M. (2001). The role of behavioral experience in judging risks. *Health Psychology, 20,* 120–126.

Hawkley, L. C., Burleson, M. H., Berntson, G. G., & Cacioppo, J. T. (2003). Loneliness in everyday life: Cardiovascular activity, psychosocial context, and health behaviors. *Journal of Personality and Social Psychology, 85,* 105–120.

Hillhouse, J. J., Stair, A. W., III, & Adler, C. M. (1996). Predictors of sunbathing and sunscreen use in college undergraduates. *Journal of Behavioral Medicine, 19,* 543–562.

Holmes, T. H., & Rahe, R. H. (1967). The social readjustment rating scale. *Journal of Psychosomatic Research, 11,* 213–218.

House, J. S., Landis, K. R., & Umberson, D. (1988). Social relationships and health. *Science, 241,* 540–545.

Jemmott, J. B., III, Jemmott, L. S., & Fong, G. (1992). Reductions in HIV risk-associated sexual behaviors among black male adolescents: Effects of an AIDS prevention intervention. *American Journal of Public Health, 82,* 372–377.

Kalichman, S. C., & Coley, B. (1996). Context framing to enhance HIV-antibody-testing messages targeted to African American women. *Health Psychology, 14,* 247–254.

Karasek, R., Baker, D., Marxer, F., Ahlbom, A., & Theorell, T. (1981). Job decision latitude, job demands, and cardiovascular disease: A prospective study of Swedish men. *American Journal of Public Health, 71,* 694–705.

Karlamangla, A. S., Singer, B. H., & Seeman, T. E. (2006). Reduction in allostatic load in older adults is associated with lower all-cause mortality risk: MacArthur studies of successful aging. *Psychosomatic Medicine, 68,* 500–507.

Kassem, N. O., & Lee, J. W. (2004). Understanding soft drink consumption among male adolescents using the theory of planned behavior. *Journal of Behavioral Medicine, 27,* 273–296.

Kessler, R. C., Kendler, K. S., Heath, A. C., Neale, M. C., & Eaves, L. J. (1992). Social support, depressed mood, and adjustment to stress: A genetic epidemiological investigation. *Journal of Personality and Social Psychology, 62,* 257–272.

Kirschbaum, C., Klauer, T., Filipp, S., & Hellhammer, D. H. (1995). Sex-specific effects of social support on cortisol and subjective responses to acute psychological stress. *Psychosomatic Medicine, 57,* 23–31.

Kivimäki, M., Head, J., Ferrie, J. E., Brunner, E., Marmot, M. G., Vahtera, J., & Shipley, M. J. (2006). Why is evidence on job strain and coronary heart disease mixed? An illustration of measurement challenges in the Whitehall II study. *Psychosomatic Medicine, 68,* 398–401.

Klohn, L. S., & Rogers, R. W. (1991). Dimensions of the severity of a health threat: The persuasive effects of visibility, time of onset, and rate of onset on young women's intentions to prevent osteoporosis. *Health Psychology, 10,* 323–329.

Kreuter, M. W., & Strecher, V. J. (1995). Changing inaccurate perceptions of health risk: Results from a randomized trial. *Health Psychology, 14,* 56–63.

Laveist, T. A., & Nuru-Jeter, A. (2002). Is doctor-patient race concordance associated with greater satisfaction with care? *Journal of Health and Social Behavior, 43,* 296–306.

Lawton, R., Conner, M., & Parker, D. (2007). Beyond cognition: Predicting health risk behaviors from instrumental and affective beliefs. *Health Psychology, 26,* 259–267.

Lazarus, R. S., & Folkman, S. (1984). *Stress, appraisal, and coping.* New York: Springer.

Lepore, S. J., & Smyth, J. M. (2002). *The writing cure: How expressive writing promotes health and emotional well-being.* Washington, DC: American Psychological Association.

Leventhal, H. (1970). Findings and theory in the study of fear communications. In L. Berkowitz (Ed.), *Advances in experimental social psychology* (Vol. 5, pp. 120–186). New York: Academic Press.

Liberman, A., & Chaiken, S. (1992). Defensive processing of personally relevant health messages. *Personality and Social Psychology Bulletin, 18,* 669–679.

Light, K. C., Grewen, K. M., & Amico, J. A. (2005). More frequent partner hugs and higher oxytocin levels are linked to lower blood pressure and heart rate in premenopausal women. *Biological Psychology, 69,* 5–21.

Linville, P. W. (1985). Self-complexity and affective extremity: Don't put all your eggs in one cognitive basket. *Social Cognition, 3,* 94–120.

Ludwick-Rosenthal, R., & Neufeld, R. W. J. (1988). Stress management during noxious medical procedures: An evaluative review of outcome studies. *Psychological Bulletin, 104,* 326–342.

Mann, T., Sherman, D., & Updegraff, J. (2004). Dispositional motivations and message framing: A test of the congruency hypothesis in college students. *Health Psychology, 23,* 330–334.

Marsland, A. L., Cohen, S., Rabin, B. S., & Manuck, S. B. (2006). Trait positive affect and antibody response to hepatitis B vaccination. *Brain, Behavior, and Immunity, 20,* 261–269.

Martin, R., & Lemos, K. (2002). From heart attacks to melanoma: Do common sense models of somatization influence symptom interpretation for female victims? *Health Psychology, 21,* 25–32.

Matthews, K. A., Gump, B. B., & Owens, J. F. (2001). Chronic stress influences cardiovascular and neuroendocrine responses during acute stress and recovery, especially in men. *Health Psychology, 20,* 403–410.

McEwen, B. S., & Stellar, E. (1993). Stress and the individual: Mechanisms leading to disease. *Archives of Internal Medicine, 153,* 2093–2101.

McGuire, W. J. (1964). Inducing resistance to persuasion: Some contemporary approaches. In L. Berkowitz (Ed.), *Advances in experimental social psychology* (Vol. 1, pp. 192–231). New York: Academic Press.

Millar, M. G., & Millar, K. (1995). Negative affective consequences of thinking about disease detection behaviors. *Health Psychology, 14*, 141–146.

Millar, M. G., & Millar, K. (1996). The effects of anxiety on response times to disease detection and health promotion behaviors. *Journal of Behavioral Medicine, 19*, 401–414.

Morgenstern, J., Irwin, T. W., Wainberg, M. L., Parsons, J. T., Muench, F., Bux, D. A., Jr., et al. (2007). A randomized controlled trial of goal choice interventions for alcohol use disorders among men who have sex with men. *Journal of Consulting and Clinical Psychology, 75*, 72–84.

Muhonen, T., & Torkelson, E. (2003). The demand-control-support model and health among women and men in similar occupations. *Journal of Behavioral Medicine, 26*, 601–613.

Murphy, D. A., Stein, J. A., Schlenger, W., Maibach, E., & National Institute of Mental Health Multisite HIV Prevention Trial Group. (2001). Conceptualizing the multidimensional nature of self-efficacy: Assessment of situational context and level of behavioral challenge to maintain safer sex. *Health Psychology, 20*, 281–290.

Naliboff, B. D., Mayer, M., Fass, R., Fitzgerald, L. Z., Chang, L., Bolus, R., & Mayer, E. A. (2004). The effect of life stress on symptoms of heartburn. *Psychosomatic Medicine, 66*, 426–434

Nemeroff, C. B., Bremner, J. D., Foa, E. B., Mayberg, H. S., North, C. S., & Stein, M. B. (2006). Posttraumatic stress disorder: A state-of-the-science review. *Journal of Psychiatric Research, 40*, 1–21.

Ogden, J. (2003). Some problems with social cognition models: A pragmatic and conceptual analysis. *Health Psychology, 22*, 424–428.

Pennebaker, J. W. (1997). *Opening up: The healing power of expressing emotions* (Revised edition). New York: Guilford Press.

Peters, E., Slovic, P., Hibbard, J. H., & Tusler, M. (2006). Why worry? Worry, risk perceptions, and willingness to act to reduce medical errors. *Health Psychology, 25*, 144–152.

Pike, J., Smith, T., Hauger, R., Nicassio, P., Patterson, T., McClintock, J., et al. (1997). Chronic life stress alters sympathetic, neuroendocrine, and immune responsivity to an acute psychological stressor in humans. *Psychosomatic Medicine, 59*, 447–457.

Polk, D. E., Cohen, S., Doyle, W. J., Skoner, D. P., & Kirschbaum, C. (2005). State and trait affect as predictors of salivary cortisol in healthy adults. *Psychoneuroendocrinology, 30*, 261–272.

Pressman, S. D., & Cohen, S. (2005). Does positive affect influence health? *Psychological Bulletin, 131*, 925–971.

Prochaska, J. O., & DiClemente, C. C. (1984). *The transtheoretical approach: Crossing traditional boundaries of therapy*. Chicago: Dow Jones/Irwin.

Raven, B. H. (1992). A power/interaction model of interpersonal influence: French and Raven thirty years later. *Journal of Social Behavior and Personality, 7,* 217–244.

Repetti, R. L., Taylor, S. E., & Saxbe, D. (2007). The influence of early socialization experiences on the development of biological systems. In J. Grusec & P. Hastings (Eds.), *Handbook of socialization* (pp. 124–152). New York, NY: Guilford Press.

Ronis, D. L. (1992). Conditional health threats: Health beliefs, decisions, and behaviors among adults. *Health Psychology, 11,* 127–134.

Rook, K. S. (1984). The negative side of social interaction: Impact on psychological well-being. *Journal of Personality and Social Psychology, 46,* 1097–1108.

Rosenstock, I. M. (1966). Why people use health services. *Milbank Memorial Fund Quarterly, 44,* 94ff.

Rosenstock, I. M. (1974). Historical origins of the health belief model. *Health Education Monographs, 2,* 328–335.

Rothman, A. J., & Salovey, P. (1997). Shaping perceptions to motivate healthy behavior: The role of message framing. *Psychological Bulletin, 121,* 3–19.

Rutledge, T., Matthews, K., Lui, L.-Y., Stone, K. L., & Cauley, J. A. (2003). Social networks and marital status predict mortality in older women: Prospective evidence from the Study of Osteoporotic Fractures (SOF). *Psychosomatic Medicine, 65,* 688–694.

Sausen, K. P., Lovallo, W. R., Pincomb, G. A., & Wilson, M. F. (1992). Cardiovascular responses to occupational stress in male medical students: A paradigm for ambulatory monitoring studies. *Health Psychology, 11,* 55–60.

Scheier, M. F., Carver, C. S., & Bridges, M. W. (1994). Distinguishing optimism from neuroticism (and trait anxiety, self-mastery, and self-esteem): A reevaluation of the Life Orientation Test. *Journal of Personality and Social Psychology, 67,* 1063–1078.

Scheier, M. F., Matthews, K. A., Owens, J., Magovern, G. J., Sr., Lefebvre, R. C., Abbott, R. A., & Carver, C. S. (1989). Dispositional optimism and recovery from coronary artery bypass surgery: The beneficial effects on physical and psychological well-being. *Journal of Personality and Social Psychology, 57,* 1024–1040.

Schroeder, D. H., & Costa, P. T., Jr. (1984). Influence of life event stress on physical illness: Substantive effects or methodological flaws? *Journal of Personality and Social Psychology, 46,* 853–863.

Schwarzer, R., & Renner, B. (2000). Social-cognitive predictors of health behavior: Action self-efficacy and coping self-efficacy. *Health Psychology, 19,* 487–495.

Seeman, T. E., McEwen, B. S., Rowe, J. W., & Singer, B. H. (2001). Allostatic load as a marker of cumulative biological risk: MacArthur studies of successful aging. *Proceedings of the National Academy of Sciences, 98,* 4770–4775.

Segerstrom, S. C. (2007). Optimism and resources: Effects on each other and on health over 10 years. *Journal of Research in Personality, 41,* 772–786.

Segerstrom, S. C., Castañeda, J. O., & Spencer, T. E. (2003). Optimism effects on cellular immunity: Testing the affective and persistence models. *Personality and Individual Differences, 35,* 1615–1624.

Self, C. A., & Rogers, R. W. (1990). Coping with threats to health: Effects of persuasive appeals on depressed, normal, and antisocial personalities. *Journal of Behavioral Medicine, 13,* 343–358.

Selye, H. (1956). *The stress of life.* New York: McGraw-Hill.

Skinner, E. A., Edge, K., Altman, J., & Sherwood, H. (2003). Searching for the structure of coping: A review and critique of category systems for classifying ways of coping. *Psychological Bulletin, 129,* 216–269.

Steele, C. M. (1988). The psychology of self-affirmation: Sustaining the integrity of the self. In L. Berkowitz (Ed.), *Advances in experimental social psychology: Vol. 21. Social psychological studies of the self: Perspectives and programs* (pp. 261–302). San Diego, CA: Academic Press.

Strecher, V. J., DeVellis, B. M., Becker, M. H., & Rosenstock, I. M. (1986). The role of self-efficacy in achieving health behavior change. *Health Education Quarterly, 13,* 73–92.

Surtees, P. G., Wainwright, N. W. J., Luben, R., Khaw, K., & Day, N. E. (2006). Mastery, sense of coherence, and mortality: Evidence of independent associations from the EPIC-Norfolk prospective cohort study. *Health Psychology, 25,* 102–110.

Sutton, S. R., & Eiser, J. R. (1984). The effect of fear-arousing communications on cigarette smoking: An expectancy-value approach. *Journal of Behavioral Medicine, 7,* 13–34.

Sutton, S., McVey, D., & Glanz, A. (1999). A comparative test of the theory of reasoned action and the theory of planned behavior in the prediction of condom use intentions in a national sample of English young people. *Health Psychology, 18,* 72–81.

Swindle, R. E., Jr., & Moos, R. H. (1992). Life domains in stressors, coping, and adjustment. In W. B. Walsh, R. Price, & K. B. Crak (Eds.), *Person environment psychology: Models and perspectives* (pp. 1–33). New York: Erlbaum.

Taylor, S. E. (2002). *The tending instinct: How nurturing is essential to who we are and how we live.* New York: Holt.

Taylor, S. E. (2009a). *Health psychology* (7th ed.). New York: McGraw-Hill.

Taylor, S. E. (2009b). Social support: A review. In H. S. Friedman (Ed.), *Oxford handbook of health psychology.* New York: Oxford University Press.

Taylor, S. E., Burklund, L. J., Eisenberger, N. I., Lehman, B. J., Hilmert, C. J., & Lieberman, M. D. (2008). Neural bases of moderation of cortisol stress responses by psychosocial resources. *Journal of Personality and Social Psychology, 95,* 197–211.

Taylor, S. E., Gonzaga, G., Klein, L. C., Hu, P., Greendale, G. A., & Seeman S. E. (2006). Relation of oxytocin to psychological stress responses and hypothalamic-pituitary-adrenocortical axis activity in older women. *Psychosomatic Medicine, 68,* 238–245.

Taylor, S. E., Klein, L. C., Lewis, B. P., Gruenewald, T. L., Gurung, R. A. R., & Updegraff, J. A.(2000). Biobehavioral responses to stress in females: Tend-and-befriend, not fight-or-flight. *Psychological Review, 107,* 411–429.

Taylor, S. E., Lerner, J. S., Sherman, D. K., Sage, R. M., & McDowell, N. K. (2003a). Are self-enhancing cognitions associated with healthy or unhealthy biological profiles? *Journal of Personality and Social Psychology, 85,* 605–615.

Taylor, S. E., Lerner, J. S., Sherman, D. K., Sage, R. M., & McDowell, N. K. (2003b). Portrait of the self-enhancer: Well-adjusted and well-liked or maladjusted and friendless? *Journal of Personality and Social Psychology, 84,* 165–176.

Taylor, S. E., & Stanton, A. (2007). Coping resources, coping processes, and mental health. *Annual Review of Clinical Psychology, 3,* 129–153.

Taylor, S. E., & Thompson, S. C. (1982). Stalking the elusive "vividness" effect. *Psychological Review, 89,* 155–181.

Taylor, S. E., Welch, W. T., Kim, H. S., & Sherman, D. K. (2007). Cultural differences in the impact of social support on psychological and biological stress responses. *Psychological Science, 18,* 831–837.

Thompson, S. C. (1981). Will it hurt less if I can control it? A complex answer to a simple question. *Psychological Bulletin, 90,* 89–101.

Thornton, B., Gibbons, F. X., & Gerrard, M. (2002). Risk perception and prototype perception: Independent processes predicting risk behaviors. *Personality and Social Psychology Bulletin, 28,* 986–999.

Tomaka, J., Blascovich, J., Kelsey, R. M., & Leitten, C. L. (1993). Subjective, physiological, and behavioral effects of threat and challenge appraisal. *Journal of Personality and Social Psychology, 6,* 248–260.

Turner, R. J., & Avison, W. R. (1992). Innovations in the measurement of life stress: Crisis theory and the significance of event resolution. *Journal of Health and Social Behavior, 33,* 36–50.

Uzark, K. C., Becker, M. H., Dielman, T. E., & Rocchini, A. P. (1987). Psychosocial predictors of compliance with a weight control intervention for obese children and adolescents. *Journal of Compliance in Health Care, 2,* 167–178.

van Ryn, M., & Fu, S. S. (2003). Paved with good intensions: Do public health and human service providers contribute to racial/ethnic disparities in health? *American Journal of Public Health, 93,* 248–255.

Verbrugge, L. M. (1983). Multiple roles and physical health of women and men. *Journal of Health and Social Behavior, 24,* 16–30.

Waldron, I., Weiss, C. C., & Hughes, M. E. (1998). Interacting effects of multiple roles on women's health. *Journal of Health and Social Behavior, 39,* 216–236.

Watson, D., & Clark, L. A. (1984). Negative affectivity: The disposition to experience aversive emotional states. *Psychological Bulletin, 96,* 465–490.

Weidner, G., Boughal, T., Connor, S. L., Pieper, C., & Mendell, N. R. (1997). Relationship of job strain to standard coronary risk factors and psychological characteristics in women and men of the family heart study. *Health Psychology, 16,* 239–247.

Weinstein, N. D., & Klein, W. M. (1995). Resistance of personal risk perceptions to debiasing interventions. *Health Psychology, 14,* 132–140.

Weinstein, N. D., Kwitel, A., McCaul, K. D., Magnan, R. E., Gerrard, M., & Gibbons, F. X. (2007). Risk perceptions: Assessment and relationship to influenza vaccination. *Health Psychology, 26,* 146–151.

Whisman, M. A., & Kwon, P. (1993). Life stress and dysphoria: The role of self-esteem and hopelessness. *Journal of Personality and Social Psychology, 65,* 1054–1060.

Wills, T. A. (1991). Social support and interpersonal relationships. In M. S. Clark (Ed.), *Prosocial behavior* (pp. 265–89). Newbury Park, CA: Sage.

World Health Organization. (1948). *Constitution of the World Health Organization.* Geneva, Switzerland: World Health Organization Basic Documents.

Wulfert, E., & Wan, C. K. (1993). Condom use: A self-efficacy model. *Health Psychology, 12,* 346–353.

Zimbardo, P., & Ebbesen, E. B. (1969). *Influencing attitudes and changing behavior.* Reading, MA: Addison-Wesley.

Chapter 20

Judgment and Decision Making

Kathleen D. Vohs and Mary Frances Luce

People's lives are saturated by judgments and decisions. You make a judgment when you see an object and think that it is good or bad or likely to happen. You make a decision when you take a course of action while not taking other actions that were possible. People make hundreds, perhaps thousands of decisions each day. Yet people are unaware of the number of choices they make each day: they think that they only make 15 food-related decisions each day. But a recent count found that people make 200 decisions each day about food alone (e.g., "At the table or on the couch?" "Eat it all or save half?") (Wansink & Sobal, 2007).

Decision making is important to study not only because it is frequent; making good decisions is essential to living the good life. In fact, good decision making may save your life. In the United States, approximately 60,000 people die each year from an incorrect diagnosis by a hospital employee (Newman-Toker & Pronovost, 2009). This ranks medical decision errors as the sixth most common cause of death in the United States—more likely to cause death than Alzheimer's disease, breast cancer, suicide, or homicide. According to autopsy reports, 5% of deaths were directly due to a misdiagnosis that, if corrected and treated, would not have led to death. Death from an incorrect diagnosis is more common than death from medication errors, yet the possibility of medication error is discussed more often. These statistics are particularly shocking in light of the fact that these mistakes are made by trained experts in medical decision making. Yet they too make decision errors that cost lives. The science of decision making is what the field of *judgment and decision making* studies.

Judgments and Decisions: How Are They Defined, Explained, and Evaluated?

Definitions

What Is a Judgment? Judgment is a broad term. Making a judgment involves perceiving objects or events and coming to a conclusion about whether they are good or bad (*valence judgments*) or likely to occur (*likelihood judgments*). A *decision* is a commitment (to oneself or publically) to an option or course of action selected from among a set of options. Decisions have outcomes, which are the circumstances or states that follow from the decision.

Decision outcomes are judged along two dimensions. Decision theorists often talk about a decision's *utility*, which is the joy, pleasure, or satisfaction that is derived from the outcome of the decision. (The study of decision making has roots in economics, which is a field dominated by mathematical models. When economists take their numbers and turn them into prose it does not typically go well; consequently there are many heavy, clunky terms in the field of judgment and decision making.) Decision outcomes that would bring about the most utility (read: satisfaction) are called *normative*, a term meaning best or right. One dominant viewpoint, shared by many economists, states that people are utility maximizers and that the normative option under any circumstance is the one that people ought to be taking. In plainer terms, people should be rational and choose what will make them most satisfied in the future. Another viewpoint, shared by many psychologists, is that people are not rational and often do not appreciate what will make them satisfied in the future. The reality is that human behavior is somewhere in between rational and irrational. In the words of Daniel Kahnemann (2003), Nobel laureate in economics, people are incompletely rational. This brings us to the question of how decision scientists explain how people make decisions.

Two Explanations of How People Make Decisions: One from Economics and One from Psychology

The predominant theory of decision making derived from economics is *subjective expected utility theory* (von Neumann & Morgenstern, 1944). Expected utility theory states that people make a decision by determining the likelihood that each option's outcome will occur and the value of the outcome in question. Then they multiply the likelihood and value for each option and compare these across options. Whichever option has the highest score (i.e , the best combination of being likely to occur and highly desirable) is the option that people should choose because it will bring them the most utility. Expected utility models make assumptions about people's preferences, which means the value they place on each decision outcomes. Expected utility theory assumes, for instance, that people value money and so the option that is expected to yield the most money is assumed to be the normative (correct) choice.

We can see expected utility theory in action when people play game shows, such as Who Wants to be a Millionaire? Take the situation in which a player answers enough questions correctly to achieve the $32,000 level. Reaching this level means that he or she is guaranteed to leave with at least $32,000—this amount cannot be taken away from them. Then the player faces a choice: end the game or continue. The player who ends the game will walk away with $32,000. Hence the option of "ending the game now" has a value of $32,000 associated with it. A player who chooses to continue, however, has a 25% chance of winning because there are four multiple choice answers from which to choose. The question's worth is $64,000. But there is a 75% chance that the player will lose, which is associated with $32,000 because of the guarantee associated with having reached this level. Faced with this choice, players always (there are no recorded accounts of this not happening, as far as we know) choose to answer the next question, even if it means arbitrarily guessing at one of the multiple choice options. This is an example of rational behavior. Can you see why?

The expected value of answering the question is $40,000 [($64,000 × 0.25) + ($32,000 × 0.75)], which is more than the $32,000 expected value ($32,000 × 1.0) from ending the game. Hence the additional likelihood that the player will answer correctly and win more money tips the scales toward the option of attempting the next question because it is associated with more money to be won and hence higher utility.

An alternate decision theory, which came out of psychology, is *prospect theory*. The title word refers to the options (prospects) that decision makers face. Prospect theory is probably the most important theory in the field of judgment and decision making.

Prospect theory created two major advances in the field of judgment and decision making (JDM). One, it used psychology to help explain when and why humans make irrational choices. Until that point, economists treated people's irrational decisions as noisy and bothersome disturbances in their elegant mathematical equations and were unconvinced that these deviations were anything meaningful. Prospect theory's use of psychology revealed that those irrational decisions are meaningful because they reveal key aspects about how the mind works. Two, prospect theory also used mathematics, which made it a vehicle to speak to economists and therefore bring to their attention the importance of psychological processes.

Prospect theory uses likelihood judgments and outcome values, as does standard expected utility theory. But prospect theory states that the values associated with outcomes are not the same for everyone or across all situations, but rather they reflect people's current standing. That is, people make judgments about the values of outcomes from a *reference point*, which is akin to a personal point of view. To predict how people will value a certain outcome, we first have to know where they stand when evaluating it. This tenet flies in the face of expected utility theory because it states that people do not perceive outcomes as having absolute values but rather think of them as worse or better (often referred to as losses or gains, respectively) from their current perspective. This aspect of prospect theory can be summarized as "everything is relative."

Reference point effects can be illustrated with the notion that people are *loss averse*. The psychological impact of losses is far greater than that of gains, even if the value of the losses and gains is exactly the same. There has been so much work on loss aversion that we can say with some certainty that people are impacted twice as much by losses as they are by gains. In the realm of money, this means that people will experience an equivalent degree of emotional intensity from losing $500 in the stock market as they will from gaining $1000 the same way. Loss aversion is part of a more general process called *bad is stronger than good* (Baumeister, Bratslavsky, Finkenauer, & Vohs, 2001). In health, learning, interpersonal interactions, sexuality, and major life decisions, those events that yield negative outcomes have a significantly greater psychological impact than equivalent events that yield positive outcomes. In the realm of interpersonal relations, for instance, one marriage scientist found that couples must say five positive comments to neutralize one negative comment they make to their partners (Gottman, 1994).

A classic finding named the endowment effect also illustrates loss aversion. Typically in these studies (e.g., Kahneman, Knetsch, & Thaler, 1990), participants come to the laboratory individually and half are given a small gift, such as a coffee mug with the university's logo on it. Other participants see the same product but are not told that it is theirs. Those who own the mug are now asked how much they would charge to sell it; those who do not own the mug are asked how much they would offer to buy it. Because random assignment to condition means that both groups overall ought to value the mug equally, it is remarkable (and in contrast to expected utility theory) that owners ask for considerably more money to sell the mug than buyers are willing to offer. We may think that it may be because buyers and owners have different motives about saving money and earning money. Yet this explanation does not explain the finding that when the same people switch roles in a 20 minute span from being owners to buyers or vice versa, they show the same pattern: people want more money to sell the mug than they themselves would offer to buy it. Endowment effect findings are interpreted in different ways with one predominant explanation being loss aversion. People feel a stronger psychological impact in losing the mug when they already own it than they do in gaining the mug when they do not own it, which demonstrates the broader theme of reference points.

What Influences Decisions?

It is generally agreed that decisions are made by considering how likely each option is to occur combined with how valuable the outcome of that option seems. Expected utility theory states that decision makers rationally judge the likelihood of an event in terms of its *base rate* (the objective tendency for any event to occur in a given circumstance) and possess stable preferences for outcomes (meaning that they value the outcome the same across time and circumstance).

In contrast, prospect theory conceptualizes decisions as resulting from decision weights and constructed preferences. The concept of decision weights states that people do not judge the likelihood or importance (these two terms encompass the notion of weight) of all outcomes similarly. For instance, some people value the style of a car they are thinking of purchasing more than its safety. But when they start to think about having children, then they might come to value safety more than style. On the likelihood front, for instance, it is well-known that people overestimate the likelihood of events that are in reality highly improbable (such as flash flooding, terrorist attacks, and winning the jackpot). This tells us that people do not think about events in terms of their objective base rates but rather overestimate the likelihood of some events happening. *Constructed preferences* means that values that people associate with different outcomes are not stable but rather can be altered by the situation. This idea led the field of judgment and decision making to study situational features that change people's preferences and, hence, their choices.

It was a shock for decision scientists 50 year ago to think that people's preferences for outcomes could change as a result of small differences in the situation—but they do. One concept that follows from constructed preferences and reference points is the idea of *sunk costs*. Standard economic theory states that no matter how much time, effort, money, energy, or emotion you have put into a cause, if it becomes clear that the outcome is no longer desirable we should no longer attempt to achieve it. People actually do otherwise. For instance, people sit through a movie they detest because they already spent money to see it. People stay in relationships that make them very unhappy because they have been in the relationship for a long period of time.

One analysis of why women stay with abusive partners concluded that sunk costs play a significant role (Rusbult & Martz, 1995). One hundred battered women were interviewed about their satisfaction and commitment to their abusive partner. These women had come to a women's shelter with fairly serious injuries (75% of them needed medical treatment on arrival). Yet some of these women would return to their abusive partners. Could the researchers predict who? The researchers asked about the resources the women had put into their relationship, namely whether the couple had children together, were married, or had been together for a long time. As predicted, having the resources that had been put into the relationship was a key factor in predicting which women would return. Women who had devoted time to raising children with the man, were married, or had been partnered with him for a longer period of time were likelier to return to the abusive man than were women who had sunk fewer resources into the relationship.

Sunk costs alter people's preferences for an outcome, making it more attractive than it would be if the decision maker had not already put resources into achieving it. Sunk cost effects are considered irrational because the money or time that was spent is gone and cannot be retrieved. Therefore, the decision maker should ignore those spent resources and decide whether to continue with the experience from that point forth as if the experience was just starting and no money, time, or effort had already been put into it.

Preferences can change because of the way that the options are described. *Framing* is an important construct in the field of judgment and decision making because it sways decision makers' preferences without changing the objective information given to the decision maker. For instance, ground beef described as 75% lean is preferred to ground beef described as 25% fat, even though those descriptions convey the same information about the meat (Levin & Gaeth, 1988).

The classic example of framing effects is Kahneman and Tversky's (1979) Asian disease problem. Participants are asked to imagine that they are policymakers deciding how to respond to a disease that threatens the health of 600 people. Some participants are told to choose between two options: one that will save 200 people for certain and the other that offers a one-third probability that all 600 people will be saved and a two-thirds probability that nobody will be saved. Other participants face two options with the same information that are framed quite differently: one that will guarantee that 400 people die versus another that offers a one-third probability that nobody will die and a two-thirds probability that all 600 people will die. If you work out the math, all of the options predict that the same number of lives are expected to be saved and lost. In principle, then, decision makers should choose the options at equal rates.

That is not what happens. The two options with certainty sway people's decisions because they bring to mind a different reference point. That is, the condition in which 200 lives are definitely going to be saved (versus a one-third chance that everyone will be saved and a two-thirds chance that everyone will die) gets people to think about an outcome that is good and certain to occur. This is called a gain frame, and people react to gain frames in general by being risk averse, meaning that they go for the certain option of 200 lives saved. However, the opposite occurs when an option promises that 400 people will definitely die (versus a one-third probability that nobody will die and a two-thirds probability that 600 people will die). This gets people to think about a bad outcome that is certain to occur. This is a loss frame, and people tend to be risk seeking in loss frames. Hence they choose the option that avoids 400 certain deaths. As this example demonstrates—and politicians have known for centuries—decisions are heavily influenced by descriptions of the options.

The *attraction effect* and *compromise effect* are also notable because they lead decision makers to choose irrationally. The attraction effect (Huber, Payne, & Puto, 1982) describes choices when people are faced with two options that are closely matched in how preferable they are. Imagine offering a group of people either donuts or chocolate ice cream. The group is indifferent overall, which means that half the people in the group will chose donuts and the other half will choose chocolate ice cream. Now imagine that a third option is introduced and in this case it is fish-flavored ice cream. The introduction of this option, which is less preferred than the other two options (even imagine that no one ever chooses this option—and that is not difficult to imagine), can shift people's choices between donuts and chocolate ice cream. The attraction effect occurs when an unwanted option—which is the fish-flavored ice cream—makes the option to which it compares most closely seem more attractive, and leads people to choose the comparably better option. In this case, it is chocolate ice cream. The key to why this is such an interesting effect is that the third option is undesirable and therefore irrelevant. Because no one would ever choose fish-flavored ice cream, all the people should still be undecided about whether they want chocolate ice cream or donuts. But all of a sudden, because of the fish-flavored ice cream (an irrelevant option), the chocolate ice cream seems more appealing.

The *compromise effect* (Simonson, 1989) arises when people are faced with options that trade off one feature for another, the most common being quality and price. In these cases, people tend to choose the option in the middle. Here is an example: a consumer choosing among hard disks with 100 GB, 150 GB, and 200 GB of space that are priced at $80, $120, and $160 would be likely to choose the 150 GB option because it gives up only some speed but also does not cost as much money. You can see the compromise effect in action when new options are added at the extremes (for instance, adding a 250 GB option priced at $200 and removing the 100 GB option) because people again tend to choose the middle option, which in this case is the 200 GB option.

You can easily see how sellers can use the compromise effect to move decision makers toward the particular products they want them to buy. In fact, restaurateurs take advantage of this effect. Where do they tend to put the wines that will make the most profit? Not at the extremes in terms of menu price but more toward the middle. Restaurateurs are known to price the wines such that the wine with the biggest markup is the second cheapest. They realize that diners want to save money but do not want to appear cheap by ordering the most inexpensive wine—diners will tend to order the second cheapest wine, and hence that is where there is a great deal of money to be made.

This next effect can change people's behavior without requiring that they actually do anything special. It involves *defaults*, which are preexisting or already-chosen options. The preexisting option may be someone else's choice (e.g., auto manufacturers' base model) or the most recent choice that the decision maker made (e.g., the station to which you left the radio turned in the car). Policymakers have determined that the default effect can be a huge help in terms of getting people to make choices that benefit society. Take, for instance, the dilemma of how to get people to donate their organs after death. One study found that changing the laws in a country such that organ donation at death was the default dramatically increased the number of organs donated, even though citizens still retained the option not to donate their organs if they so choose (Johnson & Goldstein, 2003). Other examples are more mundane but still common. When people first started using email and getting Internet accounts for services that required data protection, such as banking, the word *password* was often used as the default password. Guess what? Consumers failed to change the default password (*password*) and you can bet that thieves took advantage of it. Banks and other firms now assign unique and difficult-to-decipher passwords on the chance that the password first given to consumers remains the password for the life of that account. Establishing the basic or default option means establishing the option with which many people are likely to end up.

Decisions Evaluated: What Makes a Decision Good?

Judgment and decision-making scholars think it is important to evaluate the quality of decisions. (If you are following closely, you know that these are judgments about decisions.) Scholars separate the process by which the decision was made from its outcomes for the decision maker when judging what makes a decision good.

The Process by Which a Decision Is Made One measure of whether a decision is good is to ask whether it was a reasonably sound decision made in a reasonable amount of time. One early insight in decision science came from Herb Simon, who convinced the field of economics that people are not machines with limitless time or cognitive skills. Simon (1955) corrected the long-standing assumption in economics that people can and do devote considerable energy and time to decision making. Simon said that humans' information-processing capacities were limited even in the best of circumstances and therefore people take shortcuts when complex decisions or judgments must be made. This notion of *bounded rationality* explained when and why people make irrational decisions and it earned Simon the 1978 Nobel prize in economics. Bounded rationality leads to the judgment that (for the most part; there are exceptions) humans are good at making a "good enough" decision rather quickly, a strategy called *satisficing*, and that this probably offers a decent trade-off in terms of effort and outcomes.

Much research has demonstrated the advantages of using such decision shortcuts, called *heuristics* (e.g., Payne, Bettman, & Johnson 1993; Gigerenzer & Goldstein, 1996). Heuristics are often used when the information people are wading through is complex. The main advantage of using heuristics is that they save decision makers time. But they may be prone to decision errors. The research on heuristics is meant to show how heuristics work, but unfortunately researchers do this primarily to show how they lead people to incorrect judgments. Taking a broader view, though, it is clear that heuristics tend to result in good decisions most of the time.

If decision makers wanted to avoid using heuristics to ensure that they achieve good decision outcomes, they would instead perform thorough searches of information to come up with base rate information and objective criteria for evaluating each option's outcomes. People sometimes do this, for instance, with high-stakes choices such as deciding on a car or whether to have surgery. But as you may guess, most judgments (including many high-stakes decisions) are not made after intense information processing. Hence it is important to know the heuristics that people commonly use.

One heuristic is the tendency to diversify by not putting "all your eggs in one basket" as the colloquial saying goes. Imagine that researchers offered participants two funds into which they could invest their money (Benartzi & Thaler, 2001). One fund is made up of stocks, which are risky, and the other fund is made up of bonds, which are safe. People in this experiment generally split their money equally between the two funds, putting 50% in stocks and 50% in bonds. This behavior may suggest that these people had a goal in mind, that of having a set of funds that are, in total, moderate in risk. The researchers tested whether this was the case by offering a different group of people another two funds from which to choose: one made up of stocks and one made up of a mix of stocks and bonds (which is called a balanced fund). If the behavior of the people in the other condition reflected a moderate-risk goal, then the researchers should have seen that most of the people in this new condition put their money in the balanced fund. Instead, people again split the money 50/50 between the two funds, seemingly without having a specific investing goal. Rather, people were dividing their money equally across the options.

The diversification urge is not something that happens only when investing money. One study found that kids take Halloween treats this way (Read & Loewenstein, 1995). Trick-or-treaters arrived at a house at which the owners said that the kids could each take two candy bars, and then offered them two different types. Every trick-or-treater took one of each kind. Other ways of presenting the candy bars showed that this occurred only because the two different brands of candy bars were offered at the same time and the children were allowed to take two—"I can have two candy bars and there are two types of candy bars therefore I'll take one of each type," goes the mental shortcut. Think of shopping for groceries for the week. People tend to buy, for instance, different flavors of yogurts for breakfast, perhaps as many flavors are there are days of the work week. But there can be costs to using this rule. In the words of Eli Finkel, one of the editors of this book, at the end of the week you can find yourself stuck with that peach yogurt that you never really liked.

The Outcomes That Follow from the Decision Another way to determine what makes a decision good is whether the decision yields satisfactory outcomes. The idea is that people should make decisions about what will make them happiest. Which begs another question: Do people know what will bring them the most happiness or the least pain in the future? Unfortunately, they do not.

People are not very good at predicting what options will make them happy or the feelings they will have if certain experiences arise. *Affective forecasting* research concerns people's (in)ability to judge how they will feel in the future. People do seem to be good at predicting the valence of their feelings, that is whether they will have positive or negative experiences. They correctly predict that they will be anxious when they take their drivers' license test and happy when they get married. Where people go wrong is in predicting how intensely or long they will feel that way (Wilson & Gilbert, 2003). Although it may be nice in some circumstances to predict precisely how we will feel, there may be advantages to mispredicting our feelings. It seems that overestimating how intensely or how long we will feel a certain way has the beneficial effect of motivating people to perform behaviors that they think will bring desirable emotional states—even if they are wrong about the quality of those feelings when they reach that point (Baumeister, Vohs, DeWall, & Zhang, 2007). People who think that they will feel miserable for days if they fail an examination (or even score a B) are people who are motivated to work extra hard to avoid that outcome. Yet affective forecasting research has shown that even if those people did fail (or get a disappointing B), they would probably feel moderately sad for only a little while and not completely devastated for their rest of their lives as they might predict.

A topic related to how people make decisions about their future selves is self-control. Choices with a self-control dimension have one option typically easier in the present pitted against another option that is more difficult but better for us in the future. Self-control choices ask people to decide whether they want a better life later for some sacrifice now versus some fun in the moment. Eating healthy, not smoking (or quitting smoking), exercising, and saving money are all examples of self-control choices. It is more enjoyable to eat French fries, smoke, lie on the couch, and gamble than it is not to do these things. Yet our life satisfaction will probably be higher if people avoided the easy, indulgent option and instead opted for the option that is more challenging now but more rewarding in the future (Vohs & Baumeister, 2004).

How Do Cognitive Processes Lead to Decision Errors?

An important theme in judgment and decision making is how different types of cognitive processing might lead to different types of errors. Remember that judgment and decision-making research often compares people's decisions with what would have been the logical choice or with the option that would make people better off in the long run (i.e., normative decisions). In this section, we review some of the classic phenomena in judgment and decision making, organized into three themes to describe how cognitive processes cause decision errors.

Theme 1: Decisions Errors Follow from Not Enough Effortful Thought

The first theme is arguably the most pervasive theme in the field of judgment and decision making, namely that decision makers are unable or unwilling to put enough thought into their decisions to reach the best answers. Decision makers use a variety of cognitive strategies that range from simplistic (sometimes called intuitive) to effortful (sometimes called analytical). An influential framework is Kahneman's (Kahneman & Frederick, 2002) System 1/System 2 distinction (Table 20.1). Using System 1 means arriving at a judgment or decision relatively quickly, with little effort expended, while experiencing twinges of feelings, and using the gist of the situation. Using System 2 means arriving at a judgment or decision more slowly, after much conscious effort, perhaps while having a fully experienced emotion, and by making a detailed analysis. This section details how many of the errors in decision making come from an over-reliance on System 1 when decision makers should have been relying more on System 2.

One of the earliest demonstrations of flaws in the ability of decision makers relates to arriving at likelihood judgments. The *availability bias* occurs when decision makers judge something to be highly likely just because it is associated with information that was easy to remember. For instance, people believe that words with *r* as the first letter are more common in English than are words with *r* as the third letter (Tversky & Kahneman, 1973). Words with *r* in the third position are actually more probable. Nonetheless, it is much easier to search our

TABLE 20.1 **System 1 versus System 2: What They Are and What They Do**

System 1	*System 2*
Defining Features	
Automatic	Time-intensive
Effortless	Effortful
Parallel	Serial
Reasons by association	Reasons by application of logic and rules
Intuitive	Analytical
Experiential	Rational
Holistic	Piecemeal
Contributions to Decision Errors	
Perceptual errors: The psychological impact of losses is greater than that of gains.	Cognitive errors: Devoting much effort to deciding can hamper prediction of our own preferences.
People confuse how easy it is for information to come to mind for trying to find base rates.	At times it is better to devote less effort even if it means sacrificing decision accuracy.
People confuse the representativeness of an instance for logic.	
Feelings	
Preferences need no inferences: Feelings of good and bad arise very quickly.	Full blown emotions contain cognition and emotion and are distinguishable from one another.
Affect can automatically carry over to related decisions such as when fearful individuals make pessimistic judgments.	Negative emotions such as regret are explicitly anticipated and avoided.

memory for words marked by their first letter (the game Scattergories makes use of is) than by their third letter. The availability bias is a System 1 error, in that the feeling of how easy it was to think of that information gives decision makers the sense that the outcome is very common and they stop there and make a judgment without further cognitive work.

Another example involves asking people to estimate the number of murders per year either across a whole state or a particular city in that state. The city and state are Detroit and Michigan, and in this experiment (described in Kahneman & Frederick, 2002) some participants were asked to write down how many murders happen per year in Michigan, whereas others were asked to estimate the number of murders per year in the city of Detroit. Guess which group offered a higher number? Logically, the number of murders a year must be higher (or exactly the same) for the entire state of Michigan than for the city of Detroit because Detroit is a city in Michigan. Yet participants estimated that the median number of murders a year in Michigan was 100 compared to 200 in Detroit. (In case you are wondering about the base rates, in 2007 the actual number of murders in Michigan was 676 with 396 of those occurring in Detroit.) Participants' logically inconsistent judgments presumably arose because they drew on different information when they made their estimates. The stereotype of Detroit is of a rough, violent city with deeply poor areas, whereas the stereotype of Michigan is of a hearty Midwestern state with cold winters. Hence conjuring up different types of information about Michigan versus Detroit presumable made it seem that more murders would happen in Detroit than in Michigan. Opposing findings are found when people find it difficult to think of information. Winkielman et al. (1998) asked some participants to recall 12 events from their childhood and others to recall four childhood events. Ironically, the group that thought of 12 events later rated themselves as less capable of remembering their childhood than the participants asked to recall only four events, despite having recalled three times as many memories. Retrieving 12 events from childhood is rather difficult to do and participants let those feelings of difficulty color their self-assessments.

The *representativeness heuristic* is another shortcut that people use when making judgments about probability. It occurs when people judge an event to be probable because its appearance seems to fit the context. For instance, think about people who are asked to judge which sequence of five flips of a coin is likelier to occur: HTHHT or HHHHH (where H = heads; T = tails). The majority of people will say that the former is more likely to occur than the latter. But, statistically, both are equally probable because each flip of the coin offers a 50/50 chance of heads or tails. In decision makers' minds, though, a series of coin flips showing both heads and tails seem more representative of a random pattern than when the series shows only heads.

Another classic example of the representativeness heuristic involves information about a woman named Linda (Tversky & Kahneman, 1983). Participants read this description of Linda: "Linda is 31 years old, single, outspoken and very bright. She majored in philosophy. As a student, she was deeply concerned with issues of discrimination and social justice and also participated in antinuclear demonstrations." Participants were asked whether it is more likely that Linda was a bank teller or that Linda was a bank teller who is active in feminist causes. Participants overwhelmingly (85%) believed that Linda was likelier to be a bank teller who is active in feminist causes than only a bank teller. But, logically, an event cannot be more probable than the combination of that event and another event. Participants made a logical mistake because they were swayed by the description of Linda and were not attending to rules of logic. The idea that she was a bank teller and a feminist seemed to better represent the earlier description of Linda. If participants had not stopped their judgments after System 1 had kicked in but instead activated their System 2, they may have realized that two events cannot be more likely to occur together than one event alone.

One well-established mechanism giving rise to errors in decision making is *anchoring and adjustment*. Here, people do engage in System 2 but in insufficient amounts. A standard way to test anchoring and adjustment is to ask decision makers to first think about an arbitrary number (e.g., the last two digits of their social security number). Then they are presented with an object, for instance a bottle of wine (Ariely, Loewenstein, & Prelec, 2003). They think back to the arbitrary number and then state whether the wine is worth more or less than this number. Last, they are asked to state a specific dollar amount they are willing to pay for the object. Even though decision makers know that the number they first considered had nothing to do with the wine's worth, that initial, irrelevant number influences how much people are willing to pay. People with higher social security number endings are willing to pay more money for the wine than people with lower social security number endings. We say that decision makers do not devote enough effortful cognitive energy to this task because they "anchor" on the initial number but fail to "adjust" sufficiently. This means that they think that they have moved away from the starting point enough but they are still being swayed by it.

Anchoring and adjustment is at work in many phenomena. For instance, can you remember seeing grocery store signs near discounted items that say "Limit X"? The number that is listed is likely to become an anchor on which consumers seize when deciding how many of that item they want. The higher the number on that sign, the more items consumers are likely to buy (Wansink, Kent, & Hoch, 1998). So too are interpersonal relations affected by anchoring and adjustment. Failing to take the perspective of someone else has been said to result from people anchoring on their own viewpoint and failing to adjust enough for the perspective of others (Epley et al., 2004).

Summary

Heuristic decision strategies often sacrifice some decision accuracy but offer the benefit of reduced effort. However, putting much effort into thinking does not guarantee error-free decision outcomes, as our second theme illustrates.

Theme 2: Increased Cognitive Processing Can Cause Error

The previous section discusses research showing that decision error can result from not enough cognitive processing. This research suggests simple advice for decision makers: think more! Unfortunately for decision makers, but perhaps fortunately for judgment and decision-making scholars who need interesting questions to research, eliminating decision errors is not that easy.

This brings us to the second theme: thinking can itself cause errors. There are at least two explanations for why cognitive analysis can lead to decision error. First, some decision tasks may be inherently intuitive—meaning that the best decisions come from relying on our "gut feelings" (Hammond et al., 1987). Second, people may use cognitive processing to achieve goals that prevent them from making an accurate decision.

An influential stream of research revealed that generating reasons for why a person made his or her choice can reduce the quality of that choice. In these experiments, a decision was judged as good if it later brought the decision maker enjoyment or happiness. Wilson and Schooler (1991) told undergraduates that they were allowed to choose a poster to take home with them out of an array of posters. However, some students were first asked how they would go about choosing a poster—that is, to state the reasons for choosing a poster. Other students were simply allowed to choose. Researchers later went to the dorm rooms of the students to see whether the posters were hung on the students' walls. They saw that students who talked about how they would choose their poster were less likely to hang the poster on their walls. Wilson and colleagues argued that that this decision task relies more on feelings than cognitions and that the cognitive activity needed to express reasons for their choice made people's decisions worse.

In these types of decisions it seems that better decisions are made when the context in which people are placed when they make decisions is very similar to the context in which they will be experiencing those preferences

(Payne, Bettman, & Schkade, 1999). Coming up with reasons is not something that is typically present during later experience and therefore harms decision quality.

Analytical thought can impair decision quality when people are held accountable to others for their decisions. Simonson (1989) argued that having to justify why you made a certain choice creates "choice based on reasons," in which too much thought is placed on justifying their decisions and not enough thought is available to make the right choice. Using the attraction effect design (i.e., choosing among three options, one of which is irrelevant but closely related to one of the other two options), he told some people that they would have to tell others why they chose as they did. Other people saw the same attraction effect design and made a choice among the same three options but believed that they would not have to justify their choice. Those who were ready to justify their choice were more swayed by the irrelevant option than people who chose believing that they would not have to justify their choice. This suggests that justifying our choices can lead people to irrational decisions because they choose based on what is defensible rather than on what is logical.

Summary Although conscious thought is generally considered an important aspect of good decision making, it can go astray—and often in predictable ways. Reasons can disrupt decision making and accountability can introduce unhelpful goals.

Theme 3: Emotion versus Cognition

Although there are numerous ways to define and classify thought processes during decision making, one theme that has made inroads to judgment and decision making is whether those thoughts are emotional or cognitive. Therefore, the third theme we address is whether and how emotional decision making causes decision error.

Historically, judgment and decision-making approaches have depicted decision making as a cold, cognitive process. Yet it would be remiss to ignore the fact that many decisions are made with—if not because of—emotional input. The question of when and how emotion plays a role in decision making also implicates the intuitive versus analytical reasoning divide mentioned in Themes 1 and 2. A classic debate in the 1980s pitted two theories of emotion against each other: Robert Zajonc (1980) claimed that "preferences need no inferences" (which speaks to System 1 being active) whereas Richard Lazarus (1981) retorted with a "cognitivist's reply" (which speaks to System 2 being active). The debate can be resolved by agreeing that both routes coexist. Baumeister, Vohs, DeWall, and Zhang (2007) suggested the term *affect* for low-level, nonconscious, positive versus negative twinges and the term *emotion* for full-blown feeling states, and we use these labels in this chapter. We now discuss how each can produce decision error.

Intuitive, Affective Processes One influential model argued that decision makers' judgments about risky decisions are driven by the affect associated with the options. For instance, if positive affect arises when a decision maker thinks about skiing then this will likely increase judgments of its benefits but curtail an analysis of its riskiness. On the other hand, the negative affect connected to the idea of a nuclear power plant increases judgments of its riskiness (Slovic et al., 2007).

Sometimes getting people in an emotional mindset leads them to make erroneous decisions. One set of researchers asked some people to state how much money they wanted to donate to save one panda, whereas others were asked how much money they wanted to donate to save four. For some participants, the panda bears in question were portrayed by black dots (either one or four), whereas other participants saw adorable pictures of pandas (again, one or four). The participants who saw the pandas as black dots said that they would donate more money to save four than save one, which is a logical response. But the participants who saw the pandas as pictures pledged to donate the same amount to save one of them as they would donate to save four. The researchers, Hsee and Rottenstreich (2004), argued that portraying pandas as cute and lovable brought people into an affective mode that made them ignore quantity and treat all the pandas the same. When those same pandas were described in plain, cold, nonemotional terms, participants' decisions about how much money would be needed to save them became sensitive to quantity and they pledged more money to save more bears.

Other evidence supports the idea that being in an affective mindset changes decisions that are completely independent of the affect being felt. This is called a *misattribution* effect because people mistakenly carry over their current state (e.g., their feelings) to an unrelated judgment they are asked to make. The classic misattribution finding for emotions and decisions involved asking people to judge how happy they are with their lives. Schwarz and Clore (1983) demonstrated that people judge their lives to be happier when asked about their overall life happiness on sunny days than when they were asked the same question on rainy days. This difference presumably occurs because people use their feelings about the day's weather to make judgments about their life overall. Other research (Simonsohn, 2010) extended this weather effect to university admissions officers' judgments. On sunny days, admission officers give more weight to whether the applicant has social or extracurricular activities on his or her application whereas on overcast days they more heavily consider the applicant's academic record.

Carryover findings suggest that low-level affective states subtly alter decision makers' perceptions and goals. Work on the other route, conscious or analytical emotionality, has focused on emotion influencing decision making through how it changes decision makers' goals.

Analytical Processes Although psychological processes are often broken down into "emotional versus rational," anyone familiar with the lay concept of rumination can attest that more conscious cognitive activity does not necessarily mean less emotional experience. In fact, some emotions may be fueled by analytical processes.

Perhaps the emotion with the most sustained interest to judgment and decision-making scholars is regret. Strategies to avoiding regret are said to be analytical (not intuitive) because people engage in counterfactuals, which are mental simulations of what might happen in the future. Simonson (1992) found that asking people to think about whether they would regret a decision made them choose safer options. For instance, thinking about whether they may regret their choice led participants to prefer buying a product on sale now rather than waiting for a potentially better sale, which carries the associated risk of losing out on the discount altogether. Shoppers also chose a highly regarded brand of VCR over an unknown brand that was cheaper when reminded that they may regret their choice later. People can imagine that they will feel more regret if they made a risky decision as opposed to a safer one, so they avoid risky options so as to attenuate regret that they might feel about the decision in the future.

People put a lot of thought into the regret they feel about past behaviors too. Gilovich and Medvec (1995) asked people about what kinds of decisions they have regretted. They found that people regret mistakes that involved actions (e.g., saying the wrong thing) soon after they performed the action but regretted mistakes involving inaction (e.g., not earning a graduate degree) much later. This means that as you approach the end of life, you might regret the goals that you never pursued; but right now most of your regret revolves around acts such as getting drunk and behaving foolishly at a party last weekend.

People also need to manage the emotions that arise while making decisions and this can be a problem when the decision brings up negative emotions. Luce (1998) showed that people were more likely to choose the default option or be swayed by an irrelevant choice in the attraction effect when the decision situation itself elicited bad feelings. People seemed to be ruminating about the negative aspects of the decision situation, which led them to use features of the situation, such as whichever option was preselected, to make the choice easier.

Summary Both conscious emotion and low-level affect can cause decision errors. Low-level affect can substitute for cognitive analysis during decision making. Conscious emotions can give rise to emotion goals (e.g., avoid regret or diminish negative emotions). One final note is that emotion does not always lead to decision errors. Emotion can act as a signal of what is important to the decision maker and in that sense it can steer behaviors toward worthy goals (e.g., Baumeister et al., 2007).

Judgment and Decision Making Today: Improving Decision Quality

One major thrust emerging from the field of judgment and decision making today is to not only identify decision errors but to find corrections for them. The study of judgment and decision making has been interdisciplinary from the start, including policy-oriented practitioners as well as basic social scientists. The policy-oriented arm of judgment and decision making is what prompts scholars to find processes that will help decision makers avoid decisions errors. In judgment and decision making today, basic science and policy intersect better than ever before, applying judgment and decision-making principles to explain and aid decision problems outside the laboratory.

The field of judgment and decision making began by focusing on the debate between economists' views of "rational man" and psychologists' views of "imperfectly rational man." For many decades, the field was largely focused on identifying decision effects (e.g., framing, misattribution) that illustrated how rational decision makers were or were not. Today, the field is firmly rooted in a rich, psychological view of judgments and decisions and is shifting toward more comprehensive views of decisions as complex and flexible psychological processes (Weber & Johnson, 2009). By moving beyond debates about whether decision makers are rational, judgment and decision making is opening up to richer process explanations of decision making. The field is ripe for scholars to address how automatic (e.g., System 1) and effortful (e.g., System 2) decision processes coexist and how emotional and cognitive processes influence each other.

Richer, more comprehensive views of decision making have lent themselves to understanding the decisions that underlie important societal problems. For instance, the medical and pharmaceutical industry laments the low rate at which people take their medications. One difficult point for patients occurs when they are low on medication and need to have their prescription refilled. Multiple small steps are involved in doing this: patients have to call to order the prescription to be refilled, go to their neighborhood pharmacy, wait in line, and pay for it. Judgment and decision-making scientists know that each step means that people are less likely to follow through in getting their medicines. A series of small decisions (e.g., go to the pharmacy versus go grocery shopping) can mean that people lose sight of the importance of their health goal. To help with this, some medical plans have started shipping patients' medications to their home on a regular basis. (Patients who still want to visit the pharmacy have the option to not have their medications shipped to their homes.) These plans take advantage of the default effect, which removes all those small decisions that were once needed to get a prescription filled. The hope is that very few patients will actively choose not to have their medications shipped to their homes, which would result in many patients having their medications on hand when they need to take them.

An integration of judgment and decision-making principles with other disciplines is also at the forefront of research today. The organization to which judgment and decision-making scholars belong is the Society for Judgment and Decision Making (sjdm.org), which partners with the Society for Medical Decision Making (smdm.org) to study health care, wellness, and physician and patient decision making. Work in this area is aimed at improving health care outcomes by using clinical studies and judgment and decision-making ideas to sway patients, researchers, and the politico. Assessing health-related utility is important for these researchers, an example of which involves asking people to compare living a long time in an impaired state of health and living a shorter life in perfect health.

Recently the field has made a move toward emphasizing happiness as an appropriate goal that policy makers and decision makers ought to consider when making decisions (Diener, Sapyta, & Suh, 1998). In fact, there is a well-being index structured to take into account happiness levels in countries worldwide. Judgment and decision-making scholars want this well-being score to become as important as the gross domestic product score when world leaders judge how well countries are doing at satisfying the needs of their people.

Social Psychology Can Improve the Study of Judgment and Decision Making

Social psychology brings much to the study of judgment and decision making. Perhaps because social psychology never adhered to the notion of a perfectly rational mind, it emphasizes the importance of processes that do not neatly fit into mathematical models. Emotion and motivation are two areas to which this comment applies. Judgment and decision making would benefit from incorporating a host of emotions (other than regret) into their theories of decision making. The realization that people's decisions reflect their motivation to achieve personal and interpersonal goals is a concept not fully embraced by judgment and decision-making scholars. But this idea is quite amenable to the field of judgment and decision making because it recognizes that decisions function to maximize goals. Making use of the notion of goals in decision making will also help with the problem of integrating emotion and cognitive influences into decision making.

The field of judgment and decision making also could learn from social psychology the value in gathering seemingly isolated phenomena into overarching theories. Again perhaps because judgment and decision-making scholars were fighting against the idea that decision making is rational, they failed to adopt loftier views of the psyche and the role of judgment and decision making in it. Social psychology and judgment and decision making share common challenges in terms of the struggle between approaching science by finding phenomena and by creating unifying theories. Social psychology's success in building grander theories could provide a roadmap for the field of judgment and decision making.

Social Psychology Can Be Improved by Studying Judgment and Decision Making

Judgment and decision-making scholars have approached their discipline with an emphasis on basic phenomena, from which the field of social psychology could benefit. A similar note applies to the importance placed on attempting to correct errors, which judgment and decision making does far more than social psychology. There is at times a sense from the field of judgment and decision making that social psychology does not value either testing their theories under rich, naturalistic conditions or improving people's welfare with their science. The field of social psychology would almost surely have a greater impact on policy and people's everyday lives if it got out of the laboratory and tried to make life better for folks.

The study of social psychology could also be improved by studying judgment and decision making. Social psychology for the most part fails to grasp the importance of the act of making a decision and the impact that decision mistakes have on people's behavior. The examples of people making over 200 food-related decisions a day (but believing that they make only 15) and battered women returning to their abusive partners illustrate that decision making is exceedingly common and wildly important. Social psychological theories would be well served by tracking the decision processes that people go through and social psychologists may find new avenues for understanding their favorite topic of study.

In Closing: Big Ideas The topics and methods of study that judgment and decision-making scholars use have the potential to be applied to big ideas.

Two prominent scholars, Richard Thaler and Cass Sunstein, recently suggested a new policy of governance based in part on judgment and decision-making principles (Thaler & Sunstein, 2009). New insights on genocide came about because Paul Slovic (2007) incorporated ideas about how the emotion system reacts—actually, overreacts—to tragedy, a theory that was informed in part by social psychological ideas about emotions. Slovic found that the distress of seeing one victim is so great that adding a second victim, paradoxically, decreases the distress that people feel because the overwhelming emotion prompts them to disengage from the situation. This example highlights how social psychology and judgment and decision making can merge to provide big insights into big problems.

References

Ariely, D., Loewenstein, G., & Prelec, D. (2003). "Coherent arbitrariness": Stable demand curves without stable preferences. *Quarterly Journal of Economics, 118*, 73–105.

Baumeister, R. F., Bratslavsky, E., Finkenauer, C., & Vohs, K. D. (2001). Bad is stronger than good. *Review of General Psychology, 5*, 323–370.

Baumeister, R. F., Vohs, K. D., DeWall, N., & Zhang, L. (2007). How emotion shapes behavior: Feedback, anticipation, and reflection, rather than direct causation. *Personality and Social Psychology Review, 11*, 167–203.

Benartzi, S., & Thaler, R. H. (2001). Naive diversification strategies in defined contribution saving plans. *American Economic Review, 91*, 79–98.

Diener, E., Sapyta, J. J., & Suh, E. (1998). Subjective well-being is essential to well-being. *Psychological Inquiry, 9*, 33–37.

Epley, N., Keysar, B., Van Boven, L., & Gilovich, T. (2004). Perspective taking as egocentric anchoring and adjustment. *Journal of Personality and Social Psychology, 87*, 327–339.

Gigerenzer, G., & Goldstein, D. G., (1996). Reasoning the fast and frugal way: Models of bounded rationality. *Psychological Review, 103*, 650–669.

Gilovich, T., & Medvec, V. H. (1995). The experience of regret: What, when, and why. *Psychological Review, 102*, 379–395.

Gottman, J. (1994). *Why marriages succeed or fail.* New York: Simon & Schuster.

Hammond, K. R., Hamm, R. M., Grassia, J., & Pearson, T. (1987). Direct comparison of the efficacy of intuitive and analytical cognition in expert judgment. *IEEE Transactions, Systems, Man and Cybernetics, 17*, 753–770.

Hsee, C. K., & Rottenstreich, Y. (2004). Music, pandas, and muggers: On the affective psychology of value. *Journal of Experimental Psychology: General, 133*, 23–30.

Huber, J., Payne, J. W., & Puto, C. (1982). Adding asymmetrically dominated alternatives: Violations of regularity and the similarity hypothesis. *Journal of Consumer Research, 9*, 90–98.

Johnson, E. J., & Goldstein, D. (2003). Do defaults save lives? *Science, 302*, 1338–1339.

Kahneman, D. (2003). Tying it all together: Rules of accessibility and a two-systems view. Keynote address at the Annual Conference of Society for Judgment and Decision Making, Vancouver, Canada.

Kahneman, D., & Frederick, S. (2002). Representativeness revisited: Attribute substitution in intuitive judgment. In T. Gilovich, D. Griffin, & D. Kahneman (Eds.), *Heuristics & biases: The psychology of intuitive judgment* (pp. 49–81). New York: Cambridge University Press.

Kahneman, D., & Frederick, S. (2004). Attribute substitution in intuitive judgment. In M. Augier & J. March (Eds.), *Models of a Man: Essays in Memory of Herbert A. Simon* (pp. 411–432). Cambridge, MA: MIT Press.

Kahneman, D., Knetsch, J. L., & Thaler, R. H. (1990). Experimental tests of the endowment effect and the Coase theorem. *Journal of Political Economy, 98*, 1325–1348.

Kahneman, D., & Tversky, A. (1979). Prospect theory: An analysis of decisions under risk. *Econometrika, 47*, 263–291.

Lazarus, R. S. (1981). A cognitivist's reply to Zajonc on emotion and cognition. *American Psychologist, 36*, 222–223.

Levin, I. P., & Gaeth, G. J. (1988). How consumers are affected by the framing of attribute information before and after consuming the product. *Journal of Consumer Research, 15*, 374–386.

Luce, M.F. (1998). Choosing to avoid: Coping with negatively emotion-laden consumer decisions. *Journal of Consumer Research, 24*, 409–433.

McMackin, J., & Slovic, P. (2000). When does explicit justification impair decision making? *Applied Cognitive Psychology, 14*, 527–541.

Newman-Toker, D. E., & Pronovost, P. J. (2009). Diagnostic errors: The next frontier for patient safety. *Journal of the American Medical Association, 301*, 1060–1062.

Payne, J. W., Bettman, J. R., & Johnson, E. J. (1993). *The adaptive decision maker*. Cambridge, UK: Cambridge University Press.

Payne, J. W., Bettman, J. R. & Schkade, D. A. (1999). Measuring constructed preferences: Towards a building code. *Journal of Risk and Uncertainty, 19*, 243.

Read, D., & Loewenstein, G. (1995). Diversification bias: Explaining the discrepancy in variety seeking between combined and separated choices. *Journal of Experimental Psychology: Applied, 1*, 34–49.

Rusbult, C. E., & Martz, J. M. (1995). Remaining in an abusive relationship: An investment model analysis of nonvoluntary dependence. *Personality and Social Psychology Bulletin, 21*, 558–571.

Schwarz, N., & Clore, G. L. (1983). Mood, misattribution, and judgments of well-being: Informative and directive functions of affective states. *Journal of Personality and Social Psychology, 45*, 513–523.

Simon, H. (1955). A behavioural model of rational choice. *The Quarterly Journal of Economics, 69,* 99–118.

Simonson, I. (1989). Choice based on reasons: The case of attraction and compromise effects. *Journal of Consumer Research, 16,* 158–174.

Simonson, I. (1992). The influence of anticipating regret and responsibility on purchase decisions. *Journal of Consumer Research, 19,* 105–118.

Simonsohn, U. (2010). Weather to go to college. *The Economic Journal.* Published online July 17, 2009, http://www3.interscience.wiley.com/journal/122515169/abstract?CRETRY=1&SRETRY=0

Slovic, P. (2007). "If I look at the mass I will never act": Psychic numbing and genocide. *Judgment and Decision Making, 2,* 79–95.

Slovic, P., Finucane, M. L., Peters, E., & MacGregor, D. G. (2007). The affect heuristic. *European Journal of Operational Research, 177,* 1333–1339.

Thaler, R. H., & Sunstein, C. R. (2009). *Nudge: Improving decisions about health, wealth, and happiness.* New Haven, CT: Yale University Press.

Tversky, A., and Kahneman, D. (1973). Availability: A heuristic for judging frequency and probability. *Cognitive Psychology, 5,* 207–232.

Tversky, A., & Kahneman, D. (1983). Extensional versus intuitive reasoning: The conjunction fallacy in probability judgment. *Psychological Review, 90,* 293–315.

Vohs, K. D., & Baumeister, R.F. (2004). Understanding self-regulation: An introduction. In R.F. Baumeister & K. D. Vohs (Eds.), Handbook of self-regulation: Research, theory, and applications (pp. 1–9). New York: Guilford.

Von Neumann, J., & Morgenstern, O. (1944). *Theory of games and economic behavior.* Princeton, NJ: Princeton University Press.

Wansink, B., Kent, B. J., & Hoch, S. J. (1998). An anchoring and adjustment model of purchase quantity decisions. *Journal of Marketing Research, 19,* 71–81.

Wansink, B., & Sobal, J. (2007). Mindless eating: The 200 daily food decisions we overlook. *Environment and Behavior, 39,* 106–123.

Weber, E. U., & Johnson, E. J. (2009). Mindful judgment and decision making. *Annual Review of Psychology, 60,* 53–85.

Wilson, T. D., & Gilbert, D. T. (2003). Affective forecasting. In M. P. Zanna (Ed.), *Advances in experimental social psychology* (Vol. 35, pp. 345–411). San Diego, CA: Academic Press.

Wilson, T. D., & Schooler, J. W. (1991). Thinking too much: Introspection can reduce the quality of preferences and decisions. *Journal of Personality and Social Psychology, 60,* 181–192.

Winkielman, P., Schwartz, N., & Belli, R. F. (1998). The role of ease of retrieval and attribution in memory judgment: Judging your memory as worse despite recalling more events. *Psychological Science, 9,* 124–126.

Zajonc, R. B. (1980). Feeling and thinking: Preferences need no inferences. *American Psychologist, 35,* 151–175.

Chapter 21

Personality

Charles S. Carver

Social psychology is the part of psychology that focuses on interpersonal phenomena: how the individual's behavior is influenced by other people, present or implied. As a field, social psychology tends to fragment into broad topic areas that reflect particular "contents" of behavior: qualities such as aggression, helping, and interpersonal attraction, for example. Sometimes the contents under examination are intrinsically interpersonal in nature, as in those three examples. Sometimes the contents are fully within the individual (e.g., attitudes), but the focal interest of the social psychologist is how these aspects of the individual are influenced by, or relate to, other people.

In contrast to this, personality psychology focuses on qualities that are organized within the individual, although those internal qualities are often displayed in actions that involve other people. The stereotype of personality psychologists is that they focus on individual differences. It is often assumed for that reason that they care *only* about individual differences. That actually is not true. Personality psychologists focus partly on things that make people different from each other, but partly on things that make people the same—shared structures and dynamics. I have used the phrase *intrapersonal functioning* to refer to these shared internal properties (Carver & Scheier, 2008). Allport (1961), far more eloquently, called them a dynamic organization of psychological systems within each person that create the person's pattern of behaviors, thoughts, and feelings.

Statements about the nature of intrapersonal functioning often represent statements about the nature of people's core motivations. They are statements about what forces are at the center of people's actions, feelings, and thoughts over extended periods of time and diverse circumstances. For example, some views of personality hold that people's core motives concern relationships with significant others. Other views assume that people's core motives concern predicting and adapting better to the world. Others assume that people's central motives are the same as those of any other biological creature: obtaining rewards, avoiding threats, and reproducing.

To some extent, assumptions about core motives are captured in the phrase *human nature*. Personality psychologists, because they focus on the whole person as an entity and how that person functions over time and situations, are interested in viewpoints on personality that help capture the essence of human nature. Many people use the phrase *human nature*, but what really *is* human nature? The answer depends on whom you ask.

Personality psychologists are not the only ones interested in such issues, of course. The same issues arise in social psychology, though usually more obliquely. As social psychologists set out to study a given phenomenon, they implicitly (and sometimes explicitly) adopt one or another set of assumptions about human nature and its core motivations. They implicitly assume some model of personality as a lens for looking at how people influence each other. In this way, some view of personality (even if it is more a sketch of assumptions than an explicit theory) forms the underlying basis for an understanding of social psychological phenomena. This is one place where personality psychology intersects with social psychology, thus providing a cross-cutting perspective on social psychology.

A second point of intersection between these fields returns us to the familiar picture of personality as individual differences. It is possible for a social situation to be so potent that it forces everyone's behavior to be essentially the same, but such situations are rare. Far more common are situations that permit some degree of variation in behavior, even while exerting their own influence. When there is room for variability in behavior, it is virtually certain that part of that variability will stem from personality. Some people are more affected than others by any given situational pressure. The people who are most affected are not necessarily the same from one situation to the next, because the nature of the pressure varies across situations. Thus situational pressures interact with personality, often in subtle ways. A secondary question that always arises across the diverse content areas of social psychology is what kinds of individual differences make the phenomenon under study more likely or less likely to be displayed (Leary & Hoyle, 2009).

This chapter describes some of the viewpoints that are influential in personality psychology today. Some of them have been around for a very long time and others are more recent. Because personality psychology tends to evolve more slowly than social psychology, even the "recent" views have roots in older ideas. This chapter surveys these viewpoints in broad strokes. A good deal of detail is left out (for a more detailed look see Carver & Scheier, 2008). In each case, however, an effort has been made to portray that viewpoint in a way that allows it to serve as a backdrop for thinking about the phenomena of social psychology.

Trait Psychology and the Five-Factor Model

The easiest starting point for personality is probably the trait. The essence of this construct is ancient. The trait is both a commonsense concept and a scientific concept. Traits are dimensions of variability, which are presumed to be grounded within the person, and which are reflected in behaviors, thoughts, and emotions. All views of personality necessarily incorporate some ideas about traits, because traits are the dimensions on which individual differences exist. Although traits thus are implicit in all of personality psychology, one segment of the field has traditionally focused more on traits than have others.

The people who work in this tradition have focused particularly on the question of what traits are fundamental and what ones are less so. The process of deciding which traits are basic, along with the secondary question of how best to measure those traits and place people on the dimensions of their variability, is the crux of this approach to personality. This approach has generally been more concerned with individual differences than with core motives and dynamics, though even that statement is not universally true [for example, Eysenck (1967, 1986) addressed both themes with equal enthusiasm].

There has long been a division of opinion among trait psychologists about how best to approach the question of what traits are most basic. Eysenck (1967, 1986) argued that theorists should begin with well-developed ideas about what they want to measure and then try to measure those qualities well (this is referred to as a theoretical path of scale development). Cattell (1965, 1978) argued that researchers should determine empirically what traits form personality (an empirical path) and not impose theoretical preconceptions. In his view, deciding beforehand what traits are basic tempts you to force reality to fit your ideas. Trait theorists today tend to favor Cattell's view on this issue in principle (Goldberg, 1993), but there is some disagreement about how faithfully they have actually adhered to it in practice (Block, 1995).

The effort to let reality tell you what traits are basic is fairly complicated. It requires gathering large numbers of observations of diverse reflections of traits and then determining where there are commonalities and what those commonalities mean. Early efforts made use of the idea that languages developed in human cultures partly to convey information about what people are like. The descriptive words in various languages thus should provide a rich source of evidence about what traits are important. Important traits should be reflected in more words (this is called the lexical criterion of importance).

This is a good start, but trying to sort through thousands of descriptive words and determine their relationships to each other was a logistical nightmare. Two things changed that: the development of a methodological technique called factor analysis and the development of computers (early factor analyses were done slowly and painfully by hand, and it was hard to be sure errors did not creep in). Factor analysis allows researchers to locate commonalities easily among thousands of observations. Commonalities among ratings on descriptors are believed to reflect traits. A trait might be reflected very strongly in some descriptors and less so in many more. Even those limited reflections represent evidence that the trait is important, though, because it is implicated in many parts of the lexicon.

Despite different starting points taken by various people, a substantial consensus has emerged about what traits are basic, at least at a broad level of analysis. The emerging consensus is that the structure of personality incorporates five superordinate factors, which often are called the "five-factor model" or the "big five" (Goldberg, 1981; McCrae & Costa, 2003; Wiggins, 1996). The five factors are most commonly known by the labels Extraversion, Neuroticism, Agreeableness, Conscientiousness, and Openness to experience (McCrae & Costa, 2003).

In most views of the five factors, each is composed of subordinate traits with narrower properties. Typically the measure of the overall factor is formed of facet scales that represent the narrower traits. If the facets that contribute to the five broad traits are considered separately, the picture is more nuanced, because the facets may play different roles in behavior. (It also is far more complex than is the picture that considers only the five superordinate factors.)

Consensus on the five-factor view of individual differences does not mean unanimity. There remain staunch advocates of other frameworks. There are two three-factor models (Eysenck, 1975, 1986; Tellegen, 1985) in which elements of conscientiousness and agreeableness blend into traits that are called, respectively, Psychoticism and Constraint. There is also a six-factor model that adds honesty/humility to the five traits named above (Ashton et al., 2004), as well as an alternative-five model (Zuckerman et al., 1993) in which different facets of the five factors are emphasized. There have also been efforts to distill the five factors down to two (DeYoung, 2006; DeYoung, Peterson, & Higgins, 2001; Digman, 1997).

The next sections describe the five factors in more detail, starting with the two that have been studied the longest, and about which the greatest consensus exists. These two are also part of the three-factor models as well as the six-factor and alternative-five models.

The Two Most Consensual Factors: Extraversion and Neuroticism

The first factor is extraversion. As is true of several traits in the five-factor model, extraversion has different emphases in different measures. Sometimes extraversion is viewed as based in assertiveness, sometimes in spontaneity and energy. Sometimes it is based in dominance, confidence, and agency (Depue & Collins, 1999), and sometimes in a tendency toward positive emotions [indeed, Tellegen (1985) calls it positive emotionality]. Extraversion is often thought of as implying a sense of sociability (Watson, Clark, McIntyre, & Hamaker, 1992), but some argue that the sociability is a by-product of other features of extraversion (Lucas, Diener, Grob, Suh, & Shao, 2000). Others see the sense of agency and the sense of sociability as two separate facets of extraversion (Depue & Morrone-Strupinsky, 2005).

Whether extraversion concerns true sociability or not, it does appear to concern having social impact (Jensen-Campbell & Graziano, 2001). For example, extraverted men interact better than do introverts with women who are strangers to them (Berry & Miller, 2001), and extraverts have the firm handshake that conveys confidence (Chaplin, Phillips, Brown, Clanton, & Stein, 2000). The desire for social impact can have a more problematic side, however. For example, extraverts are less cooperative than introverts when facing a social dilemma over resources (Koole, Jager, van den Berg, Vlek, & Hofstee, 2001).

The second factor, neuroticism, concerns the ease and frequency with which the person becomes upset and distressed. Moodiness, anxiety, and depression reflect higher neuroticism. Neuroticism scales often include facets pertaining to hostility and other negative feelings, but there is also some disagreement about whether those particular negative feelings might really belong in another factor (Carver, 2004; Jang et al., 2002; Peabody & De Raad, 2002; Saucier & Goldberg, 2001). In any case, it is generally agreed that the core of neuroticism is vulnerability to subjective experiences of anxiety, worry, and general distress.

Neuroticism also has a clear impact on social behavior. It relates to more difficult interactions among married partners (Donnellan et al., 2004) and less satisfaction in the relationship. People who are highly neurotic are also more likely to distance themselves from their partners after a negative event (Bolger & Zuckerman, 1995). Neuroticism impairs academic performance (Chamorro-Premuzic &

Furnham, 2003) and it predicts a negative emotional tone when writing stories about oneself (McAdams et al., 2004).

Agreeableness, Conscientiousness, and Openness

The next factor is agreeableness. Agreeableness as a dimension is often characterized as being broadly concerned with maintaining relationships (Jensen-Campbell & Graziano, 2001). Agreeable people are friendly and helpful (John & Srivastava, 1999), empathic (Graziano, Habashi, Sheese, & Tobin, 2007), and able to inhibit their negative feelings (Graziano & Eisenberg, 1999). Having a high level of this trait seems to short-circuit aggressive responses (Meier, Robinson, & Wilkowski, 2006), because agreeable people get less angry over others' transgressions than do less agreeable people (Meier & Robinson, 2004), and they are less likely to seek revenge after being harmed (McCullough & Hoyt, 2002).

At the opposite pole is an antagonistic quality, verging on hostility (this is the other place where negative feelings of anger may belong). People low in agreeableness use displays of power to deal with social conflict more than do others (Graziano, Jensen-Campbell, & Hair, 1996) and are more prone to antisocial behavior (Miller, Lynam, & Leukefeld, 2003).

The most commonly used label for the next factor is conscientiousness. However, this label does not fully reflect the qualities of planning, persistence, and purposeful striving toward goals that are a part of it (Digman & Inouye, 1986). Other suggested names include constraint and responsibility, reflecting qualities of impulse control and reliability. Precisely what qualities are included in this trait varies considerably across measures (Roberts, Walton, & Bogg, 2005).

Conscientiousness has received a good deal of attention in recent years. Conscientious people have been found to be less likely to try to steal someone else's romantic partner and are less likely to be lured away (Schmitt & Buss, 2001). Conscientiousness has been linked to more responsive parenting of young children (Clark, Kochanska, & Ready, 2000) and to the use of negotiation as a conflict-resolution strategy (Jensen-Campbell & Graziano, 2001).

Conscientiousness also predicts various kinds of health-related behaviors (Bogg & Roberts, 2004; Roberts et al., 2005). Indeed, conscientiousness in childhood has been related to health behaviors 40 years later (Hampson, Goldberg, Vogt, & Dubanoski, 2006). Greater conscientiousness predicts avoidance of unsafe sex (Trobst, Herbst, Masters, & Costa, 2002) and other risk behaviors (Markey, Markey, & Tinsley, 2003). A recent meta-analysis links conscientiousness to longer life (Kern & Friedman, 2008), perhaps because it is associated with fewer risky behaviors and better treatment adherence. Consistent with this, conscientiousness relates to lower levels of substance abuse (Chassin et al., 2004; Lynam et al., 2003; Roberts & Bogg, 2004; Walton & Roberts, 2004).

Agreeableness and conscientiousness appear to have an important property in common. Both traits suggest a breadth of perspective on life. Many manifestations of conscientiousness imply a broad time perspective: taking future contingencies into account. Agreeableness implies a broad social perspective: taking the needs of others into account.

The fifth factor is one about which there is probably the most disagreement. The most widely used label for it is Openness to experience (Costa & McCrae, 1985). Some measures (and theories) imbue this factor with greater overtones of intelligence, however, terming it Intellect (Peabody & Goldberg, 1989). It involves curiosity, flexibility, imagination, and willingness to immerse oneself in atypical experiences (for a review of its involvement in social experience see McCrae, 1996). Openness to experience has been found to predict greater engagement with the existential challenges of life (Keyes, Shmotkin, & Ryff, 2002), to more favorable interracial attitudes (Flynn, 2005), and to greater sexual satisfaction in marriage (Donnellan et al., 2004).

Five-Factor View in Sum

In the five-factor view of personality, people can be placed on each of these dimensions according to their characteristic patterns of thoughts, feelings, and actions. The aggregation of information about the person resulting from these placements provides a reasonably good snapshot of what that person is like. In fact, the trait perspective has been called the "psychology of the stranger" (McAdams, 1992), in part because it provides the kind of information that would be important if you knew nothing about a person.

On the other hand, the phrase "psychology of the stranger" also reflects the view that this perspective does not say much about the dynamic aspects of personality. Labeling a person as sociable or dominant gives a name to what you see. But it does not tell you much about how or why the person acts that way. Others have similarly argued that this model says little about how the factors function or how they map onto any picture of human nature (Block, 1995).

This has changed to a considerable extent over the past decade and a half. Much more information has been collected on how traits function in life settings. Furthermore, several of the trait dimensions have also been linked to another model bearing on personality in which dynamics and process play a much larger role. This model is described next.

Biological Process Model

What might be characterized as a biological process model is an increasingly influential view of personality. It has roots in several places. One of them is Eysenck's version of the trait perspective. Eysenck consistently tried to ground his ideas about extraversion and neuroticism in a picture of brain functions. Another starting point is a view of early childhood temperaments. Temperaments are biologically based systems that affect broad aspects of behavior and form the basis of personality. Some personality psychologists have long been interested in temperaments (e.g., Buss & Plomin, 1975), but most work on temperaments has been done by developmental psychologists (e.g., Derryberry & Rothbart, 1997; Rothbart, Ahadi, & Evans, 2000; Rothbart, Ahadi, Hershey, & Fisher, 2001; Rothbart & Bates, 1998; Rothbart, Ellis, Rueda, & Posner, 2003; Rothbart & Posner, 1985).

Another basis for the development of a biological process model of personality is the increasing influence of a family of theories pertaining to animal behavior, psychopharmacology, and neuroscience. These viewpoints emphasize the continuity between humans and other animal species. They also focus on information obtained by research tools involving both manipulation of the nervous system by chemical means and observation of activities of the nervous system by imaging techniques.

From this biological viewpoint, it is important to understand the fundamental properties of animal self-regulation and how those properties are manifested both in the nervous system and in human personality. Three basic tendencies are considered in this section. By themselves, they yield considerable complexity. Two of them are organized tendencies to approach situations and objects that are desirable (e.g., food) and to avoid those that are dangerous (e.g., predators). These organized tendencies exist for all animals, and the regulation of these basic processes represents a core activity for humans as well.

Fitting that idea, a number of theorists have posited basic approach and avoidance temperaments as key aspects of the organization of the nervous system (see, e.g., Davidson, 1992, 1998; Depue & Collins, 1999; Caspi & Shiner, 2006; Caspi et al., 2005; Elliott & Thrash, 2002; Fowles, 1993; Gray, 1982, 1994a,b; Rothbart & Bates, 1998). Most theorists of this group believe that one set of brain structures is differentially involved in the processes by which animals organize the approach of incentives and that a second set is involved in the processes by which animals organize the avoidance of threats.

Approach

The structures involved in approach have been given several names: *activation system* (Cloninger, 1987; Fowles, 1980), *behavioral engagement system* (Depue, Krauss, & Spoont, 1987), *behavioral facilitation system* (Depue & Iacono, 1989), and *behavioral approach system* (Gray, 1987, 1990, 1994a,b), often abbreviated BAS. You might think of this system as regulating the psychological gas pedal, moving you toward what you want. It is a *go* system, a reward-seeking system (Fowles, 1980).

This set of brain structures is presumed to be involved whenever a person is pursuing an incentive. It is likely that there is differentiation such that certain parts of the brain are involved in the pursuit of food, others in the pursuit of sex, and so on (Gable, 2006; Panksepp, 1998). But some believe that the separate parts also link up to an overall BAS. Thus, the BAS is seen as a general mechanism to go after things you want. BAS doesn't rev you up in neutral, though, without an incentive in mind (Depue & Collins, 1999). It is engaged only in the active pursuit of incentives. The BAS is also held to be responsible for many kinds of positive emotions (e.g., hope, eagerness, and excitement), emotions that reflect the anticipation of getting incentives.

From temperaments emerge traits. Here is one place where the emerging biological process models intersect with the trait approach. A number of people have linked the trait of extraversion to the approach temperament (Carver, Sutton, & Scheier, 2000; Caspi & Shiner, 2006; Caspi et al., 2005; Depue & Collins, 1999; Elliott & Thrash, 2002; Rothbart & Bates, 1998). That is, some people view extraversion as reflecting the sensitivity of a general approach system. In this view, extraverts have a large appetite for incentives (particularly, though not exclusively, social incentives), whereas introverts are less drawn to incentives.

Avoidance

The structures involved in avoidance of threat have also received several names: Gray (1987, 1990, 1994a, 1994b) suggested the label behavioral inhibition system (BIS). Others have referred to an *avoidance system* (Cloninger, 1987) or *withdrawal system* (Davidson, 1988, 1992, 1995). Activity in this system may cause people to inhibit movement (especially if they are currently approaching an incentive) or to pull back from what they just encountered. You might think of this system as a psychological brake pedal, a *stop* system. Alternatively, you might think of it as a *throw-it-into-reverse* system.

The avoidance temperament is responsive to cues of punishment or danger. When this system is engaged, the person may stop and scan for further cues about the threat or may pull back. Because this system responds to threat, danger, or other to-be-avoided stimuli, it is also thought to be responsible for feelings such as anxiety, guilt, and revulsion, feelings that reflect anticipation of aversive stimuli.

Here again the biological process models intersect the trait approach. The trait of neuroticism has often been linked to the avoidance temperament (Carver et al., 2000; Caspi & Shiner, 2006; Caspi et al., 2005; Rothbart & Bates, 1998). This connection is consistent with the view that anxiety is the emotional core of neuroticism. Some people now view levels of trait neuroticism as reflecting the sensitivity of a general avoidance or withdrawal system. In this view, those high in neuroticism are very sensitive to punishment, whereas those lower in neuroticism are more indifferent to it.

Effortful Control

Another temperament posited by developmental theorists (e.g., Rothbart, Ellis, & Posner, 2004; Rothbart & Posner, 1985) is generally termed effortful control (see also Kochanska & Knaack, 2003; Nigg, 2000, 2003, 2006; Rothbart & Rueda, 2005). Effortful control develops more slowly than the approach and avoidance temperaments (Casey, Getz, & Galvan, 2008). It is superordinate to both approach and avoidance temperaments and is capable of overriding impulses that stem from those more basic temperaments. It thus acts as a supervisory system, provided sufficient mental resources are available. The label "effortful" conveys the sense that this is a planful activity, requiring the use of cognitive resources to constrain the tendency to react impulsively.

Effortful control is a construct from developmental psychology, but its features resemble those of adult self-control. Self-control is the ability to override impulses to act as well as the ability to make oneself initiate or persist in boring, difficult, or disliked activity. Self-control appears to depend on higher executive functions that are grounded in prefrontal cortical areas. Guidance of self-regulation by this temperament provides some muting of emotions and permits the organism to plan for the future and to take situational complexities into account in making behavioral decisions.

This temperament also has been linked to the five-factor model, although the connection is more complicated than for approach and avoidance. I noted earlier that agreeableness and conscientiousness both imply breadth of perspective: agreeableness involves a broad social perspective and conscientiousness a broad time perspective. Consistent with this similarity between these two traits, it has been suggested that both traits derive from the effortful control temperament (Ahadi & Rothbart, 1994; Caspi & Shiner, 2006; Jensen-Campbell et al., 2002).

Effortful control similarly reflects a breadth of perspective, enabling the person to override immediate impulses in order to optimize broader outcomes.

There is at least some evidence suggesting that effortful control relies on brain areas other than those subserving the basic approach and avoidance functions. It is often suggested that the brain structures underlying effortful control evolved more recently than those underlying the basic approach and avoidance functions. To put it in more behavioral terms, the ability to exert self-control reflects an evolutionary advance.

Biological Process View in Sum

The biological process approach to personality is an attempt to ascertain the functions a living animal needs and how those functions are reflected in personality. Approaching desired incentives and avoiding punishers are primitive necessities, although there is also room for individual variation in the strength of those motivations. These core motives—striving for things you want and avoiding harm—are surely part of human nature. Behavioral tendencies to which these motives lead are also part of personality.

Effortful control also serves important biological purposes, although perhaps not as basic as the approach and avoidance temperaments. Effortful control provides the opportunity to gain in ways that are greater than the gains that come from impulse alone. There are times when delay of gratification (or withholding an angry retort) does result in better final results, and it is those outcomes that are made possible by effortful control.

I have not mentioned the research literature bearing on neural correlates of various sorts of mental activity, or another research literature bearing on neurotransmitters and the role they play in various classes of behavior. These are very active areas of work that are clearly pertinent to the connection between personality and social psychology. However, for present purposes the points they make are refinements of this general theme: to varying degrees, people seek rewards, avoid threats, and take multiple factors into account in planning their behaviors.

Cognitive Self-Regulatory Models

The next orientation to personality I will discuss is a loose collection of views I will refer to as cognitive self-regulatory models. The biological-process view of personality emphasizes the functional systems that are required by a living biological entity. The self-regulatory models emphasize the cognitive processes that are involved in managing behavior. There are some distinct similarities between the two viewpoints, though they have very different starting points.

Goals

Cognitive self-regulatory models have roots in an expectancy-value motivational tradition. Values are qualities that are endorsed or rejected, qualities that are either positively valenced or negatively valenced. In the current incarnation of the expectancy-value viewpoint, the operative construct is most likely to be goals (Austin & Vancouver, 1996; Carver & Scheier, 1998; Elliott, 2008; Higgins, 1996; Markus & Nurius, 1986; Moskowitz & Grant, 2009). The term *value* today tends to connote qualities that are relatively abstract (Schwartz, 1992; Schwartz & Bilsky, 1990); these abstract qualities are realized in behavior by the pursuit of more concrete goals, which in turn can be broken down into subgoals.

Diverse goal-based theories hold that it is important to distinguish between motivational processes aimed at moving toward *goals* and those aimed at staying away from *threats* (Carver & Scheier, 1998; Elliott, 2008; Higgins 1996). A desired goal has a positive incentive value that pulls behavior to it. Looming harm or pain has a *dis*incentive value that pushes behavior away from it. Sometimes approach and avoidance tendencies conflict with each other, as when approaching a desired incentive also increases threat, Sometimes approach and avoidance processes are mutually supportive, as when attaining a desired incentive will simultaneously forestall something the person wants to avoid.

In goal-based views of personality, understanding the person means (in part) understanding the goals the person has, the values that motivate his or her actions (Markus & Nurius, 1986; Mischel & Shoda, 1995). Many complexities follow from this, including the extent to which people are motivated more by approach versus avoidance goals (e.g., Elliot & Sheldon, 1998; Gable & Berkman, 2008; Higgins & Tykocinski, 1992) and the extent to which people's focal goals are concrete versus abstract in nature (e.g., Liberman & Trope, 2008; Vallacher & Wegner, 1989). More obviously, even within the same behavioral context, people can pursue very different endpoints; to predict their behavior requires knowing what they are trying to do.

The emphasis on approach and avoidance motivational processes (and the importance of the distinction between these processes) is one way in which this viewpoint resembles the biological process view. A difference is that this view has generally not been concerned with the biological basis of the goal-regulation process.

Expectancies

Consistent with the expectancy-value heritage of this approach, goal-based models also typically incorporate an expectancy construct in some form or other: the sense of confidence or doubt that a given outcome will be attained successfully (e.g., Bandura, 1986; Carver & Scheier, 1998). Not every behavior produces its intended outcome; goal-directed efforts can be thwarted by impediments. Under such conditions, people's efforts are believed to be determined partly by their expectancies of success or failure (e.g., Bandura, 1986; Brehm & Self, 1989; Carver & Scheier, 1998; Eccles & Wigfield, 2002; Klinger, 1975; Wright, 1996).

People vary from context to context in their levels of confidence. Some theorists emphasize that many expectancies are domain specific and even situation specific. There also are differences among people, however, in their more generalized sense of confidence about life-in-general. This variation is what constitutes the personality dimension of optimism versus pessimism (Carver, Scheier, Miller, & Fulford, 2009; Scheier & Carver, 1992).

Abandonment and Scaling Back of Goals

Goal-based models often incorporate an element that is less obvious in biological models. When impediments to goal attainment are severe, people sometimes give up. Indeed, when goals are unattainable, it can be very important to give them up (Miller & Worsch, 2007; Wrosch, Miller, Scheier, & Brun de Pontet, 2007). The process of disengaging from goals that are beyond reach, and the negative feelings that are part of that process—sadness, despair—are adaptive and functional in such circumstances (Klinger, 1975; Nesse, 2000).

When a valued goal is abandoned, however, it is important that the person eventually take up another. The absence of a goal yields a sense of emptiness. Disengagement appears to be a valuable and adaptive response when it leads to—or is directly tied to—moving on to other goals (Wrosch et al., 2007). By taking up an attainable alternative, the person remains engaged in activities that have meaning for the self, and life continues to have purpose.

An alternative to giving up altogether is to scale the goal back to something more restricted in the same general domain. This is a kind of limited disengagement, in the sense that the initial goal no longer remains in place. It avoids a complete disengagement from the domain of behavior, however, by substituting the more restricted goal. This shift thus keeps the person involved in that area of life, at a level that holds the potential for successful outcomes. It represents an accommodation rather than a complete relinquishment.

Dual-Process Models

The collection of theories I have referred to here as cognitive self-regulation models is perhaps more diverse than any other group of theories discussed in this chapter. In many ways, placing a particular theory into this group is somewhat arbitrary. Nonetheless, this may be the place to mention dual-process, or two-mode, models in personality psychology. These models assume two levels of processing experiences: one more basic and automatic, the other more deliberative and reflective. There are many such models in social psychology (e.g., Chaiken & Trope, 1999; Lieberman, Gaunt, Gilbert, & Trope, 2002; Smith & DeCoster, 2000; Strack & Deutsch, 2004; Wilson, Lindsey, & Schooler, 2000), and there are also such models in personality psychology.

Epstein's (1973, 1985, 1990, 1994) cognitive-experiential self theory may have been the first explicitly two-mode model in contemporary psychology. Epstein started with the premise that humans experience reality via two systems. One is a symbolic processor—the rational mind. The other is associative and intuitive, and functions automatically and quickly. Epstein argued that both systems are always at work and that they jointly determine behavior.

Metcalfe and Mischel (1999) proposed a similar model, drawing on several decades of work on delay of gratification. In delay of gratification research, a choice is posed between a smaller, less desired but immediate reward, versus a larger, more desired reward later on (Mischel, 1974). Metcalfe and Mischel (1999) proposed that two systems determine the ability to restrain in this and many other contexts: a "hot" system (emotional, impulsive, reflexive, and connectionist) and a "cool" system (strategic, flexible, slower, and unemotional). How a person responds to a difficult situation depends on which system presently dominates.

One interesting thing about these models is that they share some common ground with the biological process models described earlier. In particular, the position that there is a reflective, "cool" system that processes experience symbolically and according to logical principles bears a good deal of resemblance to the concept of effortful control. As noted earlier, effortful control provides a way to optimize outcomes, with respect to both longer periods of time and the broader social context. In the same way, the reflcetive side of the mind prevents the desires of the moment from overwhelming the person's behavior.

Contextualization of Traits

Perhaps the best-known cognitive approach to personality is Mischel and Shoda's (1995) view of personality as a cognitive–affective processing system.

This label reflects the recognition that emotion plays a key role in much of cognitive experience. Mischel and Shoda, building on decades of work on social cognition, hold that people develop organizations of information about the nature of situations, other people, and the self. These schemas have a conditional property, an *if . . . then* quality. Saying that someone is aggressive does not actually mean you think the person is aggressive at every moment. It means you think he's more likely than most people to be aggressive in a certain class of situations.

Evidence from several sources supports this view. For example, in describing people we know, we often use hedges, descriptions of conditions under which we think those people act a particular way (Wright & Mischel, 1988). In fact, the better you know people, the more likely you are to think about them in conditional terms (Chen, 2003), probably because you've learned what circumstances touch off various kinds of behavior in them. People think conditionally about themselves as well, understanding that their own behavior follows an *if . . . then* principle.

To predict consistency of action, then, you need to know two things. First, you need to know how the person construes the situation (which depends on the person's mental schemas and their accessibility). Second, you need to know the person's *if . . . then* profile. The unique profile of *if . . . then* relations is a *behavioral signature* for a person's personality (Shoda, Mischel, & Wright, 1994). Even if two people tend toward the same kind of behavior, the situations that elicit that behavior may differ from one person to the other. Indeed, these profiles of *if . . . then* relations may in some sense *define* personality (Mischel, Shoda, & Mendoza-Denton, 2002).

This approach treats traits as contextualized. The trait does not exist apart from the situations that elicit behaviors that fit the trait. This is a view of traits that is very different in some ways from the perspective with which this chapter began. Yet in other ways it is entirely compatible with that perspective. The same set of traits may be equally useful in this view, but they apply in a different way. It is entirely possible—and entirely reasonable—for a person who is generally an introvert to behave in a particularly extraverted way in some circumstances (Fleeson, 2001). A person's placement on a trait dimension is not really a single point, but a frequency distribution, with a mean (what you would have thought of as the "single point") and a degree of variability.

Psychoanalysis

Now let us turn to a very old conception of personality. To people who are unfamiliar with contemporary personality psychology, the term *personality* may evoke the view of personality that was proposed over a century ago by the Austrian physician Sigmund Freud. Freud developed his ideas from clinical cases, some his own and some described to him by other therapists. He developed his view during a time in which research on personality was essentially nonexistent. As a result, his theoretical position evolved without systematic research, but rather through his own observations and intuitions.

Freud proposed a view in which primitive animalistic forces are basic to personality. He argued that their influence was generally hidden both from the person in which they were at work and from outside observers. This view was abhorrent to the Victorian society to which he was writing. It was even more shocking that the primitive animalistic forces he emphasized were focused on issues of sex and death. Freud wrote that the goal of life is death (Freud, 1955/1920), and his theory was one in which humans are obsessed with sex from infancy throughout life. In this view, most normal development is a process of disguising one's true primitive desires from oneself so as to be able to function in society.

Psychoanalysis is among the oldest set of ideas in personality psychology. In fact, some dismiss it as little more than a historical curiosity. Although parts of Freud's view of personality do seem quaint today, there are also broad themes in that viewpoint that continue to resonate today. For example, Freud was very much influenced by the writings of Darwin, who was arguing that humans are inextricably connected to a broader spectrum of animals with many characteristics in common. Among those characteristics are the fact that complex animals all eventually die, and the fact that a core motivation of all animal life is reproduction. Inasmuch as reproduction among humans entails sex, there appears to be a very sound evolutionary basis for arguing that sex is a rather important aspect of life. One might even argue that all of life before reproduction is a process of preparing the individual for reproduction.

Darwin's views were considered shocking by many people at the time he wrote (indeed, the principle of evolution and the interconnectedness of species remain controversial to some to this day). Today, however, the idea that various aspects of human behavior reflect adaptation to evolutionary pressures is widely represented throughout psychology, including personality (that broad theme is considered briefly later in this chapter). In some ways, then, Freud was ahead of his time. The sections that follow describe some of the other themes of Freud's writing that continue to resonate today.

Levels of Awareness

The part of psychoanalytic theory that is often termed the topographical model of the mind posits three levels of potential awareness of information. The conscious mind is present awareness; the preconscious is the part of the mind that contains information that is not now in consciousness but is directly accessible by voluntary search; and the unconscious is the part of the mind that is not directly accessible by voluntary search. It was the concept of the unconscious that Freud invoked in accounting for people's lack of awareness of their primitive motives and of the reasons for engaging in many of the behaviors they engage in. That is, the actions are being done for reasons that are specified only in the unconscious for one reason or another.

The notion of an unconscious region of the mind fell out of favor for quite some time. It has reemerged over the past two decades, however, in a form rather different from that portrayed in psychoanalysis. Today's version is often referred to as the "cognitive unconscious" (Hassin, Uleman, & Bargh, 2005; Kihlstrom, 1987). It acknowledges that there is in fact a good portion of the programming of the mind that is not easily accessible to awareness (and perhaps not directly accessible at all).

In part, this inaccessible portion of the mind includes what has been hardwired into the organism, such as knowing how to breathe and digest, and whatever other reflexive action patterns are built in at birth. In part, this inaccessible portion of the mind includes what is called procedural memory—information about how to engage in particular thought or action processes—which was acquired through practice and is now lost to awareness. The latter theme has been generalized to the view that information about even complex action or thought patterns that have become automatic through repetition is difficult to retrieve from memory voluntarily. Perhaps more interesting at present is the idea that those complex patterns can be triggered and executed automatically, without any awareness of their existence or their execution on the part of the person who is engaged in them (e.g., Bargh, Gollwitzer, Lee-Chai, Barndollar, & Trötschel, 2001).

In some ways, this is very similar to the unconscious postulated by Freud. In other ways it is quite different. The unconscious Freud wrote about is filled with dark secrets and hidden desires. The cognitive unconscious is, for the most part, more pedestrian. On the other hand, the part of the cognitive unconscious that has been studied the most is the part that follows from automaticity rather than from biological programming. It may be that "instinctive" aspects of human behavior that are automatic by virtue of biological inheritance are more similar to what Freud wrote about than are aspects of behavior that follow from large numbers of repetition.

In any case, the idea that people do things for reasons they are not aware of now appears beyond question. This is certainly a core theme of psychoanalysis, even if the particulars of how it happens are not entirely the same today as they once were.

Layers of Personality

Another aspect of psychoanalytic theory, often termed the structural model of personality (Freud, 1962/1923), posits three modes of functioning. Freud saw personality as having three aspects, which interweave to create the complexity of human behavior. These are not physical entities but rather three aspects of functioning, termed *id*, *ego*, and *superego*.

The id is the part of personality that exists at birth. It consists of all the inherited, instinctive, primitive aspects of personality, and it functions entirely in the unconscious. It is closely tied to basic biological processes, and is the source of all psychological energy. The id follows what is called the pleasure principle: that needs should be satisfied immediately (Freud, 1949/1940). Unsatisfied needs are aversive tension states, which should be gratified whenever they arise to release the tension. Under the pleasure principle, for example, any increase in hunger should cause an attempt to eat.

Because it is not possible to always satisfy impulses immediately, a second set of functions emerges, called ego. Ego translates fairly closely to *self*. The ego evolves from the id and harnesses part of the id's energy for its own use. The ego focuses on making sure that id impulses are expressed effectively, by taking into account the constraints of the external world. Because of this concern with the outside world, a good deal of ego functioning takes place in the conscious and preconscious regions of the mind.

The ego is said to follow the reality principle: the taking into account of external reality along with internal needs and urges. The reality principle brings a sense of rationality to behavior. Because it orients people toward the world, it leads them to weigh the risks linked to an action before acting. If the risks seem too high, the person will think of another way to meet the need. If there is no safe way to do so immediately, the person will delay it to a later, safer, or more sensible time. Thus, an important goal of the ego is to delay the discharge of the id's tension until an appropriate object or activity is found. Not prevent it, but channel it appropriately.

In other words, the ego can delay gratification. The very alert reader will have noticed a similarity between this function of the ego and effects created by the temperament of effortful control, and the function posited by cognitive models for the reflective layer of the mind. This similarity is sufficiently striking (given that the observations were made by different people across many decades of time) to suggest the theorists have been describing the same thing.

In the psychoanalytic view, as time goes on and other forces intrude on the developing child, a third mode of functioning emerges, called superego. The superego represents both an idealized way to be (ego ideal), and ways to not-be (conscience). Superego is the moral sense of personality, which tries to induce the person to adhere to high principles. This moral sense can be striking enough that some connect the upper layer of the dual-process model to the superego rather than the ego (Kochanska & Knaack, 2003). In some respects, however, what makes the superego's goals different is primarily that they are more abstract and more demanding.

Defenses

A third theme from psychoanalysis that has been maintained in mainstream psychology is the idea that people use defenses involuntarily, automatically, to protect themselves from ideas, knowledge, or desires that are threatening. In Freud's view, these defenses represent tools of the ego that permit it to do its main job of satisfying the needs of the id while avoiding problems with respect to either the constraints of external reality or the demands of the superego.

As is true of contemporary views of the unconscious, theorists after Freud have accounted for such self-protective tendencies in various ways. Today discussions of defenses would be more likely to be framed in terms of self-esteem protection. However, the theme that people avoid confronting unpleasant truths remains very much alive in personality psychology.

Attachment Patterns

Another perspective that is very influential in personality psychology today derives from a body of work in developmental psychology that had its origins in psychoanalysis, but which transformed psychoanalysis enormously. A number of post-Freudians known as object relations theorists argued that the fundamental issues in human development (and in human life more generally) do not concern sexuality (as Freud had said) but rather the relationships from one person (the infant) to another (at first, the mother or other primary caregiver).

Theories of this group share three further themes. First, a dialectic tension is assumed between processes of psychological fusion with the other and processes of separation and individuation from the other (which are involved in forming a separate identity). Thus the child (and the adult) wants to be immersed in safety and security, but also wants to have a separate existence. Second, this approach emphasizes that a person's pattern of relating to others is laid down in early childhood. Third, the patterns formed early (which can vary greatly from person to person) are assumed to recur repeatedly throughout life.

The subset of this group of theories that has come to be most influential in today's personality psychology is called attachment theory. This term is identified with Bowlby (1969, 1988) and Ainsworth (e.g., Ainsworth, Blehar, Waters, & Wall, 1978), among others. The term attachment was used initially to refer to an infant's connection with its mother. In more recent years the ideas of attachment theory have been adapted to create a broader picture of the functioning of adult personality.

Bowlby believed that the clinging and following of the infant serve the important biological purpose of keeping the infant close to the mother, thus increasing the infant's chances of survival. A basic theme in attachment theory is that mothers (and others) who are responsive to the infant create a *secure base* for it. The infant needs to know that the major person in his or her life is dependable—is there whenever needed. This sense of security gives the child a base from which to explore the world. It also provides a place of comfort (a *safe haven*) when the child is threatened.

Attachment theorists also believe that the child builds implicit mental working models of the self, others, and the nature of relationships. The model of the self can be positive or negative (or in between) as can the model of other people. How you view yourself has implications for how you behave; so does how you view the world of people around you and how you view the nature of relationships.

Research on attachment in infants led to the emergence of an analysis of individual differences in attachment pattern. Secure attachment is displayed by an appropriate distress response (not too much, but not absent either) when the mother leaves the infant, and a happy and engaged response when the mother returns. Two kinds of insecure responses also exist. An ambivalent (or resistant) infant becomes very upset when the mother leaves, and its response to the mother's return mixes approach with anger. The infant seeks contact with the mother but then angrily resists efforts to be soothed. In the avoidant pattern, the infant does not show distress when the mother leaves, and responds to her return by ignoring her. It is as though this infant expects to be abandoned and is responding by being remote.

There is at least some evidence that the patterns have a self-perpetuating quality. The clinginess mixed with rejection in the ambivalent pattern can be hard to deal with, as can the aloofness and distance of the avoidant pattern. Each of these patterns tends to cause others to react negatively. That, in turn, reconfirms the perceptions that led to the patterns in the first place. In fact, people with an insecure attachment pattern appear to distort their memory of interactions over time to make them more consistent with their working models (Feeney & Cassidy, 2003). Thus, there is a self-generated stability to the pattern over the course of time.

Hazan and Shaver (1987) took this description of infants and extrapolated it to adult social behavior, with a focus on close relationships. In this research, secure adults said that love is real and when it comes, it stays. Avoidants were less optimistic, saying that love does not last. Ambivalents said falling in love is easy and happens often to them, but they also agreed that love does not last. These responses look very much like grown-up versions of the patterns of infancy.

Other research has expanded on these findings in many directions. For example, consistent with the pattern of infancy, ambivalent undergraduates are most likely to have obsessive and dependent love relationships (Collins & Read, 1990) and to be most obsessive about lost loves (Davis, Shaver, & Vernon, 2003). Avoidants are the least likely to report being in love either in the present or in the past (Feeney & Noller, 1990). They are also the most likely to cope in self-reliant ways after a breakup (Davis et al., 2003). Those who are securely attached show the most interdependence, commitment, and trust (Mikulincer, 1998; Simpson, 1990). If they experience a breakup they turn to family and friends as safe havens (Davis et al., 2003).

There are many ways in which adult attachment can affect the course of romantic relationships, and such topics have become the focus of much research in the past few years (Mikulincer & Goodman, 2006). Indeed, in the past two decades there has been an explosion of research on wide-ranging manifestations of adult attachment patterns (Cassidy & Shaver, 2008; Feeney, 2006; Mikulincer & Goodman, 2006; Mikulincer & Shaver, 2007; Rholes & Simpson, 2004).

Issues in Adult Attachment

The proliferation of work on adult attachment has raised many issues, including how best to measure it in adults. Early studies used the three main categories from the infancy work, but another approach has also emerged. Following Bartholomew and Horowitz (1991), who began with Bowlby's notion of working models of self and other, many researchers have shifted to the assessment of two dimensions. One is a positive-versus-negative model of self (the self is worthy or not), the other is a positive versus negative model of others (others are trustworthy or not). The dimensions are termed *attachment anxiety* and *attachment avoidance*, respectively (Brennan, Clark, & Shaver, 1998). Security is represented by the combination of low on both dimensions.

It is of some interest that these dimensions have at least a little resemblance to the approach and avoidance temperaments of the biological-process approach to personality (and thus to extraversion and neuroticism; Carver, 1997). One clear difference is that the attachment patterns are specific to close relationships, whereas the approach and avoidance temperaments are quite general. Perhaps as a result of this difference in breadth, Simpson et al. (2002) found that measures of extraversion and neuroticism did not duplicate the effects of attachment patterns. Nonetheless, the resemblance remains intriguing.

Another important issue is the question of whether each person has one pattern of relating to others or many patterns for different relationships. The answer seems to be many patterns (Baldwin, Keelan, Fehr, Enns, & Koh-Rangarajoo, 1996; Cook, 2000; La Guardia, Ryan, Couchman, & Deci, 2000; Overall, Fletcher, & Friesen, 2003; Pierce & Lydon, 2001). For example, one study had participants define each of their 10 closest relationships in terms of the three categories. Across the 10 descriptions, almost everyone used at least two patterns and nearly half used all three (Baldwin et al., 1996). People also seem to have patterns of attachment to groups, distinct from their patterns for close relationships (Smith, Murphy, & Coats, 1999).

Today the attachment model of adult relationships is being explored by researchers in many different contexts. Many people now believe that the fundamental issue underlying many kinds of social behavior is the nature and quality of the bond that a given person has to a significant other. This view depends on a particular implicit view of personality: that the core dynamic of personality involves a person's perceptions of his or her relations with others (see also Andersen & Chen, 2002).

Self-Actualization, Self-Determination

Another broad approach to personality is associated with terms such as self-actualization and self-determination. One core idea in this viewpoint is that people have a natural tendency to grow and develop their capabilities in ways that maintain or enhance the true self, an idea called self-actualization (Rogers, 1959). If this tendency is allowed to express itself, the person develops in positive ways. One impediment to this is the need for acceptance by other people. Acting in ways that foster acceptance from others sometimes means acting in ways that prevent growth.

Another core idea is that people must choose how to act in the world. It is the person's task to sort out the pressures and focus on growth and development. This way of thinking is echoed in a contemporary view of personality called self-determination theory (Deci & Ryan, 1980, 1985, 1991, 2000; Ryan, 1993; Ryan & Deci, 2001). This theory (see also Chapter xxx, this volume) begins with the idea that behavior can reflect two underlying dynamics. Some actions are *self-determined*, done because the actions have intrinsic value to the actor. Other actions are *controlled*, done to gain payments or to satisfy some sort of pressure. An action can be controlled even if the control is entirely in your own mind. If you do something because you would feel guilty if you didn't do it, you are engaging in controlled behavior.

Self-determination theory holds that people want to feel a sense of autonomy in what they do. In this view, accomplishments are satisfying only if you feel a sense of self-determination in them. If you feel forced or pressured, you will be less satisfied (Grolnick & Ryan, 1989). Indeed, pressuring *yourself* to do well can reduce motivation (Ryan, 1982). People who impose conditions of worth on themselves suffer adverse consequences (see also Crocker & Knight, 2005; Crocker & Park, 2004).

In self-determination theory, people naturally strive for greater competence and greater relatedness to others (themes that I have not gone into here), and to experience their behavior as autonomous. Autonomy means "owning" whatever behavior you choose to engage in as yours. Ultimately, for you to feel comfortable choosing it, the behavior must fit your true self, and it can be hard to know whether you are forcing yourself to believe something fits when it does not. Yet that is the goal of a meaningful life.

Evolution

As noted earlier, the idea that evolutionary processes have a major influence on present-day human behavior has come to occupy an important place in psychology (see also Chapter xx, this volume) including personality psychology. The underlying idea is that behavioral tendencies can become widely represented in a population (and thus part of human nature) if those tendencies increase the rate of survival and reproduction over many generations (Barkow, Cosmides, & Tooby, 1992; Bjorklund & Pellegrini, 2002; Buss, 1995, 2005; Caporael, 2001; Heschl, 2002; Segal, 1993; Tooby & Cosmides, 1989, 1990).

This is more complicated than it sounds. Your genes are helped into the next generation by anything that helps people with a genetic makeup similar to yours (your subgroup) reproduce. Thus, if you act altruistically for a relative, it helps the relative survive, and thereby helps genes that resemble your genes survive. This kind of reasoning suggests the possibility that a tendency toward altruism is part of human nature. This idea has also been extended to suggest more broadly that our ancestors survived better by cooperating (Axelrod & Hamilton, 1981), leading some to conclude that a tendency to cooperate is part of human nature (Guisinger & Blatt, 1994; Kriegman & Knight, 1988; McCullough, Kimeldorf, & Cohen, 2008).

The evolutionary view of personality focuses closely on mating (Buss, 1991, 1994; Buss, & Schmitt, 1993; Gangestad & Simpson, 2000). Indeed, from an evolutionary view, mating is what life is all about. Mating involves competition: males competing with one another and females with one another. But the two competitions are believed to differ somewhat in their goals. Males are driven to mate widely and females to choose a mate who can provide resources (see Chapter xx, this volume).

Most psychologists believe that what we think of as personality reflects the processes of millennia of evolution. It is harder, however, to specify clearly just what properties have been selected and why. Nonetheless, many personality psychologists do continue to work at that puzzle. There could hardly be an approach to understanding the fundamentals of humanity that holds a greater claim to trying to identify human nature.

Individual Differences Revisited: Measurement

Before closing, I want to briefly mention one more issue. This is a methodological issue that is especially salient in personality psychology but also applies to work in social psychology. As noted earlier, all viewpoints on personality point partly to differences among people. To study these differences, personality psychologists have had to develop ways to measure them.

This is not as simple as it might seem. In describing the trait viewpoint, I noted a philosophical disagreement about whether to start with a theoretical reason to measure something or whether to let reality tell you what is important to measure. As a practical matter, that issue has actually affected only the trait approach to personality, which has adopted the goal of capturing all of personality. Other approaches, being more closely focused on one theme or another, have uniformly taken the theoretical path to measure development. Let's now consider the process of creating a measure a little more closely.

Suppose you had a theoretical notion about some aspect (or aspects) of personality variation and you wanted to develop a way to assess it (or them). What would you do? First you need to identify a source of relevant information. That might be self-ratings, reports of observers (people rating a person they know), or even actual behaviors that pertain to the quality of your interest. In part because self-ratings are so easy to collect, they are the most popular source. It is common to write a set of items pertaining to the trait of interest, and to collect responses on a multi-point scale indicating the extent of endorsement of what the item says (typically ranging from strong agreement to strong disagreement). If you do this, be careful that the items you write are clear and simple, that they don't combine more than one issue in any one item, and that they don't use words or phrases people will not understand.

That's easy enough so far, but that's just the start. There are many things you need to check on. If you intend to measure one and only one thing, you need to be sure that's what you are actually doing. If you intend to measure two separate things, you need to be sure that's what you are actually doing. In both cases, that means you need a factor analysis on a set of responses to your items to see what factor structure emerges from them. If you have two separate factors, do not try to treat the items as though they represent one thing, because they don't. If you have one factor, do not try to pretend you are measuring two separate properties of personality, because you aren't.

Factor analysis can reveal other things as well. Sometimes in developing a set of items you find out that some of the items are not much good: they don't correlate with the other items, or maybe everyone totally agrees (or disagrees) with them so that they give no information about differences among people. In such cases you need to throw out or revise the items and try again. Most measures go through multiple rounds of item construction and testing before they go to the next step.

There are in fact several next steps. Although the factor structure tells you something about what items go together, you also need a measure of internal reliability for each scale (which does not, by the way, substitute for the factor analysis). If you intend to measure an individual difference that is fairly stable, you need to show that it *is* fairly stable—over an interval of at least several weeks in a moderately large sample.

The hardest step is called validation. That means showing that the measure is measuring what you think it is measuring. Done properly, it means (1) correlating your measure with other measures to which it should relate (moderately strong correlations establish what is called convergent validity), (2) correlating it with measures to which it should not relate (low correlations establish what is called discriminant validity), and (3) relating scores on your measure to some behavioral index of the property you think you are measuring (that being the hardest but most important part).

After all that, you can actually use your measure. If it has only one factor you are good to go. If it has multiple factors, be careful. Try very hard to resist the impulse to make an index out of them (adding them up, or averaging them), unless they are strongly correlated with each other. Doing that can create great confusion about exactly what the index means (Carver, 1989). Under no circumstance should you treat scales as opposites unless they are fairly strongly inversely related. Once again, the resulting index is misleading rather than helpful.

Ultimately, what we learn from studies of people's behavior is only as good as our measures. Whether the measure concerns individual differences in personality or differences of some other type, the same issues apply. It is important to attend carefully to these issues as you proceed.

Conceptions of Personality in Social Behavior

As indicated at the outset, personality psychologists are interested in how best to construe human nature. Different theorists take different views of human nature as their starting points. Thus, there exist several different conceptions of what processes are fundamental to personality. The review offered in this chapter surveyed several perspectives that currently are influential in personality psychology. These perspectives are not the only possibilities (cf. Carver, 2006), but rather one person's reading of what ideas currently have the greatest influence.

When social psychologists examine a phenomenon, they do so through the lens of one or another set of assumptions, which address (in part) the core concerns underlying human action. Social psychologists in different contexts over the years have assumed widely varying dynamics as underlying the kinds of behavior on which they focused. I think it is fair to say that each of those views has also been held by some group of personality psychologists as a good way to conceptualize the central concerns of the person. In this way, ideas that are fundamental to personality psychology serve as implicit frameworks for theories of social psychology.

References

Ahadi, S. A., & Rothbart, M. K. (1994). Temperament, development and the big five. In C. F. Halverson Jr., G. A. Kohnstamm, & R. P. Martin, (Eds.), *The developing structure of temperament and personality from infancy to adulthood* (pp. 189–207). Hillsdale, NJ: Erlbaum.

Ainsworth, M. D. S., Blehar, M. C., Waters, E., & Wall, S. (1978). *Patterns of attachment: A psychological study of the strange situation.* Hillsdale, NJ: Erlbaum.

Allport, G. W. (1961). *Pattern and growth in personality.* New York: Holt, Rinehart, & Winston, Inc.

Andersen, S. M., & Chen, S. (2002). The relational self: An interpersonal social-cognitive theory. *Psychological Review*, 109, 619–645.

Ashton, M. C., Lee, K., Perugini, M., Szarota, P., de Vries, R. E., Di Blas, L., et al. (2004). A six-factor structure of personality-descriptive adjectives: Solutions from psycholexical studies in seven languages. *Journal of Personality and Social Psychology, 86*, 356–366.

Austin, J. T., & Vancouver, J. B. (1996). Goal constructs in psychology: Structure, process, and content. *Psychological Bulletin, 120*, 338–375.

Axelrod, R., & Hamilton, W. D. (1981). The evolution of cooperation. *Science, 211*, 1390–1396.

Baldwin, M. W., Keelan, J. P. R., Fehr, B., Enns, V., & Koh-Rangarajoo, E. (1996). Social-cognitive conceptualization of attachment working models: Availability and accessibility effects. *Journal of Personality and Social Psychology, 71*, 94–109.

Bandura, A. (1986). *Social foundations of thought and action: A social cognitive theory.* Englewood Cliffs, NJ: Prentice-Hall.

Bargh, J. A., Gollwitzer, P. M., Lee-Chai, A., Barndollar, K., & Trötschel, R. (2001). The automated will: Nonconscious activation and pursuit of behavioral goals. *Journal of Personality and Social Psychology, 81*, 1014–1027.

Barkow, J. H., Cosmides, L., & Tooby, J. (1992). *The adapted mind: Evolutionary psychology and the generation of culture.* New York: Oxford University Press.

Bartholomew, K., & Horowitz, L. M. (1991). Attachment styles among young adults: A test of a four-category model. *Journal of Personality and Social Psychology, 61*, 226–244.

Berry, D. S., & Miller, K. M. (2001). When boy meets girl: Attractiveness and the five-factor model in opposite-sex interactions. *Journal of Research in Personality, 35*, 62–77.

Bjorklund, D. F., & Pellegrini, A. D. (2002). *Origins of human nature: Evolutionary developmental psychology.* Washington, DC: American Psychological Association.

Block, J. (1995). A contrarian view of the five-factor approach to personality assessment. *Psychological Bulletin, 117*, 187–215.

Bogg, T., & Roberts, B. W. (2004). Conscientiousness and health-related behaviors: A meta-analysis of the leading behavioral contributors to mortality. *Psychological Bulletin*, 130, 887–919.

Bolger, N., & Zuckerman, A. (1995). A framework for studying personality in the stress process. *Journal of Personality and Social Psychology, 69*, 890–902.

Bowlby, J. (1969). *Attachment and loss: Vol. 1, Attachment.* New York: Basic Books.

Bowlby, J. (1988). *A secure base: Parent–child attachment and healthy human development.* New York: Basic Books.

Brehm, J. W., & Self, E. A. (1989). The intensity of motivation. *Annual Review of Psychology, 40*, 109–131.

Brennan, K. A., Clark, C. L., & Shaver, P. R. (1998). Self-report measurement of adult attachment: An integrative overview. In J. A. Simpson & W. S. Rholes (Eds.), *Attachment theory and close relationships* (pp. 46–76). New York: Guilford Press.

Buss, A. H., & Plomin, R. (1975). *A temperament theory of personality development.* New York: Wiley-Interscience.

Buss, D. M. (1991). Evolutionary personality psychology. *Annual Review of Psychology, 42*, 459–491.

Buss, D. M. (1994). *The evolution of desire: Strategies of human mating*. New York: Basic Books.

Buss, D. M. (1995). Evolutionary psychology: A new paradigm for psychological science. *Psychological Inquiry, 6*, 1–30.

Buss, D. M. (Ed.). (2005). *The handbook of evolutionary psychology*. New York, Wiley.

Buss, D. M., & Schmitt, D. P. (1993). Sexual strategies theory: An evolutionary perspective on human mating. *Psychological Review, 100*, 204–232.

Caporael, L. R. (2001). Evolutionary psychology: Toward a unifying theory and a hybrid science. *Annual Review of Psychology, 52*, 607–628.

Carver, C. S. (1989). How should multifaceted personality constructs be tested? Issues illustrated by self-monitoring, attributional style, and hardiness. *Journal of Personality and Social Psychology, 56*, 577–585.

Carver, C. S. (1997). Adult attachment and personality: Converging evidence and a new measure. *Personality and Social Psychology Bulletin, 23*, 865–883.

Carver, C. S. (2004). Negative affects deriving from the behavioral approach system. *Emotion, 4*, 3–22.

Carver, C. S. (2006). Assumptions about personality and core motivations as hidden partners in social psychology. In P. A. M. Van Lange (Ed.), *Bridging social psychology: Benefits of transdisciplinary approaches* (pp. 181–186). Mahwah, NJ: Erlbaum.

Carver, C. S., & Scheier, M. F. (1998). *On the self-regulation of behavior*. New York: Cambridge University Press.

Carver, C. S., & Scheier, M. F. (2008). *Perspectives on personality* (6th ed.). Boston, MA: Allyn & Bacon.

Carver, C. S., Scheier, M. F., Miller, C. J., & Fulford, D. (2009). Optimism. In C. R. Snyder & S. J. Lopez (Eds.), *Oxford handbook of positive psychology* (2nd ed., pp. 303–311). New York: Oxford University Press.

Carver, C. S., Sutton, S. K., & Scheier, M. F. (2000). Action, emotion, and personality: Emerging conceptual integration. *Personality and Social Psychology Bulletin, 26*, 741–751.

Casey, B. J., Getz, S., & Galvan, A. (2008). The adolescent brain. *Developmental Review, 28*, 62–77.

Caspi, A., Roberts, B. W., & Shiner, R. L. (2005). Personality development: Stability and change. *Annual Review of Psychology, 56*, 453–484.

Caspi, A., & Shiner, R. L. (2006). Personality development. In W. Damon & R. Lerner (Series Eds.) & N. Eisenberg (Vol. Ed.), *Handbook of child psychology*, Vol. 3. *Social, emotional, and personality development* (6th ed., pp. 300–365). New York: Wiley.

Cassidy, J., & Shaver, P. R. (Eds.). (2008). *Handbook of attachment* (2nd ed.). New York: Guilford Press.

Cattell, R. B. (1965). *The scientific analysis of personality*. Baltimore: Penguin.

Cattell, R. B. (1978). *The scientific use of factor analysis.* New York: Plenum.

Chaiken, S. L., & Trope, Y. (Eds.). (1999). *Dual-process theories in social psychology.* New York: Guilford Press.

Chamorro-Premuzic, T., & Furnham, A. (2003). Personality predicts academic performance: Evidence from two longitudinal university samples. *Journal of Research in Personality, 37,* 319–338.

Chaplin, W. F., Phillips, J. B., Brown, J. D., Clanton, N. R., & Stein, J. L. (2000). Handshaking, gender, personality, and first impressions. *Journal of Personality and Social Psychology, 79,* 110–117.

Chassin, L., Flora, D. B., & King, K. M. (2004). Trajectories of alcohol and drug use and dependence from adolescence to adulthood: The effects of familial alcoholism and personality. *Journal of Abnormal Psychology, 113,* 483–498.

Chen, S. (2003). Psychological-state theories about significant others: Implications for the content and structure of significant-other representations. *Personality and Social Psychology Bulletin, 29,* 1285–1302.

Clark, L. A., Kochanska, G., & Ready, R. (2000). Mothers' personality and its interaction with child temperament as predictors of parenting behavior. *Journal of Personality and Social Psychology, 79,* 274–285.

Cloninger, C. R. (1987). A systematic method of clinical description and classification of personality variants: A proposal. *Archives of General Psychiatry, 44,* 573–588.

Collins, N. L., & Read, S. J. (1990). Adult attachment, working models, and relationship quality in dating couples. *Journal of Personality and Social Psychology, 58,* 644–663.

Cook, W. L. (2000). Understanding attachment security in a family context. *Journal of Personality and Social Psychology, 78,* 285–294.

Costa, P. T., Jr., & McCrae, R. R. (1985). *The NEO Personality Inventory manual.* Odessa, FL: Psychological Assessment Resources, Inc.

Crocker, J., & Knight, K. M. (2005). Contingencies of self-worth. *Current Directions in Psychological Science. 14,* 200–203.

Crocker, J., & Park, L. E. (2004). The costly pursuit of self-esteem. *Psychological Bulletin, 130,* 392–414.

Davidson, R. J. (1988). EEG measures of cerebral asymmetry: Conceptual and methodological issues. *International Journal of Neuroscience, 39,* 71–89.

Davidson, R. J. (1992). Prolegomenon to the structure of emotion: Gleanings from neuropsychology. *Cognition and Emotion, 6,* 245–268.

Davidson, R. J. (1995). Cerebral asymmetry, emotion, and affective style. In R. J. Davidson & K. Hugdahl (Eds.), *Brain asymmetry* (pp. 361–387). Cambridge, MA: MIT Press.

Davidson, R. J. (1998). Affective style and affective disorders: Perspectives from affective neuroscience. *Cognition and Emotion. 12,* 307–330.

Davis, D., Shaver, P. R., & Vernon, M. L. (2003). Physical, emotional, and behavioral reactions to breaking up: The roles of gender, age, emotional involvement, and attachment style. *Personality and Social Psychology Bulletin, 29,* 871–884.

Deci, E. L., & Ryan, R. M. (1980). The empirical exploration of intrinsic motivational processes. In L. Berkowitz (Ed.), *Advances in experimental social psychology* (Vol. 13). New York: Academic Press.

Deci, E. L., & Ryan, R. M. (1985). *Intrinsic motivation and self-determination in human behavior*. New York: Plenum.

Deci, E. L., & Ryan, R. M. (1991). A motivational approach to self: Integration in personality. In R. Dienstbier (Ed.), *Nebraska symposium on motivation: Perspectives on motivation* (Vol. 38, pp. 237–288). Lincoln: University of Nebraska Press.

Deci, E. L., & Ryan, R. M. (2000). The "what" and "why" of goal pursuits: Human needs and the self-determination of behavior. *Psychological Inquiry, 11*, 227–268.

Depue, R. A., & Collins, P. F. (1999). Neurobiology of the structure of personality: Dopamine, facilitation of incentive motivation, and extraversion. *Behavioral and Brain Sciences, 22*, 491–517.

Depue, R. A., & Iacono, W. G. (1989). Neurobehavioral aspects of affective disorders. *Annual Review of Psychology, 40*, 457–492.

Depue, R. A., Krauss, S. P., & Spoont, M. R. (1987). A two-dimensional threshold model of seasonal bipolar affective disorder. In D. Magnusson & A. Öhman (Eds.), *Psychopathology: An interactional perspective* (pp. 95–123). Orlando, FL: Academic Press.

Depue, R. A., & Morrone-Strupinsky, J. V. (2005). A neurobehavioral model of affiliative bonding: Implications for conceptualizing a human trait of affiliation. *Behavioral and Brain Sciences, 28*, 313–395.

Derryberry, D., & Rothbart, M. K. (1997). Reactive and effortful processes in the organization of temperament. *Development and Psychopathology, 9*, 633–652.

DeYoung, C. G. (2006). Higher-order factors of the big five in a multi-informant sample. *Journal of Personality and Social Psychology, 91*, 1138–1151.

DeYoung, C. G., Peterson, J. B., & Higgins, D. M. (2001). Higher-order factors of the big five predict conformity: Are there neuroses of health? *Personality and Individual Differences, 33*, 533–552.

Digman, J. M. (1997). Higher-order factors of the Big Five. *Journal of Personality and Social Psychology, 73*, 1246–1256.

Digman, J. M., & Inouye, J. (1986). Further specification of the five robust factors of personality. *Journal of Personality and Social Psychology, 50*, 116–123.

Donnellan, M. B., Conger, R. D., & Bryant, C. M. (2004). The big five and enduring marriages. *Journal of Research in Personality, 38*, 481–504.

Eccles, J. S., & Wigfield, A. (2002). Motivational beliefs, values and goals. *Annual Review of Psychology*, 53, 109–132.

Elliot A. J. (Ed.). (2008). *Handbook of approach and avoidance motivation*. New York: Psychology Press.

Elliot, A. J., & Sheldon, K. M. (1998). Avoidance personal goals and the personality–illness relationship. *Journal of Personality and Social Psychology, 75*, 1282–1299.

Elliot, A. J., & Thrash, T. M. (2002). Approach–avoidance motivation in personality: Approach and avoidance temperaments and goals. *Journal of Personality and Social Psychology, 82*, 804–818.

Epstein, S. (1973). The self-concept revisited: Or a theory of a theory. *American Psychologist, 28*, 404–416.

Epstein, S. (1985). The implications of cognitive–experiential self theory for research in social psychology and personality. *Journal for the Theory of Social Behavior, 15*, 283–310.

Epstein, S. (1990). Cognitive–experiential self-theory. In L. Pervin (Ed.), *Handbook of personality: Theory and research* (pp. 165–192). New York: Guilford Press.

Epstein, S. (1994). Integration of the cognitive and the psychodynamic unconscious. *American Psychologist, 49*, 709–724.

Eysenck, H. J. (1967). *The biological basis of personality*. Springfield, IL: Charles C Thomas.

Eysenck, H. J. (1986). Models and paradigms in personality research. In A. Angleitner, A. Furnham, & G. Van Heck (Eds.), *Personality psychology in Europe*, Vol. 2: *Current trends and controversies* (pp. 213–223). Lisse, Holland: Swets & Zeitlinger.

Eysenck, H. J. (1975). *The inequality of man*. San Diego: Edits.

Feeney, B. C. (2006). An attachment theory perspective on the interplay between intrapersonal and interpersonal processes. In K. D. Vohs & E. J. Finkel (Eds.), *Self and relationships* (pp. 133–159). New York: Guilford Press.

Feeney, B. C., & Cassidy, J. A. (2003). Reconstructive memory related to adolescent-parent conflict interactions: The influence of attachment-related representations on immediate perceptions and changes in perceptions over time. *Journal of Personality and Social Psychology, 85*, 945–955.

Feeney, J. A., & Noller, P. (1990). Attachment style as a predictor of adult romantic relationships. *Journal of Personality and Social Psychology, 58*, 281–291.

Fleeson, W. (2001). Toward a structure- and process-integrated view of personality: Traits as density distributions of states. *Journal of Personality and Social Psychology, 80*, 1011–1027.

Flynn, F. J. (2005). Having an open mind: The impact of openness to experience on interracial attitudes and impression formation. *Journal of Personality and Social Psychology, 88*, 816–826.

Fowles, D. C. (1980). The three arousal model: Implications of Gray's two-factor learning theory for heart rate, electrodermal activity, and psychopathy. *Psychophysiology, 17*, 87–104.

Fowles, D. C. (1993). Biological variables in psychopathology: A psychobiological perspective. In P. B. Sutker, & H. E. Adams (Eds.), *Comprehensive handbook of psychopathology* (2nd Ed.), pp. 57–82. New York: Plenum.

Freud, S. (1955). Beyond the pleasure principle. In J. Strachey (Ed.), *The standard edition of the complete psychological works of Sigmund Freud* (Vol. 18). London: Hogarth. (Originally published, 1920.)

Freud, S. (1962). *The ego and the id*. New York: Norton. (Originally published, 1923.)

Freud, S. (1949). *An outline of psychoanalysis*. New York: Norton. (Translated by J. Strachey; originally published, 1940.)

Gable, S. L. (2006). Approach and avoidance social motives and goals. *Journal of Personality, 74*, 175–222.

Gable, S. L., & Berkman, E. T. (2008). Social motives and goals. In A. J. Elliot (Ed.), *Handbook of approach and avoidance motivation* (pp. 203–216). New York: Psychology Press.

Gangestad, S. W., & Simpson, J. A. (2000). The evolution of human mating: Trade-offs and strategic pluralism. *Behavioral and Brain Sciences, 23*, 573–587.

Goldberg, L. R. (1981). Language and individual differences: The search for universals in personality lexicons. In L. Wheeler (Ed.), *Review of personality and social psychology* (Vol. 2, pp. 141–165). Beverly Hills, CA: Sage.

Goldberg, L. R. (1993). The structure of phenotypic personality traits. *American Psychologist, 48*, 26–34.

Gray, J. A. (1982). *The neuropsychology of anxiety: An enquiry into the functions of the septo-hippocampal system*. New York: Oxford University Press.

Gray, J. A. (1987). Perspectives on anxiety and impulsivity: A commentary. *Journal of Research in Personality, 21*, 493–509.

Gray, J. A. (1990). Brain systems that mediate both emotion and cognition. *Cognition and Emotion, 4*, 269–288.

Gray, J. A. (1994a). Personality dimensions and emotion systems. In P. Ekman & R. J. Davidson (Eds.), *The nature of emotion: Fundamental questions* (pp. 329–331). New York: Oxford University Press.

Gray, J. A. (1994b). Three fundamental emotion systems. In P. Ekman & R. J. Davidson (Eds.), *The nature of emotion: Fundamental questions* (pp. 243–247). New York: Oxford University Press.

Graziano, W. G., & Eisenberg, N. H. (1999). Agreeableness as a dimension of personality. In R. Hogan, J. Johnson, & S. Briggs (Eds.), *Handbook of personality* (pp. 795–825). San Diego, CA: Academic Press.

Graziano, W. G., Habashi, M. M., Sheese, B. E., & Tobin, R. M. (2007). Agreeableness, empathy, and helping: A person X situation perspective. *Journal of Personality and Social Psychology, 93*, 583–599.

Graziano, W. G., Jensen-Campbell, L. A., & Hair, E. C. (1996). Perceiving interpersonal conflict and reacting to it: The case for agreeableness. *Journal of Personality and Social Psychology, 70*, 820–835.

Grolnick, W. S., & Ryan, R. M. (1989). Parent styles associated with children's self-regulation and competence in school. *Journal of Educational Psychology, 81*, 143–154.

Guisinger, S., & Blatt, S. J. (1994). Individuality and relatedness: Evolution of a fundamental dialectic. *American Psychologist, 49*, 104–111.

Hampson, S. E., Goldberg, L. R., Vogt, T. M., & Dubanoski, J. P. (2006). Forty years on: Teachers' assessments of children's personality traits predict self-reported health behaviors and outcomes at midlife. *Health Psychology, 25*, 57–64.

Hassin, R. R., Uleman, J. S., & Bargh, J. A. (Eds.). (2005). *The new unconscious*. New York: Oxford University Press.

Hazan, C., & Shaver, P. R. (1987). Romantic love conceptualized as an attachment process. *Journal of Personality and Social Psychology, 52*, 511–524.

Heschl, A. (2002). *The intelligent genome: On the origin of the human mind by mutation and selection*. New York: Springer.

Higgins, E. T. (1996). Ideals, oughts, and regulatory focus: Affect and motivation from distinct pains and pleasures. In P. M. Gollwitzer & J. A. Bargh (Eds.), *The psychology of action: Linking cognition and motivation to behavior* (pp. 91–114). New York: Guilford Press.

Higgins, E. T., & Tykocinski, O. (1992). Self-discrepancies and biographical memory: Personality and cognition at the level of psychological situation. *Personality and Social Psychology Bulletin, 18*, 527–535.

Jang, K. L., Livesley, W. J., Angleitner, A., Riemann, R., & Vernon, P. A. (2002). Genetic and environmental influences on the covariance of facets defining the domains of the five-factor model of personality. *Personality and Individual Differences, 33*, 83–101.

Jensen-Campbell, L. A., Adams, R., Perry, D. G., Workman, K. A., Furdella, J. Q., & Egan, S. K. (2002). Agreeableness, extraversion, and peer relations in early adolescence: Winning friends and deflecting aggression. *Journal of Research in Personality, 36*, 224–251.

Jensen-Campbell, L. A., & Graziano, W. G. (2001). Agreeableness as a moderator of interpersonal conflict. *Journal of Personality, 69*, 323–362.

John, O. P., & Srivastava, S. (1999). The big five trait taxonomy: History, measurement, and theoretical perspectives. In L. A. Pervin & O. P. John, (Eds.), *Handbook of personality: Theory and research* (2nd ed., pp. 102–138). New York: Guilford Press.

Kern, M. L., & Friedman, H. S. (2008). Do conscientious individuals live longer? A quantitative review. *Health Psychology, 27*, 505–512.

Keyes, C. L. M., Shmotkin, D., & Ryff, C. D. (2002). Optimizing well-being: The empirical encounter of two traditions. *Journal of Personality and Social Psychology, 82*, 1007–1022.

Kihlstrom, J. F. (1987). The cognitive unconscious. *Science, 237*, 1445–1452.

Klinger, E. (1975). Consequences of commitment to and disengagement from incentives. *Psychological Review, 82*, 1–25.

Kochanska, G., & Knaack, A. (2003). Effortful control as a personality characteristic of young children: Antecedents, correlates, and consequences. *Journal of Personality, 71*, 1087–1112.

Koole, S. L., Jager, W., van den Berg, A. E., Vlek, C. A. J., & Hofstee, W. K. B. (2001). On the social nature of personality: Effects of extraversion, agreeableness, and feedback about collective resource use on cooperation in a resource dilemma. *Personality and Social Psychology Bulletin, 27*, 289–301.

Kriegman, D., & Knight, C. (1988). Social evolution, psychoanalysis, and human nature. *Social Policy, 19*, 49–55.

La Guardia, J. G., Ryan, R. M., Couchman, C. E., & Deci, E. L. (2000). Within-person variation in security of attachment: A self-determination theory perspective on attachment, need fulfillment, and well-being. *Journal of Personality and Social Psychology, 79*, 367–384.

Leary, M. R., & Hoyle, R. H. (Eds.). (2009). *Handbook of individual differences in social behavior*. New York: Guilford Press.

Liberman, N., & Trope, Y. (2008). The psychology of transcending the here and now. *Science, 322*, 1201–1205.

Lieberman, M. D., Gaunt, R., Gilbert, D. T., & Trope, Y. (2002). Reflection and reflexion: A social cognitive neuroscience approach to attributional inference. In M. Zanna (Ed.), *Advances in Experimental Social Psychology* (pp. 199–249). San Diego, CA: Academic Press.

Lucas, R. E., Diener, E., Grob, A., Suh, E. M., & Shao, L. (2000). Cross-cultural evidence for the fundamental features of extraversion. *Journal of Personality and Social Psychology, 79*, 452–468.

Lynam, D. R., Leukefeld, C., & Clayton, R. R. (2003). The contribution of personality to the overlap between antisocial behavior and substance use/misuse. *Aggressive Behavior, 29*, 316–331.

Markey, C. N., Markey, P. M., & Tinsley, B. J. (2003). Personality, puberty, and preadolescent girls' risky behaviors: Examining the predictive value of the five-factor model of personality. *Journal of Research in Personality, 37*, 405–419.

Markus, H., & Nurius, P. (1986). Possible selves. *American Psychologist, 41*, 954–969.

McAdams, D. P. (1992). The five-factor model in personality: A critical appraisal. *Journal of Personality, 60*, 329–361.

McAdams, D. P., Anyidoho, N. A., Brown, C., Huang, Y. T., Kaplan, B., & Machado, M. A. (2004). Traits and stories: Links between dispositional and narrative features of personality. *Journal of Personality, 72*, 761–784.

McCrae, R. R. (1996). Social consequences of experiential openness. *Psychological Bulletin, 120*, 323–337.

McCrae, R. R., & Costa, P. T., Jr. (2003). *Personality in adulthood: A five-factor theory perspective* (2nd ed.). New York: Guilford Press.

McCullough, M. E., & Hoyt, W. T. (2002). Transgression-related motivational dispositions: Personality substrates of forgiveness and their links to the big five. *Personality and Social Psychology Bulletin, 28*, 1556–1573.

McCullough, M. E., Kimeldorf, M. B., & Cohen, A. D. (2008). An adaptation for altruism? The social causes, social effects, and social evolution of gratitude. *Current Directions in Psychological Science, 17*, 281–285.

Meier, B. P., & Robinson, M. D. (2004). Does quick to blame mean quick to anger? The role of agreeableness in dissociating blame and anger. *Personality and Social Psychology Bulletin, 30*, 856–867.

Meier, B. P., Robinson, M. D., & Wilkowski, B. M. (2006). Turning the other cheek: Agreeableness and the regulation of aggression-related primes. *Psychological Science, 17*, 136–142.

Metcalfe, J., & Mischel, W. (1999). A hot/cool-system analysis of delay of gratification: Dynamics of willpower. *Psychological Review, 106*, 3–19.

Mikulincer, M. (1998). Adult attachment style and individual differences in functional versus dysfunctional experiences of anger. *Journal of Personality and Social Psychology, 74*, 513–524.

Mikulincer, M., & Goodman, G. S. (2006). *Dynamics of romantic love: Attachment, caregiving, and sex*. New York: Guilford Press.

Mikulincer, M., & Shaver, P. R. (2007). *Attachment in adulthood: Structure, dynamics, and change*. New York: Guilford Press.

Miller, G. E., & Wrosch, C. (2007). You've gotta know when to fold 'em: Goal disengagement and systemic inflammation in adolescence. *Psychological Science, 18*, 773–777.

Miller, J. D., Lynam, D., & Leukefeld, C. (2003). Examining antisocial behavior through the lens of the five factor model of personality. *Aggressive Behavior, 29*, 497–514.

Mischel, W. (1974). Processes in delay of gratification. In L. Berkowitz (Ed.), *Advances in experimental social psychology* (Vol. 7). New York: Academic Press.

Mischel, W., & Shoda, Y. (1995). A cognitive–affective system theory of personality: Reconceptualizing situations, dispositions, and invariance in personality structure. *Psychological Review, 102*, 246–268.

Mischel, W., Shoda, Y., & Mendoza-Denton, R. (2002). Situation–behavior profiles as a locus of consistency in personality. *Current Directions in Psychological Science, 11*, 50–54.

Moskowitz, G. B., & Grant, H. (Eds.). (2009). *The psychology of goals*. New York: Guilford Press.

Nesse, R. M. (2000). Is depression an adaptation? *Archives of General Psychiatry, 57*, 14–20.

Nigg, J. T. (2000). On inhibition/disinhibition in developmental psychopathology: Views from cognitive and personality psychology as a working inhibition taxonomy. *Psychological Bulletin, 126*, 220–246.

Nigg, J. T. (2003). Response inhibition and disruptive behaviors: Toward a multiprocess conception of etiological heterogeneity for ADHD combined type and conduct disorder early-onset type. *Annals of the New York Academy of Science, 1008*, 170–182.

Nigg, J. T. (2006). Temperament and developmental psychopathology. *Journal of Child Psychology and Psychiatry, 47*, 395–422.

Overall, N. C., Fletcher, G. J. O., & Friesen, M. D. (2003). Mapping the intimate relationship mind: Comparisons between three models of attachment representations. *Personality and Social Psychology Bulletin, 29*, 1479–1493.

Panksepp, J. (1998). *Affective neuroscience: The foundations of human and animal emotions*. New York: Oxford University Press.

Peabody, D., & De Raad, B. (2002). The substantive nature of psycholexical personality factors: A comparison across languages. *Journal of Personality and Social Psychology, 83*, 983–997.

Peabody, D., & Goldberg, L. R. (1989). Some determinants of factor structures from personality-trait descriptors. *Journal of Personality and Social Psychology, 57*, 552–567.

Pierce, T., & Lydon, J. E. (2001). Global and specific relational models in the experience of social interactions. *Journal of Personality and Social Psychology, 80*, 613–631.

Rholes, W. S., & Simpson, J. A. (2004). *Adult attachment: Theory, research, and clinical implications*. New York: Guilford Press.

Roberts, B. W., & Bogg, T. (2004). A longitudinal study of the relationships between conscientiousness and the social-environmental factors and substance-use behaviors that influence health. *Journal of Personality, 72*, 325–354.

Roberts, B. W., Walton, K. E., & Bogg, T. (2005). Conscientiousness and health across the life course. *Review of General Psychology, 9*, 156–168.

Rogers, C. R. (1959). A theory of therapy, personality and interpersonal relationships, as developed in the client-centered framework. In S. Koch (Ed.), *Psychology: A study of a science* (Vol. 3, pp. 184–256). New York: McGraw-Hill.

Rothbart, M. K., Ahadi, S. A., & Evans, D. E. (2000). Temperament and personality: Origins and outcomes. *Journal of Personality and Social Psychology, 78*, 122–135.

Rothbart, M. K., Ahadi, S. A., Hershey, K., & Fisher, P. (2001). Investigations of temperament at three to seven years: The Children's Behavior Questionnaire. *Child Development, 72*, 1394–1408.

Rothbart, M. K., & Bates, J. E. (1998). Temperament. In W. Damon (Series Ed.) and N. Eisenberg (Vol. Ed.), *Handbook of child psychology: Vol. 3. Social, emotional and personality development* (5th ed., pp. 105–176). New York: Wiley.

Rothbart, M. K., Ellis, L. K., & Posner, M. I. (2004). Temperament and self-regulation. In R. F. Baumeister & K. D. Vohs, (Eds.), *Handbook of self-regulation: Research, theory, and applications* (pp. 357–370). New York: Guilford Press.

Rothbart, M. K., Ellis, L. K., Rueda, M. R., & Posner, M. I. (2003). Developing mechanisms of temperamental effortful control. *Journal of Personality, 71*, 1113–1143.

Rothbart, M. K., & Posner, M. (1985). Temperament and the development of self-regulation. In L. C. Hartlage & C. F. Telzrow, C. F. (Eds.), *The neuropsychology of individual differences: A developmental perspective* (pp. 93–123). New York: Plenum.

Rothbart, M. K., & Rueda, M. R. (2005). The development of effortful control. In U. Mayr, E. Awh, & S. Keele (Eds.), *Developing individuality in the human brain: A tribute to Michael I. Posner* (pp. 167–188). Washington, DC: American Psychological Association.

Ryan, R. M. (1982). Control and information in the intrapersonal sphere: An extension of cognitive evaluation theory. *Journal of Personality and Social Psychology, 43*, 450–461.

Ryan, R. M. (1993). Agency and organization: Intrinsic motivation, autonomy, and the self in psychological development. In J. Jacobs (Ed.), *Nebraska symposium on motivation: Developmental perspectives on motivation* (Vol. 40, pp. 1–56). Lincoln: University of Nebraska Press.

Ryan, R. M., & Deci, E. L. (2001). On happiness and human potentials: A review of research on hedonic and eudaimonic well-being. *Annual Review of Psychology, 52*, 141–166.

Saucier, G., & Goldberg, L. R. (2001). Lexical studies of indigenous personality factors: Premises, products, and prospects. *Journal of Personality, 69*, 847–879.

Scheier, M. F., & Carver, C. S. (1992). Effects of optimism on psychological and physical well-being: Theoretical overview and empirical update. *Cognitive Therapy and Research, 16*, 201–228.

Schmitt, D. P., & Buss, D. M. (2001). Human mate poaching: Tactics and temptations for infiltrating existing mateships. *Journal of Personality and Social Psychology, 80*, 894–917.

Schwartz, S. H. (1992). Universals in the content and structure of values: Theoretical advances and empirical tests in 20 countries. In M. P. Zanna (Ed.), *Advances in experimental social psychology* (pp. 1–65). San Diego, CA: Academic Press.

Schwartz, S. H., & Bilsky, W. (1990). Theory of the universal content and structure of values: Extensions and cross-cultural replications. *Journal of Personality and Social Psychology, 58*, 878–891.

Segal, N. L. (1993). Twin, sibling, and adoption methods: Tests of evolutionary hypotheses. *American Psychologist, 48*, 943–956.

Shoda, Y., Mischel, W., & Wright, J. C. (1994). Intraindividual stability in the organization and patterning of behavior: Incorporating psychological situations into the idiographic analysis of personality. *Journal of Personality and Social Psychology, 67*, 674–687.

Simpson, J. A. (1990). Influence of attachment styles on romantic relationships. *Journal of Personality and Social Psychology, 59*, 971–980.

Simpson, J. A., Rholes, W. S., Oriña, M. M., & Grich, J. (2002). Working models of attachment, support giving, and support seeking in a stressful situation. *Personality and Social Psychology Bulletin, 28*, 598–608.

Smith, E. R., & DeCoster, J. (2000). Dual-process models in social and cognitive psychology: Conceptual integration and links to underlying memory systems. *Personality and Social Psychology Review, 4*, 108–131.

Smith, E. R., Murphy, J., & Coats, S. (1999). Attachment to groups: Theory and measurement. *Journal of Personality and Social Psychology, 77*, 94–110.

Strack, F., & Deutsch, R. (2004). Reflective and impulsive determinants of social behavior. *Personality and Social Psychology Review, 8*, 220–247.

Tellegen, A. (1985). Structure of mood and personality and their relevance to assessing anxiety, with an emphasis on self-report. In A. H. Tuma & J. D. Maser (Eds.), *Anxiety and the anxiety disorders* (pp. 681–706). Hillsdale, NJ: Erlbaum.

Tooby, J., & Cosmides, L. (1989). Evolutionary psychology and the generation of culture, Part I. *Ethology and Sociobiology, 10*, 29–49.

Tooby, J., & Cosmides, L. (1990). On the universality of human nature and the uniqueness of the individual. *Journal of Personality, 58*, 17–67.

Trobst, K. K., Herbst, J. H., Masters, H. L., III, & Costa, P. T., Jr. (2002). Personality pathways to unsafe sex: Personality, condom use, and HIV risk behaviors. *Journal of Research in Personality, 36*, 117–133.

Vallacher, R. R., & Wegner, D. M. (1989). Levels of personal agency: Individual variation in action identification. *Journal of Personality and Social Psychology, 57*, 660–671.

Walton, K. E., & Roberts, B. W. (2004). On the relationship between substance use and personality traits: Abstainers are not maladjusted. *Journal of Research in Personality, 38*, 515–535.

Watson, D., Clark, L. A., McIntyre, C. W., & Hamaker, S. (1992). Affect, personality, and social activity. *Journal of Personality and Social Psychology, 63*, 1011–1025.

Wiggins, J. S. (1996). *The five-factor model of personality: Theoretical perspectives.* New York: Guilford Press.

Wilson, T. D., Lindsey, S. & Schooler, T. Y. (2000). A model of dual attitudes. *Psychological Review, 107*, 101–126.

Wright, R. A. (1996). Brehm's theory of motivation as a model of effort and cardiovascular response. In P. M. Gollwitzer & J. A. Bargh (Eds.), *The psychology of action: Linking cognition and motivation to behavior* (pp. 424–453). New York: Guilford Press.

Wright, J. C., & Mischel, W. (1988). Conditional hedges and the intuitive psychology of traits. *Journal of Personality and Social Psychology, 55*, 454–469.

Wrosch, C., Miller, G. E., Scheier, M. F., & Brun de Pontet, S. (2007). Giving up on unattainable goals: Benefits for health? *Personality and Social Psychology Bulletin, 33*, 251–265.

Zuckerman, M., Kuhlman, D. M., Joireman, J., Teta, P., & Kraft, M. (1993). A comparison of three structural models for personality: The big three, the big five, and the alternative five. *Journal of Personality and Social Psychology, 65*, 757–768.

INDEX

Note: Page numbers followed by "*f*" and "*t*" denote figures and tables, respectively.